THOMAS ARDEN IN FAVERSHAM:

THE MAN BEHIND THE MYTH

THOMAS ARDEN IN FAVERSHAM:
THE MAN BEHIND THE MYTH

Patricia Hyde

Published by The Faversham Society

1996

Published by The Faversham Society

Fleur de Lis Heritage Centre,
13 Preston Street, Faversham, Kent ME13 8NS

ISBN 0 900532 85 8

Printed by Mickle Print Ltd., Westminster Road,
Vauxhall Industrial Estate, Canterbury, Kent.
Typeset and prepared by
Patricia Hyde and Duncan Harrington
in *Microsoft Word for Windows.*
Set in 10pt. Times New Roman and printed
on matt-coated cartridge.

And hand bound by
Robert and Christine Swift, Burnt Mill, Egerton,
Ashford, Kent TN27 9AX

Limited, in a numbered edition, to
1000 copies of which 950 copies are for sale.

This copy is number

995

**For John, Tim, Steve, Sue,
Paul and Emily.**

Acknowledgements

This book is meant for the general reader, as long as he or she can stagger through all the genealogies, statistics and technical terms, which I have been unable to avoid but have always tried to explain. In particular, it is for the people of Faversham, in the hope that it will give them a greater understanding of and respect for their sixteenth-century forbears. I have therefore produced all the documents in English, even when the originals were in Latin.

I have four people to thank. First. Arthur Percival of the Faversham Society for believing against all the odds that I would eventually finish the book. He also read the script very carefully, and, from his vast local knowledge, was able to make a number of helpful comments, corrections and suggestions. Secondly, Duncan Harrington, without whose support the book certainly never would have been written. He not only transcribed most of the documents, but also went down a thousand false trails, suggested yet another source where we might find the vital clue and from time to time badgered all his friends and acquaintances with abstruse questions. Most important of all, he was always willing to go the extra mile. Thirdly, I am most grateful to Paul Wilkinson for the maps he has provided and his courtesy in allowing his transparencies to be used for the reproductions. And finally, I want to thank Richard Bradshaw for his valuable last-minute contribution.

I would also like to thank the Master and Fellows of Peterhouse, Cambridge, the Faversham Society, Lambeth Palace Library, Northampton Record Office, Norfolk Record Office, the Centre for Kentish Studies, Canterbury Cathedral Archives and the Dean and Chapter of Canterbury, the British Library Board, the Metropolitan Museum of Modern Art, New York, the Bodleian Library, Oxford, the Ordnance Survey Department, Southampton, and Rockingham Castle, Northampton for permission to publish documents and the illustrations here reproduced and I acknowledge their continuing copyright. All Public Record Office documents are crown copyright and reproduced by permission of Her Majesty's Stationery Office.

This book was inspired by Emmanuel Le Roy Ladurie's *Montaillou* and is an attempt to see how clear a picture can be drawn from available documents of the varying roles of a number of inhabitants of a small town in the first half of the sixteenth century. Also, I wanted to discover how far it is possible to recapture their sense of community. This particular town was disrupted by the dissolution of its abbey, which there can be no doubt had been an integral part of its life.

Such a picture can only be built up on a mass of detail, so that there are almost bound to be a number of errors. They are, of course, my own, and I apologise for them here and now.

Patricia Hyde

Contents

Appendices

List of Illustrations

ABBREVIATIONS

Acts & Monuments	John Foxe, *Acts and Monuments*
Add	Additional Manuscripts
adm	administration
Alum Cantab	*Alumni Cantabrigienses*
Alum Oxon	*Alumni Oxonienses*
APC	*Acts of the Privy Council*
App	appendix
Arber	*Transcripts of the Registers of the Company of Stationers of London 1554 - 1640*
Arch	Archdeaconry
Arch. Cant.	*Archaeologia Cantiana*
BL	British Library
Bodleian	Bodleian Library
Bull IHR	*Bulletin of the Institute of Historical Research*
Bullen	A. H. Bullen, *Arden of Faversham, a tragedy*
Cam Soc	Camden Society
Cant.	Canterbury
CCA	Canterbury Cathedral Archives
CCR	*Calendar of the Close Rolls*
Ch.	Charters
CKS	Centre for Kentish Studies, Maidstone
Clark, Society	P. Clark, *English Provincial Society from the Reformation to the Revolution*
Clark, Towns	P. Clark, *English Towns in Transition 1500-1700*
Coll	Collections
Commons 1509-58	S. T. Bindoff, *The House of Commons 1509-58; The History of Parliament*
Commons 1558-1603	P. W. Hasler, *The House of Commons 1558-1603; The History of Parliament*
Cons	Consistory
CPR	*Calendar of the Patent Rolls*
Cust	L. Cust, *Arden of Faversham*
DNB	*Dictionary of National Biography*
Donne	C. E. Donne, *An essay on the tragedy of Arden of Faversham*
ed,edn,eds	editor, edition, editors
EHR	*English Historical Review*
Fav	Faversham
Favward	Faversham; Wardmote book Volume 1
FIJ	*Faversham Institute Journal*
Fleay	*Biographical Chronicle of the English Drama 1559 - 1642*
fol., fols.	folio, folios
G.E.C.	*The Complete Peerage* by G. E. C.
Gent	Gentleman
Harl	Harleian MSS at BL
Hasted	E. Hasted *The History and Topographical Survey of the County of Kent*
Hazlitt	*Handbook of Popular, Poetical and Dramatic Literature of Great Britain*
HMC	Her Majesty's Commission
HMSO	Her Majesty's Stationery Office
Hyde	P. Hyde, *Henry Hatch and the battle over his will*
intro	introduction
Inq PM	Inquisition post mortem
Jacob	E. Jacob, *The History of Faversham*
JEGP	*Journal of English & Germanic Philology*
JP	Justice of the Peace
Lambeth	Lambeth Library
Lewis	J. Lewis, *The History and Antiquities of the Abbey and Church of Faversham and the Priory of Davington.*

Libr.	*The Library*
LP	*Letters and Papers of Henry VIII, foreign and domestic*
m	membrane
Mag	magazine
Monasticon	T. Southouse, *Monasticon Favershamiense in Agro Cantiano*
MS(S)	manuscript(s)
NRO	Norfolk County Record Office
no(s)	number(s)
NS	new series
OED	*Oxford English Dictionary*
Orlin	L. Orlin, *Private Matters and Public Culture in Post-Reformation England*
p., pp.	page, pages
PC	Privy Council
PCC	Prerogative Court of Canterbury
PRC	Probate Record Canterbury
PRO	Public Record Office
PROB	PCC reference at PRO
q	quire
r	recto
rec	record
RES	*Review of English Studies*
Rockingham	Rockingham Castle; Rockingham(Watson) Collection
Soc	Society
SP Dom	State Papers, Domestic
SR	Stationers Register
STC	Pollard & Redgrave, *Short Title Catalogue of English Books 1475 - 1640*
Streynsham	Rev. G. Streynsham Master, *Notes relating to the family of Streynsham*
Telfer, Abbey	Canon W. Telfer, *Faversham Abbey and its last abbot, John Caslock*
Telfer, Orphans	Canon W. Telfer, *Faversham's Court of Orphans*
TRHS	*Transactions of the Royal Historical Society*
Univ	University
UP	University Press
VCH	*The Victoria History of the counties of England*
v	verso
vol	volume
Wine	*Arden of Faversham*, ed.M. L. Wine
Youings	*Sixteenth-Century England*

Notes on Transcription

In quoting, or transcribing contemporary sources the original spelling has been retained, but capitalization has been modernized, contemporary contractions extended and sometimes punctuation modified. Documents in Latin have been rendered into English and where possible, are a literal translation.

Foreword

More than four hundred and fifty years have passed since the death of Thomas Arden in the small north Kent market town of Faversham. But fascination with the tangled web of personal relations that ended with his murder in 1551 has never waned. The anonymous domestic tragedy, 'Arden of Faversham' - published in 1592 - has been at the centre of most peoples' perception of the case, and it dramatised, or over-dramatised, what was in reality a rather sordid business. Arden is best known for the manner of his death: the victim of a conspiracy organised by his wife. It is that fact that accounts for the notoriety of the case in the sixteenth century. The murder of a husband by his wife was a horrifying, 'unnatural' reversal of the normal early modern roles of men and women: it was legally defined as petty treason. In that period any murder committed by a women was rare (there is evidence of only about twenty women convicted of murder in the surviving Kent assize records for the whole of Elizabeth's reign, 1559-1603). Even more exceptional were cases like the Arden murder: we know of just four Kent cases between 1559 and 1603 in which a woman was tried for the murder of her husband; in two of these the woman was associated with another man; in three of the four cases the victim was poisoned. In only one case, however, did the court treat the crime any differently than a simple murder: in 1591 Elizabeth Base of Waltham was convicted of murdering her husband with ratsbane; the judges in this case alone asked that she be 'executed in the manner appropriate to her crime'.[1]

In the Arden murder what was equally horrendous - and shameful - was the behaviour of Arden himself in permitting - perhaps even encouraging - his wife's infidelity. It was a tale of unmitigated evil, engendered by equal doses of greed and lust. And the results of these overturnings of moral norms provided an object lesson too dramatic to pass up for Tudor chroniclers and playwrights alike: the violent death of the cuckold who not only failed to control his wife's behaviour, but permitted her adultery for his own selfish ends; and the terrible, public punishments of the conspirators. As Patricia Hyde shows in her introduction, the Edwardian privy council (which included two men who knew and patronised Arden) rapidly determined that the perpetrators of this horrible murder should be dispatched in equally horrible ways - and as publicly as possible. She also shows that a number of misconceptions about Arden have become accepted 'history': that he was the most important man in Faversham, that he had become a substantial landowner, that he was a convinced Protestant, or that there was a wider political conspiracy against Arden. None of these was the case. In addition to giving us a more accurate account of Thomas Arden's position in Faversham society, and of his political and economic activities, Patricia Hyde, with tremendous support from Duncan Harrington, has winkled out much additional information about Arden - including his true age and birthplace. She has also provided us with a more accurate account of the textual pedigree of the 'Arden of Faversham' murder narrative - from local first-hand accounts to Stow through Holinshed to the late Elizabethan playwright. Her persistence and ingenuity in tracking down new sources for the history of Thomas Arden and of contemporary Faversham is quite remarkable. And at least as valuable for historians of 'Arden of Faversham' and for Kent historians more generally, she has provided full and accurate transcripts of all the relevant documents - readers can make up their own minds. The volume is equally a treasure trove of primary material for historians of sixteenth century towns. On both accounts the author deserves to be commended for her extraordinary efforts.

Michael Zell
University of Greenwich.

---

[1] *Calendar of Assize Records: Kent Indictments, Eliz.I*, ed. J. S. Cockburn (HMSO, 1979) nos. 578, 1200, 1779, 1957.

THOMAS ARDEN IN FAVERSHAM

Illustration overleaf:

Facsimile of an old woodcut taken from a ballad, *The complaint and lamentation of Mistresse Arden of Feversham in Kent,* and the third edition of the play published in 1633; drawing by J. W. Ebsworth (*The Kentish Garland*, Vol. 2, p. 519).

Introduction

'Arden of Feversham' continues to fascinate both scholars and the general public alike. There is, first of all, the question of the authorship of the play, published in 1592. Although many scholars think it unlikely, could it possibly have been written by either Shakespeare or Marlowe? This has been discussed again in an article by R. Fleissner in 1992 and as recently as 1993 by M. P. Jackson, who puts forward some compelling arguments in favour of his having some hand in the work.[8] 'If Shakespeare wrote Arden it is the most interesting fact in his literary development.'[9] Several companies of players visited Faversham between 1586 and 1592, the year that the play was published. It used to be thought that Shakespeare was probably in the town either with the Earl of Leicester's troupe in 1587-88 or with that of Lord Strange in 1591-92, but this is now considered by Schoenbaum to be 'a fanciful supposition'.[10] Shakespeare is not known to have belonged to any particular troupe before 1595 when he was paid as a member of the Chamberlain's group. On the other hand, Marlowe's father was born in Ospringe near Faversham and was brought up in the area before moving to Canterbury, so that Marlowe himself must have heard plenty about the murder.[11] Some modern authorities favour the view that it was written by an imitator of Thomas Kyd or by Kyd himself.[12]

'*The Tragedie of Arden of Feversham and Blackwill*' was entered in the Register of the Stationers' Company on 3 April 1592 by the London bookseller, Edward White. I have always been content to leave comment on the play, '*Arden of Feversham*', in far more capable hands than mine. However, a fortuitous meeting with Richard Bradshaw, shortly before going to press, has given me an opportunity to cast considerable doubt on the accepted premise that the author, whoever it might be, took his information from Holinshed.[13] In Appendix 21 Bradshaw has laid out his argument and evidence that *A Cruel Murder done in Kent* was an early printing of *Arden of Feversham.* As he says, M. L. Wine noted considerable scholarship focused on the play ever since it was suggested that Shakespeare was the author, but no-one until now has thought it necessary to postulate that the play appeared before the account in the Chronicle. Finding a copy of *A Cruel Murder in Kent* or *Murderous Michael* would solve the mystery; although this is somewhat unlikely. However, I hope that the present study, which seriously questions earlier authorities, will lead modern scholars to consider the question yet again.

In view of this general interest and before he sinks without trace beneath the weight of his own significance, I decided to concentrate on the historical Thomas Arden, not the Arden of the play. I think that they were quite different. This was the murder not of a king nor a queen, but of a

---

[8] R. Fleissner, 'On retaining M. Arden of Feversham: the question of titular resonance', *Analytical and Enumerative Bibliography,* NS, (1992) vi, nos 3 & 4, pp. 208-15; MacDonald P. Jackson, 'Shakespearean Features of the Poetic Style of *Arden of Faversham.*' Archiv (für das Studium der neuren Sprachen und Literaturen) (Verlag, 1993) Band 230/2, pp. 279 - 304

[9] Quoted by M.P. Jackson *op. cit.*, from *Arden of Feversham,* ed. Ronald Bayne (London, 1897/1955), p. x.

[10] S. Schoenbaum, *Shakespeare's Lives* (Oxford, 1970) has sections on Malone and Lee, who wrote about Shakespeare's membership of companies in the early 1590's; Sir E. K. Chambers, *William Shakespeare* (Oxford, 1930); J. M. Cowper, 'Notes from the records of Faversham 1560-1600', *Transactions of the Royal Historical Society,* 2nd edn. (London, 1875), pp. 218-38; a letter on 11 July 1993 from J. M. Gibson, Kent Editor of the *Records of Early English Drama* confirmed the earliest certain date as 1595.

[11] A. D. Wraight and V. Stern, *In search of Christopher Marlowe* (Chichester, 1993), p. 29; C. Nicholl, *The Reckoning* (London, 1992); W. Urry, *Christopher Marlowe and Canterbury*, ed. A. Butcher (1988).

[12] *Elizabethan drama; eight plays* ed. J. Gassner and W. Green (New York, 1990), p. 2; A. Freeman, *Thomas Kyd; facts and problems* (Oxford, 1967); P. B. Murray, *Thomas Kyd* (New York, 1969).

[13] Last May, just as this book was about to go to print, I was put in touch with Richard Bradshaw. We discovered that we had both been following the trail of Thomas Arden for some years and had both come to the same conclusion on several issues. For example, in 1993, we had both separately visited Kirtling, Cambs., where Sir Edward North lies buried.

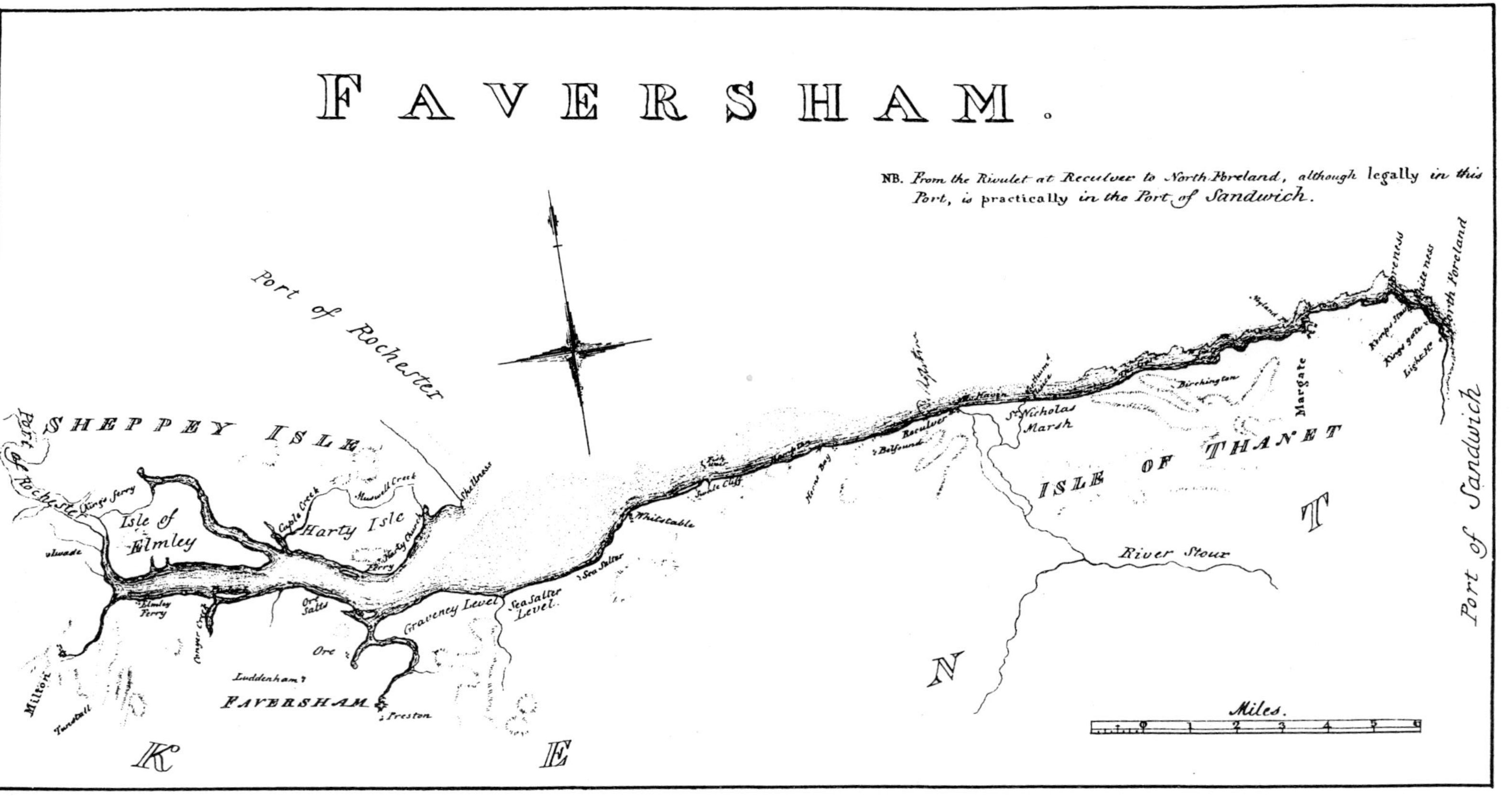

Original pen and ink nineteenth century map showing the limits of the port of Faversham, in possession of the author.

mere gentleman, a former mayor of the town. The circumstances were so involved and bizarre that they help us to learn much about the social attitudes in the period. His biography has been written a number of times and statements have been repeated time and again, which need to be investigated. I decided that it would be a good idea to re-examine all the evidence that we have. I hope to prove that Arden should be seen in his setting amongst his contemporaries in the town and cut down to size. I want to consider yet again statements that are at present taken for granted: that he was a gentleman by birth, that his wife's maiden name was Mirfyn, that he was a reformer rather than a time-server, that he acquired virtually all the property in Faversham formerly belonging to the abbey and that he was the archetype in Kent of a man who made a great fortune from the dissolution of the monasteries.

To start with, we can watch how the account of him built up, stage by stage, and now is the moment to concentrate on that. I will explain what the statements about him meant later on. Interest seems to have been aroused after 1770, when Edward Jacob reprinted the play 'With a Preface, in which some Reasons are offered in favour of its being the earliest dramatic Work of Shakespeare now remaining, and a genuine Account given of the Murder, from authentic Papers of the Time.' Debate on the authorship raged on, and, in August 1881, someone anonymous wrote an article entitled, 'Was 'Arden of Feversham' written by Shakespeare'? In the course of it he wrote that 'another gentleman lent us some manuscript notes found in a lumber room at the Dolphin Inn very many years ago, professing to be written by a Mr. Burton who represents himself in the manuscript as curious in such matters, and having collected his information from the 'auncientest people'[14].' In this manuscript Burton says that 'Arden was a gentleman, bred near Wye in Kent, and was importuned to buy the Abbey lands by Lord Cheyne, and was not aware when he bought them that several tenants had leases of different portions. He was 56 when he came to Faversham. His wife was 28, and had familiarities with Mosbie before she was married, which made her friends desirous of marrying her with Arden.' Nothing else is written about Mr Burton, but it is obvious that he had a surprisingly wide range of information and that he presents themes that will recur.

The 'Dolphin Hotel' was listed in 1878 as in Preston Street, Faversham, but earlier in the 1851 census it was given as the 'Dolphin Inn'.[15] This was first mentioned in 1764 and was pulled down in 1960. Who was Mr Burton? There were two men of that name, who, by reason of their occupation, might easily have had access to the lumber room in the inn. The first was a maltman called John Burton, who had two houses on the east side of Preston Street. When he made his will in 1820 he appointed as his executor, William Rigden, a well known brewer. However, it is unlikely that it was him, because he made his mark rather than writing his signature on his will, which probably means he was illiterate. More probably, if either of them, it was a master bricklayer, Edward Burton, who had property in Well Lane and West Street. He died in 1827, aged 68, and was buried in Faversham churchyard. There is a reference to his 'papers of moment' in his probate records. Furthermore, his son, William, was living just a few doors up from the Fleur-de-Lis, according to the census in 1851.[16]

Edward Crow wrote his manuscript notes on the town between 1847 and 1855. He said that, 'Arden was chief comptroller of the customs at Faversham and was employed in 1545 to procure a new charter for the town, with a licence to mortise the lands given by Henry Hatche, with a

[14] Mr. Burton, from eighteenth century notes recorded in *The Monthly Journal of the Faversham Institute* (August, 1881).

[15] *Kelly's Post Office Directory of Kent* 1878 p. 1409, John Joseph Rogers proprietor, No. 86; correctly should have been 38 Preston Street; 1851 Public Record Office: HO.107/1626 fol. 273 p. 8, innkeeper John Scott; HO.107/1626 fol. 282 p. 26; F. Haley, *The Inns and Taverns of Faversham*, Faversham Papers, No. 19, (1982).

[16] PRC 17/106 fol. 356; PRC 17/107 fol. 370; D. Harrington, *Faversham churchyard memorial inscriptions* 942.

grant of Market and fairs etc. and to have for his pains £20. He was also mayor in 1548 and was expelled the corporation 'by cause beying jurate and sworne to maynteyn the francheses, liberties and freedoms of the sayd towne, hath contrarye to his othe in that behalfe, gone about and labored by dy[ve]rs ways and meanes to the utermost of his p[ositio]n to infryndge and undoo the sayd francheses liberties and freedom.' It is stated in an old book that he was brought up near Wye. His arms were *ermine, a fess chequy or and azure.*' Crow was obviously using Burton's account and the town records. He also found a petition including an inventory from Arden's daughter and her husband to recover certain goods forfeited by the death of her mother. This document cannot now be found.[17]

Historians gradually built on the work of these two men. C. E. Donne in 1873 mentioned that Arden was a jurat in 1544, that he married a step-daughter of Sir Edward North, that Arden left money to charity and arranged for an annual sermon to be preached in his memory. This information came from the town records and from Arden's will. He also gave an account of the murder from Holinshed's chronicle and described how Alice and two other conspirators were charged with petty treason and explained what that meant. Fourteen years later, W. A. H. Bullen repeated the same story, but added the cost of the burning of Alice and George Bradshaw taken from the Canterbury city archives. He also referred to the report of the murder in Faversham wardmote book and added a full account of the report in Holinshed, pointing out that in one important respect it differed from the play.

We have now reached the twentieth century. In 1920 L. Cust filled in the general background and was particularly concerned with the deeds he had found at Rockingham Castle referring to Arden, his daughter, Margaret, and his neighbour, Thomas Dunkyn.[18] He also referred to Privy Council records and to the diary of the Londoner, Henry Machyn. He wrote a detailed biography of Sir Edward North and suggested that Arden worked for him in the Court of Augmentations. He thought that Arden came from a family of that name either in Warwickshire or Cheshire. He compared the accounts of the murder in Holinshed and the wardmote book and commented on how Morsby had risen to the position of steward in Holinshed. He was at pains to describe how Holinshed came to be published and was the first person to mention the account of the murder amongst the manuscripts of John Stow.

In 1966, Canon W. Telfer was mainly concerned with town records, but mentioned that Arden had lands in Sandwich. I would not always agree with his interpretation of evidence. I have had particular difficulty with his suggestion that Arden had two wives and that his son-in-law, John Bradbourne, succeeded him as Customer. A. Holt in 1970 and M. L. Wine in 1973 were mainly concerned with the play and used much the same material about the real life characters, but Wine did mention the account of the punishments in the Breviat Chronicle. Both writers referred to the differences between the play and the account in Holinshed. Wine said, 'The dramatic sureness of the playwright is most evident, however, in his characterization of the three main figures (Arden, Alice, Morsby), none of whom resembles his or her counterpart in Holinshed. He also mentioned what he called the 'accurately researched novel' by D. Davidson, who perceptively imagined that Sir Thomas Cheyne carried out an investigation after the murder.

---

17 Centre For Kentish Studies, Fa/Z41/2 p. 176.

18 J. Russell Smith, *Bibliotheca Cantiana*, (1837), p. 197; CKS, Crow MSS fa/Z41/2 p.161; .A. H. Bullen, intro., *Arden of Faversham, a tragedy* (London, 1887) p. xii, and generally, pp. iii-xx; C. E. Donne, *An essay on the tragedy of Arden of Faversham* (London, 1873); 'Arden of Faversham' ed. M. L. Wine, *The Revels Plays* (Manchester, 1973), pp. xxxv-xliv; L. Cust, 'Arden of Faversham', *Archaeologia Cantiana,* xxxiv (1920), pp. 101-38; Canon W. Telfer, 'Faversham's Court of Orphans', *Arch. Cant.*, lxxxi (1966), pp. 191-203; A. Holt, *Faversham Papers,* No. 7; S. T. Bindoff, *The House of Commons 1509-58, The History of Parliament,* 3 vols., (London, 1982), i, pp. 328-29; D. Davidson, *Feversham,* (New York, 1969).

Finally, in 1994, L. C. Orlin wrote the fullest biography yet in the first chapter of her book, *Private Matters and Public Culture in Post Reformation England.* She filled in many details about Arden's life and, in particular, was the first to publish new information about his birth-date, the Hothfield saga and John Ponet.[19]

More significantly though, she widened the whole field of discussion by asking two important questions. Why did the murder of this particular man reverberate through the centuries up to the present day and why did his wife, Alice Arden, become the personification of an evil woman? She suggests that:

"the murder of Thomas Ardern placed on the public agenda issues of private contention and consequence, in this way contributing to the reconceptualization of what we would call 'private life' in the wake of the Reformation. One public site was the 1592 theatricalization of the story. The other and inaugural site was Arden's incorporation into Holinshed's narrative, even despite the chronicler's evident unease about interrupting a history of matters of state for an account that is ' but a private matter.' "[20]

To the second question she says that she is concerned 'primarily to develop that critical awareness of the apparent scapegoating of Alyce.'[21] Elsewhere she adds, 'At the center was the agency of Alice. Alice served the cultural function of giving definition to the shape of domestic evil by marking its extreme.'[22]

These are indeed two questions that we should bear in mind throughout, but I suggest instead that it might have happened by chance. There are certain notorious murders that fascinate and horrify contemporaries, usually those which involve a number of victims. In these cases, the memory always lingers on. England is a small country, where there has been strong, central government from the Middle Ages onwards and where communication nation-wide has always been surprisingly rapid if there was anything sufficiently interesting for us to want to pass it on. Think of the plans to light the beacons at the approach of the Armada. We are therefore more likely to have a shared reaction to a notorious murder than people on a vast continent could possibly be expected to have, certainly until very recently.

In 1888 there was Jack the Ripper, who slashed five prostitutes to death in the East End. He was never caught and probably more has been written about him than about any other murderer. It has even been suggested that he might have been the Duke of Clarence. Then in 1965 there were the Moors murders. Ian Brady and Myra Hindley became involved in sadism, Nazism and pornography. They then tortured and murdered five children and young people in Yorkshire and recorded this on tape while doing so. These murders still resonate in England to such an extent that, thirty years later, it is possible that Myra Hindley will never be let out of prison alive. It is still a live issue, to be considered by the Home Secretary yet again soon. Out of idle curiosity at a meeting recently, I asked a gentleman, whom I had never met before, what he would do if she were ever set free. 'I would cheerfully kill her myself, but then I had children of the same age at the time' was his reply. We should remember this knee-jerk reaction when we come to consider the case of Alice Arden. Another gentleman, who wrote to me after my discussion with L. Orlin on Woman's Hour on the subject said, 'The idea of the female sex being especially evil can only stem from the rather odd supposition that it is really only males who commit crimes - if a female

---

19 The information about the birth date was originally located by D. Harrington, and was passed, with translations and transcripts of many other pivotal documents, to the Faversham Society prior to the publication of this book.

20 Orlin, p. 15.

21 Orlin, p. 18.

22 Orlin p. 68.

transgresses then it is unnatural and even more to be condemned.' Fair or not, politically correct or not, that still seems to be the prevailing thought amongst some people alive in England today, let alone in the sixteenth century. Brady has never aroused the same hostile reaction.

Finally, in 1994, Frederick and Rosemary West were alleged to have together murdered nine children and young women, and he another three on his own, in Cromwell Street in Gloucester. This time, reporters from all over the world sat in the street outside their house for days and days while policemen dug up body after body in the house and garden, some of them buried in concrete. The inhabitants of Gloucester became seriously alarmed that - in the future -tourists to their historic city would only make a bee-line for Cromwell Street. This very thing could be said to have happened to Arden's House in Faversham.

So there is nothing surprising in the fact that contemporaries were hypnotized by the Arden murder. In this case, it was not the number of victims that aroused horror, but the number of suspects, ten in all. It also had all the elements of a ripping yarn. In a society even more class-ridden than our own, it concerned a gentleman, who was a royal official called a customer and a former mayor, and his wife, who was the step-daughter of a Privy Councillor and great nobleman. Besides tragedy and romance, there was comedy and farce in the six botched attempts to murder him all over London and the South East, in forgetting the key to the garden gate, and in Morsby going to bed with blood-stains all over him. There was a bit of Sherlock Holmes in the 'elementary, my dear Watson' tracking down of footprints. Finally, there were not one but two miracles. First, the snow disappeared at just the right or the wrong moment, depending on your point of view. Secondly, the outline of the victim's body remained on the grass for several years for everyone to gape at. Edward Crow suggested that it was done with the help of soap ashes poured over the spot to destroy vegetation, but contemporaries were deeply impressed and repeated the tale again and again.[23] Can you wonder that everyone was astounded? Aren't you?

Given that the murder was likely to attract notoriety, how did it come to have lasting fame? I think that the reaction of the Privy Council had much to do with it. Two of its members were Sir Edward North, Thomas Arden's father-in-law, and Sir Thomas Cheyne, by right of both his offices as Treasurer of the Household and Lord Warden of the Cinque Ports. Both of them were key figures in Arden's story. The murder took place on 15 February 1551. On 5 March following, a commission of oyer and terminer - 'to hear and determine' - was appointed. Such commissions were used to inquire into the more serious offences such as murder and treason. The commission was headed by Sir Thomas Cheyne and, as I shall describe later, included a powerful group of local gentry.[24]

On the very same day, 5 March, the Privy Council sent letters arranging that two of the murderers should be punished in London, two in Canterbury and two in Faversham. Arden was, to repeat, a royal official as Customer of the town and he was also the son-in-law of a great nobleman and Privy Councillor. Furthermore, Alice and two of the servants were guilty of petty treason and their punishment was laid down by statute. A wife who killed her husband or a servant who killed his or her master was guilty of petty treason. The other group liable to this punishment, but not involved in this case, were priests who murdered a superior. This was the next most serious crime to high treason and was punishable by death.

The murderers could have been punished within the jurisdiction of the court that tried them, that is, in Faversham, which was a member of the Cinque Ports under the Head Port of Dover, which

---

23 CKS, Crow MSS Fa/Z41/2 p. 174, footnote 4.
24 See APPENDIX 1.

in turn assured the town of many privileges. Why did the Privy Council decree otherwise?[25] I think that, for reasons of its own, it wanted to make a terrible example of them and therefore dealt so spectacularly and so ferociously with them that it was scorched on men's minds for ever. The murder was remembered as much for the punishments as for the crime itself. D. Davidson realized that it was strange that Alice was burned in Canterbury and suggested that Sir Thomas Cheyne was responsible as Lord Lieutenant for Kent 1551-53 and that he was the person referred to in the Faversham wardmote book as 'by the commandement of the Kinges Majesties most honorable counsell.' In fact, the reference must be to the Privy Council.[26] Furthermore, it would still not explain why Morsby and his sister were hanged in Smithfield. I must explain that the wardmote book should be seen as something like a modern-day book of council minutes with some private documents engrossed there as well when they impinged upon the activities and welfare of the town. On 5 October 1466 at a 'wardmouth' it had been agreed by the mayor, jurats and commonality that all articles made by them 'shall be kept and held, as yt shall apere hereafter, in wrytyng.'[27]. Several wills are recorded in the wardmote books because they refer to bequests made to the town.

What prompted this action? I think that there were two reasons. First of all, two of the Privy Councillors, North and Cheyne, must have been very angry, affronted men and they were both present at the meeting on 5 March, North by name and Cheyne in his role as Mr. Treasurer, the Treasurer of the Household. He must be distinguished from William Paulet, Earl of Wiltshire, the Lord High Treasurer, who was also present.

North's step-daughter and one of his 'chefest gentlemen' had murdered a man whose patron he had been for many years. Cheyne had lost a man on whom he could rely to work in his interest in Faversham. Why, one of the botched attempts to murder Arden had even been made near Cheyne's home at Shurland.

Secondly, as L.P. Hartley said in *The Go Between,* 'The past is a foreign country; they do things differently there.' I think that the Privy Council essentially saw the murder as far more than a domestic tragedy. With justification, it was concerned with law and order. It learnt that the murderers included ex-soldiers and masterless men like Black Will, Shakebag and Bradshaw, and that attempts to murder Arden had taken place all over London and the south east.

Its reaction should be seen against the background of what else was happening in central government and in Kent during the same period. For the Privy Council this came on top of the Western Rising and Kett's rebellion in Norfolk in 1549. It was a time of tension at the very heart of government. The Protector, Edward Seymour, Duke of Somerset, had been arrested in October 1549 and released in February 1550, both at the instigation of his rival, John Dudley, Earl of Warwick, later to be Duke of Northumberland. The murder took place in the uneasy period before Somerset was again imprisoned in October 1551 and executed on 22 January following.

P.Clark has described in detail what was happening in Kent at roughly the same time, so that I shall only give only a summary of events here. There had long been tension between the conservative and radical gentry in the county. In the 1540's the conservatives were in control, wielded their power as feudal lords and made considerable use of their continuing control over the county administration. However, as M. Zell says,' religious nonconformity had a long

[25] *Acts of the Privy Council*, 1550-52, pp. 227, 229-231, 565-66.
[26] D. Davidson, *Feversham*, (Crown Publishers Inc., New York 1969), p. 374; Faversham Wardmote Book Volume 1 (Fa/Ac1) fol. 60.
[27] Favward, fol. 4v.

pedigree in Kent, and had not disappeared with the advent of the official reformation in the 1530s.'

Matters came to a head after the new foundation of Canterbury Cathedral in 1541. There were to be 12 prebendaries and 6 preachers. Cranmer deliberately chose six radicals and six conservative prebends to keep a balance. The preachers were to provide sermons in the cathedral and an itinerant ministry in the parishes. Some of these men were former monks and there was a period of religious reaction, hence the Prebendaries' Plot against Archbishop Cranmer led by Stephen Gardiner, Bishop of Winchester. As P. Collinson says, this was 'a conspiracy with national as well as local ramifications, designed not only to topple Cranmer, but also to halt the Reformation in its tracks, a dry run for the Marian reaction of ten years later.' Henry VIII rescued Cranmer and allowed him to take charge of a commission, held partly in Faversham, to investigate the plot. The depositions show that there were accusations of heresy against, among others, John Bland, one of Cranmer's chaplains, who was also vicar of Ospringe and later Adisham. There were references to sermons at Faversham and its vicar, Clement Norton, to the state of the church at Buckland, to Swan, vicar of Sheldwich, and to Robert à Stotte, curate of Davington. One of the leading members of the gentry involved was the conservative Sir Thomas Moyle, Speaker of the House of Commons in 1542. He was a typical Tudor official and MP for Rochester in 1545, 1547, 1553 and 1554 and Lynn in 1554. The plotters planned to set up a commission to deal with heresy, which would include Moyle and Sir Reginald Scott of Scot's Hall in Brabourne, both of whom were commissioners at the trial of Alice Arden and the others in 1551. Cyriak Petyt of Boughton-under-Blean had links with Moyle and was another plotter of whom more is to be heard in this story.[28]

The outbreak of war with France in 1543 led to political unrest and a host of social problems. As Clark says, 'Henry's soldiery, sick, deserting, maimed and destitute, too often returned to England by way of the Kentish ports, creating serious difficulties in East Kent.'[29] The Privy Council 'realised the danger that social distress might escalate into massive popular disorder.' In June, 1550,there was a rising when about 10,000 peasants gathered at Sittingbourne and had to be dispersed by Sir Thomas Cheyne and a force of cavalry. The following winter, there was an especially large influx of soldiers into Kent from the Continent. The following March, labourers working on the Sandwich haven project threatened to attack the town unless they were paid all their wages. P. Clark concludes that 'clearly popular disturbance was almost endemic in Edwardian Kent.'[30]

Meanwhile, the Privy Council was again alarmed, this time about a strange group who might be Anabaptists, whose very name struck fear into the hearts of magistrates all over Europe after their savagery at Munster in 1535. Suffice it to say that they were freewillers, a group of religious radicals or separatists. John Strype called them, 'the first that made separation from the Reformed Church of England.' As A. G. Dickens said in *The English Reformation,* they were 'men of erudition and open mindedness, a discussion group rather than an integrated sect under

---

[28] *Letters and Papers, Foreign and Domestic, of the reign of Henry VIII,* ed. James Brewer and others, 21 vols. and *Addenda* (London, 1864-1932), XVIII, part 2, no. 546, pp. 291-378; J. Strype, *Memorials of Archbishop Cranmer* (Oxford, 1840), pp. 142-175; G.Redworth, *In defence of the church catholic: the life of Stephen Gardiner* (Oxford, 1990), pp. 176-207; P. Clark, *English Provincial Society from the Reformation to the Revolution: Religion, Politics and Society in Kent 1500-1640* (Hassocks, 1977), pp. 49-86; M. Zell, 'The Prebendaries Plot of 1543: A reconsideration', *Journal of Ecclesiastical History,* XXVII (1976), pp. 241 -53; J. Ridley, *Thomas Cranmer* (Oxford, 1962), pp. 229-45; *A history of Canterbury Cathedral,* ed. P. Collinson, N. Ramsay and M. Sparks (Oxford, 1995), p. 161; Commons 1509-58, ii, pp. 642-44; K. Melrose, 'Annals of Ospringe', *Faversham Papers,* No. 36 (1992) pp. 10-11.

[29] Clark, Society, pp. 78-86.

[30] Clark, Society, p. 80.

imperious or charismatic leadership'.[31] They were the theological opponents of Luther, and particularly Calvin, and were known as freewillers as opposed to those who believed in predestination.

We are here concerned with two groups, one in Kent and the other in Essex, whose activities are described in detail by J. Martin.[32]. Bishop Hooper had been sent on a preaching tour against the Anabaptists in Kent and Essex in June 1550. The following Christmas a conventicle or assembly of more than 60 people from Kent and Essex met at Bocking in Essex. The Council was always alarmed by people of more than one county being involved and acting together. On 18 January 1551 a commission was appointed 'to correct and punish all anabaptists'. On 27 January and 3 February various men from Kent and Essex appeared before the Privy Council. Remember that this happened less than two weeks before Arden's murder. It must, I think, have coloured the approach of the Privy Council to it.

Surely what brings the story to life and what must have attracted the anonymous playwright are the absorbing details. Some of them, like Morsby vindicating Adam Fowle and Grene vindicating Bradshaw, are based on confessions and others come from the trial itself. How did these details reach Holinshed and thus the playwright, without a modern crime reporter sitting in the court, particularly when evidence was not often written down? I want to suggest a possible scenario step by step.

I think that, by chance, there was a man living in Faversham and present at the trial, who virtually acted in that capacity, made notes and later passed on that information to others. This man, Robert Cole of Faversham, was also a freewiller, but he was not present at the Bocking assembly. He was referred to in another document, which went to the Privy Council, dating either from 1550 or 1551. In a series of depositions about freewillers, 'John Grey saythe that Cole of Faversham apon Lammas daye laste paste saide and affirmed that the doctryne of predestynation was meter for divilles then for Christian men'. John Plume of Lenham added that, 'Umfrey Middilton being in Cole's house at Faversham apon Lammas daye he said that Adam was elected to be salvid And that all men, being then in Adams loynes were predestynate to be salvid and that ther were no reprobates and in his defence he alleaged the doctryne conteyned in the xiiii[th] article.' This shows us that Cole had a house in Faversham in 1550 or 1551, and was probably living there.

They neither of them mentioned Cole's Christian name, but John Foxe took up the story. He said that, in Mary's reign, Robert Cole and his wife and children were persecuted out of Faversham, where he apparently had a happy escape from the hands of 'Master Petyt', probably the conservative 'Cyriak Petyt' of Boughton-under-Blean, whom we last met in the Prebendaries' Plot of 1543. Petyt was 'his mortall enemye, and one that sought his lyfe.' Petyt was a JP for Kent in 1554 and MP for Winchelsea and Chippenham in the two parliaments of 1554. They apparently met in a lane not far from Faversham that was so narrow that they had to touch one another, but Cole still got past and was gone 'before the judge dyd know it was he and so the sayd Cole escaped.'[33]

Cole was next reported as based on the Sign of the Bell in Gracechurch Street in London where he brought comfort to people imprisoned for their religious beliefs in the King's Bench. Foxe

---

31 A.G.Dickens, *The English Reformation,* 2nd edn. (London, 1989), pp. 264-65.

32 J. W. Martin, *Religious Radicals in Tudor England* (London, 1989), passim.

33 APC 1550-52, pp. 197-99, 206-07; B.L. Harl. MSS 421, fols. 133-34; J. Foxe, Acts and Monuments (London, 1563) pp. 1699b, 1700a & b; Acts & Monuments, *Church Historians of England* , (G. Seeley, 1868) 3rd edn. Vol. viii, part 1, p. 384, part 2 p. 790, app. VI; C. Burrage, *The early English Dissenters 1550-1641,* (Camb. UP, 1912), I, pp. 51-52; J. W. Martin *op. cit.* pp. 10-11, 23-24, 46-49, 51-55, 64-65.

says that, 'He was a great concealer and harbourer of men. He went overseas to some of the Protestants in exile, to carry intelligence of the state of religion at home and to propound certain questions concerning religion and to know their advice ... and judgement.' He devotes a long paragraph to extolling his virtues: 'I take hym to be a man, not only rare, but a perfect Minister in deede, and worthy eternall commendation.'

He had recanted by 1554. In the 1563 edition of the *Book of Martyrs*, Foxe said that Cole assisted Thomas Bentham as a minister to the Protestant congregation in London. He left this out of subsequent editions, probably because he had discovered that Cole had been a religious radical. He disapproved of them and was ready to suppress facts about them.

On the accession of Elizabeth, Cole was collated to be Rector of St. Mary le Bow by Archbishop Parker. We know nothing of his origin. Three or possibly four priests of the same name have become so intertwined that it has become virtually impossible to disentangle them. It is usually said that the Rector of Bow came from Biggleswade in Bedfordshire and was a King's Scholar at Eton before he entered King's College, Cambridge, on 13 August 1542 at the age of 18. He was a BA in 1546-47, an MA in 1550 and a Fellow from 1545-51. I am assured by the archivist of King's College, Cambridge, that this is a mistake, because Robert Cole of Biggleswade died in 1551 and his will is entered in the Ledger Book in King's College archives.

So, John Foxe in his *Book of Martyrs* made the crucial link when he spoke of Robert Cole of Faversham, 'who is now person of Bow in London.' He called him Robert Coles. This means that Cole may have been a priest without a living present in Faversham at the same time as the conservative, litigious vicar, Clement Norton, in 1550 and 1551.

During the vestment controversy, Cole was paraded by Bishop Grindal of London as one who had conformed and was now wearing the correct canonical attire. On 12 April 1566 Archbishop Parker wrote to Sir William Cecil that 'some did refuse, but now they be induced, and they be counted sortly learned with the best of them, as one Cole of Bow Church.'

Cole made his will on 12 January 1576/7. He did not refer to Faversham, but mentioned his wife and children. He left Calvin's *Institutes* and Peter Martyr on the Romans in English to one parson friend, 'Marlorate in English uppon Matthew' to a second and his best Geneva testament in English to a third. The will was proved on 27 February 1576/7.[34]

Now to establish the link with Holinshed. This murder was, of course, a godsend to ballad-mongers. Then the antiquarian John Stow became interested in the case. As S. Booth[35] said in *The book called Holinshed's Chronicles*, 'John Stowe was one of the best and surely the most dedicated of the Elizabethan antiquaries.' There is a manuscript in the British Library, which was found among his papers, giving an account of the murder. W. H. Kelliher, formerly an assistant keeper in the Department of Manuscripts, said many years ago that the manuscript was in Stow's own hand-writing and this has been confirmed by the Folger curator of manuscripts, Laetitia Yeandle. I shall henceforth call it Stow.

M. Wine pointed out that it is almost identical in wording and in organization with the Holinshed narrative and is occasionally clearer on a point than it. Probably for political reasons, Holinshed edited out some interesting details. I suggest that this manuscript gives the earliest record of Arden's murder apart from the wardmote book of Faversham. John Stow the chronicler was born in 1525 in the parish of St. Michael's Cornhill, where, as I shall show later, Thomas Arden of Faversham leased the parsonage, which may have increased Stow's interest in him. He was a

---

34 See APPENDIX 2; Commons 1509-58, iii, pp. 96-98, 106-108.

35 S. Booth *The book called Holinshead's Chronicles (California, 1968), pp. 51, 61-66.*

tailor, who collected books from 1560 onwards. After the death in 1573 of Reginald Wolfe, the publisher, Stow bought his collections. It might be thought that the account of the murder came to Stow from John Leland, because Reginald Wolfe had inherited Leland's notes. However, Leland had become insane by 1550, a year before the murder, so that he cannot have reported it. However, John Stow was a friend of William Lambarde, the antiquarian and author of the *Perambulation of Kent*, who may have been a source. Stow died in 1605.[36]

As I shall show later, there is evidence in the manuscript that Stow was trying to reconcile various accounts. For the moment what is important is that, after Stow had written about the punishment of Arden's murderers he set down the following words in Latin: **See the charges and descriptions of the various persons and the places where they were put to death, which may be had of Master Robert Cole of Bow.**[37]

I suggest that this man Robert Cole of Bow was also our Robert Cole of Faversham, that he was present at the trial of Alice Arden and her accomplices and made notes about it very soon after. He may have been related to Cole, one of the two London grocers entertained by Alice after the murder. He tells us of Morsby clearing Adam Fowle, of Alice incriminating Bradshaw, of Bradshaw's attempts to clear himself and then of Grene clearing him in his confession, things that he could only have known if he had been at hand. He seems to me to have been a remarkable eye-witness. He lived in Faversham and must have known a number of the people involved. The personal descriptions are no doubt his. The most unusual thing about him was that he was, at that stage, basically out of sympathy with magistrates and later ministered to religious prisoners in the King's Bench. It is hard to see that he could have had a religious motive in what he did: genuine local interest seems more likely. He would have been shocked by Alice's behaviour, but who would not have been? He certainly had harsh things to say about Arden as well. He almost certainly talked to the prisoners for, without the benefit of shorthand, he could hardly have taken in all that information just listening to the trial. He developed opinions of his own as he went along, the most important being that Bradshaw was innocent, as I shall show later. He makes no comment on Arden being a reformer, which we might have expected him to do. It is worth pointing out that, if I am right, the information on which Stow's account is based is even earlier than that in the wardmote book, not the other way round. I am confident that we have contemporary notes passed from Cole to Stow, who turned them into an account. Cole even comes to us with a testimonial from John Foxe. Indeed, Stow's account now seems to me to have much in common with the accounts in *The Book of Martyrs*. Foxe tried to be as accurate as possible, even though he did not always succeed. Nevertheless, the graphic quality of his accounts profoundly influenced a whole generation of Protestants.[38]

---

[36] CKS Anonymous transcript catalogued under Arden's House; *Dictionary of National Biography*, John Stow, Raphael Holinshed, John Leland, William Lambarde; C.L. Kingsford, *A survey of London* (Oxford, 1908), intro.; W. Andrews, *England in the days of old*, (London, 1897), p. 273; S. Booth, *The book called Holinshed's Chronicles*, (The book club of California, 1968), pp. 62, 65-66.

[37] See APPENDIX 3 and see page 87 of text.

[38] See APPENDIX 2; PRO, PROB 11/59 q. 7; BL, Harl. MSS 421 fols. 133-134v; APC, NS., iii, pp. 97-99, 197, 206-7; iv, pp. 131, 138; *Alum. Cantab.* part 1, i, p. 367; C. H. Cooper and T. Cooper; *Athenae Cantabrigienses*, i, p. 364; Sir W. Sterry, *The Eton College Register* (Eton, 1943), p. 77; W. H. Frere ed., Registrum Matthei Parker 1559-75, *Cant. and York Soc*, xxxv, pp. 86, 89, 92, 93, 342, xxxvi, pp. 435-36, 839, 844, 851; J.Strype, *Annals of the Reformation etc.* (Oxford, 1824) 1, i, p. 310; *Ecclesiastical Memorials etc.* (Oxford, 1822), II, i, p. 370, III, i, pp. 224, 413, 443, III, ii, p. 63; *Life and Acts of Matthew Parker* (Oxford, 1821), i, p. 450; *Life and Acts of Edmund Grindal* (Oxford, 1821), p. 145; J. W. Martin, *Religious Radicals in Tudor England* (London, 1989), passim; C. Burrage, *The early English Dissenters 1550-1641,* 2 vols, (Cambridge, 1912), J. Foxe, *Acts and Monuments etc.*, (London, 1563), pp. 1700a, 1700b; J. Foxe, *Acts and Monuments etc.*, ed. Rev. J. Pratt, 4th edn, (London, 1577) viii, app vii; J.Foxe, *Acts and Monuments etc*., ed. G. Seeley, *The church historians of England,* (1868), III, i, p. 384; ii, p. 790, app vi; A. Townsend ed., 'The writings of John Bradford etc.', *Parker Soc.* (Cambridge, 1853), ii, pp. 133, 194, 215; A. G. Dickens, *Reformation*

Holinshed's *Chronicles of England, Scotland and Ireland* is hereafter called simply the *Chronicles.* The *Chronicles* were the brain-child of the printer and publisher Reginald Wolfe, who employed William Harrison and Raphael Holinshed to carry it out. When Wolfe died in 1573, Stow purchased many of his books. The first edition of the *Chronicles* was published in 1577, when, in M. Wine's words, Holinshed somewhat apologetically interrupted the survey of King Edward VI's reign to give an account of the murder, saying 'although otherwise it may seeme to be but a private matter and therefore as it were impertinent to this historie.' What he added is not so often quoted, 'I have thought good to set it foorth somewhat at large, having the instructions delivered to me by them, that have used some diligence to gather the true understanding of the circumstances.' He gave an account of the Arden murder, which was very similar to Stow, but lacked the interest in sources and sense of change over time that there had been there. I think it likely that Holinshed used Stow's compilation for his own version and both edited and sanitized it for justifiable fear of political consequences. As R. Bradshaw has suggested in Appendix 21 the whole play was probably performed to ridicule Roger North and the Earl of Leicester. When Holinshed died in 1580, John Stow was one of a group of men who contributed to the second edition. Another was Francis Thynne. The man usually given the credit as editor is John Hooker alias Vowell, but S. Booth thinks that the man who did the most work was Abraham Fleming, who went through the text and arranged headings and titles and so on. The continuation or volume III was entitled *The Chronicles of England, from the yeare of our Lord 1576, where Raphaell Holinshed left, supplied and continued to this present yeare 1586; by John Stow and others.* S. Booth doubts whether his contribution was that great, but comments that 'Stowe's chronicles, which he regularly amended, continued, re-issued and re-titled from 1565 to 1604, used (and were used in) every other chronicle published during the period. He was a major source for Holinshed, particularly for recent history, and for his later editions he drew on Holinshed.'

Their work was heavily censored by the Privy Council, so that they had to be extremely careful what they wrote about. Wine points out that 'the Arden narrative is precisely the same in both the first and the second editions except for 'the appearance of marginal glosses not to be found in the earlier edition of 1577, which are revealing for the moral stress that they place on passages where Holinshed's tone is essentially dispassionate and for the way that they highlight dramatic possibilities inherent in the narrative.' Although I cannot prove it, it seems to me likely that it was either John Stow or Abraham Fleming who added the marginal glosses in the second edition.

What is also worthy of comment is that in the 1587 edition, just before the account of the murder, there is a passage that may be relevant, following a symbol that is not in the 1577 edition.. In the 1577 edition, the account of the murder follows the report of the reconciliation of the Duke of Somerset and the Earl of Warwick, marked by the marriage of Seymour's daughter to Warwick's eldest son on 3 June 1550. After the account of the murder, there is a report of a meeting of Parliament from 23 January until 15 April 1552.

In the 1587 edition there are details of the appointment of an additional alderman in Southwark, where the City of London took over control in April 1550, the execution of three ring-leaders of a rebellion in Kent on 14 May following and the death on 30 July 1550 of Thomas, Lord Wriothesley, Earl of Southampton, the grandfather of Shakespeare's patron.

Studies (London, 1982), pp. 76, 435, 516, 551-52, A. G. Dickens, *The English Reformation*, 2nd edn (London, 1989), pp. 264-66, 335; J.Bruce and T. Perowne, 'Correspondence of Matthew Parker', *Parker Soc.*, (Cambridge, 1853), p. 278; Bentham, DNB; Broke, Commons 1509-58, i, pp. 506-7; E. Jacob, *The History of Faversham* (1774, Fav. Soc., 1974), p. 122; R. W. Dixon, *History of the Church of England*, 6 vols (Oxford, 1878-1902), iii, pp. 207-12.

Finally, there is a long and fulsome paragraph about Sir Andrew Judd, who founded Tonbridge School in 1553. This may have been included by Francis Thynne, who had been educated at Tonbridge and was one of the editors of the 1587 edition. Nevertheless, what is striking to us is that Judd was a close kinsman of the Ardens, because his first wife, Mary, was Edward Mirfyn's sister.

He was the son of John and Margaret Judd of Tonbridge. He went up to London, where he joined the Skinners' Company, to which the Mirfyns also belonged. He made a fortune trading in skins and furs and was a founder member of the Muscovy Company. He travelled to Russia, Spain and the Guinea coast in Africa. The geographer, Richard Hakluyt, described how Judd kept an elephant's head in his house to remind him of his travels. He was sheriff of London in 1544 and Master of the Skinners' Company in 1550-51. He was Lord Mayor in the same year and was, indeed, knighted on the very day of the murder. This is all crucial to our story, because he must at the very least have been kept well informed by the sheriffs about the hanging of Morsby and his sister, Cicely Ponder, at Smithfield. To go further, perhaps it was because he was Lord Mayor and an ally that the Privy Council chose to have them punished there. Perhaps not, but there is a whiff of the establishment closing ranks. And there is still the mystery of why the 1587 editors chose to mention him at that juncture.[39]

He died on 4 September 1558 and was buried in St. Helen's Bishopgate. His only daughter and heiress, Alice, married Thomas Smythe of Westenhanger, Kent, better known as Mr.Customer Smythe.[40]

It is not pertinent to this study, but possible links between the publisher, Reginald Wolfe, the editor, John Hooker alias Vowell, John Ponet, Bishop of Winchester, who figures later, and Robert Cole might repay further investigation. Wolfe was a native of Strasburg and a devoted Protestant, who set up a printing press in St. Paul's Churchyard, where one of the botched attempts on Thomas Arden's life was made. He was closely related to a printer called John Wolfe of Zurich, who was the host of many English Protestant refugees during Mary's reign. Hooker alias Vowell visited Strasburg on his travels, where he stayed with Peter Martyr. Ponet eventually found his way to Peter Martyr at Strasburg, where he died in August 1556. Finally, Cole went overseas to some of the Protestants in exile and left a book by Peter Martyr on the Romans in English to a friend in his will in 1577. And we now have the proximity of Edward White selling books at the Little North Door of St. Paul's.

The accepted theory is that, along came the anonymous playwright and read the story of the murder either in the first or the second edition of Holinshed. He then wrote 'Arden of Faversham', which was published in 1592. Certainly once that stage had been reached, fame for the murder was assured.

It should be stressed, as Wine points out, that neither Thomas Arden nor Alice Arden in the play resembles his or her counterpart in Holinshed. For the playwright's own purposes and with his great understanding of human nature, the Arden of the play 'represents an entirely different conception of the character' and Alice is 'no longer totally and unequivocally an evil woman.'[41]

---

[39] Mr. Richard Bradshaw, who very generously handed over his notes to me to be incorporated into my text, brought the passage here discussed to my notice.

[40] S. Rivington, *The history of Tonbridge School,* 2nd ed., (London,1898), pp. 7-19, 50,116; Rev. A. B. Beavan, *The Aldermen of the City of London,* (London, 1913), I, pp. 57, 156, II pp. lv, 30; Francis Thynne, D.N.B.; Smythe, Commons 1558-1603, III, pp. 405-406; J. Stow, *The Annales of England etc.,*(London, 1592), pp. 1015-18; A. F. Pollard, *The political history of England 1547-1603*, (London, 1910; Kraus Reprint, New York,1969), VI, pp. 46-47, 53 55-58.

[41] BL, Harl. MSS 542 fols.34-37b; DNB; *The Tragedy of Master Arden of Faversham*, ed. M. L. Wine, The Revels Plays (London, 1973) pp. xl, lxix, lxxiii, 148.

Nevertheless, the playwright weaved his magic spell and we are all still bewitched. Following Holinshed, the anonymous playwright, to great dramatic effect, concentrated only on Thomas Arden, his household and his enemies until the mayor and his watch appeared at the end. This distorts his standing in the town in real life. Clark and Hosking have estimated that there were, in 1563, only twelve years later, 1510 people in that small town, all busy leading their own lives.[42] In Archbishop Parker's visitation, returned by his official Vincent Denne on 1 December 1569, there were 278 houses and 867 communicants in the parish of Faversham.[43] According to Clark the multiplier should be 5.75, making 1598 people. We know from their wills that there were local gentry, MPs, town officers, seamen, ship-owners, corn merchants, tanners, maltsters, wax chandlers,barbers, pewterers, chandlers and so on.[44]

You would also think from the play that Thomas Arden ruled the roost, but I want to suggest that his influence came only from being the Customer and a servant of Sir Thomas Cheyne. In fact, he was neither lord of the manor nor lord of the hundred of Faversham, as the abbot had been. A hundred was an administrative division of a shire and covered a wider area than a manor. The Crown retained both these lordships until they were sold to Sir Dudley Digges of Chilham Castle, Kent, in 1630.[45]

Three things follow from this. The first is that Arden did not have the crucial manorial or feudal bond with his tenants that has been assumed. As Youings points out, 'the manor was still in 1500 and for a long time to come the key to, and the essential unit of, landownership.' Arden was just one among a number of landowners in Faversham, albeit a wealthy one. Secondly, a rental of 1532 shows that Faversham Abbey had about 300 houses in the town of which Arden acquired only 28. Lastly, the Crown must have had far more influence in Faversham than has been allowed for. The royal steward must have been at least as powerful and respected a figure there as Thomas Arden, who indeed acted merely as receiver of rents for the Crown in 1547-49.

The royal steward was William Roper, who had previously acted as the Abbey's high steward of all their lands in Kent, as his father and his grandfather had done before him. His grandfather was Sir John Fineux of Faversham and Herne in Kent, who became chief justice of the King's Bench. He is said to have been steward of 129 manors at once. When he died in 1527, he was buried in the nave of Canterbury Cathedral and left property to Faversham Abbey. His elder daughter, Jane, married John Roper, of St. Dunstan's Canterbury, who long held the office of prothonotary or clerk of the pleas of the court of King's Bench.

William Roper was their son, and he in turn married Margaret, the devoted daughter of Sir Thomas More. It is as More's 'son Roper' and hagiographer that he is remembered. He was M.P. for Bramber in 1529, Rochester in 1545 and 1547, Winchelsea in 1553, with the help of Sir Thomas Cheyne, Rochester in 1554 and Canterbury in 1555 and 1558. In 1543, like Sir Thomas Moyle and Sir Reginald Scott, he was involved in the Prebendaries' Plot against Cranmer, together with a number of men in Sir Thomas More's circle. He obviously had many interests outside Faversham, but he had a number of conservative and catholic allies in the neighbourhood. His brother, Christopher, was also an M.P. He followed his father as prothonotary of the King's Bench, an office which he in turned passed on to his son, Thomas. At a common council meeting in Faversham in 1546 it was agreed that Roper should receive a fee of £6-0-0 a year as

---

42 *Population estimates of English small towns 1550-1851*, Centre for Urban History, University of Leicester, Working paper no. 5, 1993, v, p. 77; A. Percival reckons from the rental of 1532 that the figure would be a bit higher.

43 Canterbury Cathedral Archives, DCb/Z.3.10 (2).

44 CKS: For listing of most occupations in 1616 see FA/GI/1.

45 CCA, Lit MSS B5; PRO, SC6/Ministers Accounts/Ed VI/723; LR6/113/1 m. 1v; Jacob, p. 36; J.Youings, *Sixteenth Century England* (London, 1984), p. 47.

William Roper (1495/6 - 1578) 50.69.1

Margaret Roper (1508 - 1544) 50.69.2

Miniatures painted about 1538 by Hans Holbein, the younger (1497 - 1578). Both these German miniatures are painted with watercolour on paper and have a height of 1¾ inches (4.4cm). William Roper (1495/6 - 1578) of St Dunstan's, Canterbury, Eltham, Kent, and Chelsea, Middlesex, was high steward of Faversham Abbey's lands in Kent from 1519 until 1538, and royal steward of the manor and hundred of Faversham thereafter until his death in 1578. His wife, Margaret (died 1544) was the daughter of Sir Thomas More of London and Chelsea.

steward of the King's Court of the town of Faversham. In 1571 it was decided that Humphrey Kybbett would become royal steward with the same fee of £6-0-0 a year on the death of William Roper, which happened in 1578.[46]

Roper's old friend and associate, a gentleman called John Webbe of London and Faversham, one of the More circle, seems to have acted as under-steward for a time and was sometimes referred to as steward. He was auditor there 1540-44, jurat in 1555 and mayor in 1556 until his death. He was granted his freedom in 1541. He was also linked with another M.P., Cyriak Petyt, of whom more later. He himself owed his return for Dover in 1553 and April and November 1554 to Sir Thomas Cheyne .An entry in the Dover accounts for July 1554 of the payment to Webbe of 40^s 'in part payment of his parliament wages which he received of the town of Faversham', suggests that the port, having paid Webbe and Beverley a total of £13 for their attendance in the previous autumn, persuaded Faversham to meet some of the costs in the spring of 1554. In his will, he also provided for commemorative masses at Faversham, with gifts to the poor.[47]

I suspect that if Thomas Arden had not been so spectacularly murdered, and if a play, thought possibly to be by Shakespeare, had not been written about the crime, he would long ago have been forgotten. I also doubt whether he himself was important enough in the scheme of things for any conspiracy theory about his murder to hold water. I cannot prove it but I suggest that, like many men before and since, he was murdered by his wife and her accomplices simply because he had made his will two months earlier. It is also worth pointing out at this stage that the Ardens lost virtually all connection with the town shortly after the death of their daughter, Margaret, in November 1574, so that the family were only involved there for a little over thirty years and left the town not with a bang but with a whimper.

I realise that it is always difficult to prove that a man was less important than has hitherto been assumed without appearing waspish. It would be much more agreeable to build him up as a great man. I also think that the situation in the town with the dissolution of the Abbey and the grant of a new town charter was complex and involved many other people besides Arden, so I have tried to describe some of them, but this, in turn, has involved detailed genealogy, which some may find wearisome. I felt that this was essential to give a more balanced view of Arden himself and of what was going on in the town. I think that the contribution of his contemporaries has so far been undervalued and that the concentration on one man has distorted the picture. As I said before, he should be seen in his setting. Some of the conclusions are bound to be controversial. To speed up any debate, I have provided transcripts of all the unpublished material about Thomas Arden.

As I hope to show, there are a remarkable number of sources available for the period. First there are the accounts of the murder in the wardmote book, Stow and Holinshed, which I will later consider in detail.[48] Then, as background material, Faversham has one of the most comprehensive collections of records of any town in Kent for the sixteenth century. Finally, the archives for the diocese of Canterbury possibly contain the most complete collection of probate records of any English diocese.

---

46 CKS, Fa/AC2/1 fol. 14v; PRO, E315/100 fol. 47v; Favward fol. 43; Fineux, DNB.; Roper, Commons 1509-58, iii, pp. 215-17.

47 Favward, fol. 34v; Commons 1509-58, iii pp. 564-65

48 See Chapter 10.

Chapter 1
The early years

Mr. Burton said that Arden was born in 1485-86 but it has recently come to light that, in a deposition in a court case in 1548, Arden himself said that he was then 40 years old, which means that he was born in about 1508.[49] This is important because it must surely alter our perception of him, even in the play. It means that he was only 43 years old when he was murdered, not 65-66 as he is usually depicted. In that period it is the difference between a man in his prime and a man in his declining years.

Where he was born has till now been something of a mystery. In a year-long search a daunting number of leads have been followed up. He was called Arden, Arderne or Ardern, but, as Somerset Herald confirms, surnames were reasonably fluid until about 1800, as we can see in the variations on the name of Shakespeare. It is not therefore appropriate to speak of one version rather than another as the proper one in the sixteenth century. Arden was quite a common surname and there were men called Thomas Arden all over the country. For example, there were Ardens at Aldford, Alvanley and Harden in Cheshire.[50] There was a contemporary of the same name who was a J. P. in Warwickshire [51]and another who was a citizen and clothmaker in London.[52] A third made his will in Deptford in 1557.·[53] Perhaps the most tantalizing was the fourth Thomas Arden, who lived in the parish of St. Mildred's in Canterbury with his wife, Anne, and two sons, John and Arthur. This is apparent in a chancery case concerning a mortgage in 1574.[54] This Thomas Arden died in 1568 and his wife Anne in 1574.[55] Interestingly enough, with thoughts of Shakespeare, this gentleman left all his lands in Warwickshire to his sons and his lands in Canterbury to his wife for life and then to his sons. Five daughters were mentioned. As Thomas Arden of Faversham also had property in Canterbury, in St. Paul's parish, it is just possible that this may account for Canon Telfer's story that Arden married twice, for which no evidence has yet been found.[56]

Again, stemming from Mr. Burton and Edward Crow, there has been a tradition that Arden came from 'the Arden family near Wye'. Said quickly, this sounds like a well-established family, but, although a thorough search has been made of surviving records, which include the *Old Book of Wye*, manorial and parish records, wills and visitations, only one reference to a man called Arden has been found in the area.[57] This is in that same consistory court register in which Arden gave his age as 40. In a totally different case a few folios further on concerning Myllis versus Comber on 29 January 1549, Nicholas Arden of Wye aged 23 years or thereabouts was a witness and gave a deposition concerning events in Wye.[58] Perhaps the two men were related, perhaps not.

---

49 See APPENDIX 4; CCA, Consistory Court, deposition register, DCb/X.10.3 fol. 83; Orlin, p. 21.

50 British Library, Harleian MSS. 6164, fol. 45; G. Ormerod, *The history of the county palatine and city of Chester etc.* 2nd edn., revised by Thomas Helsby, 3 vols. (1882), ii, pp. 85-86.

51 BL, Additional MSS. 5753, fols. 39, 220; LP xiv, part 2, no 236.

52 *Index to testamentary records in the Commissary Court* ed. M. Fitch, Historical Manuscripts Commission's joint publication no. 13, vol. ii, 1480-1570 (London, Her Majesty's Stationery Office, 1974).

53 CKS, Consistory Court of Rochester; Arderne, DRb/PW 5/131, DRb/PWr 16/35.

54 See APPENDIX 5; PRO, C2/Elizabeth 1/A6/31.

55 CKS, Arden, Archdeaconry Court, PRC 17/40/237, PRC 3/19/108 and 119.

56 BL, Harl. Ch. 58 H18; Telfer, Orphans, p. 195; K. Gravett, 'The Hall, Ivy Lane,' *The parish of St. Martin and St. Paul* ed. Margaret Sparks (Canterbury, 1980), passim.

57 Bodleian Library, Oxford, MS Top Kent e 4; CKS, Old book of Wye (microfilm); Bullen, p. xii; G. E. Hubbard, *The Old Book of Wye* (Derby, 1950); H. Muhlfeld, *A survey of the manor of Wye* (New York, 1933); C. S. Orwin and S. Williams, *A history of Wye church and Wye college*, (Ashford, Kent, 1913).

58 See APPENDIX 4; CCA, Consistory Court deposition register, DCb/X.10.3 fol. 96.

Perhaps someone in the eighteenth century saw that register in Canterbury and jumped to conclusions. More evidence may yet come to light, but for the moment the case rests there.

The connection that people would like to make is with Shakespeare's mother, Mary Arden of Wilmcote, or, failing that, with the Ardens of Park Hall in Warwickshire, even though these two families have not yet themselves been positively linked. Immediately after Edward Crow had spoken of Wye, he said that the arms of Arden were *ermine, a fess chequy or and azure*. These are the arms of the Ardens of Park Hall. Walter Arden died in 1502 His second son, Thomas, became bailiff of the castle and manor of Codnor, Derbyshire. Walter's eldest son, John, died in 1526, leaving a son and heir, Thomas, who was probably the J.P. whom I mentioned earlier. He died in 1563, and his fourth son, Thomas, was a student at law and died without issue, but he was probably too young to be our man. So, there were at least three Thomas Ardens in that area of Warwickshire in the period, but unfortunately no link has been established with any of them.[59]

All in all, it always seemed to me sensible to look very carefully at the story that Thomas Arden came from Norwich, which was set out in the Harleian manuscript in the British Museum which was found among the papers of John Stow. We can at least be certain that it was talking about the right man. Its heading was *'The history of a moste horrible murder commytyd at Fevershame in Kente'*. The following story was not included in either of Holinshed's printed versions of the murder.[60]

> 'There dwelt at Feversham in the county of Kent, a gentleman callyd Mastar Arden, a tall gentleman, and of a comly personage. This Ardene had a mothar dwellynge in Norwiche who went a beggynge, but he assayde all meanes posseble to kepe hir from it, which wowld not be. Notwithestondynge, he gave a stipend delyvered to Mastar Aldriche to hir use, and when Mastar Aldriche was Maior of Norwiche she was robbyd, and a princypall chest browght out into hir backsyde and certeyne lynnyn that was in it lefte scateryd abrode to the vallew of forty or fyfty shillyngs. This robery beinge commyttyd in the nyght, she, beynge deaf, hard it not. Next day, when it was knowne that she was robbed, the maior with others came to hir howse, and serchinge they found Lx^{li} (£60-0-0) lyeinge in sondry places tyed up in severall litle clowtes, not above ten grotes (40 pence) in one clowte. Than she was restreyned from her beggynge, and willed to chuse who shuld with hir porcion kepe hir durynge hir lyfe, and to have for his labour that whiche remayned of the £60-0-0 unspent at hir deathe. And so it was done. Notwithstandiynge, she nevar enjoyed after she was restreynyd from hir begginge and dyed within half a yere aftar, but many yeres aftar the deathe of hir sonne, whereof we have here to speake'.

This story seemed to be impossible when it was thought that Arden was born in 1485 or 1486, but the picture has changed now that we know that he was born in 1508, twenty three years later. Supposing that his mother was 20 years old when he was born, she would have been 63 when he was murdered and 70 and 82 respectively when John Aldrich was mayor of Norwich in 1558 and 1570 and came to her assistance 'many years after the death of her son.' Lawrence Stone

[59] Bodleian, MS Top Kent e 4 Vis. Warwickshire 1619, *Harl. Soc.* (1877), xii, p. 72; M. Eccles, *Shakespeare in Warwickshire* (Wisconsin, 1961), passim; *The Victoria History of the Counties of England, Warwickshire,* iv, pp. 45, 62-3, v, p. 188.

[60] See APPENDIX 3: BL, Harl. MSS 542, fols. 34-37b.

suggests that daughters married on the average at about 20 in the late sixteenth century. Peter Laslett puts it at 24, which would make her even older.

John Aldrich was a well-known figure in Norwich. He was the son of Thomas Aldrich, who had been mayor of Norwich in 1507. He was a mercer or grocer, who traded in wool and yarn. He became sheriff in 1551, mayor in 1557-58 and 1570-71 and member of parliament for Norwich in 1555 and 1572. What is riveting for us in view of his help for Arden's mother is his interest in poor law reform; his committees in his second parliament included one on a poor law bill modelled on the famous Norwich scheme, which he as mayor had supervised and which was widely copied. He died in 1582.[61]

So, Aldrich represented in parliament not some minor borough, but what was then the most important town in England after London. He must have been well-known, particularly for his interest in poor law reform. Surely, while in London as an M.P. in 1572, he could have told the tale of Arden's mother to his friends, who in turn told it to Stow ?

Thinking this over, it seemed to me more and more likely that Arden did indeed come from Norwich. I discovered that there was not a family of that name amongst the freemen of the city, nor anyone who was involved in city life.[62] There had, however, been people of that name living in Norwich much earlier on, and John Arden in nearby Swannington made his will in 1509.[63] In January 1993 I went to Norwich to see if I could find any mention in the city of the name Arden in the period. I therefore used the corporation records before the terrible fire at Norfolk Record Office as a telephone directory. On the last afternoon I was rewarded with an entry in the mayor's court book in 1523; 'One Arden sold a messuage in the city of Norwich to Nicholas Langham'.[64]

I planned to return in May to complete the task Two weeks before, I was idly glancing at John Pound's *Poverty and Vagrancy in Tudor England* when I suddenly noticed the following entry from the Norwich mayor's court books, which was given as an example of how much a beggar could earn;[65]

> Mayor's court book 1562-69, folio 29; 12 September 1562
>
> *Margin:* Mother Arden in all £44-3-6.
>
> This daye was brought into the Courte certeyne money of one Mother Arden who used dely to go a beggyng the parcelles wherof ensueth viz in olde grotes £29-13-4 too olde Angells in Slyppes £6-13-6 more in Slyppes £3-3-0 and in new mony £3-13-7.[66] And there was taken owte and delyvered to mother Arden 6^{s} 8^{d} of the foresayde Summe.

---

61 P. Hasler, *The House of Commons 1558-1603*, The History of Parliament, 3 vols. (London, 1981), I, p. 333; B Cozens Hardy and E. Kent, *The mayors of Norwich 1403-1835* (Norwich, 1938), pp. 56-57; L. Stone, *The family, sex and marriage in England 1500-1800* (London, 1977), p. 46. P. Laslett, *The World we have lost,* (London 1971), p. 85: Youings, p. 267.

62 P. Millican, *The Register of the freemen of Norwich* (Norwich, 1934), passim.

63 Norfolk Record Office, Consistory Court, 213 Spyltimber.

64 NRO, mayor's court book 1510-32; *Norfolk Rec. Soc.* (1986), p. lii; *Calendar of the freemen of Norwich 1317-1603*, eds J. L. Estrange & W. Rye, (London, 1883) xv i, part 1,1943; *The records of the city of Norwich,* eds. Rev. W. Hudson & J. C. Tingey, 2 vols., (Norwich, 1909-11).

65 J. Pound *Poverty and Vagrancy in Tudor England* (London, 1975), p.100.

66 *O.E.D.*, grotes = groats (4^{d}), slyppes = slips or counterfeit coins, angelles = angels or old English gold coins worth 10^{s} in Edward VI's reign.

The mayor's court dealt with the daily business of the Assembly and acted as a magistrates court in criminal jurisdiction. This entry had so much in common with the story in Stow that I had no doubt that it referred to the same person. It was at a later date than I had anticipated, because I had thought that the incident would have happened in 1558, when Aldrich was first mayor.

I went up to Norwich again and continued working through the mayor's court book. The next entry of note was;

> Mayor's court book 1562-69, folio *33;* 27 September 1563
>
> *Margin*: Mother Arden's mony and £4-0-0 for Musred put into the Tresory.
>
> Memorandum that on Mondaye the 27th daye of September Anno 1563 there was delyvered in to the Treasory by Mr William Farrour Mayor in the presens of Mr William Myngay Augusten Steward and others Souche mony as was Receyved of one Mother Arden and also £4-0-0 that was receyved of the sayde Mr. Myngaye for Musred's childerne.

The case of Musred's children was obviously quite separate. They were possibly the children of the tachemaker,[67] Henry Musred, who became a freeman on 31 May 1549. In any case, nothing more is heard of them. William Mingay was mayor in 1561 and William Ferrour in 1562 and 1575.

Then came the most important entry;

> Mayor's court book 1562-69, folio 66r; 16 January 1563
>
> *Margin:*£3-6-8 payed to Katheryne Davy the daughter of Margery Arden.
>
> Court held on Saturday 16 January Elizabeth 5 (1563), William Farrour, mayor, William Myngay, Augustine Steward, Henry Bacon, Richard Fletcher, Robert Michell. [68]
>
> This daye Katheryne Davy the wyfe of John Davy of Faversham in the Countie of Kent Cam into the Courte and gave thanks to all the howse for Souche order as was taken for one Margery Arden of Norwich her mother. And yt ys further to be understande that the sayde Katheryne have Receyved the Summe of £3-6-8 in the presens of the hole Courte as in parte of payment of £10-0-0 that Thomas Hobarde[69] stondith bounde to paye at souche tyme as she the sayde Katheryne should next Repayer and com to Norwich.

Henry Bacon was mayor in 1557 and 1566, Richard Fletcher in 1559 and Robert Michell was constable in 1561.

---

67 *O.E.D.* tache: A contrivance for fastening two parts together; a fibula, a clasp, a buckle, a hook and eye, or the like; a hook for hanging anything on..

68 'An index to Norwich city officers 1483-1835', ed. T. Hawes, *Norfolk Rec. Soc.* (1986), p. lii.

69 ~~he~~ scored through.

Mother Arden
In all £44.3.6

This daye was brought into the Courte certeyne money of one Mother Arden whoe [illegible] to ye a [illegible] [illegible] [illegible] in other partes [illegible] for [illegible] Augustine [illegible] more in [illegible] And that was taken oute and delyvered to mother Arden [illegible] aforsayde Anno

Mother Ardens money and in [illegible] put into the Treasory

Md that on Mondaye the xxvij daye of September Anno 1563 there was delyvered into the Treasorye by Mr William Ferrour mayer in the presens of Mr William Mingaye Augustine Steward & others Soume money as was receyved of one Mother Arden and also in the [illegible] that was [illegible] of the seyde Mr Mingaye for [illegible] children

folio 29 and 33 taken from Norwich Mayor's Book

Katherine Davy must surely have been Arden's sister. The mention of Faversham in the mayor's court book of Norwich must equally surely clinch the matter when coupled with a reference to an old lady who begs. It was already known that Arden had a sister, who was still alive when he made his will. He left certain lands first to his wife and then to his daughter. If his daughter died without issue then 'I will the premises do descend to my sister and to her heirs'. He did not then mention her name. In spite of a painstaking search of parish registers and wills, it has proved difficult to track down John Davy of Faversham or his wife, Katherine. There was a John Davy who was mayor in 1528 and died in 1544, whose son, Thomas, was a servant of Sir Anthony St. Leger, but I can find no link there with Katherine's husband or Arden. Equally, I have tried without success to make a connection with Richard Davy, mayor of Norwich in 1551 and 1563. All we have are some references in the Faversham wardmote book to a blacksmith called John Davy, who was presenter for Preston Street in 1555-56. He would be the man who reported offences there. When the sluice was built at the quay in 1559-60, he was paid £8-00 for 640 pounds of iron and workmanship there at 3^d^ the pound.[70]

Thomas Hubbard was probably the man who had a butcher's stall in that year. There was a John Hubbard who died in Norwich in 1536, a Thomas Hubbard of Great Ellingham in Norfolk who died in 1573 and another of the same name who died in 1586.[71]

There followed;

> Mayor's court book folio 621; Wednesday, 11 August Elizabeth 10 (1568)
>
> *Margin:* Thomas Herne Receyved £3-6-8 of Mother Arden's goods.
>
> Court held on Wednesday 11th August Elizabeth 10 (1568) before Thomas Parker Mayor, Richard Davy, Richard Fletcher, John Aldriche, Justices. [72]
>
> Whereas Thomas Herne one of the grandechilderne of Arden late of the Cittie of Norwich wedow deceased had geven hym of the goods of the sayde Arden his graundemother the Summe of £3-6-8 to be payed hym of good and Lawfull mony of Inglande This daye the sayde Thomas Herne cam into this Courte before Master Mayor and other Justices and Aldermen and confessyd and acknowledgyd hym Selfe to be fully Satisfyed contented payed and therof dothe discharge the mayor shreves cittizens and commynaltie and ther Successors by thes present for ever. In Witnes wherof the sayde Thomas have put his hande.[73]

---

70 CKS, Faversham wardmote book, Fa/AC1, fols. 67v, 68, 80v; Arch, PRC17/23 fol. 173.

71 NRO Consistory Court, 203 Huberde, 204 Godsalve, 125 Fairechilde, 536 Jarnigo; chamberlains' accounts 1551-67, fol. 264; CKS, PRC17/23/173.

72 'An index to Norwich city officers 1453-1835', ed. T. Hawes, *Norfolk Rec. Soc.* (1986), lii.

73 NRO, mayor's court book 1562-69, fols. 29, 33, 66v, 621.

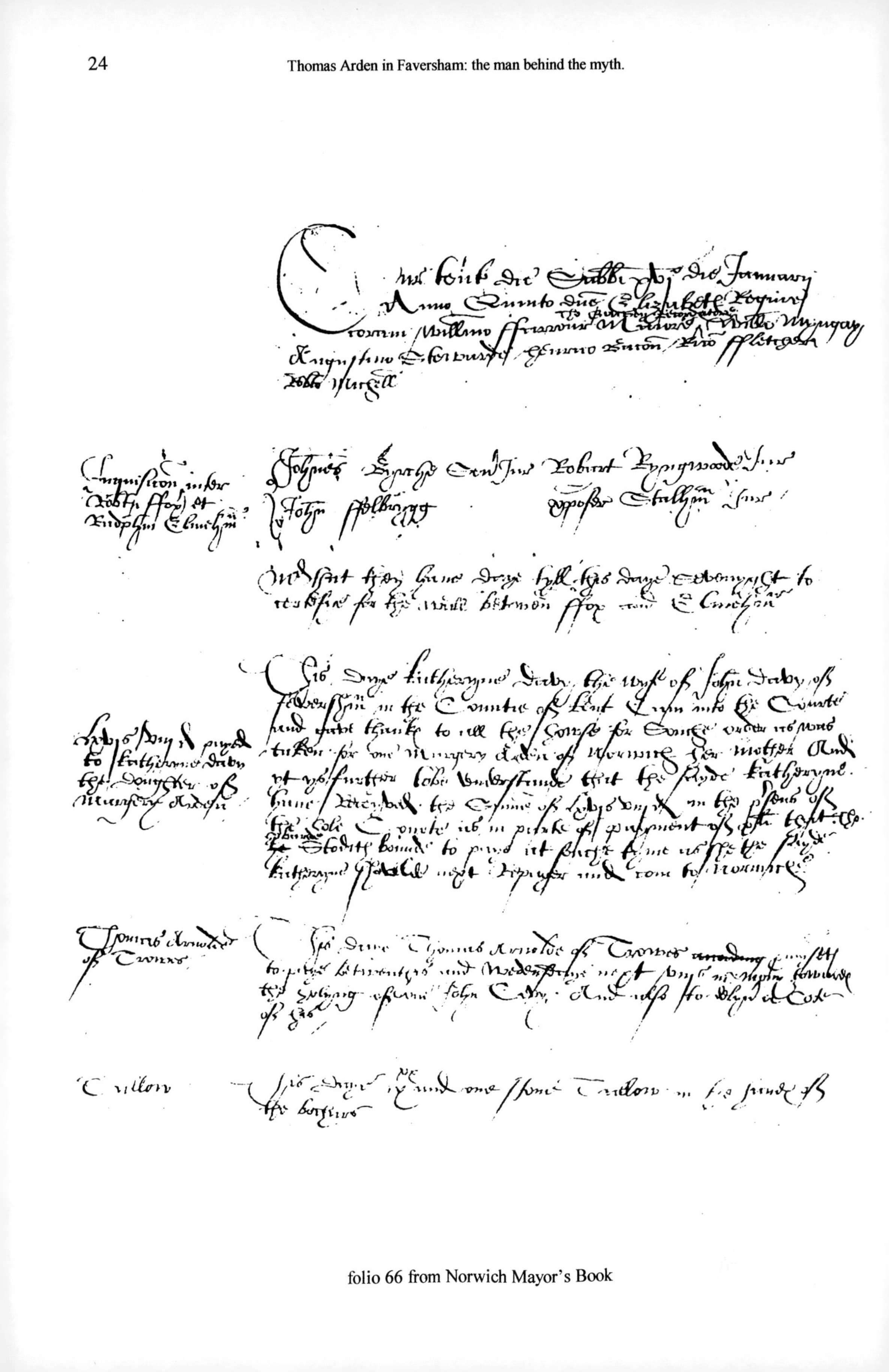

folio 66 from Norwich Mayor's Book

Thomas Parker was a brother of Matthew Parker, Archbishop of Canterbury. He was M.P. for Norwich in 1563 and mayor in 1568. Richard Davy was mayor in 1551 and 1563.[74]

Margery Arden, otherwise known as Mother Arden, received extraordinarily lenient treatment from the Norwich magistrates for begging, as these passages show and as Katherine Davy acknowledged. She may have been up to the same tricks some years earlier;

> Mayor's court book 1549-55 folio 237: 17 April Edward VI Septimo (1553)
>
> *Margin:* Mrs.Arden: clerke.
>
> Style of Wramplingham, myller, had a tolledisshe which the clerke of the market of the kinges household toke from him and lefte it here for that it was marked with the seall of the cittie.[75]

As her name is mentioned, she had possibly begged or stolen it from someone in the city and passed it on or sold it to the miller who was caught. Who knows?

Today she might be treated as a psychiatric case, because she was a woman with a home of her own who had no need to beg. She probably had more fun then than now, with the magistrates confiscating most of her ill-gotten gains, but leaving her a little something. Equally, though, she cannot be thought of as an ordinary beggar, because it must have been well known to most people in the town that she received special treatment. The citizens must surely have thought of her as a character to be humoured.

The whole episode seems at this distance to do great credit to everyone concerned. This includes Thomas Arden himself, who, according to Stow, 'assayde all meanes possible to kepe hir from it, which would not be, Not withestondynge, he have a stipend delyvered to Master Aldriche to hir use ...' It is just worth wondering in passing what effect having such a mother must have had on him, but that is perhaps the preserve of the psychoanalyst.

Why was she treated in this special way? The most likely explanation is that she was well-connected to some family that was part of the ruling élite in Norwich. As I have explained, the Ardens were not a well-known family in the town. Note in passing that her name was there spelt 'Arden'. She had a grandson called Thomas Herne, so she might have been a Herne by birth or by an earlier marriage or had another daughter married to a Herne. Hernes were indeed members of the ruling élite, but, despite an intensive investigation, a link between the Ardens and the Hernes has not yet been established apart from that given in the court book.

Margery Arden's grand-son, Thomas Herne, accepted the same sum as his aunt, Katherine Davy, had accepted five years earlier. Whether this was just a coincidence or whether it also came from Thomas Hubbard is not clear. There was a Thomas Herne who was the son of Clement Herne, who was mayor of Norwich in 1595, and, dying the following year, was buried in Norwich leaving a lot of property there. Thomas was mayor in 1604, 1609, and 1616 when he was knighted. He was a member of parliament three times between 1614 and 1625. He moved out of Norwich to Haveringland, where he died and was buried in 1637.[76] Unfortunately, this

---

[74] B. Cozens Hardy and E. A. Kent, *The mayors of Norwich 1403-1835* (Norwich, 1938), p. 59; Commons 1558-1603, iii, p. 174; 'An index to Norwich city officers 1453-1835', *Norfolk Rec. Soc.* (1986), lii, pp. 49, 52.

[75] *O.E.D.* Toll-dish:A dish or bowl of stated dimensions for measuring the toll of grain at a mill.

[76] NRO Consistory Court; Hurne 134, Goldingham 58, Fairechilde 490, Moyse alias Spicer 161, Skyppen, Malby, Prerogative Court of Canterbury F11 Welles, 85v; Vis. Norfolk 1664, *Norfolk Rec. Soc.* (1934), iv, pp. 100-01; W. Rye, *Norfolk Families* (Norwich, 1913), p. 389; 'An index to Norwich city officers 1453-1835' ed. T. Hawes,

Thomas was probably too young in 1568. His mother was Margaret, daughter of John Wise. He was the eldest son of the second marriage, but his mother's first husband, Thomas Malby, died only in 1558, so Thomas can hardly have been more than eight or nine years old in 1568. His grandfather was a husbandman of Drayton in Norfolk, who died in 1559. When his widow, Maud, died in 1573, she left her grandson Thomas 10 shillings when he reached the age of 18, which confirms that he cannot have been born before 1555. It seems unlikely that such a young child would appear before the court. There was, however, another family called Herne in Norwich, for Stephen Herne, who does not seem to have been related to the first family, died in Norwich in 1582. He had a son, Thomas, but he was then under 24 years old, so that he must have been born after 1558. This means that he, too, would only have been about ten years old, at the most, in 1568. Again, whether such a young boy would have appeared before the court is doubtful.

Finally, what comes to mind on thinking over the whole saga is the irony that Stow was wrong in saying that John Aldrich was mayor in the period shortly before Margery Arden's death, which is where my hunt began. She was presumably alive on 16 January 1563, when Katherine Davy appeared before the court, but dead by Thomas Herne's appearance on 11 August 1568. Aldrich was not mayor during that period, but only in 1557-58 and 1570-71. He was, of course, active in city politics, and was present in 1568 when Thomas Herne appeared. My weary suggestion is that this makes it all the more likely that it was John Aldrich who told the story in London, so that, when it was passed on, it was assumed that he was the central figure, because people knew that he had been mayor.

So, on the first count, Thomas Arden was not a gentleman by birth, but was probably a member of a family that was part of the merchant élite of Norwich. He is most likely to have been connected to the Hernes. Remember that his mother, Margery Arden, was Thomas Herne's grandmother. If not the Hernes, his mother must have had powerful friends, because the way she was treated was in no way typical of the way that beggars were dealt with under the Tudors.[77] Arden went to London to seek his fortune and became a gentleman *en route.* This is extremely important in view of the emphasis put on class in 'Arden of Feversham'.

Norfolk Rec. Soc.(1982), lii, pp. 82, 101; B. Cozens Hardy and E. A. Kent, *The Mayors of Norwich 1403-1835,* (Norwich, 1938), p. 65.

[77] Youings, pp. 254-78.

621

Item v s. iiij d. Inquisitio dicte de worstedweves ... that they fynde one clothe of this marke for lacke of workemanshipp v s. iiij d.

Item v s. vj d. Also they fynde one other clothe of the same marke for lacke of workemanshipp v s. vj d.

Item v s. And they do fynde one other clothe of this marke for lacke of workemanshipp v s.

Curia tenta die Martis xxix die Augusti Anno xo domine Elizabeth Regine nostre Thoma Parker Maiore Roberto Davy. Ricardo Fletcher. Johanne Aldriche Iusticiariis

Thomas Harne. Receyved xlvjs viijd of mother Ardens gyfte

Whereas Thomas Harne one of the grandchildren of Arden late of the Cittie of Norwich widdowe deceassed had geven hym of the goodes of the sayde Arden his graundmother the summe of xlvjs viijd to be payed hym of good and lawfull money of Englande This daye the sayde Thomas Harne cam into this Courte before Mr Mayor and other Justices and Aldermen and confessed and acknowledged hym selfe to be fully satisfied contented and payed and therof dothe discharge the mayor Sheriffs Cittizens and comynaltie and their successors by these presentes for ever. In witnes wherof the sayde Thomas Harne putte his hande

T H

above folio 621 from the Norwich Mayor's Book

Chapter 2
His career break through

Thomas Arden first came to public notice in 1536-37. As S. Lehmberg says, 'soon after the dissolution of the Reformation Parliament on 14 April 1536 the chief officers of Parliament were rewarded by the King. Audley (the Lord Chancellor), who had served well in both Houses, received an annuity of £300 and a dissolved priory in Colchester; Speaker Wingfield was paid £100; Chief Justices Fitzjames and Baldwin £40 and 40 marks each. Another judge, Sir Anthony Fitzherbert, and two of the King's serjeants, John Hynd and Humphrey Brown, received 30 marks; Robert Ormeston, under clerk of Parliament £10; the Lord Chancellor's clerks £5; the assistants of Edward North, Clerk of Parliament, and other for their paynes this Parliament, 20 marks.' Arden was not there mentioned by name, but, on 12 July 1537, a warrant of Richard Rich and John Onley was issued to the Treasurer of the Augmentations to pay '£6-13-4 to Thomas Arderne, one of the clerks of Edward North Esq., Clerk of the Parliament, in recompense of such pains as he and his fellows have taken in and about the writing and making of certain books of Acts of Parliament for the King's Highness concerning as well the suppressed lands as the King's Highness purchased lands'.'[78]

He now had his foot on the ladder. This was the crucial stage in his career and it is worth pointing out that in order to do such detailed and skilful work, Arden must have had a good education somewhere, though where is not yet apparent. Several articles by A.F.Pollard give some idea of the work involved in being a clerk or under-clerk in Parliament. In Norwich before the Reformation there were the cathedral schools, the episcopal grammar school, the common school and the king's school where he might have gone. From the work he did it seems probable that he was a lawyer, but it has not been possible to trace him at Oxford, Cambridge, Edinburgh, Leyden or any of the Inns of Court.[79]

So, Edward North[80] was Arden's first patron and proved to be such a pervasive influence on him that Arden made him the overseer of his will on 20 December 1550.[81] In the eighteenth century there were said to be the North coat of arms on a window in the parlour in Arden's house, proclaiming the connection. Just supposing that Arden put it there, it is worth reflecting that he would surely have been proud to add that of the Ardens of Parkhall in Warwickshire mentioned by Crow, had he had any right to do so. This, however, is all in the realm of speculation.[82] There is as yet no evidence that Arden was entitled to bear heraldic arms himself.

It is therefore worth considering North's career in some detail. He was a man of fairly humble origin, who made a successful career for himself typical of the period. He was born in 1496 at Walkeringham, Nottinghamshire. He was the son of Roger North by his wife, Christian, daughter of Richard Warcup of Sinnington and widow of Ralph Warren. He was educated at St.

---

78 S. E. Lehmberg, *The Reformation Parliament 1529-36,* (Cambridge, 1970), p. 247; Eighth Report of the Royal Commission on Historical Manuscripts; Manuscripts of His Grace the Duke of Manchester (London, HMSO, 1881) app., part 2, p. 22, noted first by L. Orlin, p. 24.

79 'The clerical organization of Parliament', *English Historical Review* (1942), lvii, pp. 31-58; 'The receivers of petitions and clerks of Parliament', EHR (1942), lvii, pp. 202-26; 'The under-clerks and the Commons journals', *Bulletin of the Institute of Historical Research* (1938), xvi, pp. 144-67; *A History of Norwich School*, ed. P. Harries (Norwich, 1991), passim. For 'A Topographical and Historical Introduction to the Inns of Court, Inns of Chancery, and Serjeants' Inns' see *Inns Ancient & Modern* by Hon. Mr. Justice Megarry. Selden Soc. 1972

80 DNB; Commons 1509-58, iii, pp. 21-23; Sir Dudley North, Some notes concerning the life of Edward, Lord North, Baron of Kirtling (1682); Lady Frances Bushby, *Three men of the Tudor time* (London, 1911); T. A. Walker, *A biographical register of Peterhouse men,* (Cambridge U.P., 1927), part 1, 304; Orlin, pp. 21-24; see Text pages 37-38.

81 CKS, Favward, fol. 280v.

82 Jacob, plate 15; Bullen, p. v.

Paul's school in London under William Lyly. He almost certainly went on to Peterhouse, Cambridge. His entry is not recorded in the college records, but nor are those of some of his contemporaries known to have been there. He was a benefactor to the college, leaving to trustees his rectory, patronage and advowson of Ellington near Grafham in Cambridgeshire with instructions to seek a royal licence to appropriate the benefice to Peterhouse, which still owns it today. There are two similar, probably contemporary, panel portraits of North, one in Hall and one in a Fellow's room, which are discussed in detail on pages 37 & 38. He was admitted to Lincoln's Inn in 1522. He obtained employment in a legal capacity with the corporation of London. He caught the attention of Sir Brian Tuke, treasurer of the chamber, and through him became clerk of parliament in survivorship. It was his marriage to the widow of two rich merchants that gave him financial security and allowed him the opportunity to speculate on the land market. On 1 January 1533, he bought the manor of Kirtling in Cambridgeshire. This was to become his principal seat and the nucleus of his estates in East Anglia and the Fenlands. He also acquired the dissolved monastery called Charterhouse in London.

His work as Clerk of the Parliaments brought North into close contact with Thomas Cromwell, for whom he was making confidential reports by 1535. This relationship was probably decisive in his appointment as treasurer to the Court of Augmentations in 1540 and chancellor in 1544. When he resigned as treasurer in 1546, he owed the crown nearly £25,000, some of which he had clearly put to his own use in accumulating other lands. Although summoned personally to account by Henry VIII he did not in the end suffer disgrace. He was returned as one of the knights of the shire for Cambridgeshire in the parliament of 1542, which is when he was probably knighted. He was appointed an executor of Henry VIII's will and was bequeathed £300.

On Edward VI's accession he was made a Privy Councillor, but was soon after forced to resign by Protector Somerset. He had his revenge a year later when he was a signatory to the letter listing the Protector's offences. As a partisan of the Duke of Northumberland, North supported Lady Jane Grey until it became clear that her cause would fail, when he submitted to Mary. Not surprisingly, she was distrustful of him. She did not renew his appointment as Privy Councillor, but raised him to the baronage as Lord North of Kirtling in 1554. The same year he was one of the people who escorted Philip of Spain from Southampton to Winchester for his marriage to Mary.

Elizabeth visited North twice at Charterhouse, but she also was wary of him and never allowed him to take an important role in the country's affairs again. He was also old and ill by then. He left a long and complicated will and died in 1564. His son and heir, Roger, married a daughter of Sir Richard Rich, who had acquired the manor of Bendysh in Essex, which had formerly belonged to Faversham Abbey. His second son, Sir Thomas North, was the translator of Plutarch in 1579 and has been described as Shakespeare's storehouse of learning.

So Arden's patron became treasurer in 1540 and chancellor in 1544 of the Court of Augmentations, which was a body created in 1536 to administer the lands, possessions and revenues of the dissolved religious houses. It should be made clear that, in spite of the statements that Arden was one of its officials by L. Cust and many others since, there is as yet no proof that this was so. W. Richardson in his detailed history of the Court of Augmentations covering the years 1536-1554, does not mention him as one of its officers.[83] Nevertheless, this is something of a quibble, because, as a clerk of parliament, he must have helped to draft the bill

[83] W. C. Richardson, *History of the Court of Augmentations 1536-54* (Louisiana State Univ., 1961); DNB; Commons 1509-58, iii, pp. 24-25.

that set it up, so that he must have had a thorough grasp of how it worked. He probably, made some powerful connections in central government in the process.[84]

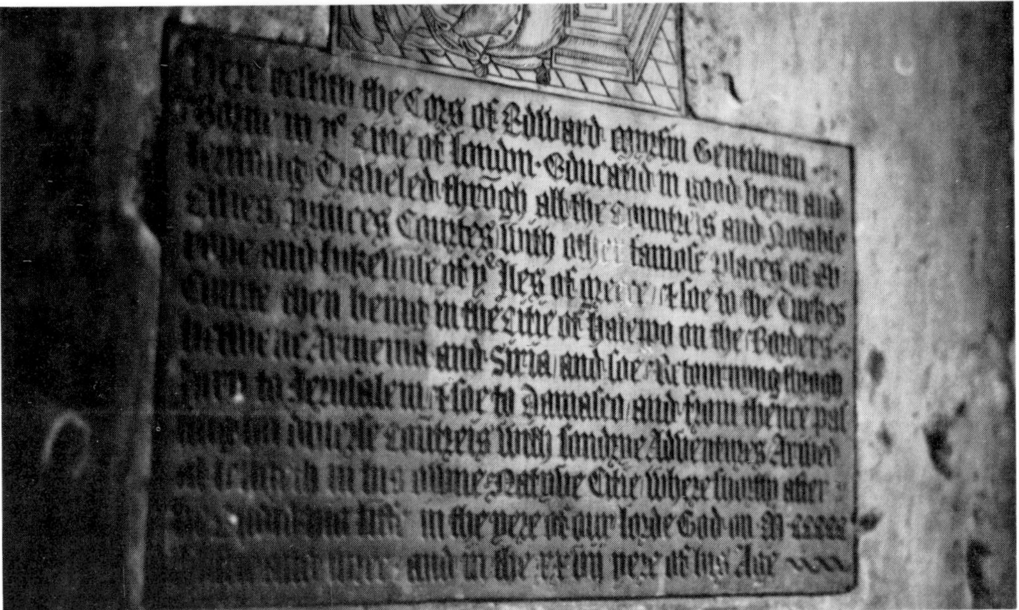

Brass of Edward Myrfin in glass cabinet on the wall of Kirtling church, Cambs. (Photo Art), detail of inscription by Don Flett RIBA.

[84] LP, xiv, part 2, no. 236 (3); Youings, pp. 160-62; Orlin, p. 25; J. Richardson, *The Local Historian's Encyclopedia* (Historical Publications, 1986), p. 189.

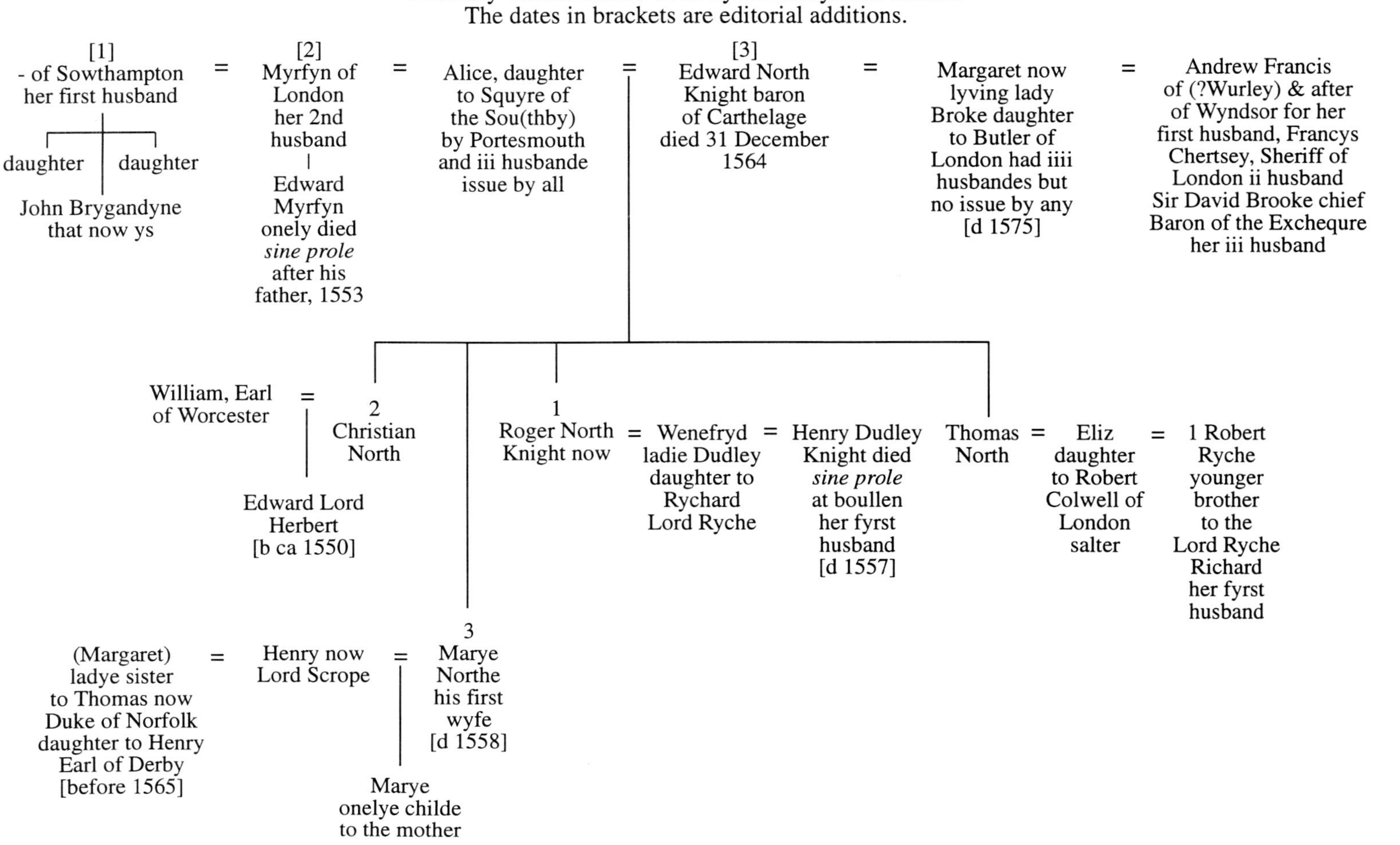
BL: Additional MSS 38133 fol. 153b Collections genealogical, legal and historical - in hands of Sir Thomas Phillips - said to be by Robert Aske who was connected with the household of the Earls of Northumberland and leader of Pilgrimage of Grace executed 1537.
Probably written before 1575 by an anonymous herald.
The dates in brackets are editorial additions.
[1] - of Sowthampton her first husband
daughter
daughter
John Brygandyne that now ys
=
[2] Myrfyn of London her 2nd husband
Edward Myrfyn onely died *sine prole* after his father, 1553
=
Alice, daughter to Squyre of the Sou(thby) by Portesmouth and iii husbande issue by all
=
[3] Edward North Knight baron of Carthelage died 31 December 1564
=
Margaret now lyving lady Broke daughter to Butler of London had iiii husbandes but no issue by any [d 1575]
=
Andrew Francis of (?Wurley) & after of Wyndsor for her first husband, Francys Chertsey, Sheriff of London ii husband Sir David Brooke chief Baron of the Exchequre her iii husband
William, Earl of Worcester
=
2 Christian North
Edward Lord Herbert [b ca 1550]
1 Roger North Knight now
=
Wenefryd ladie Dudley daughter to Rychard Lord Ryche
=
Henry Dudley Knight died *sine prole* at boullen her fyrst husband [d 1557]
Thomas North
=
Eliz daughter to Robert Colwell of London salter
=
1 Robert Ryche younger brother to the Lord Ryche Richard her fyrst husband
(Margaret) ladye sister to Thomas now Duke of Norfolk daughter to Henry Earl of Derby [before 1565]
=
Henry now Lord Scrope
=
3 Marye Northe his first wyfe [d 1558]
Marye onelye childe to the mother

Chapter 3
Marriage

North must have thought that Arden was highly talented for he not only started him off on his career but also arranged for his marriage to North's own step-daughter, Alice, though her name was never mentioned in the family histories after the murder. North and Arden arranged that Arden was to stand bound to North in a thousand marks sterling (£666) either to make her a jointure of £40 a year for life or else to appoint it to her by his last will and testament.[85] Jointure was not the same as dowry, a word with which we are more familiar. Dowry was the property which a bride brought to her groom in marriage. Jointure was the provision made by a husband for the support of his wife after his death. This is a tidy sum and gives some indication of his standing at that time. As far as we are concerned, he has only just appeared on the stage, so we have no way of knowing how North reckoned that he was good for that sum. As the daughter of a rich merchant, she must also have brought him a handsome dowry and *entrée* to the circle of the powerful North family: his sons, Sir Roger North and Sir Thomas North, and his daughters, Christian, the wife of William Somerset, third Earl of Worcester, and Mary, the wife of Henry, ninth Lord Scrope of Bolton.[86] He had already come a long way from the town elité of Norwich.

Alice is always called Alice Mirfyn, but it is clear from Edward Mirfyn's will and from a pedigree in the British Library that she was in fact Alice Brigandine. The pedigree is in a volume entitled 'Collections genealogical, legal and historical.' In the front it says that the volume was once in the hands of Sir Thomas Phillipps and that it was the work of Robert Aske, who was a servant of the Duke of Northumberland. However, he was the leader of the Pilgrimage of Grace, for which he was executed in 1537. Several of the entries relate to a later date, so that it was probably drawn up by an anonymous herald, sometime before 1575, when Margaret North died. She was 'now lyving' in this pedigree.[87]

Alice only appears as 'daughter of - of Sowthampton.' Her mother, also called Alice, was the daughter of Oliver Squire of Southby by Portsmouth. She married three times: first, John Brigandine of Southampton, then Edward Mirfyn, a citizen of London, and, finally, Edward North.

John Brigandine and his father, Robert, were almost certainly the colourful pair who appear in the state papers in the early years of the reign of Henry VIII. They were called Brigandine or Brickenden or many other variations of the same name. Robert came from Smallhithe in Tenterden in Kent, which was a member of the Cinque Ports under the head port of Rye. There was a family called Brigandine well established there over a number of years, but no direct link with our Brigandines has yet been established. However, Robert must have lived somewhere close, because Sir Edward Guildford of Halden and Hemsted, Kent, the Lord Warden of the Cinque Ports, wrote him a letter in 1523, describing him as 'my neighbour Bryganden.' There were branches of the family in Cranbrook and Maidstone in Kent, Ewhurst in Sussex and, later, Inkpen in Berkshire.

Robert Brigandine was already in the personal service of the king as a Yeoman of the Crown when he was appointed Clerk of the King's Ships on 19 May 1495, 'with 12^d a day for himself

---

85 CKS, Favward, fol. 280v.

86 DNB; Commons 1558-1603, iii, 24-25; J. H. Baker, *An introduction to English legal history*, 3rd ed., (Butterworths, 1990), p. 553.

87 I must again thank Richard Bradshaw for allowing me to incorporate his notes into this account of the Brigandine family; BL, Additional MSS 38133 fol. 153b; see Appendix 6, will of Edward Mirfyn, 1528.

and 6^d a day for his clerk, and because the king has appointed him to ride as well for the purveyance of goods and necessaries for the said ships as for the taking and arresting so often as need be, (there is) a grant to him of 3 shillings a day for every day that he so rides, out of the said customs (Exeter and Dartmouth), upon his taking oath in Chancery of the number of days he rides'. Five years earlier he had been granted a lease for seven years of subsidies on cloth sold in Kent. Later he served on commissions to seize ropes for rigging and to inspect and seize ships in Kent and Sussex. He was in trouble in 1504, when a writ was sent to the sheriff of Kent to arrest him and to order him to appear before the Barons of the Exchequer to give account of his office. He survived, and the appointment was renewed on the accession of Henry VIII in 1509. R. Bradshaw suggests that this incident may have been the inspiration for Rudyard Kipling's poem *King Henry VII and the Shipwrights*, in which he mentions Bob Brigandyne.

There are a group of letters to and from him concerning beer, iron and coal, timber, victuals, and, above all else, ship building and ship repairs. He it was who built the famous ship, the *Mary Rose*, in 1509. It was partially rebuilt and refitted in 1536. It then sank dramatically in 1545 and was excavated and raised equally dramatically with tremendous publicity in 1982 with the support of the Prince of Wales.[88]

In 1511 Brigandine was paid £129 for the conveyance of two new ships, the *Mary Rose* and the *Peter Granade*, from Portsmouth to the Thames. In 1511, he was paid for 35 coats of white and green, the king's colours, for the soldiers on the *Mary* Rose at 6^s 8^d, a coat. He also built *The Henry Grace a Dieu*,[89] which was laid down at Erith in 1512 and completed in 1514. William Bond, who worked under him, is reckoned to be the first master shipwright in the royal navy. Brigandine also built the first dry dock at Portsmouth, which was completed in 1496.

We come close to identifying Alice Arden's grandmother in an unsigned letter she wrote to her husband, 'Robert Breganden', telling him that 'she killed three of his oxen, but John Butcher's master afterwards forbade him to cut them.' She sent him by the bearer a bittern, a dozen woodcocks, a mallard, two teals and two dozen 'snytes.' We are also told that in 1511 Robert Brigandine paid Alice Brigandine for the hire of ground at Smallhithe on which *The Mary Fortune* was built. He resigned his office as Robert Briganden of Smalhed, Kent, alias of Portsmouth on 21 April 1523. Nothing more is heard of him.

Alice's father, John Brigandine, was a captain in the navy. His coat of arms as 'John Brigandine of Portsmouth' has survived. In 1510, he received a grant of 'three void tenements in great ruin and decay in the town of Portsmouth, which had come into the king's hands by the attainder of Piers Martyn.' He was master of a rowbarge,[90] a 100 ton ship *The Mawdeleyne* in Admiral Edward Howard's fleet at the battle of Camaret Bay off Brest in 1512. Prior to this he had been overseer and ruler of *The Regent* and *The Sovereign* as those two ships lay in Portsmouth Harbour awaiting departure to join Howard. Brigandine was responsible for the wages and

---

[88] F. N. M. Rule, *The Mary Rose* (Conway Maritime Press, 1982), pp. 24, 109.

[89] R. C. Anderson, 'List of English Men of War 1509-1649', *Society for Nautical Research*, Occ. publ. No. 7 (1959), says 1500 tons, built at Woolwich, she was rebuilt in 1539; J. J. College, *Ships of the Royal Navy,* Vol 1. (1969), p. 263 completed 18 June 1514, Woolwich (Erith?). Rebuilt at Portsmouth as 1,000 tons renamed Edward 1547. Burnt 27 Aug. 1553 by accident.

[90] Tom Glasgow jnr. 'Oared Vessels in the Elizabethan Navy', *Mariners Mirror*, Vol. 52 no. 4. (1966), p 374 says, "The rowbarge, in the English Navy, emerged in the latter years of Henry VIII, a few surviving to serve in Elizabeth's navy. From Anthony's Roll of 1546 it can be seen that they were small oar and sail vessels with low superstructures and a ram in the bow. However, different from brigantines, they were always assigned a tonnage figure indicating an orlop and cargo hold.' J. J. College, *Ships of the Royal Navy, A supplement to the historical index*, (1986), p. 38, Magdalen also Mawdelyn. Ship 120 tons (builder's measurements), listed 1522 , last mentioned 1525. Given as being of Deptford by R. C. Anderson, 'List of English Men of War 1509-1649', *Society for Nautical Research*, Occ. publ. No. 7 (1959).

victuals of the sailors and the safe mooring with cables of *The Regent*. Howard's brother-in-law, Sir Thomas Knyvet, was later killed when *The Regent* blew up at Camaret Bay.[91]

On 8 March 1515 a commission of oyer and terminer, that is, to hear and determine, was set up, composed of Thomas, Earl of Surrey, High Admiral, John Batemanson LLD and Christopher Middylton, Bachelor of Law and deputy of the said Earl to deal with piratical offences alleged to have been committed by John Baker, John Brigandyne and John Bristol. Two merchants of Brittany alleged that their ship had been attacked and robbed in Falmouth Harbour (in peace-time) by a ship of war whose captain was John Brigandine. Nothing more is heard of John Baker and John Bristol. In the accounts of Sir John Daunce's, who amongst other appointments was paymaster of the war, mention was later made of the cost of dinners and horsemeat for Thomas, Earl of Surrey, when he was sent to take over Brigandine's ship and the goods he had taken from Spaniards and Bretons.

Robert Brigandine was naturally alarmed by what was happening. One John Cokkes sent him an undated letter to tell him that he had done his errand to 'Mr. Gyldeforte', in other words, his neighbour, Sir Edward Guildford, who was an intimate friend of Henry VIII. Guildford bid him 'beware that ye bind not yourself to pay [any] sum of money [f]or your son in nowise, but that ye shall say unto your son's adversaries th[a]t ye will abide the awarde of Master Gyldforte and [my lor]d of Surrey etc. Thus he trusts your son's fine shall not pass 100 marks. He wishes you to be with him at Richemounte on Tuesday next and bring the names of your son's adversaries and also the things of which you bade me shew him'.

At about the same time, one Thomas Buley wrote to John Brigandine, saying that Brigandine knew now 'who was your friends and who was your foes.' Buley begged for help.saying that he had been a commander only under Brigandine and was now in sanctuary 'without ware or money for his cause.'

On 6 May 1516, a chaplain called Thomas Alen wrote a chatty letter to his master, the Earl of Shrewsbury, in which he mentioned that it was said that 'there was a ship freight in the Thames with goods of the religion of St. James.' These were the Spanish religious orders of Aragon of Alcantra and Calatrava. He went on to say that 'Anthony Villers, William Knyvet and one Brygandin, son unto him that made the King's great ship, should enter the ship at divers places, with consent of the master and the mariners, with a great company, to the number of 100 persons and above, and so depart their ways to the sea, to seek their adventures.' The last we hear of him is paying a recognisance or bond, probably for good behaviour, in 1518.[92]

The date of Brigandine's death is not known, but Alice then married Edward Mirfyn. He was the son of Sir Thomas Mirfyn, a citizen and skinner of London, who was also a leading Adventurer of London trading to the Low Countries. He took part with others in equipping ships

---

[91] College op. cit.,*Grace Dieu* 100-gun ship, 600/1,00 tons. Built at Chatham 1488. Renamed *Regent* 1489; lost 10 Aug. 1512 in action with the French off the Isle of Wight. (Was the first two-decker in the Royal Navy.)

[92] BL, Harl 5846 fol. 79v; LP1 (1509-14), no's 353, 1327, 3422, 5720 (p. 953), 5724 p. 960; I (1509), part1, g 132 (101), no's 1453 (ii, p. 663), g.632 (45); I, (1513), part 2, no.3608, p. 1500; 11, part 1, no's 235, 506, 1861; 11, part 2, pp. 1489, 1443, 1447, 1469 1487, 1489; iii, part 2, 1744, 2073, 2302, 2390, 2793, 2964, grant 2992 no. 21; Addenda, I, no's 3-13, 68 (12), 101, 136, 138, 140, 152; Calendar of Patent Rolls 1494-1509, pp. 17, 91, 92; Brigandine wills, John, 1526, Tenterden, PRC17/17 fol. 207; Robert, 1482, Tenterden, PRC17/3 fol 450; Robert, 1517, Tenterden, PRC17/13 fol. 263; Thomas, 1523/4, Ewhurst, Sussex, PROB11/21 fol 155v; Vis Berks 1532, 1566, 1623, 1665-66, *Harl. Soc.lvi*, pp. 28, 120, 179; V.C.H. Hants, V, pp. 371, 373; Commons 1509-58, II, pp. 262-63; W. L. Clowes, *The Royal Navy,* (London,1897, reprint New York, 1966), I, pp. 405, 436; M. Oppenheim, *A history of the administration of the Royal Navy, and the Merchant Shipping in relation to the Navy,* (London,1896), pp. 36, 39,53, 83; M. Oppenheim ed., Naval Accounts and Inventories of the reign of Henry VII, *Navy Rec. Soc.*,1896, xviii; F. N. M. Rule, *The Mary Rose,* (Conway Maritime Press,1982), pp. 24, 109; D. Macleane, 'A history of Pembroke College', (Oxford, 1897), *Oxford History Soc.*, XXXIII, pp. 317-19.

laden with cloth for the markets of Antwerp and Bruges, in securing armed convoys for them and in negotiating for trade privileges abroad and at home. He provided copper for the navy in 1513.[93] He came from Barway and his father was buried in Ely, both places in Cambridgeshire. This is worth remembering, because North later purchased Kirtling in the same county.

Mirfyn was Lord Mayor in 1518-19. Accounts for various processions in that year have survived, including a payment of 26^s 8^d for hiring Cardinal Wolsey's barge to accompany Mirfyn and 20^d to Richard Tegg, because they did not use his barge. There were also accounts for pageants, which included Sir Thomas a Becket; his father, Gilbert a Becket; a jewess representing his mother; the knight Tracy; one of the murderers and a gaoler with a prison for Gilbert a Becket. Another pageant concerned Our Lady and St. Elizabeth and a third a Maundy pageant. The accounts are given in full in Appendix 6.

Mirfyn left a long and elaborate will in 1523 much concerned with a settlement of £2,148-9-4 for his second wife, unsatisfactorily arranged with Sir Robert Dymoke, the King's Champion. He left property in London, Hornchurch in Essex and Downe in Kent. He remembered his son, George, who was a monk at Westminster, and made valuable bequests for religious purposes to various churches and to the Skinners' Company to arrange for a mass to be said for him and his family in the chapel over the charnel house in St. Paul's churchyard. He also left money for poor members of the Skinners' Company. After many small bequests, he left half the residue to his other three children, Edward, Mary and Frances, and half to charity. He appointed his son, Edward, and his son-in-law, Andrew Judd, as his executors, and the Bishop of London and Sir Richard Broke as his overseers. Andrew Judd, to repeat, was also a skinner, who married Mirfyn's daughter, Mary. He was the founder, in 1553, of Tonbridge School and Lord Mayor in 1550-51 and died in 1558.

Stow described the clearing away of the remains of those who were entombed at the Charnel House at St. Paul's: 'In this chapel were buried Robert Barton and Henry Barton, Mayor, and Thomas Mirfin, Mayor, all Skinners; they were entombed with their images of alabaster over them grated or coped about with iron before the said Chapel, all which was pulled down in the year 1549. The bones of the dead, couched up in a charnel under the Chapel, were conveyed from thence to Finsbury Field (by report of him who paid the carriage) amounting to more than one thousand cartloads, and there laid on a Moorish ground in short space after raised by soilage of the City upon them to bear three wind mills. The Chapel and Charnel were converted into dwelling houses, warehouses and sheds for stationers, builded before it in place of the tombs.'[94]

On 17 September 1523, Sir Thomas More wrote to Cardinal Wolsey to say that the king 'desires that Sir William Tyler should have in marriage the widow of Mr. Mirfyn, late alderman of London, whom it hath pleased God to call to his mercy. The King is anxious to have his request brought to a successful termination.' He was not successful.[95] Here apparently was a very rich man, the likely source of North's fortune. It also seems apparent that when he made his will his son, Edward, had not yet married nor was a marriage even in prospect, for it is inconceivable that the marriage of his son and heir would not have been mentioned. So, the marriage must have taken place sometime between 2 September 1523, when Sir Thomas made his will, and 3 March 1528, when his son, Edward, made his, which was proved on 11 May, following. This is an

---

[93] LP (1513), I, part 2, nos. 2668, 3613, p. 1509.

[94] See APPENDIX 6: PRO, PROB11/21, q. 13, fols. 97-99v; PRO, PROB11/22, q. 31, fol. 246; *Records of the Skinners of London,* ed., J. J. Lambert (1933), pp. 122, 134, 144-48, 153-54; Sir Richard Broke, Commons 1509-58, i, pp. 503-04; W. A. Copinger, *The manors of Suffolk* (Manchester, 1909), iv, 163; Rev. Alfred B. Beaven, *The Aldermen of the City of London,* (London, 1908), II, pp. L, 21-22, 168, 170.

[95] LP iii, part 2, no. 3340.

important document, given as an appendix, because it shows clearly that although Thomas Arden‘s wife is usually called Alice Mirfyn, she must in fact have been Alice Brigandine, a daughter of the first marriage. Edward left 'Alice Brigandine, my wife's daughter, toward her marriage £20'. He left her sister, Agnes, £6-13-4 and her brother, John, 5 marks.

He also willed to his wife, Alice, for life, the manor of Burtyns in Freckenham, Suffolk, which he already held in 1526. As she was pregnant when he drew up the will, he arranged that, should she die, Burtyns would be left to that child. Failing that, he left it to 'Alice Brigandine my wife's daughter' for life, and then to his right heirs. This arrangement surely makes it extremely unlikely that he had a daughter Alice of his own alive at the moment when he made his will. His wife was pregnant, but the child born after his death was not Alice but Edward Mirfyn, a great traveller who died in 1553, according to his memorial brass, which is one of the North family monuments in Kirtling church in Cambridgeshire.[96]

> Here restith the cors of Edward Myrfin, gentilman, borne in ye citie of London, educated in good vertue and lerning, traveled through all the countries and notable cities, princes courtes, with other famous places of Europe, and lykewise of ye Iles of Greece, and so to the Turkes courte, then being in the citie of Haleppo[97], on the borders betwene Armenia and Siria, and soe retourning through Jury to Jerusalem, and soe to Damasco, and from thence passing by diverse countries, with sondry Adventures, arrived at length in his owne Native Citie, where shortly he endid his life, in the year of Our Lorde God on MCCCCC fyfty and three, and in the XXVII yere of his age.

He was said to be 27, which would mean that he was born in 1526, that is before Edward made his will in 1528. This is a problem. Edward left half the residue to his wife, Alice, and the other half to his unborn child. He made his wife the executrix and a gentleman called Richard Bury and his brother-in-law, Andrew Judd, the overseers.

Nothing is known of Alice's sister, Agnes, but her brother, John, became a member of parliament for Huntingdon.[98] It is difficult to distinguish him from a namesake from Tenterden whose guardian was Sir Christopher Hales.[99] This man was a servant of Cromwell, and Hales was asking for him to be given the customs of Sandwich in 1539. Hales said that he had debts to settle and that he would sell £14 or £15 worth a year of his land for it. In view of Arden becoming Controller at Sandwich, it is tempting to see a connection. However, our man was certainly in royal service in the army or on embassies in Scotland, Antwerp and Germany. He and his wife, Catherine, were remembered in North's will in 1564 when a gift made earlier to them was doubled. Nothing more is heard of him.

So, on the second count, Alice Arden was the daughter of the navy captain, John Brigandine, not the merchant, Edward Mirfyn. It is now time to consider Alice's age at the time of the murder, because I suggest that she may have been closer in age to Arden than has hitherto been realized and would have been thought of as a mature, 'godly matron', as is said in the wedding service, by the time of the murder. I should stress that I am working here by arithmetic and guesswork, rather than evidence, which I would much prefer. Her brother, John, is said to have been born by 1523. In Edward Mirfyn's will, Alice seems to have been the oldest of the three children, which means that she must have been born by 1521. Mirfyn refers to her as being under the age

---

[96] G.E.C., ix, p. 651; D. and S. Lysons, *Magna Britannica*, (Cambridge, 1806-22) ii, 225; N. Pevsner, *Cambridgeshire*, (Penguin, 2nd edn., 1970), pp. 418-20; *A short guide to All Saints' Church Kirtling* (1991), p. 3

[97] Aleppo; a town in the north of Syria, capital of a Turkish province.

[98] North, PRO, PROB11/48 q. 7, fol. 54; Commons 1509-58, i, pp. 274-75.

[99] DNB.

Portrait of Sir Edward North (c.1504 - 64) of Kirtling, Cambs., and the Charterhouse, Middlesex and London. One of two portraits at Peterhouse, Cambridge. This is in Hall and the other is in a Fellow's room.

Reproduced by kind permission of the Master and Fellows of Peterhouse, Cambridge.

of marriage[100]. When Thomas Arden was murdered in 1551, his daughter and heir was said to be 13 years and four months old, born, let us say, in 1538. He and Alice must therefore have been married at least 14 years earlier, that is, in 1537, which is the very year that Arden is first heard of as North's clerk in Parliament. If this reckoning is right, Alice would have been about 16 at the time of her marriage in 1537 and 30 at the time of the murder. Based on goodness knows what evidence, Mr. Burton said that she was 28 when she came to Faversham in 1540, which would make her 39 and almost menopausal at the time of the murder.[101] Canon Telfer suggests that she was the second wife. He gives no date for the marriage and no evidence of such a marriage has yet been found.

Now that we have been introduced to most of the people involved, it is time to look at the two panel portraits of Sir Edward North at Peterhouse, Cambridge, where he had probably been educated. This photograph is of the painting in the Hall. The second, which is similar but more elaborate, is in a Fellow's room. In both paintings North has a golden chain, possibly a chain of office, round his neck and a flower in his left hand, with these arms beside him, *Azure, a lion passant or, between three fleur de lis*, for North; impaling, *Sable, on a chevron embattled between three eaglets displayed argent, 3 trefoils slipped, vert*. Willis says, 'This last bearing is wrong taken or falsely painted; for on Sir Edward North's Tomb in Kirtling church, they are quarterfoils.'[102] However, Willis and others are incorrect since the charges on the tomb at Kirtling are pansies.[103] This is confirmed in a grant of arms to Dame Alice North blazoned as '*Argent, on a chevron battelley, between three eaglets or, three paunses gules and or*'.[104] The pansy occurs sparingly in both English and French arms so that it is not surprising this error was made.[105]

The second portrait, has seven coats of arms and badges on the border of the frame. They are starting on the top left the badge of the Tudor Rose, the Tudor arms *Quarterly France Modern and England*, and the Tudor badge the portcullis. Centre left *France Modern and England quarterly within a bordure gobony azure and argent*, the arms of John de Beaufort, Earl and Marquis of Somerset, son of John of Gaunt subsequent to his legitimation[106], and centre right, *[Azure] a bend Or over all a label of three points argent* for [Scroope][107]. Bottom left North impaling Squire, bottom right the Arms of Peterhouse, *Or, three palets gules, a bordure of the last charged with eight ducal coronets, Or*, (and an indistict line to the fact the college was founded in the year of the Lord 1257). Impaling means the vertical division of a shield to

---

100 The librarian at the Guildhall library assures me that there was no fixed lawful age of marriage in the City in that period; John Brigandine, Commons 1509-58, I, p. 496.

101 Bullen, p. xii; BL, Harl 542, fol. 34.

102 R Willis, *The architectural history of the University of Cambridge and of colleges of Cambridge and Eton*, ed. J. Willis Clark, (CUP, 1886), viii, 67.

103 I am extremely grateful to Duncan Harrington who, with his great knowledge of heraldry, has contributed by far the most to this section on the portraits. Also to Major A. R. Tavener of Glebe House, Kirtling for his help, particularly in obtaining a rubbing of the charge from the tomb, and to John Titford for his assistance.

104 Barker's Grants, Stow MS. 692, folio 71 located in *Grantees of Arms named in docquets and patents to the end of the seventeenth century* Ed. W. Harry Rylands. Harleian Society, Vol. 66, (1915), p. 241. The arms are incorrectly given in W. M. Palmer, *Monumental Inscriptions and Coats of Arms from Cambridgeshire, chiefly as recorded by John Layer about 1632 and William Cole between 1742 and 1782* (1932), pp. 91-92 dated 10 Aug. 1752 taken from Add. MS 5819, pp. 115-120.

105 Henry Gough, *Glossary of Terms used in Heraldry* (1894) gives 4 examples including, *Argent, three fleur-de-lis vert on a chief azure a pansy between two fleur-de-lis or* for Woolball of London.

106 North's daughter Christian married in 1550 William Somerset, third Earl of Worcester. (Burk's Peerage 1965 under Beaufort).

107 North's daughter Mary married Henry, Lord Scroope of Bolton. Burke's Dormant & Extinct Peerages says, Henry le Scrope 9th Baron (died 1591) summoned to Parliament from 21 Oct 1555 to 4 Feb 1589 married first Alianore daughter of Edward Lord North and had by her an only daughter Mary.

incorporate two different coats of arms. The following tag is included on this painting: *Nobilis hic vere fuerat, si nobilis ullus, Qui sibi Principium Nobilitatus erat.* [This was truly a nobleman, if anyone was a nobleman, Who was in himself a fount of nobility.] In one reference his motto was quoted as 'La vertue est la seule noblesse' (Virtue is the only nobility).[108]

Sir Edward North had married firstly, about 1528, Alice widow of Edward Mirfyn, citizen and skinner of London, [*On a chevron a crescent and in the dexter chief a mullet of five points*][109] and before that of John Brigandine of Portsmouth, [*Per chevron argent and gules, in chief three crescents, and in base as many roses all counterchanged*][110] and daughter of Oliver Squire of Southby, near Portsmouth. Alice was buried on the 22 August 1560 at Kirtling and he married secondly, about 1561, Margaret widow of Sir David Brooke, Lord Chief Baron of the Exchequer (1553-58), and relict of Robert Chertsey, Alderman of London, and previously of Andrew Francis, citizen and clothworker of London, being daughter of Richard Butler of London, grocer.[111] In 1 February 1564/5 Margaret his widow was granted a coat of arms by Sir Gilbert Dethick, Garter King of Arms, emblazoned *Argent, a fess chequy azure and sable a rose between two annulets or, between six cross crosslets botonny.*[112]

The heraldry on the portraits give the arms of North impaling that of Alice, daughter of Oliver Squire and widow of Edward Mirfyn. Sir Christopher Barker, Garter King of arms granted a change in the North coat-of-arms between 1536 and 1549 from *Per pale or and azure a lion passant guardant between three fleur-de-lis counterchanged* to *Azure a lion passant or, between three fleur-de-lis or.*[113] Thus the portrait must have been made after the change in the coat of arms.

However, there remains the question of the significance of the flower in Edward North's left hand and the date 1564 painted on the portrait. North died on the 31 December 1564 at his house called the Charterhouse, London aged about 68 and was buried at Kirtling. The two visible leaves make it extremely likely that it is a carnation[114] (*Dianthus caryophyllus.* Vincent says, 'Carnation, so called from the original species being of a flesh colour (*carnis,* of flesh). Several varieties were first planted in England by the Flemings, about 1567. *Stow.*'[115]). According to Hall, 'A carnation or pink, especially when red, a symbol of betrothal, probably originating in a Flemish wedding custom. In portrait painting, especially of the 15th & 16th centuries, when held in the sitter's hand it signifies that the picture commemorates his betrothal.'[116] It would seem that the portrait must have been painted before 1560 since technically speaking, the right to impale the arms of a wife ceases at her death. However, it could be that not only the name and date but also the arms were added at a later date. The portrait is different from that in the Fellow's room showing him a lighter almost ginger beard and perhaps a more mature appearance.

---

108 Sir Bernard Burke, *The General Armory,* (London, 1884), p. 738.

109 Palmer, *op. cit.* taken from brass in Kirtling church. Burke gives for his father Thomas Mirfyn, Lord Mayor of London, *Or, on a chevron sable, a mullet argent,* crest: *A demi lion proper supporting a flag argent charged with a saltire sable.*

110 Visitation of Berks, 1532, 1566, 1623, Harleian Soc. Vol. 56 (1907) p. 179

111 *Complete Peerage*, p. 651

112 'Silver in a fece checke assure and sables a rose two anulets golde betwene vj crosse crosseletes buttonnes sables as more playnly apperethe depicted in this margent' *Miscellanea Genealogica et Heraldica*, 3rd series Vol. ii, pp. 193-94.

113 Harleian MS 586 fol. 79v, and Stow MS 692 folio 71, located through W. H. Rylands, 'Grantees of Arms named in docquets and patents to the end of the seventeenth century', *Harleian Soc.* Vol. Lxvi (1915) p. 183.

114 Often called gillyflowers at this period.

115 Benjamin Vincent, *Haydn's Dictionary of Dates* (1889)

116 James Hall, *Dictionary of subjects and symbols in Art* (Murray, 1993), p. 57. I am indebted to A. J. Edwards for this reference.

Arden's appointment as clerk to North was crucial to his career and he never forgot it. Equally, what happened in North's household possibly as early as 1537 may have been the root cause of the murder, unless a wider conspiracy theory is accepted. According to Holinshed, Arden was 'a man of a tall and comelie personage, and matched in marriage with a gentlewoman, young, tall, and well favored of shape and countenance'. What Stow adds that is not in Holinshed is the point that was crucial to Arden, namely that 'she was the lord Northes wyves dowghtar, and hir husband and she havynge therefore often recowrse to my lord Northes'. We now know that Arden was not a gentleman by birth but a self-made man from the provinces. It is therefore not in the least surprising to hear that, when his wife took a lover, Thomas Morsby, Arden mocked him for his humble origin, for he was only a step or two ahead himself. It is also clear that Morsby did not know his origins and considered him to be a gentleman. According to Stow, Morsby was 'a taylor by his occupation, a black swart man, who in procese of tyme was made one of the chefeste gentleman about the lord Northe'. The term 'gentleman' was not otherwise used about him. Edward Crow, again quoting Mr. Burton in the eighteenth century, suggests that the affair began before she was married when they were all part of North's entourage.[117] Stow speaks of an affair that broke up until she sent him silver dice and how two years after that 'he had to do with her'. He added that it continued 'a good space' before the plot to kill Arden was hatched. However long it lasted, it stretched over years. What is remarkable is how long these three people, who were mature by the standards of those days, remained trapped in the situation. Stow explains why: 'Arden perceyvinge ryght well theyr familiaritie to be muche greatar then theyr honestie, was yet so greatly gyven to seke his advauntage, and caryd so lytle how he came by it that in hope of atteynynge some benefite of the lord Northe by meanes of this Morsby who could do so muche with hym, he winked at that shamefull dysorder and bothe parmyttyd and also invited hym very often to be in his howse'. Arden's attitude as the complaisant husband seems to me completely understandable. His eye was to the main chance. He must keep his links with North, because this gave him two strings to his bow, for he had by then acquired a second patron.

Morsby seems to have spent a lot of time in Faversham. His sister, Cicely Ponder, lived close by. As we have seen, according to Stow he started life as a tailor, but rose to be 'one of the chefest gentleman about the lord Northe.' Holinshed described him as 'a tailor by occupation, a blacke swart man, servant to the lord North,' but in the play Arden called him 'a cheating steward and base minded peasant.' Class lines were not then rigid and immutable. Remember that Sir Edward North himself was of fairly humble origin. If Morsby were one of the chiefest gentlemen he should surely most of the time have been either at the Charterhouse in London or at North's country estate at Kirtling in Cambridgeshire. What was he doing in Faversham apart from having an affair with Alice? Was he really virtually commuting? If so, how? By road or by water? The customary way of travelling to London from Faversham in that period seems to have been by way of horse along the old Pilgrim's Road (from Canterbury), passing through Sittingbourne, Rainham and Rochester to Gravesend, where the journey was continued by boat along the Thames. It is noticeable in the story of the murder how often people from Faversham were up in London. This was also true in the forty-year dispute over the will of the leading Faversham merchant, Henry Hatch, who died in 1533. Alice and Morsby as star-crossed lovers receiving the sacrament on a Sunday openly in a church in London appears in Holinshed, but not in Stow.

[117] FIJ, August 1891, pp. 299-301.

Chapter 4
Another patron

By 1539 Arden had acquired another leading figure as a patron. Sir Thomas Cheyne was Lord Warden of the Cinque Ports[118] and, as such, his power-base was in Kent. This probably explains why Arden concentrated his purchases there rather than it being due to any long-standing connection of his own with the county.

In order to know more about Arden, it is essential to understand Cheyne's career as well as North's. He was a soldier and diplomat, who had property in Blackfriars, London, and Shurland in the Isle of Sheppey. Cheyne was knighted in 1512 or 1513 and was a favoured royal servant, who went on various expeditions and embassies including the Field of the Cloth of Gold in 1520. When he quarrelled in 1528 with Sir John Russell about a wardship, Henry VIII described him as 'proud and full of opprobious words', but later forgave him. Cromwell also favoured him, and it was said to have been at Cromwell's suggestion that Cheyne was made Lord Warden of the Cinque Ports on 17 May 1536, the day on which his predecessor, Anne Boleyn's brother, George, Viscount Rochford, was executed. He then became the most powerful man in Kent and his authority there was virtually unquestioned. In view of Arden's alleged Protestant views, it is worth noting that Cheyne was well known to be a religious conservative.

In 1539 he became Treasurer of the Household. During the next few years he was not only active in Kent but also attended Privy Council meetings frequently and went on a number of expeditions and embassies. Henry VIII left him £200 in his will and made him an assistant executor. He was then reappointed to all his offices by Edward VI and made the arrangements for the coronation. He was frequently present until the fall of Somerset, but thereafter stayed mainly in Kent. Surprisingly, he gave support to Lady Jane Grey but soon declared for Mary, and she sent him on a goodwill embassy to the Emperor. In 1554 he was alleged to be sympathetic to the rebel Sir Thomas Wyatt: he was at the very least dilatory. Four years later, after the fall of Calais, he was ordered to prepare Kent against invasion. He begged to resign the Wardenship, but was kept in office and in frequent correspondence with the Council. On the accession of Elizabeth, he travelled to London to swear allegiance, but died at the Tower on 16 December 1558.

Arden appeared in Cheyne's service as steward of the manor of Hothfield in Kent in 1539. It is not clear how he came to the attention of Cheyne, but it was presumably through North, because they were both prominent men and both had houses in London. It is worth noting that Arden kept up his connections with them both for the rest of his life.

Amongst the state papers in the Public Record Office there is a file of evidence accompanying a petition to Cheyne as Lord Warden by one Walter Morleyn as a pauper complaining of a conspiracy by four men to get his lands in Kent from him.[119] The first was Thomas Arden, who was under-steward to Cheyne as steward of the manor of Hothfield. Some court rolls for the manor have survived, but Arden's name has not been found on them.[120] The second was Morleyn's brother-in-law, Nicholas Sole, but he was dead by the time of the petition. The third was Thomas White alias Percy, clerk or scribe of the commissary's court at Canterbury. Fourth

---

[118] DNB; Commons 1509-58, i, pp. 634-38; Orlin, pp. 25-26; Clark, Society, pp. 54-55

[119] See APPENDIX 7: PRO, SP1/243, part 3, fols. 249-264v, attached to LP Addenda 1, part 2, no. 1514, first examined by L. Orlin, p. 25.

[120] CKS, manor of Hothfield, U455/M6-11, M13/1-3.

The ruins of Shurland, Isle of Sheppey, Kent, the home of Sir Thomas Cheyne (1482/7 - 1558), which he rebuilt between 1510 and 1518 from stone said to be taken from Chilham Castle.

Photography by Arthur Percival.

and last was John Guildford, later Sir John Guildford of Benenden, Kent, a member of Parliament.[121]

This was an extremely complicated case with a number of slightly different versions, but it is worth considering in some detail because it contains accusations against Arden very similar to those made in Faversham years later.

Morleyn proved his yeoman father Richard's will in London before 9 May 1539.[122] He alleged that Arden and Sole then persuaded him 'after a fair flattering and disarming facion' that he was in danger of praemunire because he should have proved the will in Canterbury, not London. Praemunire was a writ by which the sheriff was charged to summon a person accused of prosecuting in a foreign court a suit cognizable by the law of England, and later, of asserting or maintaining papal jurisdiction in England, thus denying the ecclesiastical supremacy of the sovereign. It is difficult to understand exactly what the problem was; whether it was simply because, as all the lands referred to in the will were in Kent, the will should therefore have been proved in Canterbury not London. Certainly the probate of Richard's will was unusual but not unknown, 'Probate of the above written testament was granted before the Lord at London on the authority of our Sovereign King'. This wording signifies that the king was present in the court. This case raises a point that Arden, as a man who had drafted parliamentary bills, would have been likely to pick up, if not to fabricate.

For whatever reason, Arden and Sole were said to have so frightened Morleyn that he agreed to hand over his lands to them temporarily. They consisted of 3½ messuages and 300 acres of land valued at £10. He agreed to it because, as they were Sir Thomas Cheyne's servants, they were much more highly respected than him. He was told that they were holding the land in trust for him, but added that, for his own safety, if anyone asked, he was to say that he had sold it to them. He gave them a bond for 100 marks. They then sent him off to White, lending him £5 to pay him, of which £1-6-8 was down payment. On his return, he was to have his lands back. Instead they sold them for £20 each to Guildford, who also impounded some of his animals.

Morleyn also alleged that Sole had said to Arden that all the country spoke evil of them, but that Arden replied, 'Hold thy peace, fool. I would we had such another bargain in hand'.

Arden in his answer said that Morleyn went to his brother-in-law, Nicholas Sole, to sell his land, saying that he 'past not greatly to kill himself being so evil handed with his neighbours'. Sole then came to Arden who in turn went to Sir Thomas Cheyne, who refused to buy the lands. They then turned to Master Henry Polsted M.P., for Bletchingley in 1547, 1553, and Guildford in 1554 and 1555, who was acting for Cromwell, who also refused the offer.[123] They then bought the land themselves, but Arden would not say what they had paid for it. As there were doubts about the title, 'to eschew great loss', they sold it to Guildford.[124]

This story sounds like a clever man outwitting 'a poor and innocent man, no worldly wiseman', but it is just worth pointing out that Morleyn was at loggerheads with his stepmother, his stepbrothers and many of his neighbours. He himself said that his neighbours owed him 'great evil will'. Finally, at a sessions at Canterbury in Michaelmas, 1541, the charge that he was a common brawler and barrator, or malicious raiser of discord, against eight of his neighbours was not proved, but he was nevertheless bound over to keep the peace.

---

121 Commons 1509-58, i, pp. 265-66; W. T. MacCaffrey, 'Place and Patronage in Elizabethan Politics', *Elizabethan Government and Society: Essays presented to Sir John Neale,* ed. S. T. Bindoff and others (London, 1961), pp. 95-126.

122 PRO, PROB 11/27/219.

123 Commons 1509-58, iii, pp. 24-27; Orlin, p. 55

124 See fols. 258v-259 on page 158.

St. Michael's Cornhill, London published in *The Churches of London*, by George Godwin (1838).

Chapter 5
Customer of Faversham and Comptroller of Sandwich

Either in 1540 or shortly afterwards Arden was appointed the king's customer for Faversham, that is, the collector of customs levied upon merchandise both imported and exported [125]. As L. Orlin rightly says, 'the appeal of the office lay in the wealth that could be and inevitably was skimmed off customs transactions and in the tax revenues that the customer (like the treasurer of Augmentations) held until they were requested of him - and could meanwhile put to private use'. Either of his patrons could have obtained the post for him, but it is more likely to have been Cheyne as Lord Warden.[126]

Sometime before September 1543, Arden was also appointed [127] the king's comptroller of the port of Sandwich, that is, he maintained a counter-roll to check the records of the customer there. Remember that it was possibly his brother-in-law, John Brigandine, who tried to buy the customership there back in 1539. Arden's appointment was renewed by Edward VI 'from the first days of the king's reign'. In November 1546 he was granted a bonus when he was given half the value of cheese which had been forfeited, which amounted to £69-13-4.[128]

As customer and comptroller, Arden had considerable authority and was entitled to respect. When he became mayor in 1548, the heading began 'Thomas Arderne chyff countroller of the kynges maiestyes custome here'. That was what distinguished him amongst his contemporaries.

One account for Arden's years as comptroller has survived, which gives us a chance to see him in action. It is said to run from 29 September 1543 to 29 September 1544, but the entries only cover the period from the 1 October to 11 April following. It deals with foreign trade to and from the ports of Sandwich, Dover, Faversham and Rochester.[129] In Sandwich, at a rough count, there were 90 ships coming into the port, mostly pinks,[130] but also the occasional ketch,[131] crayer, [132] hoy,[133] and argosy.[134] The trade was mainly with Ostend, but from time to time with Nieuwpoort, Calais, Dunkirk, Blankenburghe, Flushing and 'Armewe[135]'. The trade was in the hands of aliens or foreigners, for there were only 16 entries relating to denizens or natives. The chief goods brought into Sandwich were pockets[136] of hops, barrels of herrings and hoops for barrels. Less frequently, there were cabbages, bunches of onions, barrels of white salt, skins with wool, small firkins or casks of eels, Newland fish and staple fish.[137] Only entered rarely were

---

125 HMC, Sixth Report, (HMSO, London, 1877), p. 500;LP., xiv, part 2, no. 231.

126 Orlin, p. 28.

127 LP, xxi, part 2, no 475; J. Lewis, *Dissertation on Sandwich* (1851) passim: W. Boys, *Collections for an History of Sandwich* (Canterbury, 1792), p. 176; D. Gardiner, *Historic haven the story of Sandwich* (Derby, 1954), p. 170; G. Gray, *Sandwich,* (1907); H. C. Bentwich, *History of Sandwich*, 2nd edn. (T. F. Pain, 1972); Orlin, p. 28.

128 Calendar of the Patent Rolls preserved in the Public Record Office, London 8 June 1550, app. 1, 346; LP, xxi, part 2, grant 475 (8); Orlin, p. 30.

129 See APPENDIX 8: PRO, E122/130/15; CKS, Favward, fol. 47.

130 *O.E.D.*, A sailing vessel; originally one of small size used for coasting and fishing, described as flat bottomed and having bulging sides.

131 *O.E.D.*, A strongly built vessel of the galiot order, usually two masted and from 100 to 250 tons burden.

132 *O.E.D.*, A small trading vessel.

133 *O.E.D.*, A small vessel carrying passengers and goods especially for short distances.

134 *O.E.D.*, A merchant vessel of the largest size and burden, especially those of Ragusa and Venice.

135 Armewe is a compression of Arnemviden which is in South Holland near Ulissingen and Middleburgh; information supplied by P. Wilkinson.

136 1 pocket = 2½ cwt; A.M. Millard, *Some useful weights and measures found in the London Port Books imports only for certain years between 1588 and 1640* (PRO typescript 1960); a package in the form of a sack made of stout twill, measuring when filled 6-7 feet high and 2 feet in diameter; A. Cronk, *English Hops Glossary* (1959), passim.

137 *O.E.D.*, Fish not thoroughly cured; green fish cured with a good salt.

knit ware for Calais, a case of white glass, handguns, a barrel of black soap, cruses,[138] pieces[139] of figs, barrels of shotten fish,[140] barrels of oil and butts of malmsey and muscatel. The only export was beer, almost always 3 tuns. No doubt this was due to some regulation, but the details are not yet known.

For Faversham, there were 34 ships coming in described only as such, without giving a category. The trade was again mainly with Ostend, but also with Nieuwpoort, Flushing, Rotterdam, Brielle and once with London. There were 23 aliens involved and only 4 natives, one of whom was Adam Fowle, who was later accused of being involved in Arden's murder. In January he was exporting a hogshead of herrings in a ship from Flushing licenced to load for Boulogne. Others were Thomas Pinckeney and John Hampton, who died in 1544, leaving a second wife, two sons and four daughters. The busiest man was John Bringborne, mayor in 1535, 1542 and 1544, who died in 1545, describing himself as a merchant in his will. His widow, Katherine, later married Francis Swan of Wye in Kent. The goods brought in were again hops, hoops, herrings, herrings with roes, staple fish, shotten herrings and Bay salt. Other rarer items were tow, [141] mustard seed, winnowing fans, chairs, salmon, a 'piece of linen cloth called holland', cod and a chest of sugar candy. Exports were beer in the same quantity, broadcloth without grain and cony skins.

Faversham Abbey outer-gateway, drawn in 1756 and published by S. Hooper in Francis Grose, *The Antiquities of England and Wales* (1787)

---

[138] *O.E.D.*, An earthenware jar.
[139] Millard op. cit.; 1 piece of figs = 60lbs.
[140] *O.E.D.*, Of fish, especially herring, that has spawned, thin, emaciated and worthless.
[141] *O.E.D.*, The shorter fibres of flax and hemp separated by heckling from the fine long fibres; PRO, Bringborne, PRO, PROB11/30/29 fol. 221v; CKS Hampton, Arch., PRC 17/24/242; CKS, Fa/LB 9.

Chapter 6
Man of property

Thomas Arden is generally thought to have acquired virtually all the lands formerly belonging to the abbey and to have become in consequence the leading figure in Faversham. This was not so, but the assumption is so ingrained that I think that the only way to tackle it is painstakingly to consider his acquisitions, deal by deal. I also want to show what happened to the property thereafter in order to demonstrate that it had mostly been sold by the time that Arden's daughter, Margaret, died in 1574. To keep matters as clear and simple as possible, I will deal with the property in the following order: first, when Arden was acting as a middleman, and then his own purchases in London, Canterbury and Kent generally, Sandwich, and, finally, Faversham.

Arden gradually amassed sufficient cash to become involved in the land market, because purchases had to be paid for within six and later three months 'except by special arrangement'.[142] He acquired cash through fees as a middleman and, above all, from being customer of Faversham and comptroller of Sandwich.

Arden dealt in property, mostly between 1540 and 1545. He sometimes acted as a middleman, at other times on his own account, no doubt as the opportunity arose. When he acted for someone else, he would expect fees both for his services and for obtaining authority from the crown to transfer the land. From the records of the Court of Augmentations, Arden is shown to have been involved in the following transactions as a middleman. On 5 June 1540 he and Sir Richard Long, a member of the privy chamber, bought an estate formerly belonging to the priory of the Augustine Friars in Huntingdon, which they soon after sold to Philip Campe and his wife. On 5 September 1543 the manor of Ellenden in Seasalter and Whitstable, which had formerly belonged to Faversham Abbey, was purchased by Thomas Arden for £173-8-6 at 20 years purchase. The figure of £202-16-2 given in the printed version included other properties. At the same time he purchased a farm in the parish of Faversham and Hernhill, including the woods belonging to the same, and a marsh, part of the manor of Lesnes, which had formerly been among the possessions of Thomas Wolsey. Ellenden he sold on 3 October following to John Nedam, whose family came from Wymondley, Herts,. The marshes at Lesnes, purchased by Arden at 26 years purchase, were soon transferred to Henry Cooke, merchant tailor of London, who had previously been granted a lease in 1543. Lands in Wasperton and Heathcote in Warwickshire formerly belonging to the friary of Thelsford were granted at 22 years purchase to Arden on behalf of William Walter, a yeoman of Putney, Surrey.[143]

Arden also began to acquire property on his own account from 1540 onwards, as is clear from his will, his Inquisition *post mortem* and a document entitled 'Master Arderne's .evedences sarched' made after his death.[144] On 10 September 1550, John Modye, a grocer of London, acknowledged receipt of a whole year's rent of £2-13-4 due to Master Doctor Willoughby for the parsonage of St. Michael's, Cornhill, which Arden had leased since 20 April 1547. Modye lived in the parish of St. Leonards in Foster Lane and still held a lease of property from the Bishop of London and Westminster Abbey at his death in 1585. Willoughby was an Oxford graduate, who may also

---

142 J. Youings, *The dissolution of the monasteries* (London, 1971), p. 128; M. L. Zell 'The mid-Tudor market in Crown land in Kent', *AC*, (1981), xcvii p. 67.

143 See APPENDIX 9; PRO, E318/2/34; LP xv, grant 831 (17);, *xvii,* grant 48, xviii, part 2, grant 241 (7), 327 (7); xix, part 1, grant 610 (14), p. 372; Commons 1509-58, ii, pp. 545-46; R. H. Goodsall, *Whitstable, Seasalter and Swalecliffe,* (1938), p. 66. Orlin, pp. 28-29.

144 See APPENDIX 10: Favward, fol. 280v; PRO, C142/93 no. 111; BL, Harl. Ch. 58 H. 18, first noted by L. Orlin, p. 29 from Faversham Society material.

have been vicar of Hackney, Middlesex. He had been a physician to Anne Boleyn and lived to be nearly 100. He was looked upon kindly in his dotage by Queen Elizabeth in memory of her mother.[145] Stow said that 'Master Arden lay at a certeyn parsonage of his in London' and it was there that his servant Michael agreed to let Black Will in to murder him, but later changed his mind. In the play the setting was changed in Act 2 scene 2 and Act 3 scene 1 to Franklin's house in Aldersgate.[146] The other point worth repeating is that the antiquary John Stow was born in the parish of St. Michael's, Cornhill, and his parents were buried there, which may have given him an added interest in the Arden story.[147]

Arden concentrated on land in Kent. It is as well at this juncture for everyone to understand what is meant by the phrase 'at twenty years purchase.' After the dissolution of the monasteries, the Court of Augmentations was set up to administer property that had once belonged to them. As J.Youings explains, 'at first the commissioners' instructions were to sell at twenty years purchase, that is, for a sum equal to twenty times the net current annual value, usually the gross rental less any fixed outgoings such as bailiffs' fees. All monastic property was also sold subject to the payment of a permanent, fixed, annual rent, notionally, and usually exactly, a 'tenth' of the current annual value.' Further on she says, 'the rule laid down in 1536 was that on all grants 'of inheritance' there should be laid a tenure by knight-service of the Crown, with all that that implied in terms of the Crown's exploitation of its feudal revenues. Many owners of small, and especially new, estates thus found themselves, or rather their heirs and heiresses, objects of the attention of the Master (and from 1542 the Court) of Wards.' They would also have to buy a 'license to alienate' when they came to sell any of the property. Elsewhere, J.Youings explains that urban property, which particularly interests us, was sold at fifteen years purchase, from 1539, which was reduced to ten years, in 1543. When the Crown was short of cash in 1544, it allowed houses worth less than 40s a year to be granted in free socage or burgage, which was a free tenure without the obligation of military service.[148] How this worked out in practice can be seen in Arden's deals and will be referred to from time to time. The first thing to point out is that the price he paid varied more than has been suggested.

In 1544 he and the yeoman, William Walter of Putney, with whom he had bought lands in Warwickshire, were granted the manor of Lambertisland in Hernhill for £268-14-4 at 20 years purchase. By 8 June 1550 it belonged to Henry Crispe of Birchington, Isle of Thanet, later M.P. for Dover in 1553, Winchelsea, also in 1553, and Canterbury in 1558. Crispe was then given licence to grant it to his sons, William and John Crispe the younger, so Arden may again have been acting as a middleman.[149] Crispe was described as 'the little king of Thanet'. He had a lot of property in Faversham and the surrounding area, which he had inherited from his aunt, a widow called Margaret Horne. He was one of the executors of Cheyne's will and his son, Nicholas, married Cheyne's daughter, Frances. He is the first of five M.P.s living in the area with interests in Faversham, who have been overlooked in the relentless concentration on Arden. Another of them, Cyriak Petyt, was one of his executors.

---

145 BL, Harl. Ch. 58 H 18; PROB11/51/17, fol. 124v; J. Foster, *Alumni Oxonienses 1500-1714,* 4 vols., (Oxford, 1891-92), p. 1651; J. Strype, *The life and Acts of Archbishop Parker* (Oxford, 1821), II, p. 156; G. Godwin, *The churches of London* (London, 1838), I, pp. 1-4.

146 See APPENDIX 3: BL, Harl. MSS. 542, fols. 34-37b.

147 DNB; C. L. Kingsford, *A survey of London by John Stow* (Oxford, 1908) intro.

148 J.Youings, 'The terms of the disposal of the Devon monastic lands', 1536-58, EHR, (1954), p. 133; Youings, pp. 161-62.

149 PRO, E318/2/37; LP, xix, 1, grant 610 (14), p. 372; CPR 1549-51, iii, p. 320; Commons 1509-58, i, pp. 722-23; W. H. Ireland, *England's topographer,* or a *new and complete history of the county of Kent,* 4 vols., (G. Virtue, 1828-30), iii, pp. 559-60; DNB.

The following year, on 3 July 1545, Arden bought the manor of Otterpool in Lympne and Sellindge, which had formerly been held by Sir Thomas Wyatt and had come into the king's hands by exchange at 20 years purchase. At the same time he bought land in the parish of Saltwood and property in the suburbs of Canterbury that had formerly belonged to the Archbishop of Canterbury and St. Augustine's, Canterbury at 9 years purchase. Otterpool and the other lands were bought for £473-9-6. What happened next is not quite clear, but it looks as if he was pipped at the post, because, two months later, on 10 September 1545, the very same property in Otterpool, Saltwood and the parish of St. Paul's, Canterbury, was granted to James Hales, sergeant at law, and his wife, Margery, again for £473-9-6. James Hales, later Sir James Hales, judge, was the eldest son of John Hales of the Dungeon, near Canterbury, by Isabell, daughter of Stephen Harry. He was among those appointed to receive the Lady Anne of Cleves on her arrival at Dover (29 Dec 1539). He was called to the degree of serjeant-at-law in Trinity term 1540, and on 4 Nov 1544 was appointed king's serjeant. He was standing counsel to the corporation of Canterbury in 1541-42, and he was also counsel to Archbishop Cranmer, though from what date is not clear. He was created a knight of the Bath at the coronation of Edward VI, 20 Feb 1546-47.

In April 1549 he was placed on a commission for detecting and extirpating heresy, on 10 May following was appointed a judge of the common pleas and in the autumn of the same year sat on a mixed commission of ecclesiastics, judges, and civilians appointed to hear Bishop Bonner's appeal against his deprivation, which confirmed the sentence. He also sat on the commission appointed on 12 Dec 1550 to try Bishop Gardiner for his intrigues and practices against the reformation, and concurred in the sentence of deprivation passed against him on 14 Feb 1550-1; and he was placed on another commission specially directed against the anabaptists of Kent and Essex in January 1550-1. He was also a member of a commission of sixteen spiritual and as many temporal persons appointed on 6 Oct 1551 to examine and reform the ecclesiastical laws; and on the 26th of the same month he was appointed to hear causes in chancery during the illness of the lord chancellor, Rich. In January 1551-52 he was commissioned to assist the lord keeper, Thomas Goodrich, bishop of Ely, in the hearing of chancery matters.

In 1553 Edward VI determined to exclude both the Princess Elizabeth and the Princess Mary from the succession and settle the crown by an act of council on the Lady Jane Grey. Hales, as a member of the council, was required to affix his seal to the document, but steadily refused so to do on the ground that the succession could only be legally altered by act of parliament. On the accession of Mary (6 July 1553) he showed equal regard for strict legality by charging the justices at the assizes in Kent that the laws of Edward VI and Henry VIII against nonconformists remained in force and must not be relaxed in favour of Roman catholics. Nevertheless the queen renewed his patent of justice of the common pleas; but on his presenting himself (6 Oct) in Westminster Hall to take the oath of office Gardiner, now lord chancellor, refused to administer it on the ground that he stood not well in her grace's favour by reason of his conduct at the Kent assizes, and he was shortly afterwards committed to the King's Bench prison, whence he was removed to the Compter in Bread Street, and afterwards to the Fleet. In prison he was visited by Dr Day, bishop of Chichester; his colleague on the bench, Portman; and one Forster. He was at last so worried by their arguments that he attempted to commit suicide by opening his veins with his penknife. This intention was frustrated. He recovered and was released in April 1554, but went mad and drowned himself in a shallow stream on 4 Aug following at Thanington, near Canterbury[150].

---

150 Charles Moore, *A full enquiry into the subject of suicide*, (1790), page 316 quotes the legal arguments surrounding the reversion of leases, to Sir James and his wife, to the crown; M. L. Zell, 'Suicide in pre-industrial England', *Social History*,

Joan, the widow of Henry Hatch, stated that she had at one stage been put under great pressure to marry Hales.[151] At his death, Arden left a deed showing that he owned property in Ivy Lane in St. Paul's parish outside and near the walls of the city of Canterbury, which had formerly belonged to St. Augustine's. It had once been let to George Nicholls at will at a rent of 4s 6d. Arden had acquired it from Robert Brokelesby and Nicholas Girling, to whom it had been granted in 1547.[152] It is worth remembering here that Thomas Arden of Canterbury lived in the suburb of St. Mildred's with his wife, Anne, and sons, John and Arthur, at much the same time.[153]

In 1540 Arden acquired the five-acre site of the Carmelite friary commonly called White Friars in Sandwich. It included 'the whole church, belfry and cemetery' as well as all the messuages, houses, buildings, barns, stables, dovecotes, ponds, fish-ponds, fishery, fruit-gardens, orchards and gardens. The section is almost illegible, but Arden seems to have had to pay £36-15-6 in hand on 15 years purchase. At his death, he was said to hold property in Faversham 'together with diverse lands and tenements' in Sandwich by the service of a twentieth part of one knight's fee. It seems to me possible that Arden was hedging his bets and that it took him some time to decide whether to make Sandwich or Faversham his permanent home.[154]

In 1547 he became M.P. for the borough of Sandwich in a disputed election.[155] Possibly Protector Somerset intervened on his behalf, for as treasurer he was head of the customs administration. Possibly again this was at the request of Sir Edward North. It is, however, much more likely that it was Sir Thomas Cheyne as Lord Warden who procured the return. The election was a cause of contention as two other men, Thomas Pinnock and John Seer, who probably had the support of Archbishop Cranmer, were already elected. The mayor, Richard Still, refused to seal the indenture and returned Arden and Thomas Patche instead. After an appeal to the Protector, the Privy Council declared the second election invalid and ordered the port to pay compensation to Pinnock and Seer. The retention of the names of Arden and Patche on the revised list of members may indicate that they sat in the Commons until the Council decided against them. By the time the list was revised, Arden had been dead for nearly a year, and the fact was duly noted.[156] Apart from the land in Sandwich, the house in Canterbury and the lease of the parsonage in London, it was only in Faversham that Arden had property at the time of his death. It was there that he had made his home.

To appreciate the part that Arden played in Faversham, we have to understand something of the background. The town is built on a navigable arm of the River Swale with access to the Thames estuary and it was the first major link after Dover between the main London to Canterbury road

xi, no. 3 (Oct. 1986), p. 311; Blackstone commented [Vol. iv. B. iv. C. xiv], ' The law can only act (by way of punishment) upon what the suicide has left behind him, his reputation and his fortune; on the former, by an ignominious burial in the highway with a stake driven through the body; on the latter, by the forfeiture of all his goods and chattels to the king.' Moore says the stake through the body is local not general and makes no part in the coroner's warrant for ignominious burial.

151 See APPENDIX 20; PRO, E318/2/36; Crisp, C1/481/29; LP, xx, part 2, grant 496 (21); DNB; Ireland, op. cit. iii, pp. 559-60; R. Petty, *History of the church of St. Mary the Virgin, Sellindge* (Canterbury, 1951); H. D. Dale, *History of the parish church of St. Peter and St. Paul, Saltwood, Hythe* (Kent Messenger, 1962); *Saltwood Parish Church: one thousand years of history,* ed. O. G. Villiers (Kent Messenger, 1966); P. Hyde, 'Henry Hatch and the battle over his will', *AC*, cii, p. 121.

152 BL, Harl. Ch. 58 H 18; PRO, E318/5/181 ml, 27; LP, xxi, 2, grant 648 (22); C. Donaldson, *A short history and guide of St. Paul's Church, Canterbury* (Ramsgate, 1964); *The parish of St. Martin and St. Paul,* ed. Margaret Sparks (Canterbury, 1980).

153 See APPENDIX 5: PRO, C2/Elizabeth 1/A6/31.

154 See APPENDIX 10: PRO, E318/2/33 m. 2, C66/694 m. 26, C142/93/111; Gardiner, *op. cit.*, p. 170;. Boys, *op. cit.* p. 176; LP, xv, grant 831 (17).

155 Commons 1509-58, i, pp. 328-29, iii, pp. 69, 110, 288.

156 APC, ii, pp. 536-57.

and the sea. It is nine miles from Canterbury and forty-seven from London. There is evidence of Roman occupation and the town had royal associations dating back to 811, when it was identified as 'the king's little town of Fefresham' in a charter of Cunewulf. In 1070 William the Conqueror gave the church there and its tithes to the Abbey of St. Augustine's at Canterbury. Sixteen years later the manor of Faversham was recorded as being part of the royal demesne. In 1147 King Stephen founded a vast royal abbey there, at first Cluniac but soon Benedictine, in which he, his queen, Matilda, and his son, Eustace, were to be buried. Because he was on the losing side in the civil war, the abbey never had the significance that he had intended. Nevertheless, a borough was laid out to the south of the abbey some distance from the original settlement, and the abbey itself dominated the town for the next three hundred years or so. This was deeply resented by some townsmen, probably those of the old settlement, and there were many disputes with the abbot. By 1229 a group of townsmen had successfully applied to join the Cinque Ports with their liberties and privileges, and Faversham became a member under the Head Port of Dover. In exchange for tax exemptions, the five ports of Hastings, Romney, Hythe, Dover and Sandwich were expected to maintain fifty-seven fully crewed ships in readiness to serve as a royal navy. A private bargain probably preceded the grant of the charter. As K. Murray said, 'it is easy to guess that the reason why the men of the thirty-two haws in the king's town of Faversham agreed to help Dover by the provision of a ship, and to pay scot and lot to the Head Port, is to be found in the quarrel raging between them and the Abbot.' She suggests that its attachment to Dover rather than Sandwich was a matter of choice.[157] What is equally thought-provoking is that by the sixteenth century it is the links with Sandwich that are remarkable. In Arden's time, of course, his patron, Sir Thomas Cheyne, was Lord Warden of the Cinque Ports.[158]

The abbey was dissolved on 8 July 1538. Three years earlier, on 20 May 1535, Thomas Cromwell's nephew, Richard Cromwell alias Williams, who was a channel of communication with the minister, had been granted a £3-0-0 annuity on the manor of Faversham by the abbot and convent 'for the good council, favour and help shown before this to us and our monastery'. He married a daughter of Sir Thomas Mirfyn, the former Lord Mayor of London whom I have mentioned earlier, and he was thus a kinsman of Alice Arden and Sir Edward North. He had the grant confirmed on 10 February 1539, was knighted in 1540, sat in Parliament for Huntingdonshire in 1539 and 1542, and died in 1544. North was one of his executors and acquired the wardship of his seven year old son and heir. His great-grandson was the Protector, Oliver Cromwell.

In 1536 Cromwell wrote to the crafty old abbot, John Castlock, urging him to retire. Castlock replied at length justifying his continued tenure of office, following this with a present a month later. Two years later, Castlock wisely saw which way the wind was blowing and resigned for a fat pension worth £66-8-0 (100 marks) when the abbey's revenue was nearly £287. He did not leave a will but his brother, William Castlock, was granted the administration of his estate on 30 April 1543. William was bound with Joseph Beverley of Faversham in one hundred marks sterling and William himself died in 1550.[159]

On 10 May 1539 the site of the abbey was leased to a gentleman called John Wheler of London. This included 12 acres of grounds valued at 12^{d} an acre, Ostry garden let to Richard Fowle for 6^{s} 8^{d} a year, 9 acres attached to the brewhouse valued at 18^{s} a year, 10 acres of meadow at

157 K.M.E. Murray, *The Constitutional History of the Cinque Ports* (Manchester U.P., 1935), pp. 49-50.

158 Jacob, passim; E. Hasted, 'The parish and town of Faversham' (1798, *Faversham Papers,* no. 6, 1969); H. A. James, 'Faversham parish church' (*Faversham Papers no. 33,* 1990).

159 PRO, E315 vol. 100 p. 237; E315/100 fol. 127v; CKS, Castlock, PRC 3/9 fol. 43; LP, x, pp. 484, 627, xiii, part 1, 1339-40; Canon W. Telfer, 'Faversham abbey and its last abbot, John Caslock' (*Faversham Papers no 2,* 1965); Commons 1509-58, i, pp. 734-35.

Thornemede and 3 acres of pasture with a small tenement at 26^s a year, a 2 acre close next to the grange and dovehouse garden at 4s a year and another 6 acre close at 12^s a year. This came to a total of £3-18-8 a year and had all been part of the demesne. Nothing is known of John Wheler, though he may just possibly have been the same as the man who was appointed a doorward of Berkhamstead Castle, Herts, with two pence a day on 29 April 1540. It was noted in 1539 that the Abbot of Faversham had previously appointed Richard Fowle keeper of the outer gate of the abbey 'for good service to us'. He probably belonged to the Fowle family of Faversham, which included Adam Fowle, the inn-keeper of the Fleur de Luce and allegedly one of the assassins.[160]

Within a year, on 16 March 1540, the reversion of what was then said to be a 21 year lease was granted for £283-15-10 to Sir Thomas Cheyne, Lord Warden of the Cinque Ports.[161]He had already acquired land and marsh on the Isle of Harty with the connivance of the abbot in March, 1538. I would agree with Canon Telfer that the grant to Cheyne may have been made so that he could dismantle the abbey, for it was partially demolished immediately. Between April and June 1541 the stone was being sent to repair the defences in Calais, Ambleteuse and Guisnes; 'item in freight of stone from Faversham and St. Augustine's at Canterbury,£20'.[162]

In December 1544, possibly with his mission accomplished, Cheyne was allowed to alienate the site of the abbey to Thomas Arden, who had already acquired some other property there that had once belonged to the abbey. On 5 June 1540 Arden had been granted a messuage and land called Nethergreen, which had lately been leased to John Willoughby at a rent of £1-6-8, another leased to Richard and Dorothy Dryland near Almery Croft at a rent of £2-0-0 and two more to John Seth, one in West Street and the other, a corner tenement near the fish market, at a rent of 13^s 4^d. The rent totalled £4-0-0 and Arden bought this property for £54 at 15 years purchase, £30 down and £24 on 1 October following. In a bill four days earlier, Edward North, as treasurer of the Court of Augmentations, charged him £90-16-3 for the four messuages and the site of the late priory of Whitefriars of Sandwich. In 'Master Ardernes evedences sarched' .one of the houses in this grant is described as 'his owne mansion house'.

Nothing is known of John Willoughby unless he was the man from whom Arden later rented the house in London, but the Drylands were a well-known local family. The family history of the Drylands has not yet been satisfactorily sorted out, but Wendy McCaw is working on it. Richard Dryland of Cooksditch, son of John Dryland, had married the heiress of Thomas Frogenhale of Buckland. His second wife was Dorothy, daughter of John Mydleton alias Sampson. Known as Richard Dryland, senior, he lived in the great house at the Town Gate according to the 1532 rental and was mayor, in 1516-17, 1519-20 and 1531-32. He was one of the executors of the town's great benefactors, Henry Hatch, and was commonly thought to have been responsible for Hatch leaving his property to the town. He probably died before 1542-43, when the other Richard Dryland became mayor, but was no longer described as 'the younger.' According to the 1532 rental, the younger Richard Dryland lived in Court Street, then called North Street,. It was probably he who in 1538 was granted an annuity of ten marks out of the lands of Faversham monastery for service in the King's wars beyond the seas. He gave his age as 71 in a deposition on 9 December 1550. He made his will on 27 January 1551 and it was proved on 14 March following; he left property in Faversham, Chilham, Teynham, Luddenham, Stone, Lynsted, Davington and Harty to his two sons, both called John, and to his two daughters.

---

160 See APPENDIX 11: PRO, E313/11/146, E315/100/237, E315/402/27, E315/100/23; E318/7/265; LP, xv, grant 436 (44), grant 613 (43).

161 PRO, E313/11/146, E318/7/265; LP, xv, grant 436 (44).

162 BL, Harl. Ch. 8 H 18; LP, xiii, part 1, 585, grant 646 (64), xvi, no. 1219 (pp. 568-69); 'The chronicle of Calais', ed J. F. Nichols, *Cam.Soc.*, (1846), xxxv, p. 198.

John Seth was mayor in 1537, 1539, 1545 and 1552 and died in 1557. If his will is to be believed, it is clear that he was a wealthy man. He had a capital messuage, a messuage, two tenements, three other tenements at the key, 'a seller called the stony sellour with a lofte over yt'[163], a salt house, two wharves and a winding crane, houses at the key purchased from the former vicar, Clement Norton, a malt-house in Tanners Street called Boroughe's Hall and three flesh shambles in the market. He left silver plate and jewellery to his second wife and silver goblets to his children. The house in West Street and the corner house called Copthall, which were both let, he left for the rest of the term of years, to his son, Stephen.[164]

At his death, Arden held the site of the abbey of the king in chief for the service of the twentieth part of one knight's fee, which was the rule laid down in 1536 with all that that implied in terms of the crown's exploitation of its feudal revenues. He still held all the rest of the property mentioned above at the time of his death, except 'the house adjoining to the abbey gate', Nether Green and about half an acre of Upper Green, which he had sold on 3 August 1545 for £90 to a yeoman called Thomas Dunkyn, who was, of course, the neighbour called Dumpkin mentioned in Stow at whose house Arden had been clearing certain 'reckonings' before returning home on the night of the murder. He was mayor of the town in 1546 and probably a friend of Arden, indeed the only friend whom it has been possible to trace in spite of an intensive search. More will be said of him in connection with the murder, but he is a shadowy figure. He was probably the yeoman Thomas Dunkyn of Cranbrook who contributed £10 to the loan to the king by gentlemen in Kent in 1542. According to F.C. Dietz, this loan was more productive than any single collection of parliamentary tax had ever been, bringing £112,229 into the treasury. He was equally probably the yeoman of Clerkenwell in Middlesex who made his will on 6 July 1571. He had a wife, Juliana, but presumably no children of his own, because he left his property in Elmstead and Stowting in Kent to his numerous nieces and nephews after her death. He also arranged for his estate called Harviles in Sheldwich and Selling, otherwise unknown, to be sold and the proceeds to go to these same nephews and nieces. He remembered the poor in Elmstead, Sheldwich and, significantly, Cranbrook. He mentioned his brother, John Dunkyn of Elmstead and another brother, John Dunkyn of Boxley.[165]

It is significant that Arden himself did not appear as a contributor to that loan of 1542, presumably because he had not yet made his mark in Faversham for lack of liquidity. Several residents did contribute and they clearly must have been the leading men in the town: Laurence Manby the mayor five marks, Richard Dryland the elder £10, John David or Davy £5, John Bringborne £5, John Seth £5, William Castlock five marks, John Best forty shillings, Thomas Gate forty shillings, John Wreake forty shillings and William Marshall forty shillings. Laurence Manby died intestate in 1544 and the administration of his estate was granted to his widow, Dorothy. John David or Davy was mayor in 1528. He died in 1544, leaving a bequest to the late abbot and mentioning his son, Thomas, who was a servant of Sir Anthony Saintleger, whom he appointed one of his overseers. Joseph Beverley M.P. mentioned below was one of his executors. John Best was mayor in 1547, 1549 and 1558. The administration of the goods of John Best of Boughton-under-Blean was granted to his widow, Mary, on 3 January 1566. Thomas Gate was mayor in 1552 and died in 1560. John Wreake was mayor in 1550 and, if the

---

[163] *O.E.D.* Cellar: A store-house or store-room, whether above or below ground, for provisions; a granary, buttery, or pantry. It is impossible to determine at what period the notion of 'store-room' began to give place to that of 'underground chamber'.

[164] See APPENDIX 11: PRO, E318/2/33; CKS, U2741/T3; LP, xiv, part 1, 1355 (65); xv, grant 831 (17); Dryland, Hasted, vi, p. 287; Vis. Kent 1530-1, *Harl. Soc.*, lxxiv, p. 9; CCA, Deposition register, DCb/X.10.4.fol. 155v; CKS, PRC17/30/42v; 1559, Act Book, PRC22/4/8v; Seth, PCC 14 Wrastley, PROB11/39 q. 14 fols. 103v-105; Favward fol. 89v.

[165] PRO, C66/72 m. 39 ; PRO, PROB 11/53/271; CKS, Cons, PRC22/4 fol. 8v; Rockingham Castle, Watson (Rockingham) Collection, no. 682; *English government finance 1485-1558*, (Univ. of Illinois, 1921), p. 164; Youings, p. 162.

same man, died in 1579, leaving a large family and a lot of property in Faversham, including his principal residence in the market place. William Marshall was mayor in 1551 and he and his son, John, once leased the grange at Nethercourt from the abbot[166]. He died in 1562, leaving £47-4-2 according to his inventory. Dunkyn did not apparently hold Nether Green and half an acre in Upper Green long, because they were sold on 13 January 1568 by John and Helen Milles of Faversham to a gentleman called John Finch of Faversham for £266. Finch sold the house, Nethergreen and Uppergreen in 1577 to Thomas Stransham of St. Dunstan next the churchyard of Canterbury, Richard Dryland of Wye, gentleman, and Robert Stransham of London, gentleman. The other two released them to Robert Stransham in 1580, whose daughter married Edward Appleford, who sold it to Sir George Sondes, probably in 1671. Finch, Dryland and the two Stranshams will be described later.[167]

When Arden bought the manor of Ellenden and some land in Hernhill in 1543, he acquired a tenement called The Bear, which is still there today, though it has moved a few doors along, a shop next door called The Garret in the market and a garden at Cooksditch in the tenure of John Seth, which had previously been let to Seth for seventy years. These were rented at £1-3-4, and were to be purchased for £15-15-0 at 15 years purchase. After about a year, on 5 June 1544, Arden sold The Garret and another messuage in Court Street called The George to Anthony Aucher for £23-6-8. The Bear may have been sold with the manor of Ellenden to John Nedam and his family of Wymondley, Herts, on 3 October 1543 as it was not part of Arden's estate on his death.[168]

Anthony Aucher of Otterden is one of the names put forward by those who favour a conspiracy theory for the murder, which I will discuss later. I must in the mean time digress a while to say something of his career. He is a shadowy figure, even though he was one of three men belonging to the dozen families, who were granted half of all the Crown lands in Kent following the dissolution of the monasteries. This may be because he neither became an M. P.,nor followed the path that we might have expected.

Otterden is 6½ miles south west of Faversham, which explains why he was interested in acquiring property in the area. He came from a respectable, gentry family which had been established in Otterden since the 14th century. He married Affra, the daughter of William Cornwallis of Norfolk.

Like many another, he started his career by acting for Cromwell in his private affairs, probably about 1536. He also became a link between Cromwell and the Kentish monasteries in general, just as Richard Cromwell alias Williams did at Faversham.. Aucher thus established himself as an administrator and was rewarded with the offices of auditor and surveyor of the manors formerly belonging to the great estates of Christ Church Priory. In 1537 he was granted what P. Clark calls 'the key post of paymaster of the royal haven works at Dover'. He went on to hold, amongst other offices, receiver of the Court of Augmentations in 1544, master of the king's jewels in 1545 and surveyor at Boulogne in 1547. There was the inevitable talk of corruption from time to time.

---

[166] See APPENDIX 13.

[167] PRO, E315/96 p.58, C142/98 no. 111; CKS, Fa/JBf 10; Manby, Arch, PRC 3/10 fol. 84v; Best, Cons, PRC 22/6 fol. 29; Davy, Arch, PRC 17/23 fol. 173; Gate, Arch, PRC17/32/31; Wreake, Arch, PRC 17/43 fol. 206; Rockingham, nos. 680, 682, 678, 679, 704; Lambeth, *Carte Miscellenæ*, xxii, I, 233; CKS, Arch, PRC 17/35/138; Wine, p. 154; LP, xx, 2, 266 (36), p.124; J. Greenstreet, 'Kent contributors to a loan to the King 1542', *AC*, xi, 400; Hasted, vi, 334;
See Text pages 103-104 (conspiracy debate) & pp. 108-109 (Hothfield dispute).

[168] See APPENDIX 12: PRO, E318/2/34 m 3, m 4, m. 6; C142/93/111; CKS, Fa/JB fol. 5; LP, xviii, part 2, grant 241 (7), grant 327 (7).

In the county he was known as an active reformer, but was even more concerned with his own personal gain. Clark notes that, in the troubles there in 1550-51, William Cowley, a townsman of Sandwich, said that 'if Sir Anthony Aucher were not hanged he (Cowley) would be hanged for him.' He had no problem switching his loyalty from the Duke of Somerset to the Duke of Northumberland. He was out of favour in Mary's reign until his expertise on defence was required. He died at the siege of Calais in 1558.[169]

Not much is heard of him in Faversham. In 1541 he was granted custody of the manor of Sutton and a messuage in Faversham following the death of Richard Maycott during the minority of his three daughters. Richard was the son of Robert Maycott, who had been the abbot's steward in 1532 and had lived in what is now presumably Globe House in Abbey Street. Aucher then made the deal with Arden over The George and The Garret mentioned above. In a list of deeds drawn up after his death, 'Master Arderne's evidences serched', it appears that Aucher owed Arden and his wife or the longer liver of them 20 marks a year.

Otherwise, on 8 February 1549, the Privy Council wrote to the mayor ordering 'the sending to the Lordes oone Ashehurst, to answere to the things objected to him in the letter of Mr. Aucher of the 5th of this present'. Nothing is known of this incident, and the only time he appeared in the Faversham wardmote book in the period 1540-52 was in the chamberlains' accounts of 1545-46 on folio 242 when they included four shillings for the sergeant riding to 'Mr. Auger.'[170]

Arden at last firmly established himself in Faversham at the end of 1544 when he bought the site of the virtually demolished abbey from Cheyne. Edward Crow quoting Mr. Burton in the eighteenth century says that Arden 'was importuned to buy the abbey lands by Lord Cheyne and was not aware when he bought them that several tenants had leases of different portions'. It is impossible to trace the source of this comment, but I would not be at all surprised if it were true. Certainly it was not the great *coup* that it is usually made out to be and, furthermore, as I shall show later, he ran into problems with leases.[171] A few months later, on 24 March 1545, Arden was also granted about 25 messuages and tenements that had once belonged to the abbey. They were spread all over the town, nine in Abbey Street, which was then called Court Street, and eight in Court Street, which was then called North Street, which were names that had been used in the days of the abbey. There was also one in Preston Street, one in Middle Row and six in West Street. In addition, there was an apple garden in East Street, a storehouse in North Street, a cottage and piece of land in Preston Street, a garden, the site of a messuage and half an acre in West Street, and, finally, a well-house and two shops in the fish shambles in Middle Row.[172]

Of the eighteen tenants involved, nothing is known of eleven. We have already met John Bringborne the merchant and William Marshall. Simon Auncell had been receiver of the abbey lands in Kingsnorth before the dissolution and was mayor in 1548 until his death. His widow, Elizabeth, was the sister of Joan Hatch, in turn the widow of Henry Hatch, the leading merchant in Faversham at the time of his death in 1533. Hatch had died childless and had left all his property to the town after Joan's death. She outlived him by 40 years and was involved in a bitter struggle with the town over his will, in which Elizabeth supported her. When Joan

---

169 For other accounts of him, see, P. Clark, *English provincial society from the Reformation to the Revolution* (The Harvester Press, 1977), pp. 50, 61, 66, 79-81, 83, 105, 419n, 424n, 427n; Orlin, pp. 30, 45-46, 47-48, 50-51, 52, 56; Hasted, viii, p. 84;Burke's *Extinct and Dormant Baronetcies of England*, (1844), p. 28;F. R. H. De Boulay, *The Lordship of Canterbury*, (1966), p. 326; W. G. Richardson, *op. cit*., pp. 221, 281; LP xx, part 1, 122, part 2, 909 (33), 910 (58).

170 See APPENDIX 12 & APPENDIX 18; LP, xvi, no.1056 (21), p. 499; Maycott, PROB 11/26 q. 8; APC 1547-50, p. 389.

171 Rockingham, no. 681; LP, xix, 2, grant 800 (36); FIJ, (August, 1881), pp. 299-303.

172 See APPENDIX 12: PRO, E318/2/35.

married Sir Henry Amcotts, later Lord Mayor of London, she moved to London, while Elizabeth remained in Faversham, but they kept in touch.[173]

Joseph Beverley of Faversham was M.P. for Dover in 1547 and 1553, Winchelsea in 1554, and Dover in 1558. He was an administrator of the estate of the abbot, John Castlock, in 1543. He had property in Court Street on the west side, was an auditor of the abbey in 1535-36, was made a freeman on 20 July 1541 and was mayor in 1559. He was deeply involved in the affairs of the Cinque Ports as clerk of Dover Castle and as counsel and M.P. for the port. He died in 1561.[174]

William Norton was probably William Norton of Faversham, son of Reynold Norton of York, who married an heiress from Pouldhurst and was ancestor of the Nortons of Fordwich. He was a member of the gentry, his family was included in several visitations of Kent and he was probably mayor in 1512 and 1527. His third son, Clement, became vicar in 1535. When he died in 1549, he left lands in Chillenden, Nonington and Goodnestone. The Lambert without a Christian name may have been Thomas Lambert, the mayor in 1538.[175] John Goodhew's administration was granted to his widow, Agnes, in 1545. Reginald Smith of Boughton-under-Blean in his long will in 1559 mentioned many children and listed property in Boughton, Faversham, Ospringe and Hernhill. Finally, Robert Colwell was the son of a former mayor, Richard Colwell, who died in office in 1534. He was a member of the gentry and his family was in several visitations of Kent. He had been receiver of the farms and rents of the town for the abbey before the dissolution. He was a jurat by 1539 and bailiff from 1546 onwards, rendering his annual account. He left no will, but, when he died in 1564, administration was granted to his son, John.[176]

These then were some of the tenants of the property that Arden bought, surely not men likely to be overawed by Thomas Arden. At the time of his death there were seventeen tenants, who were said to hold their lands in free socage and not in chief which were valued above repairs at £8-0-0. When they were purchased, the auditor, William Cavendish, stated that the rents totalled £11-14-4 and it was agreed that they should be bought at ten years purchase, which came to £117-3-4. The grant was signed, significantly, by Edward North as well as Robert Southwell, the Master of the Rolls, and by Richard Rich, who had been personally involved in the dissolution of the abbey and had acquired its manor of Bendysh in Essex.

In the course of the document, the auditor, William Cavendish stated;[177]

> 'These are all the houses that the kinge's majestie hathe within the towne of Fevversham as in the right of the late Monasterye of Fevversham As by the recordes more playnelye doth appere. And what fyne or income hathe heretofore byne geven or wyll at this daye be gyven for the same ys unknowen to the audytour'.

A few years later, in the reign of Edward VI, Arden came back to the court, and, on the basis of Cavendish's comment, quoted his letters patent, saying that he had been granted all the houses that had once belonged to the abbey. He therefore claimed in addition, a shop called the pillory next to the flesh shambles at a rent of 6^{s} 8^{d}, two gardens in Preston Street at 4s and a cottage called St. Nicholas Chapel at 6^{s} 8^{d}. This makes up the bulk of the property that he left to the

[173] CKS, Auncell, Arch, PRC17/26/19; Hyde, p. 121; Jacob, p. 121.

[174] CKS, Arch, Beverley, Arch, PRC17/36/1; Commons 1509-58, i, pp. 428-29; iii, pp. 564-65.

[175] CKS, Arch, Goodhew, PRC3/11/85; Smith, Cons, PRC32/27/197; Marshall, Arch, PRC17/35/138; Norton, Arch, PRC17/26/296v; Norton; Vis. Kent 1530-1, Harl .Soc., lxxiv,p. 16; Vis. Kent 1592, Harl. Soc., lxxv, p. 139; Jacob,pp. 120-21.

[176] CKS, Arch, PRC3/11/5v; PRC3/32/27 pp.197-203; PRC3/17/29; Favward, fols. 34, 244v; Vis. Kent 1574, Harl. Soc. lxxv, p. 40, Vis Kent 1592, Harl. Soc., lxxv, p. 90; Jacob, p. 193.

[177] PRO, E318/2/35 m. 4; Commons 1509-58, i, pp. 597-99; iii, pp. 192-95, 354-56.

town in his will with the addition of two tenements in Cooksditch. The pillory was then worth eight shillings, the two gardens in Preston Street eight shillings and St. Nicholas's chapel £1-0-0. The auditor, Thomas Everard agreed that Arden should have them at ten years purchase as before, which came to £8-13-0.[178]

In view of this, it is remarkable to discover that Arden did not acquire by any means all the abbey property in the town. This is important in a study of Thomas Arden because there has until now been a false impression of his importance in Faversham based on the assumption that he did. Furthermore, the influence of the Crown in the town has been under-estimated. He acquired the site of the abbey and some other property in the town, but what he significantly did not acquire was the manor of Faversham. In an abbey rental which can be dated to 1532, which is in the cathedral archives office at Canterbury, it can be seen that the abbot held virtually the whole town, 248 messuages, 46 tenements, five cottages, 11 sites, five storehouses, two malthouses, 28 shambles, five shops, one slaughterhouse, two mills and several almshouses. There were 148 tenants for 310 houses and sites. They were spread all over the town; in Court Street, which is now Abbey Street; North Street,which is now Court Street; Preston Street; West Street and Tanners Street. Arden acquired only 28. Furthermore, there is a detailed survey of other abbey lands in the hundred in the Centre for Kentish Studies, Maidstone, which is said to be for the year 1546, but can provisionally be dated from internal evidence to 1515. This has not been studied in detail but on a rough count there were 159 free tenants holding 2,847 acres. It covered Keyborough, Westdown, Eastdown, Oare, Graveney, Ewell, Selgrave, Kingsland Street, Woodgate Leese, Badlesmere and Bakynhelde. By comparison, Arden acquired only 30 acres from the demesne.[179]

The manor remained in Crown hands, as Hasted realized. There are ministers' accounts from Michaelmas 1546 to Michaelmas 1548. In 1546 Robert Colwell was the collector of rents. and John Wylde was receiver and collector of rents for the hundred. John Wylde was possibly John Wylde of Canterbury, who died either in 1546 or 1554-55. It said quite clearly that it was the first account after the establishment of the Court of Augmentations. It is clear from the ministers' accounts in Appendix 12 that Arden was himself the collector of rents for the royal manor from September 1547 to September 1549. That is probably how he came to realize that he should have been granted a shop called the pillory, a cottage called St. Nicholas' Chapel and two gardens in Preston Street under his original patent. As already mentioned, the chief steward was William Roper, the son-in-law and hagiographer of Sir Thomas More and a well-known national figure.. The abbot had, on 6 August 1519, appointed John Roper of St. Dunstans, Canterbury, and his son, William, chief steward of all the abbeys, lordships and manors in Kent for a fee of £8-6-8 a year in succession to John Roper's father-in-law, Sir John Fineux of Faversham. After the dissolution of the abbey and the death of his father, William Roper claimed recognition of his grant at the Court of Augmentations on 14 November 1538. He thereafter acted as the royal steward and was granted £6-0-0 a year for life when the town was granted its charter in 1546. He acted as steward from 1546 till his death in 1578. He was the fourth M.P. of note in the area. He sat for Bramber in 1529 and Rochester in 1545 and 1547. In October 1553 he was returned for Winchelsea by Sir Thomas Cheyne. He then sat for Rochester in 1554 and Canterbury in 1555 and 1558. There are a series of later rentals for the manor, which show that the Crown still had 172 tenants in 1575, 198 tenants holding 243 properties in 1604, 131 holding 199 in 1608, and apparently 212 properties in 1621. The manor

---

178 See APPENDIX 12: PRO, E310/3/3, item 3.

179 See APPENDIX 17 and APPENDIX 18; CKS, U390 M37/1; PRO, SC6/Hen VIII/No. 1755, E310/3/13, item 3; SP5/1; Lambeth; ED 2006.

was sold to Sir Dudley Digges in 1630 for £3,129-13-4. His son, John, sold it to Sir George Sondes, in whose family it remains. [180]

The misunderstanding has arisen because, apart from the site and the property bought in 1540, that is Nethergreen and the messuages let to Richard Dryland and John Seth, Arden seems to have acquired property from the abbey that was mainly held in free socage, which was a tenure of lands by service of determinate quality. Such a holding was not of great benefit to the ground landlord, because it could be alienated by the tenant and inherited without restriction, subject only to a fee by the heir. In 'Master Ardernes .evedences sarched' the grant on 24 March 1545 was said to be of other houses in Faversham to hold in socage. It was described in the 1532 rental as 'to farm'. For example, in 1532 'John Sayer holdeth of the lorde to ferme (in East Street North) a garden callyd the Apple Gardyn and paith by yere 5^{s} 4^{d}', which went to support the abbey table. In 1545 the grant to Arden referred to 'the Appull Gardeyn late in the tenure of John Sayer and now of William Marshall in Eaststrete between the lands of William Marshall on the west and the high street on the east'. The alternative phrase in the 1532 rental for a messuage not to farm was as follows, 'Adam Princhett holdeth of the lorde (in East Street North) a mesuage with a garden and renth by yere to the Sexten',2^{s} 4^{d} and ½ a hen. There were nine properties to farm in Abbey (Court) Street West, 15 not to farm; four in Abbey (Court) Street East, 10 not to farm. By contrast, only two were to farm in Tanners Street, compared with 31 not to farm.[181].

The essential point is that the houses held in free socage seem by then to have become separated from the rest of the abbey property. What is important is that there was not therefore the manorial or feudal bond between Thomas Arden and his fellow townsmen that has usually been assumed. Of course he was important to them as Mr. Customer and a man of property with friends in high places, but most of them were not beholden to him. It was the Crown that could claim that loyalty, and its importance in the town for about eighty years has not been recognised. As I hope to show in a later study, Faversham was then on the verge of one of the most prosperous periods of its history and men like John Bringborne, John Seth and William Norton were not likely to be intimidated by Arden. Nor, indeed, were the men who were at one time or another abbey officials: William Roper the steward, Simon Auncell and John Wylde the receivers general, Joseph Beverley the auditor, Robert Colwell the collector of rents and George Saintleger the principal forester of Woodlese. George Saintleger may have been the younger brother of Sir Anthony Saintleger of Ulcombe and Leeds Castle in Kent, who had acquired property from the abbey.[182]

Arden had not yet completed his purchases in Faversham. At some point he bought Flood Mill, which had once belonged to the abbey and had been granted to Robert Brokilsby and Nicholas Girlington in December 1546. He possibly acquired it from them at the same time as they sold him the house in Ivy Lane, Canterbury. At his death, it was said to be worth £10 a year and to be held in free socage and, mysteriously, to be held of the royal manor of Epworth in Lincoln, which had once belonged to Epworth Priory in Axholme. After the dissolution Epworth passed to Edward Stanley, Earl of Derby. He sold the manor to the Crown on 26 June 1545. Six

---

[180] PRO, SC6/EdwardVI/233, SC6/EdwardVI/723, LR6/97/7, LR6/97/8 fol. 2v, LR6/113/1 m. 1v, E310/3/3 item 3; E315/vol. 100/47b, 96/vol 6 p. 58; Favward, fol. 43; CCA, rentals, 1575, U33; 1604, U390-M38, 1608, U390-M61/1/1, 1621, U 390-M39; CKS, will, Wylde, PRC17/24/165, PRC 32/26/101; Vis Kent 1574, *Harl. Soc* lxxv, p. 18, Vis.Kent 1619, *Harl. Soc.*xlii, p. 18; Commons 1509-58, iii, pp. 215-17; Jacob, pp. 35-36; Hasted, p. 12. See Text page 390.

[181] CCA, Lit MSS B5 fol. 7v ; S.Friar, *The Batsford companion to local history,* (London,1991), p. 356; J..Richardson, *op. cit.*, p. 25.

[182] PRO, SC6/EdwardVI/233, SC6/EdwardVI/723, LR6/97/7, LR6/97/8, LR6/113/10; Vis.Kent 1574, *Harl. Soc.* lxxv, p. 69; Commons 1509-58, iii, pp. 326-27; R.Hugh Perks, 'The hoys and after', *Fav. Mag.*, i pp. 4, 9-11.

months later, on 16 December 1545, Derby was granted lands in Eynsham, Oxfordshire, and elsewhere in lieu. The only thing that may be significant is that Sir Edward North was involved in this complicated exchange, having transferred Eynsham to the Crown on 17 May. Otherwise no link with Faversham has been established. The Augmentation documents cited earlier make it clear that the mill had long belonged to Faversham Abbey. Perhaps the explanation is that none of the jurors of Arden's inquisition *post mortem* were familiar with Faversham, which is not surprising as it was held in Bexley, Kent, but the escheator, Christopher Roper, was the brother of the steward, William Roper.[183]

Arden also bought seven acres of land in Faversham called Surrenden Croft, which was abbey land that had been granted in November 1546 to John Bellowe of Grimsby, Lincs, and John Broxholme of London. At his death, Arden was said to hold them of the king of his honor of Torrington in Devon in free socage. This is another mystery. Torrington had been granted to Henry VIII's son, Henry Fitzroy, Duke of Richmond, but reverted to the Crown on his death in 1536. Again, no connection with Faversham has yet been found and the suppression papers indicate that Surrenden Croft had always belonged to Faversham Abbey. [184]

On 8 October 1545 he took a 21 year lease for £22-0-0 a year of a wood stretching over eleven hundred acres called Faversham Blean alias Boughton Blean. There were a number of restrictions and reservations of certain trees to the Crown. The lease was later cancelled and granted to the Earl of Pembroke in 1553.[185] Finally, on 16 March 1548, he was for £50-3-4 granted the remainder of a 21 year lease of corn, barley, pigs and capons on Nethercourt and rights over Nethercourt itself formerly granted to Stephen Motte by the abbey. This grant was witnessed by Sir Edward North. Stephen Motte had been granted the freedom of the town by the mayor for free in 1542. He and John Wylde bought the manor of Lydd Court in Worth in Kent in 1544-45, but sold it again almost immediately.[186]

On 24 September 1549, Arden granted a twenty year lease to a labourer called John Baker of a small garden adjoining Baker's messuage in Preston Street at four shillings rent a year. Baker was to plant it with good fruit trees. This lease was written 'by me Thomas Arderne in my own hand, 1549', and was copied into the wardmote book when Edward Blackwell was mayor, 1563-64, no doubt as a result of the disputes between the town and Arden's daughter, Margaret. This may just have been the John Baker who left a house and garden to his daughter, Helen, in 1558.[187]

Arden sold land in Faversham at least twice. Apart from the sale of The Garret mentioned above, he sold William Garrett three acres of pasture adjoining his own property for £30 pounds in silver on 20 December 1548.[188]

By one means or another, Arden had built up his holdings in Faversham, but perhaps not as much as was at one time thought. This does also raise the question of whether or not this might be true of other places where changes in landownership on the dissolution of the monasteries have been considered on the basis of information from central records alone without reference to local sources. When Arden died, he left a will, his deeds were checked and an inquisition *post mortem* was made, so that we have a clear idea of his estate. In Faversham he had a house and

183 PRO, E318/5/181, C142/93/111, SC6/ Hen VIII 1979, 1987, 2018, 2049; LP, xx, part 2, 1068 (33), xxi, 2, grant 648 (22) p.333.

184 PRO, C142/93/111, SC6/Hen VIII 501, 502, 510, 511, 512; BL, Harl Ch.58 H.18; DNB ; LP, xxi, 2, grant 476 (96) p. 242.

185 See APPENDIX 11: BL, Harl.Ch.58 H 18; PRO, E318/33/1862; E326/12266; E315/217/68; LP, xxi, 1, 783.

186 See APPENDIX 11: PRO, E315/219/13v; E315/23/38 and 39; Favward, fol. 36; Hasted, x, p. 147.

187 Favward, fol. 105v; CKS, Arch, PRC17/33/52; see page 213.

188 CKS, Fa/JB fol. 6.

the site of the abbey which was worth annually £1-6-8 above repairs, one messuage called the Gatehouse worth 13^{s} 4^{d} with Ostry garden, a stable and nine acres let to the former abbot, John Castlock £5-6-8, a close near the grange, ten acres in Thornmead worth £4-13-4, three acres of pasture and a tenement £2-0-0, two acres called Dovehouse garden £1- 13 4. Six acres of pasture called Almery Croft, 12 acres called Outyards, Sextry land and the wash-house were worth £3-6-8. All this roughly tallies with the original grant to John Wheler, and it was held by the service of the twentieth part of a knight's fee and payment of a tenth, seven shillings a year, to the Court of Augmentations. This estate was worth £40 and was left as jointure to his wife, Alice. Next there were the messuages let to Richard Dryland and John Seth, which were said, in the inquisition, to be held together with diverse lands and tenements in Sandwich by the service of a twentieth part of a knight's fee and payment of a tenth, five English shillings a year. These made up the lands in Faversham that Arden held by knight's fee. To the town he left two tenements in Cooksditch, two gardens in Preston Street, one of which was in the tenure of Baker, which may be that referred to earlier, St. Nicholas's chapel and the pillory, which had been granted to him on his appeal under Edward VI. They were worth £2-6-0. To his daughter, Margaret, he left all the land left in free socage, the houses worth £8, Flood Mill, held of the manor of Epworth in Lincoln but not in chief, worth £40, and seven acres in Surrenden Croft held of the Honor of Torrington, but not in chief, worth 30^{s}.

All this may explain his frustration and sharp practice about leases, which in the play is centred on his treatment of Widow Cook.[189] In the list of his deeds he was also said to have the leases of Blean Wood, the parsonage of St. Michael's, Cornhill, and a parsonage from Christ Church, Canterbury for £32-0-0 a year. This was probably Faversham parsonage, on which trustees were acting for his young grandson, Nicholas Bradbourne, on 24 June 1573. They renewed a lease for 17 years at a rent of £32-6-8 . There was no mention there of property in Sandwich and the only other deed concerned Master Awcher (Sir Anthony Aucher) granting 20 marks a year to Master Arden and his wife for the terms of their lives and the longer liver.[190]

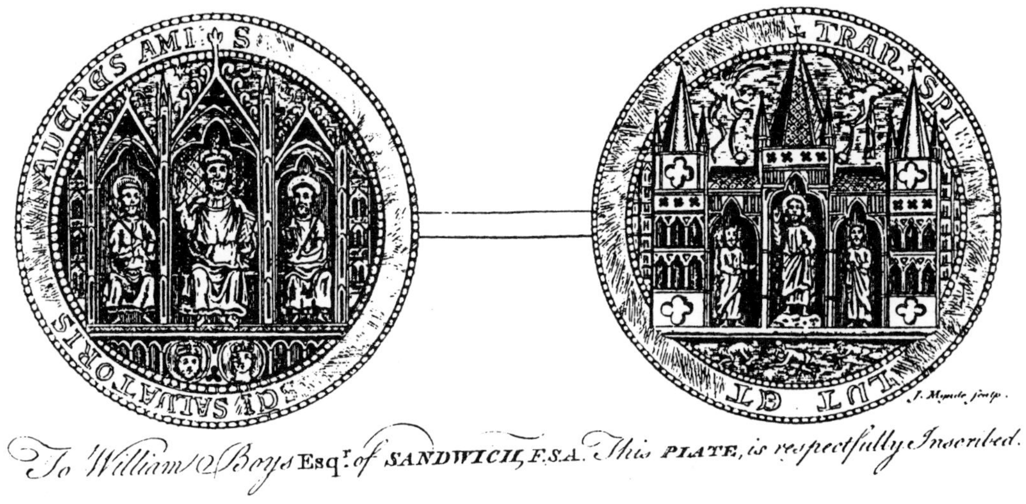

Seal of Faversham Abbey taken from Edward Jacob, *The History of Faversham,* (1774)

[189] See also pages 68, 85 and 88.
[190] BL, Harl.Ch..58H 18; CCA, Christ Church Register, DCc/Register V, fols. 255-59.

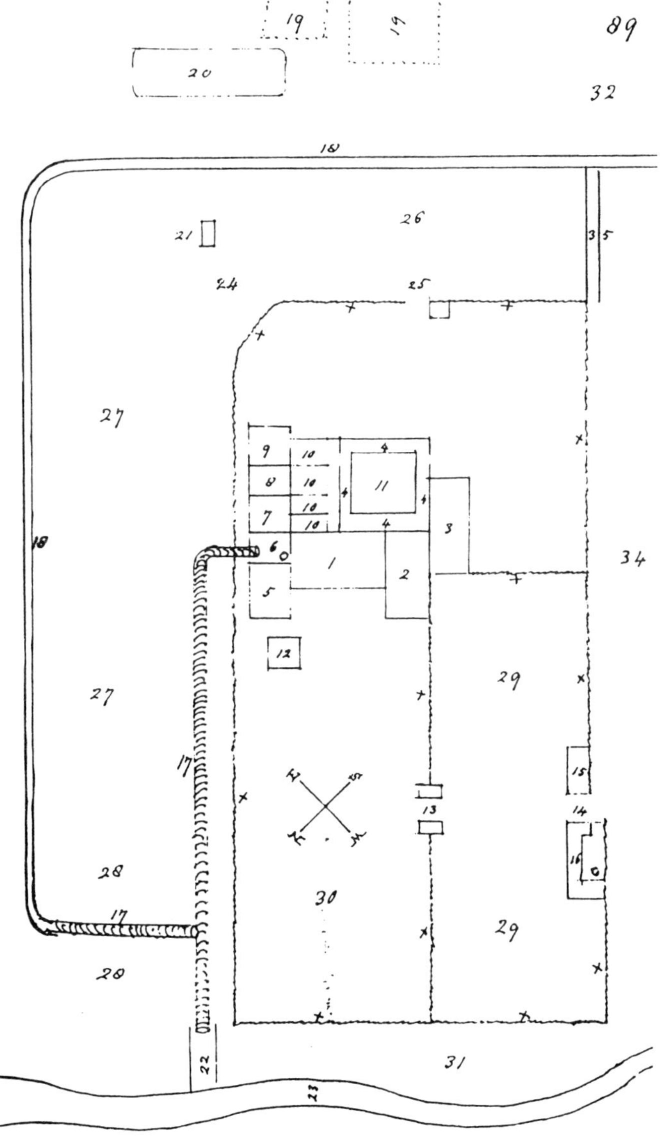

Map taken from Crow Vol. 3 page 89: The site of the Abbey previous to the reformation gathered from detached records and fragmentary ruins.

1. Refectory or Hall
2. Chapter House
3. Abbey Church
4. Cloisters
5. Calefactory or 'building of stone'
6. Kitchen and well
7-8. Bakehouse, Larder
9. Brewhouse and malthouse
10. Dormitories
11. Open quadrangle
12. Abbot's Lodgings
13. Inner gate-house
14. Town or outer gate
15. Porters Lodge
16. Almonry or Cripple Court
17. Stone sewers
18. Shooting Meadow stream
19. Site of 'The Nether Court Farm', 'The Grange' or 'Barn and Curtlege' and tenement
20. Fish-pond
21. Palfrey stables and forge
22. An outlet for the sewer
23. The creek
24. The close
25. 'The Gate House'.
26. The Ostry garden.
27. Nine acres
28. Lower Greeen
29. Upper Green
30. The Orchard
31. A swamp
32. Shooting Meadow
33. A marsh or land over flown by the tide
34. Almery Croft
35. A boundary Ditch
X. A boundary wall given in an engraving of 1735

Chapter 7
Involvement in town life

According to Crow, who was probably repeating local tradition, the town gate house of the abbey was the residence of Thomas Arden. He says, 'This house has undergone great changes since the dissolution, for in some late alterations, two other windows with double arched lights and iron bars were found in the first floor on each side of the present chimney, which is built against the old wall that runs through the present house, and is a continuance of that now standing, and which partly surrounds the 'Green Plat'[191]. These windows appear to have given light to a room in the inner side of the said wall, a portion of which building was taken down some years ago, and rebuilt with the old materials, except the bases which are very massive.' Crow goes on to say that this was undoubtedly the original porter's lodge. There is now considerable doubt about these claims. The archaeological research into the Abbey site has shown the plan by Crow to be inaccurate.[192]

'Arden's House', 80, Abbey Street, was surveyed in 1990 by Linda Rogers, and this, combined with a recent reassessment of the whole site by Sarah Pearson and Jane Wade, including Arden's Cottage at 81 Abbey Street, has shed light on the form and date of what was once a great house at the abbey gate.[193] The earliest section of the house joined the stone gate to the abbey, and includes part of a thirteenth-century chapel lying over the gate, which survived until 1772 (see the illustrations on pages 78 and 87). Whatever was originally attached to the east side of the chapel and gate was replaced in the first quarter of the sixteenth century by a grand timber-framed house. When built this seems to have consisted of a central hall flanked by projecting wings, the whole arranged in a U-shaped plan. The hall itself, which lay parallel to Abbey Street, has been demolished, but the whole of the north wing, attached to the earlier chapel, survives as Arden's House, while the front section of the south wing remains as Arden's Cottage[194]. The latter included an impressive entrance porch-cum-passage leading to the hall doorway; the kitchen and service rooms of the timber-framed house lay somewhere behind this end. Arden's House contained the private or superior rooms of the dwelling. The most important of these were the ground-floor parlour, and the great chamber above it, which was always open to its decorated crown-post roof. Both rooms had fireplaces set in a great brick stack, with oriel windows to either side overlooking the abbey grounds; these are the arched widows referred to by Crow. A small doorway opened directly into the parlour from the abbey precincts.

The puzzle about this great timber house is who built it. It has sometimes been attributed to Arden himself, who was granted the property in 1540; but the architectural style indicates an earlier date, probably between 1500 and 1525. In the rental of 1532, 'Richarde Drylande, senior gentleman holdeth of the lord to farm the greate messuage at the Town Gate with the garden thereto belonging and payith by yere 40[s] ' and it is possible that he was the builder. But the small doorway from the abbey grounds suggests that, despite largely lying outside the gate, the

[191] See map page 59; presumably Upper Green; FIJ June 1898.

[192] B. J. Philp, *Excavations at Faversham, 1965,* (1968)

[193] I am very grateful to Sarah Pearson for so willingly contributing details of her on-going researches. Linda Rogers, 'An Architectural Study of Arden's House in Faversham, Kent'. History Dissertation for the School of Architecture, Canterbury College of Art and Design, 1990.

[194] C. Hussey, 'The setting of a notorious murder', *Country Life,* 1966, pp. 76-79; A. Swaine, *Faversham: its history, its present history, its present role and the pattern for its future* (Maidstone: Kent County Council and Faversham Borough Council) 1970, p. 62 ; *Monasticon*, pp. 60-64; J. Doak, 'Arden's house', *Fav. Mag.*, i, pp. 222-23. Cust; app. p. ii; Jacob, plate 15; Bullen, p. v; *The Kentish Express,* 25 January 1957: regarding demolishing Arden's House; Orlin, pp. 35-39.

house may have been built for the abbey itself. It has sometimes been suggested that this is the site of the abbey guest-house, where John Castlock the last abbot is said to have entertained Wolsey in 1516, 1527 and 1528, as well as Henry VIIIth in 1520. Yet it is more likely that the guest-house lay inside rather than outside the gate. The one building which commonly stood beyond the gate, accessible from inside and outside, was the almonry. But in Faversham, the almonry has usually been thought to lie on the opposite side of Abbey Street. Therefore, until further information is available, the builder of the house which later became Arden's home must remain uncertain.

The photograph facing this page was taken by A. Percival in 1991 and illustrates the remains of the stone gatehouse and the parlour wing of the sixteenth-century timber-framed house. The outside of the building, before restoration in 1956, is shown in a photograph accompanying the article by J. Doak. Thomas Southouse says 'The house on the west side of the Abby gate, where the steward now dwelleth paid per annum £1-6-8. An house conveniently suitable to his employment, for the Court was kept at the Abby gate, and the street now called Abby-street, was from thence called Court-street. In this house I myself now dwell.'[195]

Before we consider Arden's involvement in town life in Faversham, it would probably be helpful to run over what we so far know of him. Born in 1508, he came from Norwich, where his mother went begging daily, but, because of the lenient way that she was treated by the authorities, she, was almost certainly related to one of the leading families in the town. He first appeared on the public scene in 1537 as one of the clerks to Edward North, Clerk of Parliament. He may have married North's step-daughter, Alice Brigandine, the same year. He never lost contact with North, but by 1539 was acting as under-steward to another patron, Sir Thomas Cheyne, who had been made Lord Warden of the Cinque Ports in 1536. Cheyne's patronage probably influenced Arden's purchase of lands in Kent. The Hothfield saga was the first of several showing Arden in an unfavourable light.

His property deals were concentrated in the period 1540-45. It was only then that he acted as a middleman, and it was in the same period that he bought the bulk of his lands in Faversham. I suggest that he hesitated for a time between making Faversham or Sandwich his home. He bought the Whitefriars site in Sandwich in 1540. Three years later he became comptroller of Sandwich and in 1547 its M.P.

It has become clear that hardly anything is as it seems in the life of Thomas Arden. This is also true of his involvement in town life. He had first bought lands there on 5 June 1540 and had been appointed customer that year or shortly after. On 3 September 1542 he was appointed a commissioner by the Crown with one John Anthony of the Isle of Thanet to gather wheat, possibly for the provision of English troops.[196] There are three separate references in the Faversham wardmote book to him being made a freeman. On folio 34v on 20 July 1541, when Lewis Marden was mayor of Faversham, Arden's name was included on a list of freemen, but with no comment beside it, as there was for the other freemen. Marden made his will on 20 February 1551 and died on 1 October following. He left lands in Marden and mills and lands in Chart next Sutton Valence. Clearly nothing came of the freedom, because three years later, on folio 37v, when the merchant John Bringborne was mayor between September 1543 and September 1544, there is a list of freemen which includes Arden. The list of mayors given in Jacob is inaccurate at this point. Arden was made a freeman by the commons and had nothing to pay. His friend, Thomas Dunkyn, was at the same time made a freeman by the mayor with

[195] Southouse, Monasticon, p. 60.
[196] APC, NS, i, pp. 28, 180.

nothing to pay. Not too much should be made of this. It was not unusual for someone who could possibly be useful to the town to be made a freeman for nothing. John Webbe M.P., the steward, was made a freeman for nothing in 1539, Joseph Beverley M.P. in 1541. John Dryland was the son of Richard Dryland of Cooksditch and was made a freeman for nothing in 1542. He was mayor in 1553 and 1555 and died in 1559, leaving as executors his brother and namesake, John, and his brother-in-law, Thomas Stransham, of whom more later. Others less well known made freemen without payment were Stephen Motte in 1542, John Goodhew at the same time as Arden and Thomas Hawkyner and Robert Elfrith in 1546. Robert Elfrith was still a member of the common council in 1558-59. Nothing is known of Thomas Hawkyner. Following that, on folio 38, in 1543-44, there is a list stating that Arden was 'made fre and geven hym by the comens'. Dunkyn was not included but nor were four others, so that it looks as if someone failed to copy the whole list into the wardmote book.[197]

In the same year that he became a freeman, 1543-44, Arden was a common councillor, otherwise described as a member of the twenty-four, twelve of whom were chosen by the mayor and jurats and twelve by the freemen. By 23 November 1544 both he and Thomas Dunkyn had been appointed to the body of jurats, who were responsible for the administration of the town with the mayor, who was annually selected from the group.[198]

It has long been realized that Arden did great service to the town when it wanted to renew its charter. He knew important people in high places, particularly Sir Edward North and Sir Thomas Cheyne, and his work as a clerk in parliament had given him experience as a draughtsman. He obviously played the leading role, but it should not be forgotten that there were others who may also have helped. There were, for instance, the five men who were of sufficient stature to become an M.P., who had some connection with Faversham. They were William Roper, John Webbe, Joseph Beverley, Cyriak Petyt and Henry Crispe. Cyriak Petyt of Boughton-under-Blean may have been a lawyer, and was a friend of John Webbe and known to William Roper and the More family circle. He was involved in the prebendaries' plot against Cranmer and he and his family were living at Boughton by May 1557 when they acquired further lands at Faversham and Graveney. He was returned for Winchelsea in April 1554 thanks to Sir Thomas Cheyne and in November 1554 thanks to official favour. He died in 1591.

In 1543 John Webbe as steward rendered an account of £3-16-10 for consulting three sergeants and one of the six clerks in Chancery concerning the attempt to save the school founded under the abbey auspices by John Cole and how to deal with the Hatch lands. Webbe had also paid for certain petitions to the king. These probably concerned the Hatch lands.[199]

It was essential for the town to obtain a new charter for two reasons. In the first place, it had to establish its claim to rights formerly enjoyed by the abbot. He had controlled the town right up to the time of the dissolution of the abbey. As late as 1531-33 the chamberlain's accounts were dealt with before the auditors in the presence of the abbot and the mayor in the hall of the abbey itself. When the abbey was dissolved, the former steward, William Roper, wrote to Sir Richard Rich, to tell him that the abbot had had the right of appointing as mayor one of three persons elected by the mayor, jurats and commonalty. He added that the mayor took an oath to do true service to the king and the monastery. Rich passed the information on to Cromwell asking

---

[197] Favward, fols. 34, 34v, 36v, 37v, 38, 41v, 74; CKS, Marden, Arch, PRC17/29/200v; Dryland, PROB11/42B/57; Vis. Kent 1530-31, *Harl Soc.* lxxiv, p. 9 ; Commons 1509-58, i, pp. 428-29, iii, pp. 564-65.

[198] Favward, fols.38, 38v.

[199] Favward, fol. 37; Commons 1509-58, i, pp. 428-29, 722-23, iii, pp. 96-98, 179-80, 215-17, 564-65.

whether the nomination should now go to the king, to Cromwell or to himself as Chancellor of the Court of Augmentations. No doubt discussions about a new charter started there.[200]

This situation had existed since 1147, when King Stephen had founded the abbey. The abbot claimed rents, reliefs, profits from the fair, market and manorial courts. He also had the right to have his corn transported to London. His right over the election of the mayor had been contested as early as 1255. In 1257 the townsmen won the arrangement which prevailed in 1538. By the end of that century they had taken advantage of the abbey's financial problems to establish a new custom of electing a mayor outright and then presenting him to the abbot for approval, but this must have lapsed. In 1511, the mayor-elect, Laurence Stransham, refused to present himself to the abbot to take his oath of office and of service to the monastery, but Abbot Castlock successfully brought a case against him in Star Chamber. In spite of a thorough search, the documents on this case have not been found.[201]

The second reason for urgency in securing a charter was Henry Hatch's bequest in 1533 of considerable property to the town on the death of his widow. He had been a merchant adventurer and leading figure in the town about whom I have written a study. The town had to establish its right to control the property. As it was, it was involved in an administrative headache and a long law-suit with the widow, but remember that it still benefits from his bequest today.[202]

The first mention of the charter came on 18 December 1544 when the chamberlains' account for 1543-44 was being considered, when charges were included of £1-12-4 for Joseph Beverley and Anthony Love 'rydynge to London with our chartours in sekynge of lerned councell apon them' sometime during the year. Love was a member of the 24 between 1559 and 1563. I suggest that a group of men in the town had been thinking about a new charter since the dissolution of the abbey in 1538. The decision was evidently taken to involve Arden as a former under-clerk of parliament and skilled administrator with good connections. This decision was so important in the life of the town that it is worth quoting in full. At a wardmote held on 3 November 1544, the same month that he became a jurat, it was agreed by the mayor, John Bringborne, the other jurats and the commonalty that 'yf Thomas Arden, gentleman, coulde purchase and optayne under the Kynge's Maiesteye's letters patentes to the use of the towne of Feversham that the seyde town myght be incorporate by the name of the mayer and comynaltey and lycense to mortyse certeyn londes [of] the seyde towne accordyng to the last wyll of Henrey Hache and allso the proffyt [of] the fayers and of the lawdayse. And the sayde lyberteys and grantes so optayned to delyver unto [the] mayer and comeners of the same towne under the Kynges maiestey letters patentes sealyd and segnyd so that the seyd mayer and comeners do not paye for the same above the rate of 20 yers purchase then yt ys agreid that the same Thomas Arden shall have in recompence of hys labor and expensys in that behalfe hade and sustaynyd twentey poundes'.[203] The document was signed by Bringborne, eight of the 11 jurats and 37 of the commonalty or general body of freemen. Some jurats did not sign. John Hampton and Laurence Manby died in the course of the year, which left the royal bailiff, Robert Colwell, and William Castlock, brother of the last abbot, either of whom might have felt constrained to stay away.

The costs continued, but it is impossible to work out exactly how much was spent. The main charges viewed in the account of John Gill and Harry Philpot on 10 December 1546 were for a cess made for purchasing the great charter. They collected £20-7-2 and 18^{s} 4^{d} from Master Castlock, John Dryland the elder, gentleman, and William Marshall, making £21-5-6 in all.

---

[200] Favward, fol. 31; LP, xiii, part 2, pp. 274, 290.
[201] Rev. G. Streynsham Master, *Notes relating to the family of Streynsham* (London, 1879), p. 10.
[202] See APPENDIX 20; Favward, fols.39v, 281v; CKS, PRC17/24/242, PRC3/10/84; Hyde, pp. 111-28.
[203] Favward, fols. 79, 82v, 85v, 92v, 104v and 281v; The figure of 20 years purchase has been checked.

They were to be allowed £13-4-6 which they had paid Arden for his charges 'of the charter'. Eighteen months later, Elizabeth, widow of the late mayor, Simon Auncell, asked to be allowed £8-16-8 for the charges of renewing the charter.[204]

Arden obtained the type of charter that the town wanted. The previous year Henry VIII had stayed one night in Faversham on his way to Boulogne. Hasted says that a humble prayer was then made to him by the inhabitants. Certainly, Thomas Hilles was paid 3^s 4^d for writing a book to be signed by the king. He was, incidentally, paid four shillings in 1548 for writing various copies and books of musters. 11^s 7^d was paid for beautifying the town against the king's coming. In addition, 35^s 4^d was spent on a present of two dozen chickens, two dozen capons and a sieve of cherries. On 27 January 1546 Faversham received its charter of incorporation. The preamble said that 'whereas before this time by many years past the governing of our whole town of Faversham in the county of Kent was left to pertain and belong to the mayor and jurats of the same town for the time being and to the late Abbot of Faversham for the time being and now after a just occasion had to search out the foundation of the occupation and tenure of the same town they are not found to be sufficiently strong and valid in the law as we have heard'. All the earlier charters had been granted either to the abbey or to the town from 1252 onwards confirming its rights as a member of the Cinque Ports. This new charter gave the names of the then mayor, the 11 jurats and the 44 freemen in whose names the town was incorporated. The mayor and jurats now not only had their former rights and privileges, but others such as the view of frankpledge and court leet, the markets and the fairs, which had belonged to the abbot. They were given the right to nominate two jurats from whom the freemen were to elect a mayor on 30 September each year. The mayor was to choose a sergeant at mace. The Hatch lands were specifically mentioned. The mayor was to be the coroner, to hold a court of clerk of the market, a court of piepowder, the assize of bread, wine and ale and a court of portmote at which fines and recoveries could be made. The court of general sessions of the peace and gaol delivery with the court leet was to be held twice a year. In addition, the mayor and jurats had the right to a common seal and to buy and sell land, notwithstanding the act of mortmain, which was the crucial right they needed in order to be able to deal with the Hatch lands. They were also to have the goods and chattels of felons and all deodands, waifs and strays, and were also allowed to establish standards for bread and other foods, to hold a market thrice weekly and annual fairs for seven days round St. Valentine's Day (14 February) and Lammas Day or the Feast of St. Peter in chains (1 August). They could also establish a gaol, admit freemen and make the same laws for the government of the town as the mayors, jurats and commonalty of Sandwich did. There had been occasional comparisons with Sandwich in Faversham's fifteenth century commonplace book, particularly in relation to the treatment of orphans, but Arden may also have been using his own special knowledge of that town.

They were to pay a yearly fee-farm of £8-0-0 to the king and £6-0-0 to William Roper, Esquire, steward of the king's court of Faversham, during his lifetime In the ministers' accounts, it was recorded that £6-0-0 had been received from the town. He was to have a fee of £8-6-8 of which £2-6-8 was to be provided by the king. After Roper's death the fee was to be allocated from the possessions of the lord king from 'this late monastery'. The incorporation was subscribed by the Chancellor of the Court of Augmentations, Sir Edward North. The mayor was to receive an annual fee of £5-0-0 and the first mayor installed under the new incorporation, the rich merchant,

[204] Favward, fols. 39v, 46 v.

John Seth, took an oath of office administered by the Lord Warden, Sir Thomas Cheyne, at the king's palace at Westminster.[205]

Arden must then have been at the height of his influence in the town. There are references to him being paid for loads of stones for paving, no doubt from from the monastic ruins. More interesting to us, though, is the matter of the fair. Stow said that 'the fayre was wont to be kepte partely in the towne, and partely in the abbey, but Arden for his owne lucre had this present yere browght it to be wholye kepte within the abbey ground, which he had purchased so that all the gaynes came to hym and none to the townesmen for the which dede he had many a curse.' This is not borne out in the town records. There were two annual week-long fairs,which were confirmed for the town by Henry VIII under the terms of incorporation. The first was on Lammas Day or the Feast of St. Peter in chains (1 August). This had been granted to the abbey by Henry II and was held on its three-and-a-half-acre green inside the outer gate, with ground rents and profits going to the abbey. There were regular payments in the town accounts over the years for bread, beer and cheese for the watch on Lammas night. At the dissolution of the abbey it was said that the fair and Nether Green were formerly leased to Robert Colwell and now to the town for £1-6-8.

The origin of St. Valentine's fair on 14 February is more obscure as it was not mentioned before 1546, so that it must have grown up by custom. After the dissolution, a ministers' account mentions 16^{s} 8^{d} for market rents 'of one fair held there of the new corporation by the jurisdiction of the late Henry VIII in the feast of St. Valentine.' It was also said that Upper Green had been leased to Ady Fould, but now to the town for £1-6-8. In 1546, Arden received five shillings rent and the town also paid eight shillings 'for charges leyd owt and watching', but it received £1-11-11½. So it continued until Arden's murder. He left the rent by will to his daughter, Margaret. In 1552 this was paid to Thomas Stransham, presumably on her behalf, because it was in turn paid later to her first husband, John Fathers, and her second husband, John Bradbourne.[206]

Arden's friend, Thomas Dunkyn, was mayor from 1546-47. He was followed by John Best, and he, in turn, by Simon Auncell, who had been the receiver of the manor of Kingsnorth and Upland for the abbey for a fee of £3-0-0 with 13^{s} 4^{d} for a gown. There is a letter from the Privy Council dated 8 November 1547 directing Auncell 'to deliver, all excuses sett aparte, in to the handes of Thomas Arderne, warden of the church of Fevershame, the pixe of silver by him of late taken from the churche, which was given thether by on(e) Hach deceassed and had ther continued by the space of 12 yeares and more'. The pyx is the vessel in which consecrated bread is kept. Auncell had been a churchwarden from 1546-47, which is no doubt when he took charge of it. The point to bear in mind is that his wife was the sister of Joan Hatch, the widow of the merchant adventurer, Henry Hatch, who had left a generous bequest to Faversham church in 1533. It included money to build and equip a jewel house of which this silver pyx must have been a part. Auncell and his family must have been particularly sad to see these gifts disappear. It is likely that Arden is mentioned by the Privy Council simply because he succeeded Auncell as churchwarden, not because they had a personal quarrel.

---

[205] PRO, SC6/EdwardVI/233 m. 16; CKS, Fa/A1 5/1, Fa/A15/3, Faversham borough custumal c1400-1740, fols. 24r-27r, concerning the custody of orphans, 1205, 1290, 1313, 1343; Mayor's parlour, charters, 1252, 1261, 1302, 1364, 1408, 1434, 1446, 1476; Favward, fols. 39v, 41v, 43, 46v; LP, xxi, part1, 48 (30) 67, grant 149 (33) 75; Hasted, pp. 17-18, 344-45; K. Murray, 'Faversham and the Cinque Ports', *TRHS* (1935), pp. 53-83.

[206] Lambeth, ED 2006; PRO, SC6/HenVIII/No1755, SC6/EdwardVI/233 m. 15; BL, Harl. 649, fol.6v; Favward, fols. 42, 42v, 62v, 65.

Under the terms of the new charter, on the death of Auncell, the jurats nominated two jurats for mayor, one of whom, Arden in this case, was elected by the other freemen. He was elected for only six months because that was the arrangement laid down in the charter which he himself had devised. It said quite clearly on 26 March 1548 that he was 'to contynue from that daye unto the last day of September then next folowyng.'[207]

Looking towards Faversham Church from W. H. Ireland, *A New & Complete History of the County of Kent* Vol. 2 (1829) opposite page 599.

[207] See APPENDIX 12 and APPENDIX 20; PRC 32/15/215; Favward, fols. 74, 78; APC, N.S., 1547-50, p. 520; Jacob, p. 193; see p. 184, Fa/AI 5/3, p. 5

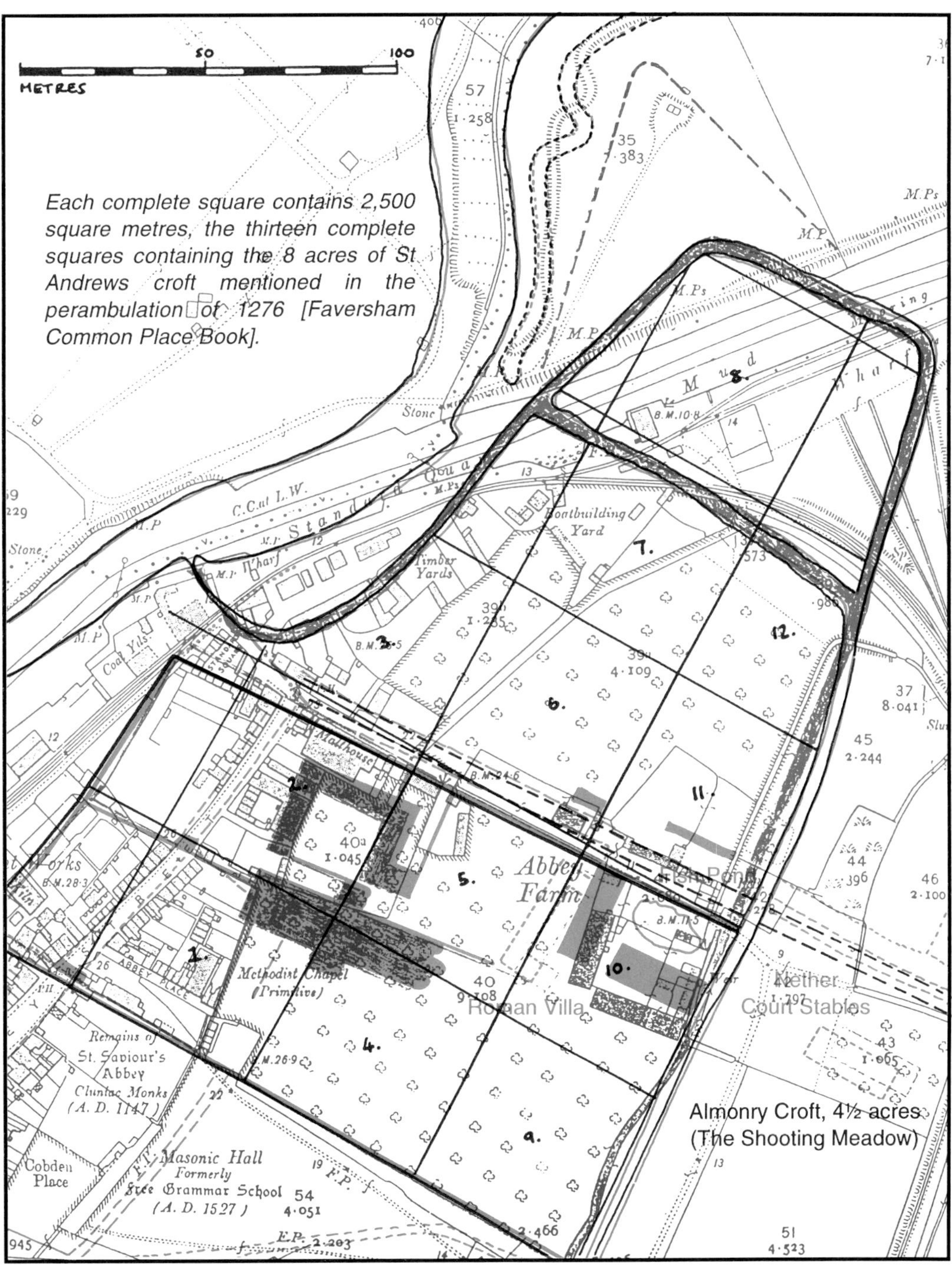

Faversham Abbey precinct area. The base drawing (grey) is derived from various archaeological and cartographic sources and superimposed upon the 1907 Ordnance Survey Map. (Copyright Ordnance Survey). The top red overlay shows a grid of 2,500 square metres, indicating the 8 acres given in the 1276 perambulation. The grid and the green overlay, which shows the buildings identified by archaeological excavation, are both based on the Jacob map of 1745-50; because of the cartographic standards the maps do not quite correspond. Information and drawings supplied by Paul Wilkinson.

Chapter 8
Mayor

So, with a great flourish in the wardmote book, Arden became mayor of Faversham on 26 March 1548. Comparing the writing there with some of his known signatures, it seems probable that this was indeed his own handwriting. It certainly says in the margin, '... in the true hand of the mayor Thomas Arden in the second year of the reign of Edward VI.' He described himself proudly as 'chief comptroller of the king's majesty's custom'. As befitted a former under-clerk of parliament, the hand-writing was more elegant and the content far more elaborate than ever before. In addition to the usual lists of jurats, common councillors, churchwardens, auditors, chamberlains and freemen, the names of porters, sealers and searchers of leather, searchers of flesh and the common meter or measurer of corn were given.[208]

Eight men were made freemen: Thomas Adryan, Robert Braban, John Greneleff, Garard Arnold, Richard Rede, Thomas Mustard, Thomas Norton and Thomas Dey. Nothing worthy of note has been discovered about Adryan, Braban, Arnold and Dey. John Grenelefe was a joiner, who died in 1563, and Thomas Norton was mayor in 1561 and died in 1564.[209] Thomas Mustard was probably the grocer who died in 1575, leaving three houses to the town. The most interesting to us is Richard Reade, who died in 1558 and whose widow, Alice, was given the right to deal with his affairs. He was surely the second husband of the widow Cooke, who had a grievance over property against Arden. He was a character in the play.[210]

The first problem Arden tackled was the vexed question of objects taken from the church. It is extremely hard at this distance to decide how many of these disputes were personal and how many were based on religious differences. They should be seen in the light of problems all over the country as a result of the legislation under Edward VI, which have been so graphically described by Eamon Duffy in *The stripping of the altars.* From a study of wills of the period, it is clear that both the church and the abbey had received many bequests before the dissolution, so that considerable sums were involved. Certainly Henry Hatch had been generous in his gifts to the treasury. In her account, Elizabeth Auncell had charged herself with £22-15-5 delivered to her husband by Master (John) Best and Thomas Stransham on the sale of the cross and silver chalice. On 17 June 1548 Arden must have arranged 'with the consent of the whole town' the sale to John Wreake of 300 quarters and 22 pounds of old latten candlesticks at £1-4-8 the hundred for £4-3-10. Wreake in turn there and then paid £3-1-0 in the presence of the town to cover 'the painting of the roodloft and the scriptures upon the same and for the scripture in the north aisle'. He therefore owed £1-2-10 for which he was discharged at the audit of the churchwardens. Wreake was one of the churchwardens in that year and it is not entirely clear whether he was acting in his official or in his private capacity. Arden then dealt with John Seth, who by then had the pyx. On 2 September 1548 Seth gave a recognisance of forty pounds to the mayor, jurats and community. It said that 'whre varyanses and sute hath ben made for and concernyng a certeyn pyxe of sylver', if he or his executors could prove its true value before six of the community by Michaelmas 1550 then the recognisance would be void. There is a note in another hand that it was sold to Seth by the consent of the whole town.

The next step that Arden took was to issue a statute for the making of laws in the town of Faversham. It ordered that only the mayor, jurats and the 24 or common council should be

---

208 See reproduction of Wardmote pages and transcripts starting on text page 274.

209 CKS, Arch., Grenelefe, PRC17/37/61, Norton, PRC17/38/86, PRC3/17/58; Vis Kent 1592, *Harl.Soc.*, lxxv, pp. 13, 39.

210 See also pages 58, 85 and 88; Favward fols. 47v-50.

called to the wardmote for the making of laws and statutes, except if the mayor called other people there. 12 of the 24 were to be chosen by the mayor, 12 by the freemen, as had long been the custom. The increase in restrictions and oligarchy was typical of towns in the period.[211]. Arden may have been carrying out the wishes of his patron, Sir Thomas Cheyne, the Lord Warden. Unlike some other members of the Cinque Ports, such as Dover, Sandwich and Rye, Faversham had long had a common council, which was even mentioned in its custumal. Wardens found such a gathering much easier to handle than an unwieldy assembly of freemen. The ports had to back successive wardens because they relied on them as a channel of communication with central government. As S. Hipkin says,' between 1550 and 1625 successive wardens put considerable effort into promoting oligarchic rule across the confederation, supporting moves originating within towns when not initiating them, and exploiting the near-client status of resulting weak oligarchic regimes in order to carve further inroads into their political independence, notably in the matter of parliamentary elections.' It is just possible that Arden's statute in 1548 was the first step in this direction.[212]

Similar things were happening in other Cinque Ports. In 1550, Cheyne attempted to revive oligarchic supremacy in Sandwich only to be rebuffed by the commonalty or general body of the town. Leading townsmen then retaliated by refusing to take office. In 1563, after Cheyne's death, there was an attempt to form a common council at Rye which was quashed by the opposition of the freemen.

Arden also arranged that if any 'persone levye any fyne of any landes, housses or tenementes within the towne that then there shalbe paid after the rate of every pounde, that the house or landes, wherof the fyne shalbe levyed shalbe worthe by year the tyme of the said fyne levyed 3^{s} 4^{d}, the summe to be levyed of the tenant of the lande by distress'. The language is obscure and bureaucratic, but I think that it applied to anyone purchasing property in the town. As I shall show later, it was probably enacted because the town was running rapidly in to debt.[213] Most such purchases in other towns were recorded in the feet of fines, which were filed in the Treasury and are to be seen in the Public Record Office. It was a privilege of the Cinque Ports to deal with these fines locally. By good fortune several hundred of these Faversham fines for the sixteenth century have survived.

Arden then arranged for the appointment of the common carrier to deal with dung and other contagious filth. He did not have to deal with stable dung or other refuse 'as of the lome and other things of the buildings and pulling down of old houses', which suggests, incidentally, that rebuilding was going on in the town in that period. Dunghills had long been a problem. In 1540-41, when Lewis Marden was mayor, a cess or tax of £5-0-0 was levied to pay for their removal. Arden said that the carrier himself was to be removable at the pleasure of the mayor, jurats and community. The refuse was to be taken twice a week wherever the mayor and three of the jurats should decide, as long as it was not more than half a mile out of town.

He next turned his attention to the wages of the parish clerk. On 3 November 1506 another reforming mayor, Robert Withiot, had set out in elaborate detail the duties of the parish clerks followed by those of the sexton. After the reformation, services were simpler and there was less for the clerks to do. Their wages were £4-0-0 each and £1-6-8 for the sexton. Because there

---

[211] See APPENDIX 14; CKS, Arch., Mustard, PRC10/8 p.155, Rede, PRC3/15 fol. 116; Jacob, p. 138; P. Clark and P. Slack, *English towns in transition 1500*-1700 (Oxford Univ. Press, 1976), pp. 127-34; E. Duffy, *The stripping of the altars* (Yale Univ. Press, 1992), pp. 448-503.

[212] S. Hipkin, 'Closing ranks; oligarchy and government at Rye, 1570-1640', *Urban History,* December 1995, vol. xxii, part 3, pp. 322-23; Clark, Society, p. 80.

[213] See APPENDIX 14.

was less to do, it was decided that there should be only one clerk who should be paid £2-13-4. The sexton was to continue on £1-6-8. The other £4-0-0 should go to the common carrier. The parishioners were to pay in the same proportions as they had done when there were two clerks.

An act for paving West Street, Preston Street and Key Lane followed. A causeway for Key Lane had been provided for in the bequest of Henry Hatch in 1533.[214] Again there were elaborate instructions. In West Street it was to run from West Broke Cross to a tenement of Godleve Prynchett, widow, in East Street. In Preston Street it ran from the Maypole to Hog Cross Well. Each house was to be paved to the middle channel, by the lessee if the lease was for more than 30 years, otherwise by the owner. The paving was to be completed by 1 November 1551. If someone did not pay, he was to forfeit the rent to the mayor and the community. These are careful arrangements which show Arden at his best. It is worth noting that the community did not choose to pave Abbey Street and Court Street first. This may have been because they led nowhere once the abbey had been dissolved. They were not paved until 1636. The townsmen no doubt concentrated on the streets where there was the most economic activity, West Street, the older and probably most commercial area of the town, Preston Street, leading to the all-important London-Dover road and Key Lane, which was crucial for traffic on the creek.. Arden was no doubt keen to encourage all this paving because he hoped to profit from his monopoly of the monastic ruins.

Hogs and swine wandering loose in the town presented a great problem. Arden introduced an act to deal with them, which nonetheless sounds far too bureaucratic to be workable and was far more elaborate than anything attempted by the town before. Calling it an act reminds us again that he had once been a clerk in parliament for the enactments in the wardmote had never been called this before. It provided that if a pig wandered without a mark, then anyone catching it had the right to seize it and the owner would have no remedy. If a pig with a mark was caught, the owner had to pay 8^{d} to the person who impounded it. If he refused to pay, a complaint could be made to the mayor. The porters were also empowered to impound hogs and swine with the same rewards. Again, if they refused to pay, owners could be committed to ward or to prison. It was also laid down that if anyone found a marked pig on his property, he could, after calling witnesses, complain to the mayor, who would send for the owner and demand the penalties. Should the owner refuse to pay, the mayor could commit him to ward. The act was not to take effect until the following Michaelmas. It was indeed simplified later at an assembly held on 4 October 1559. No hogs were to be allowed abroad on pain of 12^{d} shared between the officer and the town chamber. Officers could seize hogs without a driver and charge 12^{d}. and had to pay in the money they had collected every 15 days. Other acts and ordinances 'heretofore made and in this present booke written concernyng hogges and swyne shalbe voide and of no force and this acte only to stande in strenght'.

The final act dealt with orphans' goods, but this was not something new dreamt up by Arden, as has been suggested. The Faversham borough custumal or common-place book of the fourteenth and fifteenth centuries had a section based on similar customs at Sandwich dating from 1289-90. It said that the mayor and jurats were to assign guardians who could expect no reversion from the inheritance, that is, had nothing to gain from it. They were to restore it to the orphans when they were of full age with the approval of the mayor and jurats with expenses taken into account. If no such person could be found, some other worthy person was to be chosen. If the mayor and jurats were negligent, the Lord Warden would have free entrance to the port to deal with it. Arden merely brought this up to date. Guardians were bound to the mayor to give true account

[214] CKS, PRC 32/15/212-16.

at the child's lawful age of 21. At 18 he was to receive the goods. If the executor would not give surety, the mayor was to take it. This was to be read openly at every Lawday or else the mayor's fee was to be abated by 6^s 8^d.[215]

At the end of this recital, there came a list of signatures. This was unprecedented. Of the possible 12 jurats and 24 common councillors involved, 25 men signed. One of these was the innkeeper, Adam Fowle, allegedly one of the conspirators. He had paid 6^s 8^d to be made a freeman in 1546-47 and was a common councillor when Arden was mayor. Three jurats did not sign: Arden's friend, Thomas Dunkyn, Lewis Marden and Thomas Gate. The eight common councillors who did not sign included John Dryland and his brother in law, Thomas Stransham, who was mayor in 1554, 1556 and 1557. he was born in 1512 and he himself said that he 'had been under-steward of thier courts there under Mr. Roper and thereby frequented the said town.'[216]

In 1570 he was in charge of the Hatch suit on behalf of the town, when three jurats and the under-steward rode up to London to assist him and it was decided that some town lands would have to be sold to pay for it. He moved to Canterbury in 1575, and, two years later, with his nephew, Robert Stransham of London, he bought Nether Green and Upper Green from John Finch. He died in Canterbury in 1585. His brother, George, was lessee of the rectories of Ospringe and Preston and mayor of Faversham in 1562 and died in Faversham in 1576. William Neale was a corn merchant, who was mayor in 1560 and died in 1565, leaving a mansion house and other property in Faversham. Henry Philpott was mayor in 1564 and died in 1570, also leaving property in the town. Richard Johnson died in 1553, but nothing is known of Ralph Deacon. William Phynner or Fynner was a tenant of four houses in North Street West when Arden acquired them in 1545. He also owned one next door. It may have been pure chance that all their signatures were not there. They may have been away or ill, but there is at least a possibility that there was already a group disaffected to Arden.[217]

10 Market Place, Faversham, taken from *A guide to the Ancient Borough of Faversham*, (?1936)

[215] Favward, fols. 6v-9, 35v, 39v, 46v-50v, 57v, 97v; 104; CKS, Fa/LC 1, fols. 24v-26v; Hyde, p. 118; Walter H. Frere and William M. Kennedy, 'Visitation articles and injunctions of the period of the Reformation 1536-56', (London, 1910), *Alcuin Club Coll.* xii, p. 15; Streynsham, pp. 12-21, 54-56.

[216] CKS, Fa/LB/22, Thomas Stransham.

[217] Fowle, Favward, fols. 41v, 47; CKS, Arch, Dryland, PRC3/17/68, Neale, PRC17/39/17, PRC3/17/68, Johnson, PRC3/13/60, Philpott, PRC10/5/92, PRC17/41/21v, Stransham, PRC17/42/305; Marden, PRC17/29/200v; Streynsham, pp. 12-21, 54, 56: Clark, Society, pp. 62, 74, 421n; Duffy, *op. cit.*, pp. 438-39.

Chapter 9
Disputes

Arden's reputation as a religious reformer rests mainly on his being a witness in a deposition register two months after he stepped down as mayor. It was in an office promoted consistory court case against the vicar, Clement Norton, who was the third son of William Norton of Faversham, a member of a gentry family. Clement Norton went to Oxford in 1522 and was elected a Fellow of All Souls', where he stayed until he went to Faversham. He was therefore a colleague of Dr. John Cole, who was Warden of All Souls' from 1525 until 1528 and founded Faversham grammar school. According to Cranmer's register, Norton was admitted to Faversham on 7 August 1535 'on the presentation of William Norton gentleman for his turn'. This was his father, the man most likely to come to some arrangement with St. Augustine's. It is said that Clement was also mayor in 1536, but on what evidence is not clear. He certainly never appeared in the lists of jurats in Faversham wardmote book. He became a prominent conservative and was among the parish clergy who attended meetings in Parkhurst's rooms at which the prebendaries plot of 1543 against Cranmer was discussed. He was supported by the staunch traditionalism of a number of local landowners, not least the Roper and Hawkins families. John Bland, vicar of Ospringe, and Robert à Stotte, curate of Davington, were among his opponents, but one Swan, vicar of Sheldwich, was an ally. Norton was silenced by the church court in 1550 but became Rector of Buckland in 1556. He was last described as vicar of Faversham in Harpsfield's visitation in 1558. Two years later it was reported that 'the former vicar, Clement Norton, took away Latin books from the church which were for services in Queen Mary's time'.[218]

It was what was known as an 'office promoted' case against Norton. A suit could be commenced by anyone, who was not excommunicate or an outlaw, in the ecclesiastical courts. Suits were either civil or criminal. Civil suits, that is between party and party, were usually known as instance cases; and criminal suits as office cases, being promoted by the office of the judge either of his own mere motion through information received, from the officers of the court or from the presentments of churchwardens and sidesmen at visitations, or at the promotion of another party, called for this reason the promoter.[219] This appears to have been promoted by the parish officers. Norton had a mandate from a judge to appear in Christ Church, Canterbury, and was duly there on 31 October 1548 and ordered to appear at the next court. On 13 November Arden and eight other witnesses appeared. It was said that Norton had withdrawn the light from the altar, read the gospel in the pulpit and omitted to place 'the super-altar' on the table of the Lord. A super-altar was a sort of portable altar, a small, square hallowed stone on which, set upon an unhallowed altar, the elements for the Eucharist were consecrated. All that has survived of this case is the answers to the 24 articles objecting to the vicar of Faversham put to Arden and the other witnesses. The questions are not there and little can be gleaned from the answers themselves. The judge ordered the vicar to read the lessons at matins and evensong at the desk in the body of the church where he was wont to read them. On 3 June 1550 he was ordered not to use 'the super-altar' any more, which was a change of policy that had its origins in the latter

---

218 LPL, Register Thomas Cranmer, fol. 355v; LP, xviii, pp. 293-94; H. A. James, 'Faversham parish church', *Faversham Papers, No.33* (Faversham Soc., 1990), p. 19; B. M. Hogben, 'Preaching and reformation in Henrician Kent', *AC*, ci, pp. 169-186; M .L. Zell, 'The prebendaries plot of 1543; a reconsideration', *Journal of Ecclesiastical History,* xxvii, pp. 182-83, 241-53; P. Clark, 'Reformation and radicalism in Kentish towns 1500-53', *The urban classes, the nobility and the reformation*, ed.W. J. Mommsen (Stuttgart, 1979) pp. 107-27; A. B. Emden, *A biographical register of the University of Oxford 1501-40*, (Oxford, 1974).

219 *The Ecclesiastical Courts*: Being the report of the Commission on Ecclesiastical Courts (SPCK, 1954), pp. 13-16.

part of 1548. The King's journal for 23 May 1550, states that Sir John Gates went into Essex to see that the Bishop of London's orders, 'which touched plucking down super-altaries, altars, and such like abuses' were carried out.[220]

Arden may have been a religious reformer, but he may equally have been toeing the official or party line of 1548. Norton was a litigious fellow and was involved in other lawsuits: in 1544 and 1545 against Thomas Baker concerning the subtraction of tithes, in 1545 against William Forest of Ospringe again concerning the subtraction of tithes, on 12 June 1548 against Barbara Stransham, in May-July 1548 against Warren Fellow of Stalisfield concerning the subtraction of tithes and Faversham Mill and in the same year against William Clapham, curate, in a cause of the violation of ecclesiastical rights.[221]

What happened after getting the charter to make Arden so unpopular that he was disfranchised in December 1550? I think that some of his neighbours realized that he and Dunkyn had introduced too many changes and reforms suitable to London but not to Faversham. The town had over-stretched itself and become overwhelmed with debts, and folk held them largely responsible. To their astonishment, these same neighbours then heard that Arden and Dunkyn refused to pay the cess or tax necessary to clear these same debts. It was hardly surprising that they were angry. They may also have known that he was taking his orders from Sir Thomas Cheyne.

The town accounts were simple when they were still being audited in the abbey hall in the presence of the abbot and the mayor. In the chamberlains' accounts for Michaelmas 1530-31 the income was £8-14-9 and expenses £6-8-2, leaving a surplus of £2-6-7. The abbey was dissolved in 1538, and, three years later, the figures were £9-19-0 and £11-6-4, leaving a loss of £1-7-4. Expenses mounted with disputes over the Hatch lands, the attempt to restore the school, and, above all, the costs involved in getting a new town charter, which were £35-8-11 in 1545-46. After the charter had been granted, the town had to pay £8-0-0 a year in fee-farm to the king, which was almost the same as the town's income in 1530-31. On top of that, £6-0-0 a year had to be found for the steward and £5-0-0 a year for the mayor. In 1547-48, as well as the chamberlains' accounts, Thomas Dunkyn presented an account for £15-6-5 for making extensive repairs to the courthouse and clearing dunghills and William Marshall claimed £8-4-9 for repairing the streets at Cooksditch. What was called a roll of streets was imposed then and every year following. The crunch came in 1549-50 when John Wreake was mayor. The income came to £28-4-4½ including the usual cess. The expenses were £28-8-6, so the loss was only 4^{s} 1½^{d}. However, there followed a list of debts owed by the town in 1549, totalling £19-8-8. This included £14-13-4 owed to the king, the steward and 'for all other thinges that yere'. On top of that there was owed to 'dyvers of the comons for that they lent to the towne £3-6-8'. Then there were carters who had not been paid ten shillings for the removal of filth. All this totalled £19-8-8. More followed: £2-7-6½ for the digging and carriage of stone. There was 4^{s} 1½^{d} for 1550-51 and £2-11-8 for road repairs.

On 29 September 1550 William Marshall, another figure in the story, was elected mayor. Two months later, on 21 November, a crucial wardmote was held at which he and six out of the twelve jurats with a number of commoners were present. In view of what happened, they were either acting high-mindedly in the interest of the town or else they must be presumed to be some of

---

220 See APPENDIX 4; 'Visitation articles and injunctions of the period of the Reformation 1536-58', eds. W. H. Frere and W. M. Kennedy, *Alcuin Club Coll.*, (London, 1910), ii, pp. 241-243; J. Wickham Legg, *Ecclesiological Essays*, (London, 1905), vii, p. 29.

221 CCA, Cons, DCb/X.10.3, fols. 4, 4v, 40v, 41, 53, 67-68v, 83-87; DCb/X.10.4, fol. 175v; DCb/Y.2.3, fols. 17v, 36, 40, 51v, 58, 75-75v; DCb/Y.2.16, fols. 85v, 88, 94, 98v, 99; DCb/Y.4.8 fols. 48, 61, 65.

Arden's chief enemies in the town. They were William Marshall, Richard Dryland, Lewis Marden, John Best, Stephen Motte, John Wreake, the former mayor, and Thomas Gate. They decreed that the cess set in 1549 and organised by Dryland, Gate, Thomas Stransham and John Snothe should be paid and gathered to the use of the town. Arden and Dunkyn had clearly refused to pay it. A clause undoubtedly aimed at them said that if any man resisted the payment, then the mayor was to execute the penalty of the freeman's oath and he was to be disfranchised. Furthermore, if he was a jurat, he was to be put from the bench and disinherited for ever. Six jurats were absent: as well as Arden and Dunkyn, John Seth, John Dryland the elder, Robert Colwell and Ralph Rogers, gentleman, were not there. Rogers was a shadowy figure who had only become a jurat that year.

Marshall allowed one month, and then, on 22 December, with the full panoply of 11 jurats and 19 freemen, Thomas Dunkyn was disfranchised. Thomas Stransham and Francis Swan had replaced Arden and Dunkyn as jurats. Swan was a chamberlain when Arden was mayor. He came from Wye in Kent and married Katherine, the widow of John Bringborne, who was later a witness in the Hatch dispute. Ralph Rogers was not present nor was he ever heard of again. It was said that in spite of being a jurat with all that that meant, Dunkyn 'by dyvers wayes and meanes [had] gone about and laboured to the uttermost of his power to infrynge and undoo the said frauncheseis, liberties and freedoms. And also for his apparaunt stobourne and disobedient answeres and behavyour used to the mayor and jurates, sittyng in counsell, beyng commaunded from the benche, for certeyn reasonable causes (saying he would nott) except the mayer and jurates did violently pluck him from the same'.

After a short discussion following up Arden's reforms for orphans by appointing wardens, the assembly disfranchised Arden. Dunkyn had obviously been the noisy rebel, but it was said that Arden had 'gone aboute and labored by dyvers wayes and meanes to the utermost of his power to infrindge and undo the said frauncheses, liberties and freedoms. That therefore the said Thomas Arden shalbe deposed from the benche and no more to be juratte of the said towne. Butt from hensforth to be utterlye disfraunchesed for ever'. The oath is normally to preserve and protect the liberties - was he by any chance working for one of his patrons ? If so, it was almost certainly Sir Thomas Cheyne, who, in the very same year, 1550, 'attempted to revive oligarchic supremacy in Sandwich only to be rebuffed by the commonalty, whereupon a number of leading townsmen retaliated by refusing to take office. The Henrician oligarchy at Dover was overturned (in) about 1551.' Both these towns had strong links with Faversham in the period. Cheyne also intervened constantly in parliamentary elections in the Cinque Ports from 1547 onwards. Examples survive from Dover, New Romney, Rye and Sandwich.[222]

We should not underestimate what a serious matter this was for Arden, of whom the one thing we can be sure is that he loved power and influence. Had he been sufficiently powerful, he would certainly not have allowed it. Disfranchisement was something like a gentleman being blackballed from his London club in Victorian times. I have looked through the wardmote book from its start in 1447-48 until 1566, which is as far as it has been transcribed, and I have not found a mention of anyone else being disfranchised. Indeed, according to K. Murray, 'in 1599 Faversham indignantly asserted their right to disjurate and disfranchise at their own will and pleasure without showing any cause to the Warden, much less to his Lieutenant who had been sent to examine the case.' In 1660, following the return of Charles II, again in a political move, ten jurats were disfranchised. There are a few examples at Rye, Exeter and Norwich of the same

[222] Clark, Society, pp. 80, 424; Commons 1509-58, 1, pp. 253-64.

thing taking place. On a lighter note, Jeffery Hills of Faversham was disfranchised on 3 March 1673 for being a drunkard and for abusing the mayor, jurats and commonalty.[223]

Think what a humiliation it must have been for this to happen to the very man who had drawn up the town charter only four years earlier and had once been mayor himself. We know that he did not go willingly because, to repeat, he had 'gone about and labored by dyvers wayes and meanes to the utermost of his power to infrindge and undo the said frauncheses, liberties and freedoms.'

As P. Clark says, 'For most (towns) full incorporation served as the ultimate accolade, giving their rulers the status of representatives of the whole community. Between 1500 and 1700 no less than 160 English towns received charters of incorporation, two-thirds of them before 1600.... the dominant theme, the driving force behind these aspirations and the consequence of their achievement, was the growth of oligarchy. Charters of incorporation have been described as 'tools of an irresistible tendency towards exclusiveness'.......By the end of the century small, closed councils with members sitting for life and able to co-opt one another were, with few exceptions, the usual means of government in English towns.'

Writing of Exeter, W. MacCaffrey supports this view. He says, 'A rigidly ordered system of regulation secured the economic bases of the community. It was equally necessary to protect the whole social structure of the city by correspondingly elaborate controls. The public peace, never quite secure in this violent age, had to be preserved. Hand in hand with this task went the maintenance of the orthodoxies of politics and (what was almost the same thing) religion. And at a still more profound level, it was the obligation of the community to enforce the precepts of a morality resting upon immemorial tradition.' This was certainly the case in Faversham where the mayor, the jurats and members of the common council or 24 were the political élite, whose power and influence stretched far wider than that.[224]

So, there can be no doubt how serious the disfranchisement was for Arden. No precise reasons are given. It may have been due to an accumulation of events. First, there is the story in Stow that 'the fayre was wont to be kepte partely in the towne, and partely in the abbey, but Arden for his owne lucre had this present yere browght it to be wholye kepte within the abbey ground which he had purchased so that all the gaynes came to hym and none to the townesmen for the which dede he had many a curse'. As I have said before, it has not been possible to corroborate this from any other records. Secondly, after the heady days of obtaining the charter, the town had run into serious trouble. There were too many grand projects, like paving parts of the town and extensive repairs to the court house. There was still the charter to be paid for and new annual payments to be made to the king, the steward and the mayor. I suspect, though, that there was a deeper malaise and that Arden had been trying to mould the town council for his own purposes, probably acting on instructions from Sir Thomas Cheyne. Why, otherwise, would he have made a statute saying that only the mayor, the jurats and members of the common council should be called for the making of laws and statutes unless the mayor specifically called other people? There may have been a fight going on for control of the town and Arden may have had a long-term plan in view when he refused to pay that cess. If I am right, then both Cheyne and Arden got their comeuppance, because Arden was disfranchised by the combined efforts not only of the mayor, jurats and common council, but also of a few freemen.

---

223 CKS, Fa/AC4 fols. 117, 132; K. M. E. Murray, *The Constitutional History of the Cinque Ports,* (MUP, 1935), pp. 95-101.

224 P.Clark and P. Slack, *English Towns in Transition 1500-1700*, (Oxford Univ. Press, 1976), pp. 127-29; W. T. MacCaffrey, *Exeter 1540-1640,* (Harvard Univ. Press, 1975),pp. 38-39, 89; G. Mayhew, *Tudor Rye* (Falmer Centre for Continuing Education, Univ. of Sussex, 1987), pp. 93-94.

Just to recapitulate on the men chiefly involved; William Marshall had contributed 40^s to the loan of 1542, was mayor in 1551 and died in 1562, leaving £47-4-2 according to his inventory. Richard Dryland belonged to the family of Cooksditch, married an heiress, was granted an annuity of ten marks from the late abbey for service in the king's wars beyond the seas in 1538, was mayor in 1541 and died in 1551, leaving property in Faversham, Chilham, Teynham, Luddenham, Stone, Lynsted, Davington and Harty. Lewis Marden when mayor had planned to make Arden a freeman, though it had come to nothing. He had not signed when Arden was mayor in 1548 and died in 1551, leaving lands in Marden and lands and mills in Chart next Sutton Valence. John Best contributed 40^s to the loan of 1542 and was mayor in 1547,1549 and 1558, and had died by 1566. Stephen Motte had had a lease of Nethercourt from the abbot and had been made a freeman without payment in 1543. John Wreake contributed 40^s to the loan of 1542, was mayor in 1550 and died in 1579, leaving a large family. Finally, Thomas Gate, who contributed 40^s to the loan of 1542, was not a signatory when Arden was mayor, was mayor himself in 1552 and died in 1560. It is difficult to avoid the conclusion that these were men of substance and long-term residents.

This becomes still more evident when we turn to consider the list of people who were present at the momentous meeting in 1550 when the decision was made to disfranchise Arden and Dunkyn. There were seven men who were not present when Arden was mayor in 1548, but took part in the session in 1550. The first jurat was Lewis Marden who had had all the dunghills cleared away when he was mayor. The second was Thomas Gate. The first of the common councillors was John Snothe, a shipowner, whose son, Abraham, became the leading shipowner a generation later. William Neale was a corn merchant who was mayor in 1560 and died in 1565. The basis of Faversham's prosperity then was the transport of corn to the rapidly expanding London market. Henry Philpott was mayor in 1564 and died in 1570. Richard Johnson died in 1553, but nothing is known of William Fynner. Finally, there were the Stransham brothers, Thomas and George. Some or all of these men must have been opposed to Arden.[225]

Edward Crow realized in the middle of the nineteenth century from looking at the wardmote book that Arden was disfranchised. However, this part of his work does not seem to have been published. It was only recently that A. Percival came across the record again. In the interim, a picture of Arden as all-powerful and dominant in the town has built up. If he was all-powerful, how did his allegedly subservient fellow townsmen dare to disfranchise him? From henceforth, Arden was an outsider in the town, 'to be utterlye disfraunchesed for ever.' Alice certainly understood how serious the situation was. Later, she egged on Morsby to kill Arden, saying, 'he was so evell belovyd that no man would inquire aftar his deathe.'

The heated disputes continued after Arden's murder. On 12 November 1552, when Thomas Gate was mayor, it was decided at a common wardmote that 'as often as the mayor for the tyme being shall cause any Warmothe to be warned that all that be warned shall apere accordingly as they be warned at the owere appoynted. And as sone as the mayor shalbe sett that every man take his seatt or place quietly and therin to sytt styll withoute talkyng untyll that he shall see convenient tyme to propounde or sett forthe his mynd. And then to stonde up and declare his mynde with owtte any interruption or contradiction untyll that he hath fully declared his mynd and then to sytt in his place agayne. And that no man shall interrupte or dysquiett the parte so declaring his mynde uppon payne of forfyture 4^d. as often as it happen. And yf the parte so

[225] CKS, Arch, Neale, PRC3/17/68, Philpott, PRC17/41/21v, Johnson, PRC3/3/60, Snothe, PRC10/6 /294v, PRC3/19/32, Wreake, PRC17/43/206; CKS, Fa/LB 9.

offendyng refuse to paye the forfyte of 4^{d}. that then the mayor to commytt hym to warde untyll he hath payd the same forfett and twelve pence more for a fyne'.[226]

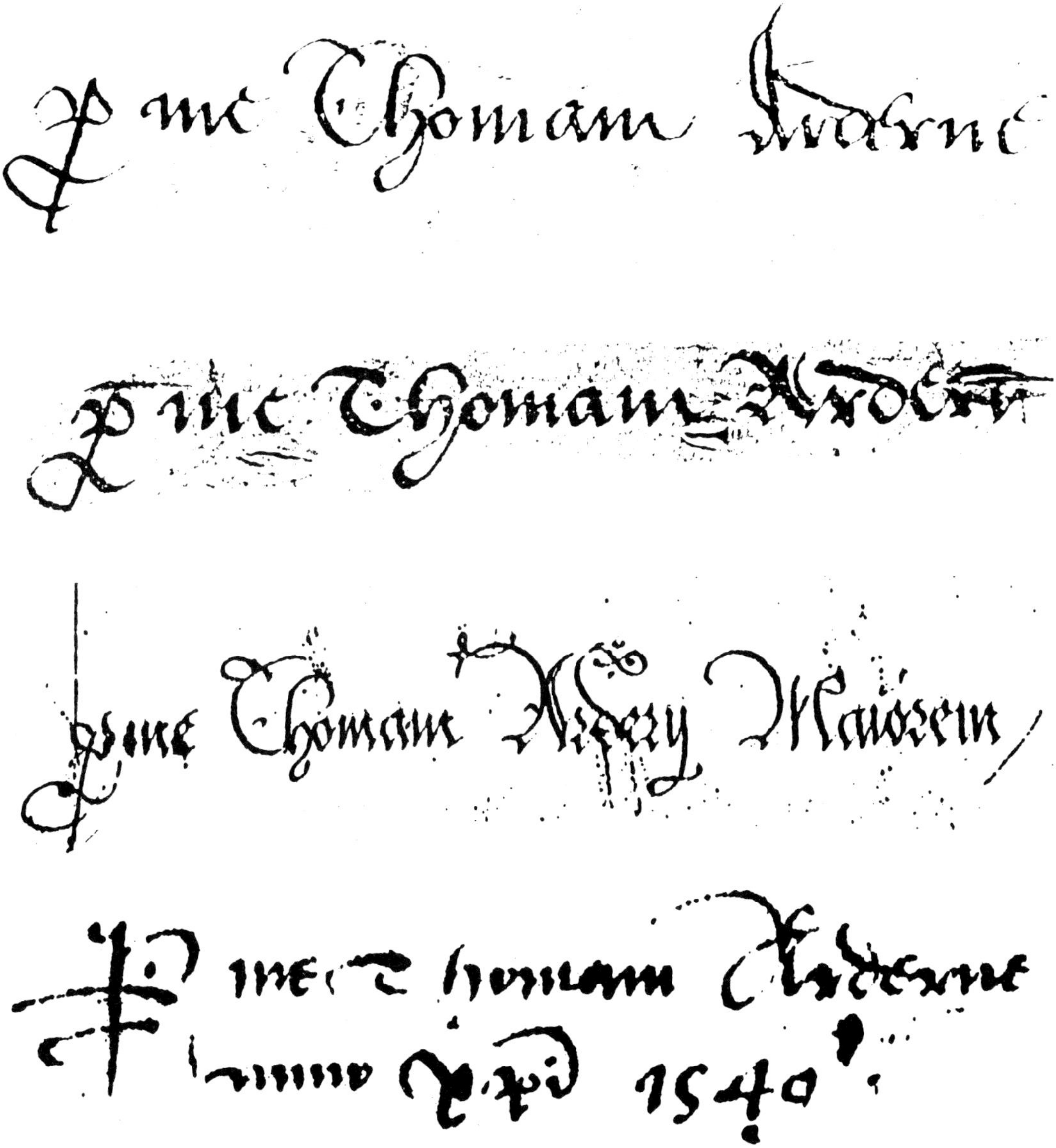

The signatures of Thomas Ardern. (1) PRO E318/2/36
(2) PRO:E318/2/37 (3)Wardmote Book CKS Fa/AC1, fol. 49v. (4) Fa/AC1 fol. 105

[226] Favward, fol. 64.

The North View of Faversham Abbey by Samuel and Nathaniel Buck in 1735 showing the inner and outer Gateways of the abbey.

KINSHIP OF ALICE WIFE OF THOMAS ARDEN[227]

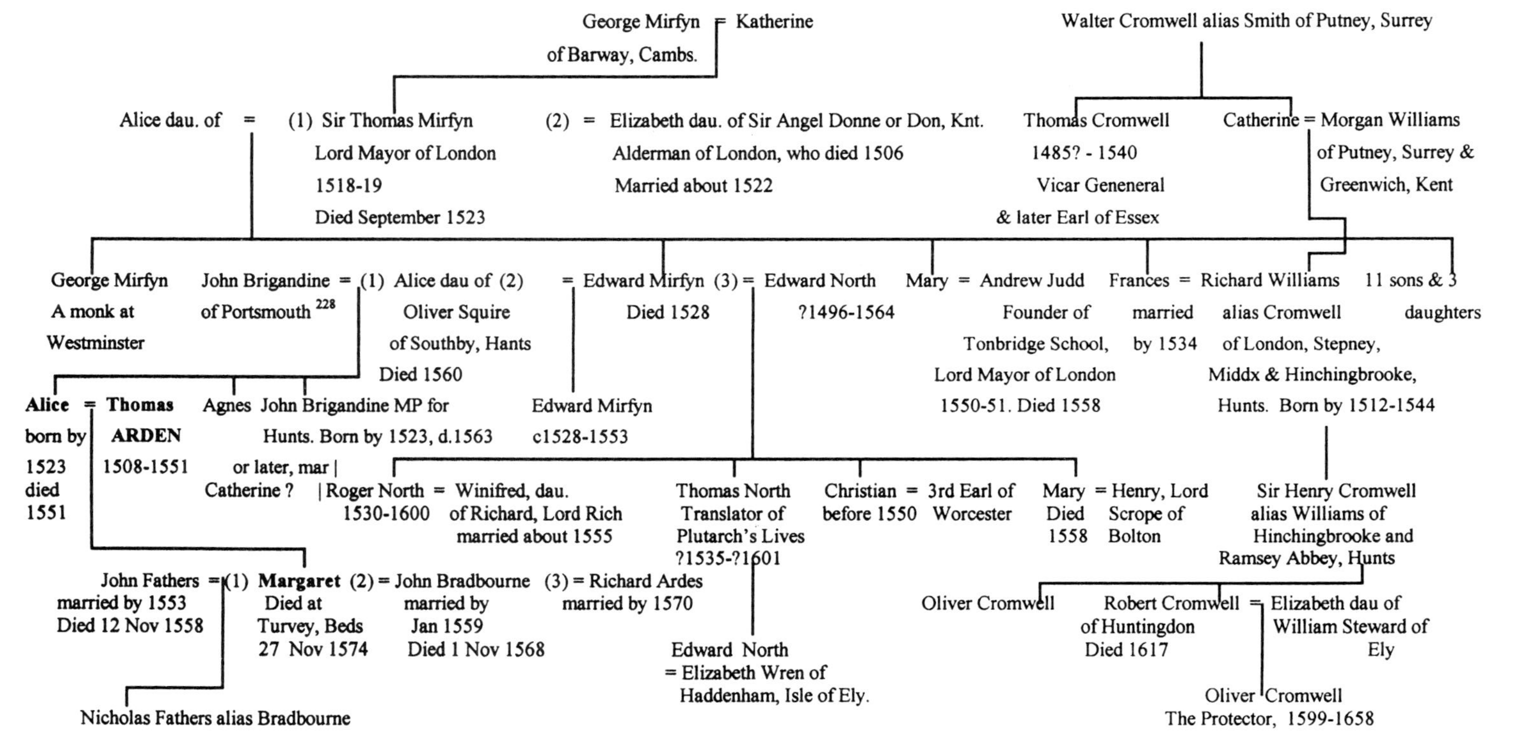

[227] PCC, PROB 11/21 fols. 97-99v, PROB 11/22 fol. 246; DNB, Burke's Peerage & Baronetage, 1978; Commons 1509-58, 1, pp. 496, 682-85; Rev. Alfred Beaven, *The Aldermen of the City of London*, (London, 1908), 11, pp. 22, 50; The Complete Peerage, iii, pp. 557-58; M. Ashley, *The Greatness of Oliver Cromwell*, (London, 1957); B. Coward, *Cromwell*, (London, 1991).

[228] John Brigandine was the son of Robert Brigandine, yeoman of the Crown by 1495, of Smallhithe, Tenterden, Kent and Portsmouth.

Chapter 10
Events leading up to the murder and the murder itself

On 20 December 1550, two days before this crucial meeting, Arden made his will. Most wills in this period were made shortly before death, but there is no indication that he was ill. If people were well, when making a will, they usually said so, 'calling to mind the suddenness of death.' They might make one if going on some hazardous journey, say, overseas, but otherwise not. What was in his mind? What was he planning to do? At this turning-point he may have been under pressure from Sir Edward North to carry out the arrangements made at the time of his marriage to North's step-daughter, Alice, in about 1537. Arden says that 'where I stand bounde to Sir Edward North knight in a thousand markes sterling to make my wife a joynture of £40-0-0 by yere for terme of her lyfe or ells to appoynt it her by my testament and last will'. Was Alice herself getting at him? He clearly had not made a settlement on her up till then because otherwise this clause would not have been necessary. Without it she would have to depend on the charity of her daughter and ultimately North. The details have been given earlier, but basically Arden allowed his wife lands as jointure worth £40 held by 1/20th part of a knight's fee as he had agreed with Sir Edward North, but he did not leave her the residue, as many husbands did. The second remarkable thing that he did was to leave some property worth £2-6-0 to the town, which, as shown earlier, he had only been granted after a petition to the Crown. What an extraordinary bequest to make when the town's élite was planning to disfranchise him only two days later. Did he really not know what was about to happen? Was he trying to curry favour?

He left money for an annual sermon and insisted that the preacher from Christ Church, Canterbury - from whom he leased Faversham parsonage - or other well-learned man, should recite his, Arden's, name as 'the causer' of that sermon. This bequest has been said to show 'his strong Protestant sympathy' and certainly it was something a Protestant was more likely than a Catholic to do. His wish to be remembered in the town is crystal clear, and this came true, though not quite in the way he expected. Perhaps he was a reformer, perhaps not. Certainly both his patrons were time-servers and Cheyne was well-known as a religious conservative to whom Cranmer had angrily written in 1537 'people in Kent dare not read God's word for fear of your threats at (as)sizes and sessions.'[229] The remainder of his property worth £22-7-8 held in free socage and the 5^{s} fee from St. Valentine's fair he left to his daughter, Margaret. He made his wife his executrix and Sir Edward North his overseer, for which he was to have Arden's best horse.[230]

Arden had less than two months to live. I suggest that his wife, Alice, had been hoping for this settlement and moment of recognition for years, possibly since her marriage in about 1537. Of course he may have granted her the jointure in an earlier will which had been destroyed, but I find the short space between the making of the will and the murder significant. Canon Telfer stated that this was Arden's second will following a second marriage. I have hunted high and low for the evidence without success. Normally there would be no way of knowing, because the first will would be destroyed when the second will was made. It is only in rare cases such as that of Henry Hatch that we can be sure, when we are told by witnesses that he was very fond of making wills and had made several of them.

---

229 Clark, Society , p 82; Commons 1509-58, i, p. 635.

230 See See APPENDIX 12: Favward, fols. 280v-281; PRO, C142/93/111.

In this account of the events leading up to the murder I will use two sources. The first is the short account in the wardmote book, which gave most of the names. The wardmote book was originally also called the mayor's book. The account comes after records concerning the mayoralty of William Marshall, which ran from September 1550 to September 1551. That was the first opportunity logically for it to appear there after the murder. Wills and deeds thought to be important to the town were entered into the wardmote book from time to time. This account was no doubt entered because the mayor, William Marshall, had been in charge of the investigations concerning the murder and was one of the quorum, that is, one of the three most important commissioners of oyer and terminer charged with the trial of Alice and the others.[231]. As the trial also took place in Faversham, we must surely therefore take this account as the closest to an official report of what was uncovered at the trial as we could possibly have. Of course, we cannot tell how far it was sanitised. The very fact that it is in the wardmote book suggests that it is the version of events which William Marshall wanted posterity to believe. That does not necessarily make it accurate nor even wholly reliable. Marshall also no doubt wanted it there because the town became responsible for the probate of Arden's will and for the murderers' goods.

The second account that I have used is Stow, who seems to have been writing from at least two different sources.[232] At the end his account is muddled and repetitive, but what is remarkable is the writer's involvement in the affair and his clear views and definite opinions on a number of the characters and events involved, which Holinshed toned down and modified. After the tale about Arden's mother, Stow described Arden as a tall man of a comely appearance. He related how he married a well-favoured young gentlewoman and a tale, meaning someone who is talked about. Holinshed had the word tall instead. She was Lord North's wife's daughter. He added that they often had recourse to Lord North's, where there was one Thomas Mosby or Morsby. He was a tailor by occupation, a black, swarthy man, who, in the process of time, was made 'one of the chiefest gentlemen about the Lord North'. There is a sense of progression here and change over time which is missing in Holinshed. It is worth noting that three of the conspirators were tailors, Morsby himself, Saunderson and Grene. Could this be significant? I have checked the records of the Merchant Taylors', but, unfortunately, they are missing for the relevant period. The word 'tailor' does not mean the owner of a business employing other hands as in its modern form. Rather it means someone belonging to a tailors' guild somewhere.

The account continued that Morsby grew familiar with Alice, 'notwithstondynge for some dyslikynge he had of hir'. He fell out with her, but she wanted to be in favour again with him and so sent him a pair of silver dice by one Adam Fowle dwelling at the Fleur de Luce in Faversham. One of Adam Fowle's ancestors may have been Richard Fowle, who held the office of porter of the great inner gate of the Abbey of Faversham. In 1543-44 Adam was exporting a hogshead of herrings in a ship from Flushing licensed to load for Boulogne. Certainly, he paid 6^{s} 8^{d} to become a freeman in 1548 and was elected to the 24 by the mayor and jurats when Arden was mayor in 1548. He signed the articles drawn up by Arden as mayor in the same year and was one of the 24 for the next three years. At some point he took a lease of Lammas Fair from the town, which he had given up by 10 February 1555. In Arden's will, he was mentioned as a tenant of 'the porter's gatehouse with the garden at 40^{s} by the yere'. His prosperous brother,

[231] See APPENDIX 1; Quorum: fixed number of members that must be present to make proceedings of assembly valid.
[232] BL, Harl. MSS. 542; APPENDIX 3.

Stephen, mentioned 'my brother Adam's children', Matthew, Thomasin and Rebecca, in his will in 1557.[233]

After the gift of the dice, Morsby resorted to Alice again and would often lie at Arden's house, so much so that within two years 'he had to do with Mistress Arden'. The wardmote book added that he did not only 'carnally keep (her) in her own house here in this town, but also fed her with delicate meats and sumptuous apparel', which gives a vivid insight into the outrage felt by the townsfolk at this virtual *ménage à trois.* This also gives an indication of how much Morsby was prepared to travel, because, surely, he had a responsible job as steward and his main place of employment must have been at North's residence at the Charterhouse in London or at Kirtling in Cambridgeshire. The wardmote book goes on to back up Stow, who asserts that Arden 'perceyvynge ryght well theyr mutuall familiaritie to be much greatar then theyr honestie, was yet so greatly gyven to seke his advauntage and caryd so little how he came by it that in hope of atteynynge some benefite of the Lord Northe by meanes of this Morsby who could do muche with hym (presumably North), he winked at that shamefull dysorder and bothe parmyttyd and also invited hym very often to be in his howse. And thus it contynuyd a good space before any practyse against Arden. At lengthe she was so inflamyd with the love of Morsby that she lothyd hir husbond and therefore wyshed, and after practysed, how to brynge hym to his end'. In other words, Arden was well aware that he was a cuckold, but accepted it for his own ends. He was not, as in the play, tortured by the thought of it.

Alice gathered her accomplices around her. She must have had charisma to attract such a loyal band. The wardmote book says that she first consulted Thomas Morsby and his sister, Cicely Ponder, and two of Arden's daily servants, another tailor called Michael Saunderson and Elizabeth Stafford. Again one wonders how a tailor came to be doing this. Stow goes on to the point where Alice consulted a painter called William Blackbourne, who was skilled at concocting poisons. Nothing more has been discovered about him. He made a poison for her, but she disobeyed instructions, so that, although it made Arden ill, he subsequently recovered. She obviously had no confidence in her fellow accomplices for she then turned to John Grene, the third tailor, who was a servant of Sir Anthony Aucher. He paid 5^{s} for his freedom in 1542-43 and in the following year there was a mysterious reference to 18^{s} 3^{d} paid for the expenses of Joseph and William Hale riding to Hampton Court concerning John Grene, tailor. He was one of the people who signed when the new charter was obtained in 1546. He was said to hate Arden because Arden had got a piece of ground at the back of the abbey extortionately from him. There had been blows and threatening words between them[234] Alice told him that anyone who would kill Arden would have £10-0-0 reward, (the wardmote book said £8-0-0). Grene had occasion to go up to London on business for Sir Anthony Aucher, who was then, as only Stow mentions, victualler to Boulogne. He asked George Bradshaw, a goldsmith of Faversham and 'a very honest man' to accompany him to Gravesend and said that he would content him for his pains. When they got to Rainham Down, they happened to see three or four serving-men coming from Leeds in Kent. Bradshaw noticed that one coming from the direction of Rochester was Black Will, a terrible ruffian with a sword and buckler, and another had a great staff over his shoulder. Bradshaw said to Grene that they were lucky to have company from Leeds, for there came as murderous a knave as any in England. If it had not been for them, they would hardly have escaped with their money and their lives. The account continued with what Grene was then thinking, as he afterwards confessed. This makes it clear that Stow was using the evidence of

233 See APPENDIX 3 and See APPENDIX 8; Favward, fols. 41v, 47, 50, 51v, 53v, 58, 280v; CKS, Arch, Fowle, PRC17/33/37; PRO, E315/100/10/237; CKS, Fa/TL2

234 Favward, fols. 37v, 39v; CKS, Fa/A1.5/3.

the prisoners' confessions for his account. Grene thought that such a man was for his purpose. It turned out that Bradshaw knew him, because he and Black Will had both served in Boulogne. Henry VIII had captured Boulogne in 1544, but his son Edward VI surrendered it back to the French in the Treaty of Boulogne on 29 March 1550, almost a year before Arden's murder. Bradshaw had been a servant of Sir Richard Cavendish, who had been comptroller of Dover in 1543, when he had a dispute over rights of authority with Sir Thomas Cheyne. He was appointed Captain of Blackness Castle near Boulogne in 1546, from which he was discharged in 1549. He may have been the Richard Cavendish, knight, who was one of the kinsfolk and co-heirs of Henry, late Duke of Suffolk, and his brother, Charles Brandon, in 1552. Black Will had been a soldier who committed many heinous murders on travellers between Boulogne and France. The wardmote book said that he came from Calais, which was then, of course, an English town.[235] After further lively conversation, Black Will agreed to go back and sup at the expense of Grene and Bradshaw at Gravesend. He renewed his acquaintance with Bradshaw, who was terrified to acknowledge him. After supper, without Bradshaw knowing, Grene and Black Will came to an agreement that if Black Will would kill Arden, he would receive £10-0-0. Grene promised to point him out the next day at St. Paul's. He then wrote a letter to Alice, telling her what had happened, thanks to Bradshaw, who in turn took this letter to Alice on his return home, knowing nothing of its contents. Grene and Black Will went up to London. Grene pointed out Arden, but he had his man with him. Black Will wanted to kill him as well, but Grene emphasized that he was one of the conspirators, though he could hardly restrain him. There were, though, so many gentlemen around Arden that he had to abandon the attempt. Saunderson was a conspirator because he wanted to marry a kinswoman of Morsby's, not, as in the play, necessarily Morsby's sister. Arden now lay at his parsonage in London, (which was St. Michael's, Cornhill), so Saunderson and Black Will agreed that Saunderson would leave the doors open, so that Black Will could murder Arden. However, Saunderson was so frightened of Black Will that he failed to leave them open. Black Will was angry at being foiled but Grene acted as a mediator and pacified him.

Arden was ready to go home. Saunderson agreed with Grene that Black Will should murder Arden at Rainham Down, but when they got to Rochester, Saunderson was again so frightened of Black Will that he deliberately made his horse lame so that he could lag behind. Arden went ahead to where Black Will lay in wait, but various gentlemen of Arden's acquaintance overtook him and accompanied him, so Black Will was foiled again.

When Arden got home he sent his man, Saunderson, as he usually did, to his patron, Sir Thomas Cheyne, Lord Warden of the Cinque Ports. Saunderson came back with a reply, which Alice took, read and kept. She told Saunderson to say to Arden that he had lost it and that Arden had better go to Sir Thomas Cheyne himself. Black Will was by then, thanks to Grene, with one George Shakebag, his old comrade in arms, in a storehouse belonging to Sir Anthony Aucher, and Alice went to see him many times and brought him meat. Unfortunately, not one shred of evidence has been found about George Shakebag or Shackebagge or Shackebacke or George Losebagg as he was called in the wardmote book.[236] They planned to lie in wait in a certain broom close between Faversham and the ferry, but Black Will waited in the wrong place. On the way to Shurland, Cheyne's home, Saunderson pretended that he had lost his purse, because, once again, he was frightened of Black Will's intentions. Arden was angry, but allowed him to return to look for it and to overtake him at the ferry. Black Will again lost him, hoped to catch him on

235 Favward, fols. 59v, 60; APC, NS, i, pp. 61, 73-74, 312, 476; CPR 1550-53, p. 225; G.E.C., xii, part I, p. 462.

236 A. Percival tells me that the name Loosbergh appears in the Brugge area telephone directory. It is just possible that Loosebag was from the Flemish-speaking area near Calais.

the return journey, but, yet again, was foiled because there were many of the Lord Warden's gentlemen accompanying Arden to Faversham.

There would have been plenty of time for all these events to take place between 20 December, when the will was made, and St. Valentine's Day. It is likely that they did take place in a short space of time because it would have been hard to hold a wayward man like Black Will, and it is clear that at this point none of the other conspirators saw themselves as murderers. They now grew more reckless and desperate. They decided that they could work the feat at St. Valentine's Fair, presumably hoping to blame it on a passer-by and to get lost in the crowds. Morsby planned to pick a quarrel at the fair in order to fight Arden, because he could not find it in himself to kill a gentleman, so he clearly knew nothing of Arden's origins. Morsby is always portrayed in Stow as a reluctant conspirator. Alice, on the other hand, egged Morsby on, saying that Arden was so evil beloved that no-one would enquire after his death. There she was wrong, but it was a reasonable assumption after all the events surrounding the disfranchisement. Here Holinshed differed from Stow. Holinshed has the story of the pair receiving the sacrament in a church one Sunday in London, but Stow does not. He, however, has a longer story based on Morsby's confession, only briefly mentioned in Holinshed. Morsby had tried to pick a quarrel with Arden riding to or from London, calling him knave, villain and cuckold, but Arden would not fight. In frustration, Morsby went off in a great fury towards the Fleur de Luce where Adam Fowle was his host. Before he got there, a messenger from Alice came begging him to return and to carry out their purpose. Holinshed went straight on with a story about Morsby's sister. In Stow there was merely a contemporary figure 1. This, I suggest, marks a plan to insert material different from the main account. Several folios on, the figure 1 is repeated and the story about Morsby's sister follows, running from 'Morsby had a sister towards the Flower de Luce where he did often host'. It said that it was in Cicely Ponder's house that the final plot was hatched. Morsby came back, and, again, there is a figure 2 to mark an intended insertion. Several folios on, there is another contemporary figure 2 and the story 'when he came back again to her she kneeled down to him, saying, if thou love me, thou would be content, seeing (as before) thou needest not to doubt no man will care'.

They conveyed Black Will into a closet at the end of the parlour in Arden's house, having sent out all the servants except the confederates. Then Morsby stood at the door in a night gown of silk. It was between 6 and 7 o'clock at night. Arden had been at the house of his neighbour, Dumpkyn alias Dunkyn, close by. They had made an end of certain reckonings between them. He came home and found Morsby standing at the door and asked if it were supper time. Morsby said, 'I thinke not, it is not redy yet'. Arden replied, 'Than let us goe and playe a game at tables in the mean ceason'. So they went straight into the parlour. As they came through the hall, Alice was walking there, and Arden said, 'how now, Mystrys Ales', but she made small answer to him. In the meantime, one of them chained the wicket door of the entry. When they came into the parlour, Morsby sat down on the bench, having his face towards the place where Black Will stood. Stow adds that Arden stood with his face towards the same. Then Michael, Arden's man, stood at his master's back holding a candle in his hand to shadow Black Will so that Arden might not see him coming forth. In the course of their play Morsby said (which seemed, according to Stow, to be a 'watchword' for Black Will's coming forth), 'Now may I take yow, see yf I will'. 'Take me', said Arden, 'which way?' With that, the terrible ruffian, Black Will, came forth, and cast a towel about his neck so as to stop his breath and strangle him. Then Morsby having at his girdle a pressing iron of 14 pounds (remember that he was a tailor) struck him on the head with the same so that he fell down and gave a great groan, in so much that they thought that they had killed him.

Then they took him and carried him away to lay him in the counting house. Only Stow has 'in the bearing of him down', because the counting house was downstairs. The pangs of death coming on him, he struggled and groaned. Then Black Will struck him a great gash with his dagger across his brow and so killed him and laid him down, taking the money out of his purse and rings from his fingers. Then Black Will said as follows, 'Now this feate is done, gyve me my monye'. So Mistress Arden gave him £10 and he 'voided' the town straight away after he had got to Grene, where he had a horse available. Then came 'this good wyfe' and with a knife gave her husband seven or eight pricks in the breast. Stow adds that she did this 'because she would make him sure'. There follows the contemporary figure 3 and an insertion a few folios on. It tells how they made the parlour clean and sent for the Londoners who had previously been invited to supper. Stow does not give their names until later, but Holinshed calls them two grocers, Prune and Cole, as well as some other Londoners There was a London grocer called Thomas Prime of St. Martin, Outwich, whose widow, Joan, was granted an administration on 15 January 1552, who might have been the man. There were two London grocers called Cole in the period. The first was Roger Cole, whose will was proved on 7 May 1561. He referred to his wife, Ellen, two daughters and several brothers and sisters. The second was Thomas Cole, a citizen and grocer of All Hallows in Honey Lane, a church close to St. Mary le Bow, where Robert Cole was the rector from 23 December 1559. His will was proved on 10 April 1571 and he left his wife, Elizabeth, as executrix.[237]

They asked after Arden but were told he was at supper in the town. Morsby's sister was called in and they were merry. After supper they played on the virginals and danced. Stow does not then mention that the daughter played on the virginals. Alice wanted them to play at tables, but they said that they must get back to their hosts or else they would be shut out of doors. How must these two men have felt when they realized that they had been so thoroughly hoodwinked? They were the Rosencrantz and Guildernstern of the affair with, no doubt, a highly coloured version of events to tell when they returned to London. They must have followed what happened after the arrest with avid interest. When they had gone, she sent away all the servants except the confederates. There are two accounts of the next episode. The first, in the text, says that they took Arden in his nightgown with his slippers on his feet to a field outside the garden joined to the abbey ground. They brought his body to the garden door, but could not find the key in half an hour, which is not in Holinshed. When they found it, they opened the door and laid the corpse in the field, which again only Stow compared to Ahab who had got Naboth's vineyard, because Arden had taken this field by violence from one Reade and his wife, who had often said to his face and in many other places with tears that she besought God for vengeance to light upon him that all men might wonder on him. This was widow Cooke, who may have been Alice Cooke, whose second husband, Richard Reade, was a mariner. When he died without leaving a will in 1559 she was granted the administration of his goods.[238]

In the meantime, there fell 'a great snow' in so much that they thought on coming into the house again that the snow would have covered 'theyr fotynge', but suddenly, 'by the good provydence of God, who would not suffer so detestable a murther to be longe hydden', it stopped snowing. The second version in contemporary figure 3 covers much the same ground, but says that the body was laid ten paces from the garden gate towards the sextry and that they laid him down upon his back straight with his slippers and between one of his slippers and his foot was a long rush which they left there. Holinshed used something of both versions.

---

237 Pryme, Commissary Ct. of London, xii, fol. 105; Cole, PROB11 /44/6, & /53/17; Thomas Cole left a book concerning accounts and details of the births and deaths of his children 1531-80, Sloane MS 1206;A.Wollaston-Hutton, Bow Church.

238 CKS, Arch, Reade, PRC3/15/116; compare pp. 58, 68 & 88.

Not considering that the snow had stopped and thinking that they were safe, again not mentioned in Holinshed, the conspirators took a cloth and wiped where it was bloody and strewed rushes about again that had been disturbed in the struggle. They cast the cloth with which they had wiped the blood and the bloody knife with which she had wounded her husband into a tub by the side of the well, where afterwards they were found. Thus, this version concludes, this wicked woman with her accomplices most shamefully murdered her own husband, who most entirely loved her all his lifetime, which is not the line that Stow had been following up till then. He may have meant that Arden loved her well enough, even though he loved his own advancement more.

There follows a second dramatic version of her encounter with the London grocers, Prime and Cole, here mentioned by name. Prime was called Prune in Holinshed, a reasonable mistake in palaeography. There is a mention of the daughter playing the virginals. Holinshed rejoins at the point where Alice made enquiries abroad about Arden, namely amongst the best in the town, but they answered that they could tell her nothing. Then she began to make an outcry and said, 'Never woman had suche neighbowrs as I have', and wept. So much so that her neighbours found her making great lamentation. Whereupon, the mayor and others came and made a search, the mayor being William Marshall, the very man who had organized Arden's disfranchisement. The modern equivalent of Alice's behaviour is when people appear on television today, apparently under great strain, asking for help in finding a close relative whom it later transpires that they themselves have murdered.

Stow continues that the fair was wont to be kept partly in the town and partly in the abbey. Arden for his own lucre had this present year brought it to be wholly kept within the abbey ground, which he had purchased, so that all the gains came to him and none to the townsmen, for the which deed he had many a curse. Then the mayor went about the fair in his search, and at length he came into the same ground where Arden lay. After a while, Prime the grocer said, 'Stay, for methinke I se one lye here'. So they looked, and, examining the body, found that Arden lay dead. Then, looking about, they found some rushes from the parlour sticking in his slippers. By diligent search they found certain footsteps, by reason of the snow, between them and the garden door.

Then the mayor said, 'Let every man stay'. Some by his commandment went about and came from the inside from the house through the garden to the place where Arden lay dead. They saw even more footsteps before them in the snow, and so it appeared plainly that he was brought along that way from the house through the garden and so into the field where he lay. They went in, and, knowing her evil behaviour in times past, they examined her, but she defied them, and said, 'I would yow showld know I am no suche woman'. Then they examined her servants. In examination, by reason of a piece of his hair and blood found about the house in the way in which they carried him and the knife which she thrust in him and the cloth with which they wiped the blood away, they all confessed the matter. Mistress Arden, seeing her husband's blood, said, 'O the blowde of God helpe me, for this blowde I have shede'. Then they were all committed to prison. After this, the mayor with others went presently to the Fleur de Luce where they found Morsby in bed. As soon as they came towards him, they noticed the blood on his hose and on his purse. Then he asked the cause of their coming. They said, 'Se here, you may understond it by thes tokens, showing him the blood on his hose and purse'. Then he confessed the deed, so he and all the others that conspired against Master Arden were laid in prison, saving Grene and Black Will, who fled, and the painter and George Shackebacke, who were gone and never heard of after. Shortly after were sessions kept at Faversham, where all these prisoners were arraigned and condemned. Then, being asked if they had any other accomplices, Mistress Arden accused

Bradshaw over the letter which he brought her sent by Grene from Gravesend, in which it was written, 'We have gotten a man for owre purpose, we may thank my brother Bradshaw, as is afore declaryd', which words had no meaning, other than that by Bradshaw's description of Black Will's qualities Grene judged him to be a proper instrument for the execution of the murder of Master Arden. Notwithstanding that, as Grene confessed at his death some years later, Bradshaw was never made privy to the plot, he was accused of being procurer of Black Will to kill Master Arden. This came wholly from misunderstanding that letter. Bradshaw asked to talk with the condemned persons, which was granted. He demanded to know whether they knew him or had had any conversation with him. They all said 'No'. Then, the letter being read out, he showed the truth of the matter. Notwithstanding this, he was condemned and suffered. The wardmote book says merely that 'and within 2 days after were apprehended and attached the foresaide Bradshawe'. So all these condemned persons were executed in various places. Michael Saunderson, Arden's man, was hanged in chains at Faversham. One of the maidens (Elizabeth Stafford) was burnt there, who pitifully bewailed her case and cried out on her mistress who brought her to this end and would not forgive her. Morsby and his sister were hanged on a gallows in Smithfield at London. Arden's wife was burned at Canterbury on 14 March 1551, only a month after the murder.

At this crucial point there follows the important sentence in Latin in Stow, which was not included in Holinshed. I have consulted the scholar, Alan Neame, about it. Translated it means:
'See the charges and the descriptions of the various persons and the places where they were put to death, which may be had of Master Robert Cole of Bow'.[239]

Now to finish Stow's account. Grene came back again years after and was hanged in the highway against Faversham between Ospringe and Boughton. Black Will the ruffian was burnt on a scaffold at Flushing in Zeeland. Adam Fowle of the Fleur de Luce in Faversham was carried up to London to prison about this matter with his legs bound under an horse because Morsby was heard to say these words, 'had it not been for Adam Fowle, I had not come to this trouble', meaning that the bringing of the silver dice for a token from Mistress Arden occasioned him to renew his familiarity with her. When the matter was well scanned, his innocence preserved him. There follows the first version of the outline of Arden's body being miraculously preserved two years later. At this point, after the main account and before the insertions, there is another sentence in Latin:

Our other esteemed observer after the burning.[240]

I suggest that Stow was commenting that the insertion had come from another eye-witness, whom unfortunately he does not name.

Then, after the insertions, the account reverts to Adam Fowle, saying that he was examined by Sir Thomas Moyle, Master (Cyriak) Petyt and Thomas Hawkyns of the Guard, who, being Papists and hating Adam Fowle for the gospel, sent him to the Marshalsea in London. This probably came from Cole, hinting at religious controversy. Holinshed made no mention of this angle.[241]. Hawkyns of the Guard was possibly Thomas Hawkins of Boughton, who died aged 101 on 15

---

[239] Vide exactores et certiorum personarum et locorum in quibus perierunt descriptiones quod a Magistro Roberto Coleo de Bow petere licet; Favward, fol. 60

[240] The abbreviated Latin, which is not clear, appears to be *nostri alius magnus contemplator post brennum.*

[241] CKS, Fa/Z 41/2, p176.

March 1587. There were verses on two brass plates fastened on an altar tomb in Boughton church, saying;

> 'King Henry theight I served which won me fame;
> Who was to me a gracious Prince always,
> And made me well to spend myne aged dayes.'

Thomas Hawkins, yeoman of the crown, had been granted a 21 year lease of the rectory of Hernhill in 1543-44.[242]

Stow continues that if Morsby at his arraignment had not discharged Fowle, he too would have suffered. A second version of Widow Cooke's story follows, saying that her husband, Reade, was a mariner who kept a tavern in the market place. The account finally comes to an end with a lengthy repetition of the miracle of the marks of Arden's body being preserved. The other repetitions concerned the arrival of the Londoners, the fall of snow, the playing of the virginals and Widow Cooke.[243]

In the foreground tomb of Edward North in Kirtling, Cambs. parish church. (Photo Art)

---

[242] Lewis, p. 29.
[243] See also pages 58, 68 and 85.

95 36

there accompanied hym so many gentlemen of my lorde wardens to feversham yt blacke
will was disapoynted, gods wonderfull providence hetherto. wen seint valentyns fayre
beinge at hand, ye conspirators thought surely to worke their feat at that tyme, mosbe thought
to picke some quarell w arden at ye fayre to fight wt hym, for he sayd he could not fynd in his
harte to kyll a gentleman, whereas mystris arden egged hym to kyll hir husbond by some
meanes, for he was so well beloved yt no man would make inquirie after his deathe / but
mosbe perceyvynge that he could not by any meanes cause arden to fight wt hym (for he
had picked a quarell wt hym cominge to or from london & callinge hym knave, villane
& cuckolde, but arden would not fight, this mosbe confessed in prison) went away
in a great fume towards ye flowredelice to adam fowles where he went to host, but or he
came thether a messenger cam to hym from mistris arden shewynge hym yt she desyred hym
of all loves to come agayne to hir & to go about ye purpose yt was in hand. so he cam backe
2 Than they conveyed blacke into ardens howse into a closet at ye end of his parlour, before this
they had sent out of ye howse all ye servants about dyvars erands, except those yt were
confederat to ye murther, Than went mosbe & stode at ye dore in a nyght gowne of silke
gyrded about hym & this was about .6. & .7. of ye clocke at nyght. Now master arden havynge
bene at a neighbours of his called dumpkyn dwellinge over agaynst his howse & their havynge
made an end of certayne rekeninges betwen them, cam home to go to supper, & findinge
mosbe standinge at ye dore asked hym yf it were suppertyme, he sayde I thinke not, it is
not redy yet. Than let us goe & playe a game at tables in ye meane ceason sayd master
arden. now they went streyght into ye parlor, and as they cam by throughe ye hall she was
walkynge ther, and master arden sayde, how now mystres ales, but she made small answer to
hym, in ye meane tyme one cheyned ye wicket dore of ye entrye. when they came into ye parlor
mosbe sat downe on ye benche havynge his face toward ye place where blacke will stode
and master arden stode wt his face toward ye same. Than mychaell his man stode at his masters
backe holdynge a candell in his hand to shadow blacke will yt arden myght by no meanes
perceyve hym cominge forthe. In their playe mosbe sayde this (whiche semyd to be a
watchworde for blacke wills cominge forthe) now may I take yow sir if I will. Take
me sayde arden whiche way, wt that the terrible ruffian blacke will cam forthe, and
cast a towell about his necke so to stope his breathe & strangle hym. Than mosbe havynge
at his gerdle a pressinge yron of .14. pound weight strake hym on ye heade wt ye same so yt
he fell downe and gave a greate grone, in so muche yt they thought that they had kylled hym.
Than they toke hym, and caried hym away to lay hym in the countinge howse and in ye beringe of hym downe, ye pangs of deathe
cominge on hym, he groned and gronyd, blacke will strake hym whereat ye throwe a great
gashe wt his dagger & so kylled hym & layd hym downe toke ye money out of his purse
& rynges from his fingars, cam out and sayd as foloweth, now this feate is done
come give me my money, so mistres arden gave hym .x. pound, and he voyded ye
towne streyght ways, after he had gone to rochester & had a horse there. Than came this
good wyfe, & wt a knyfe gave hir husbond .7. or .8. prickes in ye brest because she would
3 make hym sure. After this they toke hym as he was in his nyght gowne wt his slyppers
on his fete to cary hym into a field next ye garden joyned to ye abbey grownde. now
they brought his body to ye garden dore, but they could not find ye keye in halfe an
howre. At lengthe findinge it they opened ye dore & layde ye corps alonge in ye filde
(whiche filde he in his lyfe tyme had got by like title as ahab gat naboths vyneyard
for he had taken it frome one reade & his wyfe by vyolence, whiche often tymes had
sayd bothe to his face, & in many other places wt teares that she besought god ye plage &
vengeance myght lyght upon hym that all men myght wonder on hym) In ye meane
tyme therefell a great snowe in so muche yt they cominge in agayne into ye howse thought
that ye snow would have covered their foteinge but sodenly (by ye good providence of
god, who would not suffer so detestable a murther longe hydden) it sint snowynge
they not

Stow MS, British Library Harley 542 folio 36.

Chapter 11
The aftermath

This account can be supplemented from other records and we can reconstruct what happened to Alice and the others once they had been arrested on the order of the mayor and put into the town gaol. The wardmote book says that the prisoners were indicted and arraigned within the said town and liberties of Faversham in the Abbey Hall, 'which the said Arden purchased'. Nothing is known about which building this was, for we do not know which buildings had been destroyed by that time under instructions from Cheyne. Stow speaks of 'sessions', meaning the quarter sessions, but, in fact, it was a special assize. In the county there were two assizes each year; the first in Lent and the second in the Long Vacation. Two commissioners, who had to hold the degree of sergeant, were assigned to each circuit. The commission of general oyer and terminer was issued to the two assize judges together with the principal justices in the county concerned and commanded them to inquire into, hear and determine all offences committed in the county. In cases of felony, the jurisdiction of assizes overlapped with that of quarter sessions, but in practice, it was settled custom for capital felonies to be reserved to the assize judges. However, the Cinque Ports had special privileges. On 5 March 1551 a commission of oyer and terminer was sent to Sir Thomas Cheyne, Knight of the Garter and Lord Warden of the Cinque Ports, the mayor of Faversham, Sir Thomas Moyle, Sir Reginald Scot, Sir John Norton, Anthony Sondes, Christopher Roper and Robert Rudston. No record of this has survived on the printed patent rolls, where we would expect to find it. The original was eventually tracked down with difficulty. It survives with its royal seal among Faversham records at the Centre for Kentish Studies in Maidstone. This was a general rather than a special commission because it is expressed in general terms and there is no mention of Arden, but upon the tag attaching the royal seal to the document in a scribbled, abbreviated and difficult hand is written 'Commission of oyer and terminer upon the death of Arden'. Such a commission was appointed to inquire into the more serious offences such as murder, treason, insurrection and coining. Three of the commissioners from the following, Cheyne, the mayor, Thomas Moyle, Reginald Scott and Christopher Roper, or even two of them, were the quorum and were to be present when an enquiry was held on oath. The records were kept by the clerk of the assizes. The town had the right to hold the trial as a member of the Cinque Ports and by its new charter and it there 'adjudged for them to die'. A search has been made to see if any record of the trial can be found, but, in spite of exciting leads to Chancery and King's Bench it has not yet been traced. No assize records for Kent have survived before 1559.[244]

The commissioners made a powerful local group and it is possible to see why most of them were chosen. First there was Cheyne, the Lord Warden, and then Sir Thomas Moyle. Sir Reginald Scot was a soldier, the second son of Sir John Scot of Scot's Hall in Brabourne. He was sheriff of Kent in 1541 and later surveyor of works at Sandgate. His second wife was a daughter of Sir Brian Tuke, who had been an associate of Sir Edward North. Sir John Norton of Northwood in Milton was M.P. for Rochester in March 1553. He came of a long-established Kent family and his father was Sir John Norton of Faversham. He probably owed his return to the parliament of March 1553 to the influence of Sir Thomas Cheyne, whom he made the overseer of his will. Anthony Sondes of Throwley was a local landowner, who had married a daughter of a former Lord Chief Justice, Sir John Fineux of Faversham. Christopher Roper of Lynsted was a grandson of the same Sir John Fineux, and his brother, William, was Faversham's royal steward. Christopher was a lawyer and was put in charge of Arden's Inquisition *post mortem.* The only

---

244 See APPENDIX 1: CKS, Fa/JQc 1; Favward, fol. 60; LP xix, part I, grant 1036 (30); Lewis, ii, p. 26.

one not easy to explain is Robert Rudston of Boughton Monchelsea, who was a servant of the Wyatt family and a radical, who sat for Steyning in the parliament of 1547.[245]

The ensuing description of the procedure for a trial for treason and felony in the period is drawn from the works of J. H. Baker. Within three days after any arrest the prisoner had to be examined before a justice. At the examination the accused was accompanied by the person who arrested him and his accusers. The justice then bound over the complainants to give evidence and committed the suspect to gaol. The first business of the court was to swear and charge the grand jury. Each jury was composed of twelve or more substantial freeholders and the bulk of their findings were based on draft indictments (called 'bills') prepared by the clerk on behalf of the prosecutors. After the charge, the prosecutors and witnesses were called and sent into the grand jury room with the bills of indictment. After the indictments were found, the persons indicted were arraigned before the court. The arraignment corresponded to the pleading stage in civil suits, the reading of the indictment being in effect the declaration of the Crown. The confessions, which may have been obtained under duress, would be considered at this point. The accused was then entitled to have any irons or shackles removed, for at common law he or she was to be free from any duress during his trial. A petty jury was then impanelled. By 1550, a prisoner in capital cases was entitled at common law to 20 'peremptory' challenges. Prisoners indicted for felony were in law denied the assistance of counsel in presenting their case unless a point of law arose upon the evidence. Most criminal trials were conducted with great rapidity during very long sittings. Note that all the evidence was given orally in open court. Hearsay was regularly admitted and the written depositions could be read in evidence even though the deponent was available to give oral testimony. It was common for the constable and examining justice to give an account of their inquiries and findings. It is doubtful whether the presumption of innocence had been formulated. A recurring problem was raised by the use of accomplices' evidence. When the prisoner had been tried, the jury was asked to consider its verdict. If it was 'guilty', the clerk asked them to say what property the convict had, so that it could be seized, as happened in this case.

Before judgement was given in cases of treason or felony, there was an indispensable preliminary known as the *allocutus*. The prisoner might take the opportunity of making a necessarily futile speech in mitigation, but the legal purpose was to allow the convict to allege anything which would prevent the court from giving judgement It was at this point, according to Stow, that Alice was asked if anyone else was involved and that she incriminated Bradshaw because of the letter he had brought her from Grene, in which it was written 'We have gotten a man for owre purpose. We may thanke my brother Bradshew'. Stow says that the words only meant that Bradshaw's description of Black Will showed Grene that he was the man they needed. However, on her accusation, Bradshaw was immediately sent for to the sessions, and indicted, and a declaration was made against him, as the procurer of Black Will to kill Arden. He was then allowed to confront the other conspirators and ask them if they knew him or had ever had any conversation with him, and they all said 'No'. He was then shown the letter and explained its meaning. Nonetheless, he was condemned, but Grene confessed at his own trial the following July that Bradshaw was innocent. The wardmote book account declared him guilty because it was following the official line.

Cheyne was a member of the Privy Council, both as Treasurer of the Household and as Lord Warden. It acted very quickly, giving instructions to try to catch those conspirators who had escaped and arranging for the punishment of the rest, for it undoubtedly intended that an example

[245] Commons 1509-58, iii, pp. 26-27, 213-14, 226-27; DNB under Sir William Scott; Hasted, vi, p. 451.

should be made of them. In the middle of the sixteenth century, the Privy Council saw the murder as a threat to law and order, which is why it was one of the earliest domestic cases to achieve national notoriety. It would surely shock us even today, punch-drunk though we are. By the time that Holinshed apologized for introducing 'a private matter' into his chronicle, the surrounding circumstances had long since been forgotten.

The Privy Council already had worries about religious radicals and general public disorder in the area. It must have heard through North and Cheyne that Arden, who as customer was a royal official, had been disfranchised by his fellow townsmen. The next thing that they heard was that he had been murdered in a bizarre fashion by his wife, her lover and two servants, aided and abetted by several ex-soldiers or those dreaded 'masterless men', who had drifted back from Boulogne and Calais. The Council did not at that stage know precisely what had happened, but it sounded threatening. On the dorse of the commission to Cheyne and the others is a word which it is difficult to decipher, which may well be 'treason'. The offence against a lord preserves an interesting survival of the old Anglo Saxon idea that treason is a form of treachery.

This was enough to make the Privy Council stamp down hard and make such a savage example of the conspirators that, just as they hoped, no-one would ever forget it. Faversham must have been an unhappy place in the winter of 1550 and spring of 1551.[246]

All this must have been well known to contemporaries, who viewed the murder with the horrified fascination that we in our own time have reserved for reds under the beds and serial killers. They could not get over the number of people involved and the variety of types and places of punishment to which they were subjected. The murder is recorded in most chronicles of the period. For instance, in the earliest representation of the story outside Faversham, the chronicler in the *Breviat Chronicle* says, 'This year on S[ain]t Valentine's daye at Feversham in Kent was commytted a shamefull mourther, for one Arden a gentilman was by the consente of hys wyfe mourthered, wherfor she was brent at Canterbury, and there was one hanged in chaynes for that mourther and at Feversham was (two) hanged in chaynes, and a woman brente, and in Smithfelde was hanged one Mosby and his syster for the same murder also'. The diarist Henry Machyn wrote, 'The fourteenth day of Marche was hangyd in Smyth-feld, on John Mosbe and ys syster, for the death of a gentyll man of Feyversham, one Master Arden the custemer, and ys owne wyffe was decaul[ed] and she was burnyd at Canturbery and her sarvand hangyd ther, and two at Feyversham and on at Hospryng, and nodur in the he way to Canturbery, for the death of Master Arden of Feyversham'. Added later was 'and at Flusshyng was bernyd Blake Tome for the sam deth of M. Arden'.[247]

It is just worth remembering that the Privy Council always kept a close eye on even minor matters in towns and villages all over the country, for that was the way that Tudor and early Stuart government worked. In 1617 and 1618 letters went back and forth about an alleged conversation in Faversham concerning Thomas Napleton and again in 1619 about Richard Castle.[248]

On 3 March 1551 a letter had been sent to Christopher Roper, William Webbe, understeward of Faversham and Hawkyns of the Guard to arrest Adam Fowle and send him to London. William Webbe has not been found, but this may have been a mistake for John Webbe M.P., who was

[246] W. S. Holdsworth, *A History of English* Law, eds. A. L. Goodhart and H. G. Hanbury, 17 vols (London, 1903-22), I, p. 532; ii, pp. 449-50; J. H. Baker, *An introduction to English legal history* (London, 3rd ed. 1990), passim; J. H. Baker, 'Criminal Courts and procedure at Common Law 1550-1800' in *Crime in England 1550-1800,* ed. J. S. Cockburn (London, 1977), pp, 15-48.

[247] BL, Cotton. Vit. F.V. the original has been damaged by fire, transcribed and annotated by J. G. Nicholls, *Camden Society* 1st Series (1848), XLII 4. I owe this comment to the persistence of Duncan Harrington.

[248] Calendar State Papers Domestic 1611-18, pp. 434, 442, 457, 532, 613, 619-23, 622, 624.

certainly acting as under-steward of Faversham for his friend, William Roper, in 1552-53. In cases of treason and felony, the judgement was prescribed by law and could not be altered by the judge. On 5 March, something happened. that we are bound to find chilling. On the very day that the commission of oyer and terminer was issued, the Privy Council sent a letter to the sheriffs of London to receive from the sheriffs of Kent the widow, Cicely Ponder, and Thomas Morsby to be hanged in Smithfield. One of the Kent sheriffs was Sir Thomas Wyatt, who led the rebellion under Mary. On the same day another letter was sent to the justices of the peace in Kent, telling them how all the conspirators were to be punished; Ponder and Morsby in Smithfield, Alice Arden to be burned at Canterbury and Bradshaw hanged there in chains, Michael Saunderson to be hanged, drawn and quartered at Faversham, and Elizabeth Stafford to be burned there. A letter to the mayor of Canterbury about Alice and Bradshaw followed. There was no question here of the conspirators being innocent until proved guilty. The sentences were carried out on 14 March. The chamberlains' accounts for 1550-51 for Canterbury City included the following items: 'Item paid for the charges of the brennyng Mistress Arden and the executyon of George Bredshawe 43^{s}; Item gevyn in reward to a presentmente that brought letters for poore souldyers and execution of Mistres Arden, 16^{d} [249]

What lay behind these punishments ? I would have expected them all to be punished together within the jurisdiction of the court, but the Privy Council decreed otherwise. Morsby was the 'chiefest man' about North, whose London home was at the Charterhouse, so it was fitting that he was hanged at Smithfield as a murderer. But why was his sister, the widow Cicely Ponder, hanged there as a murderess, when she lived in Faversham and had a house there? Elizabeth Stafford and Michael Saunderson were indeed punished for petty treason in Faversham and John Grene was hanged in chains there. Above all, the final irony, why were Alice and Bradshaw, who both lived in Faversham, punished together in Canterbury, unless the Privy Council wanted to make an example of them.? In the eyes of the commission Bradshaw was particularly responsible as the procurer of Black Will. Martyrs were later burned in Canterbury from a wide area for the same reason.

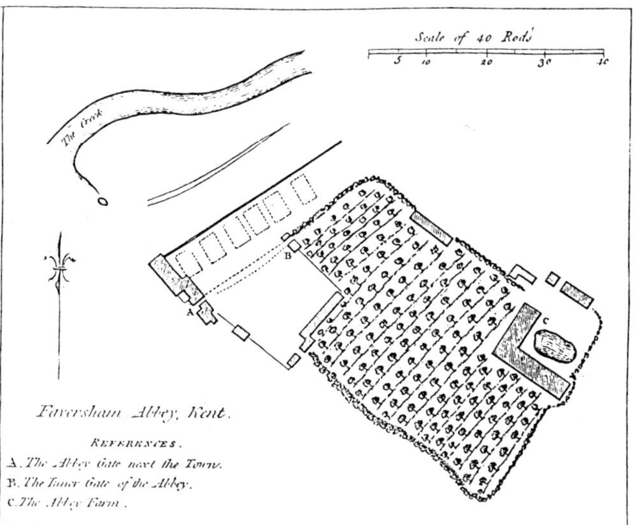

Plan of Faversham Abbey published by Francis Grose, *The Antiquities of England and Wales*, Vol 2. (1774)

[249] CCA, Canterbury city, chamberlains' accounts 1546-53, F/A14; HMSO, 9th Report, app. 154; APC 1550-52, pp. 227, 230, 231; LP xix, part 1, grant 1036 (30).

Chapter 12
Punishments

What did the punishments entail? Thomas Morsby and his sister, Cicely Ponder, were found guilty of murder. They were taken to London, imprisoned there and then taken in a cart in a public procession to Smithfield near St. Bartholomew's Hospital, where they were hanged. They may have been cut down alive or dead, but probably gave the hangman money, hoping to make sure of a quick end. Their goods were forfeited to the town.

Elizabeth Stafford was a servant of Arden and so was guilty of petty treason. She was burned at the stake in Faversham, but was probably strangled first as an act of mercy.

Michael Saunderson was another servant and was also guilty of petty treason. He was hanged, drawn and quartered in Faversham. This means that he was tied to a hurdle and drawn behind a horse from prison to the place of execution; hanged; cut down while still alive; stripped naked; his genitals cut off and stuck in his mouth; his entrails pulled out and burned; his body cut into quarters and parboiled with his head and then dispersed.[250] He probably had no estate to forfeit to the town.

John Grene was found guilty of murder and was hanged in chains in Faversham. To leave the human body unburied has, from the earliest times, been a shameful and dastardly act. This was the particular shame of being hanged in chains. After execution by hanging, the body was cut down and immersed in boiling tar or pitch, for the purpose of preservation, encased in an iron framework consisting of specially fitted chains, and suspended on a gibbet, usually near the scene of the crime. There has been some discussion about whether people were ever hanged in chains alive.[251] Blackstone says nothing about it, but William Harrison, the historian and colleague of Raphael Holinshed said in *The Description of England, 1577-87*, 'But if he be convicted of wilfull murther he is either hanged alive in chaines neere the place where the fact was committed (or else upon compassion taken first strangled with a rope) and so consumeth till his bones consume to nothing.[252] George Bradshaw suffered the same fate at Canterbury.[253] Their goods were both forfeited to the town.

Sir Edward North was present at the meeting of the Council on 5 March when the decision on the punishments was taken. To judge him by our own standards is pointless. He was a great nobleman who had lived through dangerous times, whose 'chiefest man' had just murdered his step-son-in-law and whose step-daughter had just committed the most serious crime after high treason. Without hesitation, North, like Pontius Pilate, washed his hands of her. As far as we know, the Norths had virtually no further contact with her. Sir Edward North was turned in *Arden of Faversham* into Lord Clifford for fear of offending the family. Furthermore, Alice was wiped out of the family history as a black sheep, for, when a descendant wrote a biography of

---

[250] For an illuminating account of the activities at such events see A. Neame, *The Holy Maid of Kent* (London, 1971), pp. 330-335.

[251] Neame op. cit. p. 324 quotes an example of John Bawd and Alice Wolff being hung alive in chains upon the Thames at low-water mark. This was for piracy.

[252] Murray's *New English Dictionary* (Oxford, 1919) under 'strangle'; G. Ryley Scott, *The History of Capital Punishment* (London, 1950), burning to death (strangle first) pp. 31, 33 system abandoned in 1790 for execution, drawing and quartering pp. 179-82, hanging in chains pp. 203-205; W. Harrison, *The Description of England 1577-87* in Holinshed's Chronicles II, xi, p. 184/2.

[253] For comparison, the accounts have survived for the hanging of one Robert Wyelde and his servant Alice Lynseye in 1572 at Faversham: Item paid for tymber to make the gallowes at St Anne Crosse viij[s], Item paid to Pykes the hangman iiij[s], Item paid to a laborer for making of the hooles to sett upp the gallowes in iiij[d], item for halters to hang theym wythe iiij[d]. Accounts Vouchers Fa/FAc 2/1 fol. 3

North in 1655, he mentioned that Alice Mirfyn brought him two sons by her previous marriages, not mentioning the two daughters, Alice and the unknown Agnes.[254]

What of Alice? We have another remarkable witness, who tells us what happened to her after she had been found guilty. He has been tracked down by L. Orlin, who gives us a full account of which this is only a shortened version. He was John Ponet, then bishop of Rochester and canon of Canterbury. While a Marian exile, he wrote a treatise on the theory of resistance to princes, *A Short Treatise of Politic Power*, which was published in Strasburg in 1556. He believed that one instrument of the policy of princes is the traitor. As an example, he told the story of a German king, Cacanus, who killed an Italian duke and then beseiged his city. The duke's widow, Romilda, saw Cacanus over the city wall and fell madly in love with him and promised him anything he wanted, if he would marry her. He, knowing how dangerous the invasion would be, accepted her terms. Then comes the passage that is crucial to us;

> 'And according to his promise he married her, and one night took paynes to shake up her lecherous rotten ribs. In the next morning he leaveth his chambre and her gates open free to every man; and (as some, God forgive them grace to repent in time, did to the wicked woman of Feuersham in Kent, that not long since killed her husbande) he gave every man liberty that wolde, to offer his devotion in to her corporess. So at length when he thought her tyred, and her insatiable luste somewhat staunched (for like it would never have been fully glutted), he caused her to be thrust on a stake naked, that all men might see those ugli parts, which to satisfie she was content to betraye her natural countreie: and that it should be an example to others.'[255]

What a chilling aside! Experts I have consulted seriously doubt that there would have been judicial rape. If true, I would suggest that there were three reasons why feelings had run so high that this was allowed to happen on this occasion. The first was rape and sex, on which L. Orlin has dwelt at length. The second was class, because she was the step-daughter of a nobleman, who had rejected her, leaving other men free to do what they wanted and to get at him at the same time. The third is that many people may have thought like Robert Cole that Bradshaw was innocent and that it was she who had incriminated him. There they were, a man and a woman, the man allegedly innocent, brought to Canterbury together to be punished.

How reliable could we expect John Ponet to be? I should have thought that the fact that this was an aside should give us extra confidence. Might he have been 'our other esteemed observer after the burning' mentioned by Stow?[256] He knew the area well. Born in Kent about 1514, he was educated at Queen's College, Cambridge, and became in turn, fellow, bursar and dean. He was a great scholar, particularly in greek and mathematics, and a reformer. He became chaplain to Cranmer, rector of St. Michael's, Crooked Lane in 1543, rector of Lavant in Sussex in 1545, Ashford in Kent in 1549-50, canon of Canterbury on 12 January 1546, and he was appointed proctor for the diocese in 1547.

---

254 APC, NS, iii, pp. 230-31; D. North, *Some notes concerning the life of Edward North* (1658), p. 32; Earl Jowitt, *Dictionary of English Law*, 2 vols, (1959), Orlin, pp. 80-84.

255 The spelling has been checked against the original volume.

256 See APPENDIX 3.

On 6 June 1550 he was appointed Bishop of Rochester and, as already mentioned, was one of the commissioners appointed to punish anabaptists on 18 January 1551. Two months later, on 23 March, nine days after Alice had been burned, he was appointed Bishop of Winchester. Later in the year he sat on a commission for the reformation of ecclesiastical law and was a visitor of the university of Oxford.

In Mary's reign, he was deprived, and is said to have fled at once to the continent He eventually found his way to Peter Martyr at Strasburg, where he died in August 1556.

It is intriguing that the two chief witnesses to the murder, trial and punishment of Alice and the others may both have been priests living in the area. At first, Ponet was the man in authority and Cole was one of the men he sought. In Mary's reign, they were working to the same ends: Ponet was in exile and Cole was working underground, travelling back and forth to the continent. Their paths probably crossed. In his will Cole gave 'to my entier frende Master Richard Proude nowe parson of Burton uppon Donsmore in Warwike shire a ringe of twentie shillinges Calvin's Institutions Peter Marter uppon the Romans in Englishe and to Master Sympson Marlorate in Englishe uppon Mathew and master Marshall my best Geneva Testament in Englishe'[257].

The inner, or northern most gate as viewed from the south from an engraving. Originally drawn in 1758 this print appears in a Francis Grose., *Antiquities of England and Wales*, Vol 2.

[257] See APPENDIX 2; PRO, PROB11/59/7, PROB/11/59/54; *Alum. Cantab.*,p. 111; DNB; Orlin, pp. 80-84.

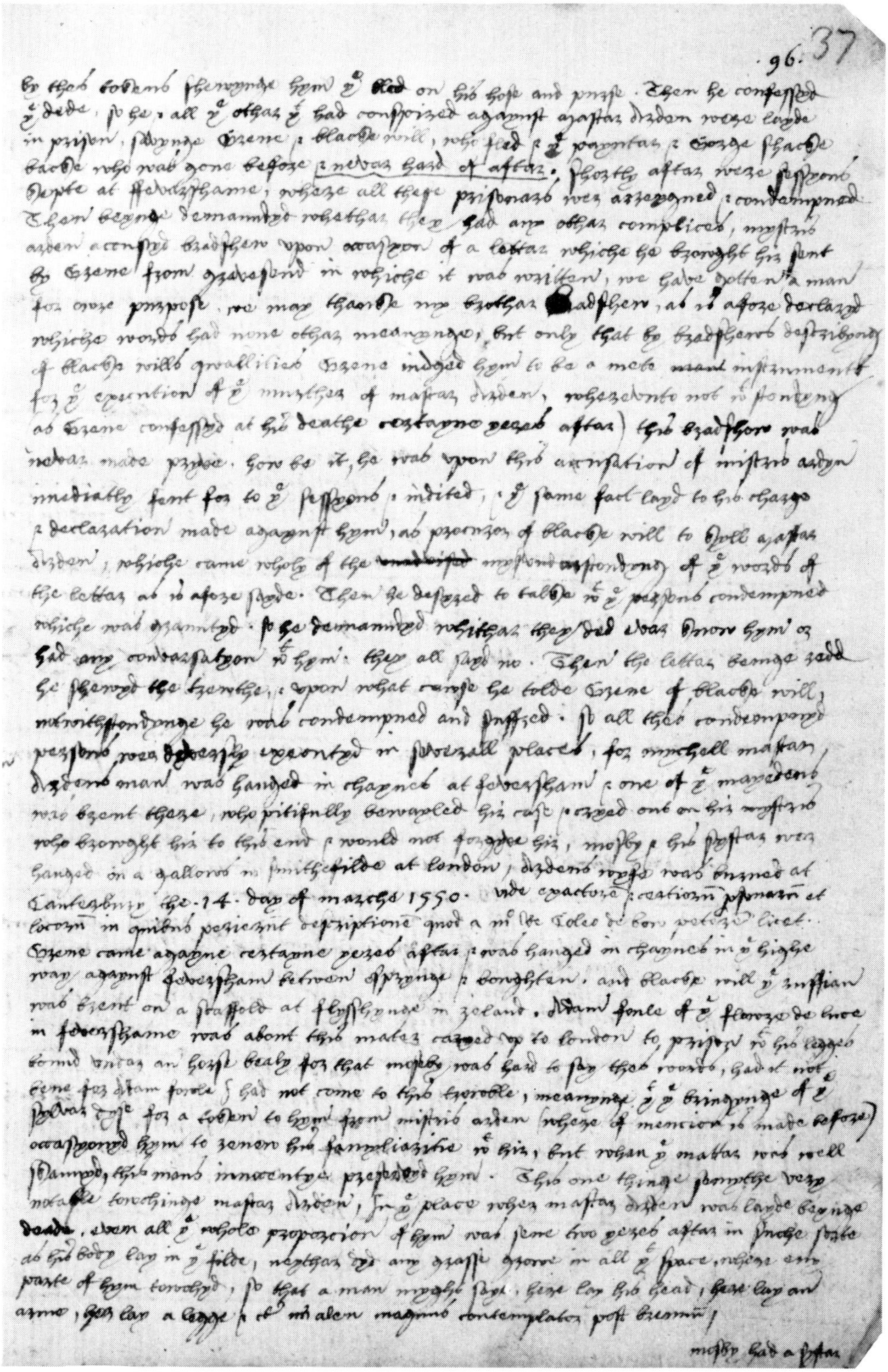
96. 37

by thes tokens shewynge hym yt [illegible] on his hose and purse. Then he confessed
ye dede, so he and all ye othar yt had conspired against mastar Arden were layde
in prison, sayinge Grene and blacke will, whiche fled and ye payntar and George shanke
backe who was gone before and nevar hard of aftar. Shortly aftar were sessions
kepte at ffeversham, where all these prisonars wer arreygned and condempned
Then beinge demaundyd whethar they had any othar complices, mistris
arden accusyd bradshaw upon occasion of a lettar whiche he broughte hir sent
by Grene from Gravesend in whiche it was written, we have gotten a man
for owre purpose, we may thanke my brothar bradshaw, as is afore declared
whiche words had none othar meanynge, but only that by bradshaws describynge
of blacke wills qualities Grene judged hym to be a mete man instrument
for ye execution of ye murthar of mastar arden, wherunto not consentynge
as Grene confessed at his deathe certayne yeres aftar) this bradshaw was
nevar made privie. How be it, he was upon this accusation of mistris arden
imediatly sent for to ye sessions and indited, and ye same fact layd to his charge
and declaration made against hym, as procuror of blacke will to kill mastar
arden, whiche came wholy of the [illegible] mysunderstondyng of ye words of
the lettar as is afore sayde. Then he desyred to talke wt ye persons condempned
whiche was grantyd. and he demaundyd whethar they did evar know hym or
had any conversation wt hym: they all sayd no. Then the lettar beinge redd
he shewyd the trewthe, and upon what cause he tolde Grene of blacke will,
notwithstondynge he was condempned and suffred. and all thes condempned
persons were diversly executed in severall places, for mychell mastar
ardens man was hanged in chaynes at feversham and one of ye maydens
was brent there, who pitifully bewayled hir case and cryed out on hir mystris
who broughte hir to this end and would not forgyve hir, mosby and his sistar wer
hanged in smithfilde at london, ardens wyfe was burned at
Canterbury the 14 day of marche 1550. vide [illegible]
[illegible]
Grene came agayne certayne yeres aftar and was hanged in chaynes in ye highe
way against feversham betwen ospringe and boughton. and blacke will ye ruffian
was brent on a scaffold at flysshinge in zeland. Adam foule of ye flowre de luce
in feversham was about this mattar caryed up to london to prison wt his legges
bound undar an horse belly for that mosby was hard to say thes words, had it not
bene for Adam foule I had not come to this trouble, meanynge yt ye bringynge of ye
silvar dyse for a token to hym from mistris arden (wherof mention is made before)
occasioned hym to renew his famyliaritie wt hir, but when ye mattar was well
stamped, this mans innocentye preserved hym. This one thinge seemythe very
notable touchinge mastar arden, in ye place wher mastar arden was layde beinge
deade, even all ye whole proporcion of hym was sene two yeres aftar in suche sorte
as his body lay in ye filde, neythar dyd any grasse growe in all ye place, where any
parte of hym touchyd, so that a man myght say, here lay his head, here lay an
arme, here lay a legge [illegible]

mosby had a sistar

Stow MS, BL: Harley 542 folio 37, showing additions to main account.

Alice, Grene and Black Will

What of Alice's final hours? Henry Machyn (1498? - 1563?), who kept a diary, called himself a merchant tailor, but his chief occupation seems to have been that of a furnisher of funerals. He recorded in his diary that 'she was decauled and she was burned at Canterbury'.[258] 'Decauled' is not a word in the Oxford English Dictionary, so that we can only hazard a guess as to what is meant. The first meaning of 'caul' is a kind of close-fitting cap, worn by women; a net for the hair: a netted cap or head-dress, often richly ornamented.' This seems hardly to be relevant or likely in this context. Another is 'the fatty membrane investing the intestines; the epiploön or omentum. A third is 'amnion or inner membrane inclosing the foetus before birth, especially this or a portion of it sometimes enveloping the head of the child at birth, superstitiously regarded as of good omen, and supposed to be a preservative against drowning.' It is obviously unwise to set too much store on the meaning of one word, but the word is there. Therefore, there seem to be two possibilities. Either her entrails were ripped out and burned for her adultery, because people believed that these had given rise to her wicked thoughts. Or, alternatively, she was pregnant by Morsby and the foetus was being torn from her and burned. Some experts think that this is highly unlikely, because a woman could normally plead 'her belly' i.e. pregnancy at the *allocutus* in her trial. She would then be examined by a jury of matrons, and, if found pregnant, would be safe until after her delivery. Feelings ran so high in this case that I would not be sure of it. If she had been pregnant she would have had an even stronger motive for murder and for her wish to marry Morsby. Another suggestion is that Machyn meant 'decolled', a word in use at the end of the sixteenth century meaning 'beheaded', perhaps standing for strangled. Women were often strangled before being burned as an act of mercy.[259] Until further evidence is forthcoming one way or another, the case must rest there.

Finally, she was burned at the stake at Canterbury and her property was forfeited to the town of Faversham. According to the authors of, *Of Bridles and Burnings*, public burnings required much organization. The platform had to be erected, and the stake with its pulley and ropes had to be adequately constructed and positioned so that, after the victim had dropped, the executioner could jump clear of the flames. Labourers were required to transport and arrange vast quantities of faggots. Pitch or tar had to be brought in and boiled up beforehand so that the victim could be covered with it to ensure thorough immolation. A priest had to be paid for his attendance. And, because this was intended to demonstrate to the public what happened to petty traitors, contingents of troops were required to control or overawe the crowds of spectators since the constables would be unable to deal with such mobs. Afterwards, the ashes were swept up and put into a sack, and, if they were not handed over to the relatives - for a cash consideration naturally - they would be thrown away. Women were conveyed to the place of execution on a sledge or hurdle.[260]

John Grene escaped with the help of one Bate, who was captured and put in the Counter, one of the prisons in the Poultry and in Bread Street. Bate promised to bring in Grene, giving a surety either to become a prisoner again or else to bring forth Grene. On 20 July following there was a warrant to the receiver of wards to pay the people who had apprehended Grene 20 marks for their costs bringing him hither and conveying him to Faversham to be hanged. On the same day a

---

258 B.L., Cotton Ms Vitellius F. v. p. 2, J.G.Nichols, *The diary of Henry Machyn*, Cam. Soc. (1848), pp.4, 315-16,. The diary spans the period July 1550 to August 1563; DNB.

259 *O.E.D.* Decoll and Decollate: to sever at the neck; to behead.

260 E.J.Binford and S. Sulman (London, 1992), pp. 44-45.

commission of gaol delivery was sent by the Council to the mayor of Faversham and certain others for the attainder of Grene, who had already been indicted, and to see him hanged in chains. A person convicted of treason or other capital felony which also resulted in the forfeiture of his goods, was said to have had his blood corrupted, or attainted, by this punishment. The original commission with the royal seal was dated 24 July and was again tracked down with difficulty among the Faversham records at Maidstone. The mayor, Moyle, Norton, Roper and Rudston were included, but Cheyne and Scott were left off, presumably because the most important steps had already been taken. According to Stow, it was Grene in his confession who exonerated George Bradshaw. A jury later said that he was hanged at Faversham on the following day, 25 July 1551 'for dyvers felonies and murders by him committyd and at the tyme of hys deathe had neyther landes, tenements, goodes nor chattelles'. Incidentally, there is a discrepancy here, because Stow says that Grene was not caught for several years.[261]

On 15 June the Privy Council sent a letter to Sir William Godolphin thanking him for his diligence in apprehending Black Will and telling him to send him under safeguard with promise of payment for the charges of the bringers. Sir William Godolphin was M.P. for Cornwall in 1539 and 1553, a leading light in Cornwall, vice-warden of the stannaries and an owner of tin mines. He had also spent a lot of time in Boulogne. Black Will must have escaped from Godolphin because the wardmote book says that he was apprehended at Flushing in Zeeland and had committed divers murders and so was scorched or half burned to death. Stow adds that it was on a scaffold. On 12 May 1553 the Privy Council informed their new agent in Flanders, Sir Philip Hoby, that Black Will was living there 'who of long times has been a notable murderer and one of the most wretched and vile persons that lives and although there be many divers causes that of conscience more than require that he be sent over to be punished, yet one special case there is the shameful murder of one Ardern, .of Faversham in Kent, which much enforces them to require earnestly that he be sent over'. The letter says that Black Will was 'stayed at Flushing by the procurement of certain servants of the Treasurer of his Majesty's household.', that is, by Sir Thomas Cheyne's men. My reading is that Cheyne was holding Black Will under the authority granted to him in the commission of oyer and terminer. The Privy Council sent Hoby copies of letters they had already issued to the bailiff and other magistrates of the Flanders port of Flushing, requesting Black Will's extradition. They ordered Hoby to speak to Mary of Hungary, Regent of Flanders, 'for her commands to the officers of that town, to deliver the culprit to those who shall be appointed to convey him to England'. On 19 May Hoby reported to the Privy Council that in his audience with the regent, she had bid farewell to the English ambassador, Sir Thomas Chamberlain, had welcomed Hoby as his successor, and had also allowed that 'although contrary to the laws of Flanders, Black Will is to be delivered up, it being a pity so abominable a murderer should escape unpunished'. The wardmote book, Stow, Holinshed and Henry Machyn all insist that Black Will was not returned to England but was burned to death in Flushing. Only the painter, William Blackbourne and Shakebag escaped.[262]

The account in the wardmote book concluded by saying that the apparel of Alice Arden, all the moveable goods of Thomas Morsby, Cecily Ponder, George Bradshaw and John Grene were seized and forfeited to the use of the said town. They amounted to £184-10-4½ over and above certain jewels, which were contained in a certain book delivered in to the treasury house. The accountants or sellers of their goods explained that there had been a loss of £60 by depression of money, but the rest was paid into the treasury. In the Crow MSS there is a copy of the goods of Master Arden which the town of Faversham had after his death. These totalled £45-5-5 and

---

[261] PRO, PC2/4, pp 236, 239, 308; APC 1550-52, pp. 285, 319; CKS, Fa/CPw 17/2, Fa/JQ 2.

[262] PRO, PC2/4, p.331; Favward, fol. 60; APC 1550-52, p. 306; Orlin, pp. 57-59.

included a number of fine ladies' dresses and a chain of gold for a gentlewoman's neck worth £3-14-9. It also mentioned two tenements in Cooksditch, a garden in Preston, a garden in the tenure of J. Caslock, the pillory in the Market Place and St. Nicholas Chapel. [263]

The Guildhall in the Market place in Faversham taken from *England's Topographer or A New & Complete History of the County of Kent* by W. H. Ireland, Vol. 2 published by G. Virtue in 1829.

[263] CKS, Fa/Z41/2, pp.176, 179.

Chapter 13
In Conclusion

'BUT YET THE PITY OF IT, IAGO! O! IAGO, THE PITY OF IT, IAGO!

The murder has the air of an implacable Greek tragedy. These were people of flesh and blood, not characters in 'Arden of Feversham.' Poor Elizabeth Stafford, the daily-servant, bewailing her fate and blaming Alice and refusing to forgive her even while dying at the stake for petty treason. Poor, craven, Michael Saunderson, the man-servant, rightly terrified of Black Will, hanged, drawn and quartered for petty treason. Poor Morsby. He had a greater standing with North than has perhaps been realized and that is why Arden allowed him to cuckold him. He had the right instincts, but was easily swayed by Alice. He wanted to give up Alice and he did not want to kill Arden except in a fair fight because Arden was a gentleman. Little did he know. He and his sister were merely hanged at Smithfield, because they were not guilty of petty treason. Poor Bradshaw, who, if Cole is to be believed, was hanged in chains as the principal villain because a phrase in a letter was misunderstood. Poor Alice, not, I think, a cold, calculating woman, but a passionate woman driven to desperation. Thousands and thousands of women today feel exactly the same about their husbands as Alice did about hers. Stow tells us that 'she was so inflamyd with the love of Mosby that she lothyd hir husband'. Have we not heard that somewhere before.? We women should weep for her, not try to whitewash her. We should use historical empathy to try to understand her in her generation, which is not ours. For women today in that situation there is ultimately divorce. For her there was no way out. Our much-vaunted woman's intuition must surely tell us that she was conscious of getting older and knew very well that she loved Morsby more than he loved her. She had no financial security until she was granted her jointure. She could expect no help from North, for he was only her step-father and Arden was his servant. Must she not, like Macbeth, have felt 'cabin'd, cribb'd (and) confin'd' in the small town of Faversham after life in a great household? Can we not see how she was driven to murder? Is that not enough? Incidentally, there are at least two other instances in the period where women followed her notorious example in hiring professional killers to dispose of unwanted husbands. And finally, poor Arden, who never quite achieved what he set out to do. He gave his embarrassing mother a stipend to stop her begging, but she went right on doing it, because that was what she enjoyed. He thought that he had hit the jackpot when he got to London, but then his marriage turned sour, and, before long, he realized that he was not quite the astute property dealer that he had meant to be. He then turned on people like Widow Cooke and Grene. He had his moment of glory getting the charter, and the whole town was elated at having at last thrown off the authority of the abbot after a bitter struggle lasting hundreds of years. Arden probably threw his weight about as mayor, which cannot have been popular. Indeed, he seems to have had only one friend in the town. With all the schemes for improvements, everyone forgot that these would have to be paid for.

The town ran into debt and then the town élite could not believe their ears when they heard that Arden did not intend to pay his share. Perhaps he was working for Sir Thomas Cheyne, perhaps not. They struck back. Linked with this was his decision to make a will, possibly because of the dispute. The stage had now been set for his murder.[264]

I must add that I do not find it surprising that there is no memorial to Arden in the parish church. Who would have offered to put it up and to pay for it? Anyway, he was probably buried in the

[264] *Crime in England 1550-1800,* ed. J. S. Cockburn (London, 1977), p. 57.

churchyard. North had washed his hands of the family. Arden's daughter, Margaret, was only thirteen years old, and as I shall show later, the appointment of Cheyne as guardian was not settled for years. Arden's affairs must have been in disarray with the town's claim on Alice's goods as a felon. Indeed, the town paid for the probate of his will. As the mayor, jurats and members of the 24 had disfranchised him only the previous December, why should they want to put up a memorial to him?

In conclusion, the important matter to decide is whether Alice and her accomplices were solely responsible for this murder or whether there was a master-mind at work behind the scenes making use of Alice for his own wider, political ends. I plump for Alice alone being responsible. The murder has some similarities with a case a year or so ago. On 19 November 1993, Mrs. Sandra Wignall was found guilty of luring her 55 year old husband into some woods on the pretext of feeding a vixen and its cubs. There she had sex with him to enable her lover and his accomplice to attack and murder him with a block of wood and a fishing knife, she, like Alice, stabbing him in the heart. The reports agreed that the motives were boredom, lust, and greed, for she had a £21,000 insurance on his life. In the same way, Alice had her jointure. There were differences, too, because Mrs.Wignall is said to have had many love affairs whereas Alice wanted only to marry Morsby, but the motives were the same. *Plus ca change, plus c'est la même chose.*[265]

The two people proposed as the master-mind are Sir Thomas Cheyne, the very man in charge of the trial, and Sir Anthony Aucher. L. Orlin favours Sir Thomas Cheyne.[266] She gives three grounds; she suggests that from Cheyne's point of view Arden had mismanaged the Morleyn affair; that, being a conservative in religion, he favoured the vicar, Clement Norton, rather than Arden, in their dispute; and that he may have known Black Will through his service in Boulogne and introduced him to Alice. For me the chief problem is that I think that Cheyne would have considered Arden small beer, just another servant or underling and in no sense a threat or or a rival. I have already shown just how many people in this area owed their promotion to Cheyne. Of course, he might have wanted to dispose of a servant, who had just been disfranchised in Faversham and was therefore of no further use to him, but, with the North connection, he would surely have hesitated to have Arden murdered. In his account of the murder, Stow says that 'after that Mastar Arden was come home he sent (as he usually did) his man to Shepey to Ser Thomas Chenyes than Lord Warden of the Cinque Portes about certayn busynes.' Surely, if Cheyne had wanted to murder him, he could so easily have arranged a discreet accident at his house at Shurland, instead of allowing the amateurish attempts that were actually made. Had he been involved, surely he would not have allowed a group of his own gentlemen to foil one of Black Will's attempts?

P.Clark favours Sir Anthony Aucher[267], one of Sir Thomas Cheyne's rivals and a reformer, which seems to me more likely. One of his men, John Grene, was a leading conspirator, and he, Black Will and Shakebag hid in one of Aucher's storehouses in Preston. Grene had a personal quarrel with Arden, who he said had unfairly evicted him from a plot of land. It is hard to see from this distance what motive Aucher would have had. As far as we know, he and Arden had only done a couple of property deals. If he had been behind the group in the town opposed to Cheyne and Arden, why would he have wanted Arden to be disposed of after his disfranchisement? More important still, if Grene was really acting on his behalf, why did he not provide him with a hired assassin instead of leaving him to flounder? He was an acknowledged expert on defence. With

265 *The Times*, 28 October and 20 November, 1993.
266 Orlin, pp. 54-62.
267 Clark, p. 83.

all his contacts in Boulogne and Dover, it would surely have been easy for him to find someone for Grene.[268]

Above all else, anyone with a conspiracy theory must surely accept that the master-mind would have kept an eagle eye on events if only because of the danger to himself of getting into serious trouble with the Privy Council. He would therefore have watched all the well-known bungling attempts to murder Arden. He would then have sat by and waited while they made a whole series of mistakes on the day of the murder. They devised the final plot at Cicely Ponder's house, but clearly failed to think it through and make any long-term plans. They thought that they would 'worke theyr feat' at St. Valentine's fair, but they failed, and they then committed the supreme folly of murdering him in his own house when two grocers and some Londoners were expected 'whiche were before the dede doynge bydde to come to suppar'. There was clearly no pre-arranged plan for the disposal of the body, even though a lot more people than usual were about because of the fair. 'When thay came to the garden gate they had forgotten the kaye but they could not find the kaye in half an houre'. They then 'toke a clout and wyped where it was blowdy and cast it and the knife into a tubbe by the wells syde, where aftarward they were found'. Alice had not even had time to think what she would say to her neighbours about where Arden was. After all, she could have said that he had suddenly been called away. As it was, her panicky reaction made discovery inevitable. I think that in modern parlance she would be described as being on a high. Morsby was then such a fool as to go to bed with 'blowde on his hose and purse'. None of us would do such a thing, but then he had not read a detective story. This does not sound to me like long-term planning by a master-mind, but more like a group of people hurtling to destruction like the Gadarene swine. This is precisely the scenario that Stow conveys.

Photograph of 'Arden's House' taken in 1991 by courtesy A. Percival.

268 Orlin, pp. 54-62; Clark, p. 83.

The end of an era

The town had not heard the end of Morsby's sister, the widow Cicely Ponder. On 9 August 1564 her daughter, Emme, wrote to the mayor of Faversham from Ipswich. She had already sent two friends and had been questioned by Master Colwell as to whether she was the heir of her mother 'which suffered in Smithfield'. Master Best and Master Norton had also been involved. Her cousin and opponent, Henry Ponder, wrote on 15 September, urging them to keep the writings until he came. It then emerged that there was a dispute going back to 1525 about a messuage in St. Clement's in Ipswich. Henry claimed that Cicely, who had been married to Emme's father, Thomas, had stolen some deeds and that these were in the treasury at Faversham. On 1 September Thomas Seckford, clearly an offical at Ipswich, asked the mayor and jurats of Faversham to hand over the evidence and writings concerning the messuage, to seal them up in a box and hand them over to Thomas Pettgrewe, who had been appointed by the bailiffs. They would settle the matter, but, if that was not possible it would go before the Court of Requests. In fact, that is what happened, and Emme and her new husband, Richard Norris, won the case. When the report of the Historical Manuscripts Commission was made on Faversham in 1877, the commissioners were puzzled to find two deeds concerning St. Clement's, Ipswich, amongst the archives. They obviously related to this case and are now at the Centre for Kentish Studies.[269]

The town was naturally far more concerned about Margaret, Arden's daughter, who, according to Arden's *Inquisition Post Mortem,* was thirteen years and four months old at his death.[270] Spare a thought for her, forced by her mother who had just murdered her father to play the virginals to entertain the two London grocers. There seems to have been confusion about what was to happen next. The town paid for the probate of Arden's will in 1552-53: 'Item paid to Master Seth the which he paid to Master Webbe in part of a more sum and for the probate of Master Thomas Arden's will, sum 6^{s} 8^{d}'. The will was copied into the wardmote book At the end was added 'Memorandum that this will is fownde in the Office fownde by the eschetor of the shire and remayneth [in] the Chaunsery under the seales of them that were jurates in the same offyce'. A thorough search has been made for it, but it has not been found.[271] The wardship and marriage of Margaret and the care of the lands took a long time to sort out. They were granted not to North but to Sir Thomas Cheyne on 14 December 1551 by an indenture in the Court of Wards and a signed bill of Edward V1, but he had no patent. At his suit, Queen Mary granted him a patent, as appeared by her signed bill, but she died before he obtained the patent, and after that he died. It was not until 6 June 1561 that his executors finally obtained the patent. Margaret would by then have been 23. Two months earlier, on 26 April, 1561, she had licence to enter on her lands and to receive the issues from the time when she attained 16.[272]

In the meantime, Margaret had married John Fathers of Faversham by 1553 and had a son, Nicholas. John died intestate on 12 November 1558 and Margaret was granted the administration of his estate. Bound with her in £310 were John Freyne of London, gentleman, and Thomas Oldfield of Faversham. The inventory was valued at £170-10-10. She married again within two months. This time it was John Bradbourne of Boughton-under-Blean, said by Hasted to have come from Derbyshire. There was a family seat at Bradbourne there. Her son was thereafter known as Nicholas Fathers alias Bradbourne. Canon Telfer said that Bradbourne

---

269 CKS, Fa/AZ 9/1, 2, 3; PRO, Req2/bundle 30, item 87, bundle 86, item 49.

270 See page 228.

271 Favward, fols. 62v, 281.

272 See APPENDIX 15: PRO, Inq. P. M., C142/172/146; CPR 1560-63, pp. 120, 128-29; CKS, PRC 3/15 fol. 67, according to Margaret's *Inquisition Post Mortem*, 1574, Margaret was granted administration of his estate on 27 November

was deputy to Arden as customer and later customer himself. In spite of a thorough search at the Public Record Office and the Centre for Kentish Studies, no evidence of this has yet come to light. By January, 1559, they were taking complicated legal measures to establish their rights to the property through an artificial legal process known as a common recovery. They aimed to bar the entail which Arden had set up in his will when he left some of the property to Margaret with remainder to his sister. It is worth dwelling on at length, because although a number of people were mentioned, it is important to remember that only the Bradbournes were really involved. On 5 January Margaret (A) was examined alone according to the customs and liberties of the town before the mayor, John Best, and other jurats. An indenture was drawn up by which all her lands were granted to Thomas Finch, gentleman, Thomas Belke and Thomas Barton (B), who were known as the tenants to the *praecipe*. Four days later, on 9 January, the Bradbournes by a fine quitclaimed their rights to the site of the monastery, 24 messuages and gardens, Flood Mill, one dovecote, two acres of land, 36 acres of meadow and 20 acres of pasture for 1,000 marks to Finch and the others. That was stage one. On 12 January, John Edmunds and Thomas Oldfield (C), who were probably lawyers, sued out a writ of entry in Le Post against (B), alleging that (C) had been dispossessed by Hugh Hunt or a man of straw. That was stage two. (B) called on (A) to warrant her title. Stage three. (A) must prove that her title was good, so she brought in the court crier to warrant it. The Bradbournes brought in Fulke David, the common vouch. Stage four. All parties asked leave to imparl or delay and when they came back, no-one could find the common vouch. Stage five. Judgement with seisin was therefore given in favour of (C), who, on 13 January, conveyed the lands to John Bradbourne in his demesne as of fee tail.

Thomas Finch had been churchwarden in the dispute over the pyx when Arden was mayor and died in 1575. Thomas Belke was mayor in 1569 and died in 1582 A fletcher called Thomas Barton was granted his freedom Nothing is known of John Edmunds but Thomas Oldfield played his part in town affairs, was present when Arden was asked to obtain the charter and when he was disfranchised and was mayor in 1565 and 1571. It seems likely from their involvement that they had previously been acting as some sort of guardians or trustees for Margaret. There is a note in the wardmote book in 1559 that John Bradbourne and Margaret his wife paid a fine in the court of £6-13-4 'of all his landes'. At a wardmote on 9 January 1560 the mayor and jurats gave John Bradbourne, gentleman, his freedom, and the said commoners gave him his fine, which was 20^{s} 'accordyng to the order late made'.[273]

In the same year, 1559, Margaret was granted a pardon by the crown for no specified reason, but this was often to do with the alienation of lands. The Bradbournes soon began to sell off some of the property. On 28 April 1561 in the portmoot they sold one messuage called the well-house and two adjacent shops for £50 to a widow called Thomasine Norton, who died in 1568. On 14 September following they sold two tenements and gardens in Tanners Street for £6 to Thomas Little, who was a chamberlain in 1554-55. Then, on 26 September 1564, they sold 17 messuages, 12 gardens, one orchard and a repository called a storehouse and a piece of land called Archerswell on the quay to a gentleman called John Finch of Faversham for £120. They went on to sell him ten acres of land and one of pasture on 20 October 1565 and, more importantly, Abbey House alias a mansion house and a malthouse on 12 October 1566. It had lately been occupied by William Segar, probably the yeoman William Saker who died in 1570. At Easter 1567 the Bradbournes sold Finch three messuages, one toft, one garden, and half an acre for 230 silver marks and on 20 September 1567 more lands including the abbey garden for

[273] PRO, Inq. P. M. C142/172/146, APPENDIX 15 p. 294; CKS, Arch, PRC3/15 fol. 67, Finch, PRC3/19/140, PRC10/8 p. 24; Belke, PRC17/44/84; Fa/JB fol.9; Favward, fols. 47v, 57v, 61v, 79v, 98, 281v; Rockingham, no. 674; Telfer, 195; Hasted, vi, p. 375; N. Pevsner, revised by E. Williamson, *Derbyshire* (Penguin, 1978), pp. 103-4.

£180. On 12 May 1568 and 12 February 1573 they received a pardon for alienating named lands in Faversham to John Finch.[274]

The Bradbournes also had disputes with the town, in the course of which they petitioned Sir William Brooke, Lord Cobham, the Lord Warden, for the return of goods and chattels seized by the corporation after Arden's death. These amounted to £45-5-5 and included several fine dresses that had belonged to Alice and a chain of gold for a gentlewoman's neck, a tablet of gold and two gold bracelets. They also claimed lands worth £24 that had been left to the town in Arden's will: two tenements in Cooksditch, a garden in Preston Street, a garden in the tenure of John Castlock, the pillory house in Market Place and St. Nicholas's chapel. The matter was evidently delegated to Roger Manwood, a judge and M.P., who wrote to both parties on 24 August, St. Bartholomew's day, arranging a meeting at his house. This was probably in 1562, because, on 30 September in that year, the Lord Warden wrote an angry letter to the mayor and jurats of Faversham because they refused to carry out an agreement that had been made. It is not known what happened to the goods and chattels, but, in view of this letter, it seems likely that they were granted to the Bradbournes. The right of the corporation to the lands was confirmed by an indenture on 23 December 1562 'for the apesing of all varyances that thereupon might arise'. On 20 December 1574 William Brooke, Lord Cobham, Lord Warden forwarded a writ concerning the value of these same lands which had once belonged to Thomas Arden.[275]

Very little is known about Bradbourne's career except that he was on a commission of sewers in 1566. He was described as John Bradbourne of Faversham when he made his will on 16 October 1568, but his inventory valued at £320-15-2 concerns a substantial house in Boughton-under-Blean. As well as leaving his wife all his household implements and plate, he left her £20 a year on condition that she made a settlement of her lands on her son, Nicholas, within three months. He was no doubt worried about the legality of the earlier arrangement. He had bought the manor of Davington in 1565-66 from Sir Henry Cheyne, but sold it two years later to Avery Giles. He left £100 to a school at Sandwich newly erected, which Roger Manwood had founded in 1563, the original building of which is now a house known as Manwood Court.[276] He also left a piece of plate worth £10 and remembrance rings made from old angels to a number of friends. He referred to Master Alcock, Master Barrey, Master Tayler, Master Pentecost, and, significantly, in view of Arden's friend in the play, someone called Master Francklinge. Robert Eyre and William Partridge were to be his executors and Master Henry Fane his supervisor. These were an impressive group of friends. Master Alcock was probably Robert Alcock of Canterbury and Marden in Kent, M.P. for Canterbury in 1563 and 1571, Richard Barrey of the Moat, Sevington, and Dover, Kent, was M.P. for Canterbury in 1563 and 1571; Henry Fane of Hadlow in Kent was M.P. for Winchelsea in 1559 and 1563. Bradbourne died on 1 November following and, two days later, on 3 November, Margaret made the settlement he required. She granted the lands to Robert Eyre, esquire, of Brenley, Boughton-under-Blean, who was M.P. for Winchelsea in 1571., Richard Barrey, Rhys Parrett, esquire, of Sandwich and Robert Fagge, gentleman, who was mayor of Faversham in 1570, to hold for Margaret for life and then for her son, Nicholas, with remainder to Thomas North, esquire, Sir Edward's second son, and his son, Edward. It is

---

[274] Finch, see p. 89;CKS, Fa/JBf 9, JBf 10, JBf 11; Rockingham, nos. 664, 675, 676, 702, 704; Arch, Norton, PRC10/3/26; Little, Favward, fol. 66; Saker, Arch, PRC10/5/123; CPR 1558-60, p. 231, 1566-68, p. 296, 1572-75, p. 8; BL, Add Ch, 45277.

[275] CKS, Crow MSS, Fa/Z41/2, 179, Fa/TC1/1, Fa/Az10, Fa/Cpw 2, Fa/Cpw 32/1, 2; Commons 1558-1603, iii, pp. 15-16.

[276] John Cavell & Brian Kennett, *A History of Sir Roger Manwood's School Sandwich 1563-1963* (London, 1963), illustration at p. 114.

touching to see Margaret trying to keep the link with the Norths which they had firmly broken. There is no mention of Arden's sister.[277]

Margaret had married again by 1570, for, on 4 February in that year, in the portmoot she and her husband, Richard Ardys, sold Flood Mill to Thomas Greenstreet for £160, and on 22 February following, they sold a garden plot to John Elfrith for £4-0-0. Nothing is known of Thomas Greenstreet, but John Elfrith was a shearman, who mentioned the plot in his will, which he made in 1571.

At this point the Crown tried to catch up with Margaret, because she had not paid the annual tenth of her income from her lands, which was due to it under the original grant. On 24 March 1573, an inquisition was held on an Exchequer writ to discover whether Margaret Arden, Margaret Bradbourne and Margaret Ardys were one and the same person and whether she had any lands in Faversham which could be seized to pay off debts owing to the queen. There is a reference to eight schedules, which have not survived. The jury could only find Thorn house and 16 acres which were let to Thomas Oldfield for £10 a year. The mayor and jurats seized these to the use of the queen. Margaret, John Milles and John Finch were all involved. In Finch's case, debts for Nether Green were said to stretch back to 1540-41. It sounds like a problem of collection equal to that recently over the poll tax.[278]

On 27 November 1574 Margaret died at Turvey in Bedfordshire. She held a principal messuage, a garden and orchard, Church mead, Abbey Green, Thorn house and twenty acres of meadow, two small tenements, Sextry meadow and Wash-house croft in Faversham. On 24 November 1584 Thomas North and his son, Edward, alienated their reversion of the lands to her son, Nicholas. This is the only known contact between the Norths and the Ardens after the murder. Four days later Nicholas had licence to alienate Thorn Quay, Abbey Green, Sextry and Washhouse Close in Faversham to John and Alice Bennett and, on 1 February 1585, lands including Almery Croft and the Bowling Green to John and Mary Storer.

On 18 August 1589 a writ was returned to the Lord Warden which declared that Nicholas Bradbourne 'has no lands, tenements, goods or cattles in the liberty of Faversham aforesaid where we are able to make knowledge of him just as in the aforesaid writ in it is demanded and required nor is found in the same'. This marked the end of an era.[279]

What happened to the rest of the property? According to Hasted, Nicholas Fathers alias Bradbourne sold most of it in 1580-81 to John Finch, who had been acquiring Arden estate lands from the Bradbournes since 1564. He was a well-established gentleman, whose family had owned an estate called Sewers in Lynsted for more than a century. The house is better known as Sewards, now Lynsted Court. .. John Finch lived in Faversham and was mayor in 1573. At the end of his life he moved to Fordwich, where he made his will on 16 February 1585. He left the manors of Goodnestone and Bayford in Sittingbourne, and 'Mowstone' [Murston], and Sewards and lands in Leysdown, Faversham, Davington and Doddington to his children. His daughter, Margaret, was married to Henry Saker, another well-known figure in Faversham, who built 82-84 Abbey Street in 1598.[280]

---

277 PRO, Inq. P M. C142/172/146; CKS, Cons, PRC28/2 fol. 105; CKS, Arch, Bradbourne, PRC32/31/164v, Cons, PRC 22/7/11; Fagge, Arch, PRC17/42/17; Hasted, vi, p. 375; CPR 1566-68, p. 217; Commons 1558-1603, i, pp. 331, 399; ii, p. 97; iii, pp. 15-17, 207.

278 CKS, Fa/JB fols. 10, 11; Fa/FAcq21 fol. 3; Fa/JC9; Fa/JB fol. 11; Fa/CPW 30 pp.3, 35; Elfrith, Arch, PRC17/41/179.

279 CKS, Fa/CPw 53; PRO, C66/1267 m. 8, 9, 12, 13.

280 CKS, Finch PRC 17/46/291; Hasted, vi, pp. 302, 334; 'Wills and other records relating to the Family of Finch transcribed by J. Greenstreet', *AC* xiii, pp. 335-36, 342; Saker, probate account, PRC 20/3 fols. 29-50, inventory PRC 28/4, fols. 7-12.

On 14 August 1577 John Finch sold the Bradbourne estate to Thomas Stransham living near the churchyard of St. Dunstan near the city of Canterbury, gentleman, Richard Dryland of Wye, gentleman, and Robert Stransham of London, gentleman.[281] Thomas Stransham, it may be remembered, was probably one of Arden's chief opponents and the man who acted for the town in the Hatch dispute. His nephew, Robert Stransham, had a distinguished career. He became a fellow of All Souls College, Oxford, and secretary to the powerful Earl of Pembroke. He followed his father, George, as lessee of the rectory of Ospringe. He had permission to build 'one faire mansion' there at his own cost within 13 years. Richard Dryland of Wye may have been acting as a kinsman or possibly because an earlier Richard Dryland had owned a house at the town gate back in 1532.[282]

On 21 November 1580 Dryland and Thomas Stransham conveyed the same property to Robert Stransham. His daughter and heiress married Edward Appleford of the Middle Temple, who eventually sold it in 1671 to Sir George Sondes of Lees Court.

At this stage it is worth setting out in full what John Finch sold to the Stranshams in 1577, in order to compare it with what Arden had once had, remembering that there had been a number of sales and purchases in the interim. There was a messuage which he then inhabited, a garden, an orchard, a barn, a stable, a small piece of land adjoining called the Upper Green, another piece called the Nether Green, another piece adjoining the channel called the Strake, a great orchard or garden enclosed with walls, a house called a long storehouse, the close adjoining, a doorway built over called the Abbey Gate, a small house adjoining the gate on the east side, the Covent Garden (9 acres) and a small house lately built there, the site and house of the late monastery, the great kitchen, the close before the doorway of the site occupied by William Saker, an acre next to the site in a place called the Sextry, a tenement, a barn and a garden now or lately occupied by Philip Peterson, a piece of pasture called the Woose adjoining the barn then or lately occupied by Edward Holt and a small piece of marsh lately enclosed adjoining the channel now or lately occupied by Thomas Pelham.[283]

In conclusion, I hope that this wealth of biographies has shown that there were between 1540 and 1550 a number of people in Faversham who felt no need to touch their forelock to Thomas Arden. They had wealth, power, influence and connections of their own. As in any small town, there were wheels within wheels. There was a persistent link with Sandwich. There was the pervasive influence of Sir Edward North and Sir Thomas Cheyne here, there, and everywhere, with Sir Richard Rich somewhere in the background. The local gentry like the Colwells, the Drylands and the Nortons were always about and took an active part in the town from time to time. There were a group of those who had been embedded in the structure of the abbey before the dissolution: William Roper, son-in-law of Sir Thomas More, Richard Cromwell alias Williams, Joseph Beverley, Simon Auncell and Thomas Hungerford of Sandwich. Another group had wide political connections in the county and were conservative in outlook: the M.P.s William Roper again, Joseph Beverley, Cyriak Petyt, John Webbe and Henry Crispe. Then there was the town's élite, mayors, ex-mayors, jurats and common councillors. Added to that there were groups linked by religious affiliations and others by kinship, though we should not forget from our own experience that we do not necessarily love other members of our own family. The important group that it is almost impossible for us to reassemble is that of people like John Bringborne and John Seth, linked by trade, the equivalent of the modern chamber of commerce:

---

281 Hasted, vi, p. 334.

282 See Stransham, p. 61, Dryland, pp. 357-58. Alum. Oxon., iv, (1891); Rev. C. W. Boase, *Register of the University of Oxford* (Oxford, 1885), i, p. 269; Ospringe Parish Magazine, June, July & August 1907.

283 Rockingham, nos. 677, 678, 679, 695, 698, 699, 702, 704; PRO, C142/172/146; C66/267/9, 13.

merchants, shipowners and ship-builders, for example. That will have been a very important group at that juncture of the town's history, when in 1559-60 it was to fulfil Henry Hatch's dream of sluicing the creek so that 'a ship with two tops', which was a three-masted ship, might come up to the crane and the town quays, heralding great prosperity for the next generation.[284] Above all else, there was the tension inherent in a vibrant town.

I suggest that we owe 'Arden of Feversham' to the happy chance that Robert Cole of Faversham and Bow happened to be in the town at the time of the murder and the trial. The case made a tremendous impact in 1551 with the accompanying threats of religious radicalism and a breakdown of law and order, but it was his vivid report of every detail that shone through later. Stow recognised its potential and made it into a coherent account, adding other material that had filtered through to him, but the surrounding circumstances were by then lost. Even when the account had been toned down by Holinshed, it sparked the imagination of the anonymous playwright. Raymond Chapman pointed out that 'the unknown author was acutely aware of the social upheavals which had taken place in his own and his father's lifetime', but the playwright was, of course, looking at it from the angle of 1592 not 1551. The more I have studied Thomas and Alice Arden, the more I have come to admire the anonymous playwright for his treatment and development of their characters for his own purposes. He has made them more subtle, more rounded and more intriguing than I think that they ever were in real life. Quite rightly he has created no character of unrelieved evil. I find them both thoroughly understandable: hard-headed, self-centred, unimaginative and desperate. We could any of us meet someone like either of them any day on a Clapham omnibus.

John Andrews, Andrew Dury and William Herbert, *A topographical Map of the county of Kent* (1769) a Section from maps 9 & 14 showing Faversham

[284] At the time of going to press Diane Davidson of Fair Oaks, California very kindly donated a microfilm copy of the first volume of the Wardmote, together with an A5 bound printout. Cursory examination has revealed on fols. 223-226v a detailed listing of everyone in the town who had given money towards the making of the sluice and an equally detailed account of the expenditure incurred in building the same. The item has been dated in a later hand 1578, but it will be necessary to verify this. See text page 481. The proposed publication of the whole Wardmote volume is well advanced.

Faversham Abbey, showing the inner (left) and outer gatehouses from William Stukeley, *Itinerarium curiosum or, an account of the Antiquityes & remarkable curiositys in nature or art observ'd in travels thro' Great Brittan illustrated with copper prints,* (London, 1724)

APPENDICES

The following documents have faithfully reproduced the spelling of the original record. However, capital letters have been given as in modern usage. All abbreviations have been expanded and all Latin rendered into English.

APPENDIX 1: Commission of Oyer and Terminer, 5 March 1551; Commission of Gaol Delivery, 24 July 1551.

FAVERSHAM BOROUGH RECORDS
FA/JQc 1 [LATIN]

Upon the tag attaching the royal seal to the document in a scribbled, abbreviated and difficult hand, 'Commission of Oyer and terminer upon the death of Arden'..

Edward the sixth by the grace of God of England France and Ireland King, defender of the faith and on earth supreme head of the church of England and Ireland. To our well-beloved and faithful adviser the right honourable Thomas Cheyney knight of the garter guardian or Warden of our Cinque Ports and to our beloved and faithful Mayor of the town of Faversham, Thomas Moyle knight, Reginald Scott knight, John Norton knight and our beloved Anthony Sandes, Christopher Roper and Robert Rudson Esquires greeting KNOW that we have assigned to you and three of anyone of you the men aforesaid Thomas Cheyney, the Mayor, Thomas Moyle, Reginald and Christopher, or two of you we wish to be of our justices to enquire upon the oaths of upright and lawful men of our town of Faversham in the county of Kent and by other ways manner and means which better to know or obtain as well within the liberty as outside by which thing to obtain the truth as far as they are able to know of whomsoever the aforesaid transgressions[285] the aforesaid insurrections rebellions unlawful assemblies and unlawful conventicles, of words, documents produced, conspiracies, false allegations, contempts, forgeries, acts of negligence, concealments, oppressions[286], riots, routs, murders, felonies, transgressions or other malefactors whomsoever and now accessories to crimes within the town aforesaid by whomsoever and whatway soever and to have made perpetrated or committed And by what or by whom to whom or of whom, when, in what way or manner and of other articles and circumstances premises and anything at all of them or any of them or any person howsoever concerning more fully the truth. And to the same aforesaid and other premises to hear and determine according to the laws and customs of our realm of England. And therefore we command you that, at certain days and places that you or three or two of anyone of you the aforesaid Thomas Cheyney, the mayor, Thomas Moyle, Reginald and Christopher shall wish to this intent diligently upon the premises to make an inquest and all and singular the premises to hear and determine and that to make and perform in the form aforesaid About to be in respect there of which to justice pertains, according to the laws and customs of our realm of England Saving to us the amerciaments[287] and other things in respect thereof belonging. Also we command by the tenor of these presents all and singular our jurats, officers and ministers within the jurisdiction and liberty of Faversham aforesaid that at certain days and places which you or three, two of anyone of you the aforesaid Thomas Cheyney, the Mayor, Thomas Moyle, Reginald and Christopher shall cause to be made known to him, cause to come before you or three, two of any one of you the aforesaid Thomas Cheyney, Mayor, Thomas Moyle, Reginald and Christopher so many and such honest and lawful men of the town aforesaid within the liberty as outside by whom the truth in the premises may be better known

[285] Latin *Mesprisionibus* Misprisons

[286] Giles Jacob, *New Law Dictionary* 7th Edition (1756)... trampling upon, or bearing down one, on pretence of law, which is unjust.

[287] *O.E.D.* the infliction of a penalty left to the 'mercy' of the inflicter: hence the imposition of an arbitary mulct or fine, originally lighter in amount than fines fixed for specific offences.

and inquired into. In testimony of which thing we have caused these our letters patent to be made. Witness me myself at Westminster the fifth day of March in the fifth year of our reign.

Marten

Faversham
[Fragment of the royal seal remaining]

Dorse: Modern hand red ink 59F[288]
(signature) Math: Denham

A commission to enquire of
Treazon__
Faversham

FAVERSHAM BOROUGH RECORDS
FA/JQC2 [LATIN]

Edward the sixth by the grace of God of England France and Ireland king defender of the faith and on earth supreme head of the church of England and Ireland. To our beloved and faithful mayor of our town of Fevarsham, Thomas Moyle knight, John Norton knight, Christopher Roper, Robert Rudston and Anthony Sandes Esquires greeting Know that we have appointed you, five , four or three or anyone of you the aforesaid mayor, Thomas Moyle, John Norton, Christopher Roper and Robert Rudston two of whom we wish to be our justices to our gaol of Fevarsham of John Grene being prisoner in the same to be delivered from this place. And therefore we command you that at a certain day which you five, four or three of anyone of you the aforesaid Mayor, Thomas Moyle, John Norton, Christopher Roper and Robert Rudson, or two to be willing to provide to summon at Fevarsham the aforesaid John Grene to be delivered In respect thereof to be made as to Justice belongs, according to the laws and customs of our realm of England. Saving our amerciaments and other things to us in respect thereof belonging. Also we command by the tenor of these presents that our sheriff of Kent that at a certain day to which you five, four or three of anyone of you the aforesaid Mayor, Thomas Moyle, John Norton, Christopher Roper and Robert Rudson, or two of you wish to be known to him to take the aforesaid John Grene and his arrest you require to come before you, five, four or three of anyone of you or two of the aforesaid Mayor, Thomas Moyle, John Norton, Christopher Roper and Robert Rudson, In testimony of which thing we have caused these letters patent to be made. Witness by me myself at Leyghes[289] the xxiiij day of July in the fifth year of our reign.

Marten

Fevarsham.

The Royal seal on the tag has become detached from the document, the tag having torn, but they are altogether in the envelope.

---

[288] Possibly Historical Manuscripts Commission number.
[289] Leighs, Essex [Leighs Lodge TL 7019].

APPENDIX 2: Will of Robert Cole, 1576; and John Foxe on Robert Cole.

PRO: PREROGATIVE COURT OF CANTERBURY WILL REGISTER ON MICROFILM PROB 11/59 FOLIO 54

IN THE NAME OF GOD AMEN The twelfe daye of January in the yeare of owre lord God 1576 and in the nynetenth yeare of the raigne of oure soveraigne ladie Elizabeth by the grace of God Quene of Englande Fraunce and Ireland defendor of the Christian faith etc. I Robert Cole clerke parson of Sainte Mary Bowe church in London beinge sicke and weake in bodie but in mynde and sowle whole and of perfecte remembraunce Thanckes be to almightie God do ordaine and make my last will and testament in manner and forme followinge That is to saye First and principally I do yelde and bequeath my sowle into the handes of Almightie God my heavenly father in whose mercie by the only meane and mearittes of his sonne Jesus Christe I truste to be saved And my bodye I will to be buried in the church and chauncell of St. Mary Bowe next unto Master William Chelsham yf so happen that I die in the same parryshe, otherwise where it shall please God to appointe As towchinge my worldly goodes my debtes beinge paide and my legacies and funeralls dischardged I give and bequeath as followeth That is I will all that I have to be soulde to the moste advauntage and the one halfe I do give to Alice Cole my beloved wife, the other halfe of all my goodes unbequeathed I do give to my welbeloved frendes Master Thomas Symson clerke and nowe parson of Saint Botolphes without Busshoppsgate in London and Master Roger Marshall of Cheame in the countie of Surrey on this condition and to this ende That they do bestowe the same in the bringing upp of my youngest sone Elcana[290] till he be able to be put to be prentice And if there be then anie thinge lefte of that is in theire handes that they do bestowe the same of those my children which they shall see to have moste nede and as may be best for theire preferment And I do give to them for a token of my goodwill fiftie shillinges a pece to make eache of them a ringe with this posie Remember to dye. I do give to my entier[291] frende Master Richard Proude nowe parson of Burton uppon Donsmore in Warwike shire a ringe of twentie shillinges, Calvins Institutions Peter Marter uppon the Romans in Englishe and to Master Sympson Marlorate in Englishe uppon Mathew and master Marshall my best Geneva Testament in Englishe Item I give to Margett Woollett the lease of my gardeine payenge the rent for it on this condition that my wife maye have the use of it to drye her cloathes for the time of her widowhood if she tarry in London els not Item I give to every one of my daughters a ringe of thirtene shillinges foure pence a pece Item I give to my goddaughter Elizabeth Stretton nowe dwellinge in Bredstrete with Master Salter twentie shillinges Item I give to my welbeloved frende Thomas Clerke of Essex my best gowne faced with budge and furred thorowe with white lambe Item I give to Ellen my mayde five shillinges To Roger my waterbearer five shillinges To Lug Clerke of Alhollowes five shillinges Item I give to Mystres Cacket thirtene shillinges foure pence to make her a ringe And I doe ordaine and make Thomas Symsonne and Roger Marshall aforesaide my sole executors of this my last will and testament And I do desire my welbeloved frendes Master Proude Master Cacket and Thomas Clerke to be good to my children and to give them good cownsaill And I do chardge them in God his name that they obey theire cownsaill as if it were I myselfe By me Robert Coles witnesse Edmunde Sympson parson of St.

[290] This is a most unusual name perhaps incorrectly copied by the clerk, possibly something like Elveva a form of Elgiva.
[291] Entier = entire *O.E.D.* of persons: wholly devoted to another, perfectly beloved.

Peters in Westchepe, Christopher Blythman. I give to Mistress Slaid my doble ringe of golde, Rafe Cackett a ringe of twentie shillinges. Be me Roberte Cole.

PROBATE was granted of this same testament at London before Master William Drewry, Doctor of Laws, Commissary of the Prerogative Court of Canterbury, the twenty seventh day of February in the year of our Lord one thousand five hundred and seventy six upon the oath of Thomas Simpson and Roger Marshall executors named in this testament to whom administration was committed etc. of the goods etc. And to exhibit a full inventory etc. and a complete account etc. Sworn in due form etc.

JOHN FOXE, *ACTES AND MONUMENTS,* FROM EDITION OF 1563[292]

Page 1694: Another Chapter of such, as by the providence of God, miraculously have been preserved from the danger in the time of persecution.

[page 1699] No lesse marvelous was the preservation of the congregation in London, which from the firste beginninge of Quene Mary, to the latter ende thereof continued, not withstanding, what so ever the malice, devise, searching and inquisition of men or streightnes of lawes could worke to the contrary. Suche was the merciful hand of the Lord, according to his accustomed godnes, ever working with his people. Of this great bountiful goodnes of the Lord many and great examples appeared in this congregation, which now I speake of. How oft, and in what great daungers dyd he deliver them.

First at Blackfriars, when they shuld have resorted to Sir Thomas Cardens house, where [*page 1700]* watch was layed for them, but yet throughe the Lordes vigilant providence the mischiefe was prevented, and they delyvered. .... In this congregation were sometimes xL somtimes one hundred, somtymes two hundred, somtymes mo[re], and somtimes lesse. About the latter tyme of Quene Marye it greatly increased, from the first beginning, which was about th[e] first entry of Quene Maryies reygne, they had divers ministers, firste maister Schamlere, then Thomas Fowle, after him maister Rowgh, then maister Austen and last maister Bentam with Robert Cole. In speaking of which persons, I cannot but something say in their justly deserved commendation, who in so daungerous a tyme, setting all things apart, not onely their goods, ease and liberty, but also neglecting their own bodyes and lives, woulde enter so venterous a charge for Christ, and in the churches cause, wherin seemeth to me to appeare the true triall of a sincere and assured faythfull minister, worthy to be preferred and have double honor in the church of Christ, wherof would to God the Churche this daye had more plentye. Althoughe to take the charge and care of Christe's flocke, at all tymes and seasons, is woorthy of muche reverence and commendation, yet in prosperity it may chaunce that respecte of lucre, ease and worldlye honour maye allure peradventure some times some men therunto: but in time of peryl and daunger, where is no lucre but losse, no gayne but payne, no life but death, no living but labour is looked [for], no safetye but miserye remayneth, there and then to enter into that yoke and function, onely upon the symple zeale and regarde of the flocke of Christe, and nothing els: He that so will do, where so ever he bee, I take hym to be a man, not onely rare, but a perfect Minister in deede, and worthy eternall commendation. But to returne agayne to Quene Maries tyme, as I have shewed the great and mercyful woorking of the Lord, in delyvering and rescuing the publycke Congregation here gathered: so neyther dyd hys providence fayle in the private cases lykewise of the ministers of he same, as in this one case of Maister Bentam (now Byshop of Lichfeld and Coventry) lyke as in many other els most evidently may be considered. For how was it possible by mans estimation, for the sayd maister Bentam to have eschued presently to have bene taken and attached, and had

[292] 4th ed., 1577, ed. Rev. J. Pratt, 8 vols (London, 1870), viii.

not the present power of the Lord, passing al[l] mens expectation, bene prest and ready to healpe his servant in suche a strayghte. The story and case is this. *[page 1701]* To this I might also adioyne the happy escape of Robert Cole, minister now of Bow in London, from the handes of maister Pettit, justice in Kent, being hys mortall enemye, and one that sought his lyfe. Who meeting hym by chaunce, in a narrow lane, not farre from Feversham, and so meeting him, that one of them must needes touche an other, yet so overcame that daunger, that hee was past and gone before the judge dyd know it was he, and so the sayd Cole escaped.

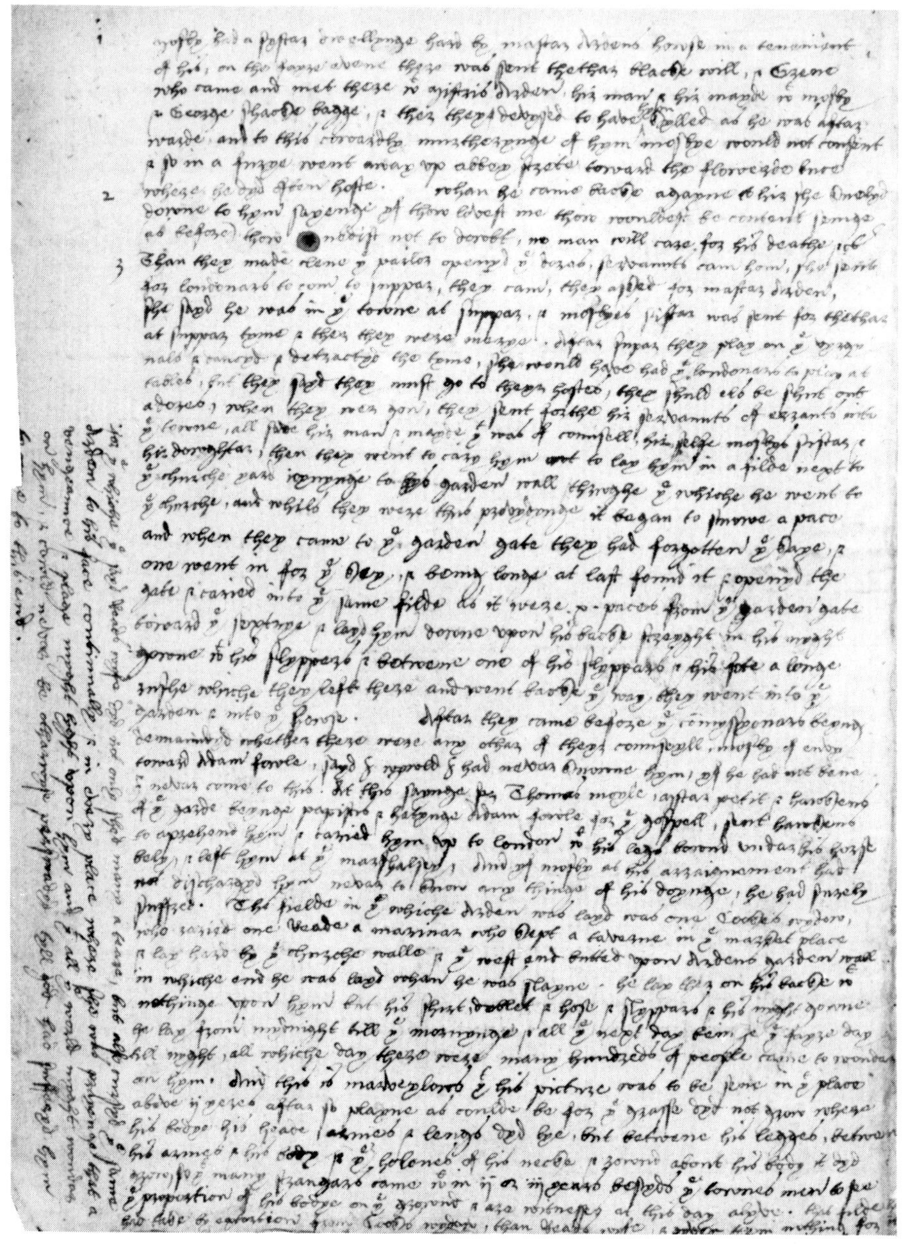

Stow MS, BL: Harley folio page 37v

Appendix 3: John Stow's Account of the Murder

Stowe's Historical and Other Collections Volume VI[293] British Library Harl MS 542. Plut XLVIII B

The[294] history of a moste horrible murder commytyd at Fevershame in Kente

There dwelt at Feversham in the county of Kent a gentleman callyd Mastar Arden, a tall[295] gentleman, and of a comly personage. This Ardene had a mothar dwellynge in Norwiche who went a beggynge, but he assayde all meanes posseble to kepe hir from it, whiche wowld not be, notwithestondynge, he gave a stipend delyvered to Mastar to hir use, and when Mastar Aldriche was maior of Norwiche she was robbyd, and a princypall chest browght out into hir backe syde[296] and certeyne lynnyn that was in it lefte scateryd abrode to the vallew of forty or fyfty shillyngs. This robery beinge commyttyd in the nyght she beynge deaf hard it not, next day whan it was knowne that she was robbed, the maior with others came to hir howse, and serchinge they found Lx£ lyeinge in sondry places tyed up in severall litle clowtes not above ten grotes in one clowte. Than she was restreyned from hir beggynge, and willed to chuse who shuld with hir porcion kepe hir durynge hir lyfe, and to have for his labowr that whiche remayned of the Lx£ unspent at hir deathe and so it was done, notwithstandynge she nevar inioyed after she was restreynyd from hir beggynge, and dyed within half a yere aftar, but many yeres aftar the deathe of hir sonne, whereof we have here to speake.

This Master Arden married a well favoryd yonge gentlewoman and a tal[e][297] who was the Lord Northes wyves dowghter, and hir husband and she havynge therefore often recowrse to my Lord Northes, ther was one Mosby, who was a taylor by his occupation, a blacke swart man, who in procese of tyme was made one of the chefeste gentlemen about the Lord Northe, and ther he grew to be familiar withe Mystris Arden notwithstondynge for some dyslykynge he had of hir, he fell out with hir, how be it she beynge very desyrows to be in favowr agayne with Mosby, sent hym a payre of sylvar dice, by one Adam Fowle dwellyng at the Flowre de Luce in Feversham. Aftar this he resorted to hir agayne and would very often tymes lye at Arden's howse. In so moche that within the space of ij yeres aftar they wer made frinds he had to do with Mistris Arden. Mastar Arden perceyvynge ryght well theyr mutuall familiaritie to be muche greatar then theyr honestie, was yet so greatly gyven to seke his advauntage, and caryd so lytle how he came by it that in hope of atteynynge some benefite of the Lord Northe by meanes of this Mosby who could do muche with hym, he winked at that shamefull dysorder and bothe parmyttyd and also invited hym very often to be in his howse. And thus it contynuyd a good space before any practyse agaynst Arden At length she was so enflamyd with the love of Mosby that she lothyd hir husbond and therefore wyshed, and aftar practysed how to brynge hym to his end, now she was acqwayntyd with a certayne payntor dwellynge in the towne of Faversham, who had skyll of poysens, whiche she demaundyd, and he[298] denyed not. Ye[a] (sayd she) but I would have suche a one, made as shuld moste spedyly dyspatche the eatar therof. Then he made hir suche one and wylled hir to put it in

[293] These are loose papers bound into a book.
[294] fol. 34. Page 93 marked in ink.
[295] *O.E.D.* in the sense of meet, becoming, seemly, proper, decent; fair, handsome.
[296] *O.E.D.* The back premises, backyard, out-buildings attached to a dwelling; also, the privy.
[297] Obscured by ink mark Holinshed p. 1703 col 2. has tall. *O.E.D.* Tale: 3b. The subject of common talk; things told so as to violate confidence or secrecy; reports of private matters not proper to be divulged; idle or michievous gossip.
[298] fol. 34v.

the botom of a poringer and then to powr mylke upon it, whiche she forgettynge powryd the mylke first and aftarward the poyson. Now Mastar Arden purposed that day to ryd to Canterbury and thowght first to breake his fast and she browght hym this mylke and butar, and he havynge eatyd a sponefull or two ther of, he muche myslykynge the collar and taste, sayd to his wyfe, Mystris Ales, what mylke have yow gyven me here? Where with she tyltyd it ovar with hir hand saynge, 'I wene nothinge can please yow.' Then as he rode to Cantorbery, he fell in a great vomittynge and a laske[299], and so porgyd upwards and downewards that he was preservyd for that tyme. Then fell she to be acqwayntyd with one Grene of Feversham, who was one of Ser Anthony Agersservauntes, and Mastar Arden had got extorciously a peace of ground from hym on the backesyde of the abbey, and ther had blowes passed betwene them and great threttyngs. Therefore she knowynge that Greene for this cawse hated Mastar Arden began to practyse with hym how to make hir husbond owt of the way, and concludyd that yf he could get any that would kyll hym, the party shuld have x$^{£}$ for a reward. This Grene havynge doyngs for Ser Antony Ager who was vitellor to Bulleyn[300] had occasyon to go up to London to his mastar, and bycawse he had some charge with hym, he desyred one Bradshow a gold smythe of Fevarsham to accompany hym to Gravesend and he would content hym for his paynes. This Bradshawe beinge a very honest man was content and rode with hym, and when they came to Raynam Doune they chansed to see iij or iiij servynge men comynge from Leedes, and than Bradshew espyed commynge up the hyll from Rochestar wards one Blacke Will a tirible ruffian with a sword and a buckler, and an other with a great stafe over his necke. Than sayde Bradshew to Grene we are happye that here comythe some company from Ledes for here commethe as murtheringe a knave as any is in England and it had not bene for them we myght have chansed to have escaped hardly of owr money and lyves, (yea thought Grene as he aftarward confessyd) such a one is for my purpose, wherefore he asked whiche, is he, yondar is he quoth[301] Bradshaw, the same that hathe the swerde and bucklar his name is Blacke Will, how know yow that, sayd Grene, Bradshow answeryd, I knowe hym at Bulleyn, when we bothe servyd, he was a souldyar and I was Ser Richard Candishes[302] man, and ther he commytted many haynous murthurs on such[303] as travayled betwene Bulleyne and Fraunce. By this tyme the othar companye of servynge men came to them, and they goynge alltogethar met with Blacke Will and his fellowe. The servyngmen knewe Black Will and salutyd hym, demaundyd whethar he went he aunsweryd, by Gods blod I know not, nor I care not but even as my staffe fallethe I goo, They sayd yf thow wilt turne backe agayne to Gravesend we will gyve the thy suppar, by God blowd sayd he, I care not, I am content, so he turnynge with them, took acqwantance of Bradshowe, sayeng fellow Bradshewe how dost thow, he unwillinge to renew acqwantance with suche a shamles ruffian, sayd, 'Why do you knowe me?' 'Ye that I do' quothe he, 'dyd not we serve in Bulleyn togethar?' 'Ye must perdon me' quoth[304] Bradshowe,. 'for I have forgoten yow.' Than Grene talked with Blacke [Will] and sayd whan yow have suppyd come to my hosteis howse at suche a signe and I will gyve you secke[305] and sugar, by Gods blode sayd he I thanke yow I will come and take it. Accordynge to promyse he came to Grene and there they made good chere. Then Blacke Will and Grene went and talked togethar aparte from Bradshaw and ther concludyd that yf Blacke Will would kyll Mastar Arden he shuld have x$^{£}$ for his labowre. Than he answeryd by Gods wounds that yf he knew hym, he

---

299 An attack of looseness of the bowels, diarrhoea.
300 Boulogne, France.
301 Written quod; this obsolete variant substituted for easier reading.
302 Query for Cavendish
303 fol. 35, page number in ink 94.
304 Written quod.
305 *O.E.D.* obsolete form of sack. Possibly a dry white wine. Shakespeare also mentions sack and sugar. See long explanation in *O.E.D.*

would dispache hym, mary[306] to morow, quoth[307] Grene I will shew hym the in Powles[308]. Then they lefte theyr talke, and Grene bad hym go to his hostes howse, and so he dyd. Then Grene wrote a lettar to Mistris Arden and amongst other things put in these words, we have got a man for owr purpose, we may thanke my brother Bradshewe. Now Bradshew not knowyng any thinge of this toke the lettar of hym, and in the mornynge departyd home agayne and delyveryd the lettar to Mystris Arden, and Grene and Blacke Will went up to London at the tyde. At the tyme apoyntyd Grene shewed Blacke Will Master Arden walkyng in Powles. Then sayd Blacke Will, what is he that goethe after hym, mary sayd Grene one of his men. Gods blowde sayd Blacke Will I will kyll them bothe, nay sayde Grene do not so for he is of counsell with us in this matar. By Gods blowd sayd he I care not for that I will kyll them bothe, nay sayd Grene in any wyse do not do so. Than Blacke Will thowght to have kyllyd Mastar Arden in Powls churche yard, but ther wer so many gentlemen that accompanyed hym to dynner that he missed of his purpose. Grene shewed all this talke to Master Ardens man, whos name was Michaell which evar after stode in dowbt of Blacke Will lest he shuld kyll hym. The cawse that this Michaell conspired with the rest agaynst his mastar was for that it was determyned he shuld mary a kynsewoman of Mosbyes. Now Mastar Arden lay at a certayn parsonage of his in London, and so Mychell his man and Grene agreyd that Blacke Will shuld come at nyght to the parsonage where he shuld find the dores open and so he myght morthar Mastar Arden. Now Mychell havynge his mastar to bed lefte open the dores accordynge to the apoyntment made before, his mastar beinge in bed asked yf he had shut the dores, and he sayd yea. Now he fearynge lest Blacke Will would kyll hym as well as his mastar aftar he was a bedde rose up agayne and shut the dores so that Blacke Will comynge thethar and fyndynge the dores shut departyd beynge disapoyntyd that tyme allso. The next day, Blacke Will cam to Grene marvelowsly chafed and vexyd bycaws he was so decyvyd, and swore wounds and blowd that where he met Arden's man he will kyll[309]hym first, for that he had so deceyvyd hym. No sayd Grene do not so for I will first know the cawse of shuttynge the dores and so pacified Blacke Will. Than Grene went and talked with Ardens man and asked why he dyd not leave open the dores accordynge to his promyse, mary sayde he I will show yow the cawse, my master dyd yesternyght that he nevar dyd before, for aftar I was a bed he rose up and shut the dores and in the morninge rated me mervellously for not shuttynge the dores, where at they war content. Arden beynge ready to goo homewards his man sayde to Grene, this nyght will my mastar goo downe, where upon it was agreed that Blacke Will shuld kyll hym on Raynam downe. When Mastar Arden cam to Rochestar his man fearinge still that Blacke Will would kyll hym with his mastar, pricked his horse of purpos, and made hym halt, to the end he myght protracte tyme, and tary behynd his mastar. So ridynge before his mastar thrwghe Rochestar, his mastar asked hym why his horse haltyd, he sayde he knew not, well quoth[310] Arden, when ye come at the smythes dwellyng before (between Rochestar and the hill fote ovar agaynst Chetham, remove his shoe and serche hym, and come aftar me . So Mastar Arden rode on and or evar he came at the place where Blacke Will layd wayte for hym there ovartoke Mastar Arden dyvars gentlemen of his acqwayntance who accompanied hym so that Blacke Will miste of his purpose After that Mastar Arden was come home he sent (as he usually dyd) his man to Shepey to Ser Thomas Chenyes than Lord Warden of the Cinque Portes about certayn busynes and at his commynge away he had a letar delyvered sent by Sir Thomas Cheney to his mastar. When he came home his mystris toke the letter and perused it and cept it and willed hir man in any wyse that he shuld tell his mastar that he had a letter delyveryd hym by Ser Thomas Cheney

306 *O.E.D.* 'why to be sure'

307 Written quod.

308 St Paul's Cathedral in London.

309 Catchword kyll duplicated fol. 35v, ink number 94.

310 Written Quod.

and had lost it, addynge that he thowght it best that his mastar went next mornynge to Ser Thomas, becawse he knewe not the mattar, he sayd he wolde and therefore he willyd his man to be stiringe betymes. Than Blacke Will lying in Preston[311] (where he and one George Shakebage his companion was kept all that while in a storehouse of Ser Anthony Ager and that by Grene and thethar came Mystris Arden to se hym and browght and sent hym meate many tymes (wayting oportunytie for his purpos) was willed in any wise to be early in the mornynge in wayte for Mastar Arden, in a certayne brome close betwene Feversham and the fery whiche Arden must nedes passe thrwghe, and ther to do his feate. Now Blacke Will stirred in the mornynge betymes, but he myst the way and tarried in a wrong place. Than Mastar Arden and his man commynge on theyr way early in the mornynge toward Shornelaw[312], as they wer almoste come to the brome close his man allwayes fearinge that Blacke Will would kyll hym with his mastar feynyd that he has lost his purce: Than sayd Arden, why thow nowghty knave, couldst thow not kepe thy purse, what was there in it? He sayd iij£, why go thy wayes back agayne sayd Arden and seke it for beinge so early as it is ther is no man stirringe, and therefore thou are swre to finde it agayne than come and overtake me at the firie, so by the meanes that Blacke Will has lost his way Arden ther esckapyd also but Blacke Will thowght he would not myse hym homewards, but there[313] accompanied hym so many gentlemen of my Lorde Wardens to Feversham that Blacke Will was disapoyntyd, Gods wonderful provydence hetharto.

Now Seint Valentyns fayre beinge at hand, the conspirators thowght surely to worke theyr feat at that tyme, Mosby thowght to picke some quarell with Arden at the fayre to fight with hym, for he sayd he could not fynd in his harte to kyll a gentleman, wher as Mystris Arden egged hym to kyll hir husband by some meanes, for he was so evell belovyd that no man would make inquire aftar his death, but Mosbye perceyvynge that he could not by any meanes cawse Arden to fight with hym (for he had piked a qwarell with hym rydynge to or from London and callynge hym knave, vyllane and cokoolde, but Arden would not fight, this much Mosby confessyd in prison) went away in a great furye towards the Flowre de Luce to Adam Fowls wher he went to hoste,[1][314] but er he came thethar a messengar cam to hym from Mistris Arden shewynge hym that she desyred hym of all loves to come agayne to hir and to go about the purpose that was in hand. So he came backe [2][315] Than they convayed Blacke Will into Arden's howse into a closet at the end of his parlowr, before this they had sent owt of the howse all the sarvauntes about dyvars errands, except those that were confederat to the morther, Then went Moseby and stode at the dore in a nyght gowne of sylke gyrdyd about hym and this was about 6 and 7 of the cloke at nyght. Now Master Arden havynge bene at a neighbowrs of his called Dimpkin dwellyng ovar agaynst his howse and thir havinge made an end of certayne reconings betwen them cam home to go to supper, and findynge Mosbye standynge at the dore asked hym yf it were suppertyme, he sayde I thinke not, it is not redy yet. Than let us goe and playe a game at tables in the meane ceason sayd Mastar Arden. Now they went streyght into the parlor and as they cam by throwghe ye hall she was walkynge ther and Master Arden sayde, how now Mystrys Ales, but she made small answer to hym, in the meane tyme one cheyned the wicket dore of the entrye. Whan they came into the parlor Mosbye sat downe on the benche havynge his face toward the place where Blacke Will stoode and Mastar Arden stood with his face toward the same. Than Mychaell his man stode at his mastars backe holdynge a candell in his hand to shadow Blacke Will that Arden myght by no

[311] Preston-next-Faversham.

[312] Shurland.

[313] fol. 36, page 95 in ink.

[314] This is the first place where Stow puts a figure to mark where material at the end different from the main account should be inserted.

[315] This is the second place where Stow puts a figure to mark where material at the end different from the main account should be inserted.

means perceyve hym commynge forthe. In theyr playe Mosbye sayde thus (whiche semyd to be a wacheworde for Black Wills comynge forthe) now may I take yow see yf I will Take me sayde Arden whiche way, with that the terrible ruffian Blacke Will cam forthe, and cast a towell about his necke so to stope his breathe and strangle hym. Than Mosby havynge at his gerdle a pressynge yron of 14 pound weight stroke hym on the heade with the same so that he fell downe and gave a great grone in so much that they thowght that they had kyllyd hym. Than they toke hym and caried hym away to lay hym in the countynge howse and in the berynge of hym downe, the pangs of deathe commynge on hym, he strugled and gronyd, Blacke Will stroke hym twharte[316] the browe a great gashe with his daggar and so kyllyd hym and layd hym downe tooke the money out of his purse and rynges from his fingars, cam out and sayd as folowythe, now this feate is done come gyve me my monye, so Mistris Arden gave him x pound, and he voydyd the towne streyght ways, aftar he had gotten to Grene and had a horse there. Than came this good wyfe, and with a knyfe gave hir husbond 7 or 8 pricks in the brest becawse she would make him sure.[3][317]

Aftar this they toke hym as he was in his nyght gowne with his slyppers on his fete to cary hym into a field without the garden ioynyd to the abbey grownde, now they brought his body to the garden dore, but they could not find the kaye in half an houre. At lengthe findynge it they openyd the dore and layde the cowrce along in the filde (whiche filede he in his lyfe tyme had got by like title as Ahab got Naboths vyneyard for he had taken it from one Reade and his wyfe by vyolence, which often tymes had sayd both to his face and in many othar places with teares that she besowght God the plage and vengeaunce myght lyght upon hym that all men myght wondar on hym) In the meane tyme there fell a great snowe in so much that they commynge in a gayne into the house thowght that the snow woulde have coveryd theyr fotynge (but sodeynly by the good provydence of God, who would not suffar so detestable a murther longe hydden) it stint[318] snowynge they[319] not consyderynge the same, but thinkynge all had been sure. Than they toke a clout and wyped where it was blowdy and strewyd agayne the russhes that was shuffled with struglynge and cast the clout with whiche they wyped the blowde and the knyfe that was blowdye where with she wounded hir husband into a tubbe by the wells syde, where aftarward they were found. Thus thys wickyd woman with hir complices most shamefully murderyd hir owne husbonde, who moste entirely loved hir all his lyfe tyme. Then she sent streght way for Pryme and Cole the grocers with othar Londonars whiche were before the dede doynge bydde to come to suppar. Whan they cam she sayd I mervayle where Mastar Arden is, well we will not tary for hym, come ye and sit downe we will go to supar, havynge supte, she sayde I merveyll where Mastar Arden is so longe I pray yow let us goe and play a game at the tables till he come, I am sure it will not be longe. So they went to the tables and hir dowghter playd on the vyrginalls and she her selfe danced till it waxed some what late and the Londonars lefte playnge, and went theyr wayes to theyr lodgynges. Than sent she abroad to make enquirie for Mastar Arden in dyvers places, namely amonge the best in the towne where he was wont to be, but they aunsweryd they could tell nothinge of hym Than she began to make an owt crye and sayde, nevar woman had suche neighbowrs as I have, and wept, in so muche that hir neighbowrs cam in and found hir makynge great lamentacion pretendynge to marvayle greatly where hir husband was, in so muche that the maior and othars came and made a searche. The fayre was wont to be kepte partely in the towne, and partely in the abbey, but Arden for his owne lucre had this present yere browght it

---

[316] *O.E.D.* thwart; to pass or extend across from side to side of; to traverse, cross.

[317] This is the third place where Stow puts a figure to mark where material at the end different from the main account should be inserted.

[318] *O.E.D.* To cut short, cease, stop.

[319] fol. 36v.

to be wholye kepte within the abbey ground which he had purchased so that all the gaynes came to hym and none to the townesmen for the which dede he had many a curse. Than the maior went about the fayre in his serche, and at lengthe came into the same grounde where as Arden lay, within a while, Prime the grocer sayd, staye for me thinke I se one lye here so they lokte and perusynge the body found it was Mastar Arden lay deade Than they lokynge about hym found some rusches of the parlowr stickynge in his slyppars, and by dyligent searche they espied certayne fotynge by meanes of the snowe betwene them and the garden dore. Then the maior sayde let every man staye, and by his commaundement went about and commynge in the insyde from the howse thrwghe the garden to the place wher Arden lay deade, they perceyved evarmore footynge before them in the snowe, and so it apperyd playnly that he was browght a longe that waye from the howse throughe the garden and so forthe into the fielde where he laye. Than they went in and knowynge hir evell behavyowr in tymes past, they examonyd hir, but she defied them, and sayd, I would yow shuld know I am no suche woman. Then they examonyd hir sarvaunts and in examination by reason of a peace of his heare and blowde found about the howse in the way by whiche they caried hym and the knyfe wherewithe she thrust hym in and the clowte wherewith they wipt the blowde awaye, they all confessyd the matter, and Mistris Arden seynge hir husbonds blowde, sayde O the blowde of God helpe me, for this blowde have I shede. Than wer they all comyttyd to prison. Aftar this the maior with othars went presently to the Flower de Luce wher they found Mosby in bed and as they came towards hym they espyed the blowde on his hose and on his purse. Than he asked the cawse of theyr comynge. They sayde se here, yow may undarstond it by[320] thes tokens shewynge hym the blod on his hose and purse. Then he confessed the dede, so he and all the othar that had conspired agaynst Master Arden were layde in prison, savynge Grene and Blacke Will, who fled and the payntar and George Shackebacke who was gone before and nevar hard of aftar. Shortly after were sessyons kepte at Fevarshame, where all these prisonars wer arreygned and condempned. Then beynge demaundyd whethar they had any othar complices, Mystris Arden accusyd Bradshew upon occasyon of a lettar whiche he brought hir sent by Grene from Gravesend in whiche it was written, we have gotten a man for owre purpose. We may thanke my brother Bradshew, as is afore declaryd which words had none other meanynge, but only that by Bradshews describyng of Blacke Wills qwallities Grene iudged hym to be a mete ~~mant~~ instrument for the execution of the murther of Mastar Arden, wherunto not withstondyng (as Grene confessyd at his deathe certayne yeres aftar) this Bradshew was nevar made pryve. How be it, he was upon this accusation of Mistris Ardyn imediatly sent for to the sessyons and indited and the same fact layd to his charge and declaration made agaynst hym, as procuror of Blacke Will to kyll Mastar Arden, whiche came wholy of the ~~unadvised~~ mysundarstondyng of the words of the lettar as is aforesayde. Then he desyred to talke with the persons condempned whiche was grauntyd, so he demaundyd whithar they did evar know hym or had any convarsatyon with hym, thay all said no. Then the lettar beinge redd he shewyd the trewthe, and upon what cawse he tolde Grene of Black Will, notwithstondynge he was condempned and suffred, so all thes condemporyd persons were dyversly executyd in severall places, for Mychell Mastar Ardens man was hanged in chaynes at Feversham and one of the mayedens was brent there, who pitifully bewayled hir case and cryed out on hir Mystris who brought hir to this end and would not forgyve hir, Mosby and his systar wer hanged on a gallows in Smithefilde at London, Ardens wyfe was burned at Canterbury the 14 day of Marche 1550

[320] fol. 37, 96 in ink.

See[321] the charges and descriptions of the various persons and the places where they were put to death, which may be had of Master Robert Cole of Bow.

Grene came agayne certyene yeres aftar and was hanged in chaynes in the highe way agaynst Feversham betwen Osprynge and Bowghten, and Blacke Will the ruffian was brent on a scaffold at Flysshynge in Zeland, Adam Fouleof the Flowre de Luce in Feversham was about this mater caried up to London to prison with his legges bound undar an horse bealy for that Moseby was hard to say these words, had it not bene for Adam Fowle I had not come to this trowble, meanynge that the bringynge of the sylvar dyse for a token to hym from Mistris Arden (whereof mencion is made before) occasyonyd hym to renew his famyliaritie with hir, but when the mattar was well skannyd, this mans innocentye preservyd hym. This one thinge semythe very notable towchinge Mastar Arden, in the place wher Mastar Arden was layde beynge deade, even all the whole proporcion of hym was sene two yeres aftar in suche sorte as his body lay in the filde, neythar dyd any grasse growe in all the space, where any parte of hym towchyd. so that a man myght saye, here lay his head,here lay an arme, her lay a legge and etc.

Our other esteemed witness after the burning[322]

1
Mosby[323] had a systar dwellynge hard by Mastar Ardens howse in a tenament of his, on the fayre even there was sent thethar Blacke Will, and Grene who came and met there with Mistris Arden hir man and hir mayde with Mosby and George Shackebagge, and ther they devysed to have hym kylled as he was aftarwarde, and to this cowardly murtherynge of hym Mosbye would not consent and so in a furye went away up Abbey Strete toward the Flower de Luce where he did often hoste.

2
Whan he came back agayne to hir she knelyd downe to hym sayenge yf thow lovest me thow wouldest be content seinge (as before) thow nedist not to dowbt, no man will care for his deathe etc.,

3
Than they made clene the parlor openyd the dores, servaunts cam hom, she sent for Londonars to com to suppar, they cam, they asked for Mastar Arden, she sayd he was in the towne at suppar, and Mosbys sister was sent for thethar at suppar tyme and ther they were merye. Aftar supar they play on the vyrgynals and dancyd and detractyd the tyme, she would have had the Londonars to play at tables, but they sayd they must go to theyr hostes, they shuld els be shut owt adores, When they were gon, they sent forthe hir servaunts on errants into the towne, all save hir man and mayde, that was of counsell, hir selfe Mosbys sistar and hir dowghtar, then they went to cary hym owt to lay hym in a filde next to the churche yard ioynynge to hys garden wall thrwghe the whiche he went to the churche, and whils they were thus provydynge it began to snowe a pace and when thay came to the garden gate they had forgotten the kaye, and one went in for the key, and being longe at last found it and openyd the gate and caried into the same filde as it were x paces from the garden gate toward the sextrye and layd hym downe upon his backe streyght in his nyght gowne with his slyppers and betwene one of his slyppars and his fote a longe rushe which they left there and went backe the way they went into the garden and into the howse.

---

321 vide exactores et certiorum personarum et locorum in quibus perierunt descriptiones quod a magistro Roberto Coleo de Bow petere licet

322 The abbreviated latin is not clear but appears to be *nostri alius magnus contemplator post brennum*.

323 fol. 37b.

Aftar they came before the commyssyonars beyng demaundyd whether there were any othar of theyr counseyll, Mosby of envy toward Adam Fowle, sayd I wowld I had nevar knowne hym, yf he had not bene I nevar come to this. At this saynge Ser Thomas Moyle, Mastar Petit and Hawkens of the garde beynge papistis and hatynge Adam Fowle for the gospell, sent Hawkens to aprehend hym and caried hym up to London with his legs bownd undar his horse bely, and left hym at the Marshalsey. And yf Mosby at his arraignement had not dischargyd hym nevar to know any thinge of his doynge, he had surely suffred. The fielde in the whiche Arden was layd was one Cookes wydow, who maried one Reade a marinar who kept a taverne in the market place and lay hard by the churche walle and the West end butted upon Ardens garden wall in whiche end he was layd when he was slayne. He lay there on his backe with nothinge upon hym but his shirt, doblet and hose and slyppars and his nyght gowne he lay from mydnight till the mornynge and all the next day beinge the fayre day till nyght, all whiche day there were many hundreds of people came to wondar on hym And this is marvelylows that his picture was to be sene in the place above ij yeres aftar so playne as coulde be for the grasse dyd not grow where his bodye his heade and armes and lengs dyd lye, but betwene his legges, betwene his armes and his body and the holoues of his necke and rownd about his body it dyd grow, so many strangars came with in ij or iij years besyds the townes man to see the proportion of his bodye on the grownd and are witnesses at this day alyve. This filde he had taken by extortion from Cooks wydow, then Reads wyfe and gyven them nothing for it[324] for the whiche the sayd Reads wyfe dyd not only shed many a teare, but also cursyd the same Arden to his face continually and in every place where she was prayenge that a vengeaunce and plage myght lyght upon hym and that all the world myght wondar over hym, and cowld nevar be otharwyse perswadyd tyll God had sufferyd hym to come to this end.

324 The rest written sideways into the margin.

APPENDIX 4: Clement Norton versus Thomas Arden and others.

Consistory Court Instance and Ex Officio Act Book (Liber 34) DCb.Y.2.3 folios 58, 75-75v 1547 to 1551

ij October [1548] [Latin]

Margin: Ex Officio cause against Norton

The vicar of Feversham had a mandate from a judge to appear in Christ Church Canterbury the last day of October to hear the further wish of the judge and so forth, the last day of October he appeared the said vicar had to appear at the next court to be examined by the judge, and so forth. xiijth [Nov.] appeared Thomas Arderne, Thomas Olphye, Thomas Tenegar, Thomas Hilles, Henry Segar, William Hochynson, Thomas Kenrycke, Thomas Bargrave, Richard Wood to whom the judge charged them to be concerned to say the truth etc., and to ......withdrawn the light from the altar and also that he has read the epistle and the gospel in the pulpit and that he has omitted to place the altar-stone[325] upon the table of the Lord under pain of law etc. ....and says that the superaltare is to be used for fyrmytie[326] of the same bycause it is a stoone, for that Chryste was a stone. Thereafter the judge [ordered] to the said vicar, that is to say, that he shall reede the lessons at Matens and evynsonge at the deske in the bodye of the churche where he was wonte to reede them

folio 75v iij June 1550

... and not to use the super-altar further.

COMMENT

The papers in ecclesiastical causes for the Consistory court of Canterbury do not survive prior to 1595. The only hope of finding the interrogatories and other papers relating to this Ex Officio case involving Clement Norton might have been in some of the early surviving precedent books. A search has been made of the catalogues of the church court records in the hope of finding such a book but nothing has come to light. It should be pointed out that the available catalogue, compiled many years ago, is badly in need of revision. There is a tiny fragment of churchwardens presentments before 1565 DCb/V/P which revealed nothing.

Depositions in Canterbury Consistory Court X.10.4 1549 to 1550[327]

folio 175v [Latin]

xvijth May 1550: The personal responses of Clement Norton, vicar of Feversham , to the ex officio articles objected to him.

To the first article he acknowledges

To the second he responds and says it contains the truth.

To the third he responds and says that it contains the truth.

---

[325] Latin superaltare, note that Latham translates this also as a portable altar.

[326] *O.E.D.* Firmity: (1) Firmness, solidity, stability. Also, moral firmness, firm allegiance, constancy. (2) A means of strengthening; an assurance.

[327] There is no mention in this volume of Thomas Ardern as a deponent.

To the fourth he responds and says that it contains the truth.
To the fifth he acknowledges the fame upon the things confessed.
Acknowledged confessed and denies to withhold any knowledge thereof.

Consistory Court of Canterbury Deposition register DCB/X.10.3 Canterbury Cathedral Archives and Library.

folio 83
Margin: Office xiijth November
Examination of witnesses upon the articles ex-officio upon the formal charge of the vicar of Faversham the xiijth November 1548.

Thomas Arderne of the parish of Feversham of free condition as he says aged xL years a witness produced, admitted, sworn and examined.

To the first[328] not examined because the party aforesaid has acknowledged.
To the second he deposes and says it contains the truth.
To the third he deposes and says its contains the truth.
To the fourth he deposes and says that sumetyme he this deponent hathe hea[r]d hym read ix lessons and otherwise he doesn't know how to depose.
To the fifth he doesn't know how to depose.
To the sixth he doesn't know how to depose of one's own hearing.
To the seventh he deposes and says it contains the truth.
To the eighth he doesn't know how to depose.
To the ninth he is not examined because the party aforesaid has acknowledged to that effect.
To the tenth he deposes and says it contains the truth.
To the eleventh he doesn't know how to depose.
To the twelfth he doesn't know how to depose.
To the thirteenth article he is not examined because the party aforesaid has acknowledged.
To the fourteenth article he is not examined because the party aforesaid has acknowledged.
To the fifteenth he says it contains the truth.
To the sixteenth he deposes and says that as oft as he hath been there he hath of[t] done it and otherwise he believes[329].
To the seventeenth he says it contains the truth.
To the eighteenth he deposes and says it contains the truth.

folio 83v
To the nineteenth he says it contains the truth.
To the twentieth he says that it contains the truth.
To the twenty first he says he doesn't know how to depose.
To the twenty second he deposes and says that it contains the truth.
To the twenty third he deposes and says that it contains the truth.

---

328 To the first article. In office promoted cases the bill of complaint is known as the article, B. L. Woodcock, *Medieval Ecclesiastical Courts in the Diocese of Canterbury* (Oxford UP, 1952)

329 crestit

To the twenty fourth he deposes and says the same is common fame etc. There is no affinity nor consanguinity nor instructions, nor learning, nor love, favour, hate, fear, nor to take care that he is victorious only that justice be done.
To the interrogatories
To the first he deposes and says that all were not putt up agaynste hym in the visitation but some sythence
To the second he says that he has deposed of his own observation and particular hearing and not by mind ?of his family
To the third

Thomas Ouldefelde of the parish of Feversham aged xxxvj years of free condition as he says a witness produced etc.

To the first he deposes and says that it contains the truth.
To the second he says it contains the truth.
To the third he deposes and says that it contains the truth.
To the fourth he deposes and says that it contains the truth.
To the fifth he does not know how to depose.
To the sixth he deposes and says that it contains the truth.
To the seventh he deposes and says that it contains the truth.
To the eighth he deposes and says that he dyd eate one bread hymself hoole and gave to the other broken.

folio 84
To the ninth he does not know how to depose.
To the tenth he deposes and says that it contains the truth.
To the eleventh he does not know how to depose.
To the twelfth he does not know how to depose.
To the thirteenth he is not examined because the party aforesaid has acknowledged.
To the fourteenth he does not know how to depose.
To the fifteenth he says it contains the truth.
To the sixteenth he says it contains the truth.
To the eighteenth he says it contains the truth.
To the nineteenth he says it contains the truth.
To the xx^th he says that it contains the truth.
To the xxj^th he does not know how to depose.
To the xxij he says it contains the truth by cause he was not at home.
To the xxiij he says it contains the truth
To the xxiiij he says he labours under the fame aforesaid and is not instructed.

xvijth day of November

Thomas Bargare of the parish of Feversham aged L years of free condition as he says a witnessed produced etc.,

To the first he says it contains the truth.
To the second he says it contains the truth.
To the third he deposes and says that it contains the truth.
To the fourth he does not know how to depose.
To the fifth he does not know how to depose.

To the sixth he does not know how to depose.
To the seventh and eighth he does not know how to depose.
To the ninth he does not know how to depose.
To the tenth he deposes and says that the said vicar saith that he can not ministre the sacramente excepte he say masse, neyther he will not.

folio 84v
To the eleventh and twelfth he does not know how to depose.
To the thirteenth not examined because the party aforesaid has acknowledged or to that effect.
To the fourteenth not examined because the party aforesaid has acknowledged.
To the fifteenth and sixteenth he deposes and he says it contains the truth.
To the seventeenth he deposes and says that he hath herde diverse sermondes there but by whois procuremente he cannot depose
To the eighteenth he deposes and says that he hath not herde the saide vicar at eny tyme encorage enyman to the reading of scripture but contrayrie he hath herd hym rebuke somme for reading of it and so forth.
To the nineteenth and twentieth he does not know how to depose.
To the xxjth he deposes and he says it contains the truth and he deposes of his own hearing.
To the xxijth he does not know how to depose.
To the xxiijth he deposes and he says it contains the truth.
To the xxiiijth he says he labours under the fame aforesaid etc. Nor is he instructed nor learned and so forth.

xvijth day of November

Richard Wood of the parish of Feversham aged xxxviij years of free condition etc. a witness produced etc.

To the first he says it contains the truth.
To the second he deposes and he says it contains the truth.
To the third he deposes and he says it contains the truth.
To the fourth he does not know how to depose nor to the fifth and nor to the sixth.
To the seventh not examined because the party aforesaid has acknowledged.
To the eighth he does not know how to depose.
To the ninth he deposes and says that they were married at Preston and otherwise he does not know how otherwise to depose.
To the tenth he deposes and he says it contains the truth.
To the eleventh and twelfth he does not know how to depose.
To the thirteenth not examined because the party aforesaid has acknowledged or to that effect.
To the fourteenth he does not know how to depose.
To the fifteenth saith that he hath not herde hym preache agaynste the usurped power of the bishopp of Rome but in reading the homylies and injunctions

folio 85
To the sixteenth he does not know how to depose and to the seventeenth
To the eighteenth he agrees with his precontest[330] Thomas Bargar

---

330 *O.E.D.* A former or previous fellow witness. Note this is an earlier reference than that given in the *O.E.D.*

To the nineteenth saith that he herde hym say that there hath bene some supersticion in the churche and otherwise he does not know
To the twentieth he says that he hath herde hym declare the true use of the sermonyes
To the xxjth he does not know how to depose nor to the xxijth.
To the xxiij he says it contains the truth.
To the xxiiij he says he labours under the particular fame aforesaid pre-deposed. Neither is he instructed nor learned and so forth, nor love, hate etc.,

xviijth November

Thomas Tenaker of the parish of Feversham aged xlv years or thereabouts of free condition a witnessed produced etc.,

To the first he says it contains the truth.
To the second he says it contains the truth.
To the third he deposes and he says it contains the truth.
To the fourth and fifth he does not know how to depose.
To the sixth he says that it contains the truth.
To the seventh he deposes and he says it contains the truth.
To the eighth he does not know how to depose nor to the ninth.
To the tenth he deposes and says that sith[ence] the aulters were pulled downe he hath not exhorted anyman to the com[munion] ~~as for as he~~ and so forth and otherwise he does not know how to depose.
To the eleventh he does not know how to depose and the twelfth.
To the thirteenth not examined because the party aforesaid has acknowledged.
To the fourteenth he deposes and he says it contains the truth.
To the fifteenth he agrees with Richard Wood his precontest

folio 85v
To the sixteenth he agrees with Thomas Arderne his precontest.
To the seventeenth he agrees with Thomas Bargar his precontest.
To the eighteenth he agrees with the said Bargar his precontest.
To the nineteenth he does not know how to depose nor to the twentieth.
To the xxjth he deposes and says that the saide vicar said unto this deponentes wife in lente laste that excepte she dyd beleve in the sacramente of the aulter meanynge the pyxe which hange over the aulter she coulde not be saved, and otherwise he does not know how to depose.
To the xxij he does not know how to depose.
To the xxiij he does not know how to depose.
To the xxiiij he labours under the particular fame aforesaid and so forth. He is not instructed or learned, nor love, favour, hate etc.,

Henry Segar of the parish of Faversham parish clerk[331] there of free condition as he says a witness produced etc.,

To the first he says it contains the truth and to the second.
To the third he says it contains the truth.

---

331 Aquebagelus - holy water clerk.

To the fourth he says that of a grete tyme he dyd not omytt iij lessons with the readinges and memories at even songe every Sonday and hollyday when ix shulde be read and he thynketh he doeth not omytt them yett.
To the fifth he says it contains the truth.
To the sixth he does not know how to depose.
To the seventh not examined because the party aforesaid has acknowledged.
To the eighth he deposes and says that when he ministreth the communion he eatith one cake hole himself and drynketh 3 suppes after the same but he breaketh itt in peces to others, and otherwise he does not know how to depose.

folio 86
To the ninth he says it contains the truth.
To the tenth he agrees with Thomas Bargar his precontest.
To the eleventh he says it contains the truth.
To the twelfth he deposes and says that one Sonday next after bartylmewe day he dyd omytt to do his dewtie concernynge the booke of buryinge and crystenynge and weddyng and so forth.
To the thirteenth he says it contains the truth.
To the fourteenth he does not know how to depose.
To the fifteenth he agrees with Richard Wood his precontest.
To the sixteenth agrees with his precontest Thomas Arderne savinge one tyme he herde hym speake agayneste supersticion, and so forth.
To the seventeenth he says it contains the truth.
To the eighteenth he does not know how to depose.
To the nineteenth he says it contains the truth and to the twentieth.
To the xxjth he does not know how to depose nor to the xxijth.
To the xxiijth he does not know how to depose.
To the xxiiijth he labours under the fame aforesaid and so forth. He is not instructed nor learnt, and so forth.

Thomas Kenrycke of the parish of Feversham aged xxx years or thereabouts of free condition as he says a witness produced etc.,

To the first he says that it contains the truth and to the second and to the third.
To the fourth he does not know how to depose nor to the fifth.
To the sixth he deposes and he says it contains the truth.
To the seventh not examined because the party aforesaid has acknowledged.
To the eighth he does not know how to depose.
To the ninth saith that one Thomas Bryce was maried at Preston, and otherwise he does not know how to depose.

folio 86v;
To the tenth he agrees with Thomas Bargar his precontest.
To the eleventh he does not know how to depose nor to the twelfth.
To the thirteenth not examined because the party aforesaid has acknowledged.
To the fourteenth he does not know how to depose.
To the fifteenth he agrees with Richard Wood his precontest.
To the sixteenth he says that it contains the truth and to the seventeenth.
To the eighteenth he does not know how to depose.
To the nineteenth he says it contains the truth and to the twentieth.

To the xxjth he does not know how to depose nor to the xxijth.
To the xxiij he says it contains the truth.
To the xxiiijth he labours under the aforesaid fame pre-deposed, and so forth.
He is not instructed, nor learned, nor love , favour and so forth.

William Huchynson of the parish of Feversham aged xxx years or thereabouts of free condition as he says, a witness produced etc.,

To the first he says that it contains the truth and to the second.
To the third he says it contains the truth.
To the fourth he does not know how to depose nor to the fifth.
To the sixth he does not know how to depose.
To the vijth he says it contains the truth
To the eighth he does not know how to depose.
To the ninth he agrees with Thomas Kenryck his precontest.
To the tenth he says it contains the truth.
To the eleventh he does not know how to depose nor to the twelfth.
To the thirteenth he does not know how to depose nor to the fourteenth.
To the fifteenth he agrees with Richard Wood his precontest.
To the sixteenth he says that it contains the truth and to the seventeenth.
To the eighteenth he says it contains the truth.
To the nineteenth he says that it contains the truth.

folio 87
To the xxth he does not know how to depose nor to the xxjth.
To the xxij he says that uppon Michaelmas day he can not tell for he was not then at home but on other daies he does not know how to depose.
To the xxiij he says it contains the truth.
To the xxiiijth he labours under the aforesaid fame pre-deposed, and so forth. He is not instructed nor learned, nor love, favour etc.

Consistory Court of Canterbury Deposition register DCb/X.10.3 Canterbury Cathedral Archives and Library.

folio 40v[332]
Norton against Waren Fellowe
Depositions ~~examination~~ Waren Fellowe of the parish of Stawlesfelde[333] made the iiijth of May [1548] concerning the subtraction of tithes

To the first he says that it ~~is~~ contains the truth

To[334] *the second to know how long a time had the said Clement Norton lived at Faversham acknowledged nevertheless and to be reputed vicar there*

---

332 The original document is a mixture of Latin and English. For convenience the translated sections are shown in italics.
333 Stalisfield.
334 Ad 2nd restit quantus temps apud Feversham habitavit dictis Clemens Norton fatetur ~~neque .... non sic~~ tamen que sit vicarius ~~vel non~~ reputatus ~~vel non~~ ibidem

To[335] *the third of the composition he did not know how to depose or how much for the minor tithes, that is to say, hay, piglets, lambs, wool and geese he acknowledged to be the tithes of the vicar there or of his deputy aforesaid within the parish of Faversham and how much for the tithe of the sixteenth part, that is to say, wheat, barley etc. ground in the mill* saith that he never knewe that any suche tithes mighte be paied to the vycar and by the name of toule, as by any other name, And he thynketh that he the saide vycar ~~oughte to~~ have ~~no corne for tithe~~ had no ~~corne~~ tithe at any tyme here to fore of that that hath corne to the myll to be grownde and that he oughte to have no suche tithe

To the 4th he the saide Fellowe thynketh that the saide vycars predecessors hath not bene in possession at any tyme of any suche tithes of toule ~~within the lymyttes~~ taken at any myll or mylles within the saide parishe *by*[336] *the name of tovet to the same mill*

And the saide Fellowe saith uppon his othe that he never ~~hearde~~ knewe of any gremente that was made by any man with the saide vycar, but by ~~the saide vicar his owne~~ reporte for the saide toule, for anye monay; or other recompence at any tyme receyvyd by the saide vicar or his predecessoures

To[337] *the fifth purgation article just as produced into court*

To[338] *the sixth acknowledged*

To[339] *the seventh purgation article just as produced into court* and saith that he dyd not entre at the annunciation of our Lady but at Maye day nexte after in the sayde yere specyfied in the libele

To[340] *the eighth acknowledged* that the myll ys rented at x£ by the yere the which same this deponente doeth pay to Master Arde[n[341]] his londelorde yerelye

To[342] *the ninth he says.....[remainder of document not transcribed].*

---

335 Ad 3rd de compositione ~~et~~ nescit deponere series quantus ad decimas minores ~~nescit deponere~~ videlicet fenum porcellos agnos lanas et aucas fatetur causae decimalis vicarii ibidem seu eius deputato infra parochia de Feversham .~~and as concernynge~~ et quantus ad decimas decime sexte partis omnium granorum videlicet frumenti ordei etc. comminuti in molendino

336 nomine tolveti eiusdem molendini. *O.E.D.* Tovet a local word of Kent evidently the same as tollfat. A measure of two pecks or half a bushel

337 Ad 5th negatium articulum ~~quantam ad preseriptum~~ pro ut ponitur

338 Ad vjth fatetur

339 Ad vijth negatium articulum ut ponitur

340 fol. 41. Ad viijth fatetur

341 There is a small portion torn off the edge of the sheet at this point and

342 Ad ixth ~~fatetur~~ dicit

APPENDIX 5: Will of Thomas Arden of Canterbury.

ARCHDEACONRY COURT OF CANTERBURY WILL REGISTER ON MICROFILM.
PRC 17/40 FOLIO 237

IN THE NAME OF GOD AMEN The xxjth day of December in the yeare of our Lord God a thowesand fyve hundrethe thre score and seaven. I Thomas Arden of the cytie of Canterbury gentleman, hole of mynde and of good and parfect remembrance ordeyne and make this my present testament here in concernynge my last wyll in manner and forme followinge, fyrst and before all other thinges I commytt me unto God and to his mercy, belevynge withe out anny doubt or mystrust that by his grace, and meryttes of Jhesus Chryste, and by the vertue of his passyon and resurrectyon I have and shall have remyssyon of my sinnes, and resurrectyon of body and soule, accordynge as it is wryten. I beleeve that my redemer lyvethe, and that in the last day I shall ryse out of the earthe and in my fleshe shall see my savyor. This my hope is leyde up in my bosome, And touchinge the wealthe of my soule, the faythe that I have taken and rehersed is suffycyent as I suppose withe out anny other mans worke or workes, my grounde and beleef is that there is but one God and one medyator betwene god and man, whiche is Jhesus Chryste so that I accompte none in heaven nor in earthe to be medyator betwene me and God, but only Jhesus Chryste, all other be petycyoners in receavynge of grace but none able to geve influence of grace, and therefore wyll I bestowe no parte of my goodes for that entente, that anny man should say or do to helpe my soule, for there in I trust only to the promysse of God, he that belevethe and is baptyzed shalbe saved, and he that belevethe not shalbe dampned. As touchinge the buryenge of my body, it avaylethe me not what so ever be done, as St. Augustyne sayethe, the funerall pompes ar rather the solace of them that lyve, then for the welthe and comforte of them that ar dead. And therefore I remytt it only to the dyscretyon of myne executors. And touchinge the distrybution of my temporall goodes, my purpose is by the grace of God to bestowe them to be accepted as the frutes of faythe, So that I not suppose that my meryttes is by good bestowing of them, but my meryttes is the faythe of Jhesus Chryste only, by whome suche workes ar good, accordynge to the woordes of our Lorde, I was hungry, and thow gavest me to eate and so forth. And it followethe, that he hath don to the leaste of my brethern he hathe don to me and so forth. And ever we shoulde consyder the true sentence, that a good worke makethe not a good man, but a good man makethe a good worke, for faythe makethe a man bothe good and righteous, for a righteous man lyvethe by faythe, and what so ever spryngethe not of faythe is synne, ITEM I geve unto Jone, Anne, Katheryne, Elizabethe, and Amy, my daughters, to every one of them, forty two pounds a peece, to be payde unto them by my executrix, when they shall accomplishe and come to the age of one and twenty yeares, or shalbe maryed. Then I wyll the overlyver of them to be the others heyer. ITEM I geve and bequethe unto John Arden my sonne and to Arthure Arden my sonne and there heyres, all my landes in Warwyckshyre, to be devyded unto them equally by even portyons immedyatly after my decease, provyded allwayes that Anne my wyffe shall have her dowry out of all my landes and the lettynge of the same at her wyll and pleasure. ITEM I wyll that my wyffe shall have and enjoy all my houses, landes and tenements within the cytie of Canterbury for the terme of her lyffe. And after her decease the same to remayne unto John and Arthure my said sonnes and there heyres equally to be devyded betwene them by even portyons. And if anny of the said sonnes do departe this worlde before the deathe of my said wyffe without heyers of his body lawfully begotten, then I wyll that the one shalbe the others heyer. ITEM I geve to Arthure my sonne my harnes and dagge. ITEM I geve also unto hym, my bay geldynge and my gowne whiche I commonly use to weare. ITEM I geve to John my sonne my gray geldynge and my gowne of sylke. ITEM I geve unto Elizabethe my daughter, and her heyres my house and lande in Postlynge when she shalbe maryed, untyll which tyme I wyll that Anne my wyffe, she kepynge the reparations, and payenge the lordes rent, shall have the profytt of itt. ITEM I ordeyne and apoynt Anne my wyffe to be my sole executyrix of this my present testament and last wyll, who I wyll in anny wyse that she shall make a true and just delyvery and satysfactyon of all suche legacyes wylled and geven by my predecessor John Cotton. And if it so fortune that my said executrix have not suffycyently to performe the said legacyes accordyngly, besydes the said legacyes conteyned in this said wyll. Then I wyll that my said executrix or her assignes shall make sale of so muche of my houses and landes in the said cytie as shall make satysfactyon of the same. The resydue of all my goodes and moveables (my dettes and legacyes fully contented and payde) I wholy geve and bequethe unto Anne my wyffe. ITEM I geve unto Thomas Cotton, George and Henry Cotton my least cheyne of goulde to be equally devyded amongest them. Also I wyll that Anne my wyffe shall pay, or cause to be payde unto Wyllyam Salmon, all suche sommes of monny as ar due, or here after shalbe due to be payde for the purchase of the house I do nowe dwell in. ITEM I geve unto Wyllyam my sarvant forty shillinges, and to John Davyson my sarvant forty shillinges, to be delyvered and payde ymmedyately after my decease. And to Rychard Bayly my sarvant forty shillinges. In wytnes where of I the said Thomas Arden to this my hande and seale have sett the xijth day of Apryll, in the tenth year of Queen Elizabeth[343].. Item I ordeyne that Jasper Nayler to be my overseer of this my wyll, unto whome I geve for his paynes there in used forty shillinges. By me Thomas Arden. These me beinge witness to this wyll John Hyll parson, Nycholas Waferer and George Powell.

[Latin] PROBATE was granted on this present above written testament before Master Vincent Denne, bachelor in law, official of the Reverend Lord Archdeacon of Canterbury the seventh day of the month of December in the year of the Lord one thousand five hundred and sixty eight upon the oaths of Nicholas Waferer and George Powell witnesses etc. With approval etc. The charge of execution of this same is committed to the executrix above named who was first duly sworn etc. Given etc.

PRO. Chancery Proceedings Elizabeth 1
C2/Elizabeth 1/A6/31

15 June in the year 16 Elizabeth 1574 *[written in top margin]*

To the right honourable Sir Nicholas Bacon knighte Lord Keper of the greate seale of Englonde

Moste humblye complayninge showe and informe unto youre lordeshippe youre dalye orators John Arderne and Arthure ~~Thomas~~ Arderne sonnes of Thomas Arderne late of the cetye of Cauntorbury gentleman deceased That whereas the saide Thomas Arderne father of your saide orators was in his lyef tyme laufully seyazed in his demmeasne as of fee of and in one mancion howse wythe the appurtenaunces scytuat lyinge and beinge in the paryshe of Sainte Myldredde the vyrgyn in the saide cetye of Caunterberye And he the saide Thomas Arderne so being of the premysses wyth the appurtenaunces seyazed as ys aforesaid dyd for the some of fyftie poundes by deede of feoffamente infeoffe one Rycharde Furnor of the cetie of Caunterbury Alderman and his heyres of and in the premysses wythe the appurtenaunces upon this condycion followinge That is

343 This date in Latin

to saye that yf he the saide Thomas Arderne his heires executours admynistrators or assigns or anye of them, dyd or sholde satysfye contente and paye or cause to be satysfied contented and paide unto the saide Rycharde Furnor his executors and assignes the saide somme of fyftye poundes at certendayes and tymes betwene them the saide Rycharde Furnour and the saide Thomas Arderne concluded and agreed uppon That then and from thensforthe the saide mortgage to be utterly voyd and of none affect and that then the saide landes and tenementes wyth the appurtenaunces there uppon to reverte and comme to the saide Thomas Arderne his heires and assignes as in his former estate After whiche the said Thomas Arderne made Anne his wief his soole executrixe of his laste will and testamente whiche saide some of fyftie poundes over and besides the some of fyve poundes for the forberinge use and intereste thereof was by the executrix of the saide Thomas paide accordingly to the saide Rycharde Furnour to his full satysfaction and contentation of all suche somes of money for whiche the saide howse and landes weere layed to mortegage for By meanes and reason whereof the saide premysses wyth the appurtenaunces and the righte of the same oughte lawfullye to dyscende and comme unto your said orators as sonnes and heyres to the saide Thomas Arderne deceasyd accordinge to the custume of gavelkynde, by vertue whereof theye entered into the same and were thereof seyezed accordingly. But so yt is righte honourable that notwithstandinge the repaymente of the saide sommes of moneye as ys aforesaide the saide Richarde Furnor by some secret practyse betwene hym and one Thomas Cranmer had and practysed pretendinge that suche some of moneye as by the said feoffmente sholde be paide was not paide at the dayes and tymes expressed in the saide feoofment hathe agaynste all righte equytie and good conscyens infeoffed the saide Thomas Cranmer and his heyres of and in the saide landes and tenementes with the appurtenaunces who by vertue thereof hathe entered into the premysses with the appurtenaunces upon whose possession your said orators have rentered whereupon the same Thomas Cranmer hathe broughte and commensed his action of trespasse agaynste your saide orators and Thomas Coxe at the common lawes of the realme, wherefore and for as muche as the saide moneye compryzed in the saide feoffmente beinge not paide to the saide Furnor at or before the dayes of paymente of the same as they surmyse the certentye of whiche is well knowen unto the said Furnour and Cranmer havinge the saide deede the premysses therefore considered maye yt please your good l[ordship] to graunte unto your saide oratores the Quenes Majesties wrytt of Subpena to be dyrected unto the saide Rycharde Furnor and Thomas Cranmer comaunding them and either of them by vertue thereof at a certen daye and under a certen payne therewith to be lymyted and appoynted personallye to be and appere before youre good lordeshippe in the Quenes Majestyes Highe Courte of Chauncerye then and there readye to answer the premysses and to abide suche further order and dyrectyon herein as to your good lordeshippe shall seme consonante to equytie and justyce And your sayde orators shall daylye praye unto Almightie God for the prosperouse preservation of youre good Lordshippe in honour longe to contenewe.

Then follows the answer of Richard Furner and Thomas Cranmer, then nexte the mandate to examine witnesses, a further copy of the bill of complaint, the replication of John Arden and Arthur Arden (sic)

APPENDIX 6:
Wills of Thomas and Edward Mirfyn.

PREROGATIVE COURT OF CANTERBURY WILL REGISTER ON MICROFILM
PROB 11/21 QUIRE 13 FOLIO 97 TO FOLIO 99V

IN THE NAME OF GOD AMEN The secunde day of the moneth of Septembre in the yere of our Lorde God a thousande fyve hundred and xxiij And in the xv yere of the reigne of King of our soveraigne Lorde king Henry the viijth by the grace of God of Inglonde and of Fraunce kynge defender of the feith and lorde of Irlande I Thomas Mirfyn citezein and alderman of the citie of London being of hole and parfite mynde and in goode memory lawde and praysing be to almighty God considering that deth is a thinge most certeyn to every man and that every man naturally shall departe out of this transitory worlde and dye and that the tyme therof is thinge moost uncerteyn Therfor I trusting through and by the merites of Jhesu Crist our saviour and redemptour to be a saved soule and a parte taker with him of the joyes of hevyn in the honour of God and for the welth of my soule and the proufit of my wife my childern and other my lovers and frendes make ordeyn and declare my testament and last will as well towching and concernyng the disposition of my soule and body landes and tenementes As of my goodes catalles and dettes in maner and fourme folowynge that is to sey First I bequeth[344] my soule to almighty God my maker and redemptour and to his moost glorious and blissed moder and virgyn lady saint Mary and unto all the holy company of hevyn And my body to be buried in the charnelhouse in Paulis church yarde in London where the body of dame Alice late my wyfe lieth buried and there where my tombe is made And I revoke repell and make frustrate and voide all other willes by me before the date of this my present will in any wise made and I will that I be honestly buried after and according to my degre And after my body be buried I will that all my debtes the which of right by lawe or conscience I owe or the tyme of my deth shall owe unto any persone or persones shalbe well and truely contented and paide at suche daies as they be payable And also yf I have doon any iniury or wronge to any persone or persones and that proved before myn executours (which I knowe noon) than I woll myn executours make to them recompence therfor And where for mariage to be had bitwene me and dame Elizabeth my wife doughter of Aungell Donne late citezein and alderman of London and Anne his wife decessed whiche Anne Sir Robert Dymmok knyght after the deth of the said Aungell Donne hir first husbonde was maried unto a writing was made remaynyng with the said Sir Robert as by me the said Thomas Mirfyn the tenour wherof ensuyth in thise wordes The xvth day of October the xjth yere of the reigne of kynge Henry the viijth It is convented and agreed bitwene Thomas Mirfyn maire of the Citie of London of the one partie and Robert Dymmok knyght on ther other partie That the said Thomas shall with the grace of God mary and take to wife Elizabeth Donne daughter and heire to Aungell Donne late Alderman of London and the said Thomas Mirfyn on this side the fest of the Nativitie of our Lorde that shalbe in the yere of our Lord MV^{C}xxij shall cause a sure and a laufull astate to be made aftyer the sure forme of the lawe unto the said Elizabeth Donne of londes rentes and tenementes to the yerely value of xl$^{£}$ clere over and above all charges for terme of lyfe of the said Elizabeth furder the said Thomas promyseth that he shal leve unto the said Elizabeth his wife yf God fortune hir to lyve after him the doble that she brought to him which summe of hir porttion amounteth MCCCLxxxiiij$^{£}$ iiij^{s} viij^{d} and x$^{£}$ gevyn to hir by hir grandame which doble shall amount MMCxLviij$^{£}$ ix^{s} iiij^{d} And also the said Thomas hath promysed that the said Elizabeth

[344] Written bequeth with a title over the top of the word it was at first thought that this was an abbreviation mark. However, closer inspection of the document shows that the scribe has put this 'flourish' over every h and as such it has been ignored.

shalbe at hir choise to chose to have the thirde parte after the custume of the citie or the somme abovewritten Also the said Thomas promyseth that if the said Elizabeth deceace afore him that she shall have C$^{£}$ to distribute and make her will of beside all hir apparrell and juelles And the said Sir Robert promiseth that he shalbe bounde to paye in three yeres next and immediatly folowing to the said Thomas MLxxiiij$^{£}$ iiij^{s} viij^{d} by even portions Also the said Thomas promyseth that the said Sir Robert shall have in his house at Saint Margaret Patens parishe the lodging that Alice Stamford dyd lye in with free entre and yssue and at all tymes to have licence to cary awaye suche stuffe as apperteneth to the said Sir Robert without contradiction of the said Thomas and Elizabeth yf there be any thinge that wantes from in the premisses it to be amended by maister Broke sergeaunt at the lawe accordinge to the true entent And after this I the said Thomas and the said Elizabeth were maried togider And where the said Sir Robert and other persones at his request were and yet stonden bounden to the chamberleyn of London and his successours by recognisaunce upon condition for the payment of the summe of MLxxiiij$^{£}$ iiij^{s} viij^{d} to Edward Donne and Fraunces Donne the children of the said Aungell then orphanes of the said citie which children ben all decessed except my said wife at the day of the said writing made and mariage bitwene me and my said wife soo that all the said hole summe of MLxxiiij$^{£}$ iiij^{s} viij^{d} was then to the use of my said wife by the survivour of hir said brethern according to the lawe and custume of the said citie of London by whiche mariage the said bonde made to the said chamberleyn of London was and is to the use of me and my said wife And howbeyt I have ben alwey redy to have made a sure astate of londes and tenementes of the yerely value of xl$^{£}$ over and above all charges and reprises to the same Dame Elizabeth my wife for terme of hir lyfe and all the residue in the said bill specified on my parte to be executed I was content yf the said Sir Robert wolde have made payment to me and my said wife of the said summe of MLxxiiij$^{£}$ iiij^{s} viij^{d} or wolde have ben bounden for the payment therof at daies reasonable in the said writing conteyned by us to have ben appoynted or at reasonable other daies sithence the said thre yeres expressed in the said writing by the said Sir Robert and me to have ben appoynted And there uppon I and my said wife of the same recognisaunce wolde have discharged the said Sir Robert and the other persones named and bounden by the same recognisaunce for the payment of the said MLxxiiij$^{£}$ iiij^{s} viij^{d} and wolde have caused the said recognisaunce to have ben made frustrate voide and cancelled which premisses to doo the said Sir Robert on his part and behalf hath refused not only contrary to his promyse in the said writing specified but also contrary to the condition of the recognisaunce Wherfor my will and mynde is yf the said Sir Robert or his executours by the assent and agrement of my said wife by her writing make payment to myn executours within six monethes next after my death of the said summe of MLxxiiij$^{£}$ iiij^{s} viij^{d} That then I will that my said wife for terme of hir lyfe shall have all my houses landes and tenementes of Merditche and Wrayttes with the appurtenaunces in the parishe of Hornechurch in the countie of Essex my manour of Downe with the appurtenaunces in the countie of Kent and those my londes and tenementes lying in the parishes of Fanchirch and Aldermary and of Saint Petyr in Cornehill with the appurtenaunces whiche ben of the clere yerely value of fourty poundes over and above all charges and reprises and better, as the thirde parte aswell of all my goodes catalles and dettes and of the said summe of Mlxxiiij$^{£}$ iiij^{s} viiij^{d} after my debtes paide funeralles and ordynary charges born and allowed after and according to the lawe and custume of the said citie or elles at the libertie of my said wife to have of myn executours the said somme of MMCxLviiij$^{£}$ ix^{s} iiij^{d} the doble that she brought with her and that I shulde have had of the said sommes to hir bilonging to have ben paide upon hir mariage according to the true meanyng of the said writing she than making a relees to myn executours of all accions suyttes and demaundes which in any wise she myght have demaunde or clayme agenst myn executours by the custume and lawe of the said citie as shalbe reasonably advised by myn executours And yf she refuse to have the said somme of MMCxLviij$^{£}$ ix^{s} iiij^{d} And will holde hir to the said thirde part of my goodes catalles and debtes in fourme beforsaid according to the lawe and custume of the said citie then she to make a release to myn executours of all actions suyttes and demaundes which in any wise she myght or then may have agenst them by reason of any promyse agreament or graunt conteyned in the forsaid writinge, the said promyse and graunt of the said manours londes and tenementes that she shuld have for terme of hir lyfe oonly except And yf the said Sir Robert and his executours pay not nor content ne paye to myn executours or their executours or their executours the said MLxxiiij$^{£}$ iiij^{s} viij^{d} within vj monethes next after my decesse but refusith the same to doo then my mynde and will is that my said gifte and bequest to my said wife aswell of the said manours landes and tenementes be utterly void and noon effect as of the said somme of MMCxLviij$^{£}$ ix^{s} iiij^{d} the doble that she brought with her when I toke hir to my wife And if the said Sir Robert or his executours content and paye within vj monethes next after my decese the said somme of Mlxxiiij$^{£}$ iiij^{s} viij^{d} Then I will and my mynde is that all the premisses be doon and executed in suche wise and fourme as before is expressed And then also I will and my mynde is that my sonne Edward Mirfyn immediately after the death of my said wife shall have all houses or tenementes Merditche or Wraittes with the appurtenaunces in the parishe of Hornechirch in the Lordship of Havering at Bowre in the countie of Essex my houses landes and tenementes in the parishe of Saint Mary Fanchirch those two newe houses in Bogerrowe lyinge in the parishe of Saint Anthonye and of Saint Johns in Walbroke whiche I late buylded to have to him and to his heires of his body laufullye begotten And for default of suche issue to be and remayn to Mary my doughter and to the heires of hir bodye laufully begotten And for default of suche issue to be and remayn to Fruncis my doughter and to the heires of hir body And for default of such issue to remayne to my right heires forever Also I geve to Mary my doughter my manour londes and tenementes with the appurtenaunces of Down in the countie of Kent To have and to holde immediately after the deathe of my said wife to my said doughter and to the heires of hir body laufully begotten And for defaulte of suche issue to be and remayn to my said sonne Edward and to the heires of his body laufully begotten And for default of suche yssue to remayne to my said doughter Fraunces and to the heires of hir body laufullye begotten And for default of such yssue to be and remayne to my right heires for ever. Also I geve and bequeth unto the said Fraunces my doughter that my tenement lying in the parishe of Aldermary in London And that my tenement lying in the parishe of Saint Peter in Cornehill To have and to holde immediately after the death of my said wife to my said doughter Fraunces and to the heires of hir body laufully begotten And for default of suche issue to be and remayne to my said doughter Mary and to the heires of hir body laufully begotten And for default of suche issue to be and remayne to my said sone Edwarde and to the heires of his body laufully begotten And for default of such issue to be and remayn to my right heires for ever And in caas yf the said Sir Robert nor his executours pay not nor doo not to be paid to the executours of me the said Thomas Myrfyn nor their executours the said Mlxxiiij$^{£}$ iiij^{s} viij^{d} within vj monethes next after my death that than my will is as before is saide that my wife shall not have the said messuages[345] londes and tenementes and other the premisses nor any parcell therof But then I will that my said children shall immediately after my death and the vj moneth expired and past have the said messuages londes and tenementes to theym in suche wise and with like remaynders as I before have declared and willed theym to have after the death of my said wife yf the said Sir Robert or his executours had paide the said MLxxiiij$^{£}$ iiij^{s} viij^{d} to myn executours within vj monethes next after my death and my said wife then to have noon of my said londes nor any of my goodes catalles and dettes but oonly after my dettes paid my funeralles and ordynary charges and expenses concernyng the same contented and paide She to have the thirde parte of that, that shall then remayn And my said children another thirde parte of the same remaynder And the other thirde parte all the residue to be myn

[345] Meases

executours for the perfourmaunce of my last wille after and according to the lawes and custumes of the said citie Also I geve and bequeth to the high awter in the parishe churche of Saint Antonyne for my offerynges omitted and forgotten in discharging of my conscience xx^s I bequeth to every each of the iiij orders of Freres in London that is to wit, the White Frers, the blak Freres, the Gray Freres and the Augustyn Freres to pray for my soule, the soules beforsaid and all christen soules and to convey my body to my burying place and to sey a trigintall of masses and to kepe a solempne dirige and masse of requiem by note in every of their said places the day of my buriall and there to pray for my soule the soules beforsaid and all Christen soules to every of the forsaid places xxvj^s viij^d Item I bequeth unto the Crossed Freres in London also to convey my body to my burying place and to sey a trentall of masses and to kepe a solempne dirige and masses of requiem by note in their place the day of my buriall there to pray for my soule and the soules aforsaid and all Christen soules xxvj^s viij^d Item I bequeth unto the Freres of Grenewiche and to the Freres at Richemont to say a trentall of masses in either of their places and to kepe a solempn dirige and masse of requiem by note in their severall places the day of my burial for my soule the soules aforsaid and all Christen soules to either place xL^s to be gevyn unto theym in money or money worth Item I bequeth unto the Charterhouse next London and to the Charterhouse at Shene[346] to kepe a solempne dirige and masse of requiem by note in either of their said places the day of my buriall for my soule the soules beforsaid and all Christen soules to every place xL^s Also I bequeth unto the brethern and sustern of the monastery of Syon to kepe a solempne dirige and masse of requiem in their churche to pray for my soule the soules beforsaid and all Christen soules the day of my burying xL^s Also I bequeth unto every prysoner being in the prisons in Newgate Ludgate both the counters in London the Marchalsee the Kynges benche in Southwerk the convicte house at Westminster to every prisoner being in the same prison houses to every of them a penny to be gevyn unto theym afore my body be buried or within iij daies after Item I bequeth unto nunnes at Stratford at Bowe to pray for my soule a cope of velwet garnisshed with orffres[347] of the value of v^£ Item I bequeth unto my sonne dane George Mirfyn monk at Westminster xx^£ to be paide him every yere iiij^£ by the handes of myn executours And if it fourtune him to decesse afore the hole somme be paid unto him then as moch as shall remayn I will it be gevyn to pouer people in almesse or in some oder deades of charitie at the discretion of myn executours for to praye for his soule Item I bequeth unto Margaret Pargetour the wife of Thomas Pargetour a blak gown and to hir husbonde another and in money to theym x^£ Also I bequeth unto every childe that she in lyve[348] whan they shall come to laufull age xL^s a pece And yf any of them dye before laufull age than I will his parte remayne amonges to other Item I bequeth unto Gilbert Hardegrave v^£ and to every each of his children xL^s to be paid within a yere after my decesse Item I bequeth unto my suster Agnes Loke the wife of Mighel Loke x^£ Item I bequeth unto Elizabeth the wife of Elyot v^£ and unto every childe that she hath xL^s Also I bequeth unto John Story the sonne of Robert Story xx^£ Item I bequeth to Mighel Loke my susters sonne xL^£ And unto every childe that he hath a lyve v^£ Item I bequeth unto John Bande beddill[349] of the crafte of Skynners to pray for my soule a blak gowne and in money xL^s Also I bequeth unto John Broun clerk of our Lady Company of the said crafte of Skynners a blak gowne

346 *Handbook to the Environs of London* by James Thorne (1876) under West Sheen, Surrey. 'Sheen was the original name of Richmond, and a royal palace stood on the West side of the present Richmond Green, between it and the River. Henry V founded in 1414 a convent of Carthusians which he called the House of Jesus of Bethlehem at Sheen. The buildings which were of great extent, stood about ¼ mile North west of the palace, and about them grew up a hamlet, which later was called West Sheen. The convent was richly endowed ....'

347 *O.E.D.* Orphrey, orfray: Gold embroidery, or any rich embroidery; with *an* and *pl.*, a piece of richly embroidered stuff.

348 sic

349 beadle

and in money xL^{s} Also I bequeth unto the chapel of Barwey[350] in the county of Cambridge where I was born and cristened in the honour of God and of Saint Nicholas a vestment and an awbe[351] with all the apparell therunto belonging for a prest to synge in of the value of xL^{s} Also I bequeth to the same chapell ij awter clothes of rede and yelowe silk one above and another beneth and ij curteyns sutable of the value of xL^{s} ij lynnen awter clothes price iiij^{s} ij newe torches price xij^{s} and xij poundes of poleyn wax to make tapers to garnysshe the said chapell Also I bequeth to an honest seculer prest to syng masse upon Sondaies and holydaies yerely in the said chapell during the space of fyve yeres next ensuyng after my decesse xL^{s} the yere summe x$^{£}$ And that the wardeyns of the said church for the tyme being provide the same yerely prest Item I bequeth unto the said awlter in the said chapell a corporase and a case[352] of the value of iij^{s} iiij^{d} a boke price x^{s} and a surpleise price iiij^{s} Also I geve and bequeth towardes the reparations and mayntenyng and supporting of the said chapell to pray for my soule my fader and moder soules my wife soule and all my childern soules xL^{s} Also I bequeth unto Saint Mary Church of Yely[353] where my fader lieth buried on whose soule Jhesus have mercy a vestment with an awbe with all thinges belonging unto a prest of the value of xL^{s} ij awter clothes price iiij^{s} a corporas and a caas of the price of iij^{s} iiij^{d} a masse boke price x^{s} ij newe torches price xij^{s} ij awterclothes of red and yelowe silk one for above the other for byneth and ij curteyns sutable of the value of xL^{s} which forsaid auterclothes and curteyns I will shalbe orderid and hangid in the North Ile of the same church by the quyre door to the entent the prestes may synge and sey masse there and to pray for my soule the soules of George and Kateryn my fader and mother my wife soule my childern soules and all Christen soules Also I bequeth to the maister and wardeyns of the guylde of Corpus Cristi of the crafte of Skynners of London and to their successours a cope a vestment with Dekyn and Subdekyn with all maner thinges to the same belonging of blak damask or blak satyn to be garnysshed with orfres and myn armes and a coope of the same suyt a coporase caase ij lynnen awter clothes a coporas and ij newe torches all of the price or value of xx$^{£}$ To the intent that the said maister and wardeyns and thir successours shall occupie yerely at myn obite to be kept in the chapell over the charnelhouse in Poles churchyarde and all the said vestmentes awter clothes cope and other thinges belonging unto the same be occupied yerely as longe as they may endure Item I bequeth towardes the sustentation repairyng and amending of the same chapell over the charnelhouse in Powlles churchyarde in my lyfe tyme or immediately after my decesse xxvj$^{£}$ xiij^{s} iiij^{d} Also I bequeth unto the parishe church of Saint Antonyne in Bogierrowe[354] in London an hole sute of vestmentes that is to sey a vestment for a prest with diacon and subdiacon and ij coopes of one sute with all other thinges bilonging unto the same of the value of four score powndes And I will that the churchyarde on the southside of Saint Agnes chapell of the said church of Saint Antonyne shalbe pavid with Brabant stone that is to sey from the East end unto the West ende of the said chapell and a faire stone of marble to be laide in the mydd of the said churchyarde with all my childern names to be graven and sett on the same stone of marble that is to sey, Thomas, John, George, Thomas, John, Fraunceis, Richard. John, Robert, Edward and Bartilmewe, Margaret, Mary and Fraunceis and that this be doon within one yere after my decesse Also I bequeth unto the maister and wardeyns of the mistery crafte or feliship of skynners of London by what name soever they be called to purches certeyn londes and tenementes laufully to theym to be conveyed for the contynuyng and mayntenyng of xij torches which I will

350 Not very clear but this is presumably Barway given in John Bartholomew *The Survey Gazetteer of the British Isles* 8th Edn. (Edinburgh, 1932) as a locality in Cambridgeshire, in Newmarket rural district.

351 *O.E.D.* Alb; A tunic or vestment of white cloth reaching to the feet, and enveloping the entire person; a variety of the surplice, but with close sleeves; worn by clerics in religious ceremonies, and by some consecrated kings.

352 Corporas, corporal, the linen cloth upon which the hosts were consecrated. They were kept in cases.

353 St Mary Ely

354 Presumably St Antholin, Budge Row, London

shalbe occupied aboute the procession of Corpus Christi which I will and charge myn executours underwritten to deliver unto the maister and Wardeyns of Skynners garnysshed with myn armes after the best maner and as myn executours shall thynk most convenient And the said maister and wardeyns of Skynners and their successours to renewe the waxe of the same torches yerely and every iiij yeres to renewe the staves[355] and to kepe theym in like maner as they were delivered to theym by the hands of myn executours which xij torches I will shalbe delivered unto theym all redy garnisshed as is aforesaid within one yere next after my decesse and over this that the maister and wardeyns of skynners for the tyme being shall cause an obite or anniversary yerely to be kept the day of my decesse or within thre daies after or within iij daies next preceding in the said chapell over the charnelhouse in Poules churcheyarde in London where my body lieth buried for me and my said wifes soules Alice and Elizabeth my childern soules and all christen soules And I will that there be yerely spent and bestowed xxvj^{s} viij^{d} sterlinges in maner and fourme folowing that is to sey to v preistes ij^{s} vj^{d} that is to sey to every each of theym vj^{d} to the curate of Saint Antonyne or his deputie there being present at the said obite or anniversary xij^{d} to the chauntry preist that usith to synge in the same chapell to syng pray and say[356] masse for my soule and the soules beforesaid xd, for two pounde tapers of waxe to brenne at my hease viij^{d} for ij half pounde tapers of wax for the aulter there to brenne and remayn viij^{d} To the maister of Corpus Christi to be there present for his commyng xxd To the iiij wardeyns of the said feliship to be there present iiij^{s} that is to sey to every of theym xij^{d} to the clerke and bedyll of the same feliship for the tyme being for bryngging of Corpus Christi cloth then unto the chapell viij^{d} that is to sey to either of iiij^{d} To xij pouer housholders of the parishe of Saint Antonyne iiij^{s} that is to sey to every of them iiij^{d} and to be spent at Skynners Hall at the commyng from the dirige for a recreation or potacion to the maister and the company with prestes and clerkes for spice bred and whitebunnes v^{s} for iiij galons of gascoyne wyne ij^{s} viij^{d} for a kilderkyn of goode ale ij^{s} and for a chese xij^{d} whiche charges of in and aboute the said obite amounten to the somme of xxvj^{s} viij^{d} And for mayntenyng of the same obite and the said twelve torches for the procession on Corpus Christi day afore rehersed which charges of both amount unto the somme of iiij marces sterlinges by yere And I bequeth and geve unto the same maister and wardeyns of Skynners to purchase lands for the contynuance of the same forever more two hundred marces and this to be doon and executed by indenture by a body corporat by my said executours or their executours to be named on the one partie and the said maister and wardeyns of Skynners on the oder partie as it shalbe advised by suche lerned counceill as myn executours or their executours shall name and appoynt Also my mynde and wille is to have an honest seculer prest to synge and say masse when he shall be dispoased for my soule my wifes soule my childern soules and all Christen soules in the parishe church of Saint Antonyne and there to be helping daily at the service in the same church and ones in the weke to sey dirige and comendations for my soule and the soules afore rehersed And my mynde and wille is that every Sonday in the yere he dispoase him to synge and say masse at the chapell over the charnelhouse in Poules churcheyard bitwene ix and x of the clok to the entent that suche men and women as shalhave myn almes may comme and here his masse and after masse to receyve their almes And the same prest to have for his salary vij$^{£}$ by the yere for the space of xv yeres next after my death till the summe of Cv$^{£}$ be clerely and fullye paide And the same Cv$^{£}$ to remayn in the handes of the said felship of Skynners in London and they to make payment unto the prest as is aforerehersed Also I bequeth unto vj pouer men and vj pouer women free of the crafte of Skynners in London yf any suche may be founde that have nede of myn almesse And for lack of suche then myn executours to take other in their rowmes and they to

[355] This would seem to follow the entry from Bailey (1721) A Torch... a staff of deal on which wax candles are stuck to be lighted on several occasions,

[356] The word is written say here but elsewhere normally sey.

have every each of theym vij^{d} every weke soo they comme to the chapell over the charnelhouse in Poulyschurch yard bitwene ix and x of the clock upon the Sonday and here masse and to pray for my soule and the soules of theym afore rehersed and to be there personally except any of theym be bedered or be syke And I will that Robert Wysbyche fishemonger a pouer man John Barbour citizen and merchant taillour of London and William Somer citizen and blacksmyth of London at the request of Sir Richard Broke knyght be thre of myn almesmen And I will one of myne executours or their executours paye unto theym after masse vij^{d} a peece as is afore rehersed during the terme of x yeres And my mynde and will is that this almes shall contynue by the space of x yeres next after my decesse untill the somme of Clxxxij$^{£}$ x^{s} be clerely gevyn amonges theym And I will that this clause also be made parfite by suche lerned counceill as myn executours or their executours shall appoynt Also I geve and bequeth unto our Lady Company of the said crafte of Skynners in London towardes the reparations of their landes soo that they make myn executours privy wherupon they shall expende it And myn executours to make payment unto theym owt of hande as the reparations be in doing x$^{£}$ Also I bequeth unto Fraunces Poulter the sonne of Richard Poulter Esquier dwelling in the countie of North[an]tes so that he by his sufficient dede release all his right and title which he shall have to the maner of Downe with the appurtenances in the countie of Kent as his fader hath doon bifore him in such wise as it shallbe advised by the counceill lerned of myn executours and to such persones as my said sonne Edwarde Mary and Fraunces my doughters shall name lxvj$^{£}$ xiij^{s} iiij^{d} Also I bequeth unto Elizabeth my wife two of my best saltes with cover my best standing cup gilt with a cover also another standing cup gilt with a cover with chekers in the botom xiiij gilt spones and all hanginges in my house reservyng suche hanginges as hagen in the parlour over the strete with the fore chambers over the strete which said hanginges I will Edward my sonne have and ij fetherbeddes and a matrasse Also I bequeth to Mary my doughter ij gilt saltes with a cover which were Maister Martyns and a doseyn of silver sponys a standing cup with a pellican Also I bequeth unto Dane George my son being a monk in Westminster a salte with sonbemes with a cover and half a doseyn spones knopped with lyons and a gilt cup Also I bequeth unto Edward my sonne two square saltes parcell gilt with a cover and a standing cup gilt with an akorne on the knoppe and a doseyn spones Also I bequeth unto Fraunces my doughter a standing cup with a maydens hede which I will shalbe kept to hir use and yf she fortune to dye I will that it shall goo remayn and be to the said crafte of Skynners And I will that it shalbe in the custodye and keping of the same crafte till she come to laufull age or elles to be maried Also I bequeth unto John Judde gentilman iij$^{£}$ vj^{s} viij^{d} and to his wyfe a ryng of golde price xx^{s} and to either of theym a blak gowne Also I bequeth unto an hundreth pour maidens mariages suche as shalbe appoynted by myn executours xxxiij$^{£}$ vj^{s} viij^{d} that is to sey to every each of theym vj^{s} viij^{d} Also I bequeth to Elizabeth Pyckman my goddoughter xx^{s} Also I bequeth to Alice Showch my goddoughter xx^{s} To Kateryn Okelir my goddoughter xx^{s} Also I bequeth to Hugh Ellys to pray for my soule vj^{s} viij^{d} Also I bequeth unto my pouer godchildren that is to sey to every of them that hath moost nede to the nombr of xx as myn executours shall thinke best vj^{s} viij^{d} Also I bequeth unto every eache of the children of Lewes Harpisfelde late mercer of London decessed when they shall come unto their lawfull age or xxj yeres or be maried xL^{s} Also I bequeth unto John Neve my servaunt to the intent that he shalbe helping to myn executours to gader in my dettes soo that my executours shall paye for his costes and charges and to pray for my soule xx$^{£}$ Also I bequeth unto Richard Waley myn apprentice iiij$^{£}$ To Thomas Potter myn apprentice xxvj^{s} viij^{d} Also to Thomas Flour my servaunt to pray for my soule xxvj^{s} viij^{d} Also I bequeth to John Forster to pray for my soule xxvj^{s} viij^{d} Item I bequeth to Robert Panck bedyll of my warde a blak gowne and to his wife another and in money xL^{s} Also I bequeth unto Jane Middelton my servaunt to pray for my soule x$^{£}$ Also I bequeth unto Elyn Atwyse myn apprentice to be delivered unto hir whan she shalbe maried or laufull age v$^{£}$ Also I bequeth unto Margaret Thorp my servaunt xxvj^{s} viij^{d} Also I bequeth unto my fermour William Coper and unto his wife and to every one of his childern to pray for my soule and all Christen soules vj^{s} viij^{d} Also I bequeth unto William Baily my fermour of Merdiche to his wife and unto every childe that he hath to pray for my soule and to every eache of theym vj^{s} viij^{d} Also I bequeth to Thomas Wrythe to his wife and to every childe that he hath to pray for my soule to every each of theym vj^{s} viij^{d} Also I bequeth unto Sir Richard Kettyll my chapleyn to pray for my soule x$^{£}$ Also I bequeth unto Elizabeth Fryth to pray for my soule vj^{s} viij^{d} Also I bequeth unto Sybill servaunt with John Judde to pray for my soule a full of ketilles[357] price iij^{s} Also I bequeth unto William Pavyour my servaunt to pray for my soule v$^{£}$ Also I bequeth unto Luce Hampshir to pray for my soule a full of ketilles price iij^{s} Item I bequeth unto Anne Taillour to pray for my soule vj^{s} viij^{d} Item I bequeth unto certeyn pour scolers aswel seculers as freres studying in divinitie in the Universitie of Cambrige towarde their exhibition to pray for my soule and all the soules aforsaid to be distributed to and amonges theym by myn executours after their good discretions C marces sterlinges THE residue of all and singuler my goodes plate catalles and dettes whatsoever they be not bequethed after my debtes well and truely paid my funeralles accomplished and this my present testament and last will entierly perfourmed I will shalbe devided in two partes and portions wherof I will the one moytie shalbe truely devided to and amonges the forsaid Edward Mary and Fraunces my childern And the other moytie therof to be dispoased in charitable dedes for the weale of my soule and all the soules above said at the discretions of myn executours And I ordeyn and make Edward Myrfyn my sonne and Andrew Judde my sonne in lawe myn executours And overseers of the same my present testament and last wille I ordeyn and make the right reverende fader in God Cutbert Bisshop of London and Sir Richard Broke knyght And I bequeth unto either of theym for his labour aide and good councill to be gevyn in the execution of this my present testament and last wille twenty poundes sterlinges Item I bequeth unto William Bailye alderman all my clokes and gownes apperteynyng to an alderman Thise being present William Danckaster curat of Saint Antonyne aforsaid William Baily Alderman John Josson Roger Bedill William Hampton Robert Waren Mighell Fitzwilliam Edward Charnok and other at the reding of the premisses Item I bequeth to Richarde Radcliff Skynnor and his wife towarde their sustentation and their eight children Liij^{s} iiij^{d}[358]

[Latin]
PROBATE of this above written testament of the deceased was granted before the aforesaid Commissary in the Cathedral church of Saint Pauls London on the xv day of the month of October in the year of the Lord one thousand five hundred and twenty three upon the oaths of the executors nominated in this testament. And with approval and registration. And administration was committed on the authority of the right reverend father of all and singular the goods rights and credits of the said deceased to the aforesaid executors to well and faithfully administer And to exhibit and full and true inventory before the feast of St. Nicholas the Bishop next coming and also to render a full and accurate account Sworn upon the Holy Gospel of God.

---

[357] *O.E.D.* Full: A set of kettles. Gives as an example 1466 taken from *Manners and household expenses in England in the thirteenth and fifteenth centuries* (Roxb. Club, 1841), 206, My mastyr paid for iij. kettelles calde a fulle, iij^{s} vj^{d}.

[358] The L in the first numeral appears to be for 50 and not simply a flourish before the number.

RECORDS OF THE SKINNERS OF LONDON,
edit. J.J.Lambert, (1933), pp. 144-48

There were Special Watches in the months of June and July on the Vigils of Festival Days and on the Festival Days themselves., in the evenings after sunset. According to Stow's Survey, there were bonfires in the streets and the wealthier people would set out tables on the Vigils, furnished with bread and drink, and on the Festival Days with meat and drink, whereunto they would invite their neighbours and passengers also to sit and be with them in great familiarity, praising God for His benefits bestowed upon them.

1518-19

Paid to 6 bowmen that went in my Lord Mayor's Watch, Mr. Mirfyn, at 6^{d} a piece the night, sum for both the nights	6^{s}
For scouring of their jackets and for drink for them both the nights	8^{d}
Paid to divers armourers dwelling in the City of London and in Southwark for 7 score men and odd in complete harness for my said Lord Mayor's Watch at 2^{s} 8^{d} a harness man for both nights	$18^{£}$-16^{s}
Paid to Seger, armourer, for 40 men in breastplates and 'mores' pikes at 16^{d} a man and for his reward 20^{d}	55^{s}
Paid to Thomas Elewe and to Israell, minstrels, one of them playing on a 'tomsell'[359] and the other of a 'flewet'[360] in the watch of my said Lord Mayor both the nights	4^{s} 8^{d}.
Paid to Hans for playing before the giant and his wife on a 'tomsell' both nights	20^{d}
For a hat for him	16^{d}
For 2 sword players both the nights, John Coke and Richard Coke, 2^{s} 8^{d}; paid to William Andrews and to John Seward, minstrels, for playing on taberettes[361] both the nights, 3^{s} 8^{d}; paid to a gunner for his labour both the nights and for 3 lbs of gunpowder that he spent, 2^{s} 4^{d}	8^{s} 8^{d}
Paid to John Bandy for the hire of 4 horses, 3 saddles and other necessaries and of a man for the Watch the first night	3^{s} 9^{d}
Paid to William Chamberlain for 6 horses for the pageants on St. Peter's even	7^{s} $5½^{d}$
Paid to Sparowe for 2 horses both the nights	16^{d}
Paid to William Thomas, my Lord of Suffolk's Armourer, for 2 horses 2 nights	2^{s}
Paid to the Armourer's servant in Southwark for leading of Tracy's horse the Knight both the nights, 8d; paid to John Hyll for leading of the Sowden's[362] horse both the nights,12d; paid for leading of the 'Jues' (Jewess's) horse and the gaoler's horse, 14^{d}	2^{s} 10^{d}
Paid to Thomas Bakehouse for playing the Martyrdom of St. Thomas with all the properties both the nights	3^{s} 4^{d}
Paid to Richard Stabyll for playing the 'Crosyer' both nights	8^{d}
Paid to Robert Johnson for playing Stracy (Tracy) the Knight both nights and to Robert Hynstok for playing the 'Jues' (Jewess) both the nights	3^{s} 6^{d}
Paid to Richard Ward for bearing the ladder for St. Thomas Pageant both the nights	

---

[359] Possibly for timbrel, *O.E.D.* A musical instrument of percussion; a tambourine or the like that could be held up in the hand.

[360] *O.E.D.* Flute: A musical wind instrument, consisting of a hollow cylinder or pipe, with holes along its length, stopped by the fingers, or by keys which are opened by the fingers. The flute of the ancients, whether single or double, was blown through a mouthpiece at the end.

[361] *O.E.D.* Tabrette obs. form tabret, a small tabor. Tabor: The earlier name of the drum; in later use (esp. since the introduction of the name *drum* in the 16th c.), A small kind of drum, used chiefly as an accompaniment to the pipe or trumpet; a taborin or tabret

[362] Lambert has (query: Soldan's or Sultan's). *O.E.D.* gives Sawden as a variant spelling of Soldan: The supreme ruler of one or other of the great Muslim powers or countries of the Middle Ages; one having the rank of Sultan.

and for cord and nails to amend the pageant by the way	10^{d}
Paid to Richard Mathewe for playing Gilberd Beckett and for his clerk both the nights	18^{d}
Paid to William Dayly for playing the gaoler both the nights	12^{d}
Paid to 6 men to bear the pageant prison for Gilbert Beckett both the nights	$7^{s}\ 4^{d}$
Paid to the Wardens of St. Giles for hiring of a pageant for the Martyrdom of St.Thomas and for having home again of the same pageant	7^{s}
Paid to the Wardens of Barking for hiring of a pageant for Our Lady and St. Elizabeth.	10^{s}
Paid to 2 maidens that were in the pageant of Our Lady and St.Elizabeth.	4^{d}
Paid to John Pycard and to Thomas Oliff, Minstrels, playing in the pageant of Our Lady and St. Elizabeth.	8^{d}
Paid to 10 boys that played the morens[363] at 2^{d} the piece	20^{d}
Paid to Halle, carpenter for making of Beckett's prison and for mending of 2 other pageants, the workmanship, board and lath, $6^{s}\ 6^{d}$; and to Mabson a day and a half, 10^{d}; and to Mr, Hanchett for board, 2^{s}	$9^{s}\ 6^{d}$
Paid for carrying a pageant from Paul's wharf unto the Prince's wardrobe	8^{d}
Paid to John Mayne for playing the sowden before the Martrydom of St. Thomas	16^{d}
Paid to William Dayly for keeping of the Pageants of St. Peter's night after the watch and for hiring of a mitre	14^{d}
Paid to Thomas Smythe's wife, the Skinner, for a brooch that was taken from her child's cap	6^{d}
Paid to Ryley for waiting on the Maundy pageant both the nights	8^{d}
Paid to a porter for keeping of the gates of the Prince's Wardrobe both the nights	8^{d}
Paid to Thomas Nelson for 12 men to bear the Maundy pageant both the nights and for drink for them by the way	$10^{s}\ 6^{d}$
Paid to 13 children playing God Almighty and His 12 Apostles, at 2 pence the piece	$2^{s}\ 2^{d}$
Paid for drink for them and singing bread	4^{d}
Paid for 13 beards and 13 diadems hired for God Almighty and the 12 Apostles	2^{s}
Paid to William Colte for Pryketts torches and tapers of wax to burn in the pageants both of St. Thomas and the Maundy for both nights	$3^{s}\ 8^{d}$
Paid to John Meret for making of scriptures about the Maundy and of other pageants	6^{d}
Paid for carrying home of a Pageant from Baynard's Castle	2^{s}
Paid to the Keeper of the Prince's Wardrobe for license to have our Pageants made there and to stand there and to be kept there after the Watch was done, $5^{s}\ 8^{d}$. Spent there in bread, ale, and candles at divers times 20^{d}	$7^{s}\ 4^{d}$

---

[363] Lambert has put query: moren, as meaning moor or negro. However, it seems more likely that this is in the form of Moorish - **morisco**, *O.E.D.* A morris dance.

PREROGATIVE COURT OF CANTERBURY WILL REGISTER ON MICROFILM. PROB 11/22 QUIRE 31 FOLIO 246.

IN THE NAME OF GOD AMEN This is the last will of me Edward Myrfyn Citizen and Skynner of London made the thirde day of Marche in the nynetenth yere of the reigne of our soveraigne Lord King Henry the eight And in the yere of our Lord god 1527 concernyng the disposition of my body and of all my londes and goodes whatsoever they be Inprimis I bequeth my soule unto Almighty God and my body to be buried at the charnel house in Powlys churchyarde where as the bodyes of Thomas and Alice my father and mother lyeth buried And I bequeth to the sustentation and repairyng of the said Chapell $8^{\pounds}$ Item I bequeth to the prest that hath the custodye of the said chapell 10^{s} Item I bequeth to the high awter of our parishe churche of Saint Andrewe Undreshafte for my oblations and tithes forgotten 10^{s} And in like wise to the high awter of Hornechurch for my tithes forgotten 20^{s} whiche parishe is in Haveryng in Essex Item I bequeth to the bilding of the churche of the said Saint Andrew Undreshafte $6^{\pounds}$ 13^{s} 4^{d} Item I forgeve John Neve of suche dett as he owith me 40^{s} Item I bequeth to John Marshall my servaunt 20^{s} Item I bequeth to every oon of the other of my servaunts that are in house with me at the houre of my death 10^{s} a pece Item I bequeth unto Alice Brygandyn my wifes doughter toward hir mariage she lyving to hir laufull age to be maried $20^{\pounds}$ And I bequeth to Agnes another of my said wifes doughters towarde hir mariage $6^{\pounds}$ 13^{s} 4^{d} And I bequethe to John Brygandyn her sonne 5 marces Item I forgeve Pargyter and his wife all suche dett as they owe me which is 33^{s} 4^{d} and further I geve to either of theym a blak gowne And I bequeth unto their childe yf he be lyving at the tyme of my deth fyve markes Item I bequeth to Richard Southwoode my two gownes furred with conye and boge and a bedde with all thinges belonging to it and a hanging of a chamber after the discretion of my wife and in money fyve markes Item I will that to suche persones as I was most famylier withall which my wife knoweth that every oon of them have a rynge for remembraunce of the value of 10^{s} Item I will that Alice my wife have all my manour of Burtyns with the appurtenaunces in the towne of Freknam in the countie of Suffolk during hir lyfe naturall and after hir deceas to remayn to the childe that she nowe goith withall and to his heires in fee symple in case the said childe be than lyving and in case that the childe wherwith she nowe goith prosper not but myscarieth or contynueth not lyfe till it commyth to laufull age or to be maried Then I will that Alice Brygandyn my wifes doughter have it for terme of hir lyfe And after her deceas to remayn to the right heires of me Edward Myrfyn Item I bequeth to Andrewe Judde my brother in lawe my gowne furred with foynes and in money fyve marces And to my suster his wife a ryng of the value of 40^{s} Item I geve to Richard Bury my jaket of blak velwet All the residue of my goodes my dettes and buriall paide I will shalbe equally devided in two partes whereof I geve the oon parte to Alice my wife and the other parte to the childe that she goyth withall which parte I will that my wife have in her custodye till the childe comme to full age she putting in for the hool parte good suertie afore the maier and his brethern And in case that she refuse it then Andrewe Judde and Richard Sper to have it putting in like suerties as aforesaid afore the maier And in caas the said childe dye afore he come to laufull age then my executour after folowing to have the said parte and portion which to be bestowed in dedes of charitie for the welthe of my soule and all Christian soules at the discretion of my said executrix And of this my last will and testament I ordeyn and make my wife sool executrix And overseers of the same Andrewe Judde my brother in lawe and Richard Bury gentilman In witnesse whereof I the said Edward have written this wille with my owne hande and subscribed my name the day and yere first abovesaid Witnesses to prove this will to be true

By me Robert West. clerk, by me Richard Cradock, by me Robert Nyssam. By me Edward Myrfyn in my proper hand

PROBATE of this above written testament of the deceased was granted before the Commissary in the Cathedral Church of St. Paul London on the 11th day of the month of May in the year of the lord one thousand five hundred and twenty eight on the oath of the relict and executrix named in this testament in the person of Master Anthony Husee proctor in this part And having been approved and those things contained therein and so forth And administration was committed as aforesaid by the Reverend Father of all and singular the goods rights and credits of the said deceased to the aforesaid executrix in the person of the said proctor to well and faithfully administer the same And to exhibit a full and faithful inventory the second day after the feast of the Holy Trinity next coming together with a complete and true account. And was sworn on the holy evangelists in the due form of law.

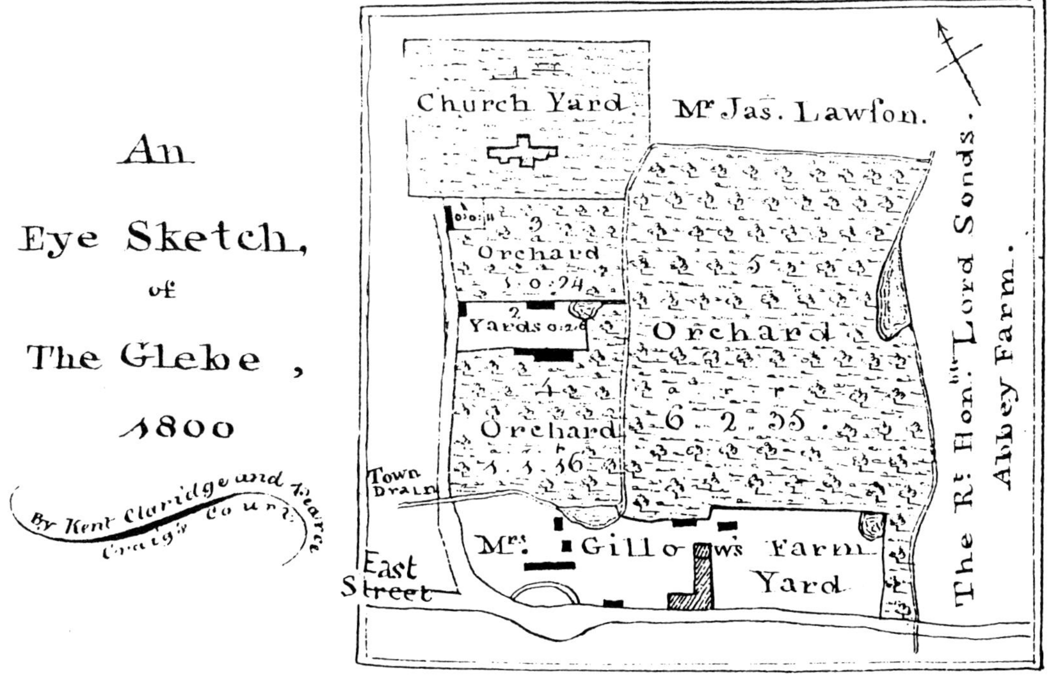

An eye sketch of Faversham Glebe 1800: CCA U63/70388

APPENDIX 7: THE HOTHFIELD DISPUTE

The Letters and Papers Foreign and Domestic of the reign of Henry VIII. Addenda Volume 1 part 2 (1932)

1514 Kent. R.O. S.P.Henry VIII, 243 f 249

File of evidences accompanying a petition to Sir Thomas Cheyney, warden of the Cinque Ports, by Walter Morleyn, who complains of a conspiracy of Mr Thomas Arden, steward of the court of Cheyne's manor of Hottefeylde, and Nicholas Sole, farmer of the said manor, with Thomas White, clerk or scribe of the commissary's court at Canterbury, to get from him his lands in Benynden, Kent. Ardern says that after the death of his father, Richard Morleyn, complainant offered to sell the lands to Sir Thomas Cheyney or to Mr Pulested for the late lord Cromwell. At sessions at Canterbury on Tuesday before Michaelmas 33 Henry VIII[364] [1541] Walter Morleyn was, as a common brawler, barrator and disturber of the peace, bound over to keep the peace. He complains also of wrongs done him by several other persons. Pp 19.

PRO: SP1/243 PART 3
folio 249 [marked Bundle 10 No. 231.[365]]

Artycles on the behalfe of Walter Marleyn of Benenden in the county of Kent

Inprimis one Richarde Mapesden of Rownden in the countie of Kente aboute three yeres nowe past forcibly toke from the said Walter out of his pasture 4 oxen and a complete weyn and a lode of woode

Item Elinour Morleyn of Rownden aforsaid widow hath taken from the said Walter in goodes and money to the value of 15$^{£}$ and above

Item Gervys Mapesden the elder of Rownden aforsaid aboute 2 yeres paste toke from the said Walter 2 keyn without any delyvere thereof, whiche Gervys might have receyved them at the pricemente of honest men

Item Richard Morleyn the elder and Thomas Big of Benenden aforsaid toke from the said Walter aboute three yeres paste 2 kien and a stere without any delyvere therof which they have solde and also cutt out their eire[366] markes for that the said Walter shulde not knowe them

Item one John Goldeforde of Benenden aforsaid gentleman is the supporter of all the said malifactors in their yvell dedes ageinst the said Walter

Item the said John Guldeforde sente for the said Walter to agree with the said Elinour and to geve her some portion in money or els he shulde not prove his fathers will at Hatefeld and for that the said Walter wolde not agree so to doo by reason of the said John Guldeford he coulde not prove his fathers will there

Item one William Allen of Benenden aforsaid hathe of the delyvere of the said Walter catall to the value of 8$^{£}$ for the whiche he hath paide but 7s 6^{d} who by supportation of the said John Guldeforde will pay no more money for the same

---

364 Further work, fol. 263, has now shown that this item in the State Papers relates to the Quarter Sessions held at Canterbury. Unfortunately nothing survives for this date.

365 This is No 1 and there are 12 items in all in the bundle.

366 For 'ear'.

folio 249 verso

Item one William Big and Laurence Daie of Benenden aforsaid have taken certen wood in the ground of the said Walter and solde it to their owne use

Item the said John Guldforde let to the said Walter his owne house and landes in the parishe of Benenden and yet nevertheles the said Elinour kepte the key of a cheife chamber thereof and locked the dore by reason whereof the said Walter loste muche goodes which were destroyed for defaute of dressinge[367]

Item furdermore the said Richarde Mapesden dwelling in the parish of Rownden whereas he did come to the feare[368] [blank] when I had solde my catall unto other men before he came and seased the cattell the which I had solde and by reason of that I coulde not gette my money, nor I have it not as yet

Here is to sertifie your honorable lordship that these be the pryncypall men with many moe that hath taken my goodes wrongfully contrary to our soveraigne lorde the kinges lawes ageinst all right and good consciens

folio 250 [369]

Interrogatoryes on the parte of Walter Morlen to be mynistred against Thomas Arden, Nicholas Sole decessid, [blank] Whyte and [blank] Guildford Esquier

Inprimis whyther thys deponent knoweth Thomas Arden Nycholas Sole while he lyved [blank] White and John Guldeford Esquier Walter Morlen of Benenden yn the county of Kent husbandman or any of them or not and howe longe hath he knowen them[370]

Item Whyther that after the dethe of Richard Morlen father to the said Walter Morlen ~~the same Walter Morlen muche~~ any contencyon arrose betwen the same Walter and his younger brethern for and concerning ~~certen~~ any londes or tenementes gyven ~~amonge theym~~ by the last wyll of the said Richard Morlen or not or ells for what cause varyance was had betwene theym or any of theym as nygh as ye can yn your consyence by commen reporte or otherwyse

Item[371] whyther the seyd Walter Morlen was seysed and yn possessyon of thre meases[372] and an half and 300 acres of lande and wood yn hys demeane as of fee yn Benenden Bedynden[373] Rovenden and Canturbury yn the county of Kent by reporte or otherwyse or not And what ys the clere yerely value of the [said][374] meases landes and tenementes with the appurtenances as farre as ye knowe or suppose yn your consyence

Item whether the said Walter Morlen lawfully proved his fathers will and testament in the Archebisshop of Canterburies Courte at London and after was put to trowble threfore before the Commyssarie of the said Archebisshop at Canterbury in the said countie of Kent or not

---

[367] *O.E.D.* Dress (1) To make straight or right; to bring into proper order; to array, make ready, prepare, tend. (12) To take away or remove anything in the process of preparing, purifying or cleansing.

[368] Fair.

[369] This is a very complex manuscript with heavy erasures and a considerable number of interlinear corrections and these themselves have interlinear corrections and passages.

[370] This last word unclear.

[371] Interlined in spaces between following entries causing confusion..

[372] For messuages.

[373] For Biddenden.

[374] Unclear word.

Item whether the seid Thomas Arden and Nycholas Sole untruely confederid themselffes togyther to deceyve the said Walter Morlen being no worldely wiseman and compossed the matter so amonge theym that they falsely and untruely so wolde bere the said Walter Morlen yn hande that he was yn daunger of a premunere[375] and that he sholde loose and forfaite his landes and goodes to the Kinges Highnes and his body to pryson bycause he proved not his fathers will before the said Commissarye of the seyd Archebyshop of Canturbury at Canturbury aforesayd or not

Item[376] whyther the said Thomas Arden and Nycholas Sole after a fayer flatteryng and disstyarmlyng[377] facion ~~a disambling fasshyon~~ promising faithfully to the said Morlen to be ~~his~~ speciall frendes to him advysed and sent the same Morlen to the seid Thomas White clerk and Officer in the seid Commissaries Courte of Canterbury for councell to save him out of the daunger of the sayd premunire or not And wyther the seyd Whyte was of cownsyll with the seyd Arden and Sole yn reherseyd matter or not

Item whether the said Thomas Arden and Nycholas Sole had before procured the said Thomas Whyte to affyrme and verifye that the said Walter Morlen was in daunger of a premunire bycause he proved not his fathers wyll in the said commissaries [courte] of Canturburie or and how ye knowe the same of your owne knowledge report or

folio 251
otherwyse

Item whether the said Thomas Arden and ~~Sole advy~~ Nycholas Sole advysed and councelled the said Morlen for the saffegard of all hys said land and goodes to put the sayd Arden and Sole ~~his landes said to putt them~~ in trust and to make unto them suche wrytinges as they shuld devise ~~for h~~ and for that no colour[378] shuld appere therin advysed ~~councelled~~ the said Morlen to saye yf ~~Master Guldeford~~ John Guldeford Esquier or any other shold ask of him whether the seyd Walter Morlen ~~he~~ had solde his londes to the said Arden and Sole to saye yes or els ~~the truste he putt them in could not take place And we shall And whether the same Arden and Sole lent to the said Morlen 5£ to agree with Master White for the discharge of the said Premunere ye or no~~ the said Arden and Sole cowlde doo the sayd Walter Morlen no good yn hys sayd matter or not or elles what other communication had the sayd Arden and Sole with the sayd Walter Morlen touchyng the sayd premisses

Item whyther the sayd Walter Morlen after the tyme that he had sayed that he put hys hole trust yn the sayd Arden and Sole the sayd Arden and Sole delyvered unto the sayd Walter Morlen 5£ sterlinges or any other other somme of money to agre with the sayd [blank] Whyte for the discharge of the seyd premunire or not

Item whether the said Thomas Arden and Nycholas Sole have ~~reported~~ confessid and sayed that the said Walter Morlen shall have his landes ageyn when he was discharged of the said premunire paying ageyn to ~~them~~ the sayd Arden and Sole the said 5£ and the charges of the wrytinges [ye or no] to be made by the sayd Arden and Sole yn that byhalf or not

---

375 *O.E.D.* Praemunire: A writ by which the sheriff is charged to summon a person accused, originally, of prosecuting in a foreign court a suit cognizable by the law of England, and later, of asserting or maintaining papal jurisdiction in England, thus denying the ecclesiastical supremacy of the sovereign.

376 Just above this is a diamond with the number 250; the number of the fol. in the bundle. fols. 250 and 251 are sewn together at the bottom of 250.

377 Interlined and confused.

378 *O.E.D.* (11) Outward appearance, show, aspect, semblance; generally that which serves to cloak or conceal the truth, or to give a show of justice to what is in itself unjustifiable.

Item whether the said Whyte ~~dyd undertake~~ by the procurement of Arden and Sole affirmed and verifyed to the said Walter Morlen that he was in a premunere that he the sayd Whyte for the somme of $4^{£}$ whereof was payed in hand 26^{s} 8^{d} the said White fully coventyd promysed graunted and agreed ~~agred~~ with the sayde Walter Morlen ~~to discharge hym out~~ that the sayd [blank] Whyte shulde clerely discharge the sayd Walter Morlen of the said premunire ~~ye~~ or not

Item whyther the sayd [blank] Whyte and John Guldeforde or any of them ~~or not~~ at any tyme were of cownsayll or confenderyd with the sayd Arden and Sole to deceyve the sayd Walter Morlen of hys said landes and tenementes or not

Item whether the said Whyte in Easter terme in the 32nd yere of the kinges reign that nowe is or elles at any other tyme dyd offer to paye ageyn to the said Morlen the said 26^{s} 8^{d} in the feast of Pentecost then next ensuing and confessid ~~he~~ that he had receyved the same 26^{s} 8^{d} in parte of payment of $4^{£}$ by the procurement of Arden and Sole to discharge the said Morlen out of a premunire And that the sayd Whyte was promysed by the said Arden and Sole or any of them at any tyme to ~~whiche they procured the said White to make Morlen byleve the same to be true ye or no~~ make the sayd Walter Morlen beleve that he was yn danger of a premunire for the sayd cause or any other cause or not or elles as nygh as ye can declare what the sayd Whyte reportyd concernyng the sayd matter

Item whether the said Arden in Easter Terme last past or any other tyme ~~reported~~ confessid and said that the same Walter Morlen was in a premunire and had ~~byn~~ undone but for him And had Walter Morlen bounde in One hundred markes for the assuraunce of his landes and ~~had~~ that a fyne was knowleged of the sayd landes which was to suer for the sayd Walter Morlen to undoe ageyn or discharge the same ~~Morlen to sue or meddyll farther therin~~ or not or elles what other communication had the sayd Whyte at that tyme or any other tyme touchyng the sayd matter as nygh as ye can or suppose yn your conscyence

folio 251 verso

Item whether the said Arden and Sole have bargayned and sold the sayd londes of Walter Morlen to John Guldeford ye[a] or not and by whose motion or procurement the sale so done

Item what money or other thynges have the sayd Arden or Sole or any of theym payed for the sayd landes and tenementes of the sayd Walter Morlen and what dayes of payment the sayd Arden and Morlen have for payment of the same

Item whether the said Sole in his lyffe confessed that he had for his rewarde of the said John Guldeford for the procuring of the sayd bargayn and sale of the said landes of the sayd Walter Morlen ~~the sayd landes~~ $20^{£}$ And that Arden for his rewarde had of the said Master Guldeford other $20^{£}$ for the same procurement of the said bargain and sale of the sayd landes

Item what hath the sayd John Guldeforde payed for the sayd landes and tenements of the sayd Walter Morlen and howe the same shalbe payed

Item whether the sayd John Guldeford hath at any tyme confessed that he hath lyke dayes of payment of the sayd Arden and Sole for payment of suche money as shalbe payed unto them for the sayd landes and tenementes of the sayd Walter Morlen as the sayd Arden and Sole had craftely gotten of the sayd Walter Morlen by suche wrytinges as the sayd Arden and Sole had untruely caused to be made and devysed for there assurance in the sayd landes and tenementes And further the sayd John Guldeford sayd that he wolde not gyve hys dayes and respyte of payement that he had of the sayd Arden and Sole for the seyd landes and tenements for

Item whether the said Sole at a courte holden at the house of the same Sole yn the lordshipp of Hotfeld by the said Arden beinge then ~~steward~~ understeward unto Sir Thomas Cheyne knight high steward there as lord of the said manor the said Sole declared and sayed to the sayd Arden under steward that all the countrey spake evill of them for the deceyving of the said Morlen of hys sayd landes and whether the same Arden then answered and sayde holde they peace fole I wold we had suche an other bargeyn in hand for all their ~~speche~~ sayings let them say what they wyll or not or elles what other wordes or communication was the oration otherwise made by the sayd Arden, Sole, Whyte, Guldeforde or any of them concerning the premysses or any of the premysses

Item whether the said Mr Guldeford confessid and sayd I have Morlen bounden for further assuraunce of the said londes in 200 markes and ~~shewed forthe the same obligation and sayde if Morlen will not knowledge a fyne I will undo him in 2 termes~~ and by the power of the sale of the sayd landes by Arden and Sole to me by Morlen and whyther then and there or elles at any other tyme the sayd John Guldeford shewyd forth any obligation or other wrytinges of the sayd Walter Morlen saying further then yf the sayd Walter Morlen and his wyffe wolde not levy a fyne of the sayd landes and tenementes with the appurtenances unto the sayd John Guyldeford for the further assuraunce of the same Then the sayd John Guldeforde wolde undo the sayd Walter Morlen within two termes and sayd make the lest frendes he can or elles what other wordes or communications had the sayd Guldeforde the sayd tyme or any other tyme for the sayd matter as ye suppose yn your conscyence

Item whyther the said maister Guldeford confessid and sayed that the daies of payment for the said londes whiche he had of Arden and Sole for the payment therof were worthe to hym 20 markes

Item wyther ye beleve yn your conscyence that the sayd Walter Morlen hath bene or ys falsely deceyved of his landes and tenementes with the appurtenaunces ageynst ryght and conscyence or not and what ys the common reporte and saying of the sayd country touchyng the sayd matter

folio 252 Latin
margin partly lost [pr]omotion by Morlyn [..]rleyn

Upon the allegation and testament aforesaid

EDWARD LEEDE of Benynden in the county of Kent servant of John Guldeforde Esquire originated in Benynden aforesaid and has lived there since the time of his birth aged 59 years of free condition a witness produced etc. of and upon the testament and allegation aforesaid Upon this testament and allegation he is examined and says upon the strength of his oath taken

That the day and yere in the testamente exhibite conteyned this deponent at the desyre of the saide Rycharde Morleyn writte and made his testamente in the howse of John Kyte of Benynden aforesaide And after the fynnyshyng of the same testamente this deponente redd yt before the saide Rycharde Morleyn in the saide John Kytes house At the writing and reading whereof there was no persone present but the saide Richarde Morleyn and this deponente And after reading therof this deponente advertysed hym to call certaine men to beare witness of yt And the saide Rycharde Morleyn saied that there but few men that he did muche meddle[379] with all Wherefore he saied that he woulde take yt with hym home and have yt redd amonge his frendes And so this deponent departed from the saide Rycharde Morleyn leving his testament with hym And this deponent saieth that aboute halfe a yere before the deathe of the saide Richarde Morleyn oone

[379] *O.E.D.* Meddle (8) .. to deal with.

Roberte Everden shewed this deponente how that he had seene and redd the testamente of Richarde Morleyn and within 8 daies after the deathe of the saide Richarde Morleyn executors named in the testamente of the saide Rycharde brought unto this deponente the testamente of the saide Richarde his father whiche testamente after this deponent had redd it and saw that there was nothing added nor mynysshed from yt, but as it was, whan this deponente did write and reade yt Wrote theise wourds

[this does not seem to follow on to the next. As this was pasted up on to a new sheet of paper the folios could easily have been reversed.]

folio 252 verso
Theis wittness Edwarde Leade Robert Everden an[d ...] in the ende of the saide testamente And he saieth that the originall testamente exhibite remayning in the registry unto hym shewed the tyme of his examination is of the proper hande of this deponente And the saide testamente which this deponente did write and rede as afore he hath deposed

[latin] And otherwise he does not know how to depose of and upon anything contained in the allegation aforesaid And he says that he is not taught, instructed nor informed about anything or in what manner to give evidence in his parte And he says that he has no consanguinity nor affinity with the parties to the suit nor the producent[380]

WILLIAM ALEYN of Benynden in the diocese of Canterbury husbandman where he has lived for 16 years, aged 62 years of free condition a witnessed produced etc of and upon the the allegation and testament aforesaid he says in the strength of his oath by him professed

That aboute a yere before the deathe of Walter Morleyn who deceased aboute Christemas last past was 12 monethes This deponente hearing that the saide Richarde Morleyn was very seeke And for because he had maryed oone of his dowghters came to see how that he did And there he fownde Richarde Mapstede who was but newly then come for the saide Richarde sayed that he was glad of his commynge and saied that he shulde here his testamente redd whiche he requyred his wyfe to sett downe whiche she so did And then the saide Richarde Mapstede at the desier of the saide Richarde Morleyn redde his testamente concerning his

[There are obviously missing pages to this depositon and allegation. It now seems possible that this may have been the Prerogative Court of Canterbury. However, there are no deposition registers surviving for this date.]

folio 253
Thes be the parcells the which my ~~father~~ mother yn lawe hathe recevyd at certeyne tymes of me
Walter Morleyn yn money and moneye worthe

In the first instance payde unto her yn the churche of
Benenden the same daye my father decessyd 3^{s} 4^{d}
Item she had of me 2 yardes and 3 quarters of whyte
clothe to make her a gowne 10^{s} 3^{d}
Item I proferred fyrsste a marke but she wolde not
receve yt but after she recevyd the moneye 13^{s} 4^{d}
Item she recevyd of Peter Evernden a marke which was

380 *O.E.D.* Producent: One who or that which produces; a producer; the party producing a witness or document under the old system of the Ecclesiastical courts.

dewe to my father $13^{s}\ 4^{d}$

Item she hadde of me at the monethese daye 2^{s}

Item she recevyd of John Bocher by the handes of Rycharde Mapesden 8^{s}

Item I delyvered her 2 kyen and she toke the profyte of them but I wyntered them and kepte and I dyd my owne (sic) and she solde the calfe of one them for $6^{s}\ 8^{d}$ and the other calfe 5^{s}, $11^{s}\ 8^{d}$

Item I dyd fynde her and her servaunte mete and drynke by the space of 5 quarters at 2^{s} every weke there bourde in the hole $7^{£}\ 10^{s}$

Item I dyd fynd her 2 sonnes mete and dryncke by the space of twelmonethe and moore at 10^{d} every weke total $41^{s}\ 10^{d}$

Item she hathe yn her custodye the chefe of all the howshold and a new pece of clothe and what she hath solde and conveyd awaye I can not tell for she doth troble me wrongfullye for I was all waye redye to paye her dewtye accordyng to my father wyll and testament therfore I besseche you accordyng to your promes to have my coostes and charges for I am able to prove my sayeng trewe

Sum total $15^{£}\ 13^{s}\ 9^{d}$ ~~$12^{£}\ 13^{s}\ 9^{d}$~~

folio 253 verso is blank

folio 254

Theyse bene the parcelles whiche my mother in lawe hathe receyved of me Walter Morleyn in monye and money worthe as herafter ensuythe, that is to say,

In the first instance paide unto her in the chirche of Benenden the same day my father deceased $3^{s}\ 4^{d}$

Item she hadde of me 2 yerdes and 3 quarters of whyte clothe to make her a gowne $10^{s}\ 4^{d}$

Item I proferryd her firste a marke but she wulde not receyve it but after she receyvid the money $13^{s}\ 4^{d}$

Item she receyvid of Petyr Everden a marke whiche money was dwe to my father $13^{s}\ 4^{d}$

Item she hadde of me at the monethes daye 2^{s}

Item she receyved of John Bocher by the handes of Richarde Mapysden 8^{s}

Item she receyvid of me 2 kyen prise 40^{s}

Item she receyvid of me 2 calves price of the oone calfe $6^{s}\ 8^{d}$ and the other calfe price 5^{s}, $11^{s}\ 8^{d}$

Item I did fynde the seid kyen wynteryng price 20^{s}

Item I did fynde her and her servaunte meate and drynke by the space of oone hole yere and a quarter at 2^{s} every weke ther bourde by all the seide tyme summe in the hole $7^{£}\ 10^{s}$

Item for the mylke of 2 kene by the space of 2 sommers after $2^{s}\ 8^{d}$ a cowe every yere summe $11^{s}\ 4^{d}$

Item delyvered her 2 busshelles of meale price 2^{s}

Item delyvered her 2 busshelles of oten malte 12^{d}
Item for lambe and veale delyvered unto her 2^{s}

folio 254 verso
Item I did fynde her 2 sonnes by the space of oone hole yere and more at 10^{d} every weke for the bourde of them bothe summe 41^{s} 10^{d}

summe to that she hathe $15^{£}$ 13^{s} 9d

Item she hathe in her custodye the chiefe of all the howsehold stuffe as brasse pewter beddyng and other movable goodes as yet not praysed with a newe piece of clothe And what she hathe solde and wastyd therof as yet I knowe not

Item I was redy at all tymes to delyver the stuffe and paye her dutye accordinge to my fathers will and testamente

folio 255

The following all scored through is almost illegible.

he was at the ...... stuffe was Rychard Marlens

Thomas Bygge, John

?first ... panne .....]

This line not crossed through:

the prys of all the stuffe that sche left ther $3^{£}$ 11^{s}

folio 255 verso blank

folio 256

In the first instance Master Guldeford aboute Whitsontyde last past distreyned the catall of Walter Morleyn for foure nobles rente of his the tenement of the said Walter whiche catall the said Master Guldeford as yet reteynith ~~them~~ and some of them hathe famyshed and ~~deade~~ are deade

the said Master Guldeford at lente before the distresses taken wolde have forgeven the said Walter Morleyn the said foure nobles rente to avoide the possession of the said tenement in the presence of Thomas Beolde of Bedynden William Allyn of Benynden and Robert Evernden of Benenden in the county of Kente

Item the said Walter Morleyn by the adwyse of his councell ~~after~~ within a quarter of a yere ~~of a yere~~ ensuyng the compounding and destyreynyng of his said catall proferred the said Master Guldeford the said 4 nobles saiyng by thise woordes Sir if it be yours here I pay it youe and upon condition that if it the lawe will adiudge me it agayn youe to repay the same Wherupon he wolde not receyve the same saiyng he had suche a pledge all redy and therupon the said Walter saide Sir if the money be due unto youe ye may receyve it and kepe it styll without any repayment of the same

Item the said Master Guldeford at Michaelmas last distreyned and compounded the said Walters cattall for 8 nobles whereupon the said Walter not onely tendered the same to the said Master Guldford as is aforsaid but also to one Master Henry Clerke keper of the pounde which money so tendred they refused and the said distresse yet detenith

Item the said Master Guldeford at the servyng of the sub pena upon hym demaunded of the said Walter why he did not replevy[381] his catall wherupon he said his councell advysed hym otherwise which Master Guldford then saide in the presence of John Hubbard that the councelles ~~of the said~~ eares of the said Walter Morleyn were worthy to be nayled unto the pilary

folio 256 verso

Item the said Master Guldeford on Fryday sennyght or Thursday sennyght last past caused Robert Evernden son of Richard Evernden and William Asshton weyver to enter into the house of the said Walter he being absent who there by the procurement of the said Master Guldeford penned up the said Walters wife his children and servauntes into a back rome of the said house so that they colde not gett out to fier nore[382] for sustenaunce untill the wife of the said Walter by chaunce founde an ax lying in the place where they were shit up wherwith she brake up a dore and so get out or els they had bene like to be famysshed

Item the said Master Guldeford at the delyveree of estate of the premisses to hym by Arden and Sole wolde have bought certen obligations of the said Walter wherin the said Arden and Sole stode bounden to the said Walter for payment of certen money which Master Guldeford then saide if any man make compleynte against me I shall lay a warraunte of good abering in his neke

Item the said Walter Morleyn on Sonday was sennyght last past chaunced home to his house and there found one Thomas Burton and John Marden keping possession thereof by the procurement of the said Master Guldeford who the said Walter then expulsed

Item the said Master Guldeford hathe solde all the premysses and his right therin in fee to one William Bygge of Benynden aforsaid

folio 257 blank folio 257v blank

folio 258

Walter Morlen plaintiff in the form of a pauper[383]

Saithe in his bill of compleinte that he being seased of certen landes in Canterbury and other tounes within the countie of Kente of the clere yerlye value of 10£ over all charges one Nicolas Sole since decessed (who had maried Margarett the syster of the said compleyante allthowg it be nott so expressed in the bill) and Thomas Arderne and Thomas White otherwise cauled Percye conspyred for the opteynyg of the premisses for the compleyante that the said White, beinge clerke in the commissarie courte att Canterburye shulde beare the plaintiff[384] in hande that the plaintiff for that he hadd nott proved the will of Richard the father of the plaintiff whose executor

[381] *O.E.D.* Replevy: a writ of Replevin: The restoration to, or recovery by, a person of goods or chattels distrained or taken from him, upon his giving security to have the matter tried in a court of justice and to return the goods if the case is decided against him.

[382] 'could not get out to make a fire or gain sustenance'

[383] This section is really very badly written and extremely difficult to decipher. 'in forma pauperis'

[384] This word and the others that follow have simply been abbrevbiated to plz

the plaintiff was shulde be indanger of the premunire whiche evill devise the said White executed and dyde accordingly wher upon the plaintiff came to the said Arderne and Sole as to his frendes for counsell and they perswaded the plaintiff for the safegard of the premisses to make suche assurance to them of the premysses as they shulde devise promysinge that upon the premunire discharged that the plaintiff shulde be suer of his said landes agene and the plaintiff upon this confidence sealed and made suche evidences and devises as the said Sole and Arderne dyd profer to the plaintiff

folio 258v

and the said Sole and Arderne with verye faire wordes delivered to the plaintiff ?5£ to agre with the said White frome the danger of the said premunire who made itt very towghe and never the les toke att the last ~~foure~~ 26s 8d in consideration ~~?afors~~ of the said discharge wherof he saithe sy[thence] restored 20s butt the said Sole and Arderne have al[low]ed the said landes to Sir John Gillforde of Benenden in Kente who kepithe the premysses and evidence from the plaintiff and takyne 20 hedd of cattell of the plaintiff pastureinge upon the premisses and haithe impounded them to the dethe of 8 of them deteynge all the resydue fore a fine and raisone of the poundage and so prayeth a subpena ageinste the said Gillford Ardene and White

Thomas Ardernes Answer

The said defendant saithe in effect that the compleynante came to the saide Nicolas Sole beinge his brother in the law and requryed hym that he wooolde hym to sell his lande sayinge that he paste[385] nott greately to kyll hym sellfe beinge so evill handed with his neighbors wher upon Sole moved this matter of sale or purchase to this defendant and this defendant moved the same to Sir Thomas Cheyneye and upon his refusell and further advice the said defendant moved the said matter of purchase to Master Poulested to the use of the late lord

folio 259

Cromewell and upon the refusell of the said Poulested the said defendant and Sole boughte the said landes butt they show nott whatt they payd for itt and further they saye that by raison they have that other nott namyng who shulde have titill 4 partes of the said landes therfor to eschue greate losse they solde itt to the saide Sir John Gillforde and so traverse all the pointes of the bill

The answer of Thomas White

Ys that the compleynante came to the said defendant beinge scribe att Canterbury and desyered to know the proces before the officiall concerninge insinuatione of the testamente of one Richard Morlye and also that the said proces myghte be transmitted to the prerogative courte of the Archebisshoppe with all the witnesses and sayyng there in and that the said defendant made answer that the said compleynante shulde be in danger of the premunire havinge no forme of appell in the said courte of the said official never the lesse the said defendant confessyythe after in his said answer that att the request of the said Arderne and Sole the defendant dyd agree with the plaintiff for the transmittyng of the said proces and that he tooke of the said plaintiff 26s 8d for the said transmittyng and to reteyne for the plaintiff a doctor and a proctor and traversythe the forme and matter of the bill that the defendant dydd sede for the plaintiff and said that the

[385] *O.E.D.* Past (4c) beyond in manner (mental state)

plaintiff was in danger of the premunire for nott provinge the will of Richard Morlye or that there was covye[386] betwene the defendant and the said Arderne and Sole and so thorowgh oute the bill

folio 259 verso blank, folio 260 and 260v, 261 and 261v are also blank

folio 262[387]

Master Ardern steward of Hottefeylde Corte servaunt unto Sir Thomas Chayne Nycholas Sole of Hottefeylde fermour unto Sir Thomas Chayney where that the said Master Arden and Nycholas Sole by their fraude and deceipte dyd deceyve Walter Morlen of Benynden by their craftynes from hys right and tytle of his landes That where the said Arden and Nycolas Sole dyd provoke the said Walter for to make sale of his landes lying in Benynden or els where unto them promysing hym that they wolde stay his landes and to make it in assuraunce for hym and that he shulde have them afterward again of them paying they their costes and charges making them resonable amendes for their labour And the said Arden and Nycholas dyd reforme and geve councell unto the said Walter that he shuld say that he has solde his said landes unto them, the whiche by his sayinges and so reportynge his landes shuld be never the further from hym And for be cause that the gentilmen and other his neighbours did owe unto the said Walter soo grete evyll wyll that they schulde have a grette dele more favour of them to make his partte more better of the said landes than they said Walter schuld be cause that they wheare my lorde warden servauntes and for be cause of that they said Walter dyd putte the seyd Arden and Nycholas Sole[388] the more in truste to have all soche right and power of his landes that he hade trustyng for to have them after warde ageyn according unto ther promasse That where upon the said Arden and Nycholas Sole dyd for to breng the seid Walter in dyspere[389] they dyd saie unto hym that there was apremynere[390] owt for hym for be cause of proving of his fathers testament wherupon that they seid Walter shulde goo unto one Master Whyte to agre with hym for to save hym from the daunger of the premynery the which the said Walter hadde proved his fathers thestament and wyll by the debyte of the Master of the rwoles and the councell of Master Doctor Hewyse before that tyme And the said Walter was sworne to agge[391] with Master Whyte for to save hym owt of the premynery wheruppon he shall geve unto the said Master Whyte so to do $4^{£}$ whereupon the seid Walter payd in hand of the said summe 26^{s} 8^{d} with[392] that the seid Master Arden Nycolas Sole upon the daye of apoyntement came downe unto [blank] for to have a sale of the said Walter of his parte of his landes wher the said Walter havyng them in mysse trust was very lothe for to delyver them eny sale there and yf he wolde so do his landes schoulde be never they further from hym or els they said that they wolde sue the said Walter of a bonde forfett unto them for the faut soo doyng in to hundred markes the whiche he the said Walter dyd not knowe that he hadde made eny soche bounde unto them soo to doo where upon the said Walter uppon ther gret wordes was faynt[393] ther for to follow ther myndes And ther the said Master Arden dyd saie that nowe we doo fynd Master Gylfordes wordes trewe for yf that we doo notte suerly bynd hym whan that you doo thyncke yne most sure of hym he wyll[394]

folio 262v is blank

---

386 Query for covert: concealment, deceit, covert conduct.

387 Bundle 10 No.231.No. 10

388 This seems to be written Cold and the next Cole

389 For despair.

390 Praemunire.

391 For agree

392 Very unclear word.

393 Unclear.

394 Page ends with a PRO diamond and the fol. number 262 and some contemporary notations.

folio 263 [Latin]

Kent,

Let it be remembered that at the General Sessions of the Peace held at Canterbury in the county aforesaid on Tuesday next before the feast of Saint Michael the Archangel in the thirty third year of the reign of Henry the Eighth by the grace of God of England and France King defendor of the faith Lord of Ireland and on earth supreme head of the English Church before James Hales knight Edward Twaytes and other justices of the Lord King in the county aforesaid to maintain the peace and also to hear and determine diverse felonies trespasses and other misdemeanors perpetrated in the same county and evidences concerning traverses to establish from trustworthy testimony without injustice in the court aforesaid

That Walter Morleyn of Benenden in the county aforesaid husbandman is a common brawler barrator and disturber of the good and peace and *defamation* not being proved it is allowed by the aforesaid justices that the aforesaid Walter now there present in court be allowed to find sufficient surety to keep the peace of the lord King and for ever according of the form of the statute etc.,

Upon which the same Walter Morleyn has taken for he himself that he will personally appear at the next General Sessions of the peace, that is to say, Tuesday after the Feast of the Epiphany of the Lord, next to be held in the aforesaid county and meanwhile to keep the peace of the lord King and for ever according to the form of the statute etc.,

And that the sum of twenty pounds is allowed upon his lands and cattles to the use of the lord King to be made and levied paid by himself anything before mentioned to do wrong and thence now lawfully communicated etc.

Let Walter Morleyn keep the peace towards Robert Gibben John Gibben Walter Everden senior William Everden alias Pynchefitche and Lawrence Daye Thomas Bygge Thomas Harryngton Richard Morleyn

folio 263 blank

folio 264

To the right honourable Sir Thomas Cheyny knyght Lord Warden of the Five Ports

In most humble wyse shewyth and compleyneth unto your good lordship your dayly orator and power bedman[395] Walter Morleyn that wher your seid besecher was and is possessid of and in diverse messuage landes and tenementes meadowes leasnes and pastures rentes reversions and services with other hereditamentes with all and singuler the appurtenaunces set and leyng in the parishe and townes of Benynden Bidyndon and Kanterbury Rovendon w[ithin] the countie of Kent the whiche landes tenementes and other the premysses ar of the cler yerly valewe of 20£ over all chargyes and he soo beyng thus seeasid oon Thomas Arden of Faversham and oon Nicholas Sole percevyng yo[ur] same besecher beyng a power and innocent man and intendyng to deseve your said besecher of his said lond causyd a *[blank]* Whit ~~beyng~~ otherwyse Persy to send for hym and your seid besecher came to hym to Canturbury aforesaid within the seid countie of Kent uppon whose commyng he thretened your seid besecher that he was in the prem[unire] and that he was utterly undone wheruppon your seid besecher went to the seid Ardern and Sole to desyre them councell and they seid in lykewyse that your seid besecher was utterly undone and thou your

395 *O.E.D.* Beadsman: .. one who prays for the soul or spiritual welfare of another.

seid besecher desired them to knowe what was best for hym ~~them~~ to doo and then they advised your seid besecher to sey that he has sold his seid lond unto them and yf he did not the kyng wold have sit and further they seid that your seid besecher shuld have his londs agayn as sone as he was discharged of the premunyre and ~~further~~ then and ther they commaundyd your seod besecher to kepe ther wordes close and yf he ~~they~~ did not the ~~kyng~~

folio 264v

and so under unlesse your party and in consideration whereof it may therfore please your [?goodly] good lordship ~~mastership~~ the premysses considerid to call before you the seyd

folio 265 is the Strelley papers

PREROGATIVE COURT OF CANTERBURY
Will Register on microfilm.
PROB 11/27 quire 27 folio 219

IN THE NAME OF GOD AMEN the 28th day of September in the yere of our Lorde God 1533 I Richard Morleyn of the parrishe of Benynden yoman being of hoole of mynde and parfet memory make my present testamment in this manner of wise Furst I bequeth my soule to allmightie God our ladye Sainte Mary and to all tholly compauny of hevyn and my bodie to be buried in the churcheyerd of the parrish churche of Sainte George the Martir of Benynden aforesaid Item I bequeth to the high aulter there for my tithes and offeringes forgotten and necligently witholden 20^{d} Item I bequeth to eche of my godchildren that beare my name 4^{d} Item I ordeigne to an honest preest to singe a trentall of thirtie masses for the helth of my soule in the churche of Benynden 10^{s} Item I wille that the costes and charges of my out burying monnethis mynde and yerees mynde be at the discretion of myne executours Item I will that my wife shall have of myn stuffe of householde and in cattall to the value of tenne poundes according to the valour that I had with hir at our mariage Item I will that Richard and Gervys my sonnes shall have the halfendeale of all my brasse and pewater spittes aundiornes[396] and trevettes[397] Item I bequeth to Jane Awsten to her mariage 40^{s} The residew of all my goodes and cattalls not bequethis nor assigned my dettis and bequestis first paid I give and bequeth them to Walter my sonne whome I make and ordeign to be myn executour.

THIS IS the last wille and ordenaunce of me the said Richard Morleyn made the day and yere above written First I will that my feoffees shall suffer Elianore my wife to have and occupy my chamber that I now lye in for one yere next after my deceace if she abide a widowe and fyre and

[396] *O.E.D.* Andiron: A utensil, consisting of an iron bar sustained horizontally at one end by an upright pillar or support usually ornamented or artistically shaped, at the other end by a short foot; a pair of these also called 'fire-dogs', being placed, one at either side of the hearth or fire-place, with the ornamental ends to the front, to support burning wood. Sometimes in a kitchen fire-place the upright support carried a rack in front for the rack to turn in.

[397] *O.E.D.* Trivet: A three-footed stand or support for a pot, kettle or other vessel placed over a fire for cooking or heating something

fleete[398] in my haule and kechin and hir easement to goo and to comme to the same and to fetche water washe and wringe and to hange hir cloathes at all tymes convenient and necessary during the said yere if she abide a widow Item I wille that my feoffees shall deliver anonne after my deceace unto Walter my sonne my meswage and gardeine called the Upper House sometyme William Morleyn and 7 peaces of land therto pertayninge with a corne mille there uppon buylded wherof the first peace of lande is called Rydett the second the Hell the third Upperestlande the fourth Netherestland the fifth Netherwoodhell the sixth Nethermeede and the seveneth Uppermeede containing by estimation thirty acres of land and also twoo other peaces of lande called Middell Marling and the Yonder Marling conteyning by estimation 12 acres of lande whether more or lesse Also more 7 peaces of lande and a gardeine whereof the first is called Netherchorfeelde Upperchorfeld Longefeeld Purtake Weryfelde the 6 acres of Wolfeham containing by estimation 40 acres of lande whethir moore or lesse Also I wille the saide Walter shalhave halfe my wood called Brosindens wood in fee simple lying and being in the parrishe of Bidendon uppon the denie[399] of Brosinden the whiche halfe of the said Wood conteyneth by estimation tenne acres of woodland and also I wille that my saide feoffees shall deliver unto Richard and Gerves my sonne when the yongest of them commeth to their age of 22 yeres equally betwixt them my principall meswage and gardeine and 3 peaces of lande therto lying called Postenfeelde Beeremeede and the Crofte and also my four peaces of lande and an aple mylle theruppon standing at the other side of the streete whereof the First is called the Hothe the second the Wood above the Hoth and the thirde the Nether Marling with the gardeine and the fourth the upper Marling conteyning by estimation 20 acres of lande and also moore 9 peaces of lande whereof one is called Nether Everyndensfeelde Everyndensfeelde with a shaw[400] to him belonging about the house Colfelde Everyndens gardeine Trowham the hell with a marle pytt and the twoo swaites conteyning 40 acres Provided alwaie that I wille Walter my sonne shalhave liberty to come and goo to fetche marle at the marle pitt in the saide lande called Swaytes to him his heires and assignes for ever Also I wille that the said Richard and Jerves shall have the other halfe of the said woodd called Brosindens Wood at their said age and if it happin anny of the said Richard and Jerves dye without heires of their bodies laufully begotten afore that they come to their said age Then I wille she (sic) shalbe others heire of them Also I will that my feofees or their assignes shall deliver unto the sonnes off Phillipp Morleyn my sonne equal betwixt them my parte of my meswage and landes called Hothes and also a peace of lande called longe hooke lying uppon the denne of Mapilsden to them their heires and assignes forever Also I wille that the profite of my howsing and tenementes in Caunterburie be to thuse and profite of Walter Richard and Gerves my sonnes unto the tyme the youngest of theim commeth to the age of 22 yeres and when the yongest of theim commeth to the age of 22 yeres then I will that they shall shifte all the said landes and tenementes equally betwixt theim and if any of theim die without heires of their bodies laufullie begotten before the tyme that the youngest of theim comme to the said age of 22 yeres Then I will that eche shall be the others heire of theim Also I will that Walter my sonne shall have the occupying of all the said landes and tenementes the whiche is before to the said Richard and Gerves before assigned unto the tyme that they come to laufull age and the profite therof in the meane tyme be to the keaping and fynding of theim And the residew above their fynding to be to the use of theim when they shall come to lawfull age Also I will that Walter Richard and Gervise my sonnes shalhave a certaine land called a Home Lane at Bektilte equally bewixt theim to their landes there as be nedeth to their partes Also I will that my right and title

[398] *O.E.D.* Fire and flet: fire and house-room.

[399] Robert Furley, *A History of the Weald of Kent* (Ashford, 1874) does not list this as an ancient dene in the parish of Biddenden. There was a dene of Brissenden in the parish of Bethersden.

[400] *O.E.D.* Shaw: A thicket, a small wood, copse or grove. Specifically s trip of wood or underwood forming the border of a field.

of my landes and woodde called Litle Dolkynden be to the use of the sonnes of Philip my sonne PROVYDED also that if Richard and Jervis die both afore their said age without heires of their bodies laufully begotten Thenne I will that all their partes of the said landes and tenementes shall remaine to Walter my sonne to his heires and assignes foever Also I wille that my feoffes deliver unto Walter my sonne my landes and tenementes at Kenchelham in Rolvynden in fee simple Item I will that my feoffees shall deliver unto Richard and Gerves my sonnes twoo peaces of lande lying in Rolvynden that I bought of the wedowe of Symon Day when that they comme to the age of 22 yeres and the profute of the same in the meane tyme be to their fynding and if any of theim die afore their said age of 22 yeres Then eche shalbe others heir of the said Richard and Gerves And if they die both afore the said age then I will it remaine to Walter my sonne to his heires and assignes in fee simple Item I will that my owtland[401] at Becktilte shall remaine equally betwixt Walter Richard Gerves my sonnes in fee simple and eche of theim to be othirs heires These witnes Edwarde Leede Robert Everynden and other

[*Latin*] Probate of the above written testament was granted before the Lord at London on the authority of our Sovereign King the ninth day of the month of May in the Year of the Lord One thousand five hundred and thirty nine on the oath of the executor in this testament nominated And approval and entering the will was entrusted with the administrator of all and singular the goods and debts of the said deceased to the aforesaid executors well and truly etc. And of a full inventory to be made etc. And also a full and true account to be returned. Sworn on the Holy Evangelists.

quire 33 folio 259

Definitive sentence in Latin read 7 November 1539

[401] *O.E.D.* Outland: The outlying land of an estate or manor. In old English and feudal tenure, that portion of the land which the lord did not retain for his own use but granted to tenants.

APPENDIX 8:
Sandwich Customs Records

INTRODUCTION

For lack of money, the Tudors had to make do without a standing army and a civil service. They had to rely almost exclusively upon the part-time services of amateur administrators. It became the usual practice to choose collectors, comptrollers and searchers from local men of standing and substance, who were frequently members of the merchant class. They must also have been people with friends in high places to nominate them for the posts. Finally, they must have come from the relatively small literate class.

The collector of customs kept a record of all shipments. When the customs had been collected, they were deposited in a chest and eventually the money was handed over to the Exchequer. Collectors were to give cockets[402] as receipts for money received.

The controller was to keep a counter roll of the shipment of goods to serve as a check on the collector's roll when both were sent to the Exchequer. The searcher had to examine the cockets and then the cargo to make sure that no goods were being smuggled out. Then he gave a bill of discharge in return for a fee, which varied with the size of the ship from 20 pence to six shillings. He had to inspect the ship's victuals to see that they were not excessive. Passengers were searched, if commoners, to see whether they had passports and gold or silver. The surveyor was controller to the searcher. Then there were clerks, deputies, troners, weighers, cranekeepers and wharfingers.

The first Book of Rates was introduced in 1507 and confirmed in 1532. At the same time it was ordered that naturalized merchants were not to enter the goods of aliens as their own. During the reign of Edward VI an act was passed to prohibit the sale of public offices by preventing the purchaser of an office from holding it for ever. Steps were frequently taken to restrict or prohibit the export of certain goods. For example, in 1554 an act was passed to restrain the carrying of corn, victuals and wood overseas.

The coastline was divided up into sections from 1275 and each section had a chief port and member ports. The old shire alignments were ignored. In the Faversham area, Sandwich was the chief port and Faversham, Dover and Rochester were the member ports.[403]

The format of the original document has been slightly changed with indenting of the merchant under the ship - this is actually adopted by the scribe in the original record on membrane two but in reverse. The membranes appear from some old numbers marked on them to be in the correct order. However, it seems that the final membrane and a portion of membrane 5 (between January and March) are missing, although there appears to be no full year for any of the ports.The whole document is in Latin with a few English words scattered through the text. The English words have been retained with their original spelling. Great care has been made to check the precise meaning of the words, since the Latin is in some instances not clear due to the highly abbreviated nature of this repetitive text.

---

402 *O.E.D.* Cocket: A document sealed by the officers of the custom-house, and delivered to merchants as a certificate that their merchandise has been duly entered and has paid duty. A recent suggestion is that the name originated in the words *quo quietus est*, 'by which he is quit', with which the Customer's receipt concluded. (S. Dowell *Hist. Taxation in Eng.* (1878) I. 171.) It is by no means clear whether the name originally belonged to the document, or to the seal which gave it validity.

403 N.S.B.Gras, *The Early English Customs' System* (Harvard UP, 1918), pp. 94-100, 105, 302; Elizabeth E. Hoon, *The Organization of the English Customs System 1696-1786*, 2nd Edn. (Newton Abbot, 1968), passim; T. S. Willan, *The English Coasting Trade 1600-1750* (Manchester UP, 1938), passim.

PRO: E122 130/15
35-36 Henry VIII Sandwich Customs[404]

SANDWICHE:

Thomas Arderne controller of the customs and subsidies of the lord King in the port and town of Sandwiche and in every single port places and creekes adjacent to the same port, that is to say, from the feast of Saint Michael the Archangel in the xxxvth [1543] year of the reign of the now King Henry VIIIth as far as the same feast of Saint Michael the Archangel then next following in the xxxvjth year of the same king that now is, at least for one whole year

Sandwiche:

Of one pynke[405] of Ostend has entered[406] the first day of October

Of James Drove alien[407] for ij pockettis[408] of hoppes weighing iiij^{C} value [*blank*]

Of one other pyncke of Osteende has entered the same day

Of Anthony Rixe alien for two pockettis of hoppes weighing v^{C} value xxxiij^{s} iiij^{d} one hundred[409] of staple fysshe value xx^{s} One half hundred bownechis[410] of rootis value xx^{d}

Of one other pincke of Ostende has entered the same day

Of James Ryfte alien for three pockettis of hoppes weighing vj^{C} value xL^{s} one half hundred of Newelande fysshe value x^{s} total L^{s}

Of one other pyncke of Ostende has entered the same day

Of Leonard Roffyne alien for one quarter of fyshe value v^{s} and one pocket of hoppes weighing ij^{C} value xiij^{s} iiij^{d} total xviij^{s} iiij^{d}

[*margin*][411] Of Henry Browne denizen[412] and merchant staple for ij thousand and xL skins complete with wool[413] laded from Sandwich towards Calais

In one catche[414] called The George of Ramysgate whereof William Charnocke is master departing the same day

---

404 Old reference JPR 2402

405 Pink *O.E.D.* A sailing vessel; originally one of small size used for coasting and fishing, described as flat bottomed and having bulging sides

406 Intrat for intravit

407 Simply given throughout as al' this according to Gras *op. cit.* is alienigena

408 Pockettis A.M. Millard, *Some useful weights and measures found in the London Port Books (imports only) for certain years between 1588 and 1640* (1960) Typescript on PRO Round Room shelves. HOPS: 1 sack = 6 cwt; 1 poake = 4 cwt; 1 pack = 3½ cwt, and 1 pocket = 2½ cwt. It would seem that the quantities remained standard for a while in that George Clinch, *English Hops, A history of cultivation and preparation for the market from the earliest times* (1919) p. 36 says 'From the accounts published in old books on the subject it is evident that there were two kinds of receptacles used for the packing and marketing of hops, namely (1) rough, common bags made of refuse hemp, fine tow and hay intermixed, and calculated to contain 2½ cwt of hops of inferior, or discoloured quality, hops of later picking; and (2) pockettis made of strong canvas, as above, with the capacity of 1½ cwt for the finest and best flavoured hops.' Anthony Cronk, *English Hops Glossary* (1959) says of the Pocket (1) package in the form of a sack made of stout twill, measuring when filled 6-7 feet high and 2 feet in diameter, (2) the quantity of hops contained in a pocket, average weight is between 1½ and 1¾ hundredweight. The poke he gives as a sack of fairly loosely woven material, capable of containing 8-10 bushels of green hops.

409 Given as tent' this would seem from later entries to be more likely to be cent[um]. Staple fish were fish not thoroughly cured; green fish cured with a good salt.

410 Later entries would suggest that this is simply bunches. R.E.Zupko, *English Weights and measures* (1968) says that bunches of onion or garlic had 25 heads.

411 There appears to be no indication as to where this should be inserted in the text.

412 Given throughout as ind for indigena

413 *Pellibus integre lanuta carcat [carcare]*: Latham, *Revised Medieval Latin Word list* says Lana Pellicia, wool on the pelt, under Pellis and under Lana Pellicia, wool on the fleece. The entry clearly indicates these are skins complete with the wool. Gras, gives *pellis lanuta* as woolfell.

Of Henry Browne merchant of the staple town of Calais for MMCCCC [2400] skins complete with wool towards the staple aforesaid

In one pincke of Osteende departing the second day of October

Of John Bage alien for three tuns[415] of berre value Lx^{s} from subsidy iij^{s}

Of one pincke of Ostende has entered the same day

Of Peter Vander alien for eight pockettis of hoppes weighing xvj^{C} value cvj^{s}

In a pincke of Ostende departing the third day of October

Of James Drobull alien for 6 pipes of berre value Lx^{s}

In a pincke of Ostende departing the fifth day of October

Of Leonard Reffene alien for three tuns of berre value Lx^{s}

In one pincke of Ostende departing the same day

Of Anthony Rixe alien for three tuns of berre value Lx^{s}

In one other pincke of Ostende departing the same day

Of James Ryfte alien for three tuns of berre value Lx^{s}

In one other pincke of Ostende departing the same day

Of Peter Vander alien for three tuns of berre value Lx^{s}

In one pincke of Donekyrke departing the ixth day of October

Of Martin Thornebolde alien for three tuns of berre

Of one pincke of Ostende has entered the same day

Of Giles Colyns alien for two pockettis of hoppes weighing CCCC value xxvj^{s} viij^{d} and one thousand hoppis value vj^{s} viij^{d} total xxxiij^{s} iiij^{d}

Of one other pincke of Ostende has entered the same day

Of Crispian Gowyne alien for one hundred of cabages value iij^{s} iiij^{d} one hundred bounches of rootis value iij^{s} iiij^{d} and one thousand hoops[416] value vj^{s} viiij^{d} total xiij^{s} iiij^{d}

Of one catche of Blanckeborowe[417] has entered the same day

Of Vincent Charles alien for one pocket of hoppes weighing CC value xiij^{s} iiij^{d} and lxxxv bounches of rootis value ij^{s} xd , total xvj^{s} ij^{d}

In one pincke of Ostende departing the xjth day of October

Giles Colyns alien for three tuns of berre value Lx^{s}

In one other pincke of Ostende departing the same day

Crispian Goweyn alien for iij tuns of berre value Lx^{s}

In one pincke of Blanckeborowe departing the same day

Of Vincent Charles alien for three tuns of berre value Lx^{s}

Of one pincke of Ostende has entered xijth day of October

Of James Drobull[418] alien for ix barrells herring[419] value Lx^{s}

Of one other Pyncke of Ostende has entered the same day

---

[414] *O.E.D.* Catch or Ketch A strongly built vessel of the galiot order, usually two masted and from 100 to 250 tons burden

[415] Dolijs: Tuns or casks. TUN: it seems clear that they are using the wine measures at this point, i.e. 1 tun/ton = 2 pipes or butts; 1 pipe = 2 hogsheads; 1 hogshead 63 gallons. The confirmation for this seems to be that further down there is a reference to 6 pipes of beer having the same value as 3 tuns.

[416] The hoppes have in the case of 'mille' been changed to hoopes; on p. 13 these are given as hoops for barrels. The quantity is always 1000s or a division and thus some entries not corrected by the scribe and spelt hoppes can be distinguished from hops which are always given in pockets

[417] Blankenberge on the coast of West Flanders, Belgium, 9 miles North of Brugge.

[418] Given elsewhere as Dorbull

[419] Allecia; this word is often badly written and highly abbreviated

Of Ludovick Harbolte alien for 6 barrells of herring value xL^{s}

Of one other pincke of Osteende has entered xiiijth day of October

Of John Bage alien for 5 barrells herring value xxxiij^{s} iiij^{d}

Of one pincke of Neweporte[420] has entered xvj day of October

Of William Scrode alien for two pockettis of hoppes weighing v^{C} ½[421] value xxxiij^{s} iiij^{d}

Of one pincke of Ostende has entered the same day

Of Francis Michaell alien for three smaller[422] pockettis of hoppes weighing v^{C} of the value of xxxvj^{s} viij^{d} and iiij barrels of herrings value xxvj^{s} viij^{d}

membrane 1 verso

Of one other pincke of Ostende has entered the same day

Of Anthony Spencer alien for two pockettis hoppes weighing iiij^{C} value xxvj^{s} viij^{d} and one barrel of herring value vj^{s} viiij^{d}

In one crayere[423] called The Leonarde of Calais[424] departing the same day

Of John Clare denizen for two gross of knit ware towards Calais aforesaid value xiij^{s} iiij^{d}

In one pincke of Ostende departing the xviij day of October

Of John Bage alien for three tuns of berre value Lx^{s}

In one pincke of Newporte departing xix day of October

Of William Scrode alien for three tuns of berre value Lx^{s}

In one pincke of Ostende departing the same day

Of Francis Mychaell alien for three tuns of berre value Lx^{s}

In one pincke of Osteende departing the same day

Of Anthony Spencer alien for three tuns of berre value Lx^{s}

Of one pincke of Dunekyrke has entered the same day

Of James Neyeman alien for five barrels of herring value xxxiij^{s} iiij^{d} the same and one thousand hops value vj^{s} viij^{d}, ij[425] small firkins of eels called pymeper elles[426] forty eight making one barrell value iij^{s} iiij^{d} and one quarter of cabages value x^{d}

Of William Arnolde denizen for one barrel of herring value vj^{s} viij^{d} and for vj small firkyns eels called pymeper elles forty eight making one barrel value x^{s}, One hundreed of crvsys[427] value iij^{s} iiij^{d}, one bounchis of rootes value xx^{d} and xx bounches onions[428] value 20^{d}

In a pincke of Osteende departing the same day

Of James Drobull alien for three tuns of berre vale Lx^{s}

In a pincke of Osteende departing the same day

---

[420] Nieuwpoort, Netherlands

[421] Simply as d'

[422] Parvius

[423] *O.E.D.*; A small trading vessell

[424] Calec

[425] ijbz p[ar]vus fyrkyns angullarne voc[ate] pymeporelles quart[o] octo facinto un barrell. In the measure of fish 1 barrel = 4 firkins. Zupko, *op. cit.* says a barrel of herrings or ells usually contained 30 gallons fully packed.

[426] As opposed to stowbe (sube) elys and Chaffte ellys; The laste of pymper elles viij£, the barelle xiiijs iiij^{d} *Book of rates 1507* Gras

[427] *O.E.D.* Cruse: a small earthen vessel for liquids; a pot, a jar or bottle; also a drinking vessel

[428] Ceparum

Of Ludovick Harbolte alien for three tuns of berre value Lx^{s}

In one pincke of Dumkyrke departing the xxvijth of October

Of James Nyeman alien for three tuns of berre value Lx^{s}

Of one pincke of Ostende has entered the same day

Of Leonard Reffyne alien for ij pockettis hoppes weighing iiij^{C} value xxvj^{s} viij^{d} and vij barrels of herrings xLvj^{s} viij^{d}

Of one other pincke of Osteende has entered the same day

Of James Ryfte alien for one pockett of hoppes weighing ij^{C} value xiij^{s} iiij^{d}, iiij barrels of herrings value xxvj^{s} viij^{d}, one hundred newelande fyshe value xx^{s}, one thousand hoppes value vj^{s} viij^{d} and one hundred bounches of rootes value iij^{s} iiij^{d}

Of one pynke of Osteende has entered xxviijth October

Of Giles Colyns alien for eight barrrels of herrings valued liij^{s} iiij^{d} and one thousand hoopes vj^{s} viij^{d}

Of one hoye of Flosshinge has entered xxix October

Of Adrian Clarcke alien for three pockettis of hoppes weighing vj^{C} value xL^{s} and x barrel of herring value lxvj^{s} viij^{d}

Of one Crayere The Blacke George of Saundewiche has entered the same day

Of William Kennedy denizen for 300 hoppes value xx^{s}

Of William Wylkynesone denizen for one case of whyte glasse value xiij^{s} iiij^{d}

Of one pincke of Osteende has entered the same day

Of Peter Vander alien for vj barrels of herrings value xL^{s} and two barrels of white salt value v^{s}

Of Cornelius Foxe denizen for iiij handeguns value xiij^{s} iiij^{d}

Of one other pincke of Ostende has entered the same day

Of John Bage alien for vj barrels of herrings value xL^{s}

Of one other pincke of Osteende has entered the same day

Of Crispian Gowyn alien for 9 barrels of herrings value Lx^{s}

In one pincke of Ostende departing the penultimate day of October

Of Leonard Reffyne alien for 3 tuns of berre value Lx^{s}

In one other pincke of Ostend departing the same day

Of James Ryfte alien for three tuns of berre value Lx^{s}

Of one pincke of Ostende has entered the ijnd day of November

Of James Drobull alien for ten barrels of herrings value lxvj^{s} viij^{d} and one thousand hoppes value vj^{s} viij^{d}

Of one other pincke of Ostende has entered the same day

Of Ludovick Harbolte alien for ten barrels of herrings value lxvj^{s}

Of one pincke of Neweporte has entered the same day

Of William Scrode alien for five barrels of herrings valued xxxiij^{s} iiij^{d}

In one pincke of Osteende departing the same day

Of Giles Colyns alien for three tuns of berre value Lx^{s}

In one hoye of Flosshing departing the same day

Of Adrian Clarke alien for three tuns of berre value Lx^{s}

In one pincke of Ostende going the third of November

membrane 2

Of Peter Vander alien for three tuns of berre value Lx^{s}

In one other pincke of Ostende departing the same day

Of John Bag alien for three tuns of berre value Lx^{s}

In one pincke of Ostende departing the vjth day of November

Of James Drobull alien for three tuns of berre value Lx^{s}

In one other pincke of Ostende departing the same day

Of Crispian Gowyne alien for three tuns of berre value Lx^{s}

In one pincke of Ostende departing the eigth of November

Of Ludovick Harbolte alien for iij tuns of berre value Lx^{s}

Of one pincke of Ostende has entered xix day of November

Of John Bage alien for ij pokettes hoppis weighing iiij^{C} value xxvj^{s} viij^{d} and iiij barrels of herrings value xxvj^{s} viij^{d}

Of one other pincke of Ostende has entered the same day

Of William Cole alien for vj barrels of herrings value xL^{s}

Of one other pincke of Ostende has entered the same day

Of James Drobull alien for viij barrels of herrings value liij^{s} iiij^{d} and one pokete of hoppes weighing ij^{C} value xiij^{s} iiij^{d}

Of one other pincke of Ostende entered the same day

Of Vincent Keyn alien for ix barrels of herrings value Lx^{s}

One other pincke of Ostende has entered the same day

Of Crispian Gowyne alien for eight barrels of herrings value liij^{s} iiij^{d} and one pockette of hoppis weighing one and a half hundredweight[429] value x^{s}

In one pincke of Ostende departing xxij day of November

Of William Cole alien for iij tuns of berre value Lx^{s}

In one other pincke of Ostende departing the same day

Of James Drobull alien for 3 tuns of berre value Lx^{s}

In one other pincke of Ostende departing the same day

Of Vincent Keyn alien for three tuns of berre value Lx^{s}

In one pincke of Ostende departing the xxiiij November

Of Crispian Gowyne alien for three tuns of berre value Lx^{s}

Of one pincke of Ostende has entered the same day

Of Ludovick Harbolte alien for five barrels of herrings value xxxiij^{s} iiij^{d} and one pockette of hoppis weighing ij^{C} value xiij^{s} iiij^{d}

Of one pincke of Ostende has entered the same day

Of James Nyeman alien for two pockettis of hoppes weighing iiij^{C} value xxvj^{s} viij^{d} and iiij barrels of herrings value xxvj^{s} viiij^{d}

Of William Arnolde denizen for iiij barrels of herrings value xxvj^{s} viij^{d} and one thousand hoppis value vj^{s} viij^{d}

Of one pincke of Neweporte has entered xxv November

Of James Blacke alien for three pockettis of hoppis weighing vj^{C} value xL^{s} ij thousand of hoopis[430] value xiij^{s} iij^{d} et ij barrels herrings value xiij^{s} iiij^{d}

Of one pincke of Ostende has entered xxvjth November

[429] C d'

[430] ijbz mille de hoopis - the second o being written over an erased p.

Of James Ryfte alien for one pockete hoppis weighing one and half hundred-weight value x^{s}, five barrells of herrings value xxxiij^{s} iiij^{d} and half a hundred Neweland fysshe value x^{s}

Of one pincke of Neweporte has entered xxvij day of November

Of Andrew Skreke for three pokettis hoppis weighing ix^{C} value Lx^{s}[431], viij barrels of herrings value liij^{s} iiij^{d} and one barrel of blake soppe value x^{s} and three barrels of white salt value vj^{s}

Of one Argusye[432] has entered the same day

Of Thomas Hewes denizen for iiij butte[433] of Malmesye and one butte of Muscadell

In one pincke of Ostende departing xxviij November

Of Ludovick Harbolte alien for three tuns of berre value Lx^{s}

In one pincke of Dounekirke departing the same day

Of James Nyeman alien for three tuns of berre vale Lx^{s}

In one pincke of Neweporte departing the xxix November

Of James Blacke alien for three tuns of berre value Lx^{s}

In one pincke of Ostende departing the last day of November

Of James Ryfte alien for three tuns of berre value Lx^{s}

Of one pincke of Ostende has entered the third of December

Of Giles Colyns alien for five barrels of herring value xxxiij^{s} iiij^{d} one thousand hoopis value vj^{s} viij^{d} and a pokette hoppes weighing one and half hundred-weight value x^{s}

In one pincke of Neweporte departing the same day

Of Andrew Sereke alien for viij pipes of berre value iiij$^{£}$

Of one pincke of Dunekyrke has entered the same day

Of Martin Fromebolde alien for viij barrels of herrings value liij^{s} iiij^{d}

Of one pincke of Ostende has entered the vth day of December

Of John Forlicke? alien for vj barrels of herrings value xL^{s} one pokete of hoppes weighing ij^{C} value xiij^{s} iiij^{d} and one thousand of hoppes value vj^{s} viij^{d}

Of one other pincke of Ostende has entered the same day

Of John Bollarde alien for viij barrels of herrings value liij^{s} iiij^{d} ij small[434] pokettis hoppis weighing CCC value xx^{s} and CC bounchis of Rootis value vj^{s} viij^{d}

In one pincke of Ostende departing the same day

membrane 2v

Of Giles Colyns alien for three tuns of berre value Lx^{s}

Of one pincke of Ostende has entered vij day of December

Of Crispian Gowyne alien for vj barrels of herrings value xL^{s}, one thousand hoopis value vj^{s} viij^{d}

Of one pincke of Ostende has entered the eighth day of December

Of Vincent Keyne for 5 barrels of herrings value xxxiij^{s} iiij^{d} and two pockettis of hoppes weighing iiij^{C} value xxvj^{s} viij^{d}

---

431 Gras p. 694 A book of rates 15 Jly 1507: Hoppys the sacke containing vii^{C} xls; Hoppys the pocke xx^{s}

432 Argosy; a merchant vessel of the largest size and burden, especially those of Ragusa and Venice.

433 Zupko; The pipe contenith a butt which is ½ of a tunne, 126 gallons.

434 Parvius

In one pynke of Ostende departing ix day of December

Of John Bollarde alien of three tuns of berre value Lx^{s}

Of one pincke of Ostende has entered the tenth day of December

Of John Bage alien for ij pokettes hoppes weighing iiij^{C} value xxvj^{s} viij^{d} et ij barrel of herrings value xiij^{s} iij^{d}

In one pincke of ~~Ostende~~ Dunekyrke departing the same day

Of Martin Thornebolde alien for three tuns of berre value Lx^{s}

In one pincke of Osteende has entered departing the same day

John Frolyke alien for three tuns of berre value Lx^{s}

In one pincke of Ostende departing xj December

Of Crispian Gowyn alien of three tuns of berre value Lx^{s}

In one pincke of Ostende departing the xij December

Of Vincent Keyne alien for three tuns of berre value Lx^{s}

In one pincke of Ostende departing the same day

Of John Bage alien for three tuns of berre value Lx^{s}

In one hoye called the Barbery of Rosyndale[435] departing the same day

Of John Rugeley denizen for vij tuns of berre upon licence granted by John Master towards foreign parts[436]

Of one hoye of Armewe has entered the same day

Of William Lotheburye denizen for eight pieces of figs[437] value x^{s} viij^{d}

Of one Argusye has entered xiij die of December

Of Thomas Syvern denizen for for two butts of Malmesey

Of Robert Morrys denizen for one butte of Malmesey

Of one pincke of Ostende has entered xvj December

Of James Drobull alien for vj barrels of herrings valued xL^{s} and two small pokettis hoppes weighjing iij^{C} value xx^{s}

Of one pincke of Neweporte has entered xx day of December

Of William Scrode alien for vj barrels of herrings value xL^{s} and one pockette of hooppes weighing ij^{C} value iij^{s} iiij^{d}

Of one pincke of Ostende has entered departing the same day

Of John Ballarde alien for ij barrels of herrings value xiij^{s} iiij^{d} one thousand of hoopes value vj^{s} viij^{d} and one hundred cabiges value iiij^{s} iiij^{d}

Of One pinke of Ostende has entered the xxj day of December

Of John Bowles alien for ij pokette hoppis weighing ij^{C} value xiij^{s} iiij^{d}, iij barrels of herrings value xx^{s} and ij barrels of white salt value iij^{s} iiij^{d}

In one pincke of Ostende has entered the same day

Of James Drobull alien for three tuns of berre value Lx^{s}

Of one pincke of Ostende has entered the same day

Of[438] Nicholas Noomes alien for ij pockettes hoppes weighing iiij^{C} value xxvj^{s} viij^{d} and v barrels of herrings value xxxiij^{s} iiij^{d}

---

435 Roosendaal, North Brabant, Netherlands.

436 Latin: versus p[ar]tes externus

437 Ficum; Millard, 1 piece of figs = 60 lbs.

438 Insert from margin

Of Anthony Spencar alien for three pokettis hoppis weighing vj^{C} value xL^{s} and vj barrels of herrings value xL^{s}

In one pincke of Ostende departing the xxij day of December

Of William Scrode alien for three tuns of berre value Lx^{s}

Of one pincke of Ostende has entered the same day

Of John Frolike alien for ij pokettis hoppis weighing iiij^{C} value xxvj^{s} viij^{d} and two barrels of herrings value xiij^{s} iiij^{d}

In one pincke of Ostende departing the same day

Of John Bollarde alien for three tuns of berre value Lx^{s}

Of one pincke of Ostende has entered xxiiijth December

Of Giles Master Jannice alien for vj barrels of herrings value xL^{s}

Of William Lathebury denizen for ij laste[439] of herring value viij$^{£}$

In one pincke of Ostende departing the same day

Of John Bowler alien for three tuns of berre value Lx^{s}

In one pincke of Ostende departing the same day

Of Nicholas Noonnes alien for three tuns of berre value Lx^{s}

In one pincke of Ostende departing ~~the same~~ xxvj day of December

Of Anthony Spencer alien for three tuns of berre value Lx^{s}

In one pincke of Ostende has entered the same day

Of John Frolyke alien for three tuns of berre value Lx^{s}

Of one pincke of Ostende has entered xj day of January

Of James Drobull alien for one laste of herring value iiij$^{£}$

In one pincke of Ostende has entered the same day

Of John Bage alien for iiij barrel of herrings value xxvj^{s} viij^{d} and two pockettes hoppis weighing v^{C} value xxxiij^{s} iiij^{d}

membrane 3

In one other pincke of Ostende has entered the same day

Of Ludovick Arbolte alien for vj barrels of herrings value xL^{s}

Of one pincke of Ostende has entered the same day

Of William Arnolde alien for vj barrels of herrings value xL^{s}

Of one pincke of Ostende departing the xv day of January

Of John Bage alien three tuns of berre vale Lx^{s}

In one pincke of Armewe departing the xvj day of January

Of William Arnoldson alien for three tuns of berre value Lx^{s}

In one pincke of Donekyrke has entered the same day

Of James Nyeman alien for vj barrels herrings value xL^{s} and one pokete of hoppes weighing 2½ hundred-weight[440] value xvj^{s} viij^{d}

Of one pincke of Ostende has entered xxvijth day of January

Of Giles Maister Jannice alien for three lastes of herring value xij$^{£}$

Of one pincke of Ostende has entered the same day

Of John Bollarde alien for three lastes of herring value xij$^{£}$

In one pincke of Ostende has entered the same day

---

[439] A last is 12 barrels. A fish barrel was normally that of an ale barrel containing 32 gallons.

[440] CC d'

William Arnold denizen for ix barrels of herrings value Lx^{s}

In one pincke of Ostende departing the same day

Of Ludovick Arbolt alien for three barrels of berre value Lx^{s}

Of one pincke of Ostende has entered the same day

Of Anthony Arbolte alien for half a laste of herrings value xL^{s}, and two pockettes hoppes weighing CC value xiij^{s} iiij^{d}

In one pincke of Ostende departing the same day

Of James Drobull alien for three tuns of berre value Lx^{s}

In one pincke of Ostende departing the same day

Of Giles Maister Jannice for three tuns of berre value Lx^{s}

In one pincke of Ostende departing the same day

Of John Bollarde alien for three tuns of berre value Lx^{s}

In one pincke of Ostend departing the same day

Of Anthony Arbolte alien for three tuns of berre value Lx^{s}

In one pincke of Neweporte departing the same day

Of James Neyeman alien for two tuns of berre value Lx^{s}

In one pincke of Neweporte has entered the tenth day of February

Of Cornelius Peterson alien of two barrels of herrings value xiij^{s} iiij^{d}, and three pockettes hoppis weighing vj^{C} d' value xliij^{s} iiij^{d}

Of one pincke of Ostende has entered the same day

Of Cornelius Nobbis alien for three barrels of herrings value xx^{s} and two pockettes hoppes weighing v^{C} value xxiij^{s} iiij^{d}

Of one pincke of Ostende has entered the same day

Of Crispian Goweyn alien for eight barrels of herrings value liij^{s} iiij^{d}

Of one pincke of Ostende has entered the same day

Of John Bage alien for five barrels of herrings value xxxiij^{s} iiij^{d} and iiij pockettis hoppis weighing viij^{C} value liij^{s} iiij^{d}

Of one pincke of Ostende has entered xxvjth day of Februray

Of Magnus[441] Peter alien for iiij barrels of herrings xxvj^{s} viiij^{d} three barrels of shottyne[442] herrings x^{s} and one pokete hoppis weighing ij^{C} value xiij^{s} iiij^{d}

Of one pincke of Ostende has entered xxj day of February

Of Giles Maister Jannice alien for ij lastis of herrings valued viij$^{£}$ and iiij pockettes hoppis weighing x^{C} value lxvj^{s} viij^{d}

Of one crayer called The Jannice of Saundewiche has entered the xxvth of February

Of John Rugelye denizen for ix barrels of herrings value Lx^{s} and six butt[443] of oyle value Lx^{s}

Of one pincke of Ostend has entered the third day of March

Of William Cornelis alien for five pokettes hoppis weighing x^{C} [value] lxvj^{s} viij^{d}

One pincke of Neweporte has entered the sixth of December

Of William Scrode alien for two barrels of herrings value xiij^{s} iiij^{d} and three pokettis hoppis weighing vj^{C} value xL^{s}

Of William Kennadye denizen for iiij butts[444] of rappe oyle value xL^{s}

---

441 The latin is Magno. Originally a Latin byname meaning 'great'.

442 *O.E.D.* Shotten, of fish, especially herring, that has spawned- thin, emaciated and worthless

443 Actually the scribe seems to have written 'B[o/a]Vns'

Of one pincke of Dunekyr[k] has entered the ninth day of March

Of Michael Thornebolde alien for two pokettis of hoppis wighing v^{C} value xxxiij^{s} iiij^{d}

Of one pincke of Ostende has entered xv die of March

Of John Roo alien for three pokettis of hoppes weighing vj^{C} value xL^{s}

Of one pincke of Ostende has entered the same day

Of Leonard Roffyne alien for iiij pokettes of hoppis weighing viij^{C} value liij^{s} iiij^{d}

Of one pincke of Ostende has entered the xxij day of March

Of Crispian Gowyn alien for ij pokettis hoppis weighing vj^{C} value xL^{s}

In one pincke of Ostende departing xxvj day of March

membrane 3v

Of Giles Maister Jannice for three pokettis of hoppis weighing viij^{C} value liij iiij^{d} and iiij barrels of herrings value xxvj^{s} viiij^{d}

Of one pincke of Ostende has entered the first day of April

Of William Cornelius alien for three [pockets[445]] of hoppis weighing viij^{C} value liij^{s} iiij^{d}

Of one pincke of Neweporte has entered the same day

Of Martin Thornebolde alien for ij barrels of herrings value xiij^{s} iiij^{d} and two pockettis hoppis weighing iiij^{C} value xxvj^{s} viij^{d}

Of one pincke of Neweporte has entered the ninth day of April

Of Cornelius Wappar alien for three pokettis of hoppis weighing vj^{C} value xL^{s} and three barrels fs'[446]

Of one pincke of Flossheing has entered the xj day of April

DOVOR

Of Cornelius Martyne alien for iiij barrel of coddisheaddis value [blank]

Of a ship of Calais[447] the second day of October

Of Oliver Skynner denizen for three pokettis of hoppis weighing vij^{C}[448] value xlvj^{s} viij^{d}

Of a ship of Dovor the same day

Of Thomas Lambert denizen for two pokettis hoppis weighing ij^{C} value xx^{s}

Of one pincke of Ostende has entered fourth day of October

Of Roger Drofte alien for three pokettis of hoppis weighing viij^{C} value Liij^{s} iiij^{d}

Of a ship of Calais the seventh day of October

Of William Doggarell denizen for one dekere[449] lethere value iiij$^{£}$ and vj dossen calfe skynnis value xx^{s} and vj^{C} sceres[450] skynnes value x^{s} and foure bakes[451] value v^{s}

---

444 The scribe appears to have written 'bvns'

445 The word appears to have been omitted.

446 The meaning of this abbreviation is uncertain perhaps 'ficus' as there is no value after the entry it would suggest that the scribe never completed the record.

447 Nave calecie.

448 Possibly vij the figure changed.

449 1 dicker equals 10 skins. A last of leather equals 20 dickers.

450 *O.E.D.* Skere, cleansed, purified.

451 *O.E.D.* Back [Du-bak] a large shallow vessell,a tub, trough, vat, cistern. especially applied to those used by brewers, dyers and picklers.

In the same pincke the eighth day of month of October

Of the same Droft for vj pipes of berre value Lx^s

Of One pincke of Ostende xij day of October

Of Roger Drofte alien for one pokete hoppes weighing [blank] value xx^s and ij^c salt fysshe value xL^s

The same pincke xiiij October

Of the same Drofte alien for three tuns of berre value Lx^s

Of one ship of Scotland[452] xvth day of the month of October

Of William Knere alien for xv diker of saltehydes called malegvye[453] total $xv^£$ and xvj barrels paid total $iiij^£$

Of Ralph[454] Hylldenizen for xxx lb of Salfforne[455] value $x^£$

Of the aforesaid ship of Scotland xviij day of October

Of Roger Wynde denizen for one pipe of berre

Of a ship of Calais the same day

Of John Morryson alien for [456] for xx bounches of oneyons and xx bounches of garlike and baskectes of crewses[457] value xj^s total xx^s

Of a ship of Dovour xx day of the month of October

Of Giles Strehe for iiij pipes of berree

Of a ship of Calais the same day

Of John Rockolles alien for one ?small trusse[458] with iiij et half[459] hosborowe[460] a lb value $ix^£$ and ij small driefattis[461] of onyon value x^s

Of one pincke of Newportexxviij day of October

Of Garred Lybore alien for two copper kettellis value $liij^s$ $iiij^d$

FEVERSHAM

Of one ship of Ostende the ninth day of October

Of James Trice alien for iiij pokettis hoppis weighing M^{lb} value $lxvj^s$ $viij^d$ one thousand hoppis value vj^s $viij^d$

In the same ship of Ostende the fifteenth day of October

Of James Trice alien for three tuns of berre vale Lx^s

In one ship of Flossheing the same day

Of John Bringeborn denizen for iij pipes of berre towards Boloyne[462] Bay value $xiij^£$ ~~xvj~~^{s} vj^s $viiij^d$ and v lastis herrings value $xxiij^£$

Of one ship of Flossheing xvij die of October

---

452 Scoti[ae].

453 Not found.

454 Rodulphe.

455 Saffron: ME 1615. Fr. *Saffron*; ult. Arab *Za'faran* An orange-red product consisting of the dried stigmas of *Crocus sativus* used for colouring confectionary and liquors for flavouring. Safflore, Safflower. 1563. Du *saffloer*; Fr. *saffleur*; early It. *safflore*. Dried petals of the *Carthamus tinctorium* and the red dye produced from them. Earlier, in 1548 the name was also used for bastard saffron, *Colchicum autumnale*.

456 This and the next line have been erased and written over again, making visibility very poor even under the ultra-violet light.

457 *O.E.D.* Cruse: a small earthern vessel for liquids; a pot jar or bottle. Also a drinking vessel.

458 Prio [last letter altered] Gras also gives *Trussum* as a bundle of cloth

459 Truss, a bundle or pack. A truss is equal to a 1/36 Load of Hay and generally weighs 52 lb. The half is simply given as d'.

460 *O.E.D.* Osnaburg: A kind of coarse linen originally made in Osnabrück, North Germany.

461 *O.E.D.* Dry-fat; a large vessel (cask,barrel, tub, box etc.) used to hold dry things.

462 Boulogne, France.

Of *Luno* Johnson alien for three lastis and a half of herrings value xiiij$^{£}$

membrane 4

In the same ship of Flosshinge the xxiiijth day of October

Of the same Lunus alien for six pipes of berre value Lx^{s}

Of one ship of Brill[463] the xxvjth day of October

Of James Williamson alien for one hundred[464] staplefysshe value xx^{s}, xv barrels of herrings with roe[465] value ciij^{s} iiij^{d} and one small chest[466] of sugar candy value ? xL^{s}

One ship of Ostende xxv day of October

Of Giles Cence alien for iiij pokettis hoppes weighing vj^{C} value three barrels of herrings with roe value xx^{s} one hundred and one quarters of stapulfysshe value xxv^{s} half a thousand[467] of hooppes value iij^{s} iiij^{d}

Of one ship of Flosshinge 29th day of October

Of John Bringeborn denizen for xv weys[468] of bay salt value x$^{£}$ one hundred fannes value xxv^{s} lx lb.towe[469] ?con.ve[470] value xx^{s}

Of one ship of Ostende xxixth day of October

Of Anthony Harbolte alien for vj barrels of herrings with roe value xL^{s} and one pokete hoppes weighing ij^{C} value xiij^{s} iij^{d}

In the aforesaid ship of Bryle the last day of October

Of James Williamson alien for three tuns of berre value Lx^{s}

Of one ship of Ostende the second day of ~~October~~ November

Of Cornelius Adamson alien for iiij barrels of herrings with roe value xxvj^{s} viij^{d} three pokettes hoppes weighing vj^{C} value xL^{s} and half a thousand hoppes for barrels value iij^{s} iiij^{d}

Of one ship of Ostende the second day of November

Of James Tace alien for ij pokettes hoppes weighing iiij^{C} value xxvj^{s} viij^{d}

In one ship of Ostende iij day of November

Of Giles Cence alien for three barrels of berre value Lx^{s}

In a ship of Ostende iiijth day of November

Of Anthony Harbolte alien for three tuns of berre value Lx^{s}

Of one ship of Flosshening vjth November

Of Nicholas Doote alien for ij laste of Herring with roe value viij$^{£}$

In a one ship of Ostend the eighth day of November

Of James Trice alien for vj pipes of berre value Lx^{s}

In one ship of Ostende the same day

Of Cornelius Adryanson alien for vj pipes of berre value Lx^{s}

Of a ship of Ostende xxvth day of November

---

463 Brielle, Netherlands sometimes The Brill, a fortified seaport town situated on the north side of the island of Voorne near the mouth of the Maas.

464 Simply C', this could also be for one hundred weight.

465 Allec' plenum = herrings with roe.

466 Cista de sugorcanndye: sugar clarified and crystallized by slow evaporation.

467 d'm^{l} de hooppes.

468 Latin *waga*, OE weight, wey. Zupko says that wey varied in size with the product as well with the region.*O.E.D.* quotes Jeake as saying of salt that it is reckoned by the hundred and wey, in 1 hundred of salt 10½ weys, in 1 wey 40 bushels.

469 Tow late ME The shorter fibres of flax and hemp separated by heckling from the fine long fibres.

470 Possibly course for coarse.

Of John Pollus alien for five barrels of herrings value xxiij^{s} iiij^{d} and iiij barrels of white salt vale x^{s}

In the same ship of Ostende the first day of December

Of the same John Poullus alien for three barrels of berre vale Lx^{s}

Of one ship of Neweport the third day of December

Of Nicholas Harbolte alien for ij pokettis hoppis weighing iij^{C} value xxvj^{s} viij^{d} three barrels of herrings with roe value xx^{s} and one thousand hoppis value vj^{s} viij^{d}

Of another ship of Neweporte the same day

Of Jasper Droite alien for three barrels of herrings with roe value xx^{s} three pokettis hoppes weighing vj^{C} value xL^{s} and one thousand hoopis[471] value vj^{s} viij^{d}

Of one ship of Ostende the eighth day of December

Of Giles[472] Cence alien for iiij pokettes of hoppes weighing viij^{C} value liij^{s} iiij^{d} three barrels of herrings value xx^{s} and one thousand hoopes value vj^{s} viij^{d}

Of One ship of Ostend xth day of December[473]

Of Vincent Gisling alien for ij pokettes hoppis weighing iiij^{C} iiij barrels of herrings with roe iiij [value not given]

Of one ship of Ostende the same day

Of Giles[474] Pansherste alien for three barrels of herrings value xx^{s} and ij pockettis hoppes weighing iiij^{C} value xxvj^{s} viij^{d}

In one ship of Neweporte xiij day of December

Of Nicholas Hellowte alien for three tuns of berre value Lx^{s}

In a ship of Neweporte the same day

Of Jasper Droye alien for three tuns of berre value Lx^{s}

In one ship of Flossheining xiiij day of December

Of Cornelius Mayson alien for six pipes of berre value Lx^{s}

In a ship of Ostende xv day of December

Of Giles Penshurste alien for three tuns of berre value Lx^{s}

In a ship of Ostende the same day

Of Giles Cence alien for three tuns of berre value Lx^{s}

In one ship of Ostende xvij day of December

Of Vincent Gyslinge alien for three barrels of berre value Lx^{s}

In a ship of Flosshing xix December

Of John Bringeborne denizen for one pipe and iiij barrels[475] of musterde sede value xij^{s}

Of a ship of Ostende xxij day of December

Of Cornelius Adryanson alien for iiij barrels of herrings valued at xxvj^{s} viij^{d} and ij pokettis hoppis weighing viij^{C} value liij^{s} iiij^{d}

In the ship aforesaid the first day of January

Of Cornelius Adrianson for three tuns of beere value Lx^{s}

In a ship of Ostende the second day of January

---

471 As with other entries the first p was erased and an O written in the space.

472 Egidio: the scribe then uses the Latin Elegius which may, in fact, once again be Giles.

473 Ship and entry for Gisling entered in the margin.

474 Elegius.

475 Abbreviated to bz.

membrane 4v

Of Giles Gowcant alien for a half a laste of herrings with roe value xL^{s}, vij pokettes hoppis weighing vj^{C} value xiij^{s} iiij^{d} and one hundred[476] stapulfysshe value xx^{s}

In the said ship the third day of January

Of the same Giles for three tuns of berre value Lx^{s}

Of a ship of Ostende the fifth day of January

Of Cornelius Nobles alien for ij pokettis hoppes weighing iiij^{C} value xxvj^{s} viij^{d} and for two barrels of herrings valued xiij^{s} iiij^{d}

In one ship of London the tenth of January

Of John Hamptone denizen for one[477] measure of a short- cloth without being made thin.

Of a ship of Flossheinge the same day

Of John Bringeborne denizen for[478] four pipes of beere licenced to load[479] towards Bolayne

Adam Fowle denizen for one hoggyshed herrings in the same ship

In a ship of Ostend xj day of January

Of Cornelius Noble alien for vj pipes of berre value Lx^{s}

Of a ship of Giles Spencer of Ostende xij day of January

Of the same Giles for iiij barrels of herrings value xxvj^{s} viij^{d} and three pokettes of hoppes weighing vj^{C} value xL^{s}

In a ship of Flossheinge the same day

Of Nicholas Doode alien for three tuns of beere value Lx^{s}

Of the ship of Ostende xix day of January

Of Giles Cence alien for viij pokettes hoppes weighing xvj^{C} value Cvj^{s} viij^{d} et viij barrel of herrings with roe value liij^{s} iiij^{d}

Of a ship of Ostende the first day of February

Of Cornelius Adrianson alien for vij barrels of herrings with roe value xlvj^{s} viij^{d}

Of a ship of Ostende vij day of February

Of Magnus Peter alien for ij pokettis hoppis weighing iiij^{C} value xxvj^{s} viij^{d}

Of another ship of Ostende the same day

Of Cornelius Ryfte alien for two pockettes hoppes weighing iiij^{C} value xxvj^{s} viiij^{d} and ij barrels of herrings xiij^{s} iiij^{d}

Of a ship of Flosshinge the same day

Of John Bringeborn denizen for viij laste of herrings value xxxij$^{£}$ and one laste barrel fysshe value iiij$^{£}$ xxiiij^{s} pecis great raysinges value xL^{s}

In a ship of Ostende ix day of February

Of Cornelius Adrianson alien for three tuns of berre value Lx^{s}

In another ship of Ostende xij day of February

Of Magnus Peter alien for three tuns of berre vale Lx^{s}

In a ship of Cornelius Rifte of Ostende the same day

---

[476] Centum, this is very difficult to see even under Ultra-violet light.

[477] Uno pannis curtis sine grac[ilare] compare *Gras* uno pannis lane curtis sine grano; pannus ad vela (sailcloth); pannus burnetti (browncloth); pannus grisius (greycloth).

[478] Rest of this entry written over an erasure.

[479] Carcand versus Bolayne.

Of the same Cornelius alien for three tuns of berre value Lx^{s}

Of a ship of Ostende iiij February

Of John Galyarde alien for xxviij barrels of herrings value ix$^{£}$ vj^{s} viij^{d}

Of a ship of Ostende xix day of February

Of James Rifte alien for xx barrels of herrings with roe value vj$^{£}$ xij^{s} iiij^{d} five barrels of shottyn herrings value xvj^{s} viij^{d} and one pokete hoppis weighing CC value xiij^{s} iiij^{d}

In one ship of Flosshinge xx day of February

Of Cornelis Baker alien for three tuns of berre value Lx^{s} and lvj dossen connye skynnes value xx^{s} and one and lvj dossen connye skynnes value xx^{s} and one measure of broadcloth without grain[480]

Of one ship of Ostende xxijth day of February

Of Crispian Oze alien for ij ~~pokettes hoppes~~ lastis of herrings with roe value viij$^{£}$ ij pockettis hoppis weighing iiij^{C} value xxvj^{s} viij^{d}

In one ship of Ostende departing the same day

Of James Ryfte alien for three barrels of berre value Lx^{s}

In one other ship of Ostende the same day

Of John Galyarde alien for three tuns of berre value Lx^{s}

Of one ship of Ostende xxvjth day of February

Of Giles Cence alien for v pokettes hoppe weighing one thousand value lxvj^{s} viij^{d}, ij [barrels] of herrings with roe value xiij^{s} iiij^{d} and one barrel of shottyn herrings value iij^{s} iiij^{d}

Of James Trice alien for v barrels of herrings value xxxiij iiij^{d} and v barrels of shottyn herrings value xvj^{s} and three pokettis hoppes weighing vj^{C} value xL^{s}

In one ship of Ostende departing the same day

Of Crispian Oze alien for three tuns of berre value Lx^{s}

Of one ship of Ostende departing ~~the same day~~ vjth day of March

Of Giles Cence alien for three tuns of berre value Lx^{s}

In another ship of Ostende the same day

Of James Trice alien for three tuns of berre value Lx^{s}

Of a ship of Ostende xij day of March

Of Cornelius Ryfte alien for iiij pokettes hoppis weighing viij^{C} value liij^{s} iiij^{d} and two dossen chayres value iiij^{s}

Of a ship of Ostende xiiij day of March

Of Cornelius Noble alien for three pokettes of hoppis weighing vj^{C} value xL^{s}

membrane 5

Of one other ship of Ostende the same day

Of Magnus Peter alien for three Pokettes of hoppes weighing vj^{C} value xL^{s}

In a ship of Ostende xviij day of March

Of Cornelius Ryfte alien for iij tuns of berre value Lx^{s}

Of One ship of Rotheredame[481] the same day

---

480 Latin: *pannis longis sine grano.*

481 Rotterdam, Netherlands.

Of John Clayson alien for two lastes of herrings and a half and half a barrell value x$^{£}$ ij barrels of salmon value xxxvj^{s} viij^{d} four pynnes[482] of samone value xviij^{s} iiij^{d}
And of Thomas Pinckeney denizen for xx barrels of herrings valued vj$^{£}$ xiij^{s} iiij^{d} one peice of holland value xiij[s] and v barrels of coddefysshe value xxxiij^{s} iiij^{d}

In a ship of Ostende xvij day of March
Of Cornelius Nobbes alien for three tuns of berre value Lx^{s}

In one other ship of Ostende the same day
Of Magnus Peter alien for three tuns of berre value Lx^{s}

In a ship of Rotheredame departing the same day
Of John Clayson for three tuns of berre value Lx^{s}

ROCHESTER

Of one pincke of Ostende the second day of the month of October
Of James Bowmes alien for two poketes hoppes weighing vij^{C}

Of the same pincke of Ostende vj day of October
Of the same James Bowmes alien for three tuns of berre value Lx^{s}

Of one pincke of Neweporte the third day of November
Of George Foyste alien for three poketes of hoppes weighing viij^{C} value

In one [the same *written above*] pincke of Neweporte the eighth day of November
Of the same George Foyste alien for three tuns of berre value Lx^{s}

Of one hoye of Flosshinge xxiijth day of November
Of Cornelius Martyne for one laste of herrings value iiij$^{£}$
Of John Tyloucye for xviij weys of bay salte value xiij$^{£}$

Of one pincke of Flossheinge xv day of November
Of William Johnson alien for one last of herrings valued iiij$^{£}$

Of one Catche of Barling xxij day of December
Of James ....ching denizen for vj laste of herring value xxiiij$^{£}$

Of one pincke of Ostende xij day of January
Of Vincent Barnarde alien for two lastes of herring value viij$^{£}$

Of one pincke of Rotheredame xvj day of January
Of John Clocysse alien for one laste of Herring value iiij$^{£}$
The same John for half a barrel of Salmond value x^{s}

Of one pincke of Ostend xix day of January
Of Peter Motes alien for one laste of herring value vj$^{£}$

In one pincke of Ostende xix day of January
Of Vincent Sernerde alien for three tuns of berre value Lx^{s}

In one pincke of Rotheredam xxijth January
Of John Cloysse alien for three tuns of berre value Lx^{s}

In one pincke of Ostende the same day
Of Peter Motes alien for three tuns of berre value Lx^{s}

---

[482] *O.E.D.* Pin (12) A small cask or keg holding half a firkin, or 4½ gallons.

membrane 6 is partly sewn to the bottom of membrane 5. Membrane 5 is cut such that there was originally writing further down. The faces of both membrane have been copied first before the dorses as this seemed to be the order.

Of one pincke of Ostende has entered xxvijth day of March

Of Giles Master Johns alien for three pockettis of hoppes weighing viij^{C} value liiij^{s} iiij^{d} and iiij barrels of herrings value xxvj^{s} viij^{d}, total [*blank*]

In another pincke of Ostende has entered the same day

Of Martin Fromebold alien for ij barrels of herrings value xiij^{s} iiij^{d} and two pockettis of hoppis weighing iiij^{C} value xxvj^{s} viij^{d}

Of one pincke of ~~Ostende~~ Neweporte has entered the ninth of April

Of Cornelius Wapper alien for three pokettis hoppis weighing vj^{C} value xL^{s} and three barrels grain[483] value vj^{s} viij^{d}

Of one pincke of Flossheninge has entered the xj day of April

Of Cornelius Martyne alien for four barrels of Coddishedes value x^{s}

Of one pincke of Ostende has entered xxviij day of April

Of Julian Roo alien for ij pokettis hoppis weighing v^{C} value xxxiij^{s} iiij^{d}

Of one pincke of Ostende has entered xxix day of April

Of Martin Fromebolde alien for two pokettis hoppes weighing iiij^{C} value xxvj^{s} viij^{d}

Of one hoye of Flossheingehas entered the sixth day of March

Of ?Paduico Cooke alien for iiij barrels of fish value xxvj^{s} viij^{d}

Of one pincke of Dunekyrke has entered the xij day of March

Of Gerrard Lyberte alien for one baskete weighing CC lb one hundred diverse pewter vessels and ancient[484] value xxiij^{s} iiij^{d}

Of one pincke of Dunekirke has entered the same day

Of Coppyne Neyeman alien for one pokette hoppis weighing CC value xiij^{s} iiij^{d} and one barrel of scastokis[485] without roe value iij^{s} iiij^{d}

One pincke of Ostende has entered the same day

Of Francis Michaell alien for ij pokettis hoppis weighing v^{C} v lb value xxxiiij^{s} iiij^{d}

Of one argusae has entered xij day of May

Of John Bowell denizen for two butts one of Malmesye tonnage

Of one pincke of Ostende has entered xiiij day of March

Of William Cornelius alien for two pokettes hoppis weighing iiij^{C} lb xxvj^{s} viij^{d}

In one ship The Mary of Saint John de Luce[486] has entered the same day

Of William Saint Martyne alien for xl tuns non-sweet wine, tonnege[487]

Of one pincke of Ostende has entered the xix day of ~~March~~ May

Of Julian Roo alien for half-hundred of Stapule fyshe and half a barrel of stapulfyshhe value xxx^{s}[488]

Of one pincke of Neweporte has entered the same day

---

483 Latin fru[mentum].

484 Latin CC lb centi diversa vasa erca et vetena. Gras *ib* vasa electri = pewter vessel.

485 Scast(or c)o (overwritten on ry?) kis non pleni stockfish without roe: cod and other gadoid fish cured by drying hard in cold air and beating with clubs or stocks.

486 Sain-Jean-de-Luz, France, department of Bassses Pyrénèes, at the mouth of the Nivelle, 7 miles from the Spanish frontier.

487 xL^{tes} [tes- is partly crossed out] dolijs vini non dulcis tonnege.

488 Changed for xxix^{s}.

Of Andreas Sereke alien for five barrels of fish value xxxiij^{s} iiij^{d} v^{C} small salte hadockes xij coppull linges and one quarter of stapul fishe value xx^{s}

Of one pincke of Dunekyrke has entered the same day

Of Martin Fromebolde alien for iij barrels fish value xx^{s}

Of another pincke of Dunekirke has entered the first day of June

Of James Neyman alien for one pokette of hoppis weighing CC lb value xiij^{s} iiij^{d} and one barrel of fish value vj^{s} viij^{d}

Of one pincke of Ostende has entered the same day

Of Cornelius Nobbes alien for one pokete of hoppis weighing CC et half-hundred of stapul fysshe value x^{s} and half-hundred of Cole fysshe[489] value vj^{s} viij^{d}

Of another pincke of Ostende has entered the same day

Of Giles Marchyns alien for ij barrels of fish value xx^{s}

Of another pincke of Ostende has entered the fifth day of June

Of Giles Maister Johns alien for CC stapul fisshe value xL^{s} and ~~xiij~~^{s} xiij cuppull lingis value xiij^{s} ... ij^{d}

Of another pincke of Ostende has entered the vj June

Of William Cornelius alien for three barrels of fish value xx^{s} one pokette of hoppis weighing CC lb value xiij^{s} iiij^{d}

Of one other pincke of Ostende has entered the viij[490] day of June

Of John Gowghe alien for vj barrels of fish value xL^{s}

Of One pincke of Neweporte has entered the same day

membrane 6 verso

The dorse of both membranes are not very clear that of membrane 5 being in a very poor state

Of Cornelius Wapper alien for ij pokettes hoppis weighing CCC lb value xx^{s} and one [barrel] of colefysshe value vj^{s} viij^{d} iiij^{CC} M bryckes[491] value xxv^{s} viij^{d} and ij thousand hoppes value x^{s}

In a pincke of Flossheing has entered the xxviij day of June

Of Ludovick Cocke for three [barrels] of fish value at xx^{s}

In one ship called The Mary Saint Johns of Barro[492] departing the xxiij day of June

Of Henry Emerson denizen for clxxv pecys lead weighing xj foder[493] value xliij$^{£}$ xvj chalderes de Newe Castyll[494] cooles value v$^{£}$ vj^{s} viij^{d} et three pokettis of Spanysshe woll weighing CCC lb value Lx^{s} and three pokettis hoppes weighing vij^{C} lb value xlvj^{s} viij^{d}

Of One hoye of Larabone has entered xxxth day of June

Of John Devyne alien for vj pecys of rasynes value xx^{s}

Of one pincke of Newport has entered the third day of July

Of Vincent Lawrence alien for iij pokettes of hoppis weighing ix^{C} lb value Lx^{s}

---

489 *O.E.D.*, **Coal-fish**. A fish (*Merlangus* or *Pollachius carbonarius*, or *Gadus virens*), allied to the Cod, so called from the dusky pigment which tinges its skin, and soils the fingers like moist coal. Found in the Northern Seas, and caught for food. (It has many local names; in U.S. called *pollock*).

490 Entry damaged, just possibly viiij.

491 This particular entry extremely difficult to read even under ultra-violet light.

492 Barrow-in-Furness, Cumbria.

493 *clxxv pecys plombis ponderis xj foder*. foder = fother = *O.E.D.* a definite weight of some specified substance - of lead now usually 19½ cwt - this was the weight at the King's Beam in 1590.

494 Newcastle-upon-Tyne, Tyne and Wear.

Of another pincke of Neweport has entered the same day

Of Cornelius Wapper alien for ij pokettis hoppis weighing v^{C} lb value xxxiij^{s} iiij^{d}

In one pincke of Neweporte departing xth day of July

Of Martin Fromebolt alien for ij tuns and a half of berre value ls

In one pincke of Ostende departing the same day

Of Julian Roo alien for three tuns of berre value Lx^{s}

Of one pincke of Dunekyrk has entered xij day of July

Of Nicholas Peke denizen for ij lastis et a half of tarre value ls and xxx pairs[495] mastes value xL^{s}

Of one pincke of Neweporte has entered the same day

Of Edward Parker denizen for ten poketes hoppes weighing xxv^{C} lb value viij$^{£}$ vj^{s} viij^{d}

Of one ship of Dunekyrke has entered the same day

Of Walter Sheterden denizen for one last and a half of tarre value xx^{s}

Of one pincke of Ostende has entered xiiij day of July

Of Leonard Roffyne for one hundred of stapull fyshe value xx^{s}

Of one pincke of Ostende has entered xvij day of July

Of Adrian Petersone alien for ~~ij~~ one pokett~~is~~ hoppis weighing iij^{C} value xx^{s} and ij barrels coddesheades value iiij^{s}

Of one pincke of Neweportehas entered the xxij day of July

Of Cornelius Petersone alien for CC stapul fysshe value xL^{s}

Of one pincke of ~~Neweporte~~ Dunekyrke has entered xxvj day of July

Of Martin Fromebolde alien for ij barrels fish value xiij^{s} and one quarter of stapul fysshe value v^{s}

Of one Crayer called The Elisabeth of Sandwiche

Whereof John Stokebrige is master departing xxvj July

Of Henry Goodyeres merchant of the staple of the town of Calais for two thousand nine hundred sixty and six skins complete with the wool towards the staple aforesaid

In one ~~new~~ Crayer called The Julian of Sandwiche whereof Robert Stone is master the last day of July

Of Henry Browne merchant of the stapull of the town of Calais for one thousand and one hundred skins complete with the wool towards the staple aforesaid

In one crayer called The James of Sandwiche whereof Thomas Shawe is master departing the same day

Of the aforesaid Henry Browne for xiiij^{C} skins complete with the wool towards the staple aforesaid

Of one pincke of Calais has entered ij day of August

membrane 5 verso

Of one pincke of Sluce[496] has entered the second day of August

Of William Clarke alien for iij pokettes hoppes weighing vj^{C} v value xL^{s} one dossen boundell fannys[497] value xx^{s} and CC lb of towe value x^{s}

---

495 Parius.

496 Sluys - Zeeland, 10m NE Bruges.

497 Most probably winnowing fans.

In one pincke of Dunekirke departing the same day

Of Martin Framebolt alien for iij tuns of berre value Lx^{s}

Of one pincke of Dunekyrke has entered the third day of August

Of James Neyeman alien for one sacke and one pokette hoppes weighing iiij^{C} lb value xxvj^{s} viij^{d} one barrel of fish value vj^{s} six cupple of stapull fysshe value iij^{s} iiij^{d}

Of one pincke of Neweporte has entered the iiij day of August

Of James Blacke alien for ij pokettis hoppes weighing iiij^{C} lb and a half value xx^{s}

Of one pincke of Ostende has entered the same day

Of Leonard Roffyne alien for one hundred of Stapul fysshe value xx^{s}, half a thousand hoopes value iij^{s} iiij^{d} and ? ij barrels of fish value xx^{s} and one hundred bounches of rootes value iij^{s} iiij^{d}

Of one pincke of Ostende has entered the same day

Of Francis Moyne alien for ij small pokettes hoppis weighing iij^{C} value xx^{s} and one thousand b[rykes] value x^{s} and half a thousand hoppes value iij^{s} iiij^{d}

Of one pincke of Ostende has entered the fifth day of August

Of Julian Roo alien for ij pokettes hoppis weighing iiij^{C} lb value xxvj^{s} viiij^{d}

Of one pinke of Neweporte entered the same day

Of Andrewe Serecke alien for three barrels ~~of berre~~ fish value xcx^{s} and one thousand brickis value v^{s}

Of one pincke of Ostende entered the same day

Of Ludovick Harbolt alien for one pockette of hoppes weighing CC lb value xiij^{s} iiij^{d}

Of one pincke of Dunekyrke entered the same day

Of Francis Butyer alien for iij barrels of fish value xx^{s}

One pincke of Neweporte departing the vjth day of August

Of James Blacke alien for three tuns of berre value Lx^{s}

Of one pincke of Ostende has entered the viijth day of August

Of Adrian Peterson alien for one pocket of hoppes weighing ij^{C} lb value xiij^{s} iiij^{d} et one thousand hoppis value vj^{s} viij^{d}

Of one pincke of Ostende has entered the same day

Of John Harbolte alien for ij barrels of fish value xiij^{s} iiij^{d} one thousand hoppes value vj^{s} viij^{d}

In one pincke of Ostende departing the same day

Of Leonard Roffyne alien for six pipes of berre value Lx^{s}

In one pincke of ~~Newe~~ Dunekyrke departing the same day

Of Francis Butyer alien for three tuns of berre value Lx^{s}

Of one pincke of Ostende departing the viij of August

end of membrane

APPENDIX 9:
Arden as broker.

ELLENDEN
PRO: E318/2/34 [Latin]
Particulars for Grants 35 Henry 8
Thomas Arderne grantee section 2 containing 7 membranes

membrane 1

County of Kent parcell of the revenues of the late monastery of Faversham in the said county

Manor of Elynnden in the said County of Kent[498]
Rents of assize there by the year 23^{s} $9\frac{1}{4}^{d}$
Rents of moveable goods (poultry) there by the year 4^{s} 9^{d}

Farm of the manor called Elynnden aforesaid with all curtilages barnes buildings closes arable and pasture containing by estimation 154 acres pertaining to the same manor or belonging lying and being in the parishes of Seasalter and Whitstable with one store of one quarter of wheat price the quarter 6^{s} 8^{d} and one quarter of barley price the quarter 3^{s} 4^{d} (Except nevertheless and always reserving all wood, and underwood) rent of assize and suit of court of the said manor appertaining in the tenure of William Baldock and John Goodhew thus to them demised by indenture dated 23rd day of September in the 27th year of the reign of King Henry the VIIIth to have from the feast of Saint Michael the Archangel next following as far as the end and term of 22 years then next following and fully to be completed rendering in respect thereof by the years $6^{£}$ at the feast of All Saints and St. Thomas the Apostle by equal portions And the said farmers and executors have annually during the term aforesaid 20 wagon-loads of wood for the fuel expended within the aforesaid manor during the term aforesaid Deductions and all and every ordinary and extraordinary charge to the charge of the lord King in accordance as in the same indenture amongst other things it plainly appears $6^{£}$

Profits of the common court[499] by estimation each year 3^{s} 4^{d}
total $7^{£}$ 11^{s} $10\frac{1}{4}^{d}$

membrane 2 (stiched to the bottom of 1)

Deductions from profits , that is to say,

deduction of rent of certain lands above charged in the title rents of assize within the sum of 23^{s} $9\frac{1}{4}^{d}$, that is to say for the lands of William Roper $17\frac{1}{4}^{d}$ for the lands of John Porte $8\frac{1}{2}^{d}$ for the lands called Lovecotes now in the hands of the lord King 10^{d} for certain lands lately of Christ Church Canterbury 7^{d} of the church of Whytestaple 10^{d} and for certain lands lately Joan Hore widow 8^{d} Which same rents have lapsed for many years that they were uncollectable[500] And

---

[498] R. H.Goodsall, *Whitstable, Seasalter and Swalecliffe* (1938) p. 66. Elyndene became the property of Robert Billesdon of Faversham, who died in 1504, leaving his manor or tenement called Elyndene with all his lands, rents and weirs, in Seasalter and Whitstable to the Abbey of Faversham for seven years, and from the income his obit (or yearly memorial service) was to be kept in the Abbey Church. After the seven years Elyndene was to be sold, and was evidently bought by Faversham Abbey, as the abbey was the owner in 1534.

[499] Custumal court: curius ibidem communibus annis per estimationem.

[500] Illemabil [?illemavil].

where the same lands situated out of what ecclesiastical community[501] they are wholly ignorant by the year 5^s ½¼

And remaining clear by the year $7^£$ 6^s $9½^d$

membrane 4 stitched to the bottom of 3 [Latin]
Margin 29th day of June in the 35th year of the reign of King Henry the Eighth by Thomas Ardern.

The yerly rent of the mannor of Elynnden and of other londes in Harnhill parcell of the possessions of the late monastery of Feversham $9^£$ 3^s $6½^d$ in respect thereof for tenth 18^s $4½^d$ And remains [clear] $8^£$ 5^s 2^d which to be purchased at 20 yerees purchase amountith to the summe of $173^£$ 8^s 6^d The yerly value of one marsche parcell of the possessions of the late monastery of Lessones[502] and after part of the possessions of the late Erle of Essex 6^s 8^d which to be purchased at 26 yeres purchase amountith to the summe of $8^£$ 13^s 4^d Also one messuage or Inne in Feversham 23^s 4^d in respect thereof for tenth 2^s 4^d And there remains clear 21^s which to be purchased at 15 yere purchase doth amounte to $15^£$ 15^s And soe the whole summe of the purchase doth amounte to the summe of $197^£$ 16^s 10^d Adde therto for the woodes $4^£$ 19^s 4^d and so the whole summe is $202^£$ 16^s 2^d

Memorandum the kinge muste discharge hym of all incumbraunces excepte leasses and the rent before reserved

signatures Richard ?Poutswell
John Williames
Walter Hendle
William Staunford

Membrane 5, a small parchment thonged at the base of the last

Memorandum that I Thomas Ardern do require to purchas of the Kinges Highnes by vertue of his commission sale the premisses beinge of the clere yerely values within written In witnes whereof I have sealed and subscribed this bill with my seale and hand the daye and yere specified in the role hereunto annexed

membrane 6

County of Kent:
The manor or tenement of Elynnden in the parishes of Seysalter and Whytstaple parcell of the possessyons of the late monasterye of Feversham in the seyd countye of Kent

Item a parcell of wode callyd the tonge woode conteyneth 5 acres, Elynnden Grove adioynyng uppon tonge woode aforeseyd conteyneth with 2 acres waste 10 acres

Item dyverse hedgerowes there conteyneth 3 acres SUMME of 18 acres whereof 2 acres wast 5 acres fallen thys yere and solde by commyssyon to Thomas Ardern gentyleman 5 acres of 7 yeres growth reservyd to William Baldocke fermour there for 20 loods of woode for fewell to be spent within the seyd manor or tenement and for woode and thornes for to repayr and amend the

501 Ex sacro coll[egio].
502 The abbey of Lesnes or Westwood was in the parish of Erith, Kent. See account VCH, Kent ii, p. 165.

hedges and fences aboute the seyd manour or tenement which he hath by covenaunt of hys indentour beryng date the 24th daye of September in the 27th yere of the reign of our soveraigne Lorde Kyng Henry the VIIIth therefore not valuyd 3 acres (12s) of 8 yeres growth and 3 acres (24s) resydue of 16 yeres growth the woode of evey acre valuyd as apperith which is in the holle 36s

The sprynges of the woode or grounde of 2 acres not valuyd bycause yt ys wast and the herbagge of the same dymysed and 10 acres not valuyd by cause they be reservyd and of 6 acres resydue ratyd yerely at 6d the acre which ys yerely in the holle 3s and amountteth after 20 yeres purchase to 60s

Likewise in hedgrowes inclosyng the landes perteynyng to the seyd manour or tenement be growing 60 okes part tymber shrude[503] and loppyd of 60 yeres growth reservyd for tymber to repayr and amend the seyd manor or tenement and other houses standing uppon the same which the kynges maiestye ys chargyd with all as apperyth by the indentour aforeseyd therfore not valuyd None

LESNES[504]

membrane 7 Latin

The value that was delivered by Henry Coke merchant taylor of London by virtue of a warrant of Richard Suthwell knight one of the General Surveyors of the lands of the lord King dated 29th day of May in the thirty fifth year of the Lord King Henry the VIIIth.

Margin underneath by Arden. At 26 yeres purchis

The marsh of the Lord King in Lyssones parcell of the manor of Lyssones in the county of Kent and a short time ago late of the monastery of Lyssones in the county aforesaid, part and parcel of the possessions late of Cardinal Thomas Wolcey attainted

Marshes of the lord King there late parcel of the manor of Lyssones aforesaid inundated by water lately at 60£ 11s 8d by the year and before they were under water for the space of 14 years no rents for the same had been paid by reason of the inundation of water aforesaid which same Henry Coke citizen and merchant taylor of London took the same marsh of the Lord King by indenture from the General Surveyor of the lands of the said Lord the king dated the 27th day of June in the 31st year of the reign of King Henry the VIIIth for the term of 31 years rendering in respect thereof by the year 6s 8d

Memorandum that the saide Marshes are parcell of the manor of Lyssones whiche manor with other was geven to Sir Rawse Sadler in ffee symple as apperythe by the kynges graunte thereof made datede at Westminster the 29th of May in the 28th year of the reign of King Henry the VIIIth And hathe the fee symple of the fysshinge of the same marshes by vertue of the same graunte

Item the saide marshes are within syx myles of the kinges manor and parkes of Grenwyche and ther be none other parkes chaces nor forests nere adjoyned unto the saide marshes to my knowleage but only Greenwyche aforesaide

---

503 *O.E.D.* **shroud** *n.*[3] [Formally identical with shroud *n.*[1], but with sense independently derived from the sense 'to cut' of the root. Cf. shred *n.*] **a.** *collect. sing. and pl.* Loppings of a tree, branches or twigs cut off. **b.** (chiefly *pl.*) A branch or bough.

Item ther hathe bene no fyne heretofore paide for the premisses to my knowleage
Item ther are no other patronages advowsyons chauntereys nor other promotions belonginge to the saide marshes nor any deductions goinge owte of the same
Item I have made no particular of the premisses to anny persons hertofore but only to the sayd Henry Coke
Item I have nott herde hertofore of anny person whiche was desyrous to purchase the saide marshes other then the saide Henry Coke now fermour there
By me J. Smyth , auditor.

OTTERPOOL, CANTERBURY.[505]

PRO: E318/2/36

Particulars for grants 37 Henry 8

Thomas Arderne grantee section 4 containing 8 membranes.

membrane 1
Memorandum that I Thomas Ardrene do require to purchase of the kynges majestie by vertue of his Graces comyssion of sale the premysses contayned in the particlers wherunto these presentes are annexid beinge of suche clere yerelye value as is comprysed in the same in wytnes wherof I have subscryvyd my name And put to my seale the threde of July in the 37th yere of the raygne of our soveraygne Lorde Kynge Henry the VIIIth by the Grace of God Kynge of Englonde Fraunce and Irelonde defendoure of the fayth and in erth of the churche of Englonde and Irelonde the supreme hedd

per me Thomas Arderne[506]

membrane 2
all Latin

County of Kent
Parcel of the lands and posessions late Thomas Wyattes now in the hands of the lord King by reason of purchase

Manor of Otterpole
Value in,
Rents of Assize of the diverse free tenants there by the year 51^{s} 5½^{d}

Farm of one mansion there well built with barns and other outhouses being in good repair with 340 acres of arable land 70 acres of pasture 20 acres of marsh and ten acres of meadow of the same manor belonging and pertaining lying in the said parishes of Lyme and Sellynge Rents of assize, profits of court, woods, underwoods and large tree enclosed lands within the park of the lord King of Osteinghanger[507] and land called Grekkes all excepted and reserved in the tenure of Thomas Harte thus to him demised by indenture by a period of years as he says rendering thence by the year 19$^{£}$ 3^{s} 4^{d}

---

[504] The ruins of Lesnes or Lessness Abbey are 1½ miles north west of Erith, Kent.
[505] Manor of Otterpool see OS Map 1 inch series TR1036.
[506] This is a very clear signature.

Profits of the the common court there by the year 12^{d}

[total] 21$^{£}$ 15^{s} 9½^{d}

Repairs,
that is to say,
Allocation of rents of certain lands there late Thomas Poynynges with 23^{d} of the value 7 hens and 1 cock surcharged to the account of 8^{s} 6½^{d} per annum within the sum of 61^{s} 5½^{d} And that there remains in the hand of the lord King by reason of the exchange with the aforesaid Thomas Poynynges knight and thus in the allocation 8^{s} 6½^{d}

Allocation of rent or quit rents arising of the late Monastery of Hyth previously entitled rents of assize amounting to 6^{s} 8^{d} by the year And which monastery being dissolved and in the hands of the lord King out which rents aforesaid there survives 6^{s} 8^{d}

[total] 15^{s} 2½^{d}
So that there remains clear by the year 21$^{£}$ 7½^{d}

interlined section
at 20 yeres profites 378$^{£}$ 5^{s} 10^{d} clear 18$^{£}$ 18^{s} 6½^{d} above this last little section Tenth[508] 42^{s} 1^{d}

The manor with the appurtenaunces above specyfyed as I have learned ys frome eny of the kynges majesties houses whereunto hys hyghnes hath eny accesse and repayre four myles and frome of his graces parkes forrests and chases foure myles what fyne or income wilbe given for the same I knowe nott what patronages advousons or other spirituall procurations do thereunto belong amonges the recordes of the tenthes doth appere This ys the fyrst particular that I have made oute of the premysses ne I do nott knowe that eny other person ys desyerous to by the same

Examined by me Richard Brasier deputy

William Cavendysshe auditor

membrane 3
County of Kent
The manor of Otterpole on the seyd countye late perteyning to Sir Thomas Wyatt knight and now in the kinges Majesties handes by reason of exchange

WESTWOOD contains with waste 8 acres
ITEM TWO other coppies woodes there conteyne 15 acres
SUM OF ACRES WHEREOF ys 23
waste and woodland destroyed 4 acres 8 acres of 10, 12 and 14 yeres growth reservid to thomas harte fermour there for his fyreboote[509] and hedgeboote which he hath byn accustomed to have in the same, one acre of 2 yeres growth (16^{d}), one acre of 3 yeres growth (2^{s}), one acre of 4 yeres growth (2^{s} 8^{d}), 4 acres of 12 yeres growth (32^{s}) And 4 acres resydue of 16 yeres growth (42^{s} 8^{d}) The wood of every acre aforeseid valuyd as apperyth which ys in the holl 4$^{£}$ 8^{d}

---

507 See account of Ostenhanger under Westenhanger; Hasted (Canterbury, 1799), viii , p.69.

508 As x^{ma}.

509 J. Richardson, *op. cit.* Firebote: The right to take wood from the commons for fuel. Hedgebote or Haybote: The right to take wood from the commons to make or repair fences.

THE SPRYNG of the wood or ground of 8 acres aforeseyd not valuyd bycause they be reservid and of 4 acres rated yerely at 4^{d} the acre bycause yt ys waste and the kinges majesties never had any profytt of the same And of 11 acres resydue rated yerely at 8^{d} the acre which ys yerely in the holle 8^{d} 8^{d} And amounteth after 20 yeres purchase to $8^{£}$ 13^{s} 4^{d}

IN THE SEYD woodes about the seytuation of the seyd mannour and in the landes perteyning to the same be growing 200 okes ashes and elmes of 60 and 80 yeres growth parte usually cropped and shred whereof 170 reservid to the seyd fermour for his housboote ploughboote carteboote and for stakes for hedgeboote to repayre and meynteyn the hedges and fences about the seyd landes And 30 resydue veluyd at 8^{d} the tree which is in the holle 20^{s}

[total] $13^{£}$ 14^{s}

examined by me David Clayton

membrane 4 Latin
County of Kent parcel of the revenues late of the Monastery of St. Augustines in the said county.

Diverse lands and tenementes lying within the suburbs of the city of Canterbury, value in,

Farm of one acre and one rod of land lying at Wynchepefelde in the tenure of the rectory of the Blessed Virgin Mary of the Castell adjoining to the lands of James Hales on the North and East side, and lands of William Yonge on the West side and a certain parcel of land called Wynchepfelde on the South side

Rendering in respect thereof by the year 21^{d} [510]

Farm of one tenement called the Blackehorse adjacent to the house of William Wygmore on the east side and the lands of Johanne Garrett widow on the West side and the kings highway on the North side and South in the tenure of John Garrarde thus to him demised by indenture as he saieth, rendering in respect thereof by the year 26^{s} 8^{d} [511]

Farm of one tenement with a garden and so forth to the same appurtaining lying and being in the parish of St. Paul near the city of Canterbury adjacent to the lands of James Peres on the West side and the lands of Richard Waler on the South side and the lands of Christopher Shorte on the North side and the kings street on the eastside in the tenure of John Kydder and Agnes his wife thus to them demised by indenture given the 6th day of July in the 30th year of the reign of King Henry the VIIIth, that is to say, from the feast of the Nativity of Saint John the Baptist last past to the end and term of 49 years and then next following and fully to be completed Rendering thence by the year 12^{d} at the feast of Nativity Saint John the Baptist as much reparations to the premisses to the charge of the farm as is shown by the said indenture 12^{d} [512]

The farm of one cottage in the same place in the parish of St. Paul near the city of Canterbury adjacent to the king's land to the East North and South sides and to the kings street on the West side in the tenure of Edward Beacher thus to him granted by letters patent under the seal of the said late Monastery given the first day of July in the 30th year of the reign of King Henry the

510 In a later hand at 20 yeres profits.
511 In a later hand at 9 [years].
512 In a later hand at 9 [years].

VIIIth for the term of his life Rendering in respect thereof by the year 12^d at the Feast of the Nativity of our Lord and the Nativity of St. John the Baptist equaliter 12^s [513]

The farm of one cottage in the same place in the parish of Saint Paul aforesaid adjacent to the kings lands on the North East and South sides and to the kings street on the West side in the tenure of William Wryght thus to him granted by the patent of the said late Monastery of Saint Augustine dated the first day of July in the 30th year of the reign of King Henry the VIIIth for the term of his life

Rendering in respect thereof by the year 12^d at the feast of the Nativity of the Lord and the Nativity of St. John the Baptist equally by the year 12^d [514]

membrane 5[515]
Farm of one tenement there in the tenure of John Wilbore thus to him demised by indenture for a term of years as he says
Rendering in respect thereof by the year 12^d at 9 [years]
Farm of one tenement in the tenure of Henry Toppyn[516] this to him demised at the will of the lord from year to year[517] rendering in respect thereof by the year 8^s[518]

Memorandum that the kynges highnes hath no landes belonging to the premysses

membrane 6 sewn to the bottom of membrane 5
These tenementes and cotagies lye nighe the Cittie of Canterburie in the parisshe of Sainte Paule aforesaide and what fyne or income wilbe gyven for the same I knowe not what patronages advousons or other speciall promotions do unto them belonge amongeste the recordes of the tenthes do appere I have not made out any particuler of the premisses but onelie this ne I do not knowe that eny other person is desierous to by the same
examined by me Richard Brasier Deputy

Rest cut through from the entry below reads 'William Cavendyssh auditor' *from the sewing marks at the bottom of the membrane it seems possible that there may have been another membrane sewn to the bottom of this at one time.*

membrane 7 [Latin]

County of Kent
Parcel of the lands and possessions lately belonging to Thomas Archbishop of Canterbury and now in the hands of the Lord King by reason of acquisition

Parish of Saltewood in the said county of Kent, value in,
Farm of diverse parcels of lands there, that is to say, 6 acres of land at Stoweparisshe hylle 2 acres of land in Oldecroft 1 acre in Halynden 2 acres at Knolle hill 3 parcels of land containing 30 acres in Mylond with a parcell of land at Denthall parcell of the lands lately in the tenure of John More Another parcel of land lately in the tenure of Thomas of Canterbury and parcel of

513 At ix [years].
514 At ix [years].
515 Sewn to the bottom of 4.
516 Marginal entry opposite entry for Toppyn.
517 De anno in annur'.
518 At ix [years].

lands there lately Ade Cottclyff and now in the tenure of Thomas Whyte so to him demised by indenture as he says, rendering in respect thereof by the year 20^{s}

later addition at 20 yeres profits $20^{£}$

These parcells of lond above specyfyed as I have learned lyeth fyve myles from eny of his graces manours wherunto hys hyghnes hath eny accesse and repayre what fyne or income wilbe gyven for the same I knowe not what patronages advousons or other speciall promotions do therunto belonge emongest the recordes of tenthes doth appere This ys the fyrst particular that I have made of the premisses ne I do nott knowe that eny other person ys desierous to by the same

Examined by me Richard Brasier deputy William Cavendyssh auditor

Third day of July in the 37th year of the reign of King Henry the VIIIth by Thomas Arden of Feversham in the county of Kent gentleman

Furst the mannour of Otterpoole in the countie of Kente parcell of the possessions lately purchased of Thomas Wyatt knyght by the yere clere $21^{£}$ $7½^{d}$

Item one acre and one roode of londe within the suberberes of the citie of Cantorburye lyeng at Winchepefeild in the tenure of [blank] late parcell of Seint Augustines in Cantorburye by the yere 21^{d}

Item the Ferme of certein parcells of lond in the parishe of [blank] in the tenure of John White late parcell of the possessions of the archbuysshop of Cantorburye by the yere 20^{s}

Total $22^{£}$ 2^{s} $4½^{d}$ which rated at 20 yeres purchase ys $442^{£}$ 7^{s} 6^{d} Adde therto for the woodes $13^{£}$ 13^{s} And so the whole somme ys $456^{£}$ 18^{d}

The yerely valowe of the tenths with there appurtenaunces lyeng within the suburbes of the citie of Cantorburye late parcell of Seint Augustines 38^{s} 8^{d}

Totall 38^{s} 8^{d} which rated at 9 yeres purchase ys $17^{£}$ 8^{s}

And so the whole somme for the purchace of all the premysses ys $473^{£}$ 9^{s} 6^{d} whereof in hand $200^{£}$ at Michaelmas $100^{£}$ and at Candlemas then next $173^{£}$ 9^{s} 6^{d}

Memorandum the kyng must discharge the premisses of all incombraunces excepte leases and excepte suche charges as the fermors are bounde to discharge by force of there indentures And also excepte suche repris as been conteined within thies particulers

Richard Southwell [servant] Edward North John Bakere
?inrolled? by John Hanbye

membrane 8 Latin
County of Kent.
Certeyne landes in the parishe of Hythe in the seyd countye dymysed to John White late parcell of the possessions of the Archbusshoppe of Canterbury and now in the Kinges Majesties hands by reason of purchase

The Trees growing in and about the seyd lanndes wyll barely suffice for stakes for hedgeboote to repare and meynteyn the hedges and fences about the same therfore not valuyd, nothing

Examined by me David Claton

LAMBERTISLAND

PRO: E318/2/37

Particulars for grants 35 Henry 8

Thomas Arderne and William Walter Grantee

[*Latin*]:
County of Kent
Parcel of the lands and possessions late belonging to the monastery or priory of Feversham in the same county.

Manor or messuage of Lambertyslande in the parish of Hernhyll in the aforesaid county, valued in,
Rents of assize of the free tenants there by the year 3^s^ 8^d^

Farm of the manor or messuage of Lambertisland with all arrable lands meadows pastures ordinarly belonging or appurtaining and also one croft called Deane Crofte and certain lands called Botrelles and Dobbys with one store[519], that is to say of 20,000, of The Pillar Tile thus demised to Daniel Cranmer by indenture under the seal of the Court of Augmentations Revenues to the Crown of the lord King dated the fifth day of December in the 34th year of the reign of King Henry the VIIIth To have to the same Daniel and his assignes from the feast of Saint Michael the Archangell and then next following as far as the end and term of 21 years Rendering in respect thereof annually, that is to say, the aforesaid manor or messuage lands pasture and store 10^£^ 2^s^ And for 1000 of tile[520] that the same Daniel holds rendering to the Lord King 40^s^ And the agreement is by the same indenture that the same farmer has hedgebote fyrebote ploughebote[521] and carte bote through delivery of the officers of the Lord King there, and also the same farmer has annually during the term aforesaid so much wood and under-wood to the costage[522] of the same farmer and to have carriage and cuttingdown[523] as much as sufficient to burn in the 11[524] tile kilns by the official of the Lord king aforesaid for the time being assigned as in the said indenture is more fully contained 22^£^ 2^s^

total 22^£^ 5^s^ 8^d^
Examined by William Cavendysshe auditor

The answere to the artycles conteyned in the lettere sent from the Commyssioners

The saide manor or messuage with the appurtenaunces as I have lernyd is from any of the kinges majesties howses whiche be kept and reservyd for the accesse of his highnes And from any of his graces parkes forestes or chases sixe miles What patronagis advousions chauntreys or other especiall promotyons are incident to the same aperithe emongist the recordes of the tenths It is of

519 *Stauro*.
520 *Tegularum*.
521 Richardson *op. cit.* Cartbote: The right to wood from the commons to make or repair carts. Ploughbote: The right to take wood from the commons to make or repair ploughs.
522 Given as *custagi*. Custage or costage; *O.E.D.* expense, expenditure, charge, cost. Or corruption of *custodia* for maintenance, preservation.
523 Latin: *prosternand'*.
524 xj le *kylnes tegularum comburere*.

the yerly valews above specyfyed What fyne or income hathe ben heretofore paid for the same I knowe not I have made owte particulers or valews of the premisses to no man but only to this bringer of thes youre letters

membrane 2 stitched to the bottom of 1
[Latin document in very poor condition]
12th day of March in the 35th year of the reign of King Henry VIIIth by Thomas Arderne and William Walter

The Manor of Lambertysland 22$^{£}$ 5^{s} 8^{d} thus by the tenth 24^{s} 7^{d} And remains clear 11$^{£}$ 13^{d} whiche rated at 20 yeres purch[ase do]the amounte to the somme of 221$^{£}$ 10^{d} adde therto for the woodes 102^{s} then the hoole is 126$^{£}$ 3^{s} [8^{d}]

Memorandum to except all the woodes to be taken in any other of the kinges woodes savyng onely in the woodes grewyng apon the premysses sold

The yerely value of certen landes and tenements in Wasperton 43^{s} Thus in tenth 4^{s} 4^{d} And there remains clear 38^{s} 8^{d} which rated at 22 yeres purches doth amounte to the somme of 42$^{£}$ 10^{s} 8^{d} Adde therto for the woodes nothing And then the hoole that the said Arden and Walter must paye is 268$^{£}$ 14^{s} 4^{d} to be paide all in the hande

Memorandum the kynge must dyscharge the byer of all incombraunces excepte leases and the rent before [ ] and except all woodes to be taken in the Bleane

William Seint John Thomas Wriothesley Richard Southwell

membrane 3 sewn on the bottom of 2

Memorandum that we Thomas Arderne gentleman and William Walter yeoman do desire to purchase of the Kinges Majestie the said messuage land tenementes closes and heredytamentes with ther appurtenaunces conteyned and specyfied in the rate and particulars herunto annexed whiche be of the same clere yerely value as in the same rate is declared in witnes wherof to this present byll wee have putt our seales the the 14th day of Marche in the 35th yere of the reigne of our sovereign Lord Henry the VIIIth by the grace of God kyng of England Fraunce and Ireland defender of the Feyth and of the churche of Englond and also of Ireland in erthe supreme hedde.

[You can see where this was originally folded at the bottom and a tag and seal passed through, on the fold and so consequently on the other side of the parchment.]

per me Thomam Ardern [525].
per me Willelmum Walter

membrane 4
County of Kent,
The Manour or messuage of Lambertisland in the seyd countye parcell of the posessions of the late monasterye or pryory of Feversham in the same countye

Oldelandes grove conteyneth 4 acres
In Colme Felde be 5 acres of wood growing by parcelles
Item there be certeyn hedgerowes sett with underwood growing by parcelles containing 6 acres

[525] A clear signature.

Summe of 15 acres whereof 5 acres of 14 yeres growth 3 acres of 20 yeres growth not valuyd but reservyd to Danyell Cranmer fermour there for hys fyerbote and hedgeboote which he hath by covenaunte as appereth by an indenture sealed with the great seale of the courte of Augmentations beryng date the 5th daye of December in the 34th yere of the reigne of our Sovereigne lorde Kinge Henry the VIIIth 2 acres of 5 yeres growth (5^{s}) 2 acres of 7 yeres growth (7^{s}) 2 acres of 10 yeres growth (10^{s}) and one acre resydue of 20 yeres growth (10^{s}) the wood of every acre aforeseyd valuyd as appereth which is in the holle 32^{s}

And the sprynge of the woode or grounde of 8 acres aforseyd not valuid bycause they be reservyd and of 7 acres resydue rated yerly at 6^{d} the acre which is yerly in the holle 3^{s} 6^{d} and amounteth after 20 yeres purchase to 3$^{£}$ 10^{s}

And in the same aboute the scytation of the seyd mannour and messuage be growinge 80 okes of 60 and 90 yeres growth moste parte cropped and shred not valued but reservyd to the seyd fermour for his ploughbote carteboote and houseboote whiche he hath by covenaunte of the seyd indenture

Totall 102^{s}
by me William Cowper

WASPERTON AND HEATHCOTE, WARWICKSHIRE

membrane 5
Latin
Parcell of the possessions late of the house of friars of Thellesforde in the County of Warwick dissolved

Lands and tenements in Wasperton and Hethcote in the county of Warwick, valued in,
Farm of five separate closes called Hethecote and of five Beys[526] built on the same which same closes lying together between the field called Wasperton Felde and the lands of the Bishop of Lichfield and Conventry in the tenure of John Venor of Wellysborne on the one parte and the lane there leading from the town of Warwick towards Newbolde on the other parte in width and extending in length from certain lands of the said Bishop in the tenure of the same John as far as the river there called Newbold Broke demised to the aforesaid John Venor by indenture under the seal of the commonality of the said late house dated the last day of March in the 28th year of the reign of King Henry the VIIIth to have and to hold to the same John and his assigns from the feast of the annunciation of the Blessed Virgin Mary next comming after the date of the said indentures as far as the end of the term of 41 years thence next following and fully to be completed rendering in respect thereof by the year 43^{s}

The answer to the articles contained in the letteres of the Kynges Commissioners

FIRSTE the premysses be of the clere yerly rente as is abovementioned And they be no parcell of any manors lordshipps or tythes whych doo excede the clere yerly valewe of 40$^{£}$

[526] J. Wright, *Dialect Dictionary* (1898). Bay: A division of space in a building between two main beams; generally applied to a barn or farm building... so a barn, of which the roof is divided by the main cross-beams into five portions, is said to be of five bay. See later under m. 6.

Item ther ys no speciall promotion[527] belongyng to the same of the kynges gyfte

Item whatte fynne or incume hath heretofore ben gevyn for the premysses I knowe not but yf they were now to be letten I thynke ther wolde be gevyn a reasonable fyne for to have a lesse of the same for the terme of 21 yeres

Item no other parson or parsons hath sued for the premysses other than the berer herof

Item the premysses doo not lye nygh any of the kynges Majesties manors or mansion howses ne doo adioyne to any of his graces parkes forests or chases whych ben reserved for the accesse and repayre of his highnes savyng that the premysses doo lye within 5 myles of Warwyk

Memorandum for wood and underwoods growing upon the premisses

by me Robert Burgoyn

membrane 6

County of Warwickshire

One house inWasperton conteyning 5 bayes with 5 closes called Hethecote and certeyne landes there in the holding of John Venour in the seyd countye parcell of the possessyons of the late pryorye or freerhowse of Thellesforde in the same countie

THERE BE growing aboute the seyd house and in the hedges aboute the seyd 5 closes and other the landes aforseyd 60 okes and elmes of 60 and 80 yeres growth moste part usually cropped and shred not valuyd but reservid to the fermour there for his houseboote ploughboote fyerboote and hedgeboote which he hath by covenaunte as appereth by an indenture beryng date the laste daye of Marche in the 28th yere of the reygne of our soveraigne Lorde Kinge Henry the VIIIth

per me William Cowper

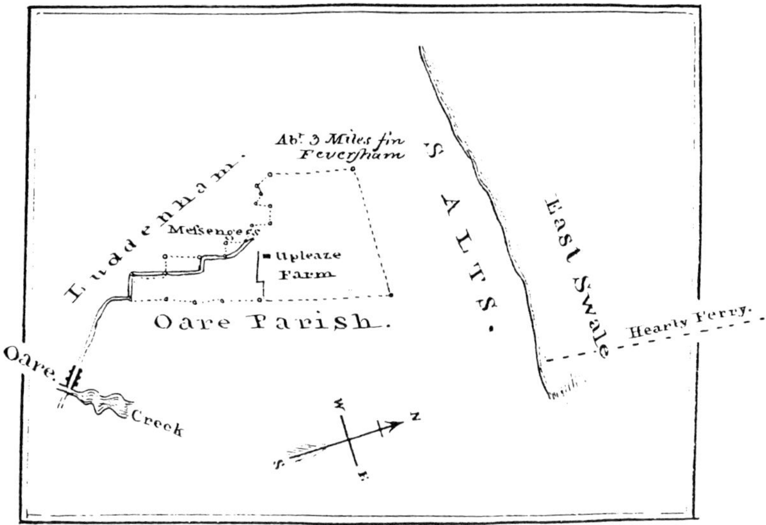

CCA: U63/70388 Part of An eye sketch of Feversham Parish dated 1800.

---

[527] *O.E.D.* Promotion: advancement in position, preferment.

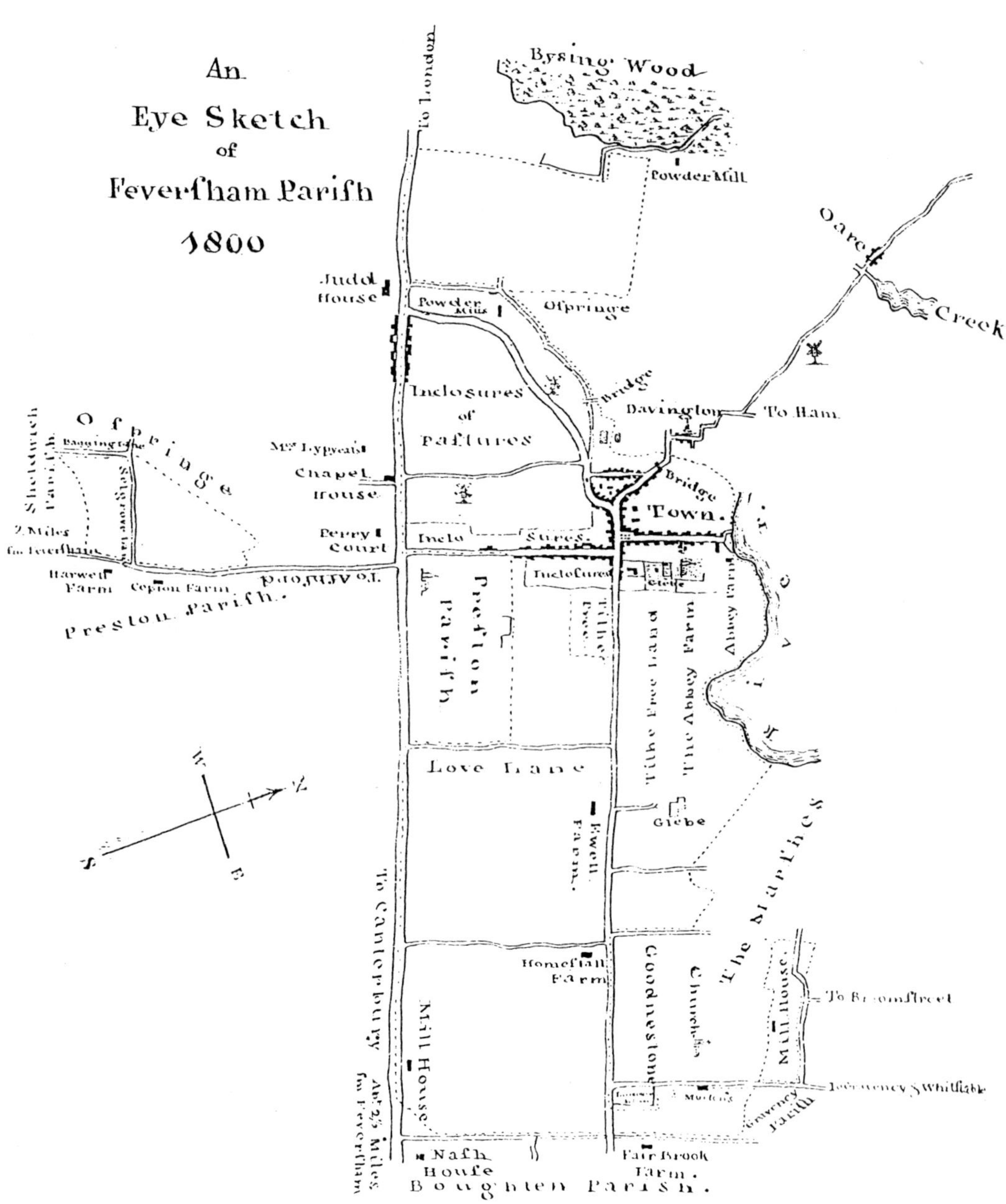

CCA: An eye sketch of Feversham Parish, 1800; CCA U63/70388.

APPENDIX 10: Grants to Arden in Canterbury and Sandwich

PRO: E318/5/181
PARTICULARS FOR GRANTS 38 HENRY 8 (CONTAINING 46 MEMBRANES)

membrane 1

Memorandum that we Robart Brokelesby and Nicholas Girlington do require to purchas of the kinges Maiestie by vertue of his graces commyssion of seale the premisses conteyned in the particulers herunto these presentes are annexed beinge of souche cler yerly value as is comprised in the same in witnes wherof to these presentes we have subscribed our names and putt our seales the vth of June in the xxxviijth yere of the reigne of our sovaraigne lorde Kinge Henry the VIIIth by the grace of God Kinge of Englound Fraunce and Ireland defendour of the faith and in earth of the churche of Englound and also of Ireland the supreme hedd

by me Robrt. Brokylesbee, Nicholas Girlington

membrane 27
[Latin]
In the county of Kent,
parcel of the revenues of the late monastery of Saint Augustine outside and near the walls of the city of Canterbury in the said county, that is to say,

In the parish of Saint Paul outside and near the walls of the city of Canterbury, the value in the farm of one garden in Ivelane there in the tenure of George Nicholls so to him demised at the will of the Lord from year to year rendering in respect thereof by the year xvj^{d}

Farm of three rods of land there in the tenure of the aforesaid George Nicholles so to him demised at the will of the lord from year to year rendering in respect thereof iij^{s} ij^{d}

[total] iiij^{s} vj^{d} at xx yeres purchis iiij$^{£}$ x^{s}

I have made a particuler of the premysses to Master Water Hendeley what fyne or income wilbe gyven for the same I knowe nott

PRO: E318/2/33
Exchequer Augmentation Office. Particulars for grants 31 Henry 8:: contains 3 membranes

The details relating to Sandwich are given on the 2nd membrane which is sewn to the foot of membrane 1.

[Latin]
Late Priory of the Franciscans[528] called Whytefryers in Sandwyche in the county of Kent

Value in,
Farm of the site of the said late priory with fruit-gardens, gardens[529] orchards and so forth and all their issues and emoluments to the same site appertaining and being within the ambit[530] and precinct to the same lately in the tenure and occupation of the late prior and convent there at the time of the dissolution of the same with xliij^{s} vij^{d} of farm for the diverse tenements and gardens to the said priory appertaining liiij^{s} vij^{d}

Reprise[531] In wages to the collector of the rents there at v^{s} by the year, that is to say, in allowance of the same for the half part ~~i~~j^{s} ~~v~~j^{d}

and there remains above lij^{s} j^{d}
for the tenth part for the lord king reserved v^{s} ij½^{d}
and there remains clear xlvj^{s} x½^{d}

Examyned by me William Cavendyshe auditor

---

528 *Fratrum minorum*
529 Ortis, gardinis. *The Medieval Latin Dictionary.*
530 *Ambitum*: *The Medieval Latin Dictionary* gives amongst other meanings for ambitus an extent or cloister. Lewis and Short, *A Latin Dictionary,* amongst the meanings of, Ambitus says 'hence the open space left round a house.' The *O.E.D.* gives as the second meaning of the word Ambit a space surrounding a house, castle, town etc.; the precincts, liberties, verge.
531 Deductions from profit.

APPENDIX 11: Grants to and leases to Arden and others in Faversham.

PRO: E315/402 FOLIO 27
COURT OF AUGMENTATIONS

[Latin] County of Kent
Faversham late monastery in the county there

Site of the late monastery aforesaid with the demesne lands there, valuation, that is to say,

Farm of the site of the of the late monastery aforesaid with gardens orchards and the owt yardes containing by estimation xij acres at xij^{d} the acre, xij^{s}

Farm of one garden there called the Ostrye gardyn demised to Richard Fowle by the year vj^{s} viij^{d}

Farm of one enclosure adjacent to the Brewhouse containing by estimation ix acres at ij^{s} the acre, xviij^{s}

Farm of one meadow called Thornemede containing x acres and j piece of pasture containing iij acres with the small tenement built upon it at ij^{s} the acre, xxvj^{s}

Farm of one close next to the Grange and one garden called the Dovehouse gerden containing ij acres at ij^{s} the acre, iiij^{s}

Farm of one close lying between the monastery there and the parish church of Faversham containing vj acres at ij^{s} the acre, xij^{s}

Sum total with vj^{s} viij^{d} for the Ostry garden, lxxviij^{s} viij^{d}

By me William Cavendysshe auditor
Made a demise to John Wheler of London gentleman

PRO: E313/11/146
AUGMENTATION OFFICE. ORIGINAL LETTERS PATENT.

This is a very large manuscript of three membranes each very approximately 24' by 36', the royal seal has been lost but the cords remain written in Latin

Translation
Henry the eighth by the Grace of God of England France and Ireland King defender of the faith and in earth of the church of England Ireland supreme head All to whom these present writings shall come Greeting WHEREAS WE made by our letters patent bearing our great seal of England given at Hamptoncourte the twenty ninth day of December in the thirty second year of our reign among other things have given and granted to Thomas Cheyne knight by the name of

Thomas Chene knight treasurer of our hospice and Warden of the Cinque Ports[532] the whole of our rectory and our church of Chilham with their rights members and appurtenances wholly in the county of Kent late the monastery of Syon ...

Further down membrane 1

And with the same we have given and by the same our letters patent have granted [*At Walden 16th March 31 Henry VIII*] to the aforesaid Thomas Cheyne thirty and four acres of our arable land with appurtenances at that time in the tenure of the Robert Coldwell lying in the field called Southfelde in Feversham in our said county of Kent And twenty and four acres of our arable land with appurtenances at that time in the tenure of the said Robert Coldwell lying at Hedgedale in the parish of Preston next Feversham in the same our county of Kent And tithes whithersoever of in and upon the said land in Southfelde aforesaid annually to issue forth, come and grow except the tithes of one acre of land thereof lying in the southern corner of the same field Which certain land and tithes in Feversham and Preston aforesaid were lately of the Monastery of Feversham in the said our county of Kent at that time dissolved formerly being and appertaining To have hold and possess the whole of the aforesaid manor of Patrickesbourne and rectory of Patrykesbourne and the aforesaid advowson to the benefice of the parish of Patrykesbourne And also the aforesaid lands tenements meadows pastures rents reversions services tithes and so forth all and singular the premises previously expressed and specified with appurtenances in Patrykesbourne , Feversham and Preston aforesaid and elsewhere in our said county of Kent to the aforesaid Thomas Cheyne and his heirs male of his body lawful begotten TO HOLD of our heirs and our successors by the service of one tenth part of one knights fee AND RENDERING in respect thereof annually to our heirs and our successors four pounds and twenty and three pence at our Court of Augmentations for the revenues of our crown at the feast of Saint Michael the Archangel each single year to pay for all rents services and demands whatsoever in respect thereof to our heirs or our successors and in what manner the rents to be paid or made according as by the same our letters patent may fully appear AND WHEREAS we made by certain other our letters patent bearing our great seal of England given at Walden the sixteenth day of March in the thirty first year of our reign extensively[533] recited that whereas we by a certain indenture made under our great seal of the Court of Augmentations revenues to our crown given at Westminster the 10th day of May in the thirty first year of our reign extensively reciting that WHEREAS WE made by a certain indenture bearing the great seal of the Court of Augmentations for the revenues of our crown given at Westminster the tenth day of May in the thirty first year of our reign by the advice and council of the said Court of Augmentations for the revenues of our crown have demised granted and to farm devised to John Wheler gentleman the house and site of the late monastery of Feversham in the county of Kent at that time dissolved together with all houses buildings barns stables dovecotes gardens orchards and *the_oute yerdes*[534] of the said late monastery containing by estimation twelve acres and one garden to the same called the Ostrey Gardeyne and one close of land adjacent to the Brewhouse there containing by estimation nine acres and also one meadow called Thornemede containing by estimation ten acres And one piece of pasture there containing by estimation three acres and one small tenement built upon the same Also one close of land adjacent to the Grange there and one garden called the Dovehouse Gardeyne containing by estimation two acres And also one close of land lying between the said late monastery and the parish church of Feversham containing by estimation six acres Which certain all and singular

532 *Quinque portuum.*
533 *Extiterit.*
534 In English.

the aforesaid gardens closes lands meadows and pasture and so forth the premises with their appurtenances lying and being in Feversham in the county aforesaid and of the said late Monastery belonging and appertaining and in the hands cultivation[535] and proper occupation of the late Abbot of the late Monastery at the time of dissolution thereof used[536] and has been occupied EXCEPT nevertheless always and to our heirs and our successors always reserved all large trees and woods upon the premisses arising and being and all such and every kind building within the site of the said late monastery which we there shall have the command to cut down and carry away. TO HAVE AND TO HOLD all and singular the premises with the appurtenances except pre-excepted to the aforesaid John and his assigns from the feast of Saint Michael the Archangel at that time the last past as far as the end and term and for the term of twenty and one years thereafter next following and fully to be completed RENDERING in respect thereof by the year to our heirs and our successors three pounds eighteen shillings and eight pence of legal money of England at the feast of the Annunciation of the Blessed Virgin Mary and Saint Michael the Archangel within one month after each of the two feast at those feasts to the court aforesaid by equal portions to be paid during the term aforesaid according as by that indenture amongst other things is fully shown AND WHEREAS WE by the same our letters patent we have given and granted to the aforesaid Thomas Cheyne knight the reversion and reversions of the aforesaid site of the said late monastery of Feversham and all and singular the aforesaid houses edifices barns stables dovecotes lands tenements and so forth all and singular the premises before expressed and specified to the aforesaid John Wheler by the indenture aforesaid as beforehand demised and the total aforesaid annual rent three pounds eighteen shillings and eight pence and the whole house and site of the said late monastery of Faversham with all and all messuages houses edifices barns stables dovecotes gardens orchards and garden land and our earth[537] as within as without and near the site enclosure surroundings neighbourhood and precinct[538] to the same late monastery belonging and also all and singular the aforesaid lands tenements meadows enclosures[539] pastures and so forth all the premises to the aforesaid John Wheler by the indenture aforesaid in the form aforesaid demised and all and all manner of great trees woods and subwoods in and upon the same lands tenements and so forth arising and being on the premises Ever as mentioned above by the same our letters patent we have given and granted to the aforesaid Thomas Cheyne all the land and our marsh called Negdowne Mershe with their appurtenances in Graveney in our said county of Kent late of the said monastery of Feversham formerly belonging and appertaining And whereas we by the same our letters patent have given and granted to the aforesaid Thomas Cheyne all and singular that messuage tenement house edifice garden curtilage and land and walls lately the priory and formerly house of the Friars Preachers[540] near Ludgate London at that time dissolved and to the same late prior or a short time ago house of the Friars Preachers lately belonging and appertaining and the liberty to enter and exit at all times[541] to that all and singular and also the reversion rents and annual profits to the same and to in respect to each parcel to this fully and wholly just as that all and singular to our hands by reason and authority of the said dissolution of the said late monastery or house a short time ago of the Friars Preachers or religious house or other authority by act of parliament or otherwise whatsoever now has become or will or ought to become in our hands at that time ought to remain and exist TO HAVE, hold and possess.

---

535 *Cultura.*
536 *Veseruat.*
537 *Sola nostra.*
538 *Septum ambitum circuitum et procinctum.*
539 *Pascuas.*
540 *Fratrum praedicatorum.*
541 *De tempore in tempus.*

Particulars for Grants of Crown Lands. 18 February 31 Henry VIII E318/7/265

[Latin] 1 membrane
County of Kent
Parcel of the possessions of the late Monastery of Feversham in the said county pertaining

Site of the said late monastery with the demesne lands[542] ... lately of the prior and convent there at the time of the dissolution of the same,

value in,
Farm of the site of the said late monastery with the demesne lands there that is to say for the farm of the site of the said late monastery with all gardens orchards and The Outegardens and other edifices there xij^{s} farm of one garden called The Ostry Gardynne vj^{s} viij^{d} Farm of viij closes adjacent The Brewehouse xviij^{s} one meadow called The Thornemede and one piece of land or pasture with small tenements built thereupon xxvj^{s} One close adjacent The Graunge and garden[543] called The Dovehouse gardenne iiij^{s} and one close lying between the same monastery and the parish church of Feversham xij^{s} so together demised by indenture under the seal of the lord King by his Court of Augmentations and revenues of his crown, in respect thereof for the year

lxxviij^{s} viij^{d}

Negdon Marshe,

value in,

Farm of this same parcel of marsh land called Negdone marshe demised to Richard Knyghte and Symon Auncelme by indenture under the seal of the convent of the said late monastery for the term of thirty years rendering by the year viij$^{£}$

[Total] xj$^{£}$ xviij^{s} viij^{d} in respect thereof

Reprise[544]
value in,
Pension annually going out of the same marsh called Negdon Marshe a payment to the vicar of Hernehill by the year xiij^{s} iiij^{d}

And there remains clear xj$^{£}$ v^{s} iiij^{d}

Further items about Middlesex and summary etc. not transcribed.

---

542 Illegible.
543 *Hortus*.
544 Deduction to be made yearly out of the estate.

PRO: E318/2/33 LATIN
PARTICULARS FOR GRANTS 31 HENRY VIII THOMAS ARDERNE GRANTEE SECTION 1 CONTAINING 3 MEMBRANES

membrane 1
County of Kent Parcel of the posessions late of the monastery of Faversham.

Margin The town of Faversham
Farm of one messuage one stable and one garden the same messuage pertaining with certain parcels of land called The Nethergrene demised to John Wylloby by indenture under the seal of the convent of the said late monastery for the term of 50 years 26^s 8^d

Farm of one messuage one garden and one dovecot in the same garden situated beside and near the closes called the Almery Croft demised to Richard Drylond and Dorothy his wife by indenture under the seal aforesaid for a term of years rendering thence by the year 40^s

The farm of two messuages within the town of Faversham of which one with a garden adjacent is situated in the street called Weststrete near the tenement in the tenure of the heirs of Richard Colwell and the other situated near The Fishemarket called The Corner tenement demised to John Seth of Feversham by indenture rendering thence by the year 13^s 4^d

Total value $4^£$

For [tenth] of the Lord the King annually reserving 8^s

And their remains clear 72^s

In a very poor illegible hand:
17th day of March in the 31st year of the reign of Henry VIIIth for Thomas Arderne
Which after 15 yeres the charge ys $54^£$
Whereof to be paid in hand $30^£$ and att the fyrst day of October the $24^£$

E318/2/34
PARTICULARS FOR GRANTS 35 HENRY 8 THOMAS ARDERNE GRANTEE SECTION 2 CONTAINING 7 MEMBRANES LATIN

membrane 3
Parish of Faversham in the county aforesaid, value in,
The farm of all that messuage called The Beare and of one shop called The Garrett adjacent to the same in the market place and one garden situated at The Cokyns dytche with all their appurtenances lying together and existing in the parish of Faversham in the tenure of John Sethe to him demised by indenture dated the last day of October in the 39th year of the reign of King Henry the VIIIth to have from the feast of St. Michael the Archangell then next following the said date as far as the end and term of 70 years next following to be fully completed rendering thence by the year 23^s 4^d at the feast of St. Michael the Archangel and the annunciation of the Blessed Virgin Mary in equal portions repairs to all the said farm as in the same indenture amongst other things is fully given
23^s 4^d

Parish of Hernehill in the said county of Kent, value in,
Farm of 6 pieces of land lying in the parish of Hernehill aforesaid called Hartangars, Upfeld, Newland, Mertynland Champney feld and Denyfelde in the tenure of Robert Broke so to him demised by indenture dated the 24th day of September in the 27th year of the reign of King Henry the VIIIth to have from the feast of St. Michael the Archangel next after the date of these presents as far as the end and term of 16 years then next ensuing and fully to be completed rendering in respect thereof by the year 29s at the feast of St. Michael the Archangel and of Saint Andrew the Apostle by equal portions. Repairs with all other charges to the charge of the lord King as in the same indenture with others is fully shown 29s

Farm of one parcel of land called Gybbotts lying in the parish of Hernehyll aforesaid in the tenure of Richard Betyll so to him demised at the will of the Lord rendering in resect thereof by the year 2^s 10^d

Farm of three acres of land called Bertons in the said parish of Hernehyll in the tenure of John Goodhewe so to him demised as the will of the lord rendering in respect thereof by the year 6^s

[total] 61^s 2^d

Sum total of the aforesaid particular $10^£$ 7s 11½d
Examined by William Cavendysshe auditor

Thys manor and parcells above specyfyed with there appurtenaunces as I have lernyd as from eny of the kynges houses whereunto hys majestie hath eny accesse and repayer 6 miles and from eny of the kynges parkes forestes and chases syxe myles They ar no parcell of eny other manor or other heredytament excedyng the clere yerely value of $40^£$ what fyne will be gyven for the same I knowe not ne can not learne There ben no patronages advousons ne chaunteries belongyng to the same I have made no particular of the premysses to eny persone only thys nor I know not that the fermers that hathe the[m] by lease or at wyll or eny other persone or persones dwellynge nere to the same wylby the premysses ne can learne

Nor on account of the woods

membrane 6

County of Kent:
One messuage callyd the beare and one shope callyd the garret therto lyeng in the markyt place and one garden lyeng at the Cokys dyche with the appurtenaunces lyeng and beyng in the parishe of Feversham in the tenure of John Sethe parcell of the possessions of the seyd late monasterye of Feversham.

NO WOODES nor trees growyng there uppon the seyd premysses. None

Six peces or parcelles of land in the parish of Hernhyll callyd Hartangars Upfeld Newland Martynlande Champneyfeld and Denysfeld in the tenure of Robert Broke

One Parcell of land called Gybbottes lyeng in the parishe of Hernehyll in the tenure of Richard Betyll

Three acres of land callyd Bertons in the seyd parishe of Hernehyll in the tenure of John Goodhewe parcell of the possessions of the seyd late monastery of Feversham

Item in hedgrowes inclosyng the seyd landes be growyng 100 okes and elmys of 40 and 60 yeres growth most part shrude[545] whereof 80 reservyd to the tenaunts there to repayr and maynteyn theyr hedges and fences aboute the same which they have hade by custome of olde tyme used therfore not valuyd and 20 resydue valuyd at 2^d the tree which ys in the holle 3^s 4^d

Summe total of all the premysses 4^£ 19s 4^d
By me William Cowper

E318/2/35
Particulars for Grants 36 Henry 8
Thomas Arderne grantee section 3 containing 4 membranes. Latin

membrane 1
Memorandum that I Thomas Arderne doo requyre to purchase of the Kinges Majestie by vertue of hys graces commyssion of sale the premysses conteyned in the particulars wherunto these present arre annexyd beyng of such yerely value as ys comprysed in the same In wytness whereof I have subscrybed my name and putt my seale the [blank] daye of [blank] in the xxxvj^th yere of our sovereigne lorde Kyng Henry the VIIIth by the grace of god of Inglond France and Yrelond defender of the fayth and in erthe of the church of Yngland and also of Yrelond the supreme hede

Thomas Arderne

membrane 2 [Latin]

County of Kent parcel of the revenues of the late monastery of Faversham

Preston Strete

Farm of one tenement there lying in Prestonne strete between the lands of George Straunsham on the South side and the lands of Robert Coldewell on the North side in the tenure of Thomas Paternoster at the will of the lord rendering in respect thereof by the year from year to year 16^s

Estestrete

Farm of one garden there lying in Eastrete North called The Appull Garden late in the tenure of John Sayere and now in the tenure of William Marshall between the lands of the same William on the West side and the kings street on the East side to whom demised by indenture for a term of years as he has said rendering in respect thereof by the year 5^s 4^d

Courtstret Easte

Farm of one messuage with garden in Courtestrete Easte late in the tenure of Richard Goslyng and now in the tenure of John Goodhewe between the lands of Thomas Ardeyne on the North side and The Churcheland on the South side to whom demised at the will of the Lord from year to year rendering in respect there by the year 13^s 4^d

Courtstrete Weste

---

545 Shroud see p. 187 & glossary.

Farm of three messuages there with three gardens lying together between the lands of Joseph [blank] on the North side and John Culverden on the South side late in the tenure of William Sandes and now in the tenure of Thomas Bargrove to him demised at the will of the lord from year to year and rendering in respect thereof by the year 20^{s}

Farm of one messuage with a garden there lying between the lands of the aforesaid Joseph Beverley on the Northside and the said John Calverdon[546]on the South side in the tenure of Henry Haffynden to whom demised at the will of the Lord rendering in respect thereof by the year 6^{s} 8^{d}

Farm of one messuage there lying between the lands of the same Joseph Beverley on the North side and John Culverden on the South side in the tenure of Quintin Bedford to whom demised at the will of the Lord from year to year and paying in respect thereof by the year 2^{s}

Farm of three messuages there with their appurtenances lying together between the lands in the tenure of Matilda Vause on the North side and William Castloke on the South side late in the tenure of [blank] Bassell and now in the tenure of Peter Quylnot to whom demised at the will of the Lord rendering in respect thereof by the year 22^{s}

Northstreet Weste

Farm of one messuage with a certain house called the Storehouse lying in Nortorthestrete[547] Weste between the lands of John North on the North side and *membrane 3* the heires of [blank] Maycote on the South side in the tenure of the said John to whom demised at the will of the Lord from year to year rendering in respect thereof by the year 8^{s}

Farm of one corner tenement there lying between the lands of Thomas Hawke on the South side and the lane there called Partrydge Lane on the Northern side late in the tenure of John Cooke and now in the tenure of Johanna Staple to whom demised at the will of the lord from year to year rendering in respect thereof by the year 15^{s}

Farm of one messuage lying in the Mydle Rowe between the lands of Richard Smyth on the south side and the gaol there on the North side late in the tenure of Richard Frende and [now] in the tenure of John Brygborne[548] to whom demised at the will of the Lord from year to year rendering in respect thereof by the year 10^{s}

Farm of one messuage there in Northstrete West lying between the lands of William Marshall on the North side and the Markett Place on the South side in the tenure of John Bryngborne to whom demised at the will of the Lord from year to year rendering in respect thereof by the year 4s

Farm of 4 messugaes with 4 gardens to the same appertaining in the same street lying between the lands of [blank] Rebarne on the North side and the lands of William Fynner on the South side in the tenure of the said William Fynner at the will of the lord from year to year, rendering in respect thereof by the year 16^{s} 8^{d}

Farm of one messuage there in the said street late in the tenure of William Belke and now in the tenure of John Bryngborne to whom demised at the will of the Lord rendering in respect thereof by the year 7^{s}

Farm of one messuage there in Northestrete Weste between the lands of Anthony Aucher on the South side and the lands of the heirs of Bourne on the North side late in the tenure of John

546 Sic.
547 So spelt for North Street.
548 So spelt.

Fynche and now in the tenure of Anthony Love to whom demised at the will of the Lord from year to year rendering in respect thereof by the year 13^{s} 4^{d}

Farm of one tenement there in the said street called the Welhouse and 2 shops in the Market place in the market called the fysshe shamble late in the tenure of John Hampton now in the tenure of Simon [blank] to whom demised at the will of the Lord from year to year rendering in respect thereof by the year 40^{s}

Westret South[549]

Farm of one cottage and one piece of land lying in Preston Strete Easte called Rotton Rowe in the tenure of William Norton at the will of the Lord from year to year rendering in respect thereof by the year 3^{s} 4^{d}

membrane 4

Farm of one corner tenement and two messuages there in Westret South and between the lands of Thomas Smyth Weste and Barnewey Lane West in the tenure of John Devyn at the will of the Lord from year to year rendering in respect thereof by the year 14s

Farm of one garden there in the street aforesaid lying between the lands of the heirs of Lambert on the East side and the kings street on the West side late in the tenure of Thomas Sayere and [now] in the tenure of [blank] Lambe widow to whom demised at the will of the lord rendering in respect thereof by the year 12^{d}

Farm of three messuages there in the same street lying between the lands of Clement Norton on the East side and the lands of George Stransham on the West side late in the tenure of Robert Uke and now in the tenure of [blank] Smyth to whom demised at the will of the Lord from year to year rendering in respect thereof by the year 12^{s}

Farm of two acres of land lying there between the land of [blank] Barley gentleman on the North side and the kings street on the South side in the tenure of Robert Coldewell rendering in respect thereof by the year 2^{s}

Westret North

Farm of one messuage there in Westrete North between the stream there on the West side in the tenure of the said Peter Grenestrete at the will of the Lord rendering in respect thereof by the year 2^{s} 8^{d}

$11^{£}$ 14s 4^{d}

on the part of William Cavendysshe Auditor

These are all the houses that the kinges majestie hathe within the towne of Feversham as in the right of the late Monasterye of Feversham, As by the recordes more playnelye doth appere, And what fyne or income hathe heretofore byne geven or wyll at this daye be gyven for the same ys unknowen to the audytour

Fourth day of December in the 36th year by Thomas Arderne gentleman

The clere yerelye valewe of the premisses ys $11^{£}$ 14s 4^{d} which rated at tenne yeres purchase dothe amounte to the somme of $117^{£}$ 3^{s} 4^{d}

Held in soccage

---

549 This heading is here, not where one might expect it, at the top of membrane 4.

Memorandum the kyng to discharge the premisses of all incombraunces excepte leases And excepte suche charges as the fermors are bounde to discharge by force of there indentures

Edward North Robert Sowthwell

Richard Ryche

Inrolled by John Hanbye

PRO: E 310/3/13 Item 3
Particulars for leases in Kent. Edward VI (53 documents).

[Latin] Parts visible only under ultra-violet light

County of Kent

Parcell of the possessions late of the Monastery of Faversham in the county aforesaid on the authority of Parliament dissolved

One shoppe garden and cottage in Faversham newly repaired of rents gathered of the said Monastery of Faversham, valued,

Farm of one shoppe called the Pyllorie in Feversham next to the fleshe shambles in the tenure of [blank] Chrisfelde and rendering by the year as claimed by Thomas Arden gentleman collector of the revenues of the said late monastery vj^{s} viij^{d}

Farm of ij gardens lying in Preston Strete in the town of Feversham adjacent to the lands of Henry Crispe Esquire on the western side and the kings way on the eastern side in the tenure of John Baker and John Castlocke and rendering by the year upon the information of the said Thomas Arden collection of the revenues of the said Priory iiij^{s}

Farm of one cottage called Saint Nicholas Chappell with the garden and yard[550] and iij virgates of land to the same adjoining in the tenure of Robert Coldwell and rendering by the year as claimed by the said Thomas Arden vj^{s} viij^{d}

xvij^{s} iiij^{d}

Memorandum the kinges Majestie our late sovereign Lorde Henrie the eight by his letters patentes date the xxiiijth daie of Marche in the xxxvjthg yere of his gracis reign did bargayne and sell geve and graunte unto Thomas Arden gentleman and to his heyres one tenemente in Preston Strete in the towne of Feversham in the tenure of Thomas Paternoster together with a garden called the Appull garden now in the tenure of Willyam Marshall lyenge in Estrete in Feversham aforesaid And also dyverse other messuages tenementes and gardens in Feversham aforeseid and particulerly mentioned in the same letters patentes And also the said Thomas Arden hathe thes generall wordes folowinge conteyned in his said letters patentes, that is to say,

[Latin] And it is lastly granted to the aforesaid Thomas Arden all and singular the other messuages tenements shops, upper rooms, gardens, curtilages, unoccupied lands, foundations, right of entry, easement, rights, profits and our hereditaments whatsoever with the whole of their

550 *Cum gardino et orto.*

appurtenances in Feversham aforesaid lately of the said monastery also now belonging or appertaining or as parcell of the possessions of the same late monastery were had known accepted or reputed to be And lastly we give and grant all the issues from the premisses from the feast of Saint Michael the Archangel then last past , as in the same letters patentes emonges other thinges dothe and may appere By reason of whiche generall wordes the seid Thomas Arden hathe perceyved and taken the issues and proffittes of the seid iij parcells before mentioned beinge xvij^{s} iiij^{d} by the yere from Michaelmas in the seid xxxvjth yere of our seid sovereign lorde Albeit the same were not conteyned in his particulers wher uppon his patent was made neyther partycularly nor specially mentioned in his seid letters patentes so that he hath not yett paid for the purchase of the same but now offrethe to paie for the premysses accordinge to a statute provided in that behalfe and desyrethe to have suche further assurance thereof as shalbe thought requysyte in this case.

Examined by me Thomas Everard auditor

For[551] as much as by the surveyase above wretten yt appereth that the said premisses be passed by generall wordes but if said Thomas Arden gentleman in the letters patents abovesaid and not certified in the particulers where[upon] the grant thereof it with other thynges was made to hym and that yet by the act in that behalfe provyded he owght to have and injoye the same according to hys sayd grant and yet to paye for the same after such rate as ys specefyed by the particulers of hys sayd graunt [whereof] appers to be by the same after the rate of x yers of which therefore of such that there sayd [make] a decree thereyn the sayd these payde after the sayd rate to the kynges majesties [crown][552] in premisses arise cometh to viij$^{£}$ xiij^{s} to be payd

Richard .?......

PRO: E315/219 FOLIO 13V

[*Latin*] [Edward the sixth by the grace of God of England France and Ireland King defender of the faith and in earth supreme head of the church of England and Ireland To all to whom this present writing shall come greeting.[553]] Know that we of the advice of the chancellor and of one of the general overseers and attorney of our court of Augmentations and revenues of our crown in the absence of Thomas Moyle knight the other of the general overseers for a payment of fifty pounds and three shillings and four pence legal money of England into the hands of the treasurer of our said court to our use by our beloved Thomas Ardern. gentleman paid we have demised granted and to farm letten and by these presents have demised granted and to farm letten to the aforesaid Thomas Arderne all that twenty one quarters of corn rase measure[554] one hundred twenty and six quarters barley rase measure of good serviceable clean and merchandisable grain and of good winnowing and twenty pigs and twelve capons which Stephen Motte and his assigns farmers of the message within The Nethercote in Faversham in the county of Kent late of the monastery of Faversham in the same county of Kent now dissolved formerly belonging and appurtaining and all lands tenements meadows pasture and hereditaments to the same messuage pertaining or with the same demised used to be leased or reputed to be with and in the name of the parcel rendering in respect thereof to us our heirs and successors annually to be paid and

551 The handwriting in this section is almost non-existent. It really is quite appalling and almost illegible.
552 This looks like sthrll.
553 Taken from fol. 1.
554 To strike off corn etc. at the level of the measure.

ought to be delivered and paid by the force and form following, that is to say, before the feast of All Saints ten quarters and a half of corn ten quarters and a half of barley and before the feast of St. Andrew twenty one quarters of barley And before the feast of the Nativity of the Lord twenty one quarters and a half or barley and before the first day of February five quarters and two measures[555] corn and twenty one quarters of corn and before the first day of March twenty one quarters of barley And before the first day of April five quarters and two measurers corn and twenty one quarters barley And between the feast of Saint Michael the Archangel and Epiphany twenty pigs And at the feast of the nativity of the lord twelve capons to have and to hold all and singular the aforesaid corn barley pigs and capons aforesaid to Thomas Arderne his executors and assigns from the feast of the annunciation of the Blessed Virgin Mary next coming unto the end and term and for the term of twenty and one years to be next following and fully to be completed Rendering annually to us our heirs and assigns thirty pounds and four shillings of legal money of England, that is to say, in accordance with any of the said quarters of the twenty one quarters of corn annually six shillings and eight pence And in accordance with the said quarters one hundred and twenty six quarters of barley annually three shillings and four pence, and in accordance with the said pigs twenty pigs annually two shillings And of and in accordance with the said capons twelve capons annually four pence at the feast of Saint Michael the Archangel and the annunciation of the Blessed Virgin Mary or within one month after each same feast to the hands of the bailiffs or receivers of the premises for the time being by equal portions to be paid during the term aforesaid PROVIDED always that immediately after the expiry and determination of the term of years expressed and specified in the indenture aforesaid to Stephen Motte granted by the late Abbot and Convent of the said late Monastery bearing date the eighth day of June in the thirtieth year of our celebrated sovereign Henry the eighth late King of England That then and next this present demise and grant to be void and to stand at nothing anything contained in this present covenant not with standing Provided also that if it shall happen that after any of the aforesaid feasts of Saint Michael and the Annunciation of the Blessed Virgin Mary the certain aforesaid payments shall be owed if they ought to be owed that then and next this our present demise and grant to be void and to have no effect anything contained in theses presents in respect thereof not withstanding Anything in statutes acts ordinances permissions proclamations or restrictions in respect thereof before this had made enacted ordinanced or provided or otherwise any other cause or material whatsoever in anything not withstanding In testimony of which thing we have caused our letters patent to be made By the witness of Edward North knight at Westminster the sixteenth day of March in the second year of our reign.

E326/12266

THIS HAS BEEN CANCELLED BY BEING SLICED THROUGH IN MANY PLACES [LATIN: 1548]

This indenture made between the most excellent principal sovereign Lord Henry by the grace of God of King of England France and Ireland defender of the faith and on earth of the church of England and Ireland supreme head on the one part and Thomas Ardern gentleman of the other part Witness that the same lord King by the advice and council of his court of Augmentations and revenues of his crown has demised granted and to farm let to the aforesaid Thomas all that our wood commonly named Feversham Blene otherwise the said Boughton Blene in the county of Kent and the whole endowments of the land and payments of the aforesaid wood containing by

555 Latin *Modios*: Liquid or dry measure Latham has ?8 Gallons.

estimation one thousand and one hundred acres lately of the Monastery of Faversham in the said county of Kent now dissolved formerly being and pertaining and lately being parcel of the possessions in respect thereof Except nevertheless and always to the said King his heirs and all his successors are reserved one thousand and two hundred oaks growing in the aforesaid wood of forty sixty and eight years of which certain one thousand and two hundred oaks each oak of forty oaks of the aforesaid one thousand and two hundred oaks to be valued at eight pence And each tree of eight hundred of which are reserved to be valued at four pence Excepted also to the same lord king similarly reserved all trees and wood growing in the aforesaid wood having been growing for over twenty years To have and to hold the aforesaid wood and the endowed lands and payments to the same wood except as pre-excepted to the aforesaid Thomas Ardern and his assigns from the feast of St. Michael the archangel last past unto the end and term of twenty and one years to be ended next following and fully to be completed Rendering annually to the said Lord the king his heirs and successors twenty and two pounds of legal money of England at the feast of annunciation of the blessed virgin Mary and Saint Michael the Archangel or within one month after both the those feasts into the hands of the general receiver of woods of the said Lord King aforesaid of the Court of Augmentations and revenues of the crown of the King to the use of the same Lord King by equal portions annually to be paid during the term aforesaid And the aforesaid Lord King has willed and by the presents has granted that he himself the heirs and successors of him the said Thomas Ardern and his assigns of all and all manner rents fees annuities and of all other charges and whatsoever their money of the premises issuing or ought to be issuing or on that account charged or answerable for profit of rent in respect thereof by the presents reserved to the use whatsoever of the parson of the time in the time will be discharged, acquitted and defended during the term aforesaid And the aforesaid Thomas Ardern grants by the presents that he himself and his assigns once so much now to fell or to be felled to make all and all manner or wood and underwood to him by the presents demised in the aforesaid wood growing during the term aforesaid And that he himself nor his assigns shall make nor cause to be made part of one cut or wood and underwood as aforesaid demised during the term aforesaid And the aforesaid Thomas Ardern further grants by the presents that he himself and his assigns after each felling in the wood aforesaid by himself or his assigns by virtue of this same indenture to be made to all the wattled fences[556] and the Sprynges of the same wood well and sufficiently to enclose and preserve as often as necessity and opportunity shall require during the term aforesaid And the twelve stadelles[557] sufficient in each acre granted in the form of the schedule and the effect of the statute in this same cause enacted and provided PROVIDED always that if it shall come to pass that the aforesaid rent to be in arrears and unpaid by the space of one month after the same should have been paid in respect thereof limited if he owe now a portion that then this present demise to be void and to have no effect anything in this present indenture contained to the contrary not with standing In witness of which thing one part to this indenture in respect of the aforesaid Thomas Ardern to remain the aforesaid Lord King his seal of the court aforesaid to this same writing to be sealed placed by appointment as commanded The other part of the same indenture in respect thereof to remain with the same lord King to which the aforesaid Thomas to have placed his seal Dated at Westminster the eighth day of October in the thirty seventh reign of our sovereign lord King

By the writ in the first instance sealed by virtue of a warrant of the council of the court aforesaid.

---

[556] *Vigultus*.

[557] *O.E.D.* Staddle: a young tree left standing, when others are cut down, for growth of timber.

PRO: E318/5/181 Particulars for grants 38 Henry 8 (containing 46 membranes) [*Latin*]

membrane 26

County of Kent, in the account of Robert Coldwell collector of the revenues of diverse farms within the town of Feversham parcel of the late monastery of Feversham in the said county of the years xxxvth, xxxvjth, and xxxvijth reign of Henry the VIIIth containing as follows, that is to say,

In money for the said account paid for diverse repairs made in and upon the mill called Flude Myll in the town aforesaid for diverse years that is to say for the years xxxvth year of the said reign lvij^{s} iiij^{d}, in the year xxxvjth liij^{s} iij^{d} and for the year xxxvijth xiij^{s} iiij^{d} in total vj$^{£}$ iiij^{s} xj^{d}

Examined by me Richard Brasier deputy to William Cavendysch auditor.

[Latin]

Parcel of the revenues of the late monastery of Faversham in the said county of Kent

The Mill called Fludmyll in the parish of Feversham, value in the farm of the mill there called Fludmyll with the ponds and banks of the rivers to the same mill appertaining except a certain parcel of land that John Elfrythe lately occupied in the tenure of Robert Joce so to him demised by indenture under the seal of the convent of the said late monastery sealed dated xxviijth day of March in the xxix year of the reign of King Henry the Eight To have from the feast of St. Michael the Archangel next to come after the date of the presents as far as the end and term of xx years then next following and fully to be completed Rendering in respect thereof by the year x$^{£}$ at the feast of the birth of the Lord, the annunciation of the Blessed Virgin Mary, Nativity of Saint John the Baptist and Saint Michael the Archangel equally. And the same Robert and assigns upon all reparation of the cogges and rowndes[558] of the said mill to be made at his own proper costs and charges and to bear all other charges of the repair to the said mill of the Abbot and Convent of the said late monastery and their successors to be made and paid at their own proper costs and charges. However, if any damage or limitation[559] to the aforesaid mill or any of their appurtenances by the aforesaid Robert or his assigns shall come to pass then and as often as the same shall occur Robert and his assigns the same damage at their own proper costs shall immediately repair and make amends as in the said indenture is more fully contained, x$^{£}$ at x yeres purchis C$^{£}$

Sum total of the particulars aforesaid x$^{£}$ iiij^{s} vj^{d}

This myll with the appurtenances above specyfied doth lye nye the towne of Feversham what fynee or income wilbe gyven for the same I knowe nott This is the fyrst particular that I have made of the premysses ne I do not knowe that any other person ys desyerous to by the same

Examined by me Richard Brasier deputy to William Cavendysch auditor

---

558 Cogges and rowndes in English.

559 *Determiet'.*

PRO: E318/33/1862
Particulars for Grants 7 Edward VI Earl of Pembroke

Grantee section 4 containing 41 membranes. [*Latin*]

membrane 2

County of Kent,

Parcel of the lands and possessions lately of the Monastery of Feversham in the county aforesaid.

value in

Farm of the lease[560] of the wood there called Feversham Bleane alias Boughton Bleane in the county aforesaid and the land endowed and accustomed to the same wood containing by estimation MC acres belonging to the said late monastery Except MDD oaks growing in the said wood aged xL years and iiij^{XX} of the same whatsoever oaks iiij^{C} oaks of the same valued at viij^{d} and each tree iiij^{XX} oaks valued to viij^{d} And except all wood growing in the wood aforesaid growing above the age of xx years. So demised to Thomas Ardern. Esquire by indenture dated viijth day of October in the xxxvijth year of the reign of King Henry the VIIIth for the term of xxj years Rendering at the feast of the annunciation of the Blessed Mary and Saint Michael the Archangel by equal portions by the year xxij$^{£}$

Rents of diverse tenants of the lord King within the aforesaid called Woodleys Money by the year xix^{s} iiij^{d} quarter

Rents issuing from certain wooded lands about The Hill called Byrche Parke now John Fogge knight by the year v^{s} xd

[total] xxiij$^{£}$ v^{s} ij^{d} quarter

Memorandum the premisses be an entyer thinge of itt selfe and no parcell of any honour or mannour Also the same ys dystante from the kinges Majesties house of Cantorburie iiij myles and these be the fyrste partyculers I have made of the same

Examined by me Thomas Wyseman deputy Auditor of the Lord King there xiij March

For my lord of Pembroke and hys Lordshipp to be bownde to answer for the landes excepted owt of the [leasse] as they shalbe receivede and ...

---

560 *Locium* should be *locagium*. However, the abbreviation mark was not very apparent. *Locus* is a place.

APPENDIX 12: Thomas Arden 's appointment to obtain a charter, his sales of property, his *inquisition post mortem* and 'Master Ardernes evidences serched.'

FAVERSHAM WARDMOTE BOOK FA/AC1 FOLIO 281V[561]

Memorandum that at the Warmemowth holden the iij daye of November Anno regni regis Henry V[III] xxxvj^{o} yt was condescendyd and agreyd by John Bryngborn Mayer and other the jurattes and Com[enalte] hyre under wrytten that yf Thomas Arden gentleman coulde ~~optayne and~~ purchase and optayne under the Kynges Maiesteyes letters patentes to the use of the towne of Feversham that the seyde towne myght be incorporate by the name of the mayer and comynaltey and lycense to mortyse certeyn londes [of[562]] the seyde towne accordyng to the last wyll of Henrey Hache ~~and allso~~ and allso the proffytes [of] the fayers and ~~lawdaye of~~ the lawdayse And the sayde lyberteys and grantes so optayned to delyver unto [the] mayer and comeners of the same towne under the Kynges maiestey ~~seale~~ letters patentes sealyd and segnyd so that the seyd mayer and comeners do not paye for the same above the rate of xx yers purchase then yt ys agreid that the same Thomas Ardern shall have in recompense of hys labor and expensys in that behalfe hade and sustaynyd twentey poundes.

Master John Bryngborn mayer Master Rychard Dryland Master Sethe Master Marden Master Beste Master Co[lwell] Master Gates Master Dunkyn Master Marshall jurates Joseph Beverley Symond Awnsell John Barber Anthoney Love Wylliam Bull John Dryland Master Wylliam Venor John Wreuke John Pullyn John Snothe Thomas Oldfylde John Harman Rychard Johnson George Stransham Rychard Bonde John Gowghe Wylliam Nele John Gyll Edward Coke Robert Joyse Wylliam Hochynson Edmond Vessey James Alcoke Robert Whythe John Coke John Colverden John Colyn Thomas Heneker Thomas Hylles Rychard Swayne John Vawter Henrey Fylpott John Umfrey Thomas Gorham Thomas Stransham Thomas Mason Raynold Mune

FAVERSHAM BOROUGH RECORDS FA/A1.5/3 THE CHARTER OF KING HENRY THE 8TH GRANTED IN THE 37TH YEAR OF HIS REIGN TO THE TOWN OF FAVERSHAM.

The[563] Charter of King Henry the eighth given to Faversham

Henry the eighth by the grace of God King of England France and Ireland defender of the Faith and in earth supreme head of the church of England and Ireland unto all unto whom these present letters shall come greeting.

WHEREAS before this time by many years past the governing of our whole town of Faversham in the county of Kent was left to pertain and belong to the mayor and jurats of the same town for the time being and to the late Abbot of Faversham for the time being and now after a just occasion

[561] This is the penultimate fol. of the volume and is very torn and dirty.

[562] Hole in the book.

[563] p. 1.

had to search out the foundation of the occupation and tenure of the same town they are not found to be sufficiently strong and valid in the law as we have heard, We now willing our loving subjects the inhabitants of the same town for the universal profit and common utility should be incorporated anew and brought into one body by these presents we do ordain make and create John Seath inhabitant within the said town to use the said office till the last day of September next to come And also by these presents we do ordain make and create the aforesaid John Seath and Richard Dryland the elder gentleman, William Castlock, Thomas Ardern, .Stephen Mott, Robert Colwell, John Dryland the elder, Lewis Marden, Thomas , William Marshall, Thomas Domikyn[564] and Simon Aunsell inhabitants in the said town jurats AND MOREOVER we will ordain and declare by these presents that the aforesaid John Seath and all other persons above named by their names[565] and John Wreak, Anthony Love, George Stransham, John Dryland the younger, Thomas Stransham, William Maycott, Thomas Oulfield, John Pullen, John Snoth, Henry Philpott, John Johnson, Richard Johnson, James Payne, John Gough, Thomas Hills, William Vinner, John Damport, Edward Vesey, John Otrington, Edward Cooke, Ralph Deacon, Thomas Mason, John Green, Thomas Tennaker, William Neale, Edward Gayle, William Wyer, Robert White, Robert Gloover, Edmund Genning, John Robinson, John Tyndall, Richard Swaine, John Collin, John Vawter, William Hall, Richard Smith, Thomas Goreham, Richard Bond, Henry Bond, John Gill, Thomas Bargrove, William Hutchinson, and John Colverden, may enjoy and use and every one of them may enjoy and use all and all manner of pre-eminences and things whatsoever which any other persons or person called Freemen or Freeman of the town of Faversham before this time have enjoyed or used, or any hath enjoyed or used. AND ALSO we will grant and ordain by these presents that the mayor and jurats of the aforesaid town for the time being or the Mayor for the time being and the greater part of the jurats of the said town for the time being may have a full authority and power for ever from time to time to admitt other persons to be jurats of the town AND ALSO that they have full power and authority for ever from time to time to admitt and assign any person or persons which shall please them to enjoy and use all and all manner of commodities and things whatsoever which any person or persons called freeman or Freemen of the town of Faversham he or they may enjoy or use AND FURTHER we will and ordain by these presents that as well the aforesaid John Seath and all other persons by these names above called as all other persons the which at any time shall be by the mayor and jurats of the town aforesaid for the time being[566] or by the mayor of the said town and the greater number of the said jurats of the said town for the time being admitted and assigned to enjoy and use the pre-eminences and commodities which the persons commonly called freemen of the town of Faversham may enjoy and use they shall be called and reputed freemen of the said town of Faversham ALSO we will and of our certain knowledge and mere motion by these presents for us our heirs and successors grant that the same mayor and jurats and other inhabitants of the same town from henceforth shall be by right and name one body by the name of the mayor jurats and commonalty of the town of Faversham in the county of Kent incorporated and erected And we incorporate those the mayor jurats and commonalty of the said town of Faversham by these presents and the body incorporated by the name of the mayor jurats and commonalty of the town of Faversham in the county of Kent and do fully ordain create make and constitute by these presents for ever to endure really and fully ALSO we will and by these presents grant to the aforesaid mayor jurats and commonalty that they may have perpetual succession AND ALSO we will and for us our heirs and successors by these presents do grant to the aforesaid mayor jurats and commonalty and their successors that the jurats of the said town

[564] Given elsewhere as Dunkyn.
[565] p. 2.
[566] p. 3.

for the time being or the major part of them for the time being from time to time every year from henceforth for ever on the last day of September in some convenient place by them to be appointed or assigned as aforesaid at their pleasures within the said town of Faversham shall name and assign and may name and assign two of the jurats of the same town for the time being to the other persons then and there present called and reputed freemen of the town of Faversham to the intent and purpose that the same other persons then[567] and there present or the greater part of them shall choose one of those two jurats so to them named and assigned to be mayor of the aforesaid town for the year then following and that he or the said two jurats so to the other persons named and assigned which by the greater number of the other persons called and reputed freemen of the town of Faversham then and there present shall be so elected he shall be mayor of the aforesaid town and shall bear the office of mayoralty of the said town for one whole year then next following the which person so elected and named to be mayor of the aforesaid town shall take a corporal oath before his next predecessor in the same office if the same his predecessor then be living and present in the aforesaid place where the aforesaid election shall be made And if his said predecessor shall be then dead or absent then before other jurats of the aforesaid town there present for a faithful execution and true exercise of his office aforesaid ALSO we will and do by these presents do grant to the aforesaid mayor jurats and commonalty and their successors for ever that if and as often as there doth happen any person being mayor of the aforesaid town to die during the term wherein he should bear his office of mayoralty of the same town or be removed from the aforesaid office within his year that then and so often the jurats of the aforesaid town or the greater part of them for the time being from time to time for ever at such time as the jurats of the same town for the time being or as it shall be thought good and fit to the greater number of them in a convenient place within the aforesaid town by them to be appointed[568] or assigned at their pleasures shall name and assign and they may name and assign two of the jurats of the said town for the time being to the other persons called and reputed freemen of the same town of Faversham then and there present to the intent and purpose that the same other persons or the greater part of them shall choose one of the said two jurats to them named and assigned to be mayor of the town aforesaid till the last day of September then next following And that the said other persons called or reputed freemen of the same town of Faversham then and there present or the greater part of them shall choose one of the said two jurats so to them named and assigned to be mayor of the said town from thenceforth until the last day of September then next following And that he of the same two jurats so named and assigned which by the greater number of the said other persons called and reputed freemen of the said town of Faversham shall be elected and chosen Mayor of the aforesaid town shall be Mayor of the aforesaid town and shall bear the office of mayoralty of the same town from thence till the last day of September then next following which persons so elected to be mayor of the said town shall take a corporal oath before the other jurats of the aforesaid town then and there present for the faithful and due execution of the said office Also we will and for us our heirs and successors by these presents do grant to the aforesaid mayor jurats and commonalty and their successors for ever that as often as it may happen that any of the aforesaid jurats of the town for the time being should die or be deprived or removed[569] from being one of the jurats of the said town that then and so often the mayor and jurats of the said town of Faversham or the Mayor of the aforesaid town and the greater part of the jurats of the aforesaid town for the time being from time to time for ever at such times as to them shall be thought good and fit in a convenient place by them to be appointed or assigned at their pleasures within the said town shall choose one or more of the other persons then called and

[567] p. 4.
[568] p. 5.
[569] p. 6.

reputed freemen of the said town of Faversham being then not[570] the jurats of the said town to be jurat or jurats of the said town ALSO we will and for us and our successors do grant by these presents to the aforesaid mayor[571] and commonalty and to their successors for ever that every mayor of the town aforesaid for the time being from time to time for ever whensoever it shall please him shall name and choose a person to be Serjeant at Mace from thence 'till the last day of September then next following for proclamations executions and other things to the office of the said Serjeant at Mace pertaining or belonging within the said town from the time of the said election of the said Serjeant at Mace until the last day of September then next following to be done and executed And the same Serjeant at Mace so named and elected may lawfully bear a Mace within the said town from the time of his election until the last day of September then next following without the let of us our heirs or successors And if and as often as any Serjeant at Mace so chosen shall die or happen to be removed from his office before the last day of September then next following his said election that then and so often the[572] mayor of the said town then being during his mayoralty shall name and choose one other person to be Serjeant at Mace within the said town until the last day of September then next following and that the said Serjeant at Mace so chosen or named may lawfully use and do in the same town all and singular things which do pertain or are reputed to pertain to the office of Serjeant at Mace until the last day of September then next following AND OF our plentiful grace certain knowledge and mere motion we will and do grant to the aforesaid mayor jurats and commonalty and their successors that the same mayor jurats and commonalty and their successors for ever, any the name of the mayor jurats and commonalty of the town of Faversham in the county of Kent may prosecute claim plead and defend in all our courts and places of our heirs and successors and elsewhere in and upon all and singular causes accounts suits demands writs complaints as well real as personal or mixed both in and upon all and singular other things causes or matters whatsoever AND ALSO that the said mayor jurats and commonalty and their successors from henceforth for ever shall have a common seal to seal all and singular charters and evidences and other writings or deeds by any means touching or concerning the same mayor jurats and commonalty and their successors and their lands and tenements goods or chattels whatsoever AND FURTHERMORE of our plentiful grace certain knowledge and mere motion for us our heirs and successors we will grant and ordain that the aforesaid Mayor jurats and[573] commonalty and their successors shall be persons able and capable in the law by the name of the mayor jurats and commonalty of the town of Faversham in the county of Kent to take receive and purchase to them and their successors for ever or otherwise at their will and pleasure manors lordships messages lands tenements and other whatsoever hereditaments liberties privileges and the jurisdictions underwritten and goods and chattels whatsoever TO HAVE AND TO HOLD to the said mayor jurats and commonalty and their successors for ever or by any other means whatsoever although the same shall be held of us our heirs and successors *in capite* and this without any other license of us our heirs or successors or any writ of ad *quod damnum Inquisitionium*, or any other thing whatsoever thereof to be obtained or prosecuted the statute of lands and tenements for mortmain not put or by any other statute act ordinance or law to the contrary in anywise notwithstanding AND FURTHER by these presents for us our heirs and successors we will and grant to the said mayor jurats and commonalty and their successors that the said mayor jurats and commonalty and their successors from henceforth for ever without let or interruption by us our heirs or assigns and lawfully and freely shall have hold and enjoy and they may have hold and enjoy all and singular manors and messuages lands tenements hereditaments goods and chattels whatsoever which before this time

[570] One of; in pencil interlined.
[571] Jurats; in pencil interlined.
[572] p. 7.
[573] p. 8.

have been given granted bequeathed or assigned to the barons of the said town or to the mayor and commonalty of Faversham or to the mayor barons and commonalty of Faversham or to the Mayor and jurats of the said town of Faversham[574] or to any of them or by any other name or by whatsoever other names or additions of names have been given granted bequeathed or assigned And that the said mayor jurats and commonalty of the town aforesaid and their successors from henceforth for ever without let or interruption of us our heirs or assigns and lawfully and freely shall have hold and enjoy all and singular manors messuages lands tenements and hereditaments goods and chattels whatsoever which before this time have been given granted bequeathed or assigned to them which were named accepted or reputed barons of the said town of Faversham or mayor and commonalty of Faversham and mayor and jurats of the town of Faversham or to any of them or by any other name or additions of names have been given granted bequeathed and assigned AND that the said mayor jurats and commonalty of the town aforesaid and their successors by the name of mayor jurat and commonalty of the aforesaid town of Faversham in the county of Kent may give alien demise grant and assign all and singular the aforesaid manors lordships messuages lands tenements and hereditaments goods and chattels whatsoever to whomsoever they will at their pleasures AND MOREOVER for us our heirs and successors we have granted and given license and by these presents do grant and give license to the aforesaid mayor jurats and commonalty of Faversham and their successors that the same mayor jurats and commonalty may lawfully and freely receive and enjoy and to have to them and their successors for ever of the gift and grant of whatsoever person or persons which will give grant alien or bequeath things unto[575] them or by any other manner by which they hold all the same lands tenements and hereditaments being in the parishes and town of Harty and Faversham in our said county of Kent and in the parishes of Icklisham Gesling Odomere and Bread in our county of Sussex and elsewhere within our said counties of Kent and Sussex which were Henry Hatches deceased in his life time or of any other person to his use TO HAVE AND TO HOLD the same lands tenements and other hereditaments with the appurtenances to the said mayor jurats and commonalty and their successors for ever of whatever person or persons the same are held the statute of mortmain or any other statute act restraint or law to the contrary notwithstanding AND FURTHERMORE by these presents we give and grant to the aforesaid mayor jurats and commonalty and their successors for ever view of Frankpledge and Leet of all and singular the inhabitants and residents and that hereafter shall be inhabitants and residents in the aforesaid town of Faversham before the mayor of the said town for the time being in a convenient place in the said town by the mayor appointed or assigned to be held twice in every year that is to say once within the month after the feast of Saint Michael the Archangel and another court within the month after the feast of Easter with all and singular things that to view of Frankpledge do pertain or hereafter may pertain by any means And all and singular amerciaments fines commodities profits emoluments and advantages[576] by any means thereof coming or growing by reason of the view of Frankpledge or let aforesaid or either of them or any ways concerning them AND ALSO the assay and assize of bread wine and ale and other victuals whatsoever in the aforesaid town and the amendment and punishment of them which shall doer or cause to be done anything against the said assize AND ALSO lands tenements goods and chattels whatsoever of felons fugitives condemned persons outlaws or by any other means judged to death within the said town being or found to be had or found and goods and chattels of felons of themselves and deodands and goods and chattels waifs and strays within the aforesaid town found or to be found or happening AND of our mere abundant grace and of our certain knowledge and mere motion we

[574] p. 9.
[575] p. 10.
[576] p. 11.

give and for us our heirs and successors by these presents do grant to the said mayor jurats and commonalty and their successors for ever authority power and license from henceforth for ever to hold before the mayor of the town aforesaid for the time being in a convenient place in the said town by the mayor of the said town for the time being to be appointed or assigned every week upon Mondays Tuesdays Wednesdays Thursdays and Fridays or oftener or seldomer at the will of the mayor of the aforesaid town of Faversham for the time being a court called the Portmote Court And all power and authority at the same court to receive the[577] acknowledgement of fines and recoveries of lands and tenements being within the said town and to hold and determine all and singular manner of assizes pleas and all other pleas actions and suits by any means touching messuages lands and tenements being within the said town AND ALSO all and all manner of pleas suits and quarrels as well real and personal as mixt and other pleas and demands whatsoever within the said town happening and arising and to make thereof due examination according to the laws of this realm of England ALSO we will and grant for us our heirs and successors by these presents that all and singular fines and recoveries the which at any time hereafter shall be levied had acknowledged or in the court aforesaid shall be valid and of force in law according to the usage had in like case in the town of Sandwich in the county aforesaid one our five ports ALSO by these presents we give and grant to the aforesaid mayor jurats and commonalty and their successors for ever as well all and singular profits amerciaments issues advantages and emoluments whatsoever of all and singular the courts aforesaid and in the same courts happening growing or arising as all and all manner of profits and customs proceeding or arising from all portages whatsoever within the town of Faversham aforesaid hereafter to be made or had AND ALSO we give and of our further knowledge and mere motion by these presents do grant for us and our heirs and successors to the aforesaid mayor jurats and commonalty and to their successors for ever as market and market place within the said town of Faversham in a place there commonly called the market place every week Wednesdays and Fridays and Saturdays and all other half holidays from henceforth for ever to be holden and kept together with all and all manner of tolls customs stallage and other profits and commodities to the market belonging or by any means appertaining AND ALSO authority and power to do and execute in the aforesaid town of Faversham all and singular things which do appertain or belong to the office of the clerk of the market. ALSO we will and grant to the said mayor jurats and commonalty and their successors for ever as well all and singular profits and emoluments which at anytime hereafter shall be received or taken of any persons or persons whatsoever who are or shall be occupiers within the said town of Faversham then not called or reputed freemen of the town of Faversham as all and singular profits and emoluments the which at any time hereafter shall be received of any persons which shall be admitted and assigned to be freemen of the said town for the same admission AND FURTHER of our plentiful grace we give and of our sure knowledge and mere motion by these presents do grant to the aforesaid mayor jurats and commonalty and their successors for ever a fair and fairs to begin every year from henceforth for ever upon the first day of August to endure for seven[578] days then next following to be holden and kept then in such convenient place within the aforesaid town of Faversham as the mayor of the same town for the time being by proclamation then to be made shall assign the fair or fairs to be holden and kept AND ALSO a fair and fairs every year from thenceforth for ever in the feast of Saint Valentine the Bishop and to endure seven days then next following to be holden and kept in such convenient place within the said town as the mayor of the same town for the time being by a proclamation then to be made shall assign the same fair and fairs to be holden and kept AND ALSO all and singular tolls stallage and also all and singular other things pertaining and

[577] p. 12.
[578] p. 14.

belonging to the Fairs by reason or occasion of the said fairs or any of them coming growing or arising And the Court of Piepowder as is commonly used to a fair or market within the realm of England And all profits issues and emoluments as well in the said courts of Piepowders as by reason and occasion of the aforesaid fairs growing coming or arising ALSO we give and grant to the aforesaid mayor jurats and commonalty and their successors for ever authority and power to make a gaol and prison in the said town[579] of Faversham in such place as it shall please them and the same as a gaol to use have and hold to them and their successors for ever The which messuages lands tenements fairs markets issues rents ands profits aforesaid view of Frankpledge courts markets and fairs and other the premises with their appurtenances are now extended to the clear yearly value of eight pounds To hold and enjoy the said messuages lands tenements view of Frankpledge courts markets fairs tolls customs privileges liberties franchises and all and singular other the premises given and granted with their appurtenances to the said mayor jurats and commonalty and their successors for ever to be holden of us our heirs and successors by fealty only in free burgage of the town of Faversham aforesaid and not in capite and yielding therefore yearly to us our heirs and successors eight pounds of lawful money of England at our court of Augmentation of the revenues of our crown to be paid every year at the feast of Saint Michael the archangel for all other rents services tenures and demands whatsoever thereof to us our heirs and successors by any means to be yielded paid and done and without any account or any other thing for the premises or any thing of the premises to us our heirs or successors to be yielded and done AND[580] MOREOVER of our especial grace we grant to the said mayor jurats and commonalty all and singular issues rents revenues and profits of all and singular the premises and every parcel thereof from the feast of Saint Michael the Archangel last past hitherto coming or growing TO HOLD to the same mayor jurats and commonalty of our gift with out account or any other thing therefore to us our heirs or successors by any means to be yielded paid or done AND MOREOVER by these presents we give and grant and confirm and ratify to the mayor jurats and commonalty and their successors for ever as well all and singular such privileges liberties franchises immunities customs authorities and acquittances as by any person occupying or using the office of mayoralty of the aforesaid town of Faversham used or exercised by any lawful means within the aforesaid town as all those things which have been given and granted by our most noble progenitors Kings of England by their several letters patents under the seal of the realm of England or by any of them to the barons of the aforesaid town of Faversham or to the mayor and commonalty of Faversham or other names or additions ALSO we will and by these presents do grant for us and our successors to the aforesaid mayor jurats and commonalty and their successors for ever that the said mayor jurats and the greater number[581] of persons inhabiting the said town of Faversham called and reputed Freemen of the town of Faversham for the time being shall have power and authority to make laws statutes and ordinances from time to time for ever for the common weal of the same town and for the wholesome government of the same And other things lawfully and freely in the aforesaid town to use and execute And also that they may change those and every of them from time [to time in pencil interlined] for ever as it shall be thought good to them in as ample manner and form as the mayor jurats and commonalty of the aforesaid town of Sandwich may justly make or at any time before this time have used AND ALSO we will and of our own sure knowledge and mere motion by these presents do grant to the aforesaid mayor jurats and commonalty of the town aforesaid that they may have and shall have these our letters patents under our great seal of England after a due manner made and sealed without fine or fee great or little to us in our hanaper or elsewhere to our use by any other means to be yielded paid

579 p. 15.
580 p. 16.
581 p. 17.

or done although no express mention be made in the presents of the true yearly value or of the certainty of the premises or any of them or of any other gifts or grants by us or any of our progenitors to the mayor jurats and commonalty of the town aforesaid before these times made And any statute act ordinance provision or restraint to the contrary thereof made done[582] ordained provided or any other thing cause or matter whatsoever in anywise notwithstanding IN WITNESS whereof we have caused these our letters patents under our seal Witness ourself at Westminster the twenty seventh day of January and in the thirty seventh year of our reign.[1546]

Faversham Borough Records
FA/JBF5

This is the final agreement made in the court of Halimote held at Faversham in the county of Kent on Thursday, that is to say the fifth day of June in the thirty sixth year of the reign of the sovereign Lord Henry the Eighth by the grace of God of England, France and Ireland King, defender of the faith and on earth of the church of England and Ireland supreme head [1544] Before John Brynbourne mayor of the town aforesaid, William Rooper Esquire steward of the lord king there, William Castlocke, John Hampton Robert Coldewell and John Best jurats of the same town and other faithful people of the lord king there present Between Anthony Aucher Esquire plaintiff and Thomas Ardern gentleman and Alice his wife deforciants of two messuages of which one called the George and the another called The Garrett and one garden with their appurtenances situated lying and being in Feversham aforesaid in respect thereof the two messuages together situated and lying in Feversham aforesaid in a certain street there called The Courtestreate otherwise Northestreate near the market and public square[583] there and the aforesaid garden similarly lying and being in Feversham aforesaid in a certain street there called the Eaststreate next to Cookes Dyche there in respect there of a plea of covenant had been summoned between them in the same court That is to say that the aforesaid Thomas and Alice have recognised the aforesaid messuages with the appurtenances to be the right of the aforesaid Anthony, as being that which the same Anthony had of the gift of the same Thomas and Alice and that he has remised and quitclaimed it for the same Thomas and Alice and the heirs of the same Alice, to the aforesaid Anthony and his heirs for ever And moreover the same Thomas and Alice furthermore have granted for themselves and their heirs of the same Alice that they themselves will warrant the aforesaid tenements with the appurtenances to the aforesaid Anthony and his heirs against all men for ever. And for this final agreement remise quitclaim and warrant the same Anthony has given the same Thomas and Alice twenty three pounds six shillings and eight pence of silver

Rockingham Castle,
Watson (Rockingham) Collection. 682.

Abstract[584]

Indenture of bargain and sale from Thomas Ardern of Faversham, gentleman to Thomas Dunkyn of Faversham, yeoman, for £90 of a messuage or tenement, barn, stable and little thatched house,

582 p. 18.

583 *Forum* but note the uncharacteristic letter r.

584 For an inaccurate transcript see *Arch. Cant.* xxxiv (1920), Appendix I, pp. 127-29.

garden 'ympaled' and piece or parcel of pasture and marsh called Nether Grene, a piece of pasture between the Crycke or Key at the Standred and a certain stone style standing at a place leading to the thorn called [ ], and all other lands now occupied by John son of William Castlocke, and a small piece of pasture in the Upper Grene on the west side of the highway adjoining the above premises (½ acre) and all trees and wood growing there. 3 August 1545.

Signed Thomam Arderne

Faversham Borough Records
FA/JBf6

Town of Faversham
This is the final agreement made in the court of Portmote there held Thursday, that is to say, the twentieth day of December in the second year of the reign of our sovereign Lord Edward the Sixth by the grace of God of England France and Ireland king, defender of the faith and on earth of the church of England and Ireland supreme head before John Best mayor there Richard Dryland senior gentleman Thomas Dunkyn Lewis Marden and John Wreuke jurates of the aforesaid town and other faithful people of the lord king then there present Between William Garrett plaintiff and Thomas Ardern and Alice his wife of three acres of pasture with appurtenances lying and being in the parish and within the jurisdiction of Faversham within the liberty of the five ports and now in the tenure of John Dryland junior gentleman, that is to say, between the messuage of William Fynner and William Nele towards East side, to the lands of the heirs of [blank] Warham towards the West side, to the lands of Henry Cryppes Esquire towards the South side, to the garden late Henry Hacche, lands of Anthony Sawnders Esquire and lands of the heirs of Lawrence Manby towards the North side, in respect thereof a plea of covenant was made thereof between them in the same court, that is to say, that the aforesaid Thomas Ardern and Alice have recognised the aforesaid land[585] with appurtenances to be the right of the aforesaid William Garrett as that which the same William had of the gift of the aforesaid Thomas Ardern and Alice and that they remised and quitclaimed it for the same Thomas and Alice and the heirs of the same Thomas to the aforesaid William Garrett and his heirs for ever And moreover the same Thomas Ardern and Alice have furthermore granted for themselves and the heirs of the same Thomas that they themselves will warrant the tenement aforesaid with appurtenances to the aforesaid William Garrett and his heirs against all men for ever And for this recognisance remise quitclaim warrant fine and agreement the same William Garrett has given to the aforesaid Thomas Ardern and Alice thirty pounds of silver.

Faversham Wardmote Book FA/AC1
folio 105v

BLAKWELL MAIOR[586]

THIS indenture made the foure and twentyth daye of September in the thyrd yere of our soveraigne Lord Edward the syxt [1549] by the grace of God king of England Fraunce and Ireland defender of the fayth and in erth supreme hedd of the churche of England and Ireland

[585] Given as tenement'.
[586] Mayor 1563.

Betwene Thomas Ardern of Faversham in the county of Kente gentleman on the one parte and John Baker of the same towne labourer on that other parte Wytnessyth that the seyd Thomas Ardern. hath demysed graunted and to ferme letten and by these presentes dymiseth and graunteth and to ferme letteth unto the seyd John Baker all that lytle gardein or orchard lying and being in Preston Strete within the towne and lybertye of Faversham aforeseid adioynyng to the gardein and messuage of the seyd John Baker there, conteynyng by estimation one yeard or rood of land and foure and fyftye fote more with the appurtenances the markes and boundes thereof every where there doth devyde and shewe To have hold and occupye the seyd gardein and orchard with all and singuler the appurtenances and the profytes commodyties and advauntages of the same unto the seyd John Baker his executours and assignes from the feast of St. Mychell the archaungell next ensuing the date hereoff unto the end and terme of twentye yeres then next following and fully to be completed and ended Yelding and paying therfore yerely duryng all the seyd terme of twentye yeres unto the seyd Thomas Arden his executours and assignes at the feastes of the annunciation of our ladye and Saint Mychell the archaungell foure shillinges of good and lawfull Englishe moneye by even portions And the seid John Baker for hym his executors and assignes and every of theym do covenaunte and graunte to and with the seyd Thomas Ardern his heires executours and assignes and with every of them by these presentes that the seid John Baker his executours or assignes shall sett and plante all the voyd grounde in the seyd gardein as sone as he or they convenyently maye wyth soch good fruites as shalbe thought mete and convenyent by the discression of the seyd John Baker his executours and assignes And so to contynue in setting and plantyng as is aforeseide there from tyme to tyme when and as often as nede shall requyre at his or their owne proper costes and charges And at their lyke costes and charges susteyne mayneteyne and kepe the necessarie closure of the seid gardein or orcharde suffycyently duryng all the terme aforeseyd And so in the ende of the seyd terme yeld and leve the same In wytnes whereof the partyes aforeseyd to this present indenture their sealles interchaungablye have putt geven the daye and yere first above wrytten

By me Thomas Arderne
in the year of Christ[587] 1549

FOLIO 280V

Master Thomas Ardens will

The xxth of December in the year 1550 and the iiijth year of the reign of King Edward VIth

THIS IS THE LAST WILL of me Thomas Arderne made the day and yere aboveseyd First where I stand bounde to Sir Edward North knight in a thousand markes sterling to make my wyfe a joynture of xL$^{£}$ by yere for terme of her lyfe, or ells to appoynt it her by my testament and last will I will that Alyce my wyfe in recompence of her said joynture, have thise parcelles of landes and tenements folowyng, to her for terme of her said lyfe naturall Furst my house wherein I dwell, the tenement adioynyng to my cartgate, late in the tenure of John Goodhewe, with the gardeyns, orchardes, dovehouse and stable belonging to the same, rated at vj$^{£}$ xiij^{s} iij^{d} by the yere Item the Abbey house in the tenour of Thomas Straunsham, at xL^{s} by the yere Item the porters gatehous with the garden in the tenure of Adam Foul at xL^{s} by the yere Item the brewhous and the great garden in the tenure of John Castlok at v$^{£}$ vj^{s} viij^{d} by the yere Item the Thorne Medowe and the house in the tenure of John Webbe; at vj$^{£}$ xiij^{s} iiij^{d} by yere Item a garden and a dovehous in the

[587] Per me Anno XPi.

tenour of William Maycote at xxxiij^{s} iiij^{d} by the yere Item the Sextry and the Uppergrene with the fruytes rated yerely at v$^{£}$ Item the Amery croft rated yerely at viij$^{£}$ Item the wasshehous croft at Liij^{s} iiij^{d} by yere Total by the year xL$^{£}$ And after her decease I will that my doughter have all the said londes and tenementes to her and to the heyres of her body laufully begotten And if she happen to dye without yssue of her bodye then I will the premysses do discend to my syster and to her heyres Item I geve to the Mayor[588] Jurates and commonalty[589] of the towne of Faversham to have to theym and their successors for evermore to bestowe uppon the releif of the pore people inhabityng within the seid towne yerely for ever ~~in Faversham Churche~~ And also uppon consideration that the said Mayor jurates and Commonalty shall cause yerely in Faversham churche for ever uppon the day of my buryall, a solempne sermon of the scripture to be made by a preacher of Crystchurch in Cantorburye or some other wellerned man and he to have for his labour, for every suche sermon, v^{s} resytyng in his sermon my name the causer of that sermon, And also resyting my said gift hereafter folowyng to the intent other good men may the rather be provoked to geve the lyke That is to saye, these parcelles folowyng Furst ij tenementes at Cokysdyche at x^{s} by the year Item a gardeyn in the tenour of Baker in Preston Strete iiij^{s} by the year Item a gardeyn in the tenour of John Castlock iiij^{s} by the year Item the pillory in the market place viij^{s} by the year Item Seynt Nicholas Chapell with the orcherd gardeyn londe and wodd belonging to the same xx^{s} by the year Item I will that myne heyres and executrix shall make suche assuraunce unto the seid Mayor Jurates and commonaltye to the use aforesaid as reason requyreth And if the said Mayor etc. Item I will to Margarete my doughter and to her heyres for ever my mylle called the Fludde Myll at x$^{£}$ by yere A peece of londe in the Abbey felde called Surrendens croft containing viij acres at xxx^{s} by yere A litell cotage at x^{s} by the yere in the tenour of Spuddell A tenement wherein John Tyknoll late dwelled at Liij^{s} iiij^{d} by yere [*a tenem*]ent in the tenure of one [*blank*] Bucknell in the Myddell rowe at xiij^{s} iiij^{d} by yere ij tenements in [tenu]r[e] of John Sede at xiij^{s} iiij^{d} by the yere, ij tenementes in the tenure of Mestres Auncell with the fysshe shambles [*lost*] xL^{s} by the yere, iij tenementes in the tenure of Master Swanne, in the Middle Rowe, at xxj^{s} viij^{d} by the yere, [*lost* - ? A tenement] late in the tenure of Henry Moore, at Parvydge[590] Lane ende at xvj^{s} by the yere, iij tenements in the ten[ure of -*lost*] [M]estres Deane, at xiiij^{s} by the yere, iij tenementes in the tenure of Reynold Smythe at xiij^{s} by the [yere] A gardeyne next Westbroke in the tenure of Huddyball, at iij^{s} iiij^{d} by the yere, A tenement in the tenure [of A]nthony [Lo]ve lying next his dwellinghouse house[591] in the marckett by the yere xx^{s}, A rent of v^{s} due to me from the Mayor Jurates and Commonalty of Faversham, for the libertye uppon the upper grene, to kepe Valentyne Fayer over, which parcelles of londes and tenementes I will that my doughter have to her, and to her heyres for ever, and the profittes of theym immedyatly after my deceasse, And of this my present testament and last wyll, I ordeyne and make Alyce my said wyfe to be myne executryx, And I ordeyne and will also, that Sir Edward North knight be myne overseer of this my present wyll and testament, and I geve him for his labour my best horse, In witnes wherof I have wrytten this present testament and last will with myne owne hande, the said xxth daye of December In the year of the Lord MDL and in the iiijth yere of the reigne of our sovereigne Lord King Edward the Syxt

By me Thomas Arderne in my proper hand

This will was wrytten in to this booke by the commaundement of Master John Seath mayer the xvth day of September in the syxt yere of the reigne of our sovereigne Lorde Kyng Edward the Syxt in the year 1552

---

588 fol. 281.

589 Abbreviated Coialtye with a tittle over the top of the oi.

590 Partridge.

Memorandum that this will is fownde in the Office fownde by the eschetor of the shire and remayneth [in] the Chaunsery under the seales of them that were jurates in the same offyce.

Marginal entry under the folio number in the top right hand corner.
All this boke was fygeryd[592] on the corner of every lefe by Thomas Norton Mayor the 10th October in the year 1561 in the third yere of Quene Elizabeth [at] which [ti]me dyvers of the sayd leavis were cut owt of the sayd bowke etc.

PRO: Writ of Diem Clausit Extremum C142/93 number 111

EDWARD[593] the sixth by the grace of God of England France and Ireland King defender of the faith and in earth the supreme head of the church of England and Ireland To his escheator in Kent, Greeting, Because Thomas Arden who held of us in chief at the time of his death, as we understand, we command that we be advised of all lands and tenements of which the same Thomas was seised in his demise as of his fee, in your bailiwick, on the day on which he died or a writ of adjournment in our hand and to preserve and take them into custody until another thereupon . And by the oath of good and lawful men of the same your bailiwick by what things truthfully we will be able better to know diligently to enquire how much land and tenements the aforesaid Thomas held of us in chief as in his demeasne as in what service in your said bailiwick, the day on which he died and how much of others and by what other services and how much land and tenements , their value by the year in all profits and on which day did the same Thomas die and who is his nearest heir and of what age. And the inquisition thereafter to be made distinct and open to us in our Chancery under your hand and seal by those will cause a summons to be made without delay and by this writ. Witness me myself at Westminster 26th May in the 5th year of our reign.

Dorse: Execution[594] of this writ is manifest in a certain inquisition indented annexed to this writ, by me Christopher Roper Escheator.

This was handed to the Court on the 8th day of October the year written below by the hand of the Escheator.[595]
Kent:
Inquisition indented held for the Lord the King at Bexley in the County aforesaid on the seventh

---

591 *Sic*.

592 An explanation for the removal of pages has not yet come to light.

593 *Latin*: Edwardus sextus dei gracia Anglie Francie et Hibernie Rex fidei defensor et in terra ecclesie anglicane et hiberne supremum caput escaetori suo in comitatu Kancie salutem Quia Thomas Arden generosus qui de nobis tenuit in capite diem clausit extremum vt accepimus tibi precipius quod omnes terras et tenementa de quibus idem Thomas fuit seisitus in dominico suo ut de feodo in balliva tua die quo obijt sive dilatio capias in manum nostram et ea salvo custodiri faciatis donec aliud inde preceperimus. Et per sacramentum proborum et legalium hominum de eadem balliva tua per quos rei veritas melius sciri poterit diligenter inquiratis quantam terrarum et tenementarum predictus Thomas tenuit de nobis in capite tam in dominico quam in servicio in dicta balliva tua dicto die quo obijt et quantum de alijs et per quod servicium et quantum terre et tenementa illa valeant per annum in omnibus exitibus et quo die idem Thomas obijt et quis propinquior heres eius sit et cuius etatis Et inquisitonem inde distincte et aperte factam nobis in Cancellariam nostram sub sigillo tuo et sigillis eorum per quos facta fuerit sine dilacione mittas et hoc breve Teste me ipso apud Westmonasterium xxvj die May anno regni nostro quinto Hever.

594 Executio istius brevis patet in quadum inquisitione [indenta] huic brevis annexis [per me] Christopher Roper Escaetore.

595 Liberatum fuit curia 8 die Octobris Anno subscripto manus escaetoris.

day of October in the fifth year of the reign of the Lord Edward the Sixth by the grace of God of England France and Ireland King, Defender of the Faith, and on earth supreme head of the church in England and Ireland Before Christopher Rooper Esquire Escheator for the said lord the King in the county aforesaid, by virtue of the same King's writ of ' diem clausit extremum'[596] after the death of Thomas Arden gentleman directed therein to the same Escheator and of one part of this inquisition stitched together who by the oath of Thomas Hynd John Borne Thomas Sedcope John Gawen John Cumbys Robert Holden William Lane Richard Halden Richard Heton John Poll Henry Chucher and Richard Shewsmythe John Taylour good and lawful men in the same county Who say upon their oath that the same Thomas Ardern was seized of for a long time before the day of his death and in his life in his demesne as of fee of and in the house and site of the late Monastery of Faversham in the county aforesaid, and of and in diverse other buildings to the same annexed and of and in twelve acres of land called the Outyerdes and the Sextry lands to the same belonging and of and in one messuage called the Gatehouse with one garden called the Ostry And of and in one stable and nine acres of land to the same adjoining now in the tenure of John Castlok And of and in one other close of land adjoining to the Graunge there and also of and in ten acres of meadow-land called the Thornemedowe And of and in one parcel of pasture containing three acres of land with one small tenement built upon now in the tenure of John Webb gentleman And of and in one garden called the Dovehouse Garden by estimation of two acres of land And of and in six acres of pasture to the same adjoining called the Amery Croft in the town of Faversham aforesaid And the jurors aforesaid furthermore say upon their oath that the same Thomas Arden was similarly seized in his demesne as of fee of and in one messuage or tenement one garden and one dovecote lately leased to Richard Dryland and Dorothy his wife next to the Amery croft in Faversham aforesaid And of and in one messuage and garden to the same annexed lately in the tenure of John Sethe lying in Westret Faversham aforesaid near the tenement of Richard Colwell And of and in one other tenement with its appurtenances called the Corner Tenement lying next to the Fyshemarket in Faversham aforesaid now in the tenure of the same John Sethe And of and in one water mill with its appurtenances called Fludmull in Faversham aforesaid and of two acres of pasture to the same adjoining And of and in seven acres with appurtenances in Faversham aforesaid called Surrenden Croft And of and in one messuage with the appurtenances lately in the tenure of John Dryland junior And of and in one messuage with appurtenances now or late in the tenure of Edward Wodd one other messuage with appurtenances now or late in the tenure of [George] Nicolson one messuage with appurtenances now in the tenure of Richard Spodell three messuages with their appurtenances now in the tenure of Thomas Oldfelde one messuage now in the tenure of Matthew Tyce two messuages in Tannerstret in Faversham aforesaid in the tenure of Peter Gylnot And of and in three messuages now in the tenure of Reginald Smyth And of and in one messuage in the tenure of Robert Keer And of and in one messuage with appurtenances now in the tenure of Anthony Love And of and in two tenements with appurtenances now in the occupation of Elizabeth Berkley and William Chesman And of and in two orchards in the separate tenures of [blank] Baker John Taylor and John Castlok And of and in one piece of ground of the blessed house built upon called The Merketcrosse now in the tenure of Elizabeth Anselme widow And furthermore the jurors aforesaid upon their oath say that the same Thomas Ardern thus of the aforesaid house and site of the said late monastery of the lands tenements meadows pastures and the rest of all the premisses with their appurtenances were seized and being of the same all and singular the aforesaid messuages lands and tenements and the rest of the premisses with their appurtenances he has declared in his will which follows amongst other things the same last will contains and specifies In the name of God Amen I Thomas Ardern of Faversham in the county of Kent

[596] 'He has closed his last day'. There is another copy of the Inquisition at PRO, E150/501/3.

gentleman [the] 20th day of December in the yere of our Lord God 1550 and in the fourth yere of the reign of our sovereigne Lord kyng Edward the Sixth make this my present testament and last wyll in manner and forme folowyng This is the last wyll of me the seid Thomas Ardern. made the day and yere aboveseid First I wyll that after my wyfes decease that my doughter have all my seid lands and tenementes to her and to the heires of her body lawfully begotten And yf she happen to dye without yssue of her bodye than I wyll the premysses to discend to my suster and to her heires Item I geve to the mayre jurattes and commynaltye of the towne of Faversham to have to them And their successors for evermore to bestowe uppon the relief of the poore people inhabytyng within the seid towne yerely for ever And also uppon consideration that the seid mayre and jurattes and commynaltye shall cause yerely for ever in Faversham churche uppon the day of my buryall a solemn sermon of scrypture to be made by a precher of Cryscherche in Caunterbery fyrst two tenementes at Cookesdyche Item a garden in the tenure of Baker in Preston Street Item a garden in the tenure of John Castlok Item the pyllory in the market place Item Seynt Nicholas Chappell with the orchard garden land and wodd belongyng to the same Item I wyll that my heres shall make such assurance unto the said Mayre jurattes and commonaltye to the use aforeseid as reason requyreth Item I wyll to Margaret my doughter and to her heires for ever my myll called Fludmyll a pece of land in the Abbeyfeld called Surrenden Croft conteynyng eight acres a tenement in the tenure of [blank] Spodell a tenement wherein John Tyknoll late dwelled a tenement in the tenure of one [blank] Buknell in myddell rowe two tenementes in the tenure of John Seede two tenementes in the tenure of Mystres Anselme with the fyshambles 3 tenementes in the tenure of Master Swan in the Myddell Rowe a tenement late in the tenure of Henry Moore at Partrydge Lane End 3 tenementes in the tenure of Mystres Deane 3 tenementes in the tenure of Reynald Smythe a garden next Westbroke in the tenure of [blank] Hodgback A tenement in the tenure of Anthony Love lying next his dwellynghouse in the market A rent of 5s due to me from the Mayre Jurattes and Commonaltye of Faversham for lybertye uppon the Upper Grene to kepe Valentyne Fayre over all which parcelles of landes and tenementes I wyll that my doughter have to her and her heires for ever the profettes of them immedyatly after my decesse as[597] amongst other things in this last will by the aforesaid jurors

---

[597] Prout inter alia in eidem ultima voluntate juratoribus predictis super captionem huius inquisicionis plenius patet Et juratores predictus dicunt super sacrum suum quod predicti domus et scitus dicti nuper monasteri cum omnibus edificijs eidem adiacent et predictis mesuagiis vocate le Gatehouse cum le Ostry Garden et predictum stabulum et novem acris terre adiacent et predictum clausum adiacent ad le Graunge decem acris prati vocate le Thornemedowe et tres acris pasture cum parvo tenemento super edificato et predictum unum ortum vocatum le Dovehouse Garden et predicti sex acris prati vocate le Amery Croft et predicti duodecem acris terre vocate le Outyerdes Sextrys and Washouse in Faversham predicto parcellarum terrarum et tenementorum predictorum tenente de domini rege in capite per servicium vicesime partis unius feodum milites Et per decimi vijs per annum annuatim solvend ad curiam augmentationum Et quod predicti domus vel scitus dicti nuper monastery valent clare per annum ultra reparis xxvjs viijd Et predictum mesuagium vocatum le Gatehouse valet per annum xiijs iiijd et predictum stabulum et novem acris terre in tenura Johannis Castlock valent clare per annum v£ vjs viijd Et quod predicti decem acris prati vocate Thornemedowe valent per annnum iiij£ xiijs iiijd Et predictum tenementum et tres acris modo in tenura predicti Johannis Tykner valent per annum xls Et predictum Gardinum vocatum le Dovehouse garden valent per annum xxxiijs iiijd Et quod predicti sex acris prati vocate le Amery Croft Sextry land et le outyerds et washouse valent per annum iij£ vjs viijd Et predictum mesuagium sive tenementum gardinum et columbare iacent in le Westret Faversham prope tenementum Richardi Colwell nuper dimisso Richardo Dryland et predictum mesuagium vocate le corner tenementum iacent iuxta le Fysshemarket in Faversham predictum tenent de dicto domino Rege in capite unacum diversis terris et tenementis in Sandwyche per servicium vicesime partis unius feodum milites et per decima quinque solidorum anglis annis solvendis ad curia augmentationum Et valent per annum ultra reparis xLs Et quod predictum molendum aquaticum vocatum Fludmyll cum predictis duabus acris prati in Faversham tenent de dicto domino Rege per fidelitatem in libero sociagio ut de Mannour suo de Epworth in comitatu Lincoln et non in capite Et valent per annum ultra reparis xl£ Et predictum septem acris terre vocati Surrenden Croft tenentur de dicto domino rege Et de honore suo de Torryton in comitatu Devon per fidelitatem tantum in libero sociagio et non in capite Et valent per annum ultra reparis xxxs Et quod predicta septem decim mesuagia super specificata in seperatis tenuris Johannis Dryland junioris Edwardi Wood Georgij Nycolson Richardi Spodell Thome Oldfeld Mathei Tyce [blank] Gayle vidue Petri Gylnot Reginaldi Smyth [blank] Anselme vidue Roberti Keer Anthonij Love Elizabethe Berkley William Chesman dua pomaria in occupatione Johannis Castlock et John Taylour et le Seynt Nicholas Chappell tenentur de dicto domino Rege in libero socagio et non in capite Et

upon the holding of this inquisition appears more fully. And the jurors aforesaid upon their oaths say that the aforesaid house and site of the said late monastery with all the buildings to the same adjoining and the aforesaid messuage called the Gatehouse with the Ostry garden and the aforesaid stable and nine acres of land adjacent and the aforesaid close adjacent to the Grange ten acres of meadow called the Thornemedowe and three acres of pasture with a small tenement built upon it and the aforesaid one garden called the Dovehouse Garden and the aforesaid six acres of meadow called the Amery Croft and the aforesaid twelve acres of land called the Outyerdes Sextrys and Washouse in Faversham aforesaid parcel of the lands and tenements aforesaid held of the lord the King in chief for the service of the twentieth part of one knight's fee. And for a tenth 7s per annum annually to be paid to the Court of Augmentations And that the aforesaid house or site of the said late monastery was of the clear annual value over and above the repairs of 26^s 8^d And the aforesaid messuage called the Gatehouse the yearly value of 13^s 4^d and the aforesaid stable and nine acres of land in the tenure of John Castlock of the clear annual value of $5^£$ 6^s 8^d And that the aforesaid ten acres of pasture called Thornemedowe of the annual value of $4^£$ 13^s 4^d And the aforesaid tenement and three acres now in the tenure of the aforesaid John Tykner of the annual value of 40^s And the aforesaid garden called the Dovehouse garden of the annual value of 33^s 4^d And that the aforesaid six acres of meadow called the Amery Croft, Sextry land and the Outyerds and the washouse of the annual value of $3^£$ 6^s 8^d And the aforesaid messuage or tenement garden and dovecote situated in Westret Faversham near the tenement of Richard Colwell lately leased to Richard Dryland and the aforesaid messuage called the corner tenement situated next to the Fysshemarket in Faversham aforesaid held of the said Lord the King in chief together with diverse lands and tenements in Sandwyche by the service of a twentieth part of one knight's fee and for a tenth five English shillings annually to be paid to the Court of Augmentations And the annual value over and above the repairs 40^s And that the aforesaid watermill called Fludmyll with the aforesaid two acres of meadow in Faversham held of the said lord the King by fealty in free socage as of his manor of Epworth in the county of Lincoln and not in chief And the yearly value over and above the repairs $40^£$ And the aforesaid seven acres of land called Surrenden Croft held of the said lord King and of his honor of Torryton in the county of Devon by fealty only in free socage and not in chief And the annual value over and above repairs 30^s And that the aforesaid seventeen messuages specified above in the separate tenures of John Dryland junior, Edward Wood, George Nycolson, Richard Spodell, Thomas Oldfeld, Matthew Tyce, [blank] Gayle widow, Peter Gylnot, Reginald Smyth, [blank] Anselme widow, Robert Keer, Anthony Love, Elizabeth Berkley, William Chesman, the two orchards in the occupation of John Castlock and John Taylour and the Saint Nicholas Chappell are held of the said lord the King in free socage and not in chief. And the annual value over and above the repairs $8^£$. And furthermore the jurors aforesaid say that the aforesaid Thomas Ardern. has or holds no other or more manors lands or tenements on the day of his death of the said lord the King in chief or otherwise holds or of others in the said county And that the said Thomas Ardern died the fifteenth day of February last past before the holding of this inquisition And that Margaret Arden is the daughter and next heir to the same Thomas and is aged at the time of the holding this inquisition thirteen years and four months and more In testimony of which things one part of this inquisition in respect of the [blank] The first of the jurors aforesaid remaining to

---

valent per annum ultra reparis viij£ Et ulterius juratores predicti dicunt quod predictus Thomas Ardern nulla alia sive plura maneria terra sive tenementa habuit seu tenuit die obitus sui de dicto domini rege in capite vel aliter tenementa sive de alijs in dicti comitatu Kantiae Et quod idem Thomas Ardern obijt quinto[decem] die Februarij ultimo preterito ante captionis huius inquisicionis Et quod Margareta Arden est filia et propinquior heres eiusdem Thome et est aetatis tempore captionis huius inquisitionis tresdecim annorum quatuor mensis et amplius In cuius rei testimonium uni parti huius inquisitionis penes [blank] primum juratorum predictorum remanent predictus escaete sigillum suum apposuit alteri vero parti penes prefatum escaetorum remanent predicti juratores sigilla sua apposuerunt Datum die anno et loco superdictis.

the aforesaid Escheator he has affixed his seal to the other true part in regard thereof by the aforesaid Escheator remains to the aforesaid jurors having affixed their seals. Dated the day year and place abovesaid.

Margin[598]: Written twice W[ards]. A copy[599] in respect thereof sent into the Court of Wards and Liberties. Walter. A copy in respect thereof sent into the Court of Exchequer

BRITISH LIBRARY, DEPARTMENT OF MANUSCRIPTS HARLEY CHARTER 58 H. 18

Dorse: The copie of the lease of the parsonage of St. Michelles and a copie of the acquitaunce for the payments of the rent. Also a note of Mr Ardernes. evidence.

Master Ardernes evidences serched.

The furst patent bering date the vth daie of June in the xxxijnd year of the late King Henry VIIIth of his owne mansion howse and diverse other howses in Feversham to have of our heirs and our successors in Chief by service of a twentieth part of one knight's fee etc.

The second patent dated the xxiiijth March in the xxxvjth year of reign of King Henry the VIIIth of other howses in Feversham to hold in soccage.

The dede from my Lord Warden dated the first of September in the xxxvjth year of the reign of King Henry the VIIIth of the howse and scite of the late Monasterye of Faversham To hold of the lord the King in Chief for the services of one twentieth part of one knight's fee etc.

Master Awchers dede to Master Arderne and his wife of xx markes by yere for terme of there lives and longer liver.

A dede under the seale of the towne of a howse in Courte strete.

A dede from Master Bellowe and Broxholme[600] of the Surrenden Crofte and other thinges. To hold in soccage.

A dede from Clement Sisley and John Leedes of one tenement in the tenure of John Driland and of other tenementes in Feversham etc. Held in soccage.

A dede from Robert Brokelsbie and Nicholas Girling[601] of a howse in Ivelane in Canterbury and of there milne called Flud Mylne. Held in soccage etc.

The[602] lease of the parsonage granted owte of Cristchurche in Canterbury paing the rent of xxxij$^{£}$ for the same

The lease of the Bleyne graunted owte of the Courte of the augmentations paing the rent of xxij$^{£}$

The copie of Master Ardernes .acquittances for the payment of his homage in the exchequer

---

598 *Marginal entry* 'scr' w bis' and some other marginal entries not clear enough to decipher.

599 *T[ra]ns[cripto] inde mittit in curia warda et liberta etc.*

600 See Court of Augmentations E 318/4/126.

601 See Court of Augmentations E318/5/181.

602 p. 2.

County of Kent

Of Thomas Arderne of a fine for his homage for the house and site of the Monastery of Faversham with others in the county aforesaid for one complete year having been respited xij^{d}

And for the fee to the Remembrancer of the Exchequer and the entry [on the record] of the same xvj^{d}

And for the Warrant of the attorney nothing[603]

Sum ij^{s} iiij^{d} received by me E.Charde

Ye must paie agayne the end of Easter the fifth year

The[604] year 1550

The copie of Master Ardernes .acquittaunce for his rent of his howse in London

Resserved the xth daie of September by me John Modye grocer of London of Master Thomas Arderne in Kent a hole yeres rent dewe unto Master Doctour Willoughbye for the rent of the parsonage of Saint Michelles in Cornehill in London dewe unto Master Doctour Willoughbye at Midsomer last past before the date hereof the somme of three and fiftie shillinges and foure pence

I the said Liij^{a} iiij^{d} by me John Modye

A note of the lease of the parsonage of St. Michelles in Cornehill

The lease berith date the xxth of Aprell in the first year of Edward VIth where by John Willoughbie clarke hath demised unto Thomas Arderne all his howse called the parsonage of Saint Michelles in Cornehill to have and to hold the said howse or parsonage to the same Thomas Arderne his executors and assignes from the fest of Saint John the Baptest next comyng unto the end and terme of the said John Willoughbie there being parson paing for the same Liij^{s} iiij^{d} by the yere the Reparations to be at the costes and chardges of the same Thomas Arderne etc.

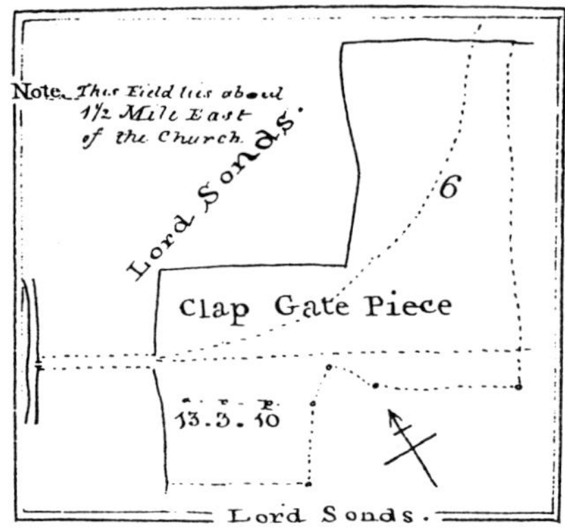

Part of 'An eye sketch of Faversham Glebe' 1800: CCA U63/70388

603 Nullus.

604 p. 3.

APPENDIX 13:
The Abbey Manor at the Dissolution and the Royal Manor of Faversham 1541-1549.

BRITISH LIBRARY
HARLEIAN ROLL G16

	The Mon[astery of? *[hole]*] Seynt Savyour in Feversham	)
The[605] pryncypall Maner)	*[hole]* county of Kent In Primis the site of the sayde	)
of Feversham)	Maner with xxx Acres by estymacion of the Demein	) iij$^{£}$
	Landes pasture medowes and Gardyns beynge in our owne	)
	haundes valued at ij^{s} le acre	)
Ferme, Rent and)	Item Receavyd for the yerely farme of the Resydewe of the	)
custume belongynge)	same maner in Corne Cattall [illegible] money and for	)
to the same)	Custume of xxij^{ti} Acres di[midiam] Rod of Land	)
maner)	belongynge to the same maner That ys to wytt in Erynge[606]	)
	Sowynge the said Acres with whete Ryppynge[607] Caryenge	) xxxvj$^{£}$
	in to the sayd Barens of the sayd Maner and tassynge[608] of	)
	the same whete Done by the Tenants of the same	)
	maner yerly by the tenure of there Landes	)
Ferme of mesuages)	Item Receavyd for the ferme of ij mesuages at the Towne	) xxvj$^{£}$
and others)	gate of Feversham and for other mesuages myll and	) xvij^{s} and
in the Towne)	Tenements in the Towne belonging to the sayd	) a quarter
of Feversham)	pryncypall maner by estimaycion yerely	) *[torn]*
Rent in the)	Item Receavyd for the yerely Rent of the Tenements and	) xxj$^{£}$ vj^{s}
same Towne)	mesuages in the sayd Towne belongynge to the maner	) xj^{d} ob and
	aforesaid	) half a
	[torn]	) qu[arter]
Rent of Uplande)	Item Receavyd for the yerely rent of	)
belongynge to the)	Upland belongynge to the pryncypall maner	) Lij$^{£}$ xj^{d}
sayd maner of)	of the sayd in Custume Cockkes hennes and	) ob quarter
Feversham)	egges all Ratyd in money	)
Casualtyes	Item Receavyd yerely by estymacyon of and for all	)
	Casualtyes of all letes and Courtes belongynge to the	)
	pryncypall maner holden within the Towne and hundred of	) viij$^{£}$

---

605 fol. 1 verso. A paper roll with the rotulets stuck together.

606 *O.E.D.* Earing: The action of ploughing.

607 Dialect variant of reaping.

608 *O.E.D.* Tass: A heap, pile stack, W. D. Parish & W. F. Shaw, *A Dictionary of Kentish Dialect* (1889) besides a heap, gives a mow of corn.

	Feversham as in fynes for Sutes mercements and Relyves) to the some of)	
Sale of wodd in the) Bleane and Bosynden) belongynge to the) foresayd princypall) maner)	Item Receavyd commonly yerely of the) forester of Bleane for Tymber and wood) sold by hym there and in Bosynden) together lyenge)	 xx$^{£}$
Ferme of the) sayd Blean)	Item Receavyd yerely by the handes of the sayd Forester for) the ferme of Wodlesse in the sayd Bleane)	 xj^{s}
Rent of the) same Blean)	Item Receavyd by the handes of the same forystер yerely) Rent of ix gates ledynge in to the sayd Bleane iij^{s} and) ix hennes pryce ij^{s} iij^{d} & Cv Egges price v^{d} q)	 v^{s} viij^{d} quarter
Profetts of Lamas) fayere)	Item Receavyd commynly yerely of the profyts of a fayre at) Lammas otherwyse callyd Ad Vincula Sancti Petri) Sum[609] of all the partyculars aforesayd CLxx$^{£}$ xiiij^{s} xj^{d} ob	 Liij^{s} iiij^{d}
Resolucyons out of) the foresayd) pryncypall manor) of Feversham)	Whereof goythe owte to the Monastery of Saynt Augtyns) without the walles of Canturbury for a yerely pencyon vj$^{£}$) xiij^{s} iiij^{d} and to the same monastery for a yerely Rent oute) of yoke of Chetham xj^{s} v^{d} summ) Sume Clare CLxiij£ x^{s} ij^{d} ob a quarter and a halfe of barley	 vij$^{£}$ iiij^{s} ix^{d}
Ferme of lande	Item Receavyd for the yerely ferme of) Londe callyd Southfeld and Hagdale)	x$^{£}$
	Item Receauvyd for the yerely ferme of Londe lyenge in) Lodgemarsshe & Weldmersshe) Sum xiij$^{£}$ vj^{s} viij^{d}	iij$^{£}$ vj^{s} viij^{d}
Ferme of Londe in the) occupyenge of Roberte) A Broke)	Item receauyd of Roberte A Broke of of Harnhill for the) yerely ferme of xvj acres and half of Lande lyenge and) adyonyng to the Landes of a mesuage or Tenement Callyd) Lambertslond)	 xx^{s}
Resolucyons out of) the sayd Landes)	Sum as yt appereth whereof goyth out for A yerely Rent for) parte of the same landes to the Canons of Saynt Stephyns) Chappell at Westminster holden of there maner of) Quenecourte in Osprenge iij^{s} iiij^{d} and to the heyres of) Mathew Martyn for the Resydew of the sayd Londes holden)	 vj^{s} viij^{d}

609 fol. 2v.

	of therė maner of Dargate xxij^{d} and a Cocke price ij^{d} in) Rent hennes iiij price le hen iij^{d} summa xij^{d} summa) Sum Clare xiij^{s} iiij^{d}	
Ferme of Cockham) and Mentylham)	Item Receavyd for the yerely ferme of Lande Callyd Cokham and Mentylham	) xLvj^{s} viij^{d})
Resolucyons out of) the sayd Cockham &) Mentylham)	Sum as yt apperyth whereof goyth out to the Archebysshoppe of Canturbury for the tyme beynge for a yerely Rent of the sayd Londes holden of hys maner of Boughton under the Bleane vij^{s} and to the Vycar of Harnhull for A yerely pencyon goynge out of the same Londes iiij^{s} viij^{d} Sum Clare xxxv^{s}	)))xj^{s} viij^{d}))
Abbatiscourte[610] in) the Isle of Hartey	Item Receavyd for the yerely ferme of the Syte of a mesuage or tenement callyd Abbattyscourte with the Lande and marsshe therto Apperteyning in the Isle of Hartey and for a marsshe there callyd Julyan marsshe Sum as it appeareth	))) xx$^{£}$ vj^{s}) viij^{d})
Resolucyons of the) sayd Abbatiscourte)	Whereof goyth out to the Sherevyes Turnne for a yerely Rent for parte of the same Londes belongynge to the sayd mesuage or Tenement ix^{d} and to the heyres of Thomas Frogenhale for A yerely Rent also out of parte of the sayd Londes iij^{s} xj^{d} ob quarter And for a Wall Scott[611]comynly yerely there xL^{s} Sum Sum Clare xviij$^{£}$ xj^{d} quarter	)))xLv^{s} viij^{d}) ob) quarter
Ferme of Prestfeld	Item Receavyd for the yerely Ferme of Lands Callyd Prestfeld Sum[612] as it appeareth	) xxx^{s} iiij^{d})
Ferme of Negdon Marsshe	Item Receavyd for the yerely ferme of A marsshe Callyd Negdon Marsshe Sum as it appeareth	)) viij$^{£}$
Resolucyons out of) the sayd Negdon) Marsshe	Whereof goythe oute for a yerely pencyon to the parson of Graveney Sum Clare vij$^{£}$ xvj^{s} viij^{d}	) iij^{s} iiij^{d})
Ferme of horsehopes)	Item Receavyd for the yerely ferme of horsehopes at	) xxxiiij^{s}

610 fol. 3v.

611 *O.E.D.* Scot: A tax levied on the inhabitants of the marshes and levels of Kent and Sussex; 1793 A. Young *Agric. Sussex* p. 22 In Pevensey, and generally in all the levels, is raised a tax by the acre, called Scot, both general and particular. The general scot is applied for the purposes of paying water-bailiffs expenses... The particular scot is applied for the.. looking after the streams and sewers. Wall Scot for the upkeep of the sea wall which protected the whole marsh....M.Teichman Derville, *The Level and the Liberty of Romney Marsh,* (London, 1936), p. 30.

612 Sum patet

and other)	Brokebrygge and for Cattyscart with other medowes there Sum[613] as it appeareth	) iiij^{d}
Resolucyons out of) the sayd horsehopes)	Whereof goythe owte for a yerely Rent to the maner of Graveney Sum Clare xxx^{s} x^{d}	) ij^{s} vj^{d})
Ferme of Goremarsshe	Item Receavyd for the yerely ferme of Goremarsshe with the Uplond thereto belongynge Sum[614] as it appereth	)) viij$^{£}$
Resolucyons out) of the sayd) Goremarsshe)	Whereof goythe out A yerely Rent to the Archebysshope of Canterbury for the tyme beynge v^{s} vj^{d} and to the vycar of Haryhull for A yerely pencion out of the same marsshe xiij^{s} iiij^{d} and for a wallscott of the sayd marsshe commynly yerely v^{s} vj^{d} Sum Clare vj$^{£}$ xv^{s} iij^{d}	))) xxiiij^{s}) ix^{d})
Ferme[615] of our) lybertes of the) See and) Snowtweyeres)	Item Receavyd by estimacyon for the yerely ferme of our Tenantes fysshynge within our lyberte of the See and for Snowtweyres wyche we have and holde of the Kynge by fee ferme Sum[616] as it appereth	))) xxxiiij^{s}) iiij^{d}
Resolucyons out of the) sayd lybertes and wayeres)	Whereof goythe oute yerely to the Kynges maner of Mylton Sum Clare xiij^{s} iiij^{d}	) xx^{s}
Ferme of the maner or) Tenement callyd) Elynden)	Item Receavyd for the yerely ferme of the maner or tenement callyd Elynden vj$^{£}$ and in Rent yerely xiij^{s} iiij^{d} in Rent hennes xij price iij^{s}	) vj$^{£}$) xvj^{s}) iiij^{d}
Sale of Tymber and) wodd there)	Item Recevyd commynly yerely for the sale of Tymber and wodd out of the woodes belongynge to the sayd maner or Tenement	)) xx^{s})
Ferme of mesuage) or Tenement) callyd Lambertislond)	Item Receavyd for the yerely ferme of the mesuage or Tenement called Lambertislond with the Londes thereto appertaynege	) xij $^{£}$) ij^{s})
Sale of Tymber and) woode there)	Item Recevyd commynly yerely for the sale of Tymber and wodd out of the woodes of the sayd mesuage or Tenement of	))

613 *Sum patet.*
614 *Sum patet.*
615 fol. 4v.
616 *Sum patet.*

Lambertislond callyd Combe Cony Grove and a grove adioynge to the sayd Tenement	) x^{s}

Sum as well of the foresayd manner or tenement callyd Elynden as of the sayd mesuage or Tenement callyd Lambertislond with the seale of Tymber and woddes as ys aforesayd xx$^{£}$ viij^{s} iiij^{d}

Out of the wyche sayd Manner or Tenemente callyd Elynden there goyth out in Rent yerely to the manor of Whytstaple x^{s} to the Prior of Crystchurche in Canturbury for A yerely rent of certayne Londes belongyng to the sayd maner or Tenement of Elynden holden of hys maner of Sesalter v^{s} and for A yerely Obyt for the soules of Robert Byllesdon gent Donor of the sayd Tenement callyd Elynden Thebald Evyas gentyllwoman and for all Christen soules x^{s} vij^{d} whereof the mayer of Feversham with ij of his brethern for the tyme beynge hathe and shalle Receave yerely for ever before the masse of the sayd Obyt xxiij^{d} That ys to saye the same mayer shalle receve by the handes of the Chaunter of the monastery of Fevershame A foresayd for the tyme beynge xiij^{d} and shall offer at the same Masse j^{d} and either of the sayd mayers Brethren shalle Receauve of the sayd Chanter v^{d} and ether of them shall Offer in hys lyke maner j^{d}

Resolucyons as well out of the foresayd Maner Elynden as of the sayd mesuage or Tenement namyd Lambertislond)	Sum as yt apperythe before wrytten Also it is ordenyd by the sayd Robert Byllesdon to be Gevyn yerely in the daye of the sayd Obit to xij power persones xij^{d} And vij^{s} viij^{d} Resydewe to be Bestowyd for waste of waxe and to priestes and clarkes Sum as yt apperyth beforesayd

Also there goythe out of the fore namyd mesuage or Tenement callyd Lambertislond together with the Landes therto appertayning for A yerely Rent of parte of the same Londes to the heyres of the foresayd Mathew Martyn holden of there sayd manor of Dargate xv^{d} ob and to the heyres of John Boyce late of Sandwyche for an Annuytye yerely goynge out as well of the foresayd maner or Tenement callyd Elynden as of the sayd messuage or Rent callyd Lambertslande x$^{£}$)

Sum Clare as well of the foresayd manor or tenement callyd Elynden as of the sayd messuage or Tenement Callyd Lambertislond with the sales of Tymber and woodes there	) ix$^{£}$ xvij^{d} ob

In Primis Ten pounds in almes money ordenyd by Kynge Stephyn and Quene Mawde his wyf to be gevyn yerely to poore pepyll perpetuall and so used for the soules for the sayd Kynge and Quene founders of the sayd monastery of Feversham foresayd and for the soules of Ewstace the sonne of them William Erle of Bulleyn and all Crysten Soulles Item every frydaye xij^{d} Sum by the yere Lij^{s} in the daye of the Natyvite of our lord god iij^{s} iiij^{d} in the Daye of the Epiphanye of our lord god iij^{s} iiij^{d} in the daye of the puryfycacyon of our Blessyd Lady the Virgin iii^{s} iiij^{d} in the Daye of the Annuncyacyon of our blessyd Lady the Virgin iij^{s} iiij^{d} uppon Palme Soundaye sondaye iij^{s} iiij^{d} uppon mawndye thursdaye x^{s} uppon Good frydaye iij^{s} iiij^{d} uppon Easter Evyns iij^{s} iiij^{d} Uppon Easter daye iij^{s} iiij^{d} The 4th daye of Maye beynge the daye of the Obit of the foresaid Quene vj^{s} viij^{d} The Daye of the Assencyon of our Saviour iij^{s} iiij^{d} in the Daye of Penticoste iij^{s} iiij^{d} Trynyte Sonndaye iij^{s} iiij^{d} in the Daye of Corpus Christi iij^{s} iiij^{d} in the daye of Saynt John

Baptist iij^{s} iiij^{d} in the daye of Peter and pawle saynts iij^{s} iiij^{d} in the daye of the Transfyguracyon of our Saviour iij^{s} iiij^{d} in the daye of the Assumpcyon of our Blessed Lady the Virgin iij^{s} iiij^{d} in the daye of the Natyvyte of our Blessed Lady the Virgin iij^{s} iiij^{d} in the daye of the
Dedication of the Churche of the sayd Monastery iij^{s} iiij^{d} in the daye of the) x$^{£}$
Exaltacyon of the holly Crosse iij^{s} iiij^{d} And in the xxiiijth daye of October beynge)
the Daye of the Obit of the sayd Kynge vj^{s} viij^{d} Sum vij$^{£}$ ij^{s} and Lviij^{s} Resydewe to be)
gevyn yerely to Bedred blynde and Lame pepole within the Towne and hundred)
of Feversham)

Item there goyth out of the fermes of the mesuages and lands before expressed by)
yere yerely for ever over and above the Obyt of Robert Byllesdon and Thebald)
Evyas Aforesayd for vij obitts [*illegible*] for our founders as yt apperythe)
by our mortelage boke to prests Clerks pore people for waste of waxe and) iiij$^{£}$ xvj^{d}
Ryngyng of Bellys)

Item[617] Receavyd for the yerely ferme of the mannor of Kynggyssnoth v$^{£}$ vj^{s} viij^{d}

Item Receavyd yerely in Rent of the tenants of the same mannor in)
money Cocks and hennyes to the somme of) xxxix^{s} ij^{d} ob

Item Receavyd of the same Tenants for the yerely ferme of Woodlese there x^{s}

The maner of) Kyngsnoth)	Item Receavyd of Antony Sentleger gent for the yerely ferme) of Vacres and one Rod of Lande inclosed in hys parke there) At Lamas otherwysse callyd Advincula sancti Petri. A Buck) or in money vj^{s} viij^{d} at the electyon of the Abbot of the) sayd monastery for the tyme beyinge)	vj^{s} viij^{d}
Sale of Tymber and) wood there)	Item Receavyd commynly yerely for the sale of Tymber and) wooddes out of the wooddes belongynge to the sayd manner) callyd Eastwell Westwell Melgrove and other there)	xxiij^{s} iiij^{d}
Resolucyons of the) sayd maner)	Sum of the sayd manner of Kyngsnoth with the sale of the) Tymber and wodde All Ratyd in money x$^{£}$ v^{s} x^{d} ob whereof) goyth out to the parson of Ulcombe for a yerely pencyon x^{s}) and to the Shryf for A yerely fynne for the Tennants of the) same manner xij^{d})	xj^{s}
	Sum Clare viij$^{£}$ xiiij^{s} x^{d} ob	
Ferehirst in the) diocese of) Canterbury)	Item Receavyd for the yerely Rent and and ferme of greate) Fereherst and lyttell Fereherst Lviij^{s} iij^{d} and in Rent henns) iiij price xij^{d})	Lix^{s}

[617] fol. 5v.

Fyrste to William Roper Esquer beynge hygh Steward of our) viij$^{£}$ vj^{s}
landes letes and Courtes within the County of Kent by yere) viij^{d}
Item to the Baylff of the Towne and lybertye of Feversham) xxj^{s} iiij^{d}
aforesayd by yere)

Item to Roberte Goldewell Receauor of the fermes and Rents)
of the same Towne of Feversham as byfore apperythe by yere) Liij^{s} iiij^{d}

Item to Symon Auncelme Receavor of the ferme and Rent of)
the manner of Kyngysnorth and Upland A foresayd by yere) iij$^{£}$ vj^{s}
iij$^{£}$ and for a Gowne xiij^{s} iiij^{d}) viij^{d}

Item to Joseph Beverley Auditor of our Accounts by yere) iij$^{£}$ vj^{s} viij^{d}

Item[618] to Thomas Hungarford gent Receavour of the fermes)
and Rents of the manner of Elynden Lambertislond the Bleane) iij$^{£}$ vj^{s}
Bosynden and other as before apperythe yerely) viij^{d}
Sum of the sayd fees xxij$^{£}$ xvj^{d}

Sum of the Temporalityes belongynge to the sayd monastery)
within the County of Kent by yere as before Apperethe)
CCLxj$^{£}$ v^{s} ij^{d} qrt half of Barley

Whereof goyth oute in Rents Resolutions) Lx$^{£}$ xix^{s}
Almesse fees and other as before apperyth) vij^{d} quarter
Sum Clare CC£ v^{s} vj^{d} ob quarter, quarter of Barely

The parsonage of) Boughton under) the Bleane)	In primis the site of the sayd parsonage with the Glebe Londes) and all manner of Tythes to the same belongynge nowe beynge) in our howne handes hathe byn lette to ferme by yere as yt apperethe by Indenture for the some of)	))) xxxvj$^{£}$)
The parsonage of) Harnhyll)	Item the site of the parsonage with all maner of Tythes to the same belongyng ys letten to ferme by yere as yt Apperethe by Indenture in corne and money for the somme of	)) x$^{£}$)
The parsonage of) Preston nexte) Feversham)	Item the Site of the sayd parsonage with all maner of Tythes to the same belongynge nowe beynge in our owne handes and hathe be letten to ferme by yere as yt appereth by Indenture for the some of	))xiij$^{£}$ vj^{s}) viij^{d})
	Sum of all the parsonages Lix$^{£}$ vj^{s} viij^{d}	

[618] fol. 6v.

Resolucyons out of the sayd Parsonages of Boughton Harnhill and Preston	Whereof goyth out to Cristchurche in Canterbury for a yerely pencyon v$^{£}$ and to the Archedeacon of Canturbury foresayd for another yerely pencyon out of the sayd parsonages xxvj^{s} viij^{d}	vj$^{£}$ vj^{s} viij^{d}
	Sum clare of all the sayd parsonage	Liij$^{£}$
Recepts of pencyons	Item receavyd for a yerely pencyon out of the Churche of Luddenham iij$^{£}$ vj^{s} viij^{d} and for a yerely pencyon out of the churche of Newynham xxxiij^{s} iiij^{d}	v$^{£}$
Oblacyons	Item Recevyd by estymacyon for all maner of oblacyons done in the monastery of Feversham	iij^{s} iiij^{d}
	Sum[619] clare of the Recepts of all the Spiritualytyes belongynge to the foresayd Monastery of Feversham	Lviij$^{£}$ iij^{s} iiij^{d}
The maner of Bendysshehall	Item Receavyd for the yerely ferme of a maner Callyd Bendysshehalle in the parissh of Radwinter in the countey of Essex for all maner of Rent services haryetes[620] fynes and sutes to the same maner belongynge or Anywysse appertayninge as it appereth by indenture for the somme of	xxxiij$^{£}$
Sale of Woodd	Item Recevyd commynly for the Sale of wodd out of the woddes there callyd Old Wodd Newewodd Bradheges Grove and other hedge rowes there	iij$^{£}$ vj^{s} iiij^{d}
	Sum of the sayd maner with the sale of the wodd	xxxvj$^{£}$ vj^{s} viij^{d}
Resolucyons pencyons fees and other out of the sayd maner of Bendysshe Hall	Whereof goyth out yerely to the Prior and Convent of Cristchurche in London for a pencyon v$^{£}$ x^{s} and to the parson of Radwynter foresayd for the yerely tenthes of the sayd maner one acre of whete in harvest price x^{s} one acre of otes price v^{s} iiij^{d} a lambe price viij^{d} a pyge price iiij^{d} and in money iij^{s} iiij^{d} Also to A Steward for a yerely fee for Kepynge of the letes and courtes of the sayd maner xiij^{s} iiij^{d} And to Edmund Burley receivour of the ferme and rents of the sayd maner for hys fee xx^{s}	xxviij$^{£}$ iij^{s} viij^{d}
	Sum clare of the whole value of the maners parsonages Lands Tenements and other Emoluments belongynge or appertaynenge to the sayd monastery as before apperethe particularly	Sum viij£ iij^{s}
		CCiiij^{XX}vj£ xij^{s} vj^{d} ob quarter,

619 fol. 7v.

620 *O.E.D.* Heriot: a feudal service, originally consisting of weapons, horses, and other military equipment restored to the lord on the death of his tenant; afterwards a render of the best beast or dead chattel of a deceased tenant due by legal custom to the lord of whom he held. At an early period this render was commuted in many cases to a fixed money payment.

a quarter and a half of barley
A tenth in respect thereof[621] xxviij£ xiij^s iij^d

PRO: E315/96 (OLD VOLUME 6) PAGE LVIIJ[622]

Memorandum that in the term of Saint Michael that is to say the eleventh day of October in the 30th year of the reign of our Lord King Henry the Eighth [1538] Joseph Beverley came into court of the said Lord of Augmentations and revenues of his crown and produced[623] there a certain indenture made and sealed under the seal of the convent of the late Monastery of Saint Saviours of Faversham now dissolved And sought that it be allowed which certain indenture the tenor following in these words

This indentour made the twenty daye of September in the xxvij yere of the reigne of our soveraigne lorde kyng Henry the viijth betwen John by the devyne provydence of God Abbot of the howse and monastery of Seynt Savour of Feversham of that one partie and Joseph Beverley of that other partie wyttenessith that the said Abbot and Convent of thir one assent full agrement and consent have gevyn and by these presentes grauntyd unto the said Joseph Beverley for the good and faithfull service to them of long tyme done in the Office of thir awdytt and other one annuyte or annuall ffee of thre powndis six shillinges and eight pence by the yere duryng the naturall lyff of the said Joseph to be had and paid to the same Joseph Beverley or to his assignes by the said Abbot and convent thir successors or assigns in manner and fourme folowyng that is to saie in the feste of the annunciation of our blessed lady the virgen xxxiij^s iiij^d In the feste of Saynt Michell the archaungell xxxiij^s iiij^d yerly as is aforsaid to be had and paide for the which said annuyte or annuall ffee of thre powndes syx shillynges and eight pence to be had and paid as before apperith yt is covenauntyd and agreid betwen the said Abbot and Convent and the said Joseph Beverley that the same Joseph by hym self or by his lawfull depute shall well and duly execute use and kepe thir said office of audytour at all tymes requysite duryng his said naturall lyff within thir said monastery at a certayn place whereof long tyme yt hath ben usid and kepte and all accomptes of receyvours rentes gatherers and other officers belongyng to thir said monastery made to the said Joseph Beverley and by him harde and examyneid shall not only them discharge and acquyte but also all soche accomptes shall ingrose and yelde up to the said Abbot and Convent thir successours or where they will assigne at the proper costis and expenses of the said Abbot or convent or thir successors all paper parchement and wrytyng concernyng to thir said office only exceptyd In wyttenes whereof to the one party of this indentour with the said Joseph Beverley remaynyng the said Abbot and Convent thir common seale have put And to this other partie of this said indentour with the said Abbot and convent remaynyng the said Joseph Beverley his seale hath putt Gevyn in the Chapiter Howse of the said Abbot and Convent the daye and yere above

[Latin] And because through due examination in this part made and had clearly by the court aforesaid the indenture aforesaid made and sealed was good faithful and without illegal compact, fraud or deceit therefore that writing by the chancellor and council of the court aforesaid is allowed. And it is ordered and decreed by the same chancellor and council that the aforesaid Joseph Beverlye to have and possess to him and his assigns until the end of his life his said office of auditor of all the manors, lands and possessions of the said late monastery and also arising from the same office an allowance and fee of three pounds six shillings and eight pence to be paid by the hands of the receiver form the issues and revenues of the said late monastery for the time

---

621 *Decima inde.*
622 Latin and lease in English.
623 *Pretulit.*

being at the feasts in the writing aforesaid limited by equal portions annually . And that the same Joseph to have so much of the arrears of the said annuity as from the time of the dissolution of the said late monastery hitherto to him is owed to be paid by the hands of the said receiver. Provided nevertheless always that if hereafter the debt now having been approved before the chancellor and council of the aforesaid court for the time being, that the aforesaid Joseph the said annuity of three pounds six shillings and eight pence by reason and by the aforementioned aforesaid script in the form aforesaid to have and possess, not to be owed that then and next this present decree to be void and of no effect in law any clause or article contained in the same to the contrary not withstanding.

❖♌❖♌❖♌❖♌❖

Court of Augmentations.
Miscellaneous Books E315/100 folio 47 verso[624].

Memorandum that in Michaelmas Term that is to say the fourteenth day of November in the thirtieth year of the reign of our present king Henry the eighth [1538] William Rooper son of John Rooper esquire deceased came into the Court of Augmentations and revenues of the Kings Majesty's Crown. And showed there a certain writing under the seal of the convent of the late monastery of Saint Saviour of Faversham made and sealed and asked that he be allowed such things by the tenor of the writing following in these words. To all to whom the present letter shall come John, by divine permission, Abbot of the Monastery of Saint Saviours of Feversham and of the convent of the same monastery Greeting, Know that we the aforesaid Abbot and convent, appoint, by papal provision, the circumspect industrious and faithful our beloved in Christ John Rooper esquire and William Rooper son of the same John with our exceeding trust have given and by these presents granted to the same John Rooper and William Rooper the office of our chief steward of all and singular our demesne, courts, lands with all and singular their appurtenances in the county of Kent to the same John Rooper and William Rooper our chief steward, make and ordain them to have exercise occupy the office of chief steward to the same John Rooper and William by them or his sufficient deputy or their sufficient deputies to the ends of their lives and the other of them living longer as long as they behave themselves in the same to have and take to the same John Rooper and William the annuity for the exercise and occupation of the aforesaid office of all and all manner of profits fees and reward to the same office from antiquity incumbent or pertaining to the same now and formerly just as John Fyneux knight late our chief steward or someone our chief steward of our demesne manors and lands with the premises by the exercise or occupation of the office aforesaid had and taken given as above and by the presents granted to the aforesaid John Rooper and William full power and authority all and singular to exercise and execute the office aforesaid to perform according to custom and to take the oath required of all and singular our bailiffs ministers officers farmers appointed and held as reeve and to hold by our precept and firmly against all men that the same John Rooper and William Rooper and with such other their deputy or deputies in the execution and occupation of the office aforesaid to be attendant, give help, be obedient and give assistance in all things just as might be proper In testimony of which thing to this our present writing we have placed our common seal by these presents. Given in our chapter house at Feversham aforesaid the sixth day of August in the eleventh year of the reign of King Henry the eighth [1519]. And because

[624] All in Latin.

through due examination in this part made and clearly had by the court aforesaid, the writing aforesaid made and sealed was good secure and without compact, fraud or deceit therefore that writing is allowed by the chancellor and council of the court aforesaid. And it is ordered and decreed by the same chancellor and council that the aforesaid William Rooper to have eight pounds six shillings and eight pence for his fee for the execution of the office aforesaid just as before the dissolution of the late monastery he had and has been by custom paid from the hands of the receiver from the issues and revenues of the said late monastery for the time being out of the issues and revenues of the said late monastery of the manors, lands and tenements of the said late monastery at the annual terms and such feasts and just as before the dissolution of the said late monastery was of custom paid by equal portions. And the said William Rooper to have so much of the arrears of the said annuity or fee of eight pounds six shillings and eight pence as from time to time of the dissolution of the said late monastery hitherto to him is owed, to be paid by the hands of the said receiver. Provided nevertheless always that if hereafter the debt now having been approved before the chancellor and council of the aforesaid court for the time being, that the aforesaid William Rooper the said office by reason and by the aforesaid script in the form aforesaid to have and to possess, not to be owed that then and next this present decree to be void and of no effect in law any clause or article contained in the same to the contrary not withstanding.

Court of Augmentations
Miscellaneous Books E315/100 folio 127v[625]

Memorandum that in Hillary Term that is to say the tenth day of February in the thirtieth year of the reign of our now sovereign Lord King Henry VIIIth [1539] Richard Crumwell esquire came into the Lord King's Court of Augmentations and revenues of his crown and produced there a certain writing made and sealed under the seal of the late convent of Saint Saviours of Feversham and sought that the same writing be allowed to him the tenor of which is as follows in these words

To all faithful Christian people to whom this present writing shall come John by divine permission Abbot of the Monastery of Saint Saviour of Feversham and the convent of the same monastery greeting in the Lord Everlasting Know that we the aforesaid Abbot and Convent with our one assent and consent have given and by these presents have granted to our beloved in Christ Richard Crumwell esquire for the good council, favour and his help shown before this to us and our monastery aforesaid and supplied and for the good advice, favour and help to us after this during the natural life of the same Richard towards our monastery aforesaid to have and to be given a certain annuity or annual fee of three pounds to be charged upon the issues and profits of our manor of Faversham in the county of Kent To have hold and to receive the said annuity or annual fee of three pounds to the same Richard at Christmas Day during the life of the same Richard annually to be paid. Know in accordance with this that we the aforesaid Abbot and Convent have given and by these presents have granted to the aforesaid Richard Crumwell that if and as often as it shall come to pass that the said annuity or annual fee of three pounds be in arrears in part or in total after any Christmas Day here afterwards ought to be paid that then and as often it shall be lawful for the aforesaid Richard Crumwell to enter into our manor of Faversham and to take distraint and distress there and so it shall be lawful from that time to take, drive and to carry off and to retain in his possession as long as the same Richard of the said annuity or annual fee and arrears to the same shall be fully paid and satisfied to him[626] In

---

[625] All in Latin.
[626] fol. cxxviij.

testimony of which thing to this present writing we have caused our common seal to be placed, given in our chapter house the twentieth day of the May in the twenty seventh year of the reign of our sovereign Lord Henry the VIIIth [1535] by the grace of God of England and France, King, defender of the faith, Lord of Ireland and on earth supreme head of the church of England and Ireland. And because through due examination in this part made and clearly had by the court aforesaid, the writing aforesaid made and sealed was good secure and without compact, fraud or deceit therefore that writing is allowed by the chancellor and council of the court aforesaid. And it is ordered and decreed by the same chancellor and council that the aforesaid Richard to have and to possess to him and his assigns until the end of his life his said annuity or annual fee of three pounds by the year from the hands of the receiver from the issues and revenues of the said late monastery for the time being out of the issues and revenues of the said late monastery at the feasts in the writing aforesaid specified by equal portions. And the said Richard to have so much of the arrears of the said annuity as from time to time of the dissolution of the said late monastery hitherto to him is owed, to be paid by the hands of the said receiver. Provided nevertheless always that if hereafter the debt now having been approved before the chancellor and council of the aforesaid court for the time being, that the aforesaid Richard the said annuity or annual rent of three pounds by reason and by the aforesaid script in the form aforesaid to have and to posses, not to be owed that then and next this present decree to be void and of no effect in law any clause or article contained in the same to the contrary not withstanding.

Court of Augmentations
Miscellaneous Books E315/100 folio 138[627]

Memorandum that in Hillary Term, that is to say, the tenth day of February in the 30th year of the reign of King Henry the Eighth [1539] Stephen Motte came into the Court of Augmentations and Revenues of the Kings Majesty's Crown and showed there a certain indenture under the seal of the convent late the monastery of Feversham in the county of Kent now dissolved made and sealed and asked that he be allowed as by a certain indenture by the tenor following in these words. This indenture made the eighth day of the monethe of June in the thirtye yere of the reign of kynge Henrye the eighte [1538] betwen John by the sufferaunce of god Abbotte of the monasterye of Seynte Savyours in Feversham and the covente of the same monasterye on the one partie and Stephen Motte of Davyngton nexte Feversham in the cowntye of Kente yoman on the other partie Witnessithe that where the seyde Abbotte and convente by ther certeyne indenture made betwene the seyde Abbotte and convente by the name of John by the sufferauns of God Abbotte of the monasterye of Seynte Savyours in Faversham and the convente of the same monasterye on the other partie and William Marchall and John Marchall by the names of William Marchall and John Marchall his sonne of the Abbye of Feversham husbondman on the other partie whose date is the one and twentye daye of June in the sevene and twentye yere of the reign of our sovereign lorde Kynge Henry the eighte [1535] by their commen assente and consente have betaken dimysed graunted and to ferme letton unto the foreseyd William Marchall and John Marchall his sonne all that their mesuage sette lyinge and beynge in the Nethercourte of the seyde monasterye withe all the barnes stables styes cartehowses and gardens to the seyd Nethercourte adioyning And allso two hundrethe twelve acres halfe an acre and halfe a rode of arable grounde medowe and pasture whereof there was of falowe and podwarelonde eighte and fouretye acres lyinge in certeyn feldes callyd Melfelde Mollysdane and Westgates withe the custome of arynge and sowinge of one and twenty acres halfe an acre and halfe a rode of lande with the corne and cornes of the seyde William and John yerelye to be sowen And with the

627 Latin and English.

custome of cuttynge downe byndynge and caryinge into the barnes and tassynge of the same of corne and cornes growynge yerely upon the same to be done yerelye by the tenantes of the same Abbotte and convente of their manor of Faversham as of olde tyme have ben used and acustomed forthwithe certeyn pastures medowes and marshes to the seyde manor adioyninge that is to seye a pasture called Catesmarshe a medowe to the same mershe adioyninge a mershe callyd Eastemarshe and the medowe nexte to the Nethercourte garthe[628] on the Sowthe parte of the same gate forthwithe the store of one and twentye quarters of whete rase measure good lawfull marchaunte and clene tryed two and fouretye quarters of barleye rase measure good lawfull marchaunte and clene tryed withe a hondrethe coppes of peasses and too hundrethe of tares and allsoo wekelye durynge the seyde terme sevene galons of ale called s[er]vauntes ale and halfe the greynes of every bruynge brued within the seide monastery forthwithe the wasshe of the same to be fette[629] by the seyde William and John or their assign at the bruehowse in the seyde monasterye excepte asmoche of the seyde greynes wasshe and effall as shall sufficientlye fynde wekelye duringe the seyde terme foure sowes and a bore Excepted furthermore and allwayes to the seyde Abbotte and convente and their successowrs reservyd the stables in the seyde Nethercourte callyd the Palfrye stables withe a lytle chambre over the porche of the same stables a lytell gardener adioyninge to the same a howse there called the forge forthwithe all rentes servyces and all other customes to the seide manor perteyninge or in anywyse belongynge The howse and closure at the Thorn a parcell of medowe conteyninge fourtene acres ledynge from the seyde to the Nethercourte gate of the seyde monasterye Excepted furthermore and allwaye reservyd of the seyde Abbotte and convente and their successours and assign sixtene fote of men in breadethe over the Easte parte of the dyche withowte the seyde medowe nowe parte of the Abbey felde aforeseyde leadynge in lengthe from the Sowthe corner of the same medowe unto the wharfe at the Thorn Excepted alsoe and moreover allweye to the seyde Abbotte and convente their successours and assign reservyd all other weys and commodityes[630] to ryde goo carye and recarye withe horse and carte over and thorowghe the seyde Nethercourte Melfelde Surrendrescrofte and other the premysses to and fro at all tymes in suche manor and fourme as the same Abbot and convente and their predecessours at any tyme before the makynge of the same indenture had used and excercysed that indenture or any thinge therin conteyned to the contrarye notwithstondinge And furthermore where it was covenaunted graunted and agreed betwene the seyde abbotte and convente and the seyde William Marshall and John his sonne that the seyde William and John or one of theym or their assign shall fette take and have durynge the seyde terme twelve lodes of fewell owte of the Bleane of the seyde Abbotte and convente where the forester of the seide Abbotte and convente or their succours shall assigne and appoynte to their owne use to be fellyd made and caryed at the propre costes and charges of the same William and John To have holde and occupye the seyde mesuage Nethercourte barnes stables styes cartehowses gardeners arable lande medowes marshes pastures custome store and other the premysses before specifyed excepte before excepted to the seyde William Marshall and John his sonne and their assign from the feaste of Seynte Mychaell the Archaungell nexte to come after the date of the seyde indenture unto the ende and terme of nyne yeres then nexte folowyng and fully to be complete as by the same indenture amonges other thynges more evydentelye maye appere the seide Abbotte and convente have nowe of and withe their commen assente and consente dimysed graunted and to ferme letten unto the seyde Stepheyn Motte and to hys assign all that their messuage aforeseyde sette lyinge and beyinge within the Nethercourte of the seyde monasterye withe all the barnes stables styes cartehowses and gardyners to the same Nethercourte adioynynge (Excepte before

[628] *O.E.D.* Garth; a small piece of enclosed ground, usually beside a house or other building, used as a yard, garden or paddock.
[629] *O.E.D.* a synonym for Fetch.
[630] fol. Cxxxviij verso.

excepted) And also two hundrethe sevene acres and a halfe acre and halfe a rode of arable grounde medowe and pasture wherof there shalbe of falowe and podware londe eighte and fouretye acres lyinge in the feldes called Melfelde Mollysdane and Westgates aforesaid to gether withe the seyde custome of arynge and sowynge of one and twenty acres halfe an acre and halfe a rode of londe with the corne and cornes of the seid Stephyn or his assign yerelye to be sowne and also withe the custome of cuttyngdowne byndinge caryinge into the barnes and tassynge the same corne or cornes growynge yerelye upon the same to be done yerelye by the tenantes of the same Abbotte and convent of their manor of Faversham (as of olde tyme hathe ben used and accustomed) Forthwithe the same pastures medowes and mershes to the seide manor adioyninge that is to seye a pasture called Catmershe a medowe to the same mershe adioyninge a mershe called Estmershe and the medowe next to the Nethercourte gate aforeseid on the Sowthe parte of the same gate forthwithe the store of one and twenty quarters of whete rase measure good lawfull marchaunte and clene tryed with an hundrethe coppes of peases two hundrethe of tearys and also wykelye duringe his terme in the premysses seven galons of ale called servauntes ale and the halfe the greynes of every brewynge in the seyde monasterye forthwithe the wasshe of the same to be sette by the seyde Stephen Motte or his assign at the bruehowse in the seyde Monasterye excepte asmoche of the seyde greynes wasshe and offall as shall sufficientlye fynde wekelye durynge the seyde terme foure sowes and a bore Excepted furthermore and allweyes to the seyde Abbotte and convente and to their successours reservyd the stables in the seyde Nethercourte called Palfreye stables withe a lyttell chambre over the porch of the same stables a lytell garden adioyninge to the same a howse there called the forge forthwithe all rentes and servyces and all other customes to the seyde manor perteyninge or in any wyse belonginge the howse and closure at the Thorn a parcell of medowe conteyninge fourtene acres leadynge from the seyde Thorn unto the Nethercourte gate of the seyde monasterye (excepted furthermore and allweye reservyd to the seyde Abbotte and convente and to their successours and assign sixtene fote men[631] in bredeathe on the Easte partie of the dyche withowte the seyde medowe nowe parte of the Abbeyfelde aforeseyde leadynge in lengthe from the Sowthe corner of the seide medowe unto the wharf at the Thorn Excepted also and moreover allweyes unto the seyde Abbotte and convent their successours and assign reservyd all otherweyes and commodytes to ryde go carye and recarye withe horse and carte over and thoroughe the seide Nethercourte Melfelde Surrendrencrofte and other the premysses to and fro at all tymes in suche manor and fourme as the same abbotte and convente and their predecessours at anytyme before the makynge of this indenture have usyd and excercysed this indenture or any thinge therin conteyned to the contrarye notwithstondinge and furthermore it is covenaunted grauntyd and agreed bitwene the side abbotte and convente and the seyde Stephyn Motte that the same Stephyn or his assign shall fette take and have yerely duringe the seyde terme twelfe loodes fewell owte of the Bleane of the seyde Abbotte and convente where the forester of the same Abbotte and convente or their successours shall assigne or appoynte to his or their owne use to be fellyd made or caryed at the propre costes and charges of the same Stephyn or his assign To have hold occupye and enioye the seyde mesuage Nethercourte barnes stables styes cartehowses gardyners arable londe medowes mershes pastures custome store and all other the premysses (excepte before excepted) unto the seyde Stephyn Motte his executors and assign from the feaste of Seynte Mychaell the Archaungell nexte aftir the expiration of the seyde former lease to the seide William Mershall and John his sonne in manor and fourme aforeseyde abovenamed and grauntyd unto the ende and terme of twentye yeres then next followynge and fullye to be completed yeldynge and payinge yerelye unto the seyde Abbotte and convente their successours and assign duringe the seyde terme one and twentye quarters of whete rase measure good lawfull marchaunte and clene tryed an hundred twentye and syxe quarters of barleye rase

[631] fol. Cxxxix.

measure good lawfull marchaunte and clene tryed and twentye lawfull bacon hogges the seyde hogges to be delyvered yerelye durynge all the seyde terme to the seyde Abbotte and convente and their successours and assign bitwen the feaste of Seynte Mychaell the Archaungell and twelfe nexte after Christmas at suche tyme or tymes or tymes as the seyde Abbotte and convente their successours and assign shall lawfullye requyre theym and nyne poundes of good and lawfull money of Englonde and sixe copull of capons yerelye to be delyvered to the seyde Abbott and convente their successours and assign before the feaste of the Nativyte of our Lorde God forthwithe all the seyde corne to be payde and delivered at the gardyners and bruehowse in the monasterye aforeseyde in manor and fourme folowynge that is to wete the feaste of All Seyntes of whete tenne quarters and a halfe rase measure good lawfull merchaunte and clene tryed of barleye tenne quarters and a halfe rase measure good lawfull merchaunte and clene tryed And before the feaste of Seynte Andrewe of barleye one and twenty quarters rase measure good lawfull mercahunte and clene tryed and before the Nativyte of our Lorde God in moneye fyve poundes sterlinge and of barley one and thirtye quarters and an halfe rase measure good lawfull marchaunte and clene tryed And before the firste daye of Februarye in moneye foure poundes sterlinge And of whete fyve quarters and two busheles rase measure good lawfull merchaunte and clene tryed of barley one and twenty quarters rase measure good lawfull merchaunte and clene tryed And before the firste daye of Aprylle of whete fyve quarters and two bussheles rase measure good lawfull merchaunte and clene tryed of barleye one and twentye quarters rase measure good lawfull merchaunte and clene tried forthwithe the seyde sixe copull of capons to be delivered[632] as is aboveseyde in full paymente of one hole yerys ferme and so yerelye bytwene feaste and feaste terme and terme as is aboveseyde lyke whete and barleye bacon hogges and capons duringe the hole terme of twentye yeres aforeseyde Allsoo the seyde Stephyn Motte covenauntethe and by theis presentes hymselfe byndethe to keepe nurryshe and fede or cause to be kepte nurryshed and fedde yerelye duringe the seide fower bullockes or kene of the Abbottes and convente aforeseyde and their succcessours withe theffall and strawe of the same Stephyn from the feaste of Seynte Andrewe the Apostell unto the feaste of Seynte George the Marteir then nexte ensuynge And if and as often as it fortune the seyde yerelye ferme of one and twenty quarters of whete one hundrethe twentye and syxe quarters of barleye twentye bacon hogges nyne poundes and sixe coppull of capons or any parte or parcell therof to be behynde and unpayde and delivered after anye feaste or daye aforeseyde in whiche it owghte to be payde and delivered That then so often it shall be lawfull to the seyde Abbotte and convente and to their successours their assign offycers and mynystres unto the seyde mesuage Nethercourte barnes stables styes cartehowses gardyners arable lande medowes mershes pastures with the appurtenaunces and other the premysses and into every parte and parcell of theym to entre and dystreyn and the distresses so there taken lawfully from thensforthe to leade dryve beare and caryeawaye and theym towardes theym to witholde and deteyn untill of the same yerelye ferme and everye whytte therof and of the arrerages of the same yf any be to gether with their hurtes costes and expenses by that occacion had and susteyned theye be fullye contentyd and payde And if it happen the same yerelye ferme or any one thynge therof to be behynde unpasyde after any of the seyde feastes or dayes in whiche as is aboveseyde it oughte to be payde by the space of one monethe and no sufficyente nor lawfull distresse in nor uppon the seyde messuage Nethercourte barnes stables styes cartehowses gardyners arable londes medowes marshes and other the premysses nor any parcell therof then it shall be lawfull to the seyde abbotte and convente and to their successours and to every of theym unto the same mesuage Nethercourte barnes stables styes cartehowses gardenes arable landes medowes mershes and other the premysses and into any parte and parcell of theym holye to reenter and theym to have ageyn and repossede as in their fourmer estate And the seyde

[632] fol. Cxxxix verso.

Stephyn his executors and assign occupyers of the same holye to expell putte owte and amove this indenture or anythinge therin conteyned to the contrarye in anywyse notwithstondinge And the seyde Stephyn Motte covenauntethe and grauntethe to and wythe the seyde Abbotte and convente by thies presentes that it shalle not be lawfull to the seyde Stephyn his executours nor assign nor any of theym to hewdowne feldowne or cutte downe loppe toppe no croppe any manner of tymber or underwoode growinge in apon and aboute the seyde londes withe the appurtenaunces or apon any parte or parcell therof duringe the seyde terme thornes and stakes for the necessarye and compotente enclosure of the premysses onlye excepted Whiche thornes and stakes notwithstondynge shalbe assigned and appoynted by the seyde abbotte and convente their successours and assign whern as as often as any suche thornes and stakes shall nede or lacke for the closure of the seyde premysses Also the seyde Stephen covenauntethe and by theis presentes unto and withe the seyde Abbotte and convente grauntethe to howse and imbarne in the howses and barnes aboveseyde and in none other place all the cornes growynge or to growe in and upon the landes aforeseyde duringe the seyde terme of twentye yeres And alsoo spredde whorle and leye abrod yerelye duringe the seyde terme upon the seyde landes all the donge offall and compose that shall happen to come ferthe of the stables barnes styes and cartehowses aforeseyde in all the seyde terme And further the seide Stephyn Motte covenauntethe and grauntethe unto[633] and withe the seyde Abbotte and convente and their successours by theis presentes that the seyde Stephyn at the ende of the terme of twentye yeres shall yelde up surrender and leave up all and singuler the seyde mesuage Nethercourte barnes stables styes gardeners landes pastures medowes and other the premysses and every parte and parcell of theym into the handes and possession of the seyde Abbotte and convente their successours and assign forthwithe the store abovewrytten together withe eighte and fourtye acres of falowe and podware landes in the foreseyde feldes called Melfelde and Westegates And the seyde abbotte and convente for theym and their successours covenaunte permytte and graunte unto and withe the seyde Stepheyn by theis presentes that they at their propre costes and expenses shall kepe susteyn and meynteyn all the seyde mesuage Nethercourte barnes stables styes cartehowses and gardeners and all other the edifycies to the same Nethercourte belongineg and every parte and parcell of theym well and sufficientelye in everye thinge repeyred aswell ageyn wynde as water durynge all the seyde terme excpte yf any hurte or harme be donne in and upon the same or any parte or parcell of theym by the necligence or oversighte of the seyde Stephyn Motte his servauntes bestes or catelles all the whiche hurtes the seyde Stephyn at his onlye coste shall repeyre and mende ageyn Also the seyde Abbotte and convente covenaunte and graunte unto and withe the seyd Stephyn Motte by thies presentes that they shall not onlye dyscharge all and everye the seyd mesuage Nethercourte barnes stables styes cartehowses gardyners arable landes medowes mershes pastures and every parte and parcell of theym of and from all manor of rente and rentes and other yerelye charges goyinge or to goo owte durynge the seyde terme of the premysses unto the chieffe lorde or lordes of the fee of the same butte alsoo all manor of tythes wherof the seyde landes and tenementes and other the premysses or any parte or parcell of theym beyinge or shalbe durynge the seyde terme yerelye charged withe the tithes or and for the foreseyde feldes called Mollysdane and Westgates allweyes excepted moore over the seyde Abbotte and convente covenaunte and graunte by theis presentes that if they or their successours at any tyme hereafter be disposed or mynded to enclose pale in or occupye the foreseyde sixtene fote of lande adioyninge to the medowe leadinge to the Thorn that the seyde Abbotte and convente and their successors shall yereleye alowe unto the seyde Stephyn Motte his executours and assign of and for the same sixtene fote of lande aftur the rate and quantityte therof as the same Stephyn payethe for the overplus of the premysses And also that the seyde Stephyn his executors and assign shall have their easemente in the barnes

[633] fol. CxL.

aforeseyde for thresshinge of their cornes and spende their offall in the curtlage there withe their beastes and have also free libertye in comming and goyinge owte for theym selfes and their servauntes with horse and carte to carye aweye their cornes there from the feaste of Seynte Mychaell the Archaungell in the ende and terme of the seide twentye yeres unto the feaste of Seynte George the Martyr then nexte and immedyately folowynge The seyde Abbotte and convente do furthermore covenaunte promytte and graunte unto and withe the seyde Stephyn Motte his executors and assign by thyes presentes that the same Stephyn Motte his executors and assign shall have remeyninge in his or their handes one hole yeres ferme of the premysses to be payde to the seyde abbotte and convente their successours or assign within one hole yere nexte and ymmedyatelye aftir the expiration of the seyde terme of twentye yerys at suche lyke dayes and feastes as is allredye before rehersed in this In wytnesse whereof to the one partie of this indenture with the seyde Stephyn Motte remeyninge the seyde abbotte and convente their commen seale have putt and to the other parte of this same indenture with the seyde Abbotte and convente[634] remeyninge the seyde Stephyn Motte his seale hathe putt gyven in the Chapiterhowse of the monasterye aforeseyde the daye and yere above wrytten.

And because through due examination in this part made and clearly had by the court that is to say the aforesaid indenture, the aforesaid writing made and sealed was good secure and without compact, fraud or deceit therefore that indenture with all and singular contained and specified in the same is allowed by the chancellor and council of the court aforesaid. Always provided that if hereafter the debt now having been approved before the chancellor and council of the aforesaid court for the time being, that the aforesaid Stephen the said demise by virtue and pretext of the aforesaid indenture in the form aforesaid to have and to possess, not to be owed, that then and next this present decree to be void and of no effect in law any clause or article contained in the same to the contrary not withstanding.

COURT OF AUGMENTATIONS
E315/23[635]

page 39

Interrogatories mynistred on the behalfe of our sovereeyne Lord the King to Thomas Asten of the countye of Kent gentleman concernyng two annuyties goyng owt of the possessions of the monasterye of Feversham And one other annuytie goyng owt of the possessions of Saynt Austyns in Canturberye

Inprimis wether this deponent knew John Castelloke late Abbot of the late dissolved monasterye of Feversham

Item what annuyties he knoweth that the same Abbott with the consent of the convent dyd graunte unto Rychard Robynson clerk charging the possessions of the same late monasterye with a clause of dystres and upon what consideracyons the same annuyties were graunted

Item wether he knew the same annuyties or any of them to be behynde unpayde before the dissolucyon of the same late monasteryes And how long he knew them to be behynde And the reason and the cause how he knew them to be behynde

page 38

---

634 fol. CxL verso.
635 Before 1547.

Depositions of Thomas Asten of the countie of Kent gent sworne and examined upon the interrogatories hereunto annexed

To the furst artycle the said deponet sworne and examynid upon his othe sayth that he knew the sayd Abbottes xxiij or xxiiij yeares before ther death

To the second he sayth upon his othe that the sayd Abbott of Feversham with the assent of the convent dyd graunte unto the sayd Rychard Robynson for terme of his lyffe two annuyties whereof the one was xij£ by the yeare and the other x£ by the yeare And that certeyne possessyons of the same house were charged with a clause of dystres for the payement of them And that the sayd Abbott of Saynte Austyns with the assent of the convent did graunte to the sayd Rychard Robynson for terme of his lyffe one annuytie of xij£ by the yere goyng owt of the manour of Northborne in the countye of Kent And that the same annuyties were graunted in consideracyon of certeyne sommes of money payd by the sayd Rychard Robynson And for the resignacyon of thre benyfyces And further sayth upon his othe that the one annuytie concernyng the Abbot of Saynt Austyns he hymselffe ingrossed And the other two annuyties the sonne of this deponent engrossed

Item to the third he upon his othe sayth that the sayd two annuyties goyng owt of the possessions of Feversham were behynde unpayd from the feast of Saynt Mychaell in the xxvjth yere of the reigne of our sovereyne Lord the king that now is untill the dissolucyon of the same late monastery And further sayth that he knoweth they were so long behynde because he hard the sayd Abbott of Feversham dyvers tymes confesse both before the dissolucyon off the same late monasterye and after as well upon a demande made by the sayd Rychard Robynson as also upon a sute made by subpena delyvered to the same Abbott by the said Rychard Robynson that he the sayd Abbott dyd owe the arrerrages of the sayd severall annuyties from the sayd feast of Saynt Mychaell And shewed this deponent the acquyttances of the sayd Rychard for the payementes made before that daye And that the sayd annuytie of xij£ goyng owt of the possessions of the sayd late monasterye of Saynt Austyns was behynde unpayde from the vjth daye of Aprill in the xxiijth yere of our sovereyne Lord the Kyng untill the dissolucyon of the sayd late monasterye whiche he knoweth to be true because upon a letter dyrected unto the sayd Abbott from one of the offycers of the courte of Augmentacyons commanding hym to certyfye how long the sayd annuytie was behynd he desyred this deponent to make answere to the same letter wherin he confessed that the sayd annuytie of xij£ was behynd unpayde from the sayd vjth daye of Aprill as is above recyted And besides he sayethe further upon his othe that the sayd Abbott of Saynt Austyns dyd dyvers tymes confesse wyles the house stode that the sayd annuytie was behynde unpayde from the sayd vjth day of Apryll

By me Thomas Astyn (his own hand)

❖♌❖♌❖♌❖

Lands of the Dissolved Religious Houses[636]

SC6/Hen. VIII/No. 1755 29-30 Hen. VIII
195 FAVERSHAM MONASTERY

Faversham: Site of the monastery, with demesne lands m 42

[636] PRO Lists and Indexes, Supplementary Series III/2.

Rents in, Mill called 'Fludmyll' with ponds, banks, and meadows pertaining thereto. m 42
Common fine of the tenants there.

Kyngesnothe (Kingsnoad in Ulcombe, co. Kent)
Rents of divers lands enclosed within the park of Anthony Seyntleger m 46
Manor of, with demesne lands
Pannage within the wood
Perquisites of courts

Southfeld and Preston Felde m 47
Arable lands in the field called 'Southfeld' in Faversham and in the parish of Preston next Faversham, with tithes.

Negdonmershe (Nagden in Graveney, Kent) m 47
Marsh lands

Weldemershe (Wildmarsh in Luddenham, co. Kent) m 47v
Marsh lands in Weldmershe in Luddenham parish

Prestfeld m 47v
Field called 'Prestfeld'

Faversham, offices of bailiff and chamberlain m 48
Amercements of the Kings Court of Portmote and amercements of bakers for breaking the assize within the liberty, in the charge of the bailiff.
Amercements of brewers, tapsters and nuisances[637], fines of occupiers of the liberties of the town and of men admitted to the liberties, contribution from four *portat[ores]* and profits of markets and '*ozago*'[638] in the charge of the chamberlain

Nethercourt, Grange called m 48v
Messuage situate in 'le Nerthercourte' with barns and other houses pertaining therto and certain lands.

Feversham
Issues of fairs within the town and liberties and two parcels of land called 'le Nether Grene' and 'le Upper Grene'.

Le Bleane m 49v
Issues of the forest of

Lambertyslonde (Lamberts Land in Dunkirk, co. Kent) m 50
Rents of land called 'Upperhawegate' and of a croft called 'Crochecrofte'
Manor called 'Lamberteslonde' with lands, meadows, etc. a croft called '[D]enys Crofte' and lands called 'Botrells and Dobbys'.

Elyndenn (Ellenden, co. Kent) m 50
Rents in manor called 'Elyngden' with arable lands, meadows etc.
Perquisites of courts.

Feversham, hundred of m 51v
Rents in the borough (burgi) of Harteye, Ore and Ewell (Ewell in Faversham, co. Kent), Selgrave (Selgrave in Faversham, co. Kent),

---

[637] Given in printed text as malefactors, however, Latin: *Nocuorum*.
[638] This is 'ozage' found elsewhere as osage for Usage; habitual use, established custom or practice, customary mode of action. For instance Favward fol. 50v.

and Oldegoldysthelde, the boroughs of Chettham(Chetham in Ospringe, co. Kent), Brumstone (Brimstone in Ospringe, co Kent), Badlysmere, Oldebouldyslande, and Rode, Graveney, Munketon (Monkton in Otterden, co. Kent) parish and Brodefelde (Bradfield in Ospringe, co. Kent) borough.[639]
Customs of certain lands for 'le Shypshottes' and 'Medeshottes.'

Goremershe
Marsh called 'Gore Mershe' and lands called 'Uplond' pertaining therto and two parcels of lands called 'Mentylsham' and 'Cockham'.

Fryttenden (Frittenden, co. Kent) m 54
Three tenements with pieces of land called 'Greate' and 'Lytell' Ferehurst in the parish of.

Benyshall (Bendysh Hall in Radwinter, Essex)
Manor of, with lands etc, and two tenements called 'Braddgys' and 'Mychelles'.

Divers small farms m 54
Lands in the parish of Hernehill with the rectory there and tithes of Denly Mershe (Denly in Hernhill, co. Kent)

Meadows called 'Saltemedys' m 55
Lands in Greatberton (?Great Burton, co. Kent)
Lands called 'Horsoppes'
Negdon Mershe[640]
Marsh called 'Lodd mershe' in the parish of Feversham, Ore and Luddenham.
Moiety of a tenement and lands called Ewellondes (Ewell in Faversham, co. Kent) and a close called 'Surrendencroft' in Feversham parish.
Seven weirs called 'Sowthewerys' and proceeds of the fishing in the sea within the liberty of the admiralty of the monastery.
Rectories of Boughton and Prestoun
Pension of tithes from the lordship of Abbotescourte and pensions from Luddenham and Newnham rectories

204 LEEDS PRIORY
SC6/Hen.VIII/No. 1757 32-33 Hen. VIII

Barn, lands, a tenement and garden in Ospringe.[641]
Lands in Badlesmere[642]
Pension from churches or rectory of .... Easlying
Rents in ... Newnham, Bokeland

[639] A. Percival suggests alternatively Boardfield in Otterden.
[640] Accounted for elsewhere on the roll.
[641] Granted by the King's Letters Patent of June 30, anno 33 Henry VIII to the Dean and Chapter of Rochester.
[642] In same grant 30 June 33 Henry VIII.

194 MONASTERY OF ST. AUGUSTINE NEAR CANTERBURY 29-30 Hen. VIII
SC6/Hen.VIII/No. 1755

Sheldwych m 21v
Rectory of, with tithes etc.

Faversham m 35v
Rectory of, with glebe lands tithes, etc.

Stone, m 37
Rectory of, with tithes, etc.

Foreign Receipts
Rents in ... Levelonde next Badylsemere

210 POSSESSIONS GRANTED BY LETTERS PATENT TO THE DEAN AND CHAPTER OF ROCHESTER 20 June 33 Hen. VIII
p. 9

Osprenge	Leeds Priory	m 44
Badlesmere	Leeds Priory	
Newenham	Leeds Priory	
Bokeland	Leeds Priory	

206 PRIORY OF CHRIST CHURCH CANTERBURY
SC6/Hen.VIII/No. 1757 32-33 Hen.VIII

Lands, tenements, woods, messuages, meadows, waters, fisheries, marshes, rents, revenues, services, knights fees, escheats, reliefs, courts leet, views of frank pledge etc., pensions, portions, tithes etc., in the towns, fields, hamlets and parishes of ....Graveney, Newneham, ... Boughton subtus Bleane, Preston iuxta Feversham ... and the parish of St. Thomas in the Isle of Hartye co. Kent

539 SOUTHWARK

Farm of the Rectory of Graveney, Kent

207 PRECEPTORY[643] OF SWINGFIELD
SC6/Hen.VIII/No.7268 32-33 Hen. VIII

Manor of Owre co. Kent, with all lands tenements etc.
Lands in Westbroke iuxta Feversham

[643] Preceptory was a subordinate community of the Knights' Templar.

Swynefeld (Swingfield)
Rents in Stallysfeld

209 BOXLEY ABBEY
SC6/Hen.VIII/ No. 1762 30-31 Hen. VIII

208 PRECEPTORY OF WEST PECKHAM

SC6/Hen. VIII/No. 7268 32-33 Hen. VIII

West Peckham, Kent m 5
Manors of West Pekham and Stallysfeld with their appurtenances ... and messuages, lands, rents, services, pensions, portions of tithes, courts leet ... in ... Stallysfeld ...

546 ROBERTSBRIDGE

SC6/Hen. VIII/ No. 3675 29-30 Hen. VIII
Farm of lands called Mershelandes and Uplands in Stone, Kent.

❖♌❖♌❖♌❖

Lambeth Palace Library, LONDON SE1 7JU

Estate Documents ED 2006[644]

folio 1: top of manuscript torn and lost

..... garden there leased to Richard [unclear] rendering per year 6^d^ 8^d^

.... in the hands of the Abbey:
It is worth in the farm of the demesne land there containing by estimation 30 acres in extent valued at 2^s^ the acre 3£

Grange called the Nethercourte
It is worth in the farm of the demesne land leased to William Marshall etc., by indenture rendering each year *[lost]*
......together with service of attendance at the hundred court of Faversham *[lost]*

Town of Faversham
It is worth in the rents of assize for tenants there per annum [?6^£^] 13^s^, 24 hens 1 cock and 1 quarter of [barley] 24£ *[lost]*

It is worth in farm of diverse messuages tenements and tofts situated within the aforesaid town with the rent of one water-mill there by the year 31^£^ 5^s^
Together with the price of 4 hens

[644] ED 2006 and former ED 2070 now to be described as ED 2006. Latin translated. Dorse of m.1: *Holdings of the Monastery* of St Augustines in Canterbury. I realised on reading it that it related to Faversham Abbey, which was not one of the holdings of St Augustines. The rectory did belong to St Augustines and that is how it may have acquired this roll.

Hundred of Faversham[645]
It is worth in rents of assize of tenants there above the price of ~~25~~ 18 hens 2 cocks 100 eggs and 1 quarter of barley by the year 57$^{£}$ 12^{s} 3^{d} [?½¼]

Note for vij hens
And in the price of ~~25~~ 18 hens at 3^{d} the hen, 2 cocks at 2^{d} the cock, 100 eggs at 20 eggs 1^{d} and one quarter of barley 3^{s} 4^{d} ~~9s 4^{d}~~ 8^{s} 7^{d} ¼

Profit of the fairs[646]
It is worth in profits of the fairs with the rent of two parcels of land called the Upper Grene and the Nether Grene within the site of the monastery aforesaid leased by indenture for the time of the fairs there, that is to say, in the Feast of St. Peter in chains and for eight days following 3$^{£}$ 3^{s} 4^{d}

Profits of the Courts
It is worth in profits issuing annually from the court of the liberties of the town of Faversham and from the Court of the Hundred there and to the [[647]] with suits of the tenants in respect whereof annually 8$^{£}$

Sowthfelde, Prestone
It is worth in the farm of 34 acres of land in The Sowthfelde and 24 acres in Prestone at Hegdale with one tithe of Sowthfelde leased by indenture rendering annually 10$^{£}$

Lodgmershe in the parish of Ore, Luddenham and Faversham
It is worth there in the farm of a tenement there and 12 acres of land called Uplande and 3^{s} 4^{d} quit of rent pertaining to the same tenement with the appurtenances and pasturage of 105 sheep in the salt marshe called Lodge mershe leased by indenture to Richard Drylande John Dryland son senior 33^{s} 4^{d}

Weldemershe
It is worth there in the farm of marsh there called Weldmershe leased by indenture rendering each year 33^{s} 4^{d}

Next Manor of Kingsnorth
Rents of Assize, Rents of demesne
Pannage in Kingsnothe wood and Eastwoode, etc.
Grange called Lamtyslande[648]
Forest called The Bleane[649]
Hernehill
Goremersh
Prestefelde
Negdonmershe
Horsehoopys
Cattystrete & Saltemedys
Gretbarton
Sowthwearys[650]
Manor of Ellynden
Greate Fereherst & Little Ferherst in the parish of Fretynden
Bendishall
Ewell

645 fol. 2.
646 Latin; nundinarum.
647 Latin; appears something like 'nu rallitatum' withan abbreviation mark over the middle.
648 fol. 3.
649 2,500 acres, sale of wood 33£ 6s 8d, pannage 11s, rent of 9 gates 5s 8d,¼ & ½ a ¼.
650 fol. 4.

Abbotyscourte:
[Note] of the farm or rent of the manor there with appurtenances we are not able to respond. In that the said manor was lately sold by the Abbot and Convent to Thomas Cheyney knight by virtue of a licence obtained from the King for that purpose.

Sum[651] of all the possessions of the temporality 311£ 17^d ½¼ ~~14s 9d~~

Spirituality

Boughton
The Rectory there is worth per year 36£

Preston
The rectory there is worth with three acres of glebe land near the parish church per year $13^£$ 11^s 8^d

Hernehill
The Rectory there is worth per year £10
And in the tithes of [ ]lynmershe 20s

Pensions Received

In the annual pension issuing out farm the Rectory of Luddenham $3^£$ 6^s 8^d

In a pension issuing out of the Rectory of Newynham by the year 33^s 4^d

Total possessions of the spiritualities $65^£$ 11^s 8^d and sum total of all the possessions of the temporalties and spiritualities £376 13s 1d ½¼

In rents received

The Abbey of Saint Augustine of Canterbury for the first demesne lands of the said monastery annually by composition 6£ 13^s 4^d

The same abbey for rent of the yoke of Chetham within the hundred 11^s 5^d

[others omitted]

Archbishop of Canterbury for land called Mentilham and Cokham to the demesne of Boughton by the year 7s

Vicar of Hernehill for the same lands by the year 4^s 8^d

Manor[652] of Graveney for land called Horsehoopes 2^s 6^d

Archbishop of Canterbury Lord of the Manor of Boughton for Goremarshe annually 5^s 6^d

[further entries omitted]

Royalties[653] belongyng to the saied Monastry

In the first place the Courte of Admyralltye with all profittes of waifes straies shipwreckes and other casualties of the Sea from the Fludmede to the beacon downe in the sea And from the beacon to Tenham flete whereof the one moyete is the archebusshoppys of Canturbury the other longyth to the Monastery And from Tenham flete to Ryde Ferye and from thens to Snowte weare

651 fol. 5.
652 fol. 6.
653 fol. 9 (pencil 8). This section mostly in English with some sections in Latin.

The nomination of the mayor of Feversham longith to the Kynges Highenes by the right of the same Monastery and to gyve hym his othe. The towne hath been accustomed to electe 2 or 3 persons which they esteme able And presente theym to the Monastery and there one to be nominated by the Abbot and the Abbot to gyve hym his othe

The[654] nombre of Free tenaunts

Free tenaunts that holde of the saied Monastery to the nombre of 360 and above

Patronages belongyng to the saied Monastery

the presentation of the parson of the parishe of Luddenham worthe by yere clare 6£ 13^s 4^d

Item the master ~~keeper~~ of an hospitall of poore people in Faversham

Knyghtyes fees none

Stocke and store in the handes of fermours the same at
Nethercorte $16^£$ 10^s
at Kyngesnothe $3^£$
att Lambtyslandes 20^s
att Ellynden 10^s
att Bendyshehall $10^£$
total $21^£$

Parkes none

Commons none

The hoole contyente of acres of woddes

Woodes belongyng to the saied Monastery by estimation 2000 [500] 30 acres [this middle figure is very badly smudged.[655]

❖♌❖♌❖♌❖

SP5/1

State Papers Domestic - Suppression papers

Kent starts at pencil fol. 97 [metal dye stamp no 78][656]

Headed: County of Kent 33 Henry VIII [22 April 1541 - 21 April 1542]

Lands[657] and possessions pertaining to the Monastery of Faversham.

Site	
Farm of the site of the said Monastery with the demesne there	78^s 8^d
Official collector of the rents of town of Faversham	
Rents of assize in Feversham	$34^£$ 20½¼^d
Rents of tenants of the will of the Lord there	$20^£$ 19^s 4^d
Rent[658] of Poultry	12^s 2^d

654 fol. 10.
655 ends at bottom of fol. 10.
656 The document is all in Latin.
657 Pencil fol. 99 metal stamp no 80.
658 *Redditus mobile*.

Farm of the mill called Floudmill by the year	10$^{£}$
Common Fines	18^{s} 4^{d}
Feversham	
Farm of one garden one stable and a messuage with	26^{s} 8^{d}
a parcell of land called the Nether Greene	40^{s}
Manor of East Kingsnorth	
Farm concession	
Hundred of Feversham	
Office of Bailiff Chamberlain of the Town of Feversham	
Rent of assise tenures in the Borough of Harte	3$^{£}$ 10^{s} 5½¼^{d}
Rents of the free tenants in the Borough of Ore	3$^{£}$ 6^{d} 1^{d}
Rents of the free tenants in the Borough of Well[659]	10$^{£}$ 6^{s} 8¼^{d}
Rents of the free tenants in Lalgrave[660] by the year	7$^{£}$ 17^{s} 9^{d}
Rents of the free tenants in Oldgoldesthelde	9$^{£}$ 9^{s} 3^{d}
Rents of the free tenants in the Borough of Chetham	40^{s}
Rents of the free tenants in the Borough of Brimstone	111^{s} 5^{d}
Rents of the free tenants in the Borough of Badlismere	31^{s} 4½¼^{d}
Rents there in the Borough of Ouldbouldsland ,	49s 8½¼^{d} half
Rents there in the Borough of Rode	46^{s} 10½¼^{d} half
Rents of the free tenants in Graveney by the year	46^{s} 9½¼^{d} half
Rents of the freee tenants in Monketon	8^{s} 10^{d}
Rents of the free tenants in the Borough of Broadfield	20^{s}
Concession[661]	2^{s} 6½ ½¼
Rent of Poultry	8^{s} 8½^{d}
Official of the Forest in the Blean	
Profits of the Forest	16^{s} 8^{d}
Increase in rent[662]	2^{s} 8^{d}
Manor of Lambitisland	
Rent of assize there	3^{s} 8^{d}
Farm of the manor	12$^{£}$ 2^{s}
Manor of Elyvnden	
Rent of assize there	23^{s} 9¼^{d}
Poultry rent	4^{s} 9^{d}
Farm of the Manor	6$^{£}$
Manor of Bendishall	
Farm there	33$^{£}$
Official Collector rents of diverse farms	
Farm of Negdon Marshe	34^{s} 6½^{d}
Farm of Marsh called Wildmarshe	33^{s} 4^{d}

659 Ewell.

660 Selgrave.

661 The abbreviated Latin is unclear.

Prestfeild	$33^{s}\ 4^{d}$
Farm of Grange called Nethercourt	$31^{£}\ 4^{s}$
Farm of the marsh called Goremarshe with the land called Mentlysham	$10^{£}$
Frittenden	$49^{s}\ 4^{d}$ concession $30^{s}\ 8^{d}$
Farm of the land in Hernehill with the farm of the rectory	$13^{£}\ 8^{s}\ 8^{d}$
Farm of the Saltmedes by the year	$26^{s}\ 8^{d}$
Greateeton by the year	6^{s}
Land called Horsoppes by the year	20^{s}
Farm of one marsh called Codmarshe in the parishes of Feversham Owre and Luddenham	$33^{s}\ 4^{d}$
Land called Ewettes with the farm of one close called Surrenden	$30^{£}\ 20\frac{1}{2}^{d}$
Southwercis by the year	$46^{s}\ 8^{d}$
Bawghton Rectory by the year	$36^{£}$ concession
Rectory of Preston	$13^{£}\ 11^{s}\ 8^{d}$ concession
Farm of the profits of the market[663] in the town and liberty of Faversham	$43^{s}\ 4^{d}$
Pension of Luddenham by the year	$46^{s}\ 8^{d}$ concession
Pension issuing out of the lordship of the Abbots Court	$40^{s}\ 8^{d}$
Farm of the site of the late monastery with the lands called Negdon Marshe by the year	$33^{s}\ 6\frac{1}{2}^{d}$
Office of Receiver General of the late monastery aforesaid	
Office of Bailiff revenues of the town of Feversham	$44^{s}\ 8\frac{1}{2}\frac{1}{4}^{d}$
Office of Collector or Chamberlain of the town of Feversham	$17^{s}\ 2\frac{1}{2}^{d}$
Hundred of Feversham	$45^{£}$ 19s $1\frac{1}{2}\frac{1}{4}^{d}$
Officer of Forrester in the Bleane	$19^{s}\ 4\frac{1}{4}^{d}$
Manor of Lambitisland	$11^{£}\ 22^{d}$
Manor of Elmern[664]	$7^{£}\ 3^{s}\ 5\frac{1}{2}^{d}$
Office of Collector of the rents of Diverse Farms	$83^{£}$ [665] $10^{s}\ 1^{d}$

662 Latin, *incrementum*; land recently bought into cultivation.

663 Latin: *nundium* can also be a fair.

664 Presumably Elverton.

665 Given as 4 score and 3.

PRO: LR6/97/7

Accounts of Thomas Spylman St. Michael the Archangel 33 Henry VIII [29 September 1541] to St. Michael the Archangel 34 Henry VIII [1542] folio 3[666]

Late monastery of Feversham in the said county of Kent

OF Ciiij^{XX} xj$^{£}$ ix^{s} iij^{d} ob. quarter received of John Wylde receiver general there of the issues of his office this year of the Lord King. He owes from the feast of St. Michael the Archangel in the thirty fourth year of the reign of King Henry VIIIth above diverse reprise in the account of the said John Wylde and other the ministers there had and paid as in the account of the same ministers.

And of xxxv^{s} received of Anthony Seyntleger knight by the annual rent to the Lord King his heirs and successors reserved named a tenth and for a tenth part of Estkyngesnothe And also for land and tenements in Sowthewark[667] parcel of the revenues of the said late monastery whilst it is existed and for the lands called Tonge parcel of [blank] and possessions of the late prior brother of the cross of Modenden whilst existing granted to the said Anthony S[...lost] for xxxv years by the year, that is to say, charged with an annual rent or tenth part for one full year ending at the feast of St. Michael the Archangel in the time of this account as above

And of Lvj^{s} of Richard R[...lost] Annual rent to the lord King and his heirs and successors for ever reserved named a tenth and for [a tenth part] of Bendysshall granted to the same Richard Rich knight at Lvj^{s} by the year that is to say, charged this year for one whole year ending at the feast of St. Michael the Archangel in the time of this account by virtue of the Letters of the lord King.

And of v^{s} of the annual rent to the Lord King and his heirs reserved named a tenth and for a tenth part of diverse messuages with gardens stables with other appurtenances to them pertaining in the town of Feversham And also for one messuage one stable and one garden with a certain parcel of land called The Nethergrene And Also for one other messuage and one garden with a dovecote in the same garden situated in Almonry Crofte granted to Thomas Arderne at v^{s} per annum, that is to say, charged this same year annual rent or tenth part for one whole year ended at the feast of St. Michael the Archangel within the time of this account.

Sum total of all the lands and possessions of the late monastery of Feversham pertaining as in this said account
Ciiij^{XX} xvj$^{£}$ v^{s} iij^{d} ob. qr.

❖ℌ❖ℌ❖ℌ❖ℌ❖ℌ❖

PRO: LR 6/97/8 FOLIO 2V
THE ACCOUNT OF THOMAS SPYLMAN ST. MICHAEL THE ARCHANGEL 35 HENRY VIII [29 SEPTEMBER 1543] TO ST. MICHAEL THE ARCHANGEL 36 HENRY VIII [1544]

[Only the section relating to the town and Ardern has been transcribed.]

And of CLix$^{£}$ vj^{s} j ob. received of John Wylde receiver general ...

---

666 The document is damaged and some of the text has been lost.

667 This appears to be the only reference to land and tenements in Southwark belonging to the monastery.

And of v^{s} received of Thomas Ardern. for annual rent to the Lord king his heirs and successors for ever reserved by the name of tenth and for a tenth part of diverse messuages with gardens and stables with other appurtenances in the town of Feversham. And also for one messuage one stable and one garden with a certain parcel of land called the Nethergrene And also for one other messuage and one garden with a dove cot in the same garden situated near Almrey crofte granted to the aforesaid Thomas Arderne for v^{s} per annum, that is to say, charged with annual rent or tenth part for one whole year ended at the feast of St. Michael the Archangel in the time of this account as aforesaid. And of ij^{s} iiij^{d} received of the aforesaid Thomas Ardern. for an annual rent to the Lord King his heirs and successors reserved named a tenth and for a tenth part of one tenement called the Bere granted to the aforesaid Thomas for ij^{s} iiij^{d} per year that is to say, charged the same annuity or tenth part for one whole year ending at the feast of St. Michael the Archangel in the time of this same account And of xiiij^{s} viij^{d} ob. received of the aforesaid Thomas Ardern. for annual rent to the lord king and his heirs and successors reserved of the manor of Elynnden granted to the aforesaid Thomas Ardern for xiiij^{s} viij^{d} ob. per annum, that is to say, charged with the annual rent or tenth part for one whole year ended the feast of St. Michael the Archangel in the time of this account as aforesaid And of iij^{s} ix^{d} ob. received of the aforesaid Thomas Ardern. for certain lands in Hernhill .....

And of xxiiij^{s} vij^{d} received of the aforesaid Thomas Ardern. of the manor of Lambertisland ...

Sum total of land and possessions of the said late manor of Feversham .... CLxvj$^{£}$ vij^{s} xd ob.

❖♌❖♌❖♌❖

PRO: SC6/EDWARD VI/233
MINISTERS ACCOUNTS 38 HENRY VIII [1546] TO 1 EDWARD VI [1547]

membrane marked D12 in pencil verso

Lands and possessions of the late Monastery of Faversham in the county of Kent.

Office of Collector of the rents of the town of Feversham

Account of Robert Cowldwell collector of the rents there from the feast of Saint Michael the Archangel in the thirty eighth year of our late lord King Henry VIIIth as far as the same feast of Saint Michael the archangel then next following in the first year of the reign of our sovereign Lord now King Edward the Sixth, that is to say, for one whole year as below,

Arrearages
None because the first account after the setting up of the Court of Augmentations and Revenues[668]

Total None

Rents of assize of the free tenants there
But received an account of xxiiij$^{£}$ xij^{s} ob. quarter of the whole rents of assize of the tenants there of whom particularly named by the account of the xxxvijth year of the reign of King Henry the VIII fully engrossed at large. To be paid at the feast of the annunciation of the Blessed Virgin

[668] The Court of Augmentations was reorganised in January 1547; Richardson, *Augmentations*, chapter 5.

Mary and Saint Michael the Archangel equally by the year. Further viij^{d} for a certain quit rent issuing of the land of the Dean and Chapter of Rochester lying at Cuthorne in the parish of Faversham That was given to the same Dean and Chapter and devised for ever just as in the foot of the account in the year next preceding

Total xxiiij$^{£}$ xij^{d} ob. qr.

Rents of the tenants at the will of the Lord there
And of xxxij^{s} ix^{d} of the whole rents of the tenants at the will of the Lord King there for the year just as of the thirtieth year of the late King Henry VIIIth is fully enrolled and by the rental in respect there of before him remaining

Sum xxij^{s} ix^{d}

m. marked in pencil D13

Poultry Rents of the tenants there
And of xij^{s} ij^{d} of the whole poultry rents of the tenants there whose names are particularised by an account of the thirty seventh year of the reign of our late King Henry the VIIIth fully written out. To be paid at the feast of the annunciation of the Blessed Virgin Mary and St. Michael the Archangel equally by the year

Farm of the Mill
And of x$^{£}$ of the farm of the mill there called Fludmylle with the ponds and banks of the rivers to the same mill pertaining except a certain parcel of land which John Elfrythe lately occupied so devised to Robert Joce this year not received. And that the late King Henry the Eighth by his Letters Patent dated the vijth day of December in the xxxviijth year of his majesties reign amongst other things has given granted and sold the said mill with appurtenances to Thomas Arden his heirs and assigns for ever to hold of the lord King and his successors for fealty to him and not in capite just as in the same letters patent is fully shown.

Total none

Common Fines
But received of xviij^{s} iiij^{d} results from the common fines of the tenants there this year as in the year proceeding.

Total xviij^{s} iiij^{d}

Profits of Court

And of pleas or profits of the courts held there this year nothing received as that none of this kind of court there

Sum total of the receipts aforesaid xxvij$^{£}$ iiij^{s} iij^{d} ob. qr.

Fealty and Pledges

The same accountant in fealty of the said accounts collected rents there to Liij^{s} iiij^{d} by the year to him granted for the term of his life by letters patent of the said Lord under the seal of the convent of the said late Monastery of Feversham that is to say in allowance this same year just as allocated in the accounts of the year preceding Liij^{s} iiij^{d} And in wages to hear and write this account and all portion of the same together with purchasing paper and parchment for engrossing the same this year just as other auditors of the king have previously ij^{s}

Total Lv^{s} iiij^{d}

Loss of rents
And in decay of rents one garden lying in Preston Street previously charged in the title of rents at the will of the Lord at iiij^{s} by the year. And that the said garden is demised to farm to John Dryland rendering in respect thereof for the year within ij^{s} vj^{d} and so in loss this year as in the years aforesaid. Nothing this year [this is not very clear and has been interlined in another hand later.]

And in loss of rent of one tenement in Feversham late in the tenure of [blank] previously charged at xxij^{d} per annum, namely in allowance this year the whole because restored into the hands of the king on account of the loss arising to the same accountants xxij^{d}

Total xxij^{d}

Total of the allocation aforesaid Lvij^{s} ij^{d} And owes xxiiij$^{£}$ vij^{s} j^{d} ob. quarter and exonerated from this ij^{d} charged upon William Wylde in the account made of the office of receiver of the lands and possessions of the said late monastery of this year just as afterwards in the same accounts And so this equal.

m. 13

Manor of Estkyngesnorth
Of any profits coming or arising of the revenues of the farm of the manor there or pertaining the whole not received because it was granted amongst other things to Anthony Saintliger knight by letters patent of the late King Henry the Eighth to have to him and his heirs male of his body lawfully begotten Holding of the said Lord King his heirs and successors in capite for service of a 20th part of one knights fee And rendering annually by the name of a tenth part of the premises which by certain other lands in the said letters patent reserved xxxv^{s} which is charged in the account of Anthony Aucher knight receiver of the lord King in the county of Kent just as there.

Total Nothing.

The Office of Chamberlain and bailiff of the town of Faversham
The account of the mayor and communality of the said town of Feversham. Bailiff and chamberlain there for the said time.

Arrears

None because the first account after the establishment of the Court of Augmentations and Revenues [of the King's Majesty's Crown.]

Total Nothing

Farm

But one account of iiij$^{£}$ of farm

Total iiij$^{£}$

Total of all the aforesaid iiij$^{£}$ who are exonerated this from this account that it is exonerated in the account of John Wylde receiver of the lands and possessions of the said last monastery just as later in the same account. And so equal.

The hundred of Faversham.

The account of John Wyld collector of the rents of the Lord king there for the time aforesaid.

Arrears.
None because this is the first account after the establishment of the Court of Augmentations and Revues.

Total Nothing.

Rents of Assize of the free tenants in the borough[669] of Hertey.
But received the account of iiij$^{£}$ xj^{s} vd ob. quarter of the total rents of assize of the free tenants there whose names are particularised by an account of the year xxxvij of the last King Henry the VIIIth fully engrossed at large To pay at the feast of annunciation of the blessed virgin Mary and St. Michael the Archangel in equal portions by the year.

Total iiij$^{£}$ xj^{s} vd ob. quarter

Rents of the free tenants of the borough of Ore.
And of iiij$^{£}$ vj^{s} j^{d} of the total rents of the free tenants there who names are particularised in an account engrossed of the xxxvijth year of the reign of the late King Henry the VIIIth To pay at the feast of the annunciation of the blessed virgin Mary and St. Michael the Archangel equally by the year.

Total iiij$^{£}$ vj^{s} j^{d}.

m. 14

Rents of the free tenants of the borough of Ewell
And of vj$^{£}$ ij^{d} quarter for all the rents of the free tenants there whose names are particularized by the account of the xxxvijth year of the reign of the late King Henry the VIIIth at large fully engrossed to be paid equally at the said terms aforesaid above xxiiij^{s} ix^{d} for the rent of the iij part of the manor of Ewell aforesaid below over leaf for the farm of the term of part of the same manor charged.

Total vj$^{£}$ ij^{d} quarter.

Rents of the free tenants in Selgrave.
And of vj$^{£}$ vj^{s} j^{d} of the total rents of the free tenants there whose names are particularized in an account of the xxxvijth year of the reign of the late King Henry the VIIIth fully engrossed at large To be paid at the said feasts of the annunciation of the Blessed Virgin Mary and St. Michael the Archangel equally by the year

Total vj$^{£}$ vj^{s} j^{d}

Rents of the free tenants in Oldgoldyscheld
And of ix$^{£}$ ix^{s} iiij^{d} of the whole rents of the free tenants there whose names are particularized on the account of the xxxvijth year of the reign of the late King Henry the VIIIth engrossed at large, to be paid at the said feasts of the annunciation of the Blessed Virgin Mary and St. Michael the Archangel in equally by the year.

Total ix$^{£}$ ix^{s} iij^{d}.

[669] *O.E.D.* Borough in the sense of township or district.; here it is meant as another word for tithing, a land division, once regarded as a tenth of a hundred run by a borsholder, Richardson, *Local Historian's Enc.*, pp. 32-33, 35, 37.

Rents of the free tenants of the borough of Chetham
And of xL^{s} of diverse messuages lands and tenements with their appurtenances that William Goldwell holds freely to pay at the said terms equally by the year.

Total xL^{s}.

Rents of the free tenants in the borough of Brumston
And of Cxj^{s} vd quarter of the whole rent of the free tenants there whose names are particularized by the account of the xxxvijth year of the late King Henry the VIIIth at large fully engrossed to be paid at the feasts of the Blessed Virgin Mary and Saint Michael the Archangel equally by the year.

Total Cxj^{s} vd quarter.

Rent of the free tenants in the borough of Badlesmere.
And of xxj^{s} iiij^{d} ob. quarter for the whole rents of the free tenants there whose names are particularized by the account of the xxxvijth year of the late King Henry the VIIIth at large fully engrossed to be paid at the said feasts of the annunciation of the Blessed Virgin Mary and St. Michael the Archangel equally by the year.

Total xxxj^{s} iiij^{d} ob. qr.

Rents of the free tenants in the borough of Oldbondisland,
And of xLix^{s} viij^{d} ob. quarter. di.[presumably here as a half of a quarter, an eighth] of the whole rents of the free tenants there whose names are particularized by the account of the xxxvijth year of the late King Henry the VIIIth at large fully engrossed will appear To be paid at said feasts of the annunciation of the Blessed Virgin Mary and St. Michael the Archangel equally by the year.

Total xLix s viij^{d} ob. qr. di.

Rents of the free tenants in the borough of Rode
And of xLvj^{s} xd ob. qr. di. for the whole of the rents of the free tenants there whose names are particularized by an account engrossed in the xxxvijth year of the late King Henry the VIIIth at large full engrossed will appear To be paid at the feasts aforesaid.

Total xLvj^{s} xd ob. qr. di.

Rents of the free tenants in Graveney
And of xLvj^{s} ix^{d} ob. qr. di. for the whole rents of the free tenants there whose names are particularized by an account of the xxxvijth year of the said late King Henry the Eighth as appears at large fully engrossed To be paid at the said terms equally by the year.

Total xLvj^{s} ix^{d} ob. qr. di.

Rents of the free tenants in the parish of Munketon
And of iij^{s} vd for the rent of certain land called Munketon Deane which Anthony Auchyer free holds to be paid at the said feast of the Annunciation of the Blessed Virgin Mary and St. Michael the Archangel equally by the year.

Total iiij^{s} vd.

Rents of the free tenants of the borough of Brodfeld.
And of xx^{s} for rents of all the free tenants in the said borough by the year to be paid at the feast of Easter and St. Michael the Archangel equally by the year.

Total xx^{s}.

New rents
And of vj^{s} viij^{d} of new rents of this quarter of grain issuing of one piece of land containing eight acres of land lying in the parish of Throwles[670] called Strakylls which Richard Lewknour free tenant just as the account or bill indented made between the late Abbot and [blank] Lewkenour father of the aforesaid Richard Lewkenour which is dated the vjth year of the said late King Henry the VIIIth.

Total vj^{s} viij^{d}.

Customary Service.
And of xviij^{d} issuing of the customary service of certain lands in the tenure of Alexander Lewkenour that is to say for The Shiphotts and Medeshottes to be paid at the said terms And of xij^{d} ob. di. qr. issuing of the customary services of certain lands in the tenure of the relict of Walter Maycott, that is to say the Shiphottes and Medeshottes, to be paid at the said terms by the year.

Total ij^{s} vj^{d} ob. di. qr.

Poultry Rents.

And of ij^{d} ob. qr of the value of Lv hens eggs arising from the poultry rents of one tenement and certain lands in the tenure of Alexander Lewkenour to be paid at the feast of Easter term by the year. And of viij^{s} iiij^{d} ob. of the whole poultry rent there whose names re particularized by the account of the xxxvijth year of the reign of the late King Henry the Eighth as appears at large fully engrossed. To be paid at the term of feast of the Lord by the year.

Total viij^{s} vij^{d} ob.

Profits of courts
And of x^{s} xd of pleas or profits of courts held there this year as appears total of the same upon this account shown and examined.

Total x^{s} xd.

SUM total of receipts aforesaid xLix$^{£}$ xij^{s} vd ob. quarter.

Fief and security.
THE same accountant in fee given to the accountant to collect the rents there at Lx^{s} by the year and by letters patent granted to him during his life, that is to say, in allocation this same year just as was allocated in the accounts and years next aforesaid Lx^{s}. And in stipend to the clerks of the audit to write this account and all the parcels of the same this year just as other audits of the lord King to have had and received ij^{s}

Total Lxij^{s}

Allowance of rents
And in allowance of the rents of assize of certain lands in the borough of Harty at Leyborowehill containing by estimation xiiij acres and one day-work parcel of the manor of Abbots Court equal to the late Abbot and Convent of the said late monastery of Feversham Thomas Cheyney knight Warden of the Cinque Ports by the kings licence in respect thereof obtained a grant previously charged at iiij^{s} xj^{d} ob by the year within the sum of x^{s} vd in the title of the borough of Hartye of

[670] Presumably Throwley.

the heirs of Thomas Frognall Which said land was purchased by the said Abbot and Convent of the said heirs of Thomas Frognall before the dissolution of the said late monastery And so in exoneration or allowance by the same for the whole time of this account and in aforesaid iij^{s} xj^{d} ob.

Total iiij^{s} xj^{d} ob.

SUM OF ALLOWANCE aforesaid Lvj^{s} xj^{d} ob. And owes xLvj$^{£}$ v^{s} vj^{d} quarter who is allowed this.

From this account which is charged upon the said William Wylde in his account made as office of receiver of this monastery just as afterwards in this same account in this year fully appears. And so it is equal.

m. 15

Office of collector of rents of diverse farms.
Accounts of John Wyld collector of the rents there for the time aforenamed.

Arrears.
None because the first account after the establishment of the Court of Augmentations and Revenues.

Total nothing.

Prestefeld
But received by this accountant xxxiij^{s} iiij^{d} of farm of a certain field called Prestefeld in the tenure and occupation of Nicholas Scott at the will of the lord rendering in respect thereof by the year as above at the feast of the annunciation of the Blessed Virgin Mary and Saint Michael the Archangel equally by the year. And of x$^{£}$ late of the farm of land lying in Southfeld and Preston this year not received and that because Thomas Cheyeney knight and the heirs male of his body lawfully procreated as in the account of the day aforesaid and a tenth part in respect thereof sold to the same lord Chayney and his heirs

Total xxxiij^{s} iiij^{d}

Farm of the Grange called Nethercourte
And of xxxix$^{£}$ iiij^{s} of farm of one messuage situated in the Nethercourt pertaining to the late monastery of Faversham with all barns and other buildings pertaining to the same messuage and also ccvij acres a half and half a rod of land in the tenure of William Marshall and John Marshall thus to them lately demised by indenture sealed under the seal of convent of the said late monastery And now in the tenure of Stephen Motte.

[*Marginal insert in English*]: Memorandum that the fermour hereof doth clayme to be allowed xL^{s} yerlye in lyke wyse as William Marshall and John Marshall late fermours there had and injoyed for the terme of there yeres according to a covenante mentioned in there indentures which covenant was that they showld have yerlye vij gallones of ale everye weke and haulf the graynes of everye bruynge together was prised at xL^{s} by yere and so to theym graunted by decree of the corte. The yeres of the which said lease be nowe expyred And ther was a lease in revertion made to oon Steven Mott for the term of xx yeres with lyke covenauntes as in the former leas was specified being also exemplified And in the same latter exemplification ther is no graunt of the said xL^{s} for recompence of the premisses which was for lacke of forseing in the attaynyng of the decree as the fermour saith wherfore he desirith order therin according to justis and conscience. [another later hand] Let it be allowed as to the other fermours was allowed for that as indenture so requyrith.

Total xxxix$^{£}$ iiij^{s}.

[*Latin*] Farm of the lands in Hernehill with farm of the rectory there.
And of ix$^{£}$ x^{s} of the farm of the rectory of Hernehill with the tithe of one marsh called Denley marshe late in the tenure of John Heler at will rendering in respect there of by the year xj$^{£}$ and now demised to Thomas Hawkyns by indenture under the seal of the Court of Augmentations and revenues of the crown by the Kings Marshall dated [blank] day of [blank] year of the late King Henry VIIIth for the term of xxj years rendering in respect thereof by the year upon the feast of the annunciation of the Blessed Virgin Mary and St. Michael the Archangel equally by the year just as in the same indenture is fully shown. And of iij^{s} iiij^{d} of the whole farm or rent of the land called Ammerye croft in the tenure of [blank] Cowldwell to be paid at the said terms equally by the year.

Total x$^{£}$ xiij^{s} iiij^{d}

Land called Ewells with the farm of one close[671] called Surrenden
And of xij$^{£}$ xx^{d} ob. of the whole rents of the lands called Ewells whose names of the tenants are particularized by the account of xxxvijth year of the reign of the late King Henry the Eighth at large fully engrossed appears to be paid at the feast of the annunciation of the Blessed Virgin Mary and St. Michael the Archangel equally by the year. And of xx^{s} late of rents of certain lands called Surrenden croft this year not received. And that because the late Lord King Henry the Eighth by his Letters Patent dated the xxiiijth day of November in the xxxviijth years of his majesty's reign amongst other things gave and granted the croft aforesaid with its appurtenances to John Belloo and his heirs for ever who released his title to Thomas Ardern.and his heirs for ever to hold of the Lord King in free socage as of the honor of Torrington in the county of Devon just as in the said letters patent fully appears.

Total xij$^{£}$ xx^{d} ob.

Southweres
But received of xxiij^{s} iiij^{d} resulting from vij fish-traps[672] called Southweres who holds at will to be paid at the feast of Easter term And of xxiij^{s} iiij^{d} issuing from the fishing[673] in the sea within the liberty of the admiralty[674] part to the demesne of the late monastery in the tenure [blank] To be paid at the terms aforesaid

Total xLvj^{s} viij^{d}

Farm issuing from the fairs within the town and liberty of Feversham
And of xxvj^{s} viij^{d} of the farm issuing from the fairs held at the feast of Saint Peter in Chains annually with the farm of one parcel of land called the Nethergrene where the same fair is accustomed to be held lately demised to Robert Cowldwell and now demised to the mayor and commonalty of Faversham by indenture to be paid yearly at the feast of the assumption of the Blessed Virgin Mary And of xxxvj^{s} viij^{d} issuing from the fairs held in the feast of St. Peter in

[671] The abbreviation is definitely *cli* where normally is cleri or circuli. The word expected was *cla* for clausa although *clis* is clausulis; clausula meaning amongst other things a close, enclosure.
[672] *Gurgit'; gurgustium.*
[673] *Piscacon'.*
[674] *Libtat' admiral'.*

Chains with the farm of one parcel of land called the Upper Grene [demised[675]] Ady Fould by indenture to be paid at the feast of the annunciation of the Blessed Virgin Mary now in the tenure of the said [mayor and commonalty[676]] of the town aforesaid And of xvj^{s} viij^{d} of market rents of one fair held there of the new co[rporation[677]] by the jurisdiction of the late Henry VIII in the feast of St. Valentine.

Total iiij$^{£}$

m. 15v

Pensions issuing from the demesne of the abbots court.
And of xL^{s} viij^{d} lately coming from certain annual pensions of the demesne of A[bbots Court[678]] late of the lord King owed in the name of tenths and tenth part of the same demesne in letters patent made to Thomas [Cheyney[679]] knight reserved this year not received And that the Lord King the late Henry the VIIIth by his letters patent dated [xth] day of September in the xxviijth year of his majesties reign amongst other things gave granted and pardoned Thomas Cheyney knight of the said annual tenths of the manor aforesaid from the feast of Saint Michael last past for ever just as in the same letters Patent is manifest.

Received later in the account of John Wylde made of the office of receiver of the late monastery of Faversham aforesaid.

SUM TOTAL of the receipts aforesaid Lxviij$^{£}$ xix^{s} ob. Of which is allocated to him ij^{s} for the stipend of the clerk of the audit for writing this account and all parcels of the same together with buy paper and parchment for this same writing and engrossing this year just as other auditors of the said lord king have received ij^{s}

And owes Lxviij$^{£}$ xvij^{s} ob. To be exonerated this from this account because charged upon the same account in the account made of the office of Receiver of Faversham this year as later in the same account is manifest.

And so quit.

Office of Forester
The account of Thomas Arden farmer and forester there for the said time. Nothing because the first after the establishment of the Court of Augmentations and Revenues.

Total nothing

Farm of Woods
But received the account of xxij$^{£}$ of the farm of all the wood there called Faversham Blene otherwise Boughton Blene in the county of Kent with the land with foundation[680] land and earth to the same wood containing by estimation one thousand and one hundred acres belonging to the said late monastery Excepting nonetheless one thousand and two hundred oaks growing in the said wood aged xL iiij^{XX} of which certain oaks forty oaks[681] of the same are valued at viij^{d} and

675 This word lost.
676 These words lost.
677 This word lost.
678 This word lost.
679 This word lost.
680 *Ac terram fund et sol ipius bosc.*
681 *Quare.*

any trees of eighty oaks[682] valued at viij^{d}. And excepting all wood growing in the aforesaid wood being above 20 years growth demised to the aforesaid Thomas Arden Esquire by indenture dated viijth day of October in the xxxvijth years of the reign of King Henry the VIIIth From the feast of St. Michael the Archangel now last past to the end of xxj years rendering in respect thereof yearly xxij$^{£}$ sterling at the feast of the annunciation of the Blessed Virgin Mary and St. Michael the Archangel equally by the year just as in the same indenture it shall full appear.

Total xxij$^{£}$

Rents called Woodleys Money
And of xix^{s} iij^{d} quarter of rents of diverse tenements of the Lord King in the forest aforesaid called Woodles money this year from the acknowledgement of the accountants

Total xix^{s} iiij^{d}

Total of him aforesaid xxij$^{£}$ xix^{s} iiij^{d} quarter of which to be allowed to him Lx s for the fee of George Sentleger principal forester there at Lx^{s} the year to him granted to him during the term of his life by letters patent under the seal of the convent of the late monastery of Faversham dated the xvth day of March in the xxviijth years of the reign of our late sovereign Lord king Henry the VIIIth by order of Edward Northe knight chancellor of the Court of Augmentations and revenues under a deed for allowing this same fee, that is to say, in allowance to the same for one whole year finishing at the birth of our Lord in the xxxviijth year of our late sovereign Lord King Henry the VIIIth by force of the said writing

Received in the account of John Wylde receiver of this same late monastery just as below is manifest.

And owes xix$^{£}$ xix^{s} iiij^{d} quarter Exonerated this by this account by which charged upon John Wylde made of his office of receiver of the late monastery just as in the same account below appears.

And so is quit

m. 16

Office of Receiver General of the said late Monastery of Feversham
Account of John Wylde receiver general of all and singular the demesne manors lands and tenements together with all other the possessions which pertained to the said late monastery or which in anyway belong, that is to say, from the Feast of St. Michael the Archangel in the xxviijth year of the reign of King Henry the VIIIth as far as the feast of St. Michael then next following in the first year of the now Lord King Edward the Sixth for one whole year just as follows:

Arrears
None because the first account after the establishment of the Court of Augmentations and Revenues.

Total Nil.

Office of Collector of rents of the town of Feversham
But received of the accountant of xxiiij$^{£}$ vij^{s} j^{d} ob. quarter by the same receiver within the time of this account of Robert Coldwell bailiff there of the issues of his same office as appears by account of this same year.

---

[682] *Quarcum.*

Total xxiiij$^{£}$ vij^{s} j^{d} ob. quarter

Office of Chamberlain of the town of Feversham aforesaid.
And of iiij$^{£}$ by the same received in the time of this account of the mayor and commonalty of the said town of the issues of the Chamberlain this year just as appears by his account of the same year.

Total iiij$^{£}$

Hundred of Feversham
And of xLvj$^{£}$ v^{s} vj^{d} quarter by the said receiver received of his own account collected there of the issues of his office this year just as his account of the same year appears.

Total xLvj$^{£}$ v^{s} vj^{d} quarter.

Office of collector of diverse farms
And of Lxviiij $^{£}$ xvij^{s} ob. received of his own account collected there of the issues of the same this year just as appears by his account of the same year

Total Lxviiij$^{£}$ xvij^{s} ob.

Office of Forester of the Bleane
And of xix$^{£}$ xix^{s} iiij^{d} quarter by him received of Thomas Arden farmer and forester of the issues of the same this year just as appears in his account of the same year.

Total xix$^{£}$ xix^{s} iiij^{d} quarter

Foreign Receipts
And of vj$^{£}$ by the said accountant received of the mayor and commonalty of the town of Feversham towards the payment of the fee of William Roper Esquire steward of the possessions of the late monastery To have a fee of viij$^{£}$ vj^{s} viiij^{d} by the year in respect thereof to be supported by the said mayor and commonalty vj$^{£}$ and by the Lord king xLvj^{s} viij^{d} from the covenant made with him by the office of the Lord King by the acknowledgement and declaration of this accountant which said sum vj$^{£}$ of the said accountant consented to be charged and the same to be charged during the life of the said William Roper and no more because the said fee of viij$^{£}$ vj^{s} viij^{d} totally afterwards allocated from the possessions of the lord King from this late monastery

Total vj$^{£}$

Sum total of the receiver aforesaid CLxix$^{£}$ ix^{s} ob. quarter

Of Which
Fees and wages
The same accountant in fee of the account as receiver general of all and singular the revenues of the same late monastery has taken possession by jurisdiction of his office exercised and occupied at iiij$^{£}$ xiij^{s} iiij^{d} by the year, that is to say, in allowance to the same for the whole year within the time of this account by force of letters patent made to Simon Auncelme dated the penultimate day of August in the xxvjth year of the reign of our late sovereign Henry the VIIIth so to him granted just as in the same letters patent appears iiij$^{£}$ xiij^{s} iiij^{d} And in fee William Roper steward and [lost] revenues to the same late monastery by decree of the Court of Augmentations and Revenues of the crown of the lord King, that is to say, in [lost] this year as in the preceding viij$^{£}$ vj^{s} viij^{d} And in stipend to the clerk of the audit to writing this [lost] and all parcels to the same this year just as other audits have had and previously received ij^{s} And in fee [lost] audit of the said late monastery at Lxvj^{s} viij^{d} by the year this year nothing because nothing paid.

Total xiij$^{£}$ ij^{s}

m. 16v

Handing over of money received for the receiver of the court of Revenues.
And in money by the said accountant handed over to Anthony Aucher knight receiver of the lord Kings court of his Augmentations and Revenue by his proper hands that is to say the vij day of May in the first year of our sovereign Lord King Edward the Sixth xx$^{£}$, the said day and year xxxiiij$^{£}$ xv^{s} iiij^{d} ob. and the ninth day of November in the same year iiij^{XX} x$^{£}$ xj^{s} jxd quarter, that is to say xxj^{s} ij^{d} ob. for a tenth of Negdonmershe by this year because by the hand of Thomas Arden farmer of the forest of the Bleane that is to say the iiijth day of June in the first year the aforesaid King xj$^{£}$ in total as appears in diverse bills of the said receiver signed and be quit CLvj$^{£}$ vij^{s} ob. quarter

Total CLvj$^{£}$ vij$^{£}$ ob. quarter.

Sum of all the allowances and payments aforesaid CLxix$^{£}$ jx^{s} ob. quarter which certain sum is coequal with the sum of the total received aforesaid And so is quit.

MINISTERS ACCOUNTS PRO: SC6/EDWARD VI/723

Feast of St. Michael the Archangel 1 Edward VI [29 September 1547] to the Feast of St. Michael the Archangel 2 Edward VI [1548]

m. 1v

Receipts of the money rents and farms in the county of Kent

Feversham:
And of CxLix$^{£}$ xj^{d} ob. by him received of Thomas Arden receiver particularly of all the possessions of the late Monastery of Feversham aforesaid issuing from his office this same year just as by the account of the said Thomas Arden of the same year.

m. 23v

Feversham:

And in an annuity or fee of Thomas Hawkyns to vij$^{£}$ by the year by the Lord King by his letters patent out of the Rectory of Boughton granted by the said late priory to have to the aforesaid Thomas and his assigns for the term of twenty one years and for this year of his term Paid at the usual feasts by equal portions that is to say in the same allowance for ij years to the feast of St. Michael in the second year as by acquittance xiiij$^{£}$

Margin: not allowed further until they have seen the letters patent for the term of years in the same specified.

And in annuity to Thomas Persey of xxx^{s} by the year from the prior and convent of the same late priory under their great seal aforesaid Thomas and his assigns granted for the term of his life each year at the feast of the annunciation and Michaelmas to be paid equally, that is to say, in allowance for one year and a half to the feast of the annunciation of the Blessed Virgin Mary within the time of this account as by aquittance xLv^{s}

And in the fee of Joseph Beverley auditor of the said late monastery at Lxvj^{s} viij^{d} by the year granted to him for the term of his life by decree of the chancellor and council of the Court of Augmentations and revenues of the crown of the said Lord King, that is to say, in allowance for the same for two years at the feast of St. Michael in the second year as was allowed in the ministers accounts for the xxxviijth year of the reign of our late sovereign Henry VIII. vj$^{£}$ xiij^{s} iiij^{d}.

And in the pension of Peter Minton at Lxvj^{s} viij^{d} by the year, Ralph Poste at iiij$^{£}$ per year to him and to each of them by letters patent under the seal of the Court of Augmentations and revenues of the crown of the Lord King during their lives. To be paid at the feasts of the annunciation of the Blessed Virgin Mary and St. Michael the Archangel equally, that is to say in this allowance for one whole year within the time of this account as by his acquitance vij$^{£}$ vj^{s} viij^{d}

And in pension of Dunstan Goodhewe at iiij$^{£}$ per year, Thomas Dewe at C^{s} per annum to them by councils[683] letters patent granted during their lives. To be paid at the said feasts of annunciation and Michael; that is to say in allowance to this same for half a year to the feast of the annunciation of the Blessed Virgin Mary in the time of this account as by his acquitance iiij$^{£}$ x^{s}

m. 24

And in money from the said accountant paid to the vicar of Hernehill for his pension issuing out of the marsh called Goremershe at xiij^{s} iiij^{d} per year that is to say in this same allowance for half a year to the feast of the annunciation Blessed Virgin Mary in the time of this account as by acquitance vj^{s} viij^{d}

And in money paid to Valentine Norton Anne Brente widow Clement Norton and William Norton for a third part of an annuity issuing out of a third part of the manor of Ewell at xxij^{s} ij^{d} ob. by the year that is to say in this allowance for two years at the feast of St. Michael in the second year of our now lord King just as was respited in the account of John Wilde bailiff of the possessions of the late Monastery of Faversham in the xxxviijth year of the late King Henry VIIIth by the power of the letters of the chancellor and council of the Court of Augmentations dated the xxixth day of June in the second year of the reign of our said sovereign Lord King Edward the Sixth by this same allowance ordered in respect of the said xliiij^{s} vd

And in money of the said account of issues of his same office this year paid to the archdeacon of Canterbury for procurations and synodals of the church of Boughton under the Blean Hernehill and Preston next Faversham appropriated of the said late Priory of Faversham by xxvj^{s} viij^{d} by the year by decree granted out of the court of the lord king Augmentations that is to say in allowance this same for 2 years at the feast St. Michael the Archangel in the second year as by acquit liij^{s} iiij^{d}

sum xxxix$^{£}$ xix^{s} vd

❖ ❖ ❖ ❖ ❖

LR 6/113/1 MEMBRANE 1v

St. Michael the Archangel 2 Edward VI [29 September 1548] to St. Michael the Archangel 3 Edward VI [1549]

---

683 Latin: *consiles*.

Receipts of the money issuing out of the mannors, rents and farm in the county of Kent

Feversham:
And of CLj$^{£}$ iij^{s} vj^{d} ob received of Thomas Ardern receiver of parcels[684] which were late the possessions of the late Monastery of Feversham aforesaid of his issues of office to him this year as by his account of the same year.

m. 8v.

Margin: Receipts of disme and annual rents reserved upon grants and letters patent of the Lord King in the said county of Kent.

Late Monastery of Faversham,
And of xxv^{s} for the same received of Anthony St. Leger for tithe of the manor of Estekingsnothe and also lands and tenements in Southwarke parcel of the revenues of the said late monastery. And for lands called Tonge parcel of the lands and possessions late of the house of Crutched Friars of Modendyne[685] to xxv^{s} by the year, that is to say, in answer for the same for the time aforesaid.

And of v^{s} for the same received of Thomas Arden gentleman for the annual reserved rent by the name of disme[686] of diverse messuages with gardens and stables and other their appurtenances in the town of Feversham and also of one messuage and one garden with dovecote in the same garden next Amerye Croft to v^{s} by the year, that is to say, in answer for the same within the time of this account.

And of ij^{s} iiij^{d} for the same received of the said Thomas Arden for disme of one tenement called the Bere in the town of Feversham at ij^{s} iiij^{d}, that is to say, in answer for the same this year.

And of xiiij^{s} viij^{d} ob. for the same received of the same Thomas Arden for disme of the manor of Elvenden to xiiij^{s} viij^{d} ob. by the year, that is to say, in answer for the same this year.

And of iij^{s} ix^{d} ob. for same received of same Thomas Arden for disme of certain lands in Hernehill to iij^{s} ix^{d} ob. by the year, that is to say,in answer for the same this year as above.

And of xxiiij^{s} vij^{d} of the same Thomas Arden for disme of the manor of Lambesland with other things at xxiiij^{s} vij^{d}, that is to say, in answer for the same this year as above.

continues with:
Payment of xxx^{s} viij^{d} by John Baker for lands in parish Brokeland and Frittendon;
William Saunders and Henry Crips Esq. xix^{s} iiij^{d} lands called Gormershe,
Thomas Cheyne, Lord Warden xxj^{s} ij^{d} ob. for disme scite with demesne land of the late Monastery of Feversham and also one marsh called Negdon Marshe,

Total vij$^{£}$ xvj^{s} vij^{d} ob.

---

684 Latin: *particule*.
685 Mottenden, approx. 11 m. North West of Ashford; St. Leger belonged to the family of that name of Leeds in Kent.
686 *O.E.D.* Disme: Besides its historical use in the senses 'tenth' and 'tithe', it is used, in the earliest English book on the subject (1608) for 'Decimal arithmetic.'

Section of map of Kent by John Speed, 1611 taken from *Theatre of the Empire of Great Britain*. (Most probably based on Symonson's map of 1596.)

APPENDIX 14
Thomas Arden as Mayor.

FAVERSHAM WARDMOTE BOOK FA/AC1

Feversham[687]

Margin: A controler Maior[688]

Thomas Arderne chyff countroller of the kynges maiestyes custome here was chosen mayour the xxvj daye of Marche in the ij^{de} yere of the reigne of our sovereigne Lorde Edward the vjth [26 March 1548[689]] by the grace of God kyng of Englonde Fraunce and Irelonde defendour of the feith and in yerth the supreme hede of the churches of Englonde and also of Yrelonde to contynue from that daye unto the last day of September then next folowyng

Names of the Jurates

Rycharde Drylonde, Thomas Dunkyn, Wylliam Castlok, Wylliam Marshall, John Seathe, Thomas Gates, John Best, Lewes Marden, John Drylonde, Robert Coldwell, Stephyn Mott, John Wreke

The names of the xxiiij^{ti}, that is to say, xij chosen by the mayour and jurates and xij by the comons

By the mayour and jurates: Nicholas Burwasshe, Wylliam Wyer, John Pullen, John Snothe, Henry Phylpott, Rauf Deacon, Edmond Vessey, Adam Fowle, John Stransham, Robert Bergrove, Wylliam Nele, Thomas Goreham

By the comons: John Drylonde, Thomas Stransham, Rychard Johnson, Antony Love, Wylliam Maycott, George Stransham, Thomas Oldfeld, John Gylle, John Johnson, John Castlok, Edward Coke, Wylliam Phynner

Churchewardens:
John Wreke, Thomas Stransham, John Pullen, Thomas Goreham

Chamberleyns:
Frances Swanne, Thomas Oldfeld

The names of Fremen made within the seyd tyme

Thomas Adryan	[*blank*]	
Robert Braban	vj^{s} viij^{d}	
John Greneleff	iij^{s} iiij^{d}	
Garard Arnold	~~xiij^{s} iiij^{d}~~	vacat
Rychard Rede	iij^{s} iiij^{d}	
Thomas Mustard	iij^{s} iiij^{d}	
Thomas Norton	vj^{s} viij^{d}	
Thomas Dey	iij^{s} iiij^{d}	

The Porters[690]
Thomas Parys, Lawrens Fynner

---

[687] fol. 47. I am very grateful to Mrs Diane Davidson for providing prints from the Wardmote microfilm made for her in 1965.
[688] Added in a later hand. It is possible that the rest of this page is in the handwriting of Thomas Arden. See text page 68.
[689] 1549 has erroneously been added in a later hand.
[690] fol. 47v

ffaversham

Thomas Ardernne Esquyer Comtroller of the kyngs maiestyes Custome here was chosen Mayor the xxv^th daye of marche in the iij^de yere of the Reygne of oure Soveraigne Lorde Edwarde the vj^th by the grace of god kyng of englonde ffraunce and Irelonde defender of the ffaith and in erth the supreme hede of the Churche of Englonde and also of Irelonde to contynue from that daye unto the last daye of September than next folowyng 1549 17

The names of the Jurate

Rycharde Drylonde
Wyllm Castlok
John Seathe
John Best
John Drylonde
Stephyn Motte

Thomas Dunkyn
Wyllm Marshall
Thomas gatis
Lewes marden
Robt Coldwell
John Wreke

The names of the xxiiij^ti Or comen chosen by the Mayor and Jurate and xij by the Comons

By the Mayor and Jurate

Nycholas Everyngsshe
Wyllm Roper
John Pullen
John Snothe
henry phylpott
Raufe Deacon
Edmonde Wesley
Adam ffowle
John Stransham
Robt Ferymore
Wyllm Nele
Thomas Gorham

By the Comons

John Drylonde
Thomas Stransham
Rycharde Johnson
Antony Love
Wyllm Marcott
George Stransham
Thomas Oldfelde
John gylle
John Johnson
John Castlok
Edwarde Coke
Wyllm phynner

Churchewardens

John Wreke
Thomas Stransham
John Pullen
Thomas Gorham

Chamberleyns

ffrances Elwaye
Thomas Oldfelde

The names of the ffremen made wtin the seyd tyme

Thomas Ardern — [illegible]
John Greneleff — [illegible]
Rycharde Tode — [illegible]
Thomas Norton — [illegible]

Robt Braban — [illegible]
Gerard Arnold — [illegible]
Thomas Stafford — [illegible]
Thomas Dey — [illegible]

Faversham Wardmote Volume 1 [Fa/AC1] folio 47 showing the first page when Thomas Arden became Mayor

The sealers and serchers of lether
John Johnson, Edward Coke

The serchers of flesshe
Nycolas Burwasshe, Gylbert Bredshawe

The comon metar of corne
[blank] Fordred

Memorandum the xvijth daye of June in the year aforesaid[691] sold to John Wreke with the consent of the whole towne at a warmouth holden at the courte halle then and there CCC quarters[692] xxij pounds of olde laten candelstykkes[693] at xxiiij^{s} viij^{d} the C summe iiij$^{£}$ iij^{s} x^{d} Wherof he payed in the presence of the towne ther iij$^{£}$ xij^{d} which seyd iij$^{£}$ xij^{d} was delyvered to paye for the peyntyng of the rodeloft and the scriptures upon the same and for the scripture in the Northe ele And so the seyd Wreke owyth to the towne xxij^{s} x^{d} which he ys bounde to paye to the thuse of the towne thys tyme twelvemoneth

In a later hand: Thys summe of xxij^{s} x^{d} was acountyd in hys acompt at the awdytt of the churche wardyns and dyschargyd of thys boke and quytt

The churchewardens,
John Wrewke, Thomas Stransam, John Pullen, Thomas Goreham

Feversham,
Margin: The recognizance of Master John Seathe for a pyxe to the towne

In the year 1548, Sunday , that is to say, 2nd day of September[694]

Memorandum that the second day of September in the second year of the reign of Edward the sixth by the grace of God of England France and Ireland King, defendor of the faith and on earth supreme head of the church of England and Ireland came John Sethe before Thomas Arderne mayor there and acknowledged he owed the aforesaid Mayor, jurats and commonalty of the town of Feversham forty pounds to be paid to the aforesaid mayor, jurats and commonalty at the feast of St. Michael the Archangel next coming and so forth and justly and so forth.

The condytion of thys recognysanse ys such that whre varyanses and sute hathe ben made for and concernyng a certeyn pyxe of sylver that yf the seyde John Sethe hys executors or assygnes delyver or cause to be delyver to the mayer jurattes and comminalte of the seyde towne to the use of the seyde pyxe or the verey true value ther of by hym to be browthe and wayde in the presense of vj of the seyde comminalte before the feast of Saynt Michell the Archangell whyche shall be in the yere of our lorde God a thowsand fyve hundreth and fyftey that then thys recognysanse to be voyde otherwyse the seyde summe of fortey poundes to be leyvyd of his goods and cattelles and so forth

(*signature*) be me John Seth

---

691 *Anno predicto*.

692 Normally a measure for grain, but it appears that one quarter weighs 4 hundred weight.

693 Presumably taken out of the parish church under the royal injunctions of Edward VI (1547) see Alcuin Club Collections XV *Visitation Artictles and Injunctions of the period of the reformation Volume II 1536-1558* by Walter Howard Frere and William McClure Kennedy (1910)

694 *Anno 1548 die dominica videlicet 2° die Septembris. Memorandum quod secundo die Septembris Anno regni domini Edwardi sexti dei gratiae Anglie et hibernie regis fidei defensoris et in terra ecclie Anglicane et Hibernice suprimi capitis secondo venit Johannes Sethe coram Thomas Ardern maiore ibidem et cognovit se debere prefato maiori jurates et comminiti de ville de Feversham quadraginta libras solvendis prefato maiori jurates et comminati in festo sancti Michaelis archiangeli proxime futuro et cetera et juste et cetera.*

Faversham Wardmote Volume 1 [Fa/AC1] folio 47v showing the second page when Thomas Arden became Mayor

[*in another hand*] This pixe brought in to the churche of Feversham by Master Thomas Fynch churchwarden which wase sold by the holl consent of the towne men

Statutes for making of Lawes within the towne of Faversham

In the 2nd year Edward VIth 1548 by the true hand of Thomas Ardern. then mayor.[695]

Margin: **The warmouth to be holden by the maiour and jurates onley**

FYRST it is ordered agreed and established by the mayer jurates and commonaltie of this towne of Faversham that to the makyng of lawes and statutes or other causes at the warmouth from hensforth none shalbe called but the mayer jurates and xxiiij except they be called thether by the mayor for speciall causes which the mayer shall open and alwayes declare to the said jurates and xxiiij before any other of the commonaltye shall come whiche xxiiij, xij to be chosen by the mayer and his brethern and the other xij by the freemen of the same as it is nowe conteyned in this great boke of the said mayer and commonaltie

Margin: **For fynes of lands purchased**

AND yt is ferther decreed, established, and ordered, that if any persone levye any fyne of any landes houses or tenementes within the towne that then there shalbe paid after the rate of every pounde, that the house or landes, whereof the fyne shalbe levyed shalbe worthe by year the tyme of the said fyne levyed ij^{s} $iiij^{d}$ the summ to be levyed of the tenant of the lande by distresse

Margin: **For the common caryour**

ITEM yt is ferther established, ordered and decreed, for ever that immediatly after the publisshing hereof that one shalbe especially by the whole assent and consent of the said towne named to be a commen caryer and a voyder of all the myre, doung and other contagious fylthes, and refuse within every strete of the said towne or their liberties, (stabledoung, and other refuse as of the lome and other thinges of the buldinges and pullyng downe of olde housses,) onely excepted Whiche said office and officer of commen caryer shalbe datif[696] and removable at the pleasure of the said Mayer jurates and comynaltie The same dounge myre fylthe and refuse to be layd by the said caryer at suche place as the said mayer and iij of the jurates shall appoynt, so the same place where the same shalbe laid do not excede half one mile out of the towne and to be caryed twyse in every weke

Margin: **For the clerkes wages**

And where as there hath bene, tyme whereof no mannys mynde hath bene to the contrarye two clerkes whiche have hadd at the equall charges of the towne $iiij^{£}$ every of theym of whiche $viij^{£}$ hath bene recowped and taken toward the fynding of one sexten $xxvj^{s}$ $viij^{d}$ for as moche as thise paymentes hath growen in consideration of such great travayll as the clerkes heretofore susteyned in the execution of their office whiche traveilles, for asmoche as they be decreased and [697] dymynisshed, so the inhabitauntes of the said towne having respect therunto have thought it mete to abate not onlely the clerkes wages but the number of clerkes And yet not mynding to have the same sommes so abated to be extincted and discharged but to remayne to good uses as the same

695 fol. 48. *In the margin* Anno 1548 manuo vero Edwardi vj^{to} ij^{o} temporare [tpe] Thome Ardern maioris.

696 Dative, *Law of an officer*; appointed so as to be removable at pleasure.

697 At this point interlined in a different hand: gods honor ?duynisshed.

did before conclude, establish and agree, that it shalbe ordeyned, and decreed, in manner and forme folowyng, That is to saye, that there shalbe no moo clerkes then one, within the said parisshe churche, And that the same clerk shall have for his wages yerely Liij^{s} iiij^{d} and that also there shalbe a sexten within the said parisshe which said sexten shall yerely have for his wages xxvj^{s} viij^{d} and the other iiij$^{£}$ sterling shall yerly for ever be paid to and for the wages of the comon caryer before rehersed And every parisshioner to paye and make contribution for the payment of the said viij$^{£}$ so appoynted, to and for the payment of the parisshe clerk, sexten and carter in lyke[698] forme and after suche severall portions as here tofore they have or any of theym have paid and bene assessed or taxed when they hadd ij clerkes and that it shalbe laufull for the mayer for the tyme beyng to commytt to warde every suche persone refusing to paye to the same as they have done before there to remayne, till they have paid ytt

An Act for pavyng of Westrete, Preston Strete and the Key Lane within the foresaid towne of Faversham.

AND yt is further by us the mayer jurates and commonaltye ordered that from hensforth for ever that the strette called Westrete shalbe paved on both sydes from West Broke Crosse to a tenement of Godleve Prynchett wedowe in Eastreate And from the Maypole in Preston strete unto Hogcrossewell And also be it enacted, that keylane shalbe paved on both sydes for ever at the charges of thise persones ensuyng, that is to say, at the costes of the lessee for the yeres the bredeth of his house, and so from thens unto the myddell chanell, if so be his interest and terme, be above xxx^{ti} yeres And if the terme be not so moche then at the charges of the owner of the freehold of the same house the bredeth of his house and from his house unto the myddell chanell The said pavyng to be done and fynysshed as abovesaid before the feaste of A Sayntes whiche shalbe in the yere of our Lorde God M^{l}DLj [1 November 1551] And if any of the said houses or that the said lane be not paved before the tyme above lymyted that then the partey that ought as above is sayd to pave the same shall not receyve any ferme or rent of his said house of the tenaunt dwelling therin notwithstonding any lease or wryting or other bonde But itt shalbe laufull for the mayor and commonaltie of the said towne and their successors to receive and levye the yerely profitt or ferme of the same house And if the owner shall inhabite the house himself that lykewyse he shall forfeyt the usuall ferme of the said house to the said mayor and commonaltye, to be levyed by way of distresse

An act for hogges and swyne

AND ferthermore it is ordeyned and established by the said mayor and jurates and commonltie that if any hogges or swyne do go a brode in any strete within the towne of Faversham or the liberties of the same out of the owners close, the same not havyng the proper marke of the owner whereby the said hogges or swyne may be knowen that what so ever persone or persones as shall or will dryve away the same hogges swyne or pygges not beyng folowed by the owner or owners their servaunt or servauntes shall have and enjoye the same to his owne propre use and behove without any contradiction of the owner or owners for the same And that suche owner or owners shalbe without any remedye or recoverye agaynst the taker or takers dryver or dryvers of suche hogges swyne or pygges and without any recompence for the same or any of theym

Another act conservyng the premisses

AND[699] ferder we ordeyne and decree that if any hogges or syne havyng the marke of the owner do go a brode in the said stretes or at the key, or the vacaunt grounde aboute the same, in

---

[698] fol. 48v.

[699] fol. 49.

orchardes pastures feldes or gardeyns within the same towne and libertie that then the owner and owners of all suche hogges and swyne shall loose and forfeyt to him or theym that will impounde and dryve theym a waye for every hogg or swyne viij^{d} And if any owners or owners of suche hogges or swyne happen to be obsynate and will nott paye the said forfeyte to the takes or dryvers of the said hogges or swyne That then upon compleynt made unto the mayer of the said towne for the tyme beyng the said mayer to take spedye order that the same takers and dryvers of suche hogges and swyne may be dyrectly aunswered of the forfeytures and penalties contened and mensioned within this estatute PROVIDED alwayes and it is also decreed and ordeyned by the said mayor jurates and comonaltie that the mayor for the tyme beyng shall have full power and aucthorytie to commaunde the porters of the said towne of faversham to dryve hogges and swyne to the pounde at all tymes whan nede shall requyre, for the ~~spedy and~~ better and spedy reformation of the runnyng a brode of the said hogges and swyne The said porters to have for their labours the lyke forfeytures as other takers ought to have by vertue of this act AND it is ordeyned by the assent a foresaid that if any porter happen to be obstynate and will not accomplisshe the said mayours commaundement That then it shalbe laufull to the said mayour to commytt suche porter or porters to warde or prysone, there to remayne without bayll or maympryse during the said mayours pleasure PROVYDED also and it is also agreed by the assent a foresaid that if any persone or persones fynding any hogges or swyne beyng marked in hys ortchard gardyn or pasture calling to him ij honest witnesses to testifie their beyng in the said ortchard gardyn or pasture ytt shalbe laufull to suche persone and persones fynding theymselfes greved in the cases before expressed to complayne to the mayour for the tyme being and yt shalbe laufull to the said mayour to sende for the owner or owners of suche hogges or swyne and to demaunde of theym the foresaid forfeytour and penalyties before said And uppon the refusall therof of the payment therof, the said mayour to have full pouer and aucthorytie to commytt suche offendour and offendours to warde there to remayne till the said complaynaunt be fully aunswered and paid This act to take effect at Mighelmas next commyng and not before.

An act for Orphans goodes

AND further we ordeyn and decree that when landes and tenementes shall discend to any orphane not beyng appoynted to any gardeyn by his father or other auncestours by whome the said landes or tenementes so discende, that the same orphane shalbe assigned by us the mayour and jurates and our successours, to suche gardeyns beyng ffreemen within the said towne of Faversham as we shall thinke mete and convenyent whiche gardeyns so assigned shall not have any title to the landes tenementes reverciones and heredytamentes discended to the same infaunt And lykewyse shall have delyvered theym or him whiche shalbe so assigned all the goodes and catalles whiche belong and apperteyn to the same infaunte to the use of the same infaunte And further he or they so assigned shalbe bounde to the mayour and jurates for the tyme beyng uppon the recept of the said landes and goodes that they shall when the enfaunt commeth to laufull age make a true accompt to the said enfaunte of suche profettes of the said landes tenementes and heredytamentes[700] of the said enfaunte wherewith he shalbe charged deductyng the necessarye charges of the said enfaunte during the tyme he remayned in keping of the same accomptant And further shall delyver the same landes unwasted to the said enfaunte and satysfye suche sommes of money as shall apperyer to remayn to be due to the said enfaunt of the said profttes and further shall delyver all the goodes and catall whiche belonged to the said enfaunte and accompte to hym for the encrease of the same goodes (if the goodes were suche wherof the encrease myght growe) And also to paye aunswere and satisfye the said encrease to the said infaunte at his laufull age of xxj yeres AND IT IS ferther agreed by the said mayour jurates and comonaltie that if any goodes

[700] fol. 49v.

or catalles be gevyn or bequethed to any infaunte within the age of xviij yeres or that he or they whoo shall receyve and kepe the said goodes or catalles to the use of any suche infaunte shall immediatly aftyer the recept of the same goodes be bounde to the mayour jurates and comonaltie with sufficient suertie that all the same goodes and catalles or the true value of theym shalbe delyvered to the said infaunte at his full aege or elles att the tyme appoynted by the gever of the said goodes or at the tyme of maryage AND yf the executour or executours administratour or any other to whose possession any suche goodes or catalles shall happen to come to the use of any suche infaunte shall refuse to putt in suche safe suertye for the safe delyverye of the said goodes according to this act That then it shalbe laufull for the mayer and jurates to take the said goodes in their handes to remayne in the treasurye house of the said towne to the use of the said infaunte or to whome suche goodes by the order of the lawe shuld perteyn unto, if the said infaunte shall happen to dye before the delyvery of the said goodes AND FERTHER yt is agredd and establisshed by the said mayour jurates and comonaltye that if the mayour for the tyme beyng shall nott cause the foresaides actes and ordynaunces (or as many of theym as shalbe then nedefull) to be redd openly at every lawdaye to be holden within the said towne to the intent the same actes may the better be hadd in execution according to the tenour of the same[701] uppon payne that the mayour for the tyme beyng shall forfeyte to the use of the said towne vj^{s} viij^{d} for evrey tyme omyttyng the same whiche vj^{s} viij^{d} shalbe defalked and a bated of the fee of the said mayour

[signatures]

per me Thomam Ardern Maiorem
by me Stephyn Mott
per me Rob[er]t Coldwell
M Wyll[ia]m Marshalles marke
per me Wylly[a]m Castloke
Be[702] me Thomas Oldfyld
By me Adam Fowlle
By me John Stransham
per me Will[ia]m Maycot
per me Johannem Castlocke
By me John Dryland
By me Anthony Love
M Wyll[ia]m Wyers marke

by me Ryc[hard] Dryland
per me Joh[ann]em Dryland
be me John Best
be me John Seth
by me John Wrewke
|—|O Thomas Gorh[a]ms marke
∴ John Gylles marke
John Polyn
X John Johnsons marke
X Edward Cokes marke
Nycholas Burwasshe marke X
Edmund Vessy
X Robart Bargars marke

Feversham[703]

The accomptes of Frauncys Swanne and Thomas Oldfeld chamberlayns ther from the fest of Sainte Michaell the archaungell in the first yere of the reigne of our sovereigne Lord Edward the sixt to the sayd fest of Saynt Michaell the archaungell then next ensuyng beyng the second yere of the reigne of our sovereigne Lord Edward the sixt by the grace of God King of ingland Fraunce and Ireland defendour of the faith and of the cherch of Ingland and allso of Ireland in earthe the supreme hedde made the xxvth day of October in the said second yere in the presence of John Seath and John Driland the elder jurates and William Meycott and Anthony Love audytours there.[704]

701 *Margin*: that the necessary actes should be ...?.... published att the laweday ... yerely.
702 fol. 50.
703 fol. 50v.
704 *Margin*; Best mayer.

First the chamberlayns charge them selffes for there first roll of [strettes]	iiij$^{£}$ xiij^{d}
Item for ther second roll	xxviij^{s} viij^{d}
Item for ther roll of them that ar not free	xxxj^{s} iiij^{d}
Item for the fynes of the Fremen of Feversham this yere	xxvj^{s} viij^{d}
Item for the osage[705] and the markett	vj^{s} x^{d}
Item they charge them selffes for the recept of money of the iij brewers of the sayd towne	iiij$^{£}$
Item for the ferme of the toune houses the signe of the Shippe the Anker and Robyn Pypers house	iij$^{£}$
Item for the toune garden at Devyngton Hill	ij^{s}
Lammas Fayer	
Item they charge them selffes for the receptes of the said fayer	iij$^{£}$ iij^{s} iiij^{d}
Item for the fines of the porters of Feversham at Lammas fayre	xx^{s}
Item they charge them selffes for felons goods taken at Sturey[706]	vij^{s} iiij^{d}
Summe	xx$^{£}$ vij^{s} iij^{d}
Wherof they axe to be alowed as foloweth	
First alowed to Master Ardern for his fee of mayralty for his time	L^{s}
Item for the stewards fees	vj$^{£}$
Item for charges on Lammas night	xij^{s} xj^{d}
Item to the kinges players	vj^{s} viij^{d}
Item in charges carryng of iij felons to Cauntorbury	iij^{s} iiij^{d}
Item for lockes to the cage and stocks	xv^{d}
Item for the sheryffes turne[707]	ij^{d}
Item[708] payd to Master Ramsey and his clerk for councell and wryting certayne bokes for our toune	xlvj^{s} viij^{d}
Item payd to the serjeant for ryding to Sandwich for to sett the co[m]position	iij^{s} iiij^{d}
Item for charges in ~~th~~ mending the pounde in the toune as it appereth by a bill	ix^{s}
Item payd for the contribucion to Dovor	xL^{s}
Item payd for the charges of the mayour of Dovor and hys company at Feversham for ther dynners	x^{s} vj^{d}
Item payd to the serjeant for his ffee	xiij^{s} iiij^{d}
Item for charges layd out by Master Arden mayour aboute the necessaryes of the toune as yt appereth by hys bill	xxxvij^{s} viij^{d}

---

705 *O.E.D.* **osage**, obs. variant of usage.

706 Query Sturry near Canterbury.

707 Sheriff's Tourn. Richardson *op. cit.* L26: Twice a year, within a month after Easter and Michaelmas, the sheriff presided at a special session of the Hundred Court. His main function was to review the Frankpledge and to see the tithings were up to strength. He also dealt with minor criminal cases but the more serious offences were dealt with by the Justices in Eyre. After the Assize of Clarendon 1166 the sheriff had the power to oversee the manorial courts in their management of Frankpledge. The effective power of the Sheriff's Tourn came to an end in 1461 when the cases formerly presided over by the sheriff were transferred to the Justices of the Peace in Quarter Sessions. The Tourn was formally abolished in 1887.

708 fol. 51.

Item payd to Master Marden for writing the confessions of
certayn felons ij^{s}
Item to the serjeant for bording of the forsayd felons iij^{s} vj^{d}
Item alowed to certayn pore men of the toune for this time vij^{s}
Item the forsayd chamberlayns aske to be alowed for desperates[709] vij^{s}
Item for the ffees of the chamberlayns xiij^{s} iiij^{d}
Item for the dynners of the audytours and other accomptauntes xviij^{s}
Item for wryting of this accompt ij^{s}
Total[710] xx$^{£}$ vij^{s} viij^{d} quytt

The baylyffes accompt or charge
First the sayd baylyf chargeth himself for the receptes of nonsutes
mercyamentes and fynes in the courtes in the sayd toune iiij$^{£}$ xviij^{s} ij^{d}

Wherof he asketh to be alowed for hys fees xiij^{s} iiij^{d}
Item for the great enquest iij^{s} iiij^{d}
Item for the afferes xvj^{d}
Item for desperates vj^{s} viij^{d}
Item payd by hym to William Noke by the consent of the audytours xxij^{s} iiij^{d}
And so he oweth Lj^{s} ij^{d}
the whyche he payd and quytt

The accomptes of Master Dunkyn of Feversham
First the sayd Master Dunkyn chargeth hymself of and for the recept of xv$^{£}$ vj^{s} v^{d}
Whereof he asketh to be alowed for certayn necessaryes aboute the seling[711] of the courtehall new translatyng of the principal wyndows there and for glasing the wyndowes and clere storyes there and for clensing of the stretes and donghilles in the toune and for other necessaryes as it appereth by a byll of the said Thomas Dunkyn
By partyculers therof xv$^{£}$ vj^{s} quytt

The accomptes of William Marshall
First the sayd Wylliam chargeth hym self for the recept of viij$^{£}$ iiij^{s} ix^{d}
Wherof he asketh to be alowed for certayne necessary reparacions
aboute Cokesdeche of the foule way there and for other necessaryes
as yt appereth by his bill viij$^{£}$ iiij^{s} ix^{d} quytt

---

[709] *O.E.D.* Desperate debt; a 'bad' debt whose recovery is past hope.
[710] *Summa.*
[711] *O.E.D.* Ceiling: (1) The action of lining the roof or walls of an apartment with boards or (more rarely) plaster etc.

APPENDIX 15:
Inquisition post mortem of Margaret Ardys, 30 April 1575; and other relevant documents.

CKS: FAVERSHAM BOROUGH RECORDS
FA/JBF9 [THERE ARE 25 DOCUMENTS IN THIS BUNDLE]

Faversham,
This is the final agreement made in the court of our sovereign Elizabeth by the grace of God of England France and Ireland Queen, defender of the faith and held there the 9th day of January in the first year of the said sovereign Queen [1559] before John Best mayor of the town aforesaid, John Wreuke, Thomas Stransham, George Stransham and Thomas Norton jurats and other faithful people then there present Between Thomas Fynche gentleman Thomas Belke and Thomas Barton querens and John Bradborn and Margaret his wife daughter and heir of Thomas Ardern gentleman deceased deforciants of twenty four messuages one water mill one dovecote twenty four gardens two acres of land thirty six acres of meadow land and twenty acres of pasture with appurtenances in Faversham aforesaid that is to say that the aforesaid John Bradborn and Margaret his wife recognize the tenements aforesaid with appurtenances to be the right of the aforesaid Thomas Fynche gentleman And that which the same Thomas with Thomas Belke and Thomas Barton had of the gift and feoffment of the aforesaid John Bradbourne and Margaret his wife And that they have remised and quitclaimed it for themselves and the heirs of the aforesaid Thomas, Thomas and Thomas and the heirs of the aforesaid Thomas Fynch for ever To hold of the chief lord of the fee and so forth And the same John and Margaret have granted and for themselves and the heirs of the same Margaret that they will warrant to the aforesaid Thomas Fynche Thomas Belke and Thomas Barton and the heirs of the aforesaid Thomas Fynche the tenement aforesaid with appurtenances against all men for ever And for this recognizance remise quitclaim fine and agreement the aforesaid Thomas Fynche Thomas Belke and Thomas Barton have given to the aforesaid John Bradbourne and Margaret his wife one thousand marks by me Thomas Stransham

Faversham
This is the final agreement made in the Court of Portmote held on Monday, being xxviijth day of April the third year of the reign of our sovereign Lady Elizabeth [1561] by the grace of God, of England France and Ireland, Queen, defender of the faith and so forth. Before William Neale mayor of the town aforesaid, John Best, Thomas Straunsham, John Wreuke, Henry Fylpott and Robert Coldwell jurats there and other faithful people then there present Between Thomasine Norton plaintiff and John Bradbourne and Margaret his wife defendant of one messuage called a wellhowse and two shops[712] to the same adjacent with their appurtenances in Faversham aforesaid And is agreed such, that is to say, that the aforesaid John Bradborn and Margaret his wife have recognized the tenements aforesaid with the appurtenances to be the right of the aforesaid Thomasine Norton and that which the same Thomasine had of gift and feoffment of the aforesaid John Bradborn and Margaret his wife And that they have remised and quitclaimed it for themselves and the heirs of the aforesaid Thomasine and her heirs for ever To hold of the chief Lord of the fee and so forth And the same John and Margaret have granted and for themselves and the heirs of the same Margaret that they will warrant to the aforesaid Thomasine and her

[712] Latin: *shopis*

heirs the tenement aforesaid against all men for ever And by the recognizance remise quitclaim fine and agreement the aforesaid Thomasine has given the same John Bradborn and Margaret his wife fifty[713] pounds of legal money of England

By me Thomas Stransham deputy of William Roper esquire steward of the aforesaid court.

Faversham
This is the final agreement made in the court of our sovereign Queen Elizabeth by the grace of God of England France and Ireland Queen, defender of the faith and so forth held there the fourteenth day of September in the fourth year of our said sovereign Queen [1562] before Thomas Norton mayor of the town aforesaid, John Best, John Wreuke, William Neale, Thomas Oldfeilde and Henry Fyllpott jurats there and other faithful subjects of the sovereign Queen there present between Thomas Lyttyll plaintiff and John Bradborn and Margaret his wife daughter and heir of Thomas Ardern gentleman deceased of two tenements two gardens to the same adjoining together situated lying and being in the town and liberty of Faversham aforesaid in a certain street there commonly called Tannere Stryte that is to say to the street[714] aforesaid towards the East to the messuage of the said Thomas Lyttyll towards the South to the tenement of Robert Elfrythe towards the North and to the common water course running there towards the West ......And for this remise quitclaim fine and concord the same Thomas Lyttyll has given the aforesaid John Bradborn and Margaret his wife six pounds of legal money of England.

Faversham Borough Records
FA/CPw 32/1

William Brooke knight, Lord of Cobham, Constable for the sovereign Queen of her Castle of Dover, Warden of Dover chancellor and admiral of the Cinque Ports and their limbs, TO all and singular mayors bailiffs and jurats of the Cinque Ports and their limbs and to each of them Greeting Four writs of the sovereign Queen of her Exchequer at Westminster to us directed and lately received which certain writs with this our mandate annexed to you and each writ by the bearer present is sent to you to observe whatsoever to perform by virtue of which certain writs and by the authority of our office aforesaid to you all and singular on behalf of the said sovereign Queen and by our authority firmly imposed we command and order that immediately after receipt of this same writ and our mandate annexed all and singular in the same writ to be specified whether satisfied or informed against by means of and on the part of the writ to be assiduously performed and carried out within the tenor and effect of their same writ So that truth and justice may be returned in respect thereof to us or our deputy at the church of Saint James the Apostle of Dover under the seal of your office on Thursday that is to say the thirteenth day of January next coming to be sent back and at that time in the same place this our mandate with one of the writs aforesaid of our sovereign Queen as above annexed And this under penalty of one hundred pounds none now to be omitted nor anyone of the writs to omit Given at the Castle aforesaid under our seal of office there the twentieth day of the month of December in the seventeen year of the reign of our most serene highness Elizabeth now Queen of England [1574]

Elizabeth by the grace of God of England France and Ireland Queen, defender of the faith and so forth To the Constable of Dover Castle or to his Deputy there Greeting Because we wish that the Barons of our Exchequer to be informed of the true yearly value of two tenements at Cookes dyche one garden in the tenure of [blank] Baker in Preston Street one garden in the tenure of

[713] The scribe has erroneously written *quinquaquingua*.
[714] Latin *plateam*.

John Castlokes and also The Pillerye in the market place and the chapel of St. Nicholas with the fruit-gardens and lands and woods to the same chapel appertaining in Faversham in the county aforesaid of which Thomas Arderne until before his death was seized in his demesne as of fee we order you that you omit nothing on account of any liberty of that right of entry and then upon the oath of good and law-worthy men of your bailiwick and by all other ways and means by which better to know or be able assiduously to enquire into the premises So that enquiry in respect thereof held distinctly and openly received to be had before the aforesaid our barons in the term of Saint Hillary to be made thereby under your and their seals And to have there then this writ . Witness E. Saunders knight at Westminster the twelfth day of November in the sixteenth year of the reign of the Queen by the rolls of account in the counting house That is to say Thomas Culpeper esquire recently in the county aforesaid auditor of [of] the revenue of his office aforesaid that is to say from the first day of March in the eighth year of the reign of the Queen that now is [1566] as far as the twelfth day of November in the same eighth year, that is by the space of half of one year and seventy four days And the writ to return in the Octave of Saint Michael.

FA/CPW 32/2

Robert Lamme	John Dewerd	John Castelocke
Rychard Tyllman	William Neale	Robert Rye
Leonard Fydge	Robert A Lee	William Pearsse
William Cademan	William Chatbourne	Thomas Harte

2 houssys at Cookes Dyeche 2^s
One gardeyn in Preston Streete nowe Master Maiors 2^s
One gardeyne in Preston Streete nowe Sir Henrie Crispes 2^s
The pyllorie 1^d
Saint Nicholas Chapple the landes the gardeyns and woodes therto belonging

Faversham Borough Records
FA/JBF 10 [13 items]

Final agreement[715] in the court of Portmote held at Faversham the fourth day of February 12 Elizabeth [1570] before Thomas Belk then mayor with John Best, Bartholomew Amys, Thomas Fynche and Robert Colwell jurats between Thomas Grynestrete plaintiff and Richard Ardys gent and Margaret his wife defendant of one water mill called the Fludmyll with all streams of water[716] all ponds river banks and also two acres of meadow land with all and singular their appurtenances to the same mill belonging and appertaining lying and being in Faversham. $160^£$. 1569

[unsigned seals missing but cuts in the fold for tags]

Final agreement in the court of Portmote held at Faversham 26th September 6 Elizabeth [1564] before Edward Blakwell gent mayor John [Best] Thomas Norton, Henry Philpott and Robert Colwell jurats between John Fynche gent plaintiff and John Bradbourne and Margaret his wife defendant of seventeen messuages twelve gardens and one orchard AND ALSO of one repository

715 Abstract.
716 Latin *aquis aquarum*.

called a storehouse called Archershwells[717] and half an acre of land lying within the town, in respect thereof one messuage one garden and one orchard adjacent in Abbey street to the tenement of Henry Fynch towards the South and to the pasture of the said John Bradborn towards the East, AND ALSO two messuage and one garden in which a certain Nicholas Surrey ?saylour[718] now inhabits called the Thornhouse and lying next to the Fyshmarkett in Faversham aforesaid towards the West and to the tenement of a certain William Brooke towards the East And the other messuage in respect thereof with a garden in which Thomas Post now inhabits in West Street to a tenement of John Wreke towards the North AND ALSO all the other messuage and garden which William Harrys now inhabits there to the market[719] there between the shop of Thomas Stransham called the Garret towards the South and to the messuage of Thomas Watman towards the North AND ALSO one other messuage with one garden lying adjacent to Partridge lane in which a certain Henry Swaylislond now lives AND ALSO one other messuage with garden adjacent in the Middle Row in which a certain Peter Holland jerkin maker now lives and lying there to the tenement of Thomasine Norton widow towards the North AND ALSO three other messuage lying in the Middlerowe next to the market there whereof two messuage to the street adjacent to the market there towards the South and to the Queens street there towards the East and West And the third messuage in respect thereof with a garden to the same messuage pertaining lying to the Queens street towards the East and West and to the tenement of John Greenstreete towards the North AND ALSO the aforesaid repository called a storehouse otherwise a certain parcel of land called Archerswell lying and being to the area[720] of the Key of Faversham aforesaid AND ALSO one messuage called the Cornerhouse and two messuages and two gardens to the same messuages adjacent lying and being in the Weststrete there to the land late of Thomas Smythe towards the West and to the lane there called Barnesey Lane towards the East AND ALSO three other messuages with three gardens adjacent to the same lying and being in the West Street aforesaid to the land late Clement Norton towards the East and to the land of Thomas Stransham towards the South AND ALSO half and acre of land in the Weststreate aforesaid to the land late [blank] Barley gentleman towards the North AND ALSO two other messuages with one garden lying and being in the Abbeystrete there lying to the other messuage of Robert Fagge towards the North In respect there of a plea of covenant is made between them in the same court, that is to say, that the aforesaid John Bradborn and Margaret his wife recognize the aforesaid messuages, gardens, orchards and repository called a storehouse and half an acre of land with appurtenances to be the right of the same John Fynche as that which the same John Fynch had of the gift of the aforesaid John Bradborn and Margaret his wife and that .....And the same John Fynche has given the aforesaid John Bradbourne and Margaret one hundred and twenty pounds of legal money of England

717 This part of the manuscript is in a very poor state and barely visible even under ultra-violet light.

718 It could be taylour but unlikely.

719 The document is very dirty and scuffed and it was only possible to read some sections with a bright light and in other places under ultra-violet.

720 Latin *partes*.

Faversham Borough Records
FA/FACQ 21[721]

folio 3 [Latin]

TO ALL CHRISTIAN PEOPLE to whom this present writing shall come Margaret Bradborne of the town of Faversham in the county of Kent widow Greeting in the Lord everlasting Know that I the aforesaid Margaret for diverse causes and considerations me specially moving and at the request and desire of John Bradbourne late my husband and for the motherly love and affection that I the aforesaid Margaret have to Nicholas Bradbourne my son have given granted handed over and by this my present writing have confirmed to Robert Eyre of the parish of Boughton under the Bleane in the county aforesaid Esquire Richard Barrey of Barham in the county aforesaid Esquire, Rice[722] Parrett of the town of Sandwiche in the county aforesaid Esquire and Robert Fagge of the town of Faversham aforesaid gentleman all and singular those messuages lands and certain hereditaments on me in this my present writing underwritten and recited, situated lying and being within the town of Faversham aforesaid and the liberty of the same town, that is to say, all that my principle messuage or tenement in which I the aforesaid Margaret now dwell situated and being in Courte Street alias Abbey Street, one garden and one orchard, one dove-cot and all the buildings and hereditaments to the same messuage or tenement being and pertaining , one parcel or close of land commonly called The Churche Mede containing by estimation ten acres of land or more or less in respect thereof to be had, one piece of pasture land called The Abbey Greane containing by estimation one acre or more or less to be had in respect thereof, one parcel of pasture land and one garden or orchard being in the same parcel of land called The Sextrey containing by estimation eight acres of land to be had more or less in respect thereof, one parcel of pasture land called The Washe House Croofte containing by estimation for acres of land to be had more or less in respect thereof, one messuage or tenement called The Thorne House and all my hereditaments to the same messuage or tenement appertaining and also all those my lands pasture and meadow called The Thorne Medowes containing by estimation twenty acres of land to be had more or less TO HAVE AND TO HOLD all and singular the aforesaid messuages lands tenements meadows and hereditaments aforesaid with all and singular their appurtenances to the aforesaid Robert Eyre Richard Barrey Rice Parrett and Robert Fagge their heirs and assigns to the use and right of possession of me the aforesaid Margaret Bradbourne and my assigns during the natural life of me that aforesaid Margaret And after the death of me the aforesaid Margaret to the use and benefit of the aforesaid Nicholas Bradbourne son of the aforesaid John Bradborne my late husband deceased and me the aforesaid Margaret and the male heirs of the body of the same Nicholas lawful begotten And for default of such offspring to the use of the heirs of the body of me the aforesaid Margaret lawfully begotten. And for default of such off-spring remainder in respect thereof to the use of Thomas North Esquire and Edward Northe son of the same Thomas their heirs and assigns for ever, of the chief lords of

---

[721] Spine 'Charters, wills, Court of Orphans' the first five binding sheets are blank. 9 un-numbered fols at start of volume rather torn and dirty, which precede the main volume which has been foliated until 411, the volume has then been reversed and from fol. 1-48 are the records of the Court of Orphans. There are also a number of sheets of loose paper, a couple of plans relating to market and market-hall tucked into the volume. In relation to the article in *Archaeologia Cantiana* Volume LXXXI, Faversham Court of Orphans by Canon W. Telfer I feel that his comments about the binding may not be correct. The fact that there is damage to the initial pages of the volume may infer that it was originally without proper boards, perhaps a parchment case. A superficial inspection shows that the volume appears to have been sewn onto strings which are threaded into the boards. The boards may have been previously used although the original calf does seem to extend over the complete volume. The outer surface of the volume is guarded with metal. The volume appears subsequently to have been repaired. The start of the index to the Court of Orphans occupies the un-numbered fols at the end of the book if viewed from the records of the Court of Orphans. fol. 1 to fol. 2v is an account of the history and statutes of the Court of Orphans.

[722] Latin given as *Risco* whereas it should be *Riceo*. Rice [Rhys] Parrot was mayor of Sandwich in 1565 [Boys p. 690] he is given in a listing of 21 May 1563 as Riche Parrott [Boys, p. 207].

that fee for services in respect thereof previously owed and of right accustomed. And I truly the aforesaid Margaret Bradbourne and my heirs of all and singular the aforesaid messages, lands, tenements, meadows and hereditaments aforesaid with all their appurtenances aforesaid to the aforesaid Robert Eyre Richard Barrey Risco Parrott (sic) and Robert Fagge their heirs and assigns to the use and benefit as above said will warrant and defend against all men for ever by these presents IN TESTIMONY of which thing to this present writing I the aforesaid Margaret Bradbourne have affixed my seal Given the third day of November in the tenth year of the reign of or sovereign lady Elizabeth [1568] by the grace of God of England, France and Ireland Queen defender of the faith and so forth.

Present at the time of the sealing and delivery of this writing and also the estate and possession of the messuages lands tenements and so forth hereditaments within written taken, had and delivered by the within named Margaret Bradbourne to the schedule effect and use within specified in the presence

William Parteriche
James Maze
William Sacre
John Milles writer

Faversham Borough Records
FA/JBF 11 (6 items)

Final agreement made in the court of our sovereign Queen Elizabeth at Faversham 22nd February 12th year of Elizabeth [1570] before Thomas Belke mayor, John Wreuke, Henry Fylpott, Thomas Fynche, Robert Fagge and Robert Collwell jurats Between John Elfryth plaintiff and Richard Ardys and Margaret his wife defendant of one parcel of land called a garden plot lying and being within the town and liberty of Faversham aforesaid near the bridge there called The Stonebrege, that is to say to the Queens street there to the South to the common water course there towards the West to the garden of the same John Elfrythe towards the North and East The same John Elfrythe has given the aforesaid Richard and Margaret four pounds of legal money of England.

By Thomas Stransham deputy of William Roper Esq. steward of the court aforesaid.

Faversham Borough Records
FA/JC9[723] [Latin]

Faversham,
Inquisition indented held there before Richard Ball mayor of the town aforesaid and the jurats there the twenty fourth day of March in the fifteenth year of our sovereign Lady Elizabeth [1573] by the grace of God of England France and Ireland Queen, defender of the faith and so forth. By virtue of a certain mandate of Lord William Brooke knight, Lord of Cobham and Constable of Dover Castle and Warden of the Cinque ports and their same limbs directed to the aforesaid

[723] There are two copies of this with seals and signatures.

Mayor and Jurats upon a writ from the sovereign Queen herself in respect of a fieri-facias[724] of the Exchequer directed to him the same Constable of her Castle of Dover and Warden of the Cinque ports aforesaid or to his deputy[725] there and this inquisition was made upon the oaths of William Okenfolde William Cumber John Neale William Neale Stephen Symmes Thomas Byrlyng William Chattborne Robert Chappman Thomas Rye Nicholas Vawter John Longley Thomas Haffenden Richard Tyllman and Hugh Boothe who say upon their oath that Margaret daughter and heir of Thomas Arderne deceased in the writ aforesaid named late wife of John Bradbourne and now wife of Richard Ardes is one and the same person and no other and not separate and that the aforesaid Richard Ardes and Margaret his wife, daughter and heir of the aforesaid Thomas Arderne named in the aforesaid in the aforesaid eight schedules of the aforesaid writ annexed did not have any goods and cattle within the town and liberty of Faversham aforesaid that can become [seized] or levied whereof he owed separately aforesaid as in the aforesaid eight schedules or any other parcel in respect thereof. And furthermore the jurors aforesaid upon their oaths say that the John Bradbourne and Margaret his wife in the lifetime of the same John Bradbourne were seized and the aforesaid Richard Ardes and Margaret his wife are now seized as in right of the said Margaret in her demesne as of fee of one messuage called The Thornehouse and sixteen acres of land next to the same messuage called The Thorne Medowes now in the occupation of the same Thomas Oldefeilde demised to the same Thomas for a certain term of years now not finished situated lying and being within the town and liberty of Faversham by rendering ten pounds annually at two annual terms, that is to say at the feast of the annunciation of the Blessed Virgin Mary and at the feast of Saint Michael the Archangel to be paid by equal portions and so that the same messuage and sixteen acres of land are of the clear value by the year over the deductions ten pounds which certain messuage and sixteen acres of land we the aforesaid mayor and jurats took possession of into the hands of the sovereign Queen to have and to hold to the use and possession of the said sovereign Queen as long as she is individually owed both by the aforesaid John Bradbourne as by the aforesaid Margaret whilst she was alone and by the aforesaid Richard Ardes and Margaret his wife after marriage between them had and celebrated in the debt of the said sovereign Queen in the aforesaid eight schedules[726] specified should be paid to the said sovereign Queen and that the aforesaid John Bradbourne in his life and the aforesaid Margaret with the aforesaid Richard Ardes and Margaret or anyone of them not having nor to have had any other more lands nor tenements within the town and liberty aforesaid In testimony of which thing the jurors to this inquisition indented have severally placed their seals, given at Faversham aforesaid the day and year above said

(signatures) Wm. Okynfold
John Nealle
Nycholas Vawter
Rycharde Tylman

Wyllyam Cumber
Robert Chapman
a mark in the form of a T *followed by the letter* S
'merchant mark' T with the ends of each arm split, and bar across ascender.

[724] *Cause to be made*; A writ wherein the sheriff is commanded that he cause to be made out of the goods and chattels of the defendant, the sum for which judgement was given.
[725] *Locum tenens*; one who holds office temporarily or who undertakes anothers professional duties during his absence.
[726] The eight schedules have not survived.

Faversham Borough Records
FA/Z41/2 page 179 Crowe MSS

A petition from Ardens daughter and her husband to recover certain goods forfeited by the death of her mother.

To the Right Honourable Sir William Brooke knight Lord Cobham Constable of Dover Castle[727] etc. most humbly complaineth John Bradbourne Gent and Margaret his wife of the town of Faversham daughter and heyer of one Thomas Ardren of Faversham deceased and sole administratrix, being under covert baron of all the goods and cattles which were the sayed Thomas Ardrens her father at the time of his death etc., of the said will made one Alyce his wyffe to be his sole executrix etc., after that by provocation and intentment of the devyll for lack of grace, the sayed Alyce confederated with others, murdred hym the said Thomas Ardren her husband, after whych by judgment of law she was burnte .... by reason whereof she was dishably'd to have or enjoy any goodes etc. ... or to administer etc.....whereupon administration was granted to one John Farther[728] deceased then husband of the said Margaret, wife to the said John Bradborne your oratour, so that the goodes etc. contained in the schedule annexed by righte without any just cause, forfaieture or occasion where hadde taken and elloyned[729] away by the mayor and jurates of the sayed town and converted to the use of their corporation etc.,

May it please your lordship etc. .. to command the said mayor etc., shall deliver them or the value of them to your orators and your said orators etc.

signed Thomas Finch, Thomas Kempe, C. Crispe and William Crowmer.

These be the parcells which the towne of Faversham had of the goods of Master Ardren after his death.

Imprimis two fayer stell glases coverd with velvete		13s	4d
Divers small parcels of cloth		6s	
Two payer of gloves layde with velvete		6s	8d
A frocke of worsted for a woman garded with velvete	2£		
An other of the same	1£		
A jackete of tawny damaske edged with feynes		10s	
page 180			
A payer of myre black hose for a man		10s	

[727] The original record cannot be found. The text has been compared with the original version of Edward Crow's *Historical Gleanings relative to the Town of Faversham and parishes adjoining,* at the Bodleian Library [Bodleian Ms Top. Kent e4 page 123]. The catalogue of the archives of the confederation of the Cinque Ports and of the Lord Warden of the Cinque Ports does not unfortunately seem to show any surving records relating to this bill of complaint. However, CP/W7 16 Sep 1574 is an agreement between Sir William Brook, Lord Cobham and the Mayors, bailiffs, jurats and barons of the Cinque Ports regarding the courts at St James Dover. See an account of the Court in Murray, *op. cit.* pp. 102-119.
Francis W.Steer, *John Philpot's Roll of the Constables of Dover Castle and Lord Warden of the Cinque Ports 1627* (1956) page 30 says that Sir William Brooke, Knight of the garter and Lord Chamberlain Lord Cobham of Cobham in Kent was made Constable of Dover Castell and Lord warden of the Cinque Ports after the death of Sir Thomas Cheney which fell in the year 1559.

[728] Archdeaconry Court of Canterbury Probate Act Book: PRC 3/15 folio 67 [Latin]: xijth November in the year of the Lord 1558. The goods of John Fathers of Faversham who died intestate administration of which was granted to Margaret to be first duly sworn etc. Bound with the said Margaret one Thomas Oldfield of Faversham and John Freyne of London gentlemen in three hundred pounds. Issued a commission to the vicar of Faversham and the rector of Ludenham to swear the relict to faithfully admininister etc. To exhibit before the feast of the Nativity of the Lord etc. Afterwards, that is to say, the same day the vicar of Faversham certified the execution of the commission etc. And the charge of administration committed to the said relict by tenor of the same. Exhibited the inventory to the value of CLxx$^{£}$ x^{s} x^{d}

[729] Aliened.

A women's cloke edged with velvete		1£		
A womens red petty coate			3s	4d
An halfe kyryle of black damaske			2s	
An old gowne for a man, new dresse etc			6s	8d
An old lether jyrkyn			1s	
An old marble coate			3s	4d
An old vardyn gale			1s	
Five smockes			10s	
Four payer long sleves			8s	
A payre of knytte hose of thread			1s	8d
A fyne cale				4d
Tow pare of knytte sleves of threed			3s	4d
A fyne neckercher			5s	
Small pieces of linnen			1s	8d
Boxe of sope			2s	
A payer of martynes			15s	
A Frenche hode playne, with all things to it		1£		
A payer of wyde black saten slevys			10s	
A payer of kyrtyll of tawny damaske			5s	
A payer of old tawny velvete slevys			1s	8d
A payer of slevys of red saten			1s	8d
A payer of blacke cut			1s	8d
A payer of tawny cut			1s	8d
A payer layed with lace			1s	8d
A face of crymson damaske			13s	4d
Imprimis a black saten purse			1s	
A frocke of black saten garded with velvete		6£	13s	4d
A frocke of tawny damaske garded with velvete		4£	16s	4d
A frocke of black guarded with lace		5£	16s	4d
A face of black taffeta			6s	8d
Two old nether bodyes, the one of tawny, the other of blacke, and a cassock of black worsted garded with velvete		2£		
A chayne of golde for a gentlewomen's neck 52s to 54s the ounce		3£	14s	9d
A tablet of gold weighed 1 ounce ½ and ½ a quarter		4£	15s	
Two braseleth of golde wayinge 1 ounce and a quarter		3£	5s	
	[Total]	£45	5	5

signed Thomas Kempe T Fynche William Crowmer

Imprimis Two tenements in Cokesditche by the year		10s	
A garden in Preston by the year		3s	
A garden in the tenure of J Caslock by the year		3s	
The pyllorie in the Market Place by the year		8s	
St. Nycholas Chappel with the chyrche yarde garden and wood belonginge to the same	1£		
	£2	4	0#

Crow Footnote 5: Jacobs MSS [730]. 'These lands were given by Arderns .will to the corporation for charitable purposes, how the law suit ended I cannot learn, but the town enjoys none of the estates now. The house near the market being long since taken down. I cannot learn at what time, perhaps on building the market place in 1575.' Note by Jacob

The chapel which stood on the site of the Chapel House was named St. Nicholas as was also the oaks estate, and might have once formed part of it.[731] See Appendix page 127[732]

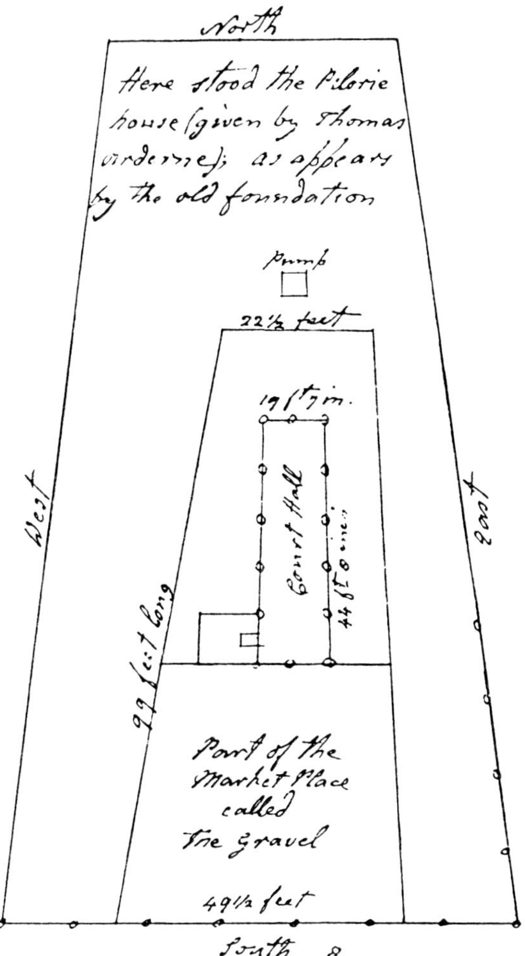

Crow MS Vol. 3, page 85, showing the foundations of the Pillory House given by Thomas Arden

[730] Crow in his preface says in a footnote to Jacobs MSS 'This book became the property of his grandson and was in his house at Chatham destroyed by fire.' The inference is that Jacob looked at this petition and that it might even have been with other Arden papers amongst his MS. Since Edward Jacob in 1770 republished the play ' with a preface .... and genuine account given of the murder, from authentic papers of the time.'

[731] In the Bodleian version: 'The Oaks estate is also named St Nicholas in old deeds and might have once formed part of this estate.'

[732] This volume was for many years at Rochester Public Library unidentified as the third volume of Crow's MSS and belongs to the Maidstone series. It is now deposited at Faversham Library.

Public Record Office, Chancery Lane, London
Inquisition Post Mortem
C142/172/146 compared with Ward 7/17 membrane 40[733]

Margin: Delivered into court the xxth day of June in the xvij year of Queen Elizabeth [1575] by the hands of William Partriche gentleman.

Kent

Inquisition indented held at Deptford Stroud in the county aforesaid the thirtieth day of April in the seventeenth year of the reign of our sovereign Lady Elizabeth by the grace of God of England France and Ireland Queen, defender of the faith etc., before Andrew Richardes Esquire Eschaetor of the said sovereign Queen in the county aforesaid BY VIRTUE of a writ of the same sovereign Queen of *diem clausit extremum* after the death of Margaret Ardys late wife of Richard Ardys gentleman , directed thereon to the same Escheator, and of one party to this same inquisition appointed upon oath Arnold Kinge, John Petley, Richard Felton, John Eton, John a Lee, William Johnson, Emery Ellery, Philip Purs, William Manninge, Walter Batt, Simon Clayton, Robert Crowe, John Hall and John Waklin good and lawful men WHO say upon their oaths that a certain Thomas Arderne before he died was seized in demesne as of fee of and in a messuage land and tenements within written, THAT IS TO SAY, of and in one principal messuage one garden one orchard and two small tenements and other buildings and hereditaments to the same messuage belonging or parcel to the same in Faversham aforesaid AND ALSO of and in one parcel of meadow called The Churche Meade containing by estimation ten acres of land AND ALSO of and in one piece of pasture called the Abbey Grene containing by estimation one acre and also of and in one parcel of pasture and one garden or orchard in the same parcel of pasture belonging called the Sextrey containing in total eight acres AND ALSO of and in one other parcel of pasture called The Washe Howse Crofte containing by estimation four acres AND ALSO of and in one other messuage or tenement called The Thornehowse and diverse other hereditaments to the same messuage belonging AND ALSO of and in twenty acres of meadow and pasture by estimation to the same messuage belonging AND SO in respect thereof being siezed he had issue Margaret Arderne. AND OF the aforesaid messuage lands tenements and hereditaments with their appurtenances the twentieth day of December in the year of the Lord 1550 in the fourth year of the reign of King Edward the sixth late King of England he declared his last will in writing here shown in evidence And by the same devised all and singular the premises with the appurtenances to the aforesaid Margaret Arderne his daughter and the heir of his body lawfully begotten remainder in respect thereof belonging to the sister of the aforesaid Thomas Arderne and his heirs AND AFTERWARDS the aforesaid Thomas Arderne at Faversham aforesaid the fifteenth day of February in the fifth year of our sovereign Lord King died seized of the premises (as previously mentioned). AFTER whose death the aforesaid Margaret by virtue of the testament aforesaid seized all and singular the premises in her demesne as of fee by entail remainder in respect thereof to the sister of the aforesaid Thomas Arderne and his heirs AND SO in respect thereof being seized she took as a husband John Fathers and having issue with one another Nicholas Fathers alias Bradborne AND THE AFORESAID John Fathers the twentieth seventh day of November in the first year of the reign of Queen Elizabeth [1558] died at Faversham in the county aforesaid AFTER whose death the aforesaid Margaret took as a husband a certain John Bradbourne Which certain John Bradborne and Margaret his wife the same Margaret by due right form according to the customs and liberties of Faversham was

[733] The document is written in Latin with a small section in English. Ward 7 was damaged along one margin and the C142 was badly stained and difficult to read even under ultra-violet light.

examined alone before John Best then Mayor of the town of Faversham aforesaid and other jurates by which certain indenture sworn aforesaid which is shown in evidence bearing date the fifth day of January in the first year of our sovereign Queen they had demised granted and confirmed to Thomas Fynche gentleman Thomas Belke and Thomas Bartone all the aforesaid messuages lands tenements and hereditaments with their appurtenances TO HAVE AND TO HOLD all and singular the premises with their appurtenances to the aforesaid Thomas Finche Thomas Belke and Thomas Bartone their heirs and assigns for ever AND AFTERWARDS that is the ninth day of January in the first year aforesaid, the aforesaid John and Margaret at Faversham aforesaid by a certain fine of all and singular the premises with appurtenances aforesaid To Thomas Finche, Thomas Belke and Thomas Bartone levied before the aforesaid John Best then mayor of the Town of Feversham aforesaid and others the jurats then there present and by that acknowledgement all their right in the tenements aforesaid to be the rights of the same Thomas Finche Thomas Belke and Thomas Bartone and that to them remised and quitclaimed OF WHICH by virtue of the aforesaid Thomas Finche Thomas Belke and Thomas Bartone were seized of all and singular the premises with their appurtenances in their demesne as of fee AND SO seized in respect thereof a certain John Edmunds and Thomas Oldfeild in a court of Portmoot of the said sovereign Queen held at Faversham aforesaid the twelfth day of the aforesaid month of January BEFORE the mayor and jurats aforesaid have affirmed a certain suit in the form and nature of a writ of the said sovereign Queen in the Post of the aforesaid messuage lands tenements and hereditaments with appurtenances towards the aforesaid Thomas Finche, Thomas Belke and Thomas Bartone WHO are to vouch to warranty in respect thereof to the aforesaid John Bradborne and Margaret his wife WHO appearing and in their proper persons vouched in respect thereof to warrant Fulke David The Common Vowche And recovery and seizin had in due right form according to the form of common recovery WHICH certain recovery was made to the use and behoof of the said John Edmundes and Thomas Oldfeild their heirs and assigns BY EFFECT of which the aforesaid John Edmundes and Thomas Oldfeild were seized of and in all and singular the premises with appurtenances in their demesne as of fee. AND SO in respect thereof being sized by a certain indenture to the aforesaid jurors this shown in evidence bearing date the thirteenth day of the aforesaid month of January demised conveyed and confirmed the aforesaid John Bradborne and Margaret his wife all and singular the premises above specified TO HAVE AND to hold all and singular the premises with their appurtenances to the aforesaid John Bradborne and Margaret his wife and the heirs of their body lawful begotten To the proper use and behoof of them John and Margaret and their heirs and assigns for ever. BY VIRTUE of which the aforesaid John Bradborne was seized in the premises in his demesne as of fee tail AND SO being seized in respect thereof the aforesaid John Bradborne of the aforesaid Messuages lands tenements and hereditaments with their appurtenances the sixteenth day of October in the year of the Lord 1568 , tenth year of the reign of our sovereign Queen declared his last will in writing as follows, ITEM I WILL that Margaret my wyffe have the use of all my howsehold implementes and my plate And I gyve unto my sayd wyffe twentye poundes yerely dueringe the terme of a certein leasse well knowen unto myne executors (yf she so longe live) to be payd by my sayd executors uppon this onely condition that my sayd wyffe shall within thre monethes next after my disceasse by good and sufficient convayaunce in lawe make or cawse to be made unto Nicholas her sonne and his heyres a good sure sufficient and lawefull estate of inheritance of and in all those landes messuages and tenementes whereof I the seyd John Bradborne togither with the seyd Margarette my wyffe are nowe lawefully seised etc., AND AFTERWARDS the aforesaid John Bradborne died at Boughton the first day of November in the tenth year of the reign of our sovereign Queen [1568] seized of the premises (as previously mentioned) without issue of his body AND THAT the aforesaid Margaret in fulfilment of the same testament , afterwards, that is to say the third day of November in the tenth year of the reign of our sovereign Queen by a certain writing shown in evidence to the jurors aforesaid bearing date the same day and year gave and granted to Robert Eyre of the parish of Boughton under the Bleane in the county aforesaid Esquire and Richard Barrey of Barrham in the county aforesaid Esquire Rhys[734] Parrett of the town of Sandwich in the county aforesaid esquire and Robert Fagge of the town of Faversham aforesaid gentleman all and singular the aforesaid messuage lands tenements and so forth the hereditaments together with all and singular their premises TO HAVE AND to hold all and singular the aforesaid messuage lands tenements and hereditaments with their appurtenances aforesaid, to the aforesaid Robert Eyer, Richard Barrey Rhys Parrette and Robert Fagge their heirs and assigns to the use and behoof of Margaret Bradborne and her assigns during the natural life of the aforesaid Margaret AND AFTER the decease of the aforesaid Margaret to the use and behoof of the aforesaid Nicholas and the heirs male of the body of the same Nicholas lawfully to be procreated AND FOR default of such issue to the use of the heirs of the body of the aforesaid Margaret lawfully to be procreated. AND FOR default of lawful issue REMAINDER in respect thereof to the use of Thomas Northe esquire and Edward North son of the same Thomas their heirs and assigns for ever BY VIRTUE of which the aforesaid Margaret was seized of the premises as of her free tenant REMAINDER in respect thereof belonging to the aforesaid Nicholas Fathers alias Bradborne and the heirs males of his body lawfully to be begotten REMAINDER in respect thereof to the aforesaid Thomas North and Edward North their heirs and assigns AND THE AFORESAID Margaret being in respect thereof so seized took as a husband a certain Richard Ardys AND AFTERWARDS, that is to say, the twenty seventh day of November in the seventeenth year of the reign of our now sovereign Queen [1574] at Turvey in the county of Bedford died. AND the aforesaid jurors say that the aforesaid Nicholas Fathers alias Bradborne is the son and heir of the aforesaid Margaret Ardys and on the day that this inquisition was taken aged sixteen years and three months ~~and more~~ AND THAT all and singular the premises held and at the time of the death of the aforesaid Margaret ought to be held of the said sovereign Queen in chief by the services of twenty parts of one knights fee AND THEY SAY moreover that the aforesaid principal messuage, garden orchard and the aforesaid parcel of meadow called the Churche Meade and the aforesaid piece of pasture called the Abbey Grene valued by the year above reprise three pounds six shillings and eight pence AND THAT the aforesaid messuage called The Thorne Howse and the aforesaid twenty acres of meadow and pasture called the Thorne Meaddowes to the same messuage belonging valued above the reprise fifty and three shillings and four pence AND THAT the aforesaid two small tenements of the aforesaid capital messuage adjoining and the aforesaid parcel of pasture called the Sextrey and the aforesaid parcel of pasture called the Washehouse crofte valued by the year above the reprise twenty six shillings and eight pence AND THEY SAY the aforesaid jurors on their oaths aforesaid that the aforesaid Margaret Ardys named in the writ aforesaid has no other messuages lands or tenements at the time of her death IN TESTIMONY OF WHICH THING to one part of this inquisition remaining in the possession of the aforesaid Escheator the said jurors have applied their seals The other true part remaining in the possession of the jurors the said Escheator has affixed his seal. Dated the day year and place above written.

734 Latin: *Riseo.*

Public Record Office, Chancery Lane, London
Patent Rolls
C66/1267 m.8 [Latin]

24 Nov. 1584

That toft The Key or wharf commonly called Thornekeye with all those arable lands meadows and pastures and salt marsh with every their appurtenances lying and being in Faversham commonly called or known by the name of Thorne Meadowe containing by estimation 20 acres and the North end one piece of land or pasture called or known by the name of Abbey Grene in our county of Kent, which is held of us in chief as is said, are able to give and grant alienation or acknowledgement for a fine or recovery in our court before our justice of the bench or any other whatsoever at the will of the same Nicholas to our beloved John Philpott to have and to hold to the same John and his heirs and his assigns for ever of our heirs and successors for the services owed and of right accustomed. And to the same John himself the aforesaid toft, the key, wharf land and tenement etc. all and singular the premises above expressed and specified with their appurtenances from the aforesaid Nicholas is able to receive and hold to him and his heirs and assigns of our heirs and successors for the services aforesaid just as the aforesaid is for ever held by the presents similar to the licence we gave and for our heirs and our successors aforesaid specially. Unwilling that the aforesaid Nicholas or his heirs or the aforesaid John or his heirs by reason of the permission of us our heirs or successors or by justices escheators sheriffs bailiffs or other our officers or ministers or our said heirs or successors whomsoever in respect thereof to interfere molest impeach or in anyway to aggravate nor anyone for them to interfere molest impeach vex or in anyway aggravate. In which thing etc. Witness by the King at Westminster xxiiij day of November.

m. 8 (next item)
... for thirteen shillings and four pence Nicholas Bradburne gentleman two pieces of land called or known by the name of Sexterye and Washouse Close containing by estimation twelve acres of land with appurtenances in Feversham in our county of Kent which are held of us in chief as grants alienation to John Bennett and Alice his wife. xxiiij November.

m. 9.
24 Nov. 1584.
.... for forty shillings paid and by virtue of our letters patent to Thomas North and Edward North his son the reversion and remainder of one capital messuage or tenement with appurtenances in Feversham and the reversion and remainder of one piece of land called Amery Croft containing by estimation ten acres and one other piece of land called Abbygrene containing by estimation one acre of land and one other piece called Thorne Medowe containing by estimation 20 acres and one other piece called Sextery and Washowse Close containing by estimation twelve acres of land with appurtenances in Feversham in the county of Kent held in chief ..... Nicholas Bradburne gentleman.

m. 13
1 Feb. 1585
... for twenty six shillings and eight pence for Nicholas Bradborne all that one capital messuage or tenement in Feversham in the county of Kent, one garden, one orchard, one dovecote with Ambrey Croft containing by estimation 10 acres more or less, and half and acre more or less called The Bowling Grene held in chief to alienate to John Storer and Mary his wife

APPENDIX 16
Life in Faversham during the final years of the Abbey from the Letters and Papers of Henry VIII

INTRODUCTION

This appendix is included simply to show the general reader the kind of contact that there was between Faversham and central government. Both major and minor matters were dealt with and we do not necessarily see the beginning or the end of an incident. We only have a snapshot. For all the details we would have to look in other places as well.

Volume I part 1 1509-14.

no. 1313. The Cinque Ports
Mandate by Sir Edward Poynings, constable of Dover Castle, warden and admiral of the Cinque Ports, to John Copuldik, his lieutenant of the said castle, and John Love, his bailiff of Faversham, to attach William Sparowe, Richard Keere, Robert Matras and Thomas Brix of Faversham, and bring them before the King and council of Westminster in the quinzaine[735] of Michaelmas next. Dover Castle 30 July 4 Hen. VIII [1512].

Volume 1 part 2

no. 2034.
Warrant to John Daunce to pay John Thurstone, master of the King's barge £15-5-4 for hire of barges and crayers to carry the guard from Greenwich to Feversham by water. Canterbury, 28 June 5 Hen. VIII (1513)

no. 2179
Payments, by Richard Smith, [a Yeoman] of the Robes, for conveying a close car, a chariot and a cart from London to Sandwich, including 1^{s} for 'a guide from my Lord Purgaynis place (George Nevill, Lord Abergavenny, in ?Mereworth, Kent) to Feversam.' 19 August 1513

2862 (7) Commissioners appointed in the Cinque Ports to levy the subsidy or tax of 1514.
Feversham: William Norton, Robert Meycote

Volume II part 2.

no. 4333.
Abbot of Feversham present at reception of [Cardinal] Campeggio on Friday 23 July 1518.

Volume III. Part 1

no. 818. The Grammar School
For the convent of St. Saviour's, Feversham, Kent. Licence to acquire lands in Kent, to the yearly value of £14, from John Cole, clerk, king's chaplain who purposes to found a free grammar school in the monastery. 16 May 1520.

no. 1177
For John, abbot, and the convent of St. Saviours, Faversham.

---

[735] *O.E.D.* Quinzaine: a period of fifteen days.

Mortmain licence to acquire lands etc. to the annual value of £10 in consideration of their granting certain land in Bride Lane for the enlargement of the ground for the king's buildings in the parish of St. Bride, London (The position of the land is fully described) 23 February 1521.

Volume III part 2.
page 1544. The King's book of payments.
To the abbot of Faversham, for grounds which the king has taken into Bridewell £100. February 1521

no. 2288. Visit of Charles V 1522.
The following persons are ordered to provide victuals: at Feversham, Ospringe and Sittingbourne, Sir John Norton, John Cheney of Sittingbourne, Crowmer, Robert Sandes.

no. 2443 Letter from Sir William Sandes to [Thomas] Wolsey.
Scarcity of beer in Calais. On his way there, he sent the king's commandment, as Wolsey directed, to Feversham and other places for speedy preparing of victuals. 16 Aug 1522.

no. 2483. A loan or 'annual grant to be [made by the] spirituality for the king's personal [expenses in] France for the recovery of the [crown] of the same.' (1522) Abbot of Faversham [John Castlock] £66-13-4

no. 3687 The loan and musters. An abbreviate[736] of the books of views and musters[737] brought into the Star Chamber. 1523. Feversham and others by John Corroll

Appendix 45 Letter from William Warham, Archbishop of Canterbury, Lord Cobham, Sir Thomas Boleyn and Sir John Norton to Thomas Wolsey. Preparation for defence. Sir John Norton and Sir William Cromor are in charge of the town and hundred of Feversham, to aid Sir William Scot etc. 29 October 1522.

Volume IV part 1
no. 459.
The retinue of Sir Edward Guyldeforde - the names of the five ports and their men -
Feversham: John Robynson, William Cryppes, Thomas Thorne, Thomas Sinnester
Musters 30 June 1524.

Volume IV part 2
no. 3192.
Commission to John, Abbot of St. Saviours, Faversham, and Sir John Norton, to ascertain the annual value of the lands of Thomas Fuller in Kent, as Sir John Mundy has an execution against them, and there is a dispute about their value. 22 June 1527.
no. 3231.
Letter from Thomas Wolsey to Henry VIII. Between Sittingbourne and Faversham I encountered the ambassador (Jerome à Lasco) from the Vayvoda[738], calling himself king of Hungary, imploring your aid against the Turks. 5 July 1527

Volume IV part 3

---

[736] *O.E.D.* To make shorter; to make an abstract or brief of; to epitomize.
[737] *O.E.D.* (2c) Of an army etc. To come together for inspection, exercise, or prepartaion for service.
[738] This word is meaningless to us, but perhaps not to Wolsey. We are, of course, assuming that the editor and printer have recorded it correctly.

no 6047.
Convocation[739]. List of persons summoned to the convocation of the province of Canterbury, 1529 John abbot of Faversham. Not * so not there in person (personaliter).

Appendix 89. Dover-receipts and charges of the corporation. [1526]
To town clerk of Dover riding to Feversham for their help to the charges of the 'burges' [burgess] of parliament.

Volume V

no. 637
Letter from Sir Thomas Crakynthorpe 'anchorite' [hermit[740]] of Faversham, to Thomas Cromwell. Is glad to hear of his welfare, and that of his household. The mayor of Feversham, the bearer of this letter, is in great hindrance and undoing from the malice of others. Begs that Cromwell will assist him, and hear what he has to say. (1531)

no. 638..
Sir Thomas Crakynthorpe 'anchorite' of Faversham ,to Thomas Cromwell
Has sent him tokens at various times, both money and capons. Sends him now by his poor sister a couple of capons, which he had better kill at once, as they will lose their fatness. Begs he will write to the abbot of St. Austin's Canterbury, for reparations to be done in the 'ancrage' of Feversham, and to give the writer yearly a load or two of wood. Recommends the suit of this poor woman, who has had a cause in the Arches[741] at Westminster Hall this four years. (1531)

no. 812.
Letter from John, Abbot of Faversham to Thomas Cromwell.
Our convent has granted to Master Hungerforth £3 annually, according to your desire, as held by the late Sir John Norton. As you have always promised to us a continuance of your favor to remedy any complaint, understand that I am marvellously annoyed with rooks, crows, choughs, and buzzards, which not only destroy my doves but the fruit of my orchard. I desire licence for my servants to have handguns and crossbows to destroy the said ravenous fowls. Faversham, 20 February [1532]. Before the last feast of All Saints I sent the king a goshawk of two cotes and a couple of spaniels. There are few better in England for pheasant and partridge. They were received by Sir Nicholas Carew.

no. 1593.
List of expenses in Dover, Sandwich and Faversham by Richard Cromwell, Ralph Sadler and others. Horsemeat at Feversham and the horsekeeper's supper 6^{s} 5^{d}. Reward to the maidens there 20^{d}. Wednesday 20[November 1532]

---

739 *O.E.D.* (3) In the church of England, a provincial synod or assembly of the clergy, constiuted by statute and called together to deliberate on ecclesiastical matters.

740 For more details of anchorites in Faversham churchyard see *Archeologia Cantiana* xi (1877), 24-39.

741 Court of Arches: The general court of appeal for the province, called for short the Court of the Province. In the Province of Canterbury this court has acquired the name of the Court of Arches, owing to the fact that from the time of Archbishop Pecham (1279-92) it sat in the Church of St Mary of the Arches or St Mary-le-Bow, to give the name by which it is generally known, in the City of London. The Court sat here, because this church with twelve other churches in the City formed a peculiar of the Archbishop of Canterbury. The peculiar had its own court, whose judge, like the judges of all the Archbishop's peculiar courts, was called a dean, the Dean of Arches. Both the Court of the Province and the local peculiar court sat in the same building, and from the time of Archbishop Warham (1503-32) the same person was appointed judge of both courts. *The Ecclesiastical Courts: Report of the Commission* (London, SPCK 1954), 8-9.

Volume VI

no. 299 iv

Thomas Cromwell - a catalogue of documents belonging to him including a supplication of the 'ancker' [anchorite] of Feversham. (1533)

Volume VII part 1

g 587 (27)

Anthony Cley of London, yeoman. Pardon for having on the 28 October 12 Hen. VIII, [1520] along with David Hareson of London, tailor, and Juliana Cley of London, spinster, stolen certain plate, clothes and ornaments, value £26, belonging to the parishioners of Feversham, Kent, in the custody of Thomas Hawkeswell, John Bolynger, Robert Fale and John Barnard, churchwardens, found at Boughton subter le Blein, Kent; and for having feloniously received other stolen goods, the property of persons unknown. Pat. 20 April 25 Hen. VIII p 2. m 33. [1534]

no. 769. In 1534 the Act of Supremacy was passed which summed up and emphasized the claims made by the English King, including that of spiritual jurisdiction. The clergy had to agree to this Royal Supremacy. St. Saviours, Feversham with 13 signatures (not listed). 1 June 1534

no. 853

Letter from Michael Mason, mayor [of ...] to Thomas Cromwell.

We have received your letter to deliver to John Godde, servant of John Hampton of Feversham, the ship 'Christopher' with cargo and one prisoner, Stephen Clayton. We took no such ship nor prisoners. She was taken by Anthony Curtoys and John Bellowe 18 June 1534.

no. 923 xxvi (pp 347-48)

Cromwell's Remembrances 1534.

Supplications in paper. Ann Sawsten, sister of the anker [anchorite] in Feversham .... The anker of Feversham.

Volume VII part 2

no. 1248.

Letter from William Grett to Lord Lisle.

Will be glad if he will pay him a little debt, as he was never so much in need. Has supplied wine etc. The bearer, Mr Beverley, will give him an acquittance. otherwise he will have to seek remedy at the King's Council. Letter dated at Faversham, 10 October 1534

no. 1480

Sir Thomas Cheyne to Thomas Cromwell.

Has caused a Flemish 'pynke' to be seized 'wherein is 25 cloths unwrought, which I have in my house. I suppose they will be forefeit.' They are worth about £5 apiece. There are also six tuns of beer, two or three barrels of candle, six 'bakyn howges'[742] and a barrel of beef. All the cloths belong to the mayor of Fefyrsham, who is but a poor man; the other baggage to the Fleming master of the ship. At my house, Friday before St. Andrew [27] November 1534.

[742] Bacon hog.

no. 1594
Faversham Abbey acknowledges the Royal Supremacy of the King.
Signed by abbot John, by Robert Faversham, prior, John Harte, sacrist, Thomas Sellyng, cellarer, John Lynstyd, precentor, Dunstan, sub-prior, and eight others. 10 December 1534.

no.1607
The Francisan Observants or Greyfriars opposed the reformation and some were implicated with the Holy Maid of Kent. The group was broken up and they were dispersed in various abbeys as if they were in prison.
Elyas Mody in Kent with the abbot of Feversham. 1534

Volume VIII
no entries

Volume IX
no. 668. The General Visitation of the Monasteries.
Letter from Richard Layton (visitor) to Thomas Cromwell
'This night I will be at Feversham Abbey.' 23 Oct. 1535

no. 830.
Richard Spery to Master Valentyn. A puzzling list as nothing else is known of either man. Obligations and discharges for victuals and billets for the year past, from port to port within the realm.
From Feversham, William Nelson for Bekensal 29th; and John Bone 28th July. 16 Nov. 1535

Volume X.
no. 484.
Letter from John (Shepey alias Castelocke), Abbot of Faversham, to Thomas Cromwell. Has received Cromwells' letters, dated 8 inst., suggesting his resignation of the house of which he has so long had the rule, because of his age and debility. Trusts he is not yet so far enfeebled but he can govern as well as ever, though he cannot so well perchance ride and journey abroad. Even if an abbot's peculiar office were to survey the possessions of his house, he took such pains in his younger years that he need to do less now; and his servants, whom he has brought up from their youth, have such experience in these worldly matters that they can supply this part. Thinks, however, the chief office and profession of an abbot is to live chaste and solitarily, to be separate from the intermeddling of worldly things, to serve God quietly, to distribute his faculties in the refreshing of poor indigent persons, to have a vigilant eye to the good order and rule of his house and the flock committed to him by God. Doubtless it would be, as Cromwell says, more to his ease to resign for a reasonable pension, and has no doubt of Cromwell's conscience therein, considering the benevolences he has always found in him. For his part, he should be contented, not being ambitious; but, considering the miserable state in which the house would be left, God forbid that he should think his office irkful or tedious. The house is much impoverished, partly by the debts left by his predecessor, who was but a right slender husband to the house, partly by the necessary repairs of the church and other buildings, and the ' innyng' of marshes which the sea had won, by lawsuits for the recovery of their rights and by dismes and subsidies to the King, amounting to more than £2,000. The house is now £400 in debt, which I might see repaid if I continued in the office six or seven years, but if I should resign, the charges of first fruits and

tenths[743] due to the King, added to the debt, would ruin the house. Christ forbid that I should so heinously offend against God and the King as to further the ruin of so godly and ancient a foundation, dedicated to St. Saviour by one of the King's progenitors, whose body, with those of his queen and son, lie buried in honorable sepulture, and are had all three in perpetual memory with continual suffrages and commendations of prayers. Considering the premises I doubt not that you will continue your accustomed favor and benevolence towards our poor monastery. At our poor monastery aforesaid 16 March 1536.

no. 627.
Letter from John, Abbot of Feversham, to Thomas Cromwell.
I thank you for your loving letters: and in consideration of the goodness you have always borne towards our poor monastery of St. Saviour, I send you a poor token. Feversham 6 April 1536.

no. 724.
Letter from John, Abbot of Feversham, to Thomas Cromwell.
I am made collector of the king's money in the diocese of Canterbury, which rises above the sum of £1,000 to be gathered out of religious houses, parsonages etc. Of this number was the late prioress of Davington, assessed to the king in 26^{s} 8^{d}; and this sum is not paid, as your servant had taken an inventory in the king's name of all the moveable goods in the said priory. I beg that the 26^{s} 8^{d} may be paid to the bearer, or that I may be discharged. Edward Crowemer, parson of Aldermairie, London, is assessed to the king £4, and on my servant demanding it of him he was referred to you. Faversham, 24 April 1536.

no. 929 iii
iij remembrances of Thomas Cromwell in his hand
Touching ... the abbot of Faversham. (no more detail)

Volume XIII, part I
no. 585.
Letter from John, Abbot of Faversham, to Thomas Cromwell.

Received by his servant, Christopher Roper, his letter, dated 15 March, and sends by the bearer the sum of the acres Sir Thomas Cheyney would have of the convent, and the value by year. Faversham 23 March 1538.

no. 254. A list of some of the larger monasteries. (1538)
' abbey of Faversham'

g 646 (64).
John, the abbot, and convent of Feversham, Kent. Licence to alienate 144 acres of land, 204 acres of fresh marsh and 10 acres of salt marsh in the parish of St. Thomas in the Isle of Hartey, near the Isle of Sheppey, Kent, to Sir Thomas Cheney. 18 March 29 Hen. VIII. (1538)

g 888 (5)
Richard Robynson clerk, confirmation of annuities granted to him

(1) By the abbey of St. Saviour for £12 out of the manor of Bendysh, Essex 1 July 19 Hen. VIII (1527)

---

[743] See page 384.

(2) By the abbey of St. Saviour for £10 out of the manor of Lambortisland, Kent. (April, 1538)

no. 1339. Feversham Abbey.
Surrender of the monastery and all its possessions in counties Kent and Essex and elsewhere in England, Wales, and the marches thereof. 8 July 30 Hen. VIII. Signed by John [Sheppey], abbot, Robert Faversham, prior; John Hartey, sacrist; Thomas Sellyng, cellarer; Dunstan Chartam[744], subprior; and four others[745]. [*see* Deputy Keeper's Eighth Report, App. II. 21]. Seal broken. Enrolled [*Cl. Roll*, p.2, No. 11] as acknowledged personally, same day, before the King in Chancery.

(2) Pensions assigned to the abbot and monks of Feversham Abbey, Kent. John Casteloke alias Sheppey, abbot, 100 marks; Robert Chillinden and Thomas Deve 5£ each; Dunstan Goddehewe, John Tailer, Ralph Post *alias* Ulcum, John Filpote and William Coyden, 4£ each; Peter Minto 3£ 6^{s} 8^{d}. Signed by Thomas Cromwell.

Decreed that pensions be made to these persons abovesaid Rychard Ryche, Thomas Pope, Robert Sowthwell.

no. 1340

Letter from John, late Abbot of Feversham, to Thomas Cromwell. In compliance with the exhortation of the king's commissioners, they have surrendered their monastery, lands, and moveables, and asks him to intercede with the King that they may be assured of some competent living. Is aged, impotent, and poor. Till they know the King's pleasure, know not not where to bestow themselves. [8 July 1538].

Volume XIII part 2

no. 24. Letter from Thomas Cranmer to Thomas Cromwell. Recommends the suit of his servant Nevell for his farm at Bowghton under the Blayne, which he had of the abbot and convent of Feversham; and which the king has commanded him to be dispossessed of. 3 August 1538.

no. 274. Letter from William Rooper to Sir Richard Ryche Consults him upon a doubt arisen by the dissolution of the monastery of Feversham, of which he is steward. The abbot and convent had among their liberties the right of appointing as mayor one of the three persons elected by the mayor, jurates and commonalty the morrow after Michaelmas; and the mayor took an oath given him by the abbot or his steward to doe true service to the king and the monastery. Asks what he is to do about it now. 3 September 1538.

no. 290. Letter from Sir Richard Rich to Thomas Cromwell. Learns by a letter, enclosed, from Master Roper steward of the late monastery of Faversham, Kent, that, the morrow after Michaelmas, the abbot there for the time used to choose the mayor for the next year out of three persons presented by the town. This liberty is now in the Court of Augmentations[746]. Desires to know whether the king will retain the nomination or remit it to Cromwell, or to the writer, as one of the officers of the said court. Desires remembrance of Master Pollerds suit and his. 6 September 1538.

---

744 The abbreviation is such that this is likely to be Chartham rather than Chartan given.

745 DK 8th Rep. App. II, 21: John Lynsted, William Frittenden [Frytynden], Ralph Ulcombe [Vltu'], Peter Sittingbourne [Sedynborne]

746 The Court of Augmentation was created in 1535 [27 Henry VII c 27] to administer the lands, possessions and revenues of the dissolved religious houses. It was dissolved and re-established by Letters Patent of 38 Henry VIII [1546-47] and

Volume XIV part I

Pensions from the Court of Augmentations.

Page 594. Richard Dryland of Feversham, Kent (for service in the King's wars beyond the sea) 10 marks annuity out of the lands of Faversham monastery. 20 September 1539

Page 597. Feversham, Kent, John Castleloke alias Shepey. 100 marks 24 July 1539
Also Robert Chillynden, Thomas Deve, John Fylpott, Peter Mynto, Dunstan Goodhewe, William Coyden, John Tayler and Ralph Post alias Ulcombe monks. 24 July 1539.

no. 610.
Letter from Sir Thomas Cheyne to Thomas Cromwell.[747]
According to the letters of your lordship and the others of the king's council delivered to me on the 23rd, I have sent to all the ports, but have only as yet got an answer from Faversham which I enclose. As soon as I hear more I will report it. 26 March 1539.

no. 708.
Letter from George Collyns in Antwerp to Thomas Wriothesley.
Crayers have come from Faversham with corn.
Antwerp 6 April 1539.

no. 1355 (65) Books of the Court of Augmentations.
Richard Dryland of Feversham, Kent (for service in the king's wars beyond the sea) 10 marks annuity out of the land of Feversham monastery 20 September 1539.

Volume XIV Part II
Thomas Cromwell's accounts, 1538, page 333, folio 117
Abbot of Veversham's servant for bringing a present 3^s 4^d

Volume XV
no. 61 Export of Corn.
William Fymer of Pheversam, mercer examined 14 Jan 1540 says (1) that, 25 may last 31 Henry VIII, William Castelocke brewer and William Belke, junior, barber, of Pheversam[748], did load 2 hoys of Flushing with grain, bought of John Goldfinch, of Faversham. This was restrained for the King by Thomas Clynton, Stephen Clynton, Peter Lawrence, John Daunell, William Borne, John Gremson, Walter Webbe and John Emerye; and Castelocke and Belke were bound to deliver it at Dover. Four days after Castlocke and Belke came to the customer's wife pretending to have unladen the grain; and so recovered their bonds. Then, at the next tide, they provided John Tylney, Henry Newman, John Bucke and others with bows, bills, and other weapons to defend them till their hoys might pass over; and so sailed into Zeeland, (2) Thomas Oldefelde, parish clerk of Faversham, and Belke, 20 June, conveyed grain in a ship of John Browne's of Whitstable to Zeeland. (3-5) John Bringborne, 21 June and 18 August, and John Umffrey, 24 June, conveyed grain to Zeeland in their own ships. (6) William Bringborne, 24 August, bought 25

---

confirmed by statute 7 Edward VI c. 2 [1553], abolished by statute 1 Mary, sess. 2. c. 10 and annexed to the Exchequer by two Letters Patent, 1 Mary, 23rd and 24th January 1553-54.

747 We cannot be sure to what this refers, but it might be to an unsatisfactory muster that he mentioned on 31 March (no. 633).

748 Hereafter given as Faversham.

'deker'[749] of leather at Bartholomew fair in London, and shipped it 'here at London' in a ship of Robert Breyes of Feversham, and bound himself in 40£ to bring it to Feversham, and not convey it beyond sea. Nevertheless he conveyed it into a ship of Dieppe at East Swale and showed the customer of Feversham 6 'deker' of country leather in his storehouse; and so got a certificate to discharge his bond. (7) Walter Webbe, Robert Cole, bailiff of Feversham, and Stephen Motte, 7 Oct, shipped grain in 2 hoys of Flushing, belonging to Adrian and Christopher Forster: witnesses, John Goldefynche, who sold them part of the grain, and John Hampton jurat of Faversham, who passed into Zeeland in one of the hoys. (8) William Belke, about 20 Nov., shipped wheat in a ship of Antwerp lying at the Fletes mouth besides Feversham, but was driven to Quenborowe Haven, where John Robinson, the mayor, seized the wheat for the King, and certified it in the Exchequer. Belke thereupon repaired to the exchequer and got John Castell and John Goldfinch, jurate of Faversham, bound for the grain to be delivered here. On 4 Dec., Goldfinch discharged half the wheat and brought it to Faversham, where he put in his own garners and the rest into a ship of John Bringborne's to go over sea; the other half Belke took over, about 15 Dec., notwithstanding the said bonds. (9) John Brinckborne, John Ambros, and William Brinckborne, 13 Nov., conveyed grain into Zeeland in the *Mawdelyn*, of Faversham, Ambros going over with it. (10) Stephen Motte and Robert Cole, 9 Dec., conveyed grain to Zeeland in Adrian Forster's Hoy; witness, John Goughe, who passed over in the hoy. (11) The same day the *Gallyon*, of Calais, was freighted with wheat, for the delivery of which at Rye John Goodale stands bound before the customer of Faversham. The said wheat is notwithstanding conveyed into Zeeland and there sold; witness, John Gough. Signed with mark. John Hudiball and Thomas Smith, of Faversham, confirm the foregoing.

Volume XVI.

no. 133 page 64.

Inventory of the implements etc. left in the king's storehouse at Dover to the use of his Grace's waterworks ... timber ...some in Faversham. 8 October 1540.

no. 724. The Privy Council: meeting at Greenwich, 14 April 1541.

John Smith, one of the King's watermen, and others, having entered a Portugal ship in Faversham road, on pretence of seizing unaccustomed merchandise, and carried away the mariners' private goods, and also brought away to London two catches laden with corn of John Antonyes, they were ordered to restore the Portugalles goods, specified in a schedule annexed to the examination, and as to the catches abide the order of the law. 14 April 1541.

no. 745 ff. 44-45. 1539-41 Creditors of the Abbey

payments by decree

9 June Edward Bartilmewe, tailor, £25 for Anne Baylye, widow and executrix of Robert Bayley, mercer, decreed 6 February debt of Faversham abbey

2 December ditto

8 February Richard Morgan executor of Robert Baylye £60 decreed 7 January debt (£75) of Faversham abbey

no. 877 page 416 Works at Calais and Guisnes 1541

' a declaration of the number of workmen and labourers, with their wages working beyond the sea on the King's Majesty's fortifications,' in the 33rd reign of Henry VIII.

---

[749] Dicker.

The estimated monthly costs of provisions of these works includes stone from Faversham and St. Augustine at Canterbury.

no. 1219 (pp. 565-569). Works at Calais.
Sir Edward Ringelay, knight, comptroller. A book of comptrolment upon the payment of the works at Calais paid by Richard a Lee, surveyor for the year beginning in the year xxxij and ending in the year of the reign of King Henry VIII, xxxiij. [similar book to no. 98, in vellum cover of 525 pages.]
Feb. - March 1541 ...stone from Maidstone and Faversham to Calais 29 Ships (8 to 20 names)
vi: 27 March to 23 April 1541
...carrying earth out of the dyke and Favershams stone from the East Juttye to Duvelin[750] Bulwark, 33 names.
vii. 24 April to 21 May 1541
...Feversham stone out of the Haven...
viii. 22 May to 18 June 1541
...'ragge' stonnes from St. Awstins [St. Augustine's Canterbury] and Feversham, ...

Volume XVII
no. 738 page 409 3 September 1542. Privy Council.
Commission delivered to John Antony and - Ardern to take up certain wheat at Faversham

no. 258 folio 16 page 129. Payments out of Augmentations
14 March Richard Robynson clerk by Doctor Leigh out of Faversham, St. Augustine's in Canterbury, Boxley and ?Ryland.
f.41, p. 134, Anne Baylye, widow, (as before) 7 November

Volume XVIII Part 1
no. 981 page 538.
Grant of Pardon to Gilbert Fitzricharde and Stephen Hochynson labourers for having 18 May 35 Henry VIII broken into the house of John Beste of Faversham and stolen two measures of corn worth $2^s 4^d$ 12 July 35 Hen. VIII (1543)

no. 436 folio 74, page 261.
Anne Baylye, widow, by Edward Bartylmewe, of London, tailor deceased decreed 6 February, Anno 31, debt of Feversham monastery, due 31 May 1542.

Volume XVIII Part 2
no. 546. Cranmer and the heretics in Kent.
These documents are concerned with the so called Prebendaries Plot of 1541-42 - a conspiracy with national as well as local ramifications designed not only to topple Cranmer but to halt the Reformation in its tracks. In the course of 80 pages the following local people and places are mentioned:

---

[750] Dublin, Dyvelin.

Archebolde of Faversham, 310.
Davington Church, 308
Thomas Hungerford of Sandwich, 299.
Sir Thomas Moyle, 297, 324, 327, 328, 335, 360.
Clement Norton, vicar of Faversham, 293, 308, 369.
Cyriak Petyt, 319, 335, 340, 356, 358.
Sermon at Faversham, preached by John Bland, 305
Sir Reginald Scott, 362.
Sir Robert a Stotte, curate of Davington, 316.
Sponer, vicar of Boughton, 291.
Swan, vicar of Sheldwich, 308.
Richard Turner, vicar of Ospringe, 335, 375.
Buckland near Faversham church, 294.

Volume XIX part 1
no. 368 page 244 folio 64.
Payments by decrees of the Court of Augmentations
6 June Anne Baylye, widow, decree 6 Feb. anno 21, debt out of Faversham, f.25
29 Jan. Anne Baylye, widow, by Edward Bartilmewe, for debt out of Feversham, decree 20 Feb. anno 31, f. 25
1544

Volume XX part 1
no. 1174 Letter from Charles Brandon, Duke of Suffolk to Sir William Paget about defence. Encloses a letter..
We shipmasters think that .... if the two beacons standing upon Whitestaple weares, the one on the north side of the channel of the East Swale, and the other on the Beacon Weare on the south side of the said channel, were taken away, no stranger dare bring a ship into the East Swale 'leading a great ship within 4 miles of Feversham.' 12 July 1545

no. 1334
Musters in Kent xxxvii Henry VIII ... from ...
the hundred of Faversham (1545), showing the numbers and description of soldiers sent to serve in the Isle of Sheppey out of the hundreds of Boughton and Fevorssham, of Maydeston and Eyhorn, of Longbrygge and Carte, of Middelton and Tenham and of Calehylle. Total 126.

Volume XXI part 2
p. 454
Map of Kentish Coast 1514.
A large pictorial coloured chart of the north coast of Kent from Margate to Faversham, showing in the higher part the East Swale and Faversham Creek etc.

Addenda Vol. I part 1

no. 46

This is the answer of Abbot of Faversham to a bill of complaint of William Osborn. Among other matters the abbot says that, for causing riots in town of Faversham, Sir Edward Poynings warden of the 'five ports' imprisoned Osborn in castle of Dover. Prays to be dismissed 'out of this court' with costs. No date.

Addenda Volume I part 2

no. 1417 page 482 & 483.

John Castlok, late Abbot of Faversham to Thomas Wyddford.

I received on 9 July your letter dated the 3rd, and as for lands that were Peter Smythes in Sedyngburne [Sittingbourne] and Milton, the said Peter and his wife, shortly after coming to dwell within the precinct of the monastery of Faversham, showed me that they had let to farm to John Cheyney all their lands there and elsewhere in Kent, reserving only a chamber in a mansion at Sedyngburne wherein their treasure and evidences remained. They showed me further that they delivered Cheyny stock and brewhouse implements together with 200£ in money, for a yearly sum which I have forgotten. After the death of Peter's wife Cheyney sent the vicar of Milton to offer me 200 marks to suffer the said Peter to come and rest with him in Sedyngburne, which I refused 'and that I suppose the said vicar will testify if he be so honest as he is noted for.' After the month's day of his wife, Peter asked me to allow my prior to ride with him to the said chamber in Sedyngburne to fetch his money, plate and evidences; and on the way they met John Cheyney at the Bekyn, a mile out of Feversham, riding towards Cantourbury, who turned back with them and suffered Peter to take away the money and plate, but 'denied him the receipt of all his evidences, saying he would keep them safe for him.' Half a year later the said Peter died, the evidence remaining still with the said John Cheyney, 'on whose souls Jesu have mercy.' Faversham, 18 July 1539. *Signed.*

*P.*1. *Add.*: at Hertrege.

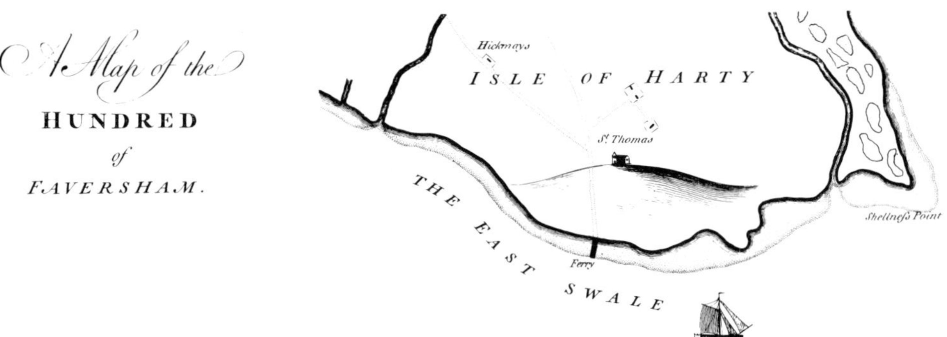

Section of the map of the Hundred of Faversham taken from, Edward Hasted, *The History and Topographical Survey of the County of Kent*. Vol. 2 (1782)

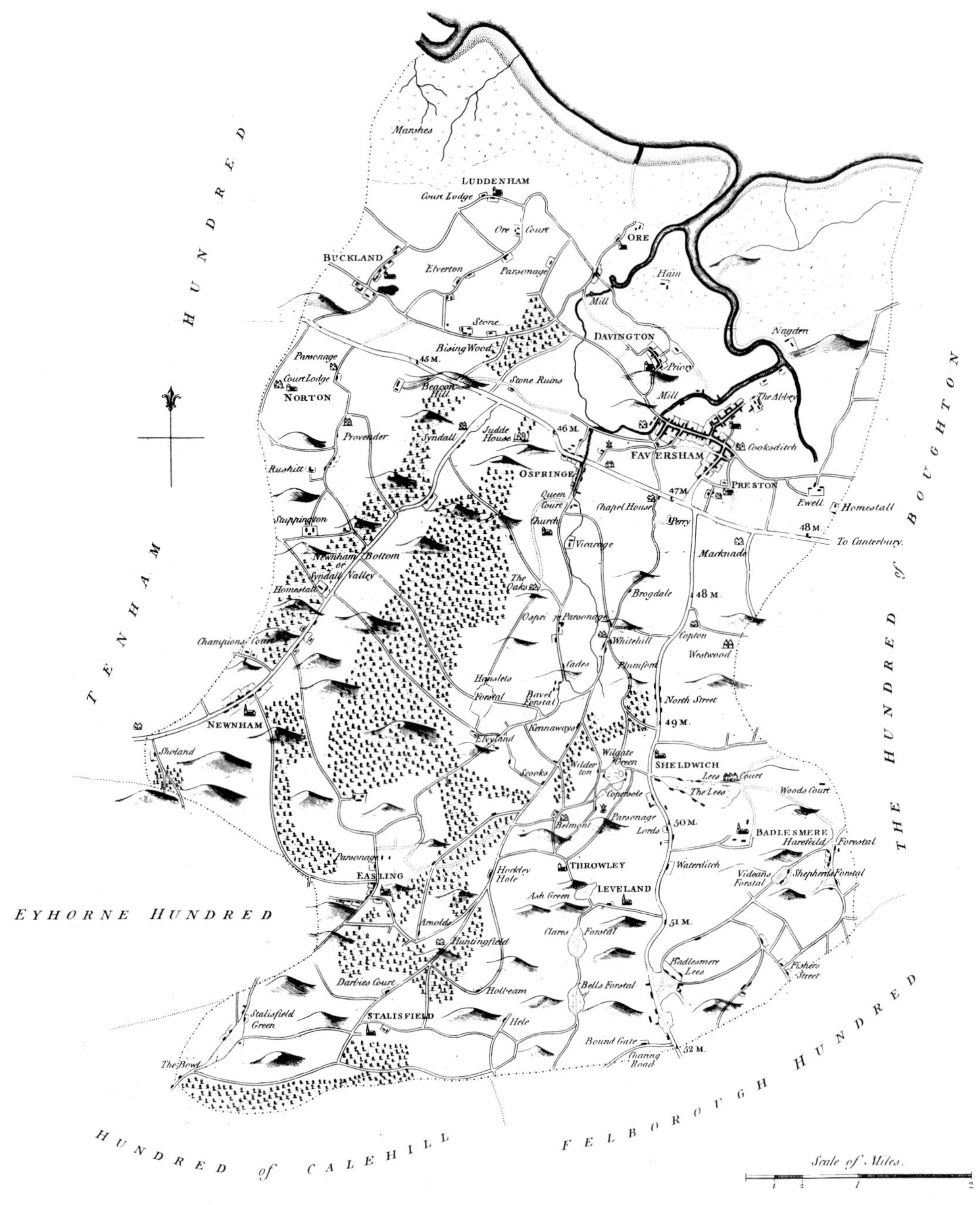

Section of the map of the Hundred of Faversham taken from, Edward Hasted, *The History and Topographical Survey of the County of Kent*. Vol. 2 (1782)

APPENDIX 17
1515 Survey of the Faversham Abbey lands in the hundred

U390 M37/1[751]

We can tell from internal evidence that this abbey survey for the hundred of Faversham was compiled in about 1515. Robert Stevynson is mentioned as vicar of Selling on page 343, but in fact, he resigned in 1514 and was replaced by John Swale. The will of William Church of Harty on page 287 was proved in 1517, that of Abraham Crowde of Harty, also on page 288, in 1516. On page 289 there is a reference to 4 acres 'lately purchased of Stephen Brayles' of Harty, whose will was proved in 1515. Furthermore, the Maison Dieu at Ospringe and the Priory of Davington are also mentioned as tenants: the Maison Dieu escheated to the Crown in 1480-81 and Davington Priory in 1535-36.

The survey was written as a fair copy, but there were minor additions in a later hand. On the inside cover amongst other notations in Latin was 'this book inspected by me Thomas Hilles 29th day of the month of November 1546.' He was probably the Thomas Hilles who paid 2^{s} 6^{d} for his freedom on 8 October 1543. The same year he was paid for the writing of a book to be signed by the King. He was later paid for many copies, including that of an acquittance to a mariner, who had bought the half hoy that was 'sumtyme John Grene's and now the town's i.e. one of Arden's assassins.[752]

Why Thomas Hilles inspected this rental in 1546, we cannot be sure. It might have been to do with obtaining the town charter in that year or equally it might have been at the request of the Court of Augmentations, which was in charge of the property. This 1515 survey would repay further study. The fields and roads named need to be related to their present day counterparts. Here and there are a few messuages whose names survive today. There should be much to interest historians of agriculture.

The survey does not seem to include the part of the hundred within the town. It does, however, give us an idea of the extent and situation of some of the rural boroughs. In particular, the borough of Ewell seems to have been extensive. The word 'borough' used in this context seems strange to us. It comes from 'borth', the Anglo-Saxon word for surety or pledge. It was the Kentish name for a district elsewhere called a tithing. Tithings were set up under the laws of Athelstan, putting men into groups of ten responsible for each other as a means of keeping the peace. It was developed in the twelfth century under the Normans as frankpledge. Each tithing had to pledge for the appearance in court of its members, to pursue and capture thieves, to bear the costs of imprisonment, to make presentments of crimes at tourns and eyres, and to pay up when they failed in any way. Twice a year from the reign of Henry II the sheriff held meetings to see that everyone was in a tithing. The head man was virtually a constable by the thirteenth century. The tithings began to decline in the late thirteenth century with improvments in royal justice, leading still later to the development of Quarter Sessions. These boroughs with their borsholders were therefore anachronisms even when the survey of 1515 was made.[753]

---

751 Deposited at the Centre for Kentish Studies.

752 Favward fols. 37v, 39v, 41v, 42v, 44, 46v, 62, 62v, 64v, 65v, 66.

753 C. I. Elton, *The Tenures of Kent* (London, 1867), p. 153; H. M. Jewell, *English Local Administration in the Middle Ages* (Newton Abbot, 1972), pp. 161-164; R. Stewart Brown, *The Serjeants of the Peace in Medieval England and Wales* (Manchester, 1936), p. 101.

This rental was one of a number of documents compiled by the abbot, John Castlock. There were also the town rentals and surveys in Literary Manuscript B5 considered in Appendix 18. There was also what is called the Leiger Book in Rockingham Castle. It is a miscellaneous register or memorandum book in which were written copies of grants, charters, wills, inquisitions, deeds and purchases. Although it deals with a longer period, most of the documents seem to have been compiled by John Castlock.

It was first called a Leiger Book by Thomas Southouse and there are some annotations by both him and his son, Filmer Southouse. It has not been transcribed for this study, because it has already been transcribed by the historian Joan Wake and I still hope that her copy may yet come to light. It was lent to the Kent Archaeological Society on 26 May 1920 and copied in the Library at Lambeth Palace by her for the society. The book itself was returned to Rockingham in 1923. The copy was used by C. R. Broughton at Lambeth for his thesis 'Faversham Abbey' in 1952. All attempts to track it down have so far proved fruitless.

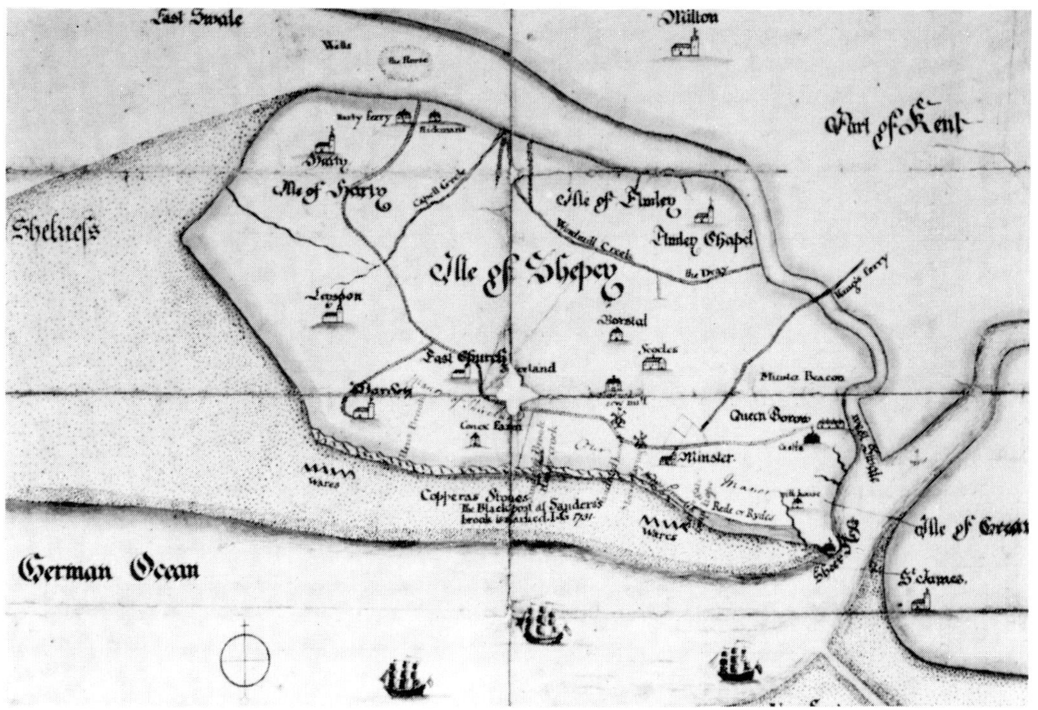

CKS: U36/P16 Island of Sheppey showing the boundaries of the manor of Minster, c. 1735.

THE SURVEY 1515

Cover late hand **'An old booke of the rents belonging to the Abby of Feversham'** and marked '12' on the spine.[754]

THE HEIRS OF THOMAS FROGENHALE hold of the Lord Abbot of Faversham as of his manor of Faversham in the hands of his tenants one marsh called Keyboroughmarsh with a hope[755] adjacent called Keyboroughmarsh hope containing 63 acres[756] of marsh and land as shown below:

In the hands of the Prioress of Davington eight acres of land called Sparows, one half acre of land lying at Brodegoredyche in the hands of Thomasine Chevyn widow, one of the heirs of Simon Champayne, 11 acres of land called New Purchased lands lying next to Brodegore, one acre lying at Keyborough hill next the lands of the Abbot of Favershamthere.

In the hands of Stephen Hayward one messuage and one piece of land called Willowes containing 10 acres lying at Keyborough hill, in the hands of the heirs of Thomas Brayles 13 acres called Brodegore croft, in the hands of the heirs of Thomas Gregory two acres of land lying at Keyboroughhill.

And in the hands of the heirs of Thomas Haywarde four acres called Brodegore lying next to Keyborowehill.

And in the hands of the Lord Abbot of Faversham 14 acres and one daywork[757] of land lying at Keyboroughhill late Thomas Oven. And pays in respect thereof each year 10^s 5^d.

THE HEIRS OF JOHN LONDON hold of the Lord Abbot of Faversham as of his manor of Faversham in the demesne one messuage one barn and one piece of land adjacent containing in itself 11 acres called Balyn one croft[758] of ground adjacent containing two acres of land and one marsh called Balyn marsh containing 50 acres and half an acre of marsh, and he holds in his hands of the heirs of Thomas Hayward seven acres of land called Lampett lying next to the king's highway[759] there towards the south and to the lands called Perry croft and to the lands called Balyn towards the north. And pay in respect thereof each year 6^s $10½^d$ [760]

---

754 The whole book, which is in Latin, has been translated. On the inside of the front cover 'iste liber pertinet ad dominus Abbati Feversham' (This book belongs to the lord Abbot of Feversham). On the pastedown in the hand of Thomas Southhouse, 'Feversham in the county of Kent, Throwleigh 1701 [Feversham in agro Cantiano, Nemo Mascitur artifex: Mea gloria Fides] insignia [drawing of the coat of arms] of the 'Prehonorabilis Ludovicus dominus de Rockingham'. It seems possible, since there is no heading to this section, that a leaf has been lost. See the comment at footnote 1008.

755 Hopa, W.E. Latham, *Revised Medieval Latin Word List*, 1965, 'hope', a piece of enclosed marshland (Essex & Kent).

756 *The Tenures of Kent* by Charles I. Elton (London 1867), page 129, 'The Kentish acre was measured in the way described by Coke ... varying indefinitely in length and breadth it was always a piece of land containing 160 perches of sixteen feet square, i.e. a fraction over 4,551 square yards. Thus 1,000 statutory acres would contain over 1,063 customary.' Thus taking the perch at sixteen feet, the canon shews the breadth of an acre for each perch in length.

Length in perches	Breadth Perches
40	4
80	2

When we know the ancient dimensions of the acre we can estimate the size of the 'day-work' which contained four perches of sixteen feet, being the fortieth part of an acre.

757 *O.E.D..daywerca* Day-work, daywork: 2. The amount of land that could be worked, ploughed, mown, etc., in a day.

758 *O.E.D.* Croft 1. A piece of enclosed ground, used for tillage or pasture; in most localities a small piece of arable land adjacent to a house. Toft and Croft a messuage with land attached. 2. A small agricultural holding worked by a peasant tenant.

759 Latin; *regia strata*.

760 Much later hand at the bottom of the page: 'olim meminisse iuvavit Filmer Southouse Favershamiensis in agro Cantiano 7° Decembris 1700' Some time ago it helped Filmer Southouse of Faversham in the County of Kent to remember 7th

THE[761] **LORD ABBOT** of Faversham holds certain lands called Dornishe crofts containing 22 acres and two dayworks and one hope adjacent partly north and lying between Balyn marsh towards the west Northmarsh towards the north and east and the said croft towards the south, total acres 22. And pays in respect thereof each year [762]

THE SAME ABBOT holds one acre one virgate[763] and one daywork of land called Hothis acre and lying between the king's highway towards the west and north the lands of the Abbot of Faversham called Forty acres towards the east and the lands of the heirs of Champeyn towards the south. Total acres one, one virgate and one daywork. And pays in respect thereof each year

STEPHEN HAYWARD AND RICHARD LAURENT feoffees for the uses and intentions and to implement the last will of Thomas Oven hold of the Lord Abbot of Faversham as of his manor of Faversham six acres of land to the benefit of the holy light[764] of the church of Hartey and lying next to Hodys and two acres thereafter called Hoddys and lying between the lands of the heirs of John Songer towards the east the king's highway towards the south the lands of the Abbot of Faversham towards the west and the lands of the same Abbot and the lands of the heirs of Thomas Oven towards the north. Total acres six. And pays to the Lord in respect thereof each year for each acre

THE HEIRS OF JOHN SONGER hold of the Lord Abbot of Faversham as of his manor of Faversham aforesaid two acres of land with a messuage standing upon called Hoddys and lying between the king's highway towards the south chirchland late Thomas Oven also called Hodyes towards the west to the lands of the heirs of Thomas Oven and the lands of Thomas Napleton towards the north and to the lands of the said Thomas Napleton towards the east. Total acres two. And pays in respect thereof to the Lord each year for each acre[765]

THOMAS NAPULTON holds of the Lord Abbot of Faversham of his manor of Faversham as aforesaid 2 acres and ½ virgate one daywork and ½ with a messuage existing upon and lying between the lands of the heirs of John Songer called Fyve Acres towards the East, the Kings way towards the South, the lands of the said heirs of John Songer containing 2 acres towards the West and the lands of the said Thomas Napulton formerly Thomas Banny towards the North. Total acres 2 and ½ virgate, 1 daywork and ½ and pays in respect thereof to the Lord for each acre each year

THE HEIRS OF JOHN SONGER hold of the Lord Abbot of Faversham as of his manor of Faversham aforesaid 5 acres of land called Rollys and lying between the Kings way towards the South, the lands of Thomas Napulton towards the West and the lands of the same Thomas and the heirs of Thomas Oven towards the North and the lands of the same heirs of Thomas Oven towards the East. Total acres 5. And pays in respect thereof to the Lord for each acre each year[766]

December 1700. *Monasticon* makes no mention of the volume, nor Fa/Z34 *Antiquities of Faversham* MS History by Filmer Southouse 1698.

[761] fol. 1v.

[762] In this and subsequent entries the value is not given.

[763] Ronald Edward Zupko, *A Dictionary of English Weights and Measures*, A measure of area for land generally synonymous with the *yardland* and in Sussex with the *wista*. Like the acreage of other superficial measures, its total acreage depended on local soil conditions, but virgates of 15, 16, 20, 24, 28, 30, 32, 40, and 60 acres (*c*.6.07 to *c*.24.30 ha) were the most common. It was generally equal to ¼ *hide* and was occasionally the sum of 2 or 3 *bovates* or 4 *farthingdales*. However, *V.C.H. Kent* Volume 3 page 322: 'It may be noted that in Kent in medieval documents the word virgate is commonly used in a third sense for a quarter of an acre, or rood.

[764] fol. 2.

[765] fol. 2v.

[766] fol. 3.

THE HEIRS OF THOMAS OVEN hold of the Lord Abbot of Faversham as of his manor of Faversham aforesaid 4 acres one virgate and 3 dayworks of land and lying between the lands of Thomas Napulton formerly Thomas Banny towards the East, the lands of the heirs of John Songer and the lands containing 6 acres lately Thomas Oven now to the use and benefit of the holy light of the church of Hartey from the gift of the same Thomas Oven towards the South, the lands of the Abbey of Faversham towards the west and formerly marsh called North Mershe towards the North. Total acres 4 and 1 virgate and 3 dayworks and pays in respect thereof to the Lord for each acre each year

THOMAS NAPULTON holds of the Lord Abbot of Faversham as of his manor of Faversham aforesaid 8 acres of meadow land and 7 dayworks formerly Thomas Banny and lying between the lands of the heirs of Thomas Oven towards the East and the lands of the heirs of Thomas Songre and the lands of the said Thomas[767] Napulton towards the South, the lands of the said heirs of Thomas Oven towards the West, and Northmershe towards the North. Total acres 8 meadow and 7 daywork. And he renders in respect thereof to the Lord for each acre each year

THE SAME THOMAS holds of the aforesaid Abbot as of his manor aforesaid 1 acre of meadow and 4 dayworks called Long Aker formerly Thomas Banny and lying between the lands of the heirs of Thomas Oven towards the East South and West and North Mershe towards the North. Total acres 1 acre meadow and 4 dayworks and pays in respect thereof to the Lord for each acre each year

THE SAME THOMAS holds of the aforesaid Abbot as of his manor aforesaid 3 acres and ½ acre and 1 virgate of meadow and 2 dayworks called 4 Akers formerly Thomas Banny and lying between the lands of the heirs of Thomas Oven called Walters towards the East, South, West and North MEMORANDUM that the said 3 acres ½ acre and 1 rood meadow and 2 dayworks lying within 30 acres and ½ acre[768] and 4 days works and ½, subsequently total acres 3 and ½ and 1 virgate meadow 2 dayworks And pays in respect thereof to the Lord for each acre each year

THE HEIRS OF THOMAS OVEN hold of the Lord Abbot of Faversham as of his manor of Faversham aforesaid 30 acres and ½ acre 4 dayworks and ½ land called Walters and Caleyse lying together between the lands of the heirs of John Songre towards the East the lands of the heirs of Thomas Oven and the lands of Richard Fayre near to Upfelde towards the South, the lands of the said heirs of John Songre and the lands of Thomas Napulton formerly Thomas Banny 30 and ½ acres 4 dayworks and ½ and pays in respect thereof to the Lord for each acre each year

THE HEIRS OF JOHN SONGRE hold of the Lord Abbot of Faversham as of his manor of Faversham aforesaid one croft of land called Upper Croft containing 6 acres 1 virgate and 3 dayworks and lying between the lands of the said heirs of John Songre which do not render to us[769] towards the East Croft of the said heirs of John Songre called Nether Croft towards the South to the lands of the heirs of Thomas Oven formerly Walters towards the West North Mershe and the lands of the said heirs of Thomas Oven towards the North. Total acres 6, 1 virgate and 3 dayworks and pays in respect thereof to the Lord for each acre each year

THE SAME HEIRS hold of the aforesaid abbot as of his manor of Faversham aforesaid one croft of land called Nether Croft containing 2 acres and 1 perch and ½ of land and lying between the lands of Richard Fayre called Leedys towards the East the Kings way and part of the lands of

---

[767] fol. 3v.
[768] fol. 4.
[769] fol. 4v.

the heirs of John Songre towards the South the lands of the said Richard Fayre called Upfelde towards the West and the lands of the said heirs of John Songre towards the North. Total acres 2, 1 perch and ½, and pays in respect thereof to the Lord for each acre each year

THE SAME HEIRS hold of the aforesaid Abbot as of his manor of[770] Faversham aforesaid one acre and ½ meadow land 3 dayworks and ½ land situated in Uppfelde between the Kings way towards the South East and South, the lands of the heirs of Thomas Oven lately Stephen Crowde and the lands of Richard Fayre towards the North. Total acres 1 and ½ perch and 3 dayworks and ½ And pays in respect thereof to the Lord for each acre each year

RICHARD FAYRE holds of the Lord Abbot of Faversham as of his manor of Faversham aforesaid 3 acres 4 dayworks and one perch called Uppfelde formerly Stephen Banny and lying between the lands of the heirs of John Songre towards the East and South the lands of the heirs of Thomas Oven called Uppfelde lately Stephen Crowde towards the West and North. Total acres 3 acres and ½, 4 dayworks and 1 perch. And pays in respect thereof to the Lord for each acre each year

THE HEIRS OF THOMAS OVEN hold of the Lord Abbot[771] of Faversham and as of his manor of Faversham aforesaid 8 acres and ½ virgate of meadow land in respect whereof 4 acres and 3 roods of land thereof called Postyng gate Crofte purchased by William Oven father of the said Thomas. And 3 acres 1 virgate and ½ thereof called Upfelde purchased by the said Thomas Oven of Habraham Crowde and all lying between the lands of Richard Fayre and the lands of the heirs of John Songre towards the East, the Kings towards the South, the lands of the said heirs of John Songre towards the West and the lands of the said heirs of Thomas Oven towards the North. Total acres 8 and ½ virgate and pays in respect thereof to the Lord for each acre each year [772]

THE WESTERN PART OF WESTDOWNE

THOMAS NAPULTON holds of the Lord Abbot of Faversham as of his manor of Faversham aforesaid 3 acres and ½ acre 4 dayworks and 1 perch in Westdowne and lying between the lands of Richard Fayre who renders to Christ Church Priory Canterbury and to the lands of the said Thomas Napulton formerly Banny who also renders to the said Priory towards the South, North Mersh towards the West lands of the said Richard Fayre lying in Westdowne towards the North and the Kings way towards the East. Total acres 3 and ½ acre 4 dayworks and 1 perch And pays in respect thereof to the Lord for each acre each year

RICHARD FAYRE holds of the Lord Abbot of Faversham as of his manor of Faversham aforesaid 6 acres and one virgate meadow one daywork and ½ land and lying between the lands of Thomas Napulton towards the South the Kings way towards the East North Marsh towards the East and the lands of the Prioress of Davington towards the North. Total acres 6, 1 virgate meadow, 1 daywork and ½ and pays in respect thereof to the Lord for each acre each year

THE[773] **LADY PRIORESS** of Davington holds there of the Lord Abbot of Faversham as of his manor of Faversham aforesaid 3 acres 1 virgate 3 dayworks and 1 perch and lying between the lands of the same prioress and the lands of Richard Fayre towards the East lands of the said Richard Fayre towards the South Northmersh and the lands of the said Richard Fayre towards the North Total acres 3 acres 1 virgate 3 dayworks and 1 perch. And pays in respect thereof to the Lord for each acre each year

770 fol. 5.
771 fol. 5v.
772 Lower half of fol. blank, fol. 6 recto and verso blank, fol. 7.
773 fol. 7v.

Dna Priorissa de Davyngton [illegible]

[illegible]

Eadem priorissa tenet de [illegible]

[illegible]

CKS: U390 M37/1 folio 7v

THE SAME PRIORESS holds of the aforesaid Abbot as of his manor aforesaid another piece of land adjacent and containing 1 acre and ½ acre 3 dayworks and 1 perch and lying between the Kings way towards the East, the lands of Richard Fayre towards the South, the lands of the said Prioress and the lands of the said Richard Fayre towards the West and the lands of Peter Songre towards the North Total acres 1 and ½ acres and 3 dayworks and 1 perch and pays in respect thereof to the Lord for each acre each year[774]

RICHARD FAYRE holds there of the Lord Abbot of Faversham as of his manor of Faversham aforesaid 1 acre 1 virgate and 4 dayworks of land formerly William Ledys and lying between the lands of Peter Songre towards the North and East the lands of the said Prioress towards the South, and Northmersh towards the West. Total acres 1 and 1 virgate and 4 dayworks. And pays in respect thereof to the Lord for each acre each year

PETER SONGRE holds of the Lord Abbot of Faversham as of his manor of Faversham aforesaid one acre of land formerly Walters lying there between the Kings way towards the East the lands of the said Prioress towards the South the lands of Richard Fayre towards the West and the lands of the said Peter towards the North. Total acres 1. And pays in respect thereof to the Lord for each acre each year

THE SAME PETER holds of the aforesaid Abbot as of his manor aforesaid 5 acres 3 virgates 3 dayworks and ½ land called Grenelese formerly Walters afterwards Thomas Mett and lying between the Kings way [775]towards the East the lands of the said Peter and the lands of the said Richard Fayre towards the South Northmershe towards the West and the lands of Thomas Hoklyng otherwise called Gregory towards the North. Total acres 5, 3 virgates 3 dayworks and ½ And pays in respect thereof to the Lord for each acre each year

THOMAS HOCKLYNG otherwise Gregory holds there of the Lord Abbot of Faversham as of his manor of Faversham aforesaid 8 acres and ½ acre ½ virgate and 1 daywork and lying between the Kings way towards the East the lands of Peter Songre called Greneleese towards the South, Northmershe towards the West and the lands of the said Prioress towards the West and North. Total 8 acres and ½, ½ virgate and 1 daywork. And pays in respect thereof to the Lord for each acre each year

THE PRIORESS OF DAVYNGTON holds of the Lord Abbot of Faversham as of his manor of Faversham aforesaid 1 acre and 1 virgate of land there and lying between the lands of the said Thomas Hoklyng[776] otherwise called Gregory towards the East and South, Northmersh towards the West and the lands of the heirs of John Songre and the lands of the said Prioress towards the North. Total acres 1. And pays in respect thereof to the Lord for each acre each year

THE HEIRS OF JOHN SONGRE holds there as of the Lord Abbot of Faversham as of his manor of Faversham aforesaid 1 acre and ½ acre 2 dayworks and 1 perch and lying between the lands of the said Thomas Hocklyng otherwise called Gregory towards the North and East, Northmershe towards the West and the lands of the said Prioress towards the South. Total acres 1 and ½ acres 2 dayworks and 1 perch. And pays in respect thereof to the Lord for each acre each year

THOMAS HOCKLYNG alias called Gregory holds of the Lord Abbot of Faversham as of his manor of Faversham aforesaid 3 virgates of meadow land 2 dayworks and lying between the lands

[774] fol. 8.
[775] fol. 8v.
[776] fol. 9.

of the said Prioress towards the North East and[777] South and the lands of the heirs of John Songre towards the West Total 3 virgates of meadow 2 dayworks. And pays in respect thereof to the Lord for each acre each year

PRIORESS OF DAVYNGTON holds of the Lord Abbot of Faversham as of his manor of Faversham aforesaid 5 acres and ½ acre, 1 virgate and 1 daywork and 1 perch of land lying between the Kings way towards the East the lands of Thomas Hocklyng otherwise called Gregory towards the South lands of the heirs of John Songre and the lands of the said Thomas Hocklyng towards the West, marsh of the said Prioress called Buttmarsh towards the North Total acres 5 and ½ 1 virgate 1 daywork and 1 perch. And pays in respect thereof to the Lord for each acre each year

THE EASTERN PART OF EASTEDOWNE

THOMAS HOCKLYNG otherwise called Gregory holds of the Lord Abbot of Faversham as of his manor of Faversham aforesaid one croft of land called Hyckescrofft containing 1 acre 1 virgate and 3[778] dayworks and lying between Buttesmarsh towards the North and East, lands of the said Thomas towards the South and lands of the Prioress of Davyngton towards the West. Total acres 1, 1 virgate and 3 dayworks. And pays in respect thereof to the Lord for each acre each year

THE PRIORESS OF DAVINGTON and Thomas Hocklyng otherwise called Gregory holds of the said Abbot of Faversham as of his manor of Faversham 8 acres and 3 virgates 3 dayworks of land and lying between the Kings way towards the West lands of the said Prioress and lands of the said Thomas towards the North, Buttmarsh and Chilsons Marsh towards the East and the lands of the Prioress towards the South. IN RESPECT WHEREOF the said Prioress holds 1 acre which lies within the said lands that is to say from Hyckes Crofte directed towards the South 11 rods and in longitude towards Buttmarsh. Total acres 8, 3 virgates and 3 dayworks. And pays in respect thereof to the Lord for each acre each year

THE[779] PRIORESS AFORESAID holds of the Lord Abbot of Faversham as of his manor of aforesaid 3 acres 3 dayworks ½ daywork and 1 perch and lying between the lands of Thomas Hocklyng otherwise called Gregory towards the North, marsh of the said Thomas called Chylsons Mersh towards the East, lands of the heirs of John Songre towards the South and the Kings way towards the West. Total acres 3, 3 dayworks and 1 perch and pays in respect thereof to the Lord for each acre each year

THOMAS HOCKLYNG otherwise called Gregory holds of the Lord Abbot of Faversham as of his manor of Faversham aforesaid 1 acre 1 virgate 2 dayworks and 1 perch and lying between the Kings way towards the West the lands of the said Prioress towards the North and East and the lands of the heirs of John Songre towards the South Total acres 1, 1 virgate 2 dayworks and 1 perch. And pays in respect thereof to the Lord for each acre each year.

THE[780] HEIRS OF SONGRE hold of the Lord Abbot of Faversham as of his manor of Faversham aforesaid 6 acres and 3 virgates and 1 perch at Upper Chylsons Dyche and lying between the lands of the Prioress of Davington towards the South, the Kings way towards the West the lands of Thomas Hocklyng otherwise called Gregory and the lands of the said Prioress

[777] fol. 9v.
[778] fol. 10.
[779] fol. 10v.
[780] fol. 11.

towards the North Total acres 6 acres 3 virgates and one perch And pays in respect thereof to the Lord for each acre each year

THE PRIORESS OF DAVYNGTON holds of the Lord Abbot of Faversham as of his manor of Faversham aforesaid 4 acres and ½ an acre and 4 dayworks of land and ½ daywork at Upper Chylsonsdyche and lying next Harflete Merssh towards the East, the lands of Richard Fayre towards the West and South, the Kings way towards the North. Total acres 4 and ½ an acre and 4 dayworks and a ½ And pays in respect thereof to the Lord for each acre each year

RICHARD[781] **FAYRE** holds of the Lord Abbot of Faversham as of his manor of Faversham 1 acre and a ½ acre land and 1 virgate of meadow-land and 1 daywork and lying between the King's way towards the West and the lands of the said Prioress towards the North and South, to the lands of the said Prioress and the lands of the said Richard Fayre towards the East. Total acres 1 and ½ an acre and 1 virgate of meadow-land and 1 daywork. And pays in respect thereof to the Lord for each acre each year

PRIORESS OF DAVYNGTON holds of the Lord Abbot of Faversham as of his manor of Faversham aforesaid 2 acres and ½ virgate and 4 dayworks and a ½ and lying between the King's way towards the West, the lands of the said Richard Fayre towards the North, East and South. Total acres 2 and ½ an acre 1 virgate and 4 dayworks and a ½. And pays in respect thereof to the Lord for each acre each year

RICHARD FAYRE holds of the Lord Abbot of Faversham as of[782] his manor of Faversham aforesaid 2 acres and ½ acre 3 dayworks and a ½ and lying between the King's way towards the West, the lands of the said Prioress towards the North, the lands of the said Richard Fayre towards the East, the common way leading from the King's way towards the West as far as Harflete Merssh towards the East and South. Total acres 2 and ½ an acre, 3 dayworks and a ½ and pays in respect thereof to the Lord for each acre each year

THE SAME RICHARD FAYRE holds of the said Abbot of Faversham as of his manor of aforesaid 5 acres and 1 virgate of land and lying between the lands of the said Prioress towards the North, Marsh of the said Richard called Harflete Merssh towards the East and lands of the same Richard towards the South and the lands of the same Richard and the lands of the said Prioress towards the West. Total acres 5 and 1 virgate and pays in respect thereof to the Lord for each acre each year.

THE SAME RICHARD FAYRE holds of the Lord Abbot as of his manor aforesaid 12 acres and a ½ virgate and lying between Harflete Mersshe towards the East [783]the lands of William Church and the lands of the said Richard towards the South, the King's way towards the West and a certain[784] way leading from the King's way towards Harflete mersshe with the lands aforesaid towards the North. Total acres 12 and ½ virgate. And pays in respect thereof to the Lord and the Office of Chamberlain for each acre each year

WILLIAM CHURCH holds of the Lord Abbot of Faversham as of his manor of Faversham aforesaid 3 acres and ½ an acre 1 virgate and a ½ and lying between the King's way towards the West and the lands of the said Richard Fayre towards the North and East and the lands of the said

---

781 fol. 11v.
782 fol. 12.
783 fol. 12v.
784 *Quandam* for quidam: just possibly *quondam* for formerly.

Richard which he pays to the Barton[785] as he says towards the South Total acres 3 and ½, 1 virgate and a ½ And pays in respect thereof to the Lord for each acre each year

RICHARD FAYRE holds of the Lord Abbot of Faversham as of his manor[786] of Faversham aforesaid 2 acres and a ½ an acre of land and ½ a daywork and 1 perch on one side East of the said 3 acres and ½ acre and 1 virgate and ½ lying beside Harflete Mersshe towards the East, the lands of the said Richard which he pays to the Barton as he says towards the South, the lands of William Church towards the West and the lands of the said Richard Fayre towards the North. Total acres 2 and ½ an acre, ½ a daywork and ½ a perch. And pays in respect thereof to the Lord for each acre each year.[787]

THE HEIRS OF THOMAS OVEN and William Church hold of the Lord Abbot of Faversham as of his manor of Faversham aforesaid 3 virgates and 1 daywork and ½ and 1 perch called Martynhayes lying between the lands of the said Prioress towards the East and 3 virgates and ½ daywork of land of the said Richard Fayre towards the South the lands of the Abbot of Faversham towards the West and the lands of the heirs of John Songre towards the North. Total 3 virgates 1 daywork and ½ and 1 perch. And pays in respect thereof to the Lord for each acre each year.

STEPHEN HAYWARD holds of the Lord Abbot of Faversham as of his manor of Faversham aforesaid 3 virgates and ½ daywork of land in one piece called Martynhayes formerly Stephen Banney before Thomas Banny his father and afterwards Stephen Napulton and lying between the lands of the Lady Prioress of Davyngton[788] called Shornefelde towards the East and South, the lands of the Abbot of Faversham towards the West and 3 roods 1 daywork and ½ daywork and 1 perch of land which the heirs of Thomas Oven and William Church hold towards the North. Total 3 virgates ½ daywork And pays in respect thereof to the land for each acre each year

PRIORESS OF DAVYNGTON holds of the Lord Abbot of Faversham as of his manor of Faversham aforesaid Shornefelde containing 20 acres and 2 dayworks and ½ and 1 and lying between the lands of the heirs of Champeyn towards the East, lands of the heirs of John Songre towards the South, the lands of William Church and the lands of the heirs of Thomas Oven and the lands of the Abbey of Faversham towards the West, the lands of William Church the lands of the heirs of John Songre and the lands of Thomas Oven North. Total acres 22, 2 dayworks and ½ and 1 perch. And pays in respect thereof to the Lord for each acre each year

THE[789] HEIRS OF THOMAS OVEN hold of the Lord Abbot of Faversham as of his manor of Faversham aforesaid 5 acres and 1 virgate of land called Newehousland and garden and lying between the lands of the Prioress of Davyngton and the lands of William Churche lately Abraham Crowde and the lands of Thomas Hocklyng otherwise called Gregory lately of the said Thomas Oven towards the East the lands of the said William Churche and the lands of the said Thomas Hocklyng towards the South, the lands of the said Prioress the lands of the said Thomas Hocklyng and the lands of the said Thomas Oven towards the West and the lands of the Abbey of Faversham towards the North Total acres 5 and 1 virgate. And pays in respect thereof to the Lord for each acre each year

WILLIAM CHURCHE holds of the Lord Abbot of Faversham as of his manor of Faversham aforesaid 3 acres[790] and ½ daywork of land lying together at a place called Newehousland and

---

785 *O.E.D.* A demesne farm; the demesne lands of a manor, not let out to tenants, but retained for the lord's own use.
786 fol. 13.
787 Remainder of fol. blank; fol. 13v.
788 fol. 14.
789 fol. 14v.
790 fol. 15.

lying between the lands of the said Prioress and the lands of the heirs of John Songre towards the East, the lands of the Abbey of Faversham containing 1 acre and 1 virgate towards the South the lands of Thomas Hocklyng otherwise called Gregory and the lands of the heirs of Thomas Oven called Garden land towards the West and lands of the said heirs of Thomas Oven towards the North. Total acres 3 and ½ And pays in respect thereof to the Lord for each acre each year

PRIORESS OF DAVYNGTON holds of the Lord Abbot of Faversham as of his manor of Faversham aforesaid 3 acres of land besides the lands of said heirs of Thomas Oven called Garden land towards the East the lands of Thomas Hocklyng otherwise called Gregory towards the South and West and the lands of the Abbey of Faversham towards the North. Total acres[791]

THOMAS HOCKLYNG otherwise called Gregory and the heirs of Thomas Oven hold of the Lord Abbot of Faversham as of his manor of Faversham aforesaid 4 acres and ½ acre of land and lying between the lands of the said heirs of Thomas Oven towards the East the lands of the said Thomas Hocklyng towards the South the lands of Stephen Hayward called Wyllowes and the lands of the said Thomas Hocklyng at Keyborough towards the West and the lands of the said Prioress containing 3 acres towards the North. Total acres 4 and ½ And pays in respect thereof for each acre each year

THE AFORESAID THOMAS HOCKLYNG otherwise called Gregory holds of the Lord Abbot of Faversham as of his manor aforesaid[792] one messuage with appurtenances and 16 acres 8 dayworks and ½ of land wherefore part thereof called Gardenlond a short time ago Elyottes containing 3 acres lying together in diverse parcels Another part thereof called Herry Rycard and the other part thereof called Brokeland a short time ago John Jekyns entirely lying between the lands of the heirs of Thomas Oven the lands of the Abbey of Faversham containing 1 virgate towards the North, the lands of the said Abbey containing 1 acre towards the East the lands of the heirs of Thomas Waller and the lands of the Prioress of Davyngton called Stangreland towards the South, lands of Prioress and lands of Stephen Hayward called the Willowes towards the West Total acres 16, 8 dayworks and a ½ And pays in respect thereof to the Lord for each acre each year

PRIORESS OF DAVYNGTON holds of the Abbot of Faversham as of his manor of Faversham aforesaid 5 acres at Stonerock[793] and lying between the lands of Richard Fayre towards the East, Master John Priour towards the South the lands of the same John towards the West and the lands of the heirs of William Brayles towards the North Total acres 5 and pays in respect thereof to the Lord for each acre each year

THOMAS BRAYLES holds of the Lord Abbot of Faversham as of his manor of Faversham aforesaid 1 acre of land on the East side of Backkesfelde and lying between the lands of the said Prioress called Stone Rock towards the East, the lands of John Pryour towards the South and the lands of the said Thomas containing 4 acres land towards the West and the lands of the heirs of William Pashley towards the North Total acres 1 And pays in respect thereof to the Lord for each acre each year

JOHN PRIOUR holds of the Lord Abbot of Faversham as of[794] his manor of Faversham aforesaid 2 acres and ½ acre, 1 daywork and ½ and 1 perch formerly Hocklyngs otherwise Gregory called Betts a short time ago Rychyngwods and lying between the lands of the said Prioress towards the East the lands of John Priour towards the South and the lands of the heirs of William Brayles

[791] fol. 15v.
[792] fol. 16.
[793] fol. 16v.
[794] fol. 17.

towards the West and North Total acres 2 and ½ an acre and 1 daywork and a ½ and 1 perch And pays in respect thereof to the Lord for each acre each year

THOMAS BRAYLES holds of the Lord Abbot of Faversham as of his manor of Faversham aforesaid 11 acres 4 dayworks and 1 perch with a messuage called Backysfelde and lying between the lands of the said Prioress called Stonerock and the lands of John Priour towards the East marsh of the said Thomas Brayles towards the South and the lands of the same Thomas and the King's way towards the West, lands of the said Thomas part of[795] Backsfelde towards the North WHEREFORE JOHN PRIOUR holds 4 acres lately purchased of Stephen Brayles And the said Thomas Brayles holds the residue Total acres 11, 4 dayworks and 1 perch And pays in respect thereof to the Lord for each acre each year

THE SAME THOMAS BRAYLES holds of the aforesaid Abbot of Faversham as of his manor aforesaid 2 acres land in Backesfelde adjoining the said 11 acres and lying between the lands of the said Thomas towards the North and East, marsh of the same Thomas towards the South and the King's way towards the West. Total acres 2. And pays in respect thereof to the Lord for each acre each year

THE[796] SAME THOMAS BRAYLES holds of the same Abbot of Faversham 4 acres of land in Backysfelde lying together between the lands of the same Thomas and the lands of John Priour towards the East lands of the said Thomas towards the South the King's way towards the West and the lands of the aforesaid Thomas which lie in the tenure of St. John Jerlin towards the North. Total acres 4, and pays in respect thereof to the Lord for each acre each year

THOMAS HOCKLYNG otherwise called Gregory holds of the Lord Abbot of Faversham as of his manor of Faversham aforesaid 4 acres of land at Peryknock formerly Walters and lying between the lands of the Abbey of Faversham towards the South West, The Hope of Abraham Crowde near to Balynmershe towards the North East and Perycrofte and lands of the heirs of Thomas Haywarde called Lampett towards the East Total acres 4, and pays in respect thereof to the Lord for each acre each year

THE LADY PRIORESS of Davyngton Peter Songre John Gregory otherwise Hocklyng Abraham Crowde hold Peryknock and lying between the lands of the Abbot of Faversham South West, The Hope of Abraham Crowde next to Belyn Marsh North East and Perycroft and lands of the heirs of Thomas Hayward called Lampett East. Wherefore the Prioress holds 3 acres on the North East side Peter Songre holds 6 acres wherefore 2 acres paid to the Monastery of Faversham [blank] John Gregory holds 4 acres and pays to the said Monastery [blank] and Abraham Crowde holds 9 acres and pays to the Poor Brothers of Harbaldowne[797]

Rents of the heirs of Thomas Frogenhall annually paid to the court of the following diverse tenements held of the same heirs at a place called Busshoppes Garden[798]

THE LADY PRIORESS of Davyngton holds of the Lord Abbot of Faversham as of his manor of Faversham aforesaid 8 acres of land lying together called Sparowes and ½ acre at Broadgoredyche And pays for the acres each year

THE SAME PRIORESS holds of the said Abbot of Faversham as of his manor of Faversham aforesaid in Keyborowe Marsshe the right of pasture of 32 sheep for each sheep each year

[795] fol. 17v.
[796] fol. 18.
[797] fol. 19 blank fol. 19v blank fol. 20.

THE HEIRS OF THOMAS WALLER hold of the Lord Abbot of Faversham as of his manor of Faversham aforesaid 11 acres of land next to Brodgore called Newpurchessyd lands for each acre each year

THE SAME HEIRS OF THOMAS Waller hold of the same Abbot as of his manor aforesaid 1 acre of land at Keyboroughhyll attached to the lands of the Abbot of Faversham[799] on the West side of The 40 acre of the same Abbot for the said acres each year

THE SAME HEIRS OF THOMAS WALLER hold of the said Abbot as of his manor aforesaid in Keyborough the right of pasture of 12 sheep for each sheep [blank]

THE LORD ABBOT of Faversham holds at Keyboroughhyll 14 acres and ½ daywork of land for the acres [blank]

STEPHEN HAYWARD holds of the Lord Abbot of Faversham as of his manor of Faversham aforesaid at Keyborow hyll 10 acres of land with one messuage standing upon it called Willowes adjoining the lands of the lady prioress of Davyngton towards the South the lands of the heirs of Thomas Waller West, lands of the said Abbot North, the lands of Thomas Gregory East And pays for the acres yearly

STEPHEN HAYWARD holds of the same Abbot of [800] Faversham as of his manor aforesaid in Keyborough Marsh the right of pasturage for 42 sheep for each sheep yearly

WILLIAM CHURCH holds of the Lord Abbot of Faversham as of his manor of Faversham aforesaid 13 acres of land called Brodgore croft aforesaid each year

WILLIAM CHURCH holds of the aforesaid Abbot as of his manor aforesaid in Keyborowe Marshe pasturage for 42 sheep for each sheep yearly

THOMAS GREGORY holds of the lord Abbot as of his manor of Faversham aforesaid at Keyborowe Hill 2 acres of land for each acre yearly

THE HEIRS OF THOMAS HAYWARD hold of the Lord Abbot of Faversham as of his manor aforesaid next to Keyborowe Hill 4 acres of land called Brodgore for each acre yearly[801]

ORE[802]

JOHN[803] NORTON knight holds of the lord Abbot of Faversham as of his manor of Faversham one messuage [later hand called Grete Howlettes] and 3 pieces of land adjacent together on the West side of the said messuage containing 16 acres between the marsh of the said John there towards the South the lands of the said John towards the West and Olde Ferywey towards the North. Total acres 16 And he renders therefore to the Lord for every acre by the year

THE SAME JOHN[804] holds of the aforesaid Abbot as of his manor aforesaid 1 acre and a half an acre of land adjoining the said messuage, the land of the said John towards the West and North

---

798 *Reddit[um] her[edum] Thome Frogenhall annuatim solvend[is] de diversis ten[emen]tibus ut sequitur ad cur[iam] ipsorum hered[um] ten[en]dum apud locu[m] voc[atis] Busshoppes Garden.*

799 fol. 20v.

800 fol. 21.

801 fol. 21v blank.

802 fol. 22. From this fol. to fol. 28 the manuscript has been collated with a translation U390.M37/2 by H.G.Hewlett, 2 Raymond Buildings, Grays Inn 10 October 1857. On the whole this proved to be reasonably accurate, with trifling errors; but he did not note additions to the original manuscript.

803 *Margin* later hand Ludnam.

804 *Margin* later hand Ludnam.

and the land of the same John containing half an acre towards the East Total acres 1½ acres. And he renders therefore to the Lord for every acre by the year

THE SAME JOHN[805] holds of the same lord Abbot of Faversham as of his manor aforesaid three acres at Forstall Marsh towards the North and East land belonging to the Maison Dieu[806] of Ospringe formerly Elliottes towards the South and the lands of the said John towards the West Be it remembered that these three acres aforesaid lie in a certain piece of land which contain 6 acres and three and a half dayworks of land Whereof the Master of the Maison Dieu of Ospringe holds three acres and three and a half dayworks as appears afterwards at this mark [+][807] formerly being two pieces. Total acres 3. And he renders therefore to the Lord for every acre by the year

THE SAME JOHN[808] holds of the aforesaid Abbot as of his manor aforesaid four and a half acres of land and 1 perch and lying between Forstall Marsh towards the North, The Fery Way and land appertaining to the Maison Dieu of Ospringe towards the West, land of the said Maison Dieu and land of the heirs of John Church towards the South. Total acres 4[809] and one perch. And he renders therefore to the Lord for every acre by the year[810]

THE SAME JOHN[811] holds of the aforesaid Abbot as of his manor aforesaid 2 acres and 4 dayworks of land adjacent between Forstall Marsh towards the East land of the Maison Dieu of Ospringe towards the South and North and land of the said John towards the West and the said two acres contain in width at the West end ten and a half perches and in length at the centre thirty and a half perches and at the East end ten and a half perches. Total acres 2 and 4 dayworks. And he renders therefore to the Lord for every acre by the year

THE SAME JOHN[812] holds of the same Abbot as of his manor aforesaid one piece of pasture enclosed near Forstall Marsh towards the West containing 1 acre 2 dayworks and ½ a daywork and lying between the lands of the heirs of John Church called Willowes towards the South and land appertaining to the messuage of Upleese towards the North and East. Total acres 1, 2½ dayworks. And he renders for the acre by the year

THE SAME JOHN[813] holds of the aforesaid Abbot as of his manor aforesaid 2 acres 3 virgates of land between the Kings highway towards the South the lands of the Maison Dieu of Ospringe called[814] Eliottes and the land of the heirs of John Church towards the West and land of [blank] Huddy called Upleese towards the North and the ancient gangway from the Kings highway and towards a curtilage and messuage of Upleese towards the East. Total acres 2 and 3 virgates. And he renders therefore to the Lord for every acre by the year

THE SAME JOHN[815] holds of the same Abbot as of his manor aforesaid one acre an a half an acre of land called Little Howlettes and lying between the land of John Chilton called Medlercroft towards the South the lands of Upleese and the common forestall[816] appertaining to Forstall marsh

---

805 *Margin* later hand Faversham.
806 fol. 22v.
807 The original has a Maltese cross see the other entry on page 324 of this text.
808 *Margin* later hand Faversham.
809 So in the MS.
810 fol. 23.
811 *Margin* later hand Faversham.
812 *Margin* later hand Faversham.
813 *Margin* later hand Faversham.
814 fol. 23v.
815 *Margin* later hand Faversham.
816 *Forstallum* W.E.Latham, *Revised Med Latin Word-List*: 'forestall','fostal' piece of land in front of building [Kent] W.D.Parish & W.F.Shaw, *A Dictionary of Kentish Dialect* (1889). FORSTALL [for.stul], FORESTAL [foa.rstul], FOSTAL [fost.ul] A farm-yard before a house; a paddock near a farm house; the house and home-building of a farm; a

towards the West and the land of Upleese towards the North and East. Total acres 1½ acres. And he renders therefore to the Lord for every acre by the year

THE[817] MASTER OF THE MAISON DIEU of Ospringe holds of the lord Abbot of Faversham as of his manor of Faversham 5 acres and ½ a perch 2 dayworks of land[818] adjacent to the said two acres of land formerly Eliottes lying between Forstall Marshe towards the East The Feryway towards the South land of the heirs of John Churche towards the West and the land of John Norton knight towards the North. An containing in width at the East end 28 perches and ½ and in the centre in length 32 perches. Total acres 5 and ½ perch, 2 dayworks. And he renders therefore to the Lord for every acre by the year

THE[819] SAME MASTER holds of the same Abbot of Faversham as of his manor of Faversham aforesaid 3 pieces of pasture containing 3 acres and 3 virgates of land lying together between [the land] of the heirs of the said John Norton towards the East and South land [blank] Huddy part of Uppleese towards the West and Forstall Marshe towards the North. Total acres 3 and 3 virgates, And he renders therefore to the Lord for every acre by the year [+][820]

THE SAME MASTER holds of the aforesaid Abbot as of his manor aforesaid 3 acres 3 dayworks and ½ daywork of land and lying between land of the said John Norton South[821] West and North and Forstall Marshe towards the East. Total acres 3, 3½ dayworks. And he renders therefore to the Lord for every acre by the year

THE[822] SAME MASTER holds of the same Abbot of Faversham as of his manor aforesaid one messuage called Eliottes containing ½ an acre 2 dayworks and ½ and lying between [blank] towards the West the land called Wyllowes towards the North and the land of the said [blank] Huddy part of Uppleese towards the East and the Kings highway towards the South. Total acres ½ an acre 2 dayworks and ½. And he renders therefore to the lord for every acre by the year

THE[823] HEIRS OF JOHN CHICCHE hold[824] of the lord Abbot of Faversham as of his manor of Faversham aforesaid the site of a messuage containing ½ an acre 2 dayworks and ½ a daywork of land called Wyllowes and lying between the lands of John Norton knight towards the North Forstall Marsh towards the West the messuage called Eliottes towards the South and the lands of [blank] Huddy towards the East. Total ½ an acre 2 dayworks and ½ daywork of land. And they render therefore to the lord for every acre by the year

THE[825] HEIRS OF JOHN CHICCHE hold of the same Abbot as of his manor aforesaid 2 acres and 1 perch of land in a certain Croft called Longgere and lying between the land formerly of Richard Eliott towards the East the common way called the Fery way towards the South and West and the lands of the said John Norton towards the North. Total acres 2 and 1 perch. And they render to the lord for every acre by the year

---

small opening in a street or lane, not large enough to be called a common As a local name, forestalls seem to have abounded in Kent; as for instance, Broken Forestall, near Buckley; Clare's Forestall, near Throwley and several others. *A manuscript note to the volume* has added Downs Forstal - Faversham.

817 *Margin* in later hand Faversham.

818 fol. 24.

819 *Margin* later hand Faversham.

820 *Margin* later hand Faversham The original cross was in the style of a Maltese cross. See the earlier mark on page 323 of this text.

821 fol. 24v.

822 *Margin* later hand Faversham.

823 *Margin* later hand Faversham.

824 fol. 25.

825 *Margin* later hand Faversham.

THE[826] **SAME HEIRS OF JOHN CHICCH** hold of the aforesaid Abbot as of his manor aforesaid 1 virgate of land in Eastdowne and lying between the land of the heirs of John Martyn towards the East[827] the land of the heirs of Richard Forstall towards the West and the land formerly Richard Eliott towards the North and a certain field called Westfelde towards the South And the said have pasture on Forstall Marsh for eight sheep. Total 1 virgate. And they render therefore to the Lord by the year

THE[828] **HEIRS OF ROBERT FEKYNHAM** now John Chilton in right of his wife hold of the Lord Abbot of Faversham as of his manor of Faversham aforesaid 3 virgates of land called Medlescroft and lying between the Kings highway towards the South West the forstall for cattle of Forstall Marshe towards the West the land of the said John Norton and the land of William Huddy Esquire towards the East. Total 3 virgates. And they render therefore to the lord by the year.

WILLIAM[829] **HUDDY** Esquire holds of the lord Abbot of Faversham[830] as of his manor of Faversham aforesaid one messuage one garden and three crofts on the South side of the said messuage containing by estimation 6 acres and one curtilage with one barn standing upon it and with the land called Uplond adjacent to the said curtilage and barn on the North and East sides containing by estimation 12 acres And the total of the said messuage, garden three crofts land curtilage barn and 12 acres of land appertaining to the said messuage and curtilage lying between the Kings Highway and the resting place for cattle which feed on Forstall Marshe towards the South lands of Upleese towards the West, Salt Marsh of the said William Huddy towards the North the land of John Norton knight called Lytell Howlettes And the forstall of Upleese towards the East. Total acres [blank] [831]

THE SAME WILLIAM HUDDY holds of the aforesaid Abbot as of his manor aforesaid one salt marsh called Upleese marshe adjacent to the said 12 acres[832] and the other lands of the said William.

THE[833] **SAME WILLIAM HUDDY** holds of the same Abbot of Faversham as of his manor aforesaid one croft of land adjacent to the said curtilage and barn on the West side containing by estimation 11 acres of land and lying between the lands of John Norton knight towards the South and West and Forstall Marsh towards the West, Salt marsh of the said William Huddy towards the North and the said messuage, garden, curtilage and barn and 12 acres towards the East Total acres 11. And he renders therefore to the lord for every acre by the year

THE[834] **SAME WILLIAM HUDDY** hold of the same Abbot as of his manor aforesaid in certain pasture of the West side near Nykerton in the Lordship of Faversham 6 acres and 1 virgate of land and lying between the lands of John Norton knight and the lands of the said William Huddy towards the North East and West And the said 6 acres and one virgate[835] of land contain in length from a certain oak called the Marke Ooke [Oak] growing on the Northside of Greteleese towards the East towards a croft of the said William Huddy towards the West 37 perches and ½. And

---

826 *Margin* later hand Faversham.
827 fol. 25v.
828 *Margin* later hand Faversham.
829 *Margin* later hand Faversham.
830 fol. 26.
831 *Margin* later hand Faversham.
832 fol. 26v.
833 *Margin* later hand Faversham.
834 *Margin* later hand Faversham.
835 fol. 27.

contains in length on the Northside from another oak called also the Marke Ooke towards the East towards the East unto a garden adjacent the messuage of Uppleese towards the West 26 perches And 6 acres and 1 virgate containing in length between the said two oaks 45 perches. And which two oaks divide the parishes of Faversham and Oore. Total acres 6 and 1 virgate. And he renders therefore to the Lord for every acre by the year

THE[836] SAME WILLIAM HUDDY holds of the aforesaid Abbot as of his manor aforesaid one piece of land called Greteleese containing by estimation 19 acres of land and lying between the field called Orefelde towards the East a certain piece of land called Bukkynberigh[837] towards the East and South, Brome Crofte towards the South a certain lane there, the land of John Chylton called Medlerscroft and the land of the said John Norton knight called Litell Owlettes towards the West and the land of the said William Huddy towards the North Whereof five and a half acres lie in the Lordship of Ore attached to the said field called Orefield containing on the South end between West and East that is to say between Orefield aforesaid and Bukkynbery croft 7 perches and a half And contains in width on the North end between West and East that is to say between next to Nekerton Pettes and a certain oak called the Marke Ooke 20 perches and a half And the residue of the said 19 acres contains in width from the said oak towards the East unto the lands of the said John Norton called Lytell Owlettes towards the West 33 perches. Total acres 19. And he renders therefore to the Lord for every acre by the year

THE[838] SAME WILLIAM HUDDY holds of the same Abbot of Faversham as of his manor aforesaid Bukkynbery Crofte containing 3 acres and 1 virgate land and lying between the land of the said William Huddy called Greteleese towards the North and West and Brome crofte towards the South Total acres 3 and 1 virgate. And he renders therefore to the Lord for every acre by the year

THE[839] SAME WILLIAM HUDDY holds of the same Abbot of Faversham as of his manor of aforesaid one croft of land called Bromecrofte containing 9 acres and 1 virgate and lying between the lands of the said William Huddy called Uppchalke towards the East and South the Kings highway adjacent to the land of the heirs of John Martyn of Dartforde West and the land of the said William Huddy called Greteleese towards the North. Total acres 9 and 1 virgate. And he renders therefore to the lord for every acre by the year

THE[840] SAME WILLIAM HUDDY holds of the aforesaid Abbot as of his manor[841] aforesaid one croft of land called Ferthyng Croft containing 4 acres and ½ which lie between a certain common lane which lies between the said croft and Greteleese towards the East the land of the heirs of Richard Martyn towards the South and West and the Kings Highway towards the North. Total acres 4 and ½. And he renders therefore to the Lord for every acre by the year

GRAVENEY[842]

THE LORD OF GRAVENEY holds of the lord Abbot of Faversham as of his manor of Faversham aforesaid one piece of land called Melfelde containing 26 acres 3 roods and 7 perches and lying between the Kings Highway towards the North the way there called Stockyslane

---

836 *Margin* later hand Faversham.
837 fol. 27v.
838 fol. 28. *Margin* later hand Faversham.
839 *Margin* in later hand Faversham.
840 *Margin* in a later hand Faversham.
841 fol. 28v.
842 fol. 29.

towards the West. Total acres 26, 3 roods and 7 perches. And he renders therefore to the lord by the year

THE HEIRS OF RICHARD COKETT now [blank] Hardyman hold of the lord Abbot of Faversham as of his manor of Faversham aforesaid one acre of land in Southfelde and lying next to Cokkes between the Kings Highway North garden of Edward Martyn called Stokys Garden and the lands of the heirs of Thomas Chicche towards the East the lands of the heirs of Robert Colwell called Chalkland towards the South and land of the heirs of John Menfelde towards the west. Total acres 1. And they render therefore to the Lord for every acre by the year.

THE[843] **HEIRS OF ROBERT COLWELL** hold of the lord Abbot of Faversham as of his manor of Faversham aforesaid in the same field one acre and ½ an acre of land called Chalkeland and lying between the said acre of land in Southfelde and the land of the aforesaid heirs of Thomas Chiche and the lands of the said Edward Martyn towards the North and a certain lane called Stokyslane towards the East and the lands of the heirs of the said Thomas Chicche towards the South and the land of the heirs of John Menfeld towards the West Total acres 1 and ½ an acre. And they render therefore to the lord for every acre by the year

THE HEIRS OF JOHN MENFELDE hold of the lord Abbot of Faversham as of his manor aforesaid in the said field 5 acres of land at Prattes lying together to the Kings Highway towards the North land of the heirs of Richard Cokett land of the heirs of Robert Colwell called Chalkeland towards the East and the land of the said heirs of Thomas Chicche towards the East and South and the land[844] of the heirs of Thomas Mett towards the West Total acres 5. And they render therefore to the Lord for every acre by the year

THE HEIRS OF THOMAS METT hold of the lord Abbot of Faversham as of his manor of Faversham aforesaid at Prattes 1 acre and ½ virgate of land and lying between the kings highway towards the North land of the heirs of John Menfelde towards the East land of the heirs of Thomas Chicche towards the South and land of the heirs of Colwell towards South and West Total acres 1 and ½ virgate. And they render therefore to the Lord for every acre by the year

THE HEIRS OF ROBERT COLWELL and the heirs of Thomas Chicche hold of the lord Abbot of Faversham as of his manor of Faversham aforesaid 3 acres and 2 dayworks ½ a daywork and 1 perch at Beawley lying together between the Kings Highway towards the North land of the heirs of the said Thomas Mett towards the East land of the heirs of Thomas Chicche towards the South and West Whereof[845] the said heirs of Thomas Chicche hold 1 virgate Total acres 3, 2 dayworks, ½ a daywork and 1 perch. And he renders therefore to the lord for every acre by the year

THE HEIRS OF THOMAS CHICCHE hold of the lord Abbot of Faversham as of his manor of Faversham aforesaid ½ an acre of land at Beawley and lying between the Kings highway towards the North land of the heirs of Robert Colwell towards the East land of the said heirs of Thomas Chicche towards the South and land of the heirs of Thomas Mett towards the West. Total ½ an acre. And they render therefore to the lord for every acre by the year

THE HEIRS OF THOMAS METT hold of the lord Abbot of Faversham as of his manor of Faversham aforesaid 2 acres 2 dayworks and ½ a daywork of land at Beawley and lying between the Kings Highway towards the North land of the heirs of Thomas[846] Chicche towards East and

---

[843] fol. 29v.
[844] fol. 30.
[845] fol. 30v.
[846] fol. 31.

South and lands of the heirs of Richard Samuell towards the West. Total acres 2, 2½ dayworks. And they render therefore to the lord for every acre by the year

THE HEIRS OF RICHARD SAMUELL holds of the lord Abbot of Faversham as of his manor of Faversham aforesaid one tenement and one garden with a parcel of land from the close annexed on the East side of the said garden demesne land of the heirs of Thomas Mett towards the East and containing 1 acre one virgate and ½ virgate and 2 dayworks of land and all lying to the Kings Highway towards the North the garden of the said heirs of Thomas Mett towards the West the land of the said heirs of Richard Samuell and the land of the heirs of John Menfeld towards the South, Total 1 acre 1 virgate ½ virgate and 2 dayworks. And they render therefore to the lord for every acre by the year

THE SAME HEIRS OF RICHARD SAMUELL hold of the aforesaid Abbot as of his manor aforesaid 4 acres 3 rood and ½ daywork of land and lying between the said garden with[847] the messuage towards the North land of the heirs of Thomas Mett towards the East land of the heirs of Thomas Chiche towards the South and lands of the heirs of John Menfelde towards the West. Total acres 3, 3 roods and ½ a daywork. And they render therefore to the lord for every acre by the year

THE HEIRS OF JOHN MENFELDE hold of the lord Abbot of Faversham as of his manor of Faversham aforesaid 1 acre and ½ an acre 2 dayworks and ½ a daywork of land and lying between the land of the heirs of Thomas Mett towards the West land of the same heirs of Thomas and land of the said heirs of Richard Samuell towards the North and East and lands of the heirs of Thomas Chicche towards the South Total an acre and ½ an acre, 2 dayworks and ½. And they render therefore to the lord for every acre by the year

THE HEIRS OF THOMAS METT hold of the lord Abbot of Faversham as of his manor of Faversham aforesaid the said messuage with the garden containing ½ an acre 1 daywork[848] ½ a daywork and 1 perch of land and lying between the Kings highway towards the North garden of the heirs of Richard Samuell towards the East parcel of the lands of the heirs of John Menfelde and the land of the said heirs of Thomas Mett towards the South the Homeway towards the West Total ½ an acre 1 daywork and ½, 1 perch. And they render therefore to the lord for every acre by the year

THE SAME HEIRS OF THOMAS METT and Richard Moyce hold of the lord Abbot of Faversham as of his manor of Faversham aforesaid 3 acres 1 virgate 2 dayworks and ½ a daywork of land and lying between the heirs of John Menfelde towards the East land of the heirs of Thomas Chicche towards the South the Sherewey towards the West garden of the said heirs of Thomas Chicche and land of the said heirs of Thomas Mett towards the North Whereof the said Richard Moyse holds ½ an acre in the East side. Total 3 acres, 1 virgate 2 dayworks and ½. And they render to the lord for each acre by the year

THE[849] HEIRS OF THOMAS CHICCHE hold of the lord Abbot of Faversham as of his manor of Faversham aforesaid parcel of a garden containing ½ rood and 2 dayworks of land lying between to Kings highway North the Homewey East and the land of the heirs of Thomas Mett South and West Total ½ a rood and 2 dayworks. And they render therefore to the lord for every acre by the year

---

847 fol. 31v.
848 fol. 32.
849 fol. 32v.

THE HEIRS OF THOMAS METT hold one garden with a barn standing upon it with a parcel of land there near the land of the heirs of Thomas Chicche annexed on the West side and containing 1 rod and 4 dayworks and lying between the Kings highway towards the North parcel of the garden of the heirs of Thomas Chicche towards the East land of the said heirs of Thomas Mett towards the South Total 1 rood and 4 dayworks. And they render therefore to the lord by the year

THE SAME HEIRS hold of the aforesaid Abbot of Faversham as of his manor[850] aforesaid 5 roods 3 dayworks and ½ daywork and 1 perch and lying between the said garden and barn towards the North the shyrewey towards the East land of the heirs of Thomas Chicche towards the South and West Total 1 acre 1 rood 3 dayworks and ½ and 1 perch. And they render to the lord by the year

THE HEIRS OF CHICCHE hold of the lord Abbot of Faversham as of his manor of Faversham 6 acres and 1 virgate of land and lying between the lands called the Conyerth[851] South marsh of the heirs themselves Southwest land of the heirs of Thomas Mett West land of the heirs of Richard Moyse land of the said heirs of Thomas Mett land of the said heirs of Thomas Chicche towards the North and land of the said heirs of Thomas Mett and the Shyrewey towards the West Total acres 6 and 1 virgate. And they render therefore to the lord for every acre by the year

THE SAME HEIRS hold 3 virgates of land of the aforesaid Abbot of Faversham[852] as of his manor of Faversham aforesaid and lying between the kings highway towards the North land of the heirs of Thomas Mett East and West land of the said heirs of Thomas Chicche towards the South Total 3 virgates. And they render to the lord by the year

THE HEIRS OF THOMAS METT hold of the lord Abbot of Faversham as of his manor of Faversham aforesaid 2 acres ½ a virgate 1 daywork and 1 perch of land and lying between the kings highway towards the North land of the heirs of Thomas Chicche towards the East and South land of the heirs of Richard Moyse West Total 2 acres ½ virgate 1 daywork and one perch. And they render therefore to the lord for every acre by the year

HEIRS OF RICHARD MOYSE hold of the said Abbot of Faversham as of his manor of Faversham aforesaid one acre of land and lying between the Kings highway towards the North, land of the heirs of Thomas Mett East land of the heirs of Thomas Chicche South and land of John Jakes West. Total 1 acre. And they render therefore to the lord for every acre by the year[853]

JOHN JAKYS holds of the lord Abbot of Faversham as of his manor of Faversham aforesaid one acre of land and lying between the Kings highway towards the North land of the heirs of Thomas Mett East land of the heirs of Thomas Chicche South and land of the heirs of John Jakys West. Total 1 ~~acre~~ rod & ½ [854]. And he renders therefore to the lord by the year

THE HEIRS OF THOMAS METT hold of the Lord Abbot of Faversham as of his manor of Faversham aforesaid ½ an acre of land lying between the lands of the heirs of Thomas Chicche East a certain marsh of the heirs themselves South land of Richard Laurent West land of John Jakys North and containing in length with the said marsh from the land of the said heirs of Thomas Chicche towards the East unto the land of the said Richard Lawrent towards the West 6 rood. Total ½ an acre. And they render by the year

---

850 fol. 33.
851 Cony-earth *O.E.D.* early form of Cony-garth, a rabbit-warren.
852 fol. 33v.
853 fol. 34.
854 Inserted in a contemporary hand.

RICHARD LAWRENT holds of the said Abbot of Faversham as of his manor aforesaid ½ an acre of land and lying between the land of the heirs[855] of Thomas Mett East, the marsh of Thomas Chicche South, land of the heirs themselves West, And containing in length with the said marsh from the said lands of the heirs of Thomas Mett towards the East unto the lands of the said heirs of Thomas Chicche towards the West 6 perches and ½. Total ½ an acre. And he renders therefore to the Lord by the year

THE HEIRS OF RICHARD MOYSE holds of the said Abbot of Faversham as of his manor of Faversham aforesaid ½ an acre 1 daywork and 1 perch lying between the Kings highway North land of the heirs of John Jakys East land of Richard Lawrent South and land of Thomas Mett West. Total ½ an acre 1 daywork and 1 perch. And they render therefore to the lord by the year.

THE HEIRS OF THOMAS METT AND THE HEIRS OF THOMAS CHICCHE hold of the lord of Abbot of Faversham as of his manor of Faversham aforesaid[856] 1 acre 4 dayworks and ½ a daywork of land lying between the Kings highway North land of the heirs of Richard Moyse and Richard Lawrent East marsh of the heirs of Thomas Chicche South and land of Richard Lawrent West Whereof the heirs of Thomas Chicche hold 1 rod And the said acre 4 dayworks and ½ contain in length with the said marsh 5 perches. Total 1 acre 4 dayworks and a ½. And they render therefore to the lord for every acre by the year

RICHARD LAWRENT holds of the lord Abbot of Faversham as of his manor of Faversham aforesaid ½ an acre of land lying between the croft of the heirs of Robert Colwell and land of the heirs of Thomas Chicche towards the West the Kings highway North land of the heirs of Thomas Mett East and the marsh of the heirs of Thomas Chicche South And containing in length with the said marsh 2 perches and 2 feet. Total ½ an acre. And he renders therefore to the lord by the year

THE[857] **HEIRS OF ROBERT COLWELL** hold of the lord Abbot of Faversham as of his manor of Faversham aforesaid in a certain croft nonetheless[858] formerly called Peykenhambrome 8 acres and ½ and ½ a rod and lying between the Kings highway called The Kings Street towards the North the land of Richard Lawrent East the marsh of the heirs of Thomas Chicche South a certain lane called Pollislane and the land of John Peryman West and North Whereof the heirs of the said Thomas Chicche hold 1 virgate of the said land on the Eastern part of the said croft. Total 8 acres and ½ and ½ a rod. And they render therefore to the lord for every acre by the year

JOHN PERYMAN holds of the lord Abbot of Faversham as of his manor aforesaid one messuage called Buttes with a garden attached containing 1 rood 1 daywork and ½ and one small croft adjacent[859] containing 12 dayworks and ½ and lying between the Kings highway North the land of the heirs of Robert Colwell East South and West. Total 1 rood, 14 dayworks. And he renders therefore to the lord by the year

THE HEIRS OF ROBERT COLWELL hold of the Lord Abbot of Faversham as of his manor of Faversham 1 rood of land attached to the said garden and croft and lying between the kings highway towards the North and the garden and croft aforesaid towards the East the lands of the heirs of Robert Colwell South and Pollislane West. Total 1 rood. And they render therefore to the lord by the year

---

[855] fol. 34v.
[856] fol. 35.
[857] fol. 35v.
[858] *Nichis* for ?*nihilominus*.
[859] fol. 36.

THE[860] BOROUGH OF EWELL

THE WARDENS OF ROCHESTER BRIDGE hold of the manor of Langdon held by the lord Abbot of Faversham as of his manor of Faversham aforesaid land pasture meadow-land and water-meadow containing 164 acres furthermore they hold of the said manor, that is to say, the demesne manor aforesaid with the land adjacent in Langdon felde containing 84 acres and lying between the Kings highway towards the West the common foot-path[861] in the same field towards the South and the Brooks towards the East and the land of the said manor towards the North. Total acres furthermore held of the manor 164. And they render therefore to the lord for every acre by the year.

THE SAME WARDENS hold of the same lord Abbot of Faversham as of his manor aforesaid another piece of land called Chalke containing 15 acres and lying besides Pottyns Brokes towards the East the land of John Bull junior called Potters towards the North, the land of Richard Lawrent called Lytille Felde and pasture of the said manor towards the West and South. Total 15 acres. And they render therefore to the Lord for every acre by the year

THE[862] SAME WARDENS hold of the aforesaid Abbot as of his manor aforesaid one piece of pasture adjacent to the said land called Chalke towards the East land called Lytill Eastfelde towards the North the kings highway West and the messuage of the said manor towards the South and containing 35 acres [rest blank]

THE SAME WARDENS hold of the aforesaid Abbot as of his manor aforesaid 38 acres of meadow-land and water-meadow adjacent to the said land called Potyns towards the East And the same wardens hold of the heirs of Edward Martyn Richard Lawrent and other tenants in respect thereof for land called Eastfelde containing 14 acres and 3 roods and lying between the Kings highway West and the land called Potters Pighthilles[863] East. Total 38 acres. And they render to the lord for every acre by the year

RICHARD DRYLAND JUNIOR holds of the lord Abbot of Faversham as of his manor of Faversham aforesaid one messuage curtilage and barn with[864] garden adjacent called Holmeston containing 4 acres. And the same person holds another 4 acres of land adjacent in Holmeston Felde on the East side of the garden. And the said 4 acres contains in width on the Northern part in a straight line towards the East from the said garden unto The Eldernstock from the said field 16 perches and 3 inches[865] And containing in length from the said Elderstok in a straight line towards the south unto the garden called Olde Makenaddes Garden 35 perches and a ½ And from the boundary of the said 35 perches and ½ in a straight line towards the East unto the garden aforesaid towards the West 20 perches and 3 inches Total 8 acres And the total lying between the land of the said Richard towards the East, Olde Makenades Garden and Collys Croft South and formerly a way there towards the West And 4 acres of land of the said Richard which lie in the parish of Graveney beside Eldernstock aforesaid towards the North. Total acres 8. And he renders to the lord for every acre by the year

---

860 fol. 36v blank, fol. 37.

861 *Co[mmun]em via[m] pedestr[um]*; M.J.Becker, *Rochester Bridge: 1387-1856* (London, 1930) pp. 36-37, 50, 66, 95-6, 105-6, 108.

862 fol. 37v.

863 *O.E.D.* Pightle: A small field or enclosure; a close or croft.

864 fol. 38.

865 *Pollic'* W.E.Latham, *Med Latin Word List* Pollex, Pollicium measure of length, inch.

THE SAME RICHARD holds of the aforesaid Abbot as of his manor aforesaid one garden[866] called Makenheddys Garden containing 5 virgates and lying between the Kings highway towards the North and the way there towards the East and the lands of the heirs of Richard Martyn towards the South and the land of the said Richard Dryland towards the West. Total 1 acre and 1 virgate. And he renders therefore to the lord for every acre by the year

THE SAME RICHARD holds of the aforesaid Abbot as of his manor aforesaid one piece of land in Ewellfelde adjacent to the said garden containing 4 acres and lying next to the Kings highway towards the North land of the heirs of Richard Martyn towards the South and West and the said garden east. Total acres 4. And he renders therefore to the lord for every acre by the year

THE SAME RICHARD holds of the aforesaid Abbot as of his manor aforesaid another piece of land there next to Holmeston land towards the East containing 4 acres and ½ lying between land of the heirs of Richard Martyn North and West and The Portewey towards the South. Total[867] 4 acres and ½. And he renders therefore to the lord for every acre by the year

THE SAME RICHARD holds of the aforesaid Abbot of Faversham as of his manor aforesaid another piece of land there besides The Portwey aforesaid towards the North and a lane called Holmeston lane towards the East garden and land of Prattesplace now Master Lenaker and the land of the heirs of Richard Martyn towards the South and The Chalke Dale towards the West And containing 16 acres

THE SAME RICHARD holds of the aforesaid Abbot of Faversham as of his manor aforesaid 1 piece of land besides Prattes place containing 8 acres and ½ of land and lying between the Kings Highway towards the South the lane called Prattyslane towards the East land of Master Lenaker lately Prattes towards the North land of the said Master Lenaker towards the West. Total 8 acres and ½. And he renders therefore to the lord for every acre by the year

THE SAME RICHARD holds of the aforesaid Abbot of Faversham as of his manor aforesaid one croft of land called Knockyng towards the East the way which leads from Holmeston[868] lane unto Knockyng North and the lane called Holmeston lane towards the West and the land of the said Master Lenaker and others adjoining towards the South. Total acres 12. And he renders therefore to the lord for every acre by the year

THE LORD OF WESTWODE holds of the lord Abbot of Faversham as of his manor of Faversham aforesaid land and tenement called Knockyng with one croft adjacent containing by estimation in total 30 acres and lying between the land called Homfelde land of Matthew Hawkyn called Bekylton and the land of the said Matthew called Bynnesfelde towards the East land called Smythfelde towards the South land called Caleyse towards the South and West land of Richard Dryland junior called Knockyng Crofte towards the West and the land called Holmstonfelde towards the North And the same lord holds the land following that is to say land of Richard Dryland junior in Lady Dane containing [blank] and for land in Croweche felde containing [blank] and for land[869] in Blobbers and Wrouges containing [blank] And for 11 acres of land in Holmston felde at Barrettyshill there formerly Richard Carpentar And for 6 acres and ½ land called Colyscrofte lying next to Holmeston lane towards the West and the way leading to the land called Knockyng towards the South and for certain land at Goldwyns And for certain land in

866 fol. 38v.
867 fol. 39.
868 fol. 39v.
869 fol. 40.

Preston Dane adjacent to Southfelde in Gatefelde next to Preston Churche containing 16 acres. Total acres 30. And he renders therefore to the lord for every acre by the year.

THE SAME LORD holds of the heirs of Robert Fekynham now John Chilton in the right of his wife for 12 acres of land next to Kekottes Hill and 8 acres at Goldwyns and for certain land at Howelettes

THE[870] HEIRS OF RICHARD MARTYN hold of the Lord Abbot of Faversham as of his manor of Faversham aforesaid one messuage curtilage and barn with the land appertaining adjacent to the said messuage on the side South and West. And the said messuage with the land adjacent containing 56 acres of land and lying between the King's highway towards the North land called Lady Dane towards the West the way called the portwey towards the south and the land called Sneggfelde towards the East Total 56 acres. And they render therefore to the lord for every acre by the year.

THE SAME HEIRS hold of the aforesaid Abbot as of his manor aforesaid a messuage with land adjacent called Sneggfelde containing 30 acres and lying between the messuage curtilage and land aforesaid towards the West, the King's highway towards the North and South next to Makenaddes Garden and also the Portwey towards the South. Total acres 30. And therefore they render to the Lord for every acre by the year

THE SAME HEIRS hold of the same Abbot as of his manor aforesaid[871] land called South Dale containing 30 acres and lying between the Portwey aforesaid towards the North the Chalke Dale and the land next Prattisfelde towards the East the Kings Highway and part of the lands of Prestesfelde towards the South land called Prestesfelde towards the West, East and South land of the heirs of Robert Fekynham now John Chilton in right of his wife West and lands called Lady Danehill towards the North. Total acres 30. And they render therefore to the lord for every acre by the year

THE SAME HEIRS hold of the aforesaid Abbot as of his manor aforesaid 7 acres adjacent to land called Prattysfelde towards the East land of Richard Dryland towards the North land called South Dale aforesaid West the Kings Highway South. Total acres 7. And they render to the lord therefore for every acre by the year

THE[872] HEIRS OF RICHARD MARTYN hold of the lord Abbot of Faversham as of his manor of Faversham aforesaid one piece of land called Fowre akers containing 6 acres of land lying between the Kings Highway South land called Honywooddes East and the Deale there North and East and part of the land called Blackland North and the lane which leads from the Kings highway unto the[873] Ewell ponddes towards the West. Total acres 8 acres. And they render therefore to the lord for every acre by the year

THE SAME HEIRS hold of the aforesaid Abbot as of his manor aforesaid another piece of land called Honywooddes containing 11 acres land called Blackland towards the North field called Goodwynston felde towards the East the Kings highway towards the South and land called the Fowre acres and the Deele aforesaid towards the West. Total acres 11. And they render therefore to the lord for every acre by the year

---

870 fol. 40v.
871 fol. 41.
872 fol. 41v the top half of the page blank.
873 fol. 42.

THE SAME HEIRS hold of the same Abbot as of his manor aforesaid another piece of land called Blackland containing 30 acres of land lying between the fields called Goodwynston felde towards the East the Marsh there towards the North and West and Ewell ponddes and pasture adjacent to the said piece of land and the lane aforesaid towards the West land called Honywooddes the Deele and the Fowre Akers aforesaid towards the South. Total Acres 30. And they render therefore to the lord for every acre by the year

THE[874] **SAME HEIRS** hold of the aforesaid Abbot of Faversham as of his manor aforesaid one acre of pasture adjacent to Blackland towards the East and South and Ewell Poondes adjacent to the said pasture and containing 8 acres of pasture and marsh in respect whereof pasture 3 acres and lying next to Blackland towards the East and South land of Richard Dryland junior land of the abbot of Faversham land of Edward Poyninges towards the West and the Mershe Dyke there towards the North Total acres [blank]

MASTER LENAKER holds of the lord Abbot of Faversham as of his manor of Faversham aforesaid one messuage and garden containing 4 acres of land and 18 acres land pertaining adjacent and wholly lying between the lane called Prattes Lane towards the East land of Richard Dryland junior and the Kings Highway towards the South and the lands of the heirs of Richard Martyn towards the West And the land of the aforesaid Richard Dryland towards the North Total acres 22. And he renders by the year

JAMES[875] **WALSYNGHAM** holds of the lord Abbot of Faversham as of his manor of Faversham aforesaid one water-mill called Holmansmell and one piece of pasture adjacent containing 3 virgates and 3 dayworks and one garden attached to the same pasture called Bodysgarden containing 3 acres and 1 virgate and wholly lying between the King's highway called Melwey East the Melle Poonde South a garden called Whites Garden and the land called Homansfelde otherwise called Brambill felde West and the land of the said James which Burton held to the fee farm towards the North Total 4 acres 3 dayworks. And he renders therefore to the lord for every acre by the year

THE SAME JAMES holds of the same Abbot as of his manor aforesaid the said garden called Whites Garden containing 3 acres and lying between the said garden called Boodes garden East the Fyssh poondes there South[876] a certain way leading unto the Fysshe Poondes West Homansfelde aforesaid towards the North Total acres 3. And he renders therefore to the Lord for every acre by the year

THE SAME JAMES holds of the aforesaid Abbot as of his manor aforesaid one field called Homansfelde otherwise called Bremylfelde containing 12 acres 3 virgates and ½ a daywork lying between the said garden called Boodes garden East Whites Garden aforesaid South a certain way leading unto the Poonde West the Forstall and other land next to his grange North Total acres 12 3 virgates and ½ a daywork. And he renders therefore to the lord for every acre by the year

THE SAME JAMES hold of the aforesaid Abbot as of his manor aforesaid one piece of pasture called the Hassock Medowe containing 3 acres [n/s] perches 1 daywork lying between the lands of the said James East pasture and land of the said James South land of the same James called Cowe Leese West the Hassock Medowe John Norton knight North Total acres 3 perches 1 daywork. And he renders therefore to the lord for every acre by the year

---

874 fol. 42v.

875 fol. 43 recto and verso blank. It is possible to clearly see the watermark of the paper which depicts, rather crudely, a unicorn.

876 fol. 44v.

THE[877] **SAME JAMES** holds of the same Abbot as of his manor aforesaid one pasture called Coweleese containing 8 acres and a ½ lying between the pasture of the said James and 3 are water East the Kings highway South and another piece of land of the said James also called Coweleese West and the Hassock medowe of the aforesaid James North Total acres 8 and ½. And he renders to the lord therefore for every acre by the year

THE SAME JAMES holds of the aforesaid Abbot as of his manor aforesaid another piece of land called Coweleese adjacent to the said pasture containing 11 acres 1 virgate and 1 daywork and lying between the said pasture towards the East, Bromston lane South and West a certain piece of land of the said James lying in Bromstonfelde called the Fowre Akers towards the West and the land of the said John Norton North Total 11 acres, 1 virgate and 1 daywork. And he renders therefore to the lord for every acre by the year

THE SAME JAMES holds of the same Abbot as of his manor aforesaid a piece of land called Fowre Acres in the field aforesaid adjacent to the said other piece called Cowe leese and containing 4 acres and lying between the said land towards the East Brumston lane aforesaid towards the South lands of the heirs of John Norwode that is to say Barley in right of his wife towards the West and the land of the said John Norton towards the North And contains in width at the North end 3 perches, ½ and 1 quarter perch And at the Southern end 11 perches Total 4 acres. And he render therefore to the lord for every acre by the year

THE SAME JAMES holds of the aforesaid Abbot of Faversham as of his manor aforesaid one piece of land called the Six Acres and containing 6 acres, ½, 3 dayworks and lying between the land called Stonerock towards the East land of the heirs of William Rose and land of the said James towards the South land of the heirs of John Norwode containing 2 acres and ½ now Barley junior in right of his wife towards the West and Bromston Lane towards the North Total acres 6 & ½ and 3 dayworks. And he renders to the lord for every acre by the year

THE SAME JAMES holds of the same Abbot one other piece of land adjacent called 8 acres at Stulpys and containing 8 acres and ½ a perch[878] 3 dayworks and lying between the King's highway towards the South, wood and land of the said James there towards the West land of the heirs of Robert Fekynham now John Chilton in the right of his wife and land of the heirs of the said John Norwodd now Barley in right of his wife North land of the feoffees of William Clerke clergyman East. Total 8 acres & ½ perch and 3 dayworks. And he renders therefore to the lord for every acre by the year

THE SAME JAMES holds of the same Abbot as of his manor aforesaid 68 acres 1 virgate and 2 dayworks of land and wood in Stondane and upon Stondanehill pertaining lying between the King's highway South the King's highway West wood of John Norton called Bysynghilles, North and West Bromstonlane North and East And the land of the said John Chilton in right of his wife next to Spryngpett and the land of the said James called Eight Acres at Stulpys East whereof the wood by estimation 1 acre at the most Total 68acres, 1 virgate and 2 dayworks. And he renders therefore to the lord for every acre by the year[879] Be it remembered that the said Abbot of the Monastery of St. Saviours of Faversham aforesaid holds between the said lands 2 acres near to the Kings Highway there towards the West [blank]

THE SAME JAMES holds of the aforesaid Abbot as of his manor aforesaid in Bromstondane one piece of land called 12 acres and containing 12 acres and 3 dayworks and lying between the

877 fol. 45.
878 fol. 46.
879 fol. 46v.

lands of John Norton South a certain lane called Bromstonlane towards the South and West land of the said John Norton North and East and containing in length between the East and West side 83 perches and in width on the East side 24 perches and in width on the West side 25 perches Total 12 acres, 3 virgates and 3 dayworks. And he renders therefore to the lord for every acre by the year

THE SAME JAMES holds of the same Abbot as of his manor aforesaid another piece of land in Bromstonsfelde called Sevyn Akers and[880] containing 6 acres 3 virgates and 1 daywork and lying between the lands of the said John Norton towards the North East South and West and King's [highway] north and containing in width on the Western side 35 perches and width on the Eastern side 47 perches Total 6 acres, 3 virgates and 1 daywork. And he renders therefore to the lord for every acre by the year

THE SAME JAMES holds of the aforesaid Abbot as of his manor aforesaid one piece of land containing 4 acres 1 virgate 2 dayworks and lying next to the lands of the Rectory of Stone and the churchyard of the church of Stone towards the West, the king's highway North and the land of the heirs of William Roose now John Wareham East and the King's Highway and ½ an acre of land of John Sennycholas formerly William Bregges towards the South Total 4 acres, 1 virgate, 2 dayworks. And he renders therefore to the Lord for every acre by the year

THE SAME JAMES holds of the same Abbot as of his manor aforesaid one acre and ½ an acre of land lying between the lands of the heirs of John Norwode South and North and a certain lane leading from the king's highway as far as the town of Osprenge East and the land of Robert Exbredge lately Hornescliffe West Total 1 acres and ½. And he renders therefore to the lord for every acre by the year.

THE[881] SAME JAMES holds of the aforesaid Abbot as of his manor aforesaid in the Neck on the Southern part of Northfelde one acre and 1 virgate of land by estimation lying between the lands of the Masyndue of Osprenge West the garden of Lady Anne Browne towards the East and land of the heirs of John Norwode towards the North Total acres 1 and 1 virgate. And he renders therefore to the lord for every acre by the year

ROBERT EXBREGGE holds of the lord Abbot of Faversham as of his manor of Faversham aforesaid in Northfelde one acre by estimation lately purchased of the said James lying in length between the King's [highway] towards the South and Bromston lane towards the North [blank]

JOHN SENNYCHOLAS holds of the said Abbot of Faversham as of his manor of Faversham aforesaid ½ an acre of land lately Bredges lying next to the land of the Rectory of Stone towards the South the churchyard of the church of Stonechurche West land of the said James North and East Total ½ an acre. And he renders therefore to the lord for every acre by the year

THE HEIRS OF JOHN NORWODE that is to say Barley in right of his wife hold of the lord Abbot of Faversham as of his manor of Faversham aforesaid 2 acres and ½ acre of land next to the lands of the said James Walsyngham called the Syx Akers towards the East[882] land of the said James called Eight Akers at Stulpys towards the South land of the heirs of Robert Fekynham that is to say John Chilton in right of his wife West, Brumston lane North. Total acres 2 and ½. And they render therefore to the lord for every acre by the year

---

[880] fol. 47.
[881] fol. 47v.
[882] fol. 48

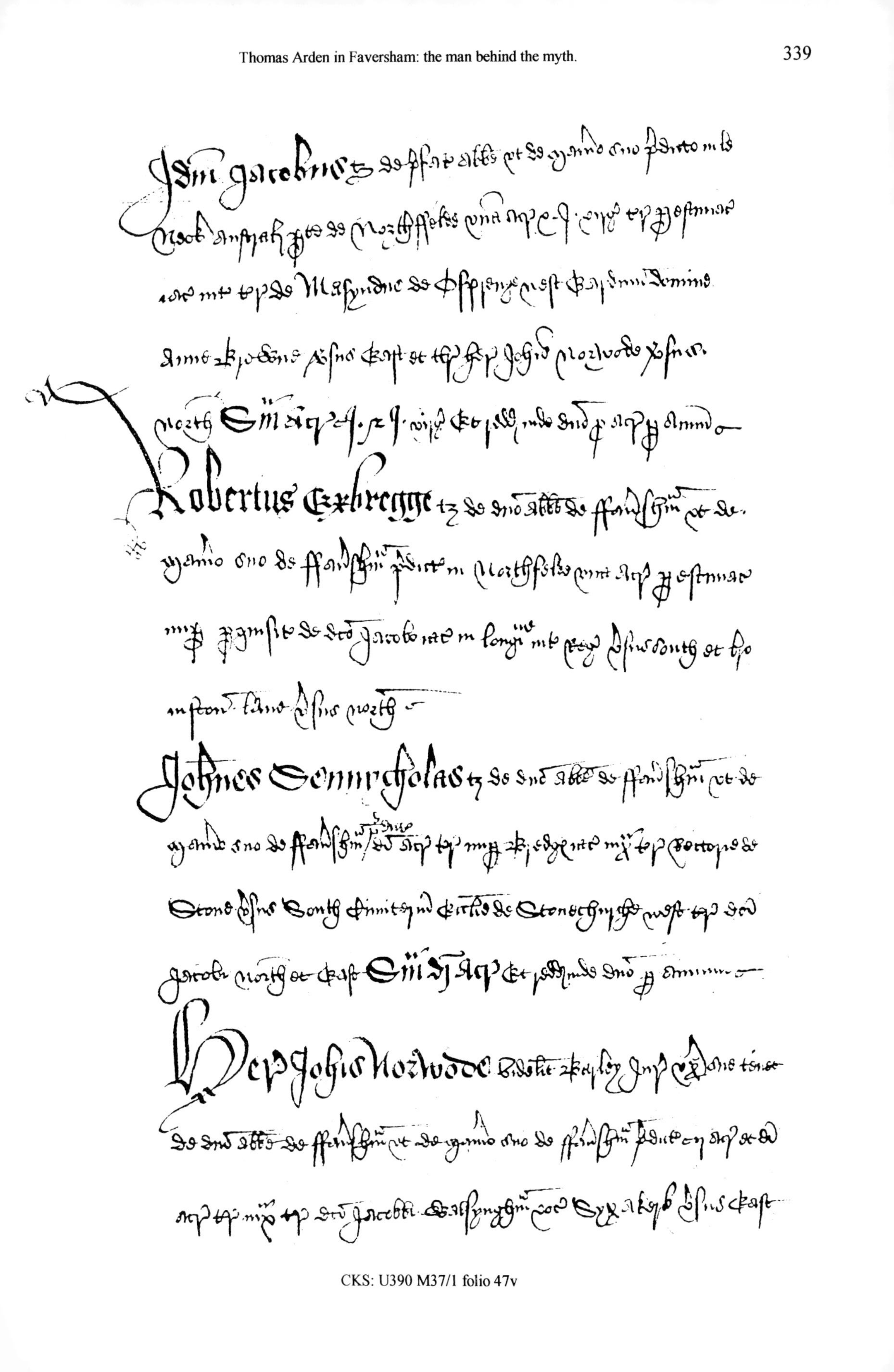

CKS: U390 M37/1 folio 47v

JOHN CHILTON in right of his wife hold of the lord Abbot of Faversham as of his manor of Faversham aforesaid 3 acres land at Spryngpett lying between the lands of the said Barley in right of his wife towards the East, land of the said James Walsyngham towards the South and West and Bromston Lane North Total acres 3. And he renders therefore to the lord for every acre by the year[883]

SELGRAVE

NORTHSTRETE ON THE EAST SIDE

INPRIMIS WILLIAM BELKE holds of the lord Abbot of Faversham as of his manor of Faversham aforesaid one croft of land called Berga[m]s hill crofte adjacent to Bargamshill ~~Croft~~ Crosse and Bargamshille Lane containing 3 acres lying between the lands of John Marche called Fyve Akers North and East and the said lane towards the South and the King's highway towards the West And containing in length with the same king's highway from the said lane towards the South unto the said John Marche called Fyve Akers 24 perches and ½ And from which lands of the said John Marche called Fyve Akers containing 8 acres. And he renders to the Court of Huntyngfelde[884] as is manifest by the rental pertaining to the same court 2^{s} 6^{d}

JOHN MARCHE holds of the Lord Abbot of Faversham as of his manor of Faversham aforesaid one croft of land called Fyve Akers containing 8 acres and lying between the land of Valentine Sowthousen lately called Ottweys and land of the lord of Westwode called Westwodfelde towards the North and the said land called Westwodefelde and the land of John Norton called Lytell Rollys towards the East and the lane in which the Cross of Bergamshill stands and land of William Belke near the cross towards the South and the King's highway[885] towards the West and containing in length with the same king's highway from the land of the said William Belke called Bargamshill Crofte towards the South unto the land of the said Valentine Sowthousen called Otweyes towards the North 22 perches and ½. And he renders to the said court of Huntyngfelde by the year 2^{s} 6^{d}

VALENTINE SOWTHOUSEN holds of the lord Abbot of Faversham as of his manor of Faversham aforesaid one messuage one garden and two crofts of land containing in total 10 acres and lying near North Street towards the West the land of John Marche called the Fyve Akers aforesaid and containing 8 acres towards the North land of the lord of Westwode East and land of the said John Marche called [blank] towards the South in respect whereof one croft there contains 2 acres & ½ and lies on the opposite side to Jacobbisfelde besides the land of the said John Marche called the Fyve Akers North. And he renders to the Monastery of St. Saviours of Faversham aforesaid for one year 7^{d} and *is bound to*[886]renders to the manor of Selgrave by the year 4s 6^{d} and the said croft of land with the messuage and garden aforesaid contains in length[887] with the king's highway from the land of the said John Marche towards the South which lies in the fee [blank] called [blank] unto the land of the said John Marche towards the North which lies in the fee [blank] called Fyve Akers 67 perches and ½ and 1 quarter

JOHN MARCHE holds of the lord Abbot of Faversham as of his manor of Faversham aforesaid one messuage with appurtenances called Halke Place *now upon*[888] the site of the messuage called

883 fol. 48v blank, then four blank fols numbered 1-4, fol. 49.
884 The Manor of Huntingfield is in the parish of Easling, see account in Hasted, vi, pp. 426-31.
885 fol. 49v.
886 Inserted in a later hand.
887 fol. 50.
888 Very convoluted abbreviation.

Harryfelde formerly Boodes of Hartey aforesaid Halke Place adjacent with garden and pasture adjoining and containing in total by estimation 4 acres and more and lying between the lands of Robert Easton lately Symondes and the land of the said John Marche towards the North land of the aid John Marche called Holmfeld otherwise Bynnefelde towards the East and land of the said John Marche called Smythes Croft towards the South and the King's highway and the site of a barn of Thomas Upton towards the West And the said site of the barn and the said 4 acres contain in length with the same king's highway from land called Smythes Croft towards the South as far as the foot-path[889] near the land called Symondes which leads to the Church of Sheldwyche towards the North 31 perches and ½. And renders to the manor of Selgrave by the year 5[s] 4 hens and 1 quarter of barley

THE SAME JOHN MARCHE holds of the aforesaid Abbot as of his manor aforesaid one croft of land called Bynnefelde and containing 9 acres and lying between the land of Robert Gaston and the land of Thomas Wode called Harfelde towards the North land of the said Thomas Woode called Wallenge felde and a certain wood called Halkewode towards the East land of the lord of Westwoode towards the South and the messuage and land aforesaid of John Marche called Halke place and Smythes Croft towards the West Total 9 acres. And he renders [blank]

THE SAME JOHN holds of the same Abbot as of his manor aforesaid one croft of land called Smythes Croft and containing 4 acres and more and lying between the said land and a messuage towards the North land called Bynnefelde otherwise Homefeld towards the East land of Valentine Sowthousen lately called Otweys towards the South the king's highway towards the West And containing in length[890] with the same king's highway from the land of the said Valentine Southousen called Chauntry land towards the South unto the land of the said John Marche towards the North 25 perches and ½ perch 4 feet. And renders for the messuage at Kyngeslondes Street called Otweys 12[d]

ROBERT EASTON holds of the lord Abbot of Faversham as of his manor of Faversham aforesaid one messuage and 4 acres of land more or less lately Robert Symondes and lying besides North Street towards the West the land of John Marche towards the South land pertaining to the manor of Harfelde North and East And containing in width from the land and with the land of Harfeld on the East side and North unto the king's street[891] towards the West 29 perches and in width with the said King's highway from the land of Harfeld aforesaid unto the land of the heirs of Thomas Upton and John Marche towards the South 18 perches and ½. Total acres [blank]

THOMAS ATWODE [holds] of the lord Abbot of Faversham as of his manor of Faversham aforesaid one messuage and curtilage called Harfeldes Messuage with two gardens adjacent to the said messuage and curtilage on the South side[892] and North and also with one small croft of land adjacent containing 4 acres And furthermore he holds another field containing 42 acres called Harfelde Homefeld and Bynnefelde also adjacent to the messuage and 4 acres of land and in total lying between the King's highway towards the West land of the manor of Selgrave called Redfeld towards the North land pertaining to the tenement of Richard Child towards the East land of the said Thomas Woode called Debyndane Wallengefeld and land of the said John Marche called Homefelde otherwise Bynnefelde towards the South and also land of Robert Easton towards the Southwest And the said field contains in length with the King's highway from the land of the said Robert Easton towards the South unto the garden of Harfelde towards the North 18 perches

889 fol. 50v.
890 fol. 51.
891. *Reg[ia] strat[a]* has been translated as king's highway throughout the text; the entry in English is *Street.*
892 fol. 51v.

and ½ And the said garden with curtilage messuage and other garden containing in length with the King's highway from the said land called Harfelde towards the South unto the field called Redfeld towards the North 25 perches

THE SAME THOMAS hold of the aforesaid Abbot as of his manor aforesaid[893] one croft of land called Debyndane containing 6 acres and lying between the field called Harfelde towards the North and five virgates of land called Oysterman part of the said messuage towards the East land which lies in Salmondesfelde also pertaining to the said messuage towards the South and land called Walengefelde towards the West [blank]

THE SAME THOMAS holds of the same Abbot as of his manor aforesaid one field called Wallengefelde containing 12 acres and lying between the aforesaid land called Debyndane towards East land which lies in Salmonds felde and parcels of wood which lie in Halkwode pertaining to the said messuage towards the South lands of John Marche towards the West and the great field called Harfelde towards the North. And for all the aforesaid parcels of land and the messuage of the Thomas At Wodde he renders by the year with the customary payments and charges 20^{s} and suit of court

THE SAME THOMAS holds of the said Abbot as of his manor aforesaid 4 acres of land in Salmondsfelde in respect whereof two acres thereof lying at[894] Halke gate beside Walengefelde And the other two acres thereof residue at Wasshpottes Deale and are in the fee of the Abbot of the Monastery of St. Augustines outside the walls of the City of Canterbury. And he renders in respect thereof to the Manor of Sellyng by the year 12^{d} And the same Thomas holds ½ an acre of wood in Halkewode

THE PRIOR OF THE CHURCH of Christ Canterbury and the heirs of John Norwode hold of the lord Abbot of Faversham as of his manor of Faversham aforesaid one field with pasturage from antiquity called Danefelde now called Redefelde and containing 55 acres and 5 dayworks and lying between the land adjacent and pertaining to the manor of Copton towards the North land of the Lord of called Brusshyngges and land called Rychardes Childe towards the East a certain field called Harfelde towards the South and the King's highway towards the West And containing in length with the same King's highway a garden of[895] Harfelde towards the South unto the land of the said Prior of the Church of Christ pertaining to the manor of Copton towards the North 99 perches and ½.

THOMAS ATWOODE VALENTINE SOUTHOSEN AND STEPHEN PETT hold Oystermannes containing in itself 4 acres and ½ and wholly lying between the King's highway towards the East land called Suttons towards the North land of Harfelde called Debyndane towards the West land of the manor of Badlismere and land of John Taylor towards the South in respect whereof the said Thomas at Wode holds thereof beside Debyndane towards the West 5 virgates and the said Valentine Southousen holds in respect thereof 2 acres and ½ And the said Stephen Pett holds in respect thereof beside Suttons 3 roods residue And contains in length with the King's highway 16 perches [blank]

VALENTINE[896] SOUTHOUSEN holds of the lord Abbot of Faversham as of his manor of Faversham aforesaid one field called Suttons formerly two fields called Dalyesfelde otherwise Delefelde now Robert Gusmer and Stephen Pett and containing 16 acres 1 rood 1 daywork and ½ and 1 perch and lying between the said land called Oystermans towards the North and the King's

---

[893] fol. 52.
[894] fol. 52v.
[895] fol. 53.
[896] fol. 53v.

highway towards the East and containing in length at the Northern end near Richardes Chylde from the King's highway towards the East just as hedge leading towards the West unto the land of the tenant called Harfelde 67 perches And containing in length at the Southern end from the King's highway towards the East just as the hedge leading with the land called Oistermannes and Debyndane unto the land of Harefelde towards the West 44 perches and containing in width in the middle of the said field between West and East 50 perches [blank]

STEPHEN[897] **JENYNS** knight hold of the aforesaid Abbot of Faversham as of his manor aforesaid a site of a tenement called Richardes Childe with 23 acres and ½ land and 1 rood or therabouts and lying between the King's highway there towards the East the land of Valentine Southousen called Suttons and Delefelde otherwise Daliesfelde towards the South land of Thomas Wode of the said tenement of Harfelde and land of the manor of Selgrave and land of the lord of Westwod called Brusshinges West and North And containing in length with the King's highway from the said land called Suttons unto the said land called Busshinges 87 perches

THE LORD OF WESTWODE holds of the same Abbot as of his manor aforesaid two pieces of land lying together at the end of Brusshinges and containing 12 acres and ½ a short time ago of the tenure of John Reede in respect whereof 1 piece of land thereof contains 11 acres and ½ and lying between the manor of Selgrave and the said piece of land of 11 acres & ½ towards the West land of the said Lord[898] of Westwod towards the North and East and containing in length from the land of the said Stephen called Richardes Childe on the southern side unto the land of the said lord of Westwode on the Northern side 24 perches And containing in width from the said piece of 11 acres and ½ on the West side unto the land of the said lord of Westwod on the Eastern side 6 perches and ½ and 1 quarter of a perch[899]

SELGRAVE
NORTHSTRETE ON THE WEST SIDE

INPRIMIS JOHN MARCHE holds of the aforesaid Abbot as of his manor aforesaid one piece of land called Six acres and containing 6 acres and lying between the lands of John himself called Hellfelde towards the North Bargamshill lane towards the South land called Sprackylles towards the West and the King's highway towards the East And containing in length with the same King's highway towards the East from Bergamshill lane aforesaid towards the South unto the land called Hellesfelde towards the North 29 perches and a quarter of a perch

THE SAME JOHN holds of the same Abbot as of his manor aforesaid one field called Hellefelde containing 7 acres and lying between the said land called Syx acres towards the South land called Sprackylles towards the West land called Jacobbisfelde towards the North the King's highway towards the East and containing in length with the same King's highway from the said land called Six Acres towards the South unto the said land called[900] Jacobbysfelde towards the North 66 perches 3 quarters of a perch and more

THE SAME JOHN Christopher Legatt and Robert Easton hold of the lord Abbot of Faversham as of his manor of Faversham aforesaid one field called Elstensfeld from antiquity called Jacobbysfelde and containing 12 acres and 1 rood lacks thereof 2 dayworks and ½ and lying beside Northstrete between the same Street towards the East land of the said John Marche called

---

[897] fol. 54.
[898] fol. 54v.
[899] Remainder of fol. blank, fol. 55.
[900] fol. 55v.

Hellefeld and land of Alexander Lewekenor called Sprakkilles towards the South land of the said Alexander called Blackedelefelde otherwise Homefelde towards the West and land of the said Christopher towards the North In respect whereof the said John Marche holds in the middle of the said field near the King's highway there 10 acres and ½ and 1 rood And the said Christopher holds thereof 3 roods on the Northern part of the said field[901] And the said Robert Easton holds 3 roods on the Southern side of the said field And containing in length with the said King's highway called North Street towards the East from the Northern part unto the Southern part 53 perches and lying with Blackedeele and Calvencroft on the Western part in length between South and North parts 57 perches And containing in width in the middle of the said field from the West unto the East 31 perches

CHRISTOPHER LEGATT holds of the lord Abbot of Faversham as of his manor aforesaid one messuage with one acre of land to the same messuage adjacent with appurtenances and between the King's highway called Northstrete towards the East land of the said Christopher and the garden of John Marche which lies in the said field towards the South land of the said Alexander Lewkenore and the garden of the lord Abbot of Faversham towards the West and the said garden and land of the said[902] Christopher lying in a certain lane leading to the said King's highway unto Lytells place towards the North And containing in width from the said lane with the King's highway unto the land of the said John Marche called Elstenfelde otherwise Jacobbisfelde towards the South 12 perches

ALEXANDER LEWKENOR holds of the lord Abbot of Faversham as of his manor of Faversham aforesaid one tenement with curtilage and garden and also certain land adjacent that is to say one field called Blakedelefelde which contains 30 acres and lying between land called the Lytill Landewe and land called Sprackkylles towards the South land called Jacobbysfelde and Calvencroft towards the east a certain lane leading from the King's highway unto the said garden and tenement and Culverhouse croft which lie towards the North and Badggyng felde towards the West

THE[903] SAME ALEXANDER holds of the same lord Abbot as of his manor aforesaid another croft thereof called Culverhouse Croft containing 28 acres and lying between the land called Stomblefeld towards the North land of William Legatt towards the North and East a certain lane leading from the King's highway unto the tenement and that tenement and also Blakdelefelde and Badgyng felde lying towards the South and the King's highway towards the West

THE SAME ALEXANDER holds of the same Abbot as of his manor aforesaid another field thereof adjacent to the said two field called Badggyngfelde containing 28 acres and lying between the said land called Culverhouse croft towards the North land called Blakedele felde and Blackdele grove towards the East Badgyng downe towards the South and the King's highway towards the West

THE SAME ALEXANDER hold of the aforesaid Abbot of his manor aforesaid another field called Calvencroft containing 2 acres ½[904] virgate 1 daywork and ½ and lying between the said field called Blakdelefelde towards the West a certain lane there towards the North and the said field called Jacobbysfelde and the garden of the lord Abbot of Faversham towards the East

THE SAME ALEXANDER holds of the aforesaid Abbot as of his manor aforesaid another field thereof residue called Sprackkilles containing 14 acres and lying between the land of John

---

901 fol. 56.
902 fol. 56v.
903 fol. 57.
904 fol. 57v.

Marche called Helfelde and the Syx acres towards the East Bargams Lane and Badgyng downe towards the South land called Lytell landowne towards the west and land called Blakedelefelde and Jacobbysfelde towards the North And the said field called Sprakkylles rendering to the Monastery of Faversham by the year 1 quarter wheat

WILLIAM LAGATT holds of the Abbot of Faversham as of his manor aforesaid one messuage with one garden called Soolys and also another[905] garden called Caleise garden and also two crofts of land lying together and containing 14 acres and more and lying between the King's highway there towards the East a certain lane leading to the said King's highway as far as Lidelles place aforesaid towards the South land of the said Alexander Lewkenore called Culverhouse felde towards the West and land of the manor of Selgrave called Stumblefelde towards the West and North. And the said messuage with the garden called Seelys containing in length from the said lane towards the South as afar as the said croft called the Homefelde North 23 perches and ½ And the said croft called the Homefelde contains in length with the King's highway from the said garden where the water well[906] is situated called Solys Garden towards the South as far as Caleyse garden towards the North 25 perches And the said garden called Caleyse garden containing in length by the King's highway from the said croft called the Homefelde towards the South as far as the field called Stumblefelde towards the North 21 perches[907]

THE PRIOR OF CHRIST CHURCH CANTERBURY and the heirs of John Norwood hold of the lord Abbot of Faversham as of his manor of Faversham aforesaid one field called Stumblefelde containing 105 acres and 3 roods lying between the land pertaining to the tenement of Lidelles called Culverhowse croft and Badgyngfelde and land of William Lagatt called Homefelde otherwise called from antiquity Westbynne and Caleyse garden towards the South Badgynglane towards the West and a certain lane there leading from the limit of Badgyngs lane aforesaid towards the forstall of Selgrave towards the North, land of William Lagatt towards the East and North and the King's highway towards the East containing in length with the same street from Caleyse garden towards the South as afar as the land of William Lagatt towards the North 75 perches.

WILLIAM LAGATT holds there of the lord Abbot of Faversham as of his manor of Faversham aforesaid 3 crofts of land pertaining containing[908] by estimation 6 acres and lying between the King's highway towards the East land of the manor of Selgrave called Stumblefelde towards the South and West and a certain way there leading from the King's highway to the limit of the forestall of Selgrave towards Badgynglane and Whytefeld[909] towards the North And containing in length from the said King's highway with forestall and lane aforesaid as far as the said land called Stumblefeld towards the West 55 perches and ½ perch and 3 feet And containing in length with the King's highway from the land called Stumblefelde towards the South as far as the Forestall of Selgrave aforesaid towards the North 28 perches. *Margin*: Let it be remembered that the Forestall of Selgrave contains in length with the King's highway between the North part 19 perches.

THE PRIOR OF CHRIST CHURCH CANTERBURY and the heirs of John Norwood hold of the lord Abbot of Faversham as of his manor of Faversham aforesaid the site of the manor of Selgrave and Northfold adjacent and lying between the said forestall and the lane which leads from the King's highway towards Badgynglane and the Whitefeld towards the South land

---

905 fol. 58.
906 *Fons*:this could also be a spring.
907 fol. 58v.
908 fol. 59.
909 Query whether this should be Whytefield see later.

called[910] Poopys and land pertaining held of Brokdale towards the West land pertaining to the manor of Pery[911] and land called Perybrome appertaining to the said manor of Selgrave towards the North and land called Stryngges East and North And King's highway towards the East And containing in length with the same King's highway from the said forestall towards the South as far as the land called S[t]ryngges towards the North 112 perches and ½

STEPHEN JENYN London[912] knight holds of the said Abbot of Faversham as of his manor of Faversham aforesaid one croft of land called Perybrome and containing 5 acres and ½ and ½ a rood and more and lying between the land called Stryngges and land called Northfelde towards the South and land pertaining to the manor of Pery towards the West and North and Homefelde towards the East[913] Be it remembered that 21 acres of land lying below the garden of the manor of Pery on the East part and 6 acres land lying below the said garden on the West part are part of the manor of Selgrave

MARGARET HORNE widow holds of the Abbot of Faversham as of his manor of Faversham aforesaid one piece of land called Stryngges and containing 8 acres of land or more and lying between the land called Northfelde South and West land pertaining to the Manor of Pery called Perybrome and Bromefelde towards the North and the King's highway towards the East And containing in length by the King's highway from the land called Northfelde towards the South as far as the land called Bromefelde towards the North 20 perches and ½ and containing in length at the Western end with the land of Northfelde 22 perches & ½ perch, 3 feet and containing in length in the middle of the said field between the West and the East, that is to say, from the land called Northfelde as far as the King's highway towards the East 56 perches And she renders[914] to the Monastery of Saint Saviours of Faversham by the year 2^{s} [915]

RYNGESLOND STREET ON THE WEST SIDE AS FAR AS WYLGARY LANE

IN THE FIRST INSTANCE THE HEIRS OF WILLIAM AT SEETH hold of the lord Abbot of Faversham as of his manor of Faversham aforesaid one croft of land and one tenement with a garden pertaining situate and lying containing in total 10 acres & ½ acre and ½ a rood of land called Otweys and lying between the King's highway towards the East land of the heirs of Thomas Amyse towards the South a certain field called Nutfelde west and land and tenement of the heirs of Robert Gyles called Bynnefelde towards the North and the said croft of land containing in length by the King's highway from the land of the said heirs of Thomas Amyse towards the South as afar as the garden and messuage aforesaid towards the North 41 perches And the said garden with the messuage contains in width with the King's highway from the said croft towards the South as far as the garden of the heirs of Robert Gyles towards the North 7 perches. And they render by the year 3^{s} 8½^{d} and suit of court And for customary payment one virgate[916] (12^{d}) and ½ (6^{d}) And for Shepeshott and[917] Medeshott [918] ½, ¼, ½-¼, ¼-¼.

TOTAL[919] 5^{s} 3^{d} ¼ ½-¼ & quarter quarter that is to say for each acre 6^{d}

---

910 fol. 59v.
911 Manor of Perry Court in the parish of Preston next Faversham, see Hasted, vi, pp.539-44.
912 London was not in the italic hand in the original.
913 fol. 60.
914 fol. 60v.
915 Remainder of fol. blank, fol. 61 blank, fol. 61v.
916 Payments above the measure of land.
917 fol. 62.
918 Ob qr di qr and quarter quarter.
919 Margin.

THE SAME HEIRS of Robert Gyles hold of the lord Abbot of Faversham as of his manor of Faversham aforesaid one messuage with garden and one croft of land called Bynnefelde adjacent to the said messuage containing in total 6 acres and 1 rood and more and lying between the King's highway towards the East the said tenement and land called Otweyes towards the South land of the said heirs of Robert Gyles and land of the lord of Leveland towards the West and a certain field called Sevyn akers otherwise Thysalltye and land of William Belk called the thre yardes towards the North and the said messuage with a garden containing in length by the King's highway from the garden of the said heirs of William At Seth towards the South as far as the land of William Belk called Napultons towards the North 20 perches and ½

WILLIAM[920] **BELKE** holds of the lord Abbot of Faversham as of his manor of Faversham aforesaid one acre of land formerly built upon called Napultons and lying between the King's highway towards the East and the land called the Three Yards towards the West and land called John Lordes Hawe towards the West and North a messuage of the said heirs of Robert Gyles towards the South and containing in length with the King's highway from the garden of the said heirs of Robert Giles towards the South as far as the said land called John Lords Hawe towards the North 21 perches

JOHANNA AT HALE formerly the wife of William Gyles holds of the lord Abbot of Faversham as of his manor of Faversham aforesaid one piece of land called an aker and also called John Lordes Hawe lying between the King's highway towards the East the said land called Napultons towards the South and East croft of land called Gyles Croft towards the West and land of the heirs of William At Seth towards the North And containing in length by the King's highway from the said land called Napultons towards the South[921] as far as the garden of the said heirs of William at Seth towards the North 9 perches and ½

THE HEIRS OF WILLIAM A SEETHE [hold] of the Abbot of Faversham as of his manor of Faversham aforesaid one messuage with outhouses and garden adjacent to them called Kenworthys messuage and containing one acre and more and lying between the King's highway towards the East land called John Lords Hawe towards the South Gylles Croft and the land called Peryham[m]e and Lyntonsfelde towards the North And containing in length by the King's highway from the land called John Lordes Hawe towards the South as afar as the land called Lyntonsfelde towards the North 41 perches and ½

THE SAME HEIRS hold of the lord Abbot of Faversham as of his manor of Faversham aforesaid one croft of land called Peryh[a]m[me] adjacent to the said messuage on the North side of the Homewey by the tenement there and containing 2 acres and more and lying between the garden the said messuage towards the East the Homewey there towards the South and land of Thomas Upton called Lyntonsfe[l]d West and North

THE[922] **HEIRS OF THOMAS UPTON** and Stephen Pett hold of the lord Abbot of Faversham as of his manor of Faversham aforesaid one field called Lyntonsfelde containing in total 12 acres of meadow-land 2 dayworks and one perch and lying between land of the Earl of Oxford towards the West and North the King's highway and land of the heirs of William att Seth called Peryham towards the East and land of the said Stephen Pett and the Homewey by the aforesaid heirs of William A Seth and another tenement there towards the South whereof the said Stephen Pett holds in respect thereof 3 virgates formerly John Lorde and lying next to the Homewey aforesaid towards the South And whereof the aforesaid 12 acres 4 acres thereof they render to the tenure of

[920] fol. 62v.
[921] fol. 63.
[922] fol. 63v.

the said heirs of William at Seth And containing in length from the lands called the Bremth[923] towards the West as far as the King's highway in a line between West and East 75 perches and ½ and containing in width with the said King's highway from the messuage and lands of the said heirs to William att Seth towards[924] the South as far as the land of the Lord of Badlysmere towards the North 26 perches

THE HEIRS OF ROBERT GYLES hold of the lord Abbot of Faversham one croft of land called Nutfelde containing 5 acres and lying between the land called Otweys towards the East land of the heirs of Thomas Amyse towards the South land of the lord of Leveland towards the West and land of the said heirs of Robert Gyles called Bynnesfelde towards the North

HEIRS OF WILLIAM AT SETHE Stephen Pett and the widow of William Gyles hold of the lord Abbot of Faversham as of his manor of Faversham aforesaid one croft of land called Kenwardes felde containing 7 akers and lying between the land of the heirs of Robert Gyles Bynnefelde towards the South and the said way called the homeway towards[925] the North land of Stephen Pett called Gylles Croft towards the East and land of the said heirs of Robert Gyles called Chistelltigh towards the West whereof the said heirs of William at Sethe hold 3 acres And the said Stephen holds thereof 3 acres and ½ And the aforesaid widow of William Giles holds ½ an acre residue which same ½ acre was formerly of the messuage of John Lorde And the meadow-land of the aforesaid Stephen Pett contains in length on the Northern end following with the way there called the Homewey from Gylles Croft on the East side as far as the said appurtenances of the said heirs of William Seeth towards the West 20 perches and ½ and the meadow-land aforesaid of the heirs of William at Seeth contains in length with the said way called the Homewey from the limit of the said 20 perches and ½ as far as the land called Thistiltye towards the West 18 perches

THE SAME HEIRS of Robert Gyles hold of the lord Abbot of Faversham as of his manor aforesaid one croft of land called Thystyltye[926] otherwise called 7 akers and containing 7 acres and lying between land of the lord of Leveland towards the South land of Stephen Pett which lies within the Bremth called Six akers towards the West the Homewey towards the North and land called Bynnefelde aforesaid towards the East And containing in length on the Northern part of the homewey from Kenwards feld as far as the land of Stephen Pett towards the West 25 perches

THE HEIRS OF WILLIAM AT SEETH hold of the Lord Abbot of Faversham as of his manor of Faversham aforesaid one croft of land called Gylles croftes likewise and containing 2 acres land and lying between Lordes hawe and the land of William Belk called the three yards towards the South messuage and the homewey of the said heirs of William at Seethe and other tenants land there towards the North field called Kenwardes felde towards the West lords hawe and garden and land[927] of Kenwards messuage towards the East in respect whereof the said heirs of William at Seeth hold ½ an acre

---

[923] J.K.Wallenberg, *The Place names of Kent* Uppsala 1934. Gives in the parish of Chislet in the Blengate Hundred, BREMTHE (lost) 13th century *The Register of St Augustine's Abbey Canterbury, commonly called the Black Book* ed. G.J.Turner & H.E.Salter, London 1915-24. I have consulted this and the entry is on page 103, and concerns a record of a case of Trespass brought in the Common Bench in Hilary Term 15 Richard II by the Abbot against Thomas Court for felling trees at Chislet on 4 October 1389. Strangely Faversham is mentioned at the bottom of page 102 in recording the holding of a heath between Blen and the great road which leads to Faversham. The actual entry reads: Gilbertus filius Roberti Cumbroce et pares eius tenent xij. acras et dimidiam que iacent inter Earnesberghe et Bremthe, vnde dant de rededitu xxvj[d]. ad ij. terminos sicut alii. ....

[924] fol. 64.

[925] fol. 64v.

[926] fol. 65

[927] fol. 65v.

WILLIAM BELKE holds of the lord Abbot of Faversham as of his manor aforesaid one piece of land called Thre Yardes containing one acre and more and lying between a certain piece of land called Napultons towards the East messuage and land of the heirs of Robert Gyles towards the South land of the same heirs called Bynnefelde towards the West land of Stephen Pett called Gylles Croft and a parcel of land of Lordis Hawe towards the North and also a parcel of land of Lordes Hawe West and North

STEPHEN PETT heirs of William at Seethe heirs of Thomas Upton and the widow of William Gyles hold of the lord one piece of land called six akers and containing 6 acres and 1 rood of land and lying between the land of the lord of Leveland South land of the said heirs of William at Seethe called Lytell Bremth and land called the Fower akers West and North and land of the said heirs of Robert Gyles[928] which is situated in Thystyll tigh[929] East in respect whereof the said Stephen Pett holds in respect thereof one acre and ½ And the said heirs of William att Seethe hold one acre and ½ And the heirs of Thomas Upton holds 2 acres And the widow of William Gyles holds 1 acre and 1 virgate residue And contains in length in the northern part from the land of Stephen Pett and other tenants with the homewey and land called Bremth as far as the land of the said heirs of William att Seeth called Fowre akers towards the West 40 perches

THE HEIRS OF WILLIAM AT SEETHE holds of the lord Abbot of Faversham as of his manor of Faversham aforesaid 2 acres of land called lytell Bremth and lying between the land of the lord of Badlysmere towards the North and the heirs of Thomas Upton called Lyntonsfelde East land of the said Stephen Pett land of the said heirs of William at Seth and Thomas Upton land of the widow of William Gyles att Seethe and also land of the said heirs of William lord of Badlismere[930] and from the land of the same lord towards the West as far as the land of the said heirs of Thomas Upton called Lyntonsfelde towards the East 39 perches

THE HEIRS OF WILLIAM AT SEETHE and the heirs of Michael Easton hold of the lord Abbot of Faversham as of his manor of Faversham aforesaid called Fowre akers and containing 4 acres 1 virgate and ½ of land lying between the land of the lord of Leveland towards the South land of the lord of Badlismere called Grete Bremth towards the North land of William Gyles which lies within the baulks[931] called the Syx akers aforesaid East land of the heirs of William at Seethe and other tenants also called the Fowre Akers towards the West in respect whereof the said heirs of William at Seethe hold in respect thereof a half part. And contains in length on the North part with the land of the lord of Badlismere from the land called the Six Akers as afar as the land of the said heirs of William at Seethe also called the Fowre akers 28 perches and ½

THE[932] **HEIRS OF WILLIAM AT SETHE** and the widow of William Gyles hold of the lord Abbot of Faversham as of his manor of Faversham aforesaid one piece of land called the Fowre akers adjacent to the said croft on the Western side and containing 4 acres and ½ an acre and 1 virgate of land and lying between the land of the lord of Leveland towards the South land of the lord of Syon towards the West land of the lord of Badlismere towards the North and land of the said heirs of Michael Easton which lie within the Fowre Akers aforesaid towards the East in respect whereof the said widow holds in respect thereof 1 rood 3 dayworks 1 perch and 4 parts of

---

928 fol. 66.

929 *O.E.D.* Tye, Tie: [ON ***teigr*** a strip of field or meadow-land, a close or paddock, which occurs frequently in names of meadows] An enclosed piece of land, enclosure, close; also, an extensive common pasture; a large common. 1670 BLOUNT *Law Dict.*, ***Tigh, Teage*** a close or enclosure, a croft ... The word Tigh is still used in Kent in the same sense. W.D.Parish & W.F.Shaw, *A Dictionary of the Kentish Dialect* (1887) Tye, Tie An extensive common pasture. Such as Waldershare Tie; Old Wives' Lees Tie. 1510 'A croft callid Wolnes Tie'. MS Accounts, St Dunstan's Canterbury.

930 fol. 66v.

931 Latin ***Limites*** can also mean lists.

932 fol. 67.

a perch[933] And containing in length with the land of the said lord of Badlismere on the Northern side from the said land of the aforesaid heirs of William at Seeth and Michael Easton also called the Fowre akers as far as the land of the said lord of Syon towards the West 33 perches

WILLIAM BELKE holds of the lord Abbot of Faversham as of[934] his manor of Faversham aforesaid one messuage with 2 gardens adjacent from both sides and with other land on the Western side and North of the said messuage and containing in total [blank] and lying between the land of the lord of Badlismere towards the South land [blank] towards the West land of Stephen Pett and land of the said William towards the North and the King's highway towards the East And the said messuage and gardens contain in length by the King's highway from the land of the said lord of Badilsmere towards the South as far as the land of the said William called Symonds felde towards the North 33 perches

THE SAME WILLIAM BELKE holds of the lord Abbot of Faversham as of his manor aforesaid one field called Symondesfelde and containing by estimation 14 acres and lying between the land of the said William towards the South land of Stephen Pett and land of the said William towards the West a certain lane called Wylgarlane[935] North the King's highway East And containing in length by the said lane from the land of the said Stephen Pett towards the West as far as the corner of the said croft near Wylgar Crosse situated between the King's highway there towards the East 56 perches And containing in width by the King's highway from the said corner beside the said cross and from the said boundary 56 perches on the Northern side as far as the garden of the said William towards the South[936]

KYNGGESLONDSTRETE ON THE EASTERN SIDE

IN THE FIRST INSTANCE THE HEIRS of Thomas Upton hold of the lord Abbot of Faversham as of his manor of Faversham aforesaid with his tenants one messuage with the site of another messuage and two gardens and two crofts of land containing 7 acres 3 virgates and ½ a daywork called Aleynsfeldes formerly John Tunhill afterwards Thomas Elsten and previously John Seman and in like manner lying between the land of William Belke towards the South the King's highway and Pettes acre towards the West land of the said heirs of Thomas Upton and land of Stephen Pett called Pettes Aker North and land of the lord of Badilsmere East And they render in respect thereof by the year 3^{s} 9d, one hen price 3^{d} and 5 eggs price a quarter. And customary payment for ½ an acre that is to say [blank] And contains in length[937] with the King's highway from the land of the said heirs of Robert Gyles towards the south as far as the land called Pettes aker towards the North 16 perches

STEPHEN PETT and the heirs of Thomas Upton hold of the lord Abbot of Faversham aforesaid one croft of land called Pettes aker containing 3 acres meadow-land 3 day works and 3 perches adjacent to the garden of the said messuage lately of the said Thomas Elsten towards the South and lying between the messuage called Kynggeslondes messuage towards the North the King's highway towards the West and land of the said heirs of Thomas Upton towards the East In respect whereof Stephen Pett holds 2 acres in 2 parcels And the said heirs of Thomas Upton hold 1 acre residue lying in the middle of the aforesaid two acres in length East and West and containing in length with the King's highway from the garden of the said heirs of Thomas Upton

---

933 iiij^{am} p[ar]te[m] p[er]tic[am].
934 fol. 67v.
935 fol. 68.
936 Remainder of fol. 68 blank and fol. 68 verso blank, fol. 69.
937 fol. 69v.

lately Thomas Elsten aforesaid towards the South as far as the messuage called Kynggeslondes[938] messuage aforesaid towards the North 21 perches

THE HEIRS OF THOMAS UPTON hold of the lord Abbot of Faversham as of his manor of Faversham aforesaid one messuage and one garden called Kynggeslonde messuage with two crofts of land adjacent to the same messuage called Long Croft otherwise Bynnefelde containing in total 12 acres 2 dayworks and ½ And rendering in respect thereof for each acre by the year 3¼^{d} and fourth part of a ¼ and more in total 1½^{d} meadow-land ½-¼ and lying between the land of the lord of Badlysmere towards the East and North land of the said heirs of Thomas Upton and land of Stephen Pett South and the King's highway West And containing in length with the said King's highway from the land called Pettes aker towards the South as far as the land called long Croft otherwise Bynnefelde site of the messuage boundary and hedge leading towards the North 21 perches And the said land called Long Croft otherwise Bynnefelde contains in length[939] with the King's highway from the said garden towards the South as far as the said land of the lord of Badlysmere towards the North 24 perches and ½

THE SAME HEIRS of Thomas Upton hold of the lord Abbot of Faversham aforesaid as of his manor of Faversham aforesaid one croft of land called Coursfelde containing 8 acres 1 virgate and ½ and ½ a daywork of land and lying between the land of the vicar of Sheldwiche lately purchased of the heirs of Rayner towards the North land of the lord of Badlysmere towards the East and South King's highway, garden and messuage of William Belk containing 3 roods and more lying within the said croft enclosed towards the West And containing in length with the said King's highway from the land of the said vicar towards the North as far as the garden of the said William Belke towards the South 39 perches And from the limit of the said 39 perches to the said garden with the messuage of the aforesaid William being upon the croft also with the King's highway as far as the side[940] of the said field towards the South 32 perches And the other side of the said field contains in length with the King's highway from the said garden towards the North as far as the land of the said lord of Badlysmere towards the South 8 perches

THE VICAR of Sheldwich holds of the lord Abbot of Faversham as of his manor of Faversham aforesaid one garden formerly built upon and one croft of land adjacent called Allards lately purchased of the heirs Reyn[er] that is to say [blank] 'tenant of a quarter virgate'[941] and [blank] his wife containing one acre and more and in like manner lying between the land of the Lord of Badlismere towards the East land of the heirs of Thomas Upton called Coursfelde towards the South and the King's highway besides Wylgarescroft towards the West and North And he renders to the tenant of Kyngeslond by the year 5^{d}

OF THE LAND AND TENEMENTS AT WODEGATE LEESE WHICH LIE THERE ON THE NORTHERN SIDE BEGINNING ON THE WESTERN SIDE

IN[942] THE FIRST PLACE John Norton knight holds of the lord Abbot of Faversham as of his manor of Faversham aforesaid one piece of land called the Breeche containing 10 acres and lying between Wodegate Leese towards the South land of the lord of Badlysmere West, Malmannesfelde North land of the said lord of Badlismere called Bonettes and land called Sekottes Croft towards the East

938 fol. 70.
939 fol. 70v.
940 fol. 71.
941 Forman[nus].

THOMAS WORMESELL holds of the lord Abbot of Faversham as of his manor of Faversham aforesaid one messuage with a garden containing ½ a virgate and more lying between the common pasture of Wodegate leese there towards the South and West land appertaining to Leese Courte called the Breeche towards the North and land called Skottes Croft towards the East And containing in length with the said pasture towards the South between the East and the West 8 perches and ½[943]

WILLIAM TAYLOR holds of the lord Abbot of Faversham as of his manor of Faversham aforesaid one croft of land called Sckottes Croft and containing by estimation one acre and lying between the said pasture towards the South the said messuage and garden of Thomas Wormsell towards the West land pertaining to Leese Courte called Breeche towards the West, land of the lord of Badlysmere towards the North the way which leads from the said pasture as far as the land called Bonettes and Malmannesfelde towards the East and containing in length with the said pasture from the said garden and messuage towards the West as far as the said way towards the East 6 perches

THE SAME WILLIAM holds of the same Abbot as of his manor aforesaid one messuage and garden lately Dane containing 1 virgate of land and more and lying between the said way towards the West land and messuage of the said Stephen Pett towards the North and West And the said pasture towards the South And containing in length with the said pasture from the said way towards the West as far as the messuage and curtilage of the said Stephen Pett towards the East 11 perches[944]

STEPHEN PETT holds of the lord Abbot of Faversham as of his manor of Faversham aforesaid one messuage with curtilage garden and one croft adjacent called Hary Kyngeslondes tenement and containing in total by estimation 7 acres and lying between the said pasture towards the South messuage and garden of William Tayllour lately Stephen Gyles and part which leads to Malmannesfeld and the land called Bonettes towards the West and the land of the lord of Badlysmere called Malmannesfeld towards the North and a certain croft of the said William called Torysfelde otherwise Pett Felde and land of Leese courte called Homefeld towards the East And the said messuage with the curtilage contains in length with the said pasture from the garden and messuage of the aforesaid William towards the West as far as the said land called Torysfelde towards the East 5 perches

WILLIAM TAYLLOUR holds of the lord Abbot of Faversham as of[945] his manor of Faversham aforesaid one croft of land called Torysfelde otherwise Pett Felde lately purchased of Stephen Gyles and containing 8 acres and 2 dayworks of land and lying between the said pasture towards the South and West and also the garden and land of Stephen Pett towards the West land of Leese Court called Homefelde towards the North land of the said Stephen Pett and land of William Bayly East In respect whereof 8 acres thereof he renders to our monastery And contains in length with the said pasture on the Western side besides the messuage of the said Stephen towards the North as far as to the corner of the said croft towards the South 15 perches and ½ just as the hedges lead as far as the land of the said Stephen and William Bayly towards the East 31 perches

STEPHEN PETT and William Bailey hold of the same Abbot as of his manor aforesaid one croft of land containing one acre and ½ and lying between the land of the said William Taillour from

942 fol. 71v.
943 fol. 72.
944 fol. 72v.
945 fol. 73.

antiquity called Torysfelde now called Pettfelde towards the West[946] land of the heirs of Laurence Croft North land and messuage of the said William Bayly towards the East And pasture of Woodgate Leese towards the South and containing in length with the same pasture from the land called Pettfelde towards the West as far as the land and messuage of the said William towards the East 10 perches and ½ In respect whereof the said Stephen Pett holds a half-part which lies beside Pettfield And he renders to the manor of Badlismere 6^{d} 1 cock and 1 hen

THOMAS BAILY holds of the lord Abbot of Faversham as of his manor of Faversham aforesaid one messuage and garden and one croft of land adjacent called Stoncse otherwise Ocnese containing in total 6 acres and ½ and more and lying between the said pasture of Wodgate Leese towards the South and the croft of land of the said Stephen and the said Thomas towards the West and land of the heirs of Laurence Crofte North and land pertaining to the messuage of Leese Courte called Homefelde towards the North and East And containing in length[947] with the said pasture from the croft of the said Stephen and Thomas towards the West as far as the land of Thomas Mason towards the East 32 perches and ½ and 1 ¼ perch

THOMAS MASON holds of the lord Abbot of Faversham as of his manor of Faversham aforesaid one messuage and one garden with the land adjacent containing in total 2 acres and ½ formerly Bakers tenement and lying between Woodgate Leese towards the South, land of Thomas Baily West and North land called Chauntry lands towards the East and containing in length with Woodgate Leese aforesaid from our land towards the West as far as the land called Chauntry landes towards the East 22 perches

CHANTRY PRIEST of Sheldwich holds of the aforesaid Abbot as of his manor aforesaid one messuage with a garden and one croft of land adjacent called Chantry Messuage containing 2 acres and ½, 2 dayworks and ½ and lying between Woodgate leese towards the South garden and croft of land of the said Thomas Mason West and one croft of land containing[948] 1 acre 1 virgate 3 dayworks and ½ pertaining to the manor of Leese Courte North and garden pertaining to the manor aforesaid towards the East

JOHN NORTON knight holds of the lord Abbot of Faversham as of his manor of Faversham aforesaid messuage of Leese Courte with the curtilage and garden adjacent to the same messuage from both sides of the said messuage and containing in total beyond the lane which leads from Woodgate Leese 4 acres and ½ lying between the land called Longham towards the East Wodgate Leese and a piece of land containing 1 acre and ½ pertaining to the said messuages South and land pertaining to the Chantry of Sheldwich and also the said acre and ½ of land called The Homefelde towards the West and land called The Fowre Akers and containing 5 acres 1 virgate and ½ towards the North and containing in length with Wodgate Leese towards the South a messuage and garden called Chantry landes[949] towards the West as far as the land also called Chantry landes towards the East 15 roods and ½ and containing in length with the land of the Chantry landes towards the East as far as the croft of land called The Fowre akers towards the North 30 roods And containing in width with The Fowre akers aforesaid The Chantry landes on the Eastern side as far as The Homefeld towards the West 19 perches

THE SAME JOHN NORTON holds of the same Abbot as of his manor aforesaid one piece of land called Longham lying on the Eastern side of the said messuage and garden containing 11 acres and ½ of meadow-land, ½ a daywork of land in respect whereof 4 acres called Chantry

---

946 fol. 73v.
947 fol. 74.
948 fol. 74v.
949 fol. 75.

landes and entirely lying near Malmannesfeld towards the North and Woodgate Leese South and the garden of Thomas Mason and the messuage, garden and croft of land of the widow of John Gyles South and East Chappell garden and parcel of land of the Chantry croft East and a field called Malmannesfelde North a certain lane leading from Wodgateleese as far as the messuage aforesaid[950] and The Hemphawe[951] and land called The Fowre akers towards the West

THOMAS MASON holds of the lord Abbot of Faversham as of his manor of Faversham aforesaid The Hemphawe adjacent to the said messuage towards the West besides Wodgate leese on the South side lately the heirs of Roger Cotyng and containing 1 virgate of meadow-land, 1 daywork and more and lying between the land of the heirs of John Gyles towards the East land of Leese Courte North and East and containing in length with Wodgate leese aforesaid 4 perches and he renders by the year 2[d]

THE WIDOW OF JOHN GILES formerly of Thomas Elsten holds of the lord Abbot of Faversham as of his manor of Faversham aforesaid one messuage and one croft of land containing in total 2 acres and ½ and 2 dayworks lying between Wodgate leese South the King's highway East land called Chantry londs North and land of Leese Courte West and containing in length with the lane leading from Wodgate leese towards the South as far as the land called chantry landes towards the North 39 perches

THE HEIRS OF LAWRENCE CROFTE hold of the lord Abbot of Faversham as of his manor[952] of Faversham aforesaid 1 acre and 1 virgate of land adjacent to the land of Thomas Bayly lying between the land pertaining to the manor of Leese Courte called Homefeld towards the North and land of the said Thomas BailyEast and South And land of the same Thomas and Stephen Pett towards the West and they render to Thomas Mason by the year 5[d]

JOHN NORTON knight holds of the lord Abbot of Faversham as of his manor of Faversham aforesaid one field called Homefield beside the said messuage and containing 16 acres and 3 virgates of meadow-land 1 daywork and ½ and lying near Malmannesfelde towards the North and land called The Fowre akers and the garden called The Hemp garden with the curtilage adjacent East and land containing 2 acres pertaining to the said messuage and land of William Baily and land of the heirs of Stephen Crofte called The Fyve Yardes towards the South the land called Torysfelde otherwise Petfeld and land of Stephen Pett pertaining to Kingeslonds tenement West[953]

THE SAME JOHN holds of the same Abbot as of his manor aforesaid one croft of land containing 1 acre 1 virgate 3 dayworks and ½ lying to the barn and garden of Leese Court towards the East land called Chantry lands South land of Thomas Baily West and The Homefeld pertaining to the said messuage of Lesse Courte towards the North

THE SAME JOHN holds of the aforesaid Abbot of Faversham as of his manor aforesaid one croft of land called The fowre akers and containing 5 acres 1 virgate and ½ and lying near Malmannesfelde towards the North the garden called The North Garden adjacent to the said messuage towards the South, land called The Homefelde West land called Malmannesfeld aforesaid West and North, land called Longham and land of the same called Chantry lands towards the East

---

[950] fol. 75v.

[951] *O.E.D.* HAW A hedge or encompassing fence; hence, a piece of ground enclosed or fenced in; a messuage; generally, a yard, close or enclosure, as in timber-haw.

[952] fol. 76.

[953] fol. 76v.

THE SAME JOHN holds of the same Abbot of Faversham as of his manor aforesaid another piece of land called Greete Rolles containing 12 acres and lying near the church of Sheldwiche and Malmannesfelde and lying between the land called Churchlond[954] towards the South the King's highway West, Bargams Lane North and Malmannesfeld East And he renders to the Court of Huntyngfelde

THE SAME JOHN holds of the same Abbot of Faversham as of his manor aforesaid one piece of land called Shortforde otherwise Shortefelde with the land called The Valey there containing in total by estimation 80 acres in respect whereof 30 acres lie between Malmannesfeld and the land called Weststrete West the King's highway North land of the said John called The Valey East and land called Chauntry Landes South And he renders in respect thereof by the year to the Monastery of St. Augustines Canterbury 25^{s} 6^{d}

THE SAME JOHN holds of the aforesaid Abbot of Faversham as of his manor aforesaid Grubbyndane with The Landdewe containing by estimation 40 acres and lying in the parish of Sellyng.

THE SAME JOHN holds of the same Abbot of Faversham as of his manor aforesaid[955] Stokkynfeld lying in the parish of Sheldwich with the wood annexed containing by estimation 14 acres and lying between a certain lane called The Sumpter Wey East, the land of Stephen Jenyns knight called Brode Reede and a parcel of wood of the said John Norton called Stokkynfelde South parcel of wood of Robert Bartlott attached to Stokkynfelde aforesaid West the King's highway leading to Danebernes North

THOMAS MASON Thomas Warmesell and Stephen Croft hold of the lord Abbot of Faversham as of his manor of Faversham aforesaid one croft of land enclosed called Stonysfelde otherwise Stonyfelde and containing by estimation 3 acres and a ½ and 1 rood and lying between the King's highway South and West and land of Leese Courte North and East In respect whereof the said Thomas Mason 5 virgates and he renders by the year 7½^{d} 1 hen and ½ And Thomas Warmsell holds 5 virgates and he renders by the year 13½^{d}[956] And the said Stephen Crofte hold the other 5 virgates remainder and renders in respect thereof by the year 7½^{d} one hen and ½

WILLIAM BELK holds of the said Abbot of Faversham as of his manor of Faversham aforesaid the site of a messuage with 8 acres in the field called Northfelde formerly Richard att Leese knight Thomas Shobbesole Sampsons and the heirs of William Shobbesole and lying between Wodgate leese towards the West and a small garden now John Gyles towards the West and North And also a lane called Danebernlane North land pertaining to the messuage of Leese Courte towards the East and land of Reginald Haywards lately Roger Cotyng South and containing in length with Wodgate Leese from the land of the said Reginald towards the South as far as the garden of the said widow towards the North 21 perches and ½ and more And the said garden contains in length with the said pasture from the limit of the said 21 perches as far as the other [957] part aforesaid 9 acres towards the North 7 perches And the other part of the 9 acres contains in length from the said garden towards the South with Wodgate leese aforesaid as far as the said lane towards the North 7 perches And also the said land called Shobbesolys containing in length with the said lane called Danebarnes from the Western corner of the said lane as far as the land of Leese Courte called [blank] towards the East 39 perches and ½[958]

---

954 fol. 77.

955 fol. 77v.

956 fol. 78.

957 fol. 78v.

958 Remainder of fol. 78v blank, 79 & 79v blank; fol. 80.

BADLISMERE

IN THE FIRST INSTANCE Thomas Turnour holds of the lord Abbot of Faversham as of his manor of Faversham aforesaid 3 acres *and ½*[959] of land in a certain croft called Augustland and lying between a certain lane called Watkyns Lane North East a croft of the heirs of John Bartilmewe called Rooke towards the West, land of John Turnour called Smythfelde otherwise Smythefelde otherwise Smythcroft towards the South and the King's highway called Grenestrete towards [n/s] and containing in length with the said lane called Watkyns Lane from the said King's highway as far as the land of the said heirs of John Bartylmew called Huntyggesdane otherwise Huntyngges Dane 26 perches and ½ and containing in width with the said King's highway towards the South 21 perches And he renders by the year for the acres 2^{d} ½, ¼ To ~~the land called Martyns formerly built upon~~ to *the table* [960] Total 10½^{d} And lying on the opposite side of the land called Dennyse Nash

JOHN TURNOUR holds of the aforesaid Abbot of Faversham as of his manor of Faversham aforesaid[961] one croft of land called Smythfelde otherwise Smyth Croft containing 5[962] acres *and a daywork*[963] and lying between the King's highway called Grenestrete towards the Southeast land of the heirs of Thomas Backe called Mabbe Croft towards the South land of Thomas Stapill called Sadilles felde Croft otherwise Seerlys felde and land of the said heirs of John Bartilmewe called The Half Aker towards the Northwest and land of the said heirs of John Bartilmewe called Huntyngges Dane and land of Thomas Turnour called Augotland towards the Northeast And renders in respect thereof to the table ~~land called Martyns~~ by the acre 2½^{d} ¼ more or less in total by the year 17½^{d} and contains in length with the said King's highway towards the South from the said lands called August otherwise Augotland towards the East as far as the said called Mabbe Crofte towards the West 20 perches and ½

THE HEIRS OF THOMAS BACK hold of the lord Abbot of Faversham as of his manor of Faversham aforesaid one croft of land called Moppis Croft otherwise Mabbe Croft and containing 5 acres and lying between the King's highway called Grenestrete towards the Southeast[964] And the lands of John Turnour called Smythe Croft towards the North and the King's highway which lies towards Ramsenn Leese West and containing in length with the said King's highway towards the South from the land of the said John Turnour called Smythefelde as far as the King's highway beside Bovyng Gate Crosse[965] 42 roods And containing in width from the said King's highway towards the South and with the other King's highway on the west side of the said crofte leading towards Ramsell Leese and also the small lane leading to Smythefelde towards the North 38 perches and ½ And lying opposite the land of the heirs of Thomas Back and land called Martyns And they render to the table by the year, in respect whereof 2 acres of the aforesaid 5 acres the Chantry Priest of Sheldwich holds

THOMAS A STAPILL holds of the lord Abbot of Faversham as of his manor aforesaid one croft of land called Seerlys Croft otherwise from antiquity called Sadelles Croft and containing 2 acres and ~~½ and more~~ *4 dayworks*[966] and lying between the King's highway towards the West land of the heirs of John Bartylmewe called[967] Meryfelde and The Hemphawe of Robert Smyth towards

---

959 Inserted later in same hand that added information from 22 onwards.
960 Added in a later hand.
961 fol. 80v.
962 Altered from 7.
963 Added in a later hand.
964 fol. 81.
965 Now called Bound Gate cross-roads.
966 Inserted by a later hand.
967 fol. 81v.

the North land of John Turnour called Smyth Croft towards the East and a certain way leading from the said King's highway as far as Smythfeld croft towards the South and containing in length with the King's highway towards the West and from the said way which leads to Smythfelde near Mabbecroft as far as the land of Robert Smyth called The Hemphawe 16 perches and ½ and more and lying opposite the land called Martyns And he renders to *the table*[968] ~~the land called Martyns~~ by the year 10^{d}

ROBERT SMYTH holds of the lord Abbot of Faversham as of his manor of Faversham aforesaid one hemphawe containing by estimation one rood and lying between the land of Thomas Stapill called Sadelles croft otherwise etc., and the common pasture called Ramselles Leese towards the South and West land of the heirs of John Bartelmewe and land of the heirs of John Bromefelde called Meryfelde towards the North and East and land of the said heirs of John Bromefelde called Half Aker towards the East And containing in length with the King's highway from the said croft called Sadelles Croft otherwise etc., as far as the aforesaid land called Meryfelde 8 perches and 1 quarter of a perch[969]

THE HEIRS OF JOHN BERTILMEWE hold of the lord Abbot of Faversham as of his manor of Faversham aforesaid one croft of land called Meryfelde containing two acres and *3 dayworks*[970] land ~~½~~, and lying between the land of the said heirs called The Rock and the land of John Turnor called Litell Croft towards the Northeast And the land of the said heirs of John Bartilmew called The Rocke towards the East land of John Bromefelde called The Half Aker towards the [n/s] and South land of Robert Smyth called the Hemphawe and common pasture of Ramselles Leese towards the South and West And they render for each acre by the year to *the table*[971] ~~to the land called Martyns~~ 3^{d} Total 7½^{d} And contains in length from the lands of the said Robert Smyth called The Hemphawe with Ramselles Leese aforesaid as far as the land of John Turnour called Lytell croft 8 perches and ½ and more.

JOHN TURNOUR holds of the lord Abbot of Faversham as of his manor of Faversham aforesaid one croft of land called Half Aker and containing in length with Ramsells Leese from the land called Meryfelde as far as the land of the said John called Bredlyngeshawe 8[972] perches And he renders to *the table* [973] ~~land called Martyns~~ by the year 2^{d}

THE SAME JOHN holds of the same Abbot as of his manor aforesaid half an acre called Bredlyngges Hawe and containing in length with Ramsells Leese from the said croft called ½ acre as far as the garden of the said John 9 perches And renders to the table by the year 2½^{d}

JOHN TURNOUR holds of the aforesaid Abbot as of his manor of Faversham aforesaid one tenement with a garden and one field adjacent called Bynnefelde and containing 6 acres and ½ and in like manner lying between the King's highway towards the West land of John Noryngton called Forefelde towards the North land of Thomas Turnour called Pettfelde towards the East land of the said John Turnour called Bredlyngges Hawe[974] which lies below his garden and tenement towards the South and containing in length with Ramsells Leese and with the said King's highway and acre called Breddlyngges Hawe aforesaid as far as the land of the said John Noryngton called Forefelde 31 perches and ½ and he renders for the tenement called Kenworthis for every acre by the year 2½^{d} ¼ and more in total[blank] *Margin* note

---

968 Inserted by a later hand.
969 fol. 82.
970 Inserted by a later hand.
971 Inserted in a later hand.
972 fol. 82v.
973 Inserted in a later hand.

JOHN[975] **NORYNGTON** holds of the lord Abbot of Faversham as of his manor of Faversham aforesaid one croft called Forefelde containing 3 acres and lying between the King's highway towards the West Webbe Croft towards the North and land of the said Thomas Turnour called Lomepett felde North and East and land of John Turnour called Bynnefelde towards the South and he renders for the tenement called Kenworthis for each acre by the year 2^{d} Total 6^{d} *Margin* Note

JOHN NORYNGTON holds of the same Abbot as of his manor aforesaid another croft of land called Webbe Croft and containing 2 acres and lying between the common pasture of Badlismere towards the North the land of Michael Easton and the land of Thomas Turnour called Lomepetfeld towards the East and the land of the said John Noryngton called Forefeld towards the South and containing in width with the said pasture just as for hedges leading as far as the aforesaid land called Lomepettfeld 10 perches and ½ and also the aforesaid 2 crofts of land containing in length with the King's highway there from the aforesaid land called Bynnefelde as far as the said common pasture of Badlismere Leese 44 perches and ½ and also containing in width also with the said pasture just as hedges leading as far as Lomepett felde[976] 23 perches and he renders for every acre by the year 2^{d} for the tenement called Kenworthis, total 4^{d} *Margin* Note

THOMAS TURNOUR and the heirs of Michael Easton hold of the lord Abbot of Faversham as of his manor of Faversham aforesaid one piece of land called Lomepett felde containing 9 acres and lying between a certain lane called Watkyns Lane and land called Dryan Croft otherwise Tryangcroft towards the East the common pasture of Badlismere towards the North a certain croft called Webbecroft and the other croft called Forefelde towards the West and a certain field called Bynnefelde and land of the heirs of John Bartylmewe called The Rock towards the South in respect whereof Thomas Turnour holds 8 acres and ½ And the Michael Easton holds ½ an acre and containing in length with the said pasture from the land called Webbe Croft and also with the said lane as far as the land called Dryancroft 57 perches And lying opposite the land called Great Watkyns and Lytell Watkyns and the tenement also called Watkyns And the said Thomas renders for the tenement called Kenworthis every acre by the year 2½^{d} ~~½ ¼ and more in total ¼ and ½~~ Total 22½^{d}

ROBERT[977] **SMYTH** of Levelond holds of the lord Abbot of Faversham as of his manor of Faversham aforesaid one croft of land called Dryancroft otherwise Tryangcroft And containing 3 acres and lying between a certain lane called Watkyns Lane towards the North and East land of the heirs of John Bartilmewe called The Rock towards the Southwest And land of Thomas Turnour called Lomepetfelde towards the West and lying in length with the said lane called Watkyns Lane from the land called Lomepetfeld as far as the said land called The Rock 35 perches and ½

THE HEIRS OF JOHN BARTILMEWE hold of the lord Abbot of Faversham as of his manor of Faversham aforesaid one croft of land called The Rock and containing 2 acres and lying between the said field called Dryancroft otherwise etc., towards the North the King's highway and the land of the said heirs of John Bartilmewe called Huncyngges Dane East and South and the land of John Turnour called Bynnefeld towards the West[978] And renders in respect thereof by

[974] Looks very like Halke.
[975] fol. 83.
[976] fol. 83v.
[977] fol. 84.
[978] fol. 84v.

the year 6^d and 1 hen to Robert Smyth karvour[979] And containing in length with the said lane from the land called Dryan croft and otherwise as far as the said land called Huncyngges Dane 3 perches And lying opposite the land called Drylandes dale otherwise Lutons Dale

THE HEIRS OF JOHN Bartilmewe hold of the Lord Abbot of Faversham as of his manor of Faversham aforesaid in Huncyngges Dane otherwise Huntyngges Dane two acres of arable and wood land in respect whereof ½ an acre is woodland lying in either part the said one acre of arable land and ½ that is to say East and West and the whole lying between the land of Thomas Turnour called Augotland towards the South land of John Turnour called Smyth Croft land of the heirs of John Bartilmewe and land of the heirs of John Bromefeld called The half acre towards the South And land of the said heirs of John Bartilmewe called Meryfeld and The Rock towards the West Augotland and Watkyns Lane towards the North East and containing in[980] length with the said lane called Watkyns Lane from the land called Augotlonds as far as The Rock 17 perches And they render by the year *to the table* ~~martyn~~ for each acre of arable land 3^d and for each acre of woodland 1^d Total $5½^d$ And lying opposite the land called Drylands Dale otherwise Lutons Dale

THE HEIRS OF JOHN BARTILMEWE and the heirs of John Bromefelde hold of the lord abbot of Faversham as of his manor of Faversham one croft of land called The Half Acre and containing one acre And lying between the land of the heirs of John Bartilmewe called Meryfelde and Huntyngges Dane North and East land of John Turnour called Smyth Croft towards the South land of Thomas Staple called Sadelles Croft and The Hemphawe of Robert Smyth towards the West And they render by the year to the land called Martyns 4^d *Margin* Martens

BAKYNHELD[981] ON THE SOUTHERN SIDE OF THE KING'S HIGHWAY THERE AS FAR AS BOUYNG GATE CROSSE

IN THE FIRST INSTANCE Reginald Backe holds of the lord Abbot of Faversham as of his manor of Faversham aforesaid one tenement called Backys tenement with gardens and diverse parcels of pasture adjacent in respect whereof one parcel thereof called Justyns Croft another piece thereof called Kyttes and another piece called Collis and containing in total 6 acres and ½ besides 2 dayworks And lying between the land of the said Reginald which he holds of the lord of Chilham called Damafeld towards the East woodland and land of the said Reginald which he also holds of the said lord towards the South land of the heirs of John Amyse called Hullond Dane towards the West and the King's highway towards the North And containing in length from the said land called Damafeld towards the East with the King's highway as far as the said land called Hullondane towards the West 50 perches and ½ and lying opposite Longfelde Forefelde and The Grete [rest blank]

THE[982] HEIRS OF JOHN AMYSE holds of the Lord Abbot of Faversham as of his manor of Faversham aforesaid 19 acres of land and wood whereof 11 acres and ½ called Hullond Dane and the residue called Hardlond and Londdewe and lying between the King's highway towards the North land of the said Reginald Backe called Justyns Croft and land of the said heirs called Bollisfelde towards the East and land of the heirs themselves land of the said Reginald and land

[979] This is presumably an English word for CARVER; One who carves wood, ivory, stone etc: a sculptor; most frequently (when not otherwise qualified) applied to one who carves in wood.

[980] fol. 85.

[981] fol. 85v blank, fol. 86.

[982] fol. 86v.

of Elianor Hawker his sister called Lytell Rameslonde towards the South and the King's highway Northwest And containing in length from the land of the said Reginald towards the East just as the King's highway circles as far as the lands of the said Reginald and Elianor his sister called Lytell Rameslond towards the West 81 perches And lying opposite Danetowne, Denysse Nassh, Watkyns Lane and Augotlond and also part of Smythfeld.

REGINALD BACKE and his said sister Elianor hold of the said Abbot of Faversham as of his manor aforesaid one field called Lytell Rameslond containing 4 acres of land lately purchased of Alexander Bodell and lying between Greete Rammeslond towards the South the King's highway called Grenestrete West, land of the heirs of John Amyse and woodland of the said heirs called Lytell Longwode towards the East And the land of the said heirs called Holonde Dane[983] North And containing in length with the said King's highway from the land of the aforesaid called Londdewe towards the East as far as the land called Grete Rammeslond towards the West 18 perches and lying opposite Smythfelde And also opposite part of Mabbe Croft.

REGINALD BACK and his said sister hold of the lord Abbot of Faversham as of his manor aforesaid one field called Grete Rammeslond lately purchased of the heirs of Thomas Amyse and containing 9 acres and lying between Chappmansfeld towards the South the King's highway called Grenestrete[984] towards the West and land called Lytell Rammeslond and woodland of the heirs of John Amyse called Longwode East and the land called Lytell Rammeslond North And containing in length from the aforesaid land called Lytell Rammeslond with the King's highway as far as the land called Chappmansfeld 27 perches and ½ And they render to the table by the year 14^{d} And lying opposite Mabbe Croft.

ALEXANDER BOODILLE holds of the lord Abbot of Faversham as of his manor of Faversham aforesaid one field called Chapmansfeld and containing 11 acres and lying between the heirs of Thomas Back called Harres Croft and Wylkyns Croft towards the South the King's highway towards the West and the land called Grete Rammeslond towards the North And woodland called Longwoode towards the East and containing in length with the said King's highway called Grenestrete from the land called Rammeslond as far as the corner of the said field and opposite Bobyng Gate Crosse 14 perches And containing in length from the said corner with the King's highway towards the West as far as the land of the heirs of Thomas Back called Harres[985] Croft towards the South 21 perches And lying opposite part of Mallecroft and Bobynggate crosse

THE HEIRS OF THOMAS BACK hold of the lord Abbot of Faversham as of his manor of Faversham aforesaid one croft of land called Harryes Croft and containing 3 acres ½ and 1 rood And lying between the land of the said heirs towards the South, the King's highway towards the West, Chapmannesfeld towards the North, and the land of the said heirs called Wylkyns Croft towards the East, and containing in length with the King's highway from the said land called Chapmannesfeld as far as the land and tenement of the said heirs towards the South 16 perches

THE HEIRS OF THOMAS BACK hold of the lord Abbot of Faversham as above is said another croft of land called Wylkyngges Croft adjacent to the said croft on the East side containing 3 acres and ½ and lying between the lands of Alexander Bodell called Chapmannesfelde towards the North, a croft of the heirs of John Amyse called Longewode East,

---

983 Dane = DEAN *O.E.D.* A vale. Now usually the deep, narrow, and wooded vale of a rivulet. One of the quotes is to the 1340 *Ayenb.* 59 Ich wille maki ye helles and ye danes. This is Dan Michel, ..*Ayenbite of Inwyt*, or, remorse of conscience. In the Kentish dialect, 1340 A.D. Edited ... with an introduction on the peculiarities of the Southern dialect. London, Trubner, for the Early English Text Society 1866 (Reprinted 1895).

984 fol. 87v.

985 fol. 88.

And[986] the land of the said heirs of Thomas Back called Bynfelde which are held of the Prior of Christ Church Canterbury towards the South And land called Harryess Croft towards the West

THE HEIRS OF THOMAS BACK hold of the lord Abbot of Faversham as of his manor aforesaid one croft of land opposite Bobyng gate Crosse beside the King's highway there in respect whereof one virgate of land and more of the said croft of land lying in the demesne of Faversham and also lying between the King's highway there East and South and residue of the said croft West and land called Martyns North And the said virgate of land contains in length on the Eastern side 9 perches and ½ And in width with the King's highway on the South side 4 perches and 1 foot

ALEXANDER BODILL holds of the lord Abbot of Faversham as of his manor of Faversham aforesaid 1 acre and ½ and one virgate of land together lying called Martyns with his tenement formerly built and lying between the land of the heirs of Thomas[987] Back towards the South, and land of the said Alexander and land of the said heirs towards the West, Ramselles Leese towards the North, and the King's highway towards the East, and containing in length by the King's highway from the land of the aforesaid heirs of Thomas Back as far as the corner of the said land called Martyns near Ramselles Leese towards the North 34 perches and ½ And the said one [acre] and a ½ and 1 virgate of land containing in width at the Northern end just as the hedges lead with Ramselles Leese between the land of the said Alexander which he holds of the lord of Thrughleygh towards the West 13 perches[988]

BAKYNHELDE ON THE NORTHERN SIDE OF THE KING'S HIGHWAY THERE

IN THE FIRST INSTANCE REGINALD BACKE holds of the lord Abbot of Faversham as of his manor of Faversham one piece of land formerly in 3 pieces now called Longfelde and one garden called Shamelles and lying together and containing in total 9 acres and ½ of meadow-land 3 dayworks 3 perches with the garden which follows and lying between a certain lane called Walters Lane otherwise called Steerelys Lane towards the East the King's highway towards the South land called Forefelde towards the West woodland called Badlysmere Park towards the North and containing in length with the said lane towards the East with the said King's highway and with Shamelles Garden aforesaid as far as the land called Gyes Hawe which is parcel of Forefelde towards the West 30 perches And containing in length with the said croft from the land called Forefelde towards the West as afar as the said lane towards the East 33 perches And lying opposite the messuage and garden called Walters and land called Sterelys Croft and Sterlys Sole towards the East And lying opposite land called Damafelde And a certain garden[989] of the said Reginald called Shamelles towards the South

REGINALD BACK holds of the said Abbot of Faversham as of his manor of Faversham aforesaid one croft called Forefelde with Gyes Hawe of which it is parcel thereof and containing in total 8 acres and ½ 1 virgate of meadow-land 2 dayworks and lying between the woodland called Badlismere Park towards the North Longfelde with Shamelles garden towards the East King's highway towards South and the land of the said Reginalds called The Greete towards the West And containing in length by the King's highway from the said garden called Shamelles garden with Gyes Hawe as far as the said land called the Greete towards the West 24 perches And lying opposite the garden and tenement of the said Reginald towards the South

---

[986] fol. 88v.

[987] fol. 89.

[988] Remainder of fol. blank, fol. 89v blank, fol. 90.

REGINALD BACKE holds of the lord Abbot of Faversham as of his manor of Faversham aforesaid 10 acres meadow-land 2 dayworks and ½ lying together called The Greete and Dane Towne formerly 3 pieces and lying between the land of the said Reginald and parcel of the croft[990] now Robert Smyth called Drylandes Grove towards the West land of the said Robert and land of the heirs of William at Hill towards the North And land with the croft of the said Reginald called Knobbill Hille otherwise Hyewode North and East And containing in length from the King's highway as the hedges lead from the land called Forefelde towards the East as far as the land called Dennyse Nassh towards the West 39 perches And lying opposite the land of Justyns Croft and Hullonde Dane towards the South

REGINALD BACK holds of the same Abbot as of his manor aforesaid one field called Dennyse Nassh and Caldhams formerly 2 pieces and containing 4 acres and ½ and ½ virgate 2 dayworks and ½ and lying with the King's highway from the land of the said Reginald towards the South as far as the lane called Watkyns Lane and the woodland of Robert Smyth towards the North and Longdane towards the East and containing in length with the King's highway towards the South between the said land and the lane 30 perches And the said field contains in length from the end of the said 30 perches with[991] the said lane as far as the land called Lintons Dale otherwise Drylandes Dale 24 perches And lying opposite Hullanddane towards the South East and also opposite Awgotland South and West

ROBERT SMYTH kerver holds of the lord Abbot of Faversham as of his manor of Faversham aforesaid Lutons Dale alias Drylandes Dale containing of arable land 7 acres and of woodland and wooded land[992] 1 acre and 3 virgates and held there adjacent to Danetowne and Dennyssnassh And holds there five virgates of arable land and 3 virgates of woodland and wooded land called Tunhill adjacent to the said Lutons Dale and Watkyns Lane and lying between the untilled land of Reginald Backe and the heirs of Hills East and Watkyns Lane South and West and the land of John Lambe called Tunhills West and land of the said John Lambe called Mawdland towards the North And the said Lutons Dale and Tunhills Crofte contain in length with the said Lane from the land called Dennysse Nassh as far as the land called Greet Watkyns 42 perches And lying opposite parte of Awgotlond[993] Huntyngges Dane and the land called The Rocke And opposite part of Drayancroft

ROBERT SMYTH holds of the same Abbot as of his manor aforesaid one croft of land called Great Watkyns Croft towards the West the common pasture of Badlismere Leese North the land of John Lambe and the land of the said Robert Smyth East and the lane called Watkyns Lane South and containing in length with the said lane from the land called Tunhilles as far as the land called Lytell Watkyns towards the North 20 perches and ½ And containing in width with the pasture of Badlismere towards the North East 19 perches And lying opposite Dryan Croft in Lomepetfelde

ROBERT SMYTH holds of the aforesaid Abbot as of his manor aforesaid a croft called Lytell Watkyns And containing one acre and more And lying between the tenement and garden of Reginald Backe called Watkyns Tenement towards the West the common pasture of Badlismere towards the North land of the said Robert Smyth called Gret Watkyns[994] towards the East and Watkyns Lane towards the South And containing in length by the said lane from the said land

---

989 fol. 90v.
990 fol. 91.
991 fol. 91v.
992 Boscabilibus.
993 fol. 92.
994 fol. 92v.

called Grete Watkyns towards the East as far as the tenement of Reginald Backe called Watkyns towards the West 9 perches And containing in width with the said pasture towards the North between the said land and tenement towards the East and West there 8 perches and lying opposite Lomepettfelde

REGINALD BACKE holds of the lord Abbot of Faversham as of his manor aforesaid one tenement and one garden called Watkyns tenement and containing by estimation 1 acre and lying between the common pasture of Badlismere Leese West and North the lane called Watkyns Lane South West and the land of Robert Smyth called Lytell Watkyns croft towards the East and containing in length by the said lane from the said land called Litell Watkyns as far as the said common pasture 16 perches and ½ And containing in width with the said pasture as far as the said land called Lytell Watkyns 9 perches And ½ And lying opposite Lomepettfelde[995]

JOHN LAMBE holds of the lord abbot of Faversham as of his manor of Faversham aforesaid one messuage with the garden and one piece of land adjacent called Bynnefelde formerly 3 pieces whereof one piece thereof where the messuage has been sited since antiquity Beldams Croft a short time ago John Dowst And containing one acre another piece thereof from antiquity called Lorkyns Croft by exchange between John Cosen and Richard Ledmede and containing also one croft another piece thereof And the 3 piece thereof residue from antiquity called Cristyne Hill a short time ago John Dowst and containing 2 acres and lying between the land of the heirs of William at Hill towards the North land of the said John called Mawdlond and land of Robert Smyth lately Richard Dryland parcel of Drylandes Dale towards the East, land of the said John Lambe called Tunhill towards the South and the common pasture of Badlismere towards the West and containing in length with the said pasture from The Stile leading to the land called Tunhills towards the South as far as the garden of the heirs of William att Hill towards the North 25 perches[996]

JOHN LAMBE holds of the lord Abbot of Faversham as of his manor of Faversham aforesaid another croft of land annexed to the said 4 acres of land on the East side called Mawdlond containing 2 acres a short time ago John Dowst and lying between the said land called Bynnefelde towards the West land of the heirs of William at Hill and land of Reginald Back towards the North land of the said heirs of William at Hill towards the East and land of Robert Smyth parcel of Lutons Dale towards the South

JOHN LAMBE holds of the same Abbot as of his manor abovesaid another piece of land a short time ago Thomas Terry lately of Threwlege before of Sheldwyche called Tunhilles adjacent to the said field called Bynnefelde towards the South and containing 2 acres of land and more And lying between the land of Robert Smyth called Lutons Dale towards the South East and West and land of the said John Lambe called Bynnefelde towards the North

THE HEIRS OF WILLIAM AT HILL hold of the Abbot of Faversham as of his manor aforesaid one croft of land called The Middle Croft and containing 2 acres of meadow-land ½ virgate with parcels of wood and lying between the land of John Lambe towards the South land called Wythisland towards the East, wood called Dowstes Grove towards the North[997]

THE HEIRS OF WILLIAM AT HILL hold of the lord Abbot of Faversham as of his manor of Faversham aforesaid one acre of land 1 daywork and ½ and 1 perch of wood called Dowsts grove and lying between the land of Robert Smyth which he holds of us towards the West, Badlismere

---

995 fol. 93.
996 fol. 93v.
997 fol. 94.

Parke towards the North land called Wythisland otherwise Wiselond towards the East, and the land of the said heirs of William at Hill called Myddell croft towards the South And contains in length with Badlismere Parke aforesaid from Wythisland aforesaid towards the East as far as the land of the said heirs towards the West 10 perches

REGINALD BACKE and the said heirs of William at Hill hold of the lord Abbot of Faversham as of his manor of Faversham aforesaid one piece of land called Wythislandes otherwise Wiseland containing 4 acres daywork and 1 perch and lying between the wood called Badlismere Parke towards the North land of the said Reginald called Knobbill Hill towards the East land of the said heirs of William at Hill and land of John Lambe towards the South and wood called Dowstes[998] Grove and land of the said heirs of William at Hill called Middell Croft towards the West and containing in length with the said Badlismere Parke from the said land called Knobbill Hill towards the East as far as the wood of the said heirs towards the west 17 perches and ½ whereof the aforesaid Reginald holds 2 acres and the said heirs of William at Hill the residue

REGINALD BACKE holds of the lord Abbot of Faversham as of his manor of Faversham aforesaid one piece of land called [*blank*] and the wood called Knobbyllhill otherwise Hyewode and containing 5 acres and 1 virgate and 1 perch and lying between the wood called Badlismere parke towards the North land of the said Reginald called Forefeld towards the East and land of the said Reginald and land of the heirs of William at Hill towards the South And land of the said Reginald and land of the said heirs called Wythis land otherwise Wiseland towards the West and containing in length with Badlismere Parke aforesaid from the said land called Wythis land towards the west as far as the said land called Forefelde towards the East 27 perches

THE HEIRS OF WILLIAM AT HILL hold of the lord Abbot of Faversham as of his manor aforesaid one[999] croft of land called Three Akers and containing 2 acres 3 roods of meadow-land 3 perches and lying between the land of the said Reginald Backe called Danetowne South, The Grete East, Knobbill Hill and Wythis land otherwise etc., towards the North And land of Robert Smyth parcel of Lutons Dane and the land of John Lambe called Mawdeland towards the West[1000]

THOMAS BREDHAM holds of the lord Abbot of Faversham as of his manor of Faversham aforesaid one messuage called Goorys with a barn curtilage and one garden adjacent containing in total one acre and one virgate of land and lying between the King's highway towards the East land called Hellcroft towards the North Gorefelde towards the West and South

THOMAS BREDHAM hold of the Lord Abbot of Faversham as of his manor of Faversham aforesaid one messuage called Goore Place with the curtilage and one barn and three gardens containing in total 4 acres and ½ whereof the said messuage curtilage and barn and one garden on the East side of the messuage contain in total one acre and a virgate of land and lying between the King's highway East the land called Hellcroft North Gorefeld West and South And another garden of the aforesaid 3 gardens South and East The second garden of the aforesaid three gardens adjacent to the said garden containing 1 acre and 5 dayworks and lying between the aforesaid King's highway[1001] East the land called Benhams South the aforesaid Garden annexed to the message aforesaid North, and The Gorefeld West and the third garden of the aforesaid three gardens containing 2 acres and 5 dayworks and lying between the land called Benhams East the land called Westmede West the King's highway South and Goorefelde West and North

---

998 fol. 94v.
999 fol. 95.
1000 Remainder of fol. blank, fol. 95v blank, fol. 96.
1001 fol. 96v.

THOMAS BREDHAM holds of the same Abbot of Faversham as of the manor aforesaid one field called Goorefeld adjacent to the said messuage containing 10 acres 3 roods 3 dayworks and ½ and lying between the land called Helcroft and the said messuage and garden East and the said three gardens and Westmede South land called Deltye and land called Longdane West and land called Wareland North

THOMAS BREDHAM holds of the lord Abbot of Faversham as of his manor of Faversham aforesaid land called Hellcroft containing five acres adjacent to the said messuage and land called Werelond adjacent to the said land called Hellcroft containing 4 acres And wholly lying between the forestall called Roode forestall East land called[1002] Isaackes and land of the heirs of John Kenett called Newelond and Warelond North land called Longdane West land called Goorefeld and the aforesaid Messuage called Gooris South

THOMAS BREDHAM holds of the same Abbot as of his manor aforesaid one parcel of enclosed land called Westmede containing 4 acres and ½ and 5 dayworks of pasture land and 2 acres and ½ wood and wooded land lying together between the King's highway South land called Deltye West land called Goorefelde North the said three gardens meadow-land of Goorysplace East

THOMAS BREDHAM holds of the lord Abbot of Faversham as of his manor before said one field called Longdane containing 27 acres whereof the wooded land ½ an acre and lying between the said land called Goorefelde and Warelond East land called Deltye and land called Boldwynes and land of the heirs of William Barbour called Axstens Lytell Croft South and the said croft and[1003] King's highway West land of Henry Norman called Bynfelde and land of Robert Norman senior and land and wood land of Thomas Spicer called Stokfeld North

ROBERT NORMAN senior holds of the Abbot of Faversham as of his manor of Faversham aforesaid 6 acres and ½ called Boldwyns and lying between the land of Thomas Beest called Deltye East, the King's highway South, the land of the said Thomas Bredham called Axstens Croft West land of the said Thomas Bredeham called Longdane North

THOMAS BREDHAM holds of the aforesaid Abbot as of his manor aforesaid one croft called Auxtens Croft containing 7 acres and ½ and lying to the land called Boldwyns East, King's highway South and West land of William Barbour junior of him called Axtens Croft and land of the said Thomas called Longdowne North[1004]

JOHN BARBOUR holds of the Lord Abbot of Faversham as of his manor of Faversham aforesaid one curtilage and barn containing ½ an acre and one daywork with one acre and ½ and 2 daywork adjacent to the said curtilage and wholly lying between the land of Thomas Spycer towards the East the land of Robert Norman and a certain lane called Werdlond Lane South the King's highway West the messuage of Thomas Merden North and West the garden of the said Thomas Merden North land of the same Thomas East and North

JOHN BARBOUR holds of the aforesaid Abbot of Faversham as of his manor abovesaid in The Dowene annexed to Gottehill 4 acres and ½ and ½ a virgate of arable land and lying together in the wood called Gotehill and Holbroke East Neweland and Wardland South wood and arable land of Thomas Merden West, Gangaker and land of Thomas Spycer called Sextrylond North[1005]

[1002] fol. 97.
[1003] fol. 97v.
[1004] fol. 98.
[1005] fol. 98v.

JOHN BARBOUR holds of the same Abbot as of his manor abovesaid one parcel of wood called Gangaker adjacent to the said wodeland towards the South and containing ½ an acre and 3 dayworks And lying between the land of Thomas Spycer West North and East

THOMAS MERDEN holds of the said lord Abbot of Faversham there as of his manor of Faversham aforesaid 2 acres one virgate and ½ of wooded-land adjoining and 3 acres and ½ and ½ a virgate of arable land and wholly lying between the aforesaid wooded-land of the said John Barbour East Wardlond South land of the said Thomas called Momyshill West Gangaker and sextryland towards the North

THOMAS MERDEN holds of the same Abbot as of his manor aforesaid a certain field called Oldboldislonde felde and Momyshill containing 11 acres[1006] and ½ virgate and lying between the land of John Barbour East and South The Downe towards the East Welfeld lane land of Robert Norman land of the heirs of Brenly North the curtilage of the said John Barbour and the garden of the said garden of Thomas Merden West[1007]

THOMAS MERDEN holds of the Lord Abbot before said one messuage curtilage barn and garden containing 1 acre and ½ besides ½ a daywork and lying between the garden of Robert Norman junior North Oldboldislond ,felde and the barn of John Barbour East the said barn curtilage of the said John Barbour South the King's highway West

THOMAS SPYCER holds of the lord Abbot of Faversham as of his manor of Faversham aforesaid two acres of land in Stokfelde called Wardlond and lying beside Longdanewode towards the South land of the heirs of William Barbour senior called Stokfelde North and East land of Robert Norman senior in Stokfelde West whereof one virgate thereof of the land wooded[1008]

ROBERT[1009] NORMAN senior holds of the Lord Abbot of Faversham as of his manor of Faversham aforesaid one acre and ½ and 3 dayworks of land in Stokfelde and lying to the land of Thomas Spycer called Longdanes Wode and the land of Thomas Bredham called Longdane towards the South the way leading to Stokfelde North and land of Henry Norman called Stokaker a short time ago Thomas Joce in Bynnfelde West land of Thomas Spycer called Wardlond towards the East

THE HEIRS OF THOMAS JOCE hold of the lord Abbot of Faversham as of his manor of Faversham aforesaid 7 acres and 3 virgates of meadow-land 2 dayworks and ½ of wooded land called Kynggesbrokes Croft and lying between the Kynggesbrokes grene towards the West the croft of Robert Norman junior called also Kynggesbrokes Croft and the croft of Thomas Best called Wodisende Croft North Croft of Simon Kempe called Skokylles Croft east and Skokylles Lane South of arable land 2 acres

ROBERT[1010] NORMAN junior holds of the lord Abbot of Faversham as of his manor aforesaid one acre of meadow land 4 dayworks and one perch at Kynggesbrokys Hill formerly William Barbour senior and lying to the King's highway there towards the West the lands of the heirs of Thomas Joce called Kynggesbrokes Croft East and South land of the heirs of John Best formerly Richard Erle called Wodsyngges Croft North

THOMAS SPICER holds of the lord Abbot of Faversham as of his manor aforesaid one acre and ½ and one virgate of meadow-land one daywork of wooded land at Wodysend and called Croft at

[1006] Corrected from 12.
[1007] fol. 99.
[1008] Boscalibus.
[1009] fol. 99v.
[1010] fol. 100.

Wodesend and lying to the land of the heirs of Brenly West the King's highway there South land of Richard Poope called Bylchewodehill North and wood of the heirs of Thomas Joce towards the East

THE HEIRS OF THOMAS JOCE hold of the aforesaid abbot as of his manor of[1011] Faversham aforesaid 2 acres land and ½, 1 virgate and one daywork of wood at Bylchwodehill and lying between the wood of the heirs of John Fogge knight North and east the King's highway South pasture and wood of Thomas Spycer and the land of Richard Poope towards the West

THOMAS BEST holds of the lord Abbot of Faversham as of his manor of Faversham one croft of wood land called Woddisendes croft containing 3 acres one virgate and 4 dayworks and lying between the King's highway East and North wood of Blean East pasture of the heirs of Thomas Joce and pasture of Robert Norman junior towards the South

THOMAS POPE holds of the lord Abbot of Faversham as of his manor of Faversham aforesaid one parcel of wood containing 5 dayworks and lying to the wood of John Best East and south the king's way leading from the Kings Broke towards the West and North[1012]

THOMAS POPE holds of the lord Abbot of Faversham as of his manor of Faversham aforesaid one piece of wooded land containing 3 virgates of meadow-land one daywork and lying to the wood of Thomas Spycer and the wood of Richard Poope towards the East the king'street called Bilchwodeland West land of the heirs of Brenly South and land of Richard Pope towards the North

~~**HENRY NORMAN** Thomas Best William Barbour junior hold of the lord Abbot of Faversham as of his manor of Faversham aforesaid one Grove~~[1013] ~~called Skokylleshill containing 3 acres lying~~ [unfinished]

THE HEIRS OF BRENLY hold of the lord Abbot of Faversham as of his manor of Faversham aforesaid 3 virgates of pasture land otherwise meadow-land 3 dayworks and ½ adjacent to Bylchwodland towards the West wooded land of Thomas Poope towards the North wooded land of Thomas Spycer towards the East the king'street towards the South[1014]

THOMAS POPE holds of the lord Abbot of Faversham as of his manor of Faversham aforesaid one piece of wooded land containing one acre and lying besides Skokilles hill to the wood of the Abbey of Faversham North and East wooded land of Simon Kempe West and the common way towards the South

HENRY NORMAN Thomas Best and William Barbour junior hold of the lord Abbot of Faversham as of his manor of Faversham aforesaid one grove called Skokilleshill containing 3 acres lying between the wood of the Abbey of Faversham East and South the way leading as far as Fyshponde towards the West the King's highway North Whereof the said Henry Norman hold 2 acres Thomas Best hold ½ an acre and the said William the other ½ an acre residue[1015]

SIMON KEMPE hold of the lord abbot of Faversham as of his manor of Faversham aforesaid at Skokillyshilles an acre and ½ and one daywork of wood lying between the lane called

---

[1011] fol. 100v.

[1012] fol. 101.

[1013] *Grovam. O.E.D.* does not give Latin for Grove in the introduction but does in one of the quotes. The definition being a small wood; a group of tree affording shade or forming avenues or walks, occuring naturally or planted for a special purpose. Groves were commonly planted by heathen peoples in honour of deities to serve as places of worship or for the reception of images.

[1014] fol. 101v.

[1015] fol. 102.

Skokilleslane towards the South the wood of the Abbey of Faversham towards the North wood of Thomas Poope towards the East and the wood of the heirs of Thomas Joce towards the West[1016]

THE HEIRS OF HENRY BULL hold of the lord Abbot of Faversham as of his manor of Faversham aforesaid one messuage and one garden at Southstrete containing ½ an acre and ½ a virgate two dayworks and ½ and lying between the land and garden of William Barbour junior East and land of the heirs William Barbour senior South land and garden of William Neele West King's highway there North whereof the said messuage and garden contains 1 virgate 3 dayworks and ½

HEIRS OF WILLIAM BARBOUR senior hold of the Abbot of Faversham as of his manor of Faversham aforesaid 3 acres of meadow-land ½ a virgate in Southfelde aforesaid and lying between the land of the heirs of Brenly and the land of Thomas Poope which lies in Southfelde East the wood of William Barbour junior called Lytell Grove South land of William Neele and land of the said William Barbour junior called Oldboldishill ,West and land of the said William Neele and the heirs of Henry Bulle and land of the said William Barbour junior which lies in Southfelde North[1017]

THE HEIRS OF BRENLEY hold there of the lord Abbot of Faversham as of his manor of Faversham aforesaid in Southfelde containing 3 virgates of land and lying between land of Thomas Poope towards the East and South land of the heirs of William Barbour senior West and land of the said heirs of William Barbour and the land of the said heirs of Brenly towards the North

THOMAS POPE holds of the lord Abbot of Faversham as of his manor of Faversham aforesaid one messuage and certain lands lying together containing in total 6 acres 1 virgate and 3 dayworks and lying at Southstreete between the messuage of Hamon Redborough land of William Barbour senior land of the heirs of John Best and the wood of William Barbour junior East, Hayes Wode and the land of William Barbour junior towards the South land of the same William Barbour junior land of the heirs of Brenly and land of the heirs of William Barbour senior West the King's highway North in respect whereof the said messuage with the garden contain ½ an acre one virgate besides 2 dayworks[1018]

WILLIAM BARBOUR junior holds of the lord Abbot of Faversham as of his manor of Faversham aforesaid 1 acre 1 virgate and 2 dayworks of land with the messuage existing upon it and lying between Southstrete towards the North land of the heirs of William Barbour which lies in Southfelde East and South land and messuage of the heirs of Henry Bull towards the West

THE HEIRS OF WILLIAM BARBOUR hold of the lord Abbot of Faversham as of his manor of Faversham aforesaid one messuage at Southstrete with 3 virgates of land and lying between the messuage and garden of William Barbour junior towards the West a foot path to the church towards the South land of the heirs of Brenly lying in Southfeld towards the East the King's highway called Southstrete North

THE HEIRS OF BRENLY hold of the lord Abbot of Faversham as of his manor aforesaid one acre of land and ½ there with parcels of gardens adjacent to the messuage of the heirs of William

[1016] Remainder of fol. blank, fol. 102v blank, fol. 103.
[1017] fol. 103v.
[1018] fol. 104.

Barbour and lying[1019] between the land of Thomas Poope towards the East and South land of the heirs of William Barbour senior West and the King's highway towards the North

THE HEIRS OF WILLIAM BARBOUR senior hold of the lord Abbot of Faversham as of his manor of Faversham aforesaid 1 acre and ½ daywork of land in Southfeld and lying between the land of the heirs of Brenly which lies in Southfelde East land of Thomas Poope in Southfelde South West and North

THE HEIRS OF BRENLY hold of the lord Abbot of Faversham as of his manor of Faversham aforesaid in Southfeld 1 acre of land in Southfelde adjacent to Underwodys Dane towards the East land of Thomas Poope South land of the heirs of William Barbour West the garden of Thomas Pope and The Hemphawe of Hamon Redborough North

THOMAS BEST holds of the lord Abbot of Faversham as of his manor of Faversham aforesaid ½ an acre of wood in Hayes Wode adjacent to Underwodes Dane towards the North the wood of William Barbour South land of Simon Kempe towards the East [1020]

ROBERT NORMAN senior holds of the lord Abbot of Faversham as of his manor aforesaid in Hayes Wode 2 pieces of wood in respect whereof one piece thereof contains ½ an acre and lies to the wood and land lately Hamon Redborough now Simon Kempe towards the North and South and wood of the said Simon West land of the said Robert called Bynnecroft East And the other piece thereof containing 1 virgate and ½ and lying between the wood of the said Simon towards the East wood of the heirs of Brenly and the wood of Hamon Redborough formerly Arnold Sare towards the South wood of William Barbour junior and the wood of Thomas Best formerly Richard Erle towards the West and land of the said Simon Kempe towards the North [1021]

HEIRS OF BRENLY hold of the lord Abbot of Faversham as of his manor of Faversham aforesaid 1 virgate 3 perches and ½ of wood there lying between the wood of the heirs of William Barbour Southwest and West and North the wood of Hamon Redborough North and the wood[1022] of Simon Kempe towards the North and East [1023]

THE HEIRS OF WILLIAM BARBOUR hold there of the same Abbot as of his manor abovesaid 2 acres 1 virgate and ½ and 1 daywork of wood and lying between Hayes ~~wode valeigh~~ steth[1024] towards the South and West the wood of William Barbour West land of Robert Norman East the wood of Simon Kempe the wood of the heirs of Brenly and the wood of the said William Barbour North and the wood of the said William Barbour towards the West [1025]

THOMAS POOPE holds of the lord Abbot of Faversham as of his manor of Faversham aforesaid ½ a virgate of wood and lying between the wood of William Barbour West North and East and the wood of the heirs of Brenley towards the South [1026]

THE HEIRS OF BRENLY hold of the lord Abbot of Faversham as of his manor of Faversham aforesaid ½ a virgate of wood and lying between the wood of Hamon Redborough towards the

1019 fol. 104v.
1020 ~~west~~ *Margin* Note fol. 105.
1021 *Margin* note.
1022 fol. 105v.
1023 *Margin* note.
1024 Written above in a later scrawl.
1025 *Margin* note.
1026 *Margin* note.

West the wood of Thomas Pope[1027] towards the North wood of William Barbour junior East and the land of the said heirs of Brenly towards the South[1028]

HAMON REDBOROUGH holds there of the lord Abbot of Faversham as of his manor of Faversham aforesaid 2 pieces of wood containing 1 virgate and two dayworks in respect whereof on piece thereof lies next to The Markestone which divides the metes and bounds of the wood of the heirs of William Barbour William Barbour junior and Robert Norman And the other piece thereof lies between the land of the said heirs of Brenly towards the South land of the said William Barbour junior Southwest wood of Thomas Best North and wood of the said William Barbour East [1029]

THOMAS BEST hold of the lord Abbot of Faversham as of his manor of Faversham aforesaid one acre of wood besides 2 dayworks formerly Cosens and Hobbnettes and lying together in two pieces between the wood of William Barbour and the wood of Hamon Redborough East Hayes Valey South wood of the said William Barbour towards the West and North and wood of Thomas Pope North[1030]

THOMAS POOPE holds there of the lord Abbot of Faversham as of his manor of Faversham aforesaid ½ a virgate of wood and lying between the wood of Thomas Best South the wood of William Barbour West North and East [1031]

THOMAS POPE holds of the lord Abbot aforesaid as of his manor before said of woodland ½ and acre three dayworks of land and one perch of land And lying between the wood of the said William Barbour South and East land of the said land of the said Thomas West and North [1032]

WILLIAM BARBOUR holds of the same Abbot as of his manor aforesaid in Hayes Wode 1 virgate and two dayworks of wood and lying between the land of Thomas Pope North the wood of Thomas Best East land of the heirs of Brenly and the land of the said William Barbour South and the land of the same William towards the West [1033]

WILLIAM BARBOUR holds of the lord Abbot of Faversham as of his manor of Faversham aforesaid an other piece of woodland adjacent there containing 6 dayworks besides 1 perch and lying between the woodland of Thomas[1034] Pope West North and East and wood of Thomas Best towards the South [1035]

WILLIAM BARBOUR holds of the lord Abbot of Faversham as of his manor of Faversham aforesaid another piece of wood adjacent containing ½ an acre 1 virgate and 6 dayworks and ½ and lying between the wood of the same William and the land of Thomas Pope towards the West the wood of the said Thomas Pope towards the West and South land of Thomas Best North wood of the said Thomas Pope East and the wood of Hamon Redborough towards the South [1036]

WILLIAM BARBOUR holds of the lord Abbot of Faversham as of his manor of Faversham aforesaid another piece of wood adjacent there containing one virgate and ½ and lying between

[1027] fol. 106.
[1028] *Margin* note.
[1029] *Margin* note.
[1030] *Margin* note fol. 106v.
[1031] *Margin* note.
[1032] *Margin* note.
[1033] *Margin* note.
[1034] fol. 107.
[1035] *Margin* note.
[1036] *Margin* note.

the wood of the heirs of William Barbour East, Hayes valeygh South, wood of the heirs of Brenly and the wood of Thomas Pope West, land of the said William North [1037]

WILLIAM BARBOUR holds of the same Abbot as of his manor aforesaid another piece of wood containing one virgate one daywork and ½ and lying between the wood of Robert Norman senior East wood of the heirs of William Barbour and wood of the said William Barbour West and wood of Thomas Best North [1038]

WILLIAM STEVYN holds of the lord Abbot of Faversham as of his manor of Faversham aforesaid at Stokilles Lane one acre and ½ and ½ a virgate of land called Mellarslond and lying next to Stokillslane aforesaid towards the north land of Thomas Spycer called Stokyllys Croft East land of the same Thomas called Southcroft South a croft of the same Thomas called Mellerslond towards the West

RICHARD POOPE holds of the lord Abbot of Faversham as of his manor of Faversham aforesaid one messuage with a garden annexed to the same messuage containing in total one acre and ½ a virgate and lying to the common street called Olboldyslond Street towards the East a messuage and curtilage of Thomas Spycer towards the South land of the same Thomas called Knollys West and Southstrete North

RICHARD POOPE holds of the same Abbot as of his manor aforesaid one garden and one piece of land opposite the said messuage containing ½ an acre and ½ a virgate besides 2 perches ~~dayworks~~ called Mellerslond and lying to the said common street towards the West and the land of Thomas Spycer also called Mellersland[1039] towards the East land of the same Thomas called The Downe towards the South and Kyngesbrokes grene towards the North

THOMAS SPICER holds of the lord Abbot of Faversham as of his manor of Faversham aforesaid three acres and 3 dayworks of arable land and wood called Cosens down at Holmebusshe and lying between Skokillys Croft towards the North the lane leading from Skokylls lane to the ffysshponde towards the East The Bo[u]ne called the Pendbo[u]ne and the land of Richard Pope called Pend South the land called Zoche towards the West in respect whereof one acre thereof of the land is arable.

THOMAS SPYCER holds of the lord Abbot of Faversham as of his manor aforesaid another piece of land called Skokyllys Croft containing 3 acres and 3 dayworks and lying to the other land called Skokyllyslond towards the North land of William Stevyn called Mellerslonde towards the West the way leading to fysshponde towards the East wood of the same Thomas Spycer towards the South[1040]

THOMAS SPICER now Richard Spycer holds of the lord Abbot of Faversham as of his manor aforesaid one piece of land called Zoche containing 2 acres and 4 dayworks and lying between a certain croft called Holmebusshe East land called Welfeld South land called The Down West land of William Stevyn called Mellarslond North in respect whereof ½ an acre of wood lies within the same close on the southern and eastern sides

THOMAS SPICER now Richard Spycerholds of the same Abbot as of his manor aforesaid two pieces of land containing 6 acres 1 virgate 3 dayworks and ½ whereof one piece thereof called The Downe contains 3 acres and ½ and 1 daywork and the other piece thereof residue called

---

1037 *Margin* note.
1038 *Margin* note fol. 107v.
1039 fol. 108.
1040 fol. 108v.

Mellerslond containing 2 acres 3 virgates 2 dayworks and ½ and lying together to the land called Welfeld towards the South Skokyllys Lane and Lynges Broke towards the North land of Richard Pope called Mellerslond King's highway and Olboldyslond Forestall towards the West land called Mellarslond and land called Zoche towards the East

THOMAS[1041] **SPYCER** now Richard Spycer holds of the lord Abbot of Faversham as of his manor aforesaid 9 acres and ½ 3 dayworks and 3 perches with diverse houses being upon it at Olboldislond called Knolles and Gouldyngges hamme and lying between the messuage and garden of Richard Pope, the King's highway, the messuage of Henry Norman lately Colwell and the Garden of the heirs of Thomas Joce towards the East Beldamsgrove South Knolles Wode West and South land of Thomas Best West and the King's highway towards the North

THOMAS SPICER holds of the lord Abbot of Faversham as of his manor of Faversham aforesaid one grove called Nether Howse Grove containing one acre 3 virgates and 3 dayworks and lying to the King's highway South the garden of the heirs of Thomas Joce and the land of the said Thomas Spycer called Knolles East Knollis wode North land called Westbynne land called Olboldislond East and a garden of Nether Howse aforesaid towards the West[1042]

THOMAS SPYCER holds of the same Abbot as of his manor aforesaid one messuage called Netherhouse with a barn and garden adjacent and the land called Olboldisland Croft and Westbynne now in one and the land called Robyns adjacent and containing 7 acres and ½ besides 2 dayworks and together lying between the King's highway towards the East the wood of the said Thomas called Nether howse grove and the wood called Knollis Wode towards the North land of Thomas Best called Underwoddes Dane towards the West land of Simon Kempe towards the South

THOMAS SPYCER and the heirs of Brenly hold of the aforesaid Abbot and of his manor before said one grove called Knollis Wode containing 3 acres and ½ one virgate and three perches and lying between the land of the said Thomas called Westbynne towards the South land of Thomas Best called Underwode Dane otherwise the said Gilys Westbynne towards the West land of the said Best called Duecroft and the garden of the same Thomas West and North land of the said Thomas Spycer called Gouldynges hame towards the North land called Knollys and a certain wood of the said Thomas Spycer[1043] called Beldams Grove towards the East Whereof the heirs of Brenly hold 1 virgate 3 dayworks and 1 perch adjacent to the lands of the said Thomas Spycer called Westbynne South and land of the said Thomas Best called Underwoddis dane South and West

THOMAS BEST holds of the lord Abbot of Faversham as of his manor of Faversham aforesaid one messuage curtilage two gardens and one croft of land called Desecroft lying to the Southstrete towards the North containing 3 acres whereof ½ an acre of wodland besides 2 dayworks and lying between the land of Thomas Spycer called Gouldyngges Hame towards the East and North and Knollys Wode East and South the common lane towards the West and Underwoddis Dane towards the South

THOMAS BEST holds of the lord Abbot of Faversham as of his manor of Faversham aforesaid one piece of land called Underwoddis Dane adjacent one garden of[1044] the aforesaid garden containing 6 acres and ½ and lying between Hayes Wode towards the South land of Thomas Pope towards the South and West the land of the heirs of Brenly North West land of Hamon

[1041] fol. 109.
[1042] fol. 109v.
[1043] fol. 110.
[1044] fol. 110v.

Redborough North land of Thomas Spycer called Westbyn towards the East, Knollyswod towards the Northeast

HAMON REDBOROUGH holds of the lord Abbot of Faversham as of his manor of Faversham aforesaid ½ an acre and 3 daywork of land with a messuage being upon it at Southstrete and lying in the King's highway towards the North a certain lane there towards the East land of Thomas Best called Erles Dane and parcel of the land of the heirs of William Barbour senior South the garden and messuage of Thomas Pope West

SIMON KEMPE holds of the lord Abbot of Faversham as of his manor of Faversham aforesaid at Olboldislond 2 acres and 1 virgate of arable land and wood land with a messuage lately Hamon Redborough and lying to the King's highway towards the East land of Robert[1045] Norman senior South, land of Thomas Best called Giles Dane and the wood of the same Thomas called Hayes Wode West land of Thomas Spycer called Westbynne and Robyns Croft North, whereof 1 virgate and ½ of the land is wooded land

ROBERT NORMAN senior holds of the lord Abbot of Faversham as of his manor of Faversham aforesaid 3 acres of land with one messuage being upon it at Olboldislonde and lying to the King's highway towards the East land lately Hamon Redborough now Simon Kempe towards the North the land of the heirs of William Barbour senior which lie in Hayes Valeigh South and the wood called Hayes Wode West

JOHN HUBBERD holds of the lord Abbot of Faversham as of his manor of Faversham aforesaid one messuage with garden and land adjacent containing in total half an acre one virgate and 3 dayworks And lying to the King's highway East land to the heirs of John[1046]

JOHN HUBBERD holds of the lord Abbot of Faversham as of his manor of Faversham aforesaid 1 virgate of land and 3 dayworks adjacent to the said messuage on the side [rest blank]

THOMAS SPYCER holds of the lord Abbot of Faversham as of his manor aforesaid 2 acres and 7 dayworks of arable land and wood at Gotehill formerly John Lanckton and lying to the lands of the heirs of William Barbour senior called Hampnettes Downe towards the South land of the said Thomas Spycer and land of the said heirs of William Barbour senior West wood of the said Thomas Spycer North and wood of Thomas Bredham and wood of Thomas Best called Gotehill towards the East Whereof one acre thereof of the land is wooded

THOMAS SPYCER holds of the lord Abbot of Faversham as of his manor[1047] of Faversham five acres and five dayworks of arable land and wood called Peende and lying between Fisshpende Broke and the wood there formerly Pryvettis and Croft land formerly John Lankton towards the East land of the heirs of William Barbour senior called Hampnettes Downe South a garden called Peend garden formerly John Stevyn now Richard Pope and embankment[1048] of Fisshpende Broke north the lane called Welfeld lane and parcel of the land of the heirs of William Barbour senior called Monyshill West whereof ½ an acre of land is wooded and the same ½ acre of wooded land with ½ acre of arable land he renders to the table the residue that is to say 4 acres he renders to the sacristan by the year 15[d]

THOMAS SPICER holds of the lord Abbot of Faversham as of his manor aforesaid 1 acre of wood a short time ago Pryvettes and lying between the land of the same Thomas formerly of the

---

1045 fol. 111.

1046 Not completed over the page fol. 111v.

1047 fol. 112.

1048 *Fossa* can also be a dike.

said Lancktons towards the South wood of the lord Abbot of Faversham called Comons[1049] towards the East the embankment of Fishpende Broke towards the North land called Sextrylond towards the West

RICHARD POOPE holds of the lord Abbot of Faversham as of his manor before said one garden next to Fisshpendbroke containing 1 acre and ½ and lying between the land of Thomas Spycer called Sextens Land towards the East and South land called Welfelde West and the land of the said Thomas Spycer called Cosens Downe towards the North and he renders to the sacristan by the year 9[d]

THE HEIRS OF THOMAS JOCE hold of the lord Abbot of Faversham as of his manor aforesaid 4 acres 1 virgate and ½ of land called Welfeld with ½ part of one there pertaining to the said land and lying between a certain lane called Welfeld lane South and West land of Thomas Spycer called The Downe North the garden of Richard Pope called The Pende East in respect whereof 1 acre and ½ thereof he renders to the sacristan by the year 6[d]

THE HEIRS OF THOMAS JOCE hold of the lord Abbot of Faversham as of his manor[1050] before said one messuage and one garden annexed containing 3 virgates and 1 perch at Olboldislonde between the King's highway South wood of Thomas Spycer West land of the said Thomas ~~Spycer Joce~~ called Knolles north a parcel of garden of the same Thomas Spycer a garden of Henry Norman formerly William Harryes East

HENRY NORMAN holds of the lord Abbot of Faversham as of his manor of Faversham before said 1 virgate and ½ daywork of land with a messuage existing upon it and lying furthermore at Olboldislond aforesaid and lying between the land of the heirs of Thomas Joce West land of Thomas Spycer called Knolles North a garden of the same Thomas towards the East and the King's highway towards the South

HENRY NORMAN holds of the lord Abbot of Faversham as of his manor aforesaid 1 piece of land called Colwellys Aker and containing 1 acre besides 5 dayworks and lying to Welfeldlane towards the East land of the heirs of Brenly towards the West land formerly[1051] Henry Hampnett and afterwards William Barbour senior called Momyshill South and the said Welfeldlane and the common forestall called Olboldislond forestall towards the North

HEIRS OF BRENLY holds of the lord Abbot of Faversham as of his manor aforesaid 2 acres of land and ½ a virgate besides 3 perches [at] Olboldislonde and lying between the forstal there North a garden of Robert Norman junior and a garden of the heirs of John Kenett West land of the said heirs of John Kenett South land of the said Robert Norman junior and land of Henry Norman formerly Colwellys towards the East

ROBERT NORMAN junior holds of the lord Abbot of Faversham as of his manor aforesaid one acre and ½ of land besides 4 dayworks at Olboldislond aforesaid with a messuage existing upon it formerly John Lanckton afterwards John Helde and lying to the King's highway to the West land of the heirs of Brenly East a garden of the heirs of William Barbour senior formerly Henry Hampnet South the forstal of Olboldislond towards the North[1052]

ROBERT NORMAN junior holds of the lord Abbot of Faversham as of his manor aforesaid three virgates and three dayworks besides one perch formerly Hampnettes and lying between

---

[1049] fol. 112v.
[1050] fol. 113.
[1051] fol. 113v.
[1052] fol. 114.

Welfeldland towards the East the land of the heirs of John Kenett towards the South land of the heirs of Brenly and land of Henry Norman called Colwellys Aker North

HENRY NORMAN holds of the lord Abbot of Faversham as of his manor aforesaid 7 acres and ½ and one virgate of land besides 5 perches with a messuage existing upon it at Olboldislond aforesaid and lying to the King's highway towards the West land of Thomas Bredham called Longdane towards the South land of Robert Norman senior called Stokfelde formerly William Norman senior East the King's highway leading to Stokfeld towards the North

PETER BEALDE holds of the lord Abbot of Faversham as of his manor of Faversham aforesaid one piece of land called Isakkys containing 3 acres 3 virgates besides 2 dayworks and 1 perch[1053] lying between the common way leading from Roode towards Boughton East Roodes Forestall and land called Helcroft South a parcel of 36 acres of land of John Kenett West land of Thomas Bredham called Helbroke towards the North whereof five acres of land is wooded

JOHN BARBOUR holds of the lord Abbot of Faversham as of his manor of Faversham aforesaid two pieces of land called Wareland and Newland and the said piece of land called Wareland containing 7 acres and ½ one daywork and ½ And the said piece called Newland contains 7 acres besides ½ a virgate and total lying together between the land of Peter Bealde called Isakkes towards the East land of Thomas Bredham called the Helcroft South land of Thomas Spycer called Wardland West and South land of Thomas Merden formerly called The Oke and Olboldislondfelde West and land of the said Thomas Merden called The Downe towards the North

WILLIAM BARBOUR junior holds of the lord Abbot of Faversham as of his manor[1054] of Faversham before said one piece of land also called Axtens Croft adjacent to the said croft containing 1 acre and ½ and lying between the King's highway west land called Longdane North and East And the said Croft aforesaid of Thomas Bredham called Axtens Croft South[1055]

THE LORD OF BADLYSMERE holds of the lord Abbot of Faversham as of his manor of Faversham before said one acre of wood next to the wood adjacent to Roodys Court towards the East land called Hikkes towne towards the South Rodefelde towards the West and land of the said Thomas Best towards the North

THOMAS BREDHAM holds of the lord Abbot of Faversham as of his manor of Faversham before said 2 pieces of arable land lying together called Hikkes towne and Chalkdeele containing 16 acres whereof 7 acres thereof formerly called Cristynefelde and lying between the King's highway East a garden and wood of Thomas Best pertaining to Rodis Courte and wood of the lord of Badlismere and also land of the said Thomas Best North and land of the said Thomas Best and others West and land of the said lord of Badlismere South whereof Hikkes towne contains 11 acres And John Hilles holds within the said land called Hikkes towne three virgates of land.

THE[1056] LORD OF BADLISMERE holds of the lord Abbot of Faversham as of his manor aforesaid 10 acres of land and ½ called Lambernelese lying next to Childenwode between the King's highway East and West Childen Wode and Crochercroft North land of Thomas Bredham and others South

---

1053 fol. 114v.

1054 fol. 115.

1055 Remainder of fol. blank; fol. 115v.

1056 fol. 116.

THOMAS BREDHAM holds of the lord Abbot of Faversham as of his manor aforesaid 12 acres of arable land in two fields lying together formerly called Childenfeldes whereof one field thereof now called Six Acres and lying between the King's highway towards the North and East land of the Lord of Badlismere called Lambernlese South and West wood of the said Lord in Childenwode ~~and Michael Halke there~~ and wood of the aforesaid Thomas Bredham and wood of Peter Beald West

THE LORD OF BADLISMERE Thomas Bredham and Peter Beald hold of the lord Abbot of Faversham as of his manor aforesaid one wood called Childenwode containing 6 acres and ½ a virgate of land and lying between the said Lord of Badlismere and the land of the said Thomas[1057] Bredham towards the South land of the same Thomas Breham called Crouchecroft towards the West the King's highway North and land of the said Thomas Bredham East whereof the said lord of Badlismere holds one acre and the said Thomas Bredham holds 3 acres and the said Peter holds 2 & ½ the residue

THOMAS BREDHAM holds of the lord Abbot of Faversham as of his manor aforesaid Crowchcroft containing 3 acres and ½ and lying between the King's highway towards the North and West And part of the wood of the said Thomas and land of the lord of Badlysmere called Lambernsleese ~~wood of the said Thomas Bredham~~ towards the South and wood of the same Thomas and ~~Thomas~~ Peter Beald towards the East Whereof the wooded land is one virgate

THOMAS BREDHAM holds of the same Abbot as of his manor above said one piece of land called Belsyers Croft containing in total one acre and ½ and lying between the lands of Peter Beald called Southfeld towards the East land of the same Peter now a garden towards the South land of said Peter formerly Perkyns towards the North and the King's highway West

THE LORD OF BADLISMERE holds of the lord Abbot of Faversham as of his manor aforesaid in Roodefeld on the Southside 9 acres and one virgate besides ½ a daywork of land and lying between the land of Thomas Bredham and the land of John Hilles called Hykkes towne and[1058] Rodefelde towards the North the King's highway towards the East and the land of Thomas Marche called Strodefelde towards the West land of the said lord towards the South

THE LORD OF BADLISMERE and Thomas Breham hold of the lord Abbot of Faversham as of his manor of Faversham aforesaid 9 acres and ½ virgate of land and wooded-land besides 1 perch of land adjacent to the said 9 acres and 1 virgate of land besides ½ a daywork and lying between the said land towards the North the King's highway towards the East land of the said lord and of others towards the South land of John Marche called Strodefelde towards the West Whereof the said Thomas Breham holds of the arable lands 3 virgates opposite Coppsole, residue held by the said lord and thereof of the wooded land one acre besides 4 dayworks

THE LORD OF BADLISMERE and Stephen Jenyns knight hold of the lord Abbot of Faversham as of his manor aforesaid 6 acres and 1 virgate and ½ of wooded land and lying between the King's highway towards the East the land of the said Lord towards the North Whereof of the land [which] is wooded 2 acres [1059]

PETER BEALD holds of the lord Abbot of Faversham as of his manor of Faversham aforesaid one messuage with two gardens and one field adjacent called Southfeld otherwise Bynnefelde containing 8 acres whereof the said field contains 6 acres and the whole lying between the King's highway South and West and a croft of land of Thomas Breham called Belsyerscroft and a garden

---

1057 fol. 116v.
1058 fol. 117.
1059 fol. 117v.

of the said Peters called Sanders Garden towards the North and land called Bealdisfelde towards the East

PETER BEALD holds of the lord Abbot of Faversham as of his manor aforesaid one croft of land called Bealdisfelde containing 9 acres and ½ and one virgate of land and lying between the land of the said Stephen Jenyns knight lately the heirs of Valentine Dryland called Fylberdisfelde towards the East the King's highway towards the South the said croft of land called Southfeld otherwise Bynnefeld Saunders Grove and the land called Welcroft towards the North

PETER BEALD holds of the lord Abbot of Faversham as of his manor of Faversham aforesaid one croft of land called Welcroft containing 3 acres ½ virgate of land and 1 daywork and lying between the land from the wood land of the said Stephen Jenyns knight called Filberdisfeld towards the East[1060] field of the said Peter called Bealdisfeld towards the South Saunders Grove aforesaid and Simons Croft towards the West and Paradise Croft towards the North whereof half an acre of land is wooded

PETER BEALDE holds of the lord Abbot of Faversham as of his manor of Faversham aforesaid one croft of land called Paradise Croft containing 1 acre and ½ and a daywork and lying between Welcroft aforesaid towards the South land called Simondiscroft towards the West the King's highway towards the North and East

PETER BEALDE holds of the same Abbot as of his manor of Faversham aforesaid one parcel of wood called Saunders Grove formerly called Sherywode containing 5 virgates of wood and lying between Saunders Garden towards the West Symons Croft towards the North Welcroft East and Bealdisfelde towards the South

PETER BEALDE holds of the aforesaid Abbot as is above said one parcel of wood lying in Childenwod containing 1 acre and ½ of one acre of wood between the King's highway towards the North the wood of Christopher Bredham towards the South East and West

PETER BEALD holds of the same Abbot of Faversham as of his manor abovesaid one acre of wood lying in Childenwode aforesaid between the land of the lord of Badlismere called Lamburnesleese towards the South and West wood of Christopher Bredeham there towards the East and North

PETER[1061] **BEALDE** holds of the lord Abbot of Faversham as of his manor of Faversham aforesaid 2 parcels of garden now inclosed in one formerly Chesys and Perkyns called Saunders garden and Chesys garden containing 1 acre and 1 virgate 1 daywork and a ½ and 1 perch whereof Chesys garden contains ½ an acre besides 1 daywork and wholly lying between the land called Bealdes Southfelde and Bredhams Croft called Belsyers Croft towards the South the King's highway West Roodys Forestall and Symonds Croft North and Saunders Grove East And Thomas Bredham enclosed the said half an acre besides 1 daywork which lies next to the King's highway towards the West

JOHN HILLES holds of the lord Abbot of Faversham as of his manor of Faversham aforesaid one acre of land and 3 virgates lately John Marche and lying between the land of Robert Stevynson vicar of Sellyng East land of Thomas Bredham South land of the Abbot of Saint Augustines Canterbury West land of the said John Hilles North and he renders by the year [blank]

1060 fol. 118.
1061 fol. 118v.

JOHN[1062] **HILLES** holds of the lord Abbot of Faversham as of his manor aforesaid three acres and 3 virgates next to The Toote lately his fathers and lying in Rodefelde between the land of the said Robert Stevynson vicar East the land of Thomas Bredham South land of John Luton and the land of the said Thomas Bredham West and the land of the same Thomas North, And he renders by the year [blank]

JOHN HILLES holds of the lord Abbot of Faversham aforesaid as of his manor abovesaid 4 acres and 1 virgate of land formerly Hamon at Millà and Robert Marche and lying between the land of the said Robert Stevynson vicar East land of Thomas Bredham South and North land of the Abbot of Saint Augustines Canterbury called Peryfelde West whereof Thomas Bredham has enclosed 2 acres and a ½ which lie next to the land of the said Thomas towards the North and Thomas Best has enclosed the residue. And for every acre he renders by the year 2^{d} ½

THOMAS BREDHAM holds of the same Abbot as of his manor aforesaid at[1063] four acres and ½ and 1 virgate of land and lying between the land of Thomas Best Northeast land of the said Thomas Bredham called Beeris South, land of John Hill and land of Robert Stevynson vicar of Sellyng West. And he renders by the year for an acre 2^{d} ½

THOMAS BREDHAM holds of the aforesaid Abbot of Faversham as of his manor before said in Rodefeld 3 acres of land and 1 virgate lying between the land of the said John Hilles and the land of the said vicar towards the South land of Thomas Best East and North land of Saint Augustines called Peryfelde West He renders for the acre by the year 2^{d} ½

THOMAS BREDHAM holds of the same Abbot as of his manor aforesaid next to Peryfelde at The Oke 2 acres and ½ virgate formerly his father's lying between John Hill South and North land of the said vicar East land of the Abbot of St. Augustines of Canterbury called Peryfelde West And he renders for an acre by the year 2^{d} ½[1064]

JOHN HILLES holds of the lord Abbot of Faversham as of his manor of Faversham aforesaid 3 acres of land and lying next to Strode Oke in Rodefelde lately his fathers and lying between the land of Thomas Bredham North and East land of the lord of Badlismere South East and land of the same lord and land of Thomas Best West And he renders for an acre by the year [blank]

JOHN HILLES holds of the lord Abbot of Faversham as of his manor of Faversham aforesaid at The Toote 1 acre and ½ lately Hamon att Mill and lying between the lands of Thomas Best East and South land of the said vicar of Sellyng and land of Thomas Bredham West and land of Thomas Best North And [he renders] for an acre by the year 2^{d} ½

ROBERT STEVYNSON vicar of Sellyng holds of the same Abbot as of his manor aforesaid at The Toote aforesaid five acres of land and ½ And lying between the land of Thomas Bredham East and South land of John Hilles and land of Thomas Bredham[1065] West and land of the said Thomas Best North And he renders for an acre by the year 2^{d} ½

ROBERT STEVENSON vicar of Sellyng holds of the lord Abbot of Faversham as above said 2 acres of land at The Tote aforesaid and lying between the land of John Hiles East the land of Thomas Best South land of the said vicar West and land of Thomas Bredham North And he renders for an acre by the year 2^{d} ½

1062 fol. 119.
1063 fol. 119v.
1064 fol. 120.
1065 fol. 120v.

JOHN HILLES holds of the aforesaid Abbot as of his manor of Faversham aforesaid three virgates of land lying within 11 acres of land called Hykkes towne lately Thomas Gylnott and lying between the land of the lord of Badlismere South and the land of Thomas Bredham East West and North

PETER BEALDE holds of the same Abbot as of his manor of Faversham aforesaid one croft of land called Benhams containing 3 acres And lying between the King's highway towards[1066] East and South the garden of Thomas Bredham lately Thomas Gylnott and the garden of the said Thomas Bredham formerly Bartlottes North

THE SAME THOMAS enclosed Peter Beald for three acres of land called Symonds feld and lying between the King's forestall West land called The Commons North Paradise Croft East Sanders Grove and Sanders Garden towards the South

THE SAME THOMAS enclosed the aforesaid Peter aforesaid ½ an acre of land called Chesys garden which lies next to the King's highway towards the West and with Sanders Garden towards the East as appears above[1067]

WILLIAM BARBOUR junior holds of the Abbot of Faversham as of his manor of Faversham aforesaid 4 acres of arable land besides ½ a virgate and 2 dayworks in Heyes Valeigh called Spynneshill and lying between the King's highway called Spynneshill Street East land of William Stevyn called Auxtens towards the South land of the heirs of William Barbour senior called Spynneshill in Hayes Valeygh aforesaid towards the West and land called Brenlylond and land of John Hubbert towards the North

WILLIAM STEVYN holds of the aforesaid Abbot as of his manor aforesaid in Hayes Valegh aforesaid 1 acre and ½, ½ a virgate and 1 daywork of arable land shortly before the barn called Auxtens lying to the land of the Abbot of Saint Augustine of Canterbury towards the West land of the heirs of William Barbour towards the East and the King's highway towards the South

THE HEIRS OF WILLIAM BARBOUR hold of the same Abbot as of his manor above said 6 acres and ½ virgate of land there next to the land of Thomas Bredham called Heggdale towards the South land of the heirs of Brenly pertaining to the church of Boughton towards the West wood of the said heirs of William Barbour[1068] called Hayes wode and parcel of the croft of Robert Norman senior towards the North and the land of William Barbour junior called Spynneshill and the land of William Stephyn called Austens towards the East

THE HEIRS OF BRENLY hold of the lord Abbot of Faversham as of his manor of Faversham aforesaid 2 acres and ½ and ½ a virgate and 3 dayworks of land there adjacent to the said 6 acres and ½ a virgate towards the East land of Thomas Bredham called Heggdale and land of John Fagg and also called Heggdale towards the South land of Hamon Redborough West wood of the heirs of William Barbour in Hayes Wode North

HAMON REDBOROUGH holds there of the lord Abbot of Faversham as of his manor aforesaid 1 acre and ½ and 2 dayworks and lying between the land of the said heirs of Brenly towards the West and East wood of the heirs of William Barbour senior parcel of Hayes Wode towards the North And land of the heirs of John Fagg called Heggdale towards the South[1069]

[1066] fol. 121.

[1067] Remainder of fol. blank, fol. 121v blank, fol. 122.

[1068] fol. 122v.

[1069] fol. 123.

THE HEIRS OF BRENLY hold there of the lord Abbot of Faversham as of his manor aforesaid of Brendley land 1 acre ½ a virgate and ½ a daywork lying between the land of the said heirs of John Fagg called Heggdale towards the South land of William Barbour junior towards the West wood of the said heirs of Brenly wood of William Barbour junior and wood of the heirs of William Barbour senior and parcel of Hayes Wode North and land of the said Hamon Redborough towards the East

WILLIAM BARBOUR holds of the same Abbot there as of his manor aforesaid 1 acre 1 daywork and ½ of land formerly Richard Erle and lying to the land of the heirs of John Fagg towards the South land of the said heirs of Brenly towards the West and East wood of the said Hamon Redborough called Hayes Wode towards the North

THE HEIRS OF BRENLY hold there of the aforesaid Abbot of Faversham as of his manor above said ½ an acre and ½ a virgate of land lying between the land of William Barbour junior towards the East[1070] land of the heirs of Henry Bulle called Heggdale towards the South and West Hayes Wode towards the North

THE HEIRS OF HENRY BULL hold of the lord Abbot of Faversham as his manor aforesaid there five virgate one daywork and a ½ and lying between the land of the said heirs of Brenly towards the East land of the said heirs of Henry Bull called Heggdale towards the South land of the heirs of Brenly towards the West wood of William Barbour junior called Hayes Wode towards the North

THE HEIRS OF BRENLY hold of the same Abbot as of his manor aforesaid at Grovehill 1 acre of land and ½ a virgate lying between the land of the heirs of William Barbour towards the West land of the heirs of Henry Bull East and Hayes Wode North

THE HEIRS OF WILLIAM BARBOUR hold of the same Abbot as of his manor of Faversham aforesaid there at Grovehill one acre of land besides 4 dayworks next to[1071] the land of William Barbour junior towards the North land of the said heirs of Brenly in Hayes Valeigh towards the East land of the said heirs of Henry Bull called Heggdale and land of the said William Barbour junior adjacent to Grubstrete towards the South land of the said William Barbour junior called Grovehill towards the West

WILLIAM BARBOUR barbour (sic) junior holds there of the lord Abbot of Faversham of his manor of Faversham aforesaid 1 acre and ½ 3 dayworks and ½ and lying between the land of the said heirs of William Barbour towards the East land of the said William Barbour junior adjacent to Grubstrete South the land of William Neele West lands of Thomas Pope and a small parcel of wood called Lytell Grove towards the North

WILLIAM BARBOUR junior holds of the same Abbot as of his manor aforesaid one small grove called Lytell Grove containing one virgate lying between the land of William Neele[1072] West the land of the heirs of William Barbour towards the North land of Thomas Poope towards the East land of the said William Barbour junior called Grovehill towards the South

WILLIAM NELLE holds of the lord abbot of Faversham as of his manor aforesaid 2 acres of land and ½ a virgate besides 3 perches lying shortly before the said Grove between the land of William Barbour junior towards the East South and West land of the heirs of William Barbour and land of the said William Barbour junior towards the North

---

1070 fol. 123v.
1071 fol. 124.
1072 fol. 124v.

WILLIAM BARBOUR junior holds of the Lord Abbot of Faversham as of his manor aforesaid one piece of land containing ½ an acre besides 1 daywork and ½ called Olboldishill lying between the land of the said William Nele called also Olboldishill towards the West and East and the land of the same William called Chesyns Hill towards the North and the land of the same William adjacent to Grubbestrete towards the South[1073]

WILLIAM NEELE holds of the lord Abbot of Faversham as of his manor before said one acre of land and ½ a virgate besides ½ a daywork of land there adjacent to the said piece of land lying between the land of the said William Barbour junior towards the North East and South land of the heirs of William Barbour senior towards the West

THE HEIRS OF WILLIAM BARBOUR senior hold of the lord Abbot of Faversham as of his manor of Faversham aforesaid at Olboldishill one garden called Cosyns Garden with arable land adjacent containing 2 acres 1 virgate and ½ of land and lying next to land of the said William Barbour junior towards the North land of William Neele called Olboldishill towards the East land of the said William Barbour junior adjacent to Grubbestrete and land of Robert Joce of Harnhill called Bonnefelde towards the South and land of the said William Barbour junior called Olboldishill towards the West and North Whereof the said garden contains ½ an acre[1074]

WILLIAM BARBOUR junior holds of the lord Abbot of Faversham as of his manor of Faversham aforesaid 2 pieces of land whereof one piece called Crouche Croft and the other piece thereof called Olboldishill now one and containing 6 acres and ½ a virgate of arable land and lying between land of the heirs of William Barbour senior at Olbodishill towards the East land of Robert Joyce of Harnehill called Bonnefeld towards the South land of William Shrubbissole called Crouchecroft and land of the heirs of Laurence Sayer towards the West a new garden of Crouchcroft and Southstrete adjacent to the said garden towards the North

WILLIAM ~~BARBOUR~~ SHRUBSOLE junior holds of the lord Abbot of Faversham as of his manor aforesaid one piece of land called Crouchecroft containing 5 virgates lately purchased of William Barbour junior called Crouche Croft South the land of the heirs of Laurence[1075] Sayer and land called Masyndewe Hawe towards the West

FEOFFEES OF RICHARD JOCE hold of the lord Abbot of Faversham as of his manor of Faversham aforesaid two pieces of land whereof one piece of land there lies next to the Masyndewe hawe containing 5 dayworks and the other piece of land thereof called Brokys Garden containing 5 virgates 3 dayworks and ½ and lying between the King's highway called Southstrete towards the North land of William Barbour junior called Crouchecroft and the garden adjacent to the said croft towards the East a garden of the same William called Cosyns garden towards the South And land of the same William called Crouche croft now made a garden towards the West

WILLIAM BARBOUR junior holds of the lord Abbot of Faversham as of his manor aforesaid one garden called Cosyns garden containing & an acre[1076] ½ a virgate and ½ a daywork and lying between the garden of the heirs of William Barbour senior and the land of William Barbour junior called Olbo[l]dishill towards the South land of the heirs of Richard Joce called Brokes garden towards the West the King's highway North a garden of the heirs of William Barbour towards the East

---

[1073] fol. 125 the following fols. have become detached and are very dirty with fol. 127 being a single detached sheet.
[1074] fol. 125v.
[1075] fol. 126.
[1076] fol. 126v.

WILLIAM BARBOUR junior holds of the same Abbot as of his manor of Faversham aforesaid one acre of land and ½ a virgate and ½ a daywork at Olboldishill and so called and lying between the land of the heirs of William Barbour senior called Southfeld towards the East land of William Neele at Olboldishill land of the said William Barbour junior and land of the heirs of William Barbour together at Olboldishill towards the South a garden of the said heirs of William Barbour called Cosyns garden West And land of the said William Neele at Olboldis Style towards the North

[1077]called Longdane North

THE SAME THOMAS holds at Gootehill of wooded land 4 acres and 2 virgates and ½ besides 1 daywork and lying between the lands of Thomas Spycer and Hampnettes Downe West, Symonds acre and land called the Down North, wood of the lord Abbot of Faversham East and wooded land called Holbroke South

THE SAME THOMAS holds at Shillynghilde of wood and wooded land by estimation 16 acres [rest blank] *margin:* Let it be remembered that here lacketh yett dyvers parcells to be sett

INSIDE BACK COVER

Second day of March made an end to this book

[*written in Latin this is in the hand of the scribe*]: hic liber sup[er]uis[us] p[er] me Thoma[m] Hilles 29 die me[n]sis noue[m]bris 1546 Translated this reads, 'This book made under my supervision Thomas Hilles 29th day of the month of November 1546' This hand is not the hand of the scribe.

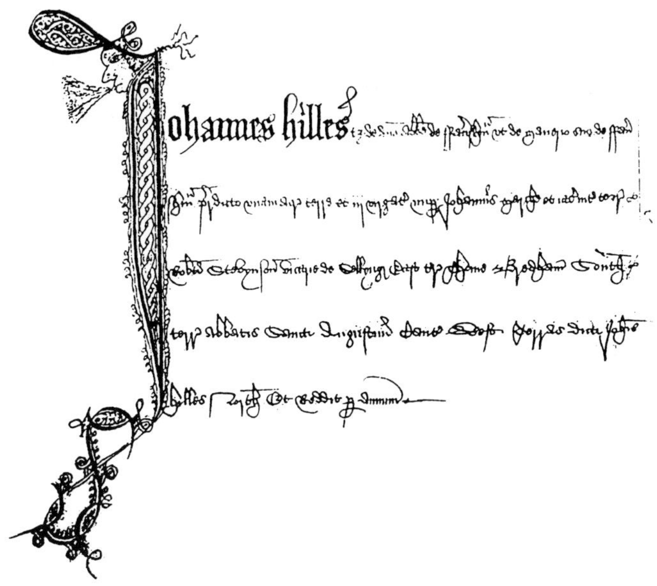

U390.M37/1 folio 118v shows the highly decorated nature of the Hilles entry perhaps indicating a relationship to the scribe.

[1077] fol. 127 This is a single sheet and doesn't appear to follow on. A close scrutiny of the fol. numbers shows them to be much later than the document.

APPENDIX 18
1532 Rental of Faversham

INTRODUCTION

This is an intriguing manuscript, Literary Manuscript B5, in Canterbury Cathedral Archives. It is a book with 38 folios and a parchment cover bearing the title 'Rentale ville of Faversham with other thynges for the town.' It consists of a rental of the town, three subsidiary rentals, a state of account of the monastery on 1 February 1499, an undated inventory of plate, linen and goods, another inventory dated 24 August 1534, and lastly, a valuation of the abbey made just before the Dissolution, which is substantially the same as that which appears in the Valor Ecclesiasticus of 1535, a detailed and exact valuation of ecclesiastical benefices. Blore transcribed the rental but only reached the end of folio 4[1078], C.R.Broughton[1079] in his M.A. thesis in 1952 entitled Faversham Abbey copied Blore and then continued the transcription. A quite separate inventory of goods and ornaments in Faversham church in 1512 has been transcribed by F. F. Giraud. An imperfect copy of it was printed by Jacob in his history of Faversham in 1774.[1080]

It is hoped to make a detailed analysis of the rentals at a later date on the lines of the work done by William Urry on the Canterbury rentals[1081]. In the meantime, it is possible to date it to 1532-33 from internal evidence, from entries relating to two tenants. The first was Thomas Perne: his will was proved on the 22 February 1531/2 and the rental refers to his heirs. The second was Henry Hatch, who was referred to as being alive in the rental, but died in May 1533. Blore was clearly also trying to date it, and put a circle around 1532 in some scribbled notes.

What is intriguing about this manuscript is therefore that it looks as if the abbot was trying to compile a document shortly before the Dissolution listing all the evidence he could find about the abbey's possessions from existing rolls and manuscripts.

The situation in 1530 was that John Castlock had long been in charge of Faversham Abbey, which had been founded in 1147 by King Stephen. John Sheppey alias Castlock received the King's writ for the restoration of the temporalities of the abbey on 17 February 1499. It was a time of crisis because the abbey was bankrupt and his aged predecessor, Walter Gore, had resigned. Castlock threw himself into restoring the estates. He said later that in his youth he had come to know so well every acre of the scattered abbey estates that he could still direct his lay agents to keep the land fully productive. He was abbot when Archbishop Warham made his visitation on 30 September 1511 with its general complaints of laxity. First came a list of the abbot and monks: Dom. Robert Faversham, prior, Dom. John Prestone, Dom. William Goodewynstone, chaplain, Dom. William Bidenden, subprior and precentor, Dom. John Boughton, sacrist, Dom. Thomas Lenham, cellarer, Dom. Thomas Barmsey, sub-cantor, Dom. Thomas Ware, Dom.William Baily, refectorer, Dom. Robert Bendisshe, Dom. John Hartey, subsacrist, Dom. William Harnehille, Dom. Thomas Sellyng. The prior said the alms were not always given to the poor, but sometimes to the monks' friends, and that women had access to the cloister and refectory. Dom. John Preston, then aged 56 years, asked to be relieved of choir service sometimes, because he had been in the monastery for 41 years. The subprior and others

---

1078 CCA: U91/219.

1079 Research has shown him to be Cyril Rawnsley Broughton. He was a Parochial Reader in the Deanery of Ospringe and in the 1952-3 Diocesan Directory shown as resident at The Cottage, Upper St Ann's Road, Faversham, he is listed 1954-57, printed September 1954 and 1957-60 printed Oct. 1957 but is not listed as a diocesan reader Deanery of Ospringe 1962-3. The thesis shows his having already gained a B.A., Dip. Th., late of St. John's College. A carbon copy of the thesis, without the illustrations, is deposited in the Cathedral Library.

1080 LP, I, part 1, no. 438; II, part 2, no. 4333; Arch. Cant. XVIII, pp. 103-113; Jacob, pp. 154-165; James, pp. 18-19.

1081 William Urry, *Canterbury under the Angevin Kings* (Athlone Press, 1967) and map folder.

said that their stipends were paid in kind instead of money, a fact which deterred men from entering religion in this house. There were complaints that obit money was not paid. One monk said the food was only half-cooked. Two complained of the harshness and arrogance of the butler. The monks lacked spare clothing, so that, when their shirts were being washed, they had to wear the same day and night. Two of the monks were said not to recite from memory. The archbishop ordered that 'the alms in meat and drink shall be given in common. That women shall not have access to the cloister and that no monk talk to a woman in the nave of the church. That the abbot shall appoint a chamberlain to give out clothing to the monks. That sufficient, well-prepared food shall be provided in the refectory. That each monk shall have a double supply of shirts and blankets. That the abbot shall pay Dom. John Barmondsey his portion of the money for Bilsingtone's obit. The abbot is not to dispense any monks from reciting. That the abbot shall pay each monk his due portion from the services for the dead. Dom. William Boughtone is to behave with modesty and charity towards his brethren. That the abbot compel Glover, the butler, to behave better towards the monks. John Barmondsey is to enjoy the same liberty as the other monks. The abbot to show the state of the house by next Easter.' The archbishop then adjourned the visitation to 1 September next or any earlier convenient day.[1082]

In 1516 Castlock entertained Wolsey on his way to France in what is said to be the fine new guest house that Gore had provided. Thomas Cromwell was then in Wolsey's service and Castlock was assiduous in cultivating an intimacy with him. In 1517 he was present at Canterbury for the visit of the papal legate.[1083]

There was a strong link between the abbey and the town. A number of townsmen made small bequests to the abbey and the abbot, whom they sometimes appointed the overseer to their wills. Others turned to the parish priest. Henry Sayer, mayor in 1501 and a yeoman of the crown, arranged in his will the following year that the abbot should be his overseer and that a chest with three locks and three keys should be delivered to the abbey for safe keeping within a month of his death. An old widow called Joanna Deve left her best coverlet to her grandson, Thomas Sellyng; a man of that name was one of the monks at the Dissolution. The residue of her moveable goods she left to the prior, Robert Faversham, to bury her. In 1532 Peter Smyth, a mercer who obtained a pardon in 1509-10, asked to be buried in the abbey before the altar of St. John the Baptist near his wife. He left many bequests to the abbey and to the abbot, whom he appointed one of his overseers. In particular he arranged for renewing the figure of the Blessed Virgin Mary and her tabernacle in her chapel and of other images in the abbey church. Two men described themselves as 'of the abbey of Faversham'. William Broke in 1527 asked to be buried there, left a 10^{s} annuity out of the lands in Lynsted called Brownys for 20 years and '£7 to buy an egle of latten to stand in the choir there to read the gospels upon after the custom of the monastery there.' Once again the abbot was to be the overseer, 'by whose counsel I will my said wife shall be ruled'. Richard Carter in 1529 asked to be buried there, left 6^{s} 8^{d} to buy a new censer, 20 pounds of wax, £7 for a yearly obit for 14 years, 26^{s} 8^{d} for one vestment and 6^{s} 8^{d} for another. He left Elizabeth Fagg, 'my bed and garments that I have in the abbey', which shows that he was living there. He appointed the abbot his overseer.[1084]

[1082] K.L. Wood-Legh, *Kentish Visitations of Archbishop William Warham and his deputies, 1511-12*. Kent Rec. Vol. XXIV (1984), pp. 33-37.

[1083] LP, XIII i, pp. 498, 585, 1322, 1339, 1340; ii, pp. 274, 290; XIV i, p. 597. Lewis, (1727). Telfer, *Abbey*; *Monasticon*; Hasted, Vol. 6 pp. 318-371.

[1084] Sayer, PRC 17/8/207v; Deve, PRC 17/14/78v; Smyth, PROB 11/21/48v; Broke, PRC 17/18/139; Carter, PRC 17/18/215; Cheseman, PRC 17/18/84; Hawkeswell, PRC 17/18/167; A Hussey, *Testamenta Cantiana* (1907), pp. 119-129 and 'Notes on Faversham Abbey from Parishioners' wills proved at Canterbury', *The Antiquary*, New Series Vol. 2, No 2 Feb. 1906, pp. 51-56.

Even in the sixteenth century, the abbot had great authority in Faversham in spite of the bitter struggle over the centuries by the townsmen to free themselves. The position of his predecessors in the Middle Ages has been described by Miss K. Murray with great clarity in her article 'Faversham and the Cinque Ports'.[1085] In the first place, from the reign of Edward I, as soon as a mayor had been elected, he had to go to the abbey for the abbot's approbation. In 1511, when a brewer called Laurence Stransham was elected, he refused to go and take the usual oath of obedience. He was the son of John Stransham of Stalisfield and Lenham, who died in 1472, and two of his own sons, George and Thomas, later became deeply involved in town affairs. The abbot subsequently sued him in the Star Chamber, where he was fined for contempt. By a decree dated 13 November 1511 he was ordered either to take the oath within eight days or pay a fine of £100. Stransham still refused to take the oath and so was committed to the Fleet Prison on the 3 February 1512 and deposed as mayor. Furthermore, Sir Edward Poynings, Lord Warden of the Cinque Ports, was ordered to arrange a new election. The freemen were to put up three men for the mayoralty so that the abbot could choose one. This was a reversion to an earlier arrangement of 1258 and one on which William Roper commented at the time of the dissolution of the abbey.[1086]

The abbot also appointed a bailiff and a steward, whose names were constantly placed after the mayor's and before the jurats. The bailiff was the abbot's deputy and without his consent nothing could be legally enacted. He was expected to be learned in the law and at one time Sir John Fineux, later Lord Chief Justice, had held the office. According to Southouse, they were wont to carry a white staff or wand in their hand. Robert Edmunds was the last before the Dissolution. The appointment continued until 1562 when Robert Coldwell agreed to accept an annuity of £1-13-4 in return for surrendering his office. The office of abbey steward was held by William Roper from 1519 until its dissolution and then he acted as royal steward until his death in 1578.[1087]

Furthermore, as late as 1531-32, the chamberlains' accounts for the town were being audited in the abbey in the presence of the abbot and the mayor. As lord of the manor, the abbot had the right to the markets and the fair on Lammas Day and to hold the manorial courts baron and courts leet. A court baron was a manorial court, which enforced the customs of the manor. It was the property of the lord and was a private jurisdiction. A court leet was a court of record and a public jurisdiction. It dealt with petty offences and was presided over by the lord or his representative. Each male over the age of 12 or 16 (depending on custom) was obliged to attend. It met at least twice a year and was responsible for the view of frankpledge: each vill or area was divided into tithings or associations of ten or twelve households, which were held corporately responsible for the behaviour of each member, a system called frankpledge. As lord of the hundred, he held the hallmote, another word for a court baron or court leet, and in the town he held a court of portmote, or borough court, as well as a court of general sessions of the peace and gaol delivery. A court of piepowder (a corruption of pied poudreux, meaning 'dusty footed' travellers) was held during the periods of the markets and fairs. The lordship also contained various fishing grounds and watercourses regulated by a water court, which were to become the subject of many disputes.[1088]

1085 TRHS, 4th series, xviii, pp. 53-84.

1086 LP XIII, p. 290; Hasted, pp. 16-18; The Rev. G. Streynsham Master, *Notes relating to the family of Streynsham* (London 1879) pp. 9-11.

1087 PRO, Court of Augmentations, E315/100 fol. 47 verso; CKS, Fa/AC2/1 fol. 14v.

1088 A bound volume presently held at the Town Hall of old manuscripts concerning '*The company or Fraternity of the Free Fishermen and Dredgermen of the manor and hundred of Faversham.*'

The abbot can be seen in a different light in his actions concerning the school. In 1521, Master John Cole, a schoolfellow of Castlock, suggested that the grammar school at the parish church should be replaced by an endowed free grammar school attached to the abbey almonry. Castlock welcomed this because the abbey was to be trustee of the endowed lands. The school was set up by an indenture dated 10 December 1526 and Castlock bought two pieces of land at Hernhill on Cole's behalf. To them he added another larger piece of land at Hernhill that had recently been given to the abbey by other local benefactors. He then asked Cole for £113, as though he had paid out money for them. Cole gave him a bond to repay him, together with all legal charges of the escheator, the law officer of the crown who had to be satisfied that land to be held under mortmain was not for any reason liable to forfeiture by the Crown. To cover these legal fees, Cole made up to £200 the overall liability under his bond. Castlock clearly satisfied the escheator for the smaller pieces of land, because he was able to sell them in 1538. The larger piece had already been conveyed by the original donors. Cole completely trusted Castlock and paid the escheator's fees on Cockham and Mentilham in Hernhill. When he paid Castlock the £200, he did not demand the return of the bond so Castlock still had it in 1538 when he showed it to the schoolmaster appointed by All Souls College, Oxford, the guarantor of the foundation. Cole had died the previous year, appointing Castlock his executor. On the back of the bond was written, 'None of the money herein mentioned paid', so Castlock claimed that he was free to sell it. He had in fact already sold the two smaller pieces. The schoolmaster felt that something was wrong and pursued the matter with some of Cole's friends. He then wrote a report to All Souls College telling them that Castlock had sold the school land at Leysdown and had also sold elms from the school's land at Ewell. According to this report, in later days, when the abbot was often at home, he dined more in his own parlour than in the refectory. Sometimes he had the prior or particular monks to dine with him in his parlour, since he could talk with them there, whereas no conversation might take place in the refectory.[1089]

According to Lewis, Castlock was one of those who in 1529 supported the invalidity of Henry's marriage. The oath of acknowledgement of the Royal Supremacy was taken on 10 December 1534 by Castlock, the prior Robert Faversham, the sacrist John Harty, the cellarer Thomas Sellyng, the precentor John Lynsted, the sub-prior Dunstan and eight others. Four years later the eight were reduced to three.

In 1535 the visitation of the abbey was carried out by Richard Layton, who reported to Cromwell on 23 October 1535 'this night I shall be at Faversham Abbey'. He found it to be in a good moral state with an income over £200, which meant that it was spared the first wave of dissolution. This was followed by the correspondence between Castlock and Cromwell mentioned earlier in the text with Castlock trying to avoid the inevitable, laying stress on the royal foundation. On 16 March 1536, Castlock said to Cromwell that 'the house is now £400 in debt, which I might see repaid if I continue in the office six or seven years ... the house is much impoverished by the debts left by [my] predecessor, who was but a right slender husband to the house, partly by the necessary repairs of the church and other buildings and the 'innyng' of marshes which the seas had won, by lawsuits for the recovery of their rights, and by dismes and subsidies to the King, amounting to more than £2,000.' One of the creditors was a London mercer called Edward Baylye. His widow, Anne, received £125 in three payments in 1541 and more until at least 1544.[1090]

[1089] Telfer, Abbey, pp. 6, 10-13; PROB 11/25/245; Hasted, pp. 8-9, 13; Jacob pp. 53-4, 134-5; A.F.Munden, *Eight Centuries of Education in Faversham*, Faversham Papers No. 9, 1972, pp. 3-7.

[1090] LP, XVI, no. 745, fols. 44-45, XVII, no. 258, fol. 41, XVIII, no. 436, fol.74, XIX, part 1, no. 368, fol.64; See Text page 301.

On 8 July 1538 the surrender of the abbey took place. Pensions were assigned as follows: John Castlock alias Sheppey, abbot 100 marks; Robert Chillenden alias Faversham £5; Thomas Deve £5; Dunstan Goodhew alias Chartham £5; John Tailer £5; Ralph Post alias Ulcombe £4; John Filpote £4; William Coyden £4 and Peter Minto £4. The monks chose local place names when they entered the monastery, no doubt based on the places they had come from.

Thomas Deve alias Sellyng, the cellarer, was possibly the grandson of Joanna Deve mentioned earlier. Joan Lull, who set up an almshouse, left 40^{s} in money towards his 'fyndyng to scole' in 1507. He received a pension of £5 and added to it the vicarage of Selling which he held with his pension until his death in 1558. The elderly Robert Chillenden alias Faversham renounced his pension to take the curacy at Sheldwich from the vicar of Faversham. He remembered his fellow monk Thomas Deve in his will, made on 16 January 1540, and died on the last day of that month.

When Thomas Arden made his will on 20 December 1550, he left the brewhouse and the great garden in the tenure of John Castlock, at £5-6-8 a year, as part of his wife's jointure. In his *Inquisition post mortem* this was described as a stable and nine acres of land. Castlock also had an orchard in free socage at a rent of 4^{s} a year. In fact he had died intestate in 1543, when the administration of his estate had been granted to his brother, William, who was bound with Joseph Beverley in 100 marks. Earlier, in 1541, one John Heyes of Faversham had left 'my maister Sir John Castlocke late Abbote of Faversham 3 sylver spones of the beste and inn money 26^{s} 8^{d}.' It is just possible that the John Taylor, who was said to hold another orchard in the *Inquisition post mortem* was the monk mentioned in the pensions.[1091]

The men who had served the abbey as officials or had been granted annuities by the abbey hastened to register their claims at the Court of Augmentations, which had been set up in 1535 to administer the lands, posessions and revenues of the dissolved religious houses. For example, on 11 October 1538, Joseph Beverley claimed the office of auditor worth £3-6-8 granted to him on 20 September 1535; on 14 November 1538 William Roper claimed the office of high steward worth £8-6-8 a year granted to him and his father on 6 August 1519; on 10 February 1539 Richard Cromwell alias Williams claimed a £3-0-0 annuity granted on 20 May 1535; Thomas Barthlette, gentleman, claimed a £1-0-0 annuity on 20 October 1538 said to have been granted 25 October 1535; finally Richard Robynson, clerk, claimed on 2 November 1538 an annuity worth £12-0-0 a year granted on 1 July 1527.[1092]

The estate at Faversham had been run as a self-contained unit. As well as the bailiff and the steward, there was a receiver of rents and leases in the town which did not accrue to any particular officer in the monastery. There was a receiver in charge of the manor of Kingsnorth fifteen miles away. There were separate officers in charge of the manor of Bendysh in Essex.

In the Valor Ecclesiaticus of 1535 the total net value of all the monastery property was as follows:

Temporalities	£200-5-6¾, three quarters of barley
Bendysh Hall, Essex	£28-3-8
Spiritualities	£58-3-4
Total;	£286-12-6¾

The spiritualities included the parsonages of Hernhill, Boughton and Preston and pensions from Luddenham and Newnham. The abbey's manor of Kingsnorth, in the parish of Ulcombe near Maidstone, was granted at the dissolution of the abbey to the St. Leger family whose land it adjoined. In 1538 Bendysh Hall was acquired by Sir Richard Rich.

[1091] Chillenden, PRC 17/22/15v; Text, 26; Broughton, 25; Castlock PRO C142/93/111; Favward, 280v; PRC 3/9/43; Heyes PRC 17/22/67v; LP, IX, 668; X, 484; Lull, PRC 17/13/338.

The Valor Ecclesiasticus does not give a true picture of the abbey estates. On 15 March 1538, just months before the Dissolution, Cromwell sent Castlock instructions through Christopher Roper to alienate 144 acres of land, 204 acres of fresh marsh and 10 acres of salt marsh in the parish of St. Thomas in the Isle of Harty to Sir Thomas Cheyne. This may have been some of the salt marsh in Harty that was left to the abbey by Richard Colwell, who was mayor in 1534 and died in 1535. He was buried in the parish church. There is furthermore, a suspicion not yet verified, that Castlock secretly disposed of other abbey lands.[1093]

For administrative purposes, as was customary, most of the rents were assigned to a particular department of the monastery, such as The Table, The Chamberlain, The Almoner, The Sacrist or Sexton, The Precentor or Chanter, The Hostilar or Guest House, King's Mill, The Chapel of St. Mary and The Altar of St. Anne, the last named both being in the abbey. Some holdings owed rent to as many as three departments. For example, the feoffees of Robert Fale owed a total of 3^{s} $8\frac{1}{2}^{d}$ and 1 hen to the table, the sacrist and the precentor for Tunbridge Croft in Tanners Street. There has not yet been time to do an analysis of the rents. These were usually in money, but occasionally hens and quarters of barley were mentioned, which probably by then had a money equivalent. Half a hen probably therefore indicates a division of property. In Archbishop Warham's visitation of 1511 the monks complained that they had to go out collecting rents and had books in which to enter their accounts. Two of them were too illiterate to keep their books.[1094]

The final question is whether or not this rental lists all the property in the town in 1532. Probably not, but the compiler made a strenuous effort to list all the other land owners, such as the Prioress of Davington, the Prior of Christ Church Canterbury, the Rectory of Faversham, the Rectory of Preston, and the heirs of Edmund Marten. Martyn of Graveney had married Joan, one of the four daughters and coheiresses of Thomas Frogenhale of Buckland and Luddenham, who died in 1505. Another was the Manor of Kingsmill, which had several houses in the town and land at Stonebridge, including the mill, which was afterwards a gunpowder mill. No. 10 Market Place, is said to have been the manor house.[1095] The compiler even went so far as to have a category 'Non Nobis' meaning not to us or not ours and gave the rent of such holding. For example, in Preston Street East, the heirs of John Barbour held a messuage called The Saracen's Head and paid 8^{d} rent, 'not ours'.

Fortunately, many late medieval, and possibly earlier, properties survive in the town and the street pattern is very much the same today. Rentals and surveys survive for 1575, 1604, 1621, 1638, 1653 and on up till a particularly full one in 1815.[1096] There are also title deeds and a memorandum or Leiger Book in the Watson (Rockingham) collection in Northampton and later street cesses and other documents, which should make it possible in due course to correlate at least some surviving properties with owners listed in the rental, that is to say, that so-and-so lived in, or, at any rate, owned this particular house which is still there for people to see. Or that on this site stood a particular building whose history is known.

There are probably not many places where this could be done. When identified, the character of the properties concerned will tell us something about the sixteenth-century and subsequent

[1092] Beverley, PRO, E315/96 p.58; Roper, PRO, E315/100/47v; Cromwell alias Williams, PRO, E315/100/127v; Barthlette, PRO, E315/100/63; Robynson, PRO, E315/100/44, E315/23 pp. 38-39.

[1093] LP XIII,I,585, g 646 (64); Jacob, pp. 120, 147.

[1094] Telfer, p. 7.

[1095] Cal. Inq. Post Mortem Hen VII, 11, no. 392; Hasted VI, p. 338; Sydney Wilson, *A guide to the town and Port of Faversham* (1936), p. 17. See illustration on page 73.

[1096] CKS, U33, U390/M38, M39, M41, M43/2.

owners. The buildings would then be documents in terms of social and economic as well as architectural history.

However, there was a wave of redevelopment in the late sixteenth century. No-one can therefore assume that because a building is timber-framed this means that it was there in 1532. Inventories, as yet mostly unexplored, would cast further light on life-styles and aspirations.

Now we can turn to the rental. This is only an opening foray on the subject. There are still some more wills and possibly a few inventories to collect. The plan is then to publish them together with a study of rental values and such aspects of interest as, for example, the market place and the shambles.

The most important thing to note about the rental is that it covered a long period from about 1490 till 1550. Clearly the abbey had not kept it up to date. Some of the people involved had died in the 1490's, while the abbot's brother, William Castlock, did not die until 1550. There were many references to heirs and feoffees, the latter being people holding property on behalf of another without specification of the uses. This is in contrast to trustees, who were people holding property on behalf of another for specified uses. It is remarkable how many owners in the rental, 23 in all, had made such an arrangement prior to their death. The legal device of 'use' had several advantages. It avoided wardship and its ramifications: lands conveyed in this way were arguably not forfeit for treason and it was a means of breaking an entail to detach 'portions' for widows, daughters and younger sons. It was stopped by the passing of the Statute of Uses in 1536. This rental illustrates how widespread the practice was.[1097]

For this rental is a list of ground rents, of owners not occupiers. For example, when John Kere of West Street North died in 1511, he left his son Richard three tenements, one being a malthouse, one a tenement in which Richard Cheseman lived and the third the one in which Peter Dutcheman lived. We do not therefore get as much information about trades and occupations in the town as we would like. We have to turn painstakingly to other sources such as the wardmote book, apprenticeship registers, wills and inventories to discover the occupation of the owners and others living in the town.

The holdings are usually described as a messuage, a tenement or a cottage, of which last there were only a few. A messuage was a dwelling and the land surrounding it, but a tenement was land held of a superior or any rented land or dwelling. In this introduction only the word house has been used, but in the rental tenements were virtually limited to Tanners Street and West Street North, the oldest part of the town. There must have been some clear distinction in the mind of the man who compiled the rental, probably the bailiff or the steward. Later the words become indistinguishable.

In all, there were 248 messuages and 46 tenements, 11 sites, three cottages in Church Lane South (53) and two others in Keylane South (29). Two slaughterhouses were in West Street North near the west quay (369). There were five storehouses; three on the north part of the quay (25, 26, 27), one with a crane; one in Keylane South and one in North Street West (59). Flood Mill (326) and King's Mill (322), which had once been used as a prison, were in Tanners Street.[1098] 28 shambles or stalls filled the market place and there were six shops there (146) and one in Middle Row (106). There was an almshouse founded by Theobald Evyas in North Street East (96) and another founded for five years by Joan Lull in Keylane South (30). Most of the ten barns were in Preston Street (50, 93, 162, 166, 186, 196, 226, 231, 232, 299). One malthouse was in North

---

[1097] Youings, pp. 53, 113, 156.

[1098] R. Pugh, *Imprisonment in medieval England* (Cambridge, 1970), pp. 130, 163-4.

Street East (94) and the other in East Street North (154), so they were close to each other. The forge was in West Street North (381).

The inns were mainly clustered around the market place. There were eleven in all; The Anchor (54), The Horn (75), The Garret (80) and The Bear (81) in North Street West; The Saracen's Head (173) in Preston Street East, The Swan (242), The Fleur de Luce (259), The Sign of the Rose (256) and The George (257) in Preston Street West; and The Ship (260) and The Grewehound[1099] (262) in West Street South.

There were 13 large houses dotted all over the town. They were described as great or principal messuages. There was the steward's house in Court Street West (1), belonging to Robert Maycott; the abbey gatehouse to Richard Dryland in Court Street East (33); one in Church Lane to Sir John Norton (49); one in North Street East to Henry Crispe (91); Cooksditch to Sir Edward Poynings (165); one in Preston Street East to Thomas Perne (182); one in Preston Street West to Simon Warmcourt (237), one in West Street South to William Norton (279); another in West Street South to Robert Fale (289); one in West Street North to John Fryer (339); and, finally, another in West Street North to John Binder (362).

As explained in the text, there were two types of holding mentioned in the rental. The first was described simply as 'Adam Princhett holdeth of the lord (in East Street North - 157) a messuage with a garden and renteth by year to the Sexton 2^{s} 4^{d} and ½ a hen.' The second was as follows 'John Sayer holdeth of the lord to farm (in East Street North - 155) a garden called the Apple Garden and payeth by year 5^{s} 4^{d}.' Most of the messuages that Thomas Arden held were of this latter type and were described in his *Inquisition post mortem* as being held in free socage. Such a holding was not of great benefit to the ground landlord, because it could be alienated by the tenant and inherited without restriction, subject only to a fee by the heir. For instance, there were nine properties to farm in Court Street West, 15 not to farm; four in Court Street East, 10 not to farm. By contrast only two were to farm in Tanners Street, compared with 31 not to farm.[1100]

Reference was sometimes made to former tenants. For example, 'Robert Fale for a lytell tenement and a lytell garden late William Clarkes and before Margery Quyllers and renteth by yere to the Prioress of Davyngton' (353a, b) in West Street North; and William Sparrowe 'as it is said holdeth of the lorde a messuage late Henry Cowpers before Ulffes' (251) in Preston Street West.

The tenant with the most holdings, 23 in all, was Robert Fale, though it should be remembered that a holding might be as large as a storehouse or as small as a stall. John Binder and Margaret Horne had 12 each, the Abbot 11, John Goodwin and William Rose 8 each, John Park, Laurence Stransham, William Norton and the wardens of the parish church 6, Simon Warmcourt 5, Robert Withiott 4 and Sir John Norton, Richard Little, Dennis Hardyman and the vicar 3. There were signs of change throughout the rental; one house made two, two houses made one, additions or augmentations to a house, a newly built house, the site of a house and so on. These will repay further investigation. My first impression is that these tenant owners mostly had a house in the town as well as other interests nearby.

The internal political structure was clear cut and similar to that in many other towns. Much of it can be confirmed in the fifteenth century custumal or common place book. Freedom of the town could be acquired in five ways, namely by patrimony, apprenticeship, marriage to the daughter of

[1099] *O.E.D.* Grewhound: A greyhound.
[1100] See page 56.

a freeman[1101], purchase and gift of the town. Freedom by purchase was quite common in this period. For instance, in 1519-20, 22 men paid fines ranging from 3^s 4^d to 10^s for the privilege. Thomas Gatte was let off his fine because the mayor gave him his freedom. In 1523-24 five men paid fines and Nicholas Westmyll was granted his for nothing. At the same time 13 men paid fines their tuition.

However, the tuitioners were an an unusual group of people. When Her Majesty's Commissioners made their report on the records of Faversham in 1877, they said that the tuitioners were natives of other places, resident in the town without right of suffrage. Edward Crow, the local historian, dug deeper and discovered that they were in fact people seeking abjuration, that is, swearing perpetual absence from the kingdom. They had probably committed a crime in their native town and paid a fine from 1^s to 6^s 8^d to the mayor, as coroner, in return for being given the right to leave the kingdom from Faversham. In 1540-41, for example, in the wardmote book, there was an entry, 'cummith before me Lewys Merden meyre oon Humfrey Taylour shomaker and entered his name for savegarde of hys bodey and for his tweyscoen xii^d.' In the borough custumal or common-place book the word 'tuition' is used in reference to felons seeking sanctuary in church. So, tuitioners were rarely heard of again. For example, in 1526-27 there were 14 tuitioners of whom no more is known.[1102]

When a man was made free of the town, he was expected to serve the town as a member of the common council, put more colourfully as a member of the 24, then as a jurat and eventually as mayor if elected. Twelve of the common council were elected by the commons and 12 by the mayor and jurats. Some men served many years without ever becoming a jurat. For instance, William Wyer was a member from 1532-33 until 1550-51 and Adam Princhett from 1516-17 until 1535-36. It was also usual for members of the 24 to act as chamberlain, auditor and churchwarden in the early stages, as Princhett and Richard Kere did.

The oath of the jurat (or twelve-man) was to assist the mayor, maintain the King's peace and the laws and customs of the town: 'you shall true recorde bere of herth and seith (dwelling), you shall true judgementes giff, you shall do right and equyte, as well to straungers as to yndwellers.'

The mayor was elected annually on 30 September. At one time, as mentioned earlier, the freemen had to put up three men for the post, one of whom the abbot chose. At another, no doubt when the standing and finances of the abbey were low, he simply needed the abbot's approbation.

[1101] An example of freedom by marriage in 1572 was when Thomas Rye was 'made frea thys yere by the maryage of hys wyfe Robert Bargrave's daughter' for nothing, CKS Fa/FAC 2/1 fol. 1.

[1102] I am grateful to Peter Tann for bringing this item by Crow to my attention; Crow MSS, Bodleian Library MS Top Kent e3 p. 99, footnote e, Crow CKS Fa/Z41/1, vol. 1, pp. 79, 81; HMC App. 6th Report, p. 500; Faversham Custumal or Commonplace Book, Fa/LC1, fols. 15r-15v; K. M. E. Murray, 'The Common-Place Book of Faversham' *Arch. Cant.* xlviii (1936), fols. 91-114; Favward fols. 26v, 34v; J. H. Baker, *Manual of Law French,* (Avebury, 1979) **tuicion**, safekeeping, protection (e.g. of sactuary).[Latin, tuitio]; Favward, fol. 13,15, 16v, 18v, 23v, 30v, 43, 58. CKS, Fa/LC1, fol. 2v. Jacob, pp. 69-74.

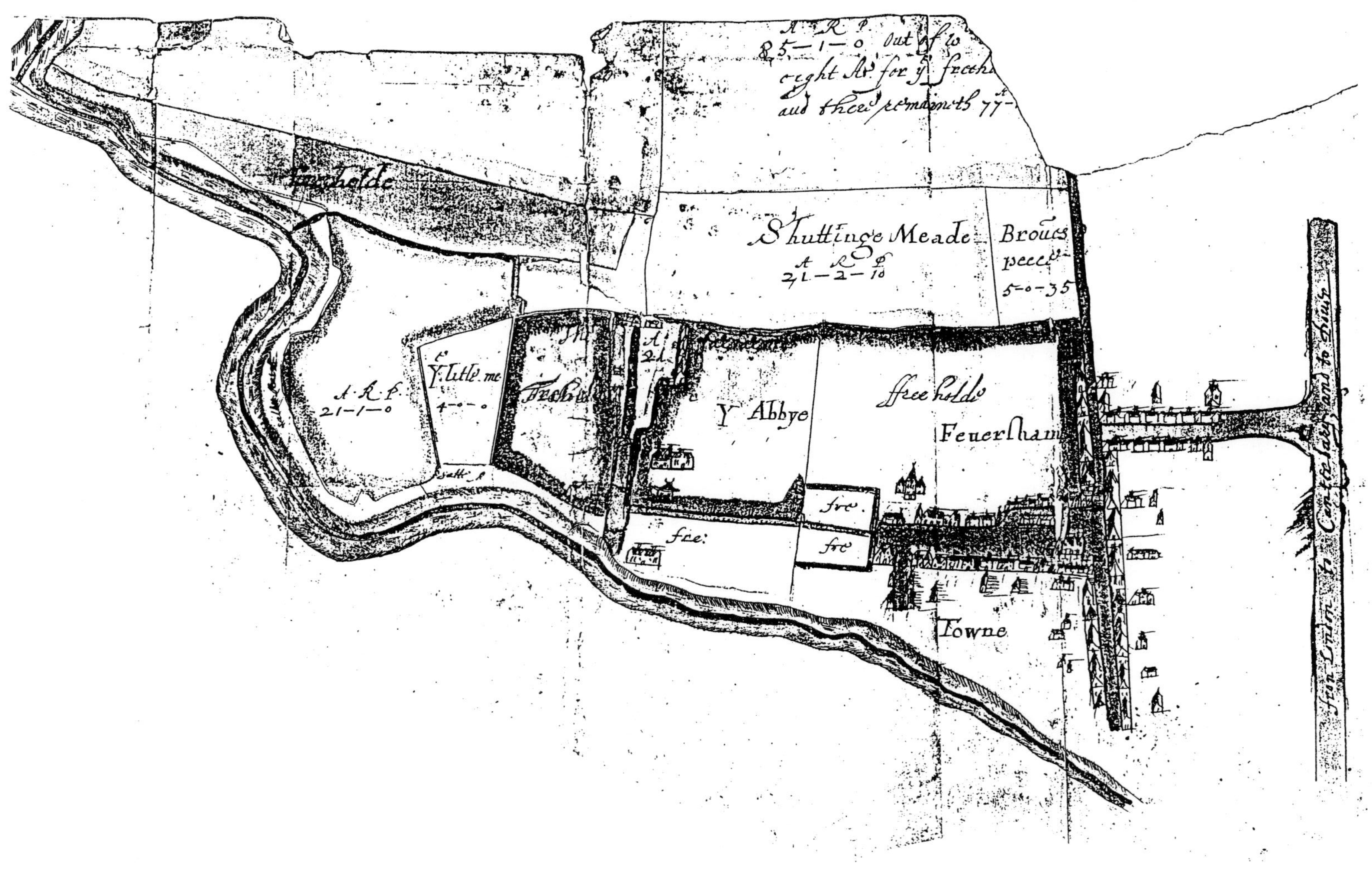

The map of Faversham Abbey lands, drawn by Elias Allen, is reproduced by kind permission from the collection at Rockingham Castle.

Churchelane Rentz

Non nob

Northstrete west

CCA: Literary MS B5 folio 3.

THE RENTAL

With this overview, it is possible to get a fair idea of the layout of the town. It is particularly helpful that in the rental each side of the street is listed separately, but it is important to remember that the street names are different from those used today.

Let us take a walk following the directions given in the rental. The compiler ingeniously managed to start at the outer abbey gate and finish at the east end of West Street, neatly contriving to make a single circuit out of the town's streets. That the compiler was anxious about the order is shown by the entries in Tanners Street West, where he put in A and B to show which entry should come first (312, 313). I must emphasize that this is simply a reconstruction of property holders, ignoring the fact that some of the tenants died as early as the 1490's and that the listing of the holdings had not been brought up to date by 1532. Furthermore, this was a list of owners not occupiers, and it is only a preliminary survey, as some of the wills have not yet been transcribed. The pinpointing of some of the tenants must therefore be tentative. Nonetheless, it is a start.[1103]

If we come out of the remains of the abbey outer gate, known as the Town Gate, walking south towards the Guildhall today, we reach not Abbey Street but Court Street. It was so called because the manorial courts were held in the upper room of the Abbey Gate, which was next to the first house on the right, the steward's house, now presumably Globe House (1). This was held by Robert Maycott, together with the almonry barn, which was the barn kept for the almoner or man who distributed alms. He died in London in 1533 and was buried in the abbey, leaving estates in Faversham, Doddington, Wichling, Newnham, Luddenham, Ospringe, Preston and Sutton next Dover. Next door (2) lived a gentleman called Thomas Grene, who was made a freeman by the mayor in 1531-32. His house was next to the lane leading to Nether Green. This immediately presents a problem. Nether Green was inside the Inner Gate and between that and the present Anchor public house. The lane referred to cannot therefore be the present Stockwell Lane, which runs down to the creek alongside Globe House. The first two entries in the rental are a bit puzzling in that perhaps their order is inverted.

A few doors down (8) lived Joseph Beverley, a gentleman who was auditor of Faversham Abbey, town clerk of Dover by 1548 and mayor of Faversham 1559-60. He was M.P. for Dover in 1547 and 1553, Winchelsea in 1554 and Dover in 1558. He died in 1561. Next door but one (10) was John Seed or Seth, a rich merchant. He was mayor in 1537, 1539, and 1545-46 the year in which the town obtained its charter. He was mayor again in 1552 and died in 1557. In his will, he left gold and silver and rich furnishings to his family and the will itself was recorded in the wardmote book because he left a bequest to the poor. He had a capital messuage, three other houses, three more at the key, 'a seller[1104] called the stony sellour with a lofte over yt', a salt house, two wharves and a winding crane, houses at the key purchased from the vicar, Clement Norton, a malt-house in Tanners Street called Boroughe's Hall and three flesh shambles in the market.[1105]

Further on (14) was Richard Friend, a waterman who paid $4^s\ 4^d$ for his fine to be a freeman in 1521-22 and became a chamberlain and a member of the 24. He died in about 1540, leaving half

---

[1103] There are several perambulations of the bounds of the town: Crow Vol iii, pp. 91-99, Faversham Public Library , Reference Collection RF 942. 23 Dav.; Faversham Borough Custumal 14v -15r; Faversham Wardmote Book 1741-1820, Part 1, CKS, Fa/AC5.

[1104] *O.E.D.* CELLAR: a store-house or store-room, whether above or below ground, for provisions.

[1105] Maycott, PROB 11/26 q 8; Beverley, Commons 1509-58, 1, 428-29, PRC 17/36/1; Seed or Seth, PROB 11/39/14 fols. 103v-105; Favward fols. 29v, 89v; Jacob, p. 102.

a boat to his widow. Next door but one (16) was described as a stone house. It has been suggested that there were timber and stone buildings of the twelfth and thirteenth century. The chances are that they were ecclesiastical or municipal in origin. Then, near the end of the street (21), came the house of Thomas Smythe, who was a merchant importing various goods in 1525-1527, mayor in 1530 and died in about 1537, leaving other houses in North Street and Tanners Street as well.

Turning into Key Lane, there were some houses and two cottages. There was also an almshouse (30) founded for five years by a great benefactor to the town, Joan, the widow of Richard Lullwho was mayor in 1490, 1491, 1493 and 1507. Richard Lull had made his will on 5 October 1506 and it was proved on 11 January 1507, making many charitable bequests and leaving bay salt and plate, lands, tenements, wharves and quays in Faversham and lands in Preston, Luddenham, Hernhill, Sheldwich, Challock and Lynsted. He even left 26^{s} 8^{d} to John Pokyll to assist his executors and supervisor. He appointed his wife, John Poleyn and John Venour his executors and Robert Withiott his supervisor.

Joan made her will a month later, on 2 February 1507, and asked to be buried beside her husband in the churchyard at Faversham. She said 'Item I will that my standyng whit covered cuppe of silver to be sold to the most avauntage by myne executours and the money thereof commyng xx^{s} to goo to the emendyng of the south ile yn the saide churche next the tresory dore.' Other plate was to be sold to pay for an antiphonar, or book, of whatever is said or sung in the choir. She left a house at the quayside for an almshouse for five years, after which it was to go to her servant, Elizabeth Knight, who was to be in charge of it. She provided a mattress, sheets and blankets as well. She arranged for an obit for Richard Lull and for a former husband, John London. She left 20^{s} for beer for the friars observant in Canterbury and a feather bed, a bolster and two pairs of sheets for her two sons Dom. Richard Faversham and Dom. John Crosse, who were monks in Christ Church, Canterbury. The residue of all 'my movable goodes shyppes and dettes' were to be divided between the relief of the poor and the 'welth of my soule.'

More significant still, there were four storehouses on the quay. John Champney had one with a crane nearby (25). He might have been the John Champneys, late of Canterbury, pewterer, who paid a five shilling fine for his freedom in 1524-25. Another (27) was held by Ralph Woolgate, who might have been the yeoman from Harty, who died in 1565. The other two (26, 28) belonged to the great merchant adventurer, Henry Hatch. Finally, there was a waterman called William More, either the man who had a house there (31) which he ordered to be sold when he made his will in 1513 or the man who paid 4^{s} 4^{d} for his fine to be a freeman in 1521-22 and became a chamberlain and member of the 24.[1106]

We then go back to the abbey and start out again walking south, this time on the left-hand side of the street. A gentleman called Richard Dryland, senior, held the great house at the Town Gate (33). How this relates to the gatehouse and Arden's house is not clear. The Drylands were a gentry family well known locally. Richard Dryland was an executor of the will of Henry Hatch and it was generally felt by contemporaries that it was he who had engineered the bequest of the Hatch lands to the town. His widow, Joan, claimed that he had persuaded her to have the will rewritten because it was 'blotted'. She claimed that the subsequent will was a forgery but she lost the case.[1107] There are some doubts about the genealogy, but a Richard Dryland was several times mayor of Faversham between 1515 and 1542. Either he or Richard Dryland, junior, was

[1106] Friend, PRC 17/22/32v; Smythe, PRC 17/21/293v; Lull, Richard, PROB 11/15 fol.133, q.17; Hatch, PRC 32/15/212; Hyde, passim; More, PRC 17/12/228v; Favward fols. 20, 23v, 24, 26v, 30v; PRO, E122/208/3.

[1107] Hyde, passim; CKS, U390.M37/1 fol.. 38

the man who died in 1550 and left estates in Faversham, Chilham, Teynham, Lynsted, Luddenham, Stone, Davington and Harty. He had lands in Ewell in the 1515 survey of the hundred. Continuing along the street we come first to the house (38) of William Venour a chamberlain and a member of the 24. John Turner (41) was probably the man who died in 1499 leaving bequests to Faversham church. He might, though, have been the John Turner listed in the subsidy rolls of 1522/3, or the boy, not yet 21, who was left a bequest of 20^{s} in the will of Thomas Sterkey in 1526. He held Smyth Croft in Badlesmere in the 1515 survey of the hundred.[1108] Next was that (42) of Edmund Marten esquire, who had paid 6^{s} 8^{d} for his fine to be a freeman in 1509-10. He also rented houses in Preston Street East where the rent went to King's Mill. He may have belonged to the Martin family of Graveney and he also may have been the man, whose executors, Richard Dryland and Roger Dounfeld, clerk, were defendants in a case about debt brought in Star Chamber by Elizabeth Sandes.[1109] Reynold Hobnett (43) had been a chamberlain in 1514-15, and then, we reach the houses of William Castlock (44, 46). It was through his brother, the abbot, that William had come to the town of Faversham and eventually died there intestate in 1550. He was a merchant, importing various goods in 1525-27 and exporting beer. He was accused with William Belke of exporting grain illegally in 1544. The administration of his estate was granted to his son, John, a beerbrewer, who was bound in 200 marks with Randolph Ordymer of Canterbury, innholder, and John Aras of Canterbury, notary public. Next door was another house described as a stone house, where William Blackborne lived. Robert Thomson left him 'my fryse cote' in his will in 1528. It is possible, but unlikely, that he was the painter, who provided Alice Arden with poison in 1551 (45).

We then turn left up Church Lane (now Church Street) as far as the church and back. The south side was mainly occupied by Sir John Norton, who had a large house (49), a barn and a curtilage there. He also came from an old gentry family well known locally and married an heiress. He held Great Howletts in Oare in the 1515 survey of the hundred. He was mayor in 1499 and 1500 and a jurat as late as 1531-32. He was a soldier and, when he died in 1534, was succeeded by his son and namesake, Sir John Norton of Northwood in Milton, Kent. Next door but one (53) was Robert Billesdon, who died in 1503, and left 6^{s} 8^{d} to the anchoress or hermit in the church of Faversham, 3^{s} 4^{d} to her woman and 20^{d} to her servant. His manor of Elyndene or Ellenden, was situated at the southern boundary of the parish of Seasalter, adjoining what was known from the seventeenth century onwards as the vill of Dunkirk.[1110] With all his lands, rents, and weirs, in Seasalter and Whitstable, he gave to the abbey of Faversham for seven years, and from the income his obit was to be kept in the abbey church.[1111] After seven years Ellenden was to be sold, and was evidently bought by Faversham Abbey, as it was the owner in 1535. The terms of his obit were given in tremendous detail in the survey of that year. On 5 September 1543 Thomas Arden received a grant in fee of lands that had belonged to Faversham Abbey which included the manor of Seasalter and Whitstable for £173-8-6 at 20 years purchase, which he alienated to John Nedam and his family from Wymondley, Herts, on 3 October following, so he was probably acting only as a broker. The later history of the manor can be traced in R. H. Goodsall's *Whitstable, Seasalter and Swalecliffe*.[1112]

[1108] From Arthur Percival; Turner, PRC 32/5/8; Sterkey, PRC 17/17/200; J. Greenstreet, Subsidy Roll of 14 Hen. VIII, AC XII, pp. 423-5; CKS, U390.M37/1 fol. 80v.

[1109] PRO: REQ 2/12/148.

[1110] Robert H. Goodsall, *Whitstable, Seasalter and Swalecliffe* (Canterbury 1938), p. 66; Biblio, p. 55; Hasted, VII, p. 33; PRO, E122/208/2; LP xix, 2, 803; Thomason, PRC 17/18/36; Favward fols. 115, 116; CKS, U390. M37/1 f22; Dunkirk first appears as a place name from at least Jan 1690/1 in the Boughton-under-Blean parish registers.

[1111] Dryland, PRC 17/30/42v; Castlock PRC 3/12/52; Norton, Common 1509-58, 111, 26; Favward fols. 12, 13, 21v, 31v, Hasted, p. 12.

[1112] Goodsall, *op. cit.* p. 66; Jacob, pp. 184-9, 193; See page 37.

The man who compiled the rental then crossed the road again to what was then not Court Street but North Street. North Street thus completed a 'trio' with East Street and West Street, missing only Preston Street as South Street. The distinction between Court Street and North Street was obviously deeply ingrained. To us it would seem sensible when compiling the rental to walk from the abbey to The Ship first down one side of the road and then back on the other side. The compiler did not feel the same way. This may mean that the two streets were laid out at different stages in the town's development. Possibly North Street belonged to the older part of the town and Court Street was part of a planned development after the foundation of the abbey in 1147. However, A. Percival still thinks that North Street was itself part of the planned development. They might simply not have been connected as they are now or there might have been some sort of obstruction such as an archway.

Crossing the street to North Street West, the house on the corner was called The Anchor (54), which was administered by the town[1114]. Thomas Blackbourne was town sergeant till about 1517 when he was given 20^{s} at a wardmote by the assent of the commonalty of the town. Next door was the house (56) of John Davy, mayor in 1528, who died in 1544. His son, Thomas, was a 'servant' of Anthony St. Leger. Proceeding along the street we come to the houses of the following people; William Best (63) was a member of the 24 in 1506 and had lands in Boughton-under-Blean and Hernhill when he died in 1512; Bartholomew Simon (65) was town crier in 1521-22, a member of the 24 in 1524-25 and left his house to his wife in 1527; William Hunt (59) had a house and storehouse when he died in 1533, and a baker called Ralph Asshebury (66) was chamberlain and a member of the 24 and had the corner plot into East Gorewell Lane, which must be Partridge Lane. Walking along past other properties the rental brings us to the doors of John Pullen (72), who was mayor in 1513, and Richard Colwell (75), mayor in 1534. Colwell was probably a descendant of Cuthbert Colwell of Yorkshire and does not seem to have been related to Robert Colwell, who was the son of William Colwell of Taunton in Somerset and later became bailiff. Richard Colwell left salt marsh in Harty to the abbey when he died in 1535 and was buried in the parish church. Some of this land may later have been granted to Sir Thomas Cheyne. Hugh Howlett (73) was a member of the 24 in 1521-22. John Bellinger (77) was mayor in 1526 and may possibly have been Richard Colwell's father-in-law, according to the visitation of 1574. Certainly Colwell was appointed one of his executors when he died in 1529 and made a long will, leaving lands in Faversham, Newnham and Minster in the Isle of Sheppey, where he lived. He left a number of bequests to churches including Faversham, where he asked to be buried and to which he left a pot of silver gilt to be made into a pax.[1115] He appointed Thomas Perne of Faversham his overseer and said that Robert Maycott the elder knew his 'will, yntent and meanyng yn every thyng' and should be consulted if there were any doubt. At the end of the street we find John Prowde, the tenant of The Bear, who had paid 3^{s} 4^{d} as a fine for his freedom in 1519-20 and became a jurat. He did not mention The Bear when he made his will on the 10 March 1533, but left the residue of his goods to his wife, Margaret, who was granted probate on the 14 May following. The existence of The Bear (81) can be pushed back to 1488

[1113] Dryland, PRC 17/30/42v; Castlock PRC 3/12/52v; Norton, Common 1509-58, iii, p. 26; Favward fols. 12, 13, 21v, 31v; Jacob, pp. 185-86; *The parish and town of Faversham* by Edward Hasted, About Faversham, No. 6, 1969, p. 12.

[1114] The Anchor was rebuilt c. 1605, remains virtually unaltered and is one of the few buildings about which we have any firm information. M. Laithwaite, 'A ship master's house at Faversham, Kent.' *Journal of Society for Post Medieval Archaeology* (London, 1969), pp. 150-161; Favward, fol. 18.

[1115] *O.E.D.* Pax: **3.** *Eccl.* A tablet of gold, silver, ivory, glass, or other material, round or quadrangular, with a projecting handle behind, bearing a representation of the Crucifixion or other sacred subject, which was kissed by the celebrating priest at Mass, and passed to the other officiating clergy and then to the congregation to be kissed; an osculatory. It came into use during the 13th c. as a symbolic substitute for the kiss of peace. In England its use died out after the Reformation; in the Roman Church it is now used in certain monastic communities on special occasions.

when a gentleman called Richard Thornbury owned both it and The Garret when he made his will in 1488.[1116]

The first house (82) in North Street East was held by Laurence Hilles. It would be pleasing to identify him with Lawrence Hilles who was formerly a merchant of Middleborough, who paid 10s for his tuition in 1524-25. Middleborough or Middleburg, capital of the Dutch province of Zeeland was on the island of Walcheren, and about 4½ miles North East of Flushing. Many Englishmen traded there in the sixteenth century and it was here on 5 October 1582 that the municipality came to an agreement with the Merchant Adventurers by which they were assured of extensive privileges and in turn became responsible for the commercial life and behaviour of the members living there, which resulted in most Englishmen moving into this community. As has been said before, 'tuition' is used in reference to felons seeking sanctuary in church. So, tuitioners were rarely heard of again and thus it is unlikely that Lawrence Hilles the tuitioner was the same person as our Lawrence Hilles , who was a merchant importing goods in 1525-27, chamberlain and a member of the common council in 1532-33 and the owner of a house in the rental in 1532.[1117]

John Cony (86) was a member of the 24 in 1524-25 and when he made his will on 23 July 1526, he left the custody of his three children to his wife, Maud, on condition that she put in a sufficient surety to the abbot and the vicar of Faversham to perform the will. They were to have 2s each for their pains. In his will, proved on 13 August 1526, he mentions having three tenements in the town.[1118]

Further along the street we come to the house of Harry Crypps (91), more usually spelt Crispe. Henry Crispe is an important figure. He had a large house in North Street and paid the abbey for an augmentation to it 'before the windows'. He was described by John Twyne as 'the little king of the Isle of Thanet', because his chief residence was in Birchington. He acquired considerable property in Faversham from his aunt, Margaret Horne. She was the sister of his father, John Crispe. She married first Henry Horne, probably of the manor of Kenardington, because that family had property in Faversham. On Horne's death on 27 August 1488 she married Edward Thomasson, who died in 1494, asking to be buried in front of the Jesus altar in Faversham church. He asked for a priest to sing for him for twenty years. In the visitation of 1511 it was claimed that she had not paid for the last two years, which she eventually did. She finally married John Wode of Whitstable, Kent, who died intestate in 1509. In a later chancery case, addressed to Thomas Wolsey, archbishop of York, cardinal, papal legate, chancellor - thus dating it between 1518 and 1529 - Crispe said that Margaret Horne had inherited lands in Faversham from her second husband, Edward Thomasson. Reckoning that she would have no heirs, she agreed to sell them to Crispe as her brother's son. He owed his election to parliament for Dover in March 1553 and Winchelsea in October 1553 to Sir Thomas Cheyne. In 1558 he sat for Canterbury with William Roper, again as a nominee. He died in 1575 and in his will granted that his wife Anne should have 'all my landes and tenementes in Feversham, Preston and Ospringe', together with other property until his son George came to his age of majority.[1119]

[1116] Davy, PRC 3/10/84v, PRC 17/23/173; Best, PRC 3/3/198, PRC 17/12/2; Symon, PRC 17/17/348v; Hunt, PRC 32/16/17; Asshebury, PRC 17/15/94; Colwell, *Vis. Kent 1574*, Harl. Soc. Lxxiv, 40-41, *Vis. Kent 1592*, Harl. Soc. Lxxv, p. 90, Jacob, p. 147; Prowde PRC 17/19/314; Favward, fols. 5v, 16v, 17, 18v, 20, 23; Hussey, *The Antiquary* op. cit., 53.

[1117] G.D.Ramsay, *The Queen's Merchants* (MUP, 1986), pp. 188-190; PRO, E122/208/3; Favward fol. 30.

[1118] Hilles, Favward fols. 24v, 30; Cony, PRC 17/17/95.

[1119] Crispe, Commons 1509-58, 1, pp. 722-23; PRO: Early Chancery Proceedings C1/481/29; LP 1, p. 438 (1 m.23); H.A. James, *Faversham Parish Church*, Faversham Paper, 1990, No. 33, pp. 17-18. PROB 11/57 q 41; F. A Crisp, *Collections relating to the Family of Crispe*, Volume 1: Abstracts of Wills and administrations in the Prerogative Court of Canterbury 1510-1760. (Private circulation, 1882).

Reynold or Reginald Lewkenor had a great void ground, a barn with a curtilage and a garden with a dovehouse (93). In 1511-12 he brought an action for 40^{s} debt against a butcher, Robert Materas, of Tanners Street East. Joan Hatch said that he had sold Hatch most of his lands in Sussex, - that is, at Icklesham, Guestling, Uden, Brede and elsewhere - and that he was another of her suitors. When he saw his hopes of marriage dashed and knew that his rival, Sir Henry Amcotts, had been privately at Faversham and was likely to succeed in his suit, she said that he sent word to Thomas Boleyn, Earl of Wiltshire, the father of Anne Boleyn. Lewkenor let him know about the alteration of her husband's will and that one of his servants, Maurice Moorcock, was next of kin to Hatch. This set the ball rolling.[1120] When Lewkenor made his will in 1541, he left bequests to Faversham church, 20^{s} for the anchorite Sir William Crakynthorpe and £3 for a conduit at the quay, hence the name Conduit Street. The actual cost of the conduit was £9-18-5, the rest of the stone and money coming from Richard Dryland of Court Street East (33) and John Seed or Seth of Court Street West (10), who was the mayor in 1546, the year that it was built.[1121]

The feoffees of William Fylpott were said to have a house (94) with a malt-house and certain gardens. He was a chamberlain and member of the 24. Unfortunately, in view of the significance of the site today as that of the late lamented Whitbread Fremlin brewery, the malthouse was not mentioned in his will, which he made in 1523.[1122]

Along the street there was an almshouse (96) founded in 1479 by Theobaud Evyas, 'the widow of Humphrey Evyas of Murston, Kent' who died in 1453-54. Her will, which she made in 1478, is a fine example of a late medieval will by a rich widow and is therefore worth quoting at length: 'In Goddys name be hytt Amen the xijth day of Apryll the yere of owre lorde God MCCCCLxxviij I **Theobaude Evyas of Feversham** in the diocise of Caunterbery wedowe of hoole mynde and remembraunce make my testament in the forme foloyng Fyrst I bequeth my soule to God almyghty to owr lady hys modyr and to all the company of hevyn and my body to be buryed withyn the monastery of Seynt Savyour in Feversham in a place ordeynyd therefor Also I ordeyne to xij pore men xij gownys of whyte cloth with whodes of the same xij schyrtys xij peyr of shoes and xij grotes[1123] to the entent that they xij pore men shal hold xij torches a bowt my corps the day of my burying and my monethes day and to pray for my soule Also I ordeyne to v pore women v blak gowyns v hodys v smokkes v kencherys v peyr shoes v grotys[1124] and vd to the entent that the v shalbe abowt my corps the dayes afor sayde to pray for my soule Also I wyll that to dayes in every weke duryng the moneth nexte after my decesse the brethren of the forsayde monastery shal synge dyryges and masse for me be noote and for my frendys and I wyll that every preste of the sayde brothren beyng at dyryge and masse for every dyryge and masse shal have vj^{d} and every novys iiij^{d}, for ryngyng at every suche dyryge and masse iiij^{d}, for wax for the sextyn there for every suche dyryge and masse iiij^{d} Of the whyche xij torches after my monethes day iiij of them shal remayne in the foresayde monastery ij to the paryssh chyrche of Feversham ij to the parysch chirch of Morston ij to the Mynster in Shepey in honowre to the priory at Davyngton and oone to the paryssh chirch of Preston besyde Faversham al the seyd torches to be occupyed oonly in the worship of the sacrement in every of the sayde chirches at the tymes of sacryng of masses in the seyde chirches Also I ordeyne to every brother of the monastery in Feversham aforeseide being a prest for al servyces be [t]hem to be doone for my soule at the day of my buryeng and monethes day besyde that ys to [t]hem lymett iij^{s} iiij^{d} And to every of the saide brotherne beyng no prest xx^{d} Also I wyl that every of vj brothern of the seide monasterie for the tyme beyng that

1120 APPENDIX 20; Hyde, passim.

1121 Lewknor, PRC 17/23/50; PRO, CP40, Roll 998 dorse.

1122 Fylpott, PROB 11/21 quire 8.

1123 *O.E.D.* The English groat coined in 1351-52 was made equal to four pence.

1124 Groats.

shalbe made prestys next after my dyscese shal have xx[d] at the day of singyng hys fyrst masses under condition that every of them shall make promys that he shal sey or do to be seide in the chapell where I shalbe buryed wekely one day in the weke duryng the fyrst yere off his presthode masse and every suche masse to say a specyall colect for me and specyally to have me in remembraunce and to pray for me and my frendys Also I wyl ther be gyvyn to xx prestys straungers that shal sey dyvyne servyce at the day of my buryeng and monethes day xx[s] every tyme to every man vj[d] To clerkes that shalbe ther for that entent at both tymys x[s] Also I wyl there be gyven in almes to poor peopyll at both tymes C[s] To clerkys that shal be there for that entent at both tymes Also I ordeyne to a newe picture to be made upon the rode of pytes in the foresay[d] monastery in Feversham xx[s] Also I wyll there be spent at my forthfare and moneythes day be the dyscretyon of myn executourys x markes for the refresshyng of gentylmen and gentylwomen that shal come to pray for my soule Also I wyll gyve to the makyng of a newe wyndowe in the chapitour hous of the seide monasterye xx[s] Also I ordeyne to the iij houses of freres in Caunterbery to pray for me xx[s] Also I bequethe to the foresayde monasterye of Feversham my grete cloth of tapstre werkes to do worship to God in thyr presbitarye and on the sepulcre next the hygh autor ther on hygh dayes Also I bequeth to John Iveas the elder an hangyng bed of red say with iij courteyns and a coveryng of the same ij peyr of shetes a hed shete a payr shetys for hys servaunt a fedyr bed a bolstar, ij pylowys a basyn and ewer a grete brasse pott halfe a dosyn of pewter vessell and ij playne borde clothes oone of workes a towell of workes Also to Thomas Evias hys brothyr too payr shetys a whyte hangyng bedde with curteyns of the same Also to John Evias the yonger the best whyte hangyng bedde with the curteyns of the same ij peyr shetys a fedurbed a bolstar a counterpoynt[1125] of tapstre workys with flowrys Also I ordeyne to the abbot and convent of the monasterye in Feversham my vestment of grene velvet enbrowdred with cotes And all that aperteyneth to the sayde vestment a chalys of sylver and gylt ij crewettes of silver a bell of sylver a paxbrede of sylver to the entente that hyt shal serve oonly to be occupyed in my chapell there I shall lye to the worship of God and Seynt John Evangelyst And I wyl that there be enbrowdred in the seyde vestment Orate pro anima Theobalde Evias[1126] Also I wyll that my crosse of goold whyche I were abowt my nek be ofred after my dyscese to the shryne of Seynt Richarde in Chycester[1127] my bedys of goolde to Seynt John hys Hed in Amyas my ryng of golld with the rubie to the sepulcre of the iij Kynges of Coleyne[1128] Also I bequeth to my systre Appultrefeld my best blak gown furred with martrons[1129] To Seynt Nycolas wyfe my blewe gown furred with grey To my goddowghtyr Thebaude Byllysdon my new blew gowne lynyd To my servaunt Julian my lynyd gown of vyolet engreyne Also I wyl that the foreseyd Thomas Iveas and John Evyas the yonger shal have al suche landys as be called purchaced londys to the maner of Easthall[1130] whyche were purchaced by me And al other londes purchaced by me in Kent owt of the libertee of the v portys to have to [t]hem and to [t]hyr heyrys in the same forme and manner as ys ordeynyd to [t]hem be the last wyll of [t]hyr fadyr made of hys purchaced londys Also I wyll that be myn executourys be bought londe to the yerely value of x[s] above all charges and repryses and with the yerely revenues and profettys therof I wyll the reparations of myne almes hous be kept the renewyng of the beddyng in the seyde house be made and the rewarde of hym that shall have the governaunces and oversyght of the seyd house to be yerly payid and this ordynaunce towchyng the sed almes house to be made fur as long to endowere as be the dyscrecyons of myne overseer myne executourys and suche councell as they shal take to [t]hem

1125 *O.E.D.* Quilt stabbed or stitched through, quilted mattress.

1126 Pray for the soul of Theobalde Evias.

1127 See J. Charles Wall, *Shrines of British Saints* (Methuen, 1905), 126-131.

1128 Cologne.

1129 *O.E.D.* The skin or fur of the animal now called marten; belonging to a certain species of *Mustela*.

1130 The manor was in the parish of Murston, Kent. Hasted, VI p. 147.

can be made Also I wyll that be myne executourys be bouth[1131] in fee as moche lande as shalbe of the yerely value of xxvj^{s} viij^{d} above and ovyr all repryses and charges or ellys that they purchace an annuytee of xxvj^{s} viij^{d} yerely to be perceyvid[1132] in fee out of londys of more value and wyth seyd xxvj^{s} viij^{d} I wyll myn yerely obite shalbe kept kept in the forsayde monasterye of Feversham by the brotherne for the tyme beyng there in this forme I wyll that the seyde xxvj^{s} and viij^{d} shall yerely be perceyvyd by the handys of the chauntour of the seyde monasterye for the tyme beyng and that he therwith shall pay yerely to every of hys brotherne beyng a prest that be both at dyrige and masse for myne obyte vj^{d} Every noves no preest iiij^{d} For wax to the sextyn ij^{s} For ryngyng x^{d} For a dyner to the brotheren vj^{s} viij^{d} And for the mayntenaunce of a taper of wax contynually to brene[1133] on the auter in the chapell there I shall lye in the tymes of hye masses to be song on holydayes in hyghe auter of the seyd monasterye iiij^{s} And to pay to every maire of Feversham for the tyme beyng comyng to the hygh masse of myn obyte and there offryng a peny there than and xiij^{d} [1134] And to every brother of ij brotherne of the mayres for the tyme beyng offryng there every of [t]hem a peny And to xij pore men comyng than and there seying at my tombe a pater noster and an ave for my soule and all crysten soules among [t]hem xij^{d} And this ordinaunce I wyll be made fur as long to endure and to be kept as kan be made by the avise and dysciecions[1135] of myn overseer myn executourys and suche councell as they shall call unto [t]hem And of this my testament and last will I make Thomas Frognhall Robert Byllesdon and John Evias the yonger myn executourys and Roger Grene overseer wyllyng that every of [t]hem shall have for [t]her labour xL^{s} The resydue of myn godys I wyll be dysposed by my seyd executours in suche maner and forme as they shall seme most expedyent for the rest of my soule and of all crysten soules.'[1136]

John Bringborne (99) was a merchant. His father, also called John, had left him the tenement in Faversham and also 'all that belongith to my craft of makyn of wax' at his death in 1515. His son played a full part in town life and was mayor in 1535, 1542 and 1544 and died in 1545. He described himself as a merchant in his will and is found importing a variety of goods in 1525-27. In his will he made a number of arrangements for his family, and appointed Richard Dryland as his overseer.[1138]

William Belke (100) paid 3^{s} 4^{d} for his freedom in 1509-10 and was a member of the 24 from 1518 to 1540. He had a croft in Selgrave in the 1515 survey of the hundred. There was a petition from the town to the King and his council in 1544, asking 'for an inquiry into the conveyance beyond the sea, contrary to the proclamation of restraint, by William Belke and William Castlock of Faversham, about May last, of two hoys laden with grain (specified) for Flushing in Zeeland, and by John Bringbourne of Faversham in July next ensuing, of his own hoy similarly laden, and by others, probably with the connivance of the searchers.' The explanation is likely to be that at a time of grain shortage the Privy Council had forbidden or limited its export, but that Belke, Castlock and Bringbourne were looking for higher prices abroad. It sounds like sour grapes on the part of other townsmen, because there were a number of such cases in the King's Bench based on information.

[1131] Bought.

[1132] *O.E.D.* Perceive: † **8.** *trans.* To receive (rents, profits, dues, etc.).

[1133] Obsolete form of burn.

[1134] Although quoted elsewhere as 12^{d} this is definitely 13^{d}, whilst the end j is partly obscured by a long descender in the line above the two short minims are clearly visible.

[1135] Decisions.

[1136] PRC 32/2/426, Proved 8 April 1479. Abstract Hussey *Notes.*

[1137] Bringborne, PROB 11/30 fol. 221v; Goldfinch PROB 11/28 q. 34; Hampton, PRC 17/24/242; Favward, fol. 12.

[1138] PRC 17/12/480; PROB 11/30/221v - q. 29; PRO: E122/208/2.

John Goldfinch (101) was a jurat and brother-in-law of Henry Hatch and had been present when Hatch's will was read out. His wife, Elizabeth, was a sister of Joan Hatch and he appointed her second husband, Sir Henry Amcotts, as governor and overseer of his children. In his will made in 1541 he left his wife, Elizabeth, his house in the market for life. He in fact had two houses, one of which was next to Hogmarket Lane. Finally, there was John Hampton (102), who was mayor in 1521 and 1532 and died in 1544. He was a merchant importing various goods in 1513-14 and 1525-27 and had two shops in the market place with the well house belonging to them.[1139]

There were eight houses in Middle Row on the side next to the gaol and several tenants were paying for 'augmentations' to the properties. The rental indicates that Middle Row then turned the corner into the present Market Street and ran as far as Hog Cross at the foot of the present Preston Street. According to A. Percival, there are still vestiges of Hog Lane, which ran at the rear of the properties on the North side of Market street. Crow records that it ceased to be a thoroughfare some time before 1712. Presumably the properties in both parts of Middle Row derive from encroachments on the market waste.The parish church had two shops there. John Kibbett (108) had lands in Faversham, Oare, Davington and Luddenham. When he died in 1542, his chief residence was in Abbey Street. His son, Humphrey, became town clerk and royal steward on the death of William Roper in 1578. A Thomas Childmell (114) was mayor in 1497 and had a lease of King's Mill and a saffron ground called Norwoodes-acre when he made his will in 1509.

We cannot be sure of the extent of the market place in 1532. We do not know whether it was just the area at present named as such, or whether it extended north into the present Court Street, as far as the junction with Quay Lane. The space is a classic linear market place. The Guildhall did not exist in 1532, and was only completed in 1574.[1140] There were three rows of shambles, tables or stalls in the market place; they seem to have been pitched longways, as it were from The Ship to The Guildhall, the first nearest West Street having ten shambles, the second nine and the third eight. Most of them were owned by just two men, John Binder (124) and John Parke (134). When John Binder made his will on 20 April 1495 he left 13^s 4^d to the work of the church of Ospringe. He also left money to the fraternity in the parish churches of Burnham and Rayleigh in Essex and the poor of Burnham. They were to be paid by a creditor, who owed him £3. He mentioned houses and tenements in West Street and lands in Preston beside Faversham, which he left to his wife, his son and daughter.[1141] William Wyer (119) was a 'servant' of a tanner called Thomas Cooke, who left him 11^s in his will in 1508. He paid a fine of 6^s for his freedom in 1519-20 and served as a member of the 24 up till 1550-51, acting as church warden in 1535-36. He was appointed an executor of the will of Avice, the widow of John Barber of the Saracen's Head in Preston Street East (173). She left the Saracen's Head to Wyer and his wife Margery, whom she does not call her daughter. In 1528 he was the overseer of the will of Robert Toppynden. Finally, in 1529, William Deryke spoke of plans for his daughter, Alice, to marry William Wyer.[1142] The Prioress of Davington had a shamble called the pudding shamble, which was empty. There were four empty shops 'under' the pillory and John Hampton had the fish shambles, important for oysters.

There were only six houses in Middle Row on the side leading from the fish market to Hog Cross. The only tenant was John Goodwin (149), who, as well as his chief residence, had seven houses

[1139] Favward fols. 24, 29v, 30, 34v; LP, xix, 2, 803; PRO, E122/130/2, E122/208/2; CKS, U390.M37/1 fol. 49.
[1140] For detailed accounts relating to the construction of what was then called the Market House in 1574 see CKS; Fa/AC2/2; Kibbett, PRC 17/22/228; Childmell, PRC 17/11/196.
[1141] PRC 32/4/38.
[1142] Cooke, PRC 17/11/50; Barber, PRC 17/17/314; Toppynden, PRC 17/17/355; Deryke, PRC 17/18/268.

in East Street and Preston Street, one in West Street and lands in Lynsted when he made his will. He was mayor in 1516 and 1520, when it was decided that because there had been a lot of controversy over jurats being put out without reason, a new rule should be made that this could only be done by the advice of the mayor, jurats and commons for a reasonable cause. He was mayor again in 1523 and died in 1531, when he was described as a brother of the abbey.[1143]

Turning left into East Street North, the feoffees of Robert Withiot (153) had a malthouse, a barn, a toft of land and a number of houses. His wife, Elizabeth, was buried in the parish church in 1502. He was an active mayor in 1506, having the will of a benefactor, James Dryland, copied into the wardmote book, drawing up regulations for the conduct of the parish clerks and the sexton and arranging for the repair of the church wall next to the Shooting Meadow. He died between 1510 and 1517. John Sayer (155) had a small house and an apple garden. He was a jurat from 1516-17 until 1539-40 and was at one time an auditor and a chamberlain and died in 1541. In his will he referred to lands and tenements in Faversham, Kingsdown, Doddington and Milstead (Mylkested). He was negotiating the purchase of a house from John Norton and mentioned 'unconsyonable and untruly delyng wyth me' about other lands. He made Richard Dryland one of his overseers, leaving anything forgotten 'to his counsel and good exhortation.' Richard Amys (156) of Preston died in 1495. Adam Princhett (157) paid $3^s 4^d$ to be a freeman in 1509-10. He was a member of the 24 from 1516-17 till 1535-36. His widow, Godleve, held the property at her death in 1558. The sexton had two houses, which he let to various men, and a garden next to Lodry Lane, which must be Church Road.

The great house at Cooksditch was held by the feoffees of Sir Edward Poynings (165) of Westenhanger, Kent. He was famous for making Poyning's Law when he went to Ireland as deputy governor, the effect of which was that all Irish legislature had to be confirmed by the English privy council. He was Lord Warden of the Cinque Ports 1509-21. He was often abroad on diplomatic missions. In 1520 he was present at the Field of the Cloth of Gold. He died in 1521.[1144]

On the opposite side of the road there was a barn, a curtilage and two gardens on the corner of East Street South. Thomas Pykering (167) paid $3^s 4^d$ fine for his freedom in 1519-20. Further along there was said to be a house belonging to the Abbot of Faversham.

Round the corner in Preston Street East, John Barber (168) was the tenant of The Saracen's Head and had other property in the town, as well at The Bull at Boughton, when he died in 1499. His widow, Avice, left The Saracen's Head to William and Margery Wyer in 1526. A widow called Elizabeth Smyth (181) had the house next to Shitborne Lane, which must be Gatefield Lane. She was the widow of John Smyth, who made his will on 1 September 1526, making bequests to his two sons and two daughters. He left 'all suche tallowe as I have within my hous at the hour of my deth' to be divided equally between his wife, Elizabeth, and son, Edmund, whom he made his sole executor. He had tenements and lands upon the den of Womanden in Smarden which he left his son, Andrew, with a contingency plan for obits in Willesborough and Faversham. The will was proved on 18 September 1526.[1145] Next to her, Thomas Perne, (182) who was mayor in 1529, had a large house, which had formerly been a number of houses. In his will in 1532, he referred to his interest in the lease of the parsonage of Ospringe, the lease of the Maison Dieu from St. John's College, Cambridge, and the lease of Huntingfield in Eastling. If there was any

---

1143 Goodwyn, PRC 17/19/234, Favward, fols. 16v, 20, 30v, 51v.

1144 Withiott, PRC 17/12/233; Sare, PRC 17/22/51; Amys, PRC 17/6/100; Godleve Princhett, PRC 17/32/26, PRC 3/15/105; Favward, fols. 12, 13, 31v, 48v, Commons 1509-58, iii, pp. 146-47.

1145 Smyth, PRC 17/17/208.

doubt about the will, Robert Maycott and Richard Colwell were to be consulted 'to whom I have showed my whole mind and intent.'

Margaret Horne (184) had a lot of property on both sides of the street. As was mentioned earlier, she was the widow of Henry Horne, Edward Thomasson and John Wode and the aunt of Henry Crispe, who had a large house in North Street East. She brought a case in Star Chamber against her neighbour, Laurence Stransham: in fact they were next door neighbours in a tenement called Mugges. She claimed that she had sown hemp but that, when it was ripe, a brewer called Laurence Stransham and other brewers and labourers stopped her collecting it. He replied that it was his garden. He was the man mentioned earlier who refused to be sworn before the abbot after being elected mayor. Further down the street, when Arnold Cowper (189) made his will on 23 August 1531, he left each monk in the abbey 6^{d} to pray for his soul. He left the rent of the house in Preston Street, which Goodman Whighthed inhabited, to Thomas and Margaret Modull until Cowper's sons, Arnold and Edward, reached the age of 20, when it was to be divided between them. The rest of his property in Faversham he left to Thomas and Margaret in fee simple, Thomas being his executor and his brother, Richard Cowper, the overseer. The will was proved on 25 October 1531. Thomas Ampner (191) was parish clerk of Preston church before his death in 1525. William Kempe (192) may have been the shoemaker who left an inventory in 1566.[1146] John Roche (193) was a member of the 24 from 1506 till 1522 and a jurat in 1523-24. He was a churchwarden in 1509-10 and 1520-21 and an auditor from 1516-17 to 1520-21. He witnessed the wills of Denyse Sole in 1503 and William Havejoy in 1510 and was one of the executors of Margery Baker in 1505. Harry Sayer, who was a rich man, a yeoman of the crown and mayor in 1501, in his will the following year left Roche 'my sergeaunt, my murrey gowne furred with black.' Roche was also left a 'russety gown furred with fox' in the will of Robert Withiot in 1511.[1147]

At the end of Preston Street East a section of the rental related to the Rectory of Preston, to which most of the rents were paid. The abbey owned the rectory, which is no doubt why it was included. John Warham (198), who had a house next to the well, was possibly John Warham of Wingham in Kent, who married Elizabeth, the daughter of William Rose, who had property in Preston Street West. One holding was next to Preston Street at the south west corner. Robert Maycott had three acres of glebeland and had to find 14 tapers for the chancel. The feoffees of Margaret Horne had two acres of land at Frydley next to the High Street. The executors of Thomas Perne had 24 acres of land at Frydley next Stokdale otherwise called Hegdale. The heirs of John Brumston (199) had an acre and a half in Bradfield called Church Field. He was probably the John Brymstone of Preston who died in 1517.

Now we turn back up Preston Street West towards the town centre. Henry Crispe had the site of a barn with three acres in Kingsfield. Humphrey Clifford (212) of Preston had a house with a garden next to 'the lane'. When he died in 1512 he left his widow eight marks out of the manor of Bobbing, left to him by his father, Alexander Clifford. William Dobbs (213) was a barber, with a house in Middle Row, two in Preston Street and one in West Street, where he died in 1506. John Love (218) was an old man when he made his will in 1516, in which he made many bequests to the abbey. He appointed the abbot and the vicar of Faversham his executors and

---

[1146] Barber, PRC 17/7/230; Perne, PRC 17/19/174; Horne, PRO STAC 2/19/154; Ampner, PRC 17/16/157; Cowper, PRC 17/19/87; Kempe, PRC 3/17/142, PRC 10/2/73; Favward, fols. 16v, 30v, 51v; The Rev. G. Streynsham Master, *Notes relating to the family of Streynsham* (London, 1879), pp. 9-11.

[1147] Favward, fols. 5v, 12, 12v, 15v, 16v, 17v, 19, 19v, 20, 23v; Sole, PRC 17/9/8; Hanejoy, PRC 17/11/245; Baker, PRC 17/10/36; Sayer, PRC 17/8/207v; Withiot, PRC 17/12/233.

arranged that all his property was to be sold to pay his debts and for the good of his soul. He died in 1518.[1148]

Further up the street, William Rose (226) was a jurat in 1506-7 and was buried in the parish church in 1509. Henry Crispe had the site of a barn with a curtilage in Kingsfield. William Norton and Simon Warmecourt each had a barn. Warmecourt (190) had a large house a little further up next to Henxhilles Lane, which must be Cross Lane. He was a brewer and died in 1496. Laurence Stransham had a house on the other side of that lane. [Thomas] Paternoster (240) witnessed the will of Richard Yalding in 1514. This property was granted to Thomas Arden in 1545.

Henry Hatch was the tenant of The Swan. John Sole (245) was mayor in 1507 when rules were made to audit the accounts of the churchwardens and to set out their duties. In 1509-10 he was an assessor for a gift to the Lord Warden. Thomas Sare (246) was a chamberlain and member of the 24. His next door neighbour, John Ealding or Yalding (247) was briefly a member of the 24. He just may have been John Ealding of Goodnestone, who made his will on 10 April 1531 leaving his wife, Agnes, and brother in law William Allen, as his executors. His will was proved on 26 May following. Next again was Richard Forman (249) alias Richard Harper, who was a commoner in 1521-22. When he died in 1527 he left his house in Preston Street to his wife for life. It was then to be sold to pay for a priest in Faversham Church to pray for the souls of his father and mother and all Christian souls 'as long as the sylver thereof will extende.'

William Sparrow (251) was made a jurat in the place of Richard Lull in 1506-7 and was still a jurat in 1509-10 when he was made an assessor for the gift to the Lord Warden. He was mayor in 1511. He witnessed the will of Elizabeth Hutson in 1505 and was a supervisor of that of Richard Jackson in 1509, for which he was given, 'my gowne off violett furred with marthrons'[1149] and 8^s 8^d. He received 20^s as an executor of the will of Thomas Childemylle of Middle Row (114). Finally, he was appointed an executor by William More of Keylane South in 1512.[1150]

William Brooke (252) was listed in the subsidy roll of 1522/23. He made his will while in the abbey of Faversham. He left £7 'to bye an egle [eagle] of laten to stand yn the queere there to rede the gospelles uppon after the custom of the monastery there.' All his lands in Faversham, Lynsted, Hernhill and Throwley he left in 1528 to his five daughters after the death of his wife.[1151]

At the far end of the street, near the market place, Henry Hatch had a house, which had formerly been called The Sign of the Rose. Next door was The George, held by the widow of Thomas Malpas (257), an entry which helps to date the rental. Thomas Malpas was a pewterer and mayor in 1496 and left a nuncupative will in 1506 in which he left everything to his wife, Elizabeth. The last house in the street was The Fleur de Luce owned by Henry Hatch. The name was carried more than 200 years ago to the house in Preston Street East belonging to Elizabeth Smyth next Shitborne Lane in 1532. After Hatch's death the Fleur-de-Lis and The George were sold to his widow's uncle, Ralph Woolgate (27).[1152] At the time of the murder the Fleur-de-Lis

---

[1148] Clifford, PRC 17/12/67v, Hasted, vi, pp. 195, 201, 205; Dobbs, PRC 17/10/124; Brymstone, PRC 17/12/568; Love, PRC 17/13/109; Warham, *Visitation of Kent 1592*, Harl. Soc. LXXV, p. 147.

[1149] *O.E.D.* Martens.

[1150] Favward fols. 5v, 12; Hutson, PRC 17/9/174v; Jackson, PRC 17/11/148; Childemylle, PRC 17/11/196v; Moore, PRC 17/12/238.

[1151] Warmecourt, PRC 17/6/215; Forman, PRC 17/17/331v, Rose, Jacob, p. 147; Broke, PRC 17/18/139, Favward, fols. 5v, 11, 12, 20, 29v; Ealdyng, PRC 17/19/158; J. Greenstreet, *The Subsidy Roll of 14 Henry VIII*, A.C., xii, pp. 423-5; Yalding, PRC 17/12/323.

[1152] CKS, Fa/LB 9.

was in the occupation of Adam Foule, who, as has been written elsewhere, was implicated and then later acquitted of being involved. We do not know whether he ever returned to the town or felt it prudent to continue life elsewhere, but at some stage John Skyrre, first elected to common council in 1567, jurat in 1572 and finally mayor in 1574, acquired the ownership of this property.[1153]

Next door in West Street was The Ship which was administered by the town. Further on was The Grewehound owned by Anthony Sondes (262), a gentleman of Throwley, who married a daughter of the former Lord Chief Justice, Sir John Fineux of Faversham and was therefore a kinsman of William Roper. Sondes was one of the men appointed to the commission of *oyer and terminer* for the trial of Alice Arden in 1551. Next door was George Awder (263), who was a member of the 24 in 1518. Richard Turner (268) was a member of the 24 from 1506-7 till 1519-20 and was described as the sergeant in 1521. The sergeant executed the mayor's commands, making all arrests and attachments, appearing at the court of portmote and all other courts. At these sessions he was responsible to the court for any further orders that might be made, levied the fines imposed and accounted to the town for the money received at the general audit. Nicholas Burwash (270) was also a member of the 24 from 1524-25 until 1551-52. He was appointed a searcher of flesh by Thomas Arden when he was mayor. Burwash was one of the witnesses when his neighbour, John Tylney (271), made his will on the 2 October 1521, leaving his property to his son, John, who was to pay sums of money as yet unpaid entered in a deed. John Burwash was also to look after his mother and John, his youngest brother, until 'he be able to helpe hymself and to get his living.' He appointed him his executor and probate was granted on 12 December following. William Penbroke alias William Coke (273) had a corner house on the west side of Bermesey Lane, which was Peases Lane in Jacob's map of 1774. Thomas Thornyvale (275) witnessed the will of William Laiston on 18 September 1527 and was the overseer to the will of his father, Robert, in 1528-29, who said he was to pay Robert's wife 6^{s} 8^{d} that he had lent him upon his wife's 'harnysed gyrdell'.[1154] John Barnard (277) was a member of the 24 from 1518 until 1532.

William Norton had a large house, which had formerly been a number of houses, an acre of ground to the south and two other houses close by. He was mayor in 1512 and 1527 and was probably the younger brother of Sir John Norton. He was a merchant importing various goods in 1525-27.[1155]

Richard Kear (286) paid a fine of 3^{s} 4^{d} for his freedom in 1509-10 and was a member of the 24 from 1516-17 until 1535-36. Next door was the property belonging to Robert Fale (289), one of the leading men in the town, who had the most holdings in the rental, 25 in all. Here he had a small house, a large one with a tenement attached, a great garden to the south and a yard of ground on the east part of the same garden. He was the abbey bailiff and a member of the 24 by 1506-07. Robert Maycott was one of his executors, the abbot was his overseer and Henry Hatch one of the witnesses to his will when he died in 1530. Fale's large house had a chamber called the officials' chamber which was elaborately furnished. When his son, also Robert, died in 1571,

---

[1153] Skyrr PRC 17/42 fol. 347. 'Item as towching my messuage or tenement called the Flower de Luese and the garden and pece or parcell of lande to the same belonginge wyth the apportenaunces scytuate lyenge and beinge in the sayd towne and lybertye of Faversham in the which I nowe inhabyte and dwell together wyth all the portalls, dores settells and weynscottes'. Portals and doors were treated as furniture and not as part of the house, and could and often were moved from one house to another. Settles where in this case probably the long wooden benches with arms and a high back probably extending to the ground still found in some old public houses even today. Wainscot in our modern age is reduced to a board of some six inches in width but at this period meant lining the walls and often the ceiling with wooden panelling.

[1154] Laiston, PRC 17/17/270; Thornvale, PRC 17/18/82v.

[1155] Malpas, PROB 11/15 fol. 92v, q.12; Favward, fols. 5v, 12, 16v, 24, 29v, 61; Tylney, PRC 17/19/240; Norton, *Vis. Kent 1592*, Harl. Soc. LXXV, p. 139; *Vis. Kent 1619*, Harl Soc., XLII, pp. 79-81; CKS, Fa/LC1 fol. 28v; PRO, E122/208/3.

he left an inventory and ordered that the wainscots and the walnut tree ceiling in the little new parlour should remain in his mansion house. His father had the lease of the parsonage of Ospringe from St. John's College, Cambridge, and a lease of the parsonage of Newnham and the manor of Monkton from the priory of Davington. He left a barn and curtilage, with the right to a ladder on the west side to do repairs, to the abbot and convent of Faversham on condition that they confirmed their grants of tenements and shambles that had not already been confirmed in writing. The vicar of Faversham was to oversee his grant of eight loads of logs for the calefactory of the abbey, 'to warme the convent of the saide monastery after the mattens there be done for ever.' If his son died before he reached the age of 18, he left £4 from his lands for finding a scholar, who had to be the son of a man living in the hundred of Faversham, and was to be appointed by the abbot and the vicar of Faversham. He set out many details about his lands and tenements. He had a storehouse at the key and left lands in Faversham, Ospringe and Boughton-under-Blean.[1156]

We have now reached Tanners Street East, where tanners were then actually living. Edward Rye (295) was sick when he made his will on 12 May 1540 and asked to be buried in Ospringe churchyard beside his father. Probate was granted on 16 September following. John Curtis (298) was a tanner. He was an old man when in 1518 he left money to the church, the abbey and the Priory of Davington. He left his son all the instruments and vessels belonging to his craft. He also left him several tenements on condition that he did not sell them. His next door neighbour was a carpenter, John Lion (299), who in 1515 left one of his small tenements to Thomas and Margaret Sheriff, who had nursed him. The other small tenement he left to his daughter. Stephen Upton (296) had a corner house 'right over agaynst' King's Mill. In this document that seems to mean 'opposite'. He had lands and tenements in Faversham, Ospringe, Stone and Buckland, which he shared amongst his four children with many remainders. He appointed William Castlock his overseer and John Barbour and Robert Kere were amongst the witnesses. He died in 1534-35. John Burston (301) in 1514 left four houses in Court Street, West Street, Tanners Street and by the market. Dennis Hardyman (305) was a jurat and had a house, gardens and barn in Tanners Street, which he left to his son in 1521. Robert Nicholas (306) was listed on the subsidy roll of 1522/3. At the end, Robert Fale held Tunbridge Croft, which his son still had in 1571.

Coming back along Tanners Street West, the vicar of Faversham had a meadow 'nigh Horsham Chartham'. A. Percival says that this meadow must have been the area round Chart Mills. The old name for the mills was Horsen Chart Mills, which is an evident corruption. Thomas Cooke was a tanner (311), who was a member of the 24 in 1506-07 and who in 1508 left his house and garden in Tanners Street to his wife. Thomas Sayer alias Lamberd (246) had three houses in West Street and one in Tanners Street, as well as a house in Sturry, when he died in 1539. He was probably a tanner, as he ordered his wife to 'leve my tanne fattes in as good condycyon men wyll saye they be worthe of the same occupacyon.' The scribe marks (312) and (313) with an A and a B showing that the tenants were listed in the wrong order in the street. It was evidently important to have it right. Richard Little (316) paid a fine of 5^{s} for his freedom in 1506-7 and was a member of the 24 by 1518-19.[1157]

Thomas Bix (320) was a commoner in 1521-22, but his name was scored through as a member of the 24 in the same year. When he made his will on 26 August 1530, he left the house he dwelt

---

[1156] Favward fols. 5v, 12, 13, 31v; Fale, PRC 17/19/111, PRC 17/41/189, Jacob, p. 131.

[1157] Rye, PRC 17/21/195; Curtis, PRC 17/13/184v; Lion, PRC 17/12/391v; Upton, PRC 17/20/149; Burston, PRC 17/12/335v; Hardyman, PRC 17/14/212; Sayer, PRC 17/21/214v; Favward, fols. 5v, 13, 16v; J. Greenstreet, Subsidy roll of 14 Hen. VIII, AC XII, p. 423b.

in to his son, Dennis, who was to pay his brother, Laurence, £5 in four years. He made both his sons executors and his neighbour, Thomas Sayer, the overseer. Ralph Symon (322) was tenant of King's Mill and paid £1-17-6 rent for him and his tenants. He was described as a citizen and fishmonger of London when he witnessed the will of William Thomas on 11 July 1523. According to Hasted, Symon brought Davington Hall and died possessed of it in 1541-42. He also bought Fishborne from Richard Dryland of Court Street East and Cooksditch. His heirs sold Davington Hall to Ralph Coppinger, who was knighted by Edward VI in 1547 for saving the royal standard from being taken at Pinkie Clough.[1158] John Norwood (323) had the little meadow on the west side of the mill and Thomas Sayer (325) a corner house against Stonebridge. Sir John Darrell (325) had a two acre meadow next to Stonebridge on the west side of the water course for a term of years. He was probably Sir John Darrell of Calehill, who died in 1509 and was buried at Little Chart. Edward Davy (326) was the tenant of Flood Mill, and the Prior of Christ Church Canterbury had a half acre meadow next to it.[1159]

Finally, we return up West Street North. The directions in the rental are here much more difficult to follow. This area between the north side of West Street and the creek was altered beyond recognition in the nineteenth century. Peter Greenstreet (328) had the site of a house next to Stonebridge and another next to it. One Fylkes, probably John Fylkes (330), had the corner house next to Mill Lane and then Peter Greenstreet had the forge with a garden and empty piece of ground and a little house as well. Greenstreet is a common name in the Faversham area. A Peter Greenstreet is listed in the subsidy roll of 1522/3. In his will of 28 February 1533/4, proved 26 September 1534, William Greenstreet of Eastling mentioned a brother, Peter. William Greenstreet also had a son, Peter, a yeoman of Plumford and Painters in Ospringe, who made his will on 5 March 1585/6, which was proved on 15 July 1586. The site of one of the messuages in West Street North was granted to Thomas Arden in 1545.[1160] Thomas Thomas (334) was a member of the 24 from 1523-24 till 1532-33. He might have been Thomas Thomas of Preston whose executor, Salmon Wilkyns, exhibited the testament, 'as the true last wishes and is sworn upon the veracity of the same' on 1 June 1550. Skot, who was either called the cowper or the cooper, (337) may have been Nicholas Skot, who was a member of the 24 in 1535-36. John Fryer (338) had a large house with another house that was now his shop. He was a chamberlain in 1531-32 and a member of the 24 between then and 1536. He was a witness to the will of Thomas Byx of Tanners Street West on 26th August 1530.[1161] William Rose (227) was a jurat in 1506-7 and died in 1509, when he was buried in the parish church.

John Bewty (126) had four houses with their gardens adjoining Hurrelane, which cannot yet be identified. He also had two stalls in the market. He was the farmer of 'Cencton' and a freeholder of Faversham when he paid 22^{s} 4^{d} for his freedom in 1524-25. John Bewty of Preston, farmer of Copton, made his traditional will in 1537, when the Reformation was well under way and just one year before the dissolution of the abbey.

> Furst I bequeth my soule to Almyghty God to his mother Saynt Mary and to all the hooly company of hevyn my body to be buryed in the church yerd of Seynt Katheryn the virgyn and marter Also I will that ther be bought iiij torches iiij tapers at the day of my burying And so to be burned in the said church at high feastes Furder more I will at the day of my

[1158] From A. Percival; Thomas, PRC 17/16/21; Hasted, vi, p. 378.

[1159] Favward, fols. 39, 40; *Vis. Kent, 1619*, Harl. Soc XLII, pp. 186-87; Hasted, vi, pp. 225, 542, VII, p. 458; Byx, PRC 17/19/47.

[1160] Information from A. Percival; James Greenstreet, *Memorials of the Ancient Kent Family of Greenstreet*; Hasted folio edn. ii, p. 753.

[1161] Favward, fols. 29v, 30, 30v; Byx, PRC 17/19/47.

burying be said trigintall of masses and likewise as many at my monethes day And likewise at my yeres day Also I will that an honest prest immediatly after my buryng be hired for to sing for me, my father and mother by the space of an yere Also I will that every poor body that is at my buryng shall have a peny to pray for me Also I geve to the reparations of the parish of Preston xx^{s} [1162] Also to the high awter for tithes forgoten and to be praid for xiij^{s} iiij^{d} ..... Item I will that ther be bestowed among poore people wher is nede xxx$^{ti\,£}$ Item I will to the Fryer of the Abbey to sing a trentall for my soule x^{s} Item to Plegger in the Marssh[1163] xL^{s} Item to my lord Abbot of Faversham to pray for me xiij^{s} iiij^{d}. The overplus of my gooddes above my legacies paid I geve to Elizabeth my wife whom I make myn executrix with John Best of Faversham to whome I geve for his labour xL^{s} And I make my overseer [blank] Marssh of Old Rumney. Witnesseth Sir Richard Malpas vicar of Preston, Thomas Harryngton, Robert Meich, Richard Bodell with others

It was proved on 26 March 1538; on 8 July following the abbey fell. Richard Yalding (247) had a corner house and garden on the east side of Hurrelane. He may have been the member of the 24 in 1506-7 and 1509-10, when he was described as Richard Yalding the younger. He may also have been a maltster, because he arranged in his will in 1514 for his wife to deliver 40 quarters of malt to Richard Dryland the elder to keep until his sons reached the age of 20. 'And the said Richard to take of the encreace thereof after his concyens for his labour.' He had eight acres of land in Faversham, Luddenham and Goodnestone. William à Bourne (350) was mayor in 1522 and referred in his will in 1540 to the house in West Street 'where John Smyth the baker dwells.' John Hardy (354) was a butcher, who was a member of the 24 in 1506-7. In his long will in 1508 he left £3 for the purchase of a silver chalice for the church. He remembered the abbey and left money for tithes forgotten in Preston, Ospringe, Luddenham and Davington. He left his servants, Thomas Chapman and Peter Hardy, all his instruments belonging to his craft in the slaughter house, that is 'wet tools, ropes, axes and cleavers, with all such other things that belongeth to the same craft.' He made several bequests of sheep and also had a small house in West Street in Ospringe, which is in fact West Street in Faversham. There are references elsewhere to people living in 'the parish of Ospringe in the town of Faversham': there was a detached portion of Ospringe on the north side of West Street astride the present North Lane. William Rowett (356) was one of the executors of John Bromfeld in 1504 and of John Hoode in 1506, but dead by the time the will was proved on 22 April 1507.[1164]

A few doors down John Bangore (357) had a house and garden on the west part 'of a certain lane' and John Shepistall a garden on the east of the same lane. John Binder (124) had a large house, a shop, half a kitchen and a curtilage, a tenement and a garden with a dovehouse next to Gorewell Lane. The half kitchen was probably a detached one and it makes me wonder how many there were still at this period. The dovehouse was probably a substantial structure like the one as Westenhanger. A dovecote was a source of fresh winter meat. He owned many of the stalls in the market place. John Kere was on the west corner of West Gorewell Lane and John Hode on the east.

John Kere (349) was a member of the 24 in 1509-10. He asked to be buried in St. Peter of Milton next Gravesend in 1511, and left lands in Faversham, Luddenham and Stalisfield. He left his son, Richard, three tenements in Faversham, one being the malthouse, one the tenement in which

[1162] It is possible that this is xxj^{s}, the second x being written partially over the j. This is followed by d which appears to be crossed through.

[1163] Query Richard Plegger of Bonnington [PRC 17/22 f 144] died 1542.

[1164] Bromfeld, PRC 17/10/176; Hoode, PRC 17/10/224; information from A. Percival.

Richard Cheseman lived and the third the one in which Peter Dutcheman lived. He also left him all his malt. To his son Robert he left another three tenements including a saffron garden near St. Stephen's pasture and Tayntors Croft, all his grain and his debts whether in money or grain, his sheep, his cows and his lands in Luddenham and Stalisfield. John Hode (367) was a husbandman who in 1507 left lands in Faversham, Herne, Swalecliffe, Chilham and Molash. He referred to a house and garden set and lying at the waterside in West Street, probably described in the rental as 'the tenement next the forsaid lane against the key, lying to a tenement at the corner of West Gorewell Lane against the north.' He also referred to his dwelling house which in the rental was 'a corner tenement on the east side of West Gorewell Lane.' Robert Mattrasse (300) had two slaughter houses with a little garden near the end of West Gorewell Lane on the west side against the key. He was a member of the 24 in 1509-10. George Mercer (370) had a garden on the east side of the lane against the key. William Hywood (375) was chamberlain in 1530-31 and a member of the 24 in 1540-41. He had a holding made up of various houses and gardens. A priest called William à Borough (380) had two houses that had formerly been one. Dom. William Borowe was described as parish priest of the Minster in Sheppey and appointed overseer in the will of Nicholas Gedding in 1505. He was possibly the son of William Barrow of Faversham, who was mayor in 1472 and left bequests to Faversham church in 1492.[1165] William Elfrith (381) paid 4^{s} fine for his freedom in 1506-7, was a collector for West Street and a member of the 24 between 1519-20 and 1531-32. So finally, we reach the corner house 'over against', meaning opposite, The Ship' held by William Bourne.[1166].

Kingsfield was shared amongst the wardens of the parish church and eight men: John Warham, Henry Hatch, William Rose, William Castlock, Laurence Stransham, Robert Fale, one Barley and Henry Crispe, who also had two holdings in Kingsfield listed under Preston Street West, one the site of a barn and three acres at rent of 3^{s} 1^{d} and the other site of a barn with a curtilage and certain lands at a rent of 7^{s} 6^{d}. It is not possible to work out the total acreage from the rental because, although 56 acres and 6 yards are mentioned, other holdings are referred to as 'a toft', 'certain lands', 'Sayntmary Aker', 'Shortforowe', 'Wadescroft' and 'Bradbroke'.

The feoffees of John Parke had 9 acres at Cutthorne, the Prior of Leeds had an acre and more and Robert Colwell half acre. This, according to A. Percival, was a field or area somewhere between the south end of Tanners Street and Ospringe Street.

There follows a rental in a different hand dealing only with the sums due to the sacrist or sexton and the chapel of St. Mary. (There is a delightful example of the duties of a sexton from St. Mary's, Sandwich. There were entries to the sexton for drink when it thundered, 'he ringing the bells to give courage to the people and putting heart into himself with that form of courage called Dutch.'[1167]) There are very few differences from the main rental. Coke the butcher in Northstreet West was said to pay a rent of 16^{s} in the main rental but 15^{s} in this. However, when the entry on folio 18 is extremely carefully examined, the last minim appears to have been deliberately erased. There is an important difference in Preston Street West. The main rental states that Henry Hatch held The Swan but this rental mentioned his feoffees, showing that it is of later date, because it was compiled after his death in May 1533.

[1165] From A. Percival; PRC 17/10/87; AC, XVIII, pp. 106, 112; TC pp. 120, 123.

[1166] Yalding, PRC 17/12/323; A Bourne, PRC 17/22/53v; Hardy, PRC 17/9/334; Kere, PROB 11/17 q. 21; Hood, PRC 17/10/224; Favward, fols. 5v, 12, 16v, 22, 23v, 25, 30, 30v, 31v, 34v; Jacob, p. 147; D.N.Durrant, *Living in the Past* (Aurum Press, 1988), p. 20; Peter and Jean Hansell, *Doves and Dovecotes*, (Millstream Books, 1988) & Peter and Jean Hansell, *Dovecotes* (Shire Publications, 1988).

[1167] I. Bulmer-Thomas, *Transactions of the Ancient Monuments Society*, N.S., VIII (1960), p. 21.

After Kingsfield, this rental refers to the rent of Upland[1168] due from Christopher Bredham for Roode.[1169] This was possibly Christopher Bredham of Molash, who died in 1537. At Selgrave,[1170] Walter Maycott's widow had a croft of land lying next to the lane leading in to Lytelles, the master, fellows and scholars of St. John's College, Cambridge had lands called Cantisdane and one Baylly of Sheldwich had a tenement. At Well, Ralph Symon, who was the tenant of King's Mill, had land in Holymston. At Oldboldisland ,the heirs of Spicer had lands at Fissheponde and the heirs of Richard Pope paid 9^{d} rent. He was possibly Richard Pope of Boughton-under-Blean, who died in 1537. Finally, in Graveney, the heirs of Peryman had a house and land called Buttes. This was possibly John Peryman of Graveney, who died in 1516. The heirs of Thomas Frogenhale, of Buckland who died in 1505, had a croft called The Rosse. He was a wealthy man and held the manors of Buckland and Luddenham and lands in Teynham, Faversham, Ospringe, Harty, Lynsted, Tong and Davington. He left four daughters and coheiresses; Elizabeth Norwood a widow, Joan, wife of Edmund Martyn of Graveney, Elizabeth (*sic*), wife of Edward Hawte of Petham and Joan Quadring, his grand-daughter, daughter of Anne and Thomas Quadring of London, mercer.[1171] Edmund Martyn and Edward Hawte were two of his executors and Dom. William Coste, vicar of Lynsted, the supervisor of his will. Coste was also one of the feoffees of his manor of Buckland, along with Sir John Fineux, Sir Thomas Kemp, John Rogers and others. Reynald Back had land called Sextry and land at Balkynhelde. Some of these place-names also appear in a 1515 survey of the abbey's holdings in the hundred.[1172]

The third rental was concerned with rents due to the chamberlain. The first difference was that the widow, Elizabeth Smyth, having a house next to Shitborne Lane in Preston Street East had remarried, this time to Thomas Sayer alias Lambert, who now held it in the right of his wife, paying a rent of 2^{s} to the chamberlain. Once again this shows that this rental was written later than the main rental. Secondly , in Kingsfield, it was not Henry Hatch but the widow, Joan Hatch, who held a toft of land next to the garden of the Fleur de Luce for a half a quarter of barley or oats.

In the Upland, Robert Easton might be Robert Easton of Preston, who died in 1539. The rent for Priestfield was 33^{s} 4^{d}. John Jury of Boughton and one named Teneker of Boughton had land at Gosompole for 6^{d} and two hens. John Jury of Boughton died in 1539-40, and there were a number of Tenacres living in Boughton in the period. Richard Lewkenor had lands called Sprakilles next to Sheldwich for a seam of wheat. A Richard Lewkenor of Throwley died in 1479.[1173] Someone surnamed Gyles had land at Lonerreddesgate. Again, there were several people of this name living in the area. Then there were lands in Harty called Johans Goore and land at Ravynshill. The final items were 'the certers house' with the adjoining grange and croft and the profits from the fair and the sea, that is Snowte weir, which were left blank. This weir,

---

[1168] *O.E.D.* (3) High ground as opposed to meadow or marsh; ground not liable to flooding.

[1169] Hasted, VI, p. 370 mentions the grant in 36 Henry VIII to Anthony St Leger, amongst other premises of a barn with appurtenances formerly belonging to the Rectory of Faversham and those tithes arising from and within the borough of Rode to hold *in capite* by knight's service. The Rectory of Faversham, which had originally belonged to St. Augustine's Abbey was after the dissolution granted in 1541 to the Dean and Chapter of Christ Church, Canterbury,as were the rectories of Boughton-under-Blean and Ticehurst in Sussex which had belonged to Faversham Abbey. It would seem that the borough of Rode covered parts of a number of parishes including Boughton-under-Blean, Faversham and Selling in which latter parish was the manor of Rhodes Court.

[1170] The manor of Selgrave in Preston by Faversham was granted to Christ Church Priory, Canterbury in 1396 to support Lady Mohun's perpetual chantry. After the dissolution it was granted in 1541 to the new foundation and continued till 1862 when transferred to the Ecclesiastical Commissioners. Arthur Hussey, *Kent Chantries* KAS Records Branch, XII (1936), p. 49. Foundation deed in *AC* XXXVIII, p. 169.

[1171] *Cal. Inq. PM* Henry VII, II, no. 392; PRC 32/8/97; Hasted, VI, pp. 57, 287, 398.

[1172] CKS: Wilson of Faversham deposit, U390.M37/1.

[1173] Easton, PRC 17/22/156, PRC 16/5/377; Jury, PRC 32/17/50; Lewkenor, PRC 17/3/246.

in the sea at Seasalter, belonged to the Abbey of Faversham, which let out the fishing rights. In October 1471 John Moys of Seasalter left his weir at the Snothe and one acre and a half of land near the church to John Moys of Dog Lane.[1174]

The last rental was for the office of the precentor. There were only these four mentioned in the main rental; the churchwardens in Middle Row, Stephen Upton and the feoffees of Robert Fale in Tanners Street East and Thomas Sayer in Tanners Street West. In addition the precentor was to receive of the beadle of the upland 5^{s} for parchments for all the courts in the year.

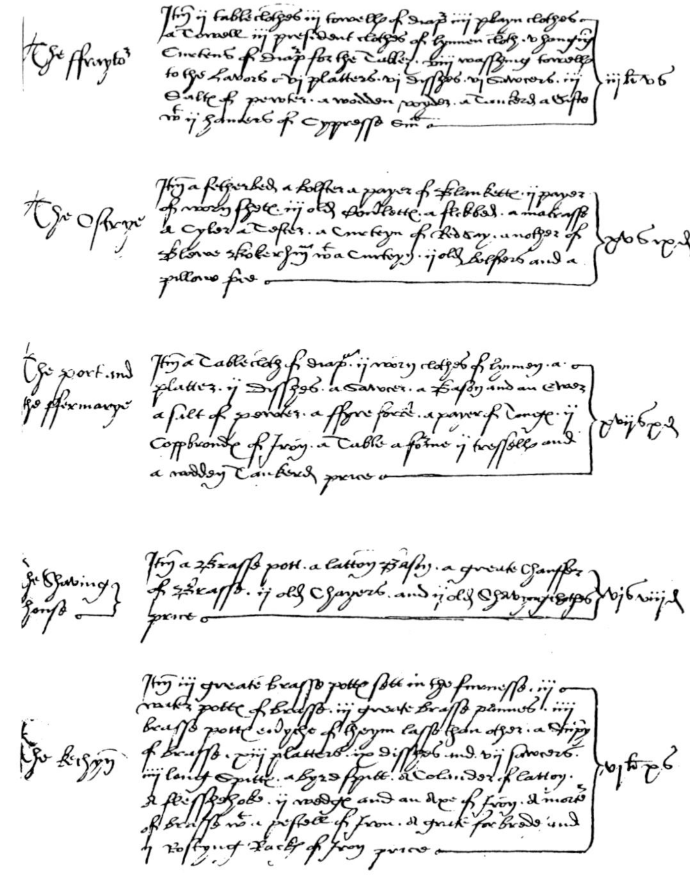

CCA: Literary MS B5 folio 26.

[1174] Robert H. Goodsall, *Whitstable*, op. cit. p. 28.

INVENTORIES AND SURVEYS

There follows the state of account of the abbey drawn up on 1 February 1499. This was presumably made following the crisis in the abbey's affairs the previous year. The abbot, Walter Gore, was a great builder and is said to have added a commodious and comfortable guest house and the Pity Rood Chapel to the abbey, but, in order to do this, savings went and income was forepledged. Then, in 1498, Henry VII called for a benevolence of £100. When he received a plea of inability, he sequestered the abbey estates and called upon Cardinal Morton to find out why the abbey was bankrupt. Gore had been elected in 1458[1175] and so must have been old and worn out. He resigned his dignity into the hands of the Archbishop on 6 September 1498 and John Castlock received the King's writ for the restoration of the temporalities of the abbey on 17 February 1499.[1176] This state of account must therefore probably be that drawn up for Cardinal Morton, and likely to be accurate.

It starts with an extent of the yearly possessions, spiritual and temporal belonging to the abbey, which will be considered with the entry in the *Valor Ecclesiasticus* of 1535. There follows the inventory of the treasures and household equipment.[1177] The treasure and plate were kept in various parts of the monastery such as the treasury, the abbot's chamber, the refectory and the gatehouse[1178] and consisted of about 60 pieces. The most prized possession was the piece of the holy cross. According to Robert of Gloucester, it had been presented by Godfrey of Boulogne to King Stephen who had in turn given it to the abbey. Godfrey had obtained it from the much larger relic of the supposed original, which had been kept in the church at Jerusalem and taken at its capture by the crusaders in 1099. This relic was enclosed in gold and set with precious stones.

The other treasures are good evidence of the pomp and splendour of the abbey and the high rank of the abbot, especially as the mitre and pontifical ring indicates that in the early days he possessed something like episcopal rank. Only the Archbishop of Canterbury had the right to visit officially. The silver cross weighed 50 ounces alone and there were in addition nine chalices and censers of silver and an ouch[1179]. Four gold rings together with the pontifical ring weighed 3½ ounces.

The bell, paxes and cruets used for the mass are presumably those left to the abbey by the will of Theobaude Evias in 1479. There were silver salt cellars and special silver spoons, having their shafts topped with a strawberry-shaped knops.[1180]

1175 Pat. 37 Hen. Vi, pt. I, m. 18 quoted in *VCH*, Kent Vol. 2 (1926), p. 141; Telfer, p. 6.

1176 Dugdale, *Monasticon Anglicanum* Vol. IV (1846), p. 570. The king's writ for the restoration of the temporalities to him is printed in Southhouse's *Monasticon Favershamiense*, p. 22. See also Lewis, p. 41. In Battely's Somner, part ii. App. p. 57, we read, it was the office of the archdeacon of Canterbury to install the abbot of Faversham, either in person or by his official; for which his fees were the abbot's palfrey, and to stay at the abbey for two nights and a day, at the abbot's expense, and to have meat and drink for ten of his suite if he chose it.

1177 Broughton, pp. 50-52.

1178 Given here as Porte.

1179 *O.E.D.* Ouch: A clasp, buckle, fibula, or brooch, for holding together the two sides of a garment; hence, a clasped necklace, bracelet, or the like; also, a buckle or brooch worn as an ornament (the chief meaning in later times). (Such nouches or ouches were often set with precious stones.)

1180 *O.E.D.* Knop: a small rounded protuberance, a knob (esp. one of ornamental character e.g. on the stem of a chalice, a candlestick etc.). In Timothy Schroder, *English Domestic Silver 1500-1900* (Penguin/National Trust 1988) a knop is described as a decorative bulbous moulding, usually placed at the mid-point of the stem of a cup. In the case of spoons it was the finial that was made decorative. There is an almost infinite range of these decorate knops, many described in wills, The apostle spoons were being made from at least the fifteenth century onwards. See Norman Gask, *Old Silver Spoons of England* (1926).

The inventory of the hostellary or guest house indicates by the difference of quality of its furnishings from that of the abbot's chamber that it was used just for casual travellers and that the more important guests were housed in special apartments in the abbot's lodging where they had the greater luxury of feather beds and linen sheets.

According to Gasquet[1181], shaving was regarded as a religious act at which psalms were generally recited. There was usually a special shaving in the shaving house on the eve of great festivals, but normally the tonsure was shaved every three weeks.

The amount of equipment in the brewhouse shows that a great deal of beer must have been brewed there, but there is nothing to connect it with the later development in Faversham of brewing as a major industry. This depended almost entirely on the excellence of its local hops and these were not introduced into England until the sixteenth century.

Nethercourt had four stables with 22 horses and four mares. On the estate were 166 hogs, three bulls, three cows, three steers, two bullocks and 669 sheep. Finally, there was the smithy.

Next there was an inventory made on 24 August 1534, the very year that the Act of First Fruits and Tenths was passed, which gave the crown financial control over the church, as I shall show below. This was again an inventory of household goods, which mentioned eight chambers in all, including 'the great chamber for estrangers next the farmarye'.

Here there is a change of handwriting and it becomes very difficult to read. There follows a brief list of customary payments and services pertaining to the abbey to be made to the infirmarer of the abbey. For example, the tenants of the manor of Selgrave, which was partly in the parish of Preston and partly in Faversham, were bound to plough, reap, carry and stack three acres of corn. There is also a reference to the manor of Knight's Place, otherwise unknown, but it was probably the Brumston estate in Davington, which passed through inheritance from John Brumston to Thomas Knight. The man who made the notes was John Wylde, who in 1546-47 in the ministers' accounts was collector of the rents of the hundred for the crown.[1182]

The chronology of the dissolution I have given in the text. The figures for the value of a monastery just prior to its dissolution are usually taken from the Valor Ecclesiasticus of 1535[1183] without further comment. However, I spent a week in August 1993 at a Latin and Palaeography Summer School on a course led by Christopher Harrison, looking in detail at the Valor and trying to decide how it was compiled and what were the pitfalls in using it. He then wrote a private pamphlet 'The Valor Ecclesiasticus: a re-appraisal' on which I have relied heavily in the following account. I think that it makes for a more lively approach if we consider the Valor in that light.

THE POLITICAL AND ECONOMIC BACKGROUND

To repeat, the Act of First Fruits and Tenths passed in 1534 gave the crown financial control over the church. It led in the following year to a great survey of both the landed and the ecclesiastical income of the English and Welsh churches. The original returns of that survey were published over 150 years ago in a six volume transcript with a one volume introduction known as the Valor

[1181] Abbot Gasquet, *English Monastic Life* (Antiquary's Books, Methuen 1904), pp. 103-104.

[1182] PRO SC 6/EdVI/233; Bibliography, pp. 69, 137, 260-61, 279-80; Vis. Kent 1574, *Harl. Soc*. LXXV, p. 18; Vis. Kent 1619, *Harl. Soc*. XLII, p. 18.

[1183] *Valor Ecclesiasticus, temp. Henrici VIII, auctoritate regia institutus*, Edited by J. Caley and Rev. J. Hunter Introduction and further 6 volumes (1810-1834) Publication of the Record Commissioners.

Ecclesiasticus. The Act of 1534 (26 Hen. 8, c.3) was one of the seminal acts which transferred power from Rome to the English Crown. First fruits, primitae or annates, were the first year's whole profits of every spiritual preferment, the tenths being a tenth part of this sum, originally payable to the pope, then after the statute to the crown and from 1703 to the commissioners of Queen Anne's bounty. Henry VIII more than doubled his annual income of £40,000 by this Act of Parliament even before he attacked the monasteries. He continued to get the new annual tax of a tenth even after the monastic property was sold.

THE COMMISSION

The 1535 survey was probably the largest land survey since the Domesday survey of 1086, because the church held between 20 and 30 per cent of all the landed wealth of England in that year. It was a much more detailed and exact valuation than the Taxation of Pope Nicholas IV of 1291, which had listed benefices the value of which was greater than six marks.[1184]

On 30 January 1535, Cromwell sent out commissions into every shire. The instructions, sent out with the commissions, were detailed, nearly 3,500 words in length, and specific. The near exclusion of clerics indicates the extent to which their authority and power within society had been eroded. The other commissioners were mainly local gentlemen, who were required to work in teams of not less than three, doubtless to prevent collusion with and/or corruption by the clerks. Some minimal outside expertise was provided by auditors, presumably out of the Exchequer, who were sent into the counties, when the survey was being written up, to help draft the returns. Amongst the 28 commissioners for Kent were Thomas Cromwell, chief secretary, Christopher Hales, the attorney general, Sir Thomas Cheyne, Anthony St. Leger of Ulcombe and John Cripis or Crispe.[1185]

THE SURVEY

The survey was made county by county, not diocese by diocese, possibly because local gentlemen were used to working together on county commissions of various kinds. The sub-unit of enquiry was the ecclesiastical rural deanery, not the secular hundred.

How was the enquiry conducted? Here the evidence is thin. What is quite clear is that the commissioners did not have the time to carry out an independent survey and must have relied on existing episcopal, monastic and cathedral rentals and the honesty of the local church officials in making their returns. The big estates would have been relatively easy to survey, but how did the commissioners find out about the parishes? According to the Kent returns, incumbents brought certificates of income to the commissioners.

THE MAKING OF THE RETURNS.

[1184] S. Ayscough and J. Calley (eds) *Taxatio Ecclesiastica Angliae et Walliae auctoritate Papae Nicholia IV, c. 1291* (Record Commission, 1802).
[1185] LP, viii, no's. 40, 49.

Experts from the Exchequer were sent to help the commissioners write up the returns. First the information was collected into books and then these were written up on parchment rolls according to a set formula. It was these written up returns which were sent to the Exchequer. The returns in general must have been accepted without question for they were written up in a two volume financial summary, and, at the same time, a best copy of the original returns, called the *Liber Regis* or King's Book, was also made literally for the King.

Kent was unusual in that some of the returns, including Faversham, were written in English, not Latin. It was also one of the first to make its returns and yet it was a month late. The returns for Bath and Wells were not sent in until 17 September. Nevertheless, the whole massive bureaucratic process from collection to writing up was completed with mind-numbing speed. There were omissions and it is important to note that the survey is not a complete list of existing parishes or churches.

Reaction to the survey

It was certainly taken seriously from the outset. As we shall see later, the monks at Faversham thought it sufficiently important to copy their return into the rental book, now Lit. MS B5 in Canterbury Cathedral Archives. Another fair copy of the Faversham return also survives as a roll in the British Library.

The records of the survey of 1535 and the Valor Ecclesiasticus.

The material collected in the survey was used in a variety of ways :

1) The original returns were subsequently published in the *Valor Ecclesiasticus*, edited by J.Caley and J.Hunter (Record Commission,1810-34).

2) A two volume transcript of the original returns, called the *Liber Regis,* was made for the king It was not a straight transcript of the original returns, as the grammatical form and the layout of the entries were different.

3) Two volumes of abstracts contemporary with the original returns were made.

4) The *Liber Valorum*, consisting of three manuscript volumes drawn up in the eighteenth century, was subsequently used by the editors of the *Valor* Ecclesiasticus as a substitute for any original returns that were missing.

5) Finally, the *Liber Decimarum* was compiled from both the original returns and from other material from the Office of First Fruits and Tenths.

The Valor Ecclesiasticus

There is internal evidence to suggest that the order in which the material is printed is not that in which it was originally arranged. It also includes some later material. A researcher should be warned that in any county return there are returns from places in other counties, and in other county returns he might find material for his own county. There is no single comprehensive index of all the volumes and the spelling of place-names provides many problems. The Liber Regis was not a straight transcript of the original returns, for the grammatical form and the layout of the entries are different

The use of the Valor Ecclesiasticus

Its use has been curiously limited, partly because the original intentions of the legislators were overtaken by events. It is used as a primary source on the monasteries just prior to their dissolution, but its value to the local historian at parish level has hardly been recognised. It is surely significant that there is no good modern guide to this record.

The great survey of 1535 is one of the most remarkable administrative achievements of an age remarkable for its administrative innovation. It is a primary source of the English church at a crucial time in its history and a major local history record. The Valor is a misused and under-used source.

Faversham Abbey

Again, a more detailed analysis will be done later. Part of the process of the compilation can be followed in the dissolution of Faversham Abbey, as there are a number of documents connected with its suppression. The first is in the printed Valor Ecclesiaticus. The second is Harleian Roll G 16 in the Manuscripts Department, British Library, which is a paper roll with the membranes joined together. This is an unusual find and is a version similar to the Valor apart from one or two scribal errors and mistakes in additions. It must therefore have been compiled at some stage in the process of drawing up the survey, although it is not clear when. The third is the version in the abbey rental book, Lit. MS B5 in Canterbury Cathedral Archives. Broughton transcribed this in his thesis on Faversham Abbey in 1952 and noted every difference from the published edition of the Valor. There were a number of minor points, but more remarkable was an item of £355-15-2 given as the sum total of the whole value of all the manors, parsonages, lands, tenements and other emoluments belonging to the said monastery of Faversham of which £75-15-11¼ went out in rents, resolutions, pensions, alms fees, to stewards, auditors and others. The first figure was not given in the Valor. The order is slightly different, too. In the Valor the sum of temporalities appears after officials' fees, in Lit. MS B5 it appears before. The final total was given as £284-15-5 and a quarter and a half of barley not £286-12-6¾ as in the Valor. Clearly the abbot knew only the figures drawn up by the commissioners on their visit, not the sums that were amended by the auditors. Edward Jacob used the version in Lit. MS B5 for his appendix VII, which was printed in his *History of Faversham.*

There were also three estate documents. The first two are in the Public Record Office: SC 6/Hen VIII/ No. 1755 in 1538-39 (A) and SP 5/1 three years later (B). The third is in Lambeth Palace Library under the heading, 'Holdings of the Monastery of St. Augustine's in Canterbury', but clearly relating to Faversham Abbey (C). St. Augustine's held the rectory of Faversham and may have acquired it in that way.

There are finally a series of ministers' accounts extending from 1542 to 1549. With such a wealth of sources it is only possible when running through the details of the estate to point out appreciable differences. It is worth remembering that these documents also varied because they placed different items together at different times.

The Valor covered the manor of Faversham and lands in Southfield, Hegdale, Lodge Marsh, Wildmarsh, Hernhill, Cockham and Mentilham, Abbot's Court in the Isle of Harty, Priestfield, Nagdon Marsh, Horsehops and Gore Marsh, which were all let out. All these were in the deanery of Ospringe. There was also the farm of the sea and Snout Weirs. Beyond this was the farm of the manor of Ellenden and the messuage of Lambert's Land in the deanery of Ospringe. There followed details of the manor of Kingsnorth in the parish of Ulcombe near Maidstone and the rent from Great Ferehurst and Little Ferehurst in the deanery of Charing. Next came the parsonages of Boughton-under-Blean, Hernhill and Preston next Faversham and receipts from the spiritualities. A list of fees of officers was followed by details of the manor of Bendysh in Essex.

First there was the site of the manor with 30 acres in demesne lands, pastures, meadows and gardens, all that was 'in our own hands', which was valued at 2^{s} an acre, a total of £3-0-0. In (B) in 1541-42 the farm of the site of the monastery with the demesne there was £3-18-8.

The first three documents referred to the customary works. They said that the yearly farm of the manor in corn, cattle, and money was worth £36-0-0. This included custom from 22 acres and a half a rood of land belonging to the manor in 'erring, sowing the said acres of wheat, ryppyng, carrying it into the barns and tassing the said wheat', all of which was done by the tenants.

The next two paragraphs in the Valor referred to various houses belonging to the abbey in the town. The first referred to the farm or lease of two houses at the town gate and to other houses and a mill, which we know to be Flood Mill, in the town amounting to £26-17-0 and a quarter of barley yearly. To this was added a rent of £21-6-11½ and a half a quarter of barley for other houses in the town. This made a total of £48-3-11½. (C) spoke of 'rents of assize', meaning fixed rents with poultry of £24-0-0 and other rents as £31-5-0, totalling £55-5-0. (B) and the ministers' accounts gave slightly different figures and referred to a decay in certain rents. Flood Mill was let at a rent of £10-0-0, but was granted on 7 December 1541 to Thomas Arden.

The yearly rent of Upland in custom, cocks, hens and eggs all rated in money was £52-1-0¾. In the Valor all the casualties of leets and courts belonging to the manor in the town and hundred and the fines for suits, amercements and reliefs amounted to £8-0-0. The figure was confirmed in (C). The forester of Blean paid £20-0-0 a year for the timber and wood that he sold from there and in Bossenden, the site of the battle which took place on 31 May 1838.[1186] He also paid 11^{s} for the farm of 'woodleese'[1187] and 5^{s} 8¼^{d} for the yearly rent of nine gates[1188] leading into the Blean. This was made up of 3^{s} in money, 9 hens price 2^{s} 3^{d} and 105 eggs price 5¼^{d}. The ministers' account in 1547-48 said that Thomas Arden was the farmer and forester of the woodland, which had been granted to him for 21 years by an indenture dated 8 October 1545. The wood contained 1,100 acres, with some trees excepted.[1189]

The fair at Lammas tide, otherwise known as the feast of St. Peter in chains, brought in £2-13-4. There is more discussion about the fair on page 78 of the text. (B) gives the total as £2-3-4 and both (A) and (C) add Nether Green and Upper Green to the total, coming to £3-3-4. The ministers' accounts in 1547-48 referred to £1-6-8 for the fair and Nether Green, which had once been let to Robert Coldwell, but was now let to the town, and £1-6-8 for the fair and Upper Green, which had once been let to Ady Fould, but was also now let to the town. It added 16^{s} 8^{d} for market rents of one fair held there by the new corporation by the jurisdiction of the late Henry VIII in the feast of St. Valentine, showing that this was a new arrangement, as I indicated in the text. The total was £4-0-0.

1186 P. G. Rogers, *Battle in Bossenden Wood* (OUP 1961) and B. Reay, *Last Rising of the Agricultural Labourers* (OUP 1990).

1187 Probably wood-leave, leave or permission to cut or procure wood.

1188 *O.E.D.* Gate: (8) a right to a run of pasturage for a cow, horse etc. i.e. 1804 *Hull Advertiser* 4 Feb. 2/3 Six gates or common rights on a common called Wilfholme.

The net total of receipts for the principal manor of Faversham after allowing for the pensions paid to St. Augustine's, Canterbury, was £163-10-2½ and a quarter and a half of barley.

Southfield and Hegdale were let for £10-0-0 and land in Lodge Marsh and Wild Marsh for £3-6-8. (C) gave more details. There were 34 acres of land in Southfield and 24 acres in Preston at Hegdale with a tithe in Southfield leased by indenture. According to Lewis, Hegdale had been granted to the town by a former bailiff, Sir John Fineux, Chief Justice of the Commmon Pleas and William Roper's grandfather. Both were granted to Sir Thomas Cheyne on 16 March 1540. Lodge Marsh was in the parishes of Oare, Luddenham and Faversham. The value in rent of a tenement there and 12 acres of land called Uplande and 3[s] 4[d] quit rent belonging to the same tenement was £1-13-4. This had pasturage for 105 sheep in the salt marsh and was leased by indenture to Richard Dryland and John Dryland, senior, his son. Wild Marsh in Stone was leased by indenture for another £1-13-4. According to Lewis, it was settled on the abbey by a group of people, possibly feoffees. It was in the tenure of John Dryland when granted to the king's servant, Anthony Aucher, in 1544.[1190]

In Hernhill there were 16½ acres adjoining Lambert's Land let to Robert a Broke for £1-0-0 from which a pension had to be paid to the canons of St. Stephen's Westminster, from their manor of Queencourt in Ospringe, and another to the heirs of Mathew Martyn for the manor of Dargate. This left 13[s] 8[d].

Cockham and Mentilham in Hernhill and Graveney were let for the clear sum of £1-15-0 after a rent paid to the Archbishop of Canterbury from his manor of Boughton-under-Blean and a pension to the vicar of Hernhill had been taken into account. According to Lewis, a group of people, possibly feoffees, gave 11 acres of land at Mentilham and 12 acres of land at Cockham to the abbey. These are the two pieces of land that the abbot, John Castlock, probably deceived John Cole about when he planned to found a school at the abbey. The incident is graphically described by Canon Telfer.

Abbot's Court in the Isle of Harty with Julian's Marsh was let for the clear sum of £18-3-0¼. According to Lewis, this was partly made up of 16 acres of land granted to the abbey by Thomas Ovyn at Keyborow Hill and another 86 acres of salt marsh called Julian Marsh granted by Richard Colwell in 1525. About three months before the dissolution of the abbey, on 23 March 1538, John Castlock wrote to Cromwell saying that he had received Cromwell's letter of 15 March by his servant, Christopher Roper, who was William Roper's brother. By the bearer he sent the sum of the acres that Sir Thomas Cheyne would have of the convent by the year. The licence to alienate 144 acres of land, 204 acres of fresh marsh and 10 acres of salt marsh in the parish of St. Thomas in the Isle of Harty, near the Isle of Sheppey, had already been granted on 18 March.

Priestfield was part of the manor of Kingsnorth and was let for £1-13-4. In the ministers' account of 1547-48 it was in the occupation of Nicholas Scott. Nagdon Marsh in Graveney was also part of the manor of Kingsnorth. It was let for the clear sum of £7-16-8 with 3[s] 4[d] going to the parson of Graveney. (B) in 1541-42 gives a lower figure of £1-14-16½, so possibly some land had been sold off by then. In 1546 Richard Fulmerston of Thetford in Norfolk was granted amongst other things a rent reserved on Nagdon Marsh in the grant to Cheyne in 1540.[1191]

[1189] For modern research into the composition and history of the woodland see, A. Wheaten, *The Ancient Woodlands of the Blean* 6th, 7th and 8th Annual Reports 1993-95.

[1190] LP Hen VIII, XV, g 436 (45), XIX, 1, g 812 (48) p. 497, Lewis, p. 38.

[1191] LP Hen VIII, XIII, part 1, no. 585, g 646 (64); XXI, 2, g 200 (24); Lewis, p. 39; Telfer, p. 11.

Horsehops at Brokebridge and Cattisscart were part of the manor of Kingsnorth and were let for £1-13-4 with 2^s 6^d due to the manor of Graveney. By 1541-42 in (B) it was valued at 20^s. On 1 November 1544 Horsoppes in Graveney in the tenure of Robert Derling was granted to William Goodyng alias Goodwyn of Writtle in Essex together with lands in Faversham, Oare and Luddenham in the tenure of Richard Dryland and his son, John, of Faversham.

Gore Marsh with lands in Hernhill called Upland was valued at £8-0-0. £1-4-9 went in a yearly rent to the Archbishop of Canterbury, a pension to the vicar of Hernhill and a wallscot or tax. According to Lewis, Sir John Fineux had granted this marsh to the abbey. In (B) Mentilham and Cockham were added to the list making a total of £10-0-0. All of these were granted on 23 November 1543 to William Sondes, one of the sons of Robert Sondes of Throwley, for £208-16-0. He had three houses lying together in Court Street West (7). Gore Marsh was then in the tenure of Richard Knight and Simon Aunsell.[1192]

The farm or rent of the tenants fishing within the abbey's liberties of the sea and for snout weirs, which were held of the king by fee farm, amounted to £1-13-4 of which £1-0-0 was paid to the king's manor of Milton. This was described in (A) as seven weirs called Sowthewerys and proceeds of the fishing in the sea within the liberty of the admiralty of the monastery. According to Lewis, in 1523-24 the weirs were let to six people at the rent of 3^s 4^d each, making a total of £1-0-0.[1193]

These are the estates that particularly concern us now. The Valor went on to describe the manor of Ellenden in the deanery of Westbere. This had been granted to the abbey by Robert Billesdon for seven years and then it was to be sold. According to Lewis, a group of people, possibly feoffees, had settled this on the abbey with 77 acres of land, 77 acres of pasture, 64 acres of wood and a quit rent of £2-0-11, 53 hens and 6 cocks in Whitstable and Seasalter. It was granted in 1543 to Thomas Arden, who sold it a month later. Lambert's Land, in what is now called Dunkirk, was also granted to him, but had passed to Henry Crispe by 1550.[1194] The manor of Kingsnorth in the deanery of Sutton was granted on 8 July 1540 to Sir Anthony St. Leger of Ulcombe.[1195]

The spiritualities followed with the three parsonages: Boughton was let for £36-0-0, Hernhill for £10-0-0 and Preston next Faversham for £13-6-8. A pension of £3-6-8 was received from the rectory of Luddenham and £1-13-4 from the rectory of Newnham. The total possessions of the spiritualities were £45-11-8.

Then came a list of the fees paid to the abbey's officials. All these people have been considered in the text and can be tracked down through the index. William Roper, esquire, high steward of 'our lands, leets and courts in Kent' received £8-6-8; the bailiff of the town and liberty of Faversham £1-1-4; Robert Coldwell, receiver of the farms and rents £2-13-4; Simon Aunsell, receiver of the manor of Kingsnorth and Upland £3-0-0 and 13^s 4^d for a gown; Joseph Beverley, auditor of the accounts £3-6-8, and Thomas Hungerford, gentleman, receiver of the farm and rents of the manor of Ellenden, Lambertsland, the Blean and Bossenden £3-6-8. The total outlay was £22-8-0.

[1192] LP Hen VIII, XVIII, 2, no. 449 g 62 p. 243, XIX, 2, g 690 (1); Lewis, p. 38.

[1193] For more details see 'The company or fraternity of the free fishermen and Dredgermen of the manor and hundred of Faversham, 1599', Faversham Borough Archives, Alexander Centre, Preston Street, Faversham.

[1194] CKS, under Hernhill map of Lambert's Land about 1825, U1005/E5.

[1195] LP Hen. VIII, XVIII, 1, no. 982 f25, p. 554; 2, g 241 (7), g 327 (7); XIX, 1, g 610 (14) p 372; Lewis, 38; CPR. Ed VI, iii, p. 320; PRC 17/9/150.

In the ministers' account of 1546-47 Robert Coldwell was still the collector of rents. John Wylde was the collector of the rents in the hundred and receiver of the late monastery. Thomas Arden was the farmer and forester of the Blean, who accounted for £3-0-0 paid to George St. Leger as principal forester in an agreement made with the abbey on 15 March 1537. Allowance was made for a fee of £8-6-8 for William Roper and £4-13-4 for Simon Aunsell.

The following year there was allowance of £7-0-0 from the rectory of Boughton, granted to Thomas Hawkyns; 30^{s} for Thomas Persey by the prior and convent; £3-6-8 for the auditor Joseph Beverley, and then pensions for presumably the last four ex-monks, £3-6-8 for Peter Minton, £4-0-0 for Ralph Poste £4-0-0, for Dunstan Goodhew and £5-0-0 for Thomas Dewe or Deve.

The account of Faversham Abbey in the Valor ended with the manor of Bendysh in Essex, which was granted to Sir Richard Rich in 1538. He and his wife sold it to Sir George Broke, Lord Cobham in 1546, eight years later.[1196]

It seems at first sight that two items were not included in the Valor. The first was the value of rents of assize of the free tenants with 18 hens, 2 cocks, 100 eggs and a quarter of barley totalling £57-12-3. These are mentioned in (B) and (C). A note was made in the latter on value: 3^{d} a hen, 2^{d} a cock, 20 eggs 1^{d} and one quarter of barley 3^{s} 4^{d}. The rents came from tenants in the boroughs of Harty, Oare, Ewell, Chetham, Brimstone, Badlesmere, Oldboldisland,, Rode and Broadfield and in Selgrave, Oldgoldyscheld, Graveney and Monkton. The boroughs were connected to the tithings. Originally, a tithing was a company of ten householders, who stood security for each other within the system called frankpledge. Each male over the age of 12 was obliged to be in a tithing. This later became a land division, once regarded as a tenth of a hundred, which was an administrative division of a shire. Representatives of tithings were called tithingman, headborough, petty constables and, in the case of Kent and particularly Faversham, borsholders.

Looking at the survey again, this item was probably covered in the Valor by the yearly rent of Upland in custom, cocks, hens and eggs all rated in money at £52-1-0¾.

The second item, recorded in (B), was the grange at Nethercourt, which was leased to William Marshall at a rent of £31-4-0 together with service at the hundred court of Faversham. In the ministers' account of 1546-47 the farm or lease of the grange came to £39-4-0 for one house in Nethercourt belonging to the abbey with all the barns and other buildings and 217½ acres and half a rod of land in the tenure of William and John Marshall, which had been granted to them by the abbey. It was now in the tenure of Stephen Motte, who claimed 40^{s} that the Marshalls had had because they should have had seven gallons of ale a week and half the grains of every brewing. Their lease had expired and Motte had the reversion for 20 years. The clause about the 40^{s} had been left out, but Motte successfully had it restored. Sir Anthony St. Leger was granted a grain rent out of the grange on 27 June 1541 and in 1558 James Bassett Esquire, one of the gentlemen of the Privy Chamber, was granted a 21 year lease which recited earlier leases and went into great details about customary services and agricultural practice. On 27 June 1570 a further 21 year lease was granted to Ralph Chamberlayne, a porter[1197] of the Tower of London. Again with many details of customs and practices.[1198]

[1196] LP Hen VIII. XIII, 1, g1519 (69), XXI, 1, g 1166 (73) p 581.

[1197] *O.E.D.* Porter; 1. a. One who has charge of a door or gate, esp. at the entrance of a fortified town or of a castle or other large building, a public institution, etc.; a gate-keeper, door-keeper, janitor.

[1198] LP Hen. VIII, XVI, p. 721, CPR 4&5 P&M, p. 284, CPR 1569-72, p.53; W. Lambarde, *A perambulation of Kent* (1570) reprinted Adams and Dart (1970), p. 19.

If it was indeed left out it was a substantial omission, £31-4-0 on the total net value of £286-12-6¾. Finally, some useful, general notes were made at the bottom of the Lambeth document relating to matters not mentioned elsewhere. First it dealt with the royalties belonging to the abbey.[1199]

> 'In the first place the Courte of Admyralltye with all profittes of waifes straies shipwreckes and other casualties of the Sea from the Fludmede to the beacon downe in the sea And from the beacon to Tenham flete whereof the one moyete is the archebusshoppys of Canturbury the other longyth to the Monastery And from Tenham flete to Ryde Ferye and from thens to Snowte weare

Secondly with the nomination of the mayor:

> 'The nomination of the mayor of Feversham longith to the Kynges Highenes by the right of the same Monastery and to gyve hym his othe. The towne hath been accustomed to electe 2 or 3 persons which they esteme able And presente theym to the Monastery and there one to be nominated by the Abbot and the Abbot to gyve hym his othe

It then gave the number of free tenants of the abbey as 360 and above. It added that there was a master of a hospital for poor people in the town, but no knight's fee. Finally the stock and store in the hands of farmers was worth £21-0-0 and there were 2530 acres of woods. A comparison with the survey of 1499 needs detailed analysis later. Many of the items are virtually the same. Land in Bride Lane in London had been granted to the King 'for the enlargement of the ground for the king's buildings' in 1521. It had consisted of a capital messuage and garden which constituted the Abbot of Faversham's London residence. It was roughly in the corner of what is now Bride Lane and New Bridge Street, but in 1521 there was no New Bridge Street and the property overlooked the River Fleet. According to John Strype, 'Bride Lane cometh out of Fleet Street by St. Bridget's Churchyard, which, with a turning passage by Bridewell and the Ditch side, falleth down to Woodmonger's Wharfs, by the Thames. This lane is of note for the many hatters there inhabiting.' Henry VIII built a fine house here for the reception of Charles V and his nobles in 1522. The abbey was allowed in return to purchase lands to the annual value of £10 elsewhere.[1200]

What of the men who bought the abbey property? I would confirm for Faversham at a humbler level of society what Michael Zell has said for Kent generally.[1201] The would-be purchasers were already on the scene before the dissolution, anxious to increase their landholdings. In 1540, when sales began in earnest, the government laid down certain rules. First, it said that all the estates were to be held by knights' service, which obliged the holder to pay wardship for an heir under 21 and the marriage of a ward as well as that of the widow. Knights' service was bitterly resented and was only abolished in 1660. Secondly, the holder was to pay a tenth of the net annual value of the property to the crown each year, though we have seen this was not easy to collect from the Arden estate. Thirdly, the holdings were to be sold at a price of twenty years purchase of the next annual value for agricultural land and fifteen years purchase for urban

---

1199 LPL ED 2006 and former ED 2070 now to be described as ED 2006. Latin & English m. 8. Dorse of m. 1: *Holdings of the Monastery of St Augustines in Canterbury*.

1200 LP Hen. VIII, III, i, no. 1177; E. G. O'Donoghue, *Bridewell Hospital: Palace, Prison, Schools*, (Bodley Head 1923), 4 etc.; Alan Stapleton, *London Lanes* (London, 1930), p. 147.

1201 M. Zell, 'The Mid-Tudor Market in Crown Land in Kent', *Arch. Cant.* xcvii pp. 53-70; J. Youings, 'The Terms of the disposal of the Devon Monastic lands 1536-58.'*EHR*, 1954, pp. 119-134.

property. In 1544, single properties worth less than 40^{s} per annum could be sold in free socage rather than knight service, as Arden did.

Three of the men belonging to the dozen families who were granted half of all the crown lands in Kent were involved in Faversham: Sir Thomas Cheyne, Anthony St. Leger and Anthony Aucher. Thomas Arden purchased abbey lands worth about £40 a year, but he was never lord of the manor nor lord of the hundred. These remained in Crown hands and he was merely one of its officials.

Most of the new landlords were already well established in the area and there was also a high degree of continuity among the actual occupiers of the estate. The abbey lands had been farmed to lay farmers long before the dissolution, and, in most cases, the sitting tenants remained in possession even as the landlords changed. As leases fell in, local men remained the obvious choice as farmers. Most lands granted by the Crown came to their new owners not only with sitting tenants, but with their rents fixed at early-sixteenth century levels. This was precisely Thomas Arden's problem, of which he was only too well aware. As Zell concludes, 'the new landowners normally had to wait several decades before they could take advantage of rising prices and land values to raise rents and fines on lands they had acquired from the crown.'

From the West Country, J. H. Bettey has said that there were 'courtiers, councillors, office-holders, royal servants of the king's household, gentry families, merchants, lawyers and officials ... many of whom were already leasing monastic lands or acting as stewards, bailiffs, auditors or receivers of rents for the monastic houses.'[1202] We can see that clearly in Faversham, where the width and depth of lay involvement in the economy of the abbey since at least 1500 is impressive. With the benefit of hindsight we might say that, quite apart from the religious issues, that was a strange state of affairs, and that, if the laymen became land-hungry, anything might happen.

1202 J.H. Bettey, *Suppression of the monasteries in the West Country,* (Alan Sutton, 1989), p. 132.

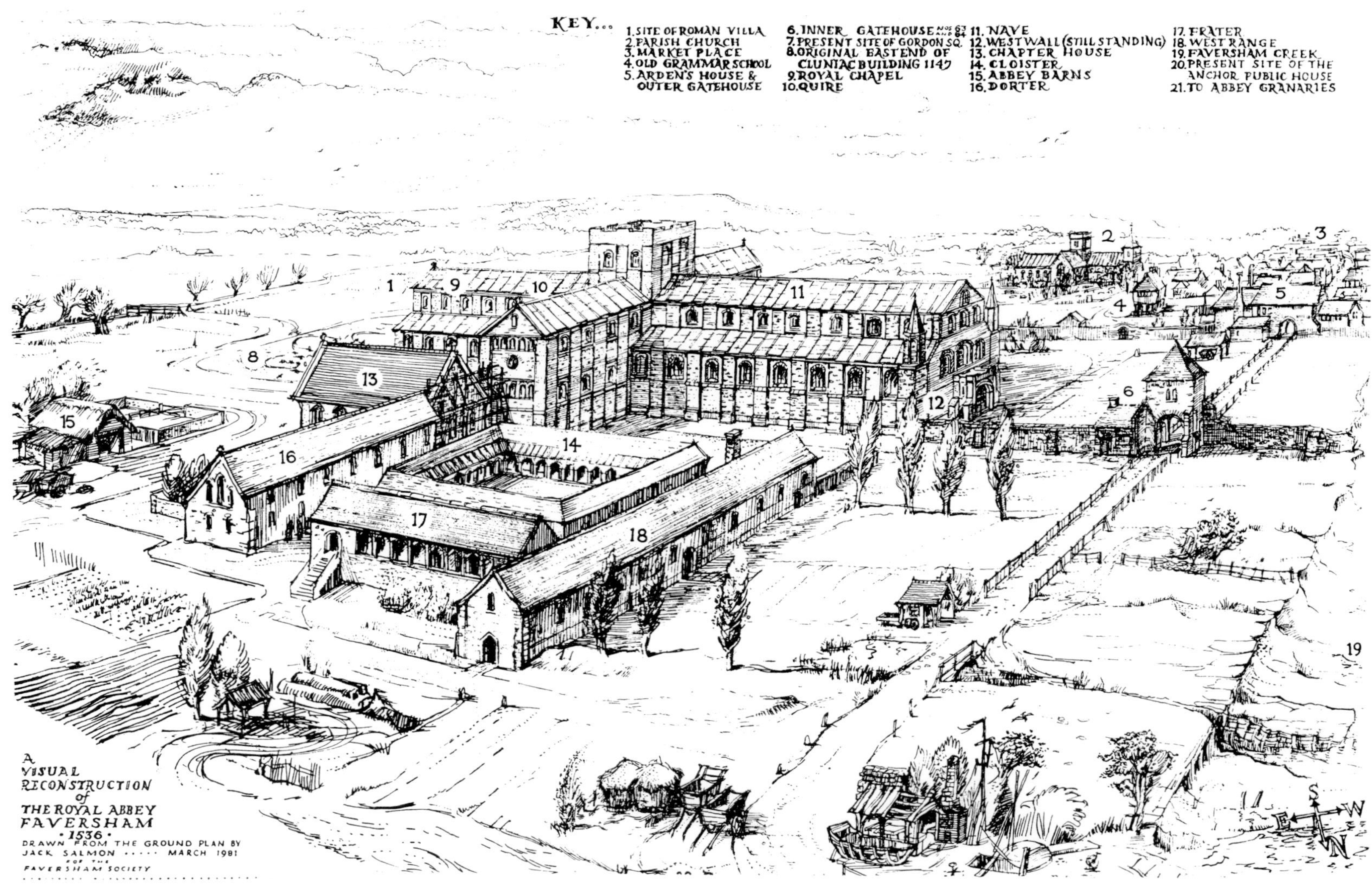
KEY...
1. SITE OF ROMAN VILLA
2. PARISH CHURCH
3. MARKET PLACE
4. OLD GRAMMAR SCHOOL
5. ARDEN'S HOUSE & OUTER GATEHOUSE
6. INNER GATEHOUSE NOS 63 AND 84
7. PRESENT SITE OF GORDON SQ.
8. ORIGINAL EASTEND OF CLUNIAC BUILDING 1147
9. ROYAL CHAPEL
10. QUIRE
11. NAVE
12. WESTWALL (STILL STANDING)
13. CHAPTER HOUSE
14. CLOISTER
15. ABBEY BARNS
16. DORTER
17. FRATER
18. WEST RANGE
19. FAVERSHAM CREEK
20. PRESENT SITE OF THE ANCHOR PUBLIC HOUSE
21. TO ABBEY GRANARIES
A VISUAL RECONSTRUCTION of THE ROYAL ABBEY FAVERSHAM · 1536 ·
DRAWN FROM THE GROUND PLAN BY JACK SALMON .... MARCH 1981
FOR THE FAVERSHAM SOCIETY
S
E
W
N

THE TRANSCRIPT

Parchment Cover:

Rentale ville of Faversham with other thynges for the towne.

There are two memoranda on the flyleaf, the top quarter of which has been cut out:

A covenaunte made the xxth day of Aprell betwyne Wyllyam Castlock of Faversham and Gorrett Gossonsone and Rycharde Hubbarde of Sandewyche for the selynge of a chamber ronde aboute and makyng of a portoll the crest albester the fasshyon of the creste of the newe bede in the sayde camber, and they to have for there payns xLvj^{s} viij^{d}, and mete drynk and logyng.

Resevyde of ?Mistress Wodds	xxx^{s}
Resevyde more	iij$^{£}$ xiij^{s} iiij^{d} for the
For the Vykar of Preston	vj^{s} vj^{d}
For Robarte Chapman	viij^{s}
Resevyd ?Sendes that	x$^{£}$

folio 1

Courtestrete West

The table[1203]	First Robert Maycotte Steward holdeth of the lorde to ferme a message and half the almonery[1204] berne and payith by yere to the table	xLvj^{s} viij^{d}	1
The table	Thomas Grene holdeth of the lorde to ferme a message next the lane ledying to the Nethergrene and payith by yere	vj^{s} viij^{d}	2
The table	Olyver Charnoke holdeth of the lorde to a ferme a message with a garden and payith by yere	xiij^{s} iiij^{d}	3
The table	James Grigge holdeth of the lorde to ferme a message and payith by yere	viij^{s}	4
The table	John Page holdeth of the lorde to ferme a message with a garden and payith by yere	xiij^{s} iiij^{d}	5
The table	Jone Hilles wedowe holdeth of the lorde to ferme a message and payith by yere	viij^{s}	6
The table	William Sondes holdeth of the lorde to ferme iij messuages with their gardeyns together lying and payith by yere	xx^{s}	7a, b, c
The table	Joseph Beverley holdeth of the lorde a message and renteth by yere	vj^{d}	8
The table	Robert Maycot junior holdeth of the lorde a message and renteth by yere	vj^{d}	9
The table	John Sede holdeth of the lorde a message and renteth by yere	vj^{d}	10
The table	The same John Sede holdeth of the lorde to ferme the site of of a message and payith by yere	xiij^{d} j hen	11
The table	John Collyn holdeth of the lorde the syte of a message and renteth by yere	viij^{d}	12
The table	The lorde holdeth the site of a message next that and lyeth voyde	viij^{d}	13

[1203] The Latin in this column, Mensa, Elemosynarye, Camerar, Fermerar, Capelle Sancte Marie etc. have been translated. There are other items in the text in Latin all of which have been translated, like gallina for hen, gallus for cock. The abbreviation used by the scribe has lead to some confusion in distinguishing which is which.

[1204] *Elmosynary*. The almoner was the officer whose duty it was to dispense alms.

The table	Richard Frende holdeth of the lorde a messuage and renteth by yere	vj^{d}	14
	Total of the first page	vj$^{£}$ v^{d}	
folio 1 verso			
The table	The heires of Robert A Fale holdeth of the lorde a messuage and renteth by yere	vj^{d}	15
The table	The same heires holdeth of the lorde another messuage next unto that called the Stonehouse[1205] and renteth by yere	xij^{d}	16
The table	Thomas Barber holdeth of the lorde to ferme iij messuages together lying and payith by yere	xxij^{s} ij hens	17a, b, c
Sacrist Chamberlain	William Castlock holdeth of the lorde a messuage with a garden and renteth by yere to the sexten vj^{d} and to the chamberlain vj^{d} the amount	xij^{d}	18
The table	The wardeyns of the parisshe churche of Faversham holdeth of the lorde ij messuages together lying and renteth by yere	ij^{s} viij^{d}	19a, b
The table	John Sede holdeth of the lorde a messuage and renteth by yere	vj^{d}	20
The table	Thomas Smyth holdeth of the lorde a messuage with a garden and renteth by yere	ij^{s} vj^{d}	21
The table Almoner	The same Thomas holdeth of the lorde a messuage next that and renteth by yere to the table xvij^{d} and to the Almoner vj^{d} the amount	xxiij^{d}	22
The table Almoner	The said Thomas Smyth holdeth of the lorde another messuage next that and renteth by yere to the table xvij^{d} and to the Almoner vj^{d} the amount	xxiij^{d}	23
The table	The heires of Roger Hall holdeth of the lorde the corner messuage of the north side of Keylane and renteth by yere, to the table xviij^{d} and to the Chamberlain xiiij^{d}. the amount	ij^{s} viij^{d}	24

<u>Messuages sett at the North part of the Key</u>

The table	John Champnes holdeth of the lorde to ferme iij messuages and a storehouse together sett with the crane there, and payith by yere	iiij^{s} j hen	25a, b, c
folio 2			
The table	Harry Hatche holdeth of the lorde there a storehouse and renteth by yere	viij^{d}	26
The table	Raffe Wolgate holdeth of the lorde there a storehouse and renteth by yere	viij^{d}	27

<u>Keylane South</u>

The table	The said Harry Hatche holdeth of the lorde another storehouse of the south part there and renteth by yere	viij^{d}	28
Kyngesmyll	The heires of Peter Reve holdeth of the lorde ij cotages and renteth by yere to the Kyngesmyll	v^{d}	29a, b
Kyngesmyll	The feoffes of Richard Lull holdeth of the lorde one messuage with a garden callyd the Almesse house and renteth by yere to the Kyngesmill	ij^{d} ob	30
Kyngesmyll	The heyres of William More, waterman, holdeth of the lorde one messuage late William Willowes, and renteth by yere to the Kynges Mylle	ij^{d} ob.	31

[1205] See page 427 for the entry relating to the Stonehouse in Courtestrete East and comment page 395 & 396.

Kyngesmyll	Item iiij messuages callyd Bollys tenementes together lying and renteth by yere to the Kyngesmyll	x^{d}	32a, b, c, d

Courtestrete Est

The table	Rycharde Drylande, senior gentleman holdeth of the lorde to ferme the greate messuage at the Town Gate with the gardyn therto belongyng and payith by yere	xL^{s}	33
The table	Rycharde Goslyng holdeth of the lorde to ferme a messuage and payith by yere	xiij^{s} iiij^{d}	34
The table	The wardens of the parisshe church of Faversham holdeth ij messuages together lying and renteth by yere	xiiij^{d}	35a, b
The table	Item the lorde holdeth a pece of voyde grounde some tyme buylded nowe[1206] in the occupying of William Sondes that was wont to pay by yere	xiiij^{s}	36

folio 2 verso

The table Chapel of St. Mary	The vycar of Faversham holdeth of the lorde a messuage somtyme ij messuages with their gardens nowe in one and renteth by yere to the table ij^{s} iij^{d}, and to the chappell of our Lady ij^{s}. The amount	iiij^{s} iiij^{d}	37a, b
The table Infirmarer	William Venour holdeth of the lorde to ferme iiij messuages with their gardens and payith by yere to the table xiiij^{s} viij^{d} and to the Infirmarer[1207] ij^{s}, the amount	xvj^{s} iiij^{d}	38a, b, c, d
The table Sacrist	The same William holdeth of the lorde ij messuages together lying and renteth by yere, to the table ij^{s} vij^{d} ob. and to the sexten ob.	ij^{s} viij^{d}	39a, b
The table	The heyres of Robert Turnour holdeth of the lorde a messuage and renteth by yere	ij^{d}	40
Rectory of Faversham	The heires of John Turnour holdeth of the lorde a messuage late William Colwels by yere to the parsonage of Faversham	viij^{d}	41
Rectory of Faversham	The heires of Edmunde Martyn holdeth of the lorde a messuage late Thomas Childmelles by yere to the parsonage aforesaid	viij^{d}	42
Rectory of Faversham	Reynold Hobnett holds of the lord a messuage late John Dunnynges senior and before that John Lyons by yere to the parsonage aforesaid	[blank]	43
[blank]	William Castlock holds of the lord ij messuages late the heires of Richard Ledmede somtyme John at Chrowche by yere	[blank]	44a, b
The table	William Blackborne holdeth of the lorde to ferme a messuage callyd the Stonehouse and payith by yere	xiiij^{s}	45
Chapel of St. Mary	William Castlock holdeth of the lorde a messuage at the Northwest corner of the Churche Lane and renteth by yere to the chappell of our Lady	xij^{d}	46
	[total of page]	v$^{£}$ viij^{s} viij^{d}	

1206 The words from *nowe ... yere xiiij*^{s} are added in slightly smaller hand but it appears to be the same scribe. It seems that the scribe wrote the document and then returned to add maginalia and some additions. For instance fol.. 1 Maycot, the scribe has added 'a mes' ' all in the same hand and ink.

1207 Given here and later as *fermerer*.

Churche Lane North

Chamberlain Chapel of St. Mary	The said William Castlock holdeth of the lorde iij messuages and renteth by yere to the Chamberlain[1208] xij^{d} and the chapel of Saint Mary xij^{d}	ij^{s}	47a, b, c
	~~The same William holdeth by ferme~~[1209]		

folio 3

Chapel of St. Mary	The vycar of Faversham holdeth of the lorde a garden adioynyng to the vycarage and renteth by yere to the chapell of our Lady	xij^{d}	48

Churche Lane South

Chapel of St. Mary	John Norton knyght holdeth of the lorde a princypall messuage next the churche yard and renteth by yere to the chapell of our Lady of Faversham	ij^{s}	49
Sacrist	The said John Norton holdeth of the lorde a bern and a courtlage to the foreseid messuage belongyng and renteth by yere to the sexten	xx^{d}	50
Almoner	The same John holdeth of the lorde a pece of grounde adioyning to a dovehouse to the said messuage belongyng and renteth by the yere to the Almoner	ij^{s}	51
Not to us[1210]	John Champneys holdeth a messuage late Robert Lacys and before Robert Billesdons by yere	To the usse of the poore bye the feoffmente made to the vycar	52
Not to us	The feoffes of Robert Byllesdon holdeth one messuage and iij cotages annexed by yere	[of Faversham] Redbourne, the maior and others	53a, b, c, d

Northstrete West

The Table Almoner	The comynaltye of the towne of Faversham holdeth of the lorde a messuage callyd the Anker and renteth by yere to the table xij^{d} and to the Almoner vj^{d}, the amount	xviij^{d}	54
The table	Thomas Blackbourne holdeth of the lorde to ferme a messuage next that and payith by yere	viij^{s}	55
The table Chamberlain	John Davy holdeth of the lorde a messuage and renteth by yere to the table xvj^{d} and to the Chamberlain xij^{d}, the amount	ij^{s} iiij^{d}	56
The table Chamberlain	The same John holdeth of the lorde another messuage and renteth by yere to the table ix^{d} and to the Chamberlain iij^{s} iiij^{d}, the amount	iiij^{s} j^{d}	57
The table	The said John holdeth of the lorde to ferme a pece of lond lying in his garden and payith by the yere	ij^{d}	58

folio 3 verso

1208 From here to the end of entry is added later in a smaller hand, probably by the same scribe.

1209 An entry of three lines scored through.

1210 Non nobis.

The table	William Hunt holdeth of the lorde to ferme a message with a storehouse to the same belongyng and paith by yere	viij^{s}	59a, b
The table	Robert Maycott senior holdeth of the lorde a message and renteth by yere	xiiij^{d}	60
The table	The same Robert holdeth of the lorde another message and renteth by yere	xij^{d}	61
The table	Harry Cryps holdeth of the lorde a message and renteth by yere	ij^{s} vj^{d}	62
The table	The heires of William Best holdeth of the lorde a message and renteth by yere	xix^{d}	63
The table	Rychard Frende holdeth of the lorde a message next that and renteth by yere	xviij^{d}	64
The table	The feoffes of Bartylmewe Symon holdeth of the lorde a message and renteth by yere	xviij^{d}	65
The table Chamberlain	The feoffes of Raff Asshebury holdeth of the lorde a message and renteth by yere to the table xij^{d} and the chamberlain xx^{d} ob. Total	ij^{s} viij^{d} ob.	66
The table	The same feoffes holdeth of the lorde a corner message and renteth by yere, to the table xij^{d} and to the chamberlain ij^{s} v^{d}, total	iij^{s} v^{d}	67
Sacrist	Coke the bocher holdeth of the sexten to ferme a corner message next Est Gorewellane and paith by yere	xvj^{s}	68
The table	Raffe Wolgate holdeth of the lorde ij messuages together lying and renteth by yere	iiij^{s} j^{d}	69a, b
The table	The heires of William Fylpott holdeth of the lorde a message and renteth by yere	vj^{d}	70
Chamberlain	Richard holdeth of the lorde a message and renteth by yere to the chamberlain	xiiij^{d}	71
The table	John Pullen senior holdeth of the lorde a message and renteth by yere	iij^{d}	72
The table	Hugh Howlett holdeth of the lorde a message and renteth by yere	vj^{d}	73
The table	Robert Maycott senior holdeth of the lorde a corner message and renteth by yere	iij^{d}	74
The table Almoner Chamberlain	Rychard Coldwell holdeth of the lorde a message callyd the Horne and renteth by yere, to the table xij^{d}, and to the almoner xij^{d} and to the chamberlain ij^{s} v^{d}, ij hens, total	iiij^{s} v^{d} ij hens	75
Chamberlain	The said Richard holdeth of the lorde another house to the same adioyning and renteth by yere to the chamberlain	iiij^{d} and j hen	76
The table	The feoffes of John Belynger holdeth of the lorde, a message and renteth by yere	xx^{d}	77
Chamberlain	William A Borne holdeth of the Priorisse of Davynton a message late David Powelles to the which message the seid William A Bourne hath purchesed an augmentacion of the lord Abbott next the strete there, and renteth by yere to the chamberlain	viij^{d} and j hen	78a, b
Infirmarer	The infirmarer holdeth a message late lett to ferme to Rychard Coldwell and payith by yere	xxx^{s}	79
The table	The lorde holdeth a message callyd the Garrett and lyeth voyde	xiij^{s} iiij^{d}	80
The table	John Prowde holdeth of the lorde to ferme a message called the Beare and payith by yere	xL^{s}	81

	[Total]	vij$^{£}$ xij^{s} vij^{d} ob	
	<u>Northstret Est</u>		
The table	Laurens Hilles holdeth of the lorde a messuage and renteth by yere	xij^{d}	82
The table	The same Laurens holdeth of the Lord another messuage next that and renteth by yere	iij^{s} iiij^{d}	83
The table	The comynaltye of the towne of Faversham holdeth of the lorde a messuage and renteth by yere	vj^{d}	84
The table	Robart Maycott senior holdeth of the lorde a messuage next that and renteth by yere	vj^{d}	85
The table	The feoffes of John Cony holdeth of the lorde a messuage and renteth by yere	viij^{d}	86
folio 4 verso			
The table Chapel of St Mary	The same feoffes holdeth of the lorde another messuage and renteth by yere, to the table xij^{d} and to the chappell of our Lady ij^{s}, total	iij^{s}	87
The table Sacrist & Chapel of St. Mary	Rychard Dryland the yongar holdeth of the lorde a messuage and renteth by yere, to the table xij^{d} and to the sexten xx^{d} and to the chapell of our Lady j^{d} and j hen, total	ij^{s} ix^{d} and j hen	88
Almoner	The said Rycharde Drylande holdeth of the lorde to fee ferme of the est parte of the forsaid messuage a pece of land and renteth by yere to the almoner	iiij^{s}	89
The table & Chapel St. Mary	Item *[blank]* holdeth of the lorde messuages late Egles and renteth by yere to the table xij^{d} and the chappell of our Lady v^{d}, total	xvij^{d}	90a, b
The table	Harry Cryps holdeth of the lorde a princypall messuage somtyme ij messuages and renteth by yere	vj^{s} ix^{d}	91
The table	The said Harry Crypps holdeth of the lorde an augmentation before the wyndowes of the said princypall messuage and payith by yere	iiij^{d}	92
The table	Reynolde Lewknor gentleman holdeth of the lorde in fee ferme a great voide grounde, a barn with a courtlage and a garden with a dovehouse and renteth by yere	xij^{d}	93a, b, c
The table Chamberlain Sacrist	The feoffes of William Fylpott holdeth of the lorde a messuage with a malthouse and certeyn garden to them belongyng and renteth by yere, to the table xiiij^{s} v^{d}, to the chamberlain iiij^{s}, and to the sacrist xiij^{d}	xix^{s} vj^{d}	94a, b, c
The table	William Norton, gentleman holdeth of the lorde a messuage and renteth by yere	xxj^{d}	95
The table	The feoffes of Thebalde Evyas holdeth of the lorde a messuage callyd the almessehouse and renteth by yere	xxj^{d}	96
The table Chamberlain	William Castlock holdeth of the lorde a messuage and renteth by yere, to the table iiij^{s}, and to the chamberlain iiij^{s}, total	viij^{s}	97

folio 5

The table	Harry Cryps holdeth of the lorde a messuage late Margarett Hoornes and renteth by yere	ix^{d}	98
The table	John Bryngbourne holdeth of the lorde a messuage and renteth by yere	v^{s} ij^{d}	99
The table Almoner	William Belk holdeth of the lorde a messuage and renteth by yere, to the table viij^{d}, and to the almoner ij^{s}, total	ij^{s} viij^{d}	100
Sacrist	John Goldfynche holdeth of the lorde a messuage and renteth by yere to the sexten	vij^{s} viij^{d}	101
The table& Chapel of St. Mary	John Hampton holdeth of the lorde to ferme ij shoppes in the market place with the welhouse to the same apperteynyng and payith by yere to the chapell of our Lady xij^{s} and to the table xxviij^{s}, total	xL^{s}	102a, b, c
Chapel of St. Mary	The forsaid John Goldfynche holdeth of the lorde a messuage next Hogmarkett lane and renteth by yere to the chappell of our Lady	iiij^{d}	103
		~~iiij~~$^{£}$ v$^{£}$ xij^{s} xj^{d}[1211]	

<u>The myddell rowe next the gaole</u>

The table	Richard Frende holdeth of the lorde to ferme a messuage and payith by yere [1212]? Memorandum Thomas [?Squyer]	xvj^{s}	104
The table Sacrist	Memorandum that William Deny holdeth of the lorde a messuage and renteth by yere, to the table xij^{d} and to the sexten ij^{s} and holdeth of the lorde to ferme an augmentacion and payith by yere iiij^{d}, total	iij^{s} iiij^{d}	105
Precentor Infirmary	The wardens of the parisshe churche of Faversham holdeth of the lorde ij shoppis nowe in one and renteth by yere to the chaunter xx^{d} and to the infermerar by yere xx^{d}, total	iij^{s} iiij^{d}	106a, b
The table	The same wardens holdeth of the lorde to ferme ij augmentacions adioynyng to the said ij shoppis and payith by yere	viij^{d}	107a, b

folio 5 verso

The table	John Kebett holdeth of the lorde a messuage and renteth by yere	ij^{s}	108
The table	The said John holdeth of the lorde to ferme an augmentacion to the same messuage adioyning and paith by yere	iiij^{d}	109
The table	Harry Hatche holdeth of the lorde a messuage and renteth by yere	ij^{s}	110
The table	The said Harry holdeth of the lorde to ferme an augmentacion to the same messuage adioyning and payith by yere	iiij^{d}	111
The table	Mawde Mylkeham holdeth of the lorde a messuage and renteth by yere	ij^{s}	112
The table	The saide Mawde holdeth of the lorde to ferme an augmentacion to the same messuage adioynyng and payith by yere	iiij^{d}	113
The table	Thomas Childmells holdeth of the lorde a messuage and renteth by yere	ij^{s}	114
The table	The said Thomas holdeth of the lorde to ferme ij augmentacions and payith by yere. Now Goodhewe holds to farm.[1213]	xiiij^{d}	115a, b
The table	John Grene tailor holdeth of the lorde to ferme a messuage and payith by yere	viij^{s}	116

[1211] Corrected and overwritten on what appears to be xij^{d}.

[1212] Interlined in another illegible hand.

[1213] This is on a line by itself in a small hand. Probably it refers to the line below.

The table	William Belk holdeth of the lorde to ferme a corner messuage and payith by yere	xij^{s}	117
		Liij^{s} vj^{d}	

<u>Shamelles in the markett place</u>

	Memorandum that ther be in the first rowe next Westrete x shamelles Whereof the		
Chamberlain	First the heires of Robert A Fale holdeth of the lorde and renteth by yere to the chamberlain	iij^{s} iiij^{d}	118

folio 6 verso

Chamberlain	William Wyer holdeth of the lorde the ij^{de} shamell and renteth by yere to the chamberlain	iiij^{d}	119
Chamberlain	The heires of Robert A Fale holdeth of the lorde iij^{de} shamell and renteth by yere to the chamberlain	ix^{d}	120
The table	Item the lorde holdeth the iiijth and lyeth voide	iiij^{d}	121
Chamberlain	Robert Coldwell holdeth the vth of the lorde and renteth by yere to the chamberlain	xx^{d}	122
The table	The same Robert holdeth of the lorde the vjth and renteth by the yere to the table	xx^{d}	123
The table	The heires of John Bynder holdeth of the lorde the vijth shamell and renteth by yere to the table	iiij^{d}	124
The table	Item the lorde holdeth the viijth shamell and lyeth voide	viij^{d}	125
Chamberlain	John Beawty late helde ~~holdeth~~ of the lorde the ixth shamell and renteth by yere to the chamberlain	iiij^{d}	126
Chamberlain	The same John holdeth of the lorde the xth shamell and renteth by yere to the chamberlain	iiij^{d}	127
		ix^{s} ix^{d}	

<u>In the seconde rowe ther is ix shamelles</u>

	whereof		
Chamberlain	The heires of Laurens Straynsham late helde of the lorde and first and renteth by yere to the chamberlain	iiij^{d}	128
The table	The heires of John Bynder holdeth of the lorde the seconde and renteth by yere to the table	ix^{d}	129
The table	The same heires holdeth of the lorde the iij^{d} shamelles and renteth by yere to the table	xij^{d}	130
The table Sacrist	The said heires holdeth of the lorde the iiijth shamelles and renteth by yere to the table ix^{d} and to the sexten iiij^{d}	xiij^{d}	131
The table	The same heires holdeth of the lorde the vth shamell and renteth by yere to the table	viij^{d}	132
	Memorandum that the said iiij shamelles of the heires of Bynder be now made in iij shamelles		

folio 6 verso

The table	The same heires holdeth of the lorde the vjth shamell and renteth by yere to the table	viij^{d}	133

Chamberlain	The heires of John Parke holdeth of the lorde the vijth shamell and renteth by yere to the chamberlain	iiij^{d}	134
Sacrist	The sexten holdeth the viij shamell and it lyeth voyde	iiij^{s}[1214]	135
The table	The ixth shamell the heires of the forsayd Bynder holdeth of the lorde and renteth by yere, to the table	vj^{d}	136
		ix^{s} iiij^{d}	

<u>In the iij^{de} rowe ther be viij shamelles</u>

	Wherof		
The table	The heires of Robert A Fale holdeth of the lorde the first and renteth by yere to the table	iij^{s} iiij^{d}	137
Chamberlain	The same heires holdeth of the lorde the ij^{de} shamell and renteth by yere to the chamberlain	iij^{s} iiij^{d}	138
Chamberlain	The heires of John Parke holdeth of the lorde the iij^{de} shamell and renteth by yere to the chamberlain	iiij^{d}	139
The table	The same heires holdeth of the lorde the iiijth and vth shamell and renteth by yere to the table	viij^{d}	140, 141
Chamberlain	The same heires holdeth of the lorde the vjth shamell and renteth by yere to the chamberlain	iiij^{d}	142
Chamberlain	The said heires holdeth of the lorde the vijth shamell and renteth by yere to the chamberlain	iiij^{d}	143
	Memorandum that v of the aforsaid shamelles ar now made but iiij as it appereth by the buyldyng of them		
folio 7			
The table	The Priorisse of Davyngton holdeth of the lorde in the markett a shamell somtyme callyd the Puddyng shamell and lyeth voide, and renteth by yere to the table	iiij^{d}	144
The table	Item the lorde holdeth a shamell adioynyng to the same and lyeth voide	iiij^{d}	145
The table	Item the lorde holdeth iiij shoppis under the pillorye and lyeth voide	vj^{s} viij^{d}	146a, b, c, d
The table	John Hampton holdeth of the lorde to ferme the fysshe shamells in the fysshemarkett with the voide grounde therunto annexed and payith by yere	xiij^{s} iiij^{d}	147a, b

<u>The myddell rowe from the fysshe markett unto Hogcrosse</u>

The table	Item the lorde holdeth a messuage callid the corner messuage nowe voide	xx^{s}	148
Almoner	The heires of John Goodwyn holdeth of the lorde a messuage and renteth by yere to the almoner	xv^{d}	149
The table	The same heires holdeth of the lord to ferme an augmentacion to the same messuage adioynyng and payith by yere	ij^{d}	150
Chamberlain Sacrist	The said heires holdeth of the lorde iiij messuages together lying and renteth by yere to the chamberlain xij^{d} to the sexten xij^{d} and to the table ij^{s}, total	iiij^{s}	151a, b, c, d

[1214] This appears to be an error, should be pence.

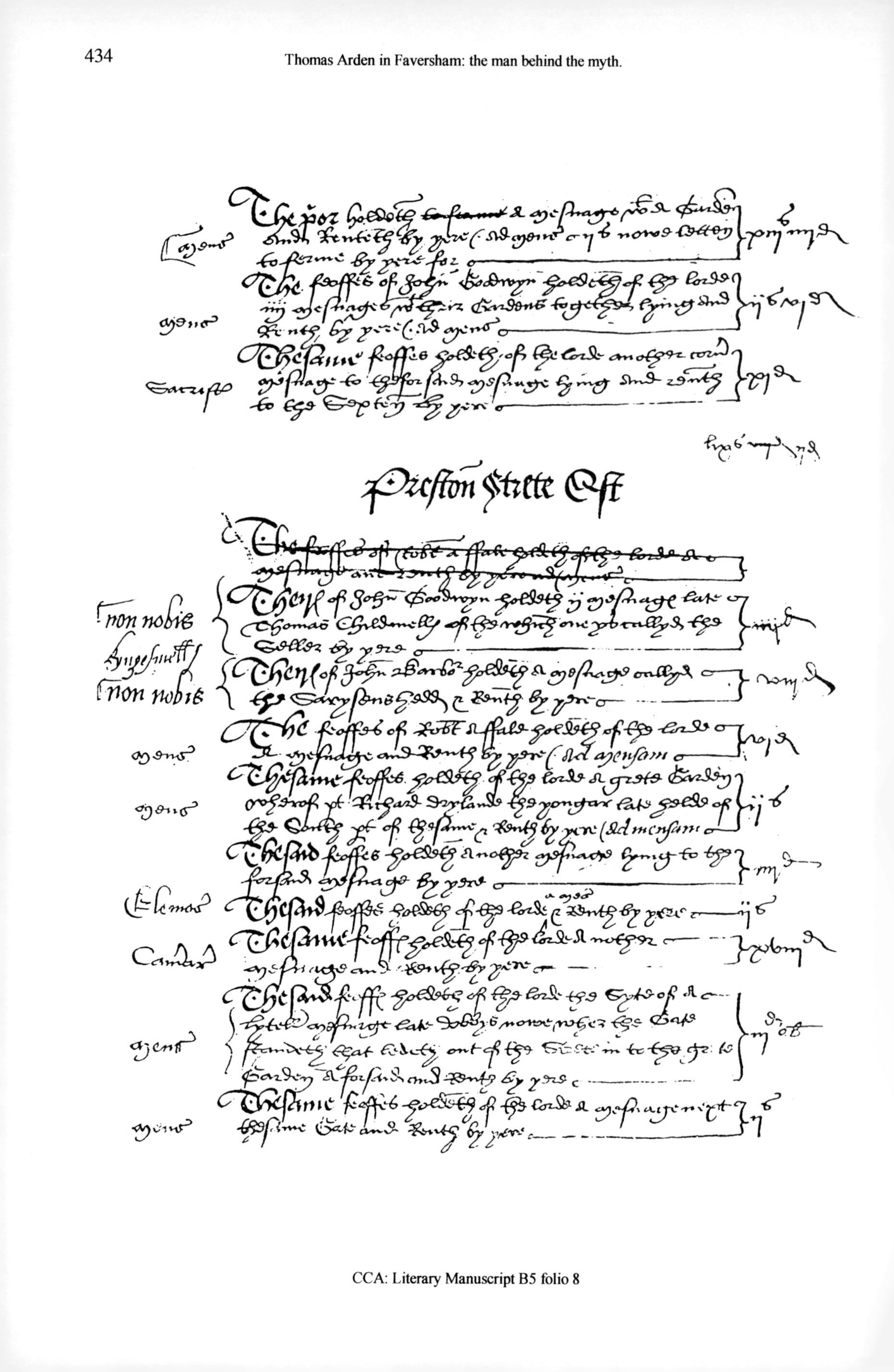

Preston Strete Est

CCA: Literary Manuscript B5 folio 8

The table	The same heires holdeth of the lorde to ferme iiij augmentacions to the to the said iiij messuages adioynyng and payith by yere	viij^{d}	152a, b, c, d
		xxvj^{s} j^{d}	
	<u>Est strete North</u>		
Almoner	The feoffes of Robert Withiott holdeth of the lorde a messuage with a garden and renteth by yere to the almoner	xxiij^{d}	153
Sacrist	The same feoffes holdeth of the lorde a malthouse and other messuages to the forsaid messuage adioynyng and renteth by yere to the sexten	ix^{d}	154a,b,c,d
folio 7 verso			
The table	John Sayer holdeth of the lorde to ferme a garden callyd the Apple Garden and payith by yere	v^{s} iiij^{d}	155
The table	The feoffes of Richard Amyse holdeth ij messuages of the lorde and renteth by yere to the table	ij^{s}	156a, b
Sacrist	Adam Princhett holdeth of the lorde a messuage with a garden and renteth by yere to the sexten	ij^{s} iiij^{d} and half a hen	157
Sacrist	The same Adam holdeth of the lorde another messuage with a garden and renteth by yere to the sexten	xvj^{d} and half a hen	158
Sacrist	The said Adam holdeth of the lorde another messuage and renteth by year to the sexten	xvj^{d} and j hen	159
Chamberlain	John Sayer holdeth of the lorde to ferme a litell messuage and a courtlage and payith by yere to the chamberlain	ij^{s} vj^{d}	160a, b
Sacrist	The feoffes of Robert Wythiott holdeth of the lorde a lytell messuage to the same courtlage adioynyng and renteth by yere to the sexten	iij^{d}	161
Almoner	The same feoffes holdeth of the lorde a barn with a lytell tofft of land to the same adioynyng and renteth by yere to the almoner	vj^{d}	162a, b
Sacrist	The sexten holdeth ij messuages and lett them to ferme to dyvers men by yere for	xj^{s}	163a, b
Sacrist	The said sexten holdeth a garden next Lodry lane and letteth it to ferme for his brother William Belk for	iij^{s} iiij^{d}	164
The table	The feoffes of Syr Edward Ponynges knyght holdeth of the lorde a princypall messuage at Cokes dyche and renteth by yere to the table	vj^{d}	165
		xxviij^{s} j^{d}	
	<u>Est strete South</u>		
The table	Item the lorde holdeth ij gardens with a barn and a courtlage nowe letten to ferme to Thomas Perne and payith by yere	xL^{s}	166a b,c,d
The table	Thomas Pykeryng holdeth of the lorde to ferme a garden plott and payith by yere	ij^{s}	167
Kyngesmyll	The heires of John Barbour holdeth a messuage sometyme occupyed for ij messuages next the messuage of the lord Abbottes of Faversham somtyme Danyelles and payith by yere	xvj^{d}	168a, b
folio 8			
The table	The prior holdeth a messuage with a garden and renteth by yere to the table ij^{s} nowe letten to ferme by yere for	xiij^{s} iiij^{d}	169
The table	The feoffes of John Goodwyn holdeth of the lorde iiij messuages with their gardens together lying and renteth by yere to the table	ij^{s} vj^{d}	170a,b,c,d

Sacrist	The same feoffes holdeth of the lorde another corner messuage to the forsaid messuage lying and renteth to the sexten by yere	xj^{d}	171
		Lix^{s} ij^{d} ~~viij^{d}~~	
	<u>Preston Strete Est</u>		
	~~The feoffes of Robert A Fale holdeth of the lorde a messuage and renteth~~ ~~by year to the table~~		
Not ours Kynges-melles	The heires of John Goodwyn holdeth ij messuages late Thomas Childmelles of which one ys callyd the Seller by yere	iiij^{d}	172a, b
Not ours	The heires of John Barbour holdeth a messuage callyd the Sarysenshedd and renteth by yere	viij^{d}	173
The table	The feoffes of Robert A Fale holdeth of the lorde a messuage and renteth by yere to the table	vj^{d}	174
The table	The same feoffes holdeth of the lorde a grete garden wherof part Richard Dryland the yongar late helde of the south part of the same and renteth by yere to the table	ij^{s}	175a, b
[blank]	The said feoffes holdeth another messuage lying to the forsaid messuage by yere	iiij^{d}	176
Almoner	The said feoffes holdeth of the lorde a messuage and renteth by yere	ij^{s}	177
Chamberlain	The same feoffes holdeth of the lorde another messuage and renteth by yere	xviij^{d}	178
The table	The said feoffes holdeth of the lorde the syte of a lytell messuage late Dobbys now wher the gate standeth that ledeth out of the strete in to the grete garden aforsaid and renteth by yere	iij^{d} ob	179
The table	The same feoffes holdeth of the lorde a messuage next the same gate and renteth by yere	ij^{s}	180
folio 8 verso			
Chamberlain	Elyzabeth Smyth widowe holdeth of the lorde a messuage next Shitborne lane and renteth by yere	ij^{s}	181
The table Almoner Sacrist	The heires of Thomas Perne holdeth of the lorde a principypall messuage somtyme dyvers messuages and renteth by yere to the table v^{s}, to the almoner xvij^{d} and j hen and to the sacrist for a yarde of grounde lying on the south est side of the said messuage and renteth by yere to the sexten vj^{d}	vj^{s} xj^{d} and j hen	182a, b, c
The table	William Norton gentleman holdeth of the lorde to ferme a ruynd messuage with a pece of land called Ratton Rowe and payith by yere	iij^{s} iiij^{d}	183
The table	The feoffes of Margarete Hoorne holdeth of the lorde the syte of half a messuage callid Mugges and renteth by yere	iiij^{d} ob	184
The table	The heires of Laurens Straynsham holdeth of the lorde the other half of the same messuage callyd Mugges and renteth by yere	iiij^{d} ob	185
The table	The same feoffes holdeth of the lorde ij barnes and a courtlage and renteth by yere	iij^{s} vj^{d}	186a, b, c
The table	The said feoffes holdeth of the lorde iij messuages together lying and renteth by yere to the table	v^{s}	187a, b, c

[blank]	Margaret Hoorne holdeth of the lorde a messuage late Rychard Roberdes and renteth to Laurens Straynsham by yere	*[blank]*	188
Kynges mill	Arnold Cowper holdeth one messuage late Thomas Fuller's somtyme Lyons	x^{d}	189
Kynges mill	The heires of Symon Warmcorte holdeth a messuage late Goldynges and renteth to Edmond Martyn by yere	vj^{d}	190
Kynges mill	Thomas Ampner holdeth a messuage late Mynces and renteth to Edmond Martyn by yere	vj^{d}	191
Kynges mill	William Kempe holdeth a messuage late the said Mynces and renteth to Edmond Martyn by yere	viij^{d}	192
Kynges mill	John Roche for a voide messuage late Benettes and renteth to the said Edmond Martyn by yere	ix^{d}	193
Kynges mill	Robert Ampner holdeth a ruynd messuage late Morys and renteth to the Edmund Martyn by yere	j^{d}	194
[blank]	Margaret Hoorne wedowe holdeth a garden and dovehouse late Rychard Ulffes and renteth to Cristyschurch by yere	*[blank]*	195
folio 9			
[blank]	The same Margarett holdeth a courtlage and ij barnes somtyme the forsaid Rychard Ulffes and renteth to the forsaid priory of Cristischurche by yere	*[blank]*	196a, b, c
Rectory of Preston	The said Margarett holdeth a messuage wher late Kersyman did dwell and renteth by yere to the parsonage of Preston	xx^{d}	197
		xxxiij^{s} xj^{d} ob.	

<u>Rectory of Preston</u>

Rectory of Preston	John Warham gentleman holdeth of the lorde a messuage next the well and renteth by yere	xx^{d}	198
Not ours	The heires of John Brumston holdeth a garden somtym buylded of old tyme William Makenades and renteth by yere	*[blank]*	199
The table	Item the lorde holdeth a garden next Preston strete at the Southwest corner and renteth by yere	iij^{s}	200
Rectory of Preston	Robert Maycott senior holdeth of the lorde to ferme iij acres of glebe lande and fyndeth xiiij tapers in the chauncell ther and payith more for the ferme of the said iij acres by yere	v^{s}	201
Rectory of Preston	The feoffes of Margaret Hoorne holdeth of the parsonage of Preston forsaid ij acres of lande at Frydley next the High strete ther and renteth by yere	xij^{d} and ij hens	202
Rectory of Preston	The executors of Thomas Perne holdeth of the lorde to ferme xxiiij acres of land at Frydley next Stokdale otherwise callyd Hegdale that was wont to rent by yere	ij^{s}	203
Rectory of Preston	The heires of John Brumston holdeth of the lorde an acre and half of lande in Bradfeld nowe callyd Churchefelde and renteth by yere	j quarter of barley	204
Rectory of	Adam at Hammeholdeth of the lorde a messuage at Westbroke nowe in	xj^{d}	205

Preston	the tenure of the heires of John Brumston and renteth by yere		
Rectory of Preston	The heires of John Bocher holdeth of the lorde a messuage and renteth by yere	vij^d	206
	xiiij^s ij^d ij hens and j quarter of barley		

Preston Strete West

[blank]	Bartholomew Symon holdeth of the lorde a messuage *[folio 9v]* with a lyttell garden lying in the upper part of Preston strete of the west part and payith to the prior of Cristischurch of Cantorbury by yere	*[blank]*	207
The table	*[blank]* Baker holdeth of the lorde a messuage with a garden and renteth by yere	xj^d and j cock	208
The table	Harry Cryps holdeth of the lorde the site of a bern with iij acres of land lying in Kyngesfelde and rent by yere	iij^s j^d	209a, b
The table	The forsaid Baker holdeth of the lord to ferme the sites of ij messuages and certeyn litell peces of lande to the same adioynyng and payith by yere	iiij^s	210a, b, c
The table	The forsaid Harry Cryps holdeth of the lorde a garden and renteth by yere	vj^d	211
Heires Martyn Kynges mill	The heires of Humfrey Clyfforde holdeth of the lorde a messuage with a garden next the lane ther south, late William Fylpottes and renteth to the heires of Edmond Martyn by yere	j^d	212
Heires Martyn Kynges mill	The wedowe of William Dobbys holdeth of the lorde a messuage with a garden late the said William's and renteth by yere to Edmond Martyn	j^d	213
Heires Martyn Kynges mill	The wardeyns of the parisshe churche of Faversham holdeth of the lorde a messuage with a lytell garden and renteth to Edmond Martyn by yere	j^d	214
Heires Martyn	Margaret Horne wedowe holdeth of the lorde a garden late Thomas Frogenhales and to Edmond Martyn by yere	iiij^d	215
The table	The same Margaret holdeth of the lorde a garden somtyme buylded late the heires of Richard Bryan by yere	vj^d	216
Prioress of Davyngton	The said Margarett holdeth a messuage and a garden late Thomas Buckes next Bryans garden agaynst the south and payith to the prioresse of Davyngton by yere	*[blank]*	217
Prioress of Davyngton	The feoffes of John Love holdeth a messuage and a garden late Thomas Byrches and before Elene Idelles	ij^d	218
The table	Robert A Fale holdeth of the lorde to ferme a garden that Margaret Hoorne late helde and payith by yere	ij^s	219

folio 10

The table	Margaret Horne holdeth of the lorde a garden late John Roberdes and renteth by yere	iij^s	220
The table	John Muddell holdeth of the lorde to ferme the syte of ij messuages and payith by yere	iiij^s	221a, b

The table	The feoffes of Arnold Coper holdeth of the lorde a messuage and renteth by yere	viij[d]	222
The table	The same feoffes holdeth of the lorde ij messuages with their gardens and renteth by yere	xiiij[d]	223
The table	The feoffes of Robert A Fale holdeth of the lorde a messuage and a garden and renteth by yere	xij[d]	224
The table	The heires of Symon Warmcourt holdeth of the lorde the site of a messuage nowe in the handes of William Norton gentylman and renteth by yere	iiij[d]	225
The table	The said heires holdeth of the lorde a barne with a courtelage called Buttry barne with stables and renteth by yere	xxij[d]	226
The table	The heires of William Rose holdeth of the lorde the sytes of ij messuages nowe a garden or courtelage and renteth by yere	xiiij[d]	227
The table	The same heires holdeth of the lorde a messuage and a garden late Stephyn Nobys and renteth by yere	ij[s] vj[d]	228
Almonary	Harry Cryps holdeth of the lorde iij messuages with their gardens and renteth by yere	ij[s]	229a, b, c
The table	The same Harry holdeth of the lorde the site of a berne with a courtlage and certeyn landes to the same lying in Kyngesfeld and renteth by yere	vij[s] vj[d]	230a, b, c
The table	William Norton gentleman holdeth of the lorde a barne and a courtlage and renteth by yere	xij[d]	231a, b
The table	The heires of Symon Warmecourte holdeth of the lorde a barne with a courtlage and renteth by yere	xij[d]	232a, b
The table	The heires of William Rose holdeth of the lorde ther site of a messuage whiche ys nowe ij gardens or a courtlage and renteth by yere	xij[d]	233
The table	The same heires holdeth of the lorde a messuage late Harry Beale's and renteth by yere	ij[s] x[d]	234
[blank]	The said heires holdeth ij messuages late John Hales by yere	*[blank]*	235a, b
[blank]	The same heires holdeth a messuage late of John Sole	*[blank]*	236
folio 10v.			
[blank]	The heires of Symond Warmecourte holdeth a pryncypall messuage next Henxhilles lane agaynst the north late Robert Henxhilles by yere	*[blank]*	237
Almonary	The feoffees of Laurens Straynsham holdeth of the lorde a messuage next Henxhilles stile south and renteth by yere	x[d]	238
The table	The same feoffes holdeth of the lorde ij messuages late Alys Rogers and renteth by yere	viij[d]	239a, b
The table	Pater Noster holdeth of the lorde to ferme a messuage with a garden and payith by yere	xvj[s]	240
Chamberlain	Robert Coldwell holdeth of the lorde a messuage and renteth by yere	ij[s] j[d] and j hen	241
The table and	Harry Hatche holdeth of the lorde a messuage callyd the Swan and renteth by yere to the table xij[d] and to the chapell of our Lady v[d], total	xvij[d]	242
[blank]	Thomas Sparrowe holdeth a lytell messuage late Waytes	*[blank]*	243

The table	Item Ho *[blank]* holdeth of the lorde a messuage late Darlandes and renteth by yere	xij^{d}	244
[blank]	John Sole holdeth a messuage late Thomas Soles his father and renteth by yere	*[blank]*	245
The table	Thomas Sayer holdeth of the lorde a messuage late John Hornesclyff and renteth by yere	xij^{d}	246
[blank]	John Ealdyng holdeth of the lorde a messuage somtyme Richard Ulffes renteth by yere	*[blank]*	247
[blank]	The same John holdeth of the lorde a messuage there annexed late *[blank]*	*[blank]*	248
[blank]	Richard Forman otherwise callyd Rycherd Harper holdeth of the lorde a messuage late John Goodwyns after Richard Seath and renteth by yere	*[blank]*	249
[blank]	The heires of John Longbredge holdeth of the lorde a messuage late Rowlande Highmore and renteth by yere	*[blank]*	250
[blank]	William Sparrowe as it is said holdeth of the lorde a messuage late Harry Cowpers before Ulffes and renteth by yere	*[blank]*	251
The table	The feoffes of William Broke holdeth of the lorde a messuage and renteth by yere	xxij^{d}	252
folio 11			
The table	The feoffes of John Goodwyn holdeth of the lorde a messuage and renteth by yere	xv^{d}	253
Kynges mill	Robert Lylley by the right of his wife holdeth of the lorde a messuage late Rychard Ulffes and renteth by yere to Kynges mill	x^{s}	254
[blank]	Geffrey Breche holdeth of the lorde a messuage somtyme John Prestons and renteth by yere	*[blank]*	255
The table	Harry Hatche holdeth of the lorde a messuage with a garden callyd somtyme the Sign of the Rose and renteth by yere	ij^{s} iiij^{d}	256
[blank]	The wedowe of Thomas Malpas holdeth of the lorde a messuage callyd the George, late Thomas Nordens and renteth by yere	*[blank]*	257
The table	John Sede holdeth of the lorde a messuage with a garden and renteth by yere	xviiij^{d}	258
The table Chamberlain	Harry Hatche holdeth of the lorde a messuage with a garden called the Fleur de luce and renteth by yere to the table xviij^{d} and to the chamberlain half a seame of barley, total	xviij^{d} and half a seame of barley	259

iij$^{£}$ xiiij^{s} ij^{d} j cock, j hen and half a quarter of barley

<u>Weststrete South</u>

The table Almoner	The Comynaltie of the towne of Faversham holdeth of the lorde a messuage callyd the Shipp and renteth by yere to the table iij^{s} v^{d}, and to the almoner vij^{d}, total	iiij^{s}	260
The table	Harry Hatche holdeth of the lorde to ferme iij messuages and a parcell of lande to them belongyng and payith by yere	xxvj^{s} viij^{d}	261a, b, c

The table	Antony Sondes gent, holdeth of the lorde a message callyd the grewehond with a tofft of land lying on the south side of the same and renteth by yere	vj^{d}	262a, b
The table Chamberlain	George Awder holdeth of the lorde message and renteth by yere, to the table ix^{d} and to the Chamberlain v^{s} total	v^{s} ix^{d}	263
The table	The feoffes of Margaret Horne holdeth of the lorde ij tenementes and renteth by yere	ij^{s} iij^{d} and j hen	264a, b
folio 11v.			
The table	Cristofer Grey holdeth of the lorde a tenement next that and renteth by yere	iiij^{s}	265
Chamberlain	John Colyn holdeth of the lorde a message and renteth by yere	x^{d}	266
Chamberlain	The same John holdeth of the lorde a message and renteth by yere	viij^{d}	267
Chamberlain	The feoffes of Richard Turnour holdeth of the lorde a message and renteth by yere	xiiij^{d}	268
Altar of St. Anne	The executors of Robert A Fale holdeth the lorde a message and renteth by yere	vj^{s} viij^{d}	269
The table	Nycholas Burwasshe holdeth of the lorde a message and renteth by yere	ij^{s}	270
Sacrist	John Tylney holdeth of the lorde message and renteth by yere	vj^{d}	271
The table	The same John holdeth of the lord another message with a cortlage at the corner of the est part of Bermesey lane and renteth by yere	ij^{s} viij^{d}	272a, b
Chamberlain	William Penbroke other wyse callyd William Coke holdeth of the lorde to ferme the corner message at the West part of Bermesey lane and payith by yere	xvj^{s}	273
Infirmary	Item the infermerar holdeth ij messuages next that and lett them to ferme by yere for	xiiij^{s} viij^{d}	274a, b
The table	Thomas Thornyvale holdeth of the lorde a message and renteth by yere to the table	vj^{d}	275
The table	The same Thomas holdeth of the lorde a message next that and renteth by yere	vj^{d}	276
The table	John Barnard holdeth of the lorde a message and renteth by yere	xiij^{d}	277
The table	The said John for ij stulpes[1215] sett at the dore of the sayd message and payith	j^{d}	278
The table and Chapel of St. Mary	William Norton gent holdeth of the lorde a princypall message which somtyme wer dyvers messuages and renteth by yere to the table viij^{s} iiij^{d}, and to the chapell of our Lady x^{d} ob. total	ix^{s} ij^{d} ob.	279a, b, c 280
The table	The said William Norton holdeth of the lorde an acre of gronde lying on the south part of the same message and renteth by yere	vj^{d}	
folio 12			
Chapel of St. Mary	The same William holdeth of the lorde ij messuages next the forsaid message and renteth by yere to the chapell of our Lady	iiij^{s} ~~vij~~^{d}	281a, b

1215 Appears as stuplez for stoop: a post or pillar.

The table	The heires of Norwod holdeth of the lorde a garden with Tayntors next Tunbridge Croft and renteth by yere	iiij^{d} ob	282
The table	The lorde holdeth in his owne handes the site of a messuage and renteth by yere	xiij^{s} iiij^{d}	283
Sacrist	The sexten holdeth ij messuages togeder sett nowe letten to ferme by yere for	xj^{s}	284a, b
The table Almoner	The feoffes of Laurens Straynsham holdeth of the lorde a messuage next them and renteth by yere, to the table vj^{d} and to the almoner vj^{d}. total	xij^{d}	285
The table Almoner	Rychard Kear holdeth of the lorde a messuage next that and renteth by yere, to the table vj^{d} and to the almoner vj^{d}, total	xij^{d}	286
The table	The same Rychard holdeth of the lorde a messuage next that and renteth by yere, to the table vj^{d} and to the almoner vj^{d}, total	xij^{d}	287
The table	The feoffes of Robert A Fale holdeth of the lorde a lytell messuage next that and renteth by yere	vj^{d}	288
The table	The said feoffes holdeth of the lorde a princypall messuage with a tenement therunto united and renteth by yere	ij^{s} j^{d}	289a, b
The table	The same feoffes holdeth of the lorde a greate garden on the south part of the said messuage and renteth by yere	xiij^{d}	290
Chapel of St. Mary	The said feoffes holdeth of the lorde a yarde of grounde on the est part of the same garden and renteth by yere to the Chapill of Our Lady	v^{d}	291
The table	The heires of John Bynder holden of the lorde a messuage and renteth by yere	xx^{d}	292
The table	Thomas Sayer holdeth of the lorde a messuage and renteth by yere	xij^{d}	293
The table	The said Thomas holdeth of the lorde to ferme a garden to the said messuage annexed and payith by yere	xij^{d}	294
		vij$^{£}$ ij^{d} and j hen	

folio 12v.

<u>Tannerstrete Est</u>

The table	Edward Rye holdeth of the lorde a messuage next the forsaid garden and renteth by yere	xviij^{d}	295
	~~Stephen Upton holdeth of the lorde a corner messuage right over against the Kynges myll and renteth by yere~~	~~v^{d}~~	
	~~The feoffes of RobertA Fale holdeth of the lorde~~		
[blank]	Johnes Curteyse holdeth a lytell tenement with a garden late *[blank]*	*[blank]*	296
[blank]	John Lyon for ij litell tenements late *[blank]*	*[blank]*	297
Precentor	Stephyn Upton holdeth of the lorde a corner messuage right over agaynst the kynges myll and renteth by yere	v^{d}	298
Almoner	The feoffes of Robert A Fale holdeth of the lorde a barn a stable and a courtlage next Yeldhall Grene and renteth by yere	viij^{d} and j hen	299a, b, c
[blank]	Robert Matrasse for a tenement with a garden adiacent	*[blank]*	300
[blank]	John Burston for a tenement with a garden	*[blank]*	301
[blank]	The wedowe of Thomas Malpas holdeth of the lorde a tenement and a garden of old tyme Thomas Gylnottes	*[blank]*	302
[blank]	The same wedowe holdeth of the lorde a tenement late of Stephyn White	*[blank]*	303

[blank]	Karolus Lacy holdeth of the lorde a tenement late Robert Olyvers	*[blank]*	304
[blank]	Denys Hardyman for a tenement somtyme John Streynshams	*[blank]*	305
[blank]	Robert Nicholas holdeth of the lorde a tenement and a garden late Symon Orwelles	*[blank]*	306
The table Precentor Sacrist	The feoffes of Robert A Fale holdeth of the lorde a croft callyd Tunbrydges Croft with the site of a barne and a courtlage and renteth by yere to the table viij^{d} ob, and to the chaunter ij^{s} viij^{d} and a henne, and to the sexten iiij^{d}. total	iij^{s} viij^{d} ob. and j hen	307a, b, c
		vj^{s} viij^{d} ob. and ij hens	
	<u>Tannerstrete West</u>		
The table Sacrist	The Vicar of Faversham holdeth of the lorde a medowe nigh Horsham Chartham and renteth by yere to the table iiij^{d} and to the sexten ij^{d}. total	vj^{d}	308
The table	The heires of Laurens Straynsham holdeth of the lorde a messuage and a garden and renteth by yere	ix^{d}	309
Almoner	The heires of Denys Hardyman holdeth the lorde a messuage and a garden and renteth by yere	xiiij^{d}	310
Sacrist	The feoffes of Thomas Coke holdeth of the lorde a messuage and renteth by yere	xviij^{d}	311
B Sacrist	®The forsaid heires of Denys Hardyman holdeth of the lorde a tenement and renteth by yere	xviiij^{d}	312
A	˯The said heieres holdeth of the lorde a voide pece of lande somtyme John Mellers late his mothers, by yere	*[blank]*	313
~~Sacrist~~ ~~Precentor~~	~~Thomas Sayer holdeth of the lorde a messuage and renteth by yere to the sexten ij^{s}, ij hennes and to the Chaunter by yere, iij^{d}, total~~	ij^{s} ~~iij^{d} and ij hennes~~	
[blank]	The heires of Thomas German holdeth of the lorde a tenement and a garden late John Exbredges and renteth to the under wrytten messuage	xij^{d}	314
Sacrist Precentor	Thomas Sayer holdeth of the lorde a messuage and renteth by yere to the sexten ij^{s}, ij hennes and to the Chaunter by yere, iij^{d}, total	ij^{s} iij^{d} and ij hennes	315
Sacrist	The feoffes of Richard Lytell holdeth of the lorde a messuage and renteth by yere	xiiij^{d}	316
The table	The same feoffes holdeth of the lorde ij tenements with their gardens and payith by yere	iij^{s} iiij^{d}	317a, b
~~Sacrist~~	~~The heires of Whitlok of Dodyngton holdeth of the lord a tenement and renteth by yere~~	vj^{d} ~~and j hen~~	
Sacrist	The said feoffes holdeth of the lorde a messuage with a garden and renteth by yere	xij^{d}, j hen	318
Sacrist	The heires of Whitlok of Dodyngton holdeth of the lord a tenement and renteth by yere	vj^{d} and j hen	319
folio 13v.			
The table	The feoffes of Thomas Bix holdeth of the lorde a messuage with a garden and renteth by yere	xvj^{d}	320
[blank]	Margaret Hoorne wedowe holdeth of the lorde a corner tenement and a garden of the South part or the Kynges myll late Edward Thompsons by yere	*[blank]*	321

The table	Raff Symon holdeth of the lorde a mill callyd the Kynges myll and renteth by yere for hym and hys tenauntes	xxxvij^{s} vj^{d}	322
[blank]	The heires of John Norwood holdeth of the lorde a lytell medowe of the west part of the forsaid mill by yere	*[blank]*	323
The table	Thomas Sayer holdeth of the lorde a corner messuage right over agenst Stonebrydge and renteth by yere	j^{d}	324
The table	The heires of John Darrell knyght holdeth of the lorde to ferme a medowe conteynyng by estymacion ij acres next Stonebrydge of the west part of the course of the water there, that holdeth by indenture for terme of yeres and renteth by yere	x^{s}	325
The table	Edward Davy, myller, holdeth of the lorde to ferm a mill callyd the Fludd myll and payith by yere	*[blank]*	326
[blank]	Prior of Cristischurche of Cantorbury for a litell medowe conteynyng half an acre lying next the Fludd myll aforsaid by yere	*[blank]*	327
		iij$^{£}$ iij^{s} vij^{d}	

<u>Westrete north from the Stone Brydge to the Signe of the Beare next to the Market place</u>

The table	Peter Grenestrete holdeth of the lorde ferme the syte of a messuage next the said Stonebrydge and payith by yere	ij^{s} viij^{d}	328
The table	The same Peter holdeth of the lorde a messuage next that and renteth by yere	viij^{d}	329
folio 14			
The table	Item *[blank]* Fylkes holdeth of the lorde the corner messuage next Mellane and renteth by yere	vj^{d}	330
The table	Peter Grenestrete holdeth of the lorde a tenement callid the Forge with a garden and a voide pece of grounde to the same lying and renteth by yere	xxij^{d}	331
The table	The same Peter holdeth of the lorde another lytell messuage and renteth by yere	iij^{d}	332
	The[1216] heires of John Darrell knyght holdeth of the lord a tenement and a garden and renteth by yere.	xij^{d}	333
The table	Thomas Thomas holdeth of the lorde a messuage and renteth by yere	ij^{s} j^{d}	334
The table	Thomas Sayer holdeth of the lorde a messuage with a garden and renteth by yere	vj^{d}	335
The table	John Sayer holdeth of the lorde a messuage wlth a garden and renteth by yere	xij^{d}	336
Altar St. Anne	Item Skot the cowper holdeth of the lorde a messuage with a garden and renteth by yere	ij^{s} iij^{d} and j henne	337
The table	John Fryer holdeth of the lorde a messuage nowe the shopp of his princypall messuage and renteth by yere	xij^{d}	338

[1216] This item written into the *Margin*.

The table	The same John holdeth of the lorde a princypall messuage and renteth by yere	xiiij^{d}	339
The table	Thomas Thomas now Edward Rye holdeth of the lorde iij messuages nowe in one messuage and renteth by yere	iiij^{d} [1217]	340a, b, c
Chamberlain	Thomas Sayer holdeth of the lorde a messuage and renteth by yere	viij^{d}	341
The table	The heires of Willlam Rose holdeth of the lorde a messuage with a garden and renteth by yere	iiij^{d}	342
Sacrist Chamberlain	John Bewtye holdeth of the lorde iiij tenements with their gardens adioynyng to Hurrelane and renteth by yere to the sexten xiiij^{d} and to the chamberlain ij^{s}, total	iij^{s} ij^{d}	343a,b,c,d
The table	The heires of Richard Ealdyng holdeth of the lorde a corner messuage and a garden on the est side of Hurlane and renteth by yere	ij^{s} vj^{d}	344
The table	The said heires holdeth of the lorde another messuage wlth a garden next that and renteth by yere	xij^{d}	345
The table	Thomas Sayer holdeth of the lorde a messuage with a garden and renteth by yere	iij^{d}	346
folio 14v.			
The table	The same Thomas holdeth of the lorde a messuage next that and renteth by yere	vj^{d}	347
The table	The same Thomas holdeth of the lorde another messuage and a garden and renteth by yere	vj^{d}	348
	~~The wedowe of Robert Deve holdeth of the lorde a tenement and garden late~~		
The table	John Kere now Richard Kere holdeth of the lorde a tenement with a garden late *[blank]*	xij^{d}	349
The table	William A Borne holdeth of the lorde a messuage ther and renteth by yere	xvij^{d}	350
[blank]	The forsaid John Kere holdeth of the lorde a messuage and a garden in the which somtyme he dwelyd of old tyme ij tenementes late his father's and *[blank]*	*[blank]*	351a, b
[blank]	The same John holdeth of the lorde a garden adiacent to a lytell tenement late theires of Margery Quyller now inclosed with pales and renteth to John Darell knight	*[blank]*	352
[blank]	Robert Fale for a lytell tenement and a lytell garden late William Clarkes and before Margery Quyllers, and renteth by yere to the Prioresse of Davyngton	xvj^{d}	353a, b
[blank]	The heires of John Hardy bocher for a tenement and a garden late William Constantynes	*[blank]*	354
[blank]	The heires of John Longbredge holdeth of the lorde a tenement in the which lately he dwellyd in late	*[blank]*	355
[blank]	The wedowe of William Rowitt holdeth of the lorde a tenement and a garden in the which he late dwellyd late	*[blank]*	356

[1217] Corrected from xvj^{d}.

[blank]	The heires of John Bangore holdeth of the lorde a tenement and a garden of the west part of a serteyn lane there late *[blank]*	*[blank]*	357
[blank]	John Shepistaill holdeth of the lorde a garden adiacent to the forsaid lane of the est part of the same lane *[blank]*	*[blank]*	358
[blank]	The same John holdeth of the lorde a tenement and a garden late *[blank]*	*[blank]*	359
[blank]	The same John for another tenement and a garden late *[blank]*	*[blank]*	360
[blank]	The same John Shepistaill for another tenement and a garden in the which John Richardson nowe inhabiteth late *[blank]*	*[blank]*	361
folio 15			
The table	The heires of John Bynder holdeth of the lorde a princypall messuage with a shopp and renteth by yere	ij^s v^d	362a, b
Chamberlain	The same heires holdeth of the lorde the half part of a kechyn and the courtlage of the same messuage next Gorewellane and renteth to the chamberlain by yere	ij^s	363a, b
The table	The said heires hold of the lorde a tenement over the north part of the same courtlage and renteth by yere	xj^d	364
The table	The same heires holdeth of the lorde a garden with a dovehouse belongyng to the said messuage and renteth by yere	vj^d	365a, b
The table	The feoffes of John Kere holdeth of the lorde a messuage at the west corner of West Gorewellane and renteth by yere	$xviij^d$	366
The table	The feoffes of John Hode holdeth of the lorde at the est corner of West Gorewellane and renteth by yere	$viij^d$	367
The table	The said feoffes holdeth of the lord another messuage in the same messuage unyte uppon the north part of the said messuage and renteth by yere	xij^d	368
[blank]	Robert Mattrasse holdeth of the lord ij stables otherwise callyd slawghter housses with a lytell garden next the garden late George Mercers before the dunghill at the end of West Gorewellane agaynst the key of the west part	*[blank]*	369a, b, c
[blank]	George Mercer for a garden next West Gorewellane of the east part agaynst the key by yere	*[blank]*	370
The table	The heires of John Hode holdeth of the lorde a tenement next the forsaid lane agaynst the key lying to a tenement at the corner of West Gorewellane agaynst the north and renteth by yere	$viij^d$	371
The table	The same heires holdeth of the lorde a corner tenement of the est part of West Gorewellane in the which the forsaid John Hode late dwellyd by yere	xij^d	372
The table	The said heires holdeth of the lorde another tenement and a garden late by yere	$viij^d$	373
Sacrist	John Bunce of Ottrenden holdeth of the lorde a messuage and renteth by yere	v^s	374
Almoner Chamberlain Hostelry	Willam Hywodd holdeth of the lorde dyuers messuages and gardens together lying and renteth by yere to the almoner $iiij^s$ ij^d and to the chamberlain v^s and to the ostrye vij^s vj^d and ij hennes	xvj^s $viij^d$ and ij hennes	375a b,c,d
folio 15v.			

[blank]	Robert Withiot holdeth of the lorde a tenement and a garden late *[blank]* and renteth by yere to the under wrytten tenement	ix^{d}	376
The table	Nowe George Awder[1218] The wedowe of Richard Flok, holdeth of the lorde a tenement and a garden and renteth with his tenant, to the table xviij^{d} and to the almoner ij^{s}, total	iij^{s} vj^{d}	377
[blank]	Robert Withiott holdeth of the lorde a tenement and a garden, late Robert Billesdons, and before Thomas Benett	*[blank]*	378
[blank]	Robert Matrasse holdeth of the lorde a tenement and a garden late in the tenure of Agnes Barough for terme of her life by yere	*[blank]*	379
Chamberlain Chapel of St. Mary	The feoffes of Syr Willam a Borough prest holdeth of the lorde ij messuages together lying somtyme but one messuage and renteth by yere to the chamberlain viij^{s} ij^{d} and the chapell of our Lady xij^{d}, total	ix^{s} ij^{d}	380
The table	William Elfrith holdeth of the lorde a messuage and renteth by yere	xij^{d}	381
Chamberlain	The same William holdeth of the lorde another tenement next that and renteth by yere	xiiij^{d} and ij hens	382
The table	William a Borne holdeth of the lorde a corner messuage right over agenst the Shipp and renteth by yere	ij^{s}	383
		iij$^{£}$ xvj^{s} j^{d} and v hens	

folio 16

Kyngisfelde[1219]

Chamberlain Sacrist	In primis John Warham gentilman holdeth of the lord iij acres and a yard of lande by estymacion and renteth by yere to the chamberlain iij^{s} iiij^{d} and to the sexten x^{d}, total	iiij^{s} j^{d}
Chamberlain	Harry Hatche holdeth of the lorde a tofft of lande next the garden of the Fleur de Luce and it conteyneth by estimacion a yard of land and renteth by yere	half a quarter of barley
The table	The wardeyns of the parishe churche of Faversham holdeth of the lorde iij acres j yarde of land and renteth by yere	vj^{d}
The table	The heires of William Rose holdeth of the lorde j acre lying at the west part of the said and renteth by yere	iiij^{d}
Chamberlain	Harry Cryps holdeth of the lorde serteyn landes by the last will of Margarett Horne lying in Kynggisfeld aforseid and renteth by yere	ix^{s}
The table	The said Harry holdeth of the lorde an acre of lande ther by the said will and renteth by yere	iiij^{d}
The table	The same Harry holdeth of the lorde by the same will vj acres of lande by estymacion and renteth by yere	ij^{s} vij^{d}
The table	William Castlock holdeth of the lorde to ferme there lying without the libertie of Faversham iij acres and payith by yere	xij^{s}
The table Sacrist	The forsaid Harry Crypps holdeth of the lorde xiij acres iij yardes of lande and renteth by yere to the table xxij^{d} ob. quarter and the sexten vj^{d} and a henne, total	ij^{s} iiij^{d} ob quarter & a henne
The table	The same Harry holdeth of the lorde iij acres of land and payith by yere	ix^{s}

1218 Inserted.

1219 The K has been illuminated with a face in the letter, and letter I in Imprimis is also illuminated.

The table	The wardens of the parisshe churche of Faversham holdeth of the lorde an acre of land callyd Saynt Mary aker and renteth by yere	xij^{d}
The table Almoner	The feoffes of Robert A Fale holdeth of the lorde by estymacion ther xij acres and renteth by yere to the table iij^{s} vj^{d} and to the almoner vj^{d}. total	iiij^{s}
The table Sacrist	The same feoffes holdeth of the lorde iiij acres and a yarde next the same and renteth by yere to the table xvij^{d} and to the sexten by yere iij^{d}, total	xx^{d}
folio 16 verso		
The table	The heires of Larens Straynsham holdeth of the lorde iij acres and renteth by yere	viij^{d} ob
Sacrist	The same heires holdeth of the lorde a pece of land next that callyd Short Forowe and renteth by yere	ix^{d}
The table	The feoffes of Robert A Fale holdeth of the lorde a crofft callyd Wadescroft and renteth by yere	ij^{s} x^{d}
The table	The heires of Barley holdeth of the lorde by the right of his wif ther iiij acres lande by estymacion callyd Bradbroke and renteth by yere	ij^{s}
	Liij^{s} ij^{d} quarter, j hen and half a quarter of barley	

Cutthorne

The table	The feoffes of John Parke holdeth of the lorde ther by estymacion ix acres of lande and renteth by yere to the table ij^{s} xj^{d}, to the sexten xij^{d} and to the chamberlain vj^{d}, total	iiij^{s} v^{d}
The table	The Priour of Ledes holdeth or the lorde an acre and more of lande and renteth by yere	viij^{d}
The table	Robart Coldwell holdeth of the lorde to ferme there half an acre of lande and payith by yere	ij^{s}
		vij^{s} j^{d} [1220]

folio 18[1221]

Annual rents pertaining to the office of sacrist
and the chapel of the Blessed Mary

Courtstrete East

Chapel of St. Mary Sacrist	The Vycar of Faversham holdeth of the lorde a messuage somtyme ij messuages with their gardens nowe in one and renteth by yere to ye chapell of our Lady	ij^{s}	37a, b.
	William Venour holdeth of the lorde ij messuages together lying and renteth by yere to the sexten	ob.	39a, b
Chapel of St. Mary	William Castlok holdeth of the lorde a messuage at the northwest corner of the Churche lane and renteth by yere to the chapell of our Lady	xij^{d}	46

Churchelane North

Chapel of St. Mary	The forseid William Castlok holdeth of the lorde iij messuages and renteth by yere to the chapell of our Lady	xij^{d}	47a, b, c

---

1220 fols. 17 and 17 verso are left blank.

1221 Here begins a different hand, clearer and finer. Having a long r there are many similarities between this hand and the various interlineations in the earlier text. The scribe uses a thorn.

Chapel of St. Mary	The Vycar of Faversham holdeth of the lorde a gardeyn adioynyng to the vycarage and renteth by yere to the chapell of our Lady	xij^{d}	48

Churchelane South

Chapel of St. Mary	John Norton knyght holdeth of the lorde a princypall messuage next the churcheyarde of Faversham and renteth by yere to the chapell of our Lady	ij^{s}	49
Sacrist	The seid John Norton holdeth of the lorde a barn and a courtlage to the seid messuage belongyng and renteth by yere to the sexten	xx^{d}	50

Northstrete West

Sacrist	Coke the bocher holdeth of the sexten to ferm a corner messuage next Estgore wellane and payith by yere to the seid sexten	xv^{s}[1222]	68

Northstrete East

Chapel of St. Mary	The feoffes of John Cony holdeth of the lorde a messuage and renteth by yere to the chapell of our Lady	ij^{s}	87

folio 18v

Sacrist & Chapel of St. Mary	Richard Dryland the yongar holdeth of the lorde a messuage and renteth by yere to the sexten xx^{d} and to the chapell of our Lady j^{d} and a henne, total	xxj^{d} and j hen	88
Chapel of St. Mary	Item *[blank]* holdeth of the lorde ij messuages late Egles and renteth by yere to the chapell of our Lady	v^{d}	90a, b
Sacrist	John Goldfynche holdeth of the lorde a messuage and renteth by yere to the sexten	vij^{s} viij^{d}	101
Chapel of St. Mary	The same John holdeth of the lorde a messuage next Hogmarkett lane and renteth by yere to the chapell of our Lady	iiij^{d}	103

The myddell rowe next the gayole

Sacrist	William Denny nowe Thomas Smyth holdeth of the lorde a messuage and rentith by yere to the sexten	ij^{s}	105

Shamelles in the Market place in the second rowe next Westrete there ar ix Shamellys

	Wherof,		
Sacrist	The sexten holdeth the viijth shamell and it lyeth voyde and renteth by yere	iiij^{s} it is empty	125

The myddell rowe from the Fysshe Markett unto Hoggcrosse

Sacrist	The heires of John Goodwyn holdeth of the lorde iiij messuages together lying and renteth by yere to the sexten	xij^{d}	149

[1222] Originally written as 16^{s} the last minim is now scarcely visible and appears to have been deliberately erased.

Eaststrete North

Sacrist	The feoffes of Robert Withiott holdeth of the lorde a malthouse and other messuages to the principall messuage adioyning and renteth to the sexten by yere	ix^{d}	154 a,b, c,d
Sacrist	Adam Princhett holdeth of the lorde a messuage with a garden and renteth by yere to the sexten	ij^{s} iiij^{d} and half a hen	157
folio 19			
Sacrist	The same Adam holdeth of the lorde another messuage with a garden and renteth by yere to the sexten	xvj^{d} and half a hen	158
Sacrist	The seid Adam holdeth of the lorde another messuage and renteth by yere, to the sexten	xvj^{d} and j hen	159
Sacrist	The feoffes of Robert Withiott holdeth of the lorde a lytell messuage next to a lytell messuage and courtlage that John Sayer holdeth of the lorde to ferme and rentith by yere to the sexten	iij^{d}	161
Sacrist	The sexten holdeth ij messuages and lettith theym to ferme to dyvers men by yere for	xj^{s}	163 a, b
	The same sexten holdeth a garden next Lodry lane and lettith it to ferme to Willyam Belk the elder by yere for	iij^{s} iiij^{d}	164

Est strete South

Sacrist	The feoffes of John Goodwyn holdeth of the lorde a corner messuage and renteth to the sexten by yere	xj^{d}	171

Preston Strete East

Sacrist	The heires of Thomas Perne holdeth of the lorde a yarde of grounde lying on the Southest syde of their princypall messuage and renteth by yere to the sexten	vj^{d}	182 a,b, c

Preston Strete West

Chapel of St. Mary	The feoffes of Henry Hatche holdeth of the lorde a messuage callyd the Swan and renteth by the yere to the chapell of our Lady	v^{d}	242

West Strete South

Sacrist	John Tylney holdeth of the lorde a messuage and renteth by yere to the sexten	vj^{d}	271
folio 19v.			
Chapel of St. Mary	William Norton gentleman holdeth of the lorde a princypall messuage somtyme dyvers messuages and renteth by yere to the chapell of our Lady	x^{d} ob.	279 a,b, c
Chapel of St. Mary	The same William holdeth of the lorde ij messuages next, the forseid messuage and renteth by yere to the chapell of our Lady	iiij^{s}	280

Sacrist	The sexten holdeth ij messuages together sett, nowe letten to ferme by yere for	xj^{s}	284 a, b
Chapel of St. Mary	The feoffes of Robert A Fale holdeth of the lorde a yarde of grounde on the east part of a great garden that lyeth on the south part of their principall messuage there renteth by yere to the chapell of our Lady	v^{d}	291

<u>Tannerstrete East</u>

Sacrist	The same feoffes holdeth of the lorde a croft callyd Tunbredges Croft with the syte of a barn and a courtlage and renteth by yere to the sexten	iiij^{d}	307 a,b, c

<u>Tannerstrete West</u>

Sacrist	The Vycar of Faversham holdeth of the lorde a medowe nygh Horsham Chartham and rentith by yere to the sexten	ij^{d}	308
Sacrist	The feoffes of Thomas Coke holdeth of the lorde a messuage renteth by yere to the sexten	xviij^{d}	311
Sacrist	The heires of Denys Hardyman holdeth of the lorde a tenement and renteth by yere	xviij^{d}	312
Sacrist	Thomas Sayer alias Lambert holdeth of the lorde a messuage and renteth by yere	ij^{s} and ij hennys	315
Sacrist	The feoffes of Richard Lytell holdeth of the lorde a messuage and renteth by yere	xiiij^{d}	316
Sacrist	The seid feoffes holdeth of the lorde a messuage with a garden and renteth by yere	xij^{d}	318
Sacrist	The heires of Whitlok of Dodyngton holdeth of the lorde a tenement and renteth by year	vj^{d} and j hen	319

<u>Westrete from the Stone bridge to the signe of the Beare next to the Market place</u>

Sacrist	John Beawty holdeth of the lorde iiij tenements with their gardens adioynyng Hurlane and renteth by.yere to the sexten	xiiij^{d}	343 a,b, c,d
folio 20			
Sacrist	John Bunce of Ottrynden holdeth of the lorde a messuage and renteth by yere	v^{s}	374
Chapel of of our Lady	The feoffes of Syr Willam A Borough preist holdeth of the lorde ij messuages together lying somtyme but one messuage and renteth by yere to the chapell	xij^{d}	380

<u>Kynggisfelde</u>

Sacrist	John Warham gentleman, holdeth of the lorde serteyn lond there and renteth by yere to the sexten	x^{d}	

Sacrist	Harry Crips holdeth of the lorde serteyn londe there and renteth by yere to the sexten	vj^{d} j hen
Sacrist	The feoffes of Robert A Fale holdeth of the lorde a pece of lond there callyd Shortforowe and renteth by yere to the sexten	ix^{d}

<u>Cutthorne</u>

[blank]	The feoffes of John Parke holdeth of the lorde there serteyn land and renteth by yere to the sexten	xij^{d}

folio 20v.

<u>Rent of Uplond to the chapell of our Lady and to the sexten as folowith</u>

<u>Roode</u>

Chapel of St. Mary	Cristofer Bredham for lande there by yere to the chapell of our Lady	ij^{d} ob.

<u>Selgrove</u>

Chapel of St. Mary	Item of the maner there to the chapell of our Lady by yere	ij^{s}
Chapel of St. Mary	Walter Maycottes wedowe for a croft of land lying next the lane ledyng in to Lytelles and renteth to the chapell of our Lady by yere	vij^{d}
[blank]	The Masters Fellowes and scolers of Seynt Johns Collage in Cambredge for landes callyd Cantisdane whiche renteth to the chapell of our Lady by yere	ij^{s}
	Item *[blank]* Baylley of Sheldwiche for a tenement and renteth by yere to the sexten	viij^{d}

<u>Well</u>

Chapel of St. Mary	Raffe Symondes for land in Holmyston and renteth to the chapell of our Lady by yere	vj^{d}

<u>Oldboldislond,</u>

Sacrist	The heires of Spycer for lond at Fissheponde and renteth by yere	xv^{d}
Sacrist	Item of *[blank]* for landes late Richard Popes and renteth by yere	ix^{d}
Sacrist	The heires of *[blank]* Joce for lande lying in Welfeld by yere	vj^{d}
Sacrist	Item for the pencyon of Luddenham by yere	iij$^{£}$ vj^{s} viij^{d}

<u>Graveney</u>

Chapel of St. Mary	Item of the heires of Peryman for a messuage and land callyd Buttes by yere	xij^{d} and iiij hennys
Sacrist	The heires of Thomas Frogenhale for a croft callyd the Rosse by yere	vj^{s}
Sacrist	Reynald Back for land callyd Sextry and land at Bakynhelde by yere	viij^{d} & j hen

folio 21

<u>Rents pertaining to the office of chamberlain</u>

<u>Courtstrete West</u>

Sacrist	The heires of Roger Hall holdeth of the lorde the corner messuage of the	xiiij^{d}

	northside of the Keylane and renteth by yere to the chamberlain		
	Churchelane northe		
[blank]	William Castlok holdeth of the lorde iij messuages and renteth by yere	xij^{d}	47a. b,c
	Northstrete West		
[blank]	John Davy holdeth of the lorde a messuage and renteth by yere	xij^{d}	56
[blank]	The same John holdeth of the lorde another messuage and renteth by yere	iij^{s} iiij^{d}	57
[blank]	The feoffes of Raffe Asshebury holdeth of the lorde a messuage and renteth by yere	xx^{d} ob.	66
[blank]	The same feoffes holdeth of the lorde a corner messuage and renteth by yere	ij^{s} v^{d}	67
[blank]	Richard Coldwell holdeth of the lorde a messuage and renteth by yere	xiiij^{d}	71
[blank]	The same Richard holdeth of the lorde a messuage callyd the Horne and renteth by yere	ij^{s} v^{d} and ij hens	75
[blank]	The seid Richard holdeth of the lorde another house to the same adioynyng and renteth by yere	iiij^{d} and j hen	76
[blank]	William A Borne holdeth of the lorde an augmentacion to his house next the strete there and rentith by yere	viij^{d} and j hen	78a, b
	Northstrete East		
[blank]	William Castlok holdeth of the lorde a messuage and renteth by yere	iiij^{s}	97
	Shamelles in the Marketplace		
	Memorandum that there are in the first rowe next Weststrete x shamelles		
	Wherof the		
[blank]	First the heires of Robert A Fale holdeth of the lorde and renteth by yere	iij^{s} iiij^{d}	118
[blank]	William Wyer holdeth of the lorde the ij^{de} shamell and renteth by yere	iiij^{d}	119
[blank]	The forseid heires of Robert A Fale holds of the lorde the iij^{d} shamell and renteth by yere	ix^{d}	120
folio 21v			
[blank]	Robert Coldwell holdeth of the lorde the vth shamell and renteth by yere	xx^{d}	122
[blank]	John Beawtye late held of the lorde the ixth Shamell and renteth by yere	iiij^{d}	126
[blank]	The same John holdeth of the lorde the xth Shamell and renteth by yere	iiij^{d}	127
	In the seconde rowe there are ix shamelles		
	Wherof the		
[blank]	First the heires of Laurence Streynsham late helde of the lorde and renteth by	iiij^{d}	128
[blank]	The heires of John Parke holdeth of the lorde the vijth shamell and renteth by yere	iiij^{d}	134
	In the iij^{d} rowe ther are viij shamelles		
	wherof		
[blank]	The heires of Robert A Fale holdeth of the lorde the ij^{de} shamell and	iij^{s} iiij^{d}	137

	renteth by yere		
[blank]	The heires of John Parke holdeth of the lorde the third shamell and renteth by yere	iiij^{d}	139
[blank]	The same heirs holdeth of the lorde the vjth Shamell and renteth by yere	iiij^{d}	142
[blank]	The seid heires holdeth of the lorde the vij shamell and renteth by yere	iiij^{d}	143

The middell rowe from the Fisshemarkett unto Hoggcross

[blank]	Item for the ferme of the Cornerhouse next the Fisshemarkett by yere	xx^{s}	148
[blank]	The heires of John Goodwyn holdeth of the lorde iiij messuages together lying and renteth by yere	xij^{d}	151a,b,c,d

East Strete North

Infirmarer Chamberlain	John Sayer holdeth of the lorde to ferme a lytell messuage and a courtlage and payeth by yere to the chamberlain	ij^{s} vj^{d}	160 a,b

Preston Strete East

[blank]	The feoffes of Robert A Fale holdeth of the lorde a messuage and renteth by yere	xviij^{d}	178
folio 22			
[blank]	Elyzabeth Smyth nowe Thomas Sayer alias Lambert by the right of the seid Elyzabeth nowe his wiff holdeth of the lorde a messuage next Shyttborne lane and renteth by yere	ij^{s}	181

Prestonstrete West

[blank]	Robert Coldewell holdeth of the lorde a messuage and renteth by yere	ij^{s} j^{d} & j hen	241
	~~Johanne Hache wedowe holdeth of the lorde a messuage with a garden called the Flour de Luce and renteth by yere xviij^{d}~~	~~halfe a seame of barley or elles~~	

Westrete South

[blank]	George Awder holdeth of the lorde a messuage and renteth by yere	v^{s}	263
[blank]	John Collyn holdeth of the lorde a messuage and renteth by yere	x^{d}	266
[blank]	The same John holdeth of the lorde another messuage and renteth by yere	viij^{d}	267
[blank]	The feoffes of Richard Turner holdeth of the lorde a messuage and renteth by yere	xiiij^{d}	268
[blank]	Willyam Penbroke alias William Coke holdeth of the lord to ferme the corner messuage at the West part of Bermesey lane and payith by yere to the chamberlain	xvj^{s}	273

Westrete North from the Stonebredge to the signe of the Beare next to the Marketplace

[blank]	Thomas Sayer alias Lambert holdeth of the lorde a messuage and renteth by yere	viij^{d}	341
[blank]	John Beawty holdeth of the lorde iiij tenementes with their gardens	ij^{s}	343a

	adioynyng to Hurlane and renteth by yere		b,c,d
[blank]	The heires of John Bynder holdeth of the lorde the half part of a kechyn and the Courtlage of the same messuage next Gorewellane and renteth by yere	ij^{s}	363 a,b
folio 22v.			
	William Highwod holdeth of the lorde dyvers messuages and gardens together lying and renteth by yere	v^{s}	375 a,b, c,d
[blank]	The feoffes of Sir William A Borough preist holdeth of the lorde ij messauges together lying somtyme but one message and renteth by yere	$viij^{s}\ ij^{d}$	380
[blank]	Willyam Elfreth holdeth of the lorde a message next to the corner messuage of William A Borne that is right over agaynst the signe of the Shipp and renteth by yere	$xiiij^{d}$ ij henys	382

<u>Kynggisfeld</u>

[blank]	John Warham holdeth of the lorde serteyn lond there and renteth by yere	$iij^{s}\ iij^{d}$
[blank]	Joan Hatche wedowe holdeth of the lorde a tofft of land there next the garden of the Flor de luce and renteth by yere	½ a ¼ of barley or oates, $xviij^{d}$
[blank]	Henry Cryps holdeth serteyn londes by the last will of Margarete Hoorne lying in Kynggisfeld aforseid and renteth by yere	ix^{s}

<u>Cutthorne</u>

	The feoffees of John Parke holdeth of the lorde there serteyn londe and renteth by yere	vj^{d}
	$v^{£}\ xvj^{s}\ xj^{d}$ ob. vij hennys half a quarter of barley	

folio 23

<u>Rent of Uplond belongyng to the chamberlain</u>

<u>Selgrave</u>

[blank]	Robert Easton for a messuage and londe by yere	vj^{d} and j hen

<u>Roode</u>

[blank]	Cristofer Bredham for landes there by yere	$iij^{s}\ j^{d}$ ob.
	~~The same Christofer for land in Ax^{s}tens felde by yere~~	~~ij^{s}~~
[blank]	Item for ferme of Preistfelde by yere	$xxxiij^{s}\ iiij^{d}$
[blank]	Item of John Jury and Teneker of Boughton for lande at Gosompole by yere	vj^{d} & ij hennys
[blank]	Richard Lewkenor for landes callyd Sprakilles next Sheldwiche by yere	a seme of whete
[blank]	Item of Gyles for land lying at Lonerreddesgate by yere	ij^{s}
[blank]	Item for landes in Hartey callyd Johans Goore by yere	$iij^{s}\ vj^{d}$
[blank]	Item for land lying at Ravynshill by yere	ij^{s}
[blank]	Item for the cyte of the certers house and the graunge therto belongyng with the Crofft to the same adioynyng by yere	x^{s}
[blank]	Item for the Fayre by yere as it happenyth	*[blank]*
[blank]	Item for the See by yere as it chaunseth	*[blank]*

Total[1223] Liiij^{s} xj^{d} ob.iij hennys j quarter of wheat
The sum total of the office of chamberlain is viij$^{£}$ xj^{s} xj^{d} x henys j quarter of whete and half a quarter of barley

folio 24

Rents pertaining to the office of Precentor

The middell rowe next the Gayole

[blank]	The Wardens of the parishe Churche of Faversham holdeth of the lorde ij shoppis, nowe in one and renteth by yere	xx^{d}	106 a,b

Tannerstrete East

[blank]	Stephyn Upton holdeth of the lorde a corner messuage right over agaynst the Kyngissmyll and renteth by yere	v^{d}	298
[blank]	The feoffees of Robert A Fale holdeth of the lorde a croft callyd Tunbredges Croft with the syte of a barn and a courtlage and renteth by yere	ij^{s} viij^{d} and a hen	307a ,b,c

Tannerstrete West

[blank][1224]	Thomas Sayer holdeth of the lorde a messuage and renteth by yere	iij^{d}	
	Item to receive of the Bedill of Uplond by yere for parchement for all the courtes in the yere	v^{s}	

folio 25[1225]

The state of account of the monastery of Saint Saviour of Faversham the first day of February in the fourteenth year of the reign of King Henry the seventh.[1499]

Margin: **The extent of the yerely possessions spirituall and temporall belonging to the said monastery**

First the parsonage of Boughton by yere xxvj$^{£}$. The parsonage of Harnhill which is Capella annexed to Boughton forseid by yere x$^{£}$. The parsonage of Preston by yere xiij$^{£}$ vj^{s} viij^{d}. The pentions of the churches of Luddenham and Newynham by yere v$^{£}$. The principall maner of Faversham with the demeane landes by yere xLij$^{£}$ xj^{s} viij^{d}. The rent of Uplond by yere Lij$^{£}$ x^{s}. The custume belonging to the said maner by yere xxij acres and half. The rent in the towne of Faversham by yere xx$^{£}$ iij^{d} ob. The ferme of the seid towne by yere vj$^{£}$ xvj^{s} iiij^{d}. The ferme of Catstart and Greate Barton, by yere xij^{s}. The ferme and rent at Frythynden by yere Lvj^{s} iij^{d}. The ferme Hartey by yere viij$^{£}$ vj^{s} viij^{d}. The ferme of Negdon by yere viij$^{£}$. The ferme of Lambertislond by yere xj$^{£}$. The maner of Kingessnoth by yere v$^{£}$ vj^{s} viij^{d}. The ferme of Wodleese there by yere x^{s}. The ferme of londe calid Horshopes by yere xiij^{s} iiij^{d}. The ferme of Wodlese in the Blean by yere xj^{s}. The ferme of Brydewell in London by yere iiij$^{£}$. The ferme of the maner of Bendissh by yere xxiiij$^{£}$. The ferme of Snowtweres by yere ij^{s} viij^{d}. The ferme of Lodgemersshe by yere xxxiij^{s} iiij^{d}.
Total CCLiij$^{£}$ xvj^{s} x^{d}. ob.

1223 At the foot of *fol. 23* in the same small hand but smaller. Fol. 23v. is blank.
1224 There is a large gap between this and the next item.
1225 A change in the handwriting at this point. The following is written in a very clear and well executed manner.

Margin: **Plate in the Thresory**.
First in the treasury one pece of the holly crosse closed in gould and sett with stones.
Item a crucifix of sylver and gilt weight L unces.
Item a myter sett with perle.
Item a staffe with a croyse . The staffe beyng sylver parcell gilt[1226] weight *[blank]* and the croyse beyng of sylver and gilt and amell[1227] weight *[blank]*.
Item a pontificall ring of gould with iiij other gould rynges weight iij unces and half.
Item ij owches[1228] of sylver and gilt. Set with perle weight j unce.
Item ix chalices with their patentes of sylver and gilt weight CL unces.
Item ij censures[1229] of sylver and gilt weight CxL unces.
Item a navett[1230] of sylver weight xvj unces. [1231]*folio 25 verso*
Item a bell of sylver and ij paxes[1232] of sylver parcell gilt weight x unces.
iiij crewettes[1233] of sylver weight xxvj unces. Total *[blank]*

Margin: **Plate in the Abbottes chamber**.
Item a standing pece all gilt with a cover weight xxx^ti^ unces. A flatt pece of sylver without a cover weight xij unces. A salt of sylver with a cover eight xvj unces. ij gilt spones weight j unce iij quarters. vj spones of sylver with knoppes lyke unto the strawberyes weight vj unces. v masours with ij covers weight xiiij unces. Total *[blank]*

Margin: **Plate in the Fraytour**.
Item vij masoures with iij covers weight Lxxxj unces. vj sylver spones weight iiij unces. Total *[blank]*

Margin: **Plate in the Porte**.
Item a masour weight ij unces. A salt of sylver with a cover weight vj unces and a half. Total *[blank]*

Margin: **Napery in the Abbottes chamber**.
First ix tableclothes, v towells, iij napkyns of diaper, price iij£ x^s^, iiij other tableclothes ij cupborde clothes, iiij towells of playncloth and iiij payers of shetes price xx^s^, a fetherbed, a coveryng of a bedd of white sylke, ij payer of blankettes, a coverlett, ij tables, vj stoles ij old hanging sayes[1234], ij bankers, vj old quysshions, xj candilstykkes. ij basons, ij ewers, a fyrepan, a chauffer,[1235] a fyreforke, ij iron copbrondes[1236] with ij payer of tressels and ij chayers price iij£ xvij^s^. Total viij£ vij^s^.
folio 26

[1226] *O.E.D.*. Parcel-gilt. Partially gilded especially of silver ware, as bowls cups etc., having the inner surface gilt.
[1227] *O.E.D.*. = Enamel.
[1228] *O.E.D.*. Ouch: A clasp, buckle, fibula or brooch for holding together the two sides of a garment.
[1229] *O.E.D.*. Censer: a vessel in which incense is burnt.
[1230] *O.E.D.*. Navet: part of a incense pan or censer box. *see 1467 Dryland will.*
[1231] At the bottom of the page here the scribe has written *verte folium*- turn the page.
[1232] *O.E.D.*. Pax, see footnote above.
[1233] *O.E.D.*. Cruets, small vessels for holding the wine and water used at the Mass, or to hold holy water for other uses.
[1234] *O.E.D.* Say: a cloth of fine texture resembling serge; in the 16th century partly of silk, subsequently entirely of wool.
[1235] *O.E.D.*. A metal basket containing fire: a small portable furnace usually of iron fitted with air-holes and a grate.
[1236] Variant of Cobborne = Cob-iron *O.E.D.* One of the irons on which a spit turns, the irons hung on the bars of a kitchen range to support the spit.

Margin: **The Fraytor.**
Item ij tableclothes iij towells of diaper, iiij playn clothes, a towell, iij president clothes of lynnen cloth, v hanging curtens of diaper for the tables, viij wasshing towells to the lavors, vj platters, vj dishes, vj sawcers, iij saltes of pewter, a wodden voyder, a tankerd, a ciste with ij hauters[1237] of Cypresse. Total iij£ v^s^.

Margin: **The Ostrye.**
Item a fetherbed, a bolster, a payer of blankettes, ij payer of worn shetes, iij old coverlettes, a flokbed, a matrasse, a cyler[1238], a tester, a curteyn of red say, another of blewe bokerham with a curteyn, ij old bolsters and a pillowe price xv^s ix^d.

Margin: **The Porte and the Fermarye.**
Item a tablecloth of diaper, ij worn clothes of lynnen, a platter, ij dishes, a sawcer, a bason and an ewer, a salt of pewter, a fyreforke, a payer of tonges, ij coppbrondes of iron, a table, a forme, ij tressells and a wodden tankerd price xvij^s x^d.

Margin: **The shaving house.**
Item a brassepott, a latton bason, a great chauffer of brasse, ij old chayers and ij old shavyng clothes. Price vj^s viij^d.

Margin: **The Kechyn.**
Item iij great brasse pottes sett in the furnesse, iij water pottes of brasse, iij greate brasse pannes, iiij brasse pottes everyche of theym lesse than other, a stup[p]y[1239] of brasse, xiij platters, ix disshes and vij sawcers, iiij long spittes. a byrd spitt, a colander of latton, a flesshehoke, ij wedges and an axe of iron, a morter of brasse with a pestell of iron, a grate for brede and ij rostyng rackes of iron. Price vj£ x^s.

folio 26v.
Margin: **The bakehouse.**
Item a great cheist for meal price vj^s viij^d. A kneding trough and other ij feble troughes price iij^s iiij^d. An iron beame and ij scales with a hundred weight and half a quartern and xiij^lb., price x^s. Total xx^s

Margin: **The brewhouse.**
Item a greate ketill of coper price vj£ xiij^s iiij^d, a greate brasse ketill price xiij^s iiij^d. A cestern of lede with other ledes waying xx hundred price the pound ob., total iiij£ iij^s iiij^d. A messhing ton and iiij yeldyng tonnes price xL^s. A brokyn coper weyng two hundred pounds price the pound j^d ob, total xxv^s. ij last of old kynderkyns price vj^s. iiij kelers. ij ryndges price iij^s vj^d. A clensyng cyve price vj^d. iiij taberdes of ledd waying a hundrith pound price the pound ob., sum iiij^s ij^d, total xv£ ix^s vj^d

1237 *O.E.D.* Cist; a small receptacle for sacred utensils carried in procession at the celebration of mystic festivals. Hauter is an obsolete form of altar. Haughte obsolete form of Hatch possibly in the sense of having two trap-doors into the base of the chest.

1238 *O.E.D.* obs. form Celure, ceiling, canopy.

1239 Written stupy with a title over the top presumably for Stupin, stuppin or Stuppnet a stew-pan or skillet. W.D. Parish & W.F. Shaw, *A Dictionary of the Kentish Dialect* (1889).

Margin: **The Nether Courte.**
Item in the first stable vj horses price vj$^{£}$. The second stable v horses price iij$^{£}$ vj^{s} viij^{d}, the iij^{de} stable v horses price xxiij^{s} iiij^{d}. The iiijth stable iiij horses price the horse v^{s}, total xx^{s}. ij horses more price xx^{s} iiij^{d}. iiij mares price of ij of them xxvj^{s} viij^{d} and the other ij price xx^{s}, and the harnesse of iiij cartes price Liij^{s} iiij^{d}. Total xvij$^{£}$ xiij^{s} iiij^{d}.

Margin: **Hogges and Shepe.**
Item a CLxvj hogges of dyvers sortes price ix$^{£}$ xviij^{s} viij^{d}. iij bulles price xxx^{s}. iij kyne, iij steeres and ij bullocks price iij$^{£}$ x^{s} and in shepe vj^{c} Lxix price xxviij$^{£}$ xvj^{s} iiij^{d}, total xxxiij$^{£}$ xv^{s}.

Margin: **The smyth.**
Item ij sledges and a hand hamer. ij fore hamers. A nayling hamer. v payer of tonges. ij prycchells. ij stemptes. ij vulliers. A gowge. ij butters. A shoyng hamer. A payer of pynsers. iij nayle tooles. A byckhorne. An andvild. A toole to hewe cartnayle. A payer of fyling tonges. A dogg of iron. A payer of billowes with a tuern and iij files price xL^{s}.

folio 27 and 27v. are blank. folio 28

The xxiiijth day of August in the xxvjth yere of the reign of King Henry the viijth an inventarye had and made of all the implementes of the Abbottes chamber and other, as here after foloweth. That is to witt. [1534]

First a greate payer of shetes of astate with the signe of the croyse and the lettir J. vj payer of fyne shetes and one shete all merked with the signe of the croyse and the lettir J. viij payer of shetes of white brussell with lyke marke. vij payer of white canvas shetes with the same marke. vj fyne pillowberes marked with the signe of the croyse and the lettires J and C. ij courser pillowberes, whereof one is marked with the croyse only, and the other with the lettir J and signe of the croyse.

Item a table cloth of diaper conteyning in length vij yardes and a half and half a quarter, and in bredeth ij yardes, marked with the signe of the croyse and the letter J. A tablecloth of diaper conteyning in length vij yardes and agreate quarter, and in bredeth ij yardes and a quarter, marked with like marke. Another tablecloth of diaper contenyning in length xj yardes and in bredeth a yarde quarter and the nayle with lyke marke. A badd tablecloth of diaper conteyning in length v yardes and a half, and in bredeth, a yarde and a half with lyke marke. A table cloth of diaper conteyning in length vj yardes and in bredeth a yarde and a half of a quarter large with lyke marke. A tablecloth of diaper good conteyning in length vj yardes large and in bredeth ij yardes and the quarter large with lyke marke. Another bad tablecloth of diaper conteyning in length iiij yardes and in bredeth a yarde and a quarter with lyke marke.

Item a towell of diaper conteyning in length xj yardes and iij quarters and in bredeth iij quarters skant with lyke marke. A bad towell of diaper conteyning in length viij yardes and a half and in bredeth half a yarde and half a quarter with lyke marke. A towell of diaper conteyning in length viij yardes skant and in bredeth half a yarde and half a quarter with lyke marke. A towell of diaper conteyning in length vij *folio 28 verso* and a half and in bredeth iij quarters and a half with lyke marke. A towell of diaper conteyning in length ix yardes iij quarters skant, and in bredeth half a yarde and half a quarter with lyke marke.

Item a playne tablecloth conteyning in length v yardes and in bredeth a yarde large with the signe of the croyse and the lettir J. Another playne tablecloth conteyning in length v yardes skant, and in bredeth a yarde with lyke marke.

Item a playne towell conteyning in length iij yardes skant and in bredeth half a yarde skant, marked with the signe of the croyse and the lettir J. A playne towell conteyning in length iij yardes skant, and in bredeth half a yarde skant with lyke marke. A playne towell conteyning in length iij yardes skant, and in bredeth half a yarde large marked with lyke marke.

Item ij coverpanes conteyning in length j yarde and j quarter skant and in bredeth iij quarters. ij other coverpanes, one conteyning in length j yarde and half a quarter and in bredeth iij quarters.

Item xix playne napkyns conteyning in length j yarde greate and in bredeth half a yarde. iiij playn napkyns more conteyning in length j yarde and half a quarter and in bredeth half a yarde. ij playne napkyns more conteyning in length j yarde and half a quarter, and in bredeth half a yard. ij playn napkyns more torn, conteyning in length iij quarters and a half, and in bredeth iij quarters. ij newe napkyns of groce canvas conteyning in length j yarde large and in bredeth iij quarters. And iij frenche napkyns myled at the endes.

Item iiij diaper napkyns, badd, conteyning in length j yarde and in bredeth iij quarters, marked with the signe of the croyse and the lettir J. And ij other diaper napkyns conteyning in length iij quarters and a half, and inbredeth half a yarde large with lyke marke.

Item a cupbordecloth of diaper conteyning in length ij yardes and iij quarters and in bredeth j yarde and j quarter and a half. Another playn cupbordcloth conteyning in length ij yardes and j quarter large, And in bredeth j yarde and half. *folio 29.*

Item iiij latton bell candilstikkes with cuppis. iiij bell candilstikkes without cuppis. iiij candilstikkes more of a lesser sort. iij candilstikks with long shankes. ij of a lesser sort with long shankkes, and a candelstik with a pyke to sett on a taper.

Item a bason and an ewer of pewter engraved. ij basons more, one bettir then another with ther ewers. And iij ewers without basons.

Item a quart pott of pewter by estymacion ij other pottes of pewter, betwene a quart and pynt. iij litell pynt pottes of pewter, sylver facion. A pottell pott of pewter, sylver facion. ij basons a biggar and a lesser. A lytell disshe of pewter, and another pewter disshe of six^{s}quare, sylver facion. vj porengers of pewter, marked with the letters T.P. and J. ij pewter disshes sylver facion, either of them with iij fete, marked with the signe of the crowne and the rose. iij greate disshes of pewter beyng six^{s}quare for spices, marked with the lettires T.P. and J. v sawcers marked with the signe of the crowne and the rose.

Item a chauffing disshe of latton with ij ryngles. ij greate chauffers, one of latton with a cover, and the other brasse without a cover. A hanging lavor of latton with an iron cheyne. iij lethern tankerdes, wherof one conteyneth a gallon the second a pottell, and the third a quarte. ij saltsellers of pewter.

Item vj quysshyns of verdure, and vj more with redd roses. ij turkey carpetts. A carpett of tappistryworke. A cupborde, ij joyned cheyres. A turned cheyre. vj newe joyned stoles and vj old joyned stoles. A counter table. A table and a forme with ij joyned tressells. A hanging of grene saye. ij pictures wherof one is of Christ the other of our Lady. ij greate andyrons. A greate fyreforke of iron. A rake of iron. ij fyre pannes, and ij payer of tongges, a biggar and a lesser.

The chamber over the Abbottes chamber.

Item a newe joyned bed with a fetherbedd therin conteyning in length ij yardes half a quarter and in bredeth j yarde and a half. A matrasse conteyning in length ij yardes and in bredeth j yarde and j quarter. A flockbed conteyning in length ij yardes and j quarter and in bredeth *folio 29v.* j yarde iij quarters and a half. A bolster conteyning in length j yarde and half, and in bredeth half a yarde large. And another bolster conteyning in length ij yardes large; and in bredeth half a yarde large.

The chappell chamber to the forseid chamber annexed.

Item in the said chamber v pottes of brasse, every of theym biggar then other, wherof the greattist hath a hole in the bottom. A lytell chauffer with a handell. A ketell and a panne with lettires bounde. A panne without lettires. A skillett with a handell. A newe joyned presse. A coverlyd with tappistryworke conteyning in length iiij yardes and half skant, and in bredeth iij yardes skant. Another coverlyd of tappistryworke with imagery conteyning in length iij yardes iij quarters and half great, in bredeth ij yardes iij quarters and half large. A coverlid of tappistryworke miled at both endes conteyning in length iij yardes greate, and in bredeth ij ayrdes and j quarter. Another coverlid of counterfete arras conteyning in length iij yardes and half and in bredeth ij yardes iij quarters. A coverlid of tappistry worke with imagery conteyning in length ij yardes iij quarters and in bredeth ij yardes. a newe quilt for a bedd conteyning in length ij yardes and in bredeth j yarde and iij quarters. A payer of wollen blanketts conteyning in length either of theym ij yardes a half and half a quarter and in bredeth j yarde and iij quarters. Another payer of wollen blanketts, either of theym conteyning in length ij yardes and a half large, and in bredeth j yarde and iij quarters. A bolster conteyning in length j yarde iij quarters skant, and in bredeth half a yarde skant. A greate pillowe covered with white fustyan conteyning in length j yard j quarter and a half and in bredeth iij quarters skant.

Item ij sawes wherof one is for cane stone and the other for wayne scott.

The chamber where Devyn lyeth.

Item in the said chamber a bedstedill. a course fetherbed *folio 30* conteyning in length ij yardes j quarter, in bredeth ij yardes. A litell bolster conteyning in length j yarde and a half and in bredeth j quarter and a half. A standing cheist with iiij fete with a lock. A litell cheist havyng iiij fete with a lock. A chest bounde with iron, havyng ij lockes and one key. A turned chayre. An hawpart for a cupborde. A presse for cappis. vij lethern bottells, wherof iij are of a gallon the pece, and the rest of pottelles.

The chamber next the entre in the Abbottes chamber.

Item in the said chamber a bedstedill, a fetherbed conteyning in length j yarde iij quarters large, and in bredeth j yarde j quarter. A fetherbed conteyning in length ij yardes and in bredeth j yarde j quarter. A mattrasse conteyning in length ij yardes, in bredeth j yarde and j quarter. A matrasse conteyning in length j yarde iij quarters, in bredeth j yarde j quarter skant. A mattrasse conteyning in length ij yardes, in bredeth j yarde and j quarter. An old tyke of a fetherbedd conteyning in length ij yardes and a half, and in bredeth ij yardes. A litell bolster conteyning in length j yarde and j quarter, in bredeth a half yarde. A bolster conteyning in length j yarde a half and a half quarter, and in bredeth a half yarde large. iij litell pillowes of flockkes covered with canvas. A coverlid of redsay conteyning in length ij yardes and a half, and in bredeth ij yardes and a half. A blankett conteyning in length ij yardes, and lykewise in bredeth.

The great chamber for Estrangers next the farmarye.

Item in the said chamber. A bedstedill. A fetherbed of downe conteyning in length iij yardes skant, in bredeth ij yardes and j quarter. A greate bolster in length j yarde and a half, and in bredeth iij quarters. A blankett of fustyan conteyning in length iij yardes skant, and in bredeth j yarde iij quarters. A wolleyn *folio 30 verso* blankett conteyning in length ij yardes j quarter skant and in bredeth j yarde iij quarters large. A coverlyd of tappistry worke, wrought with flors conteyning in length iiij yardes and j quarter, and in bredeth iij yardes and a half. ij pillowes covered with white fustyan either of theym conteyning in length iij quarters and a half, and in bredeth a half yarde large. A newe spaver of redd taffata bed with the curteynes of the same. A troclebed with an old fetherbed therin conteyning in length ij yardes j quarter large, and in bredeth j yarde iij quarters. A bolster conteyning j yarde a half and a half quarter skant and in bredeth a half yarde skant. A wolleyn blankett conteyning in length ij yardes and j quarter in bredeth ij yardes and j quarter. An old coverlyd of tappistryworke with imagery conteyning in length iiij yardes and j quarter large, and in bredeth iij yardes and j quarter large. An old carpett conteyning in length iij yardes and a half, and in bredeth j yarde, a half quarter. A table ij tressells, iij formes, ij turned chayres, ij greate cheistes with lockes and keyes. iij quysshions with rethes. A cupborde for to set on a bason and ewer. Hangyns paynted of damaske worke and another pece of stayned saye. ij awndyrons. A fyreforke. A fyre rake and an old bason of pewter.

The chamber over Dane Dunstones chamber.

Item in the said chamber ij bedstedills with iij fetherbeddes wherof one conteyunith in length ij yardes j quarter and a half, and in bredeth j yarde iij quarters and a half, the ij[de] in length ij yardes a half quarter large and in bredeth j yarde iij quarters. The iij[de] conteynith in length ij yardes j quarter and in bredeth j yarde a half large. A bolster in length j yarde, iij quarters and in bredeth j quarter and a half. Another bolster in length j yarde a half and a half quarter and bredeth a half yarde, a half quarter. Another bolster in length j yarde j quarter large, and in bredeth j quarter half large. A blankett in length ij yardes a half skant, and in bredeth ij yardes. A strayle[1240] blankett conteyning in length ij half quarter, in bredeth j yarde j quarter and a half. Another wolleyn blankett conteyning in length ij *folio 31* yardes j quarter and a half, and in bredeth ij yardes. Another wolleyn blankett conteyning in length ij yardes skant, in bredeth lykewise. A blanket conteyning in length ij yardes and in bredeth j yarde a half. An old coverlyd with imagery conteyning in length iiij yardes and in bredeth iij yardes and a half. Another old coverlyd with redd and yelowe conteyning in length iij yardes a half quarter, and in bredeth iij yardes skant. A carpett coverlett conteyning in length iij yardes quarter and a half and in bredeth ij yardes. A sparver with curteyns of redd say and grene ij old paynted clothes and a litell testor paynted. A necessarie chayre. A litell foldyng table. An old quysshion and payer of tonges.

The litell chamber next the farmary.

Item a bedstedill and an old sparver of whyte.

folio 31v. is blank, *folio 32.*[1241]

CUSTOMARY PAYMENTS AND SERVICES
PERTAINING TO THE MONASTERY OF ST. SAVIOUR OF FAVERSHAM
TO BE MADE TO THE INFIRMARER OF THE SAME MONASTERY.

In the first instance the mesne tenants of the said manor of Selgrave are bound to plough, to reap, to carry and to stack — iij acres corn

Of the tenants of the manor of Langdon are bound to plough, to reap, to carry and to stack — vj acres corn

[1240] *O.E.D.* Strail; a woollen bed-covering, a blanket.
[1241] A change of handwriting which is very difficult to read.

Of the tenants of the manor of Knightes Place are bound to plough, to reap, to carry and to stack	j acre a half
Of the tenants of the manor of Lyttles are bound to plough, to reap, to carry and to stack are bound to plough, to reap, to carry and to stack	iij acres corn
Of Thomas Kempe knight and justice, gentleman, bound to reap, to carry and to stack and half	ij acres a half a rod of corn

By John Wylde

folio 33

The certificate made of the value of all maners, parsonages, landes, tenementes, rents, pensions, tithes and other emolumentes belonging or apperteyning to the monasterye of Saynct Savyour in Faversham as here after appereth, pertycularly.

Margin:	The principall maner of Faversham in the diocese of Caunterbury and in the deanrye of Osprenge.	
	Inprimis the site of the said maner with xxx[ti] acres by estimacion of the demeane landes, pasture, medowes and gardens beyng in our owne handes, valued at ij[s] the acre, total	iij[£]
Margin:	Ferme and custume[1242] belonging to the same maner in the same deanrye	
	Item receyvid for the yerely farme of the resydue of the said maner, that is to witt, in corne, cattall, money, and for custume of xxij acres a half a rodd of land belonging to the same maner, that is to witt, in eryng sowing the said acres with whete, ryppyng, carying in, into the barnes of the said maner and tassyng of the same whete, done by the tenentes of the same maner yerely by the tenure of their landes	xxxvj[£]
Margin:	Ferme of the messuages and other in the towne of Faversham.	
	Item received for the ferme of ij messuages at the towne gate of Faversham, and for other messuages, mill and tenements in the said towne belonging to the seid princypall maner by estymacion yerely	xxvj[£] xvij[s] and a seame of barley[1243]
Margin:	Rent in the same towne.	
	Item received for the yerely rent of tenementes and messuages in the said towne belonging to maner forseid	xxj[£] vj[s] xj[d].ob. and half a quarter of barley
Margin:	Rent of the Uplond belongyng to the said maner of Faversham.	
	Item received for the yerely rent of Uplond belongyng to the principall maner forseid in custume cocks henes and egges. All rated in money	Lij[£] xj[d] ob.farthing[1244]

[1242] Val. Eccl. Henry VIII gives Ferme **Rent** and Custume.
[1243] Valor gives a quarter of barley.
[1244] *Latin*: quadrans. Valor gives Lij[£] xij[d] ob. q[a].

folio 33v.		
Margin:	Casualtyes.	
	Item received yerely by estymacion of and for all casualties of all Letes and courtes belonging to the forseid pryncipall maner holdyn within the towne and hundred of Faversham. As in fynes for sutes mercyamentes and relyves to the sum of	viij$^{£}$
Margin:	Sale of tymbir and wood in the Blean and in Bosynden belonging to the forseid principall maner	
	Item received comenly yerely of the Forester of the Blean tymbir and wood sold by hym there and in Bosynden together lying	xx$^{£}$
Margin:	Ferme of the said Blean.	
	Item received yerely by the handes of the forseid Forester for the ferme in wodlesse in the said Blean	xj^{s}
	~~Item by the handes of the same Forester for the yerely rent of ix gates ledyng intothe seyd Blean iij^{s} and ix hennes~~	
Margin:	Rent of the same Bleane.	
	Item received by the handes of the same Forester for the yerely rent of ix gates ledyng into the said Blean iij^{s} and ix hennes price ij^{s} iij^{d}. A Cv egges price v^{d} q^{a}, total	v^{s} viij^{d} q^{a}
folio 34		
Margin:	Profittes of Lamas Fayre.	
	Item received comenly yerely of the profittes of a fayre at lamas otherwise callyd Saint Peter's Chains'[1245]	Liij^{s} iiij^{d}
Margin:	Resolutions out of the forsaid principall maner off Faversham	
	Sum of all the perticulers aforseid CLxx$^{£}$ xiiiij^{s} xj^{d} ob. Wherof goith out to the Monastery of Saynct Augustynes without the walles of Cauntorbury for a yerely pension	vj$^{£}$ xiij^{s} iiij^{d}
	and to the same monastery for a yerely rent out of the yoke of Chetham xj^{s} v^{d}, sum	vij$^{£}$ iiij^{s} ix^{d}
	Clear sum	CLxiij$^{£}$ x^{s} ij^{d}. ob. j quarter and a half of barley
Margin:	Ferme of the lande	
	Item received for the yerely ferme of land callyd Southfelde and Hagdale	x$^{£}$
	Item received for the yerely ferme of land lying in Lodgemersshe and Weldmersshe	iij$^{£}$ vj^{s} viij^{d}
	Sum	xiij$^{£}$ vj^{s} viij^{d}
Margin:	Ferme of the land in the occupying of Robert Broke	
	Item received of Robert A Broke of Harnhill for the yerely ferme of xvj acres and a half of lande, lying and adjoynyng to the landes of a messuage or tenement callyd Lambertislonde	xx^{s}
Margin:	Resolutions out of the said landes.	
	Sum as it appereth. Wherof goith out for a yerely rent for part of the same	xiij^{s} viij^{d}

[1245] Sancti Petri ad vincula. 14 August. Etymologically it derives from 'loaf' and 'mass' and in the early English church it was customary to consecrate bread made from the first ripe corn on Mass on this day, probably in thanksgiving for the harvest.

landes to the Canons of Seynt Stephyns chappell at Westmynster. Holden of theirs[1246] of Quenecourte in Osprenge iij^{s} iiij^{d} and to the heires of Mathewe Martyn for the resydue of the seid londes, holden of there maner of Dargate xxij^{d}, a cock price ij^{d}, iiij hennes[1247] price the hen iij^{d}, sum xij^{d}.
Sum iij^{s}[1248] Sum vj^{s} iiij^{d}. Clear Sum

folio 34v.

Margin: Ferme of Cokham and Mentylham
Item received for the yerely ferme of lande callyd Cockham and Mentylham — xLvj^{s} viij^{d}

Margin: Resolutions out of the said Cockham and Mentilham
Sum as it appereth. Whereof goith out to the Archebisshop of Cauntorbury for the tyme beyng for a yerely rent of the saide londes, holden of his maner of Boughton-under-Blean vij^{s} and to the vicar of Harnhill for a yerely pensyon goyng out of the same landes iiijs viijd. Sum xj^{s} viij^{d}. Clear sum — xxxv^{s}

Margin: Abbottiscourte in the Ile of Hartey
Item received for the yerely ferme of the cite of a messuage or tenement callyd Abbottiscourte with the lande and mershe therto appertyenyng in the Ile of Hartey, and for a marsshe there callyd Julyan marsshe — xx$^{£}$ vj^{s} viij^{d}

Margin: Resolutions out of the saide Abbotiscourte
Sum as it appereth. Wherof goith out to the shryves turne for a yerely rent for part of the same londes belonging to the said messuage or tenement ix^{d} and to the heiers of Thomas Frogenhale for a yerely rent also out part of the said landes iiij^{s} xj^{d} ob. quarter and for a Walscott comunely yerely there xL^{s}.
Sum xLv^{s} viij ob. quarter Clear sum — xviij$^{£}$ iij^{d} quarter[1249]

Margin: Ferme of Preistfelde
Item received for the yerely ferme of lande callid Preistfeld — xxxiij^{s} iiij^{d}[1250]
Sum as it appereth

folio 35

Margin: Ferme of Necgdon Marsshe
Item received for the yerely ferme of a mersshe callyd Necgdon marsshe — viij$^{£}$

Margin: Resolutions out of the said Necgdon Marsshe
Sum as it appereth. Wherof goith out for a yerely pension to the parson of Graveney, iij^{s} iiij^{d}. Clear sum — vij$^{£}$ xvj^{s} viij^{d}

Margin: Ferme of Horshopes and other.
Item received for the yerely ferme of Horshopes at Broke Bridge, and for Catstart with other medowes there — xxxiij^{s} iiij^{d}

Margin: Resolutions out of the sayd Horshopes
Sum as it appereth. Wherof goith out for a yerely rent to the maner of Graveney ij^{s} vj^{d} Clear sum — xxx^{s} x^{d}

[1246] Val. Eccl. has 'there maner'.
[1247] Val. Eccl. gives 'rent hennes'.
[1248] Val. Eccl. omits 'Summa iij^{s}.'
[1249] Val. Eccl. gives xviij$^{£}$ xj^{d} quarter.
[1250] Val. Eccl. gives xxx^{s} iiij^{d}.

Margin: Goremarsshe[1251]

Item received for the yerely ferme of Goremarsshe with the Uplonde therto belongyng — viij$^{£}$

Margin: Resolutions out of the sayd marshe

Sum as it appereth. Whereof goith out for a yerely rent to the Archebisshopes of Cauntorburye for the tyme beyng v^{s} vj^{d}, and to the vycar of Harnhill for a yerely pension out of the same marsshe xiij^{s} iiij^{d}, and for a Walscott comunely yerely of the seid marsshe v^{s} xj^{d}. Sum xxiiij^{s} ix^{d}. Clear sum — vj$^{£}$ xv^{s} iij^{d}

folio 35v.

Margin: Ferme of our liberties of the sea and snowte weres

Item received by estymation for the yerely ferme of our tenentes fisshing within oure libertie of the sea and for snowt weres which we have and holde of the kyng by fee ferme — xxxiij^{s} iiij^{d}

Margin: Resolutions out of the said liberties and weres

Sum as it appereth. Wherof goith out yerely to the kynges maner of Mylton xx^{s} Clear sum — xiij^{s} iiij^{d}

Margin: Ferme of the maner or tenement callid Elynden in the diocese of Caunterbury and deanery of Westbere

Item received for the yerely ferme of the maner or tenement callid Elynden vj$^{£}$ and in rent yerely xiij^{s} iiij^{d} and in rent hennes xij, price iij^{s}, sum — vj$^{£}$ xvj^{s}[1252]

Margin: Sale of tymbir and wodde there.

Item received comunely yerely for the sale of tymbir and wodd out of the woddes belonging to the said maner or tenement — xx^{s}

Margin: Ferme of the messuage or tenement callid Lambertislonde

Item received for the yerely ferme of the messuage or tenement callid Lambertislondewith the londes the londes *(sic)* therto appertyning — xij$^{£}$ ij^{s}

Margin: Sale of tymbir and wodd there messuage or tenement named Lambertislonde

Item received comunely yerely for the sale of tymbir and wodd out of the woddes of the said messuage or tenement of Lambertislonde callyd Combe Conygrove, and a grove adioyning to the said tenement — x^{s}

Sum as well of the forseid maner or tenement callid Elynden as of the said messuage or tenement callid Lambertislonde with the sale of tymbir and wodd as is aforeseid is xx$^{£}$ viij^{s} iiij^{d}. Out of whiche said maner or tenement callid Elynden ther goith out in rent yerely to the maner of Whitstaple x^{s}, to the prior of Christischurche in Cantorbury for a yerely rent of certeyn londe belonging to the said maner or tenement of Elynden, holden of his maner of Seasalter v^{s}, and for a yerely obit for the soulles of Robert Billesdon gentleman donor of the seid tenement callyd Elynden, Thebalde Evyas gentylwoman, andfor all christian soulles, x^{s} vij^{d}[1253] wherof the mayre of Faversham with ij of his brethern for the tyme beying hath and shall receyve — ix$^{£}$ xvij^{d} ob.

[1251] Val. Eccl. gives 'Ferme of Goremarsshe'.

[1252] Val. Eccl. adds ...iiij^{d}.

[1253] Val. Eccl. gives v^{s} viij^{d}.

yerely for ever before the masse *[folio 36]* of the said obit xxiij^{d}, that is to say, the same mayer shall receyve by the handes of the chauntor of the monasterie in faversham foreseid for the tyme beyng xiij^{d}, and shall offer at the same masse j^{d} and either of the said mayers brethern shall receyve of the said chauntor v^{d}, and either of theym shall offer in lyke maner j^{d}. Sum as it appereth before written. Also it is ordeyned by the said Robert Billesdon to be gevyn yerely in the day of the said obit to xij power persones xij^{d} and vij^{s} viij^{d} residue to be bestowed for wast of wax, rynging of belles and to preistes and clerkes. Sum as it appereth beforesaid. Also ther goith out of the fore named messuage or tenement callid Lambertislonde together with the londes therto apperteynyng for a yerely rent of part of the same landes to the heieres of the forseid Mathewe Martyn, holden of their forsaid maner of Dargate xv^{d} ob. and to the heires of John Boyce late of Sandwiche for an annuitye yerely goyng out aswell of the forseid maner or tenement called Elynden, as of the said messuage or tenement called Lambertislonde x$^{£}$.
Sum xj$^{£}$ vj^{s} x^{d} ob.
Clear sum aswell of the forsaid maner or tenement callyd Elynden as of the said messuage or tenement callid Lambertislonde with the sales of tymbir and woddes there.

Margin: Ten poundes in Almes money ordeyned by Kyng Stephyn and Quene Mawde his wife to be gevyn yerely to power people perpetuallye, and so used for the soulles of the said kyng and quene founders of the said monastery of Faversham forseid and for the soulles of Ewstace the sonne of theym, William Erle of Boleyn and all Christen soulles. x$^{£}$.
In the first instance every Fryday xij^{d}. Sum by the yere Lij^{s} in the day of the Nativitie of our Lorde God iij^{s} iiij^{d}. In the day of the Epiphanie of our Lorde God, iij^{s} iiij^{d}. In the day of the purification of our Blissed Lady the Virgyn iij^{s} iiij^{d}. In the day of the Annunciation of our Blissed Lady the Virgyn iij^{s} iiij^{d}. Uppon Palme Sonday iij^{s} iiij^{d}. Uppon Mawndy Thursday x^{s}. Uppon Good Fryday iij^{s} iiij^{d}. Uppon Ester Evyn iij^{s} iiij^{d}. Uppon Ester day iij^{s} iiij^{d}. The iiijth day of Maye, beying the day of the obit of the forsaid Quene vj^{s} viij^{d}. In the day of The assention of our Savyour iij^{s} iiij^{d}. In the daye of Pentecoste iij^{s} iiij^{d}. Uppon Trinite Sonday iij^{s} iiij^{d}. In the day of Corporis Christi iij^{s} iiij^{d}. In the day of Saynct John Baptist iij^{s} iiij^{d}. In the day of Sayncts Petir and Paule iij^{s} iiij^{d}. In the day of the transfiguration of our Savyour Jesus iij^{s} iiij^{d}.[1254] In the day of the Natyvitie of our blissed Lady the Virgyn iij^{s} iiij^{d}. In the day of the dedication of the churche of the said monasterye iij^{s} iiij^{d}. In the day of the exaltation of the Holly Crosse iij^{s} iiij^{d}. In the day of All Sayncts iij^{s} iiij^{d}, and in the xxiiijth day of Octobir being the day of the obit of the said Kyng vj^{s} viij^{d}. Sum vij$^{£}$ ij^{s}. And the Lviij^{s} residue to be geveyn yerely to bedred, blynde and lame people within the towne and hundred of Faversham. Sum

folio 36v

[1254] Val. Eccl. gives; In the day of the Assumption of our Blissid Lady the Virgin iij^{s} iiij^{d}

	Item ther goith out of the fermes of the messuages and landes before expressed by[1255] yerely for ever over and above the obit of Robert Billesdon and Thebald Evyas forsaid for vij obbittes more for oure founders as it appereth by our mortlage boke to preistes, clerkes, power people for wast of wax and for ryngyng of belles	iij$^{£}$ xvj^{d}
	Sum	Shown
Margin:	The maner of Kynggissnoth in the diocese of Cauntorbury and in the deanry of Sutton.	
	Item received of the yerely ferme of the maner of Kinggissnoth	v$^{£}$ vj^{s} viij^{d}
	Item received yerely in rent of the tenentes of the same maner in money cockes and hennes to the sum of	xxxix^{s} ij^{d} ob.
	Item received of the said tenentes for the yerely ferme of Wodleese there	x^{s}
	Item received of Antony Sentleger gentleman for the yerely ferme of v acres and one rodd of lande inclosed in his parke there,, at Lamas otherwise called Advincla Sancti Petri, a buck, or in money vj^{s} viij^{d}. At the election of the Abbat of the said Monasterye for the tyme beying	vj^{s} viij^{d}
Margin:	Sale of tymbir and wodde there.	
	Item received comunely yerely for the sale of tymbir and wodd out of the woddes belonging to the said maner called Estwodd, Westwodde, Melgrove and other there	xxiij^{s} iiij^{d}
Margin:	Resolutions out of the said manner of Kynggissnoth.	
	Sum of the said maner of Kynggissnoth with the sale of the tymbir and wodd there all rated in money ix$^{£}$ v^{s} x^{d} ob. Wherof goith out to the persone of Ulcombe for a yerely pension x^{s}, and to the sheryve for a yerely fyne for the tenentes of the same maner xij^{d}. Sum xj^{s}. Clear sum[1256]	viij$^{£}$ x^{s} x^{d}.ob
Margin:	Fereherst in the diocese of Cantorbury forsaid and in the deanry of Charyng.	
	Item received for the yerely rent and ferme of Greate Fereherst and Litell Fereherst Lviij^{s} iij^{d} and in rent hennes iiij price xij^{d}. Sum	Lix^{s} iij^{d}.[1257]
	Sum[1258]	as shown.
	Sum of all the temporalties within the countie of Kent belonging to the forsayde monastery as before appereth	CCLix$^{£}$ xiij^{s} ix^{d}
folio 37	The parsonage of Boughton under the Bleane in the diocese of Canterbury forseid and in the deanry of Osprenge forenamed.	
Margin:	Inprimis the site of the said parsonage with the glebeland and all maner of tithes to the same belongyng, nowe beyng in our owne handes, hath been letten to ferme by yere as it appereth by indenture for the sum of	xxvj$^{£}$
Margin:	The parsonage of Harnhill in the diocese and deanry before named.	
	Item the site of the same parsonage with all maner of tithes to the same belongyng is letten to ferme by yere as it appereth by indenture in corne and money for the som of	x$^{£}$

[1255] Val. Eccl. adds 'byere' (by yere yerely).

[1256] Val. Eccl. gives xiij^{s} for x^{s}.

[1257] Val. Eccl. gives only Lix^{s}.

[1258] Val. Eccl. gives CCLxj$^{£}$ v^{s} ij^{d} ob. q^{a} quarter [and] half barley. This sum is placed after the fees.

Margin:	The parsonage of Preston next Faversham in the afore written diocese and deanry	
	Item the site of the said parsonage with all maner of tithes to the same belonging nowe beying in our owne handes hath bene letten to ferme by yere as it appereth by indenture for the sum of	xiij$^{£}$ vj^{s} viij^{d}
Margin:	Resolutions out of the said parsonages of Boughton Harnhill and Preston	
	Sum of all the said parsonages Lix$^{£}$ vj^{s} viij^{d}. Whereof goith out to Christischurche in Cauntorbury for a yerely pension v£ and to the Archedeacon of Cauntorbury forseid for another yerely pension out of the said parsonage xxvj^{s} viij^{d}. Sum vj$^{£}$ vj^{s} viij^{d}.	Liij$^{£}$
	Clear sum of all the said parsonages	
Margin:	Recepte of pensions in the above written diocese and deanry.	
	Item received for a yerely pension out of the churche of Luddenham iij$^{£}$ vj^{s} viij^{d}, and for a yerely pension out of the churche of Newynham xxxiij^{s} iiij^{d}. Sum	v$^{£}$
Margin:	Oblations	
	Item received yerely by estimation for all maner of oblations done in the monasterye of Faversham forseid	iij^{s} iiij^{d}
	Clear sum of the receptes of all the spiritualties belonging to the forseid monasterye	Lviij$^{£}$ iij^{s} iiij^{d}
folio 37v.		
Margin:	Fees	
	First to William Roper, High Stewarde of our landes letes and courtes within the countie of Kent, by yere	viij$^{£}$ vj^{s} viij^{d}
	Item to our baylif of the towne and libertie of Faversham foreseid by yere	xxj^{s} iiij^{d}
	Item to Robert Coldwell, receyvor of the farmes and rents of the same towne of Faversham as before appereth by year	Liij^{s} iiij^{d}
	Item to Symon Auncelme, receyvor of the maner of Kynggisnoth and Uplonde forsaid by yere iij$^{£}$ and for a gowne xiij^{s} iiij^{d}, sum	iij$^{£}$ xiij^{s} iiij^{d}[1259]
	Item to Joseph Beverley, awditor of our accomptes by yere	iij$^{£}$ vj^{s} viij^{d}
	Item to Thomas Hungarforde gentleman, receyvor of the fermes and rentes of the maner of Elynden, Lambertislonde and Blean, Bosynden, and other as before appereth	iij$^{£}$ vj^{s} viij^{d}
	Sum	xxij$^{£}$ viij^{s}
folio 38		
Margin:	The maner of Bendishehall, in the diocese of London, and in the deanry of Sampford in the countie of Essex	
	Item received for the yerely ferme of a maner called Bendisshehall in the parisshe of Radwynter in the countie of Essex for all maner of rentes, services, harryettes, fynes and sutes to the same maner belongyng, or in any wise apperteyning as it appereth by indenture the sum of	xxxiij$^{£}$

[1259] Val. Eccl. has iij$^{£}$ vj^{s} viij^{d}.

Margin: Sale of the wodd there

Item received comunely yerely for the sale of wodd out of the woddes there callyd Oldwod, Newewodde, Bradhedge, Grove and other hedge rowes there — iij$^{£}$ vj^{s} viij^{d}

Margin: Resolution of the said maner of Bendisshe

Sum of the said maner with the sale of the woddes there xxxvj$^{£}$ vj^{s} viij^{d}. — xxviij$^{£}$ iij^{s} viij^{d}

Wherof goith out yerely to thbe Prior and convent of Cristischurche in London for a pension v$^{£}$ x^{s}, and to the parson of Radwynter forsaid, for the yerely tithes of the said maner, one acre of whete in harvest, price x^{s}, one acre of otes price v^{s} iiij^{d}. A lambe price viij^{d}. A pigg price iiij^{d}, and in money iij^{s} iiij^{d}. Also to a steward for a yerely fee for kepyng the letes and courtes of the said maner xiij^{s} iiij^{d}, and

to Edmond Burley, receyvor of the ferme of the said maner and of the sale of woddes for his fee xxti s. Sum viij$^{£}$ iij^{s}. Clear sum

Sum of the temporalities within the countie of Essex as before appereth. Wherof goith out as is aforsaid

Sum total of the whole value of all the maners, parsonages, landes, tenements and other emolumentes belonging to the said monastery of Faversham as before appereth — CCCLv£ xv^{s} ij^{d}

Wherof goith out yerely in rentes resolute [*folio 38 verso*] pensions, almes, fees, to stewardes, awditours receyvors and other, as before appereth[1260] — Lxxv$^{£}$ xv^{s} xj^{d} q^{a}.

Clear sum of the whole yerely value of all the maners parsonages, landes, tenementes and other emolumentes belongyng or apperteynyng to the sayde monastery as before pertycularly CCLxxxiiij$^{£}$ xv^{s} v^{d} a quarter and a half of barley[1261]

4 pages then cut or torn out, then folio 39 blank

[1260] Val. Eccl. gives this figure as Lx$^{£}$ xix^{s} vij^{d} q^{a}.

[1261] Val. Eccl. gives this figure as CCiiij^{xx} vj$^{£}$ xij^{s} vj^{d} ob q^{a} a quarter and a half of barley. The tenth part in respect thereof xxviij$^{£}$ xiij^{s} iij^{d}.

Appendix 19
List of wills for tenants in the 1532 Rental

Name	*Occupation*	*Street*	*Prop-erty*	*Will*	*Date*	*Area*
Ampner R.		Preston E.	194	PRC 3/7/202	1525	Oare
Ampner T.	parish clerk	Preston E.	191	PRC 17/16/157	1525	Preston
Amys Ri.		East N.	156	PRC 17/6/100	1495	Preston
Ashbury Ra.	baker	North W.	66	PRC 17/15/94	1521	Faversham
At Ham A.		Pn. Rectory	205			
Awder Gg.		West S.	263			
Baker R.		Preston W.	208	PRC 17/8/293	1503	Faversham
Baker R.				PRC 3/7/4	1525	Stone
Bangor J.		North W.	357	PRC 17/5/106	1489	Faversham
Barber J.	innholder	Preston E.	168	PRC 17/7/30	1500	Faversham
Barker T.		Court W.	17			
Barley ?		Kingsfield				
Barnard J		West S.	277	PRC 17/20/21	1534-36	Faversham
Barough Agnes		West N.	379	PRC 3/7/51	1527	Frittenden
Barow John				PRC 16/1/33	1489	Frittenden
Barow William		West N.	380	PRC 17/5/224	1492	Faversham
Beale H.		Preston W.	234	PRC 17/12/384	1515	Faversham
Beauty J.		Market Place	126	PRC 32/17/7	1538	Preston
Bellinger John		North W.	77	PRC 17/18/224	1529	Faversham
Belke W.		North E.	100	PRC 3/7/219	1528	Sheldwich
Belke W.		North E.	100	PRC 3/11/47	1540	Faversham
Bennett T.		Preston E.	193			
Best W.		North W.	63	PRC 3/3/198	1508	Faversham
Best W.				PRC 17/12/2	1512	Faversham
Beverley John		Court W.	8	PRC 17/36/1	1561	Faversham
Billesdon R.		Church Lane S	53	PRC 17/9/150	1502	Faversham
Binder John		Market Place	124	PRC 32/4/38	1495	Faversham
Birches T.		Preston W.	218	PRC 17/3/415	1482	Sittingbourne
Bix T.		Tanners W.	320	PRC 17/19/340	1530	Faversham
Blackbourne T		North W.	55			

Blackbourne Wm		Court E.	45			
Bourne W		West N		PRC 17/22/53	1541	Faversham
Breach G.		Preston W.	255	PRC 17/13/130	1518-19	Canterbury
Broke William		Preston W	252	PRC 17/18/139	1528	Faversham
Brimstone John	gentleman	Prestn Rectory	199	PRC 17/12/568	1517	Preston
Brounston John				PRC 32/4/86	1495	Preston
Bringbourne John		North E.	99	PRC 17/12/480	1515	Faversham
Bryan R.		Preston W.	216			
Buck T.		Preston W.	217	PRC 17/12/9	1511	Faversham
Bunce J.		West N.	374	PRC 17/3/351	1481	Throwley
Burston J		Tanners E	301	PRC 17/12/335	1514	Faversham
Burwash N	yeoman	West S	270	PRC 17/18/242	1529	Pluckley
Butcher J		Prestn Rectory	206			
Castlock John	abbot	Court W	13	PRC 3/9/43	1543	Faversham
Castlock Willm		Court W	18	PRC 3/12/52	1550	Faversham
Champneys J		Key N	25	PRC 17/14/302	1521	Faversham
Charnock O		Court W	3			
Childmells Thos		Middle Row	114	PRC 17/3/253	1480	Throwley
Childmille Thos				PRC 17/11/196	1510	Faversham
Clerke William	chaplain	West N.	353	PRC 17/9/324	1508	Faversham
Clerk, William	tailor			PRC 17/12/431	1515	Faversham
Clifford Humph		Preston W.	212	PRC 17/12/67	1512	Preston
Coldwell R		Market Place	122	PRC 17/9/172	1505	Goodnestone
Coldwell Richd		North W	71			
Coldwell W		Court E	41	PRC 17/8/213	1502	Goodnestone
Collin J		Court W	12			
Coney J		North E	86	PRC 17/75/95	1526	Faversham
Constantine W	hermit	West N	354	PRC 17/10/3	1505	Ospringe
Cooke T	tanner	Tanner W	311	PRC 17/11/50	1508	Faversham
Cowper Ar		Preston E	189	PRC 17/19/87	1531	Faversham
Cripps H		North W	62			
Curtis J	tanner	Tanner E	298	PRC 17/13/185	1518	Faversham
Crouch, a' J		Court W	44	PRC 17/21/43	1537	Canterbury

Darell J	knight	Tanner W	325	PROB 11/16/24	1509	
Darland S		Preston W	244			
Derland Andrew				PRC 17/9/20	1504	Faversham
Davy Edward E	miller	Tanner W	326			
Davy John	jurat	North W	56	PRC 17/23/173	1544	Faversham
Dobbys	widow	Preston W	213			
Dobbys William	barber	Preston W	213	PRC 17/10/124	1506	Faversham
Dryland Ri (J)		North E	88			
Dryland Ri (S)		Court E	33	PRC 17/30/42	1550-1	Faversham
Dunnings J.		Court E	43	PRC 17/12/523	1516	Faversham
Eagles		North E	90			
Elfrith W		West N	381			
Evyas Th	widow	North E	96	PRC 32/2/426	1479	Faversham
Exbridge J		Tanner W	314	PRC 17/5/214	1496	Faversham
Fale R		West S	289	PRC 17/19/111	1530	Faversham
Flok Ri	widow of	West N	377			
Forman Ri		Preston W	249	PRC 17/17/331	1527	Faversham
Friend Ri		Court W	14	PRC 17/22/32	1540	Faversham
Fryer J		West N	338			
Fuller T		Preston E	189	PRC 17/6/223	1497	Faversham
Frognall Thos	esquire	Preston W	215	PRC 32/8/97	1504	Buckland
Frognall Thos				PRC 3/3/185	1505	Graveney
Fylkes John		West N	330	PRC 17/3/5	1476	Newnham
Fylkes John				PRC 17/32/187	1556	Norton
German T		Tanner W	314			
Goldfinch J		North E	101	PROB 11/28/34	1541	
Goodwin J		Middle Row	149	PRC 17/19/231	1531	Faversham
Goldings ?Ri		Preston E	190	PRC 16/1/2	1514	Faversham
Gilnott T		Tanner E	302	PRC 32/4/39	1495	Faversham
Gosling Ri		Court E	34	PRC 17/16/329	1524	Hawkhurst
Green J		Middle Row	116			

Green T	barber	Court W	2	PRC 32/4/22	1494	Faversham
Greenstreet P		West N	328			
Grey Chr.		West S	265			
Grigg Jas		Court W	4	PRC 32/21/34	1546	Sandwich
Hales J		Preston W	234	PRC 17/5/257	1490	Faversham
				PRC 16/2/319	1513	Ospringe
Hall Ro		Court W	24			
Hampton J		Market Place	147	PRC 17/24/242	1544	Faversham
Hardy J	butcher	West N	354	PRC 17/9/334	1508	Faversham
Hardyman D		Tanners E	305	PRC 17/14/212	1521	Faversham
Hatch Henry		Key N	26	PRC 32/15/212	1533	Faversham
Henxhilles R		Preston W	237	PROB 6/1/135	1568	Faversham
Highwood Wm		West N	375	PRC 17/24/21	1544	Faversham
Highmore R		Preston W	250			
Hills J	widow	Court W	6			
Hills Alice				PRC 32/3/129	1487	Faversham
Hills Juliana				PRC 32/2/411	1478-9	Sheldwich
Hills L		North E	82			
Hoad J		West N	367			
Hobnett Reg.	yeoman	Court E	43	PRC 17/12/400	1515	Faversham
Horne M		Preston E	184			
Howlett Hugh	wax chandler	North W	73	PRC 17/20/147	1535	Faversham
Hunt W		North W	59	PRC 32/8/152	1506	Boughton
Hornescliffe J		Preston W	246			
Idelles Ellen		Preston W	218			
Kersyman		Preston E	197			
Keir J		West N	349	PROB 11/17/21	1511	Faversham
Keir Ri		West S	286			
Keir R		West N	349			
Kemp W	shoemaker	Preston E	192	PRC 3/17/142 & PRC 10/2/73	1566	Faversham
Kibbet J		Middle Row	108	PRC 17/22/228	1542	Faversham

Lacy R		Chch Lane S	52	PRC 17/10/121	1506	Faversham
Lacey Chas		Tanners E	304			
Ledmede, Ri		Court W	18	PRC 17/6/242	1497	Faversham
Ledmede, T				PRC 17/8/101	1501	Faversham
Lewknor, Reg.	gentleman	North E	93	PRC 17/23/50	1540	Faversham
Lilley, R		Preston W	254			
Lilly, Margery				PRC 3/5/168 & PRC 3/7/203	1525	Gaveney
Little, Richard		Tanners W	316	PRC 17/6/103	1495	Faversham
Little, Richard				PRC 17/15/186	1523	Faversham
Longbridge, J		Preston W	250	PRC 17/10/62	1505	Ospringe
Love, John		Preston W	218	PRC 17/13/109	1514	Faversham
Lull, Richard		Keylane S	30	PROB 11/15/17	1506	Faversham
Lyon, John		Tanner E	299	PRC 16/1/3	1491-7	Faversham
Lyon, John	carpenter			PRC 17/12/391	1514	Faversham
Malpas	widow	Preston (Inn) W	257			
Malpas, Alice	widow Robert			PRC 17/12/123	1512	Faversham
Malpas, Thomas				PROB 11/15/12 & PRC 3/3/188	1506	Faversham
Martin, Emma		Court E	42			
Marten, Robert	gentleman			PRC 17/26/14	1546	Faversham & Graveney
Mattress, R		Tanners E	300			
Maycott, R (J)		Court W	9	PRC 17/27/31	1550	Ospringe
Maycott, Ro (S)		Court W	1	PROB 11/26/8	1533	Faversham
Makenades, W		Preston Rectory	199	PRC 3/6/77	1528	Ewell
Mellers, John		Tanner W	313	PRC 17/11/60	1509	Shepherdswell
Myllowe, John				PRC 3/14/82	1557	Faversham
Mercer, Gg		West N	370			
Milkham, Md	spinster	Middle Row	112			
Minces		Preston E	191			
Moore, William		Keylane S	31			
More, William	fletcher			PRC 17/12/ 239	1512	Faversham

More, William	fletcher			PRC 17/12/449	1512	Faversham
Moore, William	waterman			PRC 17/12/228	1513	Faversham
Morys, S		Preston E	194			
Mores, Agnes	widow			PRC 17/17/346	1527	Faversham
Mores, Philip				PRC 17/14/8	1519	Faversham
Muddle, J		Preston W	221			
Modyll, Thomas				PRC 17/19/264	1532	
Nicholas, R		Tanners E	306			
Nicholas, Thos				PRC 3/7/226	1529	Faversham
Norton, Sir John	knight	Church Lane S	49	PRC 3/14/107	1557	Bobbing
Norton, Wm	gentleman	North E	95	PRC 17/13/118	1518	Oare
Norton, Wm				PRC 17/26/296	1549	Chillenden
Norden, Thomas		Preston W	257			
Norton, Thomas				PRC 17/38/96	1564	Faversham
Nobys, Stephen		Preston W	228			
Norwood, J		Tanner W	323	PRC 17/30/67	1554/5	Whitstable
Oliver , R		Tanner E	304			
Orwell, Simon		Tanner E	306	PRC 16/1/6	1500	Faversham
Page, J		Court W	5			
Paternoster, T		Preston W	240			
Park, J		Market Place	134			
Penbrook, W		West S	273			
Perne, Thomas		Preston E	182	PRC 17/19/174	1532	Faversham
Philpot, Wm		North W	70	PROB 11/21/8	1523	Faversham
Pickering, T		East S	167			
Pope, Richard		Olboldisland		PRC 3/3 152 & 161	1507	Hartlip
Pope, Richard				PRC32/15/6	1527	Boughton/Blean
Poynings, E		East N	165	PROB 11/20q21	1521	Westenhanger
Powell, David		North W	78	PRC 17/13/158	1518	Faversham
Preston, J		Preston W	255	PRC 32/3/30	1485	Faversham

Princhett, A		East N	157			
Princhet, Godleve	widow			PRC 17/32/26	1558	Faversham
Proud, John		North W	81	PRC 17/19/314	1533	Faversham
Pullen, John (S)		North W	72	PRC 3/15/52	1558	Faversham
Quiller, Marg		West N	353			
Quyller, Peter				PRC 32/3/20	1484	Faversham
Reeve, P		Keylane S	29			
Richardson, Jn	tailor	West N	361	PRC 17/12/307	1514	Ospringe
Richardson, Jn				PRC 17/8/100	1501	Faversham
Roach, J		Preston E	193	PRC 3/7/198	1524	Faversham
Roberds, J		Preston W	220			
Roberdes Ri		Preston E	188			
Roberd, Clemence	widow			PRC 17/12/44	1511	Faversham
Robert, Richard				PRC 17/4/120	1487	Faversham
Rogers, Alice		Preston W	239			
Rose, W		Preston W	227			
Rowett,	widow	West N	356			
Route, John				PRC 17/3/432	1483	Faversham
Rowte, William				PRC 17/10/203	1507	Ospringe
Rye, Edward		Tanner E	295	PRC 17/21/195 & PRC 17/22/43	1540	Ospringe
Sare, John		East N	155	PRC 17/22/51	1541	Faversham
Sare, John	vicar			PRC 3/3/184	1505	Sheldwich
Sare, Thos		Preston W	246	PRC 17/21/214	1539	Faversham
Scott,	cooper	West N	337			
Seed, J		Court W	10	PROB 11/39/14	1557	Faversham
Seath, R		Preston W	249			
Sethe, Richard				PRC 32/13/129	1522	Stone/Faversham
Sethe, Robert				PRC 17/7/83	1498/9	Throwley
Sheepstail, J		West N	358			
Simon, Barth.		North W	65	PRC 17/17/348	1527/8	Faversham

Simon, Ra	miller	Tanners W	322	PROB 11/29/3	1541	
Smith, E	widow	Preston E	181	PRC 17/5/270	1490/1	Ospringe
Smith, Thomas		Court W	21	PRC 17/5/358	1493	Faversham
Smith, Thomas				PRC 17/21/293	1538	Faversham
Smythe, Thomas				PRC 17/23/150	1544	Faversham
Sole, John		Preston, W	245			
Sole, Thomas		Preston W	245	PRC 17/5/342	1492/3	Faversham
Sondes, Ann		West S	262			
Sondes, William	esquire	Court W	7	PRC 32/2/275	1473/4	Throwley
Sparrow, T		Preston W	243	PRC 17/12/553	1516	Canterbury
Stransham, L		Market Place	128			
Stransham, John		Tanner East	305	PRC 17/2/51	1472	Faversham
Thomas, Thos		West N	334	PRC 17/27/198 & PRC 3/12/18	1550	Preston
Thornevale, Tho		West S	275	PRC 32/3/3	1484	Ospringe
Thornvale, Thos				PRC 3/3/191	1506	
Tilney, John		West S	271	PRC 17/19/240	1531	Faversham
Turner, Robt		Court E	40	PRC 16/3/135 & PRC 17/16/22	1523	Faversham
Turner, John		Court E	41	PRC 32/5/8	1498/9	Faversham
Turner, Richard		West S	268	PRC 3/10/72	1541	Faversham
Ulffe, Richard		Preston W	247	PRC 17/6/115	1495	Faversham
Upton, Steph		Tanners E	296	PRC 17/20/149	1535	Faversham
Venour, Wm		Court W	38			
Waytes		Preston W	243			
Warham, John	gentleman	Preston rectory	198			
Warmcourt, Si.	brewer	Preston E	190	PRC 17/6/215	1496	Faversham
Whitlock,		Tanners W	319			
Whitloke, John				PRC 17/16/101	1524	Throwley
White, S		Tanners	303			
Withiott, Robt		East N	153	PRC 17/12/233	1511	Faversham
Willowes, Wm		Keylane S	31	PRC 17/5/39	1494	Faversham

Woolgate, Ralph	yeoman	Key N	27	PRC 17/38/39	1565	Harty
Wyer, Wm		Market place	119			
Yalding, John		Preston W	247	PRC 3/5/168	1524	Goodnestone
Yalding, John				PRC 17/19/159	1531	Goodnestone
Yalding, Richd		West N	344	PRC 17/12/322	1514	Faversham
Yalding, Richd				PRC 17/12/429	1512	Goodnestone
Yalding, Richd				PRC 17/28/27	1552	Goodnestone

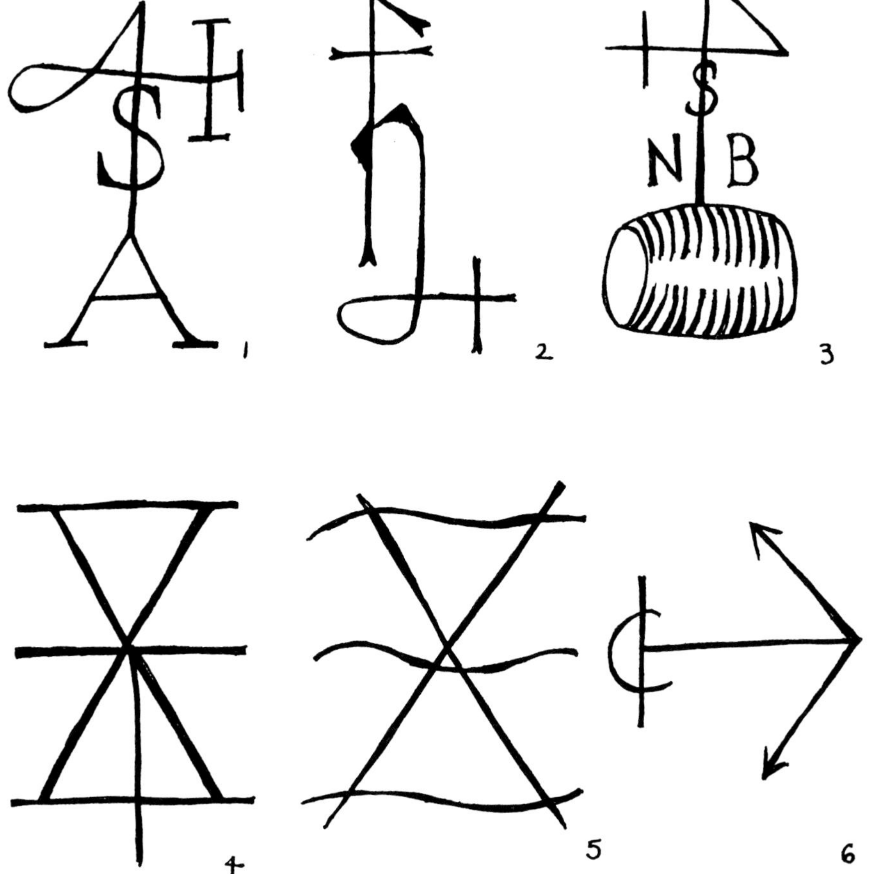

Faversham Merchants Marks:
(1) Abraham Snothe, 1585 [1262], (2) Henry Hatche, 1533 [1263], (3) Unidentified [1264] (4) John Trowtes, 1585 [1265], (5) Clement Trowtes, 1582 & 1585 [1266], (6) Robert Rye, 1582 & 1585 [1267] (by DH)

1262 Fa/JQr 6/2 no. 21.

1263 Brass in Faversham church. Kent Family History Society microfiche Vol. 1616, C174.

1264 Brass in Faversham Church associated with this mark is a badge containing a gloved hand holding a hawk, belled and on the same slab is a shield of the arms of the Haberdashers Company which were granted in 1502. KFHS microfiche C207.

1265 Fa/JQr 6/2 no. 27.

1266 Fa/JQr 6/1 no. 8, Fa/JQr 6/2; nos. 10 & 11.

1267 Fa/JQr 6/1 no. 7, Fa/JQr 6/2 no. 22.

APPENDIX 20
Henry Hatch

This is a fascinating tale on many counts.[1268] Henry Hatch was a rich, wholesale fishmonger and merchant adventurer, who dealt in merchandise worth £260 to £280 a year and also had lands worth £60 a year. He became one of the town's great benefactors. He was also a man of vision, who saw the need to sluice the creek and build a market house long before his contemporaries did. He dreamt of a ship with three masts coming up the creek to the crane.

We also see how, when he caught the plague, many townsfolk came to his sick-bed, in spite of his illness, to discuss his will, because he was childless and had decided to leave his fortune to the town after the death of his wife. He was fond of making wills and there are a bewildering number of references to copies of his will on paper and, more unusually, on parchment. Disputes over them between the town and the relatives raged on because his wife outlived him by 40 years. She could neither read nor write and had strange tales to tell about her suitors. She finally married a man who became Lord Mayor of London and lived in Fishmongers' Hall in London. There was virtually a dynasty there. We see how people from Faversham went back and forth to London to discuss the case. People in the town took sides and the whole place was divided. John Ambrose spoke of 'the common fame and voice of the county about Faversham concerning the gift.'

Finally, we watch how the town set about finding the money to fight the case in Chancery against the relatives. Each side claimed that the other was relying on a forged will. The story ends with the town winning the case in 1574 and 'making of a house over the cross that the market people might there stand dry'. Henry Hatch's dream came true. The market house 'for the benefit and ease both of the town and country' was built at last.[1269]

Henry Hatch was born in Sundridge, which is three miles west of Sevenoaks, and he left £10 under certain circumstances towards the repair of the church there. He was the son of one Henry Hatch and Alice, the daughter of a gentleman called John Parker of Kent, one of a large clan. Edward Parker of London claimed to be Hatch's nearest living relative and heir. Edward's father, Thomas Parker, had at one time been a scholar at the abbey school at Faversham and boarded with Hatch, who made very much of him and said that he was his next and dearest kinsman.

There is some doubt about the parentage of his wife, Joan, who was born at Lynsted in Kent. She might have been the daughter of one Finch of Kent; there was indeed a long established family in Lynsted of that name. It seems also possible that she was the daughter of Geoffrey Farrard or Forwood. In her will she referred to 'my brother Farrard's children', but he might have been a brother-in-law.

The position is further complicated because Joan remained on close terms with her sister, Elizabeth, who married three times: first, Mr King; then John Finch alias Goldfinch, who was descended from the Goldfinches of the North, whose four children were all mentioned in Hatch's will. Goldfinch had two houses in North Street East near Hogmarket Lane in 1532. After his

[1268] This appendix is mainly based on depositions in the law suits concerning the Hatch bequest to be found in CKS, Fa LB/2-37. I have considered them in greater detail in my article *Henry Hatch and the battle over his will*, AC, Cii (1985), pp. 111-128.

[1269] CKS, Fa/LB/18, John Ambrose. Detailed, but badly damaged, accounts of the subscription and building of the Market House are to be found in Fa/Ac2/2. From the Davidson A5 copy it has been found that these are carefully enrolled in Favward ff. 251v-256v.

death in 1541 Elizabeth married Simon Auncell. He died when mayor in 1548 and she stayed on in Faversham. When Joan moved to London, Elizabeth kept her informed about what was happening in the town. Elizabeth said in her deposition in the Chancery case following Hatch's death that she knew him four years before he married her sister and that he was married to her for about twenty years, that is, since 1513.

Hatch was variously described as a merchant or as a fishmonger, more accurately, a stockfishmonger or wholesale fishmonger. He is not mentioned in the customs records for Faversham in 1514-15, but by 1525-26 he was dealing in goods both in and out of the town. He was exporting wheat, billets of firewood, flitches of bacon and hogs shipped by the King's licence granted by Sir Edward Guldeforde, who was then Lord Warden of the Cinque Ports. At the same time Hatch was importing 2 weys of white salt, 15 pieces of raisins, 3 sorts or measures of figs, 12 barrels of rape oil, 2 butts of Rumney or sweet wine of Greek origin, 3 pipes of bastard or inferior wine, 1 last of pitch, 1 last of tar, 9 tons of iron and 3 weys of brown salt. A mixed bag. Six years later in 1531-32, he was importing quantities of staple fish or fish that was not thoroughly cured and hops.[1270]

On his brass in Faversham church there is the coat of arms of the Cinque Ports and the emblem of a fish. He is also described as a merchant adventurer, but his name has not as yet been found amongst the records of the Merchant Adventurers of London. His clerk remembered how he used 'to keep the book of account of all such merchandize as was brought from beyond the seas of as much wares as did amount to the sum of thirteen or fourteen score pounds (£260 or £280).

Considering that he was a man of obvious stature, Hatch played a remarkably small part in public affairs in Faversham, but presumably he was busy about his own affairs. On 29 September 1516 he was included in a list of the 24. In 1518-19 he became a chamberlain and in 1522-23 an auditor. It was not until 1531-32 that he became a jurat and churchwarden.[1271]

In 1533, Hatch became ill and died 14 days later, during two of which he was speechless. He was a merchant adventurer and must sometimes have run more risk of disease than most on his travels abroad. It might have been sweating sickness. One of the witnesses said that he died of plague, but Dr. Carole Rawcliffe and others whom I have consulted think that this is unlikely in view of the behaviour of those around him.[1272] Many townsfolk came to his sick-bed, in spite of his illness, in order to discuss his will, because he was childless and had decided to leave his fortune to the town after the death of his wife. Contemporaries were well aware of the horrors of plague and it is not thought likely that they would have reacted in this way even under such circumstances.

Because of the contents of this will, made during his sickness, a case was contested in Chancery forty or so years later and from the legal records that we know as much as we do about what happened in his last days.[1273] There were conflicting accounts, some supporting the town of Faversham and others favouring Hatch's nearest relative, Edward Parker, and his allies, Hatch's widow, Joan, and her nephew, Henry Goldfinch, a most important figure in the case. Henry and Joan Hatch were childless: Henry Goldfinch was the son of Joan's sister, Elizabeth. He met Hatch as a child of five, was brought up in his house and went to school in Faversham. He was in the house at the time of Hatch's death and remained with Joan thereafter, acting as her factotum, even travelling overseas for her.

1270 PRO, E122/208/2, 3; P. Clark, Society, p. 20.

1271 Favward fols. 13, 17v, 18v, 29v.

1272 At a course of 'Plague and English Society', in Rewley House, Oxford, (May 1996).

1273 PRC 32/15/212.

The case rested on whether or not Hatch was *compos mentis* when he made his will. Two witnesses said that there were various wills, both in parchment and paper, amongst Hatch's possessions. One of the men told to write it out was John Johnson alias Antony of Fordwich, and the case also hung on whether he was or was not an honest man. He was both a Protestant and a servant of Thomas Cromwell, which might be significant.

The will was then read out in the parlour and his wife ordered to lock it up. Thomas Stransham, who later acted as solicitor for Faversham, said that the will was entered into the wardmote book by (Joseph Beverley) by order of Mr Sell in the time of the mayor (Lewis) Marden in 1540. Faversham had a custom of entering wills of important townsmen, who had left bequests to the town, like Thomas Arden.[1274]

The opposition told quite a different story for they claimed that Hatch was speechless and that his memory had failed when he made that will. Joan, Elizabeth and a maidservant gave graphic accounts supporting this view. They said that John Johnson had guided his hand. The maidservant, who was living in Newington near Hythe by the time the case came to court, added that a number of people from Faversham had visited her in the preceding four years, including 'a gentleman who married Mistress Bradborne, sometimes Mr. Arderne's daughter.' This was Richard Ardys, who, she said, had threatened her that she should be brought to a book to confess her knowledge. She answered that the will must be forged because Hatch would not have forgotten her. She was married out of his house and she thought he loved her as his own sister. She and her husband were with him throughout his illness. Her husband watched over him most nights and she was there when he died.[1275]

On 6 May 1533 Hatch made, in his house, a long and incredibly complicated will with a number of contingency plans that were never needed. He asked to be buried in Faversham church, and left to it a chest bound with iron which he had bought of Henry Estey of London[1276] in which to put jewels and plate, and arranged for elaborate memorial masses. There was £10 to the repair of Sundridge church 'where I was born' and £10 to the abbey. He made bequests to the children of Joan's sister, Elizabeth, to Thomas Parker, the son of William Parker of Dartford and the children of his cousin Moorcock. He appointed as executors his wife, Joan, and Richard Dryland the elder of Abbey Street East. Dryland was later held by the relatives to be responsible for getting the estate for the town. Hatch said that he was to have £5 for his pains over the will. The abbey steward, Robert Maycott of Abbey Street West, was to be the overseer and to have 40^{s}. The residue of his goods Hatch left to his wife.

We then come to the disposition of his lands. He arranged that the inn called the Fleur de Luce and the tenement called The George were to be sold for payment of his debts and bequests. Joan was to have his dwelling house in Faversham and lands in the Isle of Harty, Kent, and in Icklesham, Guestling, Udimore and Brede in Sussex for life. After her death, one of the jurats and one of the commoners of Faversham were to be appointed by the mayor and most of the jurats and some of the commonalty to manage these lands and to give an account of them for 20 years. Hatch showed great forethought in planning how his estates should be administered and he must surely have consulted some of his fellow jurats before making these plans. He set out how this revenue was to be spent with various contingency plans: the repair of Partridge Lane and the way leading from there to the quay, the repair of common wells, the Observant Friars of Canterbury, the repair and maintenance of the haven or creek, the repair and maintenance of the parish

---

1274 Favward fol. 2.

1275 CKS, Fa/LB/13, Elizabeth Lewin.

1276 A. Percival says that this is thought to be the chest from the parish church now on display in the Fleur de Lis Heritage Centre.

church and its ornaments, allowing for a new jewel house, were all mentioned. He then went on to say that if, after 20 years, the town could obtain the King's licence of mortmain, then it could hold the lands to the maintenance of the creek, the highways within a mile of the town and the ornaments of the parish church. Mortmain meant 'dead hand'. When land was left to the church or charity, the lord, that is, the crown, lost feudal revenues like wardship and marriage. A licence therefore had to be sought and paid for permission to go ahead. Hatch said the cost of the licence could be paid for from the revenues of his estate. Again, however, he made contingency plans. If the licence could not be obtained, the lands were to be sold and the money spent on the creek, the parish church and highways.

Hatch made the will on a Tuesday and was buried the following Saturday. Six months later, just before Michaelmas (29 September), Joan Hatch rode with her brother-in-law, John Goldfinch, and her servant to Canterbury to prove the will.

In the course of the law suits that followed, Joan Hatch had a strange tale to tell. Her evidence may be suspect, but has the ring of truth in some of the background information. She said that the other executor, Richard Dryland, persuaded her to have the will rewritten because it was blotted. After the will had been proved, Sir Christopher Hales sent to her as he was riding up to London to the law term after Easter, wishing her to meet him as he came back from London at the King's High Sumpter Way' near Faversham, leading from Sittingbourne to Canterbury. Sumpter means a pack-horse or its driver. This was the continuation westwards of Lower Road leading past Stone Church to join the London Road near Beacon Hill. It is shown on 18th century maps but most of it seems to have disappeared when the railway was built in the 1850's. Just a stub remains and it is still called Sumpter Way. Sir Christopher Hales lived near Tenterden and was Master of the Rolls and an associate of Thomas Cromwell. He told her that her husband's will was not written in form of law, but was erased or blotted. He advised her to bring the will to his house at Canterbury, otherwise she would repent it. She carried the will to Canterbury and there stayed at John Johnson's house. He, it may be remembered, had probably written the will, was a Protestant and a servant of Thomas Cromwell. The next day she went with Johnson to Sir Christopher's house, where she dined and supped and handed over the will. Sir Christopher urged her to marry his kinsman, James Hales, who was later a sergeant-at-law, went mad and committed suicide in 1554. In vain, for she refused and wanted the will to be returned to her. After six days, Sir Christopher brought out the will. Because she could neither read nor write, she thought that it was the same one. She reckoned that all her troubles started there, but a lawyer in the chancery case sourly pointed out in a scribbled aside that she went 'with brother Goldfinch and man Mitchell who both could read.'

Joan claimed that Reginald Lewkenor of North Street East was also a suitor. He had sold Hatch most of the Sussex property and died in 1540.[1277] Joan alleged that when Lewkenor knew that Sir Henry Amcotts, whom she eventually married, had been privately in Faversham, he contacted Thomas Boleyn, Earl of Wiltshire, the father of Anne Boleyn. Lewkenor let him know about the alteration to her husband's will and told him that Maurice Moorcock, who was one of the earl's servants, was next of kin to Henry Hatch. On learning this, the earl sent Richard Sackville to Faversham to learn the truth of the matter. Sackville, later Sir Richard Sackville, known as Fill-sack, was a kinsman of the earl and later chancellor of the Court of Augmentations. In the Christmas holidays, he came to see Joan and said that she had been shamefully beguiled and deceived by those whom she greatly trusted.

[1277] He came from a Sussex gentry family; Berry's *Sussex Genealogies* pp. 130, 343.

After her marriage to Amcotts, the Earl of Wiltshire and Sackville came to their house in London, accusing him of withholding lands from Moorcock, an aged and poor man, threatening a law suit and claiming that the will was a forgery. The earl departed, very angrily, and, in 1538, Moorcock brought a case in the Court of Common Pleas on a plea of trespass against a tenant of Lady Amcott's in Icklesham, Sussex. The Earl of Wiltshire died soon after. Henry Amcotts said later that, if the earl had lived, he would have lost.

Moorcock renewed his suit in 1542, possibly with the connivance of Sackville. Amcotts was persuaded to fight the case and made sure that the town of Faversham joined him by contributing £6 to the case and £9 or £10 to the repair of a storehouse and the maintenance of a salt marsh. It was again said later that Richard Dryland had arranged that Amcotts should argue with Moorcock and offered on behalf of the town that it would pay money to help. Moorcock pleaded with Amcotts to be good to him, kneeling in the street before him. Amcott pitied him but Joan could never abide to hear of him. In 1539-41 there was an entry in the wardmote book: 'Item of £4-7-0 paied for and about the charges in the suite between Morecocke and Hampcottes for the title of sertyn landes in Sussex late Henry Hatch, whereof the revercyon belongith to the said towne of Faversham.'[1278]

Moorcock, as next of kin, lost the case, and in 1546 the town sought and obtained a licence in mortmain for the Hatch lands in the same year that it got its charter. Hatch's faithful clerk, Jerome Oxenbridge, said later at the age of 80 in a deposition, that 'Kynge Henry the VIIIth hym selfe dyd heere the wyll reede and grauntyd lycense of mortmayne and gave commaundment the seid wyll not to be hynderyd by no meanes.' The town heaved a sigh of relief. Joan joined them in the suit but said privately that they should have waited until she was dead. According to Jacob it costs £200.[1279]

Now came another twist in the tale. One day Sir Henry Amcotts was looking in Joan's wooden chest in her absence and found a will in paper and compared it with the other will, which he also found there under seal, and discovered that they disagreed. When he was in his counting house, he called Joan to him and read the will in paper to her and said to her in the hearing of Henry Goldfinch that he prayed God to forgive the people who had altered her husband's will. She replied that she had never heard both the wills read. Amcotts now found the Earl of Wiltshire and Master Sackville's words true and said he would not have gone to law against Moorcock as he did at a cost of £1,000 three years ago.

Amcotts died in 1554 and a description of his funeral procession is given in the diary of Henry Machyn.[1280] After his death, Sir Richard Sackville said to Joan that he could tell her more of the indirect dealing and practice of will and writings after Hatch's decease than either she or Amcotts heard or knew of. He took her by the hand and offered her £500 to be one of her executors, only to the intent that the writing concerning her husband might be performed for Hatch's kinsfolk. He also wanted a lease of some of the lands.

When Moorcock died not long after, Sackville sent for Thomas Parker, another cousin of Hatch. who was then in the Marshalsea prison. He wanted him to renew cousin Moorcock's suit, but Parker refused to do so while Joan was still alive. At the same time,. Richard Goldfinch of the Inner Temple borrowed the will that Joan had had from his brother, Henry. Richard blamed Joan for persecuting Moorcock; and this controversy went on for three years. He kept the will a long time in spite of her requests to him to return it. However, when he died in her house, his

---

1278 Favward fol. 35.

1279 Jacob, p. 132.

1280 *Diary of H. Machyn 1550-63*, Camden Society, pp. 42, 68, 70, 339.

brother, Henry recovered it. Within a year, Thomas Parker asked to see it and pulled out two other wills himself, one of paper and one of parchment. He said that the copy in parchment came from his father, William Parker, who got it from Joan six weeks after the death of Henry Hatch. A month later Thomas Parker wanted it back, but died before collecting it. Henry Goldfinch had known his son, Edward Parker, for 14 years and more because Parker lived near the Customs House where Goldfinch had reason to go for dealing with customs on merchandise and wares coming from beyond the seas.

Edward Parker eventually managed, through a friend, to persuade Goldfinch to hand over the will, which Parker then took to Canterbury to be registered.[1281] In the ensuing Chancery case, a careful collation was made of the proved will and Parker's 'original' which we will henceforth call 'Parker's will'. It was found that, for the most part 'they agree in matter, but vary in words'. After minor bequests to relatives, the proved will said that The George and The Fleur de Luce were both to be sold, but Parker's will said that The Fleur de Luce was not to be sold if fish and plate - an interesting comment on where Hatch's wealth lay - were enough to pay Mr Lewkenor for his lands in Sussex. The chief difference was that in the proved will, there was a remainder to the town after 20 years and in Parker's will after 51 years. Henry Goldfinch had a long lease on many of the Hatch lands and people in Faversham reckoned that if the town had agreed to grant him a lease of 21 years after Joan's death the case would never have been brought.

The case put for 'Parker's will' was, to repeat, that Hatch's will was made when he was past memory and had lost his speech; that John Johnson guided his hand; that the will to which the witnesses' signature were attached had been forged by Sir Christopher Hales, John Johnson and others when Joan visited Canterbury. The claim went on that Moorcock had sought to disprove the will and that Edward Parker's brother, Henry, now claimed to be the next heir.

The case against 'Parker's will' was that Hatch's will was published to the mayor and immediately recorded in the wardmote book, which agreed with it. There was a difference, not only in the lengths of sheets of paper, but also in the disposition of land in the wills. It was pointed out that Goldfinch had had Henry Hatch's will and that therefore Parker's will might very well have been forged.

On 13 October 1567 two doctors in Chancery ordered a special chest to be kept at lady Amcott's house in London with all the papers relating to Hatch's estate therein. The chest was to have three keys, one of which was to be kept by the town of Faversham, one by Edward Parker and one by Lady Amcotts. Goldfinch had charge of Lady Amcott's house and books of account and bills of debt and described how she lived in Fishmonger's Hall for 20 years before moving to Thames Street, where she had less room. She had by then become very aged and feeble. About three years before another fishmonger, Matthew Amcotts, who was a lawyer, had looked through her writings and decided that she had a good case. Her writings were in great canvas bags, which were stowed away in the chest.

The lid was so heavy with great hasps of iron and an iron bar that it needed three people to open it. Also in the chest was the plate that she used to lend to the Company of Fishmongers once in every two years when they chose the wardens.

On 13 May 1568 Edward Parker took possession of lands in Sussex in the name of his uncle Edmund, a priest, the next of kin. He then leased some of it to Henry Goldfinch who sub-let it to Thomas Paramore, who was doubtful about his position in view of the case and therefore consulted Sergeant Manwood.

The townsfolk were stunned by the turn of events, both because they had come to rely on inheriting the estate after Joan's death and because they had no money with which to fight the chancery case. They sadly recorded in the wardmote book in 1570 'the seide towne ys destytutyd of monye and especyallye for the further prosequutyng and maynteynyng of the sute agaynste Parker and mye Ladye Amcottes for and concernyng the landes late gyven to the said towne by Master Henrye Hatche late of Faversham decessyd.' They were driven to desperate remedies. First, almost all the property formerly belonging to the town was sold. Secondly, a cess or tax

[1281] 8 July 1568, PROB 6/1/135.

was charged on the inhabitants every year between 1567 and 1574. By order of the wardmote, The Ship, a storehouse on the quay, St. Nicholas's Chapel, six houses and seven pieces of land were sold. For example, the town house on the quay was sold in 1570 to Lewes Austen, who lived there.[1282]

The cesses brought in amounts varying from £20 in 1567 to £60 in 1572. They were raised on the order of the wardmote by two jurats and two or more members of the 24 or Common Council. After 8 had been collected, it was agreed that they should be entered in the town book 'that yt maye appyer what ys lente and leyed out by the inhabytaunces of the seyd towne to the entente that ther maye be satisfaction and paymente made therof agayne to the same inhabytaunces to theyr executoures and assignes when the same landes shall come to the towne after the deathe of the nowe Ladye Amcottes as heretofore hathe bynn grauntyd at dyvers warmouthes.' That was the plan, but Edward Jacob, the eighteenth century historian, said that very few of the inhabitants demanded their money back.

Three more cess lists followed in the wardmote book, the last of them on 22 December 1574. These presumably also concerned the Hatch suit. Other cesses, say for the poor, were being collected at the same time. The arithmetic of the cess lists is usually accurate and the 11 cesses raised a total of £315-11-3. With hindsight, Jacob reckoned that the corporation laid out nearly the full value of the Hatch estate in suits at law. He said, that the rents of the Hatch lands amounted to £78-2-0 in 1574 but only £60-7-4 in 1580.

The cess lists are set out in a similar manner to the muster rolls, that is, the lists of men able to serve in the militia. The muster rolls are much fuller, because they include servants as well as masters, but they usually follow the same pattern; mayor, jurats, commoners, Court Street, Preston Street, West Street and Tanners Street. No doubt because they were desperate for money, the cess lists of 1569 included outdwellers, that is, people who, although they had property in the town, were resident elsewhere, i.e. Francis Swan of Wye, Thomas Stransham of Canterbury, Thomas Hawkins of Boughton-under-Blean, John Finch of Hompston[1283], John Stransham of Eastchurch in the Isle of Sheppey, John Maycote of Ospringe and Michael Allen of Davington. There has not yet been time to analyse all these lists of inhabitants for the period. With the help of the rentals it should eventually be possible to work out where at least a few of these people in Faversham lived.[1284] F. Giraud transcribed a cess for shipping in 1596, where the same tax was applied '... as well as the inhabytants and rescyants within the libertye of the same towne bye all ...goods and ... lands and tenements as well within as without the same libertye and alsoe all the forreners with their lands and tenements lyinge within the same libertie ...'[1285] Foreigners were inhabitants resident within the liberty but not freemen. This is confirmed by a list of fines imposed in 1571 intitled, 'The fynes of the forreners inhabytyng wythin the seid towne of Faversham and occupying there nott beyng free of the same towne sessyd and taxyd bye the commoners or common councell of the same towne the xxiijth daye of Apryll beyng the Mundaye sevennyghte nexte after the feaste daye of Easter in the xiijth yere of the reygne of our sovereygne ladye Elizabethe ...'[1286]. The 1596 cess, besides listing tax payers and foreigners by streets, has a listing for 'Freemen not inhabitants'. Preliminary research would seem to suggest that some, if not all, the 'outdwellers' were non-resident freemen.

1282 CKS, Fa/AC2/1 fols. 4, 5, 7, 8, 13v, 16; Fa/LB/37.

1283 Homston Farm now Homestall Farm, Faversham. See forthcoming article by P. Hyde and D. W. Harrington, *A Faversham survey by Christopher Saxton.*

1284 Favward fols. 153-153v, 261-273; Fa/CPm 3; Fa/ZB 67; Jacob, pp. 131-34.

1285 F. Giraud, 'Cinque Ports, Faversham', *AC*, xxxii, pp. 303-11.

1286 CKS, Fa/RTf1 dated 23 April 13 Elizabeth [1571], the total came to xj$^{£}$ iiij^{s} viij^{d}.

Again in 1570 the town agreed that George Stransham, Bartholomew Amys and Thomas Belke, jurats, and the under-clerk, Humphery Kybett, should go up to London to assist Thomas Stransham, who was representing the town in the Hatch suit. Stransham had been appointed when the mayor, Robert Fagg, became ill. They appointed Richard Beste the arbitrator on the town's behalf.

In 1571 the town leased Brooke Farm in Sussex to Sir William Brooke, Lord Cobham, who was Lord Warden of the Cinque Ports, for £40 for 21 years. This was possibly to secure powerful support for the town.

Once the Chancery case had started, the town brought an action of waste against Lady Amcotts concerning her upkeep of the lands.[1287] She allegedly being very ignorant and very doubtful about which complaint she should answer made no reply and so the town got judgement.

She died in September 1573. In her will, she asked the Company of Fishmongers if they would allow her kinsman, Henry Goldfinch, to live in her dwelling house with the use of the waterside at her present rent. She also left him the lease of her houses in Faversham. She then left various household gifts to Henry and a token to her sister, Elizabeth, and various other relatives. She remembered the poor of the parish of Lynsted, where she was born. The residue she left to Henry and appointed him her executor together with her physician. She asked to be buried near her second husband in St. Michael's Crooked Lane, so that she presumably is not in Hatch's tomb in Faversham church.

The town's expenses continued to mount and everyone became extremely anxious about what was happening. Stransham asked a gentleman called Cyriak Petyt of Boughton-under-Blean, MP for Winchelsea in April 1554 and Chippenham in November 1554[1288] to go to London to see Lady Amcotts, who was now aged and impotent, and he went twice in one year. He was to find out who would have the lands and he asked her for the truth, when she, putting her hand to her mouth, making a cross, said she always, told the truth and added, 'Well I could say more.'.

Michael Lagowe of Faversham also made a deposition. He carried messages and provisions from Faversham to Lady Amcotts in London. He told the court how he was sent by Mrs Auncell to Lady Amcotts with a warning that people from the town planned to come to London in gang week (Rogation week, that is, the days before Ascension Day). Goldfinch said to him mysteriously that if Faversham would grant him the lease, 'he could so use the matter, that Parker should never have it ... I have in this house, that can quickly make him afraid.'

Goldfinch claimed that Faversham took possession of the estate after Joan's death and asked for damages. Certainly the town won the case and began to receive the income from 1574.[1289] In the same year it started to build the Market House of which Hatch had dreamed.

In 1575, the mayor, John Skyrre, put in for expenses laid out in going to London for himself and ten jurats and commoners from the town for the trial of the Hatch suit. At the end of the same year, Elizabeth Auncell made her will and died a few months later. She was living in Preston Street and remembered her son, Henry Goldfinch, and the rest of her family. She appointed Henry and Cyriak Petyt her executors. The final outcome was the agreement made between

---

[1287] There are detailed accounts of the cost of the Chancery case. For example, 'Item to Master Seriaunte Manwood and Master Seriaunte Wreye for their fees xx^{s}, Item to Smythe the proctour in the Arches hys fee iij^{s} iiij^{d}; Item paid for the coppyes of the examynations taken before Master Jones one of the examyners in the chauncerie being CxL sheets at xij^{d} a sheete vij$^{£}$, Item paid for the byndyng of the seid examynations in iiij parchment coverynges ij^{s} viij^{d}' Account Vouchers Fa/FAc 2/1 fol. 9. See *Serjerants at Law*, Selden Society Supplementary vol. 5.

[1288] Commons 1509-58, iii, pp. 96-98.

[1289] Favward fol. 179 onwards.

Faversham and Edward Parker under which Faversham was to have all Hatch's lands in Kent and Sussex. In return Parker and his heirs were to have Wykham Farm in Sussex on payment of £40.

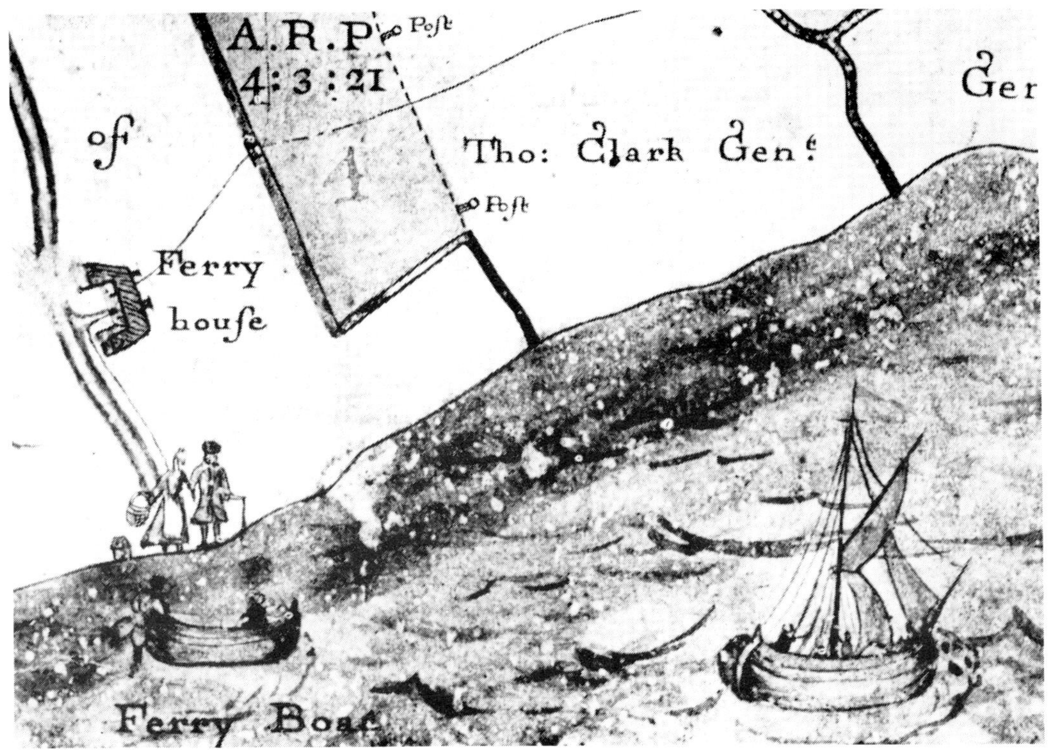

Detail showing ferry house and boat taken from a map of Harty drawn up by Jared Hill of the lands of Jacob Sawbridge in 1718. CKS: U178/P1

Faversham Borough Records
CKS: FA/ZB 67

A foolscap sheet folded in half and written on the inner pages. Endorsed: Extracts relating to Hatch's estates No. 4.

The suit about Mr Hatch's lands by him devised to the corporation of Faversham, began 36 Henry 8 and ended about 1574 near ~~between~~ 30 and ~~? 40~~ years afterwards

The corporation expended £629-18-2 in that suit; of which they raised by cesses on the inhabitants £226-12-2 and in order to repay the said inhabitants and the other demands they sold almost all the estates they then were possessed of, that is to say,

A house in Preston Street	Page 128
St. Nicholas Chappel	ditto
A piece of land	130
A house at the Key	131
An orchard at Davington	ditto
A piece of land in Preston Street	ditto
One acre of land in King's Field	ditto
Half an acre in Preston Street	ditto
A house in West Street	ditto
Another house	opposite 150
Two houses in Cook's Ditch	185
Two other parcels of land	188
The Ship tavern	ditto
A storehouse and garden at the Quay	198

N.B. The rents of Mr Hatch's estates in 1574 amounted to £73-2-0 per annum and in 1580, £60-7-4 only - at which they continued for many years.

Other page

In case the corporation could not obtain the lycense to mortmain Mr Hatch's estates, he; by his will, bequeathed them in trust to be sold and the monies arising by the sale to be disposed of as follows,

£120	to buy a suit of copes for Faversham Church
20	to buy a pair of silver candlesticks for ditto
20	to buy a pair of silver censors for ditto
240	to repair the creek of Faversham
50	to build a new market house there
40	to repair the highway between Hogcrosse and Ewell
10	to repair Church Lane
20	to the morrow masse in Faversham Church
20	in smocks and shirts to poor people of Faversham
10	to repair Sondriche church, where he was born
10	to repair Icklesham church in Sussex

£6-13-4	to repair St. Thomas's Church in Harty
5	to repair Davington church
20	to repair St. Saviour's Monastery in Faversham
5 marks	to every House of Friars Observant in Canterbury
4	i.e. 2£ to either of the Houses of Friars in Winchelsea
20	to repair the Highway from Hogcrosse to Boughton
20	to repair the Sumpter Way between St. Agnes Cross and Stone Church
10	to repair Linsted church
10	to repair the foul ways in Linstead churche
5	to repair Oare church
5	to repair Luddenham church
2	to repair Buckland church
5	to repair Wylderton Chappel[1290]
2	to repair Goodwynston church
10	to the marriages of 10 poor maidens of Linstead
10	to the like in Faversham
10	to the trustees i.e. 40s to each
£704-13-4	and the residue among the poor people of Faversham

Though it is not certain how much the residue might be for the poor of Faversham, yet it is probable the £704-13-4 was near the value of the estate, as the testator's charity, according to the fashion of the times, seems to have been chiefly extended to churches. The corporation then laid out near the full value of the estates, in the suits at law.

Another sheet in another hand
see annotations to page 190 of book has ' do not pay for the same above the rate of 20 yeres puchase...'

Another sheet
<u>Accounts 1735 to 1736</u>

The Town charge	£741-12-6	Hatch's Gifts charge	£179-12-3
Discharge	£200-14-4½	Discharge	£570-03-3
Creditor	£540-18-1½	Debtor	£390-11-0

By the accounts it appears that tho' the gift of Mr Hatch bears the title of charge yet in fact the town paid the balance of Hatch's debt of £390-11-0

(smaller hand) £300 borrowed by the town and appropriated to lessen the debt of this charity

page 161 paid a messenger to my Lord warden 2^s to give him a letter concerning the death of my Lady Amcots 1573

1290 Wallenberg p. 300; parish of Throwley. Hasted, vi, p. 454 mentions the chapel anciently connected with the manor of Wilderton.

Money paid at several times in the law suit of the for Mr Hatchs charity as taken out of the town account books

£32-9-6	129	£80-14-1	175
8-13-4		4-3-8	
7-0-0		76-9-3	185
3-0-0		15-0	157
86-12-0	149	43-4-0	163
61-16-6	150	17-8-5	
20-10-0		13-0-0	166
8-10-9	15?	235-14-5	
2-6-0	159	382-1-7	
66-13-4		617-16-0	
17-0-0		12-0-0	
5-0-0		£629-16-0	
4-10-0			
10-0-0			
47-12-2			
£382-1-7			

KING'S REMEMBRANCER CUSTOMS ACCOUNTS
PRO: E122/208/3

[Sandwich Port 22-23 Henry VIII. Particulars of account of Thomas Alcock, collector of customs and subsidies. 25 folios. Faversham commences on folio 7.]

Only the entries for Henry Hatche have been extracted. So that in the same ship may be cargoes for other merchants.

Feversham

folio 7v

Of the ship of Henry Vauster entered xiijth day of June

Of Henry Hacche denizen for vj^{C} of salt fish value vj$^{£}$ subsidy vj^{s}

folio 8v [manuscript xxij]

Of the ship of William Preston entered the same day [xxij July]

Of Henry Hacche for xv^{C} of staplefish value xv$^{£}$ subsidy xv^{s}

folio 9

Of the ship of Henry Vauster entered xxiiijth day of July

Of Henry Hacche denizen for ij^{M} stapulfish[1291] value xx$^{£}$ subsidy xx^{s}

[1291] Staple fish: Fish not thoroughly cured.

Of Christopher Vauster entered xxvjth day of July

Of Henry Hacche denizen for viij^{C} staplefish value viij$^{£}$ and vj^{C} lb hoppes value xL^{s} subsidy x^{s}

King's Remembrancer Customs Accounts E122/208/2

Particulars of account of Thomas Alcok, collector of Customs and Subsidies, 17-18 Henry VIII. *[18 folios. Faversham commences on folio 7.]*

Faversham

folio 7v

In the ship of of Garrard Bosslerd departing xxxth day of December

Of Henry Hacche denizen for xL quarters wheat value viij$^{£}$ and iiij^{M} billett value xiij^{s} iiij^{d} shippment by licence of the king. Sum viij$^{£}$ xiij^{s} iiij^{d} Subsidy viij^{s} viij^{d}

Of the same for six[1292] flicchis[1293] backon value xxj^{s} iiij^{d} and ij hogges value v^{s} iiij^{d} shipped by licence of the king granted by E.Guldeford knight. Sum xxvj^{s} viij^{d}. Customs iiij^{d} Subsidy xvj^{d}

folio 8

In the ship of William Skylman entered xixth day of January

Of Henry Haache denizen for two weys[1294] of white salt value xL^{s}, xv pieces of reysons[1295] weighing xj^{C} value xxij^{s} iij sortes of figs[1296] value xij^{s} and xij barrells of rape oyle[1297] value viij$^{£}$. Sum xj$^{£}$ xiiij^{s}. Subsidy xj^{s} viij^{d} quarter

Of the same for ij butts Rumney[1298] and three pipes of Bastard[1299] Tonage vij^{s} vj^{d}

In the ship of Peter Mawdelyn entered the same day [xxij January]

Of Henry Hacche denizen for xij barrells of rape oyle value viij$^{£}$ one last tarr value xx^{s} one last pyche[1300] value xx^{s} ix tun of iron value xviij$^{£}$ iiij weys of brown salt value Liij^{s} iiij^{d} Five sortes of figs value xx^{s} and xij pieces of reysons weighing ix^{C} value xviij^{s} Sum xxxij$^{£}$ xj^{s} iiij^{d} Subsidy xxxij^{s} vij^{d}

1292 There is a cross over this and a cross in the margin 'qr xvj' presumably for 'query 16'.

1293 R.E.Zupko, *British Weights and Measures:A History from Antiquity to the Seventeenth Century* (Wisconsin, 1977) A flitch (a side of cured hog meat) a hundred-weight of 112 avoirdupois pounds.

1294 Zupko, A wey of 42 bushels.

1295 A piece of raisins weighed 84 lbs.

1296 Zupko:A sort equals three pieces of 60lb.

1297 Zupko:Used for a lubricant, illuminant and food. A barrel of 31½ gallons.

1298 A sweet wine of Greek origin. Zupko wine a tun of 252 gallons. 2 pipes or butts equals one tun.

1299 An inferior wine.

1300 Zupko: Pitch or tar a last of 12 barrels, each barrel 31½ gallons.

FAVERSHAM BOROUGH RECORDS
CKS: FA/AC1

Heere[1301] followe all the cessys that have byn made in the towne of Faversham for the maynetenaunce of the townes sutes in lawe concernyng the landes late Master Harrye Hatches.

FAVERSHAM
A cesse made there the xxvj^th^ day of November in the tenth yere of the reigne of oure sovereigne ladye Quene Elizabeth [26 Nov. 1567] by Thomas Fynche and Rycharde Wood two of the jurattes of the seyd towne and Wylliam Sacre and Christofer Amys two of the xxiiij^th^ and Common Councell of the same towne amountyng unto the somme of xx^£^

Maior and jurattes

+	Inprimis Mr John Beste Mayor	x^s^
+	Mr Edwarde Blackewell gentleman juratte	x^s^
	Mr Thomas Stransham juratte	x^s^
+	Mr John Wreuke juratte	vj^s^ viij^d^
+	Mr Henrye Phyllpott juratte	x^s^
+	Mr George Stransham juratte	x^s^
+	Mr Thomas Oldefelde juratte	x^s^
	Mr John Maycotte juratte	x^s^
+	Mr Roberte Colwell juratte	x^s^
+	Mr Thomas Belke juratte	vj^s^ viij^d^
	Mr Thomas Fynche gentleman jurate	vj^s^ viij^d^
+	Mr Barthylmewe Amys juratte	x^s^
+	Mr Rycharde Wood juratte	x^s^
	Sum	vj^£^

The names of the xxiiij^th^

+	Wylliam Saker	viij^s^
	Mychell Allen	viij^s^
+	John Snode	ij^s^
+	Christofer Amys	iij^s^ iiij^d^
+	Humfrey Atkynson	vj^s^ viij^d^
+	Thomas Adryan	ij^s^ vj^d^
+	Rycherd Lawrence	iij^s^ iiij^d^
+	Thomas Musterde	iij^s^ iiij^d^
+	Thomas Barton	iiij^s^
+	Edwarde Russell	v^s^
+	John Mylles	ij^s^
+	Roberte Elfryth	ij^s^ viij^d^
+	John Elfrithe	ij^s^ viij^d^
+	Roberte Rye	iiij^s^
+	Wylliam Comber	iiij^s^
+	Roberte Lame	v^s^
+	John Tyndale	iij^s^ iiij^d^
+	Thomas Jerman	iiij^s^
+	Wylliam Bennett	xij^d^
+	Rychard Tylman	vij^s^
	Thomas Poaste	iij^s^ iiij^d^
+	Hugh Boothe	ij^s^ vj^d^
	Wylliam Hampton	xij^d^
+	Edwarde Harrys	vij^s^
	Summa	iiij^£^ xv^s^ viij^d^

Courtstrete

+	John Fynche gentleman	viij^s^
+	Wylliam Pecoke the younger mariner	ij^s^ viij^d^
	Thomas Hawle	iiij^s^
+	John Saben	xij^d^
+	John Dyxson	vj^d^
+	Roberte Fagge gentleman	xij^s^
+	Anne Moseley wydoe	ij^s^ vj^d^
+	Cornelys Dowman	iij^s^
+	John Fysher	iij^s^
	Roberte Hawkyns	xij^d^
+	John Ambrose	x^s^
+	Wylliam Pecoke the elder	iij^s^ iiij^d^
+	John Neale	viij^s^
+	John Johnson	iij^s^ iiij^d^
+	Thomas Waterman	iij^s^ iiij^d^
	[blank] Melcan surgeon	xij^d^
+	John Dennys	iij^s^ iiij^d^
	[blank] Cuttler	xx^d^
+	Wylliam Staples	xij^d^
+	Rychard Amys	xij^d^
	Francys Curtys	xij^d^

1301 fol. 261.

+	John Oldfeld	v^{s}
+	Rycherd Ugden	v^{s}
	Summa	iiij$^{£}$ iiij^{s} viij^{d}

Preston Streete[1302]

+	Giles Leboore	iiij^{s}
+	Wylliam Porredge	xij^{d}
+	Thomas Cole	vj^{s} viij^{d}
	Culverdens wydoe	vj^{d}
+	John Shales	ij^{s}
+	Barthylmewe Newes	vj^{d}
+	Roberte Avale	v^{s}
+	Wylliam Neale	ij^{s}
+	Edwarde Usher	vj^{d}
+	Garrattes wydoe	vj^{d}
+	Robert Medowes	vj^{d}
	Mistris Neale wydoe	xij^{d}
+	Nycholas Bull	ij^{s} vj^{d}
+	Rychard Stransham	iij^{s} iiij^{d}
	Rychard Pysyng	xij^{d}
+	Thomas Androe	vj^{d}
+	Christofer Dobynson	ij^{s} vj^{d}
+	John Mason	xij^{d}
+	Matthew Holland	xij^{d}
	Gregori Hubberd	xij^{d}
	Wylliam Okenfolde	v^{s}
	Thomas Whyte	xij^{d}
	Mistris Aunsell wydoe	iij^{s} iiij^{d}
+	Thomas Barlyng	iij^{s} iiij^{d}
+	John Skyrr	iij^{s} iiij^{d}
	Summa	Lij^{s} viij^{d}

West Strete

	Rychard Downe	xij^{d}
+	Thomas Haffenden	xij^{d}
+	Wylliam Harte	iij^{s} iiij^{d}
+	Wylliam Stephyns	xij^{d}
+	John Clarke	xij^{d}
+	Robert Chapman	xij^{d}
+	Thomas Pease	xij^{d}
+	Rychard Knyght	xij^{d}
+	Rychard Mannys	xij^{d}
	Robert Nycolles	xx^{d}
+	Thomas Byrlyng	xij^{d}
+	Giles Kydd	xx^{d}
+	Henry Bonde	vj^{s} viij^{d}
+	Thomas Rye	iij^{s} iiij^{d}
+	Stephen Symes	iij^{s} iiij^{d}
+	Larkes wydoe	vj^{d}
	Adyes wydoe	xij^{d}
+	Gregorye Wrighte	xij^{d}
+	Thomas Hawkes	xij^{d}
+	John Stone	ij^{s} vj^{d}
+	Nycholas Vawter	xij^{d}
+	Marryan Vawter wydoe	ij^{s} vj^{d}
+	Wylliam Harryson	ij^{s}
	Summa	xxxix^{s} vj^{d}

Tanner Streete

+	Wylliam Taylor	ij^{s}
	Stephen Sede	xij^{d}
+	Roberte Wyer	ij^{s}
+	John Dewarde	ij^{s} vj^{d}
+	Henrye Wrottyng	xij^{d}
+	Wylliam Vynton	xij^{d}
	Summa	ix^{s} vj^{d}
	Summa totalis	**xx$^{£}$**

Faversham[1303]

A cesse made there the xxiijth daye of November in the xjth yere of the reigne of oure sovereigne ladye Quene Elizabeth [23 Nov. 1568] ratyd uppon the enhabytantes of the seyd towne by John Beste and Thomas Oldfelde jurattes and John Snothe and Thomas Barton of the comen councell amountyng to the summe of xL$^{£}$

Maior and jurattes

+	Inprimis Mr Barthylmewe Amys mayor	xviij^{s}
+	Mr Edwarde Blackwell	xviij^{s}
+	Mr John Beste	xviij^{s}
+	Mr George Straunsham	xviij^{s}
+	Mr Thomas Oldfelde	xviij^{s}

1302 fol. 261v.

1303 fol 153v.

+	Mr Henrye Philpotte	xvj^{s} viij^{d}
+	Mr John Wreuke	xiiij^{s}
+	Mr Roberte Colwell	xvij^{s}
+	Mr Thomas Belke	xiij^{s}
+	Mr Thomas Fynch	x^{s}
+	Mr Roberte Fagge	xviij^{s}
	Summa	viij$^{£}$ xviij^{s} viij^{d}

The Names of the xxiiijth

+	Wylliam Saker	xvj^{s}
+	Edwarde Russell	xiij^{s} iiij^{d}
+	Roberte Lame	xiij^{s} iiij^{d}
+	Humfrey Atkynson	xiij^{s}
+	Rycherd Tylman	xij^{s}
+	Edward Harrys	xij^{s}
+	Wylliam Comber	x^{s}
+	Wylliam Okenfoulde	x^{s}
+	John Tyndall	ix^{s}
	Thomas Poaste	ix^{s}
+	Roberte Rye poyntmaker	viij^{s}
+	Christofer Amys	vij^{s}
+	Rycherd Laurence	vj^{s} viij^{d}
+	Thomas Jerman	vj^{s} viij^{d}
+	Thomas Barton	vj^{s}
+	John Snothe	v^{s}
+	Roberte Elfrith	v^{s}
+	Hughe Booth	v^{s}
+	John Elfrithe	v^{s}
+	Thomas Musterde	v^{s}
+	John Mylles	iiij^{s}
+	Thomas Andrian	iij^{s} iiij^{d}
	Wylliam Hampton	ij^{s}
	Summa	ix$^{£}$ vj^{s} iiij^{d}

Courte Streete

	Mistris Margerytt Bradborne wydoe	x^{s}
+	Mr John Fynche gentleman	xviij^{s}
+	Wylliam Pecoke the younger	v^{s}
	Thomas Haule	vj^{s} viij^{d}
+	John Sabyn	xx^{d}
+	Wylliam Frende	ij^{s}
+	John Dyxon	xij^{d}
+	Mr Rychard Ball	x^{s}
+	Cornelys Dowman	v^{s}
+	John Fysher	vj^{s} viij^{d}
	Roberte Hawkyns	xx^{d}
+	Roberte Rye maryner	vj^{d}
+	John Ambrose	xviij^{s}
+	Wylliam Pecoke the elder	vj^{s} viij^{d}
+	Mr Wylliam Maycott	x^{s}
+	John Neale	xiij^{s}
+	John Johnson shomaker	vj^{s}
+	Thomas Waterman	vj^{s} viij^{d}
+	John Dennys	vj^{s}
+	Wylliam Staples	xx^{d}
+	Rycherd Amys[1304]	ij^{s}
	George Bennett	xx^{d}
	Mrs Norton wydoe	x^{s}
	John Smythe	v^{s}
	Summa	vij$^{£}$ xiiij^{s} iiij^{d}

Preston Streete

+	John Skyrr	x^{s}
+	Thomas Barlyng	viij^{s}
	Mrs Aunsell wydoe	x^{s}
	Thomas Whyte	ij^{s}
	Gregorye Hubbert	iij^{s}
+	Gieles Reboure	iiij^{s}
+	Mathewe Holland	xvj^{d}
+	Wylliam Cadman	v^{s}
+	Robert Lee	xij^{d}
+	Thomas Cole	xvij^{s}
+	John Sharles	iij^{s}
+	Barthylmewe Newes	xij^{d}
	Thomas Cumber	xij^{d}
+	Roberte Falle	xij^{s}
+	Roberte Medowes	xij^{d}
+	Wylliam Neale	v^{s}
	Mrs Alyce Neale	ij^{s}
+	Henrye Hocker	xij^{d}
	Rycherd Pysyng	ij^{s}
+	Rycherd Stransham	vj^{s} viij^{d}
+	Thomas Andrewe	xij^{d}
+	Christofer Dobbynson	v^{s}
+	Nycholas Bull	iiij^{s}
+	John Musterd	xij^{d}
	John Wattes	vj^{d}

[1304] fol. 153.

	Summa	v$^{£}$ vij^{s}

Weste Streatt

+	Christofer Potter	v^{s}
	Rycherd Downe	xij^{d}
+	Thomas Harthenden	xij^{d}
+	Wylliam Harte	vj^{d}
+	Wylliam Stevens	xx^{d}
+	John Clerke wydoe	ij^{s}
+	Roberte Chapman	iij^{s} iiij^{d}
+	Thomas Payce	xij^{d}
	Rycherd Knyghte	xij^{d}
	Stephen Dodd	xij^{d}
+	Wylliam Chattborne	xij^{d}
+	Rycherd Mannys	xij^{d}
	John Ware	xij^{d}
+	Thomas Byrlyng smyth	xij^{d}
+	Geylles Kydd	iij^{s}
+	Henrye Bonde	xiij^{s}
+	Thomas Rye	viij^{s}
+	Wylliam Ogden	xij^{d}
+	Wylliam Dodd	iij^{s} iiij^{d}
+	Stephen Symes	vj^{s}
	Henrye Adys wydoe	ij^{s}
+	Gregorye Wryght	xij^{d}
+	Thomas Hawkes	xx^{d}
+	John Stone	v^{s}
+	Nycholas Vawter	v^{s}
+	Robert Whysker	ij^{s}
+	Rycherd Wode	xv^{s}
+	Wylliam Harryson	vj^{s} viij^{d}
	Thomas Bedford	xij^{d}
+	Anthonye Fynch	x^{s}
	Summa	v$^{£}$ viij^{s} viij^{d}

Tanner Streete

+	Wylliam Taylor	iij^{s}
+	Roberte Wyer	iij^{s} iiij^{d}
+	John Dewerd	vj^{s}
+	Henrye Wrottyng	ij^{s}
	Water Bucherste[1305]	xij^{d}
	Father Ponchyon	xij^{d}
	Summa	xvj^{s} iiij^{d}

The Keye

+	Fyrst Lewes Austen	ij^{s}
+	Thomas Quycke	xij^{d}
+	*[blank]* Trowtes	xij^{d}
+	John Standleye	xij^{d}
	Summa	iiij^{s}
	Summa totalis	xxxvij$^{£}$ xvj^{s} iiij^{d}

Faversham

A ceasse made the thyrde daye of June in the eleventh yere of the reygne of oure sovereigne Elizabeth by the grace of God of Ingland Fraunce and Irelande Queene defendoure of the feythe etc. [3 June 1569] ratyd uppon the inhabytauntes freemen and owt dwellers belonging to the seyd towne by John Beste Roberte Colwell Roberte Fagge jurattes Wylliam Comber Edwarde Russell; Humfreye Atkynson and Wylliam Okenfolde of the common councell amountynge to the somme of xx$^{£}$ as heerafter followethe

Maior and jurattes

+	Inprimis Mr Barthylmewe Amys mayor	ix^{s}
+	Item Mr John Best	ix^{s}
+	Mr Edwarde Blackwell	ix^{s}
+	Mr George Stransham	ix^{s}
+	Mr Thomas Oldfelde	ix^{s}
+	Mr Henrye Phylpott	viij^{s} iiij^{d}
+	Mr John Wreuke	vij^{s}
+	Mr Robert Colwell	viij^{s} vj^{d}
+	Mr Thomas Belke	vj^{s} vj^{d}
	Mr Thomas Fynche	v^{s}
+	Mr Roberte Fagge	ix^{s}
	Summa	iiij$^{£}$ ix^{s} iiij^{d}

The names of the xxiiijth

+	Fyrste of Wylliam Saker	viij^{s}
+	Edwarde Russell	vj^{s} viij^{d}
+	Roberte Lame	vj^{s} viij^{d}
+	Humfrey Atkynson	vj^{s} viij^{d}
+	Rycherd Tylman	vj^{s}
+	Edwarde Harrys	vj^{s}

1305 fol. 263.

+	Wylliam Comber	v^{s}
	Wylliam Okenfolde	v^{s}
+	John Tyndale	iiij^{s} vj^{d}
	Thomas Poast	iiij^{s} vj^{d}
+	Roberte Rye poyntmaker	vj^{s}
+	Christofer Amys	iij^{s} vj^{d}
+	Rycherd Lawrence	iij^{s} iiij^{d}
+	Thomas Jerman	iiij^{s}
+	Thomas Barton	iij^{s} iiij^{d}
+	John Snothe	iij^{s}
+	Roberte Elfrythe	ij^{s} vj^{d}
+	John Elfrythe	iij^{s}
+	Hughe Boothe	ij^{s} vj^{d}
+	Thomas Musterd	ij^{s} vj^{d}
+	John Mylles	ij^{s}
+	Thomas Audryan	ij^{s} vj^{d}
	Wylliam Hampton	xij^{d}

Courte Streete[1306]

+	Fyrste of Mr John Fynch gentleman	x^{s}
	Mr Rycherd Arddes gentleman	vj^{s}
+	Wylliam Pecocke the younger	ij^{s} viij^{d}
+	John Sabyn	xij^{d}
+	Wylliam Freende	xvj^{d}
+	John Dyxson	viij^{d}
+	Mr Rycherd Ball	ix^{s}
+	Cornelys Domer	ij^{s} vj^{d}
+	John Fysher	iij^{s} iiij^{d}
	Roberte Hawkyns	xij^{d}
+	Roberte Rye maryner	vj^{d}
+	John Ambrose	ix^{s}
+	Wylliam Pecocke the elder	iij^{s} iiij^{d}
+	Mr Wylliam Maycotte gentleman	v^{s}
+	John Neale	vj^{s} viij^{d}
+	John Johnson shoemaker	iij^{s} iiij^{d}
+	Thomas Waterman	iiij^{s}
+	John Dennys	iij^{s}
+	Wylliam Stapeles	x^{d}
+	Rycherd Amys	xij^{d}
	George Bennet	x^{d}
	John Smythe	iij^{s} iiij^{d}
+	Andrewe Newton	vj^{d}
+	Mr Smythe gentleman	v^{s}
+	John Upton	ij^{s}
+	John Standlye	viij^{d}
+	Mr Anthonye Fynch gentleman	vj^{s}
Summa		iiij$^{£}$ xij^{s} vj^{d}

Preston Strete

+	Fyrste John Skyrr	vj^{s} viij^{d}
+	Thomas Barlyng	v^{s}
	Mrs Elizabethe Ansell wydoe	vj^{s}
	Wylliam Netter	ij^{s}
	Thomas Whyghte	xij^{d}
	Gregorye Hybberd	xviij^{d}
+	Geylles Robourne wydoe	ij^{s}
+	Matthewe Hollond	xij^{d}
+	Wylliam Cademan	ij^{s} vj^{d}
+	Roberte Lee	vj^{d}
+	Thomas Colle	viij^{s}
+	John Sharles	xviij^{d}
+	Barthylmewe Newes	viij^{d}
	Thomas Comber	vj^{d}
+	Robert Falle	vj^{s} viij^{d}
+	Roberte Medowes	vj^{d}
+	John Cason	xij^{d}
+	Wylliam Neale	ij^{s} vj^{d}
	Mrs Alyce Neale wydoe	xij^{d}
+	Henrye Hocker	viij^{d}
	Rycherd Pysyng	xij^{d}
+	Rycherd Straunsham	iij^{s} iiij^{d}
+	Thomas Androwe	viij^{d}
+	Christofer Dobbynson	iij^{s}
+	Nycholas Bull	ij^{s} vj^{d}
+	John Musterd	viij^{d}
+	John Mason	xij^{d}
	Edwarde Usher	vj^{d}
+	Henrye Adys wydoe	xij^{d}
Summa		iij$^{£}$ v^{s} iiij^{d}

Weste Streatt

+	Fyrst of Christofer Potter	iij^{s} iiij^{d}
+	Thomas Harthenden	viij^{d}
+	Wylliam Harte	iij^{s}

1306 fol. 263v.

+	Wylliam Stevens	x^{d}
+	John Clarke wydoe	xij^{d}
+	Roberte Chapman	ij^{s}
	Rycherd Knyght	viij^{d}
	Stephen Dodd	vj^{d}
+	Wylliam Chattborne	xij^{d}
+	Rycherd Mannys	viij^{d}
	John Ware	viij^{d}
	Thomas Byrlyng	viij^{d}
+	Geyles Kydd	ij^{s}
+	Henrye Bonde[1307]	vj^{s} viij^{d}
+	Thomas Rye	iiij^{s}
+	Wylliam Ugden	xij^{d}
+	Wylliam Todd	ij^{s}
+	Stephen Symes	iij^{s} iiij^{d}
+	Gregorye Wryghte	vj^{d}
+	Thomas Hawkes	x^{d}
+	John Stow	ij^{s} vj^{d}
+	Nycholas Vawter	iij^{s}
+	Roberte Whysked	xij^{d}
+	Rycherd Wood	viij^{s}
+	Wylliam Harrys	iiij^{s}
	Thomas Bedford	vj^{d}
	[blank] Ponchyon	vj^{d}
+	Wylliam Vynton	xij^{d}
+	Thomas Pellam	ij^{s}
	Summa	Lvij^{s} x^{d}

Tanner Streete

+	Wylliam Taylor	xviij^{d}
+	Roberte Wyer	ij^{s}
+	John Deward	iij^{s} iiij^{d}
+	Henrye Wrottynge	xij^{d}
	Walter Bucherte	viij^{d}
	[blank] Brakenberye the myller	vj^{d}
	Summa	-

The Keye

+	Lewes Austen	xij^{d}
+	Thomas Quycke	vj^{d}
+	*[blank]* Trowghtes	vj^{d}
	Summa	ij^{s}

The Owte Dwellers

+	Fyrst of Mr Francis Swane of Wye	v^{s}
	Mr Thomas Straunsham of S. Dounstone next the cyttye of Caunterburye	v^{s}
+	Mr Thomas Hawkyns of Bowghton under the Bleane	v^{s}
+	Mr John Fynche of Homston	v^{s}
+	Mr John Straunsham of the parishe of Estchurche in the yle of Shapye	v^{s}
	Mr John Maycott of Osprynge	v^{s}
	Mychaell Allen of Davyngton	iij^{s}
	Summa	xxxiij^{s}

Summa totalis xxij$^{£}$

Faversham

A cesse made there the xxijth daye of September in the eleventhe yere of the reigne of our sovereigne ladye Quene Elizabethe [22 Sep 1569] by Henrye Phylpott and Thomas Belke jurattes and John Skyrr and Roberte Lame commoners of the seyd towne

Maior and jurattes

+	Mr Barthylmewe Amys mayor	ix^{s}
+	Mr Edwarde Blackwell	ix^{s}
+	Mr John Beste	ix^{s}
+	Mr George Straunsham	ix^{s}
+	Mr Thomas Oldefeilde	ix^{s}
+	Mr Henrye Phyllpott	viij^{s} iiij^{d}
+	Mr John Wreuke	vij^{s}
+	Mr Roberte Colwell	viij^{s} vj^{d}
+	Mr Thomas Belke[1308]	vj^{s} viij^{d}
	Mr Thomas Fynche	v^{s}
+	Mr Roberte Fagg	ix^{s}
	Summa	iiij$^{£}$ ix^{s} vj^{d}

The names of the xxiiijth

+	Wylliam Saker	viij^{s}

[1307] fol. 264.

[1308] fol. 264v.

+	Edward Russell	vj^{s} viij^{d}
+	Roberte Lame	vj^{s} viij^{d}
+	Humfrey Atkynson	vj^{s} viij^{d}
+	Rycherd Tyllman	vj^{s} viij^{d}
+	Edward Harrys	vj^{s} viij^{d}
	Wylliam Comber	vj^{s} viij^{d}
	Wylliam Okenfold	vj^{s} viij^{d}
+	John Tyndall	v^{s}
	Thomas Poste	v^{s}
+	Roberte Rye poyntmaker	vj^{s}
+	Christofer Amys	iij^{s} iiij^{d}
+	Rycherd Lawrence	iiij^{s}
+	Thomas Jerman	v^{s}
+	Thomas Barton	iiij^{s}
+	John Snothe	iij^{s} iiij^{d}
+	Roberte Elfrythe	iij^{s}
+	John Elfrithe	iij^{s} iiij^{d}
+	Hugh Boothe	iij^{s}
+	Thomas Musterd	xij^{d}
+	John Mylles	ij^{s}
+	Thomas Andryan	ij^{s} vj^{d}
	Wylliam Hampton	ij^{s}
	Summa	v$^{£}$ vij^{s} ij^{d}

Courte Strete

+	John Fynch gentleman	x^{s}
	Rycherd Ardes gentleman	vj^{s} viij^{d}
+	Wylliam Pecoke the younger	iij^{s} iiij^{d}
+	John Sabyn	xij^{d}
+	Wylliam Frynd	xvj^{d}
+	John Dyxson	viij^{d}
+	Rycherd Ball gentleman	ix^{s}
+	Cornelys Dowman	ij^{s} vj^{d}
+	John Fysher	iij^{s} iiij^{d}
	Roberte Hawkyns	xij^{d}
+	Roberte Rye maryner	vj^{d}
+	John Ambrose	ix^{s}
+	Wylliam Pecoke the elder	iij^{s} iiij^{d}
+	Wylliam Maycott gentleman	v^{s}
+	John Neale	vj^{s} viij^{d}
+	John Johnson	iij^{s} iiij^{d}
+	Thomas Smythe gentleman	vj^{s} viij^{d}
+	John Dennys	iiij^{s}
+	Thomas Waterman	iiij^{s}
+	Rycherd Amys	xij^{d}
	George Bennett	xij^{d}
	John Smythe	v^{s}
+	John Upton	ij^{s}
+	John Standleye	xij^{d}
+	Anthony Fynche gentleman	vj^{s} viij^{d}
	Summa	iiij$^{£}$ xvij^{s} vj^{d}

Preston Streete

+	John Skyrr	vj^{s} viij^{d}
+	Thomas Barlyng	v^{s}
	Mrs Aunsell wydoe	vj^{s}
	Roberte Whyghte	xij^{d}
+	Matthew Holland	xvj^{d}
+	Wylliam Cadman	ij^{s} vj^{d}
+	Roberte Alee	vj^{d}
+	Thomas Cole	viij^{s}
+	John Shales	ij^{s}
+	Barthylmewe Newes	viij^{d}
	Thomas Cumber	vj^{d}
+	Roberte A Vale	vj^{s} viij^{d}
+	Roberte Medowes	vj^{d}
+	John Cason	xij^{d}
+	Wylliam Neale	ij^{s}
	Mrs Neale wydoe	xij^{d}
+	Henrye Hocker	viij^{d}
	Rycherd Pysyng	xvj^{d}
+	Thomas Andrwe	viij^{d}
+	Rycherd Straunsham	iij^{s}
+	Christofer Dobbynson	iiij^{s}
+	Nycholas Bull[1309]	ij^{s}
+	John Musterd	viij^{d}
	Edwarde Ussher	vj^{d}
+	John Mason	xvj^{d}
	Adyes wydoe	ij^{s}
	Summa	iij$^{£}$ xviij^{d}

Weste Streete

+	Thomas Hawkes	ij^{s}
+	Thomas Haffenden	xviij^{d}
+	Wylliam Harte	iij^{s} iiij^{d}
+	Wylliam Stevens	ij^{s}
+	Roberte Chapman	ij^{s}
+	Thomas Pease	xij^{d}

[1309] fol. 265.

+	Lambert Nayeles	xij^{d}
	Steven Dodd	vj^{d}
	John Ware	xij^{d}
+	Thomas Berlyng smyth	viij^{d}
+	Gyeles Kydd	ij^{s} vj^{d}
+	Henrye Bonde	vj^{s} viij^{d}
+	Thomas Rye	v^{s}
+	Wylliam Ugden	xij^{d}
+	Wylliam Dodd	iij^{s} iiij^{d}
+	Stephen Symes	iij^{s} iiij^{d}
+	Gregorye Wryghte	xviij^{d}
+	John Stone	ij^{s} vj^{d}
	Jefferye Carpenter	vj^{d}
+	Nycholas Vawter	iij^{s} iiij^{d}
+	Roberte Whyskerd	xvj^{d}
+	Rychard Woode	viij^{s}
+	Wylliam Harrys	iij^{s} iiij^{d}
	Ponchyn the myller	xij^{d}
+	Thomas Pelham	ij^{s}
	Summa	iij$^{£}$ iiij^{d}

Tanner Streete

+	Wylliam Taylour	xviij^{d}
+	Roberte Wyer	ij^{s}
+	John Dewerd	iiij^{s}
+	Henrye Wrottyng	xvj^{d}
+	Water Buckherste	xij^{d}
	Summa	ixs xd

Keyelane

+	Lewes Austen	xij^{d}
+	Thomas Quycke	vj^{d}
	[blank] Trowttes	vj^{d}
Summa		ijs

Owte Dwellers

+	Mr John Straunsham	v^{s}
+	Mr Thomas Hawkyns	v^{s}
+	Mr John Fynche of Holmston	v^{s}
	John Ruffyn	iij^{s} iiij^{d}
+	Mr Swan	v^{s}
	Summa	xxiij^{s} iiij^{d}
Summa totalis		xxij$^{£}$ xj^{s} ij^{d}

Faversham[1310]

A ceesse there made the xth daye of November in the xijth yere of the raygne of oure sovereygne ladye Quene Elizabeth by the grace of God of Ingland Fraunce and Ireland defendour of the feythe etc. [10 Nov. 1570] by John Beste Barthylmewe Amys and Roberte Colwell jurattes and John Skyrr Wylliam Okenfolde Humfreye Atkynson Wylliam Comber Roberte Elfryth and Roberte Lame commoners of the same towne

Maior and jurattes

+	Inprimis Mr Roberte Fagg mayor	viij^{s}
+	Mr Edwarde Blackwell	viij^{s}
+	Mr John Beste	vj^{s} viij^{d}
+	Mr John Wreuke	vj^{s} viij^{d}
+	Mr George Straunsham	vj^{s} viij^{d}
+	Mr Thomas Oldefielde	vj^{s} viij^{d}
+	Mr Barthylmewe Amys	vj^{s} viij^{d}
+	Mr Thomas Belke	vj^{s} viij^{d}
+	Mr Thomas Fynche	vj^{s} viij^{d}
+	Mr Roberte Colwell	vj^{s} viij^{d}
+	Mr Thomas Smythe	vj^{s} viij^{d}
	Summa	

The names of the xxiiijth

+	Roberte Lambe	v^{s}
+	Humfery Atkynson	v^{s}
+	Rycherd Tylman	v^{s}
+	Edwarde Harrys	v^{s}
+	Wylliam Comber	v^{s}
+	Wylliam Okenfelde	v^{s}
+	John Tyndale	v^{s}
+	Roberte Rye poyntmaker	v^{s}
+	Rycherd Lawrence	iiij^{s}
+	Thomas Jerman	iiij^{s}
+	John Snothe	iij^{s}
+	Roberte Elfrythe	iij^{s}
+	John Elfrythe	ij^{s}
+	John Skyrr	v^{s}
+	John Fynche of Homston	vj^{s} viij^{d}

[1310] fol. 265v.

+	Thomas Barlyng	v^{s}
+	Thomas Cole	v^{s}
+	John Neale	v^{s}
+	Hughe Boothe	v^{s}
+	Thomas Musterd	xij^{d}
+	Thomas Barton	iij^{s} $iiij^{d}$
+	Thomas Audryan	ij^{s}
	Wylliam Hampton	iij^{s} $iiij^{d}$
+	Roberte A Vale	v^{s}
	Summa	-

Courte Streete

+	Wylliam Saker	$iiij^{s}$
+	John Fynche gentleman	$viij^{s}$
+	John Ruffyn	v^{s}
+	Wylliam Pecoke junior	ij^{s} vj^{d}
	Avery Mantle	ij^{s}
+	Wylliam Frynde	xij^{d}
+	John Dyxson	xij^{d}
+	Rycherd Ball gentleman	vij^{s}
+	Cornelys Dowman	ij^{s} vj^{d}
+	John Fysher	ij^{s}
	Roberte Hawkyns	xij^{d}
+	Anthony Fynche gentleman	$iiij^{s}$
+	Roberte Rye maryner	xij^{d}
+	John Ambrose	vij^{s}
+	John Stanleye	xij^{d}
+	Wylliam Pecoke the elder[1311]	ij^{s}
+	Humfrey Kybbott	ij^{s} vj^{d}
+	John Johnson shomaker	iij^{s} $iiij^{d}$
+	Thomas Waterman	$iiij^{s}$
+	Edwarde Masterson	iij^{s}
+	John Dennys	iij^{s}
	John Smythe	v^{s}
+	John Upton	iij^{s}
+	*[blank]* Hamond	xij^{d}
+	Wylliam Robynson	xij^{d}
+	*[blank]* Scoone	xij^{d}
+	Mrs Phylpott wydoe	iij^{s}
	Summa	

Preston Streette

	Mrs Aunsell	$iiij^{s}$
+	Matthewe Hollond	xij^{d}
+	Roberte Whyskerd	ij^{s}
+	John Shalles	xij^{d}
+	Wylliam Neale	xij^{d}
	Peter Lambyn	xij^{d}
+	Adyes wydoe	xij^{d}
+	John Cason	xij^{d}
+	Gregorye Hubberd	xij^{d}
	John Tompson hatter	xij^{d}
	Rycherd Pysyng	ij^{s}
+	Thomas Andrewe	xij^{d}
	John Rapeseed	xij^{d}
+	Christofer Dobbynson	iij^{s}
+	Nycholas Bull	ij^{s}
+	John Musterd	xij^{d}
+	John Mason	ij^{s}
+	Henrye the brewer	xij^{d}
	Summa	-

Weste Strette

+	Thomas Hawkes	ij^{s}
	Wylliam Rockerye	iij^{s}
+	Thomas Haffenden	ij^{s}
+	Wylliam Harte	ij^{s}
+	Wylliam Stevyns	xvj^{d}
+	Roberte Chapman	xvj^{d}
	Rycherd Johnson	xij^{d}
	John Ware	xij^{d}
+	*[blank]* Austen	xij^{d}
+	*[blank]* Byrlyng the smythe	xij^{d}
+	Gyles Kydd	ij^{s}
+	Wylliam Chattborne	xij^{d}
+	Henrye Bond	v^{s}
+	Thomas Rye	$iiij^{s}$
+	Steven Symes	iij^{s}
+	Lamberd Nayle	xij^{d}
+	Rycherd Mannys	xij^{d}
+	Wylliam Dodd	ij^{s} vj^{d}
+	John Stone	xvj^{d}
+	Nycholas Vawter	ij^{s}
+	Rycherd Wood	vij^{s}
+	Wylliam Harrys	ij^{s} vj^{d}
+	Thomas Pelham	ij^{s} vj^{d}
+	Wylliam Cademan	ij^{s} vj^{d}
	Summa	-

[1311] fol. 266.

Tanner Strette

+	Thomas Osborne	v^{s}
+	Leonard Fygde	iij^{s} iiij^{d}
+	John Dewerd	iij^{s}
+	Henrye Wrottyng	xij^{d}
	Wylliam Barnes	xij^{d}
+	John Holte	xij^{d}
	Summa	

Keylane

+	Lewes Austen	xij^{d}
	Henrye Asten	xij^{d}
+	Thomas Quycke	xij^{d}
	Summa	

Summa Totalis xviij$^{£}$

Faversham[1312]

A ceese made the [ ] daye of Auguste in the xiijth yere of the reygne of oure sovereygne ladye Elizabethe by the grace of God of Ingland Fraunce and Ireland Quene defendour of the feyth etc. [Aug. 1571] by John Best Thomas [*not stated*] jurattes there Wylliam Okenfold Roberte Lame Roberte Elfrythe and Rycherd Lawrence commoners of the same towne

Mayor and Jurattes

+	Inprimis Master Roberte Fagg mayor	x^{s} viij^{d}
+	Master Edwarde Blackwell	x^{s} viij^{d}
+	Mr John Beste	viij^{s} iiij^{d}
+	Mr John Wreuke	viij^{s} iiij^{d}
+	Mr George Straunsham	viij^{s} iiij^{d}
+	Mr Thomas Oldfeld	viij^{s} iiij^{d}
+	Mr Barthylmewe Amys	viij^{s} iiij^{d}
+	Mr Thomas Belke	vij^{s} viij^{d}
	Mr Thomas Fynche	vij^{s} vj^{d} [1313]
+	Mr Roberte Colwell	viij^{s} iiij^{d}
+	Mr Thomas Smythe	viij^{s} iiij^{d}
	Summa	iiij$^{£}$ xiiij^{s} viij^{d}

The names of the xxiiij

+	Roberte Lambe	vj^{s} viij^{d}
+	Humferye Atkynson	vj^{s} viij^{d}
+	Rycherd Tylman	vj^{s} viij^{d}
+	Edwarde Harrys	vj^{s} viij^{d}
+	Wylliam Comber	vj^{s} viij^{d}
	Wylliam Okenfolde	vj^{s} viij^{d}
+	John Tyndall	vj^{s} viij^{d}
+	Roberte Rye poyntmaker	vj^{s} viij^{d}
+	Rycherd Lawrence	v^{s}
+	Thomas Jerman	v^{s} vj^{d}
+	John Snode	iiij^{s}
+	Roberte Elfrythe	iiij^{s}
+	John Elfrithe	ij^{s}
+	John Skyrr	vij^{s}
+	John Fynche	x^{s}
+	Thomas Barlyng	vj^{s} viij^{d}
+	Thomas Coole	vij^{s}
+	John Neale	vj^{s} viij^{d}
+	Hugh Boothe	v^{s}
+	Thomas Musterd	xij^{d}
+	Thomas Barton	iiij^{s}
+	Thomas Audrian	xij^{d}
	Wylliam Hampton	v^{s}
+	Wydow ~~Roberte~~ A Vale	vj^{s}
	Summa	vj$^{£}$ vij^{s} iiij^{d}

Court Streete

+	Wylliam Saker	vj^{s}
+	John Fynche gentleman	x^{s} viij^{d}
+	John Ruffyn	vj^{s} viij^{d}
+	Wylliam Pecoke	iij^{s}
	Sakers wydowe	ij^{s}
+	Wylliam Frend	xij^{d}
+	John Dyxson	xvj^{d}
+	Rycherd Ball gentleman	ix^{s}
+	Cornelys Dowman	iiij^{s}
+	John Fysher	ij^{s} viij^{d}
	Roberte Hawkyns	xv^{d}
+	Anthony Fynche	*[blank]*
+	Roberte Rye maryner	xvj^{d}
+	John Ambrose	x^{s}
+	John Standeley	xvj^{d}
+	Humfrey Kybbott	iij^{s} iiij^{d}

[1312] fol. 266v.
[1313] This figure is indistinct and could be viij^{d}.

+	John Johnson	iiij^{s}
+	Thomas Waterman	vj^{s}
+	Edmonde Masterson	iiij^{s}
+	John Dennys	iiij^{s}
	John Smythe	vj^{s}
+	John Upton gentleman	iiij^{s}
+	*[blank]* Hamond[1314]	*[blank]*
+	Wylliam Robynson	xij^{d}
+	John Scoune	xvj^{d}
+	Mr Filpott	iiij^{s}
+	Peycockes wydoe	xx^{d}
Summa		v$^{£}$ xij^{s} viij^{d}

Preston Streete

	Mrs Auncell wydoe	iiij^{s} ~~v^{s} iiij^{d}~~
+	Matthew Hollond	*[blank]*
+	Roberte Whyskerd	ij^{s}
+	John Shalles	xij^{d}
+	Wylliam Neale	ij^{s}
	Peter Lambyn	xvj^{d}
	Adyes wydoe	*[blank]*
+	*[blank]* Brydg	xij^{d}
	Thomas Cumber	xij^{d}
+	John Cawson	xij^{d}
+	Wydoe Vale	vj^{s}
+	Gregorye Hubberd	xvj^{d}
	John Thomson hatter	xvj^{d}
	Rycherd Pysyng	*[blank]*
+	Thomas Andrwe	xvj^{d}
+	John Rapseede	xij^{d}
+	Christofer Dobbynson	iiij^{s}
+	Nycholas Bull	iiij^{s}
+	John Musterd	*[blank]*
+	John Mason	iij^{s} iiij^{d}
	Herry Brewer	*[blank]*
	Summa	xxxvij^{s}

Weste Streete

+	Thomas Hawkes	ij^{s}
+	*[blank]* Rockerye	iiij^{s}
+	Thomas Haffenden	iij^{s}
+	Wydoe Harte	xvj^{d}
+	Wylliam Stevens	xx^{d}
+	Roberte Chapman	ij^{s}
+	Rycherd Johnson	*[blank]*
+	John Ware	*[blank]*
+	*[blank]* Austyn	xx^{d}
+	*[blank]* Byrlyng the smyth	xvj^{d}
+	Gyeles Kydd	iij^{s} iiij^{d}
+	Wylliam Chattborne	ij^{s}
+	Henrye Bond	vj^{s}
+	Thomas Rye	vj^{s}
+	Stephen Symes	iiij^{s}
+	Lambert Nayles	xij^{d}
+	Rycherd Mannys	xij^{d}
+	Wylliam Dodd	vj^{s}
+	Gregory Wryghte	xij^{d}
+	John Dodd	ij^{s}
+	John Stone	ij^{s}
+	Nycholas Vawter	xvj^{d}
+	Thomas Furmynger	vj^{s} viij^{d}
+	Wylliam Harrys	iij^{s} iiij^{d}
+	Thomas Pelham	xij^{d}
+	Wylliam Cademan	iij^{s} iiij^{d}
Summa		iij$^{£}$ vij^{s}

Tanner Strette

+	Thomas Osborne	vj^{s} viij^{d}
+	Leonard Fygg	v^{s}
+	John Dewerd	v^{s}
+	Henrye Wrottyng	xx^{d}
	Wylliam Barnes	xx^{d}
+	John Holte	xvj^{d}

Key Lane

+	Lewes Austen	xvj^{d}
	Henrye Austen	xij^{d}
+	Thomas Quyckes	xij^{d}
Sum of both[1315]		xxiiij^{s} viij^{d}

Oute Dwellers[1316]

+	Mr Thomas Straunsham	v^{s}
+	Mr John Straunsham	v^{s}
+	Jeames Wylye	ij^{s}
+	Anthonye Wylye	ij^{s}
Summa totalis		xxiij$^{£}$ xiij^{s}

1314 fol. 267.

1315 Summa Ambus.

1316 fol. 267v.

Faversham

A ceesse made at the xjth of Februarie by Master Roberte Fagg Master Thomas Fynche jurattes Wylliam Okenfold John Neale Thomas Barlyng and Wylliam Hampton comoners of there in the xiiijth year of the reign of queen[1317] Elizabeth [11 Feb. 1572].

Mayor and jurattes

+	Inprimis Mr Thomas Oldfield mayor	x^{s}
+	Mr Edwarde Blackwell Esquyre	x^{s}
+	Mr John Beste	x^{s}
+	Mr John Wreuke	viij^{s}
+	Mr George Straunsham	viij^{s}
+	Mr Barthylmewe Amys	viij^{s}
+	Mr Roberte Fagg	x^{s}
+	Mr Thomas Belke	viij^{s}
+	Mr Roberte Coldwell	viij^{s}
+	Mr Thomas Fynche	viij^{s}
+	Mr Thomas Smythe	viij^{s}
	Summa	iiij$^{£}$ xvj^{s}

Comoners

+	Roberte Lame	vj^{s} viij^{d}
+	Humfrey Atkynson	vj^{s} viij^{d}
+	Rycherd Tyllman	vj^{s} viij^{d}
+	Edwarde Harrys	vj^{s} viij^{d}
+	Wylliam Comber	vj^{s} viij^{d}
	Wylliam Okenfolde	vj^{s} viij^{d}
+	John Tyndall	vj^{s} viij^{d}
+	Roberte Rye poyntmaker	vj^{s} viij^{d}
+	Rycherd Lawrence	v^{s}
+	Thomas Jerman	v^{s}
+	Roberte Elfrythe	iiij^{s}
+	John Skyrr	viij^{s}
+	John Fynche gentleman	viij^{s}
+	Thomas Barlyng	vj^{s} viij^{d}
+	Thomas Coole	viij^{s}
+	John Neale	vj^{s} viij^{d}
+	Hugh Boothe	v^{s}
+	Thomas Musterd	xij^{d}
	Thomas Barton	ij^{s}
+	Thomas Audryan	xij^{d}
+	Wylliam Hampton	v^{s}
+	Rycherd Ball gentleman	x^{s}
+	Thomas Waterman	vj^{s} viij^{d}
	Somme	vj$^{£}$ xv^{s} iiij^{d}

Court Street

+	Wylliam Saker	vj^{s}
+	John Fynche gentleman	x^{s}
+	Wylliam Pecocke	iiij^{s}
+	John Fysher	ij^{s}
+	Cornelys Dowman	iiij^{s}
+	Roberte Rye maryner	xij^{d}
+	Mrs Phylpott	iij^{s}
+	John Ambrose	x^{s}
+	Pecockes wydoe	x^{d}
+	Humfrey Kybbett	iij^{s}
+	John Johnson shomaker	iiij^{s}
+	Christofer Potter	vj^{s} viij^{d}
+	Snodes wydoe	xij^{d}
+	Edmund Masterson	v^{s}
+	John Dennys	iiij^{s}
	John Sntythe[1318]	vj^{s} viij^{d}
+	John Upton	iiij^{s}
	Summa	iij$^{£}$ xvj^{s}

Preston Streette[1319]

	Mrs Aunsell	v^{s} iiij^{d}
+	John Shalles	xij^{d}
+	Wylliam Neale	xx^{d}
+	John Ruffyn	vj^{s} viij^{d}
	Peter Lambyn	xvj^{d}
+	Wylliam Beesbeeche	vj^{s} viij^{d}
	John Tompson	xij^{d}
+	Thomas Androwe	xij^{d}
+	Christofer Dobbynson	iiij^{s}
+	Nycholas Bull	iiij^{s}
+	John Mason	iiij^{s}
+	Mystres Neale	xij^{d}
	Summa	xxxvij^{s} viij^{d}

[1317] Anno regine regis.

[1318] ?Smythe

[1319] fol. 268.

Weste Streete

+	Thomas Hawkes	ij^{s}
	Wylliam Rockerye	v^{s}
+	Thomas Haffenden	iij^{s}
+	Hartes wydoe	xij^{d}
+	Wylliam Stephyns	ij^{s}
+	Roberte Chapman	ij^{s}
+	Wylliam Ugden	xx^{d}
+	John Austen	xx^{d}
+	Thomas Byrlyng smythe	xvj^{d}
+	Gyeles Kydd	iij^{s} iiij^{d}
+	Wylliam Chattborne	ij^{s} vj^{d}
+	Henrye Bond	vj^{s} viij^{d}
+	Thomas Rye	vj^{s}
+	Stephyn Symmes	iiij^{s} vj^{d}
+	Lamberte Nayeles	xij^{d}
+	Wylliam Mannys	xij^{d}
+	Wylliam Todd	vj^{s} viij^{d}
+	Gregorye Wryghte	xij^{d}
+	John Dodd	iij^{s}
+	John Stone	ij^{s}
+	Nycholas Vawter	xvj^{d}
+	Thomas Furmynger	vj^{s} viij^{d}
+	Wylliam Harrys	iij^{s}
+	Thomas Pelham	xij^{d}
+	Wylliam Cademan	iij^{s} iiij^{d}
	Summa	iij$^{£}$ xij^{s} viij^{d}

Tanner Streete

+	Thomas Osborne	vj^{s} viij^{d}
+	Leonard Fygde	vj^{s} viij^{d}
+	John Deward	v^{s}
+	Henrye Wrottyng	xx^{d}
+	John Holte	xij^{d}
	Summa	xxj^{s}

Keye Lane

+	Lewes Austen	xij^{d}
+	Thomas Quycke	xij^{d}
+	John Trowtes	xij^{d}
Summa		iij^{s}

+	James Wylye	ij^{s}
+	Anthony Wylye	ij^{s} vj^{d}
+	John Holte	xij^{d}
Summa totalis		xxij$^{£}$ vij^{s} ij^{d}

Faversham[1320]

A generall ceesse made and assessyd uppon the hole inhabytaunce of the towne and libertye of Faversham accordyng to a wardmote there assessyd the xxth daye of Maye in the xiiijth yere of oure sovereygne ladye Elizabethe nowe Quene [20 May 1572] by Barthylmewe Amys Thomas Fynche and Roberte Colwell jurattes and Rychard Ball Roberte Lame Thomas Cole Roberte Elfrythe Thomas Barlyng and Wylliam Comber for the some of threescore powndes lawfull monye of Ingland accordyng to the seyd wardemote

Mayor and jurattes

+	**Inprimis** Mr Thomas Oldefield mayor	xxiij^{s} iiij^{d}
+	Mr Edwarde Blackwell	xxvj^{s} viij^{d}
+	Mr John Beste	xxiij^{s} iiij^{d}
+	Mr John Wreuke	xvj^{s}
+	Mr George Straunsham	xx^{s}
+	Mr Barthylmewe Amys	xviij^{s}
+	Mr Roberte Fagg	xxvj^{s} viij^{d}
+	Mr Thomas Belke	xvj^{s}
+	Mr Roberte Collwell	xvj^{s}
+	Mr Thomas Fynche	xvj^{s}
+	Mr Thomas Smythe	xvj^{s}
Summa		x$^{£}$ xviij^{s}

The names of the xxiiijth

+	Roberte Lambe	xv^{s}
+	Humfrey Atkynson	xvj^{s}
+	Rycherd Tylman	xv^{s}
+	Edwarde Harrys	xv^{s}
+	Wylliam Comber	xv^{s}
	Wylliam Okenfolde	xv^{s}
+	John Tyndall	xv^{s}
+	Roberte Rye poyntmaker	xv^{s}
+	Rycherd Lawrence	x^{s}
+	Thomas Jerman	x^{s}

1320 fol. 268v.

+	Roberte Elfrythe	x^{s}
+	John Skyrr	xviij^{s}
+	John Fynche gentleman	xviij^{s}
+	Thomas Barlyng	xv^{s}
+	Thomas Colle	xvj^{s}
+	John Neale	xv^{s}
+	Hugh Boothe	x^{s}
+	Thomas Barton	iiij^{s}
+	Thomas Musterd	ij^{s}
+	Thomas Andryan	ij^{s}
	Wylliam Hampton	xij^{s}
+	Rycherd Ball gentleman	xx^{s}
+	Thomas Waterman	xv^{s}
	Summa	xiiij$^{£}$ xviij^{s}

Courte Strette

+	Mr John Fynch gentleman	xxvj^{s} viij^{d}
+	Mr Roberte Mall	x^{s}
+	Mr John Woode	xv^{s}
+	Mr Thomas Brooke gentleman	x^{s}
+	Wylliam Saker	xiij^{s} iiij^{d}
+	Wylliam Pecocke	xij^{s}
	Wylliam Hawlett	ij^{s}
	Roberte Hawkyns	ij^{s}
+	John Dyxson	v^{s}
	Henrye Austen	ij^{s}
	Wylliam Mann	xij^{d}
+	John Stone[1321]	xij^{d}
	[blank] Keale	xij^{d}
+	John Fysher	iiij^{s}
+	Cornelys Dooman	vj^{s} viij^{d}
+	Roberte Rye maryner	iij^{s}
+	John Ambrose	xxvj^{s} viij^{d}
+	Christofer Potter	xx^{s}
+	John Upton	xij^{s}
+	Mrs Snothe wydoe	ij^{s}
+	Habraham Snothe	xx^{d}
+	Mrs Phylpott wydoe	vj^{s}
+	John Phylpott	v^{s}
+	John Johnson shoemaker	x^{s}
+	Edmounde Masterson	xvj^{s}
+	John Dennys	x^{s}
+	Humfrey Kybbett	*[blank]*

[1321] fol. 269.

+	*[blank]* Otterden	ij^{s}
+	Rycherd Bynyon taylor	xij^{d}
+	Gylles wydoe	xij^{d}
+	Roberte that married Rycherd Amys wydowe	xij^{d}
+	John Rockyns	ij^{s}
+	John Standleye	xij^{d}
	Nycholas Bryghte	viij^{d}
	John Bayle	xij^{d}
+	Wylliam Robynson	xij^{d}
+	Wylliam Pers shomaker	iij^{s}
+	Nycholas Turner	xij^{d}
+	Clement Oldfeld	x^{s}
+	Thomas Derton	v^{s}
+	John Hawlett	ij^{s}
	[blank] Lyvyng straunger	xxiij^{s} iiij^{d}
+	John Berrye	iij^{s} iiij^{d}
+	Thomas Surgeon	ij^{s}
+	Nycholas Adye	v^{s}
+	Lewes Austen	ij^{s} vj^{d}
+	Thomas Quycke	ij^{s}
+	John Trowtes	ij^{s}
+	James Wylye	v^{s}
+	Anthony Wylye	vj^{s} viij^{d}
	John Holte	ij^{s} vj^{d}
+	James Chylde	ij^{s}
	Audrian Isleye	ij^{s}
	Summa	xv$^{£}$ iiij^{s}

Preston Strete

	Mrs Auncell	x^{s}
	John Tompson	ij^{s}
+	Gilles Sadler wydoe	xij^{d}
+	Roberte Whysker	ij^{s}
+	John Ruffyn	xij^{s}
+	Thomas Fuggler	xij^{d}
+	John Shales	ij^{s}
+	John Musterd	xij^{d}
+	Andrwe Newton	xij^{d}
	Thomas Hall	xij^{d}
+	Bartylmewe Newes	ij^{s}
	Gregory Hubberd	ij^{s}
+	John Cason	xij^{d}
+	Artor Edgerton	xij^{d}
+	Edward Ussher	xij^{d}

+	Wylliam Bestbeeche	xv^{s}
+	Wylliam Neale	v^{s}
+	Mr Neale	ij^{s}
+	Nycholas Bull	x^{s}
+	Mother Pysynge	ij^{s} vj^{d}
+	Henrye Myller	xij^{d}
+	Thomas Androwe	iiij^{s}
+	Christofer Dobbynson	x^{s}
+	John Hawsnothe	xij^{d}
	Peter Lambenn	iiij^{s}
+	John Mason	vj^{s} viij^{d}
+	Thomas Hammon sadler[1322]	xij^{d}
+	Wylliam Mylles	ij^{s}
	John Colwell	xij^{d}
	Thomas Whyte	xij^{d}
+	John the scryvener	xij^{d}
Summa		v$^{£}$ v^{s} ij^{d}

Westreete Sowthe

+	Thomas Hawkes	v^{s}
	Wylliam Rockerye	xij^{s}
	Thomas Burwashe	xij^{d}
+	Thomas Haffenden	viij^{s}
+	Hartes wydoe	ij^{s}
+	Roberte Wylde	xij^{d}
+	Wylliam Stephens	vj^{s} viij^{d}
+	John Longleye	xij^{d}
+	Thomas Pelham	vj^{s} viij^{d}
+	Roberte Chapman	viij^{s}
	Geoffreye Comber	xij^{d}
+	Rycherd Payse	xij^{d}
+	Dorraunte the weaver	xij^{d}
+	John Deacon	xij^{d}
+	John Austen	v^{s}
+	Thomas Byrlyng[1323]	iij^{s} iiij^{d}
+	Giles Kydd v^{s}	
+	Phyllipp Peterson	xij^{d}
	Summa	iij$^{£}$ ix^{s} viij^{d}

Tanner Streete

+	Wylliam Taylor	ij^{s}
+	Thomas Gall	xij^{d}
+	John Elfrythe	ij^{s}
	Humfrey Coxe	xij^{d}
+	Edwarde Wyer	xij^{d}
	Wylliam Barnes	iij^{s} iiij^{d}
	The myller of Kyngsmyll	xij^{d}
+	Wylliam Smythe the pale clever	xij^{d}
+	Thomas Osborne	xvj^{s}
+	Leonard Fygde	xv^{s}
+	John Dewerd	xiij^{s} iiij^{d}
+	Henrye Wrattyng	v^{s}
+	John Holte	ij^{s} vj^{d}
	Reynoldes wydoe	xij^{d}
+	John Elfrythe wydoe	xij^{d}
	The myller of the Fludmyll	iij^{s} iiij^{d}
Summa		iij$^{£}$ ix^{s} vj^{d}

Weste Streete North

	[blank] Smythe the whealer	xij^{d}
	[blank] Clare the smythe	xij^{d}
	[blank] Wheston	xij^{d}
+	Rycherd Berne sherman	xij^{d}
	Rycherd Allen ropemaker	xij^{d}
	John Effyeld	xij^{d}
+	George Crosse	xij^{d}
+	Wylliam Chattborne	viij^{s}
+	Henrye Bond	xvj^{s}
+	Thomas Rye	xv^{s}
+	Stephen Symmes	xiij^{s} iiij^{d}
+	Lamberte Nayles	iij^{s}
+	Rycherd Mannys	ij^{s}
+	Wylliam Todd	xvj^{s}
+	Gregory Wryghte	iij^{s} iiij^{d}
+	John Dodd	x^{s}
+	John Stone	v^{s}
+	Nycholas Vawter	ij^{s} vj^{d}
+	Thomas Furmynger	xvj^{s}
+	Wylliam Harrys	vij^{s}
+	Wylliam Ogden	v^{s}
	Thomas Bedforde	xij^{d}
+	Wylliam Burwashe	ij^{s}
+	Wylliam Cademan	x^{s}
Summa		vij$^{£}$ ij^{s} ij^{d}

Summa totalis Lx$^{£}$ vj^{s} vj^{d}

[1322] fol. 269v.
[1323] *Marginal note*: Thys cesse of Byrlynges was paid Newes bye a forreners fyene 1577.

Faversham.[1324]
Common council held there the twenty eighth day of May in the fourteenth year of the reign of our sovereign lady Elizabeth by the grace of God of England France and Ireland queen, defender of the faith etc. [28 May 1572] By Thomas Oldefielde mayor of the town aforesaid John Best, Barthylmewe Amys, Robert Colwell, Robert Fagg, Thomas Fynche, and Thomas Smythe jurats of the town aforesaid Richard Ball, John Fynche senior, Thomas Waterman, Robert Ellfrythe, William Cumber, Edwarde Harrys, John Tyndall, Robert Lame, William Okenfolde, Thomas Barlyng John Neale, Thomas Coole, Robert Rye poynctmaker, Hugh Boothe, Richard Tyllman, Thomas Jerman, Thomas Barton, Humfrey Atkynson and John Skyrr commoners of the town aforesaid personally apprearing.

Yt ys agreayd by the seyd maior jurattes and commynaltye that all the cesses that have bynn heertofore grauntyd and cessyd in the towne of Faversham for the mayntenaunce of the townes sute agaynste Parker as concernyng the landes late gyven to the towne by Master Harrye Hatche, beyng eyghte in all shalbe entrydd in the towne booke that yt maye appyer what ys lente and leyed out by the inhabytaunces of the seyd towne to the entente that ther maye be satisfaction and paymente made therof agayne to the same inhabytaunces to theyr executoures and assignees when the same landes shall come to the towne after the deathe of the nowe ladye Amcottes as heretofore hathe bynn grauntyd at dyvers warmouthes.

Faversham[1325]
A ceesse made the laste daye of December anno regine domine nostre Elizabethe xvj° [31 Dec. 1573] uppon the inhabytaunces of the towne and libertye of Faversham aforeseyd bye John Beste and Thomas Oldefelde twoe of the jurattes of the seyd towne John Skyrr Robert Lamme Christofer Potter Edwarde Harrys fower of the commoners of the same towne accordyng to a wardmouthe holden there

The Mayor and jurattes

+	Mr John Fynche Mayor	xx^{s}
+	Mr Roberte Fagg	xx^{s}
+	Mr John Beste	xiiij^{s}
+	Mr John Wreake	xj^{s}
+	Mr George Straunsham	xviij^{s}
+	Mr Thomas Oldefielde	xj^{s}
+	Mr Thomas Belke	viij^{s}
+	Mr Thomas Fynche	x^{s}
+	Mr Roberte Collwell	x^{s}
+	Mr Thomas Smythe	viij^{s}
+	Mr Barthillmewe Amyas	xj^{s}
Summa		-

The xxiiij^{tie}

+	Roberte Lame	viij^{s}
+	Thomas Osbourne	xij^{s}
+	Rychard Tyllman	viij^{s}
+	Edwarde Harrys	ix^{s}
+	Wylliam Cumber	v^{s}
	Wylliam Okenfolde	vj^{s}
+	John Tyndale	vj^{s}
+	Roberte Rye poynctemaker	vj^{s}
+	Roberte Ellfrythe	vj^{s}
+	Christofer Potter	viij^{s}
+	John Skyrr	viij^{s}
+	Thomas Barlyng	viij^{s}

1324 fol. 270. *Latin*: Comuni concilium tenuit ibidem vicesimo octavo die may anno regni domine nostre Elizabethe dei gratiæ Anglie Fraunciae et Hibernie regine fidei defensoris etc. quarto decimo per Thomam Oldefield maiorem ville predicte Johannem Beste Bartholomum Amys Robertum Colwell Robertum Fagg Thomam Fynche et Thomam Smythe jurati ville predicte Richardum Ball Johannem Fynche seniorem Thomam Waterman Robertum Ellfrythe Willelmum Cumber Edwardum Harrys Johannem Tyndall Robertum Lame Willelmum Okenfolde Thomam Barlyng Johannem Neale Thomam Coole Robertum Rye poynctmaker Hugonem Boothe Richardum Tyllman Thomam Jerman Thomam Barton Humphridum Atkynson et Johannem Skyrr commitatu ville predicte ibidem personaliter comparentibus.

1325 fol. 270v.

+	Thomas Coole	xij^{s}
+	John Neale	viij^{s}
+	Hugh Boothe	vj^{s}
+	Thomas Musterde	xij^{d}
+	Thomas Audryan	ij^{s}
+	Thomas Furmynger	viij^{s}
+	Edmund Masterson	viij^{s}
+	Leonard Fydge	viij^{s}
+	Thomas Waterman	viij^{s}

Courte Streete

+	Wylliam Saker	x^{s}
+	Mr John Woode	xiiij^{s}
+	Mr John Fynche	xx^{s}
+	Thomas Dyerton	xij^{d}
+	Mr Kayes	xij^{s}
+	Cornelys Dowman	xij^{d}
+	John Ruffyn	v^{s}
+	Wylliam Peacocke	v^{s}
+	John Dyxson	xx^{d}
+	John Troutes	xij^{d}
+	John Ambroose	xv^{s}
+	Wylliam Hallett	ij^{s}
+	Nycholas Vawter	iiij^{s}
+	Nycholas Adye	ij^{s}
+	Mrs Blackwell	xij^{s}
+	Thomas Pellham	iij^{s}
+	Lewes Austen	xij^{d}
+	Roberte Rye maryner	ij^{s}
+	Gylles wydoe	xij^{d}
+	John Castelocke	v^{s}
+	John Berrye	ij^{s}
+	John Dennys	v^{s}
+	Edwarde Otterton	xij^{d}
+	Roberte Saunder	xij^{d}
	Mr Peter	ij^{s}
+	Wylliam Pyers	ij^{s}
+	Lawrence wydoe	iij^{s}
+	Mr Wyesse	x^{s}
+	Mrs Phyllpott	iij^{s}
+	John Phyllpott	ij^{s}
+	John Johnson	iiij^{s}

Westreete Southe[1326]

+	Thomas Hawkes	iiij^{s}
	Wylliam Rockerye	vij^{s}
+	Thomas Haffenden	v^{s}
	Ralph Halkes	ij^{s}
+	Wylliam Stephans	ij^{s}
+	John Deakon	xij^{d}
+	Roberte Chappman	iiij^{s}
+	John Austen	iiij^{s}
+	Thomas Byrlyng	ij^{s}

Tanners Streete

+	John Dewerde	viij^{s}
+	John Elldrydge	xij^{d}
	Harrye Tanner	ij^{s}
+	Edwarde Wyer	xij^{d}

Westreete Northe

+	Clemente Oldefielde	xij^{d}
	Wylliam Ball miller	xij^{d}
+	Wylliam Chattbourne	v^{s}
+	Mr Christofer Fynche	x^{s}
+	Thomas Rye	vij^{s}
+	Symses wydoe	ij^{s}
+	Lamberte Nayles	ij^{s}
+	Wylliam Dode	x^{s}
+	John Dode	iij^{s} iiij^{d}
+	Ugdens wydoe	xij^{d}
+	Stones wydoe	xij^{d}
+	Jermans wydoe	xij^{d}
+	George Croosse	xij^{d}
+	Thomas Harte	ij^{s}
+	Nycholas Pyers	xij^{d}
+	Wylliam Cademan	iiij^{s}

Preston Streete Weste

	Mrs Auncell	iiij^{s}
+	John Mason	iiij^{s}
+	John Joyner	xij^{d}
+	Christofer Dobynson	iiij^{s}
+	Thomas Andrewe	xij^{d}
	Pysynges wydoe	xij^{d}
+	Nycholas Bull	iij^{s}

[1326] fol. 271.

+	Wylliam Neale	iiij^{s}
+	Wylliam Besbeeche	vij^{s}
+	Newes the smythe	xij^{d}
+	*[blank]* Sarssens Hede	xij^{d}
+	John Shalles	xij^{d}
+	Wylliam Burwashe	xij^{d}
+	John Warde	ij^{s}
+	Jamys Wylye	ij^{s}
+	Anthonye Wylye	ij^{s}
	John Tompson capper	xij^{d}
+	Barlyng Mr Straunsham baylyffe	ij^{s}

Summa totalis

Faversham

A cesse made uppon the inhabytaunces of the seyd towne the laste daye of Maye Anno regne domine nostre Elizabeth xvj° 1574 [31 May 1574] bye John Beste John Skyrr twoe of the jurattes of the seyd towne Thomas Barlyng Christofer Potter and John Dewerde three of the commoners of the seyd towne bye the assent and consente of the maior jurattes and commynaltye of the seyd towne of Faversham at a Warmouthe holden there the xxixth daye of the seyd monythe of Maye

The Maior and jurattes

+	John Fynche mayor	xx^{s}
+	Mr Roberte Fagg	xx^{s}
+	Mr George Straunsham	xviij^{s}
+	Mr John Beste	xiiij^{s}
+	Mr John Wreake	xj^{s}
+	Mr Thomas Oldefielde	xj^{s}
+	Mr Barthyllmewe Amyas	xj^{s}
+	Mr Thomas Belke[1327]	vj^{s}
+	Mr Thomas Fynche	x^{s}
+	Mr Roberte Collwell	x^{s}
+	John Skyrr	x^{s}

The xxiiij^{tie}

+	Roberte Lame	ix^{s}
+	Thomas Osbourne	xij^{s}
+	Rycharde Tyllman	viij^{s}
+	Edwarde Harrys	ix^{s}
+	John Tyndale	vj^{s}
+	Roberte Rye poynctemaker	vj^{s}
+	Roberte Ellfrythe	vj^{s}
+	Christofer Potter	viij^{s}
+	Thomas Barlyng	ix^{s}
+	Thomas Coolle	xij^{s}
+	John Neale	viij^{s}
+	Hugh Boothe	vj^{s}
+	Thomas Musterde	xij^{d}
+	Thomas Audryan	ij^{s}
+	Thomas Furmynger	viij^{s}
+	Edmund Masterson	viij^{s}
+	Leonard Fydge	viij^{s}
+	Thomas Waterman	ix^{s}
+	John Dewerde	ix^{s}
+	Thomas Rye	viij^{s}
+	Wylliam Neale	v^{s}
+	John Castlocke	vj^{s}
+	Wylliam Rockerye	vij^{s}

Courte Streete

+	Mr John Fynche	xx^{s}
+	Wylliam Saker	x^{s}
+	Christofer Fynche	x^{s}
+	John Upton	x^{s}
+	Wylliam Peacocke	v^{s}
+	John Dyxson	xx^{d}
+	John Troutes	xij^{d}
+	Mr John Ambroose	xv^{s}
	Wylliam Hallett	ij^{s}
+	Nycholas Vawter	vj^{s}
+	Nycholas Adye	ij^{s}
+	Mr Woode	xv^{s}
+	Thomas Dyerton	xij^{d}
+	Mr Keyes	xij^{s}
+	Cornelys	xij^{d}
+	Mrs Blackwell	xij^{s}
+	Lewes Austen	xij^{d}
+	Roberte Rye maryner	ij^{s}
+	Gylles wydoe	xij^{d}
+	Mr Smale	ij^{s}
+	John Berrye	ij^{s}
+	John Dennys	v^{s}

[1327] fol. 271v.

+	Edwarde Otterton	xij^{d}
+	Roberte Saunders	xij^{d}
+	Mr Peter	ij^{s}
+	Wylliam Pyers	ij^{s}
+	Abraham Snoode	ij^{s}
+	Mr Wyesse	x^{s}
+	Mrs Phyllpott	ij^{s}
+	John Phyllpott	v^{s}
+	John Johnson	iiij^{s}

Weste Streete Southe

+	Thomas Hawkes	v^{s}
+	Thomas Haffenden	v^{s}
	Ralphe Hawes	ij^{s}
+	Wylliam Stevyns	ij^{s}
+	*[blank]* Deakon	xij^{d}
+	Roberte Chapman	iiij^{s}
+	John Austyn	v^{s}
+	Byrlynges wydoe	xij^{d}

Tanner Streete

+	Wylliam Taylour	xij^{d}
+	John Holte	xij^{d}
+	John Elldrydge	xij^{d}
+	Harrye Tanner	ij^{s} vj^{d}
+	Edwarde Wyer	xij^{d}
+	Clement Oldefielde[1328]	xij^{d}
+	Wylliam Ball myller	xij^{d}
+	Wylliam Chattbourne	vj^{s}
+	Symses wydoe	iij^{s}
+	Lambert Nayeles	ij^{s}
+	Wylliam Cumber	ij^{s}
+	*[blank]* Glasyer	xij^{d}
+	Wylliam Dode	x^{s}
+	John Dode	iiij^{s}
+	Beniamyn Markettman	ij^{s}
+	Stones wydoe	xij^{d}
+	George Croosse	xij^{d}
+	Thomas Harte	ij^{s}
+	Nycholas Pyers	xij^{d}
+	Wylliam Cademan	v^{s}

Preston Streete Weste

	Mrs Auncell	v^{s}
	[blank] Okenfoldes housse	xij^{d}
+	*[blank]* Ryppyngton	xij^{d}
+	John Mason	iij^{s}
	John Joyner	xij^{d}
+	Christofer Dobynson	v^{s}
+	Thomas Andrewe	xij^{d}
+	Pysyng & Swyfte eyther of theym	xij^{d}
+	Nycholas Bull	ij^{s}
	Edwarde Ussher	xij^{d}
+	Thomas Cooke	xij^{d}
+	Wylliam Besbeeche	x^{s}
+	*[blank]* Sarssens Hed	xij^{d}
+	*[blank]* Newes smith	xij^{d}
+	John Shalles	xij^{d}
+	Wylliam Burwashe	xx^{d}
	John Tompson capper	xij^{d}
+	John Warde	ij^{s}
+	James Wylye	ij^{s}
+	Anthony Wylye	ij^{s}
+	Barlyng Mr Straunshams baylyffe	ij^{s}

Faversham,

A cesse uppon the inhabytaunces of the seyd towne the xxijth of December in the xvijth year of the reign of our sovereign queen Elizabeth[1329] [22 Dec.] 1574 bye Thomas Oldfielde John Fynche Thomas Belke three of the jurattes of the seyd towne Edwarde Masterson Rychard Tyllman Thomas Barlyng Roberte Ellffrythe John Neale Thomas Furmynger syxe of the commoners of the seyd towne accordyng to a warmouthe holden there the xxijth of December in the xvijth year of the reign of Elizabeth.

The Maior and jurattes

+	Mr John Skyrr maior	xiij^{s} iiij^{d}
+	Mr John Wreake	xij^{s}
+	Mr John Beste	xiiij^{s}
+	Mr George Straunsham	xviij^{s}

1328 fol. 272.

1329 Anno regne domine regine nostre ... anno regne.

+	Mr Thomas Oldefielde	xij^{s}
+	Mr Barthyllmewe Amyas	xij^{s}
+	Mr Thomas Belke	vj^{s}
+	Mr Thomas Fynche	viij^{s}
+	Mr Roberte Collwell	xij^{s}
+	Mr Thomas Coole	xiiij^{s}
+	Mr John Fynche	xx^{s}
+	Mr Thomas Smythe	x^{s}
Summa		

The[1330] xxiiij^{tie}

+	Roberte Lame	x^{s}
+	Rycharde Tyllman	ix^{s}
+	Edwarde Harrys	x^{s}
+	John Tyndale	vj^{s}
+	Roberte Rye poynctemaker	v^{s}
+	Roberte Ellfrythe	vj^{s}
+	Christofer Potter	x^{s}
+	Thomas Barlyng	ix^{s}
+	John Neale	viij^{s}
+	Hugh Boothe	v^{s}
+	Thomas Audryan	ij^{s}
+	Thomas Furmynger	x^{s}
+	Leonard Fydge	ix^{s}
+	Thomas Waterman	ix^{s}
+	John Dewerde	xj^{s}
+	Thomas Rye	x^{s}
+	Wylliam Neale	v^{s}
+	John Castelocke	viij^{s}
	Wylliam Rockerye	vij^{s}
+	Christofer Fynche	x^{s}
+	Wylliam Saker	x^{s}
+	John Ellfrythe	ij^{s}
+	Edmunde Masterson	viij^{s}

Courte Streete

+	Mrs Woode wydoe	x^{s}
+	Peacockes wydoe	ij^{s}
	[blank] Byrche	viij^{s}
+	John Dyxson	ij^{s}
+	John Trowtes	xij^{d}
+	Mr John Ambroosse	xx^{s}
+	John Upton	x^{s}
+	Mr John Keyes	x^{s}
+	Mr Reynold Keyes	v^{s}
+	Nycholas Vawter	vij^{s}
+	Wylliam Hallett	ij^{s} vj^{d}
	Nycholas Adye	iij^{s} iiij^{d}
+	Thomas Chartam	xij^{d}
+	Mrs Blackwell	viij^{s}
+	Thomas Pellham	ij^{s}
+	Lewes Austen	xij^{d}
+	Roberte Rye maryner	ij^{s}
+	Abraham Snoode	v^{s}
+	Osbornes wydoe	xij^{s}
+	Michaell Smale	ij^{s}
	John Brooke	xij^{d}
+	John Berrye	ij^{s}
+	Rycherd Padnolle	xij^{d}
+	John Dennys	iiij^{s}
	Thomas Swyfte	xij^{d}
+	Mrs Phyllpottes wydoe	iij^{s}
+	John Phyllpott	iij^{s}
+	John Johnson	iiij^{s}
+	John Warde	ij^{s}
+	Wylliam Pyers	xij^{d}

Westreete

+	Thomas Hawkes	v^{s}
+	Thomas Haffenden	v^{s}
+	Nycholas Pyersse	xij^{d}
+	Wylliam Cademan	v^{s}
	Shomaker in Bartons House	xij^{d}
+	George Croosse	xij^{d}
+	John Deacon	xij^{d}
+	Roberte Chappman	iiij^{s}
+	Wylliam Stephyns	ij^{s}
+	John Doode	v^{s}
+	Beniamin Markettman	ij^{s}
+	Wylliam Doode	xij^{s}
+	Thomas Harte	ij^{s}
+	Lamberte Nayle	xij^{d}
+	Symses wydoe[1331]	ij^{s}
+	Wylliam Chattborne	vj^{s}
+	John Austen	v^{s}
+	Edwarde Wyere	xij^{d}

1330 fol. 272v.

1331 fol.. 273.

+	Clement Oldefyelde	xij^{d}
	Wylliam Ball	xij^{d}
+	Byrlynges wydoe	ij^{s}
+	Wylliam Taylour	xij^{d}
+	John Holte	xij^{d}
+	Harrye Wrottyng	ij^{s} vj^{d}
	Stephen Anderson	xij^{d}

Preston Streete

	Mrs Auncell	v^{s}
	John Tompson	xij^{d}
	George Sheparde	xij^{d}
+	Roger Ryppyngton	ij^{s}
+	John Mason	v^{s}
	John Joyner	ij^{s}
+	Christofer Dobynson	v^{s}
+	Thomas Andrewe	ij^{s}
+	Nycholas Bull	iiij^{s}
	Edwarde Ussher	xij^{d}
+	Thomas Cooke	xij^{d}
+	Wylliam Besbeche	ix^{s}
+	Edwarde Otterton	xij^{d}
+	Barthyllmewe Newes	ij^{s}
+	John Shalles	xij^{d}
+	Wylliam Burwashe	ij^{s}
+	Anthony Wyelye	ij^{s}
+	Jeames Wylye	ij^{s}
+	John Hallett	iij^{s} iiij^{d}
+	Barlyng Mr Straunshams man	iij^{s}
Summa		xxix$^{£}$ xj^{s}

Wardmote Book Fa/Ac1 folio 268.

SUMMARY TABLE OF THE HATCH ASSESSMENTS IMPOSED UPON THE INHABITANTS OF FAVERSHAM

These accounts should be treated with caution, even though their sum total and mine are very close; they reckoned that it was £315-4-0 and I came out at £315-14-7. The streets that are covered vary; for instance, the quay is sometimes mentioned, sometimes not, and West Street is broken up into West Street North, and West Street South in later accounts. More important still, simple sums are wrongly added up. For example, the short entry for the quay on 23 November 1568 is given as 4 shillings instead of 5 shillings. Some of the entries are blank and in December 1573 and May 1574 even the sum total for the year was left out.

	26 Nov 1567	23 Nov 1568	3 Jun 1569	22 Sep 1569	10 Nov 1570	Aug 1571	11 Feb 1572	20 May 1572	31 Dec 1573	31 May 1574	22 Dec 1574
Mayor & Jurats	£6-00-00	£8-18-08	£4-09-04	£4-09-06	[£3-06-00]	£4-14-08[1332]	£4-16-00	£10-18-00	[£7-01-00]	[£7-01-00]	[£7-11-04]
Commoners	£4-15-08	£9-06-04	[£4-18-02][1333]	£5-07-02	[£5-02-04]	£6-07-04[1334]	£6-15-04	£14-18-00	[£7-11-00]	[£8-10-00]	[£8-19-00]
Court Street	£4-04-08	£7-14-04[1335]	£14-12-06	£4-17-06[1336]	[£4-00-10]	£5-12-08[1337]	£3-16-00[1338]	£15-04-00[1339]	[£7-12-08]	[£8-05-08]	[£6-15-10]
Preston Street	£2-12-08[1340]	£5-07-00[1341]	£3-05-04[1342]	£3-01-06	[£1-07-00]	£1-17-00[1343]	£1-17-08	£5-05-02[1344]			[£2-14-04]
Preston St. West									[£2-02-00]	[£2-06-08]	
West Street	£1-19-06[1345]	£5-08-08[1346]	£2-17-10	£3-00-04	[£2-13-00]	£3-07-00	£3-12-08				[£3-10-06]

1332 Actual total £4-14-10.
1333 Figures in brackets denote that no total is to be found in the original text.
1334 Actual total £6-13-02.
1335 Actual total £7-14-10.
1336 Actual total £4-17-04.
1337 Actual total £4-19-07.
1338 Actual total £3-15-02.
1339 Actual total £15-03-00.
1340 Actual total £2-13-00.
1341 Actual total £5-07-06.
1342 Actual total £3-04-10.
1343 Actual total £1-15-08.
1344 Actual total £5-07-02.

West St. North								£7-02-02	[£2-12-04]		
West St. South								£3-09-08	[£1-11-00]	[£1-05-00]	
Tanners Street	£00-09-06	£00-16-04	[£00-09-00]	£00-09-10	[£00-14-04]	£1-04-08	£1-01-00	£3-09-06	[£00-12-00]	[£2-08-06]	
Quay Lane				£00-02-00							
The Quay		£00-04-00[1347]	£00-02-00		[£00-03-00]		£00-03-00				
Out Dwellers			£1-13-00	£1-03-04		[£00-14-00]	[£00-05-06]				
TOTALS	£20-00-00[1348]	£37-16-04[1349]	£22-00-00[1350]	£22-11-02[1351]	£18-00-00[1352]	£23-13-00[1353]	£22-07-02	£60-06-06	[£29-02-00]	[£29-16-10]	£29-11-00

1345 Actual total £2-00-06.
1346 Actual total £5-05-02.
1347 Actual total 5[s].
1348 Actual total £20-03-04.
1349 The total using their figures £37-15-04 and the actual total £37-13-10.
1350 Actual total £22-06-08.
1351 Actual total £22-11-08.
1352 Actual total £17-16-06.
1353 The total using their figures comes to £23-17-04 and the actual total £23-08-11.

APPENDIX 21

EDWARD WHITE, BOOKSELLER OF LONDON, HIS ASSOCIATES, AND THE FIRST PRINTING OF THE PLAY, ARDEN OF FAVERSHAM

BY RICHARD BRADSHAW[1354]

A year before Holinshed's Chronicle was published young Edward White entered *A Cruel Murder done in Kent* in the Register of the Stationers' Company. It was only the second publication to be sold in his bookstall by the Little North Door of St. Paul's, at the sign of the Gun. He paid the usual fee for a licensed first publication and left behind a copy. No copy is known to exist today but that is not unusual. Most unbound news pamphlets were shortly thumbed to shreds. White did not need entrance in the Register to print, only to protect copyright in the work.[1355] By right he now owned not only this particular published text but also the work which this text purported to represent. Copyright was conferred for his lifetime and he could sell his copyright, donate it to the Company, or pass it on to his heirs so long as they remained in the Company. But why would Edward White copyright it ? The title indicates a pamphlet not worth reprinting once the initial issue was sold and not worth holding onto if it did not sell. It has been calculated that of copies actually printed by members of the Stationers' Company a third were not entered in the Register. Was this just the overprotective act of an inexperienced bookseller or was the work something more substantial than a murder pamphlet ? Was the cruel murder in Kent the Arden murder ? At the Court of the Stationers' Company fifteen years later Edward White would establish his copyright to the first publishing of the play *Arden of Faversham* against an attempted infringement by Abell Jeffes.

M. L. Wine noted the considerable scholarship focused on the play ever since the first editor of *Arden of Faversham* raised the spectre of Shakespearian authorship. For some time it had been thought that Shakespeare acted in Faversham. The early evidence of Shakespeare's authorship seems to be that Arden was a good play and Shakespeare was around then, but most recently Professor MacDonald P. Jackson has presented logical and compelling evidence for adding the play to the Shakespeare canon.[1356] Christopher Marlowe comes in as a plausible candidate because he was born in nearby Canterbury. Kyd and Yarington have been put forward because of their attributed authorship of other murder plays. We may never know the author. Edward White, not the author, held the copyright and he did not tell us. It has been accepted, however,

[1354] The American author, who retired to London ten years ago, is an accomplished exhibiting watercolourist, graphic designer, printer and publisher. About thirty years ago he began to collect biographical information on his forebears surnamed Bradshaw and became particularly intrigued by two sixteenth century figures, Henry Bradshaw, Attorney General 1540-1553 to Henry VIII and Edward VI, and George Bradshaw, the goldsmith of Faversham in 1551. He is currently working on a biography of John Bradshaw, the regicide. He asks that it be clearly stated that he makes no pretence to academic scholarship but trusts that the contribution, which he regards as editorial work, may merit further learned study and discussion.

[1355] 'Books and Readers, 1591-94', G. B. Harrison, Libr., 4th Ser., VII, 1927; 'Laws of Elizabethan Copyright; The Stationers' View', C. J. Sisson, Libr., 5th Ser. Vol. 15, 1960; 'Is the Spanish Tragedy a Leading Case ?', Leo Kirschbaum, JEGP, xxxvii, 1938; 'Copyright of Elizabethan Plays', Leo Kirschbaum, Libr., 5th Ser, Vol. 14 -1959.

[1356] 'Shakespeare Features of the Poetic Style of Arden of Faversham', MacDonald P. Jackson, *Archiv fur das Studium de neuren Sprachen und Literaturen*, 230/2, 1993, p. 279-304; 'Material for an Edition of Arden of Faversham', Oxford, B.Litt. thesis, 1963, M. P. Jackson.

that the author took his inspiration solely from the account in Holinshed's Chronicle. Postulating any other sources has been thought to be unnecessary. As Patricia Hyde has demonstrated in this examination of the historical Thomas Arden, it is a good idea to re-examine all the evidence we have.

Unearthing a long-lost copy of *A Cruel Murder done in Kent,* or a prompt-book of the lost play called *Murderous Michael* would answer many questions but, while we await that unlikely event, much more effort needs to be expended on the contemporary evidence of Edward White and his associates. Even with this preliminary examination I hope to raise a plausible suspicion: (a) that Edward White was in a unique position to know the details of the Arden murder before Raphael Holinshed's account, (b) that *A Cruel Murder done in Kent* was the Arden story and that it was one source for a dramatic form employed in *Murderous Michael*, a lost play performed at Court in 1579, which in turn formed the basis of the more refined *Arden of Faversham* updated and expanded in light of the subsequent Holinshed account, (c) that Edward White's brother-in-law, Thomas Lodge, and perhaps one or more of his friends had a hand in both plays, (d) that *Murderous Michael* was performed before the Queen at the instigation of the Lord Chamberlain with the assistance of his Master of the Revels, Thomas Blagrave, in an effort to subtly ridicule Roger North and the Earl of Leicester, and finally, (e) that Thomas Blagrave, Edward White, Thomas Lodge and others suffered, perhaps at the hands of North and Leicester, for their involvement in the presentation of *Murderous Michael.*

It was not difficult for Edward White, Thomas Lodge, and Thomas Blagrave to gain intimate knowledge of the Arden story; knowledge independent of the Wardmote book or Holinshed's account. They had only to ask old Sir Thomas Lodge to tell the story. He was a lifelong member of the Grocers' Company and Warden in 1548.[1357] He was godfather to the son of Thomas Cole, a grocer, of Honey Lane, Allhallows in 1543.[1358] He would have known his fellow London grocers Cole and Pryme who were at Arden's house the night of the murder. They must have been full of the details and the Grocers' Hall would have buzzed with their stories. Pryme the grocer discovered Arden's body. Sir John Lion, another grocer, was the Sheriff of London who saw to the execution of Mosbie and Pounders in Smithfield. No doubt Sir Thomas witnessed the public event. There was plenty of time for Sir Thomas to tell the story. He lived until 1584. Perhaps he only asked that his friends Cole and Pryme be left out of the story. It was Holinshed who revealed their names. It is credible to link *A Cruel Murder done in Kent* with the Arden murder and to understand why Edward White would publish it.

It is also credible to suggest *Murderous Michael* must have been an early form of domestic tragedy, pioneered by the Lord Chamberlain's servants, predating two plays that we know are early domestic tragedies; *A Warning for Fair Women* and *Arden of Faversham.*[1359] Could *Murderous Michael* be about anything but a murder? But whose murder? E. K. Chambers cautiously stated that *Murderous Michael* might have been recast into *Arden of Faversham.*[1360] E. H. C. Oliphant found the suggestion was implausible because Michael Sanderson is not the most murderous character in Arden of Faversham.[1361] Oliphant ignored the obvious; the title did not always reflect the content. Besides, Roger North's half-sister could hardly have been

---

1357 *Thomas Lodge and Other Elizabethans*, Mark Eccles, (C. J. Sisson is author of 'Thomas Lodge and His Family' the first essay in this volume); *The Parish Register of St. Mary Aldermary, 1558-1754*, ed. J. L. Chester, (Harleian Soc., 1880), p. 6; *Thomas Lodge; The History of an Elizabethan Gentleman*; Nathaniel Burton Paradise; *The Worshipful Company of Grocers*, Baron Heath, 1868-69.

1358 Harl. 1206, f. 13.

1359 *The English Drama 1485-1585,* F. P. Wilson, p.146.

1360 *The Elizabethan Stage*, E. K. Chambers, iv, pp. 4, 46.

1361 'Problems of Authorship in Elizabethan Dramatic Literature', E. H. C. Oliphant, *Modern Philology*, (1911), viii, p. 420.

presented as the most murderous character in a play presented at Queen Elizabeth's court, where safety lay in subtlety.

The term 'murder-play' can be applied to these plays, specifically a kind of domestic tragedy which appeared in the late sixteenth century. Murder plays were a realistic dramatisation of some sensational crime committed in England. The audience was familiar with the basic story told in the popular murder pamphlet. We do the same today with our motion picture and television dramas of real-life murders taken from the pages of the daily newspapers. To the basic details, presented for moral purposes by the pamphleteers, the playwrights added motive, character, poetry, and stagecraft. In *A Warning for Fair Women* actors played on-stage allegorical roles of History, Tragedy, Comedy, Chastity, Lust and Divine Providence alongside the actors playing the murderers and their victim, but not in *Arden of Faversham*. *Arden* is a much more modern play. *A Warning* dramatized the 1573 murder of George Saunders committed by his wife, her lover, another woman, and her servant. The source was a pamphlet published by Henry Bynneman in 1573, and recounted by Anthony Munday in 1580. R. G. Fleay attributed authorship of *A Warning* to Thomas Lodge on the basis of certain 'coincidences of expression'. The source for *Arden of Faversham* and by inference *Murderous Michael*, may well be Holinshed's Chronicles but the two volumes must have been very expensive and thus destined for the library of a wealthy man. *A Cruel Murder done in Kent* would have been more widely circulated and therefore a more likely candidate as the source of a murder play.

We are told Arden's murder was a subject of wide-spread interest at the time. It was already a matter of popular interest before 1577. That interest could not have been generated by Holinshed alone. Some time within the year after *A Cruel Murder done in Kent* was printed, Holinshed's Chronicle was interrupted in the midst of typesetting to tell the tale. He went so far as to explain that 'I have thought it good to set it forth somewhat at large, having the instructions delivered to me by them, that have used some diligence to gather the true understanding of the circumstances'. Even after that caveat, however, he did not mention Alice Arden's kinship to the North family. Did Holinshed receive his instructions from Roger North or the Earl of Leicester who believed someone had given, or was about to give, a 'false understanding' of the circumstances ?

Early in September 1578, Roger North (half-brother of Alice Arden) entertained Queen Elizabeth at Kirtling in Cambridgeshire. She was on a royal progress from Norfolk in the company of her court. One member of the court was Thomas Radcliffe, 3rd Earl of Sussex, the Lord Chamberlain and patron of the group of stage players known as the 'Lord Chamberlain's servants'. Roger North had joined the progress before it reached Kirtling and in August he had quarrelled with Sussex in the presence of the Queen.[1362]

Elizabeth remarked that the sideboard was badly furnished with plate. North agreed and laid the blame on Sussex. Sussex 'thereupon went to Leicester and complained of the knavish behaviour of North; but Leicester deprecated the application of these words to North. Sussex answered that whatever he might think of the words, North was a great knave'. Leicester was just then on dangerous ground. He had escaped the charge of complicity in the strange death of his first wife, Amy Robsart, and he fended off rumours that he poisoned the Earl of Essex. Leicester secretly married his lover, the widow of Essex, at a private ceremony on 21st September attended by Roger North and other close friends. The marriage was carefully kept from the Queen for a year

---

[1362] *DNB*, Roger North; Thomas Radcliffe, 3rd Earl of Sussex .

although many courtiers knew the secret.[1363] No doubt Sussex, as Lord Chamberlain, made it his business to know.

Nineteen-year-old Thomas Lodge, second son of Sir Thomas Lodge, arrived in London four months before the Sussex / North quarrel.[1364] His grandfather and father were past Lord Mayors of London (in 1542/1556 and 1568 respectively) and his brother was a member of Lincoln's Inn. Thomas also entered this same inn of court in April 1577, but without any enthusiasm. The city was just that moment alive with excitement for a young man of literary bent. The Curtain and the Blackfriars theatres opened that year. The foundations of the great age of Elizabethan drama had been laid. Lodge had written well-received verse at Oxford and he soon became attached to the young reformers of the crude stage plays that exhibited no coherent plot, graphic characterisation, or poetry. Through his brother-in-law, Edward White, Thomas had access to the literary market and from his kinsman Thomas Blagrave, the Master of the Revels, he could receive encouragement in drama.

Lodge became a close friend of Robert Greene and other University Wits. Stephen Gosson, who would later attack Lodge, came to London in the same year and was soon writing plays, probably for the Earl of Leicester's company. John Lyly, who had been a fellow student with Lodge, had written his profoundly influential *Euphues, the Anatomy of Wit*. It was the lyric and narrative verse of Thomas Lodge, Samuel Daniel, Michael Drayton, Thomas Watson, and Sir Philip Sidney which inspired William Shakespeare when he arrived in London some eight years later.[1365] G. B. Harrison has said that Thomas Lodge, while not always in close touch with the reading public, 'could tell a straightforward tale well, especially when it was full of gory and horrible incident'.[1366] What better author to write a play called *Murderous Michael* ? Especially if he already had the Arden murder story told him by his father and his brother-in-law. Perhaps Blagrave approached the Lord Chamberlain with the play, or the Lord Chamberlain asked Blagrave to have to play written for his company. There are prior examples of the use of a drama for political purposes going back to the Inner Temple's production of *Gorboduc* in 1561.[1367] Hamlet echoed the plan - 'the play's the thing wherein I'll catch the conscience of the King'.

At the end of February 1579, Thomas Blagrave, was 'sent for by the Lord Chamberlain about patterns of maske'. In addition to his 'bote heir' (boat hire) Blagrave expended seven pence 'for Carriage [of] a hamper with stuff to show my Lord Chamberlain to the court and back again'. On the 3 March 1579 '*The history of Murderous Mychaell* (was) shewen at Whitehall on shrovetuesdaie at night enacted by the Lord Chamberlain servants' in the presence of the Queen. The only special prop that was specifically listed for the play was 'a painted cheste for my Lord Chamberleyns men - xvjd', but the players would have provided many of their own costumes and props.[1368]

Within a day or two of the performance Blagrave journeyed 'from the courte to Leicester howse to speak with my Lord Chamberlain'. In the summer Blagrave was passed over as permanent Master of the Revels in preference to an outsider, Edmund Tilney. Tilney received the Queen's patent for the office on 24 July 1579 but his fee ran from the previous Christmas. He and Blagrave signed accounts for the whole period 14 February 1578 to 31 October 1579. Tilney's

---

1363 *DNB*, Robert Dudley, Earl of Leicester.

1364 *DNB*, Thomas Lodge (1558 ? - 1625); *Thomas Lodge, The History of an Elizabethan Gentleman*, N. B. Paradise; *Thomas Lodge, Gentleman*, Patrick Ryan.

1365 *A Life of William Shakespeare*, Sir Sidney Lee, p 95.

1366 'Books & Readers, 1591-94', G. B. Harrison, Libr., 4th Ser., Vol. 7, 1927.

1367 'The Tragedy of Ferrex and Porrex', L. H. Courtney, NQ, 2nd Ser. X, Jul-Dec, 1860, pp. 261-263.

1368 *Documents Relating to the Office of the Revels*, A. Feuillerat, Vol. 21, pp. 303, 307, 309.

office assumed a job entirely new for the Revels Office; that of licensing plays for the stage. Blagrave returned to the post of Clerk of the Revels Office, a post he held until his death in 1603.[1369]

Between 11 September 1578 and 18 March 1579 Edward White's bookselling business declined. During the six months he entered only ballads in the Register. He published Thomas Lodge's *Epitaph of Lady Anne Lodge* in December and then not another of his brother-in-law's works until *Prosopopeia* in 1596. In all fairness it must be said that many printers and booksellers felt the chilling effect of Crown repression during this period particularly one John (or Henry) Stubbs who had his right hand cut off for publishing a widely circulated anti-Catholic pamphlet criticizing the Queen for contemplating marriage with the Duke of Anjou. His printer, Page, suffered the same fate. The Grocers' Company was warned and forbade to keep or read seditious libels in September 1579.

The Earl of Leicester opposed the Queen's marriage by every means in his power and might have been sent to the Tower had not Sussex generously protected him. Their quarrels temporarily cooled and Sussex gained some ascendancy over Leicester. By the following July the quarrel had renewed with such intensity the Queen was obliged to command them both to keep to their chambers.

Stephen Gosson had written *School of Abuse* against plays in July and dedicated it to Sir Philip Sidney who was nephew of both the Earl of Sussex and the Earl of Leicester. Sidney rejected it and replied to Gosson with *Apologie for Poetrie*. For some reason Lodge privately printed a reply to Gosson in *Honest Excuses*, about December, or possibly earlier.[1370] Lodge was not yet publicly acknowledged as a playwright but still he chose to reply; 'In the dramas, the citizen is shown the follies of many of their foolish fellow citizens - the allegory sweetens the bitter pill of knowledge - Poets were the first razors of the cities, prescribers of good laws, maintainers of religion, disturbers of the wicked, advancers of the well disposed, inventors of laws and lastly the very foot-pathes to knowledge and understanding.' He refers to his reply in *Alarm for Usurers* and said it was suppressed. The existing copy carries no title page but White would be the logical publisher and seller.

By early 1581 Lodge was in some sort of difficulty. He may be the Thomas Lodge who was called before the Privy Council to answer unspecified charges although this identification is questioned by other authorities.[1371] In September a Thomas Lodge was in King's Bench Prison, on an unknown charge, and there he was involved with a slanderous informer named Mirfin and his associate Clement Draper, to whom Lodge introduced Mirfin, when all three were prisoners together.[1372] The interjection of the name Mirfin, Alice Arden's supposed maiden name, seems ironic. In 1582 one Murfin *(sic)* seems to have hoped for a large reward in return for giving information about a fictitious Catholic plot in Ireland against the Queen. His scheme was discovered and he was compelled to make a confession in which he stated that 'being removed to the king's bench about March last was twelvemonth, he did in September following fall in acquaintance there with one Clement Draper, prisoner in the same place, by means of one Thomas Lodge, also prisoner'. Again, this Thomas Lodge is not positively identified as Thomas Lodge son of Sir Thomas Lodge, mayor of London.[1373] Positive identification seems to remain unlikely as the Register of the Privy Council June 1582 to February 1582 was destroyed by fire,

1369 *Notes on the History of the Revels Office*, E. K. Chambers.
1370 'The Missing Title of Thomas Lodge's Reply to Gosson's School of Abuse', J. D. Wilson, *Mod Lang, Rev*., III
1371 APC, 1581 1582, p. 110.
1372 *Annals of the Reformation*, J. Strype, (Oxford, 1824), Book 3, part 1, p.205.
1373 'Thomas Lodge': Edward Andrew Tenney, *Cornell Studies in English*, XXVI, 1935

but it is clear that Thomas Lodge 'lent toward the Catholic way of thought'.[1374] Edward White did not exhibit similar tendencies as evidenced by his Stationers' Register entries of John Calvin's sermons (1578), diatribes against Edmond Campion (1582), and other anti-Catholic literature (1580).

The entries in the Stationers' Register had begun to reflect a tightening of the company's licensing in 1578. No longer simply 'Licensed unto' or 'Received of him for his license' but beginning about September; 'Licensed unto him under the hands of the wardens'. The first such licensing seems to have been:

20 September 1578
Henry Bynneman Licensed unto him the entertainment of the Queens majesty in Suffolk and Norfolk; gathered by Thomas Churchyard [1375] xij$^{d.}$ and a Copie
in the margin: By the guardians under their hands[1376]

On March 20th 1581 Edward White entered a ballad by Robert Greene, *Youth seeing all his ways so troublesome..&c.*, 'Licensed under the hands of the Bishop of London and the wardens'. No copy is known. Harrison reckons Greene was 'by far the most important of the professional writers, not only for his output and ability, but because of his keen instinct for what the public wanted'.[1377]

In October 1581 Lodge, in debt and despair, contributed his Poem Dedicatory to Barnabe Rich's *Don Simonides*. Speaking of himself:

'Whose long distresse hath laid his Muse to rest
Or duld his Sprightes, or sences at the lest

....

I have the now, My Muse affords no more,
A doleful dumpe, pulls back my pleasant vaine.

In 1582 Gosson's *Plays confuted in 5 Actions..* was entered, in which he attacked Lodge as 'little better than a vagrant'. Lodge would dedicate his *Alarum Against Usurers*, describing the practices of unscrupulous money lenders, to Sir Philip Sidney in 1584. Old Sir Thomas Lodge died in that year.

R. G. Fleay assigns 1585 as the year *Arden of Faversham* was first acted publicly: 'the name Arden was just then unpopular ... Edward Arden had been executed 20th December 1583 for some treason ... As to authorship, I think there is good ground for attributing it to Kyd.'[1378] N. B. Paradise speculates that Thomas Lodge's *Wounds of the Civil War* was being performed in London repertory in 1586. Charles T. Prouty proposes 1585 as 'a reasonably safe guess' for the composition of *The Spanish Tragedy*. One other old play, *The Most Famous Chronicle History of Lier king of England and his three Daughters*, published by Edward White, but not until 1594, may have appeared on the stage about this time. William Wells, noting parallel phrases in

---

[1374] *Thomas Lodge, Gentleman*, Patrick M. Ryan

[1375] *DNB*; Thomas Churchyard (1520? - 1604), Churchyard accompanied the Queen on the Progress to Norfolk and was responsible for the entertainments. His *Churchyard's Choice* was 'a general rehearsal of warres and joyned to the same some tragedies and epitaphs' - *Epitaph on Sir William Drury* was in memory of his old commander in Ireland.

[1376] *per gardianos sub eorum manibus.*

[1377] G. B. Harrison *op. cit.*

[1378] *Biographical Chronicle of the English Drama*, F. G. Fleay, Vol. II.

Wounds of the Civil War and *Leir*, suggests Thomas Lodge and Robert Greene could be the authors.[1379]

Meanwhile Thomas Lodge removed himself from London. He sailed out at least as far as the Canaries with Grenville[1380] on 9 October 1585 in company with his cousin Thomas Loddington. He was back in London by 1588 or February 1589 when he prefixed verses to Greene's *Spanish Masquerado*. On 2 May 1591 his *Robert Duke of Normandy* was entered. In August Lodge sailed out with Cavendish and while in the Straits of Magellen he wrote *Margarite of America.* During this absence Greene supervised the publication of Lodge's *Euphues Shadow*, and completed their jointly authored play *The Looking-glass for London.* Lodge returned early in 1593 to find his friend Greene had died.

The Earl of Sussex contested with Leicester during his final years and died on 9 June 1583, much embittered at Leicester. In his last hours he regretted that his death would leave Leicester in command of the situation; 'I am now passing into another world, and must leave you to your fortunes and to the Queen's graces; but beware of the gypsie, for he will be too hard for you all; you know not the beast so well as I do'.

Sussex was succeeded first by his brother Henry the 4th Earl (d. 1593) and then by his nephew Robert (1569-1629), Lord Fitzwalter, 5th Earl (after 1593). Greene remained attached to the family of the late Earl. In 1592 Robert Greene gave his *Philomela* the subtitle *The lady Fitzwa[l]ter's Nightingale* in honour of Fitzwalter's wife. Also in 1592 Robert Greene dedicated to Fitzwalter *Euphues Shadow* by Thomas Lodge.

Leicester died in September 1588. Ben Jonson tells the story that he had given his wife 'a bottle of liquor which he willed her to use in any faintness, which she not knowing it was poison, gave him, and so he died'. Roger North addressed a letter to Burghley, praising Leicester and expressing feelings at his death. North said his own health was not so good and that he would go to Bath for a month to take the waters. From then until his death some twelve years later he suffered failing health.

We come now to Edward White's dispute over the copyright to *Arden of Faversham.* Abel Jeffes was a contentious London printer who had served his apprenticeship with Henry Bynneman during the time Holinshed's Chronicles were printed there. He had one press and in 1591 he opened a bookstall in St. Paul's Churchyard 'at the Great North Door'. From time to time the Stationers' Company assisted him and on one occasion ordered Edward White to give him a printing job.[1381] Jeffes had been fined for printing indecent material, as had Edward White. Commencing in Spring 1592 Jeffes embarked on a course of copyright infringement that would bring him into conflict with White and the Company.

When Jeffes claimed right to *Doctor Faustus* in May the Stationers' Court reached a ruling that the book should be his by some other reason than entry in the Register. Richard Orliff, perhaps a slip of the pen for Orwin in the Stationers' Register, claimed the book on the basis of a prior printing by Orwin, but Orwin had not entered it. It was probably White's book - the earliest extant copy is 1592, 'printed by T. Orwin for Edward White'.[1382] Jeffes entered the book and sold it to White four years later. Having been successful with this ruse Jeffes must have determined to try again.

[1379] 'The Authorship of 'Leir'', Wm. Wells, NQ, CLXXVII 1939, pp. 434-438.

[1380] Richard was the son of Sir Roger Greynvile who commanded and was lost in the *Mary Rose* in 1545.

[1381] see Stationers' Register transcript, 5 September 1586.

[1382] Some notes on the Stationers' Register, W. W. Gregg, Libr., N. S., vii, 1927, p. 386.

On the third of April 1592 Edward White entered *The tragedy of ARDEN of Faversham & BLACKWALL (sic)*. As is later self-evident this was a working title which was expanded in the final printing. It appears that some time before late July or early August Abel Jeffes printed an edition of Arden. In October Jeffes entered *The Spanish Tragedy*. Jeffes claimed that White had unlawfully printed his *Spanish Tragedy* and White claimed that Jeffes had done the same with his *Arden*, but we do not know in which sequence the charges were made. It is not possible to determine if Jeffes had actually printed any copies of *Spanish Tragedy* before he entered it. By the same token it is not possible to determine if any copies of Arden had been printed prior to the entry in April. Entry may have been made, in both cases, as a 'blocking' entry of title only, or with only the working manuscript as proof of copyright. White had made such a blocking entry by entering a book before it was printed on the 25th of January 1590. On that day Arnalt Cosby was executed forty-eight hours after his trial. On the very same day White entered *The arraignment and Condemnation of Arnalt Cosby for murdering Lord Burgh*. He was however blocked, or forestalled until 6 February, from entering a ballad on the same subject by R. Robinson who entered on 26 January *The sorrowful sighs of a sad soul* for the loss of Lord Burke.[1383] On a previous occasion, 14 December 1590, White entered and obtained licence for a ballad, 'upon condition that he procure this ballad lawfully authorized to print'. Booksellers and printers were not the sole source of this confusion. Authors could, and did, plagiarize from themselves and plant work on unsuspecting publishers. White had recovered damages in 1582 against Denham who had printed *The Diamond of Devotion,* part of which was lifted from White's *The Footpath of Faith leading to The Highway to Heaven*, entered 25 April 1580. It seems the author, Abraham Fleming, took *Diamond* from his own earlier work *Footpath.* Fleming, not a member of the Stationers, escaped blame. The implications of the Stationers' copyright in the work, as distinguished from the specific published version of the text, cannot be ignored.[1384]

The implication of Edward White's copyright in *A Cruel Murder done in Kent* cannot be examined without a copy, but the suspicion arises that he would easily establish his right to Arden if the subject of the two works were the same. He had less a clear-cut case against Jeffes when it came to *The Spanish Tragedy* which, I think, was probably his also. Jeffes was judged to own that book. The Jeffes vs White case has been thoroughly examined and different conclusions have been drawn.[1385] The disposition of the books at issue has been overlooked.

Although the Abel Jeffes' *Arden* was ordered to be confiscated and forfeited to the Company, the proceeds of sale to be for the benefit of the poor, no copy survives. In fact that is not what happened to whatever copies existed. The Court transcripts make it clear that the confiscated copies were sold back to Edward White, and perhaps Abel Jeffes whose name is mentioned, for eleven pounds and ten shillings. The money was put in the general account and not the account for the poor.[1386] This seems a large sum for Abel Jeffes who was just then having trouble paying his fines. I think Edward White bought all the books, destroyed any printed by Jeffes, and saved the rest. No 1592 *Arden* or *Spanish Tragedy* printed by Jeffes is known to be extant. Three 1592 copies of Arden survive, printed by Edward Allde for Edward White; the Dyce copy (V&A), the Malone (Bodleian), and the Mostyn-Perry (Huntington). One undated copy of *Spanish Tragedy* survives bearing the imprint 'Printed by Edward Allde, for Edward White ...newly

1383 G. B. Harrison *op. cit.* p. 280.
1384 'The Decrees and Ordinances of the Stationers' Company 1576-1601, W. W. Gregg, Libr. N. S. viii, 1928, p. 421.
1385 'The Spanish Tragedy; A Leading Case', W. W. Gregg, Libr., 4th Ser, vi, 1925, pp 47-56; 'Is the Spanish Tragedy a Leading Case ?', Leo Kirschbaum, JEGP, xxxvii, 1939, pp 501-512; Introduction to *The Spanish Tragedy*, Malone Soc. Reprint, 1948-49.
1386 Arber, I, p 563.

corrected and amended of such grosse faults as passed the first impression'. Leo Kirschbaum thought that White was sneering at Jeffes. If the sneer is taken to be literal then White would have possessed, or had oversight of, the original manuscript in order to gauge the 'grosse faults'. Perhaps this is another hint that White really did own both works.

Edward White died 12 January 1613 and in his long career as a London bookseller he had published works by Thomas Lodge, Robert Greene, Thomas Kyd, Anthony Munday, Thomas Churchyard, and the first printing (possibly pirated) of a play attributed to William Shakespeare; *A booke entitled a Noble Roman History of Titus Andronicus*, 1594, printed by John Danter for Edward White and Thomas Millington. No extant copy of this was know until a Swedish gentleman discovered a copy among his books in 1905. Perhaps there is hope of seeing a copy of *A Cruel Murder done in Kent* some day.

A Dictionary of Printers and Booksellers, 1557-1640, R. B. McKerrow (ed.)

EDWARD WHITE, senior, bookseller in London, 1577 - 1612; The Gun, Little North Door of St. Paul's. Son of John White of Bury St. Edmunds, Suffolk, mercer. Apprenticed to William Lobley, stationer of London, for seven years from September 29, 1565 [Arber i. 29]. Made his first entry in the Registers on January 21st, 1576/7 [Arber ii. 307]. Admitted into the Livery of the Company on June 29th 1588 [Arber ii. 866]. Edward White dealt largely in ballads and on June 25th, 1600, was fined ten shillings for selling one called *The Wife of Bath* [Arber ii 831]. He died before January 12th, 1612/13 and his widow Sarah continued the business [Arber iii. 511, 524].

Works entered by Edward White, 1576-1592, selected extracts from: A Transcript of the Registers of the Company of Stationers of London 1554-1640. Edward Arber

Note on Transcription: In quoting from Arber, I have listed only those entries that reveal something of Edward White's life and his associations prior to 3 April 1592. The spelling and capitalization for most quotations have been modernized, contemporary contractions extended, and sometimes punctuation modified.

1 July 1577 (2nd entry)	Received of Edward White for his licence to imprint A Cruel murder done in Kent	iiij^{d}. and a copie
21 July 1577 (3rd entry)	Licenced unto him The True history and faithful relation of a most horrible murder committed by Alphonse Diazius Spaniard following the example of the paracide Cain on the body of his brother Jhon Diazuis	iiij^{d}. and a copie
27 Mar 1578 (5th entry)	Received of him for his licence to imprint The lectures of the Reverend Divine Doctor JOHN CALVIN Pastor of the church of God in Geneva upon the prophet JONAS done into English by N.B. (Nathaniel Baxter)	ix^{d}. and a copie

28 June 1578 (6th entry)	Licenced unto him a ballad of one bewailing his wicked life with a caveat or warning to all young men	iiij^{d}. and a copie
	(The following two entries, while not by Edward White, are included for purposes of chronology);	
1 July 1578	Received of Master Harrison and Master Bisshop for the licensing of Raphael Holinshed's chronicle	xx^{s} and copie
15 July 1578	Thomas Woodcock obtained licence to Holinshed's Chronicles from the widow of Luke Harrison.[1387]	
30 Aug. 1578 (White's 7th entry)	Licenced unto him a doleful discourse or sorrowful sonnet made by EDWARD FALLOWES who lately suffered death at Sainct Thomas wateringe for Robberie And for his fine for printinge "the Jocund joy of the meeting of ij lovers" it being without licence and it being an undecent ballad. And also for a penitent confession to the tune of 'th[e] aged mans dump'.	
7 Apr. 1579	Licenced unto him under the hands of the warden a mirror meet for all mothers matrons and maids entitled the Mirror of modestie[1388]	vj^{d}.
3 Aug. 1579	Licenced unto him; under the hands of the wardens. Churchyards Choice[1389]	ij$^{s.}$
23 Dec. 1579	Licenced unto him under the hands of the wardens An Epitaph of the Lady ANNE LODGE by T. Lodge[1390]	iiij^{d}.
11 Apr. 1580	an epitaphe on Sir William Drury	iiij^{d}.
25 Apr. 1580	turned over to him from William Hoskins The footpath leading[to] The highway to Heaven	vij^{d}.
16 May 1580	Tolerated unto him the second earthquake in Kent	vj^{d}.
6 Oct. 1580	Licenced unto him under the bishop of LONDONS hand the description of great wonders seene the 13^{d} of Jan 1580 and fearful wind and earthquakes at Rome	vj^{d}.
5 Nov. 1580 J. Charlewood Edward White	Licenced unto him under the hands of the wardens a ballad.. .Signs & tokens seen in the air and the last Blazing Star that began the viij of Oct. 1580	iiij^{d}.
10 Nov. 1580	Licenced unto him under the wardens hands A Ringing Retreat Couragiously sounded, wherein Plays and Players are fitly Confounded	iiij^{d}.
	and a ballad iiij^{d}.[1391]	
20 Dec. 1580	Tolerated unto him by Master Watkins The English Canvazado of the Popes Croskeys (Cross Keys ?)	iiij^{d}. and a copie

[1387] *DNB*, Holinshed, Raphael; Some copies of Holinshed's Chronicles bear the imprint of John Harrison, others of George Bishop Luke or Lucas Harrison, and John Hunne...All copies were printed by Henry Bynneman. See also NQ, 6th Ser. XI, p. 269, 351.

[1388] Probably by Thomas Salter. Edward White dedicated *Mirror of Modestie* to his mother-in-law, Lady Anne Lodge, in 1579. BL has a copy of *Mirror of Modestie* by Robert Greene, printed by R. Ward, 1584, but the similarity of title is only coincidental.

[1389] See earlier footnote about Thomas Churchyard.

[1390] By Thomas Lodge (1558? - 1625). Not known to be extant. DNB and *Thomas Lodge and Other Elizabethans*; M. Eccles / C. J. Sisson; Dedicated to his mother.

[1391] By Anthony Munday (1553-1633), formerly apprenticed to John Allde, Stationer. Munday was a stage player in 1576. He journeyed from London to Rome in 1578, while still Allde's apprentice, to make capital of stories to the detriment of English Catholics, perhaps encouraged by John Charlewood and Edward White.

14 Feb. 1581	Tolerated unto him by master Watkins a Rejoinder to BRISTOWE's Reply in Defence of ALLEN's Scolle of Articles and a book of Purgatorie	vj^{d}.
20 Mar 1581	Licenced unto him under the hands of the Bishop of LONDON and the wardens, A ballad Entitled, youth seeing all his ways so Troublesome abandoning virtue and leaning to vice, Recalling his former follies with an inwards Repentence By GREENE	vj^{d}.
23 June 1581	Licenced unto him under the hands of the wardens A proper ballad Dialogue wise betweene TROYLUS and CRESSIDA	
12 Mar 1582	Licenced unto him under the hand of the Bishop of LONDON A reply to two seditious pamphlets printed the one in French the other in English Containing a defence of EDMOND CAMPION and the rest of his confederates their terrible treasons and practices against her majesty and her realm	
12 Mar 1582	Received of him for his licence to print a Discovery of EDMOND CAMPION and his confederates and their most horrible and traitorous practices against her majesty's Royal person	vj^{d}.
7 May 1582	Received of him for printing a book of physic called the pathway to health for the poor Translated and gathered by PETER LEVENS and the said Edward hath undertaken to bear and discharge all troubles that may arise for the printing thereof	xij^{d}.
7 Dec. 1584	Received of him for his licence to print A book of Cookery PROVIDED ALWAYS that if it belong already to any other man or to be collected out of any book already extant in print in English that then this licence to be void	vj^{d}.
	(and a ballad)	iiij^{d}.
1 Aug. 1586	(one entry comprising 36 ballads)	
8 Aug. 1586	(one entry of 8 books and 3 ballads)	
16 Aug. 1586	(one entry of 4 ballads)	
5 Sep. 1586	Received of him for a sackful of news being an old copy; which the said Edward is ordered to have printed by Abell Jeffes	vj^{d}.
9 Feb. 1590	Entered for his copy a book entitled GREEN's Orpharion, under master HARTWELLs hand and both the wardens	vj^{d}.
25 Jan 1590	Entered for his copy to print under the hand of Doctor Stallard and the wardens / The arraignment and Condemnation of ARNALT COSBY for murdering the lord BURGH	vj^{d}.
6 Feb. 1591	Entered for his copy under the hand of Master Cawood (a Ballad of the previous)	vj^{d}.
16 Aug. 1591	Entered for his copy under master HARTWELLs hand and master Warden Conneweys a book entitled A treatise of measuring of land by statute woodland customary and Court measure. This book is granted to Edward upon condition that it belong to no other person by some former grant and entrance	vj^{d}.

3 Apr. 1592 Entered for his copy under the hands of the Lord Bishop of London and the wardens, The tragedy of ARDEN of Faversham & BLACKWILL (strangely entered as, "BLACKWALL" according to Arber's transcription) vj^{d}.

14 May 1594
Adam Islip (lined through on the Register)
Edward White Entered also for his Copy under the hands of both the wardens a book entitled The most famous Chronicle historye of LEIRE king of England and his Three Daughters

The Dispute between Edward White and Abel Jeffes, selected extracts from; Records of the Court of the Stationers Company, 1576 to 1602 W, W, Gregg and E. Boswell

7 August (1592)

Present the	Master & Wardens	Mr. Coldock	Mr. Cooke.
	Mr. Bishop	Mr. Newbie	Mr. Allen
	Mr. Harrison	Mr. Cawood	Mr. Howe
	Mr. Watkins	Mr. Woodcock	

see Reg. A 264b (22 July) Whereas Abell Jeffes about the (blank) day of July last did Resist the search which Master Stirrop Warden Tho Dawson and Tho [Rente] man renters were appointed to make & would haue made of his printing house according to the ordinance & decrees, and for that he contemptuously proceeded in printing a book without authority contrary to our Master his commandment, and for that he refused to deliver the bar of his press neither would he deliver any Book to be brought to the hall according to the decrees. and also for that he used violence to our officer in the search. It is now therefore ordered by a full court holden this day, that for his offence he shall be committed to ward according to the ordinances and Decree in that behalf

Monday 18 December (1592)

Present	Mr. Bishop Master	Mr. Harrison	Mr. Cawood
	Mr. Conneway	Mr. Watkins	Mr. Woodcock
	Mr. Stirrop Wardens	Mr. Newbie	Richard Collins

In full court held this day. Abell Jeffes, according to the direction of the lord archbishop of Canterbury his grace, appeared and humbly aknowledged his former offense and undutyfulness, Craving pardon and favour for the same and promising hereafter to live as becometh an honest man, and to show himself obedient and dutifull in the Company, and to the ordinances thereof/
signature Abell Jeffes

STC 10711 Abell Jeffes Tho. Orwin. Yt is ordered: that if the book Doctor Faustus shall not be found in the hall
cf. ent 5 Apr.96 the book entered to Richard Oliff before Abell Jeffes claimed the same which was about May last, That then the said copy shall Remain to the said Abell as his proper copy from the time of his first claim which was about May Last as aforesaid.

fol. 456b Edw White. Whereas Edward White and Abell Jeffes have
STC 15086, Abell Jeffes. each of them offended, that is to say, Edward White in
ent. 6 Oct. 92 having printed the Spanish Tragedie belonging
to Abell Jeffes and Abell Jeffes in
cf. STC 733, having printed the Tragedie of Arden of Kent belonging to
ent. 3 Apr. 92 Edward White; it is agreed that all the books of each
impression shall be as confiscated and forfeited according
to the ordinance [be] disposed to the use of the poor of
the company for that each of them hath severally
transgressed the ordinance in the said impressions/

Edw. White. Item it is agreed that either of them shall
Abell. Jeffes pay for a fine for transgressing the
ordinance. by imprinting the said book
contrary to the orders Ten shillinge a piece.
presently or between this and our Lady day next.
see Reg.B 414b (in margin) *solut' x*^{s}. *per* Edward White in May.1593
And as touching their imprisonment for the said offence
it is Referred over till some other convenient time at the
discretion of the Master. Wardens. & Assistant
signature Edward Whit
signature Abell Jeffes

Abel Jeffes Item Abell hath promised to pay the vj^{d}. in the pound to
STC 6146 the use of the poor which he owes for Quintus Curtis

5to. February (1592/3)

present Mr. Bisshop Master Mr Watkins Mr Howe
Mr Stirrop Warden Mr Coldocke Mr Woodcock
Mr Harrison the elder Mr Newberye Richard Collins
Mr Cooke

Edwarde White Upon hearing of the matter in controversy
STC 19657-60 John Legatt between the said Edward White on one part and the said
John Legatt on the other part, concerning a book in English
ent. 27 July 92 called the Golden Chain:
It is ordered by their assent, that the said John Legatt
shall enjoy the said book, to print as his own proper copy from time to time
hereafter. And that the said Edward his executors or assignes, or any from
whom he claim the said Copy, or any other by his or their means, shall not
at any time hereafter intermeddle with the printing of the said Copy or any part
thereof. And that the said Edward shall accept and take of the said John Legatt,
all such numbers of the said books, as the said John Legatt hath now ready
printed in his hands, at the rate of iiij£ xvj^{s} the hundred. The whole sum they
amount to, at that rate to be paid, in the form following, that is to say, one third
part on the Sixth of May next, and one Third part on the Sixth of August next.
And also that the said John Legatt his executors or assignes or any other by his
or their meane, shall not at any time hereafter begin to Reprint the said book or
any part thereof, until the said Edward his executors or assignes shall have
uttered and sold, all such numbers of the said book as the said Edward shall by
vertue hereof receive of the said John as aforesaid (xxv^{tie} books only excepted)

signature Edward Whit
signature John Legate

Sunday 12 May (1594)
Edw. White. At a court held this day it is ordered
(not traced) that Edward White shall pay. v^{s}. for a fine
for printing a ballad of eating of a sheep without Licence contrary to
the ordinance the which he hath promised to deliver to Mr Warden
see Reg. B 393b (in margin) Paid as shown in the accounts of the Warden[1392]

PEDIGREE OF THOMAS LODGE

In relation to the pedigree given on the next page the *Dictionary of National Biography,* E. Grosse, and N. B. Paradise err in the marriages of either or both Sir Thomas Lodge and his son, Thomas Lodge. As a result of the first, Paradise errs in the descent of Sarah Lodge, wife to Edward White. For later findings, incorporated here, reference should be made to *Thomas Lodge,* Edward Andrews Tenney, Cornell Studies in English, (OUP, 1935), LP Hen. VIII, 1544, pt. 2, pp. 140, 455, 459, 466;1545, pt. 1, pp. 19, 107, *Thomas Lodge,* Alice Walker, RES, IX, (1939), pp. 416, 417, 419; *Thomas Lodge and Other Elizabethans,* C. J. Sissons, pp. 13, 118, App. II; Registers of St. Michael Cornhill, Harleian Soc. Register Section, VII, (1882), pp. 77, 78, 181.

THE
LAMENTA-
BLE AND TRVE TRA-
GEDIE OF M. AR-
DEN OF FEVERSHAM
IN KENT.

Who was moſt wickedlye murdered, by
the meanes of his diſloyall and wanton
wyfe, who for the loue ſhe bare to one
Moſbie, hyred two deſperat ruf-
fins Blackwill and Shakbag,
to kill him.

Wherin is ſhewed the great mal-
lice and diſcimulation of a wicked wo-
man, the vnſatiable deſire of filthie luſt
and the ſhamefull end of all
murderers.

Imprinted at London for Edward
White, dwelling at the lyttle North
dore of Paules Church at
the ſigne of the
Gun. 1592.
*

The tile page of *Arden of Feversham* printed in 1592.

[1392] *pd vt pz in compo Custod'*

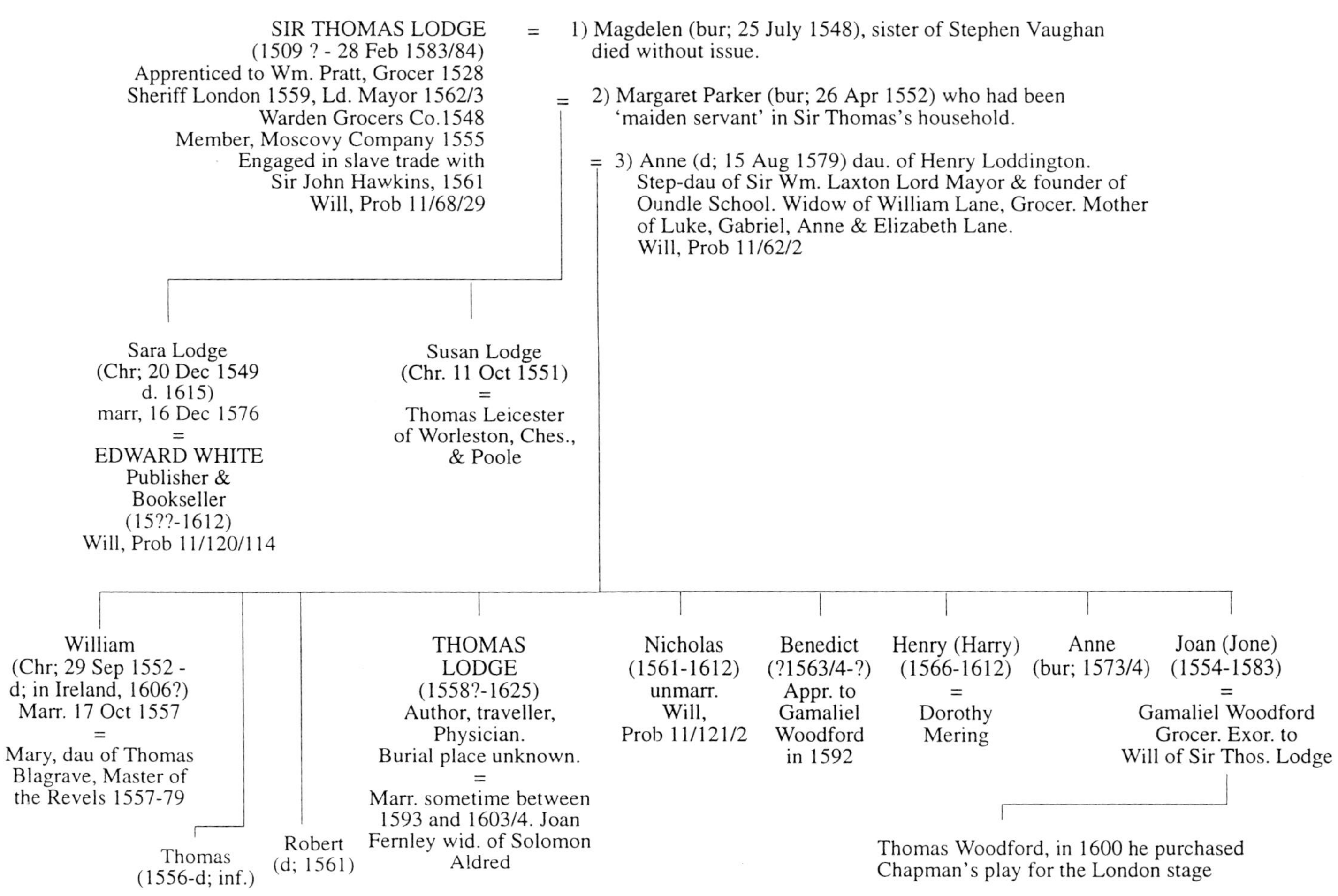
PEDIGREE OF SIR THOMAS LODGE
SIR THOMAS LODGE (1509 ? - 28 Feb 1583/84) Apprenticed to Wm. Pratt, Grocer 1528 Sheriff London 1559, Ld. Mayor 1562/3 Warden Grocers Co.1548 Member, Moscovy Company 1555 Engaged in slave trade with Sir John Hawkins, 1561 Will, Prob 11/68/29
=
1) Magdelen (bur; 25 July 1548), sister of Stephen Vaughan died without issue.
= 2) Margaret Parker (bur; 26 Apr 1552) who had been 'maiden servant' in Sir Thomas's household.
= 3) Anne (d; 15 Aug 1579) dau. of Henry Loddington. Step-dau of Sir Wm. Laxton Lord Mayor & founder of Oundle School. Widow of William Lane, Grocer. Mother of Luke, Gabriel, Anne & Elizabeth Lane. Will, Prob 11/62/2
Sara Lodge (Chr; 20 Dec 1549 d. 1615) marr, 16 Dec 1576 = EDWARD WHITE Publisher & Bookseller (15??-1612) Will, Prob 11/120/114
Susan Lodge (Chr. 11 Oct 1551) = Thomas Leicester of Worleston, Ches., & Poole
William (Chr; 29 Sep 1552 - d; in Ireland, 1606?) Marr. 17 Oct 1557 = Mary, dau of Thomas Blagrave, Master of the Revels 1557-79
Thomas (1556-d; inf.)
Robert (d; 1561)
THOMAS LODGE (1558?-1625) Author, traveller, Physician. Burial place unknown. = Marr. sometime between 1593 and 1603/4. Joan Fernley wid. of Solomon Aldred
Nicholas (1561-1612) unmarr. Will, Prob 11/121/2
Benedict (?1563/4-?) Appr. to Gamaliel Woodford in 1592
Henry (Harry) (1566-1612) = Dorothy Mering
Anne (bur; 1573/4)
Joan (Jone) (1554-1583) = Gamaliel Woodford Grocer. Exor. to Will of Sir Thos. Lodge
Thomas Woodford, in 1600 he purchased Chapman's play for the London stage

A SELECT GLOSSARY

[1393]

Alb	A tunic or vestment of white cloth reaching to the feet, and enveloping the entire person; a variety of the surplice, but with close sleeves; worn by clerics in religious ceremonies, and by some consecrated kings.
Amell	Enamel
Amerciament	The infliction of a penalty left to the 'mercy' of the inflicter; hence the imposition of an arbitrary mulct or fine, originally lighter in amount than fines for specific offences.
Andiron	An utensil, consisting of an iron bar sustained horizontally at one end by an upright pillar or support usually ornamented or artistically shaped, at the other end by a short foot; a pair of these also called 'fire-dogs', being placed, one at either side of the hearth or fire-place, with the ornamental ends to the front, to support burning wood. Sometimes in a kitchen fire-place the upright support carried a rack in front for the rack to turn in.
Angels	Angels or Old English gold coins worth 10s in Edward VI's reign.
Argosy	A merchant vessel of the largest size and burden, especially those of Ragusa and Venice.
Back	A large, shallow vessel, tub, trough, vat, cistern; especially applied to those used by brewers, dyers and picklers.
Backside	The back premises, backyard, out-buildings attached to a dwelling ; also, the privy.
Beadsman	One who prays for the soul or spiritual welfare of another.
Borough	In the sense of township or district; here it is meant as another word for tithing, a land division, once regarded as a tenth of a hundred run by a borsholder.
Cartbote	The right to wood from the commons to make or repair carts.
Carver	Presumably an English word for CARVER; one who carves wood, ivory, stone etc.; a sculptor; most frequently (when not otherwise qualified) applied to one who carves in wood.
Ceiling	The action of lining the roof or walls of an apartment with boards or (more rarely) plaster.
Censer	A vessel in which incense is burnt.
Chauffer	A metal basket containing fire; a small portable furnace usually of iron fitted with air-holes and a grate.
Cist	A small receptacle for sacred utensils carried in procession at the celebration of mystic festivals

[1393] Most of the definitions have been taken from the *Oxford English Dictionary* and *The Local Historian's Encyclopedia*; other sources are shown in the footnotes.

Coal-fish	A fish allied to the cod, so called from the dusky pigment, which tinges its skin and soils the fingers like moist coal. Found in the Northern Seas, and caught for food.
Cony-earth	An early form of cony-garth, a rabbit-warren.
Copbronde	A variant of cob-iron, one of the irons on which a spit turns, the irons hung on the bars of a kitchen range to support the spit.
Costage or Custage	An expense, expenditure, charge or cost
Counterpoint	A quilt stabbed or stitched through, a quilted mattress.
Court Baron	A manorial court ,which enforced the customs of the manor. It was the property of the lord and was a private jurisdiction.
Court Leet	It was a court of record and was a public jurisdiction. It dealt with petty offences and was presided over by the lord or his representative. Every male over the age of 12 or 16 (depending on custom) was obliged to attend. It met at least twice a year and was responsible for the view of frankpledge
Court of Piepowder	A corruption of pied poudreux, meaning 'dusty footed'. This was held during the periods of markets and fairs.
Crayer	A small trading vessel.
Croft	(1) a piece of enclosed ground, used for tillage or pasture, in most localities a small piece of arable land adjacent to a house. Toft and Croft, a messuage with land attached. (2) a small agricultural holding worked by a peasant tenant.
Cruet	A small vessel for holding the wine and water used at the Mass, or to hold holy water for other uses.
Cruse	An earthenware jar.
Cyler	An obsolete form of celure meaning ceiling or canopy
Dane	A vale, now usually the deep, narrow and wooded vale of a rivulet.
Daywork	The amount of land that could be worked, ploughed, mown etc. in a day.
Decoll, decollate	To sever at the neck; to behead.
Desperate debt	A 'bad' debt whose recovery is past hope.
Dicker	1 dicker equals 10 skins. A last of leather equals 20 dickers.
Disme	Besides its historical use in the sense of 'tenth' and 'tithe', it is used, in the earliest English book on the subject (1608), for 'Decimal arithmetic'.
Dress	To make straight or right; to bring into proper order, to array, make ready, prepare, tend.
Dry-fat	A large vessel (cask, barrel, tub, box etc.) used to hold dry things.
Earing	The action of ploughing

Elemosynary	The almoner was the officer whose duty it was to dispense alms.
Entier	Of persons; wholly devoted to another, perfectly beloved.
Escheator	He collected revenues due to the Crown from escheated estates. These occurred when the tenant died without heirs, or where the heir had not yet attained his majority, or else where the tenant had committed an offence, which incurred the forfeiture of his estate. They were abolished in 1925.
Ex officio	Prosecution in the ecclesiastical court by the court itself by virtue of its spiritual jurisdiction especially in cases of moral deliquency.
Farm	**1.** A fixed yearly amount (whether in money or in kind) payable as rent, tax, or the like (as opposed to a rent, tax, etc., of variable amount, *e.g.* one calculated at a certain proportion of the produce. (2) A fixed yearly sum accepted from a person as a composition for taxes or other moneys which he is empowered to collect; also, a fixed charge imposed on a town, county, etc., in respect of a tax or taxes to be collected within its limits. (3) The condition of being let at a fixed rent. (4) A lease. (5) Originally, a tract of land held on lease for the purpose of cultivation.
Feoffee	Person to whom freehold estate in land is conveyed by a feoffment
Fette	A synonym for Fetch.
Fire and Flet	Fire and house-room.
Firebote	The right to take wood from the commons for fuel.
Firmity	(1) firmness, solidity, stability; also, moral firmness, firm allegiance, constancy.(2) a means of strengthening; an assurance.
Flicchis	A flitch, a side of cured hog meat, a hundred-weight of 112 avoirdupois pounds.
Forestall	Piece of land in front of a building; a farm-yard before a house; a paddock near a farm house; the house and home-building of a farm; a small opening in a street or lane, not large enough to be called a common.
Frankpledge	In Anglo-Saxon times each vill or area was divided into tithings-associations of ten or twelve households, which were held corporately responsible for the behaviour of each member. The tithing was also responsible for ensuring that any member accused of an offence was available to answer the charge. This system was called Frankpledge. Representatives of tithings were called borsholders in the Faversham area.
A full of kettles	A set.
Garth	A small piece of enclosed ground, usually beside a house or other building, used as a yard, garden or paddock.
Grewehound	A greyhound.
Groat	Four pence
Groat	Equal to four pence.

Grove	A small wood; a group of trees affording shade or forming avenues or walks, occurring naturally or planted for a special purpose. Groves were commonly planted by heathens in honour of deities to serve as places of worship or for the reception of images.
Hallmote	A Court Baron or Court Leet.
Hauter	An obsolete form of altar.
Haw	A hedge or encompassing fence; a piece of ground enclosed or fenced in; a messuage; generally, a yard, close or enclosure, as in timber-haw.
Hedgebote or Haybote	The right to take wood from the commons to make or repair fences.
Heriot	A feudal service, originally consisting of weapons, horses and other military equipment restored to the lord on the death of his tenant; afterwards a render of the best beast or dead chattel of a deceased tenant due by legal custom to the lord of whom he held. At an early period this render was commuted in many cases to a fixed money payment.
Hope	A piece of enclosed marshland (Essex and Kent).
Hoy	A small vessel carrying passengers and goods, especially for short distances.
Hundred	An administrative division of a shire. The Hundred Court usually met monthly to consider criminal offences, minor ecclesiastical matters and private pleas; it also levied taxes.
Ketch	A strongly built vessel of the galiot order, usually two masted and from 100 to 250 tons burden.
Knight's Service	Originally the military support and other obligations due from a knight occupying a Knight's Fee to the Crown. It was considered to be the amount of land, which could support a and his family for a year. The obligations were later commuted to a money payment. In 1540, when sales following the dissolution of the monasteries began in earnest, the Crown said that all these estates were to be held by knight service, which obliged the holder to pay wardship for an heir under 21 and the marriage of a ward as well as that of the widow. Knight's service was bitterly resented and was finally abolished in 1660.
Knop	A small round protuberance, a knob, especially one of ornamental character, say on the stem of a chalice or candlestick.
Last	12 barrels. A fish barrel was normally that of an ale barrel containing 32 gallons.
Locum tenens	One who holds office temporarily or who undertakes another's professional duties during his absence.
Martron	The skin or fur of the animal now called marten.
Meddle	To deal with.

Messuage	A house, including garden, courtyard, orchard and outbuildings.
Mortmain	A term meaning 'dead hand'', in this case, of the Church. When land was granted by laymen to ecclesiastical bodies, it became free of escheats and reliefs etc. and this resulted in a loss of income to the manorial lord both at the time and in the foreseeable future. Legislation in 1217 and 1279 prevented this from happening .
Navet	Part of an incense pan or censer box.
Nine Gates	A gate, in this context, was the right to a run of pasturage for a cow, horse etc.
Nuncupative	A will, which is a declaration by the testator without any writing before a sufficient number of witnesses.
Orphrey	Orfray: gold embroidery, or any rich embroidery, with *an* and *pl.*, a piece of richly embroidered stuff.
Ouch	A clasp, buckle, fibula or brooch for holding together the two sides of a garment.
Outdweller	Otherwise called foreigners; people who had property in the town, even though they were resident elsewhere.
Outland	The outlying land of an estate or manor. In Old English and feudal tenure, that portion of the land which the lord did not retain for his own use but granted to tenants.
Ozage	Usage, habitual use, established custom or practice, customary mode of action.
Parcel-gilt	A partially gilded especially of silver ware, as bowls, cups etc., having the inner surface gilt.
Pax	A tablet kissed by the priest and people at the celebration of the Mass after the Agnus Dei.
Perceive	To receive rents, profits, dues etc.
Piece	1 piece of figs = 60 lbs.
Pin	A small cask or keg holding half a firkin, or 4½ gallons.
Pink	A sailing vessel ; originally one of small size used for coasting and fishing, described as flat bottomed and having bulging sides.
Ploughbote	The right to take wood from the commons to make or repair ploughs.
Pocket	1 pocket = 2½cwt; a package in the form of a sack made of stout twill, measuring when filled 6-7 feet high and 2 feet in diameter.
Portmote	The court of a borough; a borough-mote also the legal court of a sea-port town.

Praemunire	A writ by which the sheriff is charged to summon a person accused, originally, of prosecuting in a foreign court a suit cognizable by the law of England, and later, of asserting or maintaining papal jurisdiction in England, thus denying the ecclesiastical supremacy of the sovereign.
Preceptory	A subordinate community of the Knights Templars, established on one of the provincial estates of the order; hence, the estate or manor supporting this, or the buildings in which it was housed. .
Precontest	A former or previous fellow witness in the ecclesiastical courts.
Producent	One who or that which produces; a producer; the party producing a witness or document under the old system of the ecclesiastical courts.
Promotion	Advancement in position, preferment.
Quinzaine	A period of fifteen days.
Rase measure	To strike off corn etc., at the level of the measure
Replevy	A writ of replevin: the restoration to, or recovery by, a person of goods or chattels distrained or taken from him, upon his giving security to have the matter tried in a court of justice and to return the goods if the case is decided against him.
Saffron	An orange-red product consisting of the dried stigmas of <u>Crocus sativus</u> used for colouring confectionery and liquors for flavouring.
Say	A cloth of fine texture resembling serge; in the sixteenth century partly of silk, subsequently entirely of wool.
Seck	An obsolete form of sack. Said to mean only 'dry wine' in the current Eng. sense, i.e. wine 'free from sweetness and fruity flavour'; Some difficulty therefore arises from the fact that *sack* in English was often described as a sweet wine, though Shakspere's mention of 'sack and sugar' shows that it was not always such even in the 16th century. It is possible that before the recorded history of the name begins it had already been extended from the 'dry' wines of a certain class to the whole class, and had afterwards come to be applied especially to those wines of the class which were originally excluded.
Sergeant	In Faversham, the sergeant executed the mayor's commands, making all arrests and attachments, appearing at the court of portmote and all other courts. At these sessions he was responsible to the court for any further orders that might be made, levied the fines imposed and accounted to the town for the money received at the general audit.
Shaw	A thicket, a small wood, copse or grove. Specifically, a strip of wood or underwood forming the border of a field.
Sheriff's tourn	Twice a year, within a month after Easter and Michaelmas, the sheriff presided at a special session of the Hundred Court. His main function was to review the Frankpledge and to see that the tithings were up to strength. He also dealt with minor criminal cases, but the more serious offences

	were dealt with by the Justices in Eyre. After the Assize of Clarendon 1166, the sheriff had the power to oversee the manorial courts in their management of frankpledge. The effective power of the Sheriff's Tourn came to an end in 1461, when the cases formerly presided over by the sheriff were transferred to the Justices of the Peace in Quarter Sessions. The Tourn was formally abolished in 1887.
Shotten fish	Of fish, especially herring that has spawned and is thin, emaciated and worthless.
Shroud	In this sense,(a) loppings of a tree, branches or twigs cut off;(b) a branch or bough..
Skere	Cleansed, purified.
Slyppes	Slips or counterfeit coins ,
Socage	A free tenure without the obligation of military service. The holding could be alienated by the tenant and inherited without restriction, although primogeniture was the most common rule of inheritance. The heir paid a fine to enter the land. Socage was of two kinds; free socage, where the services were honourable and fixed, and villein socage, where the services were of a humbler nature and fixed.
Staddle	A young tree left standing, when others are cut down, for growth of timber.
Staple fish	Fish not thoroughly cured; green fish cured with a good salt.
Stint	To cut short, cease, stop.
Strail	A woollen bed-covering, a blanket.
Stuppy	Stupin, stuppin or stuppnet, a stew-pan or skillet.
Sumpter	A pack or baggage horse; a beast of burden. or its driver.
Tache	A contrivance for fastening two things together ; a fibula, clasp, buckle, hook and eye, or the like ; a hook for hanging anything on.
Tass	A heap, pile, stack.
Tenement	(1) A thing which is the subject of tenure, i.e. land.(2) A house, particularly a house to be let in different apartments.
Thwart	To pass or extend across from side to side of ; to traverse, cross.
Tithing	(a) Originally a company of ten householders, who stood security for each other within the system of frankpledge. Each male over the age of 12 was obliged to be in a Tithing. (b) a land division, once regarded as a tenth of a Hundred.
Toll-dish	A dish or bowl of stated dimensions for measuring the toll of grain at a mill.
Tovet	A local Kentish word, evidently the same as tollfat. A measure of two pecks or half a bushel.

Tow	The shorter fibres of flax and hemp separated by heckling from the fine long fibres.
Trivet	A three-footed stand or support for a pot, kettle or other vessel placed over a fire for cooking or heating something.
Truss	A bundle or pack. A truss is equal to a 1/36 load of hay and generally weighs 52 lbs.
Trustee	Person who holds property in trust for another.
Tuition	Originally defined as "natives of other places, resident in the town without right of suffrage" the word 'tuition' is used in reference to felons seeking sanctuary in church and thus tuitioners were in fact people seeking abjuration, that is, swearing perpetual absence from the kingdom.
Tye	An enclosed piece of land, enclosure, close; also, an extensive common pasture; a large common.
Wall Scot	A Scot was a tax levied by the acre on the inhabitants of the marshes and levels of Kent and Sussex. The general scot is applied for the purposes of paying water-bailiffs expenses, the particular scot for the looking after the streams and sewers and the wall scot for the repair and construction of the marsh walls.
Wey	Weight. It varied in size with the product as well as with the region.

BIBLIOGRAPHY

1 Manuscript sources

1. Bodleian Library	MS Top Kent e 4.	Crow MSS.
2. British Library, London	Add. Ch. 45277	Additional Charters.
	Add. MSS. 5753	Additional Manuscripts.
	Harl. Ch. 58 H 18	Harleian Charters
	Harl. MSS 421, 542, 649	Harleian Manuscripts
3. Canterbury Cathedral Archives	DCc/Register V	Christ Church Register 1573-77
	DCb/X.10 3	Consistory Court, deposition register
	CC/F/A14	Canterbury City, chamberlains' accounts 1546-53
	Lit. MS B5	Literary Manuscript
	U 33	
4. Centre for Kentish Studies	DRb /PWr	Consistory Court of Rochester Will register
	PRC 3	Archdeaconry Court of Canterbury Probate Act Books.
	PRC 10	Archdeaconry Court of Canterbury Inventory Registers.
	PRC 17	Archdeaconry Court of Canterbury Will Regs.
	PRC 22	Consistory Court of Canterbury Probate Act Books.
	PRC 28	Consistory Court of Canterbury Inventory Registers.
	PRC 32	Consistory Court of Canterbury Will Registers.
	U 2741/T3	Unofficial Collection: Deposit from University of London Library; Deeds and probate,
	U 390-M37-61	Manor of Faversham
	U 455/M	Manor of Hothfield
	Faversham Borough Records	
	Fa/A1/5/1, 3	Administrative Records, transcript of 1546 charter
	Fa/AC 1	Wardmote Book, Volume 1 1436-1583
	Fa/AC2/1	Wardmote Book, Volume 2 1570-71
	Fa/ AZ	Administrative Records, Miscellaneous
	Fa/CPW 30	The Cinque Ports; The Lord Warden, copy of writs and returns 1573-75
	Fa/CPW 53	The Cinque Ports; The Lord Warden, writs and returns concerning persons and goods 1589
	Fa/FAC	Financial Records; Accounts of the chamberlains and other officers
	Fa/FACq	Financial Records; Accounts of the public charities

	Fa/JB	Judicial Records; Borough Court of Record
	Fa/JC 9	Judicial Records; Inquests with inventories 1573
	Fa/JQc	Commissions of the Peace 1551-74
	Fa/LB 9	Legal Records;The Hatch Estate;The Corporation v Parker; depositions 1568-71
	Fa/LC 1	Photographic copy of Custumal 1400-1750
	Fa/TC 1	Corporation Deeds; four houses, five gardens and two acres 1562.
	Fa/TL.2	Fairs & the market 1555,1586, 1623, 1662
	Fa/ZB	Miscellaneous Borough Records
	Fa/Z33	Microfilm of Faversham Wardmote Vol. 1
	Fa/Z41/1 & 2	Crow MSS 1855
5. Norfolk Record Office		Mayor's court book, 1510-37, 1562-69 Chamberlains' accounts, 1551-67
6. Lambeth Palace Library	ED 2006	Estate Document.
7. Public Record Office,	C1	Chancery, Early Chancery Proceedings
	C2/Elizabeth	Chancery, Chancery Proceedings, Elizabeth I.
	C54	Chancery, Close Rolls
	C66	Chancery, Patent Rolls
	C142	Chancery, Inquisitions Post Mortem
	E122	King's Remembrancer Customs Accounts
	E310	Augmentation Office Particulars for Leases
	E313	Augmentation Office Original Letters Patent
	E315	Exchequer, Augmentation Office, Miscellaneous Books
	E318	Exchequer, Augmentation Office, Particulars for Grants of Crown Lands
	E322	Surrender of Monasteries
	E326	Ancient Deeds Series B
	LR6	Receivers' Accounts: Series I
	PROB11	Prerogative Court of Canterbury, Wills
	REQ2	Court of Requests
	SC6	Special Collections, Ministers' and Receivers' Accounts
	SP1	State Papers,Henry VIII, General Series
	SP5	Exchequer: King's Remembrancer: Miscellanea relating to the Dissolution of the Monasteries and to the General Surveyors (*Formerly* Domestic and Foreign State Papers Henry VIII Suppression Papers).
	SP10	State Papers, Domestic, Edward VI
	SP11	State Papers, Domestic, Mary
8. Rockingham Castle	Deeds, numbers 678, 679, 680, 682,704	

2 Printed books and articles

A short guide to All Saints' Church, Kirkling (1991).

Acts of the Privy Council

Andrews W., *England in Days of Old,* (London, 1897).

An introduction to English Legal History, 3rd edn. (Butterworths, 1990)

Anderson, R. C., *List of English men of war 1509-1649,* Society for Nautical Research, occ.asional publ. no. 7 (1959)

Arber, E., *Transcript of the Registers of the Company of Stationers of London, 1554 - 1640* (1875)

Baker, J. H., *Criminal courts and Procedure at Common Law 1550-1800* in *Crime in England,* ed. J. S. Cockburn, (London, 1977)

Baker, J. H., *An introduction to English Legal History,* (London, 1990), 3rd. edn.

Bettey, J.H., *Suppression of the monasteries in the West Country,* (Alan Sutton, 1989)

Beaven, Rev. A. B., *The Aldermen of the City of London,* (London, 1913)

Bentwich, H. C., *History of Sandwich* (T.F.Pain, 2nd ed., 1972)

Bindoff, S. T., The House of Commons 1509-58, *The History of Parliament,* 3 vols (London, 1982)

Boase, Rev. C. W., *Register of the University of Oxford,* (Oxford, 1885)

Booth, S., *The book called Holinshed's Chronicles*, (The Book Club of California, 1968)

Boys, W., *Collections for an History of Sandwich* (Canterbury, 1792)

Bruce, J., and Perowne, T., Correspondence of Matthew Parker, *Parker Society* (Cambridge, 1853)

Bullen, A. H., intro, *Arden of Faversham, a tragedy,* (London, 1887)

Burke, Sir B., *The General Armory,* (London, 1884).

Burke, J. B., *Extinct and Dormant Baronetcies of England*, (1844).

Burrage, C., *The Early English Dissenters 1550-1641*, 2 vols, (Cambridge, 1912)

Bushby, Lady F., *Three men of the Tudor time,* (London, 1911)

Calendar of the Patent Rolls preserved in the Public Record Office

Calendar of State Papers, Dometic, 1611-18, 1619-23.

Cavell, J. and B. Kennett, *A History of Sir Roger Manwood's School Sandwich 1563-1963,* (London, 1963),

Chambers, Sir E. K., *William Shakespeare* (Oxford, 1930)

Chambers, E. K., *The Elizabethan Stage* (1923)

Chambers, E. K., *Notes on the History of the Revels Office Under the Tudors* (1906)

Clark, P., *English provincial society from the Reformation to the Revolution* (The Harvester Press, 1977)

Clarke, P. and Slack, P., *English towns in transition1500-1700* (Oxford University Press, 1976)

Clowes, W. L., *The Royal Navy,* (London, 1897. Reprint New York, 1966)

Cockayne, G. E. ed. Vicary Gibbs and others,*The Complete Peerage*, 12 vols. (London 1910-59)

Cockburn, J. S. ed., *Crime in England 1550-1800,* (London, 1977)

Cockburn, J. S. ed., *Calendar of Assize Records: Kent Indictments, Eliz.I*, (HMSO, 1979)

Colledge, J. J., *Ships of the Royal Navy,* Vol. 1 (1969/1987) and (Vol. 3) a supplement to the historical index (1986).

Collinson, P., N. Ramsay and M. Sparks ed., *A History of Canterbury Cathedral*, (Oxford, 1995).

Cooper, C. H. and T. Cooper, *Athenae Cantabrigienses*

Copinger, W. A., *The manors of Suffolk* (Manchester, 1909)

Courtney, L. H., 'The Tragedy of Ferrex and Porrex'; *NQ, 2nd Ser, X*, (1860)

Cowper, J., W., 'Notes from the records of Faversham 1560-1600', *Transactions of the Royal Historical Society,* Vol. 1, 2nd edn, (London, 1875)

Cozens Hardy, B., and Kent, E.A., *The mayors of Norwich 1403-1835* (Norwich, 1938)

Cronk, A., *English Hops Glossary* (1959)

Cust, L., Arden of Faversham, *Archaeologia Cantiana*, XXXIV (1920)

Dale, H. D., *History of the parish church of St. Peter and St. Paul, Saltwood*, (Kent Messenger, 1962),

Davidson, D., *Feversham*, (New York, 1969)

De Boulay, F. R. H. *The Lordship of Canterbury*, (1966).

Deighton E., The Carmelite Friary at Sandwich, AC CXIV (1994), 326.

Derville, M. Teichman, *The Level and Liberty of Romney Marsh,* (London, 1936).

Dictionary of National Biography

Dickens, A. G., *The English Reformation*, 2nd ed., (London, 1989)

Dickens, A. G., *Reformation Studies* (London, 1982)

Dietz, F. C., *English government finance 1485-1558* (University of Illinois, 1921)

Dixon, R. W., *History of the Church of England from the abolition of the Roman jurisdiction*, 6 vols (Oxford, 1878-1902)

Doak, J., 'Arden's house', *Faversham Magazine,* Vol. 1.

Donaldson, C., *A short history and guide of St. Paul's church, Canterbury* (Ramsgate, 1964)

Donne, C. E., *An essay on the tragedy of Arden of Faversham* (London, 1873)

Duff, E. Gordon, *A Century of the English Book Trade* (1905)

Duffy, E., *The stripping of the altars* (Yale University Press, 1992)

Eccles, M., *Shakespeare in Warwickshire* (Wisconsin, 1961)

Eccles, Mark (and Sisson, C. J.), *Thomas Lodge and Other Elizabethans,* (1935)

Eighth Report of the Royal Commission on Historical Manuscripts; Manuscripts of His Grace the Duke of Manchester (London, Her Majesty's Stationery Office, 1881)

Elton, Charles I., *The Tenures of Kent*, (London 1867)

Emden, A. B., *A biographical Register of the University of Oxford 1501-1540*, (Oxford, 1974).

Estrange, J. L and W.Rye ed., *Calendar of the freemen of Norwich 1307-1603,* xvi, (London, 1883), part 1

Feuillerat, A., *Documents Relating to the Office of the Revels in the Time of Queen Elizabeth,* (1908)

Fitch, M. ed., *Index to testamentary records in the Commissary Court of London,* Vol. ii, 1480-1570, Historical Manuscripts Commission joint publication no 13, (London, H.M.S.O., 1974)

Fleay, F. G., *Biographical Chronicle of the English Drama, 1559 - 1642,* (1871)

Fleissner, R., On retaining M.Arden of Feversham: the question of titular resonance, *Analytical and Enumerative Bibliography*, N.S, vi, (1992)

Foster, J., *Alumni Oxonienses 1500-1714* (Oxford, 1891-2), 4 vols.

Foxe, J., *Acts and Monuments etc*, 1st edn, (London, 1563)
4th edn, (London, 1577) ed.Rev.J.Pratt
ed. G.Seeley, The church historians of England, iii, i (1868)

Freeman, A., *Thomas Kyd: facts and problems* (Oxford, 1967)

Frere, W. H., and Kennedy, W.M..Visitation articles and injunctions of the period of the Reformation 1536-58 *(Alcuin Club Collections,* 1910), 2 vols.

Frere, W.H. ed., Registrum Matthei Parker 1559-75, *Canterbury and York Society,* xxxv, xxxvi.

Friar, S., *The Batsford companion to local history,* (London, 1991)

Gardiner, D., *Historic haven; the story of Sandwich,* (Derby, 1954)

Gassner, J. and W.Green ed., *Elizabethan drama:eight plays*, (New York, 1990)

Gildersleeve, V. C., *Government Regulations of the Elizabethan Drama*, (1908)

Glasgow, T. jnr., Oared vessels in the Elizabethan Navy, *Mariner Mirror,* Vol. 52 no. 4 (1966).

Godwin G. assisted by John Britton, *The Churches of London,* (London, 1838)
Goodsall, R. H., *Whitstable, Seasalter and Swalecliffe* (1938)
Gregg, W. W., 'The Spanish Tragedy, A Leading Case'; *Library* Vol. 1, No. 1, (1925)
Gregg, W. W., 'Shakespeare and Arden of Faversham'; *Review of English Studies* Vol. XXI (1945)
Greenstreet, J., Kent contributors to a loan to the king, *Archaeologia Cantiana*, Vol. XI (1877)
Gras, N. S. B., *The Early English Customs' System,* (Harvard University Press, 1918)
Gray, G., *Sandwich,* (1907)
Harries, R. ed. *A history of Norwich school*, (Norwich, 1991)
Harrison, G. B., 'Books and Readers, 1591-94'; *Library 4th Ser*, Vol. VIII (1927)
Harvey, P. D. A., *Maps in Tudor England,* (PRO & BL, 1993)
Hasler, P. W., The House of Commons 1558-1603, *The History of Parliament*, 3 vols (London, 1981)
Hasted, E., The parish and town of Faversham, (1798, *Faversham Papers,* no.6, 1969)
Hawes, T. ed. An index to Norwich city officers 1485-1835, *Norfolk Record Society*, Vol. lii, (1986)
Hazlitt, W. C., *Handbook of the Popular, Poetical, and Dramatic Literature of Great Britain,* (1867)
Hazlitt, W. C., *Biographical Collections and Notes of Early English Literature, 1474 - 1700,* (1882)
Hogben, B. M., Preaching and Reformation in Henrician Kent, *Archaeologia Cantiana,* CI
Holdsworth, W. S., *A History of English Law,* eds.A.L.Goodhart and H.G.Hanbury, 17 vols, (Methuen, Sweet and Maxwell, 1903-22)
Holt, A., *Faversham Papers,* no.7 (1970)
Hubbard, G. E., *The old book of Wye* (Derby, 1950)
Hudson, Rev, W. and J.C.Tingey eds., *The Records of the city of Norwich,* 2 vols, (Norwich, 1909-11)
Hugh Perks, R., The hoys and after, *(Faversham Magazine), 1*
Hussey, C., The setting of a notorious murder, *Country Life* (1966)
Hyde, P., Henry Hatch and the battle over his will, *Archaeologia Cantiana, cii (1985)*
Ireland, W. H., *England's Topographer, or A new and complete history of the county of Kent* etc., (London, 1829)
Jacob, E., *The History of Faversham,* (1774, Whitstable, 1974)
James, H. A., Faversham parish church, *Faversham Papers,* no.33 (Faversham Society, 1990)
Kingsford, C. L., *A survey of London by John Stow* (Oxford, 1908)
Kirschbaum, Leo, 'Copyright of Elizabethan Plays'; *Library 5th Ser*, Vol. XIV (1959)
Kirschbaum, Leo, 'Is the Spanish Tragedy a Leading Case ?'; *Journal of English & Germanic Philology*, Vol. XXXVIII, (1939)
Lambert, J. J. ed. *Records of the Skinners of London*, (1933)
Laslett, P., *The World We Have Lost,* (London, 1971)
Lehmberg, S. E., *The Reformation Parliament 1529-36,* (Cambridge, 1970)
Letters and Papers, Foreign and Domestic, of the reign of Henry VIII, ed.J.S.Brewer and others, 21 vols and Addenda (London, 1864-1932)
Lewis, J., *Dissertation on Sandwich* (1851)
Lewis, J., *The history and antiquities of the Abbey and Church of Faversham and the Priory of Davington* (1727)
Lyon, Rev. J., *The History of the Town and Port of Dover and of Dover Castle,* 2 vols. (1814)
Lysons, D. and S., *Magna Brittanica* (Cambridge, 1806-22)
MacCaffrey, W. T., *Exeter 1540-1640* (Harvard UP, 1975)

MacCaffrey, W. T., Place and Patronage in Elizabethan Politics, *Elizabethen Government and Society: Essays presented to Sir John Neale*, ed. S.T. Bindoff, J. Hurstfield and C. H. Williams (London, 1961)

McKerrow, R. B. (ed.) *A Dictionary of Printers and Booksellers, 1557 - 1640*, (1910)

Martin, J. W., *Religious radicals in Tudor England* (London, 1989)

Mayhew, G., *Tudor Rye* (Falmer Centre for Continuing Education, Univ. Sussex, 1987)

Megarry, The Hon. Sir Robert, *Inns Ancient and Modern*, Selden Society (1972).

Melrose, K., 'Annals of Ospringe', *Faversham Papers* No. 36 (1992).

Millard, A. M., *Some useful weights and measures found in the London Port Books (imports only) for cetain years between 1588 and 1640* (1960)

Millican, P., *The register of the freemen of Norwich* (Norwich, 1934)

The Monthly Journal of the Faversham Institute from August, 1881

Muhlfeld, H., *A survey of the manor of Wye* (New York, 1933)

Murray, K. A. M., Faversham and the Cinque Ports, *Transactions of the Royal Historical Society* (1935)

Murray, P. B., *Thomas Kyd* (New York, 1969)

Naval accounts and inventories in the reign of Henry VII, ed. M.Oppenheim, *Navy Record Society* XVIII (1896)

Neame, A., *The Holy Maid of Kent,* (London, 1971)

Nosworthy, J. M., 'The Southouse Text of Arden of Faversham'; *Library*, 5th Ser, V (1950)

Nicholl, C., *The Reckoning* (London, 1992)

Nichols, J.F. ed., The chronicle of Calais,*Camden Society* Old Series Vol. 35, (1846)

Nichols, J. G., 'The diary of Henry Machyn', *Camden Society* Old Series Vol. 42, (1848)

North, Sir D., *Some notes concerning the life of Edward, Lord North, Baron of Kirtling* (1682)

O'Donoghue, E. G., *Bridewell Hospital: Palace, Prison, Schools*, (Bodley Head 1923)

Oppenheim, M., *A history of the administration of the Royal Navy and the Merchant Shipping in relation to the Navy.* (London, 1896)

Oppenheim, M., Naval accounts and inventories of the reign of Henry VII, *Navy Record Society,* Vol. XVIII (1896)

Orlin, L. C., *Private Matters and Public Culture in Post-Reformation England,* (Cornell University Press, 1994)

Ormerod, G., *The history of the county palatine and city of Chester* etc., 2nd.edn., (1882)

Orwin, C. S., and Williams, S., *A history of Wye church and Wye college* (Ashford, 1913)

Paradise, Nathaniel Burton, *Thomas Lodge; The History of an Elizabethan Gentleman,* (1931)

Petty, R., *History of the church of St Mary the Virgin Sellindge,* (Canterbury, 1951)

Pevsner, N., *Cambridgeshire* (Penguin, 2nd ed., 1970)

Philp, B., *Excavation at Faversham, 1965*, First Research Report of the Kent Archaeological Research Group's Council (W.and J. Jarvis, 1968)

Pollard, A. F., The clerical organization of Parliament, *English Historical Review*, LVII, (1942)
The receivers of petitions and clerks of Parliament, *English Historical Review*, LVII (1942)
The under-clerks and the Commons journals, *Bulletin of the Institute of Historical Research,* XVI, (1938)

Pound, J., *Poverty and Vagrancy in Tudor England* (London, 1975)

Pound, J., *Tudor and Stuart Norwich* (Phillimore, 1988)

Reay, B., *Last Rising of the Agricultural Labourers* (OUP 1990)

Redworth G., *In defence of the church catholic: the life of Stephen Gardiner* (Oxford, 1990)

Reese, Gertrude, 'Political Import of the Misfortunes of Arthur'; *Review of English Studies*, Vol. XXI (1945)

Richardson, J., *Local Historian's Encyclopedia,* (Letchworth, 1986)

Richardson, W. C., *History of the Court of Augmentations 1536-54* (Louisiana State University, 1961)

Ridley J., *Thomas Cranmer,* (Oxford, 1962)

Rogers, P. G., *Battle in Bossenden Wood,* (OUP 1961)

Rule, M., *The Mary Rose,* (Conway Maritime Press, 1982).

Ryan, Patrick, *Thomas Lodge, Gentleman,* (1958)

Rye, W., *Norfolk Families,* (Norwich, 1913)

Rylands W. H., ed. *Grantees of Arms named in docquets and patents to the end of the seventeenth century,* Harleian Society, Vol. 66, (1915).

Schoenbaum, S, *Shakespeare's Lives,* (Oxford, 1970)

Scott, G. Ryley, *The History of Capital Punishment,* (London, 1950).

Sisson, C. J., 'Laws of Elizabethan Copyright; The Stationers View'; *Library 5th Ser.*, Vol. XV (1960)

Sixth Report of the Historical Manuscripts Commission, P 61 (Her Majesty's Stationery Office, London, 1877)

Smith, J. Russell, *Bibliotheca Cantiana,* (1837)

Sparks, M., *The parish of St. Martin and St. Paul Canterbury* (Canterbury, 1980)

Southouse, T., *Monasticon Favershamiense in Agro Cantiano* (London, 1671)

Stapleton, A., *London Lanes,* (London, 1930)

Sterry, Sir W., *The Eton College Register,* (Eton, 1943)

Stone, L., *The family, sex and marriage in England 1500-1800* (London, 1977)

Streynsham Master, Rev.G., *Notes relating to the family of Streynsham* (London, 1879)

Strype, J, *Annals of the Reformation etc.,* 4 vols (London, 1709-13)

Ecclesiastical Memorials etc., 3 vols, (London, 1721)

The Life and Acts of Edmund Grindal etc., (Oxford, 1821)

The life and Acts of Matthew Parker etc., (Oxford, 1821)

Historical and Biographical Works & Annals, (1812 - 1828)

Swaine, A., *Faversham:its history, its present role and the pattern for its future* (Maidstone:Kent County Council and Faversham Borough Council, 1970)

Telfer, Canon W., Faversham's Court of Orphans, *Archaeologia Cantiana*, LXXXI (1966)

Telfer, Canon W., Faversham abbey and its last abbot, John Caslock, *Faversham Papers,* no.2, (1965)

Tenney, Edward Andrew, *Thomas Lodge*; Cornell Studies in English, Vol. XXVI, (1935)

Townsend, A. ed., The writings of John Bradford etc., *Parker Society* (Cambridge, 1853)

Urry, W., *Christopher Marlow and Canterbury*, ed. A. Butcher (1988)

Venn, J.and J. A., *Alumni Cantabrigienses* (Cambridge, 1927)

The Victoria History of the Counties of England

Vaynes, Julia H. L. de, *The Kentish Garland,* 2 vols. (Hertford, 1882)

Villiers, O. G. ed., *Saltwood Parish Church: OneThousand Years of History*, (Kent Messenger, 1966)

Visitation of Kent 1530-1, *Harleian Society,* LXXIV

1574, 1592, *Harleian Society* LXXV

1619, *Harleian Society*, XLII

The Visitation of Norfolk 1664, *Norfolk Record Society,* IV (1934)

The Visitation of Warwickshire 1619, *Harleian Society,* XII, (1877)

Walker, Alice, 'Life of Thomas Lodge'; *Review of English Studies*,Vol. IX (1933)

Watt, Robert, *Bibliotheca Britainica or general Index to British and Foreign Literature*, (1824)
Wells, William, 'The Authorship of Leir'; *Notes & Queries*, Vol. CLXXVI, (1939)
Wheaten, A. *The Ancient Woodlands of the Blean,* 6th, 7th & 8th Annual Reports (UKC, 1993-95).
Williams, G. H., *The Radical Reformation* (1972)
Willis, R., *The architectural history of the University of Cambridge and of colleges of Cambridge and Eton,* ed. J. Willis Clark, (CUP, 1886).
Wilson, F. P., *The English Drama, 1485 - 1585,* (1979)
Wilson, J. D., 'The Missing Title of Thomas Lodge's Reply to Gosson's School of Abuse'; *Modern Language Review,* Vol. III
Wine, M. L. ed.,' *The tragedy of Master* Arden of Faversham', The Revels Plays (Manchester, 1973)
Wollaston-Hutton, Rev. Arthur, *A short history and description of Bow Church Cheapside,* (London, 1908)
Wood, M., *The English Medieval House* (1965, New York, 1983)
Woodcock, B. L., *Medieval Ecclesiastical Courts in the Diocese of Canterbury,* (Oxford IP, 1952)
Wraight, A. D.and Stern, V., *In search of Christopher Marlowe* (Chichester, 1993)
Youings, J., *The dissolution of the monasteries* (London, 1971)
Youings, J., *Sixteenth Century England* (Pelican, 1984)
Zell, M. L., The prebendaries' plot of 1543; a reconsideration, *Journal of Ecclesiastical History,* XXVII, (1976)
Zell, M. L. The mid-Tudor market in Crown land in Kent, *Archaeologia Cantiana* XCVII (1981)
Zell, M. L. Suicide in pre-industrial England, *Social History,* XI, no. 3 (1986).

Map of The East Swale

COTTON CHARTER XIII. 12

It was once thought that King Henry VIII was the instigator of a series of maps for the English channel ports, which were compiled and painted about 1520[2]. Harvey says, 'they were tentatively linked with the progress of the war with France in 1513-14 and with a proposed review of defences in 1519. However, research on individual maps has tended consistently to assign them to later dates.'[3] The document reproduced here, by courtesy of the British Library, shows a small portion of this interesting map. The complete map, twenty five feet and two inches long by fifteen inches wide, was put on transparency at the request of P. Wilkinson in 1993.

The parchment roll, part picture and part map, marks the beginning of maritime surveys in this country. Involving some knowledge of geometry and perspective, it was 'painted from sight' and shows the legal extent of the customs port of Faversham as delimited by a later Exchequer commission of 1676. This area extended from the North Foreland, along the north Kent coast and up the river of Faversham to the bridge 'commonly called or known by the name of the Shire Bridge.'[4] As Harvey says, 'The two shorelines are shown with opposite horizons and the wording is one way up on one side, and the other way on the other, so that there is no 'right way up' - a common technique in drawing picture maps, suiting them for study by people on opposite sides of the table.' Harvey points out that whilst the dating of the map as 1514 is the merest guess it may be much later and 1539 is just as likely.

The portion of map illustrated here starts with a series of buildings, some possibly connected with the Key. They are separated, on the right, by the waterway leading to Cooksditch, from the Standard Key. The town crane, an enormous construction swivelled on a base firmly positioned on the key by three massive struts. The crane most probably had a winding wheel inside the structure, which would have been worked by manpower. Note the doorway leading inside the crane which gives an indication of its size. The first mention of a crane is in the Wardmote book amongst the 'Orders for the common portars' dated in 1447[5]: For the whych servysse duly to be don they shall of every tonne wyne that thay wynde vp at the key and to seller ageyne xij^{d}, and for selleryng only ffor euery barell heryng j½^{d} euery cade[6] heryng ½^{d}. Every bine[7] samon of straungers iij^{d} Every quarter whete, malte, barly or other cornys to be borne frome the howsyng off the kay syde vnto the shyp ½^{d}. And for every quarter off the forsaid graynes born from any other strete withyn the said fraunchyse to the shyp j^{d}. Item for every chalder colys iij^{d} Every quarter salt j½^{d}. And for portage of all other merchaundysse they to take after the rate of the weyght ther off.'

Moving upstream from the town quay, the stream on the left is possibly the conduit, often mentioned in the Wardmote or council meeting. The name survives as Conduit street and the town warehouse still stands as T. S. Hazard, a sea cadet training hall. The tidal limit in 1520 was at the Flood Mill shown with a huge undershot watermill, standing on a large dressed stone

---

2 The British Library Board copyright of the photograph is hereby acknowledged, and reproduced from the transparencies by courtesy of Paul Wilkinson. Some of the following information concerning the map is based on information supplied by Paul Wilkinson and D. Harrington.

3 P. D. A. Harvey, *Maps in Tudor England* (P.R.O & B.L., 1993), pp. 43-44.

4 PRO, Special Commissions and returns in the Exchequer E178/6266.

5 Faversham Wardmote Volume 1 (CKS, Fa/Z33 microfilm of original retained at Faversham Town Hall) given hereafter as *Favward*, fol. 3.

6 *O.E.D* Cade: A barrel of herrings, holding six great hundreds of six score each; afterwards 500.

7 *O.E.D* Bin: A receptacle originally of wicker or basket-work.

base. Immediately above the mill can be seen the 'shoot', designed to remove any flood-water. The triangular piece of ground thus formed came to be known in the 18th century as the Gunpowder Dock.

The tall wooden pallisading seen protecting the area beyond Flood Mill could be the remnant of a medieval defence or could be a new development to protect the embryonic gunpowder works just established in Faversham.

Coloured map of the East Swale.

Index of names and places.

Duncan Harrington has tried to ensure that this index is user friendly but readers will still have to rely on his or her native wit, particularly over different versions of the same surname and place name. Places in Kent are not prefixed by the county. Christian names have been standardised.

—À—

—A—

—D—

FAVERSHAM

FAVERSHAM

FAVERSHAM

—H—

—K—

—L—

—M—

—N—

—O—

—P—

—Q—

—R—

—U—

—Y—

—Z—

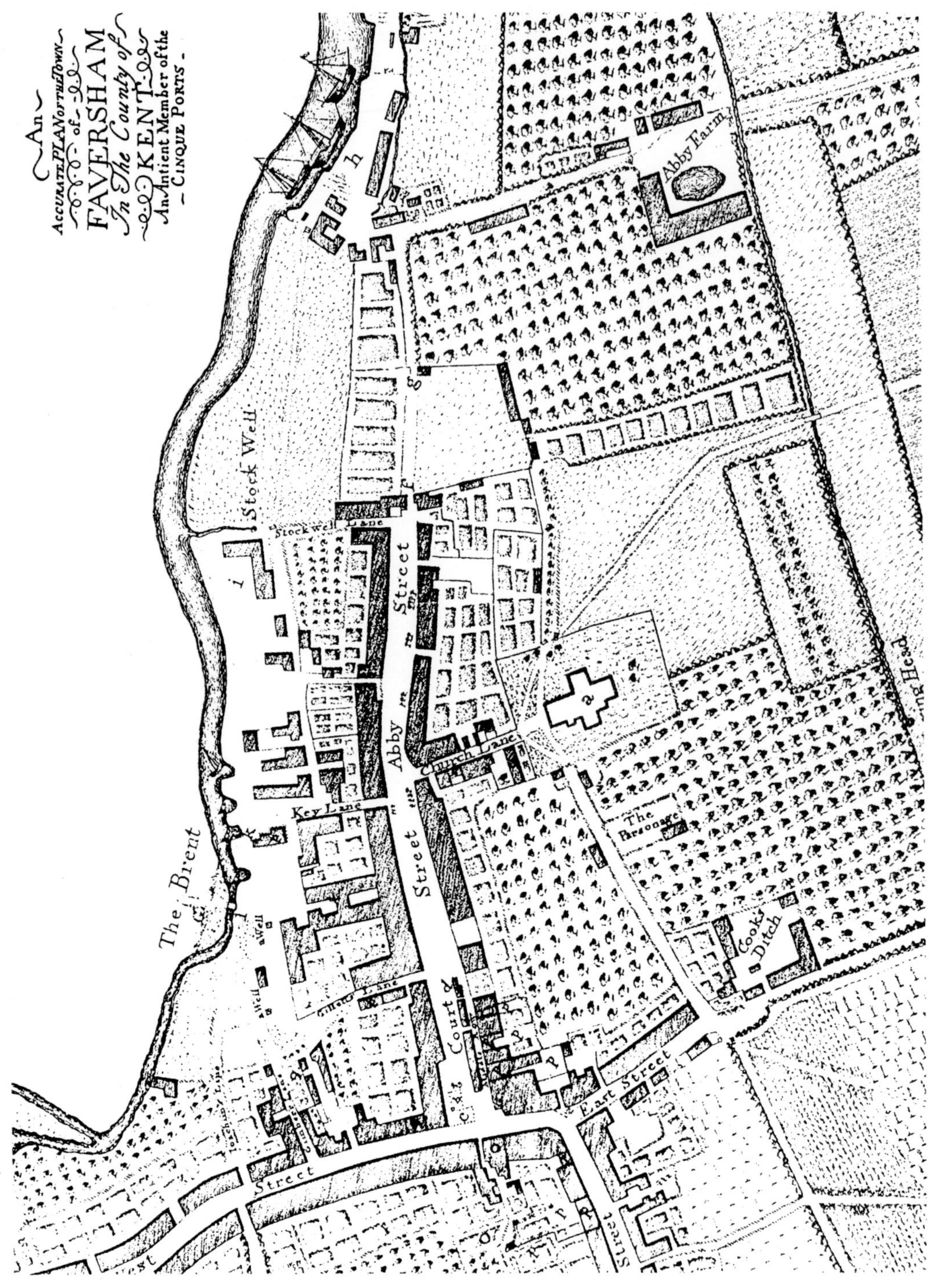

Plan of Faversham Town, I. Hilton, published by Edward Jacob, 1774.